General Equilibrium,
Overlapping Generations Models,
and Optimal Growth Theory

General Equilibrium, Overlapping Generations Models, and Optimal Growth Theory

Truman F. Bewley

Harvard University Press
Cambridge, Massachusetts
London, England
2007

Printed in the United States of America

Library of Congress Cataloging-in-Publication Data

Bewley, Truman F. (Truman Fassett), 1941–
General equilibrium, overlapping generations models, and optimal growth theory /
Truman F. Bewley.
p. cm.
Includes bibliographical references and index.
ISBN-13: 978-0-674-02288-1 (alk. paper)
ISBN-10: 0-674-02288-2 (alk. paper)
1. Equilibrium (Economics)—Textbooks. 2. Econometric models—Textbooks.
3. Economic development—Mathematical models—Textbooks. I. Title.
HB145.B49 2007
339.5—dc22 2006043512

Contents

Acknowledgments

I would like to thank Professor Roberto Baranzini of the Université de Lausanne for criticizing an early version of the introduction; Professor Herbert Scarf of Yale University for providing me with references to the applied general equilibrium theory literature; Gustavo Soares, a PhD student of economics at Yale University, for detailed critiques of an early version of the manuscript; and numerous other Yale students, including especially Mario Leonardo Chacon Barrero, a PhD student in political science, for pointing out errors in the manuscript. In addition, I am grateful to Prof. Daron Acemoglu of MIT for pointing out a logical error.

Professor Jean-Michel Courtault of the University of Franche-Comté has generously assisted me by pointing out many typographical errors in chapter 7 that have been corrected in subsequent printings.

General Equilibrium,
Overlapping Generations Models,
and Optimal Growth Theory

— 1 —

Why Study General Equilibrium?

The reader deserves a short explanation of what general equilibrium theory is and why it might be interesting. The theory provides a summary description of economic interaction in a society where people are free to pursue their own interests. The theory may be viewed as an attempt to answer the question of whether trade arranged through markets could match demands with supplies for millions of goods and services in an economically efficient way. Notice that the question is *could* trade achieve an efficient outcome, not *does* it do so. This second question is empirical, not theoretical.

The rough outlines of the general equilibrium model are easy to describe. Its participants or agents are consumer-workers and firms, and it contains a description of the motives of each of them and the constraints limiting their choices. The model's observable variables are prices and the flows of goods and services to and from each of the agents. A state of the economic system in the model is a specification of all of these flows. The flows occur through central markets that are *perfect* in the sense that each commodity has only one price, all buyers and sellers know this price, and transactions are costless. Firms choose among technically feasible flows of inputs and outputs so as to maximize the flow of profits. Consumers possess an initial allocation of goods and services, own the firms, and have utility functions specifying their satisfaction from consumption. Consumers sell their initial allocations and spend the proceeds together with the firms' profits on goods and services so as to maximize utility. The economy is said to be in *equilibrium* when all markets *clear*, that is, when the total demand for each commodity equals the total supply. Since demands and supplies depend on prices, these are part of the description of equilibrium. When time and uncertainty are included in the model, it allows borrowing, lending, and insurance. The standard model of *optimal growth* is an intertemporal general equilibrium model with no uncertainty, an infinite time horizon, and just one consumer and one firm. This model becomes the well-known *overlapping generations* model if the single consumer is replaced by a succession of consumers, each of whom lives a finite number of periods. I treat the optimal growth and overlapping generations models as special cases of the general equilibrium model.

The main conclusions of general equilibrium theory are that competitive equilibria exist and are efficient in the sense that there is no other attainable economic state that would make some consumer better off and none worse off. The assertion that competitive equilibria are efficient is called the *first welfare theorem.* A partial converse, the *second welfare theorem,* is that any efficient state can be realized as a general equilibrium occurring after lump-sum taxes and payments redistribute wealth among consumers. In the growth model, the equilibrium state not only is efficient but also is optimal in that it maximizes the single consumer's utility over all possible economic states, where a state of the economy is a time path of consumption for the consumer and of inputs and outputs for the firm. The main theorem applying to the growth model is that the optimal state converges over time to an optimal stationary state, an assertion called the *turnpike theorem.* The main theorem applying to the overlapping generations model is a version of the second welfare theorem and asserts, roughly speaking, that efficient paths for the economy can be achieved as equilibria with lump-sum taxes. If we imagine that the economy has a government, then it has debt and uses the revenue from the taxes to pay for interest on the debt. It is natural to think of the taxes as instruments of fiscal policy and the interest rate as determined by monetary policy. With this interpretation, the interest rate is not determined by equilibrium but is chosen by some public authority. The theorem asserts, roughly speaking, that fiscal and monetary policy can achieve any efficient outcome. Some of the possible efficient outcomes may have high economic growth, and others may have low growth. Efficiency does not imply high economic growth. The rate of growth is the outcome of choices made by a public authority, whether deliberately or unconsciously.

One of the attractions of general equilibrium theory is that its conclusions are deduced from simple assumptions about the basic constituents of the economic system, which are consumers, firms, and markets. The theory is reductionist in that its main conclusions are derived from premises about the behavior of the individuals in the system; most of the theory requires no assumptions on collections of individuals. Within standard general equilibrium theory, a need for nonreductionist assumptions arises only when an economy can have several equilibria. When this is so, equilibrium is not determined by the characteristics of consumers and firms; it is necessary to say that history or some unmodeled process chooses it. Apart from the difficulty arising from multiple equilibria, standard general equilibrium theory is built up entirely from microeconomic theory, which deals with the behavior of individual firms, consumers, workers, and investors. Its main assumptions are that firms maximize profits, that consumers make their sales and purchases so as to maximize a preference ordering or a utility function subject to a budget constraint, and that markets clear.

Economic equilibrium appears to have two properties that may explain some of the interest in it. First of all, in achieving equilibrium, an economy solves an extraordinarily complex computational problem—the calculation of equilibrium prices for each of millions of commodities. Probably this problem would be too difficult for any computer to solve, if it were given functions that expressed how the demands and supplies of all commodities depended on prices. The second property is that the economy performs this calculation without having to collect information about demand and supply functions; consumers' and firms' purchases and sales automatically reveal the needed information.

Despite appearances, the general equilibrium model, strictly speaking, does not have the two properties just listed. An economy's use of information and calculation of equilibrium have to do with processes, whereas general equilibrium theory deals only with equilibrium states. Because the theory does not describe a process that finds equilibrium, it does not confront the question of whether free trade could match demands and supplies in an efficient way. It is understandable that this question is not addressed, because it is not at all obvious how to model an economy's adjustment mechanisms.

Why, then, study general equilibrium theory? One reason is that the theory is the most sensible way that has been found to reduce a confusingly complicated economic reality to a structure that is simple enough to remember, analyze, and interpret. The theory also serves as a framework of thought for questions about how economies function as a whole. In addition, the model can stimulate economic insights, where by *insights* I mean short descriptions of mechanisms governing economic life. Although only careful empirical work can substantiate such insights, they are sources of useful ideas. I describe a few insights in this text, for instance, when I use the overlapping generations model to discuss the impact of fiscal and monetary policy and of social security on the steady-state capital stock. Another function of the theory is that its implications inspire empirical work by suggesting phenomena that researchers might not otherwise have thought to look for. For instance, the turnpike theorem suggests that per capita incomes in regions with similar natural resources and technology should converge toward each other as the regional economies grow. Robert Barro and Xavier Sala-i-Martin (1999, chap. 11) have tested this convergence property extensively. Another advantage of general equilibrium theory is that it focuses attention on the question of how to achieve economic efficiency. The model serves as a reference point by describing what the world could be like, but for various imperfections that prevent efficiency. Some of these imperfections have to do with externalities, where an externality is any economic influence of one economic agent on others distinct from the purchase and sale of commodities. Examples of externalities are industrial pollution or the air-freshening effects of cultivating trees. If there are externalities, equilibrium may not be efficient, and we can ask how public policy could achieve efficiency. The first welfare theorem describes the ideal situation we want the economy to imitate; we want it to achieve efficiency and to do so while spontaneously computing the efficient state. Another use for the general equilibrium model is as a basis for simulations of the whole economy that give useful estimates of its evolution over time and of the impact of changes in taxes, technology, and resources. Such simulations are studied in a subject called *applied* or *computable general equilibrium*, and it has a huge literature.[1] An obvious reason for learning general equilibrium theory is to understand the major debates in economics, many of which are expressed in the language of the theory. Probably the theory's most important use is to guide research by providing examples of conclusions that

1. There follows an incomplete list of sources on applied general equilibrium, assembled with the help of Herbert Scarf. Books that discuss the subject as a whole are Shoven and Whalley (1992) and Ginzburgh and Keyzer (1997). Collections of papers that cover diverse applications are Scarf and Shoven (1984), Pigott and Whalley (1985), and Fossati and Wiegard (2002). Books on tax incidence and tax policy are Keller (1980) and Ballard, et al. (1985). Books on international trade policy are Srinivasan and Whalley (1986) and Kehoe and Kehoe (1995). Books on economic development are Dervis, et al. (1982) and Mercenier and Srinivasan (1994).

could be drawn or might have to be modified as the underlying assumptions of the model are made more realistic.

To understand general equilibrium theory, it is important to keep in mind what it is not and what it should not be used for. First of all, it would surely be unwise to elaborate the model in order to simulate an entire economy in detail with the hope of making accurate predictions. Such simulations would require radical revision of the standard general equilibrium model since it excludes many important aspects of reality, such as externalities, imperfect markets, absence of certain markets, expectation formation, increasing returns to scale, inflexible prices, and lack of market clearance. Although many of these things are included in applied general equilibrium models, a model that included all of them and represented an economy in detail would probably be so big and complicated that no computer could handle it and economists could understand it no better than the actual economy. Successful simulations use reasonably simple models to give rough estimates.

Another caveat is that general equilibrium theory is not scientific in the sense that its main implications are not empirically testable. This statement may seem surprising, and to understand it, one must distinguish general equilibrium theory from the microeconomic theory on which it is based. The main assertions of microeconomics are testable. For instance, well-known work by Donald Brown and Rosa Matzkin (1996) tests the microeconomic assumption that consumers maximize preference orderings subject to a budget constraint. General equilibrium theory does contain testable assertions, but these require special assumptions. The turnpike theorem is an example. It requires specific assumptions and has been tested by Barro and Sala-i-Martin (1999), as was mentioned earlier. Another example is the commonsense assertion that an increase in supply reduces price. The central assumptions of general equilibrium theory do not imply this assertion, and it is easy to construct a theoretical counterexample to it. The assertion is implied, however, by models satisfying particular assumptions, and such models are testable. Werner Hildenbrand (1994) has devised such a model and has tested it extensively. In contrast, the main assertions of general equilibrium theory—the existence of equilibrium and the welfare theorems—so obviously do not apply to reality in any strict sense that they are best thought of as assertions about ideal models.

Consider the theorem that equilibria exist. First of all, it is important to understand that this theorem does not imply that actual economies are in equilibrium. The theorem cannot do so, because, like all theoretical statements, it is an assertion about a model. It would be equally illogical to argue in reverse that equilibria exist in a general equilibrium model because actual markets clear. The model and economic life are separate entities. It does make sense to check the realism of the theorem's assumptions and its assertion in order to see whether the theorem represents reality adequately. From this point of view, the theorem is inadequate. Actual markets sometimes do not clear; there are prolonged periods, namely recessions and depressions, when supply greatly exceeds demand in very important markets, namely those for various types of labor. Also the special assumptions required to prove the existence theorem are either unrealistic or difficult to test. One special assumption is that consumers spend all their income, and another is that total demand and supply for each commodity depend continuously on prices. The first assumption is inaccurate; it is not always true that actual consumers spend all their income, and that is one reason recessions occur. The other assumption may be impossible to verify. It is best to treat the equilibrium existence theorem as a proposition applying exclusively to economic models. Its significance is that it specifies conditions that may be used to check whether a particular general equilibrium model has an equilibrium.

The first welfare theorem is not scientific for similar reasons. It asserts that equilibrium states are efficient. Deviations from the conditions stated in the theorem probably prevent it from ever applying to actual economies, even if they are in equilibrium. Examples of deviations are the presence of monopoly power, imperfect markets, lack of some markets, externalities, and taxes that are not lump sum. The efficiency of general equilibrium should be thought of as an ideal that can be approximated in reality by appropriate public policies designed to overcome obstacles to efficiency, such as those just listed and lack of market clearance. For similar reasons, the second welfare theorem is also best thought of as applying only to an ideal model.

A trap to be avoided, I believe, is to accept general equilibrium theory uncritically as true. A healthier attitude is to think of the theory as tentative and to be modified as knowledge accumulates about how actual economies function. As has just been explained, only microeconomic theory should be thought testable; general equilibrium theory is a set of useful tautologies derived from microeconomics. A great deal of evidence is accumulating that the basic assertions of microeconomic theory should be adjusted. The theory has, however, the advantage that it is simple and easy to use and remember. For this reason, perhaps, many economists have long been reluctant to tamper with it. In the nineteenth century, John Stuart Mill argued that the main propositions of economics are valid because they are deduced from the self-evident premises of microeconomics.[2] More recently, Milton Friedman (1953) argued that microeconomic hypotheses should not be tested empirically, because what matters is whether the theory's implications, not its assumptions, are valid. These seemingly opposite arguments both discourage questioning of the standard microeconomic assumptions. Currently, it is common for unusual microeconomic assumptions to be labeled as ad hoc, as if only the standard assumptions were widely applicable and new ones were made up for particular applications, though it may be that the new assumptions apply more generally than do standard ones. We should keep an open mind and allow both microeconomics and theories grounded on it to evolve with increased understanding.

This text, nevertheless, uses the standard assumptions. I describe the general equilibrium model and present the propositions that form the basic structure of equilibrium theory, namely, the equilibrium existence theorem, the two welfare theorems, the turnpike theorem, application of these to the overlapping generations model, and various supporting propositions. Because interesting economic ideas can be stimulated or illustrated through simple examples, I emphasize their construction in both the text and problem sets.

This book is based on class notes for a one-semester course taught to third- and fourth-year undergraduates. I teach the same material to first-year graduate students in half a semester. More difficult sections—meant for a more advanced course—often fall at the ends of chapters.[3]

2. See Mill (1836), Blaug (1980, 68), and Hausman (1992, 124-125).

3. The advanced sections are 3.6, 3.7, 4.8, 4.9, 5.3, 6.5, 7.4, all of chapter 8, 9.6–9.9, and 10.7–10.14.

— 2 —

The General Equilibrium Model

The general equilibrium or Walrasian model results from a compromise between the needs for simplicity and realism. Although a great deal that goes on in the world is excluded, the model has the advantage that it is easy to describe and use. An important fraction of resources in a modern economy are devoted to bringing buyers and sellers together and arranging transactions, yet the perfect markets of the model require no such resources. There are no marketers, salespeople, purchasing agents, brokers, or recruiters. Because markets are perfect, there is no need for contract law or for trust to regulate transactions. Trade is exclusively in standardized commodities, though in reality a great deal of trade is in items that are to an important extent unique, such as antiques, paintings, and labor. Despite the presence of millions of managers in modern economies, it is hard to find a place for them in the model since firms are merely sets of technologies for transforming inputs into outputs. Firms have no strategies, mission statements, or problems of internal control. Individuals are assumed to want to maximize pleasure, though real human behavior is much more complicated. Although governments are major consumers in modern economies and it is possible to include them in the model, they are often excluded for simplicity of exposition.

The participants or agents in the model are firms, consumer-workers or consumers, and possibly a government. The state of the economy, called an *allocation,* is defined by the flows of goods and services to and from the agents. At first, the model will be static or timeless, so that the flows may be thought of either as stationary flows or as stocks that change hands during one period.

2.1 Commodities

A *commodity* is a good or service that is traded. Commodities are homogeneous in that all units of a given commodity are identical. Commodities are also assumed to be infinitely divisible, so that any nonnegative quantity may be traded, held, or absorbed.

It is convenient to use vector notation to keep track of flows of all commodities at once. There are N of them, indexed by $n = 1, \ldots, N$. A *commodity vector* is an N-vector, which is a sequence of N numbers, $\mathbf{x} = (x_1, \ldots, x_N)$. The component x_n is the quantity of commodity n. If the vector represents the amounts consumed by a consumer-worker, the components are nonnegative, and the vector is called a *consumption vector* or a *consumption bundle.* If the vector represents the flows of goods into and out of a firm, it is called an *input-output vector.* Consumption vectors are generally denoted by $\mathbf{x}$ and input-output vectors by $\mathbf{y}$. If the nth component, y_n, of an input-output vector $\mathbf{y}$ is nonpositive, then commodity n is an input into the production process of the firm. If y_n is nonnegative, then commodity n is an output of the firm. Notice that flows into a firm are negative whereas flows into a consumer are positive. This interpretation of the signs is a notational convention.

Throughout this text, vectors will be set in bold, variables in italic, and all other symbols in plain text. In contexts involving the use of matrix algebra, an *N-vector* is thought of an $N \times 1$ matrix, that is, one with N rows and one column. In this form, $\mathbf{x}$ would be written as

$$\mathbf{x} = \begin{pmatrix} x_1 \\ x_2 \\ \vdots \\ x_N \end{pmatrix}$$

which is known as a *column vector.* The form $\mathbf{x} = (x_1, \ldots, x_N)$ is called a *row vector.* Since I seldom use matrix algebra, I do not often distinguish row from column vectors. When I do, the vector in row form, $\mathbf{x} = (x_1, \ldots, x_N)$, is written as $\mathbf{x}^T$, the transpose of $\mathbf{x}$. When not using matrix algebra, I will write vectors in the row form, $\mathbf{x} = (x_1, \ldots, x_N)$.

2.2 Allocations

Another notational convention is that consumers are indexed by $i = 1, \ldots, I$ and firms are indexed by $j = 1, \ldots, J$, so that there are I consumers and J firms.

DEFINITION 2.1 An *allocation* consists of $(\mathbf{x}, \mathbf{y}) = (\mathbf{x}_1, \ldots, \mathbf{x}_I; \mathbf{y}_1, \ldots, \mathbf{y}_J)$, where for all i, $\mathbf{x}_i$ is an N-vector with nonnegative components and, for all j, $\mathbf{y}_j$ is an input-output vector. That is, $(\mathbf{x}, \mathbf{y}) = (x_{11}, x_{12}, \ldots, x_{1N}, x_{21}, \ldots, x_{IN}; y_{11}, y_{12}, \ldots, y_{1N}, y_{21}, \ldots, y_{JN})$, where x_{in} and y_{jn} are, respectively, consumer i's consumption and firm j's input or output of good n.

I now say just enough about consumers and firms so as to be able to define which allocations are technologically feasible. Each consumer is assumed to start with an *initial endowment,* which is a consumption bundle that may be either traded or consumed. For instance, consumers may be endowed with stocks of coal, which may be exchanged for food, or they may be endowed with their own time, which may be rented out or enjoyed as leisure. The endowment of consumer i is denoted $\mathbf{e}_i$ and has components $(e_{i1}, \ldots, e_{iN})$. If consumer i consumes the bundle $\mathbf{x}_i = (x_{i1}, \ldots, x_{iN})$, then $x_{in} - e_{in}$ is i's net absorption of good n. If $x_{in} - e_{in} < 0$, then consumer i is a net provider of $e_{in} - x_{in}$ units of commodity n. If $x_{in} - e_{in} > 0$, then the consumer is a net consumer of $x_{in} - e_{in}$ units of commodity n. Each firm j is assumed to possess certain technologies for transforming inputs into outputs. The set of these is represented by a set of possible input-output vectors, Y_j, called the firm's input-output possibility set. The set Y_j consists of N-vectors, so that if $\mathbf{y}_j \in Y_j$, then $\mathbf{y}_j = (y_{j1}, \ldots, y_{jN})$, where y_{jn} is firm j's output of commodity n, if $y_{jn} > 0$, and $-y_{jn}$ is firm j's input commodity n, if $y_{jn} < 0$.

DEFINITION 2.2 The allocation $(\mathbf{x}, \mathbf{y})$ is *feasible* if $\mathbf{y}_j \in Y_j$, and

$$\sum_{i=1}^{I} x_{in} \leq \sum_{i=1}^{I} \mathbf{e}_{in} + \sum_{j=1}^{J} y_{jn}, \tag{2.1}$$

for all n.

The left side of inequality 2.1 is total consumer demand for commodity n, the sum $\sum_{i=1}^{I} e_{in}$ is total consumer supply of the commodity, and the sum $\sum_{j=1}^{J} y_{jn}$ is its total net supply by firms.

It is possible to use vector notation to express all the N inequalities of 2.1 simultaneously with one formula. If $\mathbf{x}$ and $\mathbf{y}$ are N-vectors, then

$\mathbf{x} \geq \mathbf{y}$ means that, for all n, $x_n \geq y_n$.

$\mathbf{x} > \mathbf{y}$ means that $\mathbf{x} \geq \mathbf{y}$ and $\mathbf{x} \neq \mathbf{y}$. That is, for all n, $x_n \geq y_n$, and for some n, $x_n > y_n$.

$\mathbf{x} \gg \mathbf{y}$ means that, for all n, $x_n > y_n$.

Using this notation, inequality 2.1 may be written succinctly as

$$\sum_{i=1}^{I} \mathbf{x}_i \leq \sum_{i=1}^{I} \mathbf{e}_i + \sum_{j=1}^{J} \mathbf{y}_j.$$

Some simple examples may help you visualize the concepts just introduced. The first is an example of an input-output possibility set.

EXAMPLE 2.3 Suppose that food is produced from labor and that food and labor are the only two commodities. Since inputs are negative, the input of labor, y_L, is nonpositive. Similarly, the output of food, y_F, is nonnegative. Let f be a function expressing the production of food from labor, so that $y_F \leq f(-y_L)$. Suppose that $f(0) = 0$ and that the slope of f is positive and decreases as $-y_L$ increases. That is, nothing can be produced from nothing, output increases as input increases, and as output increases, ever greater amounts of labor are required to produce an additional unit of food. The graph of such a function is shown in figure 2.1. The input-output possibility set corresponding to the production function f is $Y = \{(y_L, y_F) \mid y_L \leq 0, y_F \leq f(-y_L)\}$. This set may be pictured by reversing the direction of the horizontal axis in this diagram, as is shown in figure 2.2.

The next example is of the feasible set for an economy with one consumer and one firm.

EXAMPLE 2.4 (The Robinson Crusoe economy) There is one consumer-worker, Robinson Crusoe, and there is one firm, owned by the same person.

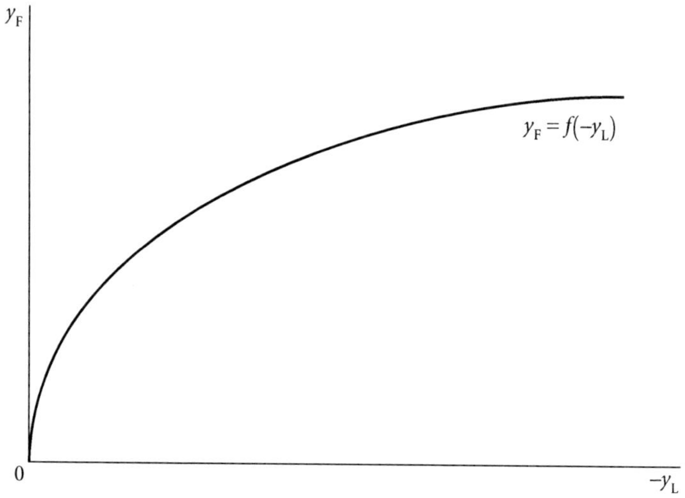

Figure 2.1 The graph of a production function

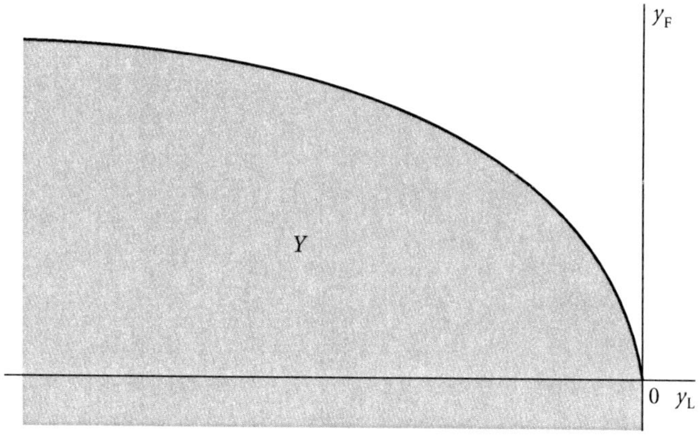

Figure 2.2 An input-output possibility set

There are two commodities, food and time for labor or leisure. Robinson's initial endowment may be any nonnegative vector $\mathbf{e} = (e_1, e_2)$. For purposes of illustration, I take it to be one unit of time, so that his endowment vector is $\mathbf{e} = (1, 0)$. The production function for food is $y_F = f(-y_L)$, where $y_L \leq 0$, since y_L is the input into food production. Robinson's input-output possibility set is $Y = \{(y_L, y_F) \mid y_L \leq 0, y_F \leq f(-y_L)\}$

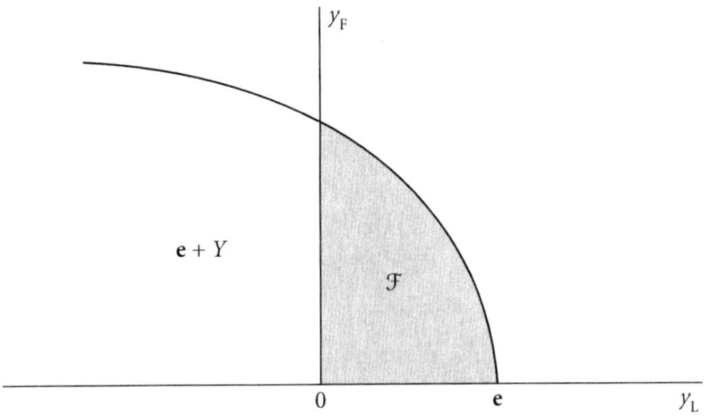

Figure 2.3 The set of feasible allocations in the Robinson Crusoe economy

and is as shown in figure 2.2. If we shift Y to the right by one unit, we obtain figure 2.3, which shows the set of feasible allocations, $\mathcal{F}$, which I now explain.

Notice that the set Y just defined is such that if $\mathbf{y}$ belongs to Y and $\mathbf{y}' \leq \mathbf{y}$, then $\mathbf{y}'$ belongs to Y. That is, Y has what is called the *free disposability property;* the economy can rid itself of surpluses of commodities at no cost. An allocation $(\mathbf{x}, \mathbf{y})$ is feasible if $\mathbf{x} \geq \mathbf{0}$ (using vector inequality notation) and if $\mathbf{x} \leq \mathbf{e} + \mathbf{y}$, where $\mathbf{y}$ belongs to Y. Among feasible allocations, $(\mathbf{x}, \mathbf{y})$, we may restrict attention to those that satisfy the equation $\mathbf{x} = \mathbf{e} + \mathbf{y}$, for suppose that $\mathbf{x} \leq \mathbf{e} + \mathbf{y}$, where $\mathbf{y}$ belongs to Y. Because Y has the free disposability property, $\mathbf{y}' = \mathbf{y} - (\mathbf{e} + \mathbf{y} - \mathbf{x})$ belongs to Y, so that $(\mathbf{x}, \mathbf{y}')$ is an allocation and satisfies the equation $\mathbf{x} = \mathbf{e} + \mathbf{y}'$. If $\mathbf{x} = \mathbf{e} + \mathbf{y}$, where $\mathbf{y}$ belongs to Y, then $(\mathbf{x}, \mathbf{y})$ is feasible if $\mathbf{x} \geq \mathbf{0}$ and also belongs to the set $\mathbf{e} + Y = \{\mathbf{e} + \mathbf{z} \mid \mathbf{z} \in Y\}$. The set of $\mathbf{x}$ satisfying these conditions is the shaded region, $\mathcal{F}$, in figure 2.3.

The following example allows one to visualize the set of feasible allocations in an economy with no production.

EXAMPLE 2.5 (The Edgeworth box economy) There are two commodities, two consumers, and no firm. Call the consumers A and B. Their endowment and consumption vectors are $\mathbf{e}_A$, $\mathbf{e}_B$, $\mathbf{x}_A$, and $\mathbf{x}_B$, respectively. The commodities are labeled 1 and 2. Using vector notation, the set of

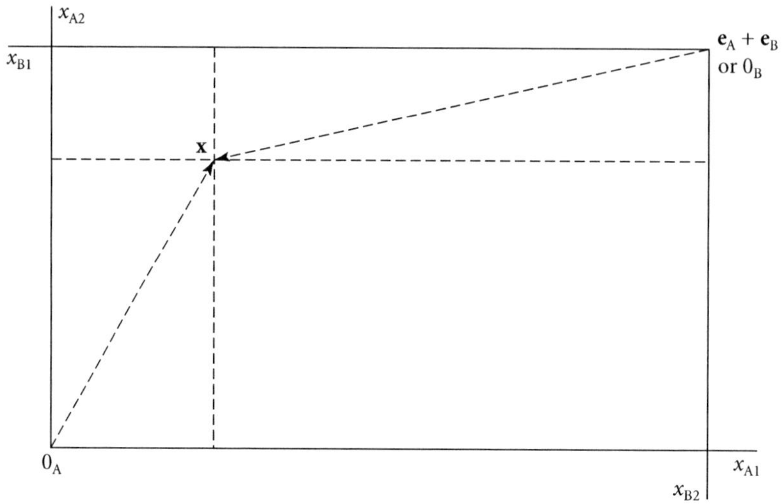

Figure 2.4 The Edgeworth box diagram

feasible allocations may be described as $\{(\mathbf{x}_A, \mathbf{x}_B) \mid \mathbf{x}_A \in \mathbb{R}^2_+, \mathbf{x}_B \in \mathbb{R}^2_+$, and $\mathbf{x}_A + \mathbf{x}_B \leq \mathbf{e}_A + \mathbf{e}_B\}$, where $\mathbb{R}^2_+$ is the set of 2-vectors with nonnegative components. For ease of visualization, consider only those feasible allocations that are such that the supply of each good equals its demand. That is, consider the set of allocations, $\{(\mathbf{x}_A, \mathbf{x}_B) \mid \mathbf{x}_A \in \mathbb{R}^2_+, \mathbf{x}_B \in \mathbb{R}^2_+$, and $\mathbf{x}_A + \mathbf{x}_B = \mathbf{e}_A + \mathbf{e}_B\}$. Then, $\mathbf{x}_A$ is part of a feasible allocation, if $\mathbf{x}_A = \mathbf{e}_A + \mathbf{e}_B - \mathbf{x}_B$, and $\mathbf{x}_B \geq \mathbf{0}$, that is, if $\mathbf{x}_A \leq \mathbf{e}_A + \mathbf{e}_B$. Such points, $\mathbf{x}_A$, are in the rectangle portrayed in figure 2.4. (The point $\mathbf{x}_A$ is indicated by $\mathbf{x}$ in the figure.) The rectangle is known as the *Edgeworth box* or the *Edgeworth-Bowley box*. Notice that an allocation is represented by a single point in the box. The point $\mathbf{0}_A$ in figure 2.4 is the origin from the point of view of person A. The point $\mathbf{0}_B$ or $\mathbf{e}_A + \mathbf{e}_B$ is the origin from the point of view of person B.

2.3 Utility Functions

It is assumed that consumer behavior is governed by a utility function, which assigns a number to each consumption bundle. Formally, such a function is written as $u\colon \mathbb{R}^N_+ \to \mathbb{R}$, where $\mathbb{R}^N_+$ is the set of all N-vectors with nonnegative components and R is the set of real numbers. Again using formal notation, $\mathbb{R}^N_+ = \{\mathbf{x} \in \mathbb{R}^N \mid \mathbf{x} \geq \mathbf{0}\}$, where $\mathbb{R}^{\mathrm{N}} = \{(x_1, \ldots, x_{\mathrm{N}}) \mid x_n$ is a number for all $n\}$ is the set of all N-vectors.

The requirement that the utility function be defined on all of $\mathbb{R}^N_+$ excludes a convenient and well-known example, the logarithmic form of the Cobb-Douglas utility function, which is $u(x_1, \ldots, x_N) = a_1 \ln(x_1) + \cdots + a_N \ln(x_N)$, where the coefficients a_n are positive numbers. This function is not defined if any of the components of x is zero. Nevertheless, the requirement that utility functions be defined on all of $\mathbb{R}^N_+$ is so useful for mathematical arguments that it is retained throughout this book.

It is not necessary to assume that actual consumers have utility functions that they are aware of. The functions are a mathematical way of representing a consumer's preferences among consumption bundles. A consumer with utility function u is said to prefer consumption bundle $\mathbf{x}$ to bundle $\mathbf{y}$ if $u(\mathbf{x}) > u(\mathbf{y})$. In this case, we write $\mathbf{x} \succ \mathbf{y}$. If $u(\mathbf{x}) \geq u(\mathbf{y})$, we say the consumer finds $\mathbf{x}$ at least as desirable as $\mathbf{y}$ and we write $\mathbf{x} \succeq \mathbf{y}$. Similarly, if $u(\mathbf{x}) = u(\mathbf{y})$, we say the consumer is indifferent between $\mathbf{x}$ and $\mathbf{y}$ and we write $\mathbf{x} \sim \mathbf{y}$. The preference relation "at least as desirable as" is what may be observed. A utility function may be inferred from the preference relation, but many different utility functions may be inferred from a given relation. For instance, the utility functions u, $2u$, and u^2 all represent the same preference relation among bundles. These functions are examples of monotone transformations of the function u.

DEFINITION 2.6 A utility function $v\colon \mathbb{R}^N_+ \to \mathbb{R}$ is said to be a *monotone transformation* of a utility function $u\colon \mathbb{R}^N_+ \to \mathbb{R}$ if $v(\mathbf{x}) = f(u(\mathbf{x}))$, for all $\mathbf{x}$, where $f\colon \mathbb{R} \to \mathbb{R}$ is an increasing function.

DEFINITION 2.7 The function $f : \mathbb{R} \to \mathbb{R}$ is *increasing,* if $f(r) > f(s)$ whenever $r > s$.

Clearly, if v is a monotone transformation of u, then $v(\mathbf{x}) \geq v(\mathbf{y})$ if and only if $u(\mathbf{x}) \geq u(\mathbf{y})$, so that v and u define the same preference ordering over consumption bundles. In fact, the converse is true, so that u and v define the same preference ordering if and only if u is a monotone transformation of v. To this extent, the utility function is not determined by the underlying preference relations.

If there are two commodities, we may visualize utility functions by using indifference curves, where an indifference curve is a level curve for the

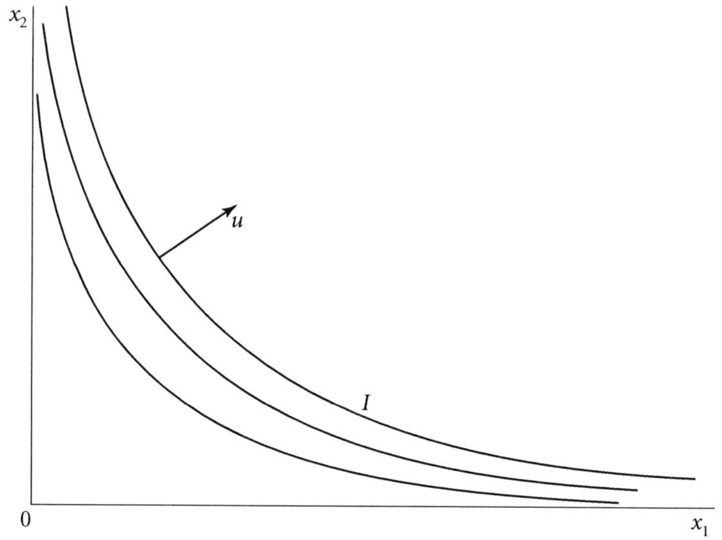

Figure 2.5 Indifference curves of a utility function

utility function. That is, it is a curve of the form $I = \{\mathbf{x} \in \mathbb{R}^2_+ \mid u(\mathbf{x}) = \mathrm{K}\}$, where K is some constant. The curve is analogous to a contour line on a hiking map, and the analogue of a utility function for the map gives altitude at each location. Figure 2.5 shows indifference curves of a utility function. If the function is increasing, the utility level increases as we move through successive indifference curves in a northeasterly direction.

DEFINITION 2.8 The function $u: \mathbb{R}^N_+ \to \mathbb{R}$ is *increasing* if $u(\mathbf{x}) > u(\mathbf{y})$ whenever $\mathbf{x} \gg \mathbf{y}$.

2.4 Economies

An economy is defined by the characteristics of its agents—the firms and consumers. These may be listed as $\mathcal{E} = ((u_i, \mathbf{e}_i)_{i=1}^I, (Y_j)_{j=1}^J)$. In this list, $\mathcal{E}$ is the economy, there are I consumers, u_i and $\mathbf{e}_i$ are, respectively, the utility function and endowment of consumer i, Y_j is the input-output possibility set of firm j, and there are J firms. The notations $(u_i, \mathbf{e}_i)_{i=1}^I$ and $(Y_j)_{j=1}^J$ are abbreviations for $((u_1, \mathbf{e}_1), (u_2, \mathbf{e}_2), \ldots, (u_I, \mathbf{e}_I))$ and $(Y_1, Y_2, \ldots, Y_J)$, respectively.

— 3 —

Economic Efficiency

Efficiency can be defined only in terms of an objective, and it is not obvious what the objective for economic efficiency should be. We can imagine many conflicting ones, including the welfare of each separate consumer, or collective objectives, such as military strength or the preservation of traditional industries and a society's culture. In general equilibrium theory, the focus is entirely on the welfare of individual consumers, and the welfare objective is taken to be either a single utility function that amalgamates those of individual consumers or a weak notion of efficiency called *Pareto optimality.*

3.1 Definition of Pareto Optimality

One allocation is said to Pareto dominate another if it makes every consumer at least as well off and at least one better off.

DEFINITION 3.1 An allocation $(\overline{\mathbf{x}}, \overline{\mathbf{y}})$ for the economy $\mathcal{E} = ((u_i, \mathbf{e}_i)_{i=1}^I, (Y_j)_{j=1}^J)$ *Pareto dominates* an allocation $(\mathbf{x}, \mathbf{y})$, if $u_i(\overline{\mathbf{x}}_i) \geq u_i(\mathbf{x}_i)$, for all i, and $u_i(\overline{\mathbf{x}}_i) > u_i(\mathbf{x}_i)$, for some i.

A feasible allocation is Pareto optimal if there exists no other feasible allocation that leaves every consumer at least as well off and makes at least one consumer better off.

DEFINITION 3.2 A feasible allocation $(\overline{\mathbf{x}}, \overline{\mathbf{y}})$ for the economy $\mathcal{E}$ is said to be *Pareto optimal* if there exists no other feasible allocation that Pareto dominates $(\overline{\mathbf{x}}, \overline{\mathbf{y}})$.

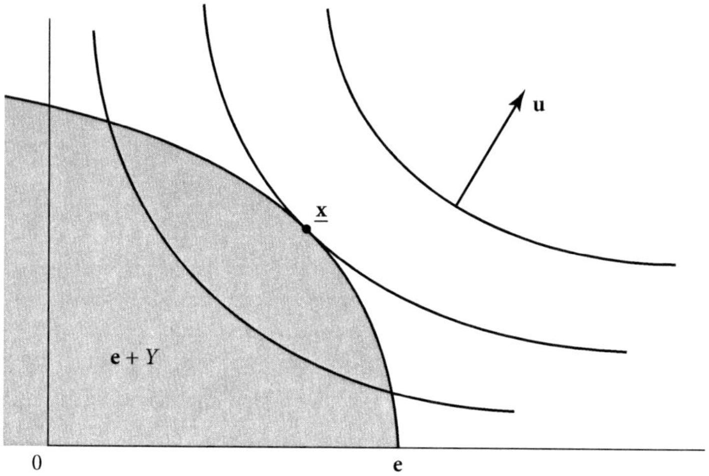

Figure 3.1 The optimal allocation in the Robinson Crusoe economy

In the Robinson Crusoe example, Pareto optimality is the same as optimality, since there is only one consumer. A Pareto optimal allocation maximizes Crusoe's utility. In figure 3.1 the unique optimal allocation is the point $\underline{\mathbf{x}}$.

In the Edgeworth box example, we may visualize the set of Pareto optima by superimposing indifference curves on the Edgeworth box diagram, as in figure 3.2. The indifference curves for consumer A are indicated by I_A and those of person B are indicated by I_B. Because allocation **y** is preferred to allocation **x** by both consumers, **x** is not economically efficient. In the Edgeworth box diagram of figure 3.3, the set of Pareto optimal allocations is the locus of points of tangency between the indifference curves and is the heavy line labeled $\mathcal{PO}$.

We see from this diagram that when there are two consumers, there may be many Pareto optimal allocations, though there is only one in the Robinson Crusoe example of figure 3.1. In the Edgeworth box example, there is a range of Pareto optima, and as we move through it, one consumer gains at the expense of the other.

Francis Edgeworth, the inventor of the box diagram, used it to describe the outcome of trade (Edgeworth, 1881). He claimed that all one can say about trade between two individuals exchanging one good for another is

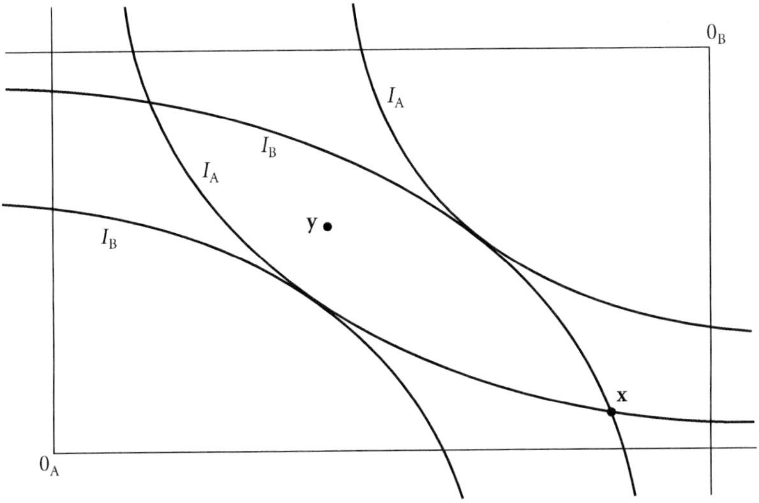

Figure 3.2 Pareto optimality in the Edgeworth box economy

that through haggling they reach an allocation that both find at least as desirable as their initial endowments and such that further trade cannot make both better off. Such an allocation is represented by a point on the section of the locus of Pareto optima between the two indifference curves through the initial allocation. In figure 3.3, the set of such points is the segment of the curve $\mathcal{PO}$ between points a and b, since the endowment point **e** represents the initial allocation. The technical term for this set is the *contract curve.*

3.2 Existence of Pareto Optimal Allocations; The Bolzano-Weierstrass Theorem

It is convenient to know conditions under which a general equilibrium model has a Pareto optimal allocation. One approach is to show that there exists a feasible allocation that maximizes the sum of the consumers' utility functions. To make this argument, we need a mathematical statement that may be unfamiliar, the Bolzano-Weierstrass theorem. The explanation of this theorem in turn rests upon several mathematical concepts, including the Cauchy sequence concept.

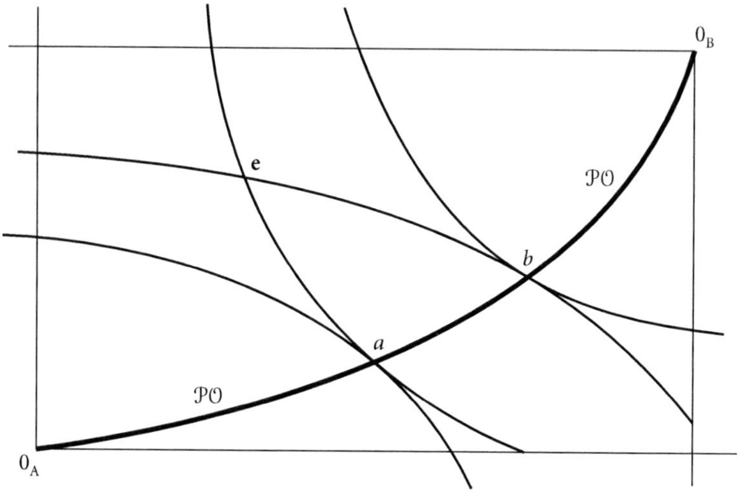

Figure 3.3 The set of Pareto optimal allocations in the Edgeworth box example

DEFINITION 3.3 A sequence of N-vectors, $\mathbf{x}_1, \mathbf{x}_2, \ldots$ is *Cauchy* if

$$\lim_{M\to\infty} \sup_{n,m\geq M} \|\mathbf{x}_n - \mathbf{x}_m\| = 0,$$

where "sup" stands for supremum and the supremum of a set of numbers is the smallest number bigger than or equal to any number in the set or is infinity if there is no number exceeding every number in the set.

In this definition, the length or norm of an N-vector $\mathbf{x}$ is $\|\mathbf{x}\| = \sqrt{x_1^2 + \cdots + x_N^2}$. A sequence $\mathbf{x}_n$ is Cauchy if for every positive number ε there exists a positive integer M such that $\|\mathbf{x}_n - \mathbf{x}_m\| < \varepsilon$, if $n \geq M$ and $m \geq M$. More loosely, $\mathbf{x}_n$ is Cauchy if its members are arbitrarily close together far enough out in the sequence.

A key property of the real numbers is that they are *complete,* which means that any Cauchy sequence of numbers converges to some number. That is, if x_n is a Cauchy sequence of numbers, then there is a number x such that $\lim_{n\to\infty} x_n = x$. The same statement applies to Cauchy sequences of N-vectors, for if $\mathbf{x}_n$ is a Cauchy sequence of N-vectors, then for each $m = 1, \ldots, N$, the mth component of $\mathbf{x}_n$, x_{nm}, is a Cauchy sequence of numbers. Therefore there is a number x_m such that $\lim_{n\to\infty} x_{nm} = x_m$. Then $\lim_{n\to\infty} \mathbf{x}_n = \mathbf{x} = (x_1, \ldots, x_N)$. The Bolzano-Weierstrass theorem is the assertion that a convergent sequence can be picked out of any bounded sequence of N-vectors. What is picked out is termed a subsequence.

DEFINITION 3.4 A *subsequence* of a sequence $\mathbf{x}_1, \mathbf{x}_2, \ldots$ consists of a sequence of the form $\mathbf{x}_{n(1)}, \mathbf{x}_{n(2)}, \mathbf{x}_{n(3)}, \ldots, \mathbf{x}_{n(k)}, \ldots$, such that $n(k) < n(k+1)$, for all k.

I require a few more definitions.

DEFINITION 3.5 A set of N-vectors A is *closed* if $\lim_{n\to\infty} \mathbf{x}_n$ belongs to A for any convergent sequence $\mathbf{x}_n$ in A.

DEFINITION 3.6 A set of N-vectors A is *bounded* if there exists a positive number b such that $\|\mathbf{x}\| \le b$, for all x in A.

DEFINITION 3.7 A set of N-vectors A is *compact* if it is closed and bounded.

For future reference, I introduce the concept of the closure of a set.

DEFINITION 3.8 If A is a set of N-vectors, the *closure* of A is the set of all limits of sequences in A, including constant sequences always equal to the same point in A.

It should be clear from this definition that A is contained in its closure. It is not hard to see that a set is closed if and only if it equals its closure.

The simple examples that follow illustrate the concepts.

EXAMPLE 3.9 The closed interval $[0, 1] = \{t \mid t$ is a real number and $0 \le t \le 1\}$ is compact.

EXAMPLE 3.10 The half-open interval $(0, 1] = \{t \mid t$ is a real number and $0 < t \le 1\}$ is not closed, since the sequence $1/n$, for $n = 1, 2, \ldots$, belongs to $(0, 1]$ and converges to zero and yet zero does not belong to the set. Hence, $(0, 1]$ is not compact, though it is bounded. The closure of $(0, 1]$ is the closed interval $[0, 1]$.

EXAMPLE 3.11 The interval $[0, \infty) = \{t \mid t$ is a real number and $0 \le t < \infty\}$ is closed but is not bounded and so is not compact.

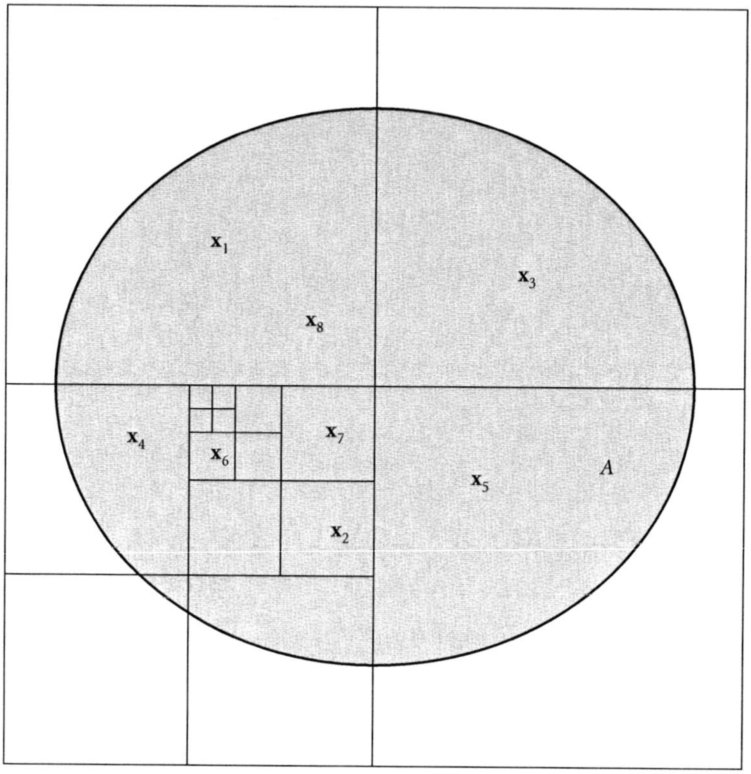

Figure 3.4 Successive partitions of the set A

BOLZANO-WEIERSTRASS THEOREM 3.12 Any sequence in a compact set of N-vectors, A, has a subsequence that converges to a point in A.

Proof. The proof is easily explained using figure 3.4, where the shaded oval represents the set A. Let $\mathbf{x}_n$ be a sequence in A, for $n = 1, 2, \ldots$. Because the set A is bounded, it is contained in some cube. Call it C_1. Divide C_1 into 2^N congruent subcubes by dividing C_1 in half along each of the N orthogonal coordinate directions. Because C_1 contains the entire sequence $\mathbf{x}_n$, one of the 2^N subcubes contains $\mathbf{x}_n$, for infinitely many values of n. Call this subcube C_2. Proceed by induction on the index of the subcube. Suppose we have defined $C_1, C_2, \ldots, C_K$, so that each contains infinitely many members of the sequence $\mathbf{x}_n$, and for $k = 1, \ldots, k$, each C_{k+1} is one of 2^N subcubes of the cube C_k. Divide C_K into 2^N congruent subcubes and choose one of them containing $\mathbf{x}_n$, for infinitely many values of n. Call the subcube C_{K+1}. I have defined by induction on K a sequence of cubes, C_k, such that for all $k = 1, 2, \ldots$, the cube C_{k+1} is contained in C_k, each cube C_k contains $\mathbf{x}_n$, for infinitely many values of n, and the diameter of the cube C_k converges to zero as k goes to infinity.

I now define the subsequence $\mathbf{x}_{n(k)}$, for $k = 1, 2, \ldots$. Let $\mathbf{x}_{n(1)}$ be a member of C_1. Having defined $\mathbf{x}_{n(1)}, \mathbf{x}_{n(2)}, \ldots, \mathbf{x}_{n(k)}$, where $\mathbf{x}_{n(m)}$ belongs to C_m, for all m, and $n(1) < n(2) < \cdots < n(k)$, let $\mathbf{x}_{n(k+1)}$ be a member of the sequence $\mathbf{x}_n$ in C_{k+1} such that $n(k+1) > n(k)$. Such an $\mathbf{x}_{n(k+1)}$ exists because C_{k+1} contains infinitely many members of the sequence $\mathbf{x}_n$. By induction on k, I have defined a subsequence $\mathbf{x}_{n(k)}$ of the sequence x_n such that $\mathbf{x}_{n(k)}$ belongs to $C_{n(k)}$, for all k. Since $C_{n(m)} \subset C_{n(k)}$, if $m > k$, it follows that $\mathbf{x}_{n(m)} \in C_{n(k)}$, if $m > k$. Because the diameter of $C_{n(k)}$ shrinks to zero as k goes to infinity, the subsequence $\mathbf{x}_{n(k)}$ is Cauchy and so converges. Because the set A is closed, the limit of $\mathbf{x}_{n(k)}$ belongs to A. ▪

For our purposes, the most important consequence of the Bolzano-Weierstrass theorem is that any continuous function achieves a maximum and a minimum on a compact set. Before stating this result, I define continuity.

DEFINITION 3.13 Let A be a set of N-vectors, and let $f: A \to \mathbb{R}^K$ be a function, where K is a positive integer. Then f is *continuous*, if $\lim_{n\to\infty} f(\mathbf{x}_n) = f(\lim_{n\to\infty} \mathbf{x}_n)$, whenever $\mathbf{x}_n$ is a sequence in A converging to a point in A.

PROPOSITION 3.14 If A is a nonempty compact set of N-vectors, any continuous function $f: A \to \mathbb{R}$ achieves a minimum and a maximum on A.

Proof. I do the proof for the maximum. The assertion for the minimum then follows, because

$$\min_{\mathbf{x}\in A} f(\mathbf{x}) = -\max_{\mathbf{x}\in A}(-f(\mathbf{x})).$$

I must show that there exists a vector $\mathbf{a}$ in A such that $f(\mathbf{a}) \geq f(\mathbf{x})$, for all $\mathbf{x}$ in A. Let $\bar{\mathbf{r}} = \sup\{f(\mathbf{x}) \mid \mathbf{x} \text{ is in } A\}$. First of all, I show by contradiction that $\bar{r} < \infty$. Suppose that $\bar{\mathbf{r}} = \infty$. Then, for every positive integer n, there is $\mathbf{x}_n$, in A such that $f(\mathbf{x}_n) > n$. Because A is compact, the sequence $\mathbf{x}_n$ has a subsequence, $\mathbf{x}_{n(k)}$, that converges to a point $\overline{\mathbf{x}}$ in A. Therefore,

$$\lim_{k\to\infty} f(\mathbf{x}_{n(k)}) = f(\lim_{k\to\infty} \mathbf{x}_{n(k)}) = f(\overline{\mathbf{x}}) < \infty,$$

which is impossible, because the sequence $f(x_{n(k)})$ is unbounded.

I may now complete the proof. For each positive integer n, let $\mathbf{x}_n$ be a member of A such that $f(\mathbf{x}_n) > \overline{r} - \frac{1}{n}$. Such an $\mathbf{x}_n$ exists, because if it did not, $\sup\{f(\mathbf{x}) \mid \mathbf{x} \text{ is in } A\}$ would be less than $\overline{r}$. By the Bolzano-Weierstrass theorem, the sequence $\mathbf{x}_n$ has a convergent subsequence, $\mathbf{x}_{n(k)}$, that converges to a point $\mathbf{a}$ in A. Clearly $\lim_{k\to\infty} f(\mathbf{x}_{n(k)}) = \overline{r}$, since $\overline{r} \geq f(x_{n(k)}) > \overline{r} - \frac{1}{n(k)}$, for all k, and $n(k)$ goes to infinity as k goes to infinity. Since f is continuous, $\lim_{k\to\infty} f(\mathbf{x}_{n(k)}) = f(\lim_{k\to\infty} \mathbf{x}_{n(k)}) = f(\mathbf{a})$. In summary,

$$f(\mathbf{a}) = \lim_{k\to\infty} f(\mathbf{x}_{n(k)}) = \overline{r},$$

so that f achieves a maximum on A at $\mathbf{a}$. ▪

The following theorem on the existence of Pareto optimal allocations is an immediate consequence of proposition 3.14.

THEOREM 3.15 If the set of feasible allocations for an economy $\mathcal{E} = ((u_i, \mathbf{e}_i)_{i=1}^{I}, (Y_j)_{j=1}^{J})$ is compact and nonempty and if its utility functions are continuous, then it has a Pareto optimal allocation.

Conditions guaranteeing the compactness and nonemptiness of the set of feasible allocations will be presented in section 3.7. The assumption that the utility functions are continuous is made for mathematical convenience. It is hard to say what continuity implies about economic behavior since most actual choices are from a finite set of alternatives.

Proof. Let $\mathcal{F}$ be the set of feasible allocations, and let $U: \mathcal{F} \to \mathbb{R}$ be defined by

$$U(\mathbf{x}, \mathbf{y}) = \sum_{i=1}^{I} u_i(\mathbf{x}_i).$$

Since U is the sum of continuous functions, it is continuous. Since $\mathcal{F}$ is compact and nonempty, proposition 3.14 implies that there is a feasible allocation that maximizes U. This allocation is Pareto optimal because U would have a higher value at any allocation that Pareto dominated it. ▪

(Q) I agree that (x,y) P.D. (x',y') ⇒ U(x,y) > U(x',y')
but U(x,y) > U(x',y) ⇏ (x,y) P.D. (x',y') ?

3.3 The Utility Possibility Frontier

The Edgeworth box diagram in figure 3.3 makes clear that the consumers' relative utility levels can vary widely among Pareto optimal allocations. Another way to express this variation is by means of the frontier of the utility possibility set. This set consists of vectors of utility levels that the economy can achieve. In order to define the set, consider the mapping

$$u(\mathbf{x}, \mathbf{y}) = (u_1(\mathbf{x}_1), u_2(\mathbf{x}_2), \ldots, u_I(\mathbf{x}_I))$$

from feasible allocations $(\mathbf{x}, \mathbf{y})$ to I-vectors of utility levels. The utility possibility set consists of the image of this map and all vectors less than or equal to points in this image. The utility possibility frontier is the set of vectors that are not dominated in the vector sense by any other vector in the utility possibility set. The more formal definitions follow.

DEFINITION 3.16 The *utility possibility set* of the economy

$$\mathcal{E} = ((u_i, \mathbf{e}_i)_{i=1}^{I}, (Y_j)_{j=1}^{J})$$

is $\mathcal{U} = \{(v_1, \ldots, v_I) \mid$ there is a feasible allocation $(\mathbf{x}, \mathbf{y})$ such that $v_i \leq u_i(\mathbf{x}_i)$, for all $i\}$.

DEFINITION 3.17 The *utility possibility frontier* is the set $\mathcal{UF} = \{\overline{\mathbf{v}} = (\overline{v}_1, \ldots, \overline{v}_I) \in \mathcal{U} \mid$ there is no $\mathbf{v} \in \mathcal{U}$ such that $\mathbf{v} > \overline{\mathbf{v}}\}$.

The utility possibility frontier is the image under the map $u(\mathbf{x}, \mathbf{y})$ of the set of Pareto optimal allocations. That is, the I-vector $\mathbf{v}$ belongs to $\mathcal{UF}$, if and only if there is a Pareto optimal allocation $(\mathbf{x}, \mathbf{y})$, such that $v_i = u_i(\mathbf{x}_i)$, for all i. The utility possibility set and frontier are illustrated in figure 3.5 for the Edgeworth box example.

The curve labeled $\mathcal{PO}$ on the left in figure 3.5 is the set of Pareto optimal allocations, and the part of that curve between the points **a** and **b** is the contract curve. On the right, the shaded set $\mathcal{U}$ is the utility possibility set, and the curve $\mathcal{UF}$ is the utility possibility frontier. The mapping indicated by the curved arrow labeled u is the mapping $u(\mathbf{x}, \mathbf{y})$ carrying the set of feasible allocations to a subset of $\mathcal{U}$. This mapping carries the set of Pareto optima, the curve $\mathcal{PO}$ on the left, onto the curved part of the utility possibility frontier, $\mathcal{UF}$, on the right.

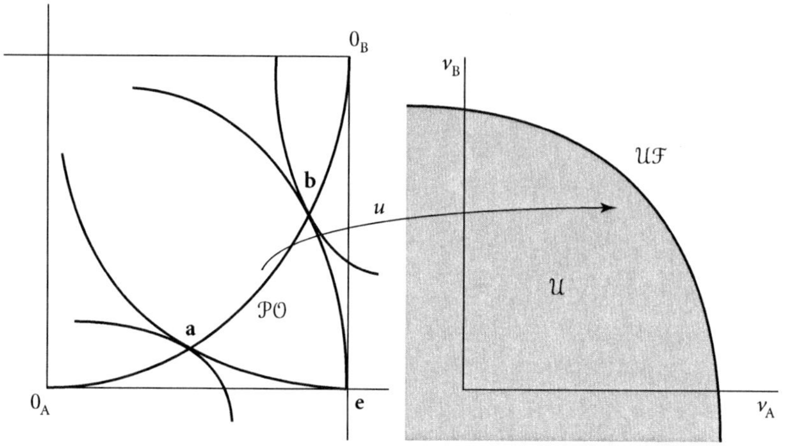

Figure 3.5 Generation of the utility possibility set in the Edgeworth box example

3.4 The Calculation of Pareto Optima; Homogeneous Functions

I now explain how to calculate the optimal allocation in the Robinson Crusoe example as well as the set of Pareto optimal allocations and the utility possibility frontier in simple two-dimensional Edgeworth box examples.

As is clear from figure 3.1, the optimal allocation in the Robinson Crusoe example is at the point of tangency between the frontier of the set of feasible points and one of Robinson's indifference curves. Suppose that the feasible set is described as $\mathbf{e} + \{(y_1, y_2) \mid y_1 \leq 0 \text{ and } y_2 \leq f(-y_1)\}$, where $\mathbf{e} = (e_1, e_2)$ is Robinson's initial endowment, the first good is the input, the second is the output, and f is a differentiable production function with a positive derivative that decreases as $-y_1$ increases. Recall that the input is written as $-y_1$ rather than as y_1 because input quantities are negative. The slope of the frontier of the feasible set at the point $\mathbf{e} + (y_1, f(-y_1))$ is $-\frac{df(-y_1)}{dy}$. The number $\frac{df(-y_1)}{dy}$ is known as the *marginal rate of transformation* between commodities 1 and 2 and is abbreviated as $\text{MRT}(y_1)$. Assuming that Robinson's utility function, u, is differentiable, we can calculate the slope of an indifference curve at the consumption point (x_1, x_2) by differentiating the equation

$$u(x_1, x_2(x_1)) = \text{constant}$$

with respect to x_1, where the graph of the function $x_2(x_1)$ is an indifference curve for the consumer. The result is

$$\frac{\partial u(x_1, x_2(x_1))}{\partial x_1} + \frac{\partial u(x_1, x_2(x_1))}{\partial x_2}\frac{dx_2(x_1)}{dx_1} = 0,$$

so that the slope of the indifference curve, $\frac{dx_2(x_1)}{dx_1}$, equals

$$-\frac{\dfrac{\partial u(x_1, x_2)}{\partial x_1}}{\dfrac{\partial u(x_1, x_2)}{\partial x_2}}.$$

The number

$$\frac{\dfrac{\partial u(x_1, x_2)}{\partial x_1}}{\dfrac{\partial u(x_1, x_2)}{\partial x_2}}$$

is known as the *marginal rate of substitution* between commodities 1 and 2 and is abbreviated as $\mathrm{MRS}(x_1, x_2)$. The optimum may be found by solving the equation

$$\mathrm{MRT}(y_1) = \mathrm{MRS}(x_1, x_2),$$

which is

$$\frac{df(-y_1)}{dy} = \frac{\dfrac{\partial u(x_1, x_2)}{\partial x_1}}{\dfrac{\partial u(x_1, x_2)}{\partial x_2}}$$

at a feasible allocation. That is, the optimal allocation is feasible and equates the marginal rate of transformation to the marginal rate of substitution. Feasibility is defined by the equations $x_1 = e_1 + y_1$ and $x_2 = e_2 + y_2$. Therefore, the optimum may be found by solving the equation

$$\frac{df(-y_1)}{dy} = \frac{\dfrac{\partial u(e_1 + y_1, e_2 + f(-y_1))}{\partial x_1}}{\dfrac{\partial u(e_1 + y_1, e_2 + f(-y_1))}{\partial x_2}}. \tag{3.1}$$

EXAMPLE 3.18 Let the endowment be $\mathbf{e} = (1, 0)$, and let $f(-y_1) = 2\sqrt{-y_1}$, and $u(x_1, x_2) = 2\sqrt{x_1 x_2}$. Then, equation 3.1 becomes

$$\frac{1}{\sqrt{-y_1}} = \frac{\dfrac{\sqrt{2\sqrt{-y_1}}}{\sqrt{1+y_1}}}{\dfrac{\sqrt{1+y_1}}{\sqrt{2\sqrt{-y_1}}}} = \frac{2\sqrt{-y_1}}{1+y_1},$$

which reduces to the equation

$$1 + y_1 = -2y_1,$$

so that $y_1 = -\frac{1}{3}$, and so $x_1 = \frac{2}{3}$, and $x_2 = y_2 = \frac{2\sqrt{3}}{3}$.

Turning to the Edgeworth box example, we see from figure 3.2 that at a Pareto optimal allocation, the indifference curves of the two consumers are tangent. Since the slope of an indifference curve is the negative of the marginal rate of substitution, we must find a feasible allocation where the marginal rates of substitution are equal. Let $(u_A, \mathbf{e}_A)$ and $(u_B, \mathbf{e}_B)$ be the utility function and endowment of consumers A and B, respectively, and assume that the utility functions are differentiable. Equating the marginal rates of substitution, we obtain the equation

$$\frac{\dfrac{\partial u_A(x_{A1}, x_{A2})}{\partial x_1}}{\dfrac{\partial u_A(x_{A1}, x_{A2})}{\partial x_2}} = \frac{\dfrac{\partial u_B(x_{B1}, x_{B2})}{\partial x_1}}{\dfrac{\partial u_B(x_{B1}, x_{B2})}{\partial x_2}}. \tag{3.2}$$

The equations describing feasibility are $x_{A1} + x_{B1} = e_{A1} + e_{B1}$ and $x_{A2} + x_{B2} = e_{A2} + e_{B2}$. Substituting these equations into equation 3.2, we obtain

$$\frac{\dfrac{\partial u_A(x_{A1}, x_{A2})}{\partial x_1}}{\dfrac{\partial u_A(x_{A1}, x_{A2})}{\partial x_2}} = \frac{\dfrac{\partial u_B(e_{A1} + e_{B1} - x_{A1}, e_{A2} + e_{B2} - x_{A2})}{\partial x_1}}{\dfrac{\partial u_B(e_{A1} + e_{B1} - x_{A1}, e_{A2} + e_{B2} - x_{A2})}{\partial x_2}}. \tag{3.3}$$

Since this is one equation in the two unknowns x_{A1} and x_{A2}, it defines x_{A2} implicitly as a function of x_{A1} and so defines the set of Pareto optimal allocations in the Edgeworth box. Only in some cases can we solve explicitly for x_{A2} as a function of x_{A1}.

The utility possibility frontier is the set of vectors (v_A, v_B) of the form $(v_A, v_B) = (u_A(x_{A1}, x_{A2}), u_B(x_{B1}, x_{B2}))$, where $((x_{A1}, x_{A2}), (x_{B1}, x_{B2}))$ is a Pareto optimal allocation. It is not always possible to solve explicitly for v_B as a function of v_A.

EXAMPLE 3.19 Let $\mathbf{e}_A = (1, 0)$, $\mathbf{e}_B = (0, 1)$, and $u_A(x_1, x_2) = \sqrt{x_1 x_2} = u_B(x_1, x_2)$.

In this example, equation 3.3 becomes

$$\frac{\sqrt{\frac{x_{A2}}{x_{A1}}}}{\sqrt{\frac{x_{A1}}{x_{A2}}}} = \frac{\sqrt{\frac{1-x_{A2}}{1-x_{A1}}}}{\sqrt{\frac{1-x_{A1}}{1-x_{A2}}}},$$

which reduces to the equation

$$\frac{x_{A2}}{x_{A1}} = \frac{1-x_{A2}}{1-x_{A1}}.$$

The solution of this equation is

$$x_{A2} = x_{A1}.$$

Hence, $x_{B1} = 1 - x_{A1} = 1 - x_{A2} = x_{B2}$. The set of Pareto optima is the diagonal, $\mathcal{PO}$, of the Edgeworth box pictured in figure 3.6. The initial endowment allocation is indicated by $\mathbf{e}$.

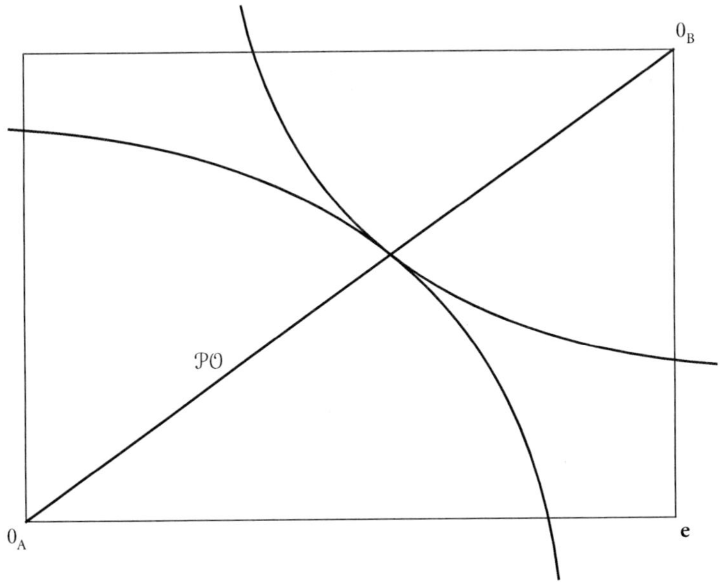

Figure 3.6 The set of Pareto optima in example 3.19

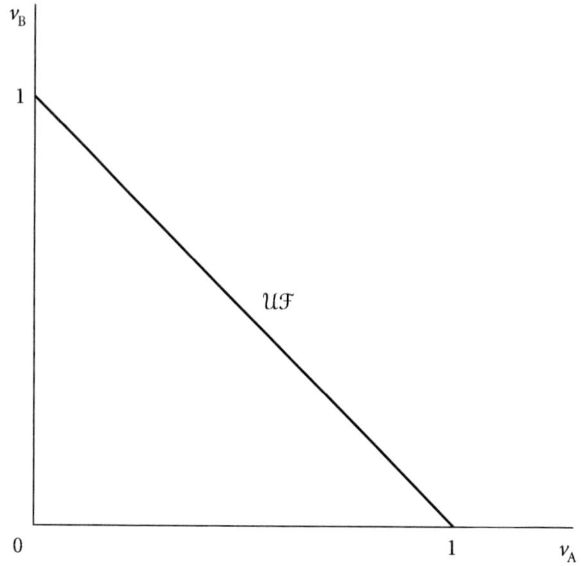

Figure 3.7 The utility possibility frontier in example 3.19

To solve for the utility possibility frontier, notice that if $x_{A1} = x_{A2} = t$, then $v_A = u_A(t, t) = t$, and $x_{B1} = x_{B2} = 1 - t$, so that $v_B = u_B(1 - t, 1 - t) = 1 - t$. Therefore, the equation $v_B = 1 - v_A$ defines the utility possibility frontier, where $0 \leq t \leq 1$. This frontier, $\mathcal{UF}$, is shown in figure 3.7.

Slight changes in example 3.19 create an example in which the utility possibility frontier is defined only implicitly.

EXAMPLE 3.20 Let $\mathbf{e}_A = (1, 0)$, $\mathbf{e}_B = (0, 1)$, and $u_A(x_1, x_2) = x_1^{1/3} x_2^{2/3}$, and $u_B(x_1, x_2) = x_1^{2/3} x_2^{1/3}$.

Equation 3.3 now implies that

$$\frac{1}{2} \frac{x_{A2}}{x_{A1}} = 2 \frac{1 - x_{A2}}{1 - x_{A1}},$$

which simplifies to

$$x_{A2} = \frac{4x_{A1}}{1 + 3x_{A1}}. \tag{3.4}$$

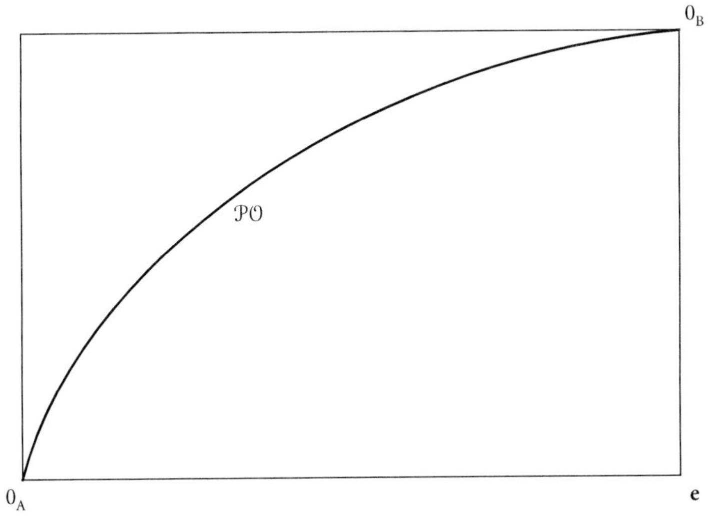

Figure 3.8 The set of Pareto optima

Equation 3.4 describes the set of Pareto optima. The set of Pareto optimal allocations may be expressed in terms of the parameter x_{A1} as

$$\left\{\left(x_{A1}, \frac{4x_{A1}}{1+3x_{A1}}, 1-x_{A1}, \frac{1-x_{A1}}{1+3x_{A1}}\right) \mid 0 \le x_{A1} \le 1\right\},$$

where $\left(x_{A1}, \frac{4x_{A1}}{1+3x_{A1}}\right)$ is the allocation to person A and $\left(1-x_{A1}, \frac{1-x_{A1}}{1+3x_{A1}}\right)$ is the allocation to person B. The set of Pareto optimal allocations is portrayed in figure 3.8. By substitution into the utility functions, we find that the utility levels of persons A and B at the Pareto optimum

$$\left(x_{A1}, \frac{4x_{A1}}{1+3x_{A1}}, 1-x_{A1}, \frac{1-x_{A1}}{1+3x_{A1}}\right) \text{ are } v_A = \frac{4^{\frac{2}{3}}x_{A1}}{(1+3x_{A1})^{\frac{2}{3}}}$$

and

$$v_B = \frac{1-x_{A1}}{(1+3x_{A1})^{\frac{1}{3}}}.$$

These formulas for v_A and v_B express the utility possibility frontier as functions of the parameter x_{A1}. There is, however, no simple formula expressing v_B as a function of v_A. The utility possibility frontier is nevertheless a simple curve concave to the origin, like the curve $\mathcal{UF}$ in figure 3.9.

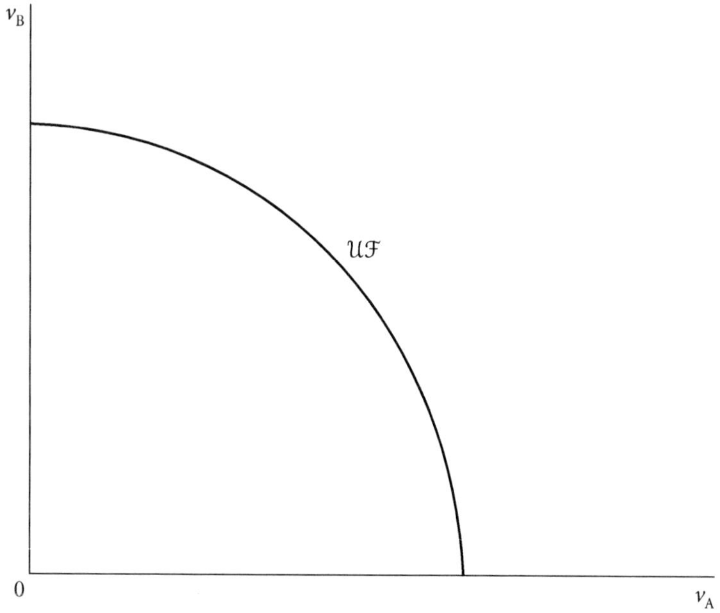

Figure 3.9 The utility possibility frontier

The previous two examples illustrate general principles that can be used as shortcuts in computing the set of Pareto optimal allocations in examples. The utility functions in the examples are homothetic, a concept I now define. The definition requires first of all the definition of homogeneity.

DEFINITION 3.21 The function $f: \mathbb{R}_+^N \to \mathbb{R}$ is *homogeneous* of degree b, where b is a number, if $f(t\mathbf{x}) = t^b f(\mathbf{x})$, for all N-vectors $\mathbf{x}$ and for all nonnegative numbers t.

The definition means that the graph of f over the ray from the origin and through the nonzero vector $\mathbf{x}$ is the graph of a function of the form $g(t) = At^b$, where A is a number. This ray is $\{t\mathbf{x} \mid t \text{ is a nonnegative number}\}$. A function that is homogeneous of degree 0 is constant along a ray. If f is homogeneous of degree b and $b \neq 0$, then $f(0) = 0$.

DEFINITION 3.22 A function $f: \mathbb{R}_+^N \to \mathbb{R}$ is *homothetic* if some monotone transformation of f is homogeneous of degree 1.

Recall that $g\colon \mathbb{R}^N_+ \to \mathbb{R}$ is a monotone transformation of f if $g(\mathbf{x}) = h(f(\mathbf{x}))$, for all $\mathbf{x}$, where $h\colon \mathbb{R} \to \mathbb{R}$ is increasing. A function $f\colon \mathbb{R}^N_+ \to \mathbb{R}$ is homothetic if it is homogeneous of positive degree, for suppose that f is homogeneous of degree b, where $b \neq 0$. Then $g(\mathbf{x}) = \text{sgn}(b)[f(\mathbf{x})]^{1/b}$ is homogeneous of degree 1, since

$$g(t\mathbf{x}) = \text{sgn}(b)[f(t\mathbf{x})]^{1/b} = \text{sgn}(b)[t^b f(\mathbf{x})]^{1/b} = t(\text{sgn}(b))[f(\mathbf{x})]^{1/b} = tg(\mathbf{x}).$$

(The function $\text{sgn}(b)$ equals 1 if b is positive and -1 if b is negative.) Since the function $h\colon \mathbb{R} \to \mathbb{R}$ defined by $h(s) = \text{sgn}(b)s^{1/b}$ is an increasing function and $g(\mathbf{x}) = h(f(\mathbf{x}))$, it follows that f is homothetic.

If u is homothetic, all indifference sets may be obtained from one indifference set by radial projection. This remark may be visualized when $N = 2$ by imagining an indifference curve, I, and then shrinking it inward toward zero or expanding it outward from zero by multiplying each vector in I by a fixed number t. This transformation is obtained by multiplying each of the coordinates by t. If u is homothetic, the new curve is also an indifference curve for u. Figure 3.10 illustrates such an outward expansion. Indifference

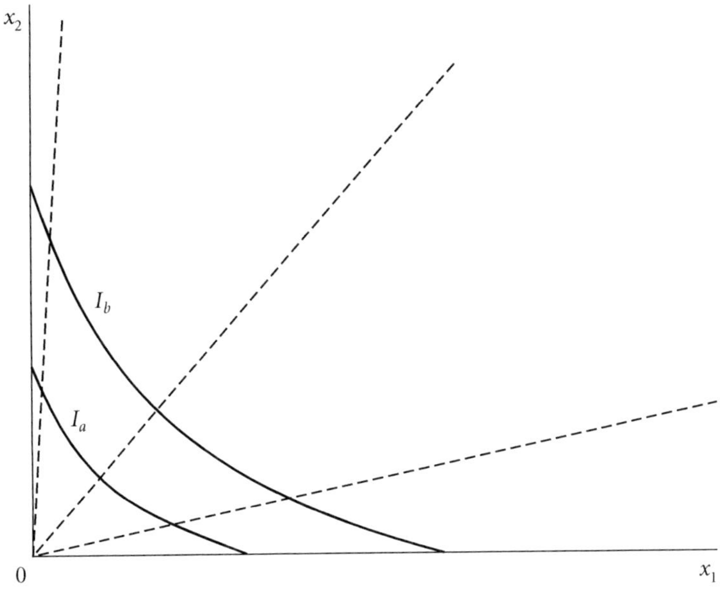

Figure 3.10 Indifference curves of a homothetic utility function

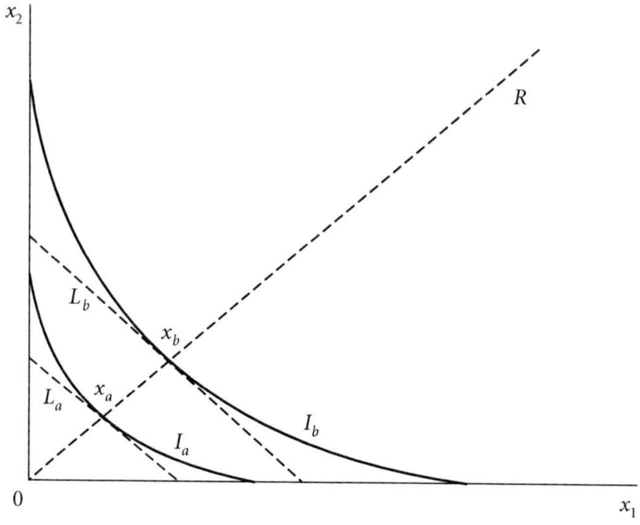

Figure 3.11 Constancy of the marginal rates of substitution along rays, when the utility function is homogeneous

curve I_b is twice as far from the origin as indifference curve I_a. If the utility function, u, is homothetic, any outward expansion or inward shrinking of the indifference curve I_a is still an indifference curve of u.

If the utility function, u, is homothetic, then the slopes of its indifference curves or its marginal rates of substitution are constant along rays through the origin, such as the dotted lines in figure 3.10. This point is further illustrated in figure 3.11. The indifference curve I_b is a doubling of indifference curve I_a. That is, the vectors y in I_b are of the form $2\mathbf{x}$, for some vector $\mathbf{x}$ in I_a. The lines L_a and L_b are tangent to I_a and I_b, respectively, at the points where these indifference curves intersect the ray, R, through $\mathbf{0}$. If we double L_a by multiplying each vector in it by 2, we obtain a new straight line, L_b, parallel to L_a and intersecting the ray R at a point, $\mathbf{x}_b$ on I_b. Clearly, L_b is tangent to I_b at $\mathbf{x}_b$. It follows that the slopes of I_a and I_b at the points, $\mathbf{x}_a$ and $\mathbf{x}_b$, respectively, are the same, since these slopes are the same as those of L_a and L_b, respectively.

The same point may be made by applying calculus to a differentiable utility function $u: \mathbb{R}^N_+ \rightarrow \mathbb{R}$. In the next paragraph, I will show that the partial derivatives, $\frac{\partial u(x)}{\partial x_n}$, are constant along rays through the origin if u is homogeneous of degree 1. It follows that if u is homogeneous of degree 1, the marginal rates of substitution,

$$\frac{\dfrac{\partial u(x_1, \ldots, x_N)}{\partial x_n}}{\dfrac{\partial u(x_1, \ldots, x_N)}{\partial x_k}}$$

are constant along rays through the origin. If u is homothetic, some monotone transformation of u is homogeneous of degree 1, and so for that monotone transformation the marginal rates of substitution are constant along rays through the origin. Since monotone transformations do not change indifference curves, the marginal rates of substitution of any homothetic utility function are constant along rays through **0**.

The following string of equations demonstrates the statement that the partial derivatives of u are constant along rays through **0** if u is homogeneous of degree 1. For any positive number t,

$$t\frac{\partial u(\mathbf{y})}{\partial y_n}\bigg|_{y=tx} = \frac{\partial u(t\mathbf{x})}{\partial x_n} = \frac{\partial t u(\mathbf{x})}{\partial x} = t\frac{\partial u(\mathbf{x})}{\partial x_n}, \tag{3.5}$$

where the symbol

$$\frac{\partial u(\mathbf{y})}{\partial y_n}\bigg|_{y=tx}$$

represents the partial derivative of $u(y_1, \ldots, y_N)$ with respect to its nth variable, y_n, at the point $(y_1, \ldots, y_N) = (tx_1, \ldots, tx_N)$. The symbol $\frac{\partial u(t\mathbf{x})}{\partial x_n}$ is the partial derivative of the function $u(tx_1, tx_2, \ldots, tx_N)$ with respect to x_n. By the chain rule for differentiation,

$$\frac{\partial u(t\mathbf{x})}{\partial x_n} = t\frac{\partial u(\mathbf{y})}{\partial y_n}\bigg|_{y=tx},$$

which is the first of equations 3.5. Canceling t from the extreme left and right of each of equations 3.5, we see that

$$\frac{\partial u(\mathbf{y})}{\partial y_n}\bigg|_{y=tx} = \frac{\partial u(\mathbf{x})}{\partial x_n},$$

so that the nth partial derivative of u is constant along the ray through **0** and **x**.

Suppose that the homothetic utility function $u: \mathbb{R}^2_+ \to \mathbb{R}$ is such that the marginal rate of substitution decreases along an indifference curve as

x_1 increases and x_2 decreases, so that the curve gets progressively flatter as you move to the right. If for some positive number K the equation $\text{MRS}(x_1, x_2) = K$ has a solution, then the vectors (x_1, x_2) satisfying this equation belong to a unique ray through the origin. If the marginal rate of substitution is constant along part of an indifference curve, then the vectors $(x_1.x_2)$ satisfying the equation may belong to a set of rays. For instance, if $u(x_1, x_2) = x_1 + x_2$, then every vector in the positive quadrant $\mathbb{R}^2_+$ satisfies the equation $\text{MRS}(x_1, x_2) = 1$, and no vectors satisfy the equation $\text{MRS}(x_1, x_2) = K$, for $K \neq 1$.

Consider an Edgeworth box economy where both consumers have homothetic utility functions such that the marginal rates of substitution decrease along indifference curves as x_1 increases. At a Pareto optimal allocation, the two consumers' allocations must coincide in the box and their marginal rates of substitution must be the same at that allocation. Suppose that the marginal rates of substitution equal some value, K. The points at which the marginal rates of substitution for consumers A and B equal K lie on rays R_A and R_B, respectively, as pictured in figure 3.12. The curves I_A

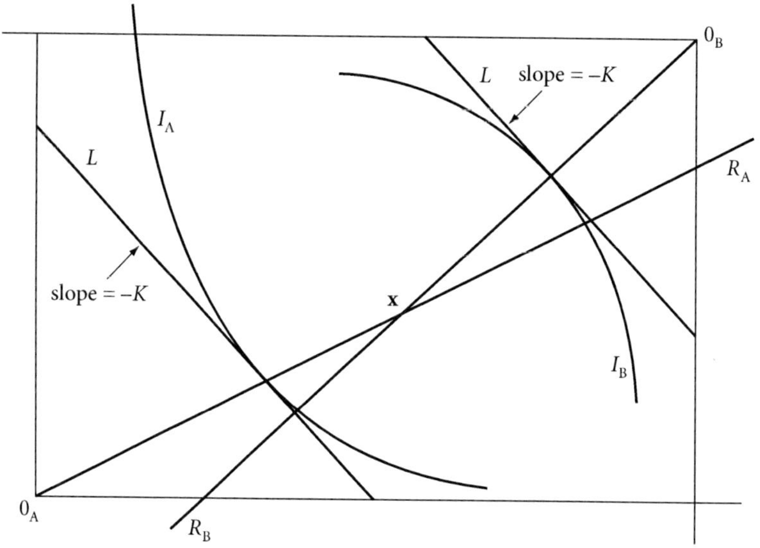

Figure 3.12 Determination of a Pareto optimal allocation when both consumers have homothetic utility functions

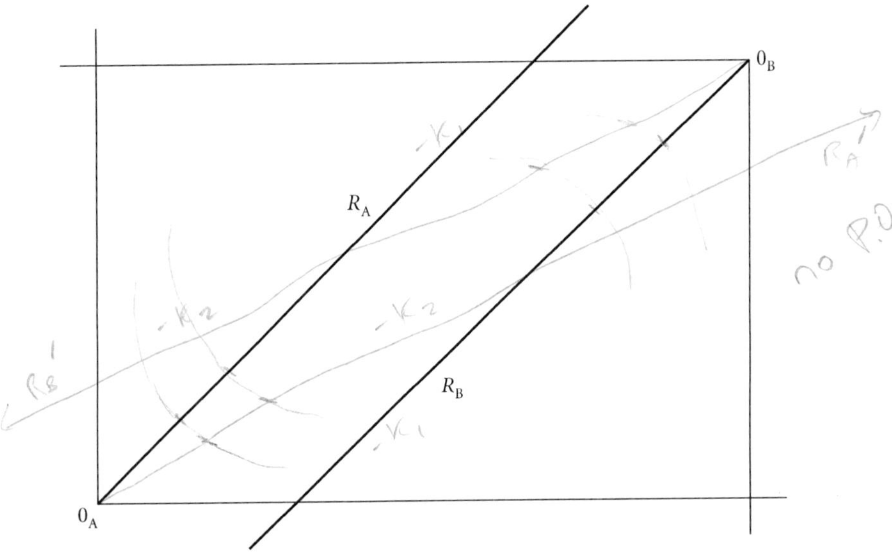

Figure 3.13 Lines of constant marginal rates of substitution when both consumers have the same homothetic utility function

and I_B are indifference curves for consumers A and B, respectively, tangent to the straight lines, L, of slope $-K$. The point $\mathbf{x}$ is the only Pareto optimal allocation with marginal rate of substitution K.

If both consumers have homothetic utility functions one of which is a monotone transformation of the other, then the rays R_A and R_B are parallel, as in figure 3.13. Parallel rays can have a point in common only if they coincide, and if they do, they intersect along a diagonal of the Edgeworth box, as in figure 3.14. In example 3.19, both consumers had the same homothetic utility function, so that we know without having to make any calculations that the set of Pareto optimal allocations equals the diagonal of the Edgeworth box. The set of Pareto optimal allocations could be larger than the diagonal if the indifference curves of the two consumers contained straight line segments. For instance, if the utility function of each consumer is $u(x_1, x_2) = x_1 + x_2$, then the set of Pareto optimal allocations is the whole Edgeworth box.

The approach just explained may be applied to calculate the set of Pareto optimal allocations in Edgeworth box examples such as example 3.20. In

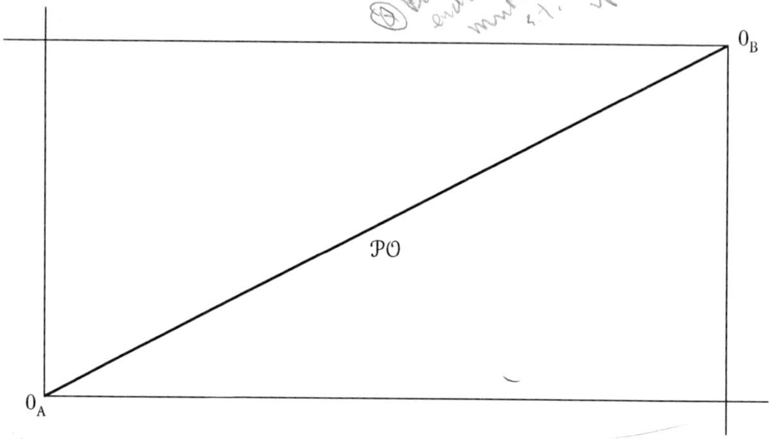

Figure 3.14 Pareto optimal allocations when both consumers have the same homothetic utility function

this example, the equation

$$\left(\frac{\partial u_{\mathrm{A}}(x_1, x_2(x_1))}{\partial x_2}\right)^{-1} \frac{\partial u_{\mathrm{A}}(x_1, x_2(x_1))}{\partial x_1} = K$$

yields

$$x_{\mathrm{A}2} = 2Kx_{\mathrm{A}1}.$$

Similarly, the equation

$$\left(\frac{\partial u_{\mathrm{B}}(x_1, x_2(x_1))}{\partial x_2}\right)^{-1} \frac{\partial u_{\mathrm{B}}(x_1, x_2(x_1))}{\partial x_1} = K$$

yields

$$2x_{B2} = Kx_{\mathrm{B}1}.$$

Feasibility requires that

$$x_{\mathrm{A}1} + x_{\mathrm{B}1} = 1 \text{ and } x_{\mathrm{A}2} + x_{\mathrm{B}2} = 1.$$

Solving these four simultaneous linear equations, we obtain

$$x_{A1} = \frac{2-K}{3K}, \; x_{A2} = \frac{4-2K}{3}$$
$$x_{B1} = \frac{4K-2}{3K}, \; x_{B2} = \frac{2K-1}{3}. \tag{3.6}$$

Since all the consumption allocations must be nonnegative, it follows that

$$\frac{1}{2} \leq K \leq 2.$$

As K varies over this interval, equations 3.6 sweep out the set of Pareto optimal allocations in example 3.20.

The utility functions in examples 3.19 and 3.20 are homothetic functions of a class known as Cobb-Douglas utility functions. A *Cobb-Douglas* utility function has the form

$$u(x_1, \ldots, x_N) = x_1^{a_1} x_2^{a_2} \ldots x_N^{a_N},$$

where $a_n > 0$, for all n. Since the natural logarithm function is increasing, the function

$$v(x_1, \ldots, x_N) = \ln(u(x_1, \ldots, x_N)) = a_1 \ln x_1 + \cdots + a_N \ln x_N$$

defines the same preference ordering. The function v is also referred to as a Cobb-Douglas function and is normally easier to use than the exponential form u.

A nondifferentiable but convenient homothetic utility function is the *Leontief* utility function, which has the form

$$u(x_1, \ldots, x_N) = \min(a_1 x_1, \ldots, a_N x_N),$$

where $a_n > 0$, for all n. The indifference curves of such a function appear in figure 3.15. Figure 3.16 depicts the set of Pareto optimal allocations for a particular case of an Edgeworth box economy in which both consumers have Leontief utility functions. The shaded areas are the Pareto optimal allocations. The shape of the set of Pareto optimal allocations depends on the parameters of the utility functions of the two consumers.

Linear functions are another class of simple homothetic utility functions. A *linear* utility function is of the form $u(x_1, \ldots, x_N) = a_1 x_1 + \cdots + a_N x_N$,

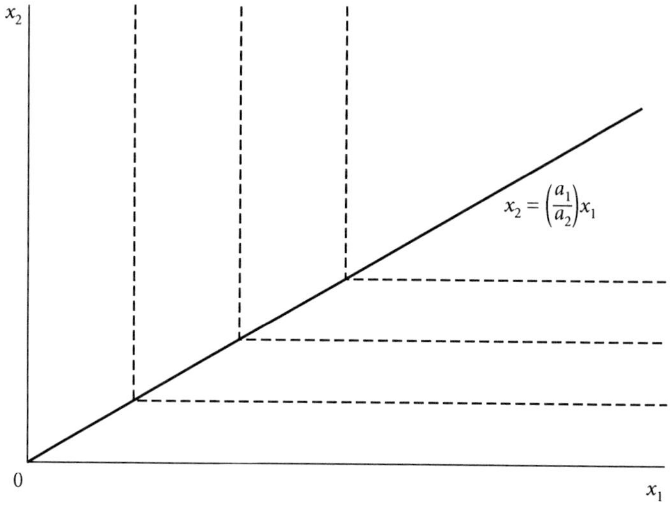

Figure 3.15 Indifference curves of a Leontief utility function

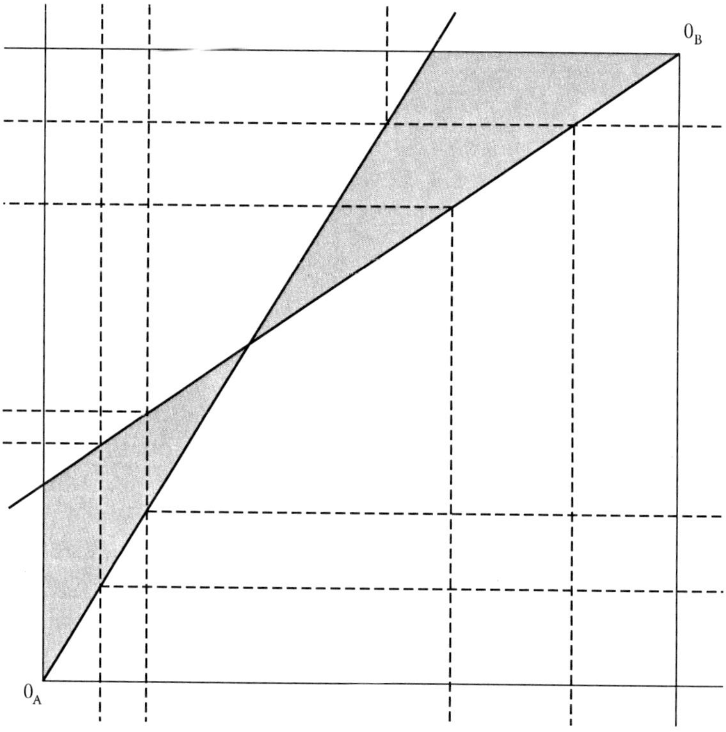

Figure 3.16 The set of Pareto optima when both consumers have Leontief utility functions

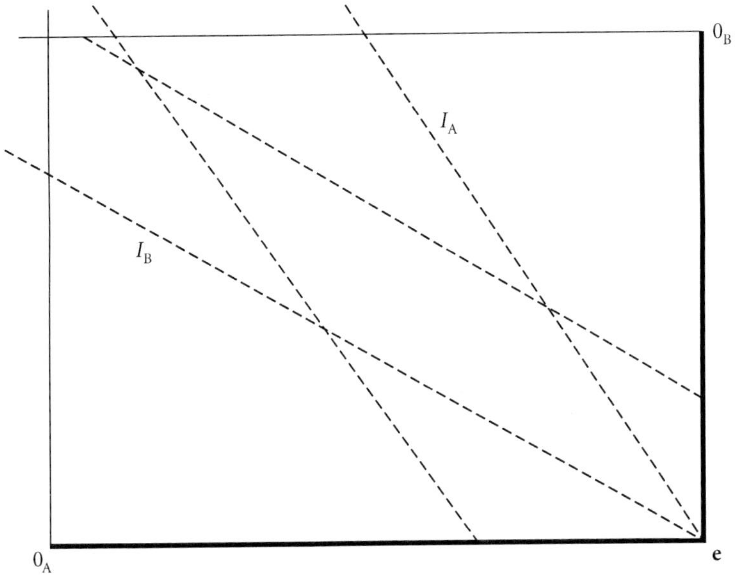

Figure 3.17 Pareto optimal allocations with linear utilities when consumer A has a greater relative preference for commodity 1

where a_n is a nonnegative number, for all n. Consider an Edgeworth box economy with utility functions and endowments

$$u_A(x_1, x_2) = a_{A1}x_1 + a_{A2}x_2, \mathbf{e}_A = (1, 0),$$
$$u_B(x_1, x_2) = a_{B1}x_1 + a_{B2}x_2, \text{ and } \mathbf{e}_B = (0, 1),$$

where $a_{A1} > 0$, $a_{A2} > 0$, $a_{B1} > 0$, and $a_{B2} > 0$. Figure 3.17 shows the Pareto optimal allocations for the case $a_{A1}/a_{A2} > a_{B1}/a_{B2}$. The parallel indifference curves of consumer A and B are the dashed lines labeled I_A and I_B, respectively. The set of Pareto optimal allocations consists of the heavy line segments $\mathbf{0}_A\mathbf{e}$ and $\mathbf{e0}_B$, where $\mathbf{e}$ is the initial endowment allocation. In order to see that the Pareto optimal allocations are as shown, fix attention on an indifference curve of one person, say consumer A, and maximize the utility of the other consumer along that curve. When you do so, you arrive at a point on an edge of the box.

Figure 3.18 illustrates the case $a_{A1}/a_{A2} < a_{B1}/a_{B2}$. The set of Pareto optima consists of the heavy line segments $\mathbf{0}_A\mathbf{E}$ and $\mathbf{E0}_B$.

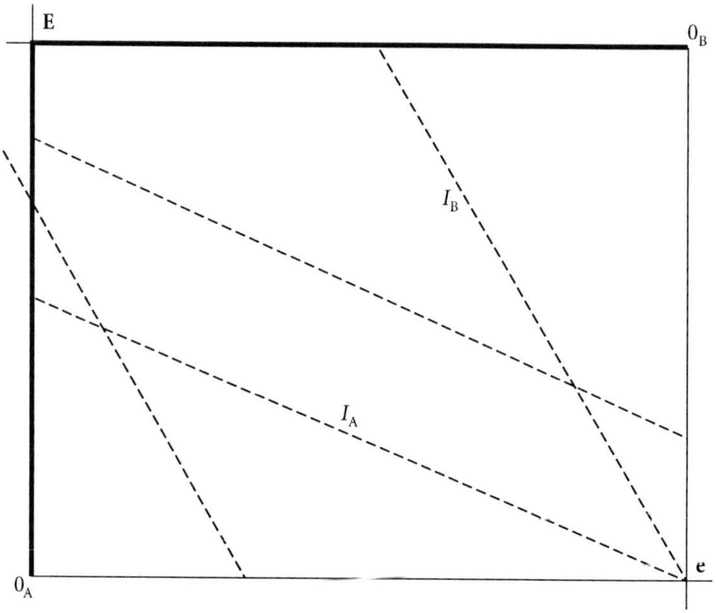

Figure 3.18 Pareto optimal allocations with linear utilities when consumer B has a greater relative preference for commodity 1

3.5 Pareto Optimality and Optimality: Minkowski's Separation Theorem

Under special assumptions, an allocation is Pareto optimal if and only if it is optimal with respect to a social objective function that is a weighted sum of consumers' utilities, $\sum_{i=1}^{I} a_i u_i(\mathbf{x}_i)$, in which the weights, a_i, are non-negative numbers, not all of which are zero. The function $\sum_{i=1}^{I} a_i u_i(\mathbf{x}_i)$ is a social welfare function in that it assigns to each allocation a number indicating aggregate welfare. (A *social welfare function* is a function $W: \mathcal{A} \to \mathbb{R}$, where $\mathcal{A}$ is the set of allocations.) As the welfare weights, $(a_1, \ldots, a_I)$, vary, the corresponding Pareto optimal allocations sweep out the entire utility possibility frontier.

It is easy to see that an allocation that is optimal in this sense is Pareto optimal.

PROPOSITION 3.23 Suppose that $(\overline{\mathbf{x}}, \overline{\mathbf{y}})$ is a feasible allocation for the economy $\mathcal{E} = ((u_i, \mathbf{e}_i)_{i=1}^{I}, (Y_j)_{j=1}^{J})$ that solves the problem

$$\max_{\substack{(x,\,y)\text{ is a feasible}\\ \text{allocation}}} \sum_{i=1}^{I} a_i u_i(\mathbf{x}_i),$$

where $a_i > 0$, for all i. Then, $(\overline{\mathbf{x}}, \overline{\mathbf{y}})$ is Pareto optimal.

Proof. If $(\overline{\mathbf{x}}, \overline{\mathbf{y}})$ is not Pareto optimal, then it is Pareto dominated by a feasible allocation $(\mathbf{x}, \mathbf{y})$. Since the a_i's are all positive, it follows that $\sum_{i=1}^{I} a_i u_i(\mathbf{x}_i) > \sum_{i=1}^{I} a_i u_i(\overline{\mathbf{x}}_i)$, so that the allocation $(\overline{\mathbf{x}}, \overline{\mathbf{y}})$ does not maximize the welfare function $\sum_{i=1}^{I} a_i u_i$. This contradiction proves the proposition. ▪

I now describe mathematics required for the proof of a converse to this proposition. The first concept is the dot product.

DEFINITION 3.24 If $\mathbf{x}$ and $\mathbf{y}$ are N-vectors, then the *dot product* or *inner product* of $\mathbf{x}$ and $\mathbf{y}$ is $\mathbf{x}.\mathbf{y} = \sum_{n=1}^{N} x_n y_n$.

If we were to use matrix notation, then we would consider vectors to be column vectors and could write the dot product of $\mathbf{x}$ and $\mathbf{y}$ as $\mathbf{x}.\mathbf{y} = \mathbf{x}^T\mathbf{y}$, where $\mathbf{x}^T$ is the transpose of $\mathbf{x}$. Clearly if a and b are numbers, $\mathbf{x}.(a\mathbf{y} + b\mathbf{z}) = a\mathbf{x}.\mathbf{y} + b\mathbf{x}.\mathbf{z} = (a\mathbf{y} + b\mathbf{z}).\mathbf{x}$. The dot product has a geometric interpretation. It is not hard to show that the cosine of the angle between the vectors $\mathbf{x}$ and $\mathbf{y}$ equals $\frac{\mathbf{x}.\mathbf{y}}{\|\mathbf{x}\|\,\|\mathbf{y}\|}$, where $\|\mathbf{x}\| = \sqrt{\mathbf{x}.\mathbf{x}} = \sqrt{x_1^2 + \cdots + x_N^2}$ is the length of $\mathbf{x}$. Since $\mathbf{x}$ and $\mathbf{y}$ are perpendicular if and only if the cosine of the angle between them is zero, it follows that $\mathbf{x}$ and $\mathbf{y}$ are perpendicular or orthogonal if and only if $\mathbf{x}.\mathbf{y} = 0$. Fix an N-vector $\mathbf{q}$ and consider the function $f(\mathbf{x}) = \mathbf{q}.\mathbf{x}$, which assigns the number $\mathbf{q}.\mathbf{x}$ to the N-vector $\mathbf{x}$. If $\mathbf{q}.\mathbf{x} = \mathbf{q}.\mathbf{y}$, then $\mathbf{q}.(\mathbf{x} - \mathbf{y}) = 0$, so that $\mathbf{q}$ is orthogonal to the vector $\mathbf{x} - \mathbf{y}$. If r is a number, then a level set, $\{\mathbf{x} \mid \mathbf{q}.\mathbf{x} = r\}$, of the function f is a flat set of vectors and is called a *hyperplane.* It is orthogonal to $\mathbf{q}$ in the sense that $\{\mathbf{x} \mid \mathbf{q}.\mathbf{x} = r\} = \{\mathbf{x} \mid \mathbf{q}.\mathbf{x} = 0\} + \overline{\mathbf{x}}$, where $\overline{\mathbf{x}}$ is any vector such that $\mathbf{q}.\overline{\mathbf{x}} = r$. If $q_n \neq 0$, then the hyperplane $\{\mathbf{x} \mid \mathbf{q}.\mathbf{x} = r\}$ intersects the nth coordinate axis at the point where the nth coordinate equals $\frac{r}{q_n}$. The vectors of the form $t\mathbf{q}$, where t is a number, form a line through the origin, and as t increases, the point $t\mathbf{q}$ moves along this line in the direction from 0 to $\mathbf{q}$. This line intersects the hyperplane $\{\mathbf{x} \mid \mathbf{q}.\mathbf{x} = r\}$ at the point $\frac{r}{\mathbf{q}.\mathbf{q}}\mathbf{q}$, so that as r increases, the hyperplane intersects the ray at a point that moves along the ray in the direction from 0 to $\mathbf{q}$. The hyperplane $\{\mathbf{x} \mid \mathbf{p}.\mathbf{x} = r\}$ is the boundary between

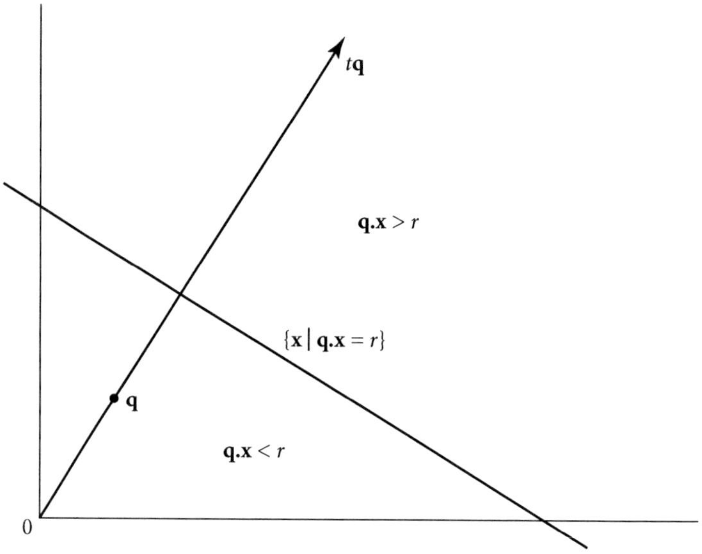

Figure 3.19 A level curve for the dot product function

two halves of $\mathbb{R}^N$, one where $\mathbf{p}.\mathbf{x} > r$ and one where $\mathbf{p}.\mathbf{x} < r$. If $N = 2$, the hyperplane is itself a line. Figure 3.19 shows this line and the ray through $\mathbf{q}$.

Suppose that B is a set of N-vectors and that b is a vector in B that solves the problem

$$\max_{x \in B} \mathbf{q}.\mathbf{x}.$$

Then the hyperplane $\{\mathbf{x} \mid \mathbf{q}.\mathbf{x} = \mathbf{q}.\mathbf{b}\}$ is tangent to B at the point $\mathbf{b}$ and is the hyperplane orthogonal to $\mathbf{q}$ and touching B that is furthest in the direction from $\mathbf{0}$ to $\mathbf{q}$. Figure 3.20 illustrates the relation between $\mathbf{q}$, $\mathbf{b}$, and B when $N = 2$.

The welfare function $\mathrm{W}(\mathbf{x}, \mathbf{y}) = \sum_{i=1}^{I} a_i u_i(\mathbf{x}_i)$, where $(\mathbf{x}, \mathbf{y})$ is an allocation, may be viewed as the composition of two functions, namely $u: \mathcal{A} \to \mathbb{R}^I$, defined as $u(\mathbf{x}, \mathbf{y}) = (u_1(\mathbf{x}_1), \ldots, u_I(\mathbf{x}_I))$, followed by $f: \mathbb{R}^I \to \mathbb{R}$, defined as $f(\mathbf{v}) = \mathbf{a}.\mathbf{v} = \sum_{i=1}^{I} a_i v_i$, where $\mathcal{A}$ is the set of allocations. That is, $\mathrm{W}(\mathbf{x}, \mathbf{y}) = f(u(\mathbf{x}, \mathbf{y}))$. Let V be the image of the feasible allocations under the mapping u. That is, $V = \{u(\mathbf{x}, \mathbf{y}) \mid (\mathbf{x}, \mathbf{y}) \text{ is a feasible allocation}\}$. I will show that the allocation $(\overline{\mathbf{x}}, \overline{\mathbf{y}})$ solves the problem.

$$\max_{\substack{(x,\, y) \text{ is a feasible} \\ \text{allocation}}} \mathrm{W}(\mathbf{x}, \mathbf{y}),$$

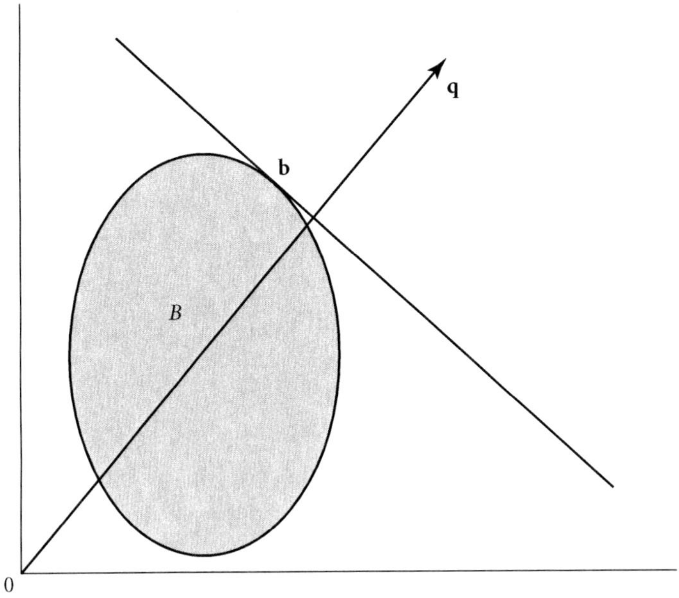

Figure 3.20 Maximization of the dot product over a set

if and only if the I-vector $\overline{\mathbf{v}} = u(\overline{\mathbf{x}}, \overline{\mathbf{y}})$ solves the problem $\max_{\mathbf{v} \in V} f(\mathbf{v})$. If $\mathbf{a}.\overline{\mathbf{v}} = f(\overline{\mathbf{v}}) \geq f(\mathbf{v}) = \mathbf{a}.\mathbf{v}$, for all $\mathbf{v} = \mathrm{u}(\mathbf{x}, \mathbf{y})$ in V, then

$$\mathrm{W}(\overline{\mathbf{x}}, \overline{\mathbf{y}}) = f(u(\overline{\mathbf{x}}, \overline{\mathbf{y}})) = f(\overline{\mathbf{v}}) \geq f(\mathbf{v}) = f(u(\mathbf{x}, \mathbf{y})) = \mathrm{W}(\mathbf{x}, \mathbf{y}),$$

for any feasible allocation $(\mathbf{x}, \mathbf{y})$. Similarly if $\mathrm{W}(\overline{\mathbf{x}}, \overline{\mathbf{y}}) \geq \mathrm{W}(\mathbf{x}, \mathbf{y})$, for all feasible allocations $(\mathbf{x}, \mathbf{y})$, then, for any $\mathbf{v} = \mathrm{u}(\mathbf{x}, \mathbf{y})$ in V,

$$f(\overline{\mathbf{v}}) = f(u(\overline{\mathbf{x}}, \overline{\mathbf{y}})) = \mathrm{W}(\overline{\mathbf{x}}, \overline{\mathbf{y}}) \geq \mathrm{W}(\mathbf{x}, \mathbf{y}) = f(u(\mathbf{x}, \mathbf{y})) = f(\mathbf{v}).$$

Because $\overline{\mathbf{v}}$ solves the problem $\max_{\mathbf{v} \in V} f(\mathbf{v})$, it follows that the hyperplane in $\mathbb{R}^I$, $\{\mathbf{v} \mid \mathbf{a}.\mathbf{v} = \mathbf{a}.\overline{\mathbf{v}}\}$, is tangent to V at $\overline{\mathbf{v}}$.

The utility possibility set $\mathcal{U}$ is simply V together with every point in $\mathbb{R}^I$ dominated by points in V in the sense of vector inequality. Therefore if $(\overline{\mathbf{x}}, \overline{\mathbf{y}})$ is the feasible allocation that maximizes $\mathrm{W}(\mathbf{x}, \mathbf{y})$, then $\mathcal{U}$ is tangent to the hyperplane $\{\mathbf{v} \mid \mathbf{a}.\mathbf{v} = \mathbf{a}.\overline{\mathbf{v}}\}$ at $\overline{\mathbf{v}} = u(\overline{\mathbf{x}}, \overline{\mathbf{y}})$.

The geometry of the situation may be visualized in the Edgeworth box model as in figure 3.21. It may be seen from this figure that the vector $\overline{\mathbf{v}}$ in the utility possibility set $\mathcal{U}$ maximizes the function $a_1 v_1 + a_2 v_2$ over the set of possible utility vectors, $\mathbf{v} = (v_1, v_2)$. The vector $\overline{\mathbf{v}}$ corresponds

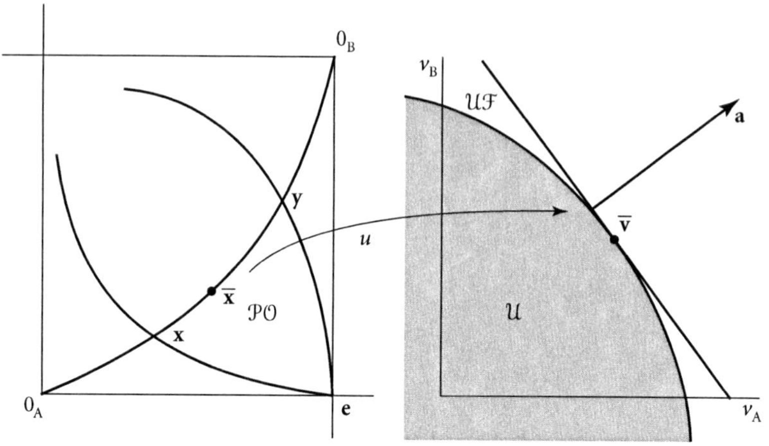

Figure 3.21 Dot product maximization over a utility possibility set

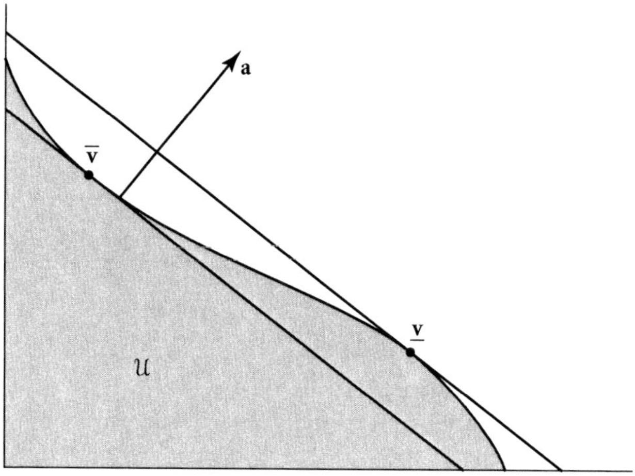

Figure 3.22 Dot product maximization over a utility possibility set that does not bulge outward

to the feasible allocation $\overline{\mathbf{x}}$ in the sense that $u_A(\overline{\mathbf{x}}_A) = \overline{\mathbf{v}}_A$ and $u_B(\overline{\mathbf{x}}_B) = \overline{\mathbf{v}}_B$. The allocation $\overline{\mathbf{x}}$ maximizes the social welfare function $a_A u_A(\mathbf{x}_A) + a_B u_B(\mathbf{x}_B)$ over feasible allocations $\mathbf{x} = (\mathbf{x}_A, \mathbf{x}_B)$. Figure 3.21 illustrates a possible approach to proving a converse of proposition 3.23.

The assertion of this converse may be false if the utility possibility set $\mathcal{U}$ does not bulge outward, as is illustrated in figure 3.22. There are points

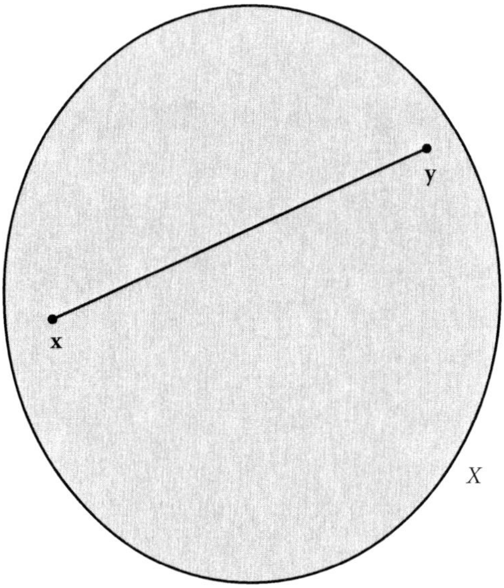

Figure 3.23 A convex set

in the set $\mathcal{U}$ above any line through the point $\overline{\mathbf{v}}$ and perpendicular to a vector **a**. For the particular vector **a** shown in the diagram, the point $\underline{\mathbf{v}}$, not $\overline{\mathbf{v}}$, maximizes the function $\mathbf{a}.\mathbf{v}$ as $\mathbf{v}$ varies over $\mathcal{U}$. We need to make assumptions that guarantee that $\mathcal{U}$ does not have any coves, as the set $\mathcal{U}$ in figure 3.22 does. The absence of coves and holes is known as *convexity.*

DEFINITION 3.25 A set X of N-vectors is said to be *convex,* if for all $\mathbf{x}$ and $\mathbf{y}$ in X and for all α such that $0 < \alpha < 1$, the vector $\alpha\mathbf{x} + (1 - \alpha)\mathbf{y}$ belongs to X.

Since the vector $\alpha\mathbf{x} + (1 - \alpha)\mathbf{y}$ may be written as $\mathbf{y} + \alpha(\mathbf{x} - \mathbf{y})$, we see that $\alpha\mathbf{x} + (1 - \alpha)\mathbf{y}$ is on the straight line segment between $\mathbf{x}$ and $\mathbf{y}$ and moves from $\mathbf{y}$ toward $\mathbf{x}$ as α increases from 0 to 1. The line segment is illustrated in figure 3.23. The set Y in figure 3.24 is not convex.

The next example shows that the utility possibility set of an economy may not be convex.

EXAMPLE 3.26 There are two consumers, no firms, and one commodity. The endowment of each consumer is 1/2, and the utility function of each is $u_A(x) = u_B(x) = x^2$. The utility possibility frontier is

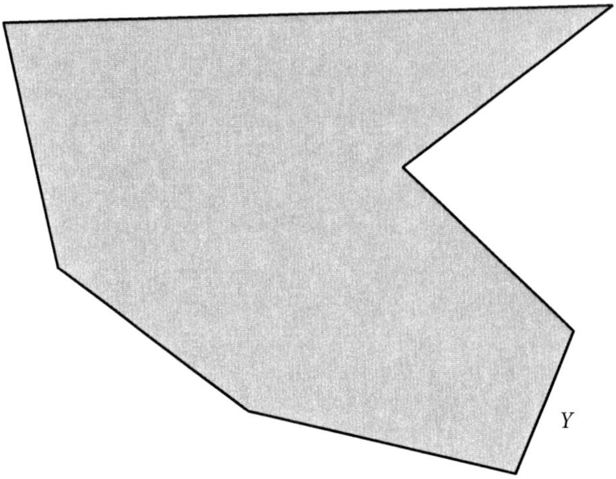

Figure 3.24 A nonconvex set

$$\mathcal{UF} = \{(x_A^2, (1 - x_A)^2) \mid 0 \leq x_A \leq 1\} = \{(v_A, v_B) \mid v_A \geq 0, v_B \geq 0, \text{ and } \sqrt{v_A} + \sqrt{v_B} = 1\}.$$

Figure 3.25 shows this frontier and the corresponding utility possibility set.

The reason the utility possibility set in this example is not convex is that the slope of the consumers' utility function increases as consumption increases. We will see shortly that if the slope decreases, then the utility possibility set is convex. If the slope decreased, the function would be what is known as *concave*. For functions of one or more variables, the precise definition of concavity is as follows.

DEFINITION 3.27 If X is a convex set of N-vectors and $f: X \to \mathbb{R}$, then f is *concave* if

$$f(\alpha\mathbf{x} + (1 - \alpha)\mathbf{y}) \geq \alpha f(\mathbf{x}) + (1 - \alpha) f(\mathbf{y}),$$

for all $\mathbf{x}$ and $\mathbf{y}$ in X and for all α such that $0 \leq \alpha \leq 1$.

Figure 3.26 portrays the graph of a concave function f from the non-negative real numbers to the real numbers. As is illustrated by the shaded area in the figure, a function is concave if and only if all the points on or below the graph of f form a convex set. Clearly an affine function is concave,

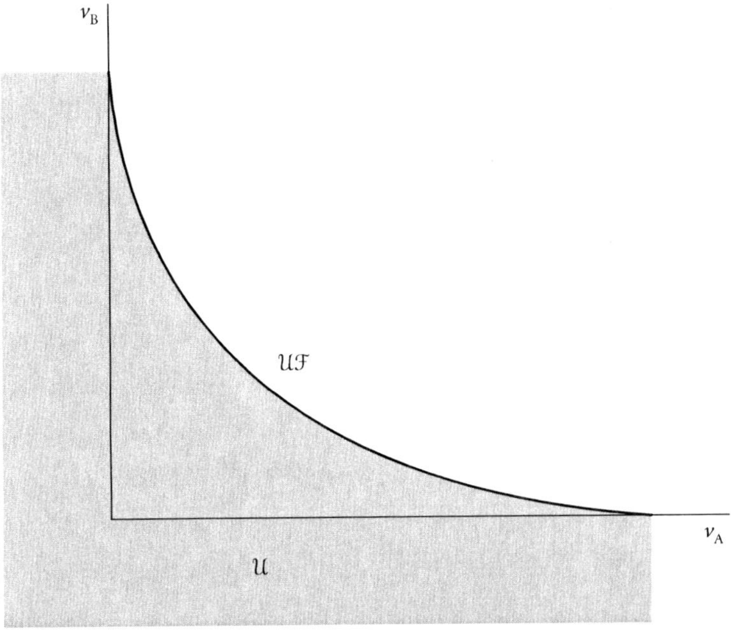

Figure 3.25 A nonconvex utility possibility set

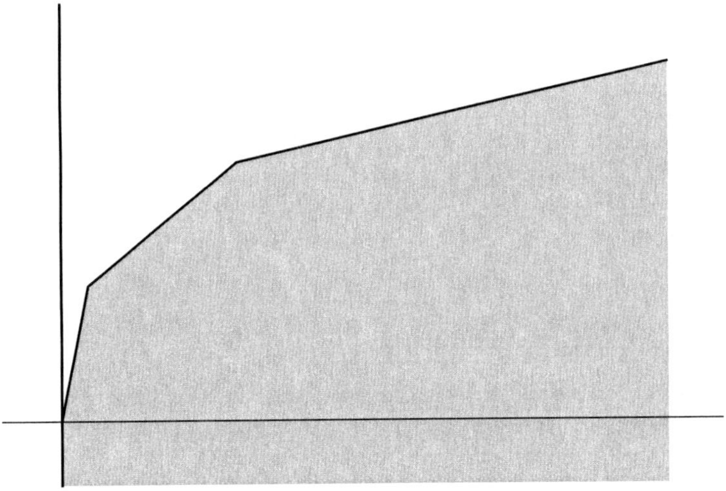

Figure 3.26 The graph of a concave function

where a function f is *affine* if

$$f(\alpha\mathbf{x} + (1-\alpha)\mathbf{y}) = \alpha f(\mathbf{x}) + (1-\alpha) f(\mathbf{y}),$$

for all $\mathbf{x}$ and $\mathbf{y}$ in X and for all α such that $0 \le \alpha \le 1$. The function f is affine if and only if it is of the form $f(\mathbf{x}) = \mathbf{a}.\mathbf{x} + \mathbf{b}$, where $\mathbf{a}$ and $\mathbf{b}$ are N-vectors.

If the function f is twice differentiable, it is possible to characterize its concavity in terms of its second derivative. To do so, I need the concepts of the *interior of a set* and *definiteness of matrices.*

DEFINITION 3.28 If X is a set of N-vectors, the *interior* of X, written as int X, is

$$\{\mathbf{x} \in X \mid \text{ for some } \varepsilon > 0, \mathbf{y} \text{ belongs to } X, \text{ if } \|\mathbf{y} - \mathbf{x}\| < \varepsilon\}.$$

A point $\mathbf{x}$ belongs to the interior of the set X if a ball centered at $\mathbf{x}$ of small enough radius is contained entirely within X. The following examples illustrate the concept. The interior of the closed ball of 2-vectors about zero of radius 1, $\{(x_1, x_2) \in \mathbb{R}^2 \mid \sqrt{x_1^2 + x_2^2} \le 1\}$, is $\{(x_1, x_2) \in \mathbb{R}^2 \mid \sqrt{x_1^2 + x_2^2} < 1\}$. The interior of the closed square of 2-vectors, $\{(x_1, x_2) \in \mathbb{R}^2 \mid -1 \le x_1 \le 1 \text{ and } -1 \le x_2 \le 1\}$, is $\{(x_1, x_2) \in \mathbb{R}^2 \mid -1 < x_1 < 1 \text{ and } -1 < x_2 < 1\}$. In both examples, the sets equal their interiors plus their boundary lines or curves. The set $\{(x_1, x_2) \in \mathbb{R}^2 \mid x_1 + x_2 = 1\}$ has no interior.

DEFINITION 3.29 An $N \times N$ matrix, A, is *positive definite* if $\mathbf{v}^T A\mathbf{v} = \sum_{n=1}^N \sum_{k=1}^N v_n a_{nk} v_k > 0$, for every nonzero N-vector $\mathbf{v}$. The matrix is *positive semidefinite* if $\mathbf{v}^T A\mathbf{v} \ge 0$, for every N-vector $\mathbf{v}$. Similarly, A is *negative definite* if $\mathbf{v}^T A\mathbf{v} < 0$, for all nonzero N-vectors $\mathbf{v}$, and A is *negative semidefinite* if $\mathbf{v}^T A\mathbf{v} \le 0$, for every N-vector $\mathbf{v}$.

The notation $\mathbf{v}^T A\mathbf{v}$ indicates the number obtained when the matrix A is multiplied on the left by the row vector $\mathbf{v}^T$ and on the right by the column vector $\mathbf{v}$.

I will need to use vector and matrix notation in order to describe the first and second derivatives of a function of N variables. Let $f: X \to \mathbb{R}$ be a differentiable function, where X is a subset of $\mathbb{R}^N$ with nonempty interior. Then

$$Df(\mathbf{x}) = \left(\frac{\partial f(\mathbf{x})}{\partial x_1}, \ldots, \frac{\partial f(\mathbf{x})}{\partial x_N}\right)$$

is the vector of first partial derivatives of f with respect to its N variables. It is customary to think of this vector as a row vector. If f is twice differentiable, then

$$D^2 f(\mathbf{x}) = \begin{pmatrix} \frac{\partial^2 f(\mathbf{x})}{\partial x_1 \partial x_1} & \cdots & & \frac{\partial^2 f(\mathbf{x})}{\partial x_1 \partial x_N} \\ \vdots & \frac{\partial^2 f(\mathbf{x})}{\partial x_n \partial x_k} & \cdots & \vdots \\ \vdots & & \ddots & \vdots \\ \frac{\partial^2 f(\mathbf{x})}{\partial x_N \partial x_1} & \cdots & & \frac{\partial^2 f(\mathbf{x})}{\partial x_N \partial x_N} \end{pmatrix}$$

is the $N \times N$ matrix of second partial derivatives of f with respect to its variables. If f has only one variable, so that $N = 1$, then $Df(x) = \frac{df(x)}{dx}$ is the first derivative of f at x, $D^2 f(x) = \frac{d^2 f(x)}{dx^2}$ is the second derivative of f at x, $D^2 f(x)$ is negative definite if $\frac{d^2 f(x)}{dx^2} < 0$, and $D^2 f(x)$ is negative semidefinite if $\frac{d^2 f(x)}{dx^2} \leq 0$.

LEMMA 3.30 If X is a convex set of N-vectors and $f\colon X \to \mathbb{R}$ is twice differentiable, then f is concave if the matrix $D^2 f(\mathbf{x})$ is negative semidefinite, for all $\mathbf{x}$. If f is concave, then $D^2 f(\mathbf{x})$ is negative semidefinite, for all $\mathbf{x}$ in the interior of X.

Proof. Suppose, first of all, that $N = 1$, so that X is a subset of the real numbers. Suppose that x and y are in X and that $y < x$. For t such that $0 \leq t \leq 1$, let

$$g(t) = f(tx + (1-t)y) - (tf(x) + (1-t)f(y)). \tag{3.7}$$

Observe that $g(0) = g(1) = 0$. Assume that $D^2 f(x)$ is negative semidefinite, so that $\frac{d^2 f(x)}{dx^2} \leq 0$. In order to show that f is concave, I must show that $g(t) \geq 0$, for all t between 0 and 1. The proof is by contradiction. Suppose that $g(\alpha) < 0$, for some α between 0 and 1. By the mean value theorem of calculus, there exist $\underline{t}$ and $\overline{t}$ such that $0 < \underline{t} < \alpha < \overline{t} < 1$ and

$$g(\alpha) = g(\alpha) - g(0) = \frac{dg(\underline{t})}{dt}\alpha \text{ and} \tag{3.8}$$

$$-g(\alpha) = g(1) - g(\alpha) = \frac{dg(\overline{t})}{dt}(1-\alpha). \tag{3.9}$$

Since $\alpha > 0$, equation 3.8 implies that $\frac{dg(\underline{t})}{dt} < 0$, and, since $\alpha < 1$, equation 3.9 implies that $\frac{dg(\bar{t})}{dt} > 0$. Another application of the mean value theorem implies that $\frac{d^2g(t)}{dt^2} > 0$, for some t such that $\underline{t} < t < \bar{t}$. However, $\frac{d^2g(t)}{dt^2} = \frac{d^2f(tx+(1-t)y)}{dz^2}(x-y)^2 \le 0$, where z is the variable of the function f. This contradiction proves that $g(t) \ge 0$, for all t between 0 and 1, and hence that f is concave.

I continue to assume that $N = 1$ and show that if f is concave, then $D^2 f(x)$ is negative semidefinite, for all x in the interior of X. Suppose to the contrary that $\frac{d^2f(a)}{dx^2} > 0$, for some a in the interior of X. Because f is twice differentiable, Taylor's theorem implies that

$$f(x) = f(a) + \frac{df(a)}{dx}(x-a) + \frac{d^2f(a)}{dx^2}(x-a)^2 + o[(x-a)^2],$$

where o indicates a function with the property that $\lim_{y\to 0} \frac{o(y)}{y} = 0$. Let

$$g(x) = f(a) + \frac{df(a)}{dx}(x-a) + \frac{d^2f(a)}{dx^2}(x-a)^2.$$

Then,

$$\frac{g(a-\varepsilon)+g(a+\varepsilon)}{2} - g(a) = \frac{d^2f(a)}{dx^2}\varepsilon^2 > 0,$$

and $a-\varepsilon$ and $a+\varepsilon$ belong to X if ε is sufficiently small, since a belongs to the interior of X. Since

$$\frac{f(a-\varepsilon)+f(a+\varepsilon)}{2} - f(a) - \left[\frac{g(a-\varepsilon)+g(a+\varepsilon)}{2} - g(a)\right] = o(\varepsilon^2),$$

it follows that

$$\frac{f(a-\varepsilon)+f(a+\varepsilon)}{2} - f(a) > 0,$$

if ε is sufficiently small. Since this inequality contradicts the concavity of f, it must be that $\frac{d^2f(a)}{dx^2} \le 0$, for all a in the interior of X.

Suppose now that $N > 1$. Assume that $D^2 f(\mathbf{x})$ is negative semidefinite, for all $\mathbf{x}$. Let $\mathbf{x}$ and $\mathbf{y}$ belong to X, and for each t such that $0 \le t \le 1$, let $g(t)$ be defined by equation 3.7. In order to show that f is concave, I must show that $g(t) \ge 0$, for all t between 0 and 1. The function g is a twice-differentiable function of a single variable, and

$$\frac{d^2g(t)}{dt^2} = (\mathbf{x}-\mathbf{y})^T D^2 f(t\mathbf{x}+(1-t)\mathbf{y})(\mathbf{x}-\mathbf{y}) \le 0,$$

where the inequality follows because the matrix $D^2 f(t\mathbf{x} + (1-t)\mathbf{y})$ is negative semidefinite. Therefore, by the proof just given for the case $N = 1$, $g(t) \geq 0$, for all t between 0 and 1, and hence f is concave.

Assume that f is concave. I must show that $D^2 f(\mathbf{x})$ is negative semidefinite, for all $\mathbf{x}$ in the interior of X. If $D^2 f(\mathbf{x})$ is not negative semidefinite for some $\mathbf{x}$ in the interior of X, then there exists an N-vector $\mathbf{v}$ such that $\mathbf{v}^T D^2 f(x)\mathbf{v} > 0$. If ε is a sufficiently small positive number, then $\mathbf{a} - \varepsilon\mathbf{v}$ and $\mathbf{a} + \varepsilon\mathbf{v}$ both belong to X, since $\mathbf{a}$ is in the interior of X. Let $g(t) = f(\mathbf{a} + t\mathbf{v})$. Since g is twice differentiable and is concave, the lemma for the case $N = 1$ implies that $0 \geq \frac{d^2 g(0)}{dt^2} = \mathbf{v}^T D^2 f(\mathbf{a})\mathbf{v}$, contrary to hypothesis. This contradiction proves that $D^2 f(\mathbf{x})$ is negative semidefinite, for all $\mathbf{x}$ in the interior of X. ■

It is now possible to state a converse to proposition 3.23.

THEOREM 3.31 Assume that the economy $\mathcal{E} = ((u_i, \mathbf{e}_i)_{i=1}^{I}, (Y_j)_{j=1}^{J})$ is such that

1. for all j, Y_j is convex, and
2. for all i, $u_i\colon \mathbb{R}_+^N \to \mathbb{R}$ is concave.

If $(\overline{\mathbf{x}}, \overline{\mathbf{y}})$ is a Pareto optimal allocation, then there exists an I-vector, $\mathbf{a}$, such that $\mathbf{a} > 0$ and $(\overline{\mathbf{x}}, \overline{\mathbf{y}})$ solves the problem

$$\max_{\substack{(x,\, y) \text{ is a feasible} \\ \text{allocation}}} \sum_{i=1}^{I} a_i u_i(\mathbf{x}_i).$$

Observe that some of the components of the vector $\mathbf{a}$ in theorem 3.31 may be zero, so that the theorem is not, strictly speaking, a converse to proposition 3.23, where all the components of $\mathbf{a}$ are positive.

If the vector $\mathbf{a}$ satisfies the conditions of theorem 3.31, then so does the vector $t\mathbf{a}$, for any positive number t. Since $\mathbf{a} > 0$, $\sum_{i=1}^{I} a_i > 0$, so that the vector $(1/\sum_{i=1}^{I} a_i)\mathbf{a}$ satisfies the conditions of the theorem. Therefore we may assume that $\sum_{i=1}^{I} a_i = 1$, in which case the welfare function $\sum_{i=1}^{I} a_i u_i(x_i)$ is a weighted average of the utilities of the consumers. Thus the theorem asserts that any Pareto optimal allocation maximizes some weighted average of the consumers' utilities.

The assumption that the input-output possibility sets Y_j are convex intuitively means that returns to scale are nowhere increasing and that distinct production processes do not interfere with each other. Suppose that $\underline{\mathbf{y}}$ and $\overline{\mathbf{y}}$ belong to Y_j and that α is a number between 0 and 1. If the returns to scale are not increasing, then it should be possible to scale back production from $\underline{\mathbf{y}}$ to $\alpha\underline{\mathbf{y}}$, that is, to shrink all inputs and outputs by the factor α. Therefore, $\alpha\underline{\mathbf{y}}$ should belong to Y_j. Similarly, $(1-\alpha)\overline{\mathbf{y}}$ belongs to Y_j. If we think of $\alpha\underline{\mathbf{y}}$ and $(1-\alpha)\overline{\mathbf{y}}$ as the outcomes of separate production processes and if processes do not interfere with each other, then $\alpha\underline{\mathbf{y}} + (1-\alpha)\overline{\mathbf{y}}$ is producible and so belongs to Y_j.

The assumption that the utility functions are concave can be interpreted in terms of choices among risky alternatives, a topic presented in section 7.3.

The statement of theorem 3.31 should not be thought of as an assertion about economic reality but about economic models. It would be nearly impossible to measure consumers' preferences, to verify that they could be represented by concave utility functions, and to check that an allocation thought to be Pareto optimal maximized a weighted sum of these functions. Theorem 3.31 is important because it is a convenient tool for analyzing Pareto optimal and equilibrium allocations. It, in effect, reduces an economy with many consumers to one with a single consumer who has initial endowment $\mathbf{e} = \sum_{i=1}^{I} \mathbf{e}_i$ and utility function

$$U(\mathbf{x}) = \max_{\mathbf{x}_i \in \mathbb{R}^N_+,\ \text{for } i=1,\ldots,I} \sum_{i-1}^{I} a_i u_i(\mathbf{x}_i)$$

$$\text{s.t.} \quad \sum_{i=1}^{I} \mathbf{x}_i = \mathbf{x}.$$

The proof of theorem 3.31 requires the following assertion.

LEMMA 3.32 Under the assumptions of theorem 3.31, the utility possibility set,

$$\mathcal{U} = \{\mathbf{v} \in \mathbb{R}^I \mid \text{there exists a feasible allocation } (\mathbf{x}, \mathbf{y}) \text{ such that } v_i \le u_i(\mathbf{x}_i), \text{ for all } i\},$$

of $\mathcal{E}$ is convex.

Although the utility possibility set $\mathcal{U}$ is convex, the set $V = \{(u_1(\mathbf{x}_1), \ldots, u_I(\mathbf{x}_I) \mid (\mathbf{x}, \mathbf{y}))$ is a feasible allocation$\}$ may not be convex under the conditions of the lemma. It is for this reason that the utility possibility set is defined to be $\mathcal{U}$ rather than V.

Proof. Let $\underline{\mathbf{v}}$ and $\overline{\mathbf{v}}$ belong to $\mathcal{U}$ and let α be such that $0 \leq \alpha \leq 1$. I must show that $\mathbf{v} = \alpha\underline{v} + (1-\alpha)\overline{v}$ belongs to $\mathcal{U}$. By the definition of $\mathcal{U}$, there exist feasible allocations $(\underline{\mathbf{x}}, \underline{\mathbf{y}})$ and $(\overline{\mathbf{x}}, \overline{\mathbf{y}})$ such that $\underline{\mathrm{v}}_i \leq u_i(\underline{\mathbf{x}}_i)$ and $\overline{\mathrm{v}}_i \leq u_i(\overline{\mathbf{x}}_i)$, for all i. Consider the allocation $(\mathbf{x}, \mathbf{y}) = \alpha(\underline{\mathbf{x}}, \underline{\mathbf{y}}) + (1-\alpha)(\overline{\mathbf{x}}, \overline{\mathbf{y}})$. I show that the allocation $(\mathbf{x}, \mathbf{y})$ is feasible. First of all, $\mathbf{x}_i \geq \mathbf{0}$, for all i, since $\mathbf{x}_i = \alpha\underline{\mathbf{x}}_i + (1-\alpha)\overline{\mathbf{x}}_i$ and $\underline{\mathbf{x}}_i \geq \mathbf{0}$ and $\overline{\mathbf{x}}_i \geq \mathbf{0}$. Also, $\mathbf{y}_j \in y_j$, for all j, because Y_j is a convex set and $\underline{\mathbf{y}}_j$ and $\overline{\mathbf{y}}_j$ both belong to Y_j and $\mathbf{y}_j = \alpha\underline{\mathbf{y}}_j + (1-\alpha)\overline{\mathbf{y}}_j$. In addition,

$$\begin{aligned}
\sum_{i=1}^{I} \mathbf{x}_i &= \alpha \sum_{i=1}^{I} \underline{\mathbf{x}}_i + (1-\alpha) \sum_{i=1}^{I} \overline{\mathbf{x}}_i \\
&\leq \alpha\Big(\sum_i \mathbf{e}_i + \sum_i \underline{\mathbf{y}}_i\Big) + (1-\alpha)\left(\sum_i \mathbf{e}_i + \sum_i \overline{\mathbf{y}}_i\right) \\
&= \sum_i \mathbf{e}_i + \sum_i (\alpha\underline{\mathbf{y}}_i + (1-\alpha)\overline{\mathbf{y}}_i) \\
&= \sum_i \mathbf{e}_i + \sum_j \mathbf{y}_j,
\end{aligned}$$

where the inequality follows from the feasibility of the allocations $(\underline{\mathbf{x}}, \underline{\mathbf{y}})$ and $(\overline{\mathbf{x}}, \overline{\mathbf{y}})$. Finally,

$$\begin{aligned}
v_i = \alpha\underline{\mathrm{v}}_i + (1-)\overline{\mathrm{v}}_i &\leq \alpha u_i(\underline{\mathbf{x}}_i) + (1-\alpha)u_i(\overline{\mathbf{x}}_i) \\
&\leq u_i(\alpha\underline{\mathbf{x}}_i + (1-\alpha)\overline{\mathbf{x}}_i) = u_i(\mathbf{x}_i),
\end{aligned}$$

for all i, where the second inequality follows from the concavity of u_i. Therefore, $\mathbf{v}$ belongs to $\mathcal{U}$. ▪

The proof of theorem 3.31 is an application of Minkowski's separation theorem, a theorem that underlies a great deal of mathematical economics. To state this theorem, I need to define two new concepts.

DEFINITION 3.33 An N-vector $\mathbf{a}$ is said to *separate* the sets of N-vectors, X and Y, if $\mathbf{a} \neq 0$ and $\mathbf{a}.\mathbf{x} \leq \mathbf{a}.\mathbf{y}$, for all $\mathbf{x}$ in X and $\mathbf{y}$ in Y.

In figure 3.27, the vector $\mathbf{a}$ separates X from Y. Notice that if the vector $\mathbf{a}$ separates X from Y, then a straight line, H, perpendicular to $\mathbf{a}$ lies between X and Y. In dimensions higher than 2, if the vector $\mathbf{a}$ separates X from Y, then there is a hyperplane of the form $H = \{\mathbf{x} \in \mathbb{R}^N \mid \mathbf{a}.\mathbf{x} = r\}$ that comes between X and Y, though it may touch one or both sets on their

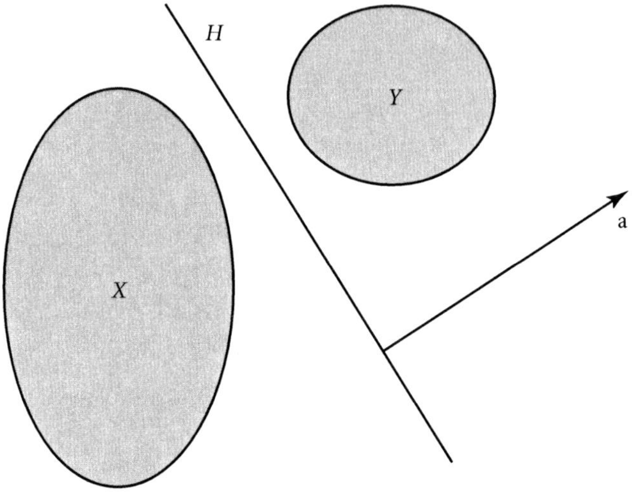

Figure 3.27 Separation of sets

boundaries. Because the set H comes between X and Y, it is said to be a *separating hyperplane.*

Minkowski's separation theorem says that two sets of N-vectors may be separated if they are convex and if one set does not intersect the interior of the other.

MINKOWSKI'S SEPARATION THEOREM 3.34 Let X and Y be convex sets of N-vectors and suppose that int X is not empty and that Y does not intersect int X. Then, there exists a nonzero N-vector, **a**, that separates X from Y.

This theorem is also known as the *theorem of the separating hyperplane.*

The examples that follow illustrate the need for the assumptions made in the theorem. Figure 3.28 shows how the theorem may fail to be valid if X or Y is not convex.

Figure 3.29 shows that one of X and Y should have nonempty interior for Minkowski's separation theorem to apply. Both X and Y are convex. Neither has an interior, so that neither set intersects the interior of the other. The sets clearly cannot be separated.

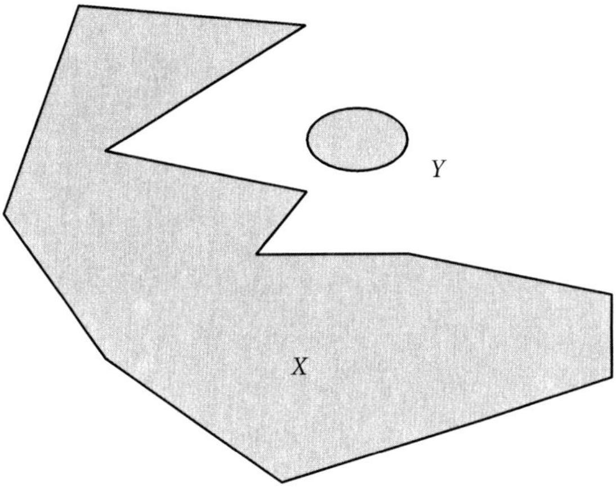

Figure 3.28 Disjoint but inseparable nonconvex sets

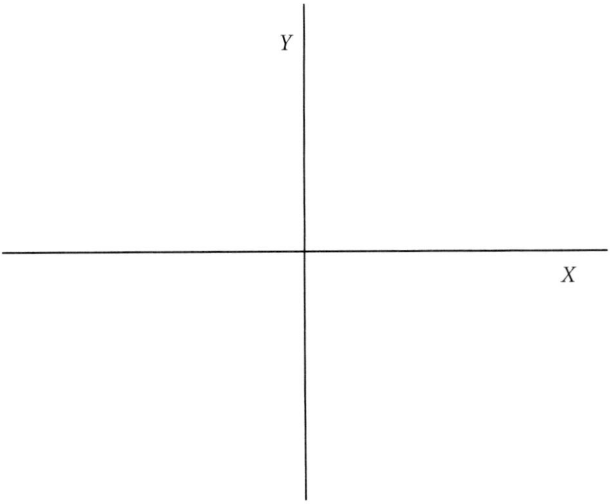

Figure 3.29 Inseparable convex sets with empty interior

Figure 3.30 shows that a stronger separation theorem may exist. (It does.) In the figure, X and Y may be separated, yet the theorem does not apply, because both sets have empty interiors.

I now turn to the proof of theorem 3.31.

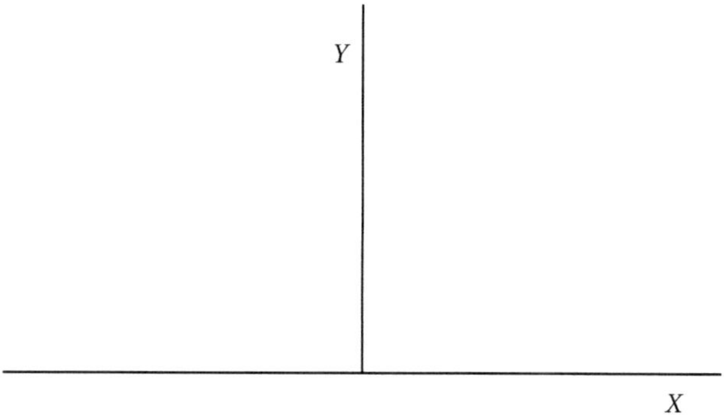

Figure 3.30 Separable convex sets with empty interior

Proof of Theorem 3.31. Let $\mathcal{U}$ be the utility possibility set for the economy, and let

$$\Gamma = \{\mathbf{v} \in \mathbb{R}^I \mid \mathbf{v} \geq \overline{\mathbf{v}}\},$$

where $\overline{\mathbf{v}} = (u_1(\overline{\mathbf{x}}_1), u_2(\overline{\mathbf{x}}_2), \ldots, u_I(\overline{\mathbf{x}}_I))$ and $(\overline{\mathbf{x}}, \overline{\mathbf{y}})$ is the given Pareto optimal allocation.

I show that the only point in the intersection of $\mathcal{U}$ and Γ is the vector $\overline{\mathbf{v}}$. Clearly $\overline{\mathbf{v}}$ belongs to both these sets. Suppose that some vector other than $\overline{\mathbf{v}}$, call it $\mathbf{w}$, belongs to both $\mathcal{U}$ and Γ. Because $\mathbf{w}$ belongs to $\mathcal{U}$, there is a feasible allocation $(\mathbf{x}, \mathbf{y})$ such that $w_i \leq u_i(\mathbf{x}_i)$, for all i. Because $\mathbf{w} \neq \overline{\mathbf{v}}$ and $\mathbf{w}$ belongs to Γ, it follows that $\mathbf{w} > \overline{\mathbf{v}}$. Therefore, $u_i(\mathbf{x}_i) \geq u_i(\overline{\mathbf{x}}_i)$, for all i, and $u_i(\mathbf{x}_i) > u_i(\overline{\mathbf{x}}_i)$, for some i. Hence, the allocation $(\mathbf{x}, \mathbf{y})$ Pareto dominates the allocation $(\overline{\mathbf{x}}, \overline{\mathbf{y}})$, and so $(\overline{\mathbf{x}}, \overline{\mathbf{y}})$ is not Pareto optimal, contrary to hypothesis. This contradiction establishes that the intersection of $\mathcal{U}$ and Γ equals $\overline{\mathbf{v}}$.

I now verify that we may apply Minkowski's separation theorem. Because $\overline{\mathbf{v}}$ is the intersection of $\mathcal{U}$ and Γ, and $\overline{\mathbf{v}}$ does not belong to the interior of Γ, it follows that $\mathcal{U}$ does not intersect the interior of Γ. The interior of Γ is not empty, since it contains any vector $\mathbf{w}$ such that $\mathbf{w} \gg \overline{\mathbf{v}}$. The set $\mathcal{U}$ is convex by the lemma 3.32, and it is obvious that Γ is convex. Hence, all the assumptions of Minkowski's separation theorem are satisfied. Minkowski's theorem implies that there exists a nonzero I-vector, $\mathbf{a}$, such that $\mathbf{a}.\mathbf{w} \geq \mathbf{a}.\mathbf{v}$, for all $\mathbf{w}$ in Γ and all $\mathbf{v}$ in $\mathcal{U}$. The separation argument is illustrated in figure 3.31.

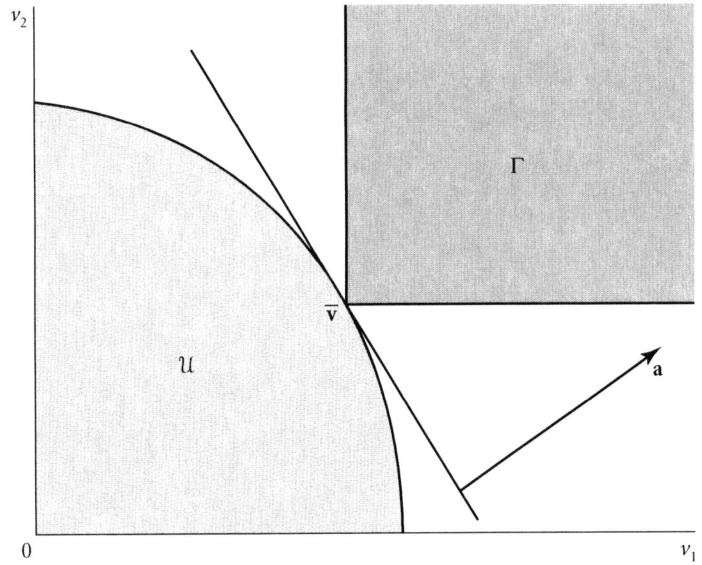

Figure 3.31 The sets separated in the proof that welfare weights exist

I show that $\mathbf{a} > \mathbf{0}$. Since $\mathbf{a} \neq \mathbf{0}$, it is sufficient to prove that $\mathbf{a} \geq \mathbf{0}$. I show that $a_1 \geq 0$. The vector $\overline{\mathbf{v}} + (1, 0, \ldots, 0)$ belongs to Γ, and $\overline{\mathbf{v}}$ belongs to $\mathcal{U}$. Therefore,

$$\mathbf{a}.\overline{\mathbf{v}} + a_1 = \mathbf{a}.(\overline{\mathbf{v}} + (1, 0, \ldots, 0)) \geq \mathbf{a}.\overline{\mathbf{v}},$$

by the separating property of the vector $\mathbf{a}$. Therefore $a_1 \geq 0$. Since the same argument applies to any component of $\mathbf{a}$, it follows that $\mathbf{a} \geq 0$.

I next show that

$$\sum_i a_i u_i(\overline{\mathbf{x}}_i) \geq \sum_i a_i u_i(\mathbf{x}_i),$$

for all feasible allocations $(\mathbf{x}, \mathbf{y})$. The vector $\overline{\mathbf{v}}$ belongs to Γ, and if $\mathbf{v} = (u_1(\mathbf{x}_1), \ldots, u_I(\mathbf{x}_I))$, where $(\mathbf{x}, \mathbf{y})$ is any feasible allocation, then $\mathbf{v}$ belongs to $\mathcal{U}$. Hence, by the separating property of the vector $\mathbf{a}$,

$$\mathbf{a}.\overline{\mathbf{v}} \geq \mathbf{a}.\mathbf{v},$$

which is the same as saying that

$$\sum_i a_i u_i(\overline{\mathbf{x}}_i) \geq \sum_i a_i u_i(\mathbf{x}_i). \quad \blacksquare$$

It is natural to ask how in simple examples to calculate welfare weights $a_1, \ldots, a_I$ associated with a Pareto optimal allocation, $(\overline{\mathbf{x}}, \overline{\mathbf{y}})$, as in theorem 3.31. Assume that there is no production and that the utility functions have positive first derivatives, so that a Pareto optimal allocation satisfies the feasibility constraints with equality. Suppose that the weights $a_1, \ldots, a_I$ are such that the Pareto optimal allocation $\overline{\mathbf{x}}$ solves the problem

$$\max_{\substack{(x,\,y)\text{ is a feasible}\\ \text{allocation}}} \sum_{i=1}^{I} a_i u_i(x_i).$$

This problem may be written as

$$\max_{\mathbf{x}_1 \in \mathbb{R}^N_+, \ldots, \mathbf{x}_{I-1} \in \mathbb{R}^N_+} \left[\sum_{i=1}^{I-1} a_i u_i(\mathbf{x}_i) + a_I u_I(\mathbf{e}_1 + \cdots + \mathbf{e}_I - \mathbf{x}_1 - \cdots - \mathbf{x}_{I-1}) \right]$$

If the u_i are differentiable and $\overline{x}_{i1} > 0$ for all i, then the first-order conditions for this problem imply that

$$a_i \frac{\partial u_i(\overline{x}_{i1}, \ldots, \overline{x}_{iN})}{\partial x_1} = a_I \frac{\partial u_I(\overline{x}_{I1}, \ldots, \overline{x}_{IN})}{\partial x_1},$$

for $i = 1, \ldots, I - 1$, so that

$$a_i = a_I \frac{\dfrac{\partial u_I(\overline{x}_{I1}, \ldots, \overline{x}_{IN})}{\partial x_1}}{\dfrac{\partial u_i(\overline{x}_{i1}, \ldots, \overline{x}_{iN})}{\partial x_1}},$$

for $i = 1, \ldots, I - 1$. If $a_I = 0$, then $a_i = 0$ for all i, which is impossible since $\mathbf{a} \neq 0$. Since $a_I > 0$, we may set a_I equal to any positive number, and these equations determine $a_1, \ldots, a_{I-1}$.

EXAMPLE 3.35 Consider the Edgeworth box economy with $\mathbf{e}_A = (1, 0)$, $\mathbf{e}_B = (0, 1)$, $u_A(x_1, x_2) = 8x_1^{1/8}x_2^{3/8} = u_B(x_1, x_2)$. Because both consumers have the same homothetic utility function, we know that the allocation $(\overline{\mathbf{x}}_A, \overline{\mathbf{x}}_B) = ((1/3, 1/3), (2/3, 2/3))$ is Pareto optimal. Set a_B equal to 1 and let

$$a_A = \frac{\dfrac{\partial u_B(2/3, 2/3)}{\partial \mathbf{x}_1}}{\dfrac{\partial u_A(1/3, 1/3)}{\partial \mathbf{x}_1}} = \frac{\dfrac{(2/3)^{3/8}}{(2/3)^{7/8}}}{\dfrac{(1/3)^{3/8}}{(1/3)^{7/8}}} = \frac{\dfrac{1}{\sqrt{2/3}}}{\dfrac{1}{\sqrt{1/3}}} = \frac{\sqrt{2}}{2}.$$

Then the allocation $(\overline{\mathbf{x}}_A, \overline{\mathbf{x}}_B)$ maximizes the welfare function $\frac{\sqrt{2}}{2}u_A(\mathbf{x}_A) + u_B(\mathbf{x}_B)$ over all feasible allocations.

The significance of theorem 3.31 is that it provides a tool for economic analysis. For instance, it is much easier to analyze the impact of economic change on welfare optima than on competitive equilibria. Equilibrium will not be introduced until the next chapter, but it represents the outcome of economic interaction through competitive markets. It is therefore natural to ask what the impact of a change in some economic parameter, such as a technology, an endowment, or a utility function, would be on equilibrium. Equilibria of economies with more than one consumer, however, can be nonunique and can jump discontinuously and erratically in response to a change in a parameter. An example of such behavior appears in section 4.9. Because of this behavior and the difficulty of calculating equilibria, it is difficult to analyze the impact of parameter changes on equilibria. It may not be appropriate, however, to focus on equilibrium when considering economic change. Any Pareto optimal allocation can be realized as a competitive equilibrium with lump-sum taxes and subsidies, as is explained in section 5.2. There are reasons that it is plausible to assume that utility functions are concave. If we make this assumption, theorem 3.31 implies that any Pareto optimal allocation maximizes a weighted average of consumers' utility functions, and the allocation can also be realized as that of an equilibrium with lump-sum taxes and subsidies. Economists who estimate the impact of parameter changes on economic outcomes are usually interested in the impact on welfare, and that can be measured by a welfare function, such as a weighted average of consumer utilities. If a government had the same welfare objective in mind, it could adjust the taxes and subsidies to keep the state of the economy near its welfare optimum as parameters changed. Hence it may be more appropriate to estimate the impact of change on the welfare optimum than on equilibrium. Under somewhat plausible assumptions, welfare optima, unlike equilibria, are unique and even depend continuously on economic parameters. The assumptions are that utility functions be strictly increasing and strictly concave and that input-output possibility sets be strictly convex. The latter assumption is the least plausible of the three.

DEFINITION 3.36 If X is a set of N-vectors and $f: X \to \mathbb{R}$, then f is said to be *strictly increasing* if $f(\mathbf{x}) > f(\mathbf{y})$ whenever $\mathbf{x} > \mathbf{y}$.

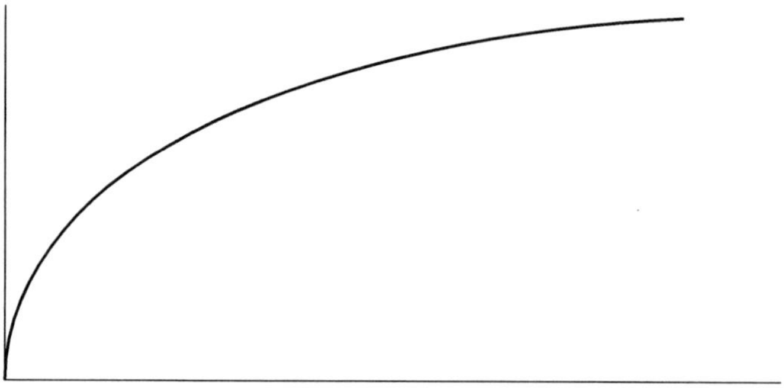

Figure 3.32 The graph of a strictly concave function

A strictly increasing function is increasing, as "increasing" is defined in definition 2.8. The function $u\colon \mathbb{R}^2_+ \to \mathbb{R}$ defined by $u(x_1, x_2) = x_1 + x_2$ is strictly increasing. The function $u\colon \mathbb{R}^2_+ \to \mathbb{R}$ defined by $u(x_1, x_2) - x_1 x_2$ is increasing but not strictly increasing, because it does not increase along the coordinate axes. It equals zero on both axes.

DEFINITION 3.37 If X is a convex set of N-vectors and $f\colon X \to \mathbb{R}$, then f is *strictly concave* if

$$f(\alpha\mathbf{x} + (1-\alpha)\mathbf{y}) > \alpha f(\mathbf{x}) + (1-\alpha) f(\mathbf{y}),$$

for all $\mathbf{x}$ and $\mathbf{y}$ in X such that $\mathbf{x} \neq \mathbf{y}$ and for all α such that $0 < \alpha < 1$.

It is clear from the definition that all strictly concave functions are concave. Figure 3.32 portrays a strictly concave function, and it may be compared with the graph of the concave but not strictly concave function in figure 3.26. If a utility function $u\colon \mathbb{R}^2 \to \mathbb{R}$ is strictly concave and increasing, then every indifference curve for u flattens as you move to the right along it. An analogue of lemma 3.30 applies to strict concavity with a nearly identical proof.

LEMMA 3.38 If X is convex and $f\colon X \to \mathbb{R}$ is twice differentiable, then it is strictly concave if the matrix $D^2 f(\mathbf{x})$ is negative definite, for all $\mathbf{x}$.

Although lemma 3.30 says that negative semidefiniteness of $D^2 f(\mathbf{x})$ is a necessary condition for concavity, the negative definiteness of $D^2 f(\mathbf{x})$ is

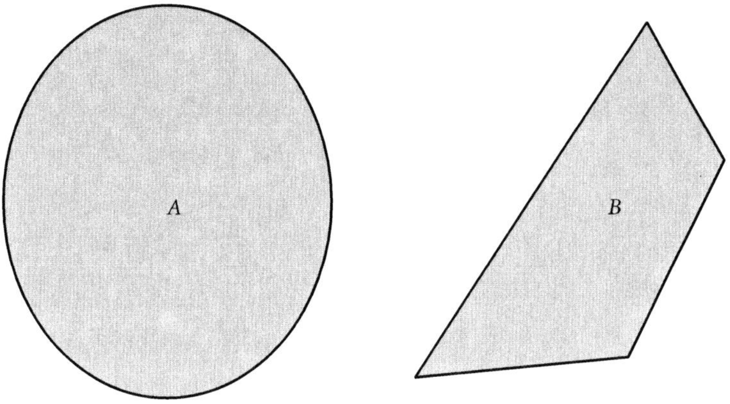

Figure 3.33 A strictly convex set and a convex but not strictly convex set

not a necessary condition for strict concavity. For example, the function $f(x) = -x^4$ is strictly concave, yet $\frac{d^2 f(0)}{dx^2} = 0$.

DEFINITION 3.39 A set Y of N-vectors is *strictly convex* if whenever $\mathbf{x}$ and $\mathbf{y}$ are distinct points in Y and $0 < \alpha < 1$, the point $\alpha\mathbf{x} + (1 - \alpha)\mathbf{y}$ belongs to the interior of Y.

The set A in figure 3.33 is strictly convex, whereas the set B is convex but not strictly convex.

THEOREM 3.40 Assume that the economy $\mathcal{E} = ((u_i, \mathbf{e}_i)_{i=1}^I, (Y_j)_{j=1}^J)$ is such that

1. for all j, Y_j is strictly convex, and
2. for all i, $u_i\colon \mathbb{R}_+^N \to \mathbb{R}$ is strictly concave and strictly increasing.

Then there is at most one allocation that maximizes the welfare function

$$\max_{\substack{(\mathbf{x},\mathbf{y}) \text{ is a feasible} \\ \text{allocation}}} \sum_{i=1}^{I} a_i u_i(\mathbf{x}_i),$$

provided $a_i > 0$, for all i.

Proof. Suppose that the allocations $(\overline{\mathbf{x}}, \overline{\mathbf{y}})$ and $(\underline{\mathbf{x}}, \underline{\mathbf{y}})$ are distinct and both maximize the above welfare function. Because both allocations achieve the welfare maximum, it follows that

$$\sum_{i=1}^{I} a_i u_i(\overline{\mathbf{x}}_i) = \sum_{i=1}^{I} a_i u_i(\underline{\mathbf{x}}_i).$$

Because the input-output possibility sets Y_j are convex, the allocation $(\mathbf{x}, \mathbf{y}) = \frac{1}{2}(\underline{\mathbf{x}}, \underline{\mathbf{y}}) + \frac{1}{2}(\underline{\mathbf{x}}, \underline{\mathbf{y}})$ is feasible. Because u_i is concave, $u_i(\mathbf{x}_i) \geq \frac{1}{2}u_i(\overline{\mathbf{x}}_i) + \frac{1}{2}u_i(\underline{\mathbf{x}}_i)$, for all i. Because $(\overline{\mathbf{x}}, \overline{\mathbf{y}}) \neq (\underline{\mathbf{x}}, \underline{\mathbf{y}})$, $\overline{\mathbf{x}}_i \neq \underline{\mathbf{x}}_i$, for some i, or $\overline{\mathbf{y}}_j \neq \underline{\mathbf{y}}_j$, for some j. If $\overline{\mathbf{x}}_i \neq \underline{\mathbf{x}}_i$, for some i, then since $a_i > 0$, for all i, it follows that

$$\sum_{i=1}^{I} a_i u_i(\mathbf{x}_i) > \frac{1}{2}\sum_{i=1}^{I} a_i u_i(\overline{\mathbf{x}}_i) + \frac{1}{2}\sum_{i=1}^{I} a_i u_i(\underline{\mathbf{x}}_i) = \sum_{i=1}^{I} a_i u_i(\underline{\mathbf{x}}_i),$$

which contradicts the optimality of $(\underline{\mathbf{x}}, \underline{\mathbf{y}})$. If $\overline{\mathbf{y}}_j \neq \underline{\mathbf{y}}_j$, for some j, say for $j = 1$, then $\mathbf{y}_1$ belongs to the interior of Y_1, since Y_1 is strictly convex. It follows that if the positive number ε is sufficiently small, then $\mathbf{y}_1 + \varepsilon I \mathbf{e} \in Y_1$, where $\mathbf{e}$ is the N-vector $(1, 1, \ldots, 1)$. It follows that the allocation $(\mathbf{x}^*, \mathbf{y}^*)$ is feasible, where $\mathbf{x}_i^* = \mathbf{x}_i + \varepsilon\mathbf{e}$, for all i, $\mathbf{y}_1^* = \mathbf{y}_1 + \varepsilon I\mathbf{e}$, and $\mathbf{y}_j^* = \mathbf{y}_j$, for $j \geq 2$. Since the utility functions are strictly increasing, it follows that

$$\sum_{i=1}^{I} a_i u_i(\mathbf{x}_i^*) > \sum_{i=1}^{I} a_i u_i(\mathbf{x}_i) \geq \sum_{i=1}^{I} a_i u_i(\underline{\mathbf{x}}_i),$$

which contradicts the optimality of $(\underline{\mathbf{x}}, \underline{\mathbf{y}})$. This contradiction proves the theorem. ■

Under the assumptions of theorem 3.40, the optimal allocation depends continuously on parameters of the economy, though I do not state or prove this assertion formally.

According to theorem 3.31, every point on the utility possibility frontier maximizes a weighted sum of utilities given some choice of welfare weights. Provided the economy satisfies certain additional assumptions, the converse statement is true. That is, given any nonnegative and nonzero vector of welfare weights, $\mathbf{a} = (a_1, \ldots, a_I)$, a unique point on the utility possibility frontier maximizes the weighted sum of utilities using these weights. The needed assumptions are that the set of feasible allocations be compact and nonempty and that consumers' utility functions be continuous, strictly increasing, and strictly concave.

I sketch the proof that under these assumptions a unique point on the utility possibility frontier corresponds to every vector of welfare weights,

$\mathbf{a} = (a_1, a_2, \ldots, a_I)$, such that $\mathbf{a} > \mathbf{0}$. If the set of feasible allocations is compact and the utility functions are continuous, then proposition 3.14 implies that there is a feasible allocation that maximizes the welfare function $\sum_{i=1}^{I} a_i u_i(\mathbf{x}_i)$ among all feasible allocations. If the utility functions are strictly concave, all allocations $(\mathbf{x}, \mathbf{y})$ that achieve the maximum have the same vector of utility levels, $\mathbf{v} = (u_1(\mathbf{x}_1), \ldots, u_I(\mathbf{x}_I))$. Call this vector of utility levels $\overline{\mathbf{v}}(\mathbf{a})$. We know from proposition 3.23 that a maximizing allocation is Pareto optimal, if $a_i > 0$, for all i. If the utility functions are strictly increasing, a maximizing allocation is Pareto optimal, even if some of the components of $\mathbf{a}$ are zero. Therefore, $\overline{\mathbf{v}}(\mathbf{a})$ belongs to the utility possibility frontier, $\mathcal{UF}$, and $\overline{\mathbf{v}}$ is a function from the set of welfare weights to $\mathcal{UF}$.

We can go further. Clearly,

$$\sum_{i=1}^{I} a_i u_i(\mathbf{x}_i) \geq \sum_{i=1}^{I} a_i u_i(\underline{\mathbf{x}}_i),$$

if and only if

$$\sum_{i=1}^{I} t a_i u_i(\mathbf{x}_i) \geq \sum_{i=1}^{I} t a_i u_i(\underline{\mathbf{x}}_i),$$

for any positive number t. Therefore, the feasible allocation $(\mathbf{x}, \mathbf{y})$ maximizes the welfare function $\sum_{i=1}^{I} a_i u_i(\mathbf{x}_i)$ if and only if it maximizes the welfare function $\sum_{i=1}^{I} t a_i u_i(\mathbf{x}_i)$. That is, $\overline{\mathbf{v}}(\mathbf{a}) = \overline{\mathbf{v}}(t\mathbf{a})$, for all $t > 0$. If $\mathbf{a}$ is any welfare weight vector, let $\underline{\mathbf{a}} = (\sum_{i=1}^{I} a_i)^{-1}\mathbf{a}$. Then, $\overline{\mathbf{v}}(\underline{\mathbf{a}}) = \overline{\mathbf{v}}(\mathbf{a})$, where the sum of the components of $\underline{\mathbf{a}}$ is 1. The set of nonnegative I-vectors with components that sum to 1 is known as the $I - 1$ dimensional simplex and is denoted Δ^{I-1}. Formally,

$$\Delta^{I-1} = \{\mathbf{a} \in \mathbb{R}_+^I \mid \sum_{i=1}^{I} a_i = 1\}$$

The $I - 1$ simplex Δ^{I-1} is the set of relative welfare weights.

Theorem 3.31 says that if $\mathbf{v}$ belongs to the utility possibility frontier $\mathcal{UF}$, then there exists a vector of welfare weights, $\mathbf{a} = (a_1, \ldots, a_I)$, such that $\mathbf{v} = \overline{\mathbf{v}}(\mathbf{a})$. Hence, by the argument of the previous paragraph, for every vector $\mathbf{v}$ in $\mathcal{UF}$, there exists a vector $\mathbf{a}$ in Δ^{I-1} such that $\mathbf{v} = \overline{\mathbf{v}}(\mathbf{a})$. That is, $\overline{\mathbf{v}}$ maps Δ^{I-1} onto $\mathcal{UF}$. The function $\overline{\mathbf{v}}: \Delta^{I-1} \to \mathcal{UF}$ is not necessarily one to one, however. The statement that $\overline{\mathbf{v}}$ is "onto" is a way of saying that by varying the relative welfare weights, we may obtain through welfare maximization every point on the utility possibility frontier. In case the reader does not know what it means for a function to be one to one or onto, I give formal definitions.

DEFINITION 3.41 A function $f: A \to B$ is said to be *one to one* or *injective* if $f(a) \neq f(a')$ whenever $a \neq a'$.

DEFINITION 3.42 A function $f: A \to B$ is said to be *onto* or *surjective* if for every b in B, there is an a in A such that $b = f(a)$.

I now make rigorous the argument just outlined. The first step is to show that if utility functions are strictly increasing, then an allocation that maximizes the welfare function $\sum_{i=1}^{I} a_i u_i(\mathbf{x}_i)$ is Pareto optimal, even if some of the weights a_i are zero. Recall that proposition 3.23 applies to the case in which all these weights are positive.

PROPOSITION 3.43 Suppose that the utility functions of the economy $\mathcal{E} = ((u_i, \mathbf{e}_i)_{i=1}^{I}, (Y_j)_{j=1}^{J})$ are strictly increasing and that the allocation $(\overline{\mathbf{x}}, \overline{\mathbf{y}})$ solves the problem

$$\max \left\{ \sum_{i=1}^{I} a_i u_i(\mathbf{x}_i) \mid (\mathbf{x}, \mathbf{y}) \text{ is a feasible allocation} \right\},$$

where $\mathbf{a} = (a_1, \ldots, a_I) > \mathbf{0}$. Then, for all i, $\overline{\mathbf{x}}_i = \mathbf{0}$, if $a_i = 0$, and the allocation $(\overline{\mathbf{x}}, \overline{\mathbf{y}})$ is Pareto optimal.

The assumption that the utility functions are strictly increasing is plausible, as it means that consumers prefer more to less. The assumption implies that noxious commodities, such as garbage, are excluded from the model as well as commodities such as air that are naturally in such abundance that consumers do not need more of them.

Proof of Proposition 3.43. Suppose that $a_i = 0$, for some i. Without loss of generality, I may assume that $i = 1$. Since $\mathbf{a} > \mathbf{0}$, $a_i > 0$, for some i. Again without loss of generality, I may assume that $a_2 > 0$. I show that $\overline{\mathbf{x}}_1 = \mathbf{0}$. Suppose, to the contrary, that $\overline{\mathbf{x}}_1 \neq \mathbf{0}$. Since $\overline{\mathbf{x}}_1 \geq \mathbf{0}$, it follows that $\overline{\mathbf{x}}_1 > \mathbf{0}$. Define the allocation $(\mathbf{x}, \mathbf{y})$ by the equations $\mathbf{x}_1 = \mathbf{0}$, $\mathbf{x}_2 = \overline{\mathbf{x}}_2 + \overline{\mathbf{x}}_1$, $\mathbf{x}_i = \overline{\mathbf{x}}_i)$, if $i > 2$, and $\mathbf{y} = \overline{\mathbf{y}}$. The allocation $(\mathbf{x}, \mathbf{y})$ is feasible, for it is obtained from the allocation $(\overline{\mathbf{x}}, \overline{\mathbf{y}})$ by giving consumer 2 the consumption allocated to consumer 1. Because u_2 is strictly increasing and $\overline{\mathbf{x}}_1 > \mathbf{0}$, it follows that $u_2(\mathbf{x}_2) = u_2(\overline{\mathbf{x}}_2 + \overline{\mathbf{x}}_1) > u_2(\overline{\mathbf{x}}_2)$. Since $a_1 = 0$ and $a_2 > 0$, it follows that $\sum_{i=1}^{I} a_i u_i(\mathbf{x}_i) > \sum_{i=1}^{I} a_i u_i(\overline{\mathbf{x}}_i)$. Since this inequality contradicts the optimality of $(\overline{\mathbf{x}}, \overline{\mathbf{y}})$, it follows that $\overline{\mathbf{x}}_1 = \mathbf{0}$. This proves that for all i, $\overline{\mathbf{x}}_i = \mathbf{0}$, if $a_i = 0$.

I now show that $(\overline{\mathbf{x}}, \overline{\mathbf{y}})$ is Pareto optimal. Suppose the contrary, so that a feasible allocation, $(\mathbf{x}, \mathbf{y})$, Pareto dominates $(\overline{\mathbf{x}}, \overline{\mathbf{y}})$. By the definition of Pareto dominance, $u_i(\mathbf{x}_i) \geq u_i(\overline{\mathbf{x}}_i)$, for all i. Therefore, $\sum_{i=1}^{I} a_i u_i(\mathbf{x}_i) \geq \sum_{i=1}^{I} a_i u_i(\overline{\mathbf{x}}_i)$. Since the allocation $(\overline{\mathbf{x}}, \overline{\mathbf{y}})$ maximizes the welfare function $\sum_{i=1}^{I} a_i u_i(\mathbf{x}_i)$, it cannot be the case that $\sum_{i=1}^{I} a_i u_i(\mathbf{x}_i) > \sum_{i=1}^{I} a_i u_i(\overline{\mathbf{x}}_i)$, and so $\sum_{i=1}^{I} a_i u_i(\mathbf{x}_i) = \sum_{i=1}^{I} a_i u_i(\overline{\mathbf{x}}_i)$. In addition, $u_i(\mathbf{x}_i) = u_i(\overline{\mathbf{x}}_i)$, for all i such that $a_i > 0$, for otherwise $\sum_{i=1}^{I} a_i u_i(\mathbf{x}_i) > \sum_{i=1}^{I} a_i u_i(\overline{\mathbf{x}}_i)$. Therefore, $a_i = 0$ and, hence, $\overline{\mathbf{x}}_i = \mathbf{0}$, if i is such that $u_i(\mathbf{x}_i) > u_i(\overline{\mathbf{x}}_i)$. Because $(\mathbf{x}, \mathbf{y})$ Pareto dominates $(\overline{\mathbf{x}}, \overline{\mathbf{y}})$, $u_i(\mathbf{x}_i) > u_i(\overline{\mathbf{x}}_i)$, for some i. Without loss of generality, I may assume that $u_1(\mathbf{x}_1) > u_1(\overline{\mathbf{x}}_1)$. Because $u_1(\mathbf{x}_1) > u_1(\overline{\mathbf{x}}_1)$, it follows that $\mathbf{x}_1 > \mathbf{0}$. Since $\mathbf{a} > \mathbf{0}$, there is some i such that $a_i > 0$. Without loss of generality, I may assume that $a_2 > 0$. Define the allocation $(\underline{\mathbf{x}}, \underline{\mathbf{y}})$ by the equations $\underline{\mathbf{x}}_1 = \mathbf{0}$, $\underline{\mathbf{x}}_2 = \mathbf{x}_2 + \mathbf{x}_1$, $\underline{\mathbf{x}}_i = \mathbf{x}_i$, if $i > 2$, and $\underline{\mathbf{y}} = \mathbf{y}$. This allocation is clearly feasible. Since $a_1 = 0$ and $a_2 > 0$ and u_2 is strictly increasing, it follows that $\sum_{i=1}^{I} a_i u_i(\underline{\mathbf{x}}_i) > \sum_{i=1}^{I} a_i u_i(\mathbf{x}_i) = \sum_{i=1}^{I} a_i u_i(\overline{\mathbf{x}}_i)$, which contradicts the optimality of the allocation $(\overline{\mathbf{x}}, \overline{\mathbf{y}})$. This contradiction proves that $(\overline{\mathbf{x}}, \overline{\mathbf{y}})$ is Pareto optimal. ▪

The second step of the argument outlined earlier is to show that if utility functions are strictly concave, then all feasible allocations that maximize the welfare function $\sum_{i=1}^{I} a_i u_i(\mathbf{x}_i)$ have the same vector of utility levels.

PROPOSITION 3.44 Suppose that the economy $\mathcal{E} = ((u_i, \mathbf{e}_i)_{i=1}^{I}, (Y_j)_{j=1}^{J})$ is such that the utility functions u_i are continuous, strictly concave, and strictly increasing, for all i; the production possibility sets Y_j are convex, for all j; and the set of feasible allocations is compact. Suppose also that $\mathbf{a} > \mathbf{0}$, where $\mathbf{a}$ is the vector of welfare weights $(a_1, \ldots, a_I)$. Then, the problem

$$\max_{x, y} \sum_{i=1}^{I} a_i u_i(\mathbf{x}_i) \qquad (3.10)$$

$$\text{s.t.} \quad (\mathbf{x}, \mathbf{y}) \text{ is a feasible allocation}$$

has a solution and all solutions have the same consumption vector $\mathbf{x}$, so that the vector $\overline{\mathbf{v}}(\mathbf{a}) = (u_1(\mathbf{x}_1), \ldots, u_I(\mathbf{x}_I))$ is uniquely defined.

Proof. Because the function $\sum_{i=1}^{I} a_i u_i(\mathbf{x}_i)$ is continuous and the set of feasible allocations is compact, proposition 3.14 implies that there exists an allocation $(\underline{\mathbf{x}}, \underline{\mathbf{y}})$ that solves problem 3.10. I will show that if $(\overline{\mathbf{x}}, \overline{\mathbf{y}})$ is another solution of problem 3.10, then $\overline{\mathbf{x}}_i = \underline{\mathbf{x}}_i$, for all i. Suppose to the contrary that $\overline{\mathbf{x}}_i \neq \underline{\mathbf{x}}_i$, for some i. Because both $(\underline{\mathbf{x}}, \underline{\mathbf{y}})$ and $(\overline{\mathbf{x}}, \overline{\mathbf{y}})$ solve problem 3.10, it follows that

$$W = \sum_{i=1}^{I} a_i u_i(\underline{\mathbf{x}}_i) = \sum_{i=1}^{I} a_i u_i(\overline{\mathbf{x}}_i),$$

where W is the maximum value of the objective function of problem 3.10.

We know from proposition 3.43 that $\overline{\mathbf{x}}_i = \underline{\mathbf{x}}_i = \mathbf{0}$, if i is such that $a_i = 0$. Therefore, $a_i > 0$, if $\overline{\mathbf{x}}_i \neq \underline{\mathbf{x}}_i$.

Let $(\mathbf{x}, \mathbf{y})$ be the allocation defined by the formulas $\mathbf{x}_i = \frac{1}{2}\underline{\mathbf{x}}_i + \frac{1}{2}\overline{\mathbf{x}}_i$, for all i, and $\mathbf{y}_j = \frac{1}{2}\underline{\mathbf{y}}_j + \frac{1}{2}\overline{\mathbf{y}}_j$, for all j. I show that the allocation $(\mathbf{x}, \mathbf{y})$ is feasible. Because the production possibility sets are convex and $\underline{\mathbf{y}}_j$ and $\overline{\mathbf{y}}_j$ both belong to Y_j, it follows that $\mathbf{y}_j$ belongs to Y_j, for all j. Also,

$$\begin{aligned}\sum_{i=1}^{I} \mathbf{x}_i &= \sum_{i=1}^{I} \left(\frac{1}{2}\underline{\mathbf{x}}_i + \frac{1}{2}\overline{\mathbf{x}}_i\right) = \frac{1}{2}\sum_{i=1}^{I} \underline{\mathbf{x}}_i + \frac{1}{2}\sum_{i=1}^{I} \overline{\mathbf{x}}_i \\ &\leq \frac{1}{2}\left(\sum_{i=1}^{I} \mathbf{e}_i + \sum_{j=1}^{J} \underline{\mathbf{y}}_j\right) + \frac{1}{2}\left(\sum_{i=1}^{I} \mathbf{e}_i + \sum_{j=1}^{J} \overline{\mathbf{y}}_j\right) \\ &= \sum_{i=1}^{I} \mathbf{e}_i + \sum_{j=1}^{J} \left(\frac{1}{2}\underline{\mathbf{y}}_j + \frac{1}{2}\overline{\mathbf{y}}_j\right) = \sum_{i=1}^{I} \mathbf{e}_i + \sum_{j=1}^{J} \mathbf{y}_j,\end{aligned}$$

so that all the conditions for feasibility apply.

We now see that

$$\begin{aligned}W &\geq \sum_{i=1}^{I} a_i u_i(\mathbf{x}_i) = \sum_{i=1}^{I} a_i u_i\left(\frac{1}{2}\underline{\mathbf{x}}_i + \frac{1}{2}\overline{\mathbf{x}}_i\right) > \sum_{i=1}^{I} a_i \left(\frac{1}{2}u_i(\underline{\mathbf{x}}_i) + \frac{1}{2}u_i(\overline{\mathbf{x}}_i)\right) \\ &= \frac{1}{2}\sum_{i=1}^{I} a_i u_i(\underline{\mathbf{x}}_i) + \frac{1}{2}\sum_{i=1}^{I} a_i u_i(\overline{\mathbf{x}}_i) = \frac{1}{2}W + \frac{1}{2}W = W, \qquad (3.11)\end{aligned}$$

where the first inequality is valid because $(\mathbf{x}, \mathbf{y})$ is feasible and W is the maximum value of the objective function of problem 3.10. The second inequality is valid because the utility functions u_i are strictly concave and $\overline{\mathbf{x}}_i \neq \underline{\mathbf{x}}_i$, for some i such that $a_i > 0$. Because inequality 3.11 is impossible, $\overline{\mathbf{x}}_i = \underline{\mathbf{x}}_i$, for all i, and hence the consumption allocation $\mathbf{x}$ is uniquely determined in any solution $(\mathbf{x}, \mathbf{y})$ of problem 3.10. ▪

The next proposition summarizes what has been learned so far in this section.

PROPOSITION 3.45 Suppose that the economy $\mathcal{E} = ((u_i, \mathbf{e}_i)_{i=1}^{I}, (Y_j)_{j=1}^{J})$ is such that the utility functions u_i are continuous, strictly increasing, and strictly concave, for all i; the production possibility sets Y_j are convex, for all j; and the set of feasible allocations is compact. Then, there is a surjective function $\overline{\mathbf{v}}: \Delta^{I-1} \to \mathcal{UF}$, defined by the equation

$$\overline{\mathbf{v}}(a) = (u_1(\overline{\mathbf{x}}_1), \ldots, u_I(\overline{\mathbf{x}}_I)),$$

for each $\mathbf{a}$ in Δ^{I-1}, where $(\overline{\mathbf{x}}, \overline{\mathbf{y}})$ is any feasible allocation that solves the problem

$$\max_{(\overline{\mathbf{x}}, \overline{\mathbf{y}})} \sum_{i=1}^{I} a_i u_i(\mathbf{x}_i)$$

$$\text{s.t.} \quad (\overline{\mathbf{x}}, \overline{\mathbf{y}}) \text{ is a feasible allocation.}$$

The following example shows that $\overline{\mathbf{v}}$ may not be injective.

EXAMPLE 3.46 There are two consumers, A and B. There is one commodity and no firm. Each consumer is endowed with one unit of the one commodity, and each has utility function u defined by the formula

$$u(x) = \begin{cases} 2\sqrt{x}, & \text{if } 0 \leq x \leq 1, \\ 1 + \sqrt{x}, & \text{if } x \geq 1. \end{cases}$$

This utility function is strictly concave but has a kink at $x = 1$. Its graph is shown in figure 3.34. The set of Pareto optimal allocations is $\mathcal{PO} = \{(x_A, x_B) \mid 0 \leq x_A \leq 2 \text{ and } x_A + x_B = 2\}$. It is easy to calculate that the utility possibility frontier is

$$\begin{aligned} \mathcal{UF} &= \{(u(x_A), u(x_B)) \mid (x_A, x_B) \text{ is in } \mathcal{PO}\} \\ &= \Bigg\{ (v_A, v_B) \mid v_B = 1 + \sqrt{2 - \frac{v_A^2}{4}}, \text{ if } 0 \leq v_A \leq 2, \\ &\qquad \text{and } v_B = 2\sqrt{2 - (v_A - 1)^2}, \text{ if } 2 \leq v_A \leq 1 + \sqrt{2} \Bigg\}. \end{aligned}$$

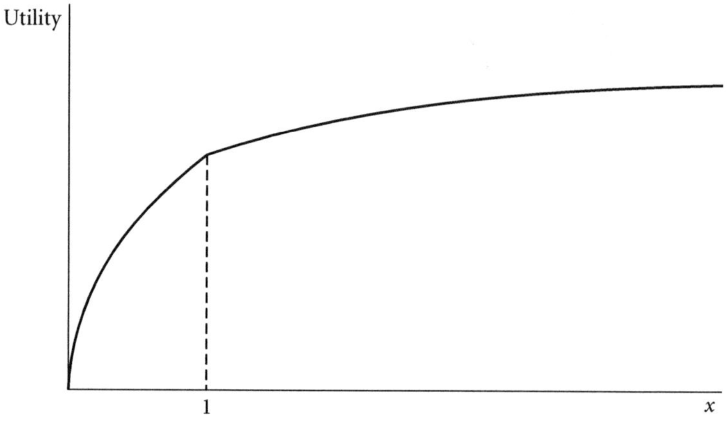

Figure 3.34 The utility function of example 3.46

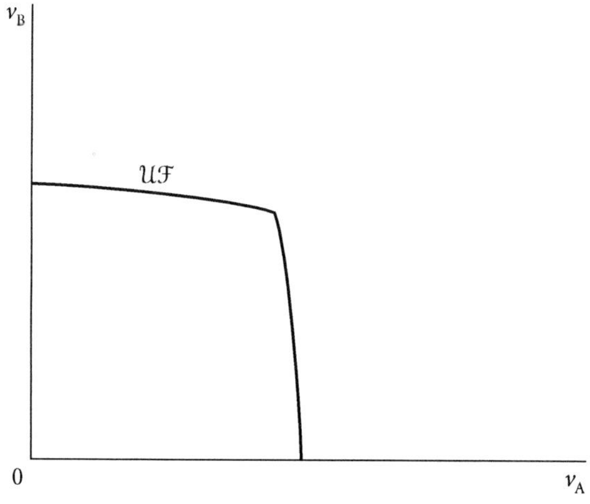

Figure 3.35 A kinked utility possibility frontier

The frontier $\mathcal{UF}$ has a kink at the point $(v_A, v_B) = (2, 2)$, as is portrayed in figure 3.35. If we let $v_B(v_A)$ be the function of which the graph is $\mathcal{UF}$, then we see that at the kink point where $v_A = 2$, the derivative from the left of $v_B(v_A)$ is $-\frac{1}{2}$. The derivative from the right at the same point is -2. It follows that the welfare function $a_A v_A + a_B v_B$ achieves a maximum over the utility possibility frontier $\mathcal{UF}$ at the point $(v_A, v_B) = (2, 2)$ whenever $\frac{1}{2} \leq \frac{a_A}{a_B} \leq 2$. Therefore, the function $\overline{\mathbf{v}}$ from Δ^1 to $\mathcal{UF}$ is not injective.

3.6 The Structure of the Utility Possibility Frontier

In the previous section, we saw that welfare maximization associates, surjectively, a point on the utility possibility frontier $\mathcal{UF}$ with every vector of relative welfare weights in Δ^{I-1}. We can also associate points in $\mathcal{UF}$ with points in Δ^{I-1} by means of a function that is continuous, surjective, injective, and that has a continuous inverse. That is, the sets Δ^{I-1} and $\mathcal{UF}$ are the same, up to a continuous deformation. Before making a rigorous argument, I describe the function informally. If we add constants to the utility functions of each of the consumers, we do not change the set of Pareto optimal allocations and we merely displace the utility possibility frontier $\mathcal{UF}$ by the vector of these constants. Therefore, we may subtract $u_i(\mathbf{0})$ from the utility function u_i, for each i, without changing the shape of $\mathcal{UF}$. If we do so, then each consumer's utility of the vector $\mathbf{0}$ is zero, that is, $u_i(\mathbf{0}) = 0$, for all i. If we assume that the utility functions are increasing, then $u_i(\mathbf{x}) \geq 0$, for all consumption bundles $\mathbf{x}$, and $\mathcal{UF}$ consists of nonnegative I-vectors and is contained in $\mathbb{R}^I_+$, as is the $I - 1$ simplex Δ^{I-1}. If $\mathbf{v}$ is a vector in $\mathcal{UF}$ and $\mathbf{v} \neq \mathbf{0}$, then there is a unique ray from the origin through $\mathbf{v}$, and this ray intersects the simplex Δ^{I-1} at a unique point; call it $\pi(\mathbf{v})$. The projection, π, of $\mathcal{UF}$ onto Δ^{I-1} along rays through the origin establishes a one-to-one correspondence between these two sets, provided all the vectors in $\mathcal{UF}$ are nonzero. Since every one-to-one and onto function has an inverse, π has an inverse, π^{-1}. Both the function π and its inverse are continuous functions under standard assumptions on the economy $\mathcal{E}$. Figure 3.36 pictures the projection just described.

Before describing formally the properties of π, I state an assumption that implies that the utility possibility frontier contains a vector every component of which is positive.

DEFINITION 3.47 The economy $\mathcal{E} = ((u_i, \mathbf{e}_i)_{i=1}^I, (Y_j)_{j=1}^J)$ is *productive* if it has a feasible allocation $(\mathbf{x}, \mathbf{y})$ such that $\sum_{i=1}^I \mathbf{x}_i \gg \mathbf{0}$.

THEOREM 3.48 Suppose that the economy $\mathcal{E} = ((u_i, \mathbf{e}_i)_{i=1}^I, (Y_j)_{j=1}^J)$ satisfies the four assumptions below.

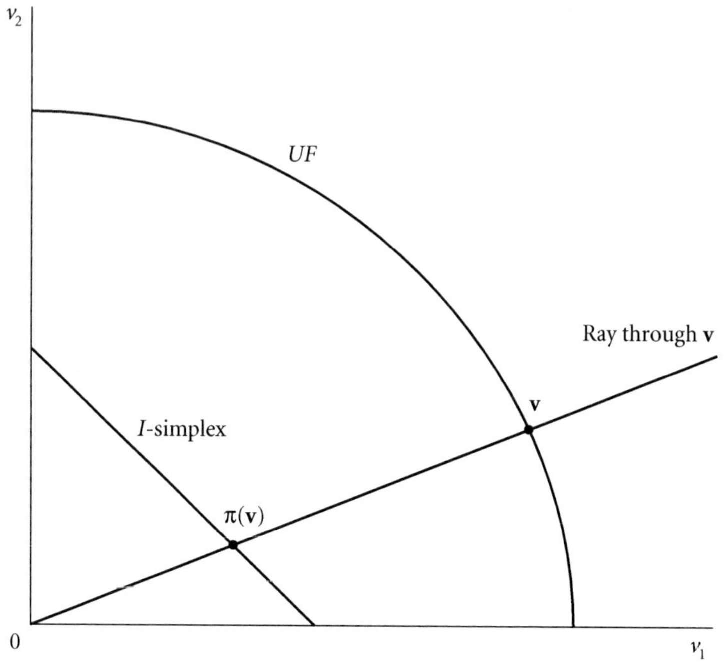

Figure 3.36 The radial projection, π, of $\mathcal{UF}$ onto Δ^{I-1}

1. For every i, u_i is continuous and strictly increasing and is such that $u_i(\mathbf{0}) = 0$.
2. For every j, Y_j is convex.
3. The set of feasible allocations $\mathcal{F}$ is compact.
4. $\mathcal{E}$ is productive.

Then, the utility possibility frontier $\mathcal{UF}$ is nonempty; the radial projection $\pi: \mathcal{UF} \to \Delta^{I-1}$ is one to one, onto, and continuous; and its inverse function, $\pi^{-1}: \Delta^{I-1} \to \mathcal{UF}$, is continuous.

In proving this theorem, I use the next lemma.

LEMMA 3.49 Suppose that A is a compact set of N-vectors, B is a set of K-vectors, and the function $f: A \to B$ is continuous, one to one, and onto. Then the inverse function, $f^{-1}: B \to A$, is continuous.

Proof. It must be shown that if $\mathbf{b}_n$ is an infinite sequence in B that converges to a point $\mathbf{b}$ in B, then the sequence $f^{-1}(\mathbf{b}_n)$ converges to $f^{-1}(\mathbf{b})$. Assume that $f^{-1}(\mathbf{b}_n)$ does not converge to $f^{-1}(\mathbf{b})$. Because $f^{-1}(\mathbf{b}_n)$ does not converge to $f^{-1}(\mathbf{b})$, there exists a positive number ε such that $\|f^{-1}(\mathbf{b}_n) - f^{-1}(\mathbf{b})\| > \varepsilon$, for infinitely many values of n. If we ignore the members of the sequence $f^{-1}(\mathbf{b}_n)$ such that $\|f^{-1}(\mathbf{b}_n) - f^{-1}(\mathbf{b})\| \leq \varepsilon$, we obtain a new sequence, which I may again call $f^{-1}(\mathbf{b}_n)$, such that $\|f^{-1}(\mathbf{b}_n) - f^{-1}(\mathbf{b})\| > \varepsilon$, for all n. Since A is compact, the Bolzano-Weierstrass theorem implies that the sequence $f^{-1}(\mathbf{b}_n)$ has a subsequence $f^{-1}(\mathbf{b}_{n(k)})$ that converges to a point $\mathbf{a}$ in A. Since $\|f^{-1}(\mathbf{b}_{n(k)}) - f^{-1}(\mathbf{b})\| > \varepsilon$, for all k, it follows that $\|\mathbf{a} - f^{-1}(\mathbf{b})\| \geq \varepsilon$. Since the function f is continuous, the sequence $\mathbf{b}_n$ converges to $f(\mathbf{a})$. Because $\mathbf{b}_{n(k)}$ is a subsequence of the sequence $\mathbf{b}_n$ that converges to $\mathbf{b}$, it follows that $\mathbf{b}_{n(k)}$ converges to $\mathbf{b}$ and hence that $\mathbf{b} = f(\mathbf{a})$ and so $f^{-1}(\mathbf{b}) = \mathbf{a}$. However, $f^{-1}(\mathbf{b}) \neq \mathbf{a}$, since $\|\mathbf{a} - f^{-1}(\mathbf{b})\| \geq \varepsilon > 0$. This contradiction completes the proof. ▪

Proof of Theorem 3.48. I show that the inverse function $\pi^{-1}: \Delta^{I-1} \to \mathcal{UF}$ exists and is continuous. It will follow that both π and π^{-1} are one to one and onto. Since Δ^{I-1} is compact, it will follow from lemma 3.49 that $\pi = (\pi^{-1})^{-1}$ is continuous. The proof proceeds by a series of easy steps. During the proof, I refer to an I-vector $\mathbf{v}$ as *attainable* if $\mathbf{v} = u(\mathbf{x}, \mathbf{y})$, where $u(\mathbf{x}, \mathbf{y}) = (u_1(\mathbf{x}_1), u_2(\mathbf{x}_2), \ldots, u_I(\mathbf{x}_I))$ and $(\mathbf{x}, \mathbf{y})$ is a feasible allocation.

Step 1 If $\mathbf{v}$ is attainable, then $\mathbf{v} \geq \mathbf{0}$.

Proof Let $(\mathbf{x}, \mathbf{y})$ be a feasible allocation such that $\mathbf{v} = u(\mathbf{x}, \mathbf{y})$. For all i, $\mathbf{x}_i \geq \mathbf{0}$. Therefore, $v_i = u_i(\mathbf{x}_i) \geq u_i(\mathbf{0}) = 0$, since u_i is strictly increasing.

Step 2 If $\mathbf{v}$ is attainable and $\underline{\mathbf{v}}$ is an I-vector such that $\mathbf{0} \leq \underline{\mathbf{v}} \leq \mathbf{v}$, then $\underline{\mathbf{v}}$ is attainable.

Proof Let $(\mathbf{x}, \mathbf{y})$ be a feasible allocation such that $\mathbf{v} = u(\mathbf{x}, \mathbf{y})$. Since u_i is continuous, $u_i(t\mathbf{x}_i)$ varies continuously from 0 to $u_i(\mathbf{x}_i)$ as t varies from 0 to 1. By the intermediate value theorem of elementary analysis, for each i, there exists a number t_i such that $0 \leq t_i \leq 1$ and $u_i(t_i\mathbf{x}_i) = \underline{\mathbf{v}}_i$. Let $\underline{\mathbf{x}}_i = t_i\mathbf{x}_i$ and $\underline{\mathbf{x}} = (\underline{\mathbf{x}}_1, \ldots, \underline{\mathbf{x}}_I)$. The allocation $(\underline{\mathbf{x}}, \mathbf{y})$ is feasible, since

$$\sum_{i=1}^{I} \underline{\mathbf{x}}_i \leq \sum_{i=1}^{I} \mathbf{x}_i \leq \sum_{i=1}^{I} \mathbf{e}_i + \sum_{j=1}^{J} \mathbf{y}_j.$$

By construction, $\underline{\mathbf{v}} = u(\underline{\mathbf{x}}, \mathbf{y})$, so $\underline{\mathbf{v}}$ is attainable.

Step 3 If $\mathbf{v}$ is attainable and $\underline{\mathbf{v}}$ is a nonnegative I-vector such that $\mathbf{v} > \underline{\mathbf{v}}$, then there exists an attainable vector $\overline{\mathbf{v}}$ such that $\overline{\mathbf{v}} \gg \underline{\mathbf{v}}$.

Proof Let $(\mathbf{x}, \mathbf{y})$ be a feasible allocation such that $\mathbf{v} = u(\mathbf{x}, \mathbf{y})$. Since $\mathbf{v} > \underline{\mathbf{v}}$, $v_i > \underline{v}_i$, for some i. Without loss of generality, I may assume that $v_1 > \underline{v}_1$, Since $u_1(\mathbf{x}_1) = v_1 > \underline{v}_1 \geq 0$, it follows that $\mathbf{x}_1 > \mathbf{0}$. Since u_1 is continuous and strictly increasing, I may choose t between 0 and 1 and so close to 1 that $u_1(t\mathbf{x}_1) > \underline{v}_1$. Let $\overline{\mathbf{x}}_1 = t\mathbf{x}_1$. For $i > 1$, let $\overline{\mathbf{x}}_i = \mathbf{x}_i + \frac{1-t}{I-1}\mathbf{x}_1$. And let $\overline{\mathbf{x}} = (\overline{x}_1, \ldots, \overline{x}_I)$. The allocation $(\overline{\mathbf{x}}, \mathbf{y})$ is feasible, since it is obtained by taking the vector $(1-t)\mathbf{x}_1$ away from consumer 1 and distributing it uniformly among the other consumers. Let $\overline{\mathbf{v}} = u(\overline{\mathbf{x}}, \mathbf{y})$. Since u_i is strictly increasing, for all i, it follows that $\overline{\mathbf{v}} \gg \underline{\mathbf{v}}$.

Step 4 There exists an attainable vector $\mathbf{v}$ such that $\mathbf{v} \gg \mathbf{0}$.

Proof Since the economy $\mathcal{E}$ is productive, there is a feasible allocation $(\mathbf{x}, \mathbf{y})$ such that $\sum_{i=1}^{I} \mathbf{x}_i \gg \mathbf{0}$. Since I may redistribute consumption among consumers, I may assume that $\mathbf{x}_i \gg \mathbf{0}$, for all i. Let $\mathbf{v} = u(\mathbf{x}, \mathbf{y})$. Then, $v_i = u_i(\mathbf{x}_i) > u_i(\mathbf{0}) = 0$, for all i, since u_i is strictly increasing, for all i.

Step 5 If $\mathbf{b}$ belongs to Δ^{I-1}, then there is a vector $\mathbf{v}$ on the utility possibility frontier, $\mathcal{UF}$, such that $\mathbf{v} = t\mathbf{b}$, for some positive number t.

Proof Consider the welfare function of allocations defined by the formula

$$W_b(\mathbf{x}, \mathbf{y}) = \min\left(\frac{u_1(\mathbf{x}_1)}{b_1}, \frac{u_2(\mathbf{x}_2)}{b_2} \ldots, \frac{u_I(\mathbf{x}_I)}{b_I}\right),$$

where $\frac{u_i(\mathbf{x}_i)}{b_i}$ is defined to be infinity if $b_i = 0$. Since W_b is a continuous function of $(\mathbf{x}, \mathbf{y})$ and the set of feasible allocations is compact, proposition 3.14 implies that W_b achieves a finite maximum at some feasible allocation $(\mathbf{x}, \mathbf{y})$. By the definition of W_b, $u_i(\mathbf{x}) \geq W_b(\mathbf{x}, \mathbf{y})b_i$, for all i, or in vector notation, $u(\mathbf{x}, \mathbf{y}) \geq W_b(\mathbf{x}, \mathbf{y})\mathbf{b}$. In fact, $u(\mathbf{x}, \mathbf{y}) = W_b(\mathbf{x}, \mathbf{y})\mathbf{b}$, for if $u(\mathbf{x}, \mathbf{y}) > W_b(\mathbf{x}, \mathbf{y})\mathbf{b}$, then by step 3, there exists a feasible allocation $(\overline{\mathbf{x}}, \overline{\mathbf{y}})$ such that $u(\overline{\mathbf{x}}, \overline{\mathbf{y}}) \gg W_b(\mathbf{x}, \mathbf{y})\mathbf{b}$. Then, $W_b(\overline{\mathbf{x}}, \overline{\mathbf{y}}) > W_b(\mathbf{x}, \mathbf{y})$, which contradicts the maximality of $(\mathbf{x}, \mathbf{y})$. The same argument implies that there is no feasible allocation $(\mathbf{x}', \mathbf{y}')$ such that $u(\mathbf{x}', \mathbf{y}') > u(\mathbf{x}, \mathbf{y})$. Therefore, $\mathbf{v} = u(\mathbf{x}, \mathbf{y})$ belongs to the utility possibility frontier. It has just been shown that

$\mathbf{v} = t\mathbf{b}$, where $t = W_b(\mathbf{x}, \mathbf{y})$. Furthermore, $t > 0$ because by step 4 there exists a feasible allocation $(\underline{\mathbf{x}}, \underline{\mathbf{y}})$ such that $u(\underline{\mathbf{x}}, \underline{\mathbf{y}}) \gg 0$, so that $t = W_b(\mathbf{x}, \mathbf{y}) \geq W_b(\overline{\mathbf{x}}, \overline{\mathbf{y}}) > 0$. This completes the proof of step 5.

The next step of the proof of theorem 3.48 implies that $\pi^{-1}: \Delta^{I-1} \to \mathcal{UF}$ is a function.

Step 6 If $\mathbf{b}$ belongs to Δ^{I-1}, there is at most one number t such that $t\mathbf{b}$ is on the utility possibility frontier, $\mathcal{UF}$.

Proof Suppose that both $t\mathbf{b}$ and $t'\mathbf{b}$ belong to the utility possibility frontier, where $t > t'$. Since $t\mathbf{b} > t'\mathbf{b}$, $t'\mathbf{b}$ is by definition not on the utility possibility frontier. Therefore, there can be only one number t such that $t\mathbf{b}$ is on the frontier.

Step 7 The function π^{-1} is continuous.

Proof Let $\mathbf{b}^n$ be a sequence in Δ^{I-1} converging to a point $\mathbf{b}$ in Δ^{I-1}. Let t be a positive number and, for each n, let t_n be a positive number such that $t\mathbf{b}$ and $t_n\mathbf{b}^n$, respectively, belong to the utility possibility frontier. Then, $t\mathbf{b} = \pi^{-1}(\mathbf{b})$ and $t_n\mathbf{b}^n = \pi^{-1}(\mathbf{b}^n)$, for all n, so that in order to prove that π^{-1} is continuous it is sufficient to show that $\lim_{n\to\infty} t_n = t$.

For all n, it is not the case that $t_n\mathbf{b}^n > t\mathbf{b}$, for otherwise the vector $t\mathbf{b}$ would not be on the utility possibility frontier. Therefore, for every n, either $t_n\mathbf{b}^n = t\mathbf{b}$ or $t_n\mathbf{b}_i^n < t\mathbf{b}_i$, for some i. If $t_n\mathbf{b}^n = t\mathbf{b}$, then $t_n = t$ and $\mathbf{b}^n = \mathbf{b}$. If $t_n b_i^n < t b_i$, then $b_i > 0$ and $t > 0$. Therefore, either $t_n = t$ or

$$t_n < t \max_i \left\{ \frac{b_i}{b_i^n} \mid i \text{ is such that } b_i > 0 \right\}.$$

Since $\lim_{n\to\infty} \mathbf{b}^n = \mathbf{b}$, it follows that

$$\lim_{n\to\infty} \max_i \left\{ \frac{b_i}{b_i^n} \mid i \text{ is such that } b_i > 0 \right\} = 1.$$

Therefore, for any positive number ε, there exists a positive integer N such that $t_n < t + \varepsilon$, if $n \geq N$.

To demonstrate that $\lim_{n\to\infty} t_n = t$, it remains to be shown that for any positive number ε, there exists a positive integer N such that $t_n > t - \varepsilon$, if $n \geq N$. The proof is by contradiction. If the statement is false, there exists a positive number ε such that $t_n \leq t - \varepsilon$, for infinitely many values of n. That is, there is a subsequence $t_{n(k)}$, such that $t_{n(k)} \leq$

$t - \varepsilon$, for all nonnegative integers k. Since $t_{n(k)}$ belongs to the compact interval $[0, t - \varepsilon]$ for each k, the Bolzano-Weierstrass theorem implies that there exists a convergent subsequence of the subsequence $t_{n(k)}$. Call the new subsequence $t_{n(k)}$ again, and let $\underline{t} = \lim_{k\to\infty} t_{n(k)}$. Then, $0 \le \underline{t} \le t - \varepsilon$. Since $\underline{t}\mathbf{b} < t\mathbf{b}$, step 3 implies that there is an attainable vector $\overline{\mathbf{v}}$, such that $\underline{t}\mathbf{b} \ll \overline{\mathbf{v}}$. Since $\lim_{k\to\infty} t_{n(k)}\mathbf{b}^{n(k)} = \underline{t}\mathbf{b}$, it follows that $t_{n(k)}\mathbf{b}^{n(k)} \ll \overline{\mathbf{v}}$, if k is sufficiently large. This last inequality is impossible, since $t_{n(k)}\mathbf{b}^{n(k)}$ belongs to the utility possibility frontier, for all k. This contradiction proves that $t_n > t - \varepsilon$, for sufficiently large n, and so proves that $\lim_{n\to\infty} t_n = t$ and hence that π^{-1} is continous.

■

3.7 Compactness of the Set of Feasible Allocations

A central assumption in the material presented thus far has been that the set of feasible allocations is compact, and I now state assumptions about the production possibility sets that imply this compactness property. Such assumptions make it easy to verify compactness for particular models. One assumption that is obviously required is that the production possibility sets be closed, for otherwise, as the following example shows, the feasible allocations may not form a closed set and therefore may not be compact.

EXAMPLE 3.50 Consider the Robinson Crusoe economy with initial endowment $\mathbf{e} = (1, 0)$ and input-output possibility set $Y = \{(y_1, y_2) \mid y_1 \le 0,$ and $y_2 < -y_1\}$. The set of feasible consumption allocations is

$$C = \{(x_1, x_2) \mid x_1 \ge 0, x_2 \ge 0, x_1 + x_2 < 1\},$$

which is not closed. These sets are portrayed in figure 3.37. The dotted line of slope -1 is not part of the sets C or $\mathbf{e} + Y = \{\mathbf{e} + \mathbf{y} \mid \mathbf{y} \in Y\}$.

Compactness of the feasible allocations also depends on the relation of production possibility sets to each other. There follows an example with two production possibility sets in which the set of feasible allocations is unbounded.

EXAMPLE 3.51 The economy has two commodities, one consumer with initial endowment $\mathbf{e} = \mathbf{0}$, and production possibility sets Y_1 and Y_2, where

$$Y_1 = \{(y_1, y_2) \mid y_2 \le 0 \text{ and } y_1 \le -2y_2\}$$

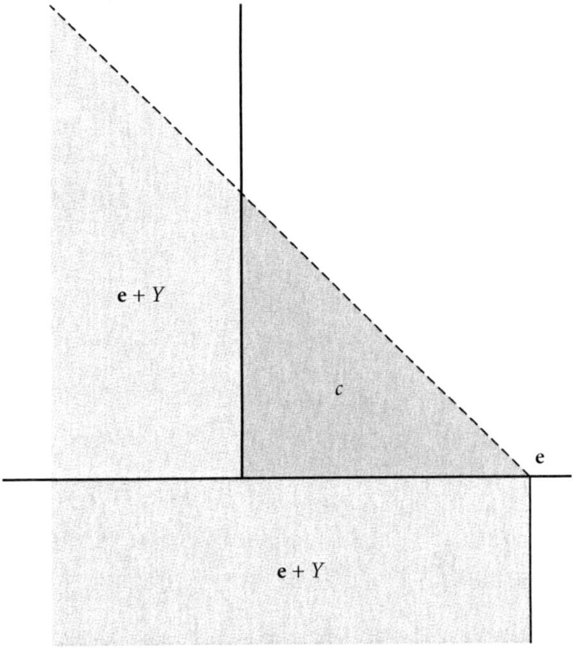

Figure 3.37 A nonclosed input-output possibility set and set of feasible allocations

and

$$Y_2 = \{(y_1, y_2) \mid y_1 \leq 0 \text{ and } y_2 \leq -2y_1\}.$$

It is feasible for the consumer to consume any nonnegative quantities of both commodities, so that the set of feasible allocations is unbounded. The input-output possibility sets are shown in figure 3.38. It should be clear that any vector in the nonnegative orthant may be obtained as the sum of a vector from each of the two production possibility sets.

It is possible for the production possibility sets to be closed and for the set of feasible allocations not to be closed, even though it is bounded. This possibility is illustrated by the next example.

EXAMPLE 3.52 The economy has two commodities, one consumer with initial endowment $\mathbf{e} = \mathbf{0}$, and production possibility sets Y_1 and Y_2, where

$$Y_1 = \left\{(y_1, y_2) \mid y_2 \leq 0 \text{ and } y_1 \leq 1 - y_2 - \frac{1}{1 - y_2}\right\}$$

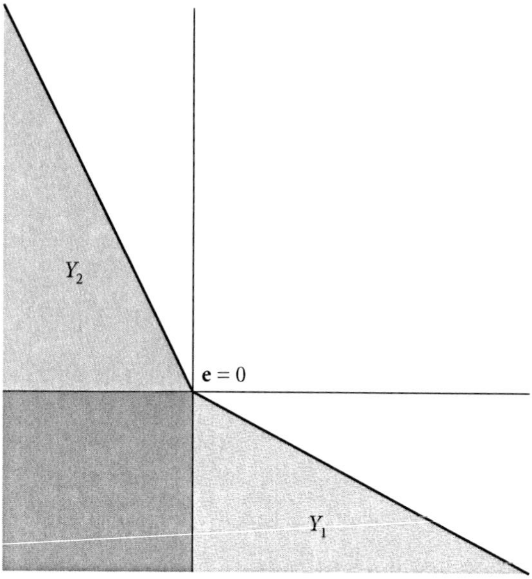

Figure 3.38 Unbounded set of feasible allocations

and

$$Y_2 = \left\{ (y_1, y_2) \mid y_2 \leq 0 \text{ and } y_2 \leq 1 - y_1 - \frac{1}{1 - y_1} \right\}.$$

These sets are clearly closed. The set of feasible consumption allocations is

$$C = \left\{ (x_1, x_2) \mid x_1 \geq 0, x_2 \geq 0, \text{ and } x_1 + x_2 < 2 \right\},$$

which is not closed. The sets are pictured in figure 3.39.

The assumptions of the next theorem exclude the above counterexamples. To state the theorem, I need the notion of the sum of sets.

DEFINITION 3.53 If A and B are set of N-vectors, then $A + B = \{\mathbf{a} + \mathbf{b} \mid \mathbf{a} \in A \text{ and } \mathbf{b} \in B\}$

THEOREM 3.54 In the economy $\mathcal{E} = ((u_i, \mathbf{e}_i)_{i=1}^{I}, (Y_j)_{j=1}^{J})$, let $Y = \sum_{j=1}^{J} Y_j = Y_1 + \cdots + Y_J$. Assume that

1. for all j, Y_j is closed, convex, and contains the vector $\mathbf{0}$,

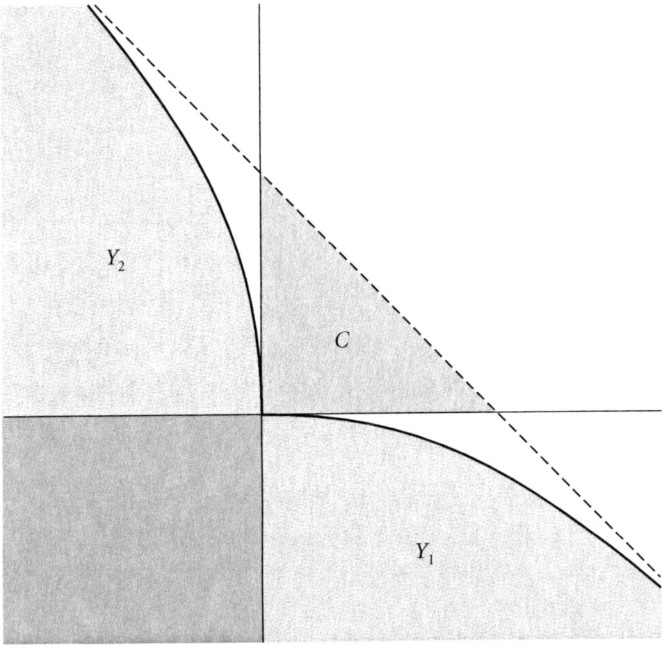

Figure 3.39 A bounded nonclosed set of feasible allocations

2. $Y \cap \mathbb{R}^N_+ = \{\mathbf{0}\}$, and
3. $Y \cap (-Y) = \{\mathbf{0}\}$.

Then the set of feasible allocations of $\mathcal{E}$ is compact and nonempty.

The assumption that $\mathbf{0}$ belongs to Y_j means that firm j can withdraw from the economy by doing nothing. In particular, the firm is not endowed with any capital equipment the maintenance of which requires inputs. The second and third assumptions are plausible. The total input-output possibility set, Y, is the set of input-output vectors producible or technically feasible for the economy as a whole, and the second assumption means that the economy can produce no output without some input. The third assumption means that the economy's production is not reversible. If the vector $\mathbf{y}$ belonged to both Y and $-Y$, then $-\mathbf{y}$ would also belong to Y, and $-\mathbf{y}$ is the reverse of $\mathbf{y}$ in the sense that the outputs in $\mathbf{y}$ are the inputs in $-\mathbf{y}$

and vice versa; both $\mathbf{y}$ and its reverse, $-\mathbf{y}$, would be possible input-output vectors.

Proof. The set of feasible allocations is nonempty because it contains the zero allocation such that $\mathbf{x}_i = \mathbf{0}$, for all i, and $\mathbf{y}_j = \mathbf{0}$, for all j.

In order to see that the set of feasible allocations is closed, let $(\mathbf{x}^n, \mathbf{y}^n)$ be a sequence of feasible allocations that converges to $(\mathbf{x}, \mathbf{y})$. I must verify that $(\mathbf{x}, \mathbf{y})$ is a feasible allocation. We know that $\mathbf{x}_i \geq \mathbf{0}$, for all i, because $\mathbf{x}_i^n \geq \mathbf{0}$, for all i and n, and $\mathbf{x}_i^n$ converges to $\mathbf{x}_i$, for all i, as n goes to infinity. Similarly, $\mathbf{y}_j$ belongs to Y_j, because Y_j is closed and $\mathbf{y}_j^n$ belongs to Y_j, for all j and n, and $\lim_{n\to\infty} \mathbf{y}_j^n = \overline{\mathbf{y}}_j$. Therefore, $(\mathbf{x}, \mathbf{y})$ is an allocation. Passing to the limit with n in the inequality $\sum_{i=1}^{I}(\mathbf{x}_i^n - \mathbf{e}_i) \leq \sum_{j=1}^{J} \mathbf{y}_j^n$, we see that $\sum_{i=1}^{I}(\mathbf{x}_i - \mathbf{e}_i) \leq \sum_{j=1}^{J} \mathbf{y}_j$, so that $(\mathbf{x}, \mathbf{y})$ is feasible.

It remains to prove that the set of feasible allocations is bounded. I assume that $(\mathbf{x}^n, \mathbf{y}^n)$ is an unbounded sequence of feasible allocations and obtain a contradiction. I show that the sequence of vectors $\mathbf{y}_j^n$ is unbounded, for some j, again by contradiction. If the sequence $\mathbf{y}_j^n$ is bounded, for all j, then the sequence $\sum_{j=1}^{J} \mathbf{y}_j^n$ is bounded and hence there is a vector $\overline{\mathbf{y}}$ such that $\sum_{j=1}^{J} \mathbf{y}_j^n \leq \overline{\mathbf{y}}$, for all n. Therefore, for all i and n, $\mathbf{0} \leq \mathbf{x}_i^n \leq \sum_{k=1}^{I} \mathbf{x}_k^n \leq \sum_{k=1}^{I} \mathbf{e}_k + \sum_{j=1}^{J} \mathbf{y}_j^n \leq \sum_{k=1}^{I} \mathbf{e}_k + \overline{\mathbf{y}}$, and hence the sequence $\mathbf{x}_i^n$ is bounded, for all i. This proves that at least one of the sequences $\mathbf{y}_j^n$ is unbounded.

I now work toward another contradiction that will prove that the set of feasible allocations is bounded. For each n, let $j(n)$ be such that $\|\mathbf{y}_{j(n)}^n\| = \max_j \|\mathbf{y}_j^n\|$. Since the sequence $\mathbf{y}_j^n$ is unbounded, for some j, it follows that for one of the indices j, $j(n) = j$, for infinitely many values of n. Without loss of generality, I may assume that this value of j is 1. Let $n(k)$ be the subsequence of integers n that picks out those values of n for which $j(n) = 1$, so that $j(n(k)) = 1$, for all k. For simplicity of notation, I drop the k from the subsequence $n(k)$, so that $j(n) = 1$, for all n. We know that $\|\mathbf{y}_j^n\| \leq \|\mathbf{y}_1^n\|$, for all n and j, and that the sequence $\mathbf{y}_1^n$ is unbounded. By passing again to a subsequence and calling it $\mathbf{y}_1^n$ again, I may assume that $\lim_{n\to\infty} \|\mathbf{y}_1^n\| = \infty$. For each j and n, let $\overline{\mathbf{y}}_j^n = \frac{\mathbf{y}_j^n}{\|\mathbf{y}_1^n\|}$. Then, $\|\overline{\mathbf{y}}_j^n\| \leq 1$, for all n and j, and $\|\overline{\mathbf{y}}_1^n\| = 1$, for all n. Also, $\overline{\mathbf{y}}_j^n$ belongs to Y_j, for all j, because Y_j is convex, $\mathbf{0}$ and $\mathbf{y}_j^n$ belong to Y_j, and $\overline{\mathbf{y}}_j^n$ is a convex combination of $\mathbf{0}$ and $\mathbf{y}_j$. The sequence $(\overline{\mathbf{y}}_1^n, \overline{\mathbf{y}}_2^n, \ldots, \overline{\mathbf{y}}_J^n)$ is bounded, so that by the Bolzano-Weierstrass theorem it has a convergent subsequence, which I call $(\overline{\mathbf{y}}_1^n, \overline{\mathbf{y}}_2^n, \ldots, \overline{\mathbf{y}}_J^n)$ again. Let $(\overline{\mathbf{y}}_1, \overline{\mathbf{y}}_2, \ldots, \overline{\mathbf{y}}_J)$ be the limit of this subsequence, so that $\lim_{n\to\infty} \overline{\mathbf{y}}_j^n = \overline{\mathbf{y}}_j$, for all j. Because the sets Y_j are closed and $\overline{\mathbf{y}}_j^n$ belongs to Y_j, it follows that $\overline{\mathbf{y}}_j$ belongs to Y_j, for all j. Because $\|\overline{\mathbf{y}}_j^n\| \leq 1$, for all j and n, it follows that $\|\overline{\mathbf{y}}_j\| \leq 1$, for all j. Similarly, $\|\overline{\mathbf{y}}_1\| = 1$, since $\|\overline{\mathbf{y}}_1^n\| = 1$, for all n.

I show that $\sum_{j=1}^J \overline{\mathbf{y}}_j \geq \mathbf{0}$. Because the allocation $(\mathbf{x}^n, \mathbf{y}^n)$ is feasible,

$$\sum_{i=1}^I \mathbf{e}_i + \sum_{j=1}^J \mathbf{y}_j^n \geq \sum_{i=1}^I \mathbf{x}_i^n \geq \mathbf{0},$$

so that

$$\frac{\sum_{i=1}^I \mathbf{e}_i}{\|\mathbf{y}_1^n\|} + \frac{\sum_{j=1}^J \mathbf{y}_j^n}{\|\mathbf{y}_1^n\|} \geq \frac{\sum_{i=1}^I \mathbf{x}_i^n}{\|\mathbf{y}_1^n\|} \geq \mathbf{0}.$$

If we let $\overline{\mathbf{y}}_j^n = \frac{\mathbf{y}_j^n}{\|\mathbf{y}_1^n\|}$, for all j, this inequality becomes

$$\frac{\sum_{i=1}^I \mathbf{e}_i}{\|\mathbf{y}_1^n\|} + \sum_{j=1}^J \overline{\mathbf{y}}_j^n \geq \frac{\sum_{i=1}^I \mathbf{x}_i^n}{\|\mathbf{y}_1^n\|} \geq \mathbf{0}. \tag{3.12}$$

Since $\lim_{n\to\infty} \|\mathbf{y}_1^n\| = \infty$, it follows that

$$\lim_{n\to\infty} \frac{\sum_{i=1}^I \mathbf{e}_i}{\|\mathbf{y}_1^n\|} = \mathbf{0}. \tag{3.13}$$

Since $\lim_{n\to\infty} \overline{\mathbf{y}}_j^n = \overline{\mathbf{y}}_j$, for all j, inequality 3.12 and equation 3.13 imply that

$$\sum_{j=1}^J \overline{\mathbf{y}}_j = \lim_{n\to\infty} \left[\frac{\sum_{i=1}^I \mathbf{e}_i}{\|\mathbf{y}_1^n\|} + \sum_{j=1}^J \overline{\mathbf{y}}_j^n \right] \geq \limsup_{n\to\infty} \left[\frac{\sum_{i=1}^I \mathbf{x}_j^n}{\|\mathbf{y}_1^n\|} \right] \geq \mathbf{0}.$$

This inequality and the second assumption of the theorem imply that $\sum_{j=1}^J \overline{\mathbf{y}}_j = \mathbf{0}$. Therefore, $\overline{\mathbf{y}}_1 = -\sum_{j=2}^J \overline{\mathbf{y}}_j$. Since $\|\overline{\mathbf{y}}_1\| = 1$ it follows that $\overline{\mathbf{y}}_1 \neq \mathbf{0}$ and so $\sum_{j=2}^J \overline{\mathbf{y}}_j \neq \mathbf{0}$. Because $\mathbf{0}$ belongs to Y_j, for all j, it follows that $\overline{\mathbf{y}}_1 = \overline{\mathbf{y}}_1 + \mathbf{0} + \cdots + \mathbf{0}$ belongs to Y and similarly that $-\overline{\mathbf{y}}_1 = \sum_{j=2}^J \overline{\mathbf{y}}_j = \mathbf{0} + \sum_{j=2}^J \overline{\mathbf{y}}_j$ belongs to Y. Therefore, $\overline{\mathbf{y}}_1$ and $-\overline{\mathbf{y}}_1$ both belong to Y, so that by the third assumption of the theorem, $\overline{\mathbf{y}}_1 = \mathbf{0}$, which is impossible. This contradiction proves that the set of feasible allocations is bounded. ▪

Problem Set

1. Consider the Edgeworth box economy where the endowment of consumer A is (1, 0) and the endowment of consumer B is (0, 1). For each of the following three cases, find and sketch the set of Pareto optimal allocations and the utility possibility set and find the allocations that maximize the sum of the utilities of the two consumers. By "sketch the set of Pareto optimal allocations," I mean find the coordinates of a few points on the utility possibility frontier and fill in the remaining part of the curve. In maximizing the sum of the utilities in part (b), use the symmetry of the problem. In order to see where the sum of the utilities is maximized, it is important to have a fairly accurate sketch of the utility possibility set.

(a) $u_A(x_1, x_2) = \sqrt{x_1 x_2}$ and $u_B(x_1, x_2) = \sqrt{x_1 x_2}$.
(b) $u_A(x_1, x_2) = x_1^{1/6} x_2^{1/3}$ and $u_B(x_1, x_2) = x_1^{1/3} x_2^{1/6}$.
(c) $u_A(x_1, x_2) = x_1 x_2^2$ and $u_B(x_1, x_2) = x_1^2 x_2$.

2. Find the optimum allocation and draw the feasible set for each of the following three Robinson Crusoe economies, where L is the input of labor, ℓ is the consumption of leisure, x is the consumption of food, and y is the production of food. Indicate Crusoe's indifference curves and the optimum on the drawing. In a commodity vector, the first component is labor–leisure time and the second is food.

(a) $y = f(L) = 2L$, $\mathbf{e} = (1, 0)$, $u(\ell, x) = \ell^{2/3} x^{2/3}$.
(b) $y = f(L) = L$, $e = (1, 0)$, $u(\ell, x) = \min(\ell, 2x)$.
(c) $y = f(L) = 3\sqrt{L}$, $\mathbf{e} = (1, 0)$, $u(\ell, x) = \ell + 2x$.

3. For each of the three following Edgeworth box examples, calculate and draw an accurate picture of the set of

$$V = \left\{(u_A(\mathbf{x}_A), u_B(\mathbf{x}_B)) \mid \mathbf{x}_A \in \mathbb{R}^2_+, \mathbf{x}_B \in \mathbb{R}^2_+, \text{ and } \mathbf{x}_A + \mathbf{x}_B = \mathbf{e}_A + \mathbf{e}_B\right\}$$

and of

$$\mathcal{U} = \left\{(v_A, v_B) \mid \text{ there is a feasible allocation } (\mathbf{x}_A, \mathbf{x}_B) \text{ such that } v_A \le u_A(\mathbf{x}_A) \text{ and } v_B \le u_B(\mathbf{x}_B)\right\}.$$

(a) $\mathbf{e}_A = (1, 0)$, $\mathbf{e}_B = (0, 1)$, $u_A(x_1, x_2) = 3x_1 + x_2$, $u_B(x_1, x_2) = x_1 + 3x_2$.
(b) $\mathbf{e}_A = (1, 0)$, $\mathbf{e}_B = (0, 1)$, $u_A(x_1, x_2) = \min(x_1, 2x_2)$, $u_B(x_1, x_2) = \min(2x_1, x_2)$.

(c) $\mathbf{e}_A = (1, 0)$, $\mathbf{e}_B = (0, 1)$, $u_A(x_1, x_2) = \sqrt{x_1 x_2}$, $u_B(x_1, x_2) = x_1 + 3x_2$.

4. For the Edgeworth box economies listed below (i) find the set of feasible allocations and the set of Pareto optimal allocations and show them on a box diagram, (ii) find a Pareto optimal allocation $\overline{\mathbf{x}} = (\overline{\mathbf{x}}_A, \overline{\mathbf{x}}_B)$ that gives the consumers equal utility, that is, is such that $u_A(\overline{\mathbf{x}}_A) = u_B(\overline{\mathbf{x}}_B)$, (iii) indicate the endowment allocation $\mathbf{e}$ and the allocation $\overline{\mathbf{x}}$ on the box diagram, (iv) find and draw the utility possibility set and indicate the utility vectors corresponding to the endowment allocation and to the allocation $\overline{\mathbf{x}}$, and (v) find all vectors of the form $\mathbf{a} = (a_A, a_B)$, such that $\mathbf{a} > 0$ and $a_A u_A(\overline{\mathbf{x}}_A) + a_B u_B(\overline{\mathbf{x}}_B) \geq a_A u_A(\mathbf{x}_A) + a_B u_B(\mathbf{x}_B)$, for all feasible allocations $\mathbf{x} = (\mathbf{x}_A, \mathbf{x}_B)$.

(a) $\mathbf{e}_A = (1, 0)$, $\mathbf{e}_B = (0, 1)$, $u_A(x_1, x_2) = \sqrt{x_1 x_2} = u_B(x_1, x_2)$.

(b) $\mathbf{e}_A = (0, 1)$, $\mathbf{e}_B = (1, 0)$, $u_A(x_1, x_2) = 2x_1 + x_2$, $u_B(x_1, x_2) = x_1 + 2x_2$.

(c) $\mathbf{e}_A = (2, 0)$, $\mathbf{e}_B = (0, 1)$, $u_A(x_1, x_2) = x_1 + x_2 = u_B(x_1, x_2)$.

(d) $\mathbf{e}_A = (1, 0)$, $\mathbf{e}_B = (0, 1)$, $u_A(x_1, x_2) = \min(2x_1, x_2)$, $u_B(x_1, x_2) = \min(x_1, 2x_2)$.

(e) $\mathbf{e}_A = (1, 0)$, $\mathbf{e}_B = (0, 2)$, $u_A(x_1, x_2) = \min(x_1, x_2) = u_B(x_1, x_2)$.

5. For the Edgeworth box economies listed below, find a number a_B such that the Pareto optimal allocation with $x_{A1} = 1/2$ maximizes the welfare function $u_A(x_{A1}, x_{A2}) + a_B u_B(x_{B1}, x_{B2})$ among all feasible allocations.

(a) $\mathbf{e}_A = (1, 0)$, $\mathbf{e}_B = (0, 1)$, $u_A(x_1, x_2) = 2\sqrt{x_1} + \sqrt{x_2}$, $u_B(x_1, x_2) = x_1 + 2x_2$.

(b) $\mathbf{e}_A = (1, 0)$, $\mathbf{e}_B = (0, 1)$, $u_A(x_1, x_2) = x_1^{1/3} x_2^{2/3}$, $u_B(x_1, x_2) = \sqrt{x_1 x_2}$.

6. Let $\mathbf{y} \in \mathbb{R}^N$. Prove that $\|\mathbf{x} - \mathbf{y}\|$ is a continuous function of $\mathbf{x}$. (Hint: Use the triangle inequality. That is, use the fact that $\|\mathbf{x} + \mathbf{y}\| \leq \|\mathbf{x}\| + \|\mathbf{y}\|$.)

7. Prove that if $\mathbf{y} \in \mathbb{R}^N$ and C is a closed set in $\mathbb{R}^N$, then there is a point in C that is closest to $\mathbf{y}$, that is, there is a vector $\mathbf{z} \in C$ such that $\|\mathbf{y} - \mathbf{z}\| \leq \|\mathbf{y} - \mathbf{x}\|$, for all $\mathbf{x} \in C$.

8. Suppose that C is convex and closed. You know from problem 7 that if the vector $\mathbf{y}$ in $\mathbb{R}^N$ does not belong to C, then there is a vector $\mathbf{z}$ in C which is closest to $\mathbf{y}$. Let $\mathbf{x}$ be a vector in C not equal to $\mathbf{z}$.

(a) Show that $\frac{d}{dt} \|\mathbf{y} - [\mathbf{z} + t(\mathbf{x} - \mathbf{z})]\|^2 \,|_{t=0} \geq 0$, where the notation means that the derivative is evaluated at $t = 0$.
(b) Use part (a) to show that $(\mathbf{y} - \mathbf{z}).\mathbf{z} \geq (\mathbf{y} - \mathbf{z}).\mathbf{x}$, for all $\mathbf{x}$ in C.
(c) Use part (b) to show that $(\mathbf{y} - \mathbf{z}).\mathbf{y} > (\mathbf{y} - \mathbf{z}).\mathbf{x}$, for all $\mathbf{x}$ in C.

You have shown that if C is compact and convex and $\mathbf{y}$ does not belong to C, then there exists a nonzero N-vector $\mathbf{w}$ such that $\mathbf{w}.\mathbf{y} > \mathbf{w}.\mathbf{x}$, for all $\mathbf{x}$ in C. This is a special case of Minkowski's separation theorem.

— 4 —

Competitive Equilibrium

One of the main accomplishments of general equilibrium theory is simply the definition of equilibrium. Although this achievement may seem modest, alternative definitions can be imagined, and the one that has been settled on has the advantages of being easy to remember and use and of capturing important aspects of economic life. It gives economists a simple common domain of discourse. Economic life is so varied and complex that models can become unmanageable if they include too many facets of reality.

4.1 The Definition of Competitive Equilibrium

In order to define equilibrium, we need a unit of account for evaluating purchases and sales. Its size is arbitrary. It may be thought of as money, but it lacks specific properties of actual money. For instance, no one in the model holds balances of unit of account. The price of commodity n in terms of the unit of account is denoted by p_n, and the vector of N prices is $\mathbf{p} = (p_1, p_2, \ldots, p_N)$. When I speak of a price vector, I mean an N-vector $\mathbf{p}$ such that $\mathbf{p} > 0$. That is, every price is nonnegative and at least one is positive. Given the price p_n, the value of x_n units of commodity n is $p_n x_n$. The value or cost of a bundle $\mathbf{x} = (x_1, \ldots, x_N)$ is the sum of the values of the quantities of each commodity, namely $p_1 x_1 + p_2 x_2 + \cdots + p_N x_N$. This sum may be written in an abbreviated form as $\mathbf{p}.\mathbf{x} = \sum_{n=1}^{N} p_n x_n$, where $\mathbf{p}$ is the N-vector of prices and $\mathbf{p}.\mathbf{x}$ is the dot product of $\mathbf{p}$ and $\mathbf{x}$ defined in definition 3.24 (in section 3.5). If $\mathbf{y}$ is an input-output possibility vector, then $\mathbf{p}.\mathbf{y}$ is the profit generated by $\mathbf{y}$ at prices $\mathbf{p} = (p_1, p_2, \ldots, p_N)$, as may be seen when $\mathbf{p}.\mathbf{y}$ is decomposed as follows:

$$\mathbf{p}.\mathbf{y} \sum_{n:y_n>0} p_n y_n + \sum_{n:y_n \leq 0} p_n y_n = \text{total revenues} - \text{total costs}.$$

It is assumed in the general equilibrium model that firms maximize profits. That is, each firm j solves the problem

$$\max_{\mathbf{y}\in Y_j} \mathbf{p}.\mathbf{y}.$$

The maximum profits are denoted by $\pi_j(\mathbf{p})$. That is,

$$\pi_j(\mathbf{p}) = \sup_{\mathbf{y}\in Y_j} \mathbf{p}.\mathbf{y}.$$

The set of profit maximizing vectors in Y_j is denoted by $\eta_j(\mathbf{p})$, so that

$$\eta_j(\mathbf{p}) = \{\mathbf{y} \in Y_j \mid \mathbf{p}.\mathbf{y} = \pi_j(\mathbf{p})\}.$$

It is assumed that firm j chooses some input-output vector in the set $\eta_j(\mathbf{p})$, though we cannot say which point is selected, if $\eta_j(\mathbf{p})$ contains more than one point. Figure 4.1 shows the profit maximizing point $\eta(\mathbf{p})$ in an example with two commodities. The line perpendicular to the price vector $\mathbf{p}$ through $\eta(\mathbf{p})$ is a line of constant profits, called an *isoprofit* line. Its intersection with the coordinate axes give profits measured in commodities 1 and 2, $\frac{\pi(\mathbf{p})}{p_1}$ and $\frac{\pi(\mathbf{p})}{p_2}$, respectively.

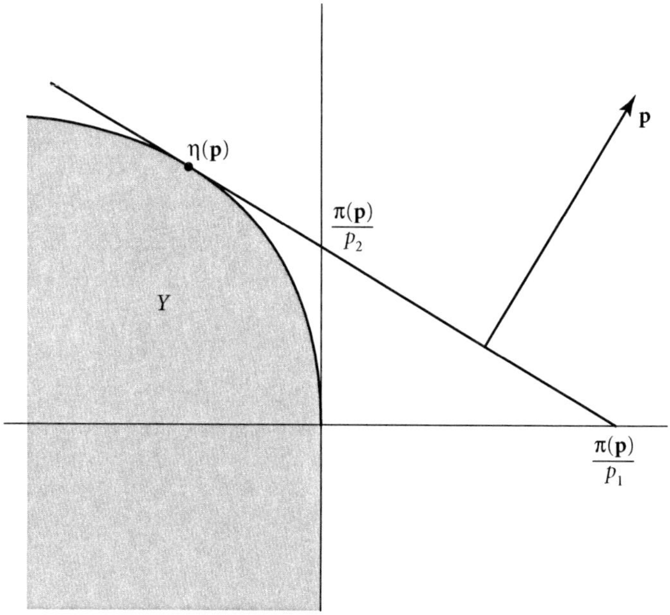

Figure 4.1 Profit maximization

Profits must be paid to someone, and I assume that they go to consumers, according to shares they own of the firms. It is possible to have profits be earned by one or more governments, but I do not include governments. The symbol Θ_{ij} denotes the share of consumer i in firm j. The numbers Θ_{ij} are nonnegative, and all the shares in a particular firm sum to 1. Formally,

$$\Theta_{ij} \geq 0, \text{ for all } i \text{ and } j, \text{ and for all } j, \sum_{i=1}^{I} \Theta_{ij} = 1.$$

If the price vector is $\mathbf{p}$, then consumer i receives $\Theta_{ij}\pi_j(\mathbf{p})$ in profits from firm j, and consumer i's total income from profits from all firms is $\sum_{j=1}^{J} \Theta_{ij}\pi_j(\mathbf{p})$. The description of an economy includes the parameters Θ_{ij}. That is, an economy $\mathcal{E}$ consists of the list

$$\mathcal{E} = ((u_i, \mathbf{e}_i)_{i=1}^{I}, (Y_j)_{j=1}^{J}, (\Theta_{ij})_{i=1,\ j=1}^{I\quad J}).$$

It is assumed that consumers can spend no more than they earn. If $\mathbf{e}_i$ is consumer i's endowment vector, the inner product $\mathbf{p}.\mathbf{e}_i$ is the value of $\mathbf{e}_i$ in terms of unit of account. Given a price vector $\mathbf{p}$, the *total income or wealth* of consumer i is

$$w_i(\mathbf{p}) = \mathbf{p}.\mathbf{e}_i + \sum_{j=1}^{J} \Theta_{ij}\pi_j(\mathbf{p}),$$

which is the value of the endowment plus the value of the consumer's share of profits from each of the firms. The set of consumption bundles that a consumer can purchase when prices are $\mathbf{p}$ is the *budget set,* defined as

$$\beta_i(\mathbf{p}) = \left\{\mathbf{x} \in \mathbb{R}_+^N \mid \mathbf{p}.\mathbf{x} \leq w_i(\mathbf{p})\right\}.$$

Figure 4.2 shows a budget set for a consumer when there are two commodities. The distance from A to B is the consumer's share of the profits of all firms measured in good 1, namely, $\frac{\sum_{j=1}^{J} \theta_{ij}\pi_j(\mathbf{p})}{p_1}$. The distance from 0 to A is the value of the consumer's initial endowment, $\mathbf{e}$, measured in good 1, $\frac{\mathbf{p}.\mathbf{e}}{p_1}$.

In equilibrium, consumers choose a consumption bundle in their budget sets so as to maximize their utility. That is, each consumer i solves the problem

$$\max_{\mathbf{x} \in \beta_i(\mathbf{p})} u_i(\mathbf{x}).$$

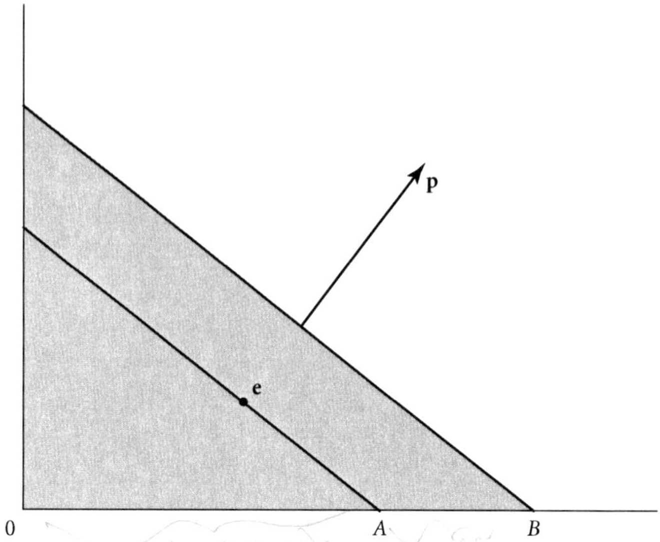

Figure 4.2 A consumer's budget set

The set of utility-maximizing vectors in the budget set is called the *consumer's demand set* or *Walrasian demand set* and is denoted $\xi_i(\mathbf{p})$. That is,

$$\xi_i(\mathbf{p}) = \{\mathbf{x} \subset \beta_i(\mathbf{p}) \mid u_i(\mathbf{x}) \geq u_i(\underline{\mathbf{x}}), \text{ for all } \underline{\mathbf{x}} \in \beta_i(\mathbf{p})\}.$$

Figure 4.3 shows a demand set with more than one point, the interval from A to B. The number w is the consumer's wealth or income measured in unit of account. The curve I is the consumer's indifference curve through the set of utility-maximizing points in the budget set.

An equilibrium is a feasible allocation together with a price vector such that in the allocation every firm maximizes profits at the given prices and every consumer maximizes utility within his or her budget set. In addition, commodities cost nothing if their supply exceeds demand. The formal definition is as follows.

DEFINITION 4.1 A *competitive* or *Walrasian equilibrium* for an economy

$$\mathcal{E} = ((u_i, \mathbf{e}_i)_{i=1}^{I}, (Y_j)_{j=1}^{J}, (\Theta_{ij})_{i=1,\ j=1}^{I\ \ \ \ J})$$

consists of $(\overline{\mathbf{x}}, \overline{\mathbf{y}}, \mathbf{p})$, where

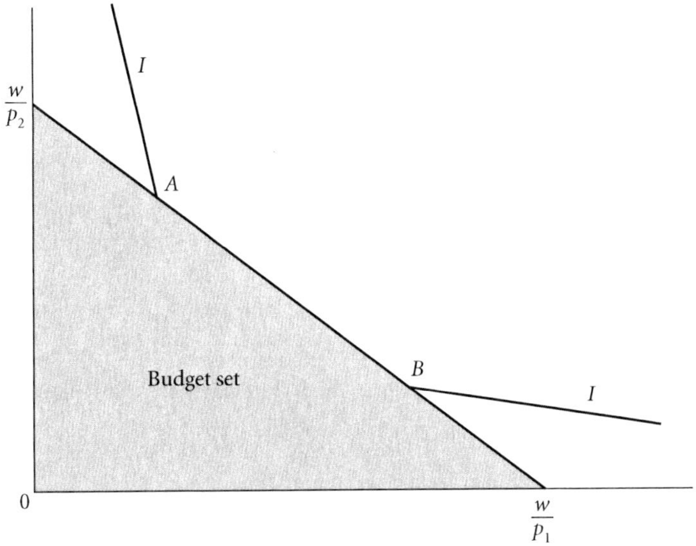

Figure 4.3 The demand set for a consumer

1. $(\overline{\mathbf{x}}, \overline{\mathbf{y}})$ is a feasible allocation
2. $\mathbf{p}$ is a price vector (that is, $\mathbf{p}$ is an N-vector such that $\mathbf{p} > 0$)
3. for all j, $\overline{\mathbf{y}}_j \in \eta_j(\mathbf{p})$
4. for all i, $\overline{\mathbf{x}}_i \in \xi_i(\mathbf{p})$
5. for all n, $p_n = 0$, if $\sum_{i=1}^{I} \overline{x}_{in} < e_{in} + \sum_{j=1}^{J} \overline{y}_{jn}$

The feasibility of the allocation $(\overline{\mathbf{x}}, \overline{\mathbf{y}})$ implies that supply is at least as great as demand in all markets. Condition (5) implies that the price is zero of any good for which supply exceeds demand. It is in this sense that all markets clear in equilibrium.

Competitive equilibrium is easy to visualize in the Robinson Crusoe and Edgeworth box examples. Equilibrium in the Crusoe example is illustrated in figure 4.4. The price vector is $\mathbf{p} = (w, p_F)$, where w is the wage and p_F is the price of food. The two straight lines of negative slope in the figure are perpendicular to $\mathbf{p}$ and represent consumption bundles of constant value in terms of unit of account. The distance $0\mathbf{e}$ from the origin, 0, to the initial endowment, $\mathbf{e}$, is Robinson's initial endowment of labor–leisure time. The distance $0A$ is the value of the endowment measured in food.

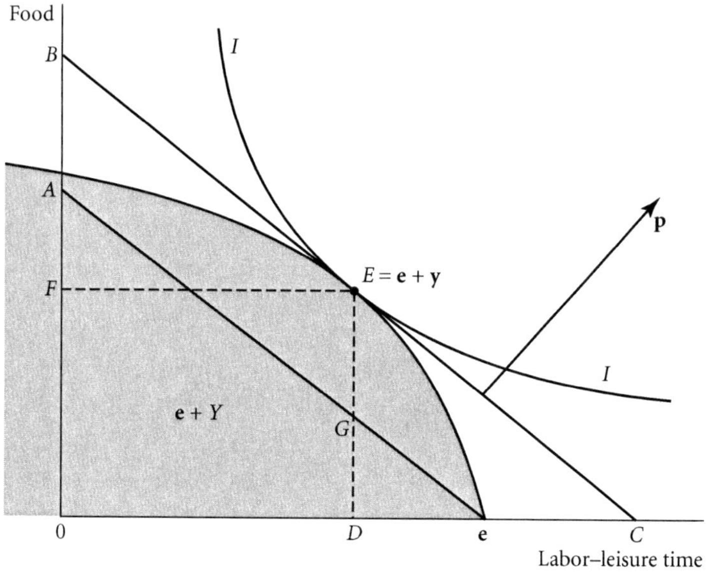

Figure 4.4 Equilibrium in the Robinson Crusoe example

That is, $0A$ and $0\mathbf{e}$ have the same value at the prices w and p_{F}. At the equilibrium allocation, E, Robinson, as a firm, uses $D\mathbf{e}$ units of labor to produce $DE = 0\mathrm{F}$ units of food. The value of the labor input, $D\mathbf{e}$, in terms of food is DG. Profits, measured in food, equal food sales, DE, minus the cost of labor, DG. That is, profits measured in food are $GE = AB$. Profits measured in labor or leisure are $\mathbf{e}C$, which is sales measured in labor, DC, minus the labor input, $D\mathbf{e}$. At the equilibrium point, E, Robinson consumes $0D$ units of leisure and $0F$ units of food. The value of Robinson's total income, measured in labor–leisure time, is $0C$, which consists of the endowment, $0\mathbf{e}$, plus profits, $\mathbf{e}C$. The value of Robinson's total income, measured in food, is $0B$, which consists of the value of the endowment, $0A$, plus the value of profits, AB. Robinson's budget set is the triangle $0BC$. His utility-maximizing point in the budget set is E, where an indifference curve, I, is tangent to the budget frontier, BC. The point E is $\mathbf{e}$ plus the profit maximizing input-output vector, $\mathbf{y}$, in the possibility set, Y. Because $\mathbf{y}$ maximizes profits, the budget frontier, BC, is tangent to $\mathbf{e} + Y$ at the point E.

Q what decides $\bar{p}$ vector? It's an endogenous var in Robinson Crusoe model, right?

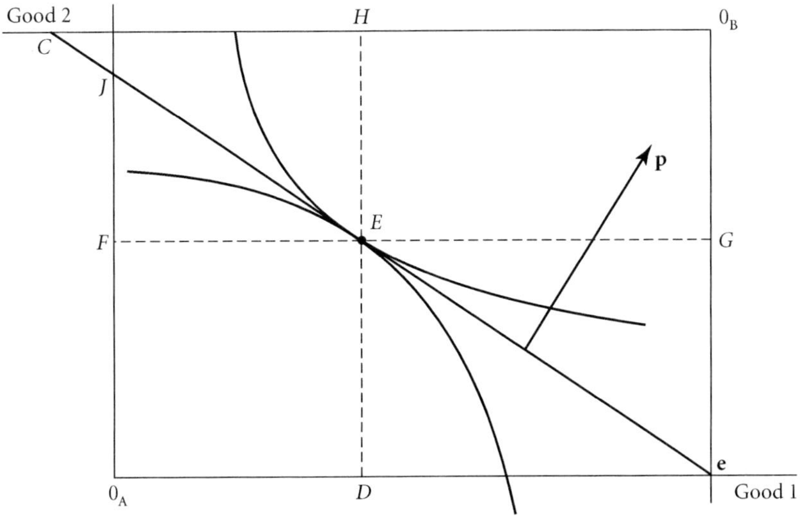

Figure 4.5 Equilibrium in the Edgeworth box example

Figure 4.5 illustrates equilibrium in the Edgeworth box example. In the equilibrium, consumer A consumes $0_A D$ units of good 1 and $0_A F$ units of good 2. The point E is the best point in consumer A's budget set, which is the triangle $0_A J\mathbf{e}$. Consumer B consumes EG units of good 1 and EH units of good 2. This consumption bundle is the best point in consumer B's budget set, $0_B\mathbf{e}C$. Notice that the budget set of consumer B contains infeasible points outside the box, such as the point C. Infeasible bundles may belong to budget sets, because consumers consider what they can afford, not what is available, when they choose consumption bundles so as to maximize utility.

The concept of equilibrium may perhaps be grasped more firmly by considering demand and supply in the above examples at nonequilibrium prices. Figure 4.6 shows a disequilibrium price vector for the Robinson Crusoe example. In the figure, the price of labor–leisure time is too high relative to that of food. The demand point is $\mathbf{x}$ and the supply point is $\mathbf{e} + \mathbf{y}$. There is an excess demand EF of food and an excess supply CD of labor–leisure time. Notice that the vector, $\mathbf{x} - \mathbf{e} - \mathbf{y}$, from $\mathbf{e} + \mathbf{y}$ to $\mathbf{x}$ is perpendicular to the price vector $\mathbf{p}$. This vector is termed the *excess-demand vector.* The orthogonality of the price and excess-demand vectors

how to visualize Edgeworth box if $e_A = (0, 0.5)$ & $e_B = (0.5, 0.5)$

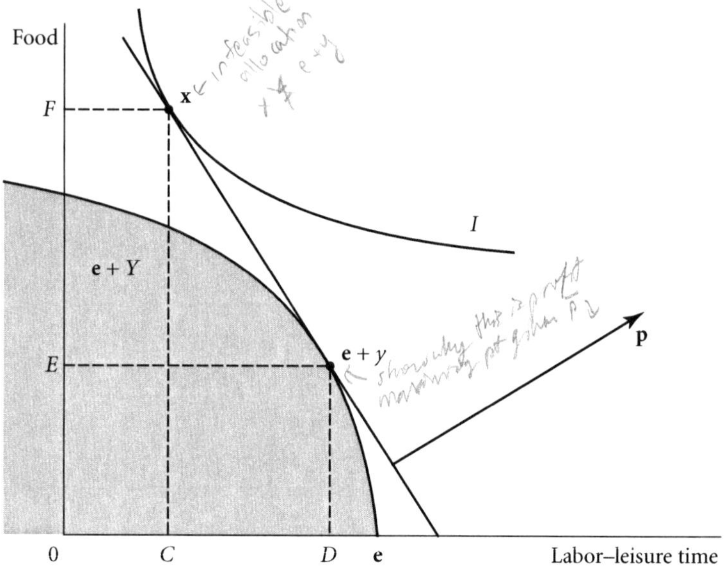

Figure 4.6 Nonequilibrium prices in the Robinson Crusoe example

is termed Walras' law and will be discussed in the next section. Notice also that we could arrive at equilibrium in the example by raising the price of the commodity in excess demand, which is food, relative to the price of the commodity in excess supply, which is labor–leisure time. That this should be so makes sense intuitively, since we imagine that prices should rise for commodities in excess demand and fall for those in excess supply. The reverse situation is shown in figure 4.7, where supply exceeds demand for food and is less than demand for labor–leisure time. Notice that the price of food is too high relative to that of labor–leisure time and that the excess-demand vector, $\mathbf{x} - \mathbf{e} - \mathbf{y}$, is again perpendicular to $\mathbf{p}$.

Figure 4.8 shows demands at nonequilibrium prices in the Edgeworth box example. Consumer A's demand point is $\mathbf{x}_A$, and that of consumer B is $\mathbf{x}_B$. There is an excess demand for good 2 of $x_{A2} + x_{B2} - e_{A2} - e_{B2}$ and an excess supply of good 1 of $e_{A1} + e_{B1} - x_{A1} - x_{B1}$, and the price of, good 2 is too low relative to that good 1. The excess-demand vector, $\mathbf{x}_A + \mathbf{x}_B - (\mathbf{e}_A + \mathbf{e}_B) = \mathbf{x}_A - (\mathbf{e}_A + \mathbf{e}_B - \mathbf{x}_B)$, is the vector from $\mathbf{x}_B$ to $\mathbf{x}_A$ in the figure since the vector $\mathbf{e}_A + \mathbf{e}_B - \mathbf{x}_B$ is labeled as $\mathbf{x}_B$ in the figure. The excess-demand vector is again perpendicular to the price vector $\mathbf{p}$.

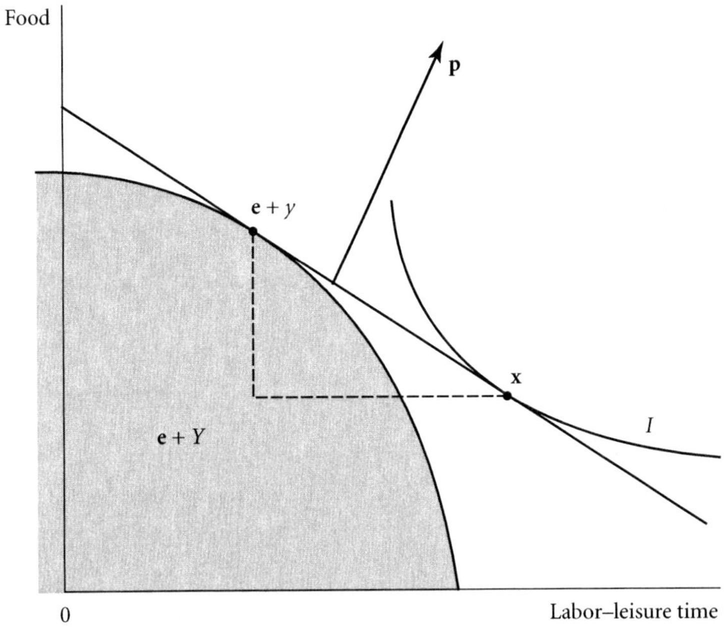

Figure 4.7 Non-equilibrium prices in the Robinson Crusoe example

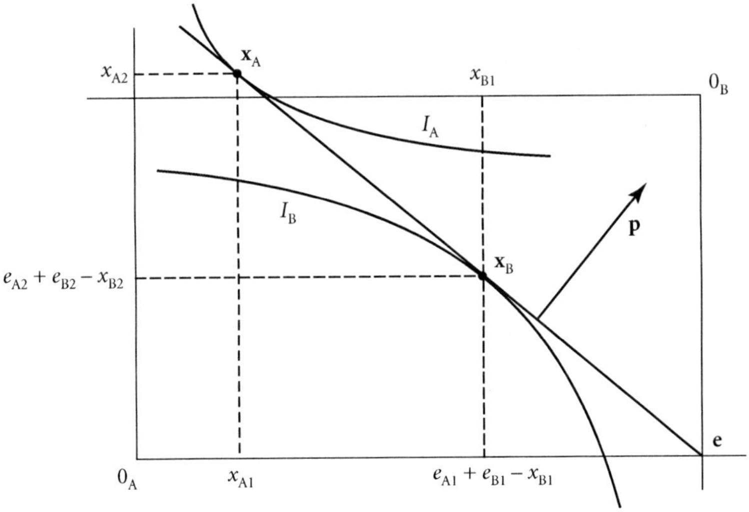

Figure 4.8 Nonequilibrium prices in the Edgeworth box example

Equilibrium may be achieved by raising the price of the good in excess demand, good 2, relative to that of the good in excess supply, good 1.

4.2 Properties of Market Excess Demand and Equilibrium

The market excess demand set is $z(\mathbf{p}) = \sum_{i=1}^{I}(\xi_i(\mathbf{p}) - \mathbf{e}_i) - \sum_{j=1}^{J} \eta_j(\mathbf{p})$, the difference between the market demand set, $\sum_{i=1}^{I} \xi_i(\mathbf{p})$, and the market supply set, $\sum_{i=1}^{I} \mathbf{e}_i + \sum_{j=1}^{J} \eta_j(\mathbf{p})$. The set $z(\mathbf{p})$ may contain many points, so that $\mathbf{z}$ is not necessarily a function. In this section, I describe useful properties of market excess demand and equilibrium. First of all, I show that market excess demand is homogeneous of degree 0, in the sense that $z(t\mathbf{p}) = z(\mathbf{p})$, for all positive numbers t. At the same time, I show that $((\mathbf{x}, \mathbf{y}), \mathbf{p})$ is an equilibrium if and only if $((\mathbf{x}, \mathbf{y}), t\mathbf{p})$ is one, for all positive numbers t. Hence, equilibrium depends only on the direction of the price vector and not on its length. That is, equilibrium depends only on relative and not on absolute prices. The relative prices at price vector $\mathbf{p}$ are the ratios $\frac{p_n}{p_k}$, for any n and k between 1 and N. These are well defined as long as $p_k \neq 0$. The relative prices at the price vector $t\mathbf{p}$ are the same as those at $\mathbf{p}$, since $tp_n/tp_k = p_n/p_k$.

As a first step toward showing that $z(\mathbf{p})$ is homogeneous of degree 0, I show that if Y_j is an input-output possibility set, the set of profit maximizing points, $\eta_j(\mathbf{p})$, is homogeneous of degree 0, in the sense that $\eta_j(t\mathbf{p}) = \eta_j(\mathbf{p})$, for all price vectors $\mathbf{p}$ and for all positive numbers t. The vector $\mathbf{y}$ belongs to $\eta_j(\mathbf{p})$, if and only if $\mathbf{p}.\mathbf{y} \geq \mathbf{p}.\mathbf{y}'$, for all $\mathbf{y}'$ in Y_j. Therefore, if $t > 0$, $t\mathbf{p}.\mathbf{y} \geq t\mathbf{p}.\mathbf{y}'$, for all $\mathbf{y}'$, which is true if and only if $\mathbf{y}$ belongs to $\eta_j(t\mathbf{p})$. That is, $\eta_j(\mathbf{p}) = \eta_j(t\mathbf{p})$ and so η_j is homogeneous of degree 0.

It is clear that the profit function π is homogeneous of degree 1, for

$$\pi(t\mathbf{p}) = \sup_{y \in Y_j} t\mathbf{p}.\mathbf{y} = t \sup_{y \in Y_j} \mathbf{p}.\mathbf{y} = t\pi(\mathbf{p}),$$

for all nonnegative numbers t and for all price vectors $\mathbf{p}$.

Recall that the income of consumer i is $w_i(\mathbf{p}) = \mathbf{p}.\mathbf{e}_i + \sum_{j=1}^{J} \Theta_{ij}\pi_j(\mathbf{p})$. The function w_i is homogeneous of degree 1, because

$$\begin{aligned} w_i(t\mathbf{p}) &= t\mathbf{p}.\mathbf{e}_i + \sum_{j=1}^{J} \Theta_{ij}\pi_j(t\mathbf{p}) = t\mathbf{p}.\mathbf{e}_i + \sum_{j=1}^{J} \Theta_{ij}t\pi_j(\mathbf{p}) \\ &= t[\mathbf{p}.\mathbf{e}_i + \sum_{j=1}^{J} \Theta_{ij}\pi_j(\mathbf{p})] = tw_i(\mathbf{p}). \end{aligned}$$

The budget set, $\beta_i(\mathbf{p})$, is homogeneous of degree 0 when thought of as a multiple-valued function of $\mathbf{p}$. Notice that if $\mathbf{x}$ belongs to $\mathbb{R}^N_+$, then it belongs to $\beta_i(\mathbf{p})$ if and only if $\mathbf{p.x} \leq w_i(\mathbf{p})$, which is true if and only if $t\mathbf{p.x} \leq t w_i(\mathbf{p}) = w_i(t\mathbf{p})$, for any $t > 0$, since w_i is homogeneous of degree 1. Therefore, $\mathbf{x}$ belongs to $\beta_i(t\mathbf{p})$. Similarly, $\mathbf{x}$ belongs to $\beta_i(\mathbf{p})$ if $\mathbf{x}$ belongs to $\beta_i(t\mathbf{p})$, so that $\beta_i(\mathbf{p}) = \beta_i(t\mathbf{p})$ and β_i is homogeneous of degree 0, as is to be shown.

The demand set, $\xi_i(\mathbf{p})$, is the set of points in the budget set, $\beta_i(\mathbf{p})$, that maximize consumer i's utility function, u_i. Because $\beta_i(\mathbf{p}) = \beta_i(t\mathbf{p})$, it follows that $\xi_i(\mathbf{p})$ is also the set of points that maximize u_i over the set $\beta_i(t\mathbf{p})$, and so $\xi_i(\mathbf{p}) = \xi_i(t\mathbf{p})$ and ξ_i is homogeneous of degree 0.

Because all the summands appearing in the definition of $z(\mathbf{p})$ are homogeneous of degree 0, $z(\mathbf{p}) = \sum_{i=1}^{I}(\xi_i(\mathbf{p}) - \mathbf{e}_i) - \sum_{j=1}^{J} \eta_j(\mathbf{p})$ is homogeneous of degree 0. Similarly, it is easy to see that equilibrium depends only on relative prices. Recall from definition 4.1 that the vector $((\overline{\mathbf{x}}, \overline{\mathbf{y}}), \mathbf{p})$ is an equilibrium, if and only if $(\overline{\mathbf{x}}, \overline{\mathbf{y}})$ is a feasible allocation; $\mathbf{p}$ is a price vector; $\overline{\mathbf{x}}_i \in \xi_i(\mathbf{p})$, for all i; $\overline{\mathbf{y}}_j \in \eta_j(\mathbf{p})$, for all j; and for all n, $p_n = 0$, if $\sum_{i=1}^{I} \overline{\mathbf{x}}_{in} < \sum_{i=1}^{I} \mathbf{e}_{in} + \sum_{j=1}^{J} \overline{\mathbf{y}}_{jn}$. If we replace $\mathbf{p}$ by $t\mathbf{p}$, where $t > 0$, then $\overline{\mathbf{x}}_i \in \xi_i(t\mathbf{p})$, for all i; $\overline{\mathbf{y}}_j \in \eta_j(t\mathbf{p})$, for all j; and all the other conditions obtain that are required for $((\overline{\mathbf{x}}, \overline{\mathbf{y}}), t\mathbf{p})$ to be an equilibrium.

Because equilibrium depends only on the direction of the price vector, not its length, we can choose its length arbitrarily. For instance, we can require that equilibrium prices sum to 1, so that the equilibrium price vector belongs to the price simplex, which is defined to be

$$\Delta^{N-1} = \{\mathbf{p} \in \mathbb{R}^N_+ \mid \sum_{n=1}^{N} p_n = 1\}.$$

Similarly, we might require that equilibrium price vectors belong to the $N - 1$ dimensional sphere of radius 1, so that they belong to the set

$$\mathrm{S}^{\mathrm{N}-1}_+ = \{\mathbf{p} \in \mathbb{R}^N_+ \mid \sum_{n=1}^{N} p_n^2 = 1\}.$$

The simplex and unit sphere are shown in figures 4.9 and 4.10, respectively, for the case of two commodities.

I turn now to Walras' law, which asserts that the value of market excess demand is zero at any price vector. More formally, for all price vectors $\mathbf{p}$,

$$\mathbf{p.z} = 0, \tag{4.1}$$

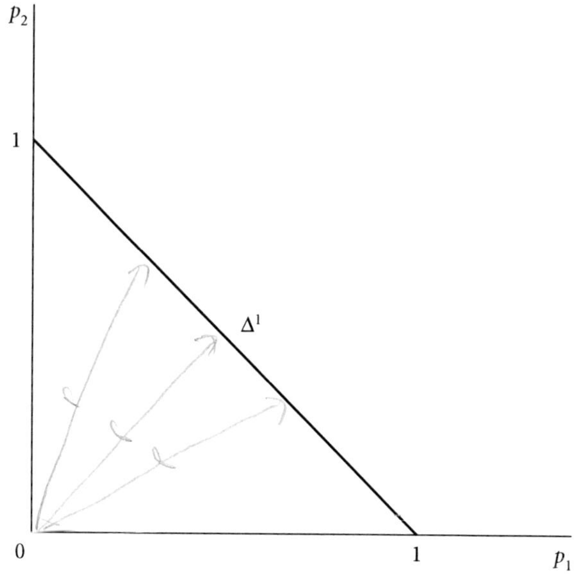

Figure 4.9 The price simplex

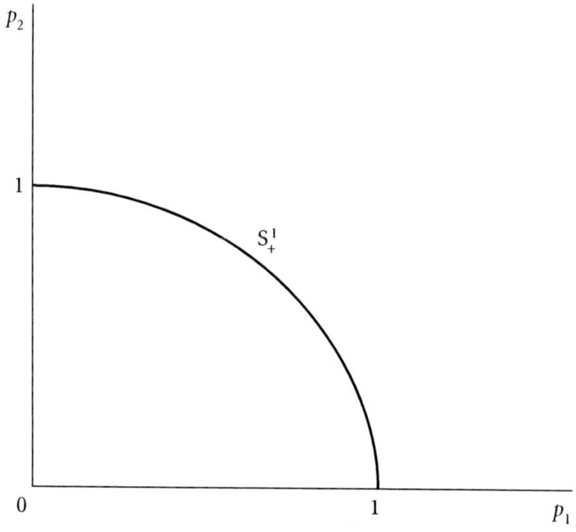

Figure 4.10 Price on the unit sphere

for all $\mathbf{z}$ in $z(\mathbf{p})$. Walras' law implies that there cannot be excess demand or excess supply for all commodities simultaneously. Thus, if $\mathbf{z}$ is in $z(\mathbf{p})$ and if commodity n is in excess supply and has positive price (that is, $z_n < 0$ and $p_n > 0$), then some other commodity m is in excess demand and has positive price (i.e., $z_m > 0$ and $p_m > 0$). Observe that Walras' law applies for all price vectors $\mathbf{p}$, not just for equilibrium price vectors. Clearly, equation 4.1 applies if $\mathbf{p}$ is an equilibrium price vector and $\mathbf{z}$ is the market excess demand corresponding to an equilibrium allocation, for in this case $z_n \leq 0$, for all n, and $p_n = 0$, if $z_n < 0$. If we think of an economic recession as corresponding to a state in which all commodities are in excess supply, then Walras' law implies that an economy in recession cannot be in equilibrium.

In order to state Walras' law precisely, I need to define a property of utility functions called *local nonsatiation.*

DEFINITION 4.2 A utility function $u: \mathbb{R}^N_+ \to \mathbb{R}$ is said to be *locally nonsatiated* if for every $\mathbf{x}$ in $\mathbb{R}^N_+$ and every positive number ε, there exists an $\mathbf{x}'$ in $\mathbb{R}^N_+$ such that $\|\mathbf{x}' - \mathbf{x}\| < \varepsilon$ and $u(\mathbf{x}') > u(\mathbf{x})$.

A utility function is locally nonsatiated if it is increasing, where increasing is defined as in definition 2.8 (section 2.3). If $\mathbf{x}$ is a nonnegative N-vector and ε is a positive number, then there is a vector $\mathbf{x}'$ such that $\mathbf{x}' \gg \mathbf{x}$ and $\|\mathbf{x}' - \mathbf{x}\| < \varepsilon$. Because u is increasing, $u(\mathbf{x}') > u(\mathbf{x})$. An example of a utility function that is not locally nonsatiated is $u: \mathbb{R}^2_+ \to \mathbb{R}$ defined by $u(x_1, x_2) = -(x_1 - 1)^2 - (x_2 - 1)^2$, which reaches a maximum at $(x_1, x_2) = (1, 1)$ and is therefore satiated there.

WALRAS' LAW THEOREM 4.3 If u_i is locally nonsatiated, for all i, then, for every price vector, $\mathbf{p}$,

$$\mathbf{p}.\left(\sum_{i=1}^{I}(\mathbf{x}_i - \mathbf{e}_i) - \sum_{j=1}^{J}\mathbf{y}_j\right) = 0,$$

if $\mathbf{x}_i \in \xi_i(\mathbf{p})$, for all i, and $\mathbf{y}_j \in \eta_j(\mathbf{p})$, for all j.

Observe that Walras' law applies at all price vectors, not just at equilibrium price vectors.

To prove Walras' Law, I need the following lemma, which says that consumers with locally nonsatiated utility functions spend all their income.

LEMMA 4.4 If u_i is locally nonsatiated, then $\mathbf{p}.\mathbf{x} = w_i(\mathbf{p})$, for all $\mathbf{x}$ in $\xi_i(\mathbf{p})$ and for all price vectors, $\mathbf{p}$.

Proof. Because $\mathbf{x} \in \xi(\mathbf{p})$, we know that $\mathbf{p}.\mathbf{x} \le w_i(\mathbf{p})$, so that $\mathbf{p}.\mathbf{x} < w_i(\mathbf{p})$, if $\mathbf{p}.\mathbf{x} \neq w_i(\mathbf{p})$. In this case, by the local nonsatiation of u_i, there exists an $\mathbf{x}'$ such that $u_i(\mathbf{x}') > u_i(\mathbf{x})$ and $\mathbf{x}'$ is so close to $\mathbf{x}$ that $\mathbf{p}.\mathbf{x}' < w_i(\mathbf{p})$. Hence, there is a point in consumer i's budget set strictly preferred by consumer i to $\mathbf{x}$, and this assertion contradicts the assumption that $\mathbf{x}$ belongs to $\xi_i(\mathbf{p})$. ■

Proof of Walras' Law. The idea of the proof is as follows. If all consumers have locally nonsatiated utility functions, then they spend all their income. Hence, the total value of all consumer demands equals the total of all consumer income. This income equals the income from profits and endowments, and the total value of these is the total value of all supply.

The formal proof of Walras' law is the string of equations that follows.

$$\mathbf{p}\cdot\left(\sum_i(\mathbf{x}_i - \mathbf{e}_i) - \sum_j \mathbf{y}_j\right) = \sum_i(\mathbf{p}.\mathbf{x}_i - \mathbf{p}.\mathbf{e}_i) - \sum_j \mathbf{p}\cdot\mathbf{y}_j$$

$$= \sum_i(w(\mathbf{p}) - \mathbf{p}.\mathbf{e}_i) - \sum_j \mathbf{p}\cdot\mathbf{y}_j$$

$$= \sum_i(\mathbf{p}.\mathbf{e}_i + \sum_j \Theta_{ij}\pi_j(\mathbf{p}) - \mathbf{p}.\mathbf{e}_i) - \sum_j \mathbf{p}\cdot\mathbf{y}_j$$

$$= \sum_i(\mathbf{p}.\mathbf{e}_i + \sum_j \Theta_{ij}\mathbf{p}\cdot\mathbf{y}_j - \mathbf{p}.\mathbf{e}_i) - \sum_j \mathbf{p}\cdot\mathbf{y}_j$$

$$= \sum_j\sum_i \Theta_{ij}\mathbf{p}\cdot\mathbf{y}_j - \sum_j \mathbf{p}\cdot\mathbf{y}_j = \sum_j \mathbf{p}\cdot\mathbf{y}_j - \sum_j \mathbf{p}\cdot\mathbf{y}_j = 0,$$

where the second equation follows from lemma 4.4 and the next-to-last equation follows from the condition that

$$\sum_i \Theta_{ij} = 1,$$

for all j. ■

Walras' law has a geometric interpretation, for it implies that an excess-demand vector **z** in $z(\mathbf{p})$ is orthogonal to the price vector **p**. The orthogonality is illustrated for the Robinson Crusoe and Edgeworth box economies in figures 4.6, 4.7, and 4.8 in section 4.1. This geometric interpretation underlies the standard proof of the existence of general equilibrium. In order to visualize the idea of the proof, normalize prices so that they are of length 1, that is, so that they belong to S_+^{N-1}. Because **z** is orthogonal to p, it is tangent to this sphere. Imagine moving the price vector in the direction of **z** and hence along the surface of the sphere. Such a movement has some intuitive appeal, since it involves raising the prices of commodities in excess demand (those for which $z_n > 0$) and lowering the prices of commodities in excess supply (those for which $z_n < 0$). Equilibrium is shown to exist by proving that this movement has a rest point and that the rest point is an equilibrium price vector.

The argument may be illustrated diagrammatically when there are two commodities. Then price vectors lie on a quarter circle of radius 1, S_+^1, as in figure 4.11. Assume that market excess demand is a function, so that $z(\mathbf{p})$ contains exactly one point. If the price vector moves in the direction of $z(\mathbf{p})$, then in the figure it moves along the circle toward the northwest. Equilibrium is reached either at a point where $z(\mathbf{p})$ equals 0 or at the point $(0, 1)$, which is the northwest endpoint of S_+^1. At this endpoint, the excess-demand vector $z(\mathbf{p})$ must be horizontal and pointing to the left, which means that there is excess supply of the first commodity ($z_1(\mathbf{p}) < 0$) and no excess supply of or demand for the second commodity ($z_2(\mathbf{p}) = 0$). It is permissible in equilibrium for $z_1(\mathbf{p})$ to be negative at the price vector $\mathbf{p} = (0, 1)$, since $p_1 = 0$. Similarly, there could be an equilibrium at the southeast endpoint of the quarter circle, if the excess-demand vector pointed straight down at that point. It should make sense intuitively that if there is no equilibrium at either end of the quarter circle, then there is one somewhere between the ends, provided $z(\mathbf{p})$ changes continuously as **p** changes.

As was mentioned earlier, Walras' law implies that excess supply for any commodity is matched by excess demand for some other commodity. This assertion is contradicted by common observation of reality, for in recessions or depressions there is a clear excess supply of almost every commodity, and especially of labor. The reason that Walras' law does not apply in such circumstances is that people cannot always sell all they want to. For instance, people may not be able to sell their labor at any price. An unstated

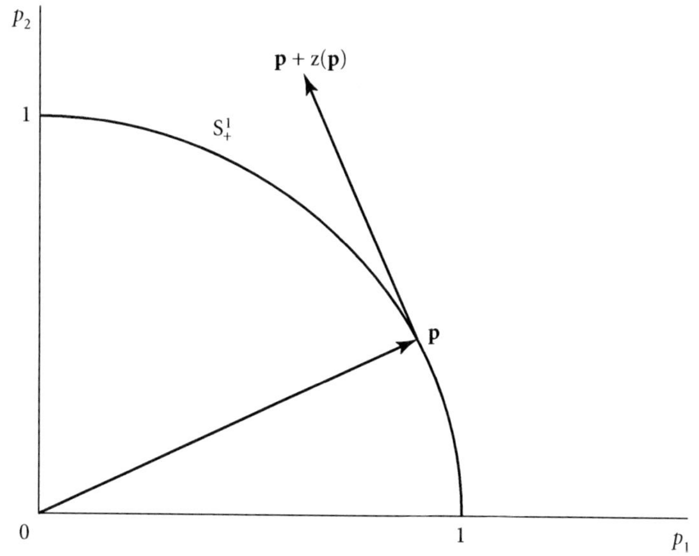

Figure 4.11 A consequence of Walras' law

assumption of the general equilibrium model is that individual buyers and sellers can buy or sell all they want at the market price.

4.3 Offer Curves

Offer curves are useful tools for visualizing equilibria in Edgeworth box models. If there are two commodities, the offer curve of a consumer with initial endowment vector **e** and utility function u is $\{\mathbf{x} \mid \mathbf{x} \in \xi(\mathbf{p}), \mathbf{p}$ is a price vector$\}$, where $\xi(\mathbf{p})$ is the set of solutions of the problem

$$\max_{\mathbf{x} \in \mathbb{R}^2_+} u(\mathbf{x})$$

$$\text{s.t.} \quad \mathbf{p}.\mathbf{x} \leq \mathbf{p}.\mathbf{e}.$$

The offer curve is the image of the map that carries price vectors to the consumer's demand set, $\xi(\mathbf{p})$.

Figure 4.12 shows an offer curve, $\mathcal{O}$, together with two indifference curves of the utility function u. The offer curve is the solid curve, and the indifference curves are dashed. Notice that the offer curve everywhere lies on or to the northeast of the indifference curve through the endowment point **e**. This is so because consumers can always buy their endowment

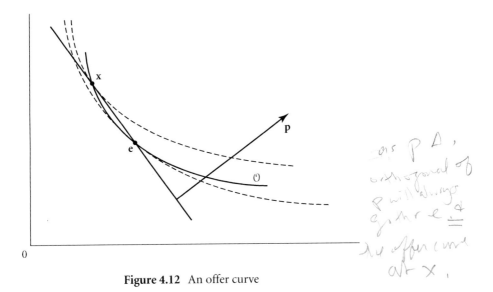

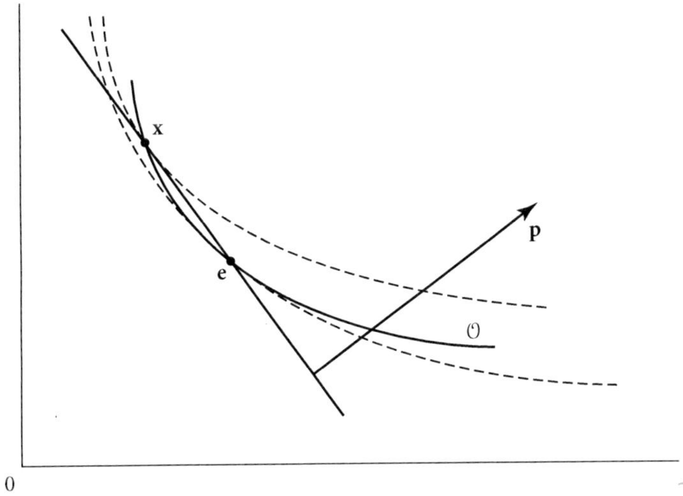

Figure 4.12 An offer curve

point, so that any demand vector in $\xi(\mathbf{p})$ is at least as desired as the endowment point **e**. Any point, **x**, on the offer curve corresponding to price vector **p** is a utility-maximizing point in the budget set determined by **p** and **e**.

In the Edgeworth box economy, equilibrium allocations occur at points where the offer curves of the two consumers intersect, when the offer curves are drawn relative to the origins of the respective consumers. Although the offer curves intersect at the endowment point, this point is an equilibrium allocation only if the offer curves are tangent there. The relation between equilibrium and offer curves is illustrated in figure 4.13. Again, the dashed curves are indifference curves, and the solid ones, $\mathcal{O}_A$ and $\mathcal{O}_B$, are the offer curves of consumers A and B, respectively. There is a unique equilibrium allocation at point E.

In Figure 4.14, offer curves are used to illustrate the possibility that an economy may have more than one equilibrium relative price vector. The equilibrium allocations are E_1, E_2, and E_3 with corresponding equilibrium price vectors p_1, p_2, and p_3.

Figure 4.15 illustrates an economy with a continuum of equilibrium allocations along the curved line segment CD.

In the Edgeworth box economy of figure 4.16, the endowment point, **e**, is an equilibrium allocation and is the only such allocation.

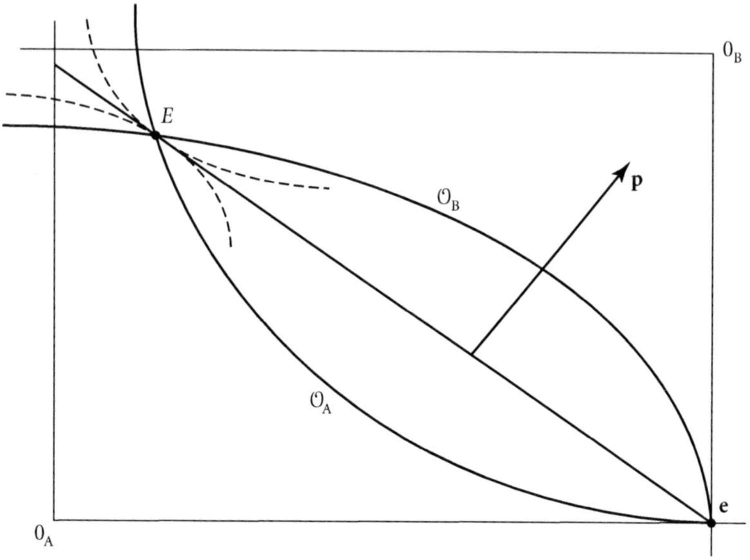

Figure 4.13 Equilibrium and offer curves

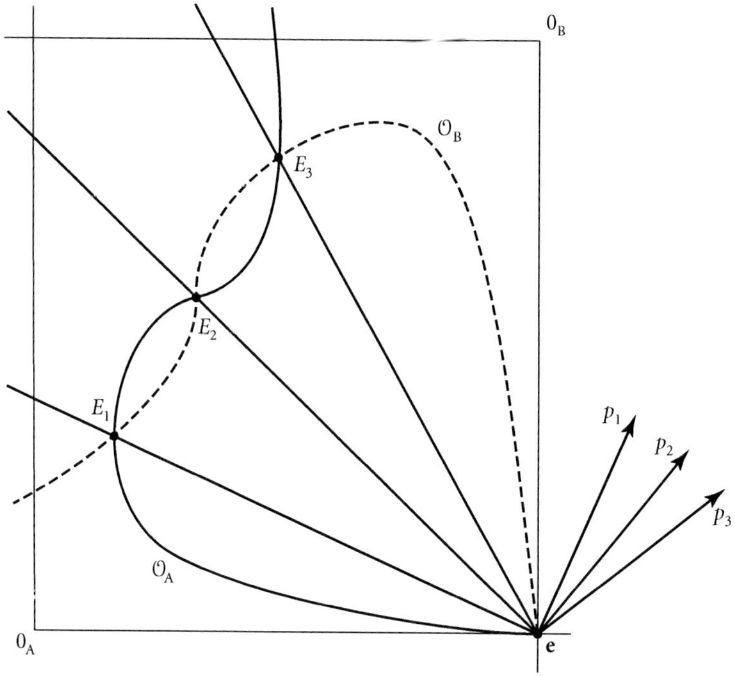

Figure 4.14 An economy with three equilibria

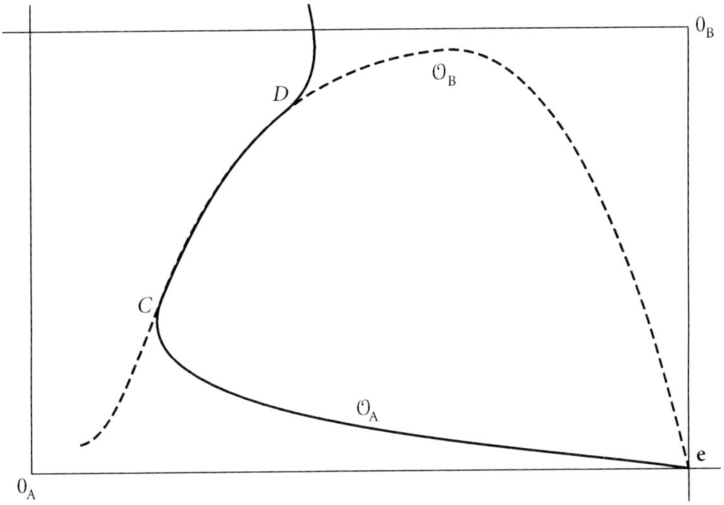

Figure 4.15 An economy with a continuum of equilibria

4.4 Equilibrium with Constant Returns to Scale

An important property of equilibrium is that the profits of a firm are zero if it has constant returns to scale. A production function $f: \mathbb{R}^N_+ \to [0, \infty)$ has *constant returns to scale* if it is homogeneous of degree 1, that is, if $f(t\mathbf{x}) = tf(\mathbf{x})$, for all $t \geq 0$. If an input-output possibility set rather than a production function describes technology, then constant returns to scale corresponds to the production possibility set being a cone.

DEFINITION 4.5 A subset Y of $\mathbb{R}^N$ is a *cone* if, for any nonnegative number t, $t\mathbf{y}$ belongs to Y, whenever $\mathbf{y}$ belongs to Y.

The set Y is a cone if and only if it contains all rays from zero through any nonzero member of Y. Any cone contains the zero vector $\mathbf{0}$.

I show that a production function f is homogeneous of degree 1 if and only if the corresponding input-output possibility set $Y = \{(-\mathbf{x}, y) \mid \mathbf{x} \in \mathbb{R}^N_+ \text{ and } y \leq f(\mathbf{x})\}$ is a cone, so that Y being a cone generalizes the concept of the constant returns to scale from production functions to input-output possibility sets. Suppose that f is homogeneous of degree 1, and let $t \geq 0$. Then $(-\mathbf{x}, \mathbf{y})$ belongs to Y only if $\mathbf{y} \leq f(\mathbf{x})$, which is true only if $t\mathbf{y} \leq tf(\mathbf{x}) = f(t\mathbf{x})$, where the equation follows from the homogeneity of f.

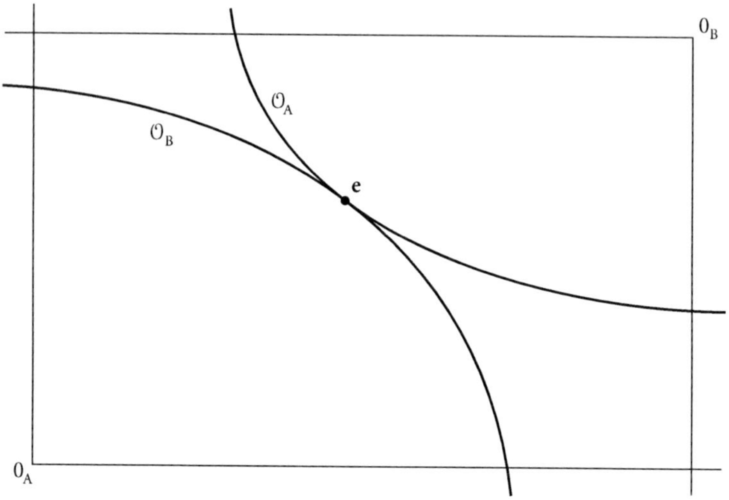

Figure 4.16 An Edgeworth box economy where the initial endowment point is an equilibrium allocation

Since $t\mathbf{y} \leq f(t\mathbf{x})$, it follows that $t(-\mathbf{x}, \mathbf{y})$ belongs to Y, so that Y is a cone. Suppose that Y is a cone, and let t be a positive number. Then, for any $\mathbf{x}$ in $\mathbb{R}^N_+$, $(-\mathbf{x}, f(\mathbf{x}))$ belongs to Y, so that $(-t\mathbf{x}, tf(\mathbf{x}))$ belongs to Y, since Y is a cone. Therefore by the definition of Y, $tf(\mathbf{x}) \leq f(t\mathbf{x})$. Similarly $(-t\mathbf{x}, f(t\mathbf{x}))$ belongs to Y, so that $(-\mathbf{x}, \frac{1}{t}f(t\mathbf{x}))$ belongs to Y and hence $\frac{1}{t}f(t\mathbf{x}) \leq f(\mathbf{x})$. Therefore, $f(t\mathbf{x}) \leq tf(\mathbf{x})$ and hence $tf(\mathbf{x}) \leq f(t\mathbf{x}) \leq tf(\mathbf{x})$ and so $f(t\mathbf{x}) = tf(\mathbf{x})$. It remains to be shown that $f(\mathbf{0}) = 0$. We know that $f(\mathbf{0}) \geq 0$, so that if $f(\mathbf{0}) \neq 0$, then $f(\mathbf{0}) > 0$. Suppose that $f(\mathbf{0}) > 0$. By the definition of Y, $(\mathbf{0}, f(\mathbf{0}))$ belongs to Y. Since Y is a cone, $t(\mathbf{0}, f(\mathbf{0})) = (\mathbf{0}, tf(\mathbf{0}))$ belongs to Y if $t > 0$. Therefore $tf(\mathbf{0}) \leq f(\mathbf{0})$, for all $t > 0$, which is impossible. This contradiction proves that $f(\mathbf{0}) = 0$.

Figure 4.17 shows an example of an input-output possibility set that is a cone and hence exhibits constant returns to scale. If we superimpose price vectors on this figure, as in figure 4.18, we see that profits are unbounded or zero, depending on whether the price vector is more vertical than or at least as vertical as the vector that is normal to the frontier of Y. If the price vector is more vertical than the normal, as is $\mathbf{p}''$, then there is no profit maximizing input-output vector and profits may be made arbitrarily large by moving out in the northwest direction along the frontier of Y. If the price vector is normal to the frontier, as is $\mathbf{p}$, then any point on the frontier is

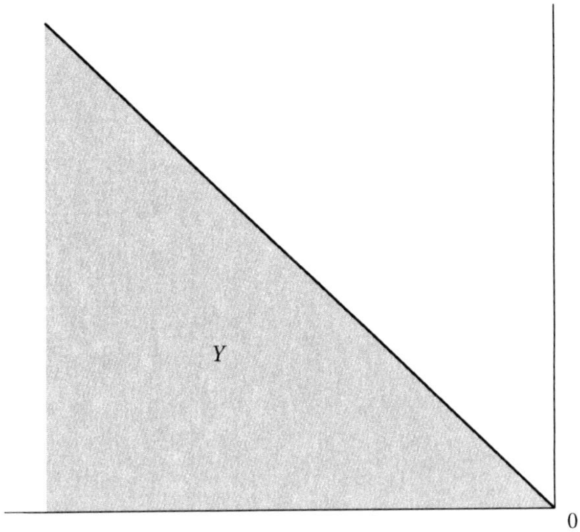

Figure 4.17 Constant returns to scale in production

profit maximizing, and maximum profits are zero. If the price vector is less vertical than the normal, as is $\mathbf{p}'$, then $\mathbf{0}$ is the only profit maximizing vector, and maximum profits are zero. The dotted lines in the figure are isoprofit lines at price vectors $\mathbf{p}'$ and $\mathbf{p}''$. The next proposition formally links zero profits to constant returns to scale.

PROPOSITION 4.6 If $Y \subset \mathbb{R}^N$ is a nonempty cone and $\mathbf{p}$ is a nonzero N-vector, then

$$\pi(\mathbf{p}) = \sup_{\mathbf{y} \in Y} \mathbf{p}.\mathbf{y}$$

is either infinity or zero.

Proof. Because Y is a cone, it contains the vector $\mathbf{0}$, and $\pi(\mathbf{p}) \geq \mathbf{p}.\mathbf{0} = 0$. Suppose that $\pi(\mathbf{p}) > 0$. Then $\mathbf{p}.\mathbf{y} > 0$, for some $\mathbf{y}$ in Y. Since Y is a cone, $t\mathbf{y}$ belongs to Y, for all $t > 0$. Therefore, $\pi(\mathbf{p}) \geq \mathbf{p}.(t\mathbf{y}) = t\mathbf{p}.\mathbf{y}$, for any positive number t. Letting t go to infinity, we see that $\pi(\mathbf{p}) = \infty$. ■

This proposition implies that if input-output possibility sets are cones, then profits must be zero in equilibrium, since they cannot be infinite. The idea is illustrated in figure 4.19, which shows a Robinson Crusoe economy with constant returns to scale in production. Crusoe's budget line goes

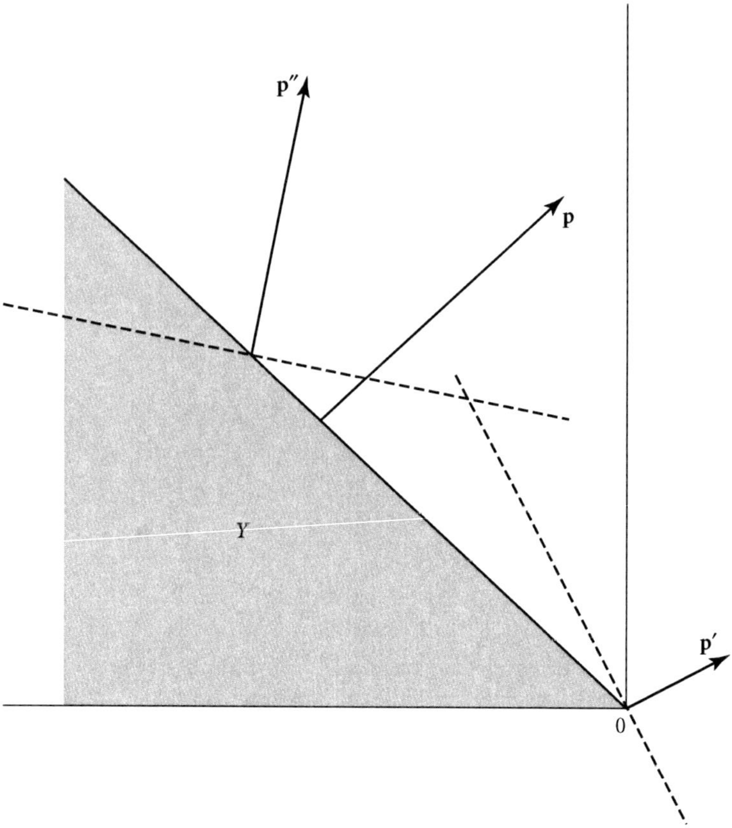

Figure 4.18 Profits with constant returns to scale

through his endowment point **e**, because all his income is earned from the sale of his endowment of labor–leisure time.

When there is only one output and the technology may be expressed by a differentiable production function, Euler's equation provides another way to see that there are zero profits when returns to scale are constant. Let the production function be $y = f(x_1, x_2, \ldots, x_N)$, where y is the quantity of output and x_n is the quantity of input n, and assume that f is differentiable and homogeneous of degree 1. The profit-maximization problem corresponding to this production function is

$$\max_{x_1 \geq 0, \ldots, x_N \geq 0} [pf(x_1, \ldots, x_N) - (w_1 x_1 + \cdots + w_N x_N)],$$

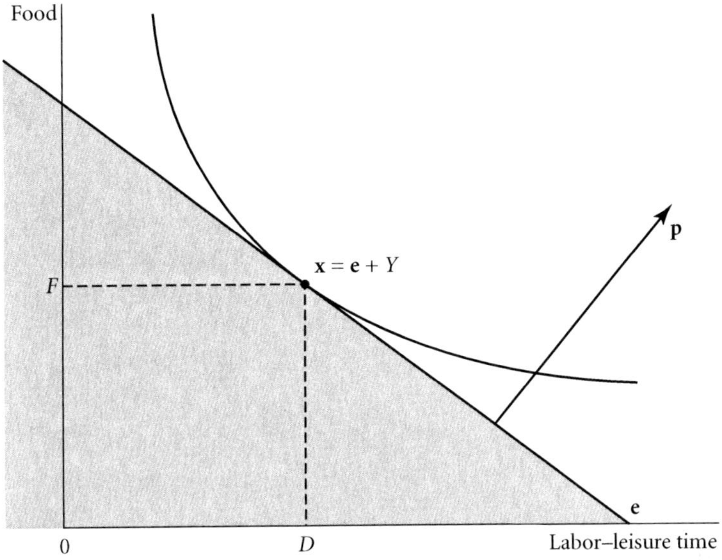

Figure 4.19 A Robinson Crusoe economy with constant returns to scale

where p is the price of the output and w_n is the price of the nth input, for all n. Since f is differentiable, the first-order conditions for this optimization problem are that, for all n,

$$w_n = p\frac{\partial f(x_1, \ldots, x_N)}{\partial x_n},$$

provided $x_n > 0$. Therefore,

$$w_n x_n = p\frac{\partial f(x_1, \ldots, x_n)}{\partial x_n} x_n. \tag{4.2}$$

That is, the total payments to each factor of production equals the value of its marginal product times the amount of the factor used in production. If we differentiate the equation $tf(x_1, \ldots, x_n) = f(tx_1, \ldots, tx_N)$ with respect to t at $t = 1$, we obtain

$$f(x_1, \ldots, x_N) = \frac{\partial f(x_1, \ldots, x_N)}{\partial x_1} x_1 + \cdots + \frac{\partial f(x_1, \ldots, x_N)}{\partial x_N} x_N, \tag{4.3}$$

an equation known as *Euler's equation*. If we substitute equation 4.2, for each n, into equation 4.3, we obtain

$$pf(x_1, \ldots, x_N) = w_1 x_1 + \cdots + w_N x_N.$$

That is, the revenue from sales of the product equals the sum of all payments to factors of production, so that maximum profits are zero.

4.5 Computation of Competitive Equilibrium in Simple Examples

I describe the computation of equilibrium in examples with no production and with simple forms of homothetic utility functions—the Cobb-Douglas, Leontief, and linear ones. Some of the computations involve the method of Lagrange multipliers, which I now review.

Consider the constrained maximization problem

$$\max_{\mathbf{x}\in\mathbb{R}^N_+} f(\mathbf{x})$$

$$\text{s.t.} \quad g(\mathbf{x}) = w,$$

where f and g are differentiable functions and w is a number. The function f is the objective function, the function g is the constraint function, and the equation $g(\mathbf{x}) = w$ is the constraint. If the maximum is attained at $\overline{\mathbf{x}}$, where $\overline{\mathbf{x}} \gg 0$, then there exists a number λ, called the *Lagrange multiplier*, such that

$$\frac{\partial f(\overline{\mathbf{x}})}{\partial x_n} = \lambda \frac{\partial g(\overline{\mathbf{x}})}{\partial x_n},$$

for $n = 1, \ldots, N$. This assertion may be written as $Df(\overline{\mathbf{x}}) = \lambda Dg(\overline{\mathbf{x}})$, where

$$Df(\overline{\mathbf{x}}) = \left(\frac{\partial f(\overline{\mathbf{x}})}{\partial x_1}, \ldots, \frac{\partial f(\overline{\mathbf{x}})}{\partial x_N}\right)$$

and

$$Dg(\overline{\mathbf{x}}) = \left(\frac{\partial g(\overline{\mathbf{x}})}{\partial x_1}, \ldots, \frac{\partial g(\overline{\mathbf{x}})}{\partial x_N}\right)$$

are the derivatives or gradients of f and g, respectively, at $\overline{\mathbf{x}}$. Hence the gradients of f and g lie on the same line, provided $\lambda \neq 0$. Necessary conditions for optimality are

$$g(x_1, \ldots, x_N) = w$$

and

$$\frac{\partial f(x_1, \ldots, x_N)}{\partial x_n} = \lambda \frac{\partial f(x_1, \ldots, x_N)}{\partial x_n},$$

for $n = 1, \ldots, N$. The latter N equations are known as *first-order conditions.* These equations together with the previous one form $N + 1$ equations in the $N + 1$ unknowns $x_1, \ldots, x_N$ and λ. These equations may be summarized using the Lagrangian function

$$\mathcal{L}(x_1, \ldots, x_N, \lambda) = f(x_1, \ldots, x_N) - \lambda[g(x_1, \ldots, x_N) - w].$$

The equations are

$$\frac{\partial \mathcal{L}}{\partial x_n} = 0,$$

for $n = 1, \ldots, N$, and

$$\frac{\partial \mathcal{L}}{\partial \lambda} = 0.$$

If we let

$$V(w) = \max_{\mathbf{x} \geq 0} f(\mathbf{x}) \text{ s.t. } \quad g(\mathbf{x}) = w,$$

then $\lambda = \frac{dV(w)}{dw}$. That is, the Lagrange multiplier is the rate at which the maximized value of the objective function increases as the right-hand side of the constraint increases.

I now apply the method of Lagrange multipliers to the problem of maximizing a utility function, $u(\mathbf{x})$, subject to a budget constraint, $\mathbf{p}.\mathbf{x} = w$. That is, I consider the problem

$$\max_{x_1 \geq 0, \ldots, x_N \geq 0} \quad u(x_1, \ldots, x_N)$$
$$\text{s.t.} \quad p_1 x_1 + \cdots + p_N x_N = w.$$

The Lagrangian is $\mathcal{L}(\mathbf{x}, \lambda) = u(\mathbf{x}) - \lambda \mathbf{p}.\mathbf{x}$. If the optimum occurs at $\overline{\mathbf{x}}$, where $\overline{\mathbf{x}} \gg 0$, then the necessary conditions for optimality are

$$\frac{\partial u(\overline{x}_1, \ldots, \overline{x}_N)}{\partial x_n} = \lambda p_n,$$

for $n = 1, \ldots, N$, and

$$p_1 \overline{x}_1 + \cdots + p_N \overline{x}_N = w.$$

The Lagrange multiplier is the rate at which the constrained maximum utility increases as the income or wealth w increases. For this reason, the multiplier is called the *marginal utility* of income or wealth.

I apply this method to the utility maximization with a Cobb-Douglas utility function, which, you may recall, has the form $u(x_1, \ldots, x_N) = x_1^{a_1} x_2^{a_2} \ldots x_N^{a_N}$ or $v(x_1, \ldots, x_N) = \ln(u(x_1, \ldots, x_N)) = a_1 \ln(x_1) + \cdots + a_N \ln(x_N)$, where $a_n > 0$, for all n. The utility functions u and v determine the same demand, since v is a monotone transformation of u. In order to calculate the demand function for a consumer with a Cobb-Douglas utility function, consider the consumer's maximization problem

$$\max[a_1 \ln(x_1) + \cdots + a_N \ln(x_N)]$$
$$\text{s.t.} \quad \sum_{n=1}^{N} p_n x_n = w.$$

The first-order conditions are obtained by forming the Lagrangian,

$$\mathcal{L} = a_1 \ln(x_1) + \cdots + a_N \ln(x_N) - \lambda[p_1 x_1 + \cdots + p_N x_N]$$

and calculating the equations

$$\frac{\partial \mathcal{L}}{\partial x_n} = 0,$$

for all n. These equations are

$$\frac{a_n}{x_n} = \lambda p_n,$$

for all n, which are the same as

$$p_n x_n = \lambda^{-1} a_n, \tag{4.4}$$

provided $\lambda > 0$, which turns out to be the case. By adding these equations over n, we obtain the equation

$$w = \sum_{n=1}^{N} p_n x_n = \lambda^{-1} \sum_{n=1}^{N} a_n,$$

which is the same as

$$\lambda^{-1} = \frac{w}{\sum_n a_n}. \tag{4.5}$$

Substituting equation 4.5 into equation 4.4, we obtain

$$p_n x_n = \frac{a_n}{\sum_{k=1}^{N} a_k} w,$$

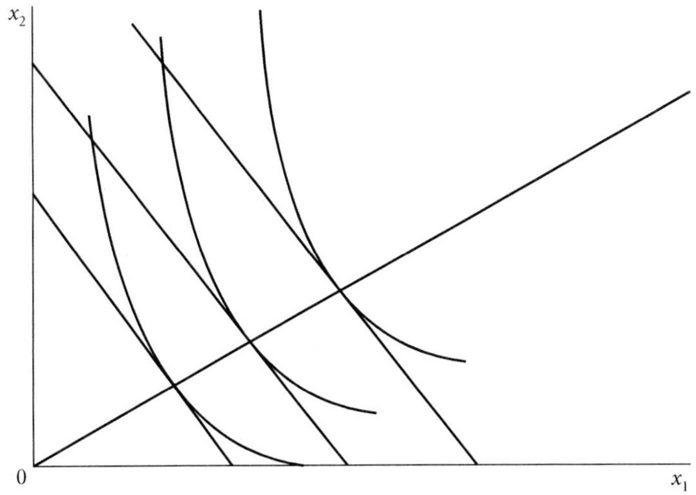

Figure 4.20 Income-expansion line for the Cobb-Douglas case

which is the same as

$$x_n = \frac{a_n}{\sum_{k=1}^{N} a_k} \frac{w}{p_n},$$

provided $p_n > 0$. Notice that the proportion of income spent on commodity n is $\frac{a_n}{\sum_k a_k}$.

If there are two goods and if prices are constant, then, as income w varies, the demand point moves along the ray defined by the equation $x_2 = (a_2/a_1)(p_1/p_2)x_1$, as pictured in figure 4.20. The ray is called an income-expansion line for this utility function. In general, an *income-expansion line* is the set of points $\mathbf{x} = (x_1, x_2)$ that solve the problem

$$\max_{\mathbf{x} \in \mathbb{R}^2_+} u(x_1, x_2)$$

$$p_1x_1 + p_2x_2 = w,$$

for some positive number w. If u is homothetic and the indifference curves of u become flatter and flatter as x_1 increases and x_2 decreases, then the income-expansion line is a ray through the origin, as in figure 4.20.

Returning to the Cobb-Douglas case, suppose that the income, w, is the value of the endowment vector, $\mathbf{e}$, so that $w = \mathbf{p}.\mathbf{e}$. Assume that the

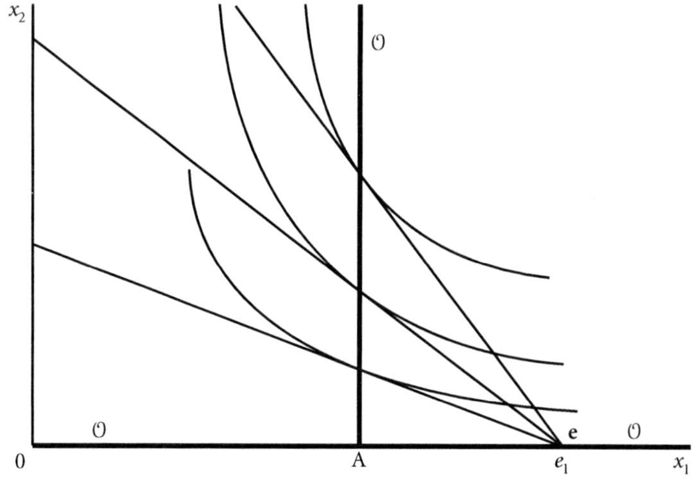

Figure 4.21 Offer curve for Cobb-Douglas utility with endowment only of commodity 1

consumer's endowment contains only one of the commodities, say, commodity 1. Then, $e = (e_1, 0, \ldots, 0)$, where $e_1 > 0$, and the demand, x_1, for commodity 1 satisfies the equation

$$p_1 x_1 = \frac{a_1}{a_1 + a_2 + \cdots + a_N} p_1 e_1.$$

If p_1 is positive, I may cancel it from both sides of this equation and obtain

$$x_1 = \frac{a_1}{a_1 + a_2 + \cdots + a_N} e_1. \tag{4.6}$$

If $N = 2$, equation 4.6 defines the part of the offer curve $\mathcal{O}$ of the consumer that is shown in figure 4.21 as the vertical line $\mathcal{O}$ over the point A, which has coordinates $\left(\frac{a_1}{a_1+a_2} e_1, 0\right)$. The offer curve also includes the nonnegative part of the horizontal axis, since this is the budget set if the price of good 1 is 0, and the consumer is indifferent among all points in the budget set.

It is easy to calculate an equilibrium allocation for an Edgeworth box economy in which both of the consumers possess only one commodity initially. Suppose that the economy is

$$u_A(x_1, x_2) = x_1^a x_2^{1-a}, \ \mathbf{e}_A = (1, 0),$$

$$u_B(x_1, x_2) = x_1^b x_2^{1-b}, \text{ and } \mathbf{e}_B = (0, 1),$$

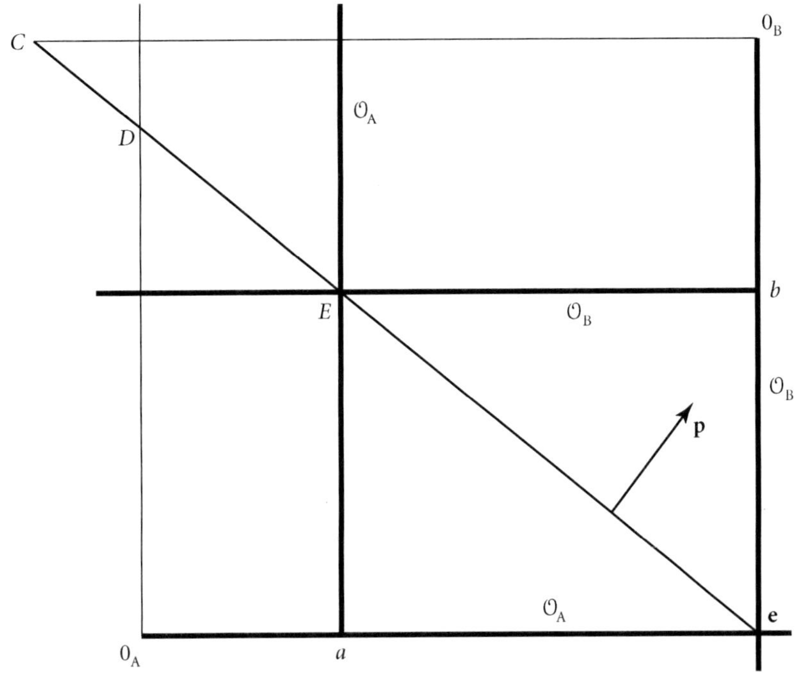

Figure 4.22 Equilibrium in Edgeworth box with Cobb-Douglas utilities and each consumer owning only one commodity initially

where the numbers a and b lie between 0 and 1. If $(\mathbf{x}_A, \mathbf{x}_B)$ is the equilibrium allocation, then $x_{A1} = a$, so that $x_{B1} = e_{A1} + e_{B1} - x_{A1} = 1 - a$. Similarly, $x_{B2} = 1 - b$, so that $x_{A2} = b$. We may compute the equilibrium prices as follows. Since any equilibrium price vector, $\mathbf{p}$, may be replaced by $t\mathbf{p}$, for any positive t, we may normalize the equilibrium price vector so that $p_1 + p_2 = 1$. The equilibrium allocation satisfies the budget constraint, $\mathbf{p}.\mathbf{x}_A = \mathbf{p}.\mathbf{e}_A$, so that $p_1 a + p_2 b = p_1$. Substituting $p_2 = 1 - p_1$ into this last equation, we obtain $p_1 a + (1 - p_1)b = p_1$, which implies that $p_1 = \frac{b}{1-a+b}$ and hence $p_2 = \frac{1-a}{1-a+b}$. The equilibrium is pictured in figure 4.22. The equilibrium allocation is at point E. The budget set of consumer A is the triangle $0_A D\mathbf{e}$, and that of consumer B is the triangle $0_B\mathbf{e}C$.

It is not hard to calculate equilibrium allocations in Edgeworth box economies with Cobb-Douglas utility functions, even when consumers possess some of both commodities initially. Suppose that the utility functions are as just stated and that the endowments are $\mathbf{e}_A = (e_{A1}, e_{A2})$ and $\mathbf{e}_B = (e_{B1}, e_{B2})$. Then, the demands for commodity 1 are determined by the equations

$$\begin{aligned} p_1 x_{A1} &= a[p_1 e_{A1} + (1 - p_1)e_{A2}] \quad \text{and} \\ p_1 x_{B1} &= b[p_1 e_{B1} + (1 - p_1)e_{B2}]. \end{aligned} \tag{4.7}$$

By adding the previous two equations and substituting the feasibility condition, we see that

$$\begin{aligned} p_1(e_{A1} + e_{B1}) = p_1(x_{A1} + x_{B1}) = a[p_1 e_{A1} + (1 - p_1)e_{A2}] \\ + b[p_1 e_{B1} + (1 - p_1)e_{B2}], \end{aligned} \tag{4.8}$$

which is a linear equation in p_1. Once p_1 has been calculated, p_2 is known, since it is assumed that the two prices sum to 1. Given p_1 and p_2, the consumer demands x_{A1} and x_{B1} may be calculated by substitution into equations 4.7, and the demands x_{A2} and x_{B2} can be obtained from similar equations.

I now turn to the case of Leontief utility functions. Recall that these functions have the form $u(x_1, \ldots, x_N) = \min(a_1 x_1, \ldots, a_N x_N)$, where $a_n > 0$, for all n. Consider the problem

$$\max_{x_1 \geq 0, x_2 \geq 0} \min(a_1 x_1, a_2 x_2)$$
$$\text{s.t.} \quad p_1 x_1 + p_2 x_2 = w,$$

where a_1 and a_2 are positive numbers. The solution is obtained by solving the two equations given by the budget condition, $p_1 x_1 + p_2 x_2 - w$, and the condition, $a_1 x_1 = a_2 x_2$, satisfied at the optimum. These demands are

$$x_1 = \frac{a_2 w}{a_2 p_1 + a_1 p_2} \text{ and } x_2 = \frac{a_1 w}{a_2 p_1 + a_1 p_2}.$$

The solution is pictured in figure 4.23. The demand point is at A, and the dashed lines are indifference curves. The person's offer curve is the heavy angled line that includes the nonnegative half of the horizontal axis, the part of the line labeled $x_2 = (a_1/a_2)x_1$ from the origin to point B, and the vertical half of the line going upward from point B. The income-expansion line is the line defined by the equation $x_2 = (a_1/a_2)x_1$, provided both prices are positive. If $p_2 = 0$, then what corresponds to the income-expansion line is the region on and above the line defined by the equation $x_2 = (a_1/a_2)x_1$. Similarly if $p_1 = 0$, then what corresponds to the income-expansion line is the region on and below this line.

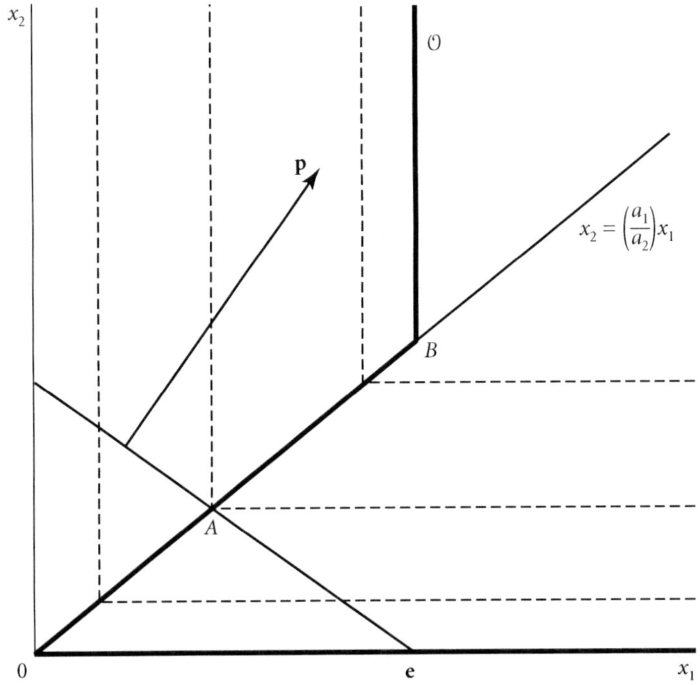

Figure 4.23 Offer curve with Leontief utility

Figure 4.24 depicts equilibrium in an Edgeworth box economy where both consumers have Leontief utility functions. The shaded areas are the Pareto optimal allocations, and, as before, the dashed lines are indifference curves. The configuration of the set of Pareto optimal and equilibrium allocations depends on the particular choices of the two Leontief utility functions.

Figure 4.25 shows another Edgeworth box example, where the total endowment of commodity 2 exceeds that of commodity 1 and where each consumer has the Leontief utility function $u(x_1, x_2) = \min(x_1, x_2)$. The shaded area again represents the Pareto optimal allocations. The equilibrium allocations are the interval along the right-hand side of the box from point C to $\mathbf{0}_B$, and the equilibrium price vector is $\mathbf{p} = (1, 0)$. We may think of the commodities as left shoes and right shoes, with left shoes on the

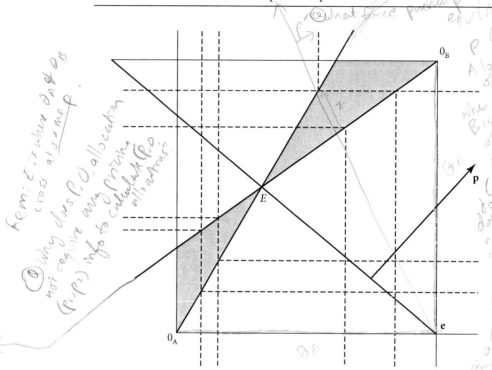

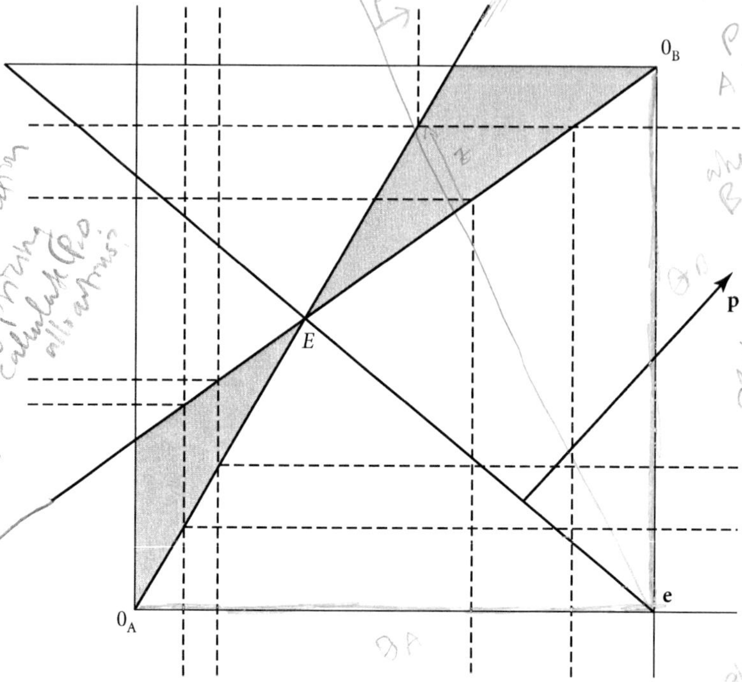

Figure 4.24 Equilibrium in an Edgeworth box economy with Leontief utility functions

vertical axis. Shoes are wanted only in pairs, and because there are more left than right shoes, the price of left shoes is zero.

Calculations with linear utility functions are very simple. Recall that a linear utility function is of the form $u(x_1, x_2) = a_1x_1 + a_2x_2$, where $a_1 > 0$ and $a_2 > 0$. Maximizing this function subject to the budget constraint $p_1x_1 + p_2x_2 = w$, we see that $x_2 = 0$ and $x_1 = w/p_1$, if $p_2/p_1 > a_2/a_1$ and $x_2 = w/p_2$ and $x_1 = 0$, if $p_2/p_1 < a_2/a_1$. The set of utility-maximizing points is the entire budget line $\{(x_1, x_2) \geq \mathbf{0} \mid p_1x_1 + p_2x_2 = w\}$ if $p_2/p_1 = a_2/a_1$. The case $p_2/p_1 > a_2/a_1$ is illustrated in figure 4.26. The dashed lines are indifference curves, and demand is at point A. The income-expansion line is the nonnegative part of the horizontal coordinate axis if $p_2/p_1 > a_2/a_1$ and is the nonnegative part of the vertical axis if $p_2/p_1 < a_2/a_1$. If $p_2/p_1 = a_2/a_1$, then what corresponds to the income-expansion line is the entire nonnegative orthant.

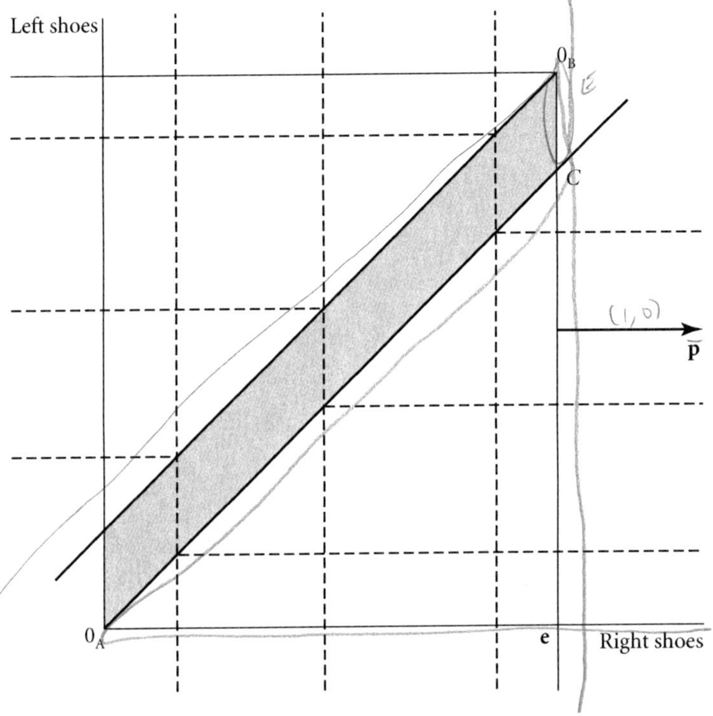

Figure 4.25 Left-shoe, right-shoe example

Consider the following Edgeworth box economy with linear utility functions:

$$u_A(x_1, x_2) = a_{A1}x_1 + a_{A2}x_2,\ \mathbf{e}_A = (1, 0),$$
$$u_B(x_1, x_2) = a_{B1}x_1 + a_{B2}x_2,\ \text{and } \mathbf{e}_B = (0, 1).$$

The case $a_{B2}/a_{B1} > a_{A2}/a_{A1}$ is illustrated in figure 4.27. The unique equilibrium allocation is the endowment point, **e**. Any price vector, **p**, satisfying the inequalities $a_{B2}/a_{B1} \geq p_2/p_1 \geq a_{A2}/a_{A1}$ is an equilibrium price vector. One such vector is indicated in the figure. The indifference curves of consumers A and B are labeled I_A and I_B, respectively.

Figure 4.28 illustrates the case $a_{B2}/a_{B1} < a_{A2}/a_{A1}$. The sole equilibrium allocation is at E. The equilibrium relative-price vector, **p**, is also unique. At another relative price vector, such as $\overline{\mathbf{p}}$, consumers A and B choose distinct bundles, namely C and D, respectively.

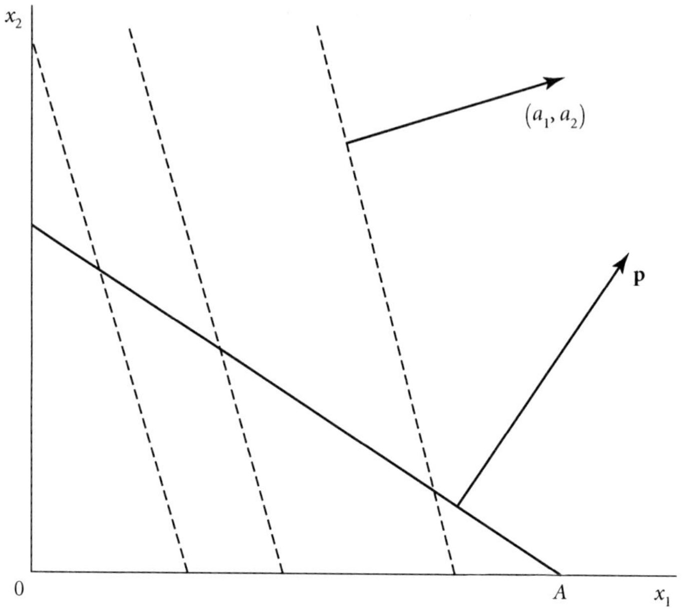

Figure 4.26 Demand with linear utility

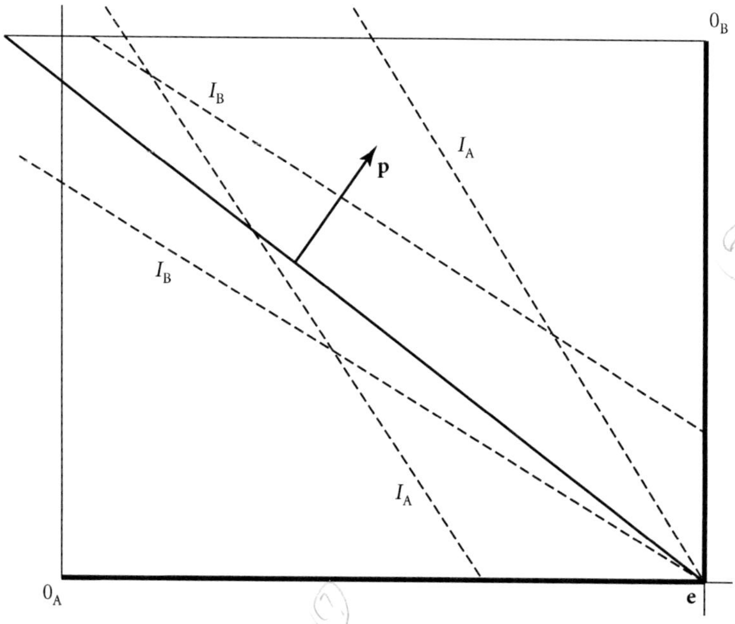

Figure 4.27 Equilibrium in the Edgeworth box with linear utility functions when consumer A has a greater relative preference for commodity 1

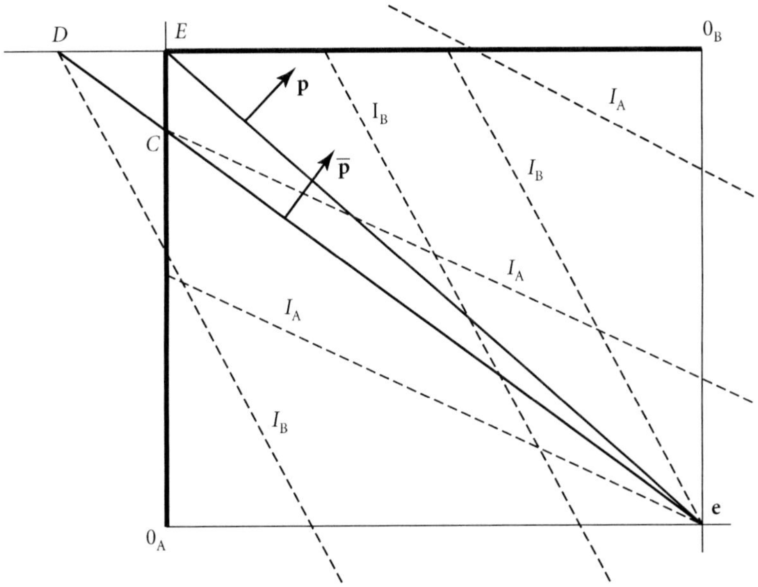

Figure 4.28 Equilibrium in the Edgeworth box with linear utility functions when consumer B has a greater relative preference for commodity 1

4.6 Aggregate Input-Output Possibility Sets

I turn to the study of production processes that operate simultaneously. It may help the reader's intuition to visualize two firms that use the same two inputs to produce single outputs. Suppose that firms A and B use inputs 1 and 2 to produce output according to the production functions $f_A : \mathbb{R}^2_+ \to \mathbb{R}$ and $f_B : \mathbb{R}^2_+ \to \mathbb{R}$, respectively. The two firms may be producing the same or different commodities. Suppose that there are fixed amounts, e_1 and e_2, respectively, of inputs 1 and 2 available to be used in production by the two firms. Then the situation is exactly analogous to the problem of allocating fixed amounts of two consumption goods between two consumers, A and B, with utility functions, f_A and f_B, respectively. The production problem may be represented by an Edgeworth box diagram with horizontal length e_1 and vertical height e_2. It is sufficient to relabel the axes as production inputs, as in figure 4.29, where x_{A1}, x_{A2}, x_{B1}, and x_{B2} are the inputs of commodities 1 and 2 used by firms A and B, respectively. The curves corresponding to consumers' indifference curves are called *isoquants*, which are

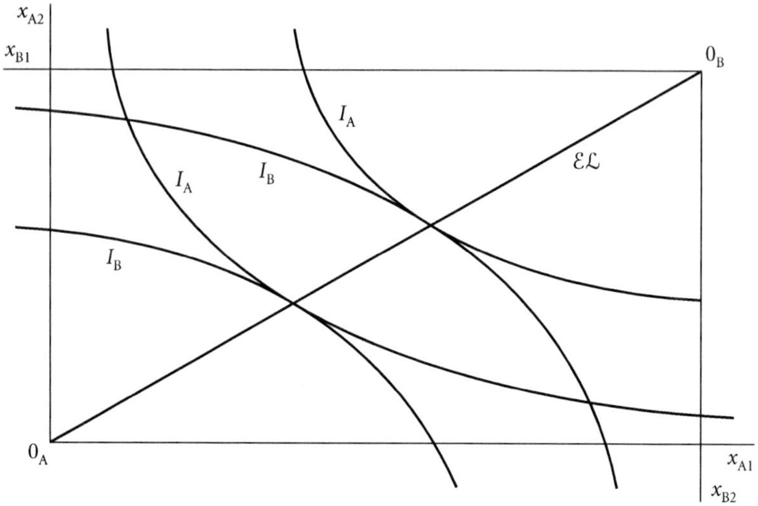

Figure 4.29 Efficient allocation of inputs between two firms

curves of constant output. An isoquant is a set of points (x_1, x_2) that satisfy the equation $f_A(x_1, x_2) = \text{constant}$ or the equation $f_B(x_1, x_2) = \text{constant}$. Efficient allocations of inputs to the two firms occur at points of tangency of the isoquants, and the set of tangencies is the *efficiency locus*, labeled $\mathcal{EL}$ in figure 4.29. It is the set of efficient allocations of the two inputs to the production of commodities A and B. An allocation is efficient if no other allocation yields at least as much output from both firms and more from at least one of them. If both firms maximize profits at the same prices, then they minimize the costs of producing the outputs they choose to produce. If a firm chooses inputs so as to minimize costs, then it chooses a point on an isoquant that has the lowest cost. The input levels for one firm can be represented as points in the nonnegative orthant, $\mathbb{R}^2_+$, and the points of constant cost satisfy an equation of the form $p_1x_1 + p_2x_2 = \text{constant}$, where p_1 and p_2 are the prices of inputs 1 and 2, respectively. These points are a straight line segment analogous to the budget line of a consumer and termed an *isocost line.* The point on an isoquant of lowest cost is tangent to such an isocost line, just as the indifference curve of a consumer is tangent to the budget line at the point where he or she maximizes utility. Point $\mathbf{x}$ is such a point of tangency in figure 4.30. If firms A and B face the same input prices and allocate the inputs between them by choosing quantities that maximize profits, then they minimize costs and so choose a point, such as $\mathbf{x}$ in the box

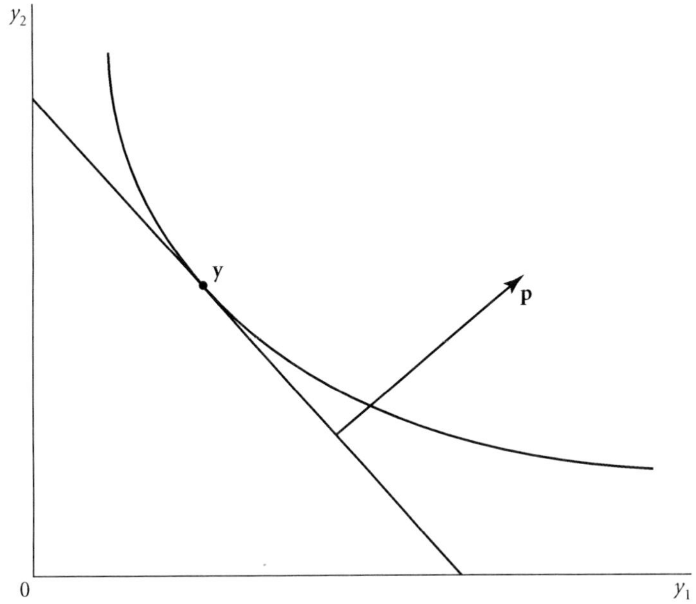

Figure 4.30 Cost-minimizing pair of inputs

diagram of figure 4.31, at which their isoquants are tangent to a common constant cost line and hence are tangent to each other. It follows that the input allocation is efficient.

The efficiency of this input allocation is a special case of the more general assertion that if there are many firms and every one of them maximizes profits, then the aggregate input-output vector of all firms is efficient, provided all prices are positive. As a first step toward making this statement rigorous, I define efficiency.

DEFINITION 4.7 The point $\overline{\mathbf{y}}$ in an input-output possibility set Y (or in an output possibility set Y) is said to be *efficient* in Y, if there exists no $\mathbf{y}$ in Y such that $\mathbf{y} > \overline{\mathbf{y}}$.

A key statement is as follows.

PROPOSITION 4.8 If $p \gg 0$ and if the vector $\overline{\mathbf{y}}$ in the input-output possibility set Y (or in the output possibility set Y) is such that $\mathbf{p}.\overline{\mathbf{y}} \geq \mathbf{p}.\mathbf{y}$, for all $\mathbf{y}$ in Y, then $\overline{\mathbf{y}}$ is efficient in Y.

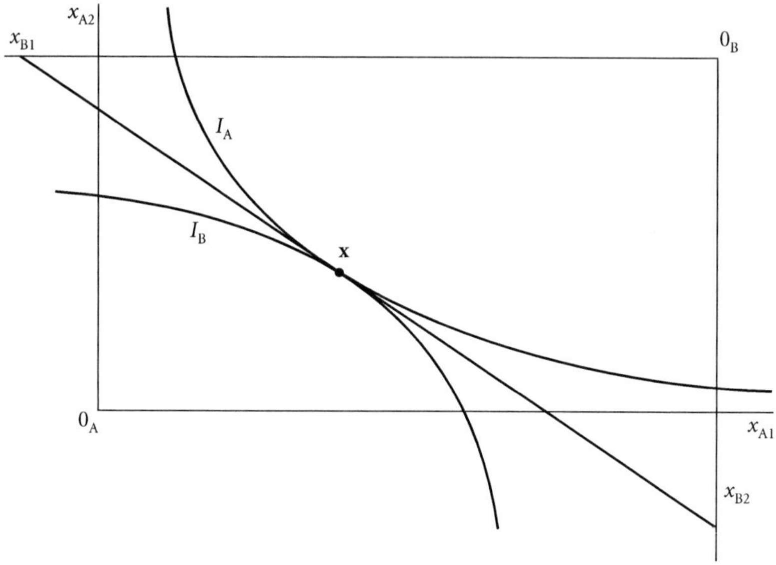

Figure 4.31 Efficient and profit maximizing input allocation

Proof. Suppose that $\overline{\mathbf{y}}$ is not efficient, so that there exists $\mathbf{y}$ in Y such that $\mathbf{y} > \overline{\mathbf{y}}$. Since $\mathbf{p} \gg 0$, $\mathbf{p}.\mathbf{y} > \mathbf{p}.\overline{\mathbf{y}}$, contrary to the assumption that $\overline{\mathbf{y}}$ maximizes profits over Y. ▪

Just as the utility possibility frontier corresponds to the set of Pareto optimal allocations, as in figure 3.5, an efficiency frontier or output possibility frontier corresponds to the locus of efficient allocations in figure 4.29. The efficiency frontier is the northeast boundary of the output possibility set, which is the set of pairs of outputs from firms A and B, respectively, that are less than or equal to some pair that can be produced from the given inputs. The efficiency frontier is labeled $\mathcal{EF}$ in figure 4.32, the locus of efficient input allocations is labeled $\mathcal{EL}$, and the output possibility set is labeled $\mathcal{OP}$. The outputs of commodities A and B are labeled y_A and y_B, respectively. The function f from inputs to outputs is defined by the equation

$$f(x_{A1}, x_{A2}, x_{B1}, x_{B2}) = (f_A(x_{A1}, x_{A2}), f_B(x_{B1}, x_{B2})) = (y_A, y_B).$$

We know that in the case of two consumers with concave utility functions, for every point, $\overline{\mathbf{v}}$, on the utility possibility frontier, there is a nonnegative 2-vector, $\mathbf{a}$, such that $\mathbf{a}.\overline{\mathbf{v}} \geq \mathbf{a}.\mathbf{v}$, for all v in the utility possibility

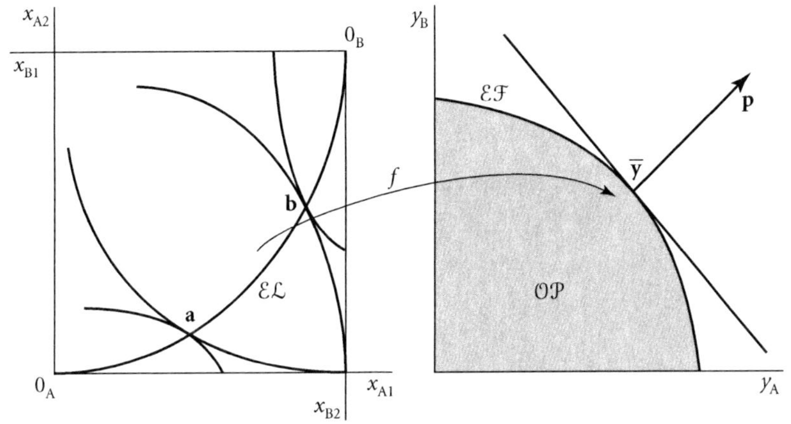

Figure 4.32 The efficiency frontier

set. Similarly, if the production functions f_A and f_B are concave, then for every point $\bar{\mathbf{y}} = (\bar{y}_A, \bar{y}_B)$ on the efficiency frontier in figure 4.32, there is a nonnegative 2-vector, $\mathbf{p}$, such that $\mathbf{p}.\bar{\mathbf{y}} \geq \mathbf{p}.\mathbf{y}$, for every vector $\mathbf{y}$ in the output possibility set, $\mathcal{OP}$. The vector $\mathbf{p}$ may be interpreted as a price vector. According to this interpretation, the point $\bar{\mathbf{y}}$ is the output vector with the highest value at the price vector $\mathbf{p}$.

A more general assertion is possible. To state it, I define the total or aggregate input-output possibility set associated with input-output possibility sets $Y_1, Y_2, \ldots, Y_J$ to be the sum $Y = \sum_{j=1}^{J} Y_j$, where $\sum_{j=1}^{J} Y_j = \{\sum_{j=1}^{J} \mathbf{y}_j \mid \mathbf{y}_j \in Y_j, \text{ for all } j\}$. The set Y represents the set of input-output vectors that may be obtained by operating all the technologies simultaneously, provided they do not interact or interfere with each other. What I show next is that if the Y_j are convex, then any efficient point in Y maximizes profits at some price vector $\mathbf{p}$. It is easy to verify that if the sets Y_j are all convex, then the set Y is convex as well, so that the following proposition applies to an aggregate-production possibility set derived from convex individual-production possibility sets.

PROPOSITION 4.9 If the input-output possibility set Y is convex and $\bar{\mathbf{y}}$ is an efficient point of Y, then there exists a price vector $\mathbf{p}$ such that $\mathbf{p} > \mathbf{0}$ and $\mathbf{p}.\bar{\mathbf{y}} \geq \mathbf{p}.\mathbf{y}$, for all y in Y.

Proof. The proof of this proposition is just like that of theorem 3.31, which asserts that every point on the utility possibility frontier maximizes a weighted average of the consumers' utilities. Let $\Gamma = \{\mathbf{z} \in \mathbb{R}^N \mid \mathbf{z} \geq \overline{\mathbf{y}}\}$ and observe that Γ is nonempty and convex, has nonempty interior, and intersects Y only at the point $\overline{\mathbf{y}}$. Therefore, Minkowski's separation theorem implies that there exists a nonzero vector $\mathbf{p}$ such that $\mathbf{p.z} \geq \mathbf{p.y}$, for all $\mathbf{z}$ in Γ and $\mathbf{y}$ in Y. Because of the form of Γ, $\mathbf{p} \geq \mathbf{0}$, and because $\mathbf{p} \neq \mathbf{0}$, $\mathbf{p} > \mathbf{0}$. Because $\overline{\mathbf{y}}$ belongs to Γ, $\mathbf{p}\overline{\mathbf{y}} \geq \mathbf{p.y}$, for all y in Y. ▪

The decentralization theorem asserts that if the point $\overline{\mathbf{y}}$ in an aggregate-production possibility set maximizes profits, then each of the corresponding input-output vectors of the J firms maximizes the profits of that firm.

DECENTRALIZATION THEOREM 4.10[1] The vector $\overline{\mathbf{y}} \in Y = \sum_{j=1}^{J} Y_j$ solves the problem

$$\max_{y \in Y} \mathbf{p.y}, \tag{4.9}$$

if and only if $\overline{\mathbf{y}} = \sum_{j=1}^{J} \overline{\mathbf{y}}_j$, where, for each j, $\overline{\mathbf{y}}_j$ solves the problem

$$\max_{y \in Y_j} \mathbf{p.y}. \tag{4.10}$$

Proof. Suppose that $\overline{\mathbf{y}}_j$ solves problem 4.10, for all j. Let $\overline{\mathbf{y}} = \sum_{j=1}^{J} \overline{\mathbf{y}}_j$ and suppose that $\mathbf{y} = \sum_{j=1}^{J} \mathbf{y}_j$ is an arbitrary vector in Y, where $\mathbf{y}_j \in Y_j$, for all j. Then,

$$\mathbf{p.y} = \mathbf{p.} \sum_{j=1}^{J} \mathbf{y}_j = \sum_{j=1}^{J} \mathbf{p.y}_j \leq \sum_{j=1}^{J} \mathbf{p.}\overline{\mathbf{y}}_j = \mathbf{p.} \sum_{j=1}^{J} \overline{\mathbf{y}}_j = \mathbf{p.}\overline{\mathbf{y}},$$

where the inequality follows from the assumption that $\overline{\mathbf{y}}_j$ solves problem 4.10, for all j. It follows that $\overline{\mathbf{y}}$ solves problem 4.9.

In order to prove the converse, suppose that $\overline{\mathbf{y}}$ solves problem 4.9. By the definition of Y, $\overline{\mathbf{y}} = \sum_{j=1}^{J} \overline{\mathbf{y}}_j$, where $\overline{\mathbf{y}}_j \in Y_j$, for all j. I show that $\overline{\mathbf{y}}_j$ solves problem 4.10, for each j. Without loss of generality, let $j = 1$. I must show that if $\mathbf{y}_1$ is an arbitrary member of Y_1, then $\mathbf{p.}\overline{\mathbf{y}}_1 \geq \mathbf{p.y}_1$. The vector

1. This theorem is the work of Koopmans (1957, 12).

$\mathbf{y}_1 + \overline{\mathbf{y}}_2 + \cdots + \overline{\mathbf{y}}_J$ belongs to Y, by the definition of Y. Because $\overline{\mathbf{y}}$ solves problem 4.9, it follows that

$$\begin{aligned}\mathbf{p}.\overline{\mathbf{y}}_1 + \mathbf{p}.\overline{\mathbf{y}}_2 + \cdots + \mathbf{p}.\overline{\mathbf{y}}_j &= \mathbf{p}.\overline{\mathbf{y}} \\ &\geq \mathbf{p}.(\mathbf{y}_1 + \overline{\mathbf{y}}_2 + \cdots + \overline{\mathbf{y}}_J) = \mathbf{p}.\mathbf{y}_1 + \mathbf{p}.\overline{\mathbf{y}}_2 + \cdots + \mathbf{p}.\overline{\mathbf{y}}_J.\end{aligned}$$

Canceling like terms from the extreme sides of this inequality, we see that $\mathbf{p}.\overline{\mathbf{y}}_1 \geq \mathbf{p}.\mathbf{y}_1$, as is to be proved. ▪

The decentralization theorem and propositions 4.8 and 4.9 come close to asserting that a vector **y** in an aggregate production possibility set is efficient if and only if there is a price vector **p** such that **y** is the sum of vectors in the input-output possibility sets of the individual firms that maximize profits at the price vector **p**. The "if" part of this statement applies, however, only if $\mathbf{p} \gg \mathbf{0}$.

I now discuss some consequences of constant returns to scale. Recall from section 4.4 that an input-output possibility set exhibits constant returns to scale if it is a cone and then maximum profits are zero. This assertion implies that if the input-output possibility set Y is a cone and profits at price vector **p** are maximized at a nonzero vector **y** in Y, then **p** is orthogonal to the ray from zero through **y**, where this ray is $\{t\mathbf{y} \mid t \geq 0\}$. If an economy is such that every firm's input-output possibility set is a cone, then the equilibrium price vector is orthogonal to one such ray for each firm that produces a positive amount of some commodity. This orthogonality condition restricts the equilibrium price vector and may even determine it uniquely up to a multiplicative constant. For instance, the price vector is unique in this sense if every production process produces only one commodity, every commodity is produced except one, this nonproduced commodity is used as an input in the production of every commodity, and it is possible for the economy to provide a positive amount of every commodity for consumption. The one nonproduced commodity is a primary input, which may be thought of as labor. I now explain and prove this assertion, which is known as the *nonsubstitution theorem*.

This theorem is probably best understood by visualizing the case where there are two produced commodities, labeled 1 and 2. Assume that, for $n = 1$ and 2, the production function for good n, $f_n\colon \mathbb{R}^2_+ \to \mathbb{R}$, is homogeneous of degree 1, concave, and strictly increasing. Assume that the third commodity is labor, write the input of labor into the production of good

n as L_n, and let y_{nm} denote the input of commodity m into the production of good n, where m equals 1 or 2, n equals 1 or 2, $n \neq m$, and where $L_n \leq 0$ and $y_{nm} \leq 0$. Then the output of good 1 is $y_1 = f_1(-y_{12}, -L_1)$, and the output of good 2 is $y_2 = f_2(-y_{21}, -L_2)$. The output of good 1 net of the amount used as an input into production is $f_1(-y_{12}, -L_1) + y_{21}$, and the net output of good 2 is $f_2(-y_{21}, -L_2) + y_{12}$. Assume that there is one unit of labor available, so that $L_1 + L_2 = -1$, and that the inputs can be chosen so that a positive amount of each produced good is available for consumption. The latter assumption means that L_1, y_{12}, and y_{21} can be chosen so that $f_1(-y_{12}, -L_1) + y_{21} > 0$ and $f_2(-y_{21}, 1 + L_1) + y_{12} > 0$. We can see how the two production processes create total output by plotting the functions $y_1 = f_1(-y_{12}, 1)$ and $y_2 = f_2(-y_{21}, 1)$ on the same graph with good 1 on the abscissa and good 2 on the ordinate. Since inputs are negative and outputs are positive, the graph of $y_1 = f_1(-y_{12}, 1)$ appears in the fourth quadrant and the graph of $y_2 = f_2(-y_{21}, 1)$ appears in the

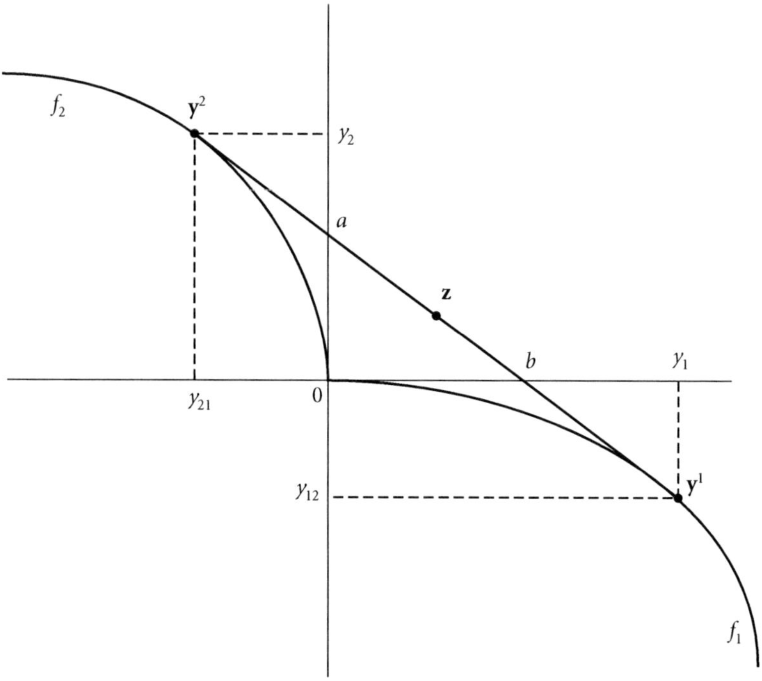

Figure 4.33 Nonsubstitution illustrated

second quadrant, as in figure 4.33. The vector $\mathbf{y}^1 = (y_1, y_{12})$ is such that $y_1 = f_1(-y_{12}, 1)$, and the vector $\mathbf{y}^2 = (y_{21}, y_2)$ is such that $y_2 = f_2(-y_{21}, 1)$. The point $\mathbf{z}$ is the average of points $\mathbf{y}^1$ and $\mathbf{y}^2$, and so $\mathbf{z} = \left(\frac{y_1+y_{21}}{2}, \frac{y_2+y_{12}}{2}\right)$. Suppose that a half unit of labor and $-y_{12}/2$ units of good 2 are devoted to the production of good 1. Since f_1 is homogeneous of degree 1, the output of good 1 is $f_1(-y_{12}/2, 1/2) = f_1(-y_{12}, 1)/2 = y_1/2$. Similarly, if a half unit of labor and $-y_{21}/2$ units of good 1 are devoted the production of good 2, then the output of good 2 is $y_2/2$. Therefore the vector of the two net outputs is $\left(\frac{y_1+y_{21}}{2}, \frac{y_2+y_{12}}{2}\right)$, which is $\mathbf{z}$. That is, $\mathbf{z}$ is the vector of net outputs that results from applying half the amount of inputs to each commodity as are used at the points $\mathbf{y}^1$ and $\mathbf{y}^2$, respectively. Similarly, any point on the straight line between $\mathbf{y}^1$ and $\mathbf{y}^2$ can be obtained in a similar fashion as a vector of net outputs resulting from using one unit of labor in total and using each produced commodity as an input in the production of the other. Any such point can be represented as $\alpha\mathbf{y}^1 + (1-\alpha)\mathbf{y}^2$, where $0 \leq \alpha \leq 1$. This point can be realized as a vector of net outputs by devoting α units of labor and $-\alpha y_{12}$ units of good 2 to the production of good 1 and $(1-\alpha)$ units of labor and $-(1-\alpha)y_{21}$ units of good 1 to the production of good 2.

To understand better the significance of the straight line from $\mathbf{y}^1$ to $\mathbf{y}^2$, add a third axis representing labor to figure 4.33, with the positive direction coming out of the page, as in figure 4.34. Since there is one unit of labor available, the point one unit along the labor axis from the origin is labeled as the endowment point $\mathbf{e}$. We may associate with the production of good 1 the input-output possibility set

$$Y_1 = \{(y_1, y_{12}, L_1) \mid y_{12} \leq 0, L_1 \leq 0, \text{ and } y_1 \leq f_1(-y_{12}, -L_1)\}.$$

Similarly, we may associate with the production of commodity 2 the input-output possibility set

$$Y_2 = \{(y_{21}, y_2, L_2) \mid y_{21} \leq 0, L_2 \leq 0, \text{ and } y_2 \leq f_2(-y_{21}, -L_2)\}.$$

In figure 4.34, the set $\mathbf{e} + Y_1$ is the set of all points on or below the surface formed by all rays from $\mathbf{e}$ through points on the curve f_1, which is the graph of the function $y_1 = f_1(-y_{12}, 1)$. Similarly, $\mathbf{e} + Y_2$ is the set of points on or below the surface formed by all rays from $\mathbf{e}$ through points on the curve f_2, which is the graph of the function $y_2 = f_2(-y_{21}, 1)$. The curves

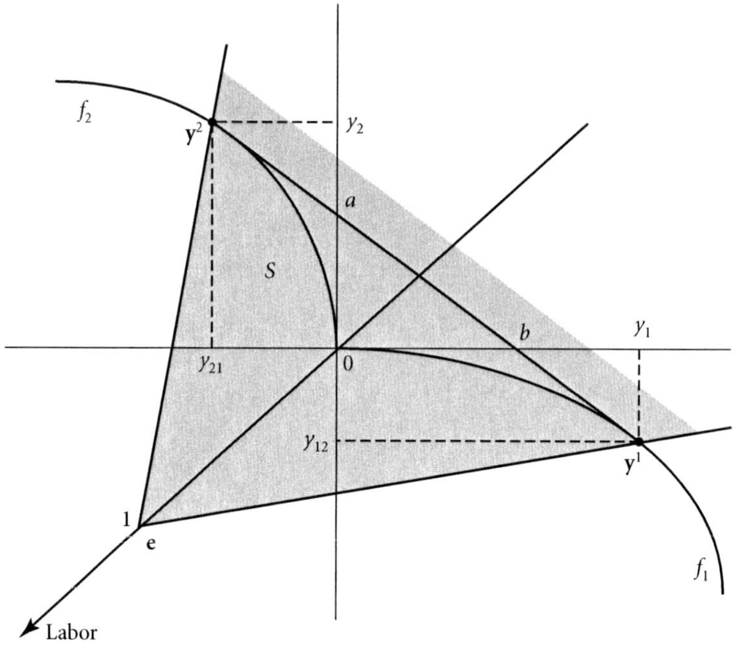

Figure 4.34 Nonsubstitution in three dimensions

f_1 and f_2 are the intersections of the surfaces of the sets $\mathbf{e} + Y_1$ and $\mathbf{e} + Y_2$, respectively, with the plane defined by the equation $L = 0$. The set $\mathbf{e} + Y_1 + Y_2$, which is the aggregate input-output possibility set plus $\mathbf{e}$, is the set of all points on or below the surfaces formed by all rays from $\mathbf{e}$ through points on f_1, f_2, and the straight line segment from $\mathbf{y}^1$ to $\mathbf{y}^2$. Therefore a portion of the surface of $\mathbf{e} + Y_1 + Y_2$ is flat, namely the shaded section, S, from the ray from $\mathbf{e}$ through $\mathbf{y}^1$ to the ray from $\mathbf{e}$ through $\mathbf{y}^2$ The line segment from point a to b in figures 4.33 and 4.34 is, therefore, the output possibility frontier for the economy endowed with one unit of labor. Points on this segment are the net outputs available for consumption that can be provided by the economy.

Suppose now that the economy is in equilibrium with price vector $\mathbf{p}$, both produced commodities are desirable and are consumed, and no labor is consumed as leisure. Then nothing will be wasted, and the economy will produce at a point on the production possibility frontier, so that the aggregate input-output vector plus $\mathbf{e}$ will be at a point in the interior of the flat surface, S. In the equilibrium, both firms maximize profits, so that by the decentralization theorem the aggregate input-output vector maximizes profits over the aggregate input-output possibility set, $Y_1 + Y_2$. Therefore the equilibrium price vector must be orthogonal to the surface S, which means that it is unique up to a multiplicative constant. This is the assertion of the nonsubstitution theorem.

I will prove a version of this theorem for a model with N commodities. The main difficulty in proving the result is the demonstration that the aggregate input-output possibility set has a flat section on its surface that includes in its interior the points at which an equilibrium would operate. I make this step using a theorem from linear activity or input-output analysis, which I now describe briefly. In linear activity analysis, it is assumed that a production process may be described by a single N-vector, $\mathbf{a} = (a_1, \ldots, a_N)$. If the process is operated at unit level, then a_n units of commodity n are produced, if a_n is positive, and $-a_n$ units of commodity n are used as an input, if a_n is negative. In a linear activity model, there are several linear production processes, and the model is represented by a matrix or table, where the entry a_{nm} in the nth row and mth column represents the nth coefficient of the mth activity or process. That is, if the mth process is operated at unit level, $-a_{nm}$ is the amount of commodity n absorbed if it is an input and a_{nm} is the amount of commodity n produced if it is an output.

I will consider linear activity models where only one commodity is produced by each process and there is only one process for producing each commodity. If it is assumed that when a process is operated at unit level one unit of commodity is produced, then the process can be represented by the vector of inputs, which I may represent as nonnegative. With this approach in mind, let a_{mn} be the nonnegative quantity of commodity m that is used to produce commodity n and let $\mathbf{a}_n = (a_{1n}, a_{2n}, \ldots, a_{Nn})$. Then the activity vector describing the process producing commodity n is the vector $\mathbf{e}_n - \mathbf{a}_n$, where $\mathbf{e}_n$ is the nth standard unit basis vector defined by $e_{nn} = 1$ and $e_{nm} = 0$, if $n \neq m$. Assume that $a_{nn} = 0$, for all n, so that commodities are not used to produce themselves. Then if the nth production process operates at level x_n, for each n, the total output of each commodity m is x_m, and the total usage of commodity m as an input in the production of all commodities is $\sum_{m=1}^{N} x_n a_{mn}$. Hence the total output of commodity m net of its use as an input is $x_m - \sum_{m=1}^{N} x_n a_{mn}$. Let A be the $N \times N$ matrix with entry a_{mn} in row m and column n, and let $\mathbf{x}$ be the N-vector with component n equal to x_n. (The vector $\mathbf{x}$ should not be confused with a consumption vector. It is the vector of total output levels or the vector of levels of activity use.) Note that the nth column of A is the vector $\mathbf{a}_n$, viewed as a column vector. Then the N-vector of output levels net of inputs is $(I - A)\mathbf{x}$, where $\mathbf{x}$ is thought of as a column vector and I is the $N \times N$ identity matrix.

DEFINITION 4.11 The $N \times N$ input matrix A is *productive* if there exists an N-vector $\mathbf{x}$ such that $(I - A)\mathbf{x} \gg \mathbf{x}$.

Clearly if $(I - A)\mathbf{x} \gg \mathbf{0}$, then $\mathbf{x} \gg \mathbf{0}$, since the net output of each commodity can be positive only if the total output of each is positive.

THEOREM 4.12 A is productive if and only if the matrix $I - A$ is invertible. In this case, $(I - A)^{-1} = \sum_{k=0}^{\infty} A^k$, and this matrix is nonnegative.

Proof. Suppose that A is productive. Then for some N-vector $\mathbf{x}$, $(I - A)\mathbf{x} = \mathbf{c}$, where $\mathbf{c} \gg \mathbf{0}$. The sequence of sums of matrices, $I + A + A^2 + \cdots + A^k$, is nonnegative and nondecreasing in k, since the kth power of a nonnegative matrix is nonnegative. Therefore, $\lim_{k\to\infty}[I + A + A^2 + \cdots + A^k]$ exists, provided the sequence of matrices $I + A + A^2 + \cdots + A^k$ is bounded. Because $\mathbf{c} = (I - A)\mathbf{x}$, it follows that

$$
\begin{aligned}
(I + A + A^2 + \cdots + A^k)\mathbf{c} &= (I + A + A^2 + \cdots + A^k)(I - A)\mathbf{x} \\
&= (I - A^{k+1})\mathbf{x} \leq \mathbf{x}.
\end{aligned}
$$

Since $\mathbf{c} \gg \mathbf{0}$, it follows that the sequence $I + A + A^2 + \cdots + A^k$ is bounded and hence $\lim_{k\to\infty}(I + A + A^2 + \cdots + A^k)$ exists, so that $\lim_{k\to\infty} A^k = \mathbf{0}$ and hence

$$
\lim_{k\to\infty} (I - A)(I + A + A^2 + \cdots + A^k) = \lim_{k\to\infty} (I - A^{k+1}) = I.
$$

Therefore $\sum_{k=0}^{\infty} A^k = (I - A)^{-1}$ and is clearly nonnegative. This proves the "only if" part of the theorem.

In order to prove the converse, suppose that $I - A^{-1}$ exists. If the N-vector $\mathbf{c}$ is such that $\mathbf{c} \gg 0$, then there exists an N-vector $\mathbf{x}$ such that $(I - A)\mathbf{x} = \mathbf{c}$, namely, $\mathbf{x} = (I - A)^{-1}\mathbf{c}$. Therefore, A is productive and by an argument already made, $(I - A)^{-1} = \sum_{k=0}^{\infty} A^k$. ▪

I now state the nonsubstitution theorem.

NONSUBSTITUTION THEOREM 4.13[2] Suppose that the input-output possibility sets $Y_1, \ldots, Y_J$ satisfy the conditions that follow.

1. Commodities $1, 2, \ldots, N$ are produced, and commodity $N + 1$ is the unique nonproduced commodity or primary input. Call this primary input labor.
2. Each input-output production possibility set, Y_j, is devoted to the production of one produced commodity. That is, for each j, there is an n such that $1 \leq n \leq N$ and for every $\mathbf{y}$ in Y_j, $y_m \leq 0$, if $m \neq n$.
3. Production requires labor. That is, for each j, if $\mathbf{y}$ belongs to Y_j and $y_n > 0$, for some $n \leq N$, then $y_{N+1} < 0$.
4. For each j, Y_j is a convex cone.
5. There is an efficient point $\overline{\mathbf{y}}$ in $Y = \sum_{j=1}^{J} Y_j$, such that $\overline{y}_n > 0$, for $n = 1, \ldots, N$.

Up to a multiplicative constant, there is one and only one price vector $\mathbf{p}$ such that if $\underline{\mathbf{y}}$ is an efficient point of Y and $\underline{y}_n > 0$, for $n = 1, \ldots, N$, then $\mathbf{p}.\underline{\mathbf{y}} \geq \mathbf{p}.\mathbf{y}$, for all $\mathbf{y}$ in Y.

This theorem says that if an economy satisfying the assumptions of the theorem were in an equilibrium where some of every produced commodity was consumed, then the relative prices of labor and all the produced commodities would be unique. The theorem can be loosely interpreted as justifying a labor theory of value. The assumptions of the theorem are unrealistically restrictive, however. For instance, in reality there are other primary inputs besides labor (such as land, water, and minerals), there are many types of labor, and many commodities are produced jointly with other commodities.

Proof of Theorem 4.13. Let $\overline{\mathbf{y}}$ be as in assumption (5) of the theorem. I show that I may assume that $\overline{y}_{N+1} = -1$. Since $\overline{y}_n > 0$, for $n = 1, \ldots, N$, assumption (3) of the theorem implies that $\overline{y}_{N+1} < 0$. Since Y is a cone, the vector $\overline{\mathbf{z}} = \frac{1}{(-\overline{y}_{N+1})}\overline{\mathbf{y}}$ belongs to Y. Since $\overline{\mathbf{y}}$ is efficient, $\overline{\mathbf{z}}$ is also efficient. Clearly $\overline{z}_n > 0$, for $n = 1, \ldots, N$. Since $\overline{z}_{N+1} = -1$, I may assume that $\overline{y}_{N+1} = -1$.

2. This theorem is the work of Samuelson (1951).

Since every Y_j is convex by assumption (4), Y is convex. Since $\overline{\mathbf{y}}$ is an efficient point of Y, proposition 4.9 implies that there exists an $(N+1)$-vector $\mathbf{p}$ such that $\mathbf{p} > 0$ and $\mathbf{p}.\overline{\mathbf{y}} \geq \mathbf{p}.\mathbf{y}$, for every $\mathbf{y}$ in Y.

Since every Y_j is a cone by assumption (4), Y is a cone. Therefore proposition 4.6 implies that $\mathbf{p}.\overline{\mathbf{y}} = 0$. By the definition of Y, $\overline{\mathbf{y}} = \sum_{j=1}^{J} \overline{\mathbf{y}}_j$, where $\overline{\mathbf{y}}_j \in Y_j$, for every j. By the decentralization theorem 4.10, for every j, $\mathbf{p}.\overline{\mathbf{y}}_j \geq \mathbf{p}.\mathbf{y}$, for every $\mathbf{y}$ in Y_j. Since Y_j is a cone, $\mathbf{p}.\overline{\mathbf{y}}_j = 0$.

I show that $\mathbf{p} \gg 0$. First I show that $P_{N+1} > 0$. Since $\mathbf{p}.\overline{\mathbf{y}} = 0$, $p_{N+1}(-y_{N+1}) = \sum_{n=1}^{N} p_n \overline{y}_n$. If $p_{N+1} = 0$, then $\sum_{n=1}^{N} p_n \overline{y}_n = 0$. Since $\overline{y}_n > 0$, for $n = 1, \ldots, N$, it would then follow that $p_1 = \cdots = p_N = 0$, which is impossible since $\mathbf{p} > \mathbf{0}$. This proves that $p_{N+1} > 0$. I next show that $p_n > 0$, for $n = 1, \ldots, N$. Fix n such that $1 \leq n \leq N$. Since $\overline{y}_n = \sum_{j=1}^{J} \overline{y}_{jn}$, where $\overline{\mathbf{y}}_j \in Y_j$, for all j, it follows that $\overline{y}_{jn} > 0$, for some j. By assumption (2) of the theorem, $\overline{y}_{jm} \leq 0$, if $m \neq n$, and by assumption (3), $\overline{y}_{j,N+1} < 0$. Since $\mathbf{p}.\overline{\mathbf{y}}_j = 0$, $p_n \overline{y}_{jn} = \sum_{m \neq n} p_m(-\overline{y}_{jm}) \geq p_{N+1}(-\overline{y}_{j,N+1}) > 0$. This inequality implies that $p_n > 0$.

I now reduce our problem to one for an input-output model. For each $n = 1, \ldots, N$, let $J(n) = \{j \mid \overline{y}_{jn} > 0\}$. Since $\overline{y}_n > 0$, $J(n)$ is not empty, for every n. Since $\mathbf{p} \gg 0$ and $\mathbf{p}.\overline{\mathbf{y}}_j = 0$, for all j, for any j either $\overline{\mathbf{y}}_j = 0$ or $\overline{y}_{jn} > 0$, for some n. Therefore $\overline{\mathbf{y}}_j = 0$, if j does not belong to $\bigcup_{n=1}^{N} J(n)$. Let $\overline{\mathbf{y}}^n = \sum_{j \in J(n)} \overline{\mathbf{y}}_j$. Then $\sum_{n=1}^{N} \overline{\mathbf{y}}^n = \overline{\mathbf{y}}$, and for all n, $\overline{y}_n^n > 0$, $\overline{y}_{N+1}^n < 0$, $\overline{y}_m^n \leq 0$, if $m \neq n$, and $\mathbf{p}.\overline{\mathbf{y}}^n = 0$. For each n, let $\overline{\mathbf{z}}^n = \frac{1}{(-\overline{y}_{N+1})} \overline{\mathbf{y}}^n$. Since the sets Y_j are all cones, it follows that $\overline{\mathbf{z}}^n \in \sum_{j \in J(n)} Y_j$, $\overline{z}_n^n > 0$, $\overline{z}_{N+1}^n = -1$, $\overline{y}_m^n \leq 0$, if $m \neq n$, and $\mathbf{p}.\overline{\mathbf{z}}^n = 0$. Also $\sum_{n=1}^{N} (-\overline{y}_{N+1}^n) \overline{\mathbf{z}}^n = \sum_{n=1}^{N} \overline{\mathbf{y}}^n = \overline{\mathbf{y}}$. It is important to note that since the Y_j are cones, each Y_j contains the vector $\mathbf{0}$, so that $\sum_{j \in J(n)} Y_j$ is contained in the set $\sum_{j=1}^{J} Y_j = Y$, and hence each $\overline{\mathbf{z}}^n$ belongs to Y.

I next choose the units of the commodities $1, \ldots, N$, so that $\overline{z}_n^n = 1$ for all n. This choice of units may be accomplished by dividing the nth component of each vector in the commodity space $\mathbb{R}^{N+1}$ by $\overline{z}_n^n$, where $\overline{\mathbf{z}}^n$ is the vector defined in the previous paragraph. It remains true after this change of units that $\sum_{n=1}^{N} (-\overline{y}_{N+1}^n) \overline{\mathbf{z}}^n = \overline{\mathbf{y}}$ and $\sum_{j=1}^{J} \overline{y}_{jn} = \overline{y}_n > 0$, for $n = 1, \ldots, N$.

For each m and n such that $1 \leq m, n \leq N$, let

$$a_{mn} = \begin{cases} -\overline{z}_m^n, & m \neq n, \\ 0, & \text{if } m = n. \end{cases}$$

Let A be the $N \times N$ matrix with (m, n)th entry a_{mn}. Let $\mathbf{x}$ be the N-vector defined by the equation $x_n = -\overline{y}^n_{N+1}$, for all n. Then using matrix notation $(I - A)\mathbf{x}$ is the vector of the first N components of $\sum_{n=1}^N (-\overline{y}^n_{N+1})\overline{\mathbf{z}}^n = \overline{\mathbf{y}}$, and these components are all positive by hypothesis. Therefore, the matrix A is productive and theorem 4.12 implies that the matrix $(I - A)$ is invertible and that $(I - A)^{-1}$ is nonnegative.

I now show that all efficient vectors in Y with positive outputs of all produced commodities lie in a flat subset of Y that is part of an N-dimensional hyperplane in $\mathbb{R}^{N+1}$. Let $\mathbf{e}_n$ be the nth standard basis vector of $\mathbb{R}^N$ (the vector with nth component equal to 1 and all other components equal to 0), and let $\mathbf{x}^n = (I - A)^{-1}\mathbf{e}_n$. Then $\mathbf{x}^n > \mathbf{0}$ and $(I - A)\mathbf{x}^n = \mathbf{e}_n$. Since $\mathbf{x}^n > \mathbf{0}$, it follows that $\sum_{m=1}^N x^n_m > 0$ and so $t_n = \left(\sum_{m=1}^N x^n_m\right)^{-1}$ is well defined. Let $\overline{\mathbf{x}}^n = t_n \mathbf{x}^n$, so that $(1 - A)\overline{\mathbf{x}}^n = t_n \mathbf{e}_n$ and $\sum_{m=1}^N \overline{x}^n_m = 1$. Since the mth column of the matrix $(I - A)$ is the vector of the first N components of the $(N + 1)$-vector $\overline{\mathbf{z}}^n$ and the last component of $\overline{\mathbf{z}}^n$ is -1, it follows that $\overline{\mathbf{q}}^n = \sum_{m=1}^N \overline{x}^n_m \overline{\mathbf{z}}^m$ is the vector whose nth component is the positive number t_n, whose $(N + 1)$st component is -1, and whose other components are all 0. Since each vector $\overline{\mathbf{z}}^m$ belongs to Y and Y is convex, it follows that every $\overline{\mathbf{q}}^n$ belongs to Y. Since $\mathbf{p}.\overline{\mathbf{z}}^m = 0$, for all m, it follows that $\mathbf{p}.\overline{\mathbf{q}}^n = 0$, for all n. Since $\mathbf{p} \gg \mathbf{0}$ and $\mathbf{p}.\mathbf{y} \leq 0$, for all $\mathbf{y}$ in Y, proposition 4.8 implies that every $\overline{\mathbf{q}}^n$ is an efficient point of Y. Observe that $p_n \overline{q}^n_n - p_{N+1} = \mathbf{p}.\overline{\mathbf{q}}^n = 0$, so that $p_{N+1} = p_n \overline{q}^n_n$.

I show that if $\mathbf{y}$ in $\mathbb{R}^{N+1}$ is such that $y_{N+1} = -1$, $y_n \geq 0$, if $n = 1, \ldots, N$, and $\mathbf{p}.\mathbf{y} = 0$, then $\mathbf{y}$ is a convex combination of $\overline{\mathbf{q}}^1, \ldots, \overline{\mathbf{q}}^N$. Since $\mathbf{p}.\mathbf{y} = 0$ and $y_{N+1} = -1$, it follows that $p_{N+1} = \sum_{n=1}^N p_n y_n$. Let $\alpha_n = \frac{p_n y_n}{p_{N+1}}$. Then, $\alpha_n \geq 0$, for all n, and $\sum_{n=1}^N \alpha_n = 1$. Because $p_{N+1} = p_n \overline{q}^n_n$, it follows that $\alpha_n = \frac{y_n}{\overline{q}^n_n}$, so that $\sum_{m=1}^N \alpha_m \overline{q}^m_n = \alpha_n \overline{q}^n_n = y_n$, if $n = 1, \ldots, N$, and $\sum_{m=1}^N \alpha_m \overline{q}^m_{N+1} = -\sum_{m=1}^N \alpha_m = -1 = y_{N+1}$. Therefore $\sum_{m=1}^N \alpha_m \overline{\mathbf{q}}^m = \mathbf{y}$.

Since $\overline{q}^n \in Y$, for all n, and Y is convex, the argument of the previous paragraph implies that $\mathbf{y}$ belongs to Y, if $y_{N+1} = -1$, $y_n \geq 0$, if $n = 1, \ldots, N$, and $\mathbf{p}.\mathbf{y} = 0$. Any such $\mathbf{y}$ is efficient by proposition 4.8, since $\mathbf{p}.\mathbf{y} = 0 = \max_{\mathbf{y} \in Y}$ and $\mathbf{p} \gg 0$.

Since Y is a convex cone, the set $Z = \left\{\sum_{n=1}^N r_n \overline{\mathbf{q}}^n \mid r_n \geq 0, \text{ for all } n\right\}$ is contained in Y, and all points in Z are efficient by proposition 4.8, because $\mathbf{p} \gg \mathbf{0}$ and $\mathbf{p}.\mathbf{z} = 0$, for all $\mathbf{z}$ in Z. It should be clear from what has been said that

$$Z = \{\mathbf{z} \in \mathbb{R}^{n+1} \mid z_{N+1} < 0, z_n \geq 0, \text{ for } n = 1, \ldots, N, \text{ and } \mathbf{p}.\mathbf{z} = 0\}.$$

Suppose that $\mathbf{y}$ is an efficient vector in Y and is such that $y_n > 0$, if $n = 1, \ldots, N$. Assumption (3) of the theorem implies that $y_{N+1} < 0$. Because $\overline{\mathbf{y}}$ maximizes profits in Y at the price vector $\mathbf{p}$ and $\mathbf{p}.\overline{\mathbf{y}} = 0$, it follows that $\mathbf{p}.\mathbf{y} \leq 0$. If $\mathbf{p}.\mathbf{y} < 0$, then $\mathbf{z} = \mathbf{y} - \frac{(\mathbf{p}.\mathbf{y})\mathbf{e}}{\mathbf{p}.\mathbf{e}}$ belongs to Z, where $\mathbf{e} = (1, 1, \ldots, 1, 0) \in \mathbb{R}^{N+1}$. Since Z is a subset of Y and $\mathbf{z} > \mathbf{y}$, $\mathbf{y}$ is not efficient. This contradiction proves that $\mathbf{p}.\mathbf{y} = 0$ and so Z contains all efficient points $\mathbf{y}$ in Y such that $y_n > 0$, if $n = 1, \ldots, N$.

The set Z is a subset of the N-dimensional hyperplane in $\mathbb{R}^{N+1}$ spanned by the linearly independent vectors $\overline{\mathbf{q}}^1, \ldots, \overline{\mathbf{q}}^N$, which is the same as the hyperplane H defined by the equation $\mathbf{p}.\mathbf{y} = 0$. If the vector $\mathbf{y}$ in Y is efficient and is such that $y_n > 0$, for $n = 1, \ldots, N$, then $\mathbf{y}$ is in the interior of the set Z within H. Any price vector $\overline{\mathbf{p}}$ such that $\overline{\mathbf{p}}.\mathbf{y} \geq \overline{\mathbf{p}}.\underline{\mathbf{y}}$, for all $\underline{\mathbf{y}}$ in Y, is such that $\overline{\mathbf{p}}.\mathbf{y} \geq \overline{\mathbf{p}}.\underline{\mathbf{y}}$, for all $\underline{\mathbf{y}}$ in H, since $\mathbf{y}$ belongs to the interior of Z within H. Therefore $\overline{\mathbf{p}}$ is a multiple of $\mathbf{p}$, as is to be proved. ▪

4.7 An Incomplete Theorem on the Existence of Equilibrium

I now explain how ideas presented in section 4.2 may be used to prove the existence of an equilibrium price vector. In that section, I showed that the market excess-demand set, $z(\mathbf{p})$, is homogeneous of degree 0 and satisfies Walras' law. I prove here that if market excess demand is a continuous function of prices, then there exists a vector, $\overline{\mathbf{p}}$, such that, for all n, $z_n(\overline{\mathbf{p}}) \leq 0$ and $\overline{p}_n = 0$, if $z_n(\overline{\mathbf{p}}) < 0$. This vector $\overline{\mathbf{p}}$ is an equilibrium price vector. The resulting theorem on the existence of equilibrium is incomplete, because the assumptions are about an endogenous object, the excess-demand function, rather than about the fundamental exogenous objects defining a model, namely, utility functions, endowments, and input-output possibility sets. It is easy to make up examples of economic models for which excess demand does not exist at some prices. For instance, if a consumer has a strictly increasing utility function and a nonnegative income and if the price of one of the commodities is zero, then his or her demand is unbounded, so that market excess demand is not defined. A complete existence theorem is stated in section 4.8 and proved using the theorem given here. A somewhat better theorem is stated in section 5.3 and proved using a different approach.

Before going further, some insight can be gained into the significance of the homogeneity of excess demand and of Walras' law by counting equations and unknowns. Suppose that for every price vector $\mathbf{p}$, the demand sets, $\xi_i(\mathbf{p})$, and supply sets, $\eta_j(\mathbf{p})$, are single points, so that ξ_i and η_j are functions, for all i and j. Then, the equilibrium price vector, $\mathbf{p}$, may be thought of as N unknowns, $(p_1, p_2, \ldots, p_N)$, that satisfy the N-equations

$$\begin{aligned}
&\sum_{i=1}^{I} [\xi_{i1}(p_1, \ldots, p_N) - e_{i1}] - \sum_{j=1}^{J} \eta_{j1}(p_1, \ldots, p_N) = 0 \\
&\sum_{i=1}^{I} [\xi_{i2}(p_1, \ldots, p_N) - e_{i2}] - \sum_{j=1}^{J} \eta_{j2}(p_1, \ldots, p_N) = 0 \\
&\vdots \\
&\sum_{i=1}^{I} [\xi_{iN}(p_1, \ldots, p_N) - e_{iN}] - \sum_{j=1}^{J} \eta_{jN}(p_1, \ldots, p_N) = 0.
\end{aligned} \tag{4.11}$$

Since the functions ξ_i and η_j are homogeneous of degree 0, if $(p_1, p_2, \ldots, p_N)$ solves this system so does $(tp_1, tp_2, \ldots, tp_N)$, for any positive number t, and hence the system is underdetermined. We can create an inhomogeneous system by adding an equation, such as

$$\sum_{n=1}^{N} p_n = 1, \tag{4.12}$$

that normalizes prices. The system of equations 4.11 and 4.12 seems overdetermined, for there are $N + 1$ equations in N unknowns. Walras' law, however, implies that one of the equations in system 4.11 is redundant, since the law says that if we multiply the nth equation by the nth price and add the resulting equations, the left-hand sides sum to zero for any price vector $(p_1, p_2, \ldots, p_N)$. For instance, if $(p_1, p_2, \ldots, p_N)$ solves all but the kth equation of system 4.11 and if $p_k > 0$, then the kth equation is automatically satisfied as well, since

$$\sum_{i=1}^{I} [\xi_{ik}(p_1, \ldots, p_N) - e_{ik}] - \sum_{j=1}^{J} \eta_{jk}(p_1, \ldots, p_N) =$$

$$- p_k^{-1} \sum_{n \neq k} p_n \left\{ \sum_{i=1}^{I} [\xi_{in}(p_1, \ldots, p_N) - e_{in}] - \sum_{j=1}^{J} \eta_{jn}(p_1, \ldots, p_N) \right\} = 0.$$

Therefore for the N unknowns, there are exactly N independent equations, namely, equation 4.12 plus $N - 1$ of the equations 4.11.

The formal statement of the theorem to be proved follows.

EQUILIRIUM EXISTENCE THEOREM 4.14 Let $z\colon \{\mathbf{p} \in \mathbb{R}^N_+ \mid \mathbf{p} > 0\} \to \mathbb{R}^N$ be such that

1. $\mathbf{p}.z(\mathbf{p}) = 0$, for all $\mathbf{p}$
2. z is a continuous function

Then, there exists an N-vector $\overline{\mathbf{p}}$ such that $\overline{\mathbf{p}} > \mathbf{0}$, $z(\overline{\mathbf{p}}) \leq \mathbf{0}$, and, for all n, $\overline{p}_n = 0$, if $z_n(\overline{p}) < 0$.

The proof uses the Brouwer fixed point theorem, where a fixed point of a function is defined as follows.

DEFINITION 4.15 If $f\colon X \to X$ is a function, a *fixed point* of f is a point $\overline{\mathbf{x}} \in X$, such that $\overline{\mathbf{x}} = f(\overline{\mathbf{x}})$.

BROUWER FIXED POINT THEOREM 4.16 Any continuous function from a nonempty, compact, and convex subset of $\mathbb{R}^N$ to itself has a fixed point.

Let $f\colon X \to X$ be the function to which this theorem applies. I give examples to show why each of the assumptions of the Brouwer fixed point theorem are needed. Recall that a compact set is closed and bounded.

EXAMPLE 4.17 (Why X must be closed.) Let $X = (0, 1]$ and $f(x) = x/2$. The set X is convex and bounded but not closed, f is continuous, and f has no fixed point.

EXAMPLE 4.18 (Why X must be bounded.) Let $X = [0, \infty)$ and $f(x) = x + 1$. The set X is convex and closed but not bounded, f is continuous, and f has no fixed point.

EXAMPLE 4.19 (Why X must be convex.) Let $X = \{\mathbf{x} \in \mathbb{R}^2 \mid \|\mathbf{x}\| = 1\}$ and $f(\mathbf{x}) = -\mathbf{x}$. The set X is compact but not convex, f is continuous, and f has no fixed point.

EXAMPLE 4.20 (Why f must be continuous.) Let $X = [0, 1]$ and

$$f(x) = \begin{cases} 1, & \text{if } 0 \leq x \leq 0.5, \\ 0, & \text{if } 0.5 < x \leq 1. \end{cases}$$

The set X is compact and convex, but f is not continuous and has no fixed point.

Proof of Theorem 4.14.[3] Restrict the price vector $\mathbf{p}$ to the set

$$\Delta^{N-1} = \{\mathbf{p} \in \mathbb{R}_+^N \mid \sum_{n=1}^{N} p_n = 1\},$$

so that $z\colon \Delta^{N-1} \to \mathbb{R}^N$ is such that z is continuous and $\mathbf{p}.z(\mathbf{p}) = 0$, for all $\mathbf{p}$. I show that there exists a $\overline{\mathbf{p}} \in \Delta^{N-1}$ such that $z(\overline{\mathbf{p}}) \leq \mathbf{0}$ and, for all n, $\overline{p}_n = 0$, if $z_n(\overline{\mathbf{p}}) < 0$. By Walras' law, $0 = \overline{\mathbf{p}}.z(\overline{\mathbf{p}}) = \sum_{n=1}^{N} \overline{p}_n z_n(\overline{\mathbf{p}})$. Therefore if $z_n(\overline{\mathbf{p}}) \leq 0$, for all n, then, $\overline{p}_n = 0$, for any n such that $z_n(\overline{\mathbf{p}}) < 0$. Hence, it is enough to show that $z(\overline{\mathbf{p}}) \leq \mathbf{0}$.

Let $g\colon \Delta^{N-1} \to \mathbb{R}_+^N$ be defined by the equation $g_n(\mathbf{p}) = \max(0, p_n + z_n(\mathbf{p}))$, for all n and $\mathbf{p}$. First of all, I show that $g(\mathbf{p}) > \mathbf{0}$, for all $\mathbf{p}$. Since $g(\mathbf{p}) \geq \mathbf{0}$, it is sufficient to show that $g(\mathbf{p}) \neq \mathbf{0}$. This is so because

$$\mathbf{p}.g(\mathbf{p}) \geq \mathbf{p}.(\mathbf{p} + z(\mathbf{p})) = \mathbf{p}.\mathbf{p} + \mathbf{p}.z(\mathbf{p}) = \mathbf{p}.\mathbf{p} > 0,$$

where the first inequality holds because $\mathbf{p} \geq \mathbf{0}$ and $g(\mathbf{p}) \geq \mathbf{p} + z(\mathbf{p})$ and the last equation follows from Walras' law.

Let the function $f\colon \Delta^{N-1} \to \Delta^{N-1}$ be defined by the equation

$$f(\mathbf{p}) = \frac{g(\mathbf{p})}{\sum_{n=1}^{N} g_n(\mathbf{p})}.$$

This function is well defined, because $g(\mathbf{p}) > \mathbf{0}$ and so $\sum_{n=1}^{N} g_n(\mathbf{p}) > 0$.

Since f is continuous and Δ^{N-1} is compact, nonempty, and convex, the function f has a fixed point, $\overline{\mathbf{p}}$ by the Brouwer fixed point theorem. Because $\overline{\mathbf{p}} = f(\overline{\mathbf{p}})$, it follows that $\overline{\mathbf{p}} = \lambda g(\overline{\mathbf{p}})$, for some positive number λ. I show that $\lambda = 1$. By the definition of g,

$$\overline{p}_n = \lambda \max(0, \overline{p}_n + z_n(\overline{\mathbf{p}})),$$

for all n. Hence $\overline{p}_n = 0$, whenever $\max(0, \overline{p}_n + z(\overline{\mathbf{p}})) = 0$, and so

$$\overline{p}_n \max(0, \overline{p}_n + z_n(\overline{\mathbf{p}})) = \overline{p}_n(\overline{p}_n + z_n(\overline{\mathbf{p}})),$$

for all n. We thus have thc following equations.

3. This proof follows closely the argument in Debreu (1959, 82–83).

$$\overline{\mathbf{p}}.g(\overline{\mathbf{p}}) = \sum_{n=1}^{N} \overline{p}_n \max(0, \overline{p}_n + z(\overline{\mathbf{p}})) = \sum_{n=1}^{N} \overline{p}_n(\overline{p}_n + z_n(\overline{\mathbf{p}}))$$
$$= \overline{\mathbf{p}}.(\overline{\mathbf{p}} + z(\overline{\mathbf{p}})) = \overline{\mathbf{p}}.\overline{\mathbf{p}} + \overline{\mathbf{p}}.z(\overline{\mathbf{p}}) = \overline{\mathbf{p}}.\overline{\mathbf{p}},$$

where the last equation follows from Walras' law. Therefore,

$$\overline{\mathbf{p}}.\overline{\mathbf{p}} = \overline{\mathbf{p}}.(\lambda g(\overline{\mathbf{p}})) = \lambda \overline{\mathbf{p}}.g(\overline{\mathbf{p}}) = \lambda(\overline{\mathbf{p}}.\overline{\mathbf{p}} + \overline{\mathbf{p}}.z(\overline{\mathbf{p}})) = \lambda \overline{\mathbf{p}}.\overline{\mathbf{p}},$$

which in turn implies that $\lambda = 1$, and hence $\overline{\mathbf{p}} = g(\overline{\mathbf{p}})$ or

$$\overline{p}_n = \max(0, \overline{p}_n + z_n(\overline{\mathbf{p}})),$$

for all n. This equation is impossible if $z_n(\overline{\mathbf{p}}) > 0$, for any n. Hence $z_n(\overline{\mathbf{p}}) \leq 0$, for all n, as was to be proved. This completes the proof of the theorem. ▪

The progression from $\mathbf{p}$ to $\mathbf{p} + z(\mathbf{p})$ to $g(\mathbf{p})$ to $f(\mathbf{p})$ may be seen in figure 4.35 for two price vectors, $\mathbf{p}$ and $\overline{\mathbf{p}}$.

Theorem 4.14 is used in the next section as a step in the proof of a proper equilibrium existence result, where assumptions are made only about utility functions, endowments, and input-output possibility sets. The theorem is not likely, however, to apply to any reasonable economic model, for excess demand may not be defined for all price vectors, as was pointed out earlier.

Before going on, I define conditions under which demand $\xi_i(\mathbf{p})$ and supply $\eta_j(\mathbf{p})$ have at most one value, so that market excess demand is single valued when it is defined. The key condition for consumer demand is that utility functions be strictly quasi-concave.

DEFINITION 4.21 A utility function $u: \mathbb{R}^N_+ \to \mathbb{R}$ is said to be *strictly quasi-concave* if for all x and y in $\mathbb{R}^N_+$ and for all α such that $0 < \alpha < 1$, $u(\alpha x + (1-\alpha)y) > \min(u(x), u(y))$.

If u is strictly quasi-concave and continuous, then for an number v, $\{\mathbf{x} \mid u(\mathbf{x}) \geq v\}$ is strictly convex, where the strict convexity of sets is defined in definition 3.39 (in section 3.5).

PROPOSITION 4.22 In any economy

$$\mathcal{E} = ((u_i \mathbf{e}_i)_{i=1}^{I}, (Y_j)_{j=1}^{J}, (\Theta_{ij})_{i=1}^{I}{}_{j=1}^{J}),$$

if the utility function of consumer i is strictly quasi-concave, then $\xi_i(\mathbf{p})$ contains at most one point, for every price vector $\mathbf{p}$.

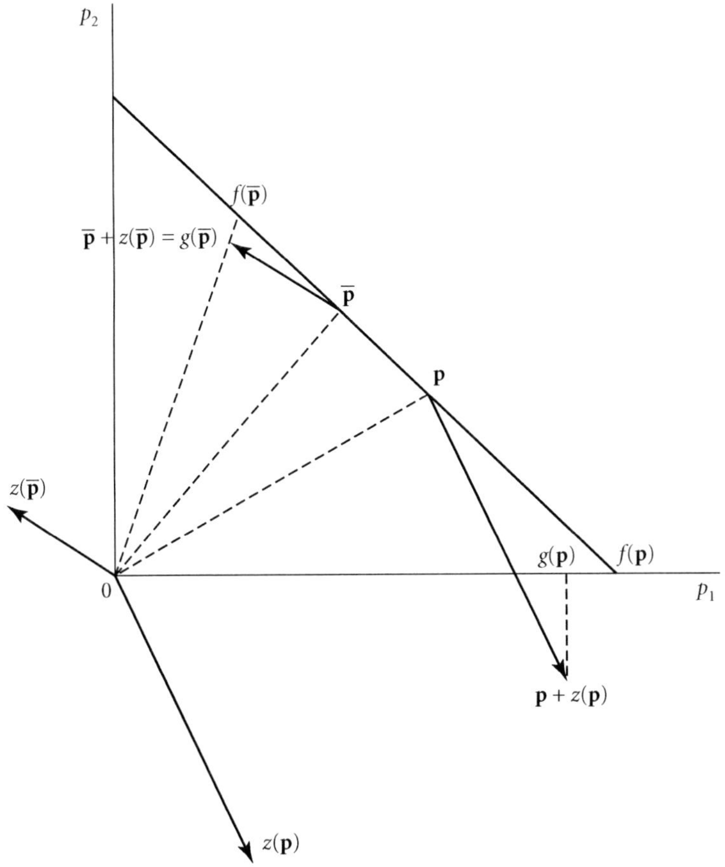

Figure 4.35 The fixed point mapping

Proof. Suppose that $\xi_i(\mathbf{p})$ contains two distinct vectors, $\overline{\mathbf{x}}$ and $\underline{\mathbf{x}}$. Since $\overline{\mathbf{x}}$ and $\underline{\mathbf{x}}$ maximize utility over consumer i's budget set, $\beta_i(\mathbf{p})$, it follows that $u_i(\overline{\mathbf{x}}) = u_i(\underline{\mathbf{x}})$. Also, $\overline{\mathbf{x}}$ and $\underline{\mathbf{x}}$ both belong to $\beta_i(\mathbf{p})$. Since this budget set is convex, the vector $\mathbf{x} = \frac{1}{2}\overline{\mathbf{x}} + \frac{1}{2}\underline{\mathbf{x}}$ belongs to it as well. Since u_i is strictly quasi-convex, $u_i(\mathbf{x}) > \min(u_i(\overline{\mathbf{x}}), u_i(\underline{\mathbf{x}})) = u_i(\overline{\mathbf{x}})$, which is impossible, since $\overline{\mathbf{x}}$ is a utility maximizing point in the budget set. ▪

The corresponding assertion for firms requires strict convexity of input-output possibility sets.

PROPOSITION 4.23 In any economy

$$\mathcal{E} = ((u_i \mathbf{e}_i)_{i=1}^I, (Y_j)_{j=1}^J, (\Theta_{ij})_{i=1,\ j=1}^{I\ \ \ J}),$$

if the input-output possibility set Y_j is strictly convex, then $\eta_j(\mathbf{p})$ has at most one point for every price vector $\mathbf{p}$.

Proof. Suppose that $\eta_j(\mathbf{p})$ contains two distinct vectors $\overline{\mathbf{y}}$ and $\underline{\mathbf{y}}$. Since $\overline{\mathbf{y}}$ and $\underline{\mathbf{y}}$ maximize profits over Y_j, $\mathbf{p}.\overline{\mathbf{y}} = \mathbf{p}.\underline{\mathbf{y}}$. Since Y_j is strictly convex, the vector $\mathbf{y} = \frac{1}{2}\overline{\mathbf{y}} + \frac{1}{2}\underline{\mathbf{y}}$ belongs to the interior of Y_j, so that for a sufficiently small positive number ε, $\mathbf{y} + \varepsilon\mathbf{p}$ belongs to Y_j. But then $\mathbf{p}.(\mathbf{y} + \varepsilon\mathbf{p}) = \mathbf{p}.\mathbf{y} + \varepsilon\mathbf{p}.\mathbf{p} > \mathbf{p}.\mathbf{y} = \frac{1}{2}\mathbf{p}.\overline{\mathbf{y}} + \frac{1}{2}\mathbf{p}.\underline{\mathbf{y}} = \mathbf{p}.\underline{\mathbf{y}}$, which contradicts the assumption that $\underline{\mathbf{y}}$ maximizes profits over Y_j. ▪

Although the assumptions of propositions 4.22 and 4.23 may not be convincing, they do give conditions on a model that guarantee that demands and supplies are single valued when they are defined.

4.8 A Complete Theorem on the Existence of Equilibrium

Theorem 4.14 may be applied to prove the following statement.

EQUILIBRIUM EXISTENCE THEOREM 4.24 In the economy

$$\mathcal{E} = ((u_i \mathbf{e}_i)_{i=1}^I, (Y_j)_{j=1}^J, (\Theta_{ij})_{i=1,\ j=1}^{I\ \ \ J}),$$

let $Y = \sum_{j=1}^J Y_j$ and assume that

1. for all j, Y_j is closed, strictly convex, and contains $\mathbf{0}$
2. $Y \cap \mathbb{R}_+^N = \{\mathbf{0}\}$
3. $Y \cap (-Y) = \{\mathbf{0}\}$
4. for all i, u_i is strictly increasing, strictly quasi-concave, and continuous
5. for all i, $\mathbf{e}_i \gg \mathbf{0}$

Then there exists an equilibrium $(\overline{\mathbf{x}}, \overline{\mathbf{y}}, \mathbf{p})$.

Proof.[4] The outline of the proof is as follows. By theorem 3.54 (in section 3.7), the set of feasible allocations is compact and nonempty. Because the set of feasible allocations is bounded, I can place an upper limit on the amount of any commodity available to any firm or consumer. The resulting truncated input-output and budget sets are compact, and the supply and demand vectors defined from them exist for all price vectors. Theorem 4.14 applies to the corresponding truncated, market excess demand function, so that there exists a price vector at which the truncated excess demand for no commodity is positive. The last step is to verify that this price vector is an equilibrium price vector for the economy with no truncation.

Because the set of feasible allocations is bounded, there exists a positive number B such that if $(\mathbf{x}, \mathbf{y})$ is a feasible allocation, then $| x_{in} |< B$ and $| y_{jn} |< B$, for all i, j, and n. The truncated input-output possibility sets are defined to be $Y_j^T = \{\mathbf{y} \in Y_j \mid \|\mathbf{y}\| \leq B\sqrt{N}\}$, for each j. For each j and each $\mathbf{p} \in \Delta^{N-1}$, let $\pi_j^T(\mathbf{p}) = \sup_{\mathbf{y} \in Y_j^T} \mathbf{p}.\mathbf{y}$. and let $\eta_j^T(\mathbf{p}) = \{\mathbf{y} \in Y_j^T \mid \mathbf{p}.\mathbf{y} = \pi_j^T(\mathbf{p})\}$. Since Y_j^T is compact and nonempty, $\eta_j^T(\mathbf{p})$ is nonempty and so $\pi_j^T(\mathbf{p}) = \mathbf{p}.\mathbf{y}$, for some $\mathbf{y} \in Y_j^T$. Since Y_j^T is strictly convex, $\eta_j^T(\mathbf{p})$ contains a single point by proposition 4.23, so that η_j^T is a function. Observe that if $\mathbf{p} \in \Delta^{N-1}$ and $\mathbf{y} \in Y_j^T$, then $\mathbf{p}.\mathbf{y} \leq \mathbf{p}.\left(\frac{B\sqrt{N}}{\|\mathbf{p}\|}\mathbf{p}\right) = B\sqrt{N}\|\mathbf{p}\| \leq B\sqrt{N}$. Therefore,

$$\pi_j^T(\mathbf{p}) \leq B\sqrt{N}, \tag{4.13}$$

for $\mathbf{p} \in \Delta^{N-1}$.

I now turn to the definition of the truncated consumer budget sets. For each i and each $\mathbf{p} \in \Delta^{N-1}$, the wealth of consumer i in the truncated economy is $w_i^T(\mathbf{p}) = \mathbf{p}.\mathbf{e}_i + \sum_{j=1}^J \Theta_{ij}\pi_j^T(\mathbf{p})$. In order to define an appropriate truncation of the budget set, I need an upper bound on this wealth. Since $(\mathbf{x}, \mathbf{y}) = (\mathbf{e}_1, \ldots, \mathbf{e}_I, \mathbf{0}, \ldots, \mathbf{0})$ is a feasible allocation, it follows that $| e_{in} |< B$, for all i and n, and hence $\mathbf{p}.\mathbf{e}_i < B$, if $\mathbf{p} \in \Delta^{N-1}$. Therefore inequality 4.13 implies that

$$w_i^T(\mathbf{p}) \leq \mathbf{p}.\mathbf{e}_i + \sum_{j=1}^{J} \pi_j^T(\mathbf{p}) < B + JB\sqrt{N}, \tag{4.14}$$

for all i and for $\mathbf{p} \in \Delta^{N-1}$ Since I need Walras' law to apply to the truncated consumer demand, there should be points in the truncated commodity

4. This proof is based on that of Debreu (1959), section 7 of chapter 5.

space that cost at least as much as the consumer's income. For this reason, consumer i's truncated budget set at price vector **p** is defined to be $\beta_i^T(\mathbf{p}) = \{\mathbf{x} \in \mathbb{R}_+^N \mid\mid x_n \mid\leq B + JB\sqrt{N}$, for all n, and $\mathbf{p}.\mathbf{x} \leq w_i^T(\mathbf{p})\}$. This budget set is clearly compact and convex. I show that it is nonempty. Because each Y_j^T contains the zero vector, $\pi_j^T(\mathbf{p}) \geq 0$, for all j. Since $\mathbf{e}_i \gg \mathbf{0}$, $\mathbf{p}.\mathbf{e}_i > 0$, for all **p** such that $\mathbf{p} > \mathbf{0}$. Therefore for such **p**,

$$w_i^T(\mathbf{p}) \geq \mathbf{p}.\mathbf{e}_i > 0 \tag{4.15}$$

and so $\beta_i^T(\mathbf{p})$ is nonempty.

The truncated demand of consumer i is defined to be

$$\xi_i^T(\mathbf{p}) = \{\mathbf{x} \in \beta_i^T(\mathbf{p}) \mid u_i(\mathbf{x}) \geq u_i(\underline{\mathbf{x}}),\ \text{ for all } \underline{\mathbf{x}} \in \beta_i^T(\mathbf{p})\}.$$

Since $\beta_i^T(\mathbf{p})$ is compact and nonempty and u_i is continuous, it follows that $\xi_i^T(\mathbf{p})$ is nonempty. Since u_i is strictly quasi-concave and β_i^T is convex, a slight extension of proposition 4.22 implies that $\xi_i^T(\mathbf{p})$ contains a single point and hence ξ_i^T is a function.

I next show that

$$\mathbf{p}.\xi_i^T(\mathbf{p}) = w_i^T(\mathbf{p}), \tag{4.16}$$

for all i, an assertion needed to prove that Walras' law applies to the truncated, market excess demand to which theorem 4.14 applies. Since $\xi_i^T(\mathbf{p}) \in \beta_i^T(\mathbf{p})$, $\mathbf{p}.\xi_i^T(\mathbf{p}) \leq w_i^T(\mathbf{p})$. Suppose that $\mathbf{p}.\xi_i^T(\mathbf{p}) < w_i^T(\mathbf{p})$. By the definition of $\beta_i^T(\mathbf{p})$, $\xi_i^T(\mathbf{p}) \leq (B + JB\sqrt{N})\mathbf{e}$, where **e** is the N-vector $(1, 1, \ldots, 1)$. If $\mathbf{p} \in \Delta^{N-1}$, then $\mathbf{p}.\xi_i^T(\mathbf{p}) < w_i^T(\mathbf{p}) < (B + JB\sqrt{N}) = \mathbf{p}.(B + JB\sqrt{N})\mathbf{e}$, where the second inequality is inequality 4.14. Hence $\xi_i^T(\mathbf{p}) \neq (B + JB\sqrt{N})\mathbf{e}$ and so $\xi_i^T(\mathbf{p}) < (B + JB\sqrt{N})\mathbf{e}$. Therefore for a sufficiently small positive number α,

$$\mathbf{p}.\{\xi_i^T(\mathbf{p}) + \alpha[(B + JB\sqrt{N})\mathbf{e} - \xi_i^T(\mathbf{p})]\} < w_i^T(\mathbf{p}),$$

so that $\xi_i^T(\mathbf{p}) + \alpha[(B + JB\sqrt{N})\mathbf{e} - \xi_i^T(\mathbf{p})]$ belongs to $\beta_i^T(\mathbf{p})$. Since u_i is strictly increasing,

$$u_i(\xi_i^T(\mathbf{p}) + \alpha[(B + JB\sqrt{N})\mathbf{e} - \xi_i^T(\mathbf{p})]) > u_i(\xi_i^T(\mathbf{p})),$$

which is impossible since $\xi_i^T(\mathbf{p})$ is the point in $\beta_i^T(\mathbf{p})$ that maximizes u_i. This completes the proof that $\mathbf{p}.\xi_i^T(\mathbf{p}) = w_i^T(\mathbf{p})$.

To apply theorem 4.14 to the truncated, market excess demand, I need to show that it is continuous. To this end, I show that η_j^T is a continuous function, for each j. Let $\mathbf{p}^k$ be a sequence in Δ^{N-1} such that $\lim_{k\to\infty} \mathbf{p}^k = \mathbf{p}$. I must show that $\lim_{k\to\infty} \eta_j^T(\mathbf{p}^k) = \eta_j^T(\mathbf{p})$. If $\eta_j^T(\mathbf{p}^k)$ does not converge to $\eta_j^T(\mathbf{p})$, then for some positive number ε, $\|\eta_j^T(\mathbf{p}^k) - \eta_j^T(\mathbf{p})\| > \varepsilon$, for infinitely many k, so that there is a subsequence, which I again call $\eta_j^T(\mathbf{p}^k)$, such that $\|\eta_j^T(\mathbf{p}^k) - \eta_j^T(\mathbf{p})\| > \varepsilon$, for all k. Since Y_j^T is compact, I may assume, by the Bolzano-Weierstrass theorem, that the sequence $\eta_j^T(\mathbf{p}^k)$ converges to some vector $\mathbf{y} \in Y_j^T$. Passing to the limit in the equality $\|\eta_j^T(\mathbf{p}^k) - \eta_j^T(\mathbf{p})\| \geq \varepsilon$, we see that $\|\mathbf{y} - \eta_j^T(\mathbf{p})\| \geq \varepsilon$, so that $\mathbf{y} \neq \eta_j^T(\mathbf{p})$. Therefore, $\mathbf{p}.\eta_j^T(\mathbf{p}) > \mathbf{p}.\mathbf{y}$, since $\eta_j^T(\mathbf{p})$ is the unique point in Y_j^T that maximizes $\mathbf{p}.\mathbf{y}$. Since $\lim_{k\to\infty} \mathbf{p}^k.\eta_j^T(\mathbf{p}) = \mathbf{p}.\eta_j^T(\mathbf{p})$ and $\lim_{k\to\infty} \mathbf{p}^k.\eta_j^T(\mathbf{p}^k) = \mathbf{p}.\mathbf{y}$, it follows that $\mathbf{p}^k.\eta_j^T(\mathbf{p}) > \mathbf{p}^k.\eta_j^T(\mathbf{p}^k)$, for k sufficiently large, which contradicts the definition of $\eta_j^T(\mathbf{p}^k)$. This contradiction proves that $\lim_{k\to\infty} \eta_j^T(\mathbf{p}^k) = \eta_j^T(\mathbf{p})$ and hence that η_j^T is continuous.

I next show that ξ_i^T is a continuous function for each i. First of all, because each η_j^T is continuous, it follows that

$$w_i^T(\mathbf{p}) = \mathbf{p}.\mathbf{e}_i + \sum_{j=1}^{J} \Theta_{ij}\mathbf{p}.\eta_j^T(\mathbf{p})$$

is a continuous function of $\mathbf{p}$. I must show that if $\mathbf{p}^k$ is a sequence in Δ^{N-1} that converges to $\mathbf{p}$, then $\xi_i^T(\mathbf{p}^k)$ converges to $\xi_i^T(\mathbf{p})$. If $\xi_i^T(\mathbf{p}^k)$ does not converge to $\xi_i^T(\mathbf{p})$ then there is a positive number ε such that $\|\xi_i^T(\mathbf{p}^k) - \xi_i^T(\mathbf{p})\| > \varepsilon$, for infinitely many k. By passing to a subsequence, I may assume that this inequality applies for all k. The truncated demands $\xi_i^T(\mathbf{p}^k)$ belong to the compact set $\{\mathbf{x} \in \mathbb{R}_+^N \mid |x_n| \leq B + JB\sqrt{N}, \text{ for all } n\}$. Therefore, by the Bolzano-Weierstrass theorem, I may assume that the sequence $\xi_i^T(\mathbf{p}^k)$ converges to some $\mathbf{x}$ in this set. Since $\mathbf{p}.\xi_i^T(\mathbf{p}^k) \leq w_i^T(\mathbf{p}^k)$, for all k, and w_i^T is a continuous function, it follows that $\mathbf{p}.\mathbf{x} \leq w_i^T(\mathbf{p})$ and hence $\mathbf{x} \in \beta_i^T(\mathbf{p})$. Since $\|\xi_i^T(\mathbf{p}^k) - \xi_i^T(\mathbf{p})\| > \varepsilon$, for all k, it follows by passage to the limit that $\|\mathbf{x} - \xi_i^T(\mathbf{p})\| \geq \varepsilon$ and hence $\mathbf{x} \neq \xi_i^T(\mathbf{p})$ and so $u_i(\xi_i^T(\mathbf{p})) > u_i(\mathbf{x})$, since $\xi_i^T(\mathbf{p})$ is the unique point in $\beta_i^T(\mathbf{p})$ that maximizes u_i. If $\alpha$is such that $0 < \alpha < 1$ and α is sufficiently close to 1, then $u_i(\alpha\xi_i^T(\mathbf{p})) > u_i(\mathbf{x})$. Since $\mathbf{p}.\xi_i^T(\mathbf{p}) = w_i^T(\mathbf{p}) > 0$ by equation 4.16 and inequality 4.15, it follows that $\mathbf{p}.(\alpha\xi_i^T(\mathbf{p})) = \alpha\mathbf{p}.\xi_i^T(\mathbf{p}) < \mathbf{p}.w_i^T(\mathbf{p})$. Hence, if k is sufficiently large, $\mathbf{p}^k.(\alpha\xi_i^T(\mathbf{p})) < \mathbf{p}^k.w_i^T(\mathbf{p}^k)$ and so $\alpha\xi_i^T(\mathbf{p}) \in \beta_i^T(\mathbf{p}^k)$. Similarly for k sufficiently large, $u_i(\alpha\xi_i^T(\mathbf{p})) > u_i(\xi_i^T(\mathbf{p}^k))$, since u_i is a continuous function and $\lim_{k\to\infty} \xi_i^T(\mathbf{p}^k) = \mathbf{x}$. This last inequality contradicts the definition of $\xi_i^T(\mathbf{p}^k)$, and this contradiction proves that $\lim_{k\to\infty} \xi_i^T(\mathbf{p}^k) = \xi_i^T(\mathbf{p})$ and hence that ξ_i^T is a continuous function.

I define the truncated, market excess demand to be

$$z^T(\mathbf{p}) = \sum_{i=1}^{I}[\xi_i^T(\mathbf{p}) - \mathbf{e}_i] - \sum_{j=1}^{J} \eta_j^T(\mathbf{p}).$$

Since by equation 4.16 $\mathbf{p}.\xi_i^T(\mathbf{p}) = w_i^T(\mathbf{p})$, for all i, it follows that $\mathbf{p}.z^T(\mathbf{p}) = 0$, for all $\mathbf{p} > \mathbf{0}$. That is, z^T satisfies Walras' law. Since ξ_i^T and η_j^T are continuous, z^T is continuous. Therefore theorem 4.14 implies that there exists a price vector $\overline{\mathbf{p}}$ such that $\overline{\mathbf{p}} > \mathbf{0}$, $z^T(\overline{\mathbf{p}}) \leq \mathbf{0}$, and, for all n, $\overline{p}_n = 0$, if $z_n^T(\overline{\mathbf{p}}) < 0$. Let $\overline{\mathbf{x}}_i = \xi_i^T(\overline{\mathbf{p}})$, for each i, and let $\overline{\mathbf{y}}_j = \eta_j^T(\overline{\mathbf{p}})$, for each j.

I show that $(\overline{\mathbf{x}}, \overline{\mathbf{y}}, \overline{\mathbf{p}})$ is an equilibrium. First of all,

$$\sum_{i=1}^{I}(\overline{\mathbf{x}}_i - \mathbf{e}_i) - \sum_{j=1}^{J}\overline{\mathbf{y}}_i = \sum_{i=1}^{I}[\xi_i^T(\overline{\mathbf{p}}) - \mathbf{e}_i] - \sum_{j=1}^{J}\eta_j^T(\overline{\mathbf{p}}) = z^T(\overline{\mathbf{p}}) \leq 0,$$

so that $(\overline{\mathbf{x}}, \overline{\mathbf{y}})$ is a feasible allocation. Since $\overline{p}_n = 0$, if $z_n^T(\overline{\mathbf{p}}) < 0$, for all n, it follows that, for all n, $\overline{p}_n = 0$, if $\sum_{i=1}^{I}(\overline{x}_{in} - e_{in}) - \sum_{j=1}^{J}\overline{y}_{jn} < 0$. Because the allocation $(\overline{\mathbf{x}}, \overline{\mathbf{y}})$ is feasible, $|\,\overline{x}_{in}\,| < B$ and $|\,\overline{y}_{jn}\,| < B$, for all i, j, and n.

I show that $\overline{\mathbf{y}}_i = \eta_i(\overline{\mathbf{p}})$, for all j. If $\overline{\mathbf{y}}_j \neq \eta_j(\overline{\mathbf{p}})$, then there exists a $\mathbf{y} \in Y_j$ such that $\overline{\mathbf{p}}.\mathbf{y} > \overline{\mathbf{p}}.\overline{\mathbf{y}}_j$. Since $|\,\overline{y}_{jn}\,| < B$, for all n, if ε is a sufficiently small positive number, $|\,\varepsilon y_n + (1 - \varepsilon)\overline{y}_{jn}\,| \leq B$, for all n, and so, since Y_j is convex, $\varepsilon\mathbf{y} + (1-\varepsilon)\overline{\mathbf{y}}_j \in Y_j^T$. However, $\mathbf{p}.(\varepsilon\mathbf{y} + (1-\varepsilon)\overline{\mathbf{y}}_j) = \varepsilon\mathbf{p}.\mathbf{y} + (1-\varepsilon)\mathbf{p}.\overline{\mathbf{y}}_j > \mathbf{p}.\overline{\mathbf{y}}_j$, which is impossible, since $\overline{\mathbf{y}}_j = \eta_j^T(\overline{\mathbf{p}})$. This contradiction proves that $\overline{\mathbf{y}}_j = \eta_j(\overline{\mathbf{p}})$. It follows that $\pi_j^T(\overline{\mathbf{p}}) = \overline{\mathbf{p}}.\overline{\mathbf{y}}_j = \pi_j(\overline{\mathbf{p}})$ and so

$$w_i^T(\overline{\mathbf{p}}) = w_i(\overline{\mathbf{p}}), \tag{4.17}$$

for all i.

I next show that $\overline{\mathbf{x}}_i = \xi_i(\overline{\mathbf{p}})$, for all i. Suppose that $\overline{\mathbf{x}}_i \neq \xi_i(\overline{\mathbf{p}})$. Then for some $\mathbf{x} \in \beta_i(\overline{\mathbf{p}})$, $u_i(\mathbf{x}) > u_i(\overline{\mathbf{x}})$. Since $|\,x_{in}\,| < B$, for all n, if ε is a sufficiently small positive number, then $|\,\varepsilon x_n + (1-\varepsilon)\overline{x}_{in}\,| \leq B$, for all n. Since

$$\begin{aligned}\overline{\mathbf{p}}.(\varepsilon\mathbf{x} + (1-\varepsilon)\overline{\mathbf{x}}_i) &= \varepsilon\overline{\mathbf{p}}.\mathbf{x} + (1-\varepsilon)\overline{\mathbf{p}}.\overline{\mathbf{x}}_i \leq \varepsilon w_i(\overline{\mathbf{p}}) + (1-\varepsilon)w_i^T(\mathbf{p})\\ &= \varepsilon w_i^T(\overline{\mathbf{p}}) + (1-\varepsilon)w_i^T(\overline{\mathbf{p}}) = w_i^T(\overline{\mathbf{p}}),\end{aligned}$$

where the second equation follows from equation 4.17. Hence $\varepsilon\mathbf{x} + (1-\varepsilon)\overline{\mathbf{x}}_i \in \beta_i^T(\mathbf{p})$. Since u_i is strictly quasi-concave, $u_i(\varepsilon\mathbf{x} + (1-\varepsilon)\overline{\mathbf{x}}_i) >$

$\min(u_i(\mathbf{x}_i), u_i(\overline{\mathbf{x}}_i)) = u_i(\overline{\mathbf{x}}_i)$. This inequality contradicts the assumption that $\overline{\mathbf{x}}_i = \xi_i^T(\mathbf{p})$. I have shown that $(\overline{\mathbf{x}}, \overline{\mathbf{y}}, \overline{\mathbf{p}})$ has all the properties of an equilibrium. ▪

The theorem just proved has a number drawbacks. The assumptions that utility functions are strictly quasi-concave and strictly increasing are unnecessarily restrictive, as is the assumption that input-output possibility sets are strictly convex and that endowments are strictly positive. There is a literature proving stronger existence theorems. Section 5.3 contains a somewhat stronger existence theorem, though the point of that section is not the strength of the theorem but its method of proof.

4.9 An Example of Discontinuous Behavior of Equilibria

In comparative static analysis, assertions are made about how equilibria respond to changes in the values of parameters governing an economy's description. Unfortunately equilibria may depend so perversely and discontinuously on such parameters that general comparative static statements may be impossible. Equilibrium depends continuously on parameters only under special assumptions. There follows an example in which equilibrium varies discontinuously with consumers' endowments.

EXAMPLE 4.25 The example is of an Edgeworth box economy. The parameter varied is consumer A's endowment of good 1. Consumer B's endowment of good 1 is such that the total endowment remains constant; the endowment of consumer A is $\mathbf{e}_{\mathrm{A}} = (e_{A1}, 0)$, and that of consumer B is $\mathbf{e}_{\mathrm{B}} = (10 - e_{A1}, 10)$, so that the total endowment of each good is 10. The utility function of consumer B is

$$u_{\mathrm{B}}(x_1, x_2) = \min(x_1, x_2),$$

and that of consumer A is

$$u_{\mathrm{A}}(x_1, x_2) = \begin{cases} 2x_1 - 1, & \text{if } x_2 \geq x_1 - 1 \text{ and } x_1 \geq 3.25, \\ x_1 + x_2, & \text{if } x_1 + x_2 \leq 5 \text{ or } x_2 \leq x_1 - 1, \\ \dfrac{x_1 + x_2 - 5}{1 + 2(x_2 - x_1 + 1)} + 5, & \text{if } x_1 + x_2 \geq 5 \\ & \text{and if } x_2 \geq x_1 - 1 \text{ and } x_1 \leq 3.25. \end{cases} \tag{4.18}$$

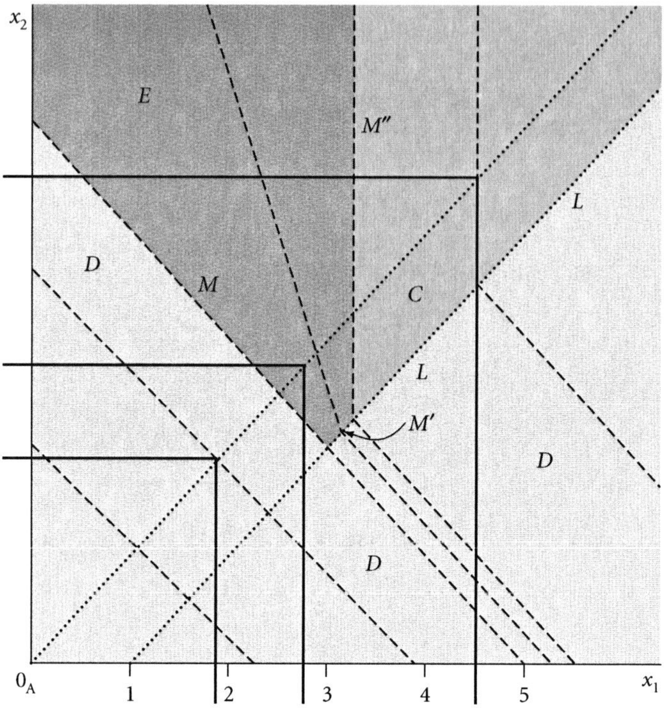

Figure 4.36 The Edgeworth box diagram for example 4.25

The southwest part of the Edgeworth box diagram for the example is pictured in figure 4.36. The dashed lines in the figure are indifference curves for consumer A, and the solid lines are indifference curves for consumer B. The dotted lines of slope 1 are guide lines used in defining the indifference curves for the two consumers.

I verify that the u_A is consistently defined and hence is continuous. Consider the region C defined by the inequalities

$$x_2 \geq x_1 - 1 \text{ and } x_1 \geq 3.25,$$

and the region D defined by the inequality

$$x_2 \leq x_1 - 1 \text{ or } x_1 + x_2 \leq 5.$$

These regions meet along the half line L defined by the formulas

$$x_2 = x_1 - 1,\ x_1 \geq 3.25$$

In region D and along line L,

$$u_A(x_1, x_2) = x_1 + x_2 = x_1 + x_1 - 1 = 2x_1 - 1,$$

which is the value of $u_A(x_1, x_2)$ in region C, so that the u_A is consistently defined over these two regions.

The region E, defined by the inequalities

$$x_1 + x_2 \geq 5,\ x_2 \geq x_1 - 1,\ \text{and}\ x_1 \leq 3.25,$$

intersects each of the other two regions. It meets region D along the line segment M, defined by the formulas

$$x_1 + x_2 = 5,\ 0 \leq x_1 \leq 3,$$

and along line segment M', defined by the formulas

$$x_2 = x_1 - 1 \text{ and } 3 \leq x_1 \leq 3.25.$$

In region D, $u_A(x_1, x_2) = x + 1 + x_2$. This function equals 5 along line segment M, and along M the function u_A as defined in region E also equals 5, as is evident from equation 4.18. Along line segment M', u_A equals $x_1 + x_2$ in both regions D and E. Region E meets region C along line segment M'' defined by the formulas

$$x_1 = 3.25 \text{ and } x_2 \geq 2.25.$$

The function u_A of region C equals 5.5 along line segment M'', and u_A as defined in region E, equals

$$\frac{x_1 - 1.75}{1 + 2(x_2 - 2.25)} + 5 = \frac{x_2 - 1.75}{2(x_2 - 1.75)} + 5 = 5.5,$$

so that u_A is defined consistently on the union of regions C and E. The function u_A is continuous, because it is defined by consistent formulas that are continuous on each of a finite number of closed regions of definition.

It is now possible to describe the equilibria. Prices will be normalized so that $p_1 = 1$. If $0 \leq e_{A1} \leq 5$, then there is an equilibrium with $p_2 = 1$ and $\mathbf{x}_A = \left(\frac{e_{A1}}{2}, \frac{e_{A1}}{2}\right)$, as should be clear from figure 4.36. If $e_{A1} \geq 3.25$, there is an equilibrium with $p_2 = 0$ and $\mathbf{x}_A$ equal to any member of the set $\{(e_{A1}, x_2) \mid e_{A1} - 1 \leq x_2 \leq e_{A1}\}$.

There are also equilibria where the allocation to consumer A lies in the region E. In order to define these equilibria, let $u_A(x_1, x_2) = \Theta + 5$ in region E, where

$$\Theta = \frac{x_1 + x_2 - 5}{1 + 2(x_2 - x_1 + 1)}.$$

Solving for x_2, we find that

$$x_2 = \frac{1 + 2\Theta}{1 - 2\Theta}x_1 + \frac{5 + 3\Theta}{1 - 2\Theta}.$$

That is, the indifference curve of consumer A for utility level $\Theta + 5$ is a straight line segment in region E with slope $-\frac{1+2\Theta}{1-2\Theta}$. From figure 4.36, it is clear that any equilibrium allocation for consumer A in region E is of the form $x_A = (x, x)$. Then,

$$u_A(x, x) = \frac{2x - 5}{3} + 5 = \Theta + 5,$$

where

$$\Theta = \frac{2x - 5}{3}. \tag{4.19}$$

If the equilibrium price vector is $(p_1, p_2) = (1, p_2)$, then the equation for consumer A's budget line is

$$x_2 = -p_1^{-1}x_1 + p_2^{-1}e_{At},$$

and so

$$-p_2^{-1} = -\frac{1 + 2\Theta}{1 - 2\Theta}$$

or

$$p_2 = \frac{1 - 2\Theta}{1 + 2\Theta}. \tag{4.20}$$

If we substitute equation 4.19 into equation 4.20 and solve for x, we obtain

$$x = \frac{13 + 7p_2}{4(1 + p_2)}. \tag{4.21}$$

Consumer A's budget equation for the equilibrium at $\mathbf{x}_A = (x, x)$ is

$$(1 + p_2)x = e_{A1}. \tag{4.22}$$

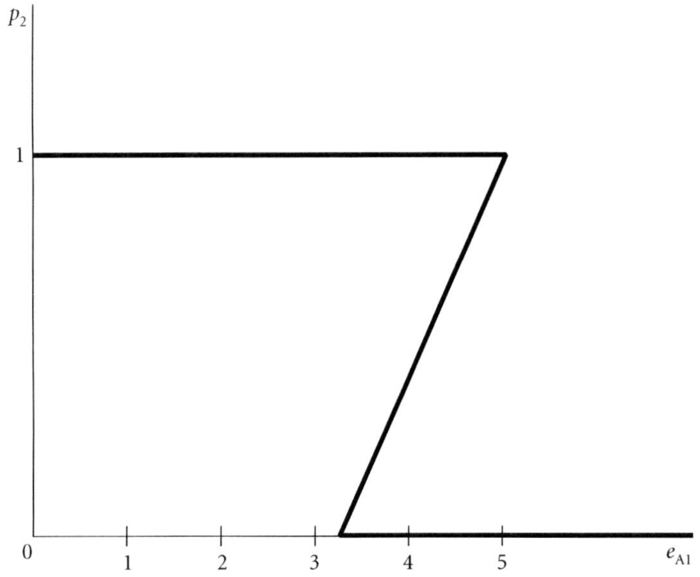

Figure 4.37 Graph of the multivalued equilibrium function for example 4.25

If we substitute equation 4.21 into equation 4.22 and solve for p_2, we find that

$$p_2 = \frac{4e_{A1} - 13}{7}. \tag{4.23}$$

Equation 4.23 defines an equilibrium price p_2, for every value of e_{A1} from 3.25 to 5. If $e_{A1} = 5$, then $p_2 = 1$, and if $e_{A1} = 3.25$, then $p_2 = 0$. The relation between e_{A1} and p_2 is expressed by a multivalued function, the graph of which is portrayed in figure 4.37. Notice that if $e_{A1} < 3.25$, then there is only one equilibrium price vector, namely $(p_1, p_2) = (1, 1)$. Similarly, if $e_{A1} > 5$, there is only one equilibrium price vector, (1, 0). If $3.25 < e_{A1} < 5$, there are three equilibrium price vectors, namely (1, 0), $\left(1, \frac{4e_{A1}-13}{7}\right)$, and (1, 1). If $e_{A1} = 3.25$ or $e_{A1} = 5$, there are two equilibrium price vectors, (1, 0) and (1, 1). Imagine that $3.25 < e_{A1} < 5$ and that we decrease e_{A1} while keeping the equilibrium price vector at (1, 0) or $\left(1, \frac{4e_{A1}-13}{7}\right)$. When e_{A1} arrives at 3.25, these two price vectors come together at (1, 0), and when e_{A1} passes 3.25, the equilibrium at (1, 0) disappears and the equilibrium price vector must jump to (1, 1). It is in this sense that the relation between the parameter e_{A1} and the price vector is discontinuous.

For purposes of exposition, the example has indifference curves composed of straight line segments. With more work, a similar example can be created with utility functions that are strictly increasing and strictly concave.

Problem Set

1. Solve

$$\max_{x_1 \geq 0, x_2 \geq 0} \left(\sqrt{x_1} + \sqrt{x_2}\right)^2$$
$$\text{s.t.} \quad p_1 x_1 + p_2 x_2 = w.$$

2. Calculate a consumer's demand for goods 1 and 2 as a function of p_1 and p_2—the prices of goods 1 and 2, respectively, when the consumer's utility function and initial endowment are as below. Draw the offer curve in each case.

(a) $u(x_1, x_2) = x_1^5 x_2^2$, $\mathbf{e} = (10, 0)$
(b) $u(x_1, x_2) = \min(5x_1, 2x_2)$, $\mathbf{e} = (10, 0)$
(c) $u(x_1, x_2) = 5x_1 + 2x_2$, $\mathbf{e} = (10, 0)$
(d) $u(x_1, x_2) = \ln(x_1) + \ln(x_2)$, $\mathbf{e} = (1, 1)$

3. Suppose that the production function for good 3 is

$$y_3 = \left(\sqrt{-y_1} + \sqrt{-y_2}\right)^2,$$

where commodities 1 and 2 are the inputs, $y_1 \leq 0$, and $y_2 \leq 0$. Let $\mathbf{p} = (p_1, p_2, p_3)$ be the vector of prices of the three commodities, where $\mathbf{p} \gg 0$.

(a) For what price vectors $\mathbf{p}$ is $\pi(\mathbf{p}) < \infty$, where $\pi(\mathbf{p})$ is the supremum of the possible profits?
(b) Find $\pi(\mathbf{p})$ and $\eta(\mathbf{p})$, for all price vectors, where $\eta(\mathbf{p})$ is the set of profit maximizing input-output vectors.

4. In cases (a) and (b) below, find $\pi(\mathbf{p})$ and $\eta(\mathbf{p})$ for any vector $\mathbf{p}$ of appropriate dimension and such that $\mathbf{p} > 0$, where $\pi(\mathbf{p}) = \sup_{\mathbf{y} \in Y} \mathbf{p}.\mathbf{y}$ and $\eta(\mathbf{p}) = \{\mathbf{y} \in Y \mid \mathbf{p}.\mathbf{y} = \pi(\mathbf{p})\}$.

(a) $Y = \{(y_1, y_2, y_3) \mid y_1 \leq 0,\ y_2 \leq 0, \text{ and } 0 \leq y_3 \leq (-y_1)^{1/4}(-y_2)^{1/2}\}$

(b) $Y = \{(y_1, y_2, y_3, y_4) \mid y_1 \geq 0,\ y_2 \geq 0,\ y_3 \leq 0,\ y_4 \leq 0, \text{ and } y_1^2 + y_2^2 \leq \sqrt{y_3 y_4}\}$

5. Consider the Robinson Crusoe economy with utility function

$$u(x_1, x_2) = \ln(x_1) + 2\ln(x_2),$$

endowment vector $\mathbf{e} = (1, 0)$, and production function

$$y_2 = -2y_1,$$

where x_1 and x_2 are the consumptions of commodities 1 and 2, respectively, and (y_1, y_2) is the input-output vector of Robinson Crusoe's firm. Find all equilibria with the price of the first good equal to 1.

6. (a) Consider the Edgeworth box economy with utility functions

$$u_A(x_1, x_2) = 3x_1 + x_2 \text{ and}$$
$$u_B(x_1, x_2) = x_1 + 3x_2$$

and endowment vectors $\mathbf{e}_A = (2, 0)$ and $\mathbf{e}_B = (0, 2)$. Find all equilibria with the price of the first good equal to one.

(b) Consider the Edgeworth box economy with utility functions

$$u_A(x_1, x_2) = x_1 + 3x_2 \text{ and}$$
$$u_B(x_1, x_2) = 3x_1 + x_2$$

and endowment vectors $\mathbf{e}_A = (2, 0)$ and $\mathbf{e}_B = (0, 2)$. Find all equilibria with the price of the first good equal to one.

7. Consider the Edgeworth box economy where

$$\mathbf{e}_A = (12, 0),\ \mathbf{e}_B = (0, 12) \text{ and}$$
$$u_A(x_1, x_2) = u_B(x_1, x_2) = x_1^{1/3} x_2^{2/3}.$$

(a) Calculate and draw accurately the offer curves for each consumer.

(b) Find all competitive equilibria with the price of the first good equal to 1.

8. Consider the following Edgeworth box economy.

$$u_A(x_1, x_2) = \frac{1}{3}\ln(x_1) + \frac{2}{3}\ln(x_2),\ \mathbf{e}_A = (18, 0),$$

$$u_B(x_1, x_2) = \frac{1}{2}\ln(x_1) + \frac{1}{2}\ln(x_2),\ \mathbf{e}_B = (0, 20).$$

Find all competitive equilibria with prices that sum to 1.

9. Consider an Edgeworth box economy[5] with utility functions $u_A(x_1, x_2) = \min(3x_1, x_2)$ and $u_B(x_1, x_2) = \min(x_1, 3x_2)$.

(a) Find the unique equilibrium when $\mathbf{e}_A = (4, 0)$ and $\mathbf{e}_B = (0, 4)$ and the price of good 1 equal to 1. Compute the utility of person A at the equilibrium.

(b) Find the unique equilibrium when $\mathbf{e}_A = (6, 0)$ and $\mathbf{e}_B = (0, 4)$ and the price of good 1 equal to 1.

(c) Compute the utility of person A at the equilibrium of part (b) and compare it with his utility in the equilibrium of part (a). Is there anything paradoxical about your finding? Can you explain intuitively why person A's utility level changes in the way that it does from part (a) to part (b)?

10. Consider the following Edgeworth box economy.

$$u_A(x_1, x_2) = \left(\sqrt{x_1} + 2\sqrt{x_2}\right)^2 = u_B(x_1, x_2),$$
$$\mathbf{e}_A = (4, 1),\ \mathbf{e}_B = (1, 4).$$

(a) Find the set of Pareto optimal allocations and draw it in a box diagram. Indicate the endowment point.

(b) Find the utility possibility frontier and draw it.

(c) Find a competitive equilibrium with the price of good 1 equal to 1.

(d) Find positive numbers a_A and a_B such that the competitive equilibrium allocation maximizes the welfare function $a_A u_A(x_{A1}, x_{A2}) + a_B u_B(x_{B1}, x_{B2})$ over the set of feasible allocations $(\mathbf{x}_A, \mathbf{x}_B)$.

11. Consider the following Edgeworth box economy.

$$u_A(x_1, x_2) = \min(4x_1, x_2), \qquad u_B(x_1, x_2) = 4x_1 + x_2,$$
$$\mathbf{e}_A = (0, 4), \qquad \mathbf{e}_B = (4, 0).$$

Do the following for this economy.

(a) Show the set of Pareto optimal allocations in a box diagram.

(b) Make a precise drawing of the utility possibility frontier.

(c) Compute a general equilibrium such that the sum of the prices is 1. Show the equilibrium allocation in a box diagram. Show the utility vector corresponding to the equilibrium allocation on a diagram of the utility possibility frontier.

(d) Compute nonnegative numbers a_A and a_B such that the equilibrium allocation maximizes the welfare function

5. I owe this problem to a personal communication from Professor Herbert Scarf.

$$a_A u_A(x_{A1}, x_{A2}) + a_B u_B(x_{B1}, x_{B2}).$$

12. Consider the following model with two consumers, A and B, and with two commodities, 1 and 2.

$$u_A(x_1, x_2) = x_1 + \ln(x_2), \qquad u_B(x_1, x_2) = x_1 + 2\ln(x_2),$$
$$\mathbf{e}_A = (e_{A1}, e_{A2}), \qquad \mathbf{e}_B = (e_{B1}, e_{B2}).$$

Assume that $e_{A1} > 10$, $e_{B1} > 10$, $e_{A2} > 0$, $e_{B2} > 0$, and $|e_{A2} + e_{B2}| \leq 1$.

(a) Compute an equilibrium where the price of good 1 is 1. The equilibrium price of good 2 and the equilibrium allocations will be formulas in terms of the endowments. (Hint: The endowments of good 1 are so large that each consumer consumes a positive amount of good 1 in equilibrium.)

(b) Show that the price of good 2 and the consumer's consumption of good 2 depend only on $e_{A2} + e_{B2}$.

13. Compute an equilibrium for the following economy with labor, two produced goods, two consumers, A and B, and two firms, 1 and 2. In commodity vectors, the first component is labor–leisure time, the second component is the first produced good, and the third is the second produced good.

$$\mathbf{e}_A = (2, 0, 0),\ u_A(\ell, x_1, x_2) = \ell + x_1 + x_2,\ \Theta_{A1} = 1,\ \Theta_{A2} = 0,$$
$$\mathbf{e}_B(2, 0, 0),\ u_B(\ell, x_1, x_2) = \ell x_1^2 x_2^3,\ \Theta_{B1} = 0,\ \Theta_{B2} = 1,$$
$$y_1 = 2\sqrt{L_1},\ y_2 = 2\sqrt{L_2},$$

where y_1 and y_2 are the outputs of produced goods 1 and 2, respectively, and L_1 and L_2 are the inputs of labor into the production of goods 1 and 2, respectively. Let the price of labor be 1. (Hint: Use the fact that person A's utility function is linear to guess the equilibrium price vector.)

14. Compute an equilibrium for the following economy.

$$u_A(x_1, x_2) = x_1^{3/7} x_2^{4/7} = u_B(x_1, x_2),$$
$$\mathbf{e}_A = \mathbf{e}_B = \mathbf{0},$$
$$Y_1 = \{(y_1, y_2) \mid y_1 \geq 0,\ 0 \leq y_2 \leq 3 - y_1\},$$
$$Y_2 = \left\{(y_1, y_2) \mid y_1 \geq 0,\ 0 \leq y_2 \leq 4 - \frac{2y_1}{5}\right\},$$
$$\Theta_{A1} = 1,\ \Theta_{A2} = 0,\ \Theta_{B1} = 0,\ \Theta_{B2} = 1.$$

(Hint: Compute the total output possibility set. Use the fact that both consumers have the same Cobb-Douglas utility function.)

15. Suppose that there is one input, labor (L), and that there are two outputs, goods 1 and 2. The production function for good 1 is $y_1 = f_1(L)$, and the production function for good 2 is $y_2 = f_2(L)$. There is one unit of labor available for use in the production of goods 1 or 2. Calculate a formula for the total output possibility set for goods 1 and 2 and draw it when

(a) $f_1(L) = L$ and $f_2(L) = 2L$.
(b) $f_1(L) = \sqrt{L}$ and $f_2(L) = 2\sqrt{L}$.

16. There are two primary inputs, labor (L) and land (T), and two outputs, goods 1 and 2. The production function of good 1 is

$$y_1 = L^{1/4}T^{3/4},$$

and the production function for good 2 is

$$y_2 = L^{3/4}T^{1/4}.$$

There is one unit of labor and one unit of land available for the production of goods 1 and 2.

(a) Sketch in a box diagram and compute a formula for the set of efficient allocations of land and labor to the production of goods 1 and 2.
(b) Sketch the total output possibility set for goods 1 and 2.
(c) What allocation of labor and land to the production of the two outputs maximizes the sum of the two outputs, $y_1 + y_2$?

17. There is one primary good, labor, and there are two outputs, goods 1 and 2. Good 1 is used as an input in the production of good 2 and good 2 is used as an input in the production of good 1. The production function for good 1 is $y_1 = f_1(y_{12}, L)$, where y_{12} is the amount of good 2 used as an input in the production of good 1. The production function for good 2 is $y_2 = f_2(y_{21}, L)$, where y_{21} is the amount of good 1 used in the production of good 2. There is one unit of labor to use in the production of goods 1 or 2.

(a) Compute a formula for the total output possibility set for goods 1 and 2 and draw it when

$$f_1(y_{12}, L) = \min(2y_{12}, L) \text{ and}$$
$$f_2(y_{21}, L) = \min(3y_{21}, L).$$

(b) Suppose that the price of labor is 1. What are the prices of goods 1 and 2 such that when each production process is operated so as to maximize profits at these prices, the two processes together can produce a positive total amount of each of goods 1 and 2 while using the one unit of labor available?

18. An economy with two produced commodities and labor has linear production processes represented by activity vectors $(-1, -1, 3)$ and $(-1, 2, -1)$, where the first commodity is labor. If the price of labor is one, what are the prices of the other two commodities in a competitive equilibrium in which positive amounts of both the second and third goods are consumed?

19. There are two primary goods, goods 1 and 2, and there are two produced goods, goods 3 and 4. There is an endowment of one unit of each of the primary goods. The production functions for goods 3 and 4 are, respectively,

$$f_3(y_1, y_2) = \min(2y_1, y_2) \text{ and } f_4(y_1, y_2) = \min(y_1, 2y_2).$$

(a) In a box diagram, indicate the set of efficient allocations of goods 1 and 2 to the production of goods 3 and 4.

(b) Draw the output possibility set for goods 3 and 4.

(c) Suppose that equal positive quantities of goods 3 and 4 are produced at a point, $\underline{z}$, on the output possibility frontier for goods 3 and 4. If the price of good 4 is 1, what are the possible prices of goods 1, 2, and 3, such that the point $\underline{z}$ would be produced if both production processes were operated so as to maximize profits at these prices and if no more than the endowments of goods 1 and 2 were used in production?

20. Think of a society with three commodities—food, wood, and labor. It has four linear activities, described by the following matrix.

	Activity 1	*Activity 2*	*Activity 3*	*Activity 4*
Food	5	7	−5	−3
Wood	−2	−6	12	10
Labor	−1	−1	−1	−1

The society has one unit of labor available.

(a) Plot the society's output possibility frontier for food and wood.

(b) Suppose the society consumes both food and wood and that all commodities are priced so that activities are operated so as to maximize profits at those prices. If production is organized efficiently, what must the prices of food and wood be in terms of labor?

21. Consider the following linear activity model. There are two produced goods, food and wood, and two primary inputs, labor and land. One unit of each of labor and land are available. There are three activities, with coefficient vectors given in the following table.

	Activity 1	*Activity 2*	*Activity 3*
Food	6	6	−1
Wood	−1	−1	6
Labor	−2	−1	−2
Land	−1	−2	−1

(a) Find the production possibility frontier between food and wood.

(b) Draw the frontier.

(c) What are the prices of food, wood, and land in terms of labor if prices are such that profits are maximized and twice as much food is produced as wood?

22. Suppose that steel (S) is produced from coal (C) and labor (L) according to the production function $S = 2\sqrt{CL}$, and coal is produced from steel and labor according to the production function $C = \sqrt{SL}$ There is one unit of labor available for coal and steel production. Find the production possibility frontier for coal and steel.

23. Two people live on separate islands, Houtt and Coutt. Each person is endowed with one unit of labor. There are two produced goods, cloth and food. The utility function of each person is

$$u(x_F, x_C) = \frac{\ln(x_F)}{4} + \frac{3\ln(x_C)}{4},$$

where the notation should be obvious. On Houtt Island, the production functions for food and cloth are

$$y_F = 20L \text{ and } y_C = 10L,$$

respectively, where again the notation should be obvious. On Coutt Island, the production functions for food and cloth are

$$y_F = 10L \text{ and } y_C = 20L.$$

The two people cannot trade in food, cloth, or labor.

(a) Compute the output possibility frontiers for food and cloth for the two islands separately, assuming that each island can use only the labor of the person on that island.
(b) Compute an equilibrium for each island separately with the price of labor equal to 1 on both islands.
(c) Compute the utility of Houtt and Coutt in the equilibrium. (This is the maximum each can obtain without trade.)

Now suppose that Houtt and Coutt can trade cloth and food freely but still cannot trade labor. That is, neither can go work on the other's island.

(d) What is the output possibility frontier for food and cloth now?
(e) Compute a competitive equilibrium with free trade. Be sure to specify the production of Houtt and Coutt of each good. Let the price of Houtt's labor be 1. Be sure to specify all prices, including the price of Coutt's labor.
(f) What are the utility levels of Houtt and Coutt in the equilibrium with trade? Compare these utility levels with those from part (c).

24. Robinson Crusoe and Friday live on separate islands and produce two goods, food and cloth using two factors of production, labor (L) and land (T). The utility functions of both Crusoe and Friday are

$$u(x_F, x_C) = x_F x_C.$$

where the notation should be obvious. The production function for food is

$$y_F = 4L^{3/4}T^{1/4}.$$

The production function for cloth is

$$y_C = 4L^{1/4}T^{3/4}.$$

Crusoe is endowed with two units of labor and one of land. Friday is endowed with one unit of labor and two of land.

(a) Suppose there is *no* trade between the islands. Compute separate equilibria for Crusoe and Friday, letting the labor of each be the unit of account on his own island.

(b) Suppose there is *free* trade between the islands in cloth and food but *no trade* in labor and land. Compute the equilibrium for the two islands together with the labor of Crusoe as the unit of account. (Hint: Use the symmetry of the problem.)

25. Consider an Edgeworth box economy with endowments $\mathbf{e}_A = (1, 0)$ and $\mathbf{e}_B = (0, 1)$ and utility functions $u_A(x_1, x_2)$ and $u_B(x_1, x_2)$, where u_A and u_B are continuous and strictly quasi-concave.

(a) Can an equilibrium exist if both utility functions are everywhere strictly decreasing with respect to x_1 and x_2?

(b) Does an equilibrium necessarily exist if both u_A and u_B are decreasing with respect to x_1 and increasing with respect to x_2?

(c) Does an equilibrium necessarily exist if u_A is decreasing with respect to x_1 and increasing with respect to x_2, and u_B is increasing with respect to x_1 and decreasing with respect to x_2?

26. (a) Which of the functions, z: $\{x \in \mathbb{R}^N \mid x > 0\} \to \mathbb{R}^N$, listed below could be the aggregate or market excess-demand function for an economy in the sense that they are homogeneous of degree 0 and satisfy Walras' Law?

(i) $z(p_1, p_2) = \dfrac{(p_1, p_2)}{\|p\|}$.

(ii) $z(p_1, p_2) = \left(\dfrac{p_2 - p_1}{p_1}, \dfrac{p_1 - p_2}{p_2}\right)$.

(iii) $z(p_1, p_2) = \dfrac{(p_2, -p_1)}{p_1 + p_2}$.

(iv) $z(p_1, p_2) = \dfrac{(p_2, -p_1)}{p.p}$.

(b) For each of the four functions above that could be the excess demand function for an economy, find an equilibrium price vector.

27. Three next-door neighbors put up flagpoles. The flagpole height chosen by each neighbor depends continuously on the heights chosen by the other two. (For instance, having too tall a pole compared to the neighbors would be ostentatious, whereas having one too short would look stingy.) A town ordinance imposes an upper limit of 100 feet on flagpole heights. The choices of flagpole heights are in equilibrium when no one wishes to change the height of their flagpole. Prove that there exists an equilibrium.

28. Suppose a stock-market analyst publishes forecasts of the prices of N stocks one month ahead. He or she knows that the price of the nth stock, p_n, is influenced by the forecast, the influence being expressed by the continuous functions $p_n = f_n(q, \ldots, q_N)$, for $n = 1, \ldots, N$ and where q_n is the forecast of the price of the nth stock. Assume that $f_n(q_1, \ldots, q_N) > 0$, for all $q_1, \ldots q_N$, and that there is a $\overline{Q} > 0$ such that $f_n(q_1, \ldots, q_N) < \overline{Q}$, for all $q_1, \ldots, q_N$. Prove that the market analyst can make a correct forecast if he or she knows the functions f_n.

29. Suppose that the pure exchange economy $\mathcal{E} = ((u_i, \mathbf{e}_i)_{i=1}^I)$ satisfies the following assumptions: (i) Each utility function depends directly on the price vector $\mathbf{p}$ as well as on the consumption vector $\mathbf{x}_i$, so that consumer i's utility is $u_i(\mathbf{x}_i, \mathbf{p})$. Hence $u_i: \mathbb{R}^N_+ \times (\mathbb{R}^N_+ \backslash \{0\}) \rightarrow \mathbb{R}$. (ii) For each i, u_i is continuous with respect to both $\mathbf{p}$ and $\mathbf{x}_i$ and is strictly increasing and strictly concave with respect to $\mathbf{x}_i$. (iii) For each i, $\mathbf{e}_i \gg 0$.

(a) Prove that $\mathcal{E}$ satisfies Walras' law.

(b) Prove that $\mathcal{E}$ has a competitive equilibrium.

(c) Either prove or give a counterexample to the statement that any competitive equilibrium $(\mathbf{x}, \mathbf{p})$ for $\mathcal{E}$ is Pareto optimal.

— 5 —

The Welfare Theorems

The first welfare theorem is probably the assertion that economists are most proud of. It is the statement that competitive equilibrium allocations are Pareto optimal. A complementary assertion is the second welfare theorem, which states that any Pareto optimal allocation can be achieved as the allocation of a competitive equilibrium after an appropriate lump-sum redistribution of wealth among consumers. As was mentioned in chapter 1, these assertions are best thought of as referring to an ideal world that can perhaps be approximated in reality by means of suitable government policies. The assertions are also useful tools in the analysis of equilibrium. In section 5.3, I use the second welfare theorem to prove the existence of equilibrium, and in chapters 9 and 10 we will see that the relations between optimality and equilibrium give insight into the overlapping generations model.

5.1 The First Welfare Theorem

The intuition underlying the first welfare theorem may be seen by considering equilibria in the Robinson Crusoe and Edgeworth box economies, illustrated in figures 5.1 and 5.2, respectively. In both figures, sets of points preferred by a consumer to the equilibrium allocation are shaded. In figure 5.1, we see that the set of points preferred to the equilibrium allocation, E, does not intersect the feasible set, $\mathcal{F}$, so that no feasible allocation is preferred to E. In figure 5.2, we see that the set of points preferred by either consumer to the equilibrium allocation does not intersect the set of points at least as desired as that allocation by the other consumer. Therefore no feasible allocation can Pareto dominate E.

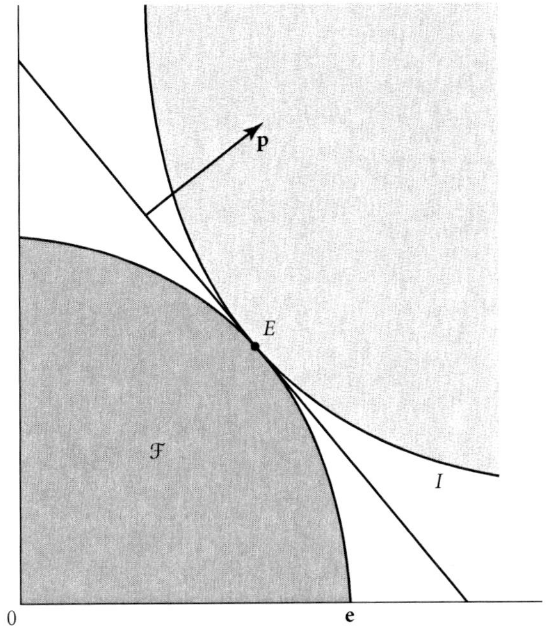

Figure 5.1 Equilibrium and optimality in the Robinson Crusoe economy

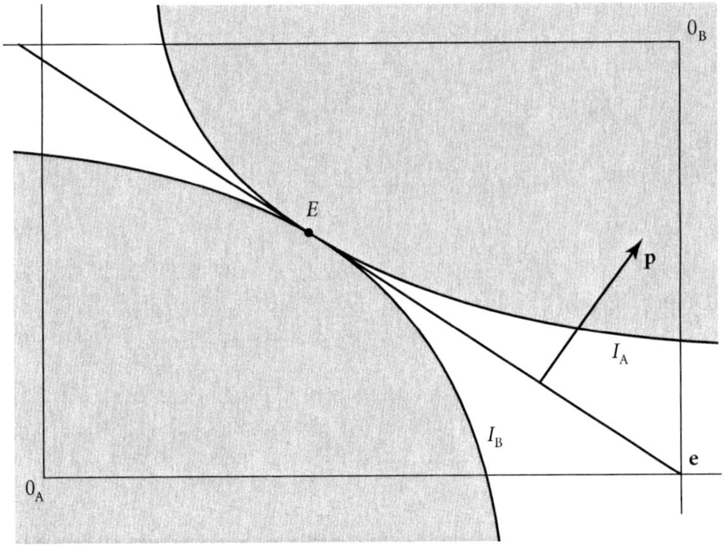

Figure 5.2 Equilibrium and optimality in the Edgeworth box economy

Some condition is necessary for the validity of the first welfare theorem, for it is easy to construct a counterexample to the unconditional statement that equilibrium allocations are Pareto optimal.

EXAMPLE 5.1 (Equilibrium allocations may not be Pareto optimal.) Let an Edgeworth box economy have utility functions $u_A(x_1, x_2) = 0$ and $u_B(x_1, x_2) = x_1 x_2$ and endowments $\mathbf{e}_A = (2, 0)$ and $\mathbf{e}_B = (0, 2)$. Then, the allocation $\overline{\mathbf{x}}_A = \overline{\mathbf{x}}_B = (1, 1)$ and the price vector $\mathbf{p} = (1, 1)$ form an equilibrium. Nevertheless, the allocation $\mathbf{x}_A = (0, 0)$, $\mathbf{x}_B = (2, 2)$ Pareto dominates the allocation $(\overline{\mathbf{x}}_A, \overline{\mathbf{x}}_B)$, because consumer A does not mind losing one unit of each good to consumer B.

The first welfare theorem fails in this example, because consumer A is indifferent between all allocations. Such blanket indifference is impossible if utility functions have the property of local nonsatiation defined in definition 4.2 (in section 4.2), and this property turns out to be enough to ensure that all equilibrium allocations are Pareto optimal.

FIRST WELFARE THEOREM 5.2 If the economy $\mathcal{E} = ((u_i, e_i)_{i=1}^{I}, (Y_j)_{j=1}^{J}, (\Theta_{ij})_{i=1,}^{I}\,{}_{j=1}^{J})$ is such that u_i is locally nonsatiated, for all i, then any equilibrium allocation is Pareto optimal.

Proof. Let $(\overline{\mathbf{x}}, \overline{\mathbf{y}}, \mathbf{p})$ be an equilibrium, and suppose that $(\overline{\mathbf{x}}, \overline{\mathbf{y}})$ is not Pareto optimal. Then, there exists a feasible allocation, $(\mathbf{x}, \mathbf{y})$, that Pareto dominates $(\overline{\mathbf{x}}, \overline{\mathbf{y}})$, so that $u_i(\mathbf{x}_i) \geq u_i(\overline{\mathbf{x}}_i)$, for all i, and $u_i(\mathbf{x}_i) > u_i(\overline{\mathbf{x}}_i)$, for some i. If $u_i(\mathbf{x}_i) > u_i(\overline{\mathbf{x}}_i)$, then $\mathbf{p}.\mathbf{x}_i > w_i(\mathbf{p})$, since $\overline{\mathbf{x}}_i$ solves the problem

$$\max_{\mathbf{x} \in \mathbb{R}^N_+} u_i(\mathbf{x})$$
$$\text{s.t.} \quad \mathbf{p}.\mathbf{x} \leq w_i(\mathbf{p}).$$

I show that if $u_i(\mathbf{x}_i) = u_i(\overline{\mathbf{x}}_i)$, then $\mathbf{p}.\mathbf{x}_i \geq w_i(\mathbf{p})$. If on the contrary $\mathbf{p}.\mathbf{x}_i < w_i(\mathbf{p})$, then by local nonsatiation there exists a vector $\mathbf{x}'$ in $\mathbb{R}^N_+$ such that $u_i(\mathbf{x}') > u_i(\mathbf{x}) \geq u_i(\overline{\mathbf{x}}_i)$ and such that $\mathbf{x}'$ is so close to $\mathbf{x}_i$ that $\mathbf{p}.\mathbf{x}_i < w_i(\mathbf{p})$. This assertion contradicts the assumption that $\overline{\mathbf{x}}_i$ solves the problem

$$\max_{\mathbf{x} \in \mathbb{R}^N_+} u_i(\mathbf{x})$$
$$\text{s.t.} \quad \mathbf{p}.\mathbf{x} \leq w_i(\mathbf{p}).$$

In summary, $\mathbf{p}.\mathbf{x}_i \geq w_i(\mathbf{p})$, for all i, and $\mathbf{p}.\mathbf{x}_i > w_i(\mathbf{p})$, for some i. Summing these inequalities over i, we see that

$$\sum_{i=1}^{I} \mathbf{p}.\mathbf{x}_i > \sum_{i=1}^{I} w_i(\mathbf{p}). \tag{5.1}$$

However,

$$\begin{aligned}
\sum_{i=1}^{I} w_i(\mathbf{p}) &= \sum_{i=1}^{I}\left(\mathbf{p}.\mathbf{e}_i + \sum_{j=1}^{J} \Theta_{ij}\mathbf{p}.\overline{\mathbf{y}}_j\right) = \sum_{i=1}^{I} \mathbf{p}.\mathbf{e}_i + \sum_{j=1}^{J}\left(\sum_{i=1}^{I} \Theta_{ij}\right)\mathbf{p}.\overline{\mathbf{y}}_j \\
&= \sum_{i=1}^{I} \mathbf{p}.\mathbf{e}_i + \sum_{j=1}^{J} \mathbf{p}.\overline{\mathbf{y}}_j \geq \sum_{i=1}^{I} \mathbf{p}.\mathbf{e}_i + \sum_{j=1}^{J} \mathbf{p}.\mathbf{y}_j \qquad (5.2) \\
&= \mathbf{p}.\left(\sum_{i=1}^{I} \mathbf{e}_i + \sum_{j=1}^{J} \mathbf{y}_j\right),
\end{aligned}$$

where the third equation follows from the assumption that $\sum_{i=1}^{I} \Theta_{ij} = 1$, for all j, and the inequality follows from the fact that each $\overline{\mathbf{y}}_j$ maximizes profits over Y_j at price vector $\mathbf{p}$. Inequalities 5.1 and 5.2 imply, however, that

$$\mathbf{p}.\sum_{i=1}^{I} \mathbf{x}_i > \mathbf{p}.\left(\sum_{i=1}^{I} \mathbf{e}_i + \sum_{j=1}^{J} \mathbf{y}_j\right),$$

and this inequality is impossible since $\mathbf{p} > \mathbf{0}$ and the feasibility of $(\mathbf{x}, \mathbf{y})$ implies that $\sum_{i=1}^{I} \mathbf{x}_i \leq \sum_{i=1}^{I} \mathbf{e}_i + \sum_{j=1}^{J} \mathbf{y}_j$. This contradiction proves the theorem. ▪

An important implicit assumption underlying the first welfare theorem is that there are no external effects. An *external effect* is an interaction among consumers and firms other than the exchange of commodities and that affects utilities or input-output possibilities. For short, external effects are called *externalities*. An example of a negative externality among consumers would be the annoyance caused to a consumer by the smoke from a neighbor's backyard barbecue. The pleasure derived from the same neighbor's flower garden would be a positive externality. Sports or commercial fishermen can have a negative external effect on the production possibilities of another commercial fisherman by reducing the number of fish available.

If two construction companies employ the same carpenters on different projects or shifts, one company can have a positive external effect on the other by improving the carpenters' skills.

In economies with externalities, equilibria may exist but not be Pareto optimal, as the following examples show.

EXAMPLE 5.3 Consider the Robinson Crusoe economy with utility function $u(\ell, x) = \ell x$, endowment equal to $\mathbf{e} = (3/2, 0)$, and production function equal to $y = f(L, x) = Lx$, where ℓ is leisure consumption, L is labor input, y is food output, and x is food consumption. The variable x appears in the production function not as an input but as an external effect. Eating more makes Robinson more productive.

I show that in equilibrium, $x = 0$. Suppose the price of labor is positive. We may then normalize it to be 1. If x is positive, then L is positive as well in equilibrium and Robinson's firm solves the profit-maximization problem

$$\max_{L \geq 0}(qLx - L),$$

where q is the price of food. Since L is positive at the maximum, $qx = 1$, so that $q = 1/x$. As a consumer, Robinson solves the problem

$$\max_{\ell \geq 0, z \geq 0} \ \ell z$$

$$\text{s.t.} \quad pz + \ell \leq 3/2,$$

where z is a dummy variable that equals x in equilibrium. The solution of this problem is $\ell = \frac{3}{4}$ and $z = \frac{3}{4q} = \frac{3}{4}x$. Since $z = x$, the equation $z = \frac{3}{4}x$ can be valid only if $z = x = 0$. Suppose that the price of labor is 0. Then the price of output must be positive, and we may normalize it to be 1. If x is positive, then the firm's profit-maximization problem,

$$\max_{\mathrm{L} \geq 0} \mathrm{L}x,$$

has no solution. Therefore $x = 0$.

We may let the equilibrium price vector be $\mathbf{p} = (0, 1)$. Robinson's budget set is then the nonnegative part of the horizontal axis. Since he is indifferent to all points on it, we may assume that he chooses the point $(3/2, 0)$. The resulting equilibrium allocation $\ell = 3/2$, $x = y = \mathrm{L} = 0$ is not Pareto optimal, for it gives Robinson 0 utility and the feasible allocation $\ell = 1/2$, $y = x = \mathrm{L} = 1$ gives Robinson 1/2 units of utility.

EXAMPLE 5.4 Consider the Edgeworth box economy with $\mathbf{e}_A = (2, 0)$, $\mathbf{e}_B = (0, 2)$, $u_A(x_{A1}, x_{A2}, x_{B1}) = x_{A1}x_{A2} - x_{B1}$, and $u_B(x_{B1}, x_{B2}) = x_{B1}x_{B2}$. Consumer B's consumption of good 1 causes consumer A discomfort. An equilibrium is $\overline{\mathbf{x}}_A = \overline{\mathbf{x}}_B = (1, 1)$ and $\mathbf{p} = (1, 1)$. The equilibrium allocation is not Pareto optimal, however, for it is Pareto dominated by the feasible allocation $\mathbf{x}_A = \left(\frac{5}{4}, \frac{2}{3}\right)$, $\mathbf{x}_B = \left(\frac{3}{4}, \frac{4}{3}\right)$, since $u_A\left(\frac{5}{4}, \frac{2}{3}, \frac{3}{4}\right) = \frac{5}{4}\frac{2}{3} - \frac{3}{4} = \frac{1}{12} > 0 = u_A(1, 1, 1)$ and $u_B\left(\frac{3}{4}, \frac{4}{3}\right) = 1 = u_B(1, 1)$.

5.2 The Second Welfare Theorem

The second welfare theorem is nearly a converse of the first. It may be visualized in an Edgeworth box, as in figure 5.3. The Pareto optimal allocation $\overline{\mathbf{x}}$ in the figure is that of an equilibrium, if a lump-sum transfer payment from person A to person B shifts the budget line from the dashed line going through the endowment to the solid line tangent to the two indifference curves through point $\overline{\mathbf{x}}$. The idea of the theorem is that any Pareto optimal

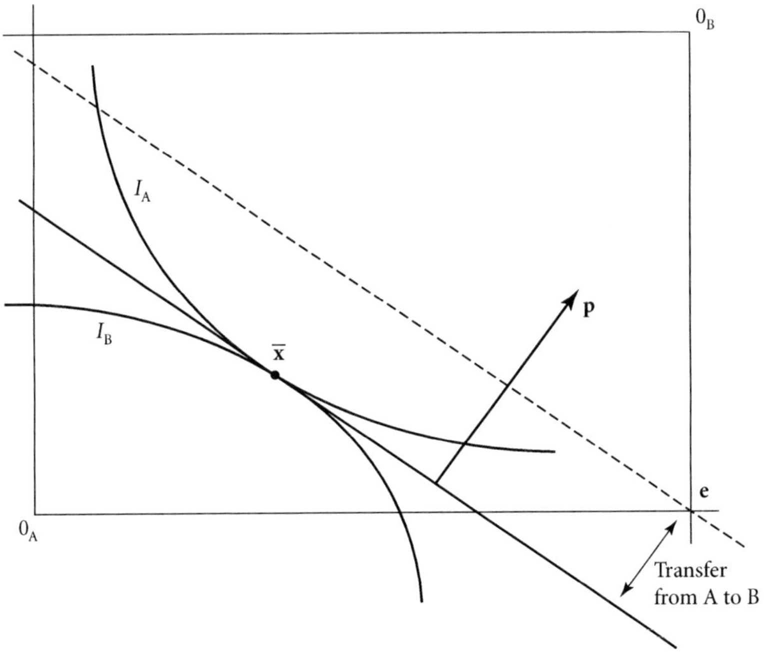

Figure 5.3 An equilibrium with transfer payments

allocation, $\overline{\mathbf{x}}$, can be achieved as an equilibrium by using a transfer payment to shift a budget line of the appropriate slope.

Formally, an equilibrium with transfer payments is defined as follows.

DEFINITION 5.5 $(\overline{\mathbf{x}}, \overline{\mathbf{y}}, \mathbf{p}, \boldsymbol{\tau})$ is a *competitive equilibrium with transfer payments* for the economy $\mathcal{E} = ((u_i, e_i)_{i=1}^I, (Y_j)_{j=1}^J, (\Theta_{ij})_{i=1,}^I{}_{j=1}^J)$, if

1. $(\overline{\mathbf{x}}, \overline{\mathbf{y}})$ is a feasible allocation
2. $\mathbf{p} \in \mathbb{R}_+^N$ and $\mathbf{p} > 0$
3. $\boldsymbol{\tau} = (\tau_1, \tau_2, \ldots, \tau_I) \in \mathbb{R}^I$
4. for all j, $p.\overline{\mathbf{y}}_j \geq p.\mathbf{y}$, for all $\mathbf{y}$ in Y_j
5. for all i, $\overline{\mathbf{x}}_i$ solves the problem

$$\max_{\mathbf{x} \in \mathbb{R}_+^N} u_i(\mathbf{x})$$
$$\text{s.t.} \quad p.\mathbf{x} \leq w_i(\mathbf{p}) - \tau_i,$$

where $w_i(\mathbf{p}) = \mathbf{p}.\mathbf{e}_i + \sum_{j=1}^J \Theta_{ij}\mathbf{p}.\overline{\mathbf{y}}_j$

6. for all n, $p_n = 0$, if $\sum_{i=1}^I \overline{x}_{in} < \sum_{i=1}^I e_{in} + \sum_{j=1}^J \overline{y}_{jn}$

The quantity τ_i is a lump-sum transfer payment made by consumer i to other consumers. An equilibrium with transfer payments is an ordinary competitive equilibrium in the sense of definition 4.1 if the transfer payments are all zero, that is, if $\boldsymbol{\tau} = \mathbf{0}$. The next proposition says that if utility functions are nonsatiated, then in equilibrium, transfer payments sum to zero, so that they redistribute wealth among consumers. This implies that in Robinson Crusoe models, there can be no transfer payments in equilibria with transfer payments; Robinson has no other consumer with whom to make transfers. In such models, equilibria with transfer payments are ordinary equilibria.

PROPOSITION 5.6 If u_i is locally nonsatiated, for all i, then $\sum_{i=1}^I \tau_i = 0$, for any equilibrium with transfer payments $(\overline{\mathbf{x}}, \overline{\mathbf{y}}, \mathbf{p}, \boldsymbol{\tau})$.

Proof. Because the allocation $(\overline{\mathbf{x}}, \overline{\mathbf{y}})$ is feasible, condition (6) of definition 5.5 of an equilibrium with transfer payments implies that

$$\mathbf{p}.\left[\sum_{i=1}^I (\overline{\mathbf{x}}_i - \mathbf{e}_i) - \sum_{j=1}^J \overline{\mathbf{y}}_j\right] = 0.$$

Because u_i is locally nonsatiated, lemma 4.4 (in section 4.2) implies that

$$\mathbf{p}.\overline{\mathbf{x}}_i = \mathbf{p}.\mathbf{e}_i + \sum_{j=1}^{J} \Theta_{ij}\mathbf{p}.\overline{\mathbf{y}}_j - \tau_i,$$

for all i. These equations imply that

$$0 = \mathbf{p}.\left[\sum_{i=1}^{I}(\overline{\mathbf{x}}_i - \mathbf{e}_i) - \sum_{j=1}^{J}\overline{\mathbf{y}}_j\right]_{ij} = \mathbf{p}.\left[\sum_{i=1}^{I}(\overline{\mathbf{x}}_i - \mathbf{e}_i) - \sum_{j=1}^{J}\sum_{i=1}^{I}\Theta_{ij}\overline{\mathbf{y}}_j\right]$$

$$= \sum_{i=1}^{I}\left[\mathbf{p}.(\overline{\mathbf{x}}_i - \mathbf{e}_i) - \sum_{j=1}^{J}\Theta_{ij}\mathbf{p}.\overline{\mathbf{y}}_j\right] = -\sum_{i=1}^{I}\tau_i,$$

where the second equation follows from the assumption that $\sum_{i=1}^{I}\Theta_{ij} = 1$, for all j. ■

It is easy to check that the proof of the first welfare theorem applies to equilibria with transfer payments, so that the following proposition is valid.

PROPOSITION 5.7 If the utility functions u_i is locally nonsatiated, for all i, then the allocation, $(\overline{\mathbf{x}}, \overline{\mathbf{y}})$, of an equilibrium with transfer payments, $(\overline{\mathbf{x}}, \overline{\mathbf{y}}, \mathbf{p}, \boldsymbol{\tau})$, is Pareto optimal.

A rigorous version of the second welfare theorem requires several assumptions, and the examples that follow illustrate why the assumptions are needed.

EXAMPLE 5.8 (Production possibility sets must be convex.) Figure 5.4 represents a Robinson Crusoe economy. Because utility over the budget set must be maximized at $\overline{\mathbf{x}}$, equilibrium price vectors must be in the direction of $\mathbf{p}$. Because Y is not convex, profits are not maximized at $\overline{\mathbf{x}}$.

EXAMPLE 5.9 (Preferred sets must be convex.) I use the Robinson Crusoe example portrayed in figure 5.5. Because profits must be maximized at $\overline{\mathbf{x}}$, on $\mathbf{e} + Y$, the equilibrium price vector, $\mathbf{p}$, must be in the direction shown. At such a price vector, $\overline{\mathbf{x}}$ is not the point in the budget set with maximum utility. Points such as $\mathbf{x}$ in the budget set are preferred to $\overline{\mathbf{x}}$.

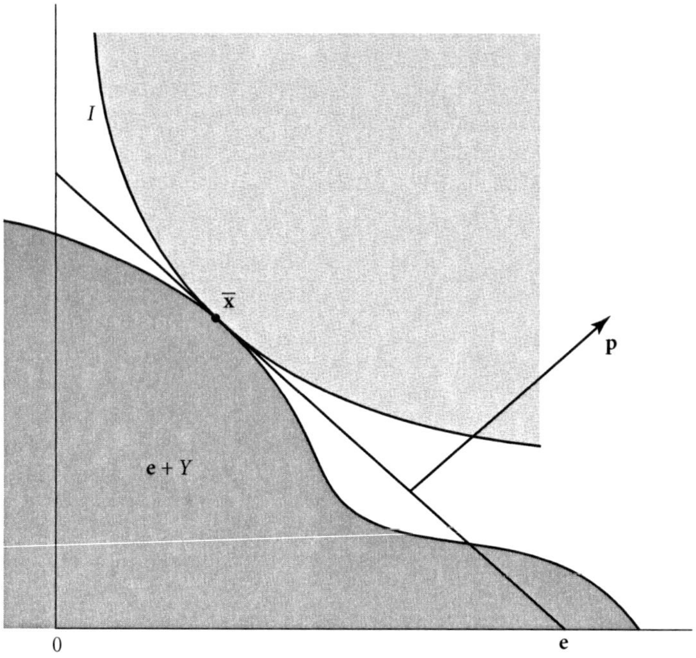

Figure 5.4 Failure of the second welfare theorem with a nonconvex input-output possibility set

EXAMPLE 5.10 (Utility functions must be continuous.) Let

$$u(x_1, x_2) = \begin{cases} x_1 + x_2, & \text{if } x_1 + x_2 < 4 \\ x_1 + 2x_2, & \text{if } x_1 + x_2 \geq 4. \end{cases}$$

Notice that the set of points preferred to any point is convex, but u is not continuous at the line segment $\{(x_1, x_2) \mid x_1 \geq 0, x_2 \geq 0 \text{ and } x_1 + x_2 = 4\}$, the dashed line in figure 5.6. Consider the Robinson Crusoe economy with utility function u, with endowment (3, 0) and with input-output possibility set

$$Y = \{(y_1, y_2) \mid y_1 \leq 0, y_2 \leq 2\sqrt{-y_1}\}.$$

Then, the allocation $(\overline{\mathbf{x}}, \overline{\mathbf{y}})$ with $(\overline{x}_1, \overline{x}_2) = (2, 2)$ and $(\overline{y}_1, \overline{y}_2) = (-1, 2)$ is Pareto optimal but is not the allocation of an equilibrium with transfer payments, as figure 5.6 makes clear. In the figure, indifference curves are labeled as I. An equilibrium price vector would have to be of the form $\mathbf{p} = (a, a)$, for some positive number a. At such a price vector, the budget

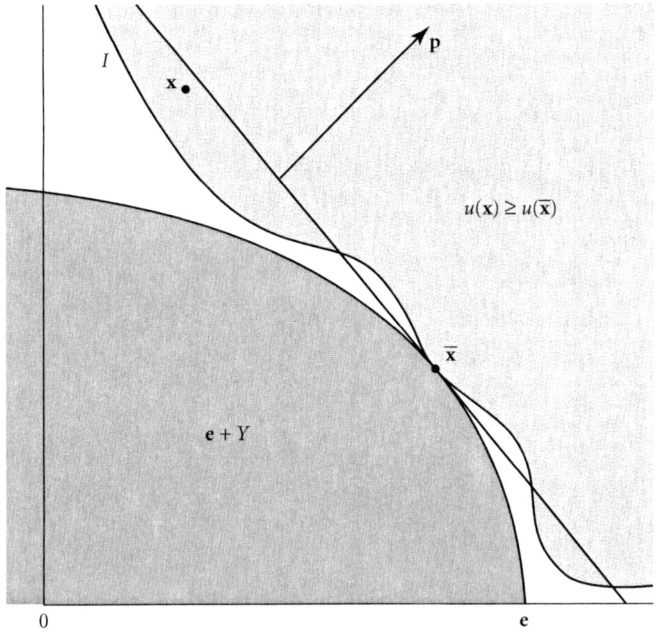

Figure 5.5 Failure of the second welfare theorem with a nonconvex preferred set

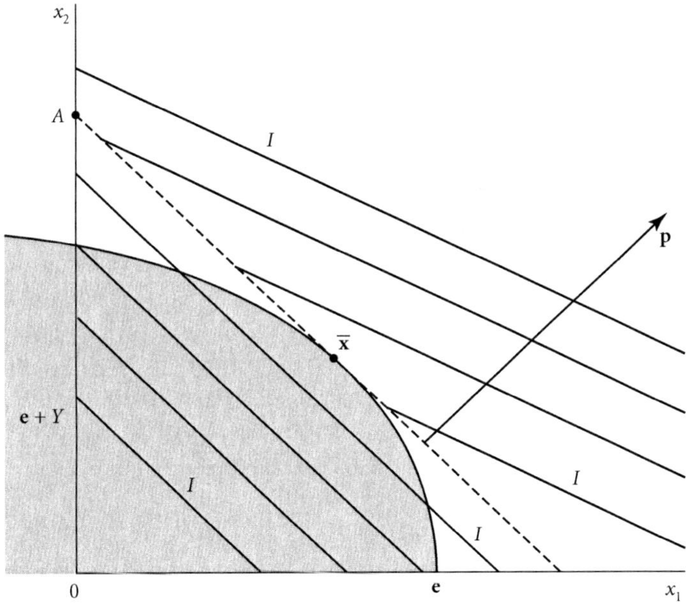

Figure 5.6 Failure of the second welfare theorem with discontinuous utility function

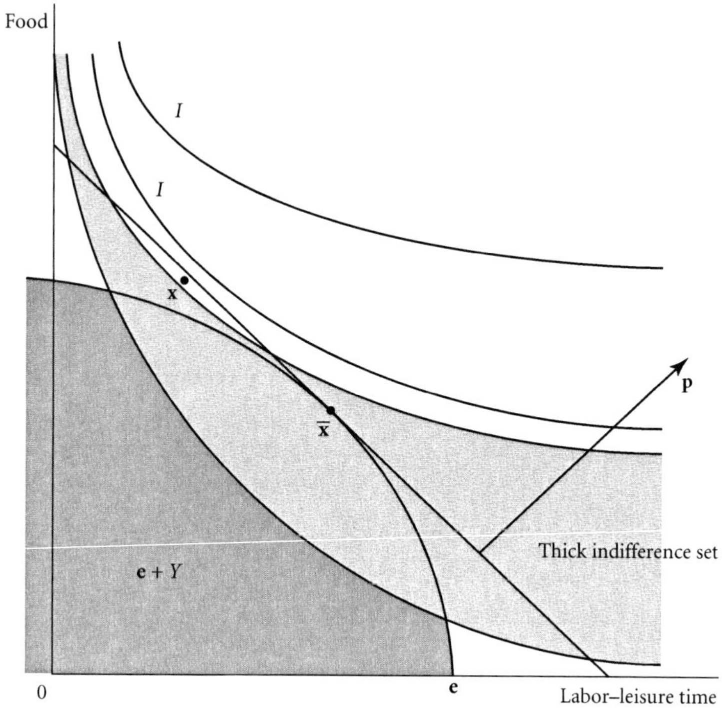

Figure 5.7 Failure of the second welfare theorem with a locally satiated utility function

line of the consumer, which is the dashed line in the figure, is tangent to $\mathbf{e} + Y$ at the point $\overline{\mathbf{x}}$, but the point of highest utility on this budget line is A, not $\overline{\mathbf{x}}$.

EXAMPLE 5.11 (Utility functions must be locally nonsatiated.) Figure 5.7 describes a Robinson Crusoe economy in which the preferred sets and the production possibility set are convex. There is, however, an area of points with the same utility, the thick indifference set shaded by light gray. Thin indifference curves are labeled I. The point $\overline{\mathbf{x}}$ represents a Pareto optimal allocation that is on the frontier of the production possibility set but is inside the thick indifference set. If $\overline{\mathbf{x}}$ is the allocation of an equilibrium with transfer payments, the price equilibrium vector must be in the direction of the vector $\mathbf{p}$ that is shown, because profit must be maximized at the point $\overline{\mathbf{x}}$ over the set $\mathbf{e} + Y$. There are points, such as $\mathbf{x}$, preferred to $\overline{\mathbf{x}}$ and in the budget set defined by this price vector and $\overline{\mathbf{x}}$.

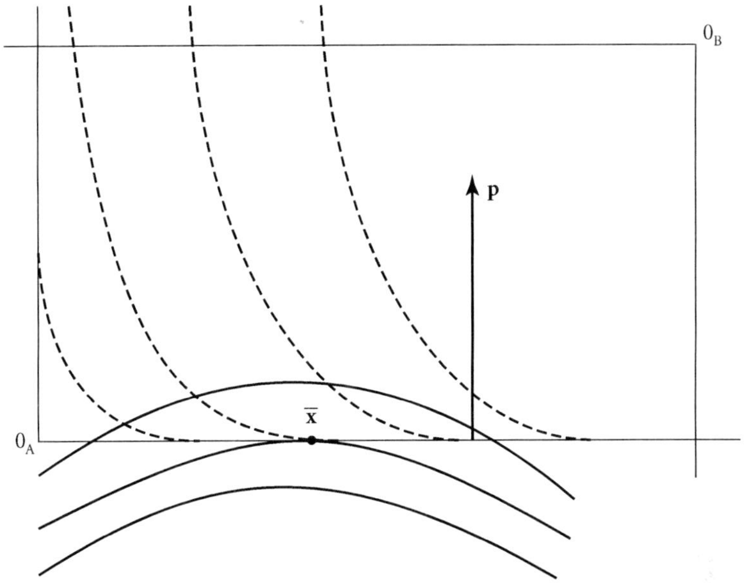

Figure 5.8 Failure of the second welfare theorem with consumption vectors that are not strictly positive

EXAMPLE 5.12 (Consumption vectors must be strictly positive or the utility functions must be strictly increasing.) Figure 5.8 portrays an Edgeworth box economy with a Pareto optimal allocation at $\overline{\mathbf{x}}$. The indifference curves of consumer A are dashed curves, and those of consumer B are solid curves. Vertical price vectors such as $\mathbf{p}$ are the only ones that make $\overline{\mathbf{x}}_B$ the best point for person B in the budget set that has a budget line through $\overline{\mathbf{x}}_B$ and orthogonal to $\mathbf{p}$. Person A's budget set at this price vector is the non-negative part of the horizontal coordinate axis through 0_A, and person A has no utility maximizing point in this set. Therefore, the allocation $\overline{\mathbf{x}}$ is not the allocation of an equilibrium with transfer payments.

To state the second welfare theorem, I need to define a property of utility functions that guarantees that all preferred sets are convex.

DEFINITION 5.13 A utility function $u: \mathbb{R}^N_+ \rightarrow \mathbb{R}$ is *quasi-concave* if for all numbers v, $\{\mathbf{x} \in \mathbb{R}^N_+ \mid u(\mathbf{x}) \geq v\}$, is convex.

Quasi-concavity is weaker than strict quasi-concavity, defined in definition 4.21 (in section 4.7). If u is quasi-concave, then for every number v, the preferred set $\{\mathbf{x} \in \mathbb{R}^N_+ \mid u(\mathbf{x}) > v\}$ is convex, for suppose that $u(\overline{\mathbf{x}}) > v$, $u(\underline{\mathbf{x}}) > v$, and $0 \le \alpha \le 1$. Because u is quasi-concave,

$$u(\alpha\overline{\mathbf{x}} + (1-\alpha)\underline{\mathbf{x}}) \ge \min(u(\overline{\mathbf{x}}), u(\underline{\mathbf{x}})) > v.$$

SECOND WELFARE THEOREM 5.14 Assume that the economy

$$\mathcal{E} = \left((u_i, e_i)_{i=1}^{I}, (Y_j)_{j=1}^{J}, (\Theta_{ij})_{i=1,\ j=1}^{I\quad J}\right)$$

is such that

1. for all i, u_i is a continuous, locally nonsatiated, and quasi-concave
2. for all j, Y_j is convex

If $(\overline{\mathbf{x}}, \overline{\mathbf{y}})$ is a Pareto optimal allocation such that $\overline{\mathbf{x}}_i \gg 0$, for all i, then there exists a price vector, $\mathbf{p}$, and an I-vector of transfer payments, $\boldsymbol{\tau}$, such that $(\overline{\mathbf{x}}, \overline{\mathbf{y}}, \mathbf{p}, \boldsymbol{\tau})$ is an equilibrium with transfer payments.

The second welfare theorem has a social engineering interpretation. A government could use lump-sum taxes and subsidies of individuals to guide competitive equilibrium to any desired Pareto optimal allocation. A government would, of course, have to know a great deal about individuals' preferences, firms' technologies, and available resources in order to determine precisely how large lump-sum payments should be to arrive at a particular Pareto optimal outcome. Although it is unrealistic to imagine that governments have so much information, they might have enough information to bring economies near the desired Pareto optima.

Proof of Theorem 5.14. The proof is presented in a series of easy steps.

Step 1 I apply Minkowski's separation theorem. For each i, let $\mathcal{P}_i = \{\mathbf{x} \in \mathbb{R}^N_+ \mid u_i(\mathbf{x}) > u_i(\overline{\mathbf{x}}_i)\}$. Because u_i is locally nonsatiated, $\mathcal{P}_i$ is not empty. Let $\mathcal{P} = \sum_{i=1}^{I}(\mathcal{P}_i - \mathbf{e}_i)$ and let $Y = \sum_{j=1}^{J} Y_j - \mathbb{R}^N_+$. ($Y$ is the total input-output possibility set for the economy minus all possible excess supply vectors.) The sets $\mathcal{P}$ and Y do not intersect, for suppose that $\mathcal{P}$ and Y have a point in common. Then there exist vectors $\mathbf{x}_i \in \mathcal{P}_i$, for $i = 1, \ldots, I$, and vectors $\mathbf{b} \in \mathbb{R}^N_+$ and $\mathbf{y}_j \in Y_j$, for $j = 1, \ldots, J$, such that $\sum_i(\mathbf{x}_i - \mathbf{e}_i) = \sum_j \mathbf{y}_j - \mathbf{b}$. Hence $\sum_i(\mathbf{x}_i - \mathbf{e}_i) \le \sum_j \mathbf{y}_j$, and so $(\mathbf{x}, \mathbf{y})$ is a feasible allocation. Furthermore, $(\mathbf{x}, \mathbf{y})$ Pareto dominates $(\overline{\mathbf{x}}, \overline{\mathbf{y}})$, because $(\mathbf{x}, \mathbf{y})$ is feasible and $u_i(\mathbf{x}_i) > u_i(\overline{\mathbf{x}}_i)$, for all i. Because $(\overline{\mathbf{x}}, \overline{\mathbf{y}})$ is Pareto dominated, it cannot be Pareto optimal, contrary to assumption. This proves that $\mathcal{P}$ and Y do not intersect. The set $\mathcal{P}_i$ is convex, for all i, because u_i is quasi-concave. It follows that $\mathcal{P}$ is convex. Similarly, Y is convex, because each of the sets Y_j is convex. In addition, int Y is not empty, since int $\mathbb{R}^N_+$ is not empty. In summary, all the assumptions of Minkowski's separation theorem apply to $\mathcal{P}$ and Y, so that there exists a nonzero N-vector, $\mathbf{p}$, such that $\mathbf{p.x} \geq \mathbf{p.y}$, for all $\mathbf{x}$ in $\mathcal{P}$ and all $\mathbf{y}$ in Y.

Step 2 I show that $\mathbf{p} > 0$. It is sufficient to show that $\mathbf{p} \geq 0$, since $\mathbf{p} \neq \mathbf{0}$. Suppose that it is not the case that $\mathbf{p} > 0$. Then, $p_n < 0$, for some n, say for $n = 1$. Because $Y = \sum_{j=1}^{J} Y_j - \mathbb{R}^N_+$, it follows that

$$\sum_j \overline{\mathbf{y}}_j - (T, 0, \ldots, 0) \in Y,$$

for any $T > 0$. Hence, if $\mathbf{x}$ is an arbitrary point in $\mathcal{P}$, then

$$\mathbf{p.x} \geq \mathbf{p.}\left[\sum_j \overline{\mathbf{y}}_j - (T, 0, \ldots, 0)\right] = \mathbf{p.}\sum_j \overline{\mathbf{y}}_j - T p_i.$$

Since $p_1 < 0$, the right-hand side of the above inequality goes to infinity as T goes to infinity. Since the left-hand side is finite, there is a contradiction. This completes the proof that $\mathbf{p} > \mathbf{0}$.

Step 3 I show that $\mathbf{p.}\sum(\overline{\mathbf{x}}_i - \mathbf{e}_i) \geq \mathbf{p.}\sum_j \mathbf{y}_j$, if $\mathbf{y}_j \in Y_j$, for all j. Because the utility functions u_i are locally nonsatiated, there exists, for each i, a sequence $\mathbf{x}_i^k$, where $k = 1, 2, \ldots,$ such that $u_i(\mathbf{x}_i^k) > u_i(\overline{\mathbf{x}}_i)$ for all i and k, and $\lim_{k\to\infty} \mathbf{x}_i^k = \overline{\mathbf{x}}$, for all i. It follows from the separating property of $\mathbf{p}$ that

$$\mathbf{p.}\sum_i(\mathbf{x}_i^k - \mathbf{e}_i) \geq \mathbf{p.}\sum_j \mathbf{y}_i,$$

if $\mathbf{y}_j \in Y_j$, for all j. Passing to the limit with respect to k, we see that

$$\mathbf{p.}\sum_i(\overline{\mathbf{x}}_i - \mathbf{e}_i) \geq \mathbf{p.}\sum_j \mathbf{y}_j, \tag{5.3}$$

as was to be proved.

Step 4 I show that $\mathbf{p.}\sum_i(\overline{\mathbf{x}}_i - \mathbf{e}_i) = \mathbf{p.}\sum_j \overline{\mathbf{y}}_j$. Letting $\mathbf{y}_j = \overline{\mathbf{y}}_j$, for all j, in inequality 5.3, we see that $\mathbf{p.}\sum_i(\overline{\mathbf{x}}_i - \mathbf{e}_i) \geq \mathbf{p.}\sum_j \overline{\mathbf{y}}_j$. Since $(\overline{\mathbf{x}}, \overline{\mathbf{y}})$ is a feasible allocation, it follows that $\sum_i \overline{\mathbf{x}}_i \leq \sum_i \mathbf{e}_i + \sum_j \overline{\mathbf{y}}_j$. Since $\mathbf{p} \geq \mathbf{0}$, it follows that $\mathbf{p.}\sum_i(\overline{\mathbf{x}}_i - \mathbf{e}_i) \geq \mathbf{p.}\sum_j \overline{\mathbf{y}}_j$. Therefore, $\mathbf{p.}\sum_i(\overline{\mathbf{x}}_i - \mathbf{e}_i) = \mathbf{p.}\sum_j \overline{\mathbf{y}}_j$.

Step 5 I show that, for all j, $\mathbf{p}.\overline{\mathbf{y}}_j \geq \mathbf{p}.\mathbf{y}_j$, for all $\mathbf{y}_j \in Y_j$. That is, firm j's profits are maximized at $\overline{\mathbf{y}}_j$, for all j. Without loss of generality, we may let $j = 1$. By the results of steps 3 and 4,

$$\mathbf{p}.\overline{\mathbf{y}}_1 + \sum_{j=2}^{J} \mathbf{p}.\overline{\mathbf{y}}_j = \mathbf{p}.\sum_{j=1}^{J} \overline{\mathbf{y}}_j = \mathbf{p}.\sum_{i=1}^{I} (\overline{\mathbf{x}}_i - \mathbf{e}_i) \geq \mathbf{p}.\left(\mathbf{y}_1 + \sum_{j=2}^{J} \overline{\mathbf{y}}_j\right)$$
$$= \mathbf{p}.\mathbf{y}_1 + \sum_{j=2}^{J} \mathbf{p}.\overline{\mathbf{y}}_j,$$

if $\mathbf{y}_1 \in Y_1$. Canceling like terms from both sides of this inequality, we see that

$$\mathbf{p}.\overline{\mathbf{y}}_1 \geq \mathbf{p}.\mathbf{y}_1,$$

so that firm 1 maximizes profits at $\overline{\mathbf{y}}_1$.

To finish the proof of the theorem, I must show that, for all i, $\mathbf{p}.\mathbf{x}_i > \mathbf{p}.\overline{\mathbf{x}}_i$, if $u_i(\mathbf{x}_i) > u_i(\overline{\mathbf{x}}_i)$. The next step is part of the proof of this assertion.

Step 6 I show that, for all i, if $\mathbf{x}_i$ is such that $u_i(\mathbf{x}_i) > u_i(\overline{\mathbf{x}}_i)$, then $\mathbf{p}.\mathbf{x}_i \geq \mathbf{p}.\overline{\mathbf{x}}_i$. Without loss of generality, assume that $i = 1$. For $i = 2, \ldots, I$, let $\mathbf{x}_i^k$, for $k = 1, 2, \ldots$, be a sequence such that $u_i(\mathbf{x}_i^k) > u_i(\overline{\mathbf{x}}_i)$, for all k, and $\lim_{k\to\infty} \mathbf{x}_i^k = \overline{\mathbf{x}}_i$. (As in step 3, such sequences exist because the utility functions are locally nonsatiated.) Then, $\mathbf{x}_i^k \in \mathcal{P}_i$, for all $i \geq 2$. By assumption $\mathbf{x}_1 \in \mathcal{P}_1$, so that $\mathbf{x}_1 - \mathbf{e}_1 + \sum_{i=2}^{I}(\mathbf{x}_i^k - \mathbf{e}_i) \in \mathcal{P}$. Therefore, the separating property of $\mathbf{p}$ implies that

$$\mathbf{p}.(\mathbf{x}_1 - \mathbf{e}_1) + \mathbf{p}.\sum_{i=2}^{I}(\mathbf{x}_i^k - \mathbf{e}_i) = \mathbf{p}.\left(\mathbf{x}_1 - \mathbf{e}_1 + \sum_{i=2}^{I}(\mathbf{x}_i^k - \mathbf{e}_i)\right)$$
$$\geq \mathbf{p}.\sum_{j=1}^{J} \overline{\mathbf{y}}_j.$$

Passing to the limit with respect to k, we see that

$$\mathbf{p}.(\mathbf{x}_1 - \mathbf{e}_1) + \mathbf{p}.\sum_{i=2}^{I}(\overline{\mathbf{x}}_i - \mathbf{e}_i) \geq \mathbf{p}.\sum_{j=1}^{J} \overline{\mathbf{y}}_j$$
$$= \mathbf{p}.(\overline{\mathbf{x}}_1 - \mathbf{e}_1) + \mathbf{p}.\sum_{i=2}^{I}(\overline{\mathbf{x}}_i - \mathbf{e}_i),$$

where the equation follows from step 4. Canceling like terms from both sides of this inequality, we see that $\mathbf{p}.\mathbf{x}_1 \geq \mathbf{p}.\overline{\mathbf{x}}_1$, as was to be shown.

Step 7 I may now show that, for all i, $\mathbf{p}.\mathbf{x}_i > \mathbf{p}.\overline{\mathbf{x}}_i$, if $\mathbf{x}_i$ is such that $u_i(\mathbf{x}_i) > u_i(\overline{\mathbf{x}}_i)$. Without loss of generality, assume that $i = 1$. By step 6, $\mathbf{p}.\mathbf{x}_1 \geq \mathbf{p}.\overline{\mathbf{x}}_1$. Therefore, if it is not the case that $\mathbf{p}.\mathbf{x}_1 > \mathbf{p}.\overline{\mathbf{x}}_1$, then $\mathbf{p}.\mathbf{x}_1 = \mathbf{p}.\overline{\mathbf{x}}_1$. Suppose that $\mathbf{p}.\mathbf{x}_1 = \mathbf{p}.\overline{\mathbf{x}}_1$. By an assumption in the statement of the theorem, $\overline{\mathbf{x}}_1 \gg 0$, and since $\mathbf{p} > 0$, it follows that $\mathbf{p}.\overline{\mathbf{x}}_1 > 0$. Let t be any positive number less than 1. Then, $\mathbf{p}.(t\mathbf{x}_1) = t\mathbf{p}.\mathbf{x}_1 = t\mathbf{p}.\overline{\mathbf{x}}_1 < \mathbf{p}.\overline{\mathbf{x}}_1$, where the inequality is strict because $\mathbf{p}.\overline{\mathbf{x}}_1 > 0$. Since u_i is continuous and $u_i(\mathbf{x}_1) > u_1(\overline{\mathbf{x}}_1)$, it follows that if t is close enough to 1, then $u_i(t\mathbf{x}_1) > u_1(\overline{\mathbf{x}}_1)$. Since $u_1(t\mathbf{x}_1) > u_1(\overline{\mathbf{x}}_1)$, step 6 implies that $\mathbf{p}.(t\mathbf{x}_1) \geq \mathbf{p}.\overline{\mathbf{x}}_1$, contrary to the earlier assertion that $\mathbf{p}.(t\mathbf{x}_1) < \mathbf{p}.\overline{\mathbf{x}}_1$. This contradiction shows that $\mathbf{p}.\mathbf{x}_1 \geq \mathbf{p}.\overline{\mathbf{x}}_1$, as was to be proved.

The argument of step 7 is illustrated by figure 5.9.

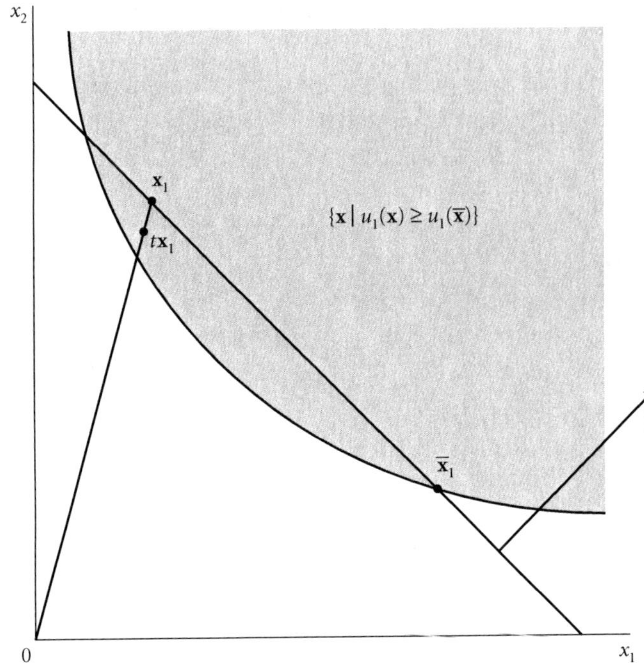

Figure 5.9 The use of local nonsatiation to prove that utility is maximized over the budget set

Step 8 Let consumer i's transfer payment be $\tau_i = \mathbf{p}.\mathbf{e}_i + \sum_j \Theta_{ij} \cdot \mathbf{p}.\overline{\mathbf{y}}_j - \mathbf{p}.\overline{\mathbf{x}}_i = w_i(\mathbf{p}) - \mathbf{p}.\overline{\mathbf{x}}_i$, for all i. This definition guarantees that $\overline{\mathbf{x}}_i$ satisfies with equality consumer i's budget constraint for an equilibrium with transfer payment τ_i. Since step 7 implies that any consumption bundle preferred to $\overline{\mathbf{x}}_i$ violates the budget constraint, it must be that $\overline{\mathbf{x}}_i$ solves the problem

$$\max_{\mathbf{x} \in \mathbb{R}^N_+} u(\mathbf{x})$$

$$\text{s.t.} \quad \mathbf{p}.\mathbf{x} \leq w_i(\mathbf{p}) - \tau_i.$$

Step 9 I show that for any n, $p_n = 0$, if $\sum_i \overline{\mathbf{x}}_{in} < \sum_i e_{in} + \sum_j \overline{y}_{jn}$. This assertion is true, because $\sum_i \overline{\mathbf{x}}_{in} \leq \sum_i e_{in} + \sum_j \overline{y}_{jn}$ and $p_n \geq 0$, for all n, and because

$$\sum_n p_n \sum_i \overline{x}_{in} = \sum_n p_n \left(\sum_i e_{in} + \sum_j y_{jn} \right), \tag{5.4}$$

by step 4. If there were an n such that $\sum_i \overline{x}_{in} < \sum_i e_{in} + \sum_j \overline{y}_{jn}$ and $p_n > 0$, then equation 5.4 could not apply. This completes the proof of step 9.

Step 9 verifies condition (6) of the definition of an equilibrium with transfer payments. All the conditions of an equilibrium with transfer payments have been verified, so that the proof of theorem 5.14 is complete. ▪

The assumption in theorem 5.14 that $\overline{\mathbf{x}}_i \gg \mathbf{0}$, for all i, seems unrealistic, since in actual economic life each individual consumes a positive quantity of only a small fraction of the goods available. This assumption is not necessary if we assume that utility functions are strictly increasing (definition 3.36 in section 3.5) and that the economy is productive in that it can produce a positive amount of every commodity (definition 3.47 in section 3.6). An economy is *productive* if it has a feasible allocation $(\mathbf{x}, \mathbf{y})$ such that $\sum_{i=1}^{I} \mathbf{x}_i \gg 0$.

THEOREM 5.15 Assume that the economy

$$\mathcal{E} = \left((u_i, e_i)_{i=1}^{I}, (Y_j)_{j=1}^{J}, (\Theta_{ij})_{i=1,\ j=1}^{I \quad J} \right)$$

is such that

1. for all i, u_i is continuous, strictly increasing, and quasi-concave
2. for all j, Y_j is convex
3. $\mathcal{E}$ is productive

If $(\overline{\mathbf{x}}, \overline{\mathbf{y}})$ is a Pareto optimal allocation, then there exists a price vector, $\mathbf{p}$, and an I-vector of transfer payments, $\boldsymbol{\tau}$, such that $(\overline{\mathbf{x}}, \overline{\mathbf{y}}, \mathbf{p}, \boldsymbol{\tau})$ is an equilibrium with transfer payments. Furthermore, the price vector $\mathbf{p}$ is strictly positive, that is, $\mathbf{p} \gg \mathbf{0}$.

Proof. Because the utility functions are strictly increasing, they are locally nonsatiated. Therefore, all the steps of the proof of theorem 5.14 except step 7 apply, since they make use of local nonsatiation but do not use the assumption that $\overline{\mathbf{x}}_i \gg 0$, for all i. Because $\mathcal{E}$ is productive, there exists a feasible allocation $(\mathbf{x}, \mathbf{y})$ such that $\sum_{i=1}^{I} \mathbf{e}_i + \sum_{j=1}^{J} \mathbf{y}_j \gg \mathbf{0}$. Let $\mathbf{p}$ be the price vector whose existence is proved in step 1 of the proof of theorem 5.14. By step 5 of that proof, $\overline{\mathbf{y}}_j$ maximizes profits in Y_j at price vector $\mathbf{p}$, for all j, so that

$$\mathbf{p}.\left(\sum_{i=1}^{I} \mathbf{e}_i + \sum_{j=1}^{J} \overline{\mathbf{y}}_j\right) \geq \mathbf{p}.\left(\sum_{i=1}^{I} \mathbf{e}_i + \sum_{j=1}^{J} \mathbf{y}_j\right) > 0,$$

where the strict inequality applies because $\mathbf{p} > 0$. Because $\mathbf{p}.\sum_{i=1}^{I} \overline{\mathbf{x}}_i = \mathbf{p}.\left(\sum_{i=1}^{I} \mathbf{e}_i + \sum_{j=1}^{J} \overline{\mathbf{y}}_j\right)$ by step 4 of the proof of theorem 5.14, it follows that $\mathbf{p}.\sum_{i=1}^{I} \overline{\mathbf{x}}_i > 0$. Therefore, $\mathbf{p}.\overline{\mathbf{x}}_i > 0$, for some i. Without loss of generality, I may assume that $i = 1$, so that $\mathbf{p}.\overline{\mathbf{x}}_1 > 0$. In step 7 of the proof of theorem 5.14, the assumption that $\overline{\mathbf{x}}_i \gg 0$ was used only to establish that $\mathbf{p}.\overline{\mathbf{x}}_1 > 0$. Since we know that $\mathbf{p}.\overline{\mathbf{x}}_1 > 0$, the argument of step 7 applies to consumer 1 and implies that $\mathbf{p}.\mathbf{x}_1 > \mathbf{p}.\overline{\mathbf{x}}_1$, if $u_1(\mathbf{x}_1) > u_1(\overline{\mathbf{x}}_1)$.

I show that $\mathbf{p} \gg \mathbf{0}$. If it is not true that $\mathbf{p} \gg \mathbf{0}$, then $p_n = 0$, for some n. Without loss of generality, I may assume that $p_1 = 0$. Because u_1 is strictly increasing, $u_1(\mathbf{x}_1) > u(\overline{\mathbf{x}}_1)$, where $\mathbf{x}_1 = \overline{\mathbf{x}}_1 + (1, 0, 0, \ldots, 0)$. Because $p_1 = 0$, it follows that $\mathbf{p}.\mathbf{x}_1 = \mathbf{p}.\overline{\mathbf{x}}_1$, contrary to the assertion of step 7, which I have just shown applies to consumer 1. This proves that $\mathbf{p} \gg \mathbf{0}$.

I show that the assertion of step 7 applies to all consumers. That is, for all i, $\mathbf{p}.\mathbf{x}_i > \mathbf{p}.\overline{\mathbf{x}}_i$, if $\mathbf{x}_i$ is such that $u_i(\mathbf{x}_i) > u_i(\overline{\mathbf{x}}_i)$. Suppose that $\overline{\mathbf{x}}_i = \mathbf{0}$. Then, if $\mathbf{x}_i$ is such that $u_i(\mathbf{x}_i) > u_i(\overline{\mathbf{x}}_i)$, it must be that $\mathbf{x}_i > 0$. Because $\mathbf{p} \gg \mathbf{0}$, it follows that $\mathbf{p}.\mathbf{x}_i > 0 = \mathbf{p}.\overline{\mathbf{x}}_1$. If $\overline{\mathbf{x}}_i > \mathbf{0}$, then $\mathbf{p}.\overline{\mathbf{x}}_i > 0$ and the argument of step 7 applies and proves that $u_i(\mathbf{x}_i) > u_i(\overline{\mathbf{x}}_i)$. This completes the proof of the theorem. ■

The argument in the second paragraph of the proof of theorem 5.15 proves the following statement as well.

PROPOSITION 5.16 If u_i is continuous, strictly increasing, and quasi-concave, for all i, then any price vector, $\mathbf{p}$, of an equilibrium with transfer payments, $(\overline{\mathbf{x}}, \overline{\mathbf{y}}, \mathbf{p}, \boldsymbol{\tau})$, is such that $\mathbf{p} \gg \mathbf{0}$.

5.3 Another Complete Theorem on the Existence of Equilibrium

I state and prove an equilibrium existence theorem that generalizes theorem 4.24 (in section 4.8), by replacing strict quasi-concavity of utility by quasi-concavity and strict convexity of input-output possibility sets by convexity. In addition, the strict positivity of endowments is replaced by the assumption that the economy is productivc. Thc main reason for presenting this theorem is as a pretext for introducing two new analytical tools. One is the Kakutani fixed point theorem, which is a generalization of the Brouwer fixed point theorem to set-valued functions. The other is an approach to proving the existence of equilibrium that is a fixed point argument on consumers' utility levels rather than on price vectors.

Before stating and proving the existence theorem, I givc thc idca of thc argument by using the Edgeworth box example pictured in figure 5.10. The set of Pareto optimal allocations is labelled $\mathcal{PO}$, and the line L is a line of slope 1 through the endowment point $\mathbf{e}$. By the second welfare theorem, for every Pareto optimal allocation, $\mathbf{x}$, there is a price vector, $\mathbf{p}$, such that $\mathbf{x}$ and $\mathbf{p}$, together with lump-sum transfers, form an equilibrium with transfer payments. Normalize $\mathbf{p}$ so that $p_1 + p_2 = 1$, and, for the moment, assume that there is only one such $\mathbf{p}$. The budget line through $\mathbf{x}$ orthogonal to $\mathbf{p}$ intersects the line L at a point, $f(\mathbf{x})$. The difference, $f(\mathbf{x}) - \mathbf{e}$, is a multiple of the vector $(1, 1)$. That is, $f(\mathbf{x}) - \mathbf{e} = t(\mathbf{x})(1, 1)$. Since $t(\mathbf{x}) = t(\mathbf{x})\mathbf{p}.(1, 1) = \mathbf{p}.t(\mathbf{x})(1, 1) = \mathbf{p}.(f(\mathbf{x}) - \mathbf{e}) = \mathbf{p}.f(\mathbf{x}) - \mathbf{p}.\mathbf{e} = \mathbf{p}.\mathbf{x}_A - \mathbf{p}.\mathbf{e}_A = -\tau_A = \tau_B$, the quantity $t(\mathbf{x})$ is just the transfer payment made by consumer B in the equilibrium with transfer payments. The pair $(\mathbf{x}, \mathbf{p})$ forms an equilibrium if and only if $f(\mathbf{x}) = \mathbf{e}$, that is, if and only if $t(\mathbf{x}) = 0$. If $u_A(\mathbf{x}) \le u_A(\mathbf{e}_A)$, then $f(\mathbf{x})$ is southwest of the point $\mathbf{e}$ and $t(\mathbf{x})$ is nonpositive. If $u_B(\mathbf{x}) \le u_B(\mathbf{e}_B)$, then $f(\mathbf{x})$ is northeast of $\mathbf{e}$ and $t(\mathbf{x})$ is

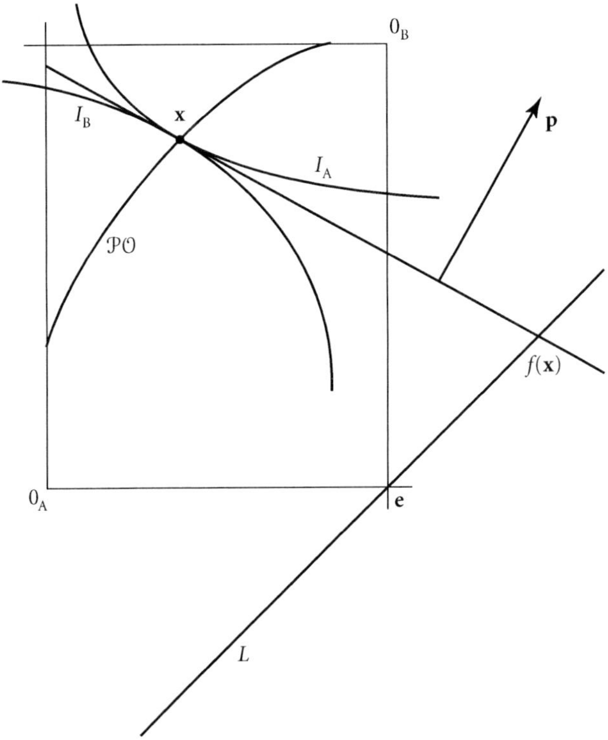

Figure 5.10 The transfer payments mapping

nonnegative, as is shown in figure 5.10. If the function t is continuous, then $t(\mathbf{x})$ must equal zero for some $\mathbf{x}$, and $\mathbf{x}$ is an equilibrium allocation.

Although the argument just given cannot be extended directly to economies with many consumers and commodities, it can be recast in a way that does generalize. Assume that the utility functions are normalized, so that $u_A(\mathbf{0}) = u_A(\mathbf{0}) = 0$. We know from theorem 3.48 (in section 3.6) that under appropriate assumptions the radial projection, π, is a continuous function from the utility possibility frontier, $\mathcal{UF}$, onto the simplex Δ^1 and has a continuous inverse π^{-1} Given a utility vector $\mathbf{v}$ in $\mathcal{UF}$, let $\mathbf{X}(\mathbf{v})$ be a Pareto optimal allocation such that $u_A(\mathbf{X}_A(\mathbf{v})) = \mathbf{v}_A$ and $u_B(\mathbf{X}_B(\mathbf{v})) = \mathbf{v}_B$, and assume that enough assumptions are made so that $\mathbf{X}(\mathbf{v})$ is unique. Again, if $\mathbf{x}$ is a Pareto optimal allocation, there are $\mathbf{p}$ and $\boldsymbol{\tau}$ such that $(\mathbf{x}, \mathbf{p}, \boldsymbol{\tau})$ is an equilibrium with transfer payments, with prices normalized so that $p_1 + p_2 = 1$. Assume that given this normalization, $\mathbf{p}$ and $\boldsymbol{\tau}$ are unique. Let $\boldsymbol{\tau}(\mathbf{x})$ be the unique vector of transfer payments associated with $\mathbf{x}$ in this way. Since the transfer payments sum to zero, it follows that $\boldsymbol{\tau}(\mathbf{x})$ belongs to the line $H = \{(t_A, t_B) \mid t_A + t_B = 0\}$. Given a vector $\mathbf{t} = (t_A, t_B)$ in H and a vector $\mathbf{b}$ in Δ^1, let $g(\mathbf{b}, \mathbf{t})$ be the point in Δ^1 closest to $\mathbf{b} + \mathbf{t}$. The composition of all these functions, $h(\mathbf{b}) = g(\mathbf{b}, \boldsymbol{\tau}(\mathbf{X}(\pi^{-1}(\mathbf{b}))))$, is a function from Δ^1 to itself, which, by the Brouwer fixed point theorem 4.16 in (section 4.7), has a fixed point, provided h is continuous. I sketch an argument showing that if $\mathbf{b} \in \Delta^1$ is a fixed point of h, then $\mathbf{x} = \mathbf{X}(\pi^{-1}(\mathbf{b}))$ is an equilibrium allocation. It is enough to show that $\boldsymbol{\tau}(\mathbf{X}(\pi^{-1}(\mathbf{b}))) = \mathbf{0}$, since $\mathbf{x} = \mathbf{X}(\pi^{-1}(\mathbf{b}))$ is an equilibrium allocation if and only if $\boldsymbol{\tau}(\mathbf{X}(\pi^{-1}(\mathbf{b}))) = \mathbf{0}$. If $\mathbf{b}$ belongs to the interior of Δ^1, then $\mathbf{b}$ can be a fixed point of h only if $\boldsymbol{\tau}(\mathbf{X}(\pi^{-1}(\mathbf{b}))) = \mathbf{0}$. Suppose that $\mathbf{b}$ is one of the two endpoints of Δ^1. Then, $b_A = 0$ or $b_B = 0$, so that $u_A(\mathbf{x}_A) = 0$ or $u_B(\mathbf{x}_B) = 0$. If $b_A = 0$ and $u_A(\mathbf{x}_A) = 0$, then $u_A(\mathbf{e}_A) \geq u_A(\mathbf{x}_A)$, so that $\mathbf{p}.\mathbf{e}_A \geq \mathbf{p}.\mathbf{x}_A$ and hence

$$\tau_A(\mathbf{X}(\pi^{-1}(\mathbf{b}))) = \tau_A(\mathbf{x}) = \mathbf{p}.\mathbf{e}_A - \mathbf{p}.\mathbf{x}_A \geq 0.$$

Since $\mathbf{b}$ is the closest point in Δ^1 to $\mathbf{b} + \boldsymbol{\tau}(\mathbf{X}(\pi^{-1}(\mathbf{b})))$, it follows that $\tau_A(\mathbf{X}(\pi^{-1}(\mathbf{b}))) = 0$ and hence $\boldsymbol{\tau}(\mathbf{X}(\pi^{-1}(\mathbf{b}))) = \mathbf{0}$. A similar argument applies if $b_B = 0$, so that $\boldsymbol{\tau}(\mathbf{X}(\pi^{-1}(\mathbf{b}))) = \mathbf{0}$, no matter where $\mathbf{b}$ lies in Δ^1.

In the discussion above, I have assumed that corresponding to every utility vector in $\mathcal{UF}$, there corresponds a unique Pareto optimal allocation $\mathbf{X}(\mathbf{v})$, such that $u_A(X_A(\mathbf{v})) = v_A$ and $u_B(X_B(\mathbf{v})) = v_B$, and to every Pareto optimal allocation $\mathbf{x}$, there corresponds a unique equilibrium with transfer payments, $(\mathbf{x}, \mathbf{p}, \boldsymbol{\tau})$, when the price vector is normalized so that prices sum to 1. These assumptions apply only under very restrictive conditions. Under more natural assumptions, there may be many Pareto optimal allocations $\mathbf{X}(\mathbf{v})$ and many equilibria with transfer payments, $(\mathbf{x}, \mathbf{p}, \boldsymbol{\tau})$, corresponding to a Pareto optimal allocation $\mathbf{x}$. The difficulties in generalizing the argument of the previous paragraph stem from the fact that the function $\boldsymbol{\tau}(\mathbf{X}(\pi^{-1}(\mathbf{b})))$ and hence h may be multiple valued.

Functions with multiple values are called correspondences.

DEFINITION 5.17 If X and Y are sets, a *correspondence*, $f: X \to Y$, associates a subset of Y, $f(\mathbf{x})$, with every member $\mathbf{x}$ of X.

If $f: X \to Y$ is a correspondence, the subset $f(\mathbf{x})$ may be empty, may equal the entire set Y, or may be any intermediate subset. Just as with functions, it is sometimes helpful to think of the graph of a correspondence.

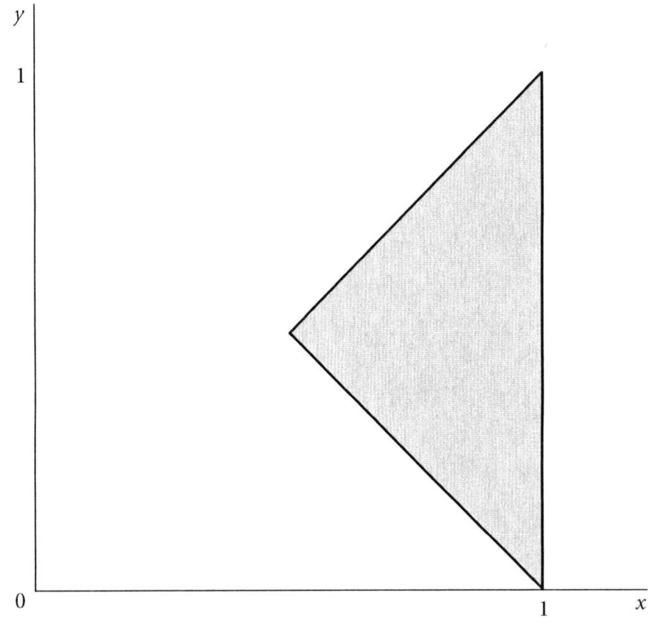

Figure 5.11 The graph of a correspondence

DEFINITION 5.18 The *graph* of the correspondence, $f: X \to Y$, is

$$\{(\mathbf{x}, \mathbf{y}) \mid \mathbf{x} \in X \text{ and } \mathbf{y} \in f(\mathbf{x})\}.$$

Figure 5.11 shows the graph of the correspondence f: $[0, 1] \to [0, 1]$ defined by the equation $f(x) = \{y \mid 1 - x \leq y \leq x\}$. Notice that $f(x)$ may be empty or may equal the whole interval $[0, 1]$.

The proof of the existence of equilibrium requires a fixed point theorem for correspondences.

DEFINITION 5.19 A *fixed point* of a correspondence f: $X \to X$ is an x in X such that x belongs to $f(x)$.

A generalization of the Brouwer fixed point theorem to correspondences should say that if X is compact and convex and f: $X \to X$ is continuous, then f has a fixed point. To state such a theorem, we require a notion of continuity for correspondences. Since the graph of a continuous function is a closed set, it makes sense to think of a correspondence as continuous if its graph is closed.

DEFINITION 5.20 If X is a subset of $\mathbb{R}^N$ and Y is a subset of $\mathbb{R}^K$ and if $f: X \to Y$ is a correspondence, then f has *closed graph* if the graph of f is a closed subset of $X \times Y$.

Notice that the graph of f is closed only within $X \times Y$. It may not be closed within $\mathbb{R}^N \times \mathbb{R}^K$, if the sets X and Y are not both closed. The graph of $f: X \to Y$ is closed if for every sequence $\mathbf{x}_1, \mathbf{x}_2, \ldots$ in X that converges to a point $\mathbf{x}$ in X and for every sequence $\mathbf{y}_1, \mathbf{y}_2, \ldots$ in Y such that $\mathbf{y}_n \in f(\mathbf{x}_n)$, for all n, and $\mathbf{y}_1, \mathbf{y}_2, \ldots$ converges to a point $\mathbf{y}$ in Y, it is true that $\mathbf{y} \in f(\mathbf{x})$.

A function $f: X \to Y$ has closed graph if it is continuous, but the next example shows that f is not necessarily continuous if its graph is closed.

EXAMPLE 5.21 The function $f: [0, \infty) \to [0, \infty)$ defined by the equation

$$f(x) = \begin{cases} \dfrac{1}{x}, & \text{if } x > 0 \text{ and} \\ 0, & \text{if } x = 0 \end{cases}$$

has closed graph but is not continuous at 0.

A function $f: X \to Y$ with closed graph is continuous, however, if Y is compact.

PROPOSITION 5.22 Let $f: X \to Y$ be a function with closed graph, where X and Y are subsets of $\mathbb{R}^N$. If Y is compact, then f is continuous.

Proof. It is sufficient to show that $\lim_{n \to \infty} f(\mathbf{x}_n) = f(\mathbf{x})$, if $\mathbf{x}_n$ is a sequence in X converging to $\mathbf{x}$. Let $\mathbf{x}_n$ be such a sequence, and suppose to the contrary that $f(\mathbf{x}_n)$ does not converge to $f(\mathbf{x})$ as n goes to infinity. Then there exists a positive number, ε, and a subsequence of $\mathbf{x}_n$, call it $\mathbf{x}_{n(k)}$, for $k = 1, 2, \ldots$, such that $\|f(\mathbf{x}_{n(k)}) - f(\mathbf{x})\| \geq \varepsilon$, for all k. Because $\mathbf{x}_{n(k)}$ is a subsequence of $\mathbf{x}_n$ and $\mathbf{x}_n$ converges to $\mathbf{x}$, it follows that $\mathbf{x}_{n(k)}$ does so as well. Because Y is compact, it follows from the Bolzano-Weierstrass theorem that a subsequence of $f(\mathbf{x}_{n(k)})$, which I again call $f(\mathbf{x}_{n(k)})$, converges to some point $\mathbf{y}$. Since $\|f(\mathbf{x}_{n(k)}) - f(\mathbf{x})\| \geq \varepsilon$, for all k, $\|\mathbf{y} - f(\mathbf{x})\| \geq \varepsilon$.

Since f has closed graph and is a function, $\mathbf{y} = f(\mathbf{x})$, which is impossible, since $\varepsilon > 0$. This contradiction proves the proposition. ■

For our purposes, having closed graph is not a strong enough notion of continuity for correspondences. The following example shows that having closed graph does not guarantee the existence of a fixed point.

EXAMPLE 5.23 (In order to have a fixed point, a correspondence must be convex valued.) Let $f: [0, 1] \to [0, 1]$ be defined by the equation

$$f(x) = \begin{cases} \{1\}, & \text{if } 0 \leq x < 0.5, \\ \{0, 1\}, & \text{if } x = 0.5, \text{ and} \\ \{0\}, & \text{if } 0.5 < x \leq 1. \end{cases}$$

This correspondence f has no fixed point, as may be seen from its graph in figure 5.12. The graph of f is indicated with heavy lines and is clearly a closed set. There is no fixed point, because the graph does not intersect the dashed diagonal line.

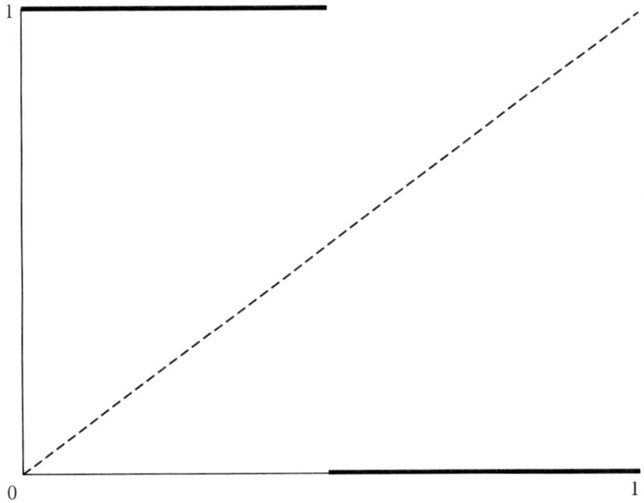

Figure 5.12 A correspondence with closed graph that has no fixed point

As indicated by the title of the previous example, $f(x)$ must be convex, for all x, if f is to have a fixed point. In addition, $f(x)$ must be nonempty, for all x, since f may have no fixed point if $f(x)$ can be empty. The proof of the existence of an equilibrium uses the following generalization of the Brouwer fixed point theorem 4.16 in (section 4.7).

KAKUTANI FIXED POINT THEOREM 5.24 The correspondence $f: X \to X$ has a fixed point provided

1. X is a compact, convex, and nonempty subset of $\mathbb{R}^N$
2. f has closed graph
3. $f(\mathbf{x})$ is convex and nonempty, for all $\mathbf{x}$

The Kakutani fixed point theorem generalizes the Brouwer theorem. If $f: X \to X$ is a function, a fixed point of f thought of as a correspondence is also a fixed point of f as a function. If f is continuous, it has closed graph, and $f(\mathbf{x})$, being a single point, is convex and nonempty, for all x.

The next theorem is a typical equilibrium existence theorem, of which there are many versions. Recall that an economy is productive if it can produce a positive amount of every good (definition 3.47 in section 3.6).

EQUILIBRIUM EXISTENCE THEOREM 5.25 The economy

$$\mathcal{E} = \left((u_i, \mathbf{e}_i)_{i=1}^I, (Y_j)_{j=1}^J, (\Theta_{ij})_{i=1}^I{}_{, j=1}^{J}\right)$$

has an equilibrium, $(\overline{\mathbf{x}}, \overline{\mathbf{y}}, \mathbf{p})$, provided

1. for all i, u_i is continuous, strictly increasing, and quasi-concave
2. for all j, Y_j is closed, convex, and contains the vector $\mathbf{0}$
3. $Y \cap \mathbb{R}^N_+ = \{\mathbf{0}\}$
4. $Y \cap (-Y) = \{\mathbf{0}\}$
5. $\mathcal{E}$ is productive

In the proof of this theorem, I will make use of the notion of the Cartesian product of sets.

DEFINITION 5.26 If A and B are sets, $A \times B = \{(a, b) \mid a \in A \text{ and } b \in B\}$ is known as the *Cartesian product* of the sets A and B.

Proof of Theorem 5.25. Since the economy $\mathcal{E}$ satisfies the conditions of theorem 3.54 (in section 3.7), its feasible allocations form a compact and nonempty set. We may normalize the utility functions u_i so that $u_i(\mathbf{0}) = 0$, for all i. With this condition and because the feasible allocations are compact, $\mathcal{E}$ satisfies the assumptions of theorem 3.48 (in section 3.6), so that the radial projection $\pi: \mathcal{UF} \to \Delta^{I-1}$ has a continuous inverse, π^{-1}, where $\mathcal{UF}$ is the economy's utility possibility frontier.

Let $\mathbf{v}$ belong to $\mathcal{UF}$ and let $(\mathbf{x}, \mathbf{y})$ be a feasible allocation such that $u(\mathbf{x}, \mathbf{y}) = \mathbf{v}$, where $u(\mathbf{x}, \mathbf{y}) = (u_1(\mathbf{x}_1), \ldots, u_I(\mathbf{x}_I))$. Since $\mathbf{v}$ belongs to $\mathcal{UF}$, $(\mathbf{x}, \mathbf{y})$ is Pareto optimal. Because $\mathcal{E}$ satisfies the assumptions of theorem 5.14 (in section 5.2), there exists a price vector $\mathbf{p}$ and a vector of transfer payments $\boldsymbol{\tau}$ such that $(\mathbf{x}, \mathbf{y}, \mathbf{p}, \boldsymbol{\tau})$ is an equilibrium with transfer payments.

I now show that no ambiguity is caused by the possibility that more than one Pareto optimal allocation $(\mathbf{x}, \mathbf{y})$ may correspond to an I-vector $\mathbf{v}$ in $\mathcal{UF}$. Let $(\underline{\mathbf{x}}, \underline{\mathbf{y}})$ and $(\overline{\mathbf{x}}, \overline{\mathbf{y}})$ be two such allocations, and let $\mathbf{p}$ and $\boldsymbol{\tau}$ be such that $(\underline{\mathbf{x}}, \underline{\mathbf{y}}, \mathbf{p}, \boldsymbol{\tau})$ is an equilibrium with transfer payments. I show that $(\overline{\mathbf{x}}, \overline{\mathbf{y}}, \mathbf{p}, \boldsymbol{\tau})$ is also an equilibrium with transfer payments and furthermore that

$$\mathbf{p}.\overline{\mathbf{x}}_i = \mathbf{p}.\mathbf{e}_i + \sum_{j=1}^{J} \Theta_{ij}\mathbf{p}.\overline{\mathbf{y}}_j - \tau_i = \mathbf{p}.\mathbf{e}_i + \sum_{j=1}^{J} \Theta_{ij}\mathbf{p}.\underline{\mathbf{y}}_j - \tau_i = \mathbf{p}.\underline{\mathbf{x}}_i, \qquad (5.5)$$

for all i. Because the utility functions u_i are strictly increasing and the allocation $(\overline{\mathbf{x}}, \overline{\mathbf{y}})$ is Pareto optimal, it follows that

$$\sum_{i=1}^{I} \overline{\mathbf{x}}_i = \sum_{i=1}^{I} \mathbf{e}_i + \sum_{j=1}^{J} \overline{\mathbf{y}}_j, \qquad (5.6)$$

for if $\sum_{i=1}^{I} \overline{\mathbf{x}}_i < \sum_{i=1}^{I} \mathbf{e}_i + \sum_{j=1}^{J} \overline{\mathbf{y}}_j$, it would be possible to increase the utility of all consumers by distributing the difference $\sum_{i=1}^{I} \mathbf{e}_i + \sum_{j=1}^{J} \overline{\mathbf{y}}_j = \sum_{i=1}^{I} \overline{\mathbf{x}}_i$ among them. Because $(\underline{\mathbf{x}}, \underline{\mathbf{y}}, \mathbf{p}, \boldsymbol{\tau})$ is an equilibrium with transfer payments and $u_i(\overline{\mathbf{x}}_i) = v_i = u_i(\underline{\mathbf{x}}_i)$, for all i, it follows that

$$\mathbf{p}.\overline{\mathbf{x}}_i \geq \mathbf{p}.\underline{\mathbf{x}}_i, \qquad (5.7)$$

for all i. Because u_i is strictly increasing, $\underline{\mathbf{x}}_i$ satisfies the budget constraint of the equilibrium $(\underline{\mathbf{x}}, \underline{\mathbf{y}}, \mathbf{p}, \boldsymbol{\tau})$ with equality, for otherwise it would be possible for consumer i to achieve higher utility within the budget set by increasing the consumption of some commodity. Therefore,

$$\mathbf{p}.\underline{\mathbf{x}}_i = \mathbf{p}.\mathbf{e}_i + \sum_{j=1}^{J} \Theta_{ij}\mathbf{p}.\underline{\mathbf{y}}_j - \tau_i, \tag{5.8}$$

for all i. Because $\underline{\mathbf{y}}_j$ maximizes profits over Y_j at the price vector $\mathbf{p}$, for all j, it follows that

$$\mathbf{p}.\mathbf{e}_i + \sum_{j=1}^{J} \Theta_{ij}\mathbf{p}.\underline{\mathbf{y}}_j - \tau_i \geq \mathbf{p}.\mathbf{e}_i + \sum_{j=1}^{J} \Theta_{ij}\mathbf{p}.\overline{\mathbf{y}}_j - \tau_i, \tag{5.9}$$

for all i. Inequalities 5.7–5.9 imply that

$$\mathbf{p}.\overline{\mathbf{x}}_i \geq \mathbf{p}.\underline{\mathbf{x}}_i = \mathbf{p}.\mathbf{e}_i + \sum_{j=1}^{J} \Theta_{ij}\mathbf{p}.\underline{\mathbf{y}}_j - \tau_i \geq \mathbf{p}.\mathbf{e}_i + \sum_{j=1}^{J} \Theta_{ij}\mathbf{p}.\overline{\mathbf{y}}_j - \tau_i, \tag{5.10}$$

for all i. If we sum the inequalities 5.10 over i and make use of equation 5.6, we find that

$$\begin{aligned} &\mathbf{p}.\left(\sum_{i=1}^{I} \mathbf{e}_i + \sum_{j=1}^{J} \overline{\mathbf{y}}_j\right) = \mathbf{p}.\sum_{i=1}^{I} \overline{\mathbf{x}}_i = \sum_{i=1}^{I} \mathbf{p}.\overline{\mathbf{x}}_i \\ &\geq \sum_{i=1}^{I}\left(\mathbf{p}.\mathbf{e}_i + \sum_{j=1}^{J} \Theta_{ij}\mathbf{p}.\overline{\mathbf{y}}_j - \tau_i\right) \\ &= \mathbf{p}.\left(\sum_{i=1}^{I} \mathbf{e}_i + \sum_{j=1}^{J}\sum_{i=1}^{I} \Theta_{ij}\overline{\mathbf{y}}_j\right) - \sum_{i=1}^{I} \tau_i = \mathbf{p}.\left(\sum_{i=1}^{I} \mathbf{e}_i + \sum_{j=1}^{J} \overline{\mathbf{y}}_j\right), \end{aligned} \tag{5.11}$$

where the last equation follows because $\sum_{i=1}^{I} \Theta_{ij} = 1$ by assumption and because $\sum_{i=1}^{I} \tau_i = 0$ by proposition 5.6 (in section 5.2). Since the left- and right-hand sides of inequality 5.11 are equal, we must have equality throughout, and therefore we must have equality throughout 5.10. These equations imply equation 5.5.

Since $\mathbf{p}.\overline{\mathbf{x}}_i = \mathbf{p}.\mathbf{e}_i + \sum_{j=1}^{J} \Theta_{ij}\mathbf{p}.\overline{\mathbf{y}}_j - \tau_i$, for all i, $\overline{\mathbf{x}}_i$ satisfies the budget condition for an equilibrium $(\overline{\mathbf{x}}, \overline{\mathbf{y}}, \mathbf{p}, \boldsymbol{\tau})$ with equality. I now show that $(\overline{\mathbf{x}}, \overline{\mathbf{y}}, \mathbf{p}, \boldsymbol{\tau})$ satisfies the other conditions for an equilibrium with transfer payments. If $\mathbf{x}_i$ is such that $u_i(\mathbf{x}_i) > u_i(\overline{\mathbf{x}}_i)$, then $u_i(\mathbf{x}_i) > u_i(\underline{\mathbf{x}}_i)$, since $u_i(\overline{\mathbf{x}}_i) = u_i(\underline{\mathbf{x}}_i)$. Since $(\underline{\mathbf{x}}, \underline{\mathbf{y}}, \mathbf{p}, \boldsymbol{\tau})$ is an equilibrium with transfer payments,

$$\mathbf{p}.\mathbf{x}_i > \mathbf{p}.\mathbf{e}_i + \sum_{j=1}^{J} \Theta_{ij}\mathbf{p}.\underline{\mathbf{y}}_j - \tau_i.$$

Inequality 5.9 therefore implies that

$$\mathbf{p}.\mathbf{x}_i > \mathbf{p}.\mathbf{e}_i + \sum_{j=1}^{J} \Theta_{ij}\mathbf{p}.\overline{\mathbf{y}}_j - \tau_i,$$

so that $\overline{\mathbf{x}}_i$ maximizes u_i over consumer i's budget set in the possible equilibrium with transfer payments $(\overline{\mathbf{x}}, \overline{\mathbf{y}}, \mathbf{p}, \boldsymbol{\tau})$. The only condition of equilibrium that remains to be verified is that $\overline{\mathbf{y}}_j$ maximizes profits over Y_j at the price vector $\mathbf{p}$. Summing the central equation of equations 5.5 over i, we find that

$$\mathbf{p}.\sum_{i=1}^{I} \mathbf{e}_i + \sum_{j=1}^{J}\sum_{i=1}^{I} \Theta_{ij}\mathbf{p}.\overline{\mathbf{y}}_j = \mathbf{p}.\sum_{i=1}^{I} \mathbf{e}_i + \sum_{j=1}^{J}\sum_{i=1}^{I} \Theta_{ij}\mathbf{p}.\underline{\mathbf{y}}_j. \qquad (5.12)$$

Canceling the terms $\mathbf{p}.\sum_{i=1}^{I} \mathbf{e}_i$ from both sides of equation 5.12 and making use of the equation $\sum_{i=1}^{I} \Theta_{ij} = 1$, we see that

$$\sum_{j=1}^{J} \mathbf{p}.\overline{\mathbf{y}}_j = \sum_{j=1}^{J} \mathbf{p}.\underline{\mathbf{y}}_j. \qquad (5.13)$$

Since $\mathbf{p}.\overline{\mathbf{y}}_j \leq \mathbf{p}.\underline{\mathbf{y}}_j$, for all j, by profit maximization in the equilibrium $(\underline{\mathbf{x}}, \underline{\mathbf{y}}, \mathbf{p}, \boldsymbol{\tau})$, equation 5.13 implies that

$$\mathbf{p}.\overline{\mathbf{y}}_j = \mathbf{p}.\underline{\mathbf{y}}_j, \qquad (5.14)$$

for all j. Since $\underline{\mathbf{y}}_j$ maximizes profits at the price vector $\mathbf{p}$, it follows that $\overline{\mathbf{y}}_j$ does so as well. This completes the proof that $(\overline{\mathbf{x}}, \overline{\mathbf{y}}, \mathbf{p}, \boldsymbol{\tau})$ is an equilibrium with transfer payments.

If $\mathbf{v}$ belongs to $\mathcal{UF}$, let $T(\mathbf{v})$ be the set of all transfer payment vectors $\boldsymbol{\tau} = (\tau_1, \tau_2, \ldots, \tau_I)$ for an equilibrium with transfer payments $(\mathbf{x}, \mathbf{y}, \mathbf{p}, \boldsymbol{\tau})$, such that $u(\mathbf{x}, \mathbf{y}) = \mathbf{v}$. Theorem 5.14 (in section 5.2) implies that $T(\mathbf{v})$ is not empty. The next step is to show that $T(\mathbf{v})$ is a convex set, for all $\mathbf{v}$. If $(\mathbf{x}, \mathbf{y})$ is a Pareto optimal allocation such that $u(\mathbf{x}, \mathbf{y}) = \mathbf{v}$, let $P(\mathbf{x}, \mathbf{y})$ be the set of price vectors $\mathbf{p}$ such that $\sum_{n=1}^{N} p_n = 1$ and, for some vector of transfer payments, $\boldsymbol{\tau}$, $(\mathbf{x}, \mathbf{y}, \mathbf{p}, \boldsymbol{\tau})$ is an equilibrium with transfer payments. I have shown that if $(\mathbf{x}, \mathbf{y}, \mathbf{p}, \boldsymbol{\tau})$ is an equilibrium with transfer payments, then $(\underline{\mathbf{x}}, \underline{\mathbf{y}}, \mathbf{p}, \boldsymbol{\tau})$ is an equilibrium with transfer payments, for any feasible allocation $(\underline{\mathbf{x}}, \underline{\mathbf{y}})$ such that $u(\underline{\mathbf{x}}, \underline{\mathbf{y}}) = \mathbf{v}$. Therefore, the set $P(\mathbf{x}, \mathbf{y})$ depends only on $\mathbf{v}$, and I may write it as $P(\mathbf{v})$. Since $(\mathbf{x}, \mathbf{y}, \mathbf{p}, \boldsymbol{\tau})$ is an equilibrium with transfer payments, for each i,

$$\tau_i = \mathbf{p}.(\mathbf{e}_i - \mathbf{x}_i) + \sum_{j=1}^{J} \Theta_{ij}\mathbf{p}.\mathbf{y}_j. \tag{5.15}$$

Equations 5.5 and 5.14 imply that the quantities $\mathbf{p}.\mathbf{x}_i$ and $\mathbf{p}.\mathbf{y}_j$ are independent of the feasible allocation $(\mathbf{x}, \mathbf{y})$ such that $u(\mathbf{x}, \mathbf{y}) = \mathbf{v}$. Hence, equation 5.15 implies that the transfer payments τ_i are also independent of $(\mathbf{x}, \mathbf{y})$, and so I may write

$$\begin{aligned} T(\mathbf{v}) = \Bigg\{ \Bigg(& \mathbf{p}. \left[(\mathbf{e}_1 - \mathbf{x}_1) + \sum_{j=1}^{J} \Theta_{1j}\mathbf{y}_j \right], \ldots, \\ & \mathbf{p}. \left[(\mathbf{e}_I - \mathbf{x}_I) + \sum_{j=1}^{J} \Theta_{Ij}\mathbf{y}_j \right] \Bigg) \mid \mathbf{p} \in P(\mathbf{v}) \Bigg\}, \end{aligned} \tag{5.16}$$

where $(\mathbf{x}, \mathbf{y})$ is any feasible allocation such that $u(\mathbf{x}, \mathbf{y}) = \mathbf{v}$. Hence, in order to show that $T(\mathbf{v})$ is a convex set, it is sufficient to show that the set $P(\mathbf{v})$ is convex. Fix a feasible allocation $(\underline{\mathbf{x}}, \underline{\mathbf{y}})$ such that $u(\underline{\mathbf{x}}, \underline{\mathbf{y}}) = \mathbf{v}$. The N-vector $\mathbf{p}$ belongs to $P(\mathbf{v})$ if and only if $\mathbf{p} \in \Delta^{N-1}$ and, for all i, $\mathbf{p}.\mathbf{x}_i > \mathbf{p}.\underline{\mathbf{x}}_i$, whenever $u_i(\mathbf{x}_i) > u_i(\underline{\mathbf{x}}_i)$ and, for all j, $\mathbf{p}.\underline{\mathbf{y}}_j \geq \mathbf{p}.\mathbf{y}_j$, for any $\mathbf{y}_j \in Y_j$. It should be clear that if $\mathbf{p}$ and $\mathbf{q}$ are price vectors that satisfy these conditions, then $\alpha\mathbf{p} + (1-\alpha)\mathbf{q}$ satisfies them, for any α such that $0 \leq \alpha \leq 1$. Therefore, $P(\mathbf{v})$ and hence $T(\mathbf{v})$ are convex.

It is important that the correspondence T is bounded. That is, there is a positive number B, such that $\|\boldsymbol{\tau}\| < B$, for any vector $\boldsymbol{\tau}$ in $T(\mathbf{v})$ and for any $\mathbf{v}$ in $\mathcal{UF}$. The boundedness of T is a consequence of equation 5.16, the boundedness of the set of feasible allocations, and the fact that the price vectors in equation 5.16 belong to the bounded set Δ^{N-1}.

The final major task is to verify that the correspondence T has closed graph. Let $\mathbf{v}^n$ be a sequence of points in $\mathcal{UF}$ converging to a point $\mathbf{v}$ in $\mathcal{UF}$ and, for each n, let $\boldsymbol{\tau}^n$ be a member of $T(\mathbf{v}^n)$ and suppose that the sequence $\boldsymbol{\tau}^n$ converges to $\boldsymbol{\tau}$. I must show that $\boldsymbol{\tau}$ belongs to $T(\mathbf{v})$. Because $\boldsymbol{\tau}^n$ belongs to $T(\mathbf{v}^n)$, there exists a price vector $\mathbf{p}^n$ and a feasible allocation $(\mathbf{x}^n, \mathbf{y}^n)$ such that $(\mathbf{x}^n, \mathbf{y}^n, \mathbf{p}^n, \boldsymbol{\tau}^n)$ is an equilibrium with transfer payments and $\mathbf{p}^n \in \Delta^{N-1}$. The sequence $(\mathbf{x}^n, \mathbf{y}^n, \mathbf{p}^n, \boldsymbol{\tau}^n)$ is bounded, because the allocations $(\mathbf{x}^n, \mathbf{y}^n)$ belong to the compact set of allocations that are feasible, the price vectors $\mathbf{p}^n$ belong to the compact set Δ^{N-1}, and the vectors of transfer payments $\boldsymbol{\tau}^n$ belong to the range of the correspondence T, which I showed to be bounded in the previous paragraph. Therefore, by the Bolzano-Weierstrass theorem, the sequence $(\mathbf{x}^n, \mathbf{y}^n, \mathbf{p}^n, \boldsymbol{\tau}^n)$ has a convergent subsequence, which I again call $(\mathbf{x}^n, \mathbf{y}^n, \mathbf{p}^n, \boldsymbol{\tau}^n)$. Let $(\underline{\mathbf{x}}, \underline{\mathbf{y}}, \mathbf{p}, \boldsymbol{\tau})$ be the limit of this sequence. I prove that $(\underline{\mathbf{x}}, \underline{\mathbf{y}}, \mathbf{p}, \boldsymbol{\tau})$ is an equilibrium with transfer payments.

Because the input-output possibility sets Y_j are closed, it is easy to verify that $(\underline{\mathbf{x}}, \underline{\mathbf{y}})$ is a feasible allocation.

Because $\tau_i^n = \mathbf{p}^n.(\mathbf{e}_i - \mathbf{x}_i^n) + \sum_{j=1}^J \Theta_{ij}\mathbf{p}^n.\mathbf{y}_j^n$, for all i and n, it follows by passage to the limit that

$$\tau_i = \mathbf{p}.(\mathbf{e}_i - \underline{\mathbf{x}}_i) + \sum_{j=1}^J \Theta_{ij}\mathbf{p}.\underline{\mathbf{y}}_j, \tag{5.17}$$

for all i. Therefore, for each i, the consumption bundle $\underline{\mathbf{x}}_i$ satisfies the budget condition for an equilibrium with transfer payments, $(\underline{\mathbf{x}}, \underline{\mathbf{y}}, \mathbf{p}, \boldsymbol{\tau})$.

I verify that for all j, $\underline{\mathbf{y}}_j$ maximizes profits in Y_j at the price vector $\mathbf{p}$. Let $\mathbf{y}_j$ belong to Y_j. For each n, $\mathbf{y}_j^n$ maximizes profits in Y_j at the price vector $\mathbf{p}^n$, so that

$$\mathbf{p}^n.\mathbf{y}_j^n \geq \mathbf{p}^n.\mathbf{y}_j. \tag{5.18}$$

Passing to the limit in inequality 5.18, we see that $\mathbf{p}.\underline{\mathbf{y}}_j \geq \mathbf{p}.\mathbf{y}_j$ and hence $\underline{\mathbf{y}}_j$ maximizes profits.

I next verify that for all i, $\underline{\mathbf{x}}_i$ maximizes u_i over the budget set defined by $(\underline{\mathbf{y}}, \mathbf{p}, \boldsymbol{\tau})$. First of all, I show that, for all i, if $\mathbf{x}_i$ is such that $u_i(\mathbf{x}_i) > u_i(\underline{\mathbf{x}}_i)$, then $p.\mathbf{x}_i \geq p.\underline{\mathbf{x}}_i$. Because $\mathbf{x}_i^n$ converges to $\underline{\mathbf{x}}_i$ as n goes to infinity, $u_i(\mathbf{x}_i) > u_i(\mathbf{x}_i^n)$,for sufficiently large n. Because $(\mathbf{x}^n, \mathbf{y}^n, \mathbf{p}^n, \boldsymbol{\tau}^n)$ is an equilibrium with transfer payments,

$$\mathbf{p}^n.\mathbf{x}_i > \mathbf{p}^n.\mathbf{x}_i^n, \tag{5.19}$$

if n is so large that $u_i(\mathbf{x}_i) > u_i(\mathbf{x}_i^n)$. Passing to the limit in inequality 5.19, we see that $\mathbf{p}.\mathbf{x}_i \geq \mathbf{p}.\underline{\mathbf{x}}_i$, as was to be proved.

I have just verified step 6 in the proof of theorem 5.14 (in section 5.2). Because the utility functions u_i are strictly increasing and $\mathcal{E}$ is productive, the arguments in steps 7 and 9 of that proof demonstrate that $(\underline{\mathbf{x}}, \underline{\mathbf{y}}, \mathbf{p}, \boldsymbol{\tau})$ is an equilibrium with transfer payments.

The allocation $(\underline{\mathbf{x}}, \underline{\mathbf{y}})$ satisfies the equation $u(\underline{\mathbf{x}}, \underline{\mathbf{y}}) = \mathbf{v}$, because $u(\mathbf{x}^n, \mathbf{y}^n) = \mathbf{v}^n$, for all n, and the function u is continuous and $\lim_{n\to\infty} \mathbf{v}^n = \mathbf{v}$. Because $u(\underline{\mathbf{x}}, \underline{\mathbf{y}}) = \mathbf{v}$ and $(\underline{\mathbf{x}}, \underline{\mathbf{y}}, \mathbf{p}, \boldsymbol{\tau})$ is an equilibrium with transfer payments, it follows that $\boldsymbol{\tau}$ belongs to $T(\mathbf{v})$. This completes the proof that the correspondence T has closed graph.

I am now in a position to use the Kakutani fixed point theorem (theorem 5.24) to complete the proof of the existence of an equilibrium. It has already been shown that there exists a positive number B, such that $\|\boldsymbol{\tau}\| < B$, for any vector $\boldsymbol{\tau}$ in $T(\mathbf{v})$ and for any $\mathbf{v}$ in $\mathcal{UF}$. Let $K = \{\boldsymbol{\tau} \in \mathbb{R}^I \mid \sum_{i=1}^{I} \tau_i = 0$ and $\|\boldsymbol{\tau}\| \leq B\}$. By definition, K is compact and convex. Let $M\colon K \to \Delta^{I-1}$ be the correspondence defined by the equation

$$M(\boldsymbol{\tau}) = \{\underline{\mathbf{b}} \in \Delta^{I-1} \mid \underline{\mathbf{b}}.\boldsymbol{\tau} \geq \mathbf{b}.\boldsymbol{\tau}, \ \text{for all } \mathbf{b} \in \Delta^{I-1}\}.$$

If $\mathbf{b}$ belongs to Δ^{I-1} and $\boldsymbol{\tau}$ belongs to K, then $\mathbf{b}.\boldsymbol{\tau}$ is a weighted average of the components of $\boldsymbol{\tau}$ with weights specified by the components of $\mathbf{b}$. The vector $\mathbf{b}$ belongs to $M(\boldsymbol{\tau})$ if and only if its weights are such as to maximize the weighted average $\mathbf{b}.\boldsymbol{\tau}$. Therefore, any vector in $M(\boldsymbol{\tau})$ puts all the weight on the largest components of $\boldsymbol{\tau}$. In other words, $b_i > 0$ only if i is such that $\tau_i \geq \tau_k$, for $k = 1, \ldots, I$. For any $\boldsymbol{\tau}$ in K, $\sum_{i=1}^{I} \tau_i = 0$, so that some component of $\boldsymbol{\tau}$ is positive if any component is negative. Therefore, the following statement is true:

$$\text{If } \mathbf{b} \text{ belongs to } M(\boldsymbol{\tau}), \text{ then } \tau_i < 0 \text{ implies that } b_i = 0. \qquad (5.20)$$

In addition, it is easy to verify that the correspondence M has closed graph and that $M(\boldsymbol{\tau})$ is nonempty and convex, for any $\boldsymbol{\tau}$ in K.

Let the correspondence $F\colon \Delta^{I-1} \times K \to \Delta^{I-1} \times K$ be defined by the equation $F(\mathbf{b}, \boldsymbol{\tau}) = M(\boldsymbol{\tau}) \times T(\pi^{-1}(\mathbf{b}))$. The set $\Delta^{I-1} \times K$ is compact and convex, because it is the Cartesian product of compact and convex sets, where the Cartesian product is described in definition 5.26. Similarly, F has closed graph and $F(\mathbf{b}, \boldsymbol{\tau})$ is convex and nonempty for all $(\mathbf{b}, \boldsymbol{\tau})$, because the component correspondences M and $T \cdot \pi^{-1}$ have the same properties, where $T \circ \pi^{-1}$ is the composition of T and π^{-1}. That is, $T \circ \pi^{-1}(\mathbf{b}) = T(\pi^{-1}(\mathbf{b}))$. It is easy to check that $T \circ \pi^{-1}$ has closed graph, because T has closed graph and π^{-1} is a continuous function. In summary, F satisfies the assumptions of the Kakutani fixed point theorem, so that F has a fixed point. That is, there exists $\underline{\mathbf{b}} \in \Delta^{I-1}$ and $\boldsymbol{\tau} \in K$, such that $\underline{\mathbf{b}} \in M(\boldsymbol{\tau})$ and

$\boldsymbol{\tau} \in T(\pi^{-1}(\underline{\mathbf{b}}))$. Let $(\underline{\mathbf{x}}, \underline{\mathbf{y}}, \mathbf{p}, \boldsymbol{\tau})$ be the equilibrium with transfer payments such that $u(\underline{\mathbf{x}}, \underline{\mathbf{y}}) = \pi^{-1}(\underline{\mathbf{b}})$ and $\mathbf{p} \in \Delta^{N-1}$.

I show that $(\underline{\mathbf{x}}, \underline{\mathbf{y}}, \mathbf{p})$ is an equilibrium without transfer payments by proving that $\boldsymbol{\tau} = \mathbf{0}$. Because $\sum_{i=1}^{I} \tau_i = 0$, it is sufficient to prove that $\boldsymbol{\tau} \geq \mathbf{0}$. Suppose to the contrary that $\tau_i < 0$, for some i. Because $\underline{\mathbf{b}} \in M(\boldsymbol{\tau})$, statement 5.20 implies that $\underline{b}_i = 0$, so that component i of $\pi^{-1}(\underline{\mathbf{b}})$ is zero, since π is the radial projection of $\mathcal{UF}$ onto Δ^{I-1}. This ith component is simply $u_i(\underline{\mathbf{x}}_i)$, so that $u_i(\underline{\mathbf{x}}_i) = 0$. Since u_i is strictly increasing, it follows that $\underline{\mathbf{x}}_i = \mathbf{0}$. Since $\mathbf{e}_i \geq \mathbf{0}$, it follows that $\mathbf{p}.\mathbf{e}_i \geq 0$. Since $\mathbf{0}$ belongs to Y_j, for all j, $\mathbf{p}.\underline{\mathbf{y}}_i \geq \mathbf{p}.\mathbf{0} = 0$, for all j. Therefore, $\tau_i = \mathbf{p}.\mathbf{e}_i + \sum_{j=1}^{J} \Theta_{ij}\underline{\mathbf{y}}_j - \mathbf{p}.\underline{\mathbf{x}}_i \geq 0$, contrary to hypothesis. This contradiction proves that $\boldsymbol{\tau} = \mathbf{0}$ and hence that $(\underline{\mathbf{x}}, \underline{\mathbf{y}}, \mathbf{p})$ is an equilibrium. ■

Problem Set

1. Consider the Edgeworth box economy with $\mathbf{e}_A = (1, 0)$, $\mathbf{e}_B = (0, 1)$, $u_A(x_1, x_2) = \min(4x_1, x_2)$, and $u_B(x_1, x_2) = x_1 + 2x_2$. Find the equilibrium with transfer payments, $(\mathbf{x}, \mathbf{p}, \boldsymbol{\tau})$, that has $u_B(x_{B1}, x_{B2}) = 1$ and $p_1 = 1$.

2. Consider the following economy with three commodities (1, 2, and 3), two firms (2 and 3), and two consumers (A and B).

$$u_A(x_1, x_2, x_3) = \ln(x_2) + \ln(x_3) = u_B(x_1, x_2, x_3).$$
$$\mathbf{e}_A = (2, 0, 0).\mathbf{e}_B = (0, 0, 0).$$

Firm 2 produces good 2 from good 1 with the production function $y_2 = 2(-y_{21})$, where $y_{21} \leq 0$ and y_{21} is firm 2's input of good 1. Firm 3 produces good 3 from good 1 with the production function $y_3 = -y_{31}$, where $y_{31} \leq 0$ and y_{31} is firm 3's input of good 1. (Notice that there are constant returns to scale in production, so that there are no profits in equilibrium and hence no need to assign ownership shares to consumers.)

(a) Compute an allocation that maximizes the sum of the utilities of the two consumers.

(b) Find an equilibrium with transfer payments the allocation of which is the one calculated in part (a). Let the price of good 1 be 1.

3. Consider the Edgeworth box economy with $\mathbf{e}_A = (1, 0)$, $\mathbf{e}_B = (0, 1)$, $u_A(x_1, x_2) = x_1^{1/3} x_2^{2/3} = u_B(x_1, x_2)$. Calculate the function τ from $\Delta^1 = \{(v_A, v_B) \in \mathbb{R}^2_+ \mid v_A + v_B = 1\}$ to $H = \{(t_1, t_2) \in \mathbb{R}^1 \mid t_1 + t_2 = 0\}$ and defined by the equation

$$\tau(v_A, v_B) = (\tau_A, \tau_B) = (\mathbf{p}.(\mathbf{e}_A - \mathbf{x}_A), \mathbf{p}.(\mathbf{e}_B - \mathbf{x}_B)),$$

where $(\mathbf{x}_A, \mathbf{x}_B)$ is a Pareto optimal allocation such that $(u_A(\mathbf{x}_A), u_B(\mathbf{x}_B)) = \lambda(v_A, v_B)$, for some positive number λ, and $\mathbf{p}$ is a price vector such that $((\mathbf{x}_A, \mathbf{x}_B), \mathbf{p}, (\tau_A, \tau_B))$ is an equilibrium with transfer payments and $p_1 + p_2 = 1$.

4. Suppose that $(\overline{\mathbf{x}}, \overline{\mathbf{y}}, \overline{\mathbf{p}})$ is a competitive equilibrium for an economy $((u_i, \mathbf{e}_i)_{i=1}^I, (Y_j)_{j=1}^J, (\Theta_{ij}))$ with locally nonsatiated utility functions. Let Y_0 be another input-output possibility set containing 0 and satisfying

$$\max_{\mathbf{y} \in Y_0} \overline{\mathbf{p}}.\mathbf{y} = 0,$$

and let $(\mathbf{x}, \mathbf{y}, \mathbf{p})$ be an equilibrium for the economy $((u_i, \mathbf{e}_i)_{i=1}^I, (Y_j)_{j=0}^J, (\Theta_{ij}))$, which is the original economy with Y_0 adjoined. Is it possible that $(\mathbf{x}, \mathbf{y})$ Pareto dominates the allocation $(\overline{\mathbf{x}}, \overline{\mathbf{y}})$? In other words, is it possible to use a new production process earning zero profit to make everyone at least as well off and someone better off? Demonstratc your answer by means of a proof or counter example.[1]

5. Consider an economy with two consumers, two goods, and no firms. The endowment vectors of consumers A and B are $\mathbf{e}_A$ and $\mathbf{e}_B$, respectively, where $\mathbf{e}_A \gg 0$ and $\mathbf{e}_B \gg 0$. Assume that the utility of each consumer depends on the consumption of the other consumer as well as on his or her own consumption. That is, each consumer cares about what the other consumes, out of sympathy, envy, or because the other's consumption interferes with or helps his or her own life. For instance, each neighbor might want the other to paint his or her house, but dislike smoke from his or her barbecue. Such effects are known as consumption externalities. More formally, if $\mathbf{x}_A$ and $\mathbf{x}_B$ are the consumption bundles of consumers A and B, respectively, then their utilities are $u_A(\mathbf{x}_A, \mathbf{x}_B)$ and $u_B(\mathbf{x}_A, \mathbf{x}_B)$, respectively. Assume that u_A and u_B are continuous and that for $i =$ A and B, u_i is strictly

1. I owe this problem to a personal communication from Professor Herbert Scarf.

increasing and strictly concave with respect to $\mathbf{x}_i$. (That is, $u_A(\mathbf{x}_A, \mathbf{x}_B)$ is both strictly increasing and strictly concave with respect to $\mathbf{x}_A$ but not necessarily so with respect to $\mathbf{x}_B$, and the symmetric statement applies to u_B.) In an equilibrium, consumer A chooses $\mathbf{x}_A$ to solve the problem.

$$\max_{\mathbf{x} \in \mathbb{R}^2_+} u_A(\mathbf{x}, \mathbf{x}_B)$$

$$\text{s.t.} \quad \mathbf{p}.\mathbf{x} \leq \mathbf{p}.\mathbf{e}_A.$$

That is, consumer A holds $\mathbf{x}_B$ fixed when considering how to choose $\mathbf{x}_A$. Similarly, consumer B chooses $\mathbf{x}_B$ to solve the problem

$$\max_{\mathbf{x} \in \mathbb{R}^2_+} u_B(\mathbf{x}_A, \mathbf{x})$$

$$\text{s.t.} \quad \mathbf{p}.\mathbf{x} \leq \mathbf{p}.\mathbf{e}_B.$$

In addition, the market excess demand for each good is nonpositive and the price of any good in excess supply is zero.

(a) Prove that an equilibrium exists.

(b) Is an equilibrium allocation Pareto optimal? Give a proof or counterexample.

6. Let $E = \mathcal{E} = ((u_i, \mathbf{e}_i)_{i=1}^I)$ be a pure trade economy such that every utility function, u_i, is strictly increasing. Let $(\overline{\mathbf{x}}, \mathbf{p})$ be a competitive equilibrium for this economy. Now consider dividing the set of consumers into two disjoint groups, G_1 and G_2, where the union of G_1 and G_2 is the entire set of I consumers of $\mathcal{E}$ and each of G_1 and G_2 contains at least two people. Let $(\overline{\mathbf{x}}^1, \mathbf{p}^1)$ and $(\overline{\mathbf{x}}^2, \mathbf{p}^2)$ be competitive equilibria for the economies consisting of the people in G_1 and G_2, respectively.

(a) Show that $(\overline{\mathbf{x}}^1, \overline{\mathbf{x}}^2)$ is a feasible allocation for $\mathcal{E}$.

(b) Is it possible for $(\overline{\mathbf{x}}^1, \overline{\mathbf{x}}^2)$ to Pareto dominate $\overline{\mathbf{x}}$? Give an example to show that $(\overline{\mathbf{x}}^1, \overline{\mathbf{x}}^2)$ may Pareto dominate $\overline{\mathbf{x}}$ or prove that $(\overline{\mathbf{x}}^1, \overline{\mathbf{x}}^2)$ cannot Pareto dominate $\overline{\mathbf{x}}$.

7. Consider an economy with I consumers and N goods, where, for all i, the endowment vector of consumer i is $\mathbf{e}_i$, and the utility function of each consumer i is of the form

$$u_i(x_i, \sum_{k=1}^{I} x_k),$$

where $\mathbf{x}_i$ is the consumption vector of the ith consumer. Assume that u_i is increasing with respect to the components of $\mathbf{x}_i$.

(a) Define a notion of competitive equilibrium.

(b) Is an equilibrium allocation necessarily Pareto optimal? Give an argument.

8. There are I consumers and one good, which may be used for public or private consumption. Each consumer is endowed with one unit of the good and divides this one unit between public and private consumption. That is, each consumer i, for $i = 1, \ldots, I$, chooses x_i, where $0 \leq x_i \leq 1$, and the total amount available for public consumption is $g = x_1 + x_2 + \cdots + x_I$. For all i, the utility function of consumer n is $u_i(1 - x_i, g)$, where u_i is continuous, strictly increasing, and strictly concave. In equilibrium, each consumer knows the choice of x_i for all other consumers and chooses her or his personal consumption and contribution to public consumption so as to maximize her or his own utility.

(a) Describe the equilibrium formally.

(b) Prove that an equilibrium exists.

(c) Either prove that the equilibrium is Pareto optimal or show that it may not be by means of a counterexample.

— 6 —

The Kuhn-Tucker Approach to General Equilibrium Theory

We know that under appropriate conditions the allocation of a competitive equilibrium with or without transfer payments is Pareto optimal and that a Pareto optimal allocation maximizes a weighted sum of consumers' utility functions. It follows that an equilibrium allocation maximizes a welfare function that is a weighted sum of the consumers' utility functions. We can deepen our understanding of this last result by using the Kuhn-Tucker theorem to interpret it. This approach reveals that the weight given each consumer's utility in the welfare function may be set equal to the inverse of his or her marginal utility of unit of account in the equilibrium. If these are the welfare weights, then the equilibrium price of each commodity is the rate at which aggregate welfare increases as the supply of that commodity increases. Before stating and proving these assertions formally, I explain the Kuhn-Tucker theorem.

6.1 Kuhn-Tucker Theorem

The Kuhn-Tucker theorem is, roughly speaking, an application of the method of Lagrange multipliers to maximization problems with a concave objective function and constraints described by a convex set and convex functions. Convex functions are like concave ones turned upside down.

DEFINITION 6.1 If X is a convex set of N-vectors and $f: X \to \mathbb{R}$, then f is *convex* if

$$f(\alpha \mathbf{x} + (1-\alpha)\mathbf{y}) \leq \alpha f(\mathbf{x}) + (1-\alpha) f(\mathbf{y}),$$

for all $\mathbf{x}$ and $\mathbf{y}$ in X and for all α such that $0 \leq \alpha \leq 1$.

A function f is convex if and only if the function $-f$ is concave, as may be seen by comparing the definition of convexity with that of concavity (definition 3.27 in section 3.5). Affine functions are both concave and convex, recalling that an affine function, f, is one of the form $f(\mathbf{x}) = \mathbf{a}.\mathbf{x} + \mathbf{b}$, where $\mathbf{a}$ and $\mathbf{b}$ are N-vectors. The theorem characterizes solutions to the following problem:

$$\max_{x \in X} f(\mathbf{x})$$
$$\text{s.t.} \quad g_k(\mathbf{x}) \le \overline{a}_k, \text{ for } k = 1, \ldots, K, \tag{6.1}$$

where X is a convex set of N-vectors, $f: X \to (-\infty, \infty)$ is concave, and, for $k = 1, \ldots, K$, $g_k: X \to (-\infty, \infty)$ is convex and $\overline{a}_k$ is a number.

An economic example of such a problem is utility maximization over a budget set, namely,

$$\max_{\mathbf{x} \in \mathbb{R}^N_+} u(\mathbf{x})$$
$$\text{s.t.} \quad p.\mathbf{x} \le w,$$

where u is a concave function. Many applications involve the allocation of resources among productive activities. In these applications, the quantity, x_n, is the level at which the nth activity operates, $f(\mathbf{x}) = f(x_1, \ldots, x_N)$ is either output or profit from the operation of the activities, $g_k(\mathbf{x}) = g_k(x_1, \ldots, x_N)$ is the amount of the kth resource absorbed when the activities operate at levels $x_1, \ldots, x_N$, and $\overline{a}_k$ is the amount of the kth resource available. In discussions of the Kuhn-Tucker theorem, the constraint $g_k(\mathbf{x}) \le \overline{a}_k$ is often referred to as the kth resource constraint, the quantity $\overline{a}_k$ is referred to as the amount of the kth resource, and the K-vector $\overline{\mathbf{a}}$ is called the resource vector.

The statement of the theorem uses the concept of feasibility.

DEFINITION 6.2 An N-vector x is said to be *feasible* for problem 6.1 if $\mathbf{x}$ belongs to X and $\mathbf{x}$ satisfies the inequalities

$$g_k(\mathbf{x}) \le \overline{a}_k,$$

for $k = 1, \ldots, K$.

THE KUHN-TUCKER THEOREM 6.3[1] Assume that X is a convex set of N-vectors, $f: X \to (-\infty, \infty)$ is concave, and, for $k = 1, \ldots, K$, $g_k: X \to (-\infty, \infty)$ is convex. Suppose that $\overline{\mathbf{x}}$ is feasible for problem 6.1 and that there exist nonnegative numbers $\lambda_1, \ldots, \lambda_K$ such that

1. See Kuhn and Tucker (1951).

1. for all k, $\lambda_k = 0$, if $g_k(\overline{\mathbf{x}}) < \overline{a}_k$
2. $\overline{\mathbf{x}}$ solves the maximization problem

$$\max_{\mathbf{x} \in X} \left[f(\mathbf{x}) - \sum_{k=1}^{K} \lambda_k g_k(\mathbf{x}) \right]$$

Then, $\overline{\mathbf{x}}$ solves problem 6.1.

Suppose that $\overline{\mathbf{x}}$ solves problem 6.1 and that the following *constraint qualification* is satisfied:

3. There exists a vector $\underline{\mathbf{x}} \in X$ such that $g_k(\underline{\mathbf{x}}) < \overline{a}_k$, for all k.

Then, there exist nonnegative numbers, $\lambda_1, \ldots, \lambda_K$, such that conditions (1) and (2) above apply.

The conditions in (1) in the Kuhn-Tucker theorem are known as the *complementary slackness conditions.* The function

$$\mathcal{L}(\mathbf{x}, \lambda) = f(\mathbf{x}) - \sum_{k=1}^{K} \lambda_k g_k(\mathbf{x})$$

is known as the *Lagrangian,* and the numbers λ_k are called *Kuhn-Tucker coefficients.* They are analogous to Lagrange multipliers. The Lagrangian is concave because f is concave, the λ_k are nonnegative, and the functions g_k are convex. Notice that the only constraint in the problem

$$\max_{\mathbf{x} \in X} \left[f(\mathbf{x}) - \sum_{k=1}^{K} \lambda_k g_k(\mathbf{x}) \right]$$

is that $\mathbf{x}$ belongs to X. The Kuhn-Tucker theorem reduces a constrained maximization problem to one that is nearly unconstrained or completely unconstrained if $X = \mathbb{R}^N$.

The following is a counterexample to the existence of Kuhn-Tucker coefficients when the constraint qualification is not satisfied.

EXAMPLE 6.4 Consider the problem

$$\max_{\mathbf{x} \in \mathbb{R}^2} x_2$$

$$\text{s.t.} \quad -x_1 + x_2^2 \leq 0$$

$$x_1 + x_2^2 \leq 0.$$

This example does not satisfy the constraint qualification, because $\mathbf{x} = \mathbf{0}$ is the only feasible vector. Because $\mathbf{0}$ is the only feasible point, it is also the optimum. There are no nonnegative numbers λ_1 and λ_2 such that $\mathbf{x} = \mathbf{0}$ and λ_1, and λ_2 satisfy condition (2) of theorem 6.3, for suppose there were. Then, $\mathbf{x} = \mathbf{0}$ would solve the problem

$$\max_{\mathbf{x} \in \mathbb{R}^2} \left[x_2 - \lambda_1(-x_1 + x_2^2) - \lambda_2(x_1 + x_2^2)\right],$$

and the derivative of the objective function of this problem would be zero at $\mathbf{x} = \mathbf{0}$. Setting the partial derivative with respect to x_2 equal to zero at $x_2 = 0$, we find that $1 - 2(\lambda_1 + \lambda_2)0 = 0$, which is impossible.

Figure 6.1 should make clear why the Kuhn-Tucker theorem does not apply to this example. In labeling this figure, I let $f(\mathbf{x}) = x_2$, $g_1(\mathbf{x}) = -x_1 + x_2^2$, and $g_2(\mathbf{x}) = x_1 + x_2^2$. The region where $-x_1 + x_2^2 \leq 0$ is labeled as $g_1(\mathbf{x}) \leq 0$, and the region where $x_1 + x_2^2 \leq 0$ is labeled as $g_2(\mathbf{x}) \leq 0$. The Lagrangian is $f(\mathbf{x}) - \lambda_1 g_1(\mathbf{x}) - \lambda_s g_2(\mathbf{x})$. If condition (2) is satisfied, then the derivative of the Lagrangian is 0 at $\mathbf{x} = \mathbf{0}$. That is, $Df(\mathbf{0}) =$

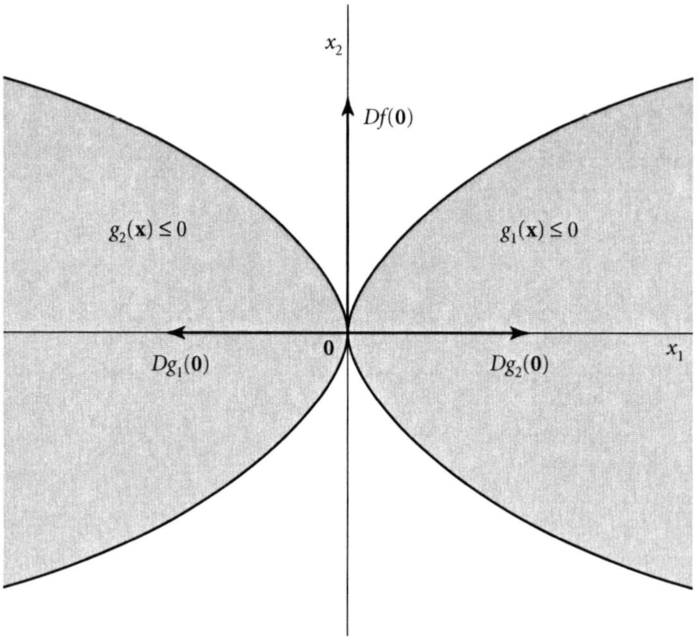

Figure 6.1 A constraint set that does not satisfy the constraint qualification

$\lambda_1 Dg_1(\mathbf{0}) + \lambda_2 Dg_2(\mathbf{0})$. The derivative $Df(\mathbf{0})$ points straight upward, and $Dg_1(\mathbf{0})$ and $Dg_2(\mathbf{0})$ are horizontal. Since a vertical vector cannot be a linear combination of horizontal vectors, condition (2) cannot be satisfied.

The situation changes when example 6.4 is modified so as to satisfy the constraint qualification, as in the next example.

EXAMPLE 6.5 Consider the problem

$$\max_{\mathbf{x} \in \mathbb{R}^2} x_2$$

$$\text{s.t.} \quad -x_1 + x_2^2 \leq 1$$

$$x_1 + x_2^2 \leq 1.$$

The solution to this problem is $\mathbf{x} = (0, 1)$. If $\lambda_1 = \lambda_2 = \frac{1}{4}$, the solution $\mathbf{x} = (0, 1)$ maximizes the Lagrangian $x_2 - \frac{1}{4}(-x_1 + x_2^2) - \frac{1}{4}(x_1 + x_2^2)$, and so the problem satisfies condition (2) of theorem 6.3. The derivative of the Lagrangian is 0 at (0, 1), because $Df(1, 0) = (0, 1) = \frac{1}{4}(-1, 2) + \frac{1}{4}(1, 2) = \frac{1}{4}Dg_1(0, 1) + \frac{1}{4}Dg_2(0, 1)$.

The constraints are pictured in figure 6.2. The figure shows vectors pointing in the direction of the derivatives $Dg_1(0, 1)$ and $Dg_2(0, 1)$ of the constraint functions at the optimum point (0, 1) as well as a vertical vector corresponding to the derivative of the objective function, $Df(0, 1)$. The derivatives $Dg_1(0, 1)$ and $Dg_2(0, 1)$ are orthogonal at (0, 1) to the boundaries of the corresponding constraint sets, $\{\mathbf{x} \mid g_1(\mathbf{x}) \leq 1\}$ and $\{\mathbf{x} \mid g_2(\mathbf{x}) \leq 1\}$. Clearly, $Df(0, 1)$ may be written as a linear combination of $Dg_1(0, 1)$ and $Dg_2(0, 1)$ with positive coefficients, as is required by condition (2) of theorem 6.3.

The next example illustrates another reason for assuming the constraint qualification.

EXAMPLE 6.6 Consider the problem

$$\max_{x \in [0, \infty)} \sqrt{x}$$

$$\text{s.t.} \quad x \leq 0.$$

This example clearly does not satisfy the constraint qualification, because 0 is the only feasible point. As the unique feasible point, 0 is necessarily optimal. However, 0 does not satisfy condition (2) of theorem 6.3, for suppose there were a positive number λ such that $x = 0$ maximized the Lagrangian $\sqrt{x} - \lambda x$ among all nonnegative numbers. Then, the derivative

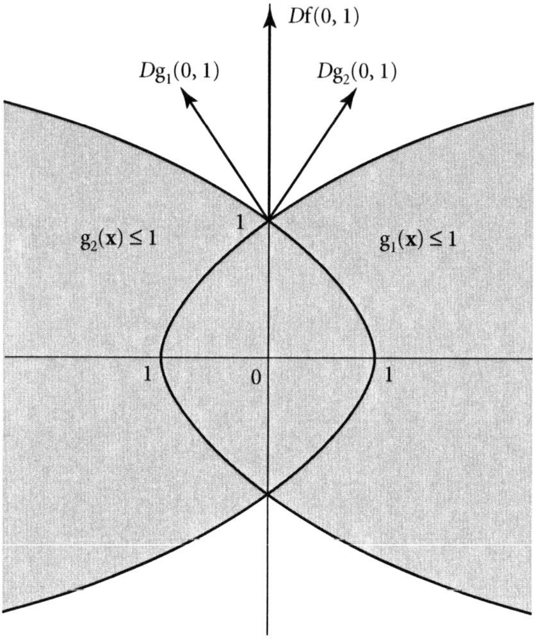

Figure 6.2 A constraint set that does satisfy the constraint qualification

of the Lagrangian at $x = 0$ should be no more than 0, but this derivative equals $\frac{1}{2\sqrt{x}}\,|_{x=0} - \lambda$, which is infinity for any value of λ. This contradiction proves that the example does not satisfy condition (2). The difficulty is that the objective function has infinite slope at the optimum point.

6.2 Kuhn-Tucker Coefficients

Perhaps the most interesting aspect of the Kuhn-Tucker theorem is the interpretation of the coefficients. Each Kuhn-Tucker coefficient, λ_k, equals the rate at which the maximum value of problem 6.1 increases as the amount of the kth resource, $\overline{a}_k$, increases. To make sense of this statement, I need the notion of a value function.

DEFINITION 6.7 The *value function* $V: A \to \mathbb{R}$ is defined by the equation

$$V(a_1, \ldots, a_k) = \sup_{\mathbf{x} \in X} f(\mathbf{x})$$

$$\text{s.t.} \quad g_k(\mathbf{x}) \leq a_k, \quad \text{for } k = 1, \ldots, K,$$

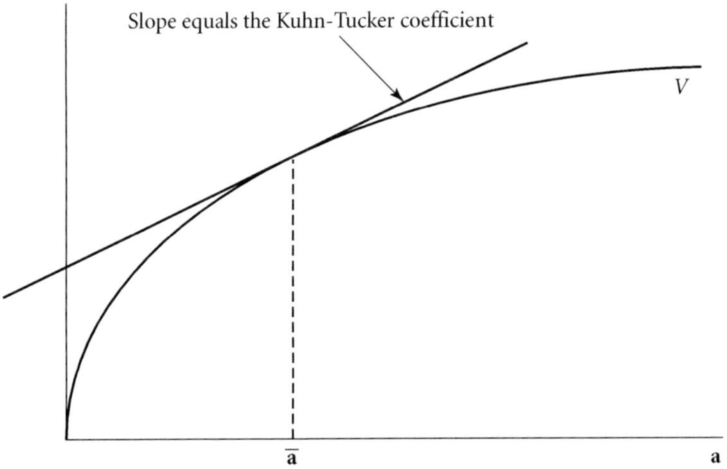

Figure 6.3 The Kuhn-Tucker coefficient is the slope of the value function.

where the domain of V is $A = \{\mathbf{a} \in \mathbb{R}^K \mid \text{for some } \mathbf{x} \in X, g_k(\mathbf{x}) \leq a_k, \text{ for } k = 1, \ldots, K\}$.

If the value function is differentiable, then the Kuhn-Tucker coefficient λ_k is the slope of the value function V with respect to a_k,

$$\frac{\partial V(\overline{\mathbf{a}})}{\partial a_k} = \lambda_k,$$

and we may visualize the relation between the value function and the Kuhn-Tucker coefficient as in figure 6.3. If the value function is not differentiable, then the Kuhn-Tucker coefficient is the slope of a line tangent to the graph of the value function. Figure 6.4 illustrates the case where V has no slope at $\overline{\mathbf{a}}$. The slope of a tangent line as in figure 6.4 is termed a *subgradient* of V.

DEFINITION 6.8 If $V\colon A \to \mathbb{R}$, where A is a subset of $\mathbb{R}^K$, then the vector $\boldsymbol{\lambda} = (\lambda_1, \ldots, \lambda_K)$ is a *subgradient* of V at $\overline{\mathbf{a}}$ in A if

$$V(\mathbf{a}) \leq V(\overline{\mathbf{a}}) + \sum_{k=1}^{K} \lambda_k (a_k - \overline{a}_k), \tag{6.2}$$

for all $\mathbf{a}$ in A.

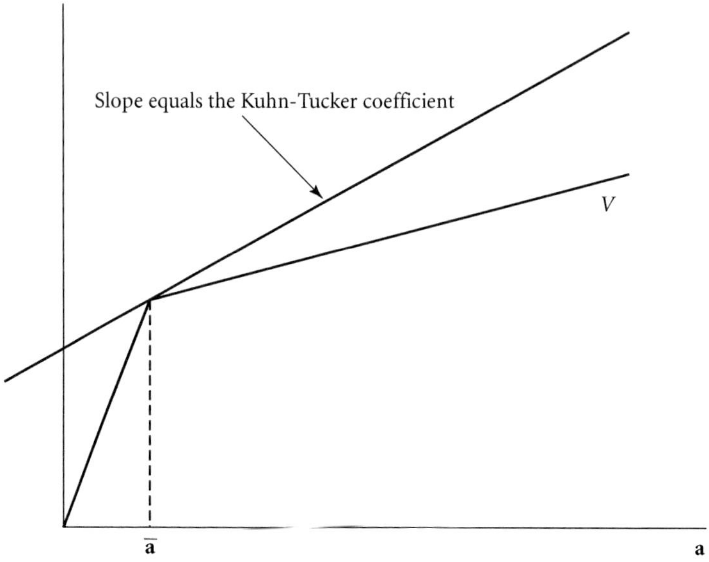

Figure 6.4 The Kuhn-Tucker coefficient is the slope of a line tangent to the value function.

There may be many subgradients of V at a point $\bar{\mathbf{a}}$, as there are in figure 6.4. If V is differentiable, however, the subgradient is unique and equals the derivative, as is easy to check.

The next proposition is the assertion, roughly speaking, that the vector $\boldsymbol{\lambda} = (\lambda_1, \ldots, \lambda_K)$ is a vector of Kuhn-Tucker coefficients if and only if it is a subgradient of the value function.

PROPOSITION 6.9 Suppose that $\bar{\mathbf{x}}$ solves problem 6.1, for all k. Then, $\bar{\mathbf{x}}$ and $\boldsymbol{\lambda} = (\lambda_1, \ldots, \lambda_K)$ satisfy conditions (1) and (2) of the Kuhn-Tucker theorem 6.3 and $\boldsymbol{\lambda} \geq 0$, if and only if $\boldsymbol{\lambda}$ is a subgradient of the value function V at $\bar{\mathbf{a}}$.

Proof. Suppose that $\bar{\mathbf{x}}$ and $\boldsymbol{\lambda} = (\lambda_1, \ldots, \lambda_K)$ satisfy conditions (1) and (2) of the Kuhn-Tucker theorem and that $\boldsymbol{\lambda} \geq 0$. To show that $\boldsymbol{\lambda}$ is a subgradient of V at $\bar{\mathbf{a}}$, I must show that inequality 6.2 holds for any K-vector $\mathbf{a}$ in A. This inequality may be rewritten as

$$V(\bar{\mathbf{a}}) - \sum_{k=1}^{K} \lambda_k \bar{a}_k \geq V(\mathbf{a}) - \sum_{k=1}^{K} \lambda_k a_k. \tag{6.3}$$

Let **a** be an arbitrary vector in A. Because **a** belongs to A, there exists a vector **x** in X such that $g_k(\mathbf{x}) \le a_k$, for all k. Because $\overline{\mathbf{x}}$ solves problem 6.1 with resource vector $\overline{\mathbf{a}}$,

$$V(\overline{\mathbf{a}}) = f(\overline{\mathbf{x}}). \tag{6.4}$$

I show that $\lambda_k g_k(\overline{\mathbf{x}}) = \lambda_k \overline{a}_k$, for all k. Because $\overline{\mathbf{x}}$ is feasible, $g_k(\overline{\mathbf{x}}) \le \overline{a}_k$, for all k. Furthermore, if k is such that $g_k(\overline{\mathbf{x}}) < \overline{a}_k$, then $\lambda_k = 0$ by the complementary slackness condition (1) of theorem 6.3 and hence $\lambda_k g_k(\overline{\mathbf{x}}) = 0 = \lambda_k \overline{a}_k$. Therefore, for all k, $\lambda_k g_k(\overline{\mathbf{x}}) = \lambda_k \overline{a}_k$, whether $g_k(\overline{\mathbf{x}}) = \overline{a}_k$ or $g_i(\overline{\mathbf{x}}) < \overline{a}_k$, as was to be shown. Hence,

$$\sum_{k=1}^{K} \lambda_k g_k(\overline{\mathbf{x}}) = \sum_{k=1}^{K} \lambda_k \overline{a}_k. \tag{6.5}$$

It now follows that

$$\begin{aligned} V(\overline{\mathbf{a}}) - \sum_{k=1}^{K} \lambda_k \overline{a}_k = f(\overline{\mathbf{x}}) - \sum_{k=1}^{K} \lambda_k g_k(\overline{\mathbf{x}}) \ge f(\mathbf{x}) \\ - \sum_{k=1}^{K} \lambda_k g_k(\mathbf{x}) \ge f(\mathbf{x}) - \sum_{k=1}^{K} \lambda_k a_k. \end{aligned} \tag{6.6}$$

The equation in 6.6 follows from equations 6.4 and 6.5. The first inequality of 6.6 follows from condition (2) of theorem 6.3. The second inequality holds because the numbers λ_k are nonnegative and $g_k(\mathbf{x}) \le a_k$, for all k.

By definition, $V(\mathbf{a})$ is the supremum of all the numbers $f(\mathbf{x})$, for vectors **x** in X satisfying $g_k(\mathbf{x}) \le a_k$, for all k. Therefore, inequality 6.6 implies inequality 6.3. This completes the proof that $\boldsymbol{\lambda} = (\lambda_1, \ldots, \lambda_k)$ is a subgradient of V at $\overline{\mathbf{a}}$.

I now prove the converse, that if $\boldsymbol{\lambda} = (\lambda_1, \ldots, \lambda_k)$ is a subgradient of V at $\overline{\mathbf{a}}$, then $\boldsymbol{\lambda}$ and $\overline{\mathbf{x}}$ satisfy conditions (1) and (2) of theorem 6.3 and $\boldsymbol{\lambda} \ge 0$. To prove that $\boldsymbol{\lambda} \ge 0$, it is sufficient to show that V is nondecreasing. A vector **x** that is feasible for problem 6.1 remains feasible if we increase any of the components of the K-vector **a** so that $V(\mathbf{a})$, which is the supremum of $f(\mathbf{x})$ over all feasible vectors **x**, cannot decrease when components of **a** increase. Therefore, $V(\mathbf{a})$ is nowhere decreasing with respect to **a**.

I next demonstrate the complementary slackness property, condition (1) of theorem 6.3. Suppose that $g_k(\overline{\mathbf{x}}) < \overline{a}_k$, for some k. Without loss of generality, we may assume that $k = 1$. Let the positive number ε be so small that $g_1(\overline{\mathbf{x}}) < \overline{a}_1 - \varepsilon$, and let $\mathbf{a} = (\overline{a}_1 - \varepsilon, \overline{a}_2, \ldots, \overline{a}_k)$. Because $\mathbf{a} < \overline{\mathbf{a}}$, it follows that $V(\mathbf{a}) \le V(\overline{\mathbf{a}})$. However, the vector $\overline{\mathbf{x}}$ is feasible with resource vector **a**, so that $V(\mathbf{a}) \geq f(\overline{\mathbf{x}}) = V(\overline{\mathbf{a}})$. It follows from the two preceding inequalities that $V(\mathbf{a}) = V(\overline{\mathbf{a}})$. Because $\boldsymbol{\lambda}$ is a subgradient of V at $\overline{\mathbf{a}}$, it follows that

$$V(\mathbf{a}) \leq V(\overline{\mathbf{a}}) + \sum_{k=1}^{K} \lambda_k (a_k - \overline{a}_k) = V(\overline{\mathbf{a}}) - \lambda_1 \varepsilon. \tag{6.7}$$

Since $V(\mathbf{a}) = V(\overline{\mathbf{a}})$ and $\varepsilon > 0$ and $\lambda_1 \geq 0$, inequality 6.7 is valid only if $\lambda_1 = 0$. This completes the proof of the complementary slackness condition (1).

It remains to verify condition (2), which is the statement that

$$f(\overline{\mathbf{x}}) - \sum_{k=1}^{K} \lambda_k g_k(\overline{\mathbf{x}}) \geq f(\mathbf{x}) - \sum_{k=1}^{K} \lambda_k g_k(\mathbf{x}), \tag{6.8}$$

for any $\mathbf{x}$ in X. Fix $\mathbf{x}$ in X and let the K-vector **a** be defined by the equations $a_k = g_k(\mathbf{x})$, for all k. We know that $f(\overline{\mathbf{x}}) = V(\overline{\mathbf{a}})$. By an argument made earlier, the complementary slackness condition implies that $\sum_{k=1}^{K} \lambda_k g_k(\overline{\mathbf{x}}) = \sum_{k=1}^{K} \lambda_k \overline{a}_k$. Therefore,

$$f(\overline{\mathbf{x}}) - \sum_{k=1}^{K} \lambda_k g_k(\overline{\mathbf{x}}) = V(\overline{\mathbf{a}}) - \sum_{k=1}^{K} \lambda_k \overline{a}_k. \tag{6.9}$$

We also know that

$$V(\overline{\mathbf{a}}) - \sum_{k=1}^{K} \lambda_k \overline{a}_k \geq V(\mathbf{a}) - \sum_{k=1}^{K} \lambda_k a_k, \tag{6.10}$$

because $\boldsymbol{\lambda}$ is a subgradient of V at $\overline{\mathbf{a}}$. Since $V(\mathbf{a})$ is the supremum of numbers $f(\mathbf{z})$, for vectors $\mathbf{z}$ that are feasible at the K-vector **a**, we know that $V(\mathbf{a}) \geq f(\mathbf{x})$. Because $a_k = g_k(\mathbf{x})$, for all k, it follows that

$$V(\mathbf{a}) - \sum_{k=1}^{K} \lambda_k a_k \geq f(\mathbf{x}) - \sum_{k=1}^{K} \lambda_k g_k(\mathbf{x}). \tag{6.11}$$

Inequalities 6.9, 6.10, and 6.11 together imply inequality 6.8. This completes the proof that condition (2) is satisfied when λ is a subgradient of V at $\overline{\mathbf{a}}$. ■

In figures 6.3 and 6.4, the value function is drawn as concave. The next proposition says that this representation is correct.

PROPOSITION 6.10 The value function $V: A \to \mathbb{R}$ for problem 6.1 is concave, and the set A is convex.

Proof. Let $\underline{\mathbf{a}} = (\underline{a}_1, \ldots, \underline{a}_K)$ and $\overline{\mathbf{a}} = (\overline{a}_1, \ldots, \overline{a}_K)$ belong to A, and let α be such that $0 \leq \alpha \leq 1$. Let ε be a small positive number. By the definitions of A and V, there exist $\underline{\mathbf{x}}$ and $\overline{\mathbf{x}}$ in X such that $g_k(\underline{\mathbf{x}}) \leq \underline{\mathbf{a}}_k$ and $g_k(\overline{\mathbf{a}}) \leq \overline{\mathbf{a}}_k$, for all k, $f(\underline{\mathbf{x}}) > V(\underline{\mathbf{a}}) - \varepsilon$, and $f(\overline{\mathbf{x}}) > V(\overline{\mathbf{a}}) - \varepsilon$. Since X is convex, $\alpha\underline{\mathbf{x}} + (1 - \alpha)\overline{\mathbf{x}}$ belongs to X. The constraints with resource vector $\alpha\underline{\mathbf{a}} + (1 - \alpha)\overline{\mathbf{a}}$ are satisfied by the vector $\alpha\underline{\mathbf{x}} + (1 - \alpha)\overline{\mathbf{x}}$, since the convexity of the functions g_k implies that

$$g_k(\alpha\underline{\mathbf{x}} + (1 - \alpha)\overline{\mathbf{x}}) \leq \alpha g_k(\underline{\mathbf{x}}) + (1 - \alpha) g_k(\overline{\mathbf{x}}) \leq \alpha\underline{\mathbf{a}}_k + (1 - \alpha)\overline{a}_k,$$

for all k. Therefore, $\alpha\underline{\mathbf{a}} + (1 - \alpha)\overline{\mathbf{a}}$ belongs to A, and so A is convex.

Finally,

$$\begin{aligned} V(\alpha\underline{\mathbf{a}} + (1 - \alpha)\overline{\mathbf{a}}) &\geq f(\alpha\underline{\mathbf{x}} + (1 - \alpha)\overline{\mathbf{x}}) \\ &\geq \alpha f(\underline{\mathbf{x}}) + (1 - \alpha) f(\overline{\mathbf{x}}) > \alpha V(\underline{\mathbf{a}}) + (1 - \alpha) V(\overline{\mathbf{a}}) - \varepsilon, \end{aligned}$$

where the second inequality follows from the concavity of f. Since ε is arbitrarily small,

$$V(\alpha\underline{\mathbf{a}} + (1 - \alpha)\overline{\mathbf{a}}) \geq \alpha V(\underline{\mathbf{a}}) + (1 - \alpha) V(\overline{\mathbf{a}}),$$

as was to be proved. ▪

6.3 The Kuhn-Tucker Interpretation of Competitive Equilibrium

I now use the Kuhn-Tucker theorem to relate equilibrium to welfare maximization. I will use the following assumptions about the economy $\mathcal{E} = ((u_i, \mathbf{e}_i)_{i=1}^I, (Y_j)_{j=1}^J, (\Theta_{ij})_{i=1}^I{}_{j=1}^J)$.

ASSUMPTION 6.11 For all i, u_i is concave and strictly increasing.

ASSUMPTION 6.12 For all j, Y_j is closed, convex, and contains the vector $\mathbf{0}$.

ASSUMPTION 6.13 $\mathcal{E}$ is productive.

Productiveness is defined in definition 3.47 (section 3.6). (An economy $\mathcal{E}$ is *productive* if it has a feasible allocation $(\mathbf{x}, \mathbf{y})$ such that $\sum_{i=1}^I \mathbf{x}_i \gg \mathbf{0}$.)

The next proposition is an application of the Kuhn-Tucker theorem to the consumer's maximization problem.

PROPOSITION 6.14 Suppose that u satisfies assumption 6.11. If $w \geq 0$, $\mathbf{p} \in \mathbb{R}^N$, and $\mathbf{p} \gg \mathbf{0}$, then the N-vector $\overline{\mathbf{x}}$ solves the problem

$$\begin{aligned} &\max_{\mathbf{x} \in \mathbb{R}^N_+} u(\mathbf{x}) \\ &\text{s.t.} \quad \mathbf{p}.\mathbf{x} \leq w, \end{aligned} \tag{6.12}$$

if there exists a nonnegative number λ, such that $\lambda = 0$, if $\mathbf{p}.\overline{\mathbf{x}} < w$, and such that $\overline{\mathbf{x}}$ solves the problem

$$\max_{\mathbf{x} \in \mathbb{R}^N_+} [u(\mathbf{x}) - \lambda \mathbf{p}.\mathbf{x}]. \tag{6.13}$$

If $w > 0$ and if $\overline{\mathbf{x}}$ solves problem 6.12, then $\mathbf{p}.\overline{\mathbf{x}} = w$ and there exists a positive number λ, such that $\mathbf{x}$ solves problem 6.13.

The Kuhn-Tucker coefficient, λ, appearing in proposition 6.14 is the rate at which the consumer's maximized utility increases as the income or wealth, w, increases. For this reason, λ is called the *consumer's marginal utility of wealth* or sometimes the *marginal utility of unit of account or of money,* even when there is no money in the model. The units of λ are utiles per unit of account, where a *utile* is a unit of utility.

Proof of Proposition 6.14. The first assertion of the proposition follows directly from the sufficiency part of the Kuhn-Tucker theorem. If $w > 0$, problem 6.12 satisfies the constraint qualification and the Kuhn-Tucker theorem implies the second assertion of the proposition. I demonstrate that $p.\overline{\mathbf{x}} = w$ and $\lambda > 0$. It is enough to show that $\lambda > 0$, for by the Kuhn-Tucker theorem, $\lambda = 0$, if $p.\overline{\mathbf{x}} < w$. The Kuhn-Tucker theorem implies that $\lambda \geq 0$. If $\lambda = 0$, then problem 6.13 has no solution, since u is strictly increasing. Therefore λ must be positive. ▪

I now apply the Kuhn-Tucker theorem to the welfare-maximization problem

$$\max_{\substack{(x,\, y) \text{ is a feasible} \\ \text{allocation}}} \sum_{i=1}^{I} a_i u_i(x_i), \tag{6.14}$$

where $a_i > 0$, for all i.

THEOREM 6.15 Suppose that the economy $\mathcal{E}$ satisfies assumptions 6.11 and 6.12. If $(\overline{\mathbf{x}}, \overline{\mathbf{y}}, \mathbf{p}, \boldsymbol{\tau})$ is an equilibrium with transfer payments such that $\mathbf{p}.\overline{\mathbf{x}}_i > 0$, for all i, then $(\overline{\mathbf{x}}, \overline{\mathbf{y}})$ solves problem 6.14, where, for all i, a_i^{-1} is consumer i's marginal utility of wealth in the equilibrium.

Suppose that in addition $\mathcal{E}$ satisfies assumption 6.13. If $(\overline{\mathbf{x}}, \overline{\mathbf{y}})$ solves problem 6.14, then there exist a price vector $\mathbf{p}$ and a vector $\boldsymbol{\tau} = (\tau_1, \ldots, \tau_I)$ such that $(\overline{\mathbf{x}}, \overline{\mathbf{y}}, \mathbf{p}, \boldsymbol{\tau})$ is an equilibrium with transfer payments. In this equilibrium, a_i^{-1} is consumer i's marginal utility of wealth, for all i.

Proof. First of all, problem 6.14 may be rewritten as

$$\begin{aligned} &\max_{\mathbf{x}_i \in \mathbb{R}_+^N, \mathbf{y}_j \in Y_j, \text{ for all } i, j} \sum_{i=1}^{I} a_i u_i(\mathbf{x}_i) \\ &\text{s.t.} \quad \sum_{i=1}^{I} x_{in} - \sum_{j=1}^{J} y_{jn} \le \sum_{i=1}^{I} e_{in}, \quad \text{for } n = 1, 2, \ldots, N, \end{aligned} \tag{6.15}$$

where $a_i > 0$, for all i.

Suppose that $(\overline{\mathbf{x}}, \overline{\mathbf{y}}, \mathbf{p}, \boldsymbol{\tau})$ is an equilibrium with transfer payments and that $\mathbf{p}.\overline{\mathbf{x}}_i > 0$, for all i. By the definition of equilibrium, for each i, $\overline{\mathbf{x}}_i$ solves the problem

$$\max_{\mathbf{x} \in \mathbb{R}_+^N} u_i(\mathbf{x})$$
$$\text{s.t.} \quad \mathbf{p}.\mathbf{x} \le w_i(\mathbf{p}) - \tau_i,$$

where $w_i(\mathbf{p}) = \mathbf{p}.\mathbf{e}_i + \sum_{j=1}^{J} \Theta_{ij}\mathbf{p}.\overline{\mathbf{y}}_j$. Therefore, $\mathbf{p}.\mathbf{e}_i + \sum_{j=1}^{J} \Theta_{ij}\mathbf{p}.\overline{\mathbf{y}}_j \ge \mathbf{p}.\overline{\mathbf{x}}_i > 0$, for all i. By proposition 6.14, for each i, there exists a positive number λ_i such that $\overline{\mathbf{x}}_i$ solves the problem

$$\max_{\mathbf{x} \in \mathbb{R}_+^N} [u_i(\mathbf{x}) - \lambda_i \mathbf{p}.\mathbf{x}].$$

Since $\lambda_i > 0$, we may let $a_i = \lambda_i^{-1}$ and write this problem as

$$\max_{\mathbf{x} \in \mathbb{R}_+^N} [u_i(\mathbf{x}) - a_i^{-1}\mathbf{p}.\mathbf{x}].$$

Therefore, $\overline{\mathbf{x}}_i$ solves the problem

$$\max_{\mathbf{x} \in \mathbb{R}_+^N} [a_i u_i(\mathbf{x}) - \mathbf{p}.\mathbf{x}].$$

By the definition of equilibrium, for all j, $\overline{\mathbf{y}}_j$ solves the problem

$$\max_{\mathbf{y}\in Y_j} \mathbf{p}.\mathbf{y}.$$

The previous two statements imply that $(\overline{\mathbf{x}}, \overline{\mathbf{y}})$ solves the problem

$$\max_{\substack{\mathbf{x}_i\in \mathbb{R}^N_+,\text{ for all } i\\ \mathbf{y}_i\in Y_j,\text{ for all } j}} \left[\sum_{i=1}^{I} a_i u_i(\mathbf{x}_i) - \mathbf{p}.\left(\sum_{i=1}^{I} \mathbf{x}_i - \sum_{j=1}^{J} \mathbf{y}_j\right)\right].$$

That is, the allocation $(\overline{\mathbf{x}}, \overline{\mathbf{y}})$ maximizes the Lagrangian corresponding to problem 6.15. One of the conditions of competitive equilibrium is that, for each n, $p_n = 0$, if $\sum_{i=1}^{I} \overline{x}_{\text{in}} - \sum_{j=1}^{J} \overline{y}_{jn} < \sum_{i=1}^{I} e_{\text{in}}$. Therefore, the numbers $\overline{x}_{\text{in}}$, $\overline{y}_{jn}$, and p_n satisfy the complementary slackness conditions for problem 6.15. Hence the Kuhn-Tucker theorem implies that the allocation $(\overline{\mathbf{x}}, \overline{\mathbf{y}})$ solves that problem, which is the same as problem 6.14.

I now prove the second part of the theorem. I show that problem 6.15 satisfies the constraint qualification. Because $\mathcal{E}$ is productive, there exists a feasible allocation, $(\mathbf{x}, \mathbf{y})$, such that $\sum_{i=1}^{I} \mathbf{x}_i \gg \mathbf{0}$. The allocation $(\frac{\mathbf{x}}{2}, \mathbf{y})$ is not only feasible but satisfies the strict inequalities $\sum_{i=1}^{I} \frac{x_{\text{in}}}{2} - \sum_{j=1}^{J} y_{jn} < \sum_{i=1}^{I} e_{\text{in}}$, for all n. Hence, problem 6.15 satisfies the constraint qualification.

Suppose that $(\overline{\mathbf{x}}, \overline{\mathbf{y}})$ solves problem 6.15. Because problem 6.15 satisfies the constraint qualification, the Kuhn-Tucker theorem applies, with the convex set X equal to $\left(\sum_{i=1}^{I} \mathbb{R}^N_+\right) \times \left(\sum_{j=1}^{J} Y_j\right)$. Therefore, there exist nonnegative numbers p_n, for $n = 1, \ldots, N$, such that, for all n, $p_n = 0$, if $\sum_{i=1}^{I} \overline{x}_{\text{in}} + \sum_{j=1}^{J} \overline{y}_{jn} < \sum_{i=1}^{I} e_{\text{in}}$ and $(\overline{\mathbf{x}}, \overline{\mathbf{y}})$ solves the problem

$$\max_{\substack{\mathbf{x}_i\in \mathbb{R}^N_+,\text{ for all } i\\ \mathbf{y}_i\in Y_j,\text{ for all } j}} \left[\sum_{i=1}^{I} a_i u_i(\mathbf{x}_i) - \mathbf{p}.\left(\sum_{i=1}^{I} \mathbf{x}_i - \sum_{j=1}^{J} \mathbf{y}_j\right)\right]. \tag{6.16}$$

By focusing on where $\mathbf{x}_i$ appears in problem 6.16, we see that, for each i, $\overline{\mathbf{x}}_i$ solves the problem $\max_{\mathbf{x}\in\mathbb{R}^N_+}[a_i u_i(\mathbf{x}) - \mathbf{p}.\mathbf{x}]$, which may be written as $\max_{\mathbf{x}\in\mathbb{R}^N_+}[u_i(\mathbf{x}) - a_i^{-1}\mathbf{p}.\mathbf{x}]$, since $a_i > 0$. Let $\tau_i = \mathbf{p}.(\mathbf{e}_i - \overline{\mathbf{x}}_i) + \sum_{j=1}^{J} \Theta_{ij}$ $\mathbf{p}.\overline{\mathbf{y}}_j$, so that $\mathbf{p}.\overline{\mathbf{x}}_i = \mathbf{p}.\mathbf{e}_i + \sum_{j=1}^{J} \Theta_{ij}\mathbf{p}.\overline{\mathbf{y}}_j - \tau_i$. Proposition 6.14 implies that $\overline{\mathbf{x}}_i$ solves the problem

$$\max_{\mathbf{x}\in\mathbb{R}^N_+} u_i(\mathbf{x})$$
$$\text{s.t.} \quad \mathbf{p}.\mathbf{x} \le \mathbf{p}.\mathbf{e}_i + \sum_{j=1}^{J} \Theta_{ij}\mathbf{p}.\overline{\mathbf{y}}_j - \tau_i, \tag{6.17}$$

which is consumer i's maximization problem in an equilibrium with transfer payments $\boldsymbol{\tau} = (\tau_1, \ldots, \tau_I)$. The number a_i^{-1} is consumer i's marginal utility of wealth in problem 6.17.

By focusing on the way $\mathbf{y}_u$ appears in problem 6.16, we see that, for each j, $\overline{\mathbf{y}}_j$ solves the profit maximization problem

$$\max_{\mathbf{y}\in Y_j} \mathbf{p}.\mathbf{y} \tag{6.18}$$

that appears in the definition of an equilibrium with transfer payments.

The allocation $(\overline{\mathbf{x}}, \overline{\mathbf{y}})$ is feasible because it solves problem 6.15 and so satisfies its constraints. We know by the Kuhn-Tucker theorem that, for all n, $p_n = 0$, if $\sum_{i=1}^{I} \overline{x}_{in} - \sum_{j=1}^{J} \overline{y}_{jn} < \sum_{i=1}^{I} e_{in}$. Therefore, $(\overline{\mathbf{x}}, \overline{\mathbf{y}}, \mathbf{p}, \boldsymbol{\tau})$ satisfies all the conditions for an equilibrium with transfer payments. This completes the proof of the first two assertions of the theorem. ▪

If $(\overline{\mathbf{x}}, \overline{\mathbf{y}}, \mathbf{p}, \boldsymbol{\tau})$ is an equilibrium with transfer payments such that $(\overline{\mathbf{x}}, \overline{\mathbf{y}})$ solves problem 6.14, then we may write the objective function of that problem as $\sum_{i=1}^{I} \lambda_i^{-1} u_i(\mathbf{x}_i)$, where λ_i is consumer i's marginal utility of wealth in the equilibrium $(\overline{\mathbf{x}}, \overline{\mathbf{y}}, \mathbf{p}, \boldsymbol{\tau})$. Since the units of λ_i are consumer i utiles per unit of account, the units of $\lambda_i^{-1} u_i(\mathbf{x}_i)$ and hence of $\sum_{i=1}^{I} \lambda_i^{-1} u_i(\mathbf{x}_i)$ are the unit of account; welfare is measured in units of account. According to the interpretation of the Kuhn-Tucker coefficients described in section 6.2, the prices p_n are the rate at which welfare increases as the endowment of commodity n, $\sum_{i=1}^{I} e_{in}$, increases. This interpretation is consistent with the units; the units of welfare are the same as the units of account, so that the units of p_n as a Kuhn-Tucker coefficient are units of account per unit of commodity n, which are also the units of p_n interpreted as a price.

An economic interpretation of the condition of equilibrium that $p_n = 0$ when $\sum_{i=1}^{I} \overline{x}_{in} - \sum_{j=1}^{J} \overline{y}_{jn} < \sum_{i=1}^{I} e_{in}$ is that commodities in excess supply are free. Theorem 6.15 shows that this condition may also be interpreted as a complementary slackness condition for welfare-maximization problem 6.14.

There is an alternative proof of the part of theorem 6.15 that asserts that an equilibrium allocation maximizes a weighted average of the consumers' utility functions, where the weights are the inverses of the consumers' marginal utilities of wealth in the equilibrium. The proof uses what is called the *value loss method,* which is similar to the proof of the sufficiency of the Kuhn-Tucker conditions for optimality. Though this method adds little in the context of finite dimensional models, it is quite useful when dealing with infinite dimensional models arising in growth theory and the overlapping generations model. In such contexts, it replaces the Kuhn-Tucker theorem, which does not have an easy extension to infinite dimensional problems. I introduce the method here, in order to show its meaning in finite dimensional models.

As in theorem 6.15, let $(\overline{\mathbf{x}}, \overline{\mathbf{y}}, \mathbf{p}, \boldsymbol{\tau})$ be an equilibrium and suppose that $\mathbf{p}.\overline{\mathbf{x}}_i > 0$, for all i, and that assumptions 6.11 and 6.12 apply. By proposition 6.14, each consumer i has a marginal utility of wealth, λ_i, in the equilibrium. Because u_i is strictly increasing, $\lambda_i > 0$. Since u_i is concave, $\overline{\mathbf{x}}_i$ solves the problem

$$\max_{\mathbf{x} \in \mathbb{R}^N_+} [u_i(\mathbf{x}) - \lambda_i \mathbf{p}.\mathbf{x}]$$

and hence solves the problem

$$\max_{\mathbf{x} \in \mathbb{R}^N_+} [\lambda_i^{-1} u_i(\mathbf{x}) - \mathbf{p}.\mathbf{x}],$$

for all i. Because of profit maximization, $\overline{\mathbf{y}}_j$ solves the problem

$$\max_{\mathbf{y} \in Y_j} \mathbf{p}.\mathbf{y},$$

for all j. For each i, let the value loss of consumer i, $\mathcal{L}_i: \mathbb{R}^N_+ \to \mathbb{R}$, be defined by the equation

$$\mathcal{L}_i(\mathbf{x}) = \left[\lambda_i^{-1} u_i(\overline{\mathbf{x}}_i) - \mathbf{p}.\overline{\mathbf{x}}_i\right] - \left[\lambda_i^{-1} u_i(\mathbf{x}_i) - \mathbf{p}.\mathbf{x}_i\right].$$

Clearly, $\mathcal{L}_i(\mathbf{x}) \geq 0$, for all $\mathbf{x}$ and i. Similarly, let the value loss for each firm j, $\mathcal{L}_j: Y_j \to \mathbb{R}$, be defined by the equation

$$\mathcal{L}_j(\mathbf{y}) = \mathbf{p}.\overline{\mathbf{y}}_j - \mathbf{p}.\mathbf{y}.$$

Again, $\mathcal{L}_j(\mathbf{y}) \geq 0$, for all $\mathbf{y} \in Y_j$ and for all j.

I show that if $(\mathbf{x}, \mathbf{y})$ is a feasible allocation, then $\sum_{i=1}^{I} \lambda_i^{-1}[u_i(\overline{\mathbf{x}}_i) - u_i(\mathbf{x}_i)] \geq 0$, so that $(\overline{\mathbf{x}}, \overline{\mathbf{y}})$ solves the problem

$$\max_{\substack{(\mathbf{x},\,\mathbf{y})\text{ is a feasible}\\ \text{allocation}}} \sum_{i=1}^{I} \lambda_i^{-1} u_i(\mathbf{x}_i).$$

Because the value losses are nonnegative, it follows that for any feasible allocation, $(\mathbf{x}, \mathbf{y})$,

$$\begin{aligned}
0 &\le \sum_{i=1}^{I} \mathcal{L}_i(\mathbf{x}_i) + \sum_{j=1}^{J} \mathcal{L}_j(\mathbf{y}_j) \\
&= \sum_{i=1}^{I} \left\{ \left[\lambda_i^{-1} u_i(\overline{\mathbf{x}}_i) - \mathbf{p}.\overline{\mathbf{x}}_i\right] - \left[\lambda_i^{-1} u_i(\mathbf{x}_i) - \mathbf{p}.\mathbf{x}_i\right] \right\} + \sum_{j=1}^{J} (\mathbf{p}.\overline{\mathbf{y}}_j - \mathbf{p}.\mathbf{y}_j) \\
&= \sum_{i=1}^{I} \lambda_i^{-1} \left[u_i(\overline{\mathbf{x}}_i) - u_i(\mathbf{x}_i)\right] + \mathbf{p}.\left(\sum_{i=1}^{I} \mathbf{x}_i - \sum_{j=1}^{J} \mathbf{y}_j\right) \\
&\quad - \mathbf{p}.\left(\sum_{i=1}^{I} \overline{\mathbf{x}}_i - \sum_{j=1}^{J} \overline{\mathbf{y}}_j\right) \\
&= \sum_{i=1}^{I} \lambda_i^{-1} \left[u_i(\overline{\mathbf{x}}_i) - u_i(\mathbf{x}_i)\right] + \mathbf{p}.\left(\sum_{i=1}^{I} \mathbf{x}_i - \sum_{i=1}^{I} \mathbf{e}_i - \sum_{j=1}^{J} \mathbf{y}_j\right) \\
&\quad - \mathbf{p}.\left(\sum_{i=1}^{I} \overline{\mathbf{x}}_i - \sum_{i=1}^{I} \mathbf{e}_i \sum_{j=1}^{J} \overline{\mathbf{y}}_j\right) \\
&\le \sum_{i=1}^{I} \lambda_i^{-1} \left[u_i(\overline{\mathbf{x}}_i) - u_i(\mathbf{x}_i)\right],
\end{aligned}$$

where the last inequality is valid for the following two reasons. First, $\mathbf{p} \ge 0$ and $\sum_{i=1}^{I} \mathbf{x}_i - \sum_{i=1}^{I} \mathbf{e}_i - \sum_{j=1}^{J} \mathbf{y}_j \le 0$, by the feasibility of the allocation $(\mathbf{x}, \mathbf{y})$. Second, $\mathbf{p}.\left(\sum_{i=1}^{I} \overline{\mathbf{x}}_i - \sum_{i=1}^{I} \mathbf{e}_i - \sum_{j=1}^{J} \overline{\mathbf{y}}_j\right) = 0$, since the allocation $(\overline{\mathbf{x}}, \overline{\mathbf{y}})$ is feasible and the equilibrium price of any commodity in excess supply is 0. This completes the proof.

It is important to realize that the marginal utilities of wealth a_i^{-1} appearing in theorem 6.15 depend on the equilibrium. It is not possible to prove the existence of an equilibrium by showing that a welfare function of the form $\sum_{i=1}^{I} a_i u_i(\mathbf{x}_i)$ has a maximum, for we do not know what the welfare weights a_i should be until we know the equilibrium $(\overline{\mathbf{x}}, \overline{\mathbf{y}}, \mathbf{p})$. If an economy has more than one equilibrium, each equilibrium allocation may maximize a different welfare function. (It is possible to prove that an equilibrium exists by making a fixed point argument on the welfare weights, $(a_1, a_2, \ldots, a_I)$. See Negishi [1960].)

If an equilibrium $(\overline{\mathbf{x}}, \overline{\mathbf{y}}, \mathbf{p})$ maximizes a welfare function of the form $\sum_{i=1}^{I} \lambda_i^{-1} u_i(\mathbf{x}_i)$, the equilibrium may be interpreted as that of an economy with a single consumer who receives all the profit from all the firms and has initial endowment $\mathbf{e} = \sum_{i=1}^{I} \mathbf{e}_i$ and utility function

$$U(\mathbf{x}) = \max \left\{ \sum_{i=1}^{I} \lambda_i^{-1} u_i(\mathbf{x}_i) \mid \sum_{i=1}^{I} \mathbf{x}_i = \mathbf{x} \right\}.$$

The budget set of the consumer in this equilibrium is

$$\left\{ \mathbf{x} \in \mathbb{R}_+^N \mid \mathbf{p}.\mathbf{x} \leq \mathbf{p}.\sum_{i=1}^{I} \mathbf{e}_i + \mathbf{p}.\sum_{j=1}^{J} \overline{\mathbf{y}}_j \right\}.$$

Theorem 6.15 is what is known as an *aggregation theorem* because all consumers are aggregated into a single consumer.

The following example illustrates how to compute the welfare weights corresponding to an equilibrium.

EXAMPLE 6.16 Consider the following Edgeworth box example.

$$u_A(x_1, x_2) = \frac{1}{4}\ln(x_1) + \frac{3}{4}\ln(x_2),$$

$$u_B(x_1, x_2) = \frac{2}{3}\ln(x_1) + \frac{1}{3}\ln(x_2),$$

$$\mathbf{e}_A = (2, 0), \text{ and } \mathbf{e}_B = (0, 2).$$

Proceeding as in section 4.5 and using equation 4.6 from there, I may calculate that there is a unique equilibrium allocation

$$\overline{x}_{A1} = \frac{1}{2}, \overline{x}_{A2} = \frac{4}{3},$$

$$\overline{x}_{B1} = \frac{3}{2}, \overline{x}_{B2} = \frac{2}{3},$$

with prices

$$p_1 = \frac{8}{17}, \text{ and } p_2 = \frac{9}{17}.$$

The equation

$$\frac{\partial u_A(\overline{\mathbf{x}}_A)}{\partial x_1} = \lambda_A p_1$$

implies that

$$\frac{1}{4}\frac{1}{\overline{x}_{A1}} = \lambda_A p_1,$$

so that

$$\lambda_A = \frac{17}{16},$$

where λ_A is consumer A's marginal utility of wealth in the equilibrium $(\overline{\mathbf{x}}_A, \overline{\mathbf{x}}_B, \mathbf{p})$. Similarly, the equation

$$\frac{\partial u_B(\overline{\mathbf{x}}_B)}{\partial x_2} = \lambda_B p_2$$

implies that

$$\lambda_B = \frac{17}{18}.$$

Therefore, the equilibrium allocation maximizes the welfare function

$$\lambda_A^{-1} u_A(\mathbf{x}_A) + \lambda_B^{-1} u_B(\mathbf{x}_B) = \frac{16}{17} u_A(\mathbf{x}_A) + \frac{18}{17} u_B(\mathbf{x}_B).$$

The prices $p_1 = \frac{8}{17}$ and $p_2 = \frac{9}{17}$ measure the rate at which the maximized welfare, $\frac{16}{17} u_A(\mathbf{x}_A) + \frac{18}{17} u_B(\mathbf{x}_B)$, increases as the total endowments of commodities 1 and 2, respectively, increase.

The welfare weight vector, $\mathbf{a} = (\lambda_A^{-1}, \lambda_B^{-1}) = \left(\frac{16}{17}, \frac{18}{17}\right)$, is perpendicular to the utility possibility frontier, $\mathcal{UF}$, for the economy at utility vector

$$U = (u_A(\overline{\mathbf{x}}_A), u_B(\overline{\mathbf{x}}_B)) = \left[\frac{1}{4}\ln\left(\frac{1}{2}\right) + \frac{3}{4}\ln\left(\frac{4}{3}\right), \frac{2}{3}\ln\left(\frac{3}{2}\right) + \frac{1}{3}\ln\left(\frac{2}{3}\right)\right],$$

because the inner product $\mathbf{a}.\mathbf{v} = \lambda_A^{-1} v_A + \lambda_B^{-1} v_B$ is maximized among all vectors $\mathbf{v}$ in the utility possibility set at the utility vector U. The orthogonality of the vector $\mathbf{a}$ to the slope of $\mathcal{UF}$ at U is portrayed in figure 6.5.

The next example shows why it is necessary to require in theorem 6.15 that $\mathbf{p}.\overline{\mathbf{x}}_i > 0$, for all i.

EXAMPLE 6.17 Let there be two consumers (A and B), one commodity, and no firm. The utility function and initial endowment of each consumer

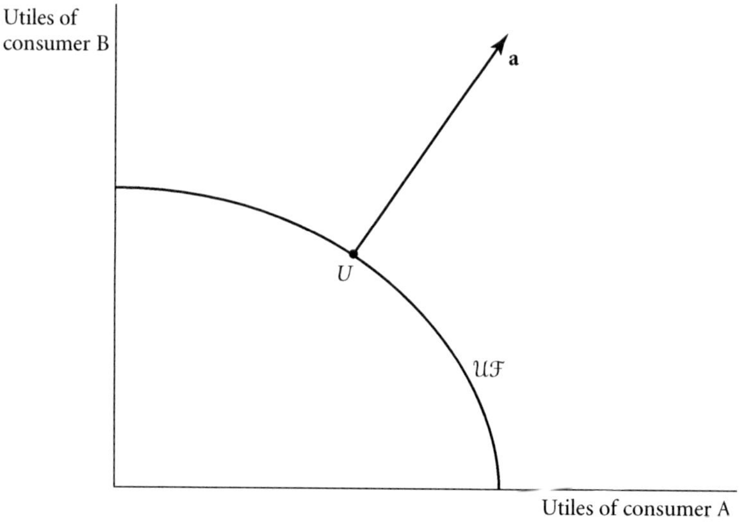

Figure 6.5 The utility possibility frontier and the vector welfare weights

are $u(x) = \sqrt{x}$ and $e = 1$, respectively. The allocation $x_A = 2$, $x_B = 0$ is Pareto optimal, and $(x_A, x_B, p, \tau_A, \tau_B) = (2, 0, 1, -1, 1)$ is an equilibrium with transfer payments. The allocation (2, 0), however, does not maximize a welfare function that gives positive weight to both consumers, for suppose that $a_A\sqrt{x_A} + a_B\sqrt{x_B}$ were such a welfare function, with $a_A > 0$ and $a_B > 0$. If we maximize this welfare function subject to the constraint $x_A + x_B \leq 2$, we find that $x_B = \frac{2a_B^2}{a_A^2+a_B^2}$, which is positive, contrary to the hypothesis that $x_B = 0$.

6.4 The Differentiable Case

If the functions appearing in the Kuhn-Tucker theorem are differentiable, it may be restated in terms of conditions involving derivatives. The validity of the restatement follows from the next proposition, which may be familiar to many readers and has been used implicitly in computing examples.

PROPOSITION 6.18 Let $F: X \to \mathbb{R}$ be a concave and differentiable function, where $X = \{\mathbf{x} \in \mathbb{R}^N \mid x_n \geq 0, \text{ if } n \leq M\}$ and where $M \leq N$. F is maximized at $\overline{\mathbf{x}} \in X$, if and only if, for all $n \leq M$,

$$\frac{\partial F(\overline{\mathbf{x}})}{\partial x_n} \leq 0, \text{ with equality if } \overline{x}_n > 0,$$

and (6.19)

$$\frac{\partial F(\overline{\mathbf{x}})}{\partial x_n} = 0,$$

for all $n > M$.

Proof. It is should be well known from calculus that the conditions of 6.19 apply if F attains a maximum at $\overline{\mathbf{x}}$. I show the converse, that the conditions of 6.19 imply that F attains a maximum at $\overline{\mathbf{x}}$. Let $\mathbf{x}$ be any vector in X, and suppose that $0 \leq \alpha \leq 1$. Then

$$\begin{aligned} F(\overline{\mathbf{x}} + \alpha(\mathbf{x} - \overline{\mathbf{x}})) &= F(\alpha\mathbf{x} + (1-\alpha)\overline{\mathbf{x}}) \geq \alpha F(\mathbf{x}) + (1-\alpha)F(\overline{\mathbf{x}}) \\ &= F(\overline{\mathbf{x}}) + \alpha\left[F(\mathbf{x}) - F(\overline{\mathbf{x}})\right], \end{aligned} \tag{6.20}$$

where the inequality follows from the concavity of F. Therefore,

$$\begin{aligned} 0 \geq \sum_{n=1}^{N} \frac{\partial F(\overline{\mathbf{x}})}{\partial x_n}(x_n - \overline{x}_n) &= \frac{d}{d\alpha} F(\overline{\mathbf{x}} + \alpha(\mathbf{x} - \overline{\mathbf{x}}))\Big|_{\alpha=0} \\ &= \lim_{\alpha \to 0} \frac{F(\overline{\mathbf{x}} + \alpha(\mathbf{x} - \overline{\mathbf{x}})) - F(\overline{\mathbf{x}})}{\alpha} \geq F(\mathbf{x}) - F(\overline{\mathbf{x}}). \end{aligned} \tag{6.21}$$

The first inequality in 6.21 follows from conditions 6.19, because if $\frac{\partial F(\overline{\mathbf{x}})}{\partial x_n} < 0$, then $n \leq M$ and $\overline{x} = 0$ and so $x_n \geq \overline{x}_n$ and hence $\frac{\partial F(\overline{\mathbf{x}})}{\partial x_n}(x_n - \overline{x}_n) \leq 0$. The second inequality in 6.21 is a consequence of inequality 6.20. Since $F(\mathbf{x}) \leq F(\overline{\mathbf{x}})$ and $\mathbf{x}$ is an arbitrary vector in X, F achieves its maximum value at $\overline{\mathbf{x}}$. ▪

The version of the Kuhn-Tucker theorem involving derivatives is as follows.

DIFFERENTIABLE VERSION OF THE KUHN-TUCKER THEOREM 6.19 Suppose that $f: X \to (-\infty, \infty)$ is concave and differentiable and $g_k: X \to (-\infty, \infty)$ is convex and differentiable, for $k = 1, \ldots, K$, where $X = \{\mathbf{x} \in \mathbb{R}^N \mid x_n \geq 0, \text{ if } n \leq M\}$ and $M \leq N$. Then, the vector $\overline{\mathbf{x}} \in X$ solves the problem

$$\begin{aligned} &\max_{x \in X} f(\mathbf{x}) \\ &\text{s.t.} \quad g_k(\mathbf{x}) \leq a_k, \quad \text{for } k = 1, \ldots, K, \end{aligned} \tag{6.22}$$

if there exist nonnegative numbers $\lambda_1, \ldots, \lambda_K$ such that

1. for all k, $\lambda_k = 0$, if $g_k(\overline{\mathbf{x}}) < a_k$
2. for all n, $\frac{\partial f(\overline{\mathbf{x}})}{\partial x_n} \leq \sum_{k=1}^{K} \lambda_k \frac{\partial g_k(\overline{\mathbf{x}})}{\partial x_n}$, with equality if $\overline{x}_n > 0$ or $n > M$

Suppose that there exists an $\underline{\mathbf{x}}$ such that $g_k(\underline{\mathbf{x}}) < a_k$, for all k, and that $\overline{\mathbf{x}}$ in X solves problem 6.22. Then, there exist nonnegative numbers $\lambda_1, \ldots, \lambda_K$ such that conditions (1) and (2) above apply.

Proof. Suppose that $\overline{\mathbf{x}}$ in X satisfies conditions (1) and (2) of the theorem. Condition (1) of theorem 6.19 is the same as condition (1) of theorem 6.3 (in section 6.1). By proposition 6.18, condition (2) of theorem 6.19 implies that $\overline{\mathbf{x}}$ solves the problem

$$\max_{\mathbf{x} \in X} \left[f(\mathbf{x}) - \sum_{k=1}^{K} \lambda_k g_k(\mathbf{x}) \right], \tag{6.23}$$

which is condition (2) of theorem 6.3. Therefore, theorem 6.3 implies that $\overline{\mathbf{x}}$ solves problem 6.22.

Suppose that there exists an $\underline{\mathbf{x}}$ in X such that $g_k(\underline{\mathbf{x}}) < a_k$, for all k, and that $\overline{\mathbf{x}}$ in X solves problem 6.22. Then by theorem 6.3, there exist nonnegative numbers $\lambda_1, \ldots, \lambda_K$ such that condition (1) applies and $\overline{\mathbf{x}}$ solves problem 6.23. Because $\overline{\mathbf{x}}$ solves problem 6.23, proposition 6.18 implies that condition (2) above applies. ▪

Conditions (1) and (2) of theorem 6.19 are known as *first-order conditions.* Another way to see the connection between Pareto optimality, welfare maximization, and equilibrium is to compare the first-order, complementary slackness, and feasibility conditions corresponding to each. To simplify matters, I deal only with economies that have no production. In doing so, I continue to apply assumptions 6.11 and 6.13 (in section 6.3) and add the following assumption.

ASSUMPTION 6.20 For each i, the function $u_i: \mathbb{R}_+^N \rightarrow \mathbb{R}$ is differentiable.

In proving theorem 6.15, I showed that, under assumptions made here, the following welfare-maximization problem satisfies the constraint qualification:

$$\max_x \sum_{i=1}^{I} a_i u_i(\mathbf{x}_i)$$
$$\text{s.t.} \quad \sum_{i=1}^{I} x_{\text{in}} \le \sum_{i=1}^{I} e_{\text{in}}, \text{ for } n = 1, \ldots, N, \tag{6.24}$$

where $a_i > 0$, for all i. Therefore, theorem 6.19 implies that the allocation $\overline{\mathbf{x}}$ maximizes the welfare function if and only if there exist Kuhn-Tucker coefficients $p_1, \ldots, p_N$, such that these coefficients and the allocation $\overline{\mathbf{x}}$ satisfy conditions 6.25–6.28 below.

$$\overline{\mathbf{x}}_i \ge 0, \text{ for all } i. \tag{6.25}$$

$$\sum_{i=1}^{I} (\overline{x}_{\text{in}} - e_{\text{in}}) \le 0, \text{ for all } n. \tag{6.26}$$

$$\text{For all } n,\ p_n \ge 0, \text{ with } p_n = 0, \text{ if } \sum_{i=1}^{I} (\overline{x}_{\text{in}} - e_{\text{in}}) < 0. \tag{6.27}$$

$$\text{For all } i \text{ and } n,\ a_i \frac{\partial u_i(\overline{\mathbf{x}}_i)}{\partial x_n} \le p_n, \text{ with equality, if } \overline{x}_{\text{in}} > 0. \tag{6.28}$$

Conditions 6.25 and 6.26 define feasibility of the allocation $\overline{\mathbf{x}}$. The conditions in 6.27 are the complementary slackness conditions for the Kuhn-Tucker coefficients, p_n. Condition 6.28 is the first-order condition for maximization of the Lagrangian

$$\sum_{i=1}^{I} a_i u_i(\mathbf{x}_i) - \sum_{n=1}^{N} p_n \sum_{i=1}^{I} x_{\text{in}}.$$

These conditions imply those characterizing an equilibrium with transfer payments. Let $\lambda_i = a_i^{-1}$, so that condition 6.28 becomes

$$\text{for all } i,\ \frac{\partial u_i(\overline{\mathbf{x}}_i)}{\partial x_n} \le \lambda_i p_n, \text{ with equality, if } \overline{x}_{\text{in}} > 0. \tag{6.29}$$

If we adjoin the equations defining the transfer payments,

$$\tau_i = p.(\mathbf{e}_i - \overline{\mathbf{x}}_i), \tag{6.30}$$

for all i, we see that theorem 6.19 implies that $(\overline{\mathbf{x}}, \mathbf{p}, \boldsymbol{\tau})$ is an equilibrium with transfer payments, provided it and the coefficients $\lambda_1, \ldots, \lambda_I$ satisfy conditions 6.25–6.27, 6.29, and 6.30. The coefficients $\lambda_1, \ldots, \lambda_I$ are the

Lagrange multipliers or Kuhn-Tucker coefficients for utility maximization over the budget sets. Once again, conditions 6.25 and 6.26 define feasibility of the allocation $\overline{\mathbf{x}}$. Condition 6.27 is the condition in the definition of equilibrium that says that commodities in excess supply have zero value. Conditions 6.29 and 6.30 imply that, for each i, $\overline{\mathbf{x}}_i$ solves consumer i's utility-maximization problem

$$\max_{\mathbf{x}\in\mathbb{R}^N_+} u_i(\mathbf{x})$$
$$\text{s.t.} \quad p.\mathbf{x} \le p.\mathbf{e}_i - \tau_i.$$

(Since $\lambda_i > 0$ and by the definition of τ_i the budget equation is satisfied with equality, we do not need a complementary slackness condition of the form $\lambda_i = 0$, if $\mathbf{p}.\overline{\mathbf{x}}_i < \mathbf{p}.\mathbf{e}_i + \sum_{j=1}^{J} \Theta_{ij}\mathbf{p}.\overline{\mathbf{y}}_i - \tau_i$.)

Conversely, if $\mathbf{p}.\mathbf{e}_i - \tau_i > 0$, for all i, in the equilibrium with transfer payments, $(\overline{\mathbf{x}}, \mathbf{p}, \boldsymbol{\tau})$, then each consumer's utility-maximization problem satisfies the constraint qualification. Thus theorem 6.19 may be applied to show that for each i, there exists a Kuhn-Tucker coefficient, λ_i, for consumer i's utility-maximization problem such that the equilibrium together with $\lambda_1, \ldots, \lambda_I$ satisfy conditions 6.25–6.27, 6.29, and 6.30. Because the utility functions are strictly increasing, the λ_i are positive, so that inequality 6.29 may be transformed into inequality 6.28 by letting $a_i^{-1} = \lambda_i$. Therefore, the conditions implied by an equilibrium with transfer payments are those for a welfare maximum.

In conclusion, an allocation that solves problem 6.24 is an equilibrium with transfer payments in which the marginal utility of income of each consumer i is a_i^{-1}. Furthermore, if $(\mathbf{x}, \mathbf{p}, \boldsymbol{\tau})$ is an equilibrium with transfer payments such that $\mathbf{p}.\mathbf{e}_i - \tau_i > 0$, for all i, then $\mathbf{x}$ solves problem 6.24 with $a_i = \lambda_i^{-1}$, for all i, where λ_i is consumer i's marginal utility of income in the equilibrium.

By using somewhat different reasoning, it is possible to derive a similar set of conditions implying that a Pareto optimal allocation is the allocation of an equilibrium with transfer payments. If the allocation $\overline{\mathbf{x}}$ is Pareto optimal, then it maximizes the utility of consumer 1, subject to the constraint that the utility of each of the other consumers be no lower than the level achieved in the allocation $\overline{\mathbf{x}}$. That is, $\overline{\mathbf{x}}$ solves the problem

$$\max_{\mathbf{x}} u_1(\mathbf{x}_1)$$
$$\text{s.t.} \quad \mathbf{x} \text{ is a feasible allocation and} \tag{6.31}$$
$$u_i(\mathbf{x}_i) \ge v_i, \quad \text{for } i \ge 2,$$

where $v_i = u_i(\overline{\mathbf{x}}_i)$, for all i. Problem 6.31 may be rewritten as

$$\begin{aligned} \max_{\mathbf{x}_i \in \mathbb{R}^N_+, \text{ for all } i,} \quad & u_1(\mathbf{x}_1) \\ \text{s.t.} \quad & \sum_{i=1}^{I} (x_{in} - e_{in}) \leq 0, \text{ for } n = 1, \ldots, N, \text{ and} \\ & -u_i(\mathbf{x}_i) \leq -v_i, \text{ for } i = 2, \ldots, I. \end{aligned} \tag{6.32}$$

Because the utility functions u_i are concave, the function $-u_i$ is convex, so that all the constraint functions are convex.

I show that problem 6.32 satisfies the constraint qualification under the assumption that $\overline{\mathbf{x}}_1 > \mathbf{0}$.

Let $\mathbf{x}^1$ be the allocation defined by the equations

$$\mathbf{x}_1^1 = \mathbf{0} \quad \text{and} \quad \mathbf{x}_1^1 = \overline{\mathbf{x}}_i + \frac{\overline{\mathbf{x}}_1}{I - 1},$$

for $i \geq 2$. The allocation $\mathbf{x}^1$ is feasible since it is obtained by redistributing consumer 1's consumption in the feasible allocation $\overline{\mathbf{x}}$ to the other consumers. Since the utility functions are assumed to be strictly increasing and $\overline{\mathbf{x}}_1 > \mathbf{0}$, $u_i(\mathbf{x}_i^1) > u_i(\overline{\mathbf{x}}_i) = v_i$, for all $i \geq 2$. Since by assumption 6.13, the economy is productive, there exists an allocation $\underline{\mathbf{x}}$ such that

$$\sum_{i=1}^{I} (\underline{x}_{in} - e_{in}) < 0,$$

for all n. Let $\mathbf{x}^2 = \varepsilon \underline{\mathbf{x}} + (1 - \varepsilon)\mathbf{x}^1$, where ε is a positive number that is so small that $u_i(\mathbf{x}_i^2) > v_i$, for all $i \geq 2$. Then,

$$\sum_{i=1}^{I} (x_{in}^2 - e_{in}) < 0,$$

for all n, so that problem 6.32 satisfies the constraint qualification.

I now apply theorem 6.19 to problem 6.32. For each n, let p_n be the Kuhn-Tucker coefficient corresponding to the constraint $\sum_{i=1}^{I}(x_{in} - e_{in}) \leq 0$. For each $i \geq 2$, let a_i be the Kuhn-Tucker coefficient corresponding to the constraint $-u_i(\mathbf{x}_i) \leq -v_i$. With this notation, the Lagrangian of problem 6.32 is

$$u_1(\mathbf{x}_1) + \sum_{i=2}^{I} a_i u_i(\mathbf{x}_i) - \mathbf{p} \cdot \sum_{i=1}^{I} (\mathbf{x}_i - \mathbf{e}_i),$$

which is the same as the Lagrangian for the welfare-maximization problem 6.24 with $a_1 = 1$. Therefore, the Pareto optimal allocation satisfies conditions 6.25–6.28, with the understanding that $a_1 = 1$. We may apply the reasoning used before to pass from these conditions to those for an equilibrium with transfer payments, provided $a_i > 0$, for all $i \geq 2$.

I verify that, for $i \geq 2$, $a_i > 0$, provided $\overline{\mathbf{x}}_i > 0$. Without loss of generality, let $i = 2$. In problem 6.32, fix the right-hand sides of all the constraints except the constraint $-u_2(\mathbf{x}_2) \leq -v_2$. That is, allow v_2 to vary, but fix $v_i = u(\overline{\mathbf{x}}_i)$, for $i > 2$. Let $V_2(-v_2)$ be the value function of problem 6.32 as a function of v_2. The coefficient a_2 is a subgradient of V_2 at $v_2 = u_2(\overline{\mathbf{x}}_2)$. Because u_2 is strictly increasing and $\overline{\mathbf{x}}_2 > 0$, it follows that $u_2(\overline{\mathbf{x}}_2) > u_2(\mathbf{0})$. Because V_2 is concave,

$$V_2(-u_2(\mathbf{0})) \leq V_2(-u_2(\overline{\mathbf{x}}_2)) + a_2\left[-u_2(\mathbf{0}) + u_2(\overline{\mathbf{x}}_2)\right],$$

so that

$$a_2 \geq \frac{V_2(-u_2(\mathbf{0})) - V_2(-u_2(\overline{\mathbf{x}}_2))}{u_2(\overline{\mathbf{x}}_2) - u_2(\mathbf{0})}. \tag{6.33}$$

We know that

$$V_2(-u_2(\overline{\mathbf{x}}_2)) = u_1(\overline{\mathbf{x}}_1). \tag{6.34}$$

I may obtain a feasible solution for problem 6.32 with $v_2 = u_2(\mathbf{0})$ by giving consumer 2's consumption bundle to consumer 1. That is, I may replace the allocation $\overline{\mathbf{x}}$ with the allocation $\mathbf{x}$ defined by the equations $\mathbf{x}_1 = \overline{\mathbf{x}}_1 + \overline{\mathbf{x}}_2$, $\mathbf{x}_2 = 0$, and $\mathbf{x}_i = \overline{\mathbf{x}}_i$, for $i > 2$. Then,

$$V_2(-u_2(\mathbf{0})) \geq u_1(\mathbf{x}_1) = u_1(\overline{\mathbf{x}}_1 + \overline{\mathbf{x}}_2). \tag{6.35}$$

Because u_i is strictly increasing and $\overline{\mathbf{x}}_2 > \mathbf{0}$,

$$u_1(\overline{\mathbf{x}}_1 + \overline{\mathbf{x}}_2) - u_1(\overline{\mathbf{x}}_1) > 0. \tag{6.36}$$

Inequalities and equations 6.33–6.36 imply that

$$a_2 \geq \frac{u_1(\overline{\mathbf{x}}_1 + \overline{\mathbf{x}}_2) - u_1(\overline{\mathbf{x}}_1)}{u_2(\overline{\mathbf{x}}_2) - u_2(\mathbf{0})} > 0.$$

This completes the proof that $a_i > 0$, for all $i \geq 2$ such that $\overline{\mathbf{x}}_i > \mathbf{0}$. It follows, therefore, that $\overline{\mathbf{x}}$ is the allocation of an equilibrium with transfer payments, $(\overline{\mathbf{x}}, \mathbf{p}, \boldsymbol{\tau})$, provided $\overline{\mathbf{x}}_i > 0$, for all **i**.

6.5 Proof of the Kuhn-Tucker Theorem

I repeat the statement of the Kuhn-Tucker theorem for ease of referral when reading its proof.

THE KUHN-TUCKER THEOREM Let $f: X \to (-\infty, \infty)$ be concave, and, for $k = 1, \ldots, K$, let $g_k: X \to (-\infty, \infty)$ be a convex function, where X is a convex set of N-vectors. For each $k = 1, \ldots, K$, let $\overline{a}_k$ be a number. Suppose that $\overline{\mathbf{x}}$ in X is such that $g_k(\overline{\mathbf{x}}) \leq \overline{a}_k$, for $k = 1, \ldots, K$, and that there exist nonnegative numbers $\lambda_1, \ldots, \lambda_K$ such that

1. for all k, $\lambda_k = 0$, if $g_k(\overline{\mathbf{x}}) < \overline{a}_k$
2. $\overline{\mathbf{x}}$ solves the maximization problem

$$\max_{\mathbf{x} \in X} \left[f(\mathbf{x}) - \sum_{k=1}^{K} \lambda_k g_k(\mathbf{x}) \right]$$

Then, $\overline{\mathbf{x}}$ solves the problem

$$\begin{aligned} &\max_{\mathbf{x} \in X} f(\mathbf{x}) \\ &\text{s.t.} \quad g_k(\mathbf{x}) \leq a_k, \quad \text{for } k = 1, \ldots, K. \end{aligned} \tag{6.37}$$

Suppose that $\overline{\mathbf{x}}$ solves problem 6.37 and assume the following *constraint qualification:*

3. There exists an $\underline{\mathbf{x}}$ in X such that $g_k(\underline{\mathbf{x}}) < \overline{a}_k$, for all k.

Then, there exist nonnegative numbers $\lambda_1, \ldots, \lambda_K$ such that conditions (1) and (2) above apply.

Proof. Recall from definition 6.2 (in section 6.1) that a vector $\mathbf{x}$ in X is said to be feasible if it satisfies the constraints of problem 6.37.

I first prove that the stated conditions are sufficient for optimality. That is, if $\overline{\mathbf{x}}$ is feasible and there exist nonnegative numbers $\lambda, \ldots, \lambda_K$ that together with $\overline{\mathbf{x}}$ satisfy conditions (1) and (2), then $f(\overline{\mathbf{x}}) \geq f(\mathbf{x})$, for any feasible vector $\mathbf{x}$. The complementary slackness conditions of (1) imply that $\lambda_k g_k(\overline{\mathbf{x}}) = \lambda_k \overline{a}_k$, for all k, so that

$$\sum_{k=1}^{K} \lambda_k g_k(\overline{\mathbf{x}}) = \sum_{k=1}^{K} \lambda_k \overline{a}_k. \tag{6.38}$$

Therefore,

$$\begin{aligned} f(\overline{\mathbf{x}}) - \sum_{k=1}^{K} \lambda_k \overline{a}_k &= f(\overline{\mathbf{x}}) - \sum_{k=1}^{K} \lambda_k g_k(\overline{\mathbf{x}}) \\ &\geq f(\mathbf{x}) - \sum_{k=1}^{K} \lambda_k g_k(\mathbf{x}) \geq f(\mathbf{x}) - \sum_{k=1}^{K} \lambda_k \overline{a}_k, \end{aligned} \tag{6.39}$$

where the equation in inequality 6.39 follows from equation 6.38, the first inequality follows from condition (2) of the theorem, and the second inequality follows from the nonnegativity of the λ_k and from the inequalities $g_k(\mathbf{x}) \leq \overline{a}_k$, for all k. Canceling the sum $\sum_{k=1}^{K} \lambda_k \overline{a}_k$ from the extreme left- and right-hand sides of inequality 6.39, we see that $f(\overline{\mathbf{x}}) \geq f(\mathbf{x})$, as was to be proved.

It remains to be proved that the stated conditions are necessary for optimality, if the constraint qualification applies. That is, I must show that if $\overline{\mathbf{x}}$ solves problem 6.37, then there exist nonnegative numbers $\lambda_1, \ldots, \lambda_K$ such that conditions (1) and (2) of the theorem apply. Recall from definition 6.7 (in section 6.2) that $V(\mathbf{a})$ is the supremum of possible values of the objective function of problem 6.37, when the right-hand sides of the constraints are $\mathbf{a} = (a_1, \ldots, a_K)$, and that the function V is defined for $\mathbf{a}$ belonging to the set A of K-vectors for which the constraints of problem 6.37 have a feasible solution. By proposition 6.9 (in section 6.2), it is sufficient to prove that the value function, V, has a subgradient $\boldsymbol{\lambda} = (\lambda_1, \ldots, \lambda_K)$ at $\overline{\mathbf{a}}$. The argument that V has a subgradient is an application of Minkowski's separation theorem 3.34 (in section 3.5).

Let $Z = \{(\mathbf{a}, t) \mid \mathbf{a} \in A, t \leq V(\mathbf{a})\}$ and let $B = \{(\mathbf{a}, t) \mid \mathbf{a} \in \mathbb{R}^K, \mathbf{a} \leq \overline{\mathbf{a}},$ and $t \geq V(\overline{\mathbf{a}})\}$. The set Z is the set of all points on or below the graph of V. This set is convex, because, by proposition 6.10 (in section 6.2), the function V is concave and the set A is convex. It is clear from the definition of B that it is convex and has nonempty interior. Because V is nondecreasing, the set Z does not intersect the interior of B. Figure 6.6 should help you visualize these sets.

It follows from Minkowski's separation theorem that there exists a nonzero $(K+1)-$ vector $\mathbf{v} = (v_1, \ldots, v_K, s)$ such that

$$\mathbf{v}.\mathbf{b} \leq \mathbf{v}.\mathbf{z}, \quad \text{for all } \mathbf{b} \text{ in B and } \mathbf{z} \text{ in Z.} \tag{6.40}$$

I show that $v_k \geq 0$, for all k. Without loss of generality, I may let $k = 1$. Let $\mathbf{a} = \overline{\mathbf{a}} + (1, 0, \ldots, 0)$. Because V is nondecreasing, $V(\mathbf{a}) \geq \mathbf{V}(\overline{\mathbf{a}})$.

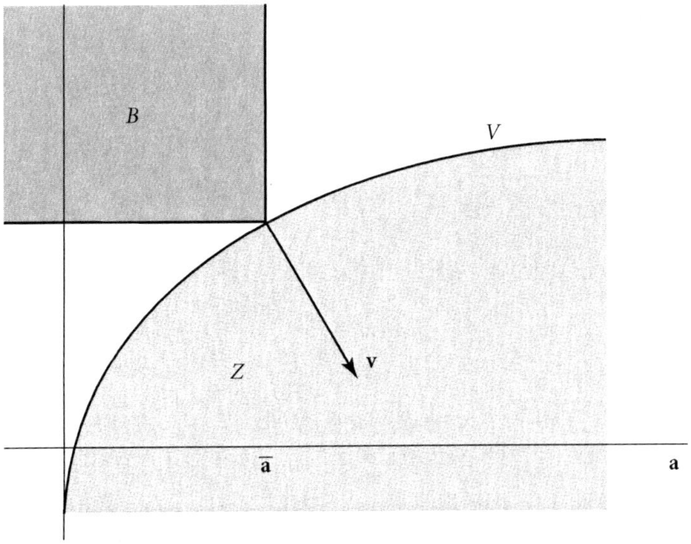

Figure 6.6 The sets to be separated

Therefore, $(\mathbf{a}, V(\bar{\mathbf{a}}))$ belongs to Z, by the definition of Z. Because $(\bar{\mathbf{a}}, V(\bar{\mathbf{a}}))$ belongs to B, inequality 6.40 implies that

$$\mathbf{v}.(\bar{\mathbf{a}}, V(\bar{\mathbf{a}})) \leq \mathbf{v}.(\mathbf{a}, V(\bar{\mathbf{a}})).$$

By the definition of **a**,

$$\mathbf{v}.(\mathbf{a}, V(\bar{\mathbf{a}})) = \mathbf{v}.(\bar{\mathbf{a}}, V(\bar{\mathbf{a}})) + v_1.$$

Substituting this equation into the previous inequality, we see that

$$\mathbf{v}.(\bar{\mathbf{a}}, V(\bar{\mathbf{a}})) \leq \mathbf{v}.(\bar{\mathbf{a}}, V(\bar{\mathbf{a}})) + v_1,$$

which implies that $v_1 \geq 0$, as was to be proved.

I next show that $s \leq 0$. By the definitions of B and Z, $(\bar{\mathbf{a}}, V(\bar{\mathbf{a}}) + 1)$ belongs to B, and $(\bar{\mathbf{a}}, V(\bar{\mathbf{a}}))$ belongs to Z. Therefore,

$$\mathbf{v}.(\bar{\mathbf{a}}, V(\bar{\mathbf{a}}) + 1) \leq \mathbf{v}.(\bar{\mathbf{a}}, V(\bar{\mathbf{a}})),$$

which implies that

$$\mathbf{v}.(\bar{\mathbf{a}}, V(\bar{\mathbf{a}})) + s \leq \mathbf{v}.(\bar{\mathbf{a}}, V(\bar{\mathbf{a}})),$$

so that $s \leq 0$.

I now show that $s < 0$. Since $s \leq 0$, it follows that $s = 0$, if s is not less than 0. Suppose that $s = 0$. The constraint qualification implies that there exists an $\underline{\mathbf{a}}$ in A such that $\overline{\mathbf{a}} \gg \underline{\mathbf{a}}$. Since

$$(\overline{\mathbf{a}}, V(\overline{\mathbf{a}})) \in B \text{ and } (\underline{\mathbf{a}}, V(\underline{\mathbf{a}})) \in Z,$$

inequality 6.40 implies that

$$\mathbf{v}.(\overline{\mathbf{a}}, V(\overline{\mathbf{a}})) \leq \mathbf{v}.(\underline{\mathbf{a}}, V(\underline{\mathbf{a}}))$$

which, because $s = 0$, implies that

$$\sum_{k=1}^{K} v_k \overline{a}_k \leq \sum_{k=1}^{K} v_k \underline{a}_k.$$

Because $\overline{\mathbf{a}} \gg \underline{\mathbf{a}}$ and $\mathbf{v} \geq 0$, it follows that $v_k = 0$, for $k = 1, \ldots, K$. Hence, $\mathbf{v} = 0$, since $s = 0$. This is impossible, since $\mathbf{v} \neq 0$. This contradiction proves that $s < 0$.

For each k, let $\lambda_k = \frac{V_k}{-s}$. Then, $\lambda_k \geq 0$, for all k, and the vector $\mathbf{v}$ may be replaced, as a separating vector, by the vector $(\lambda_1, \ldots, \lambda_K, -1) = \frac{1}{-s}\mathbf{v}$. That is,

$$(\lambda_1, \ldots, \lambda_K, -1).\mathbf{b} \leq (\lambda_1, \ldots, \lambda_K, -1).\mathbf{z}, \quad \text{for all } \mathbf{b} \text{ in } B \text{ and } \mathbf{z} \text{ in } Z. \tag{6.41}$$

I show that the vector $\boldsymbol{\lambda} = (\lambda_1, \ldots, \lambda_K)$ is a subgradient of V at $\overline{\mathbf{a}}$. That is, if $\mathbf{a}$ is in A, then

$$V(\mathbf{a}) \leq V(\overline{\mathbf{a}}) + \sum_k \lambda_k (a_k - \overline{a}_k) \tag{6.42}$$

In order to see that this inequality applies, notice that $(\overline{\mathbf{a}}, V(\overline{\mathbf{a}})) \in B$ and $(\mathbf{a}, V(\mathbf{a})) \in Z$, so that by inequality 6.41

$$(\lambda_1, \ldots, \lambda_K, -1).(\overline{\mathbf{a}}, V(\overline{\mathbf{a}})) \leq (\lambda_1, \ldots, \lambda_K, -1).(\mathbf{a}, V(\mathbf{a})).$$

That is,

$$\sum_k \lambda_k \overline{a}_k - V(\overline{\mathbf{a}}) \leq \sum_k \lambda_k a_k - V(\mathbf{a}),$$

which is the same as inequality 6.42. ▪

Problem Set

1. Compute the marginal utility of wealth, λ, for a consumer with endowment $\mathbf{e} = (2, 5)$ when prices are $(p_1, p_2) = (2, 3)$ and with the following utility functions:

(a) $u(x_1, x_2) = x_1^{1/4} x_2^{1/2}$
(b) $u(x_1, x_2) = 4x_1 + x_2$
(c) $u(x_1, x_2) = 4x_1 + 6x_2$
(d) $u(x_1, x_2) = \min(3x_1, x_2)$
(e) $u(x_1, x_2) = \sqrt{\min(6x_1 + x_2, 2x_1 + 7x_2)}$

(Hint: One approach is to compute

$$V(w) = \max_{x_1 \geq 0, x_2 \geq 0} \; u(x_1, x_2)$$
$$\text{s.t.} \quad 2x_1 + 3x_2 \leq w.$$

Then $\lambda = \frac{dV(19)}{dw}$.)

2. Consider the following Edgeworth box example:

$$e_A = (2, 0), \, u_A(x_1, x_2) = 2\sqrt{x_1 x_2},$$
$$e_B = (0, 5), \, u_B(x_1, x_2) = 2\ln(x_1) + \ln(x_2).$$

(a) Compute a competitive equilibrium with the price of commodity 1 equal to 1.
(b) Compute the marginal utilities of unit of account for each consumer in the equilibrium.
(c) Use these marginal utilities to compute weights a_A and a_B such that the equilibrium allocation maximizes the welfare function

$$a_A u_A(x_{A1}.x_{B2}) + a_B u_B(x_{B1}, x_{B2})$$

among all feasible allocations.

3. For the economies listed below, do the following:

(a) Compute a competitive equilibrium $(\overline{\mathbf{x}}_A, \overline{\mathbf{x}}_B, \mathbf{p})$ such that $p_1 + p_2 = 1$.
(b) Find positive numbers a_A and a_B such that the equilibrium allocation $(\overline{\mathbf{x}}_A, \overline{\mathbf{x}}_B)$ solves the problem

$$\max_{(\mathbf{x}_A, \mathbf{x}_B) \geq \mathbf{0}} \left[a_A u_A(\mathbf{x}_A) + a_B u_B(\mathbf{x}_B)\right]$$
$$\text{s.t,} \quad \mathbf{x}_A + \mathbf{x}_B \leq \mathbf{e}_A + \mathbf{e}_B$$

and such that, for $n = 1$ and 2,

$$p_n = \frac{\partial V(e_{A1} + e_{B1}, e_{A2} + e_{B2})}{\partial E_n},$$

where

$$V(E_1, E_2) = \max_{(\mathbf{x}_A, \mathbf{x}_B) \geq \mathbf{0}} \left[a_A u_A(\mathbf{x}_A) + a_B u_B(\mathbf{x}_B)\right]$$

$$\text{s.t.} \quad \mathbf{x}_A + \mathbf{x}_B \leq (E_1, E_2).$$

(i) $u_A(x_1, x_2) = x_1^{1/3} x_2^{2/3} = u_B(x_1, x_2)$, $\mathbf{e}_A = (12, 0)$, and $\mathbf{e}_B = (0, 12)$.
(ii) $u_A(x_1, x_2) = \min(x_1, x_2) = u_B(x_1, x_2)$, $\mathbf{e}_A = (4, 1)$, and $\mathbf{e}_B = (0, 1)$.
(iii) $u_A(x_1, x_2) = x_1 + 2x_2$, $u_B(x_1, x_2), = 2x_1 + x_2$, $\mathbf{e}_A = (2, 0)$, $\mathbf{e}_B = (0, 1)$.
(iv) $u_A(x_1, x_2) = x_1^{6/7} x_2^{1/7}$, $\mathbf{e}_A = (7, 0)$, $u_B(x_1, x_2) = x_1^{3/7} x_2^{4/7}$, $\mathbf{e}_B = (7, 0)$, and $u_C(x_1, x_2) = x_1^{4/5} x_2^{1/5}$, $\mathbf{e}_C = (0, 10)$.
(v) $u_A(x_1, x_2) = \frac{1}{6} \ln(x_1) + \frac{1}{3} \ln(x_2)$, $\mathbf{e}_A = (1, 2)$, $u_B(x_1, x_2) = \frac{1}{3} \ln(x_1) + \frac{1}{6} \ln(x_2)$, $\mathbf{e}_B = (2, 1)$.
(vi) $u_A(x_1, x_2) = \min(x_1 + 2x_2, 2x_1 + x_2)$, $\mathbf{e}_A = (1, 1)$, $u_B(x_1, x_2) = \sqrt{\min(x_1 + 8x_2, 2x_1 + 3x_2)}$, $\mathbf{e}_B = (3, 1)$.

4. Consider a consumer who purchases two goods, 1 and 2. The consumer's utility function is

$$u(x_1, x_2) = \sqrt{x_1 x_2}.$$

The consumer's wealth is w, where $w > 0$. The price of each good is 1. Suppose that good 1 is rationed, so that the consumer can buy no more than r units of it, where $r \geq 0$.

(a) Describe the consumer's utility-maximization problem formally as a constrained maximization problem with two constraints.
(b) What is the optimum quantity of each good purchased as a function of w and r?
(c) Compute the consumer's maximized utility, $V(w, r)$, as a function of w and r.
(d) As a function of w and r, what are the consumer's marginal utilities of wealth, λ, and of ration tickets, γ?
(e) Suppose the consumer could buy on the black market more ration tickets for good 1 at a price of q per ticket. As a function of w and r, what is the minimum value of q such that the consumer would

not buy any ration tickets, assuming that the ration tickets could be sold in arbitrarily small units? (Hint: Consider the units in which λ, γ, and q are measured.)

(f) Show that if $w > 0$, then this value of q diverges to infinity as r converges to zero.

5. Let $u(x_1, x_2, x_3) = (x_1 x_2 x_3)^{1/3}$. Suppose that $p_1 = p_2 = p_3 = 1$ and that $w = 6$ and that good 1 is rationed, so that the consumer can buy no more than one unit of it.

(a) Compute the demands for goods 1, 2, and 3.

(b) Suppose there is a black market for good 1. For what black market prices q would the consumer buy no more than the one unit of good 1 received at price of 1 under rationing?

(c) Suppose there was no black market. For what price p would the consumer be willing to pay for more ration tickets, assuming that the tickets could be sold in arbitrarily small units?

6. A firm has two processes for producing a good, X. Each process uses five chemicals: A, B, C, D, and E. The first process, when operated at unit level, produces 3 tons of X and uses 5, 4, 3, 2, and 1 tons of chemicals A, B, C, D, and E, respectively. If the process is operated at level a, where $a > 0$, it uses $5a$, $4a$, $3a$, $2a$, and a tons of the chemicals, respectively, and produces $3a$ tons of X. The second process, when operated at unit level, produces 4 tons of X and uses 1, 2, 3, 4, and 5 tons, respectively, of chemicals A, B, C, D, and E. If this process is operated at level a, where $a > 0$, it uses a, $2a$, $3a$, $4a$, and $5a$ tons, respectively, of the chemicals and produces $4a$ tons of X. The company has available 26 tons of each of chemicals A and E, 22 tons of each of chemicals B and D, and 21 tons of chemical C. The price of X is \$100 per ton.

(a) What is the maximum amount of X the firm can produce? (Hint: The requirement that no more than a certain amount of each be used places a linear constraint on the outputs, y_1 and y_2, produced by the two processes. Calculate and graph these constraints for each resource. The answer should then be obvious.)

(b) At this optimum, how much is produced by each process?

(c) What is the maximum price the firm is willing to pay for additional marginal amounts of each chemical? (Hint: Calculate the Kuhn-Tucker coefficients corresponding to each resource constraint.)

7. You are given the following economy with two consumers, two firms, and three commodities.

$Y_I = \{(-t, 2t, t) \mid t \geq 0\}$.

$Y_{II} = \{(-t, t, 3t) \mid t \geq 0\}$.

$\mathbf{e}_\mathrm{A} = (2, 0, 0)$. $\quad u_\mathrm{A}(x_1, x_2, x_3) = \ln(x_1) + 2\ln(x_2) + 2\ln(x_3)$.

$\mathbf{e}_\mathrm{B} = (0, 0, 0)$. $\quad u_\mathrm{B}(x_1, x_2, x_3) = 2\ln(x_1) + 2\ln(x_2) + \ln(x_3)$.

Consider the following value function of a welfare-maximization problem.

$$V(e_1, e_2, e_3) = \max_{\substack{\mathbf{x}_\mathrm{A} \in \mathbb{R}^3_+,\, \mathbf{x}_\mathrm{B} \in \mathbb{R}^3_+,\\ \mathbf{y}_I \in Y_I,\, \mathbf{y}_{II} \in Y_{II}}} [u_\mathrm{A}(\mathbf{x}_\mathrm{A}) + u_\mathrm{B}(\mathbf{x}_\mathrm{B})]$$

$$\text{s.t.} \quad \mathbf{x}_\mathrm{A} + \mathbf{x}_\mathrm{B} \leq \mathbf{y}_I + \mathbf{y}_{II} + (e_1, e_2, e_3).$$

Find a subgradient for V at the point $(e_1, e_2, e_3) = \mathbf{e}_\mathrm{A} + \mathbf{e}_\mathrm{B} = (2, 0, 0)$. (Hint: Start by computing equilibrium relative prices. There is no need to compute an equilibrium. Remember that transfer payments may be freely adjusted.)

8. I introduce a government into a pure trade or exchange economy, $((u_i, \mathbf{e}_i)_{i=1}^I)$. (An economy with no production is said to be a *pure trade economy* or an *exchange economy*.) The government chooses a consumption bundle $\mathbf{g} \in \mathbb{R}^N_+$. An allocation consists of $(\mathbf{x}, \mathbf{g}) = (\mathbf{x}_1, \ldots, \mathbf{x}_I, \mathbf{g})$. It is feasible if $\mathbf{g} + \sum_{i=1}^I \mathbf{x}_i \leq \sum_{i=1}^I \mathbf{e}_i$. For each i, u_i depends on $\mathbf{x}_i$ and $\mathbf{g}$, so that consumer i's utility is $u_i(\mathbf{x}_i, \mathbf{g})$. Assume that for each i, u_i is differentiable, concave, and strictly increasing.

(a) Define Pareto optimality of a feasible allocation.

(b) Show that if $(\overline{\mathbf{x}}, \overline{\mathbf{g}})$ is a Pareto optimal allocation, then there exists an I-vector $\mathbf{a}$ such that $\mathbf{a} > 0$ and $(\overline{\mathbf{x}}, \overline{\mathbf{g}})$ solves the problem

$$\max_{\substack{(x,\, y) \text{ is a feasible}\\ \text{allocation}}} \sum_{i=1}^I a_i u_i(x_i, g).$$

(c) Show that if $(\overline{\mathbf{x}}, \overline{\mathbf{g}})$ is a Pareto optimal allocation such that $\overline{\mathbf{x}}_i \gg 0$, for all i, and $\overline{\mathbf{g}} \gg 0$, then there exists an N-vector $\mathbf{q}$ such that $\mathbf{q} \gg 0$, $a_i \frac{\partial u_i(\overline{\mathbf{x}}_i, \overline{\mathbf{g}})}{\partial x_n} = q_n$, for all i and n, and $\sum_{i=1}^I a_i \frac{\partial(\overline{\mathbf{x}}_i, \overline{\mathbf{g}})}{\partial g_n} = q_n$, for all n, where the a_i are as in part (b).[2]

2. This problem is based on the work of Paul Samuelson on public expenditures (1954, 1955).

— 7 —

Arrow-Debreu Equilibrium

The Arrow-Debreu model incorporates time and uncertainty in general equilibrium theory in a way that preserves the theory's main conclusions but at the cost of making the unrealistic assumption that all trading takes place at one initial moment, before anything other than trade occurs. Time and uncertainty are included by collapsing the entire future into a fictitious present. Despite this drawback, the model enriches the theory and its interpretation, for the extreme restriction on trading may be replaced by more plausible assumptions.

7.1 The Arrow-Debreu Model

The Arrow-Debreu approach requires a model of uncertainty and the passage of time. Uncertainty is represented by using a set of states, S, called the *states of the world.* I usually assume that S is a finite set, though a valid theory exists with an infinite set S. Each state s in S is a complete description of everything that is relevant to the situation studied. It should be imagined that only one state, s, actually occurs. What people observe are *events,* and these are subsets of S. Not all subsets of S are included as events, but only those that are considered to be observable. It is assumed that if A and B are events, then $A \cup B$, $A \cap B$, and $S \backslash A = \{s \in S \mid s \notin A\}$ are events as well. The set of events may or may not include subsets consisting of a single state. It is assumed that the whole set, S, and the empty set, $\emptyset$, are events. Probabilities are assigned to events by means of a function p, from the set of events to the unit interval, $[0, 1]$. If A is an event, $p(A)$ is, roughly speaking, the proportion of times that A would occur if the circumstances generating the observation were repeated a great many times. If $p(A) = 1$, then A

would always occur, and if $p(A) = 0$, A would never occur. It is assumed that $p(S) = 1$ and that $p(A \cup B) = p(A) + p(B)$, if A and B are disjoint events. These two assumptions imply that $p(\emptyset) = 0$. If S is a finite set, then the probability of an event is the sum of the probabilities of the individual states in the event, provided these states are themselves events. If there are infinitely many states, it may not be possible to build up the probabilities of all events from those of individual states. The following examples illustrate these notions.

EXAMPLE 7.1 You toss a fair coin twice. The set of states is

$$S = \{(H, H), (H, T), (T, H), (T, T)\},$$

where H represents heads and T represents tails. The state (H, T) represents heads on the first toss and tails on the second. Each state, (x, y), may be thought of as an event $\{(x, y)\}$, where x and y can be either H or T. The probability of each state is 1/4, so that $p((H, H)) = 1/4$ and so on. The set of events is the set of all possible subsets of S. The event of heads on the second toss is $\{(H, H), (T, H)\}$, and the probability of this event is $p((H, H)) + p((T, H)) = 1/4 + 1/4 = 1/2$.

EXAMPLE 7.2 A coin is tossed twice by an unknown mechanism, and you are told the number of times heads comes up. The set of states is as in the previous example, but the observable events are only the empty set, $\emptyset$, the whole set, S, and the sets $\{(T, T)\}$, $\{(H, T), (T, H)\}$, and $\{(H, H)\}$. It makes sense to assign probabilities only to these observable sets, since the mechanism generating the tosses is unknown.

EXAMPLE 7.3 A number is chosen from the interval $[0, 1]$ with uniform probability. The set of states is $[0, 1]$. Events are what is known as Lebesgue measurable subsets of $[0, 1]$. It includes all intervals, such as $[a, b]$, as well as many other sets, but does not include all subsets of $[0, 1]$. The probability of any single state, $\{s\}$ is zero, whereas the probability of the interval $[a, b]$ is $b - a$, if $b \geq a$. If $b > a$, the probability of $[a, b]$ cannot, therefore, be the sum of the probabilities of the individual states in $[a, b]$.

In example 7.1, events occur in a temporal sequence; there is a first toss, and there is a second toss. The set of states is the set of histories of what occurs. These histories may be described by a tree diagram, as in figure

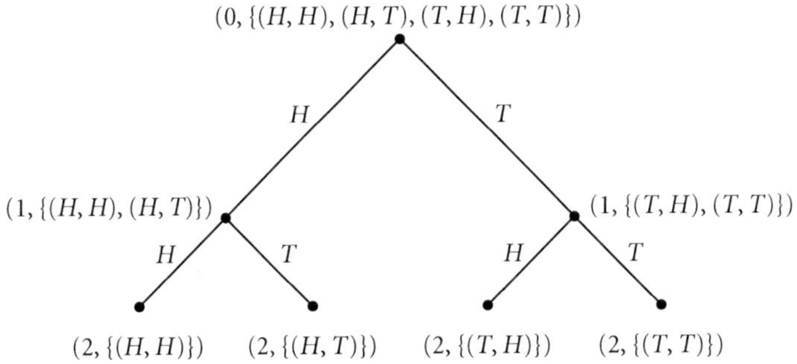

Figure 7.1 A dated event tree

7.1. The nodes in the figure correspond to what are called *dated events*. The dated event $(0, \{(H, H), (H, T), (T, H), (T, T)\})$ is the situation at time 0 before anything has happened. The dated event $(1, \{(T, H), (T, T)\})$ is the situation at time 1 occurring after tails occurred at time 0. The dated event $(2, \{(H, T)\})$ is the situation at time 2 after heads occurred at time 0 and tails at time 1.

I now describe terminology and notation that permits discussion of general dated events.

DEFINITION 7.4 A *partition* of a set S is a set, $\mathcal{S}$, of nonempty subsets of S that are mutually disjoint and whose union is S. That is, $A \cap B = \emptyset$, for any distinct members, A and B, of $\mathcal{S}$, and $\cup_{A \in \mathcal{S}} A = S$.

DEFINITION 7.5 If $\mathcal{F}$ and $\mathcal{S}$ are partitions of S, $\mathcal{F}$ *refines* $\mathcal{S}$ if every A in $\mathcal{S}$ is a union ofsets in $\mathcal{F}$. That is, for every A in $\mathcal{S}$, the sets in $\mathcal{F}$ that are subsets of A form a partition of A.

Partitions can be used to express the revelation of information over time. Suppose that the information is revealed over periods $t = 0, 1, \ldots, T$ and that S is the set of possible states of the world. The amount of information available at time t is represented by a partition, $\mathcal{S}_t$, of S. If nothing is forgotten, so that information increases over time, then $\mathcal{S}_{t+1}$ refines $\mathcal{S}_t$, for all t. The partition $\mathcal{S}_t$ is the set of events that occur up to time t. Suppose that such a sequence of partitions, $\mathcal{S}_t$, is given, for $t = 0, 1, \ldots, T$.

DEFINITION 7.6 The *set of dated events*, Γ, equals $\{(t, A) \mid 0 \leq t \leq T, A \in \mathcal{S}_t, \text{ for all } t\}$, where in a pair (t, A) the letter t is the date of occurrence of the event A.

There are as many dated events for period t as there are events in $\mathcal{S}_t$. Since $\mathcal{S}_0$ may contain many events, there may be many dated events for period 0. Imagine that all the agents in an economy observe the same events, and let the dated event set, Γ, be as above. Finally, imagine that the same N commodities are available in each dated event.

DEFINITION 7.7 A *contingent claim* is an agreement to deliver or receive an amount of a specified commodity in a specified dated event.

The set of all vectors of quantities of commodities in dated events is

$$\mathbb{R}^{\Gamma \times N} = \{\mathbf{x}: \Gamma \times \{1, \ldots, N\} \rightarrow \mathbb{R}\} = \{\mathbf{x}: \Gamma \rightarrow \mathbb{R}^N\},$$

where $\Gamma \times N$ denotes the Cartesian product of the sets Γ and $\{1, 2, \ldots, N\}$. That is, $\Gamma \times N = \{((t, A), n) \mid (t, A) \in \Gamma \text{ and } n = 1, 2, \ldots, N\}$. (The Cartesian product is defined in definition 5.26 (section 5.3).) A typical component of a vector $\mathbf{x}$ in $\mathbb{R}^{\Gamma \times N}$ is $x_{(t,A),n}$, where (t, A) is a dated event in Γ and n is one of the N commodities. If S is finite, the sets Γ and $\Gamma \times N$ are finite as well.

Imagine that trade in all the contingent claims occurs at a moment, time -1, just preceding time 0, that trade is made against a single unit of account, and that no trade occurs after the initial moment when trade in contingent claims occurs. In periods $0, 1, \ldots, T$, deliveries are made and taken according to the contingent contracts purchased and sold at time -1. Trade occurs at time -1 for commodities in all dated events of any given period t, even though only one of those events is actually realized.

Imagine an economy where all trading is in contingent claims. In such an economy, if you wanted to buy 5 pounds of wild bird food on a certain winter day (but only if there had been snow on the ground for at least a week), the purchase would be arranged beforehand on a market for bird food, at that date and when there had been snow on the ground for at least a week. An economy where all trades are arranged through forward contingent trades is said to be *Arrow-Debreu* or to have *complete markets.* To model such an economy, let the input-output possibility set, Y_j of the

jth firm be a subset of $\mathbb{R}^{\Gamma \times N}$, for each j, and for each consumer i, let the utility function be $u_i : \mathbb{R}_+^{\Gamma \times N} \to \mathbb{R}$ and the endowment be $\mathbf{e}_i \in \mathbb{R}_+^{\Gamma \times N}$, where $\mathbb{R}_+^{\Gamma \times N}$ is the set of all vectors in $\mathbb{R}^{\Gamma \times N}$ with nonnegative components. An equilibrium in such a model is termed an *Arrow-Debreu equilibrium.* It is denoted by $(\mathbf{x}, \mathbf{y}, \mathbf{p})$, where $(\mathbf{x}, \mathbf{y})$ is a feasible allocation and $\mathbf{p} \in \mathbb{R}_+^{\Gamma \times N}$ is a price vector. We know from the first welfare theorem 5.2 (in section 5.1) that if the utility functions are locally nonsatiated, then any equilibrium allocation is Pareto optimal. The Pareto optimality of Arrow-Debreu equilibria explains economists' interest in them.

The following example should clarify the meaning of the concept.

EXAMPLE 7.8 There are two periods, 0 and 1, two states in the second period, a and b, and the events are $\{a\}$ and $\{b\}$. The dated events are $(0, \{a, b\})$, $(1, \{a\})$, and $(1, \{b\})$. Let $\{a, b\} = S$. There is one firm, one consumer, and one commodity in each dated event, so that this is a Robinson Crusoe economy. The consumer is endowed with one unit of the good in period 0 and none in period 1 in either state. That is, the consumer's initial endowment is

$$\mathbf{e} = (e_{(0,S)}, e_{(1,a)}, e_{(1,b)}) = (1, 0, 0),$$

where I use $(1, a)$ and $(1, b)$ to stand for $(1, \{a\})$ and $(1, \{b\})$, respectively. Each of the two states a and b has probability one-half, the consumer has utility $\ln(x)$ for consumption of x units of the good in any state, and the consumer's utility is the sum of the utility from consumption in period 0 and the expected utility from consumption in period 1. That is, the consumer's utility function is

$$u(x_{(0,S)}, x_{(1,a)}, x_{(1,b)}) = \ln(x_{(0,S)}) + \frac{1}{2}\ln(x_{(1,a)}) + \frac{1}{2}\ln(x_{(1,b)}).$$

The firm's output is $\sqrt{-y_{(0,S)}}$ in dated event $(1, a)$, and $-y_{(0,S)}$ in dated event $(1, b)$, where $-y_{(0,S)}$ is the firm's input of the good in period 0.

Since the Arrow-Debreu equilibrium allocation in this example is Pareto optimal, it is optimal, so that the equilibrium allocation is the optimal one. That is, in order to calculate the equilibrium allocation, we must solve the problem

Note: b/c RobCru, thus AD eq must be CE, P.O., & WMP ∴ book uses WMP to solve (I'm sure UMP, PMP could have equivalently been used).

$$\max_{x_{(0,S)}, x_{(1,a)}, x_{(1,b)}, y_{(0,S)}} \left[\ln(x_{(0,S)}) + \frac{1}{2}\ln(x_{(1,a)}) + \frac{1}{2}\ln(x_{(1,b)}) \right]$$

$$\text{s.t.} \quad y_{(0,S)} \le 0,$$

$$0 \le x_{(0,S)} \le 1 + y_{(0,S)},$$

$$0 \le x_{(1,a)} \le \sqrt{-y_{(0,S)}}, \text{ and}$$

$$0 \le x_{(1,b)} \le -y_{(0,S)}.$$

Solving this problem, we find that $x_{(0,S)} = \frac{4}{7}$, $x_{(1,a)} = \sqrt{\frac{3}{7}}$, $x_{(1,b)} = \frac{3}{7}$, and $y_{(0,S)} = -\frac{3}{7}$. In calculating Arrow-Debreu prices, I normalize them so that $p_{(0,S)} = 1$. A first-order condition for the consumer's utility-maximization problem over a budget constraint is

$$\frac{\partial u(x_{(0,S)}, x_{(1,a)}, x_{(1,b)})}{\partial x_{(0,S)}} = \lambda p_{(0,S)},$$

where λ is the consumer's marginal utility of unit of account. This equation implies that

$$\lambda = \frac{1}{x_{(0,S)}} = \frac{7}{4}.$$

Another first-order condition for the consumer's maximization problem is

$$\frac{\partial u(x_{(0,S)}, x_{(1,a)}, x_{(1,b)})}{\partial x_{(1,a)}} = \lambda p_{(1,a)},$$

which implies that

$$\frac{1}{2}\frac{1}{x_{(1,a)}} = \lambda p_{(1,a)},$$

and hence

$$p_{(1,a)} = \frac{2\sqrt{21}}{21}.$$

Similarly, the first-order condition

$$\frac{\partial u(x_{(0,S)}, x_{(1,a)}, x_{(1,b)})}{\partial x_{(1,b)}} = \lambda p_{(1,b)},$$

implies that

$$\frac{1}{2}\frac{1}{x_{(1,b)}} = \partial p_{(1,b)},$$

and hence that

$$p_{(1,b)} = \frac{2}{3}.$$

There are two important things to notice about this example. First of all, the prices for the good in the dated events $(1, a)$ and $(1, b)$ are not proportional to the events' probabilities, though the consumer maximizes the expected utility of consumption in period 2. The probabilities of the two events are equal, yet $p_{(1,a)} = \frac{2}{\sqrt{21}} < \frac{2}{3} = p_{(1,b)}$. Because more of the good is available in dated event $(1, a)$ than $(1, b)$, the good is cheaper in event $(1, a)$. The second thing to notice is that the firm does not need to know the probabilities of the events in order to maximize its profits. It need only know the Arrow-Debreu prices. The firm's profit-maximization problem is

$$\max_{y_{(0,S)} \geq 0} \left[p_{(0,S)} y_{(0,S)} + p_{(1,a)}\sqrt{-y_{(0,S)}} + p_{(1,b)}(-y_{(0,S)})\right]$$

$$= \max_{y_{(0,S)} \geq 0} \left[y_{(0,S)} + \frac{2}{\sqrt{21}}\sqrt{-y_{(0,S)}} + \frac{2}{3}(-y_{(0,S)})\right].$$

The probabilities appear nowhere in this expression. This feature of the model does not correspond to reality, because executives of actual firms are preoccupied with trying to predict the future. They cannot, however, buy their inputs and sell their outputs on markets for contingent claims. If they could do so, they would, no doubt, care little about the likelihoods of the various future events.

7.2 Arrow Equilibrium

I now present an idea of Kenneth Arrow (1953) that makes Pareto optimality of equilibrium with uncertainty seem somewhat more feasible than it might otherwise appear. The Arrow-Debreu equilibrium strains our credulity, for not only does it require that all trading occur at an initial moment, but people must trade on an enormous number of markets at that time. Suppose that $\mathcal{S}_0 = \{S\}$ and that for every time period t, every member of the set of events, $\mathcal{S}_t$, contains two members of the partition $\mathcal{S}_{t+1}$. Suppose also that there are N goods in each dated event and that $t = 0, 1, \ldots, T$. Then there are N types of contingent claim for period 0, $2N$ for period 1, $4N$ for period 2, and $2^t N$ for period t. Since the number of events in

$\mathcal{S}_t$ is 2^t, the total number of contingent claims markets and prices at time -1 is

$$N \sum_{t=0}^{T} 2^t,$$

which quickly becomes huge as T grows.

We can reduce the number of contingent claims markets that open in the model by assuming that during every dated event, agents trade in current goods and services and in one period forward contingent contracts for unit of account in the dated events of the succeeding period. This arrangement requires that there be a different unit of account for each dated event. This scheme reduces the number of markets on which trade actually occurs, though the number of potential markets is even greater than in the Arrow-Debreu model. In the above example, trade would occur on N markets for goods in every period and on two markets for contingent claims in each of the first T periods, so that the total number of markets on which trade occurred would be

$$N(T+1) + 2T.$$

If T is large, this number is considerably less than the number, $N \sum_{t=0}^{T} 2^t$, of markets that open in an Arrow-Debreu equilibrium. The number of markets on which trade potentially could occur in an Arrow equilibrium is $N \sum_{t=0}^{T} 2^t + 2 \sum_{t=0}^{T-1} 2^t$. We will see that if the allocation of an Arrow equilibrium is to be Pareto optimal, then all traders must know at time 0 not only current prices but what all prices would be on potential markets if the dated events of those markets occurred. This foreknowledge is a form of rational expectations and requires knowledge of $N \sum_{t=0}^{T} 2^t + 2 \sum_{t=0}^{T-1} 2^t$ current and potential prices. This number exceeds by $2 \sum_{t=0}^{T-1} 2^t$ the number of prices in an Arrow-Debreu equilibrium.

Though the realization of Arrow-Debreu and Arrow equilibria requires different practical arrangements, the equilibria are equivalent in that they generate the same allocations. I need some new notation in order to explain the relation between the two concepts of equilibrium and to define an Arrow equilibrium formally. Let us start with an Arrow-Debreu equilibrium, $(\mathbf{x}, \mathbf{y}, \mathbf{p})$. The vector of Arrow prices for commodities bought and sold in dated event (t, A) is $\mathbf{P}_{(t,A)}$, which is a nonnegative N-vector that is proportional to the vector $\mathbf{p}_{(t,A)} = (p_{(t,A),n})_{n=1}^{N}$. That is,

$$\mathbf{P}_{(t,A)} = b_{(t,A)}\mathbf{p}_{(t,A)}, \tag{7.1}$$

where $b_{(t,A)} > 0$. The price $P_{(t,A),n}$ is the price in an Arrow equilibrium of one unit of commodity n in dated event (t, A) in terms of the unit of account or money of that dated event. The number $b_{(t,A)}$ is determined by the choice of unit of account of dated event (t, A) and is arbitrary unless other restrictions are added to the model. I use the term *(t, A)-dollars* to refer to the unit of account of dated event (t, A). I use the term *Arrow-Debreu dollars* to refer to the unit of account of period -1 in the Arrow-Debreu equilibrium. The units of $P_{(t,A),n}$ are (t, A)-dollars per unit of good n. The units of $p_{(t,A),n}$ are Arrow-Debreu dollars per unit of good n. Equation 7.1 makes it clear that the units of $b_{(t,A)}$ are (t, A)-dollars per Arrow-Debreu dollar. In what follows, I write a dated event at time t as $(t, A(t))$ in order to emphasize that $A(t) \in \mathcal{S}_t$.

I next define the one-period forward contingent prices for unit of account in the Arrow equilibrium. The price $q_{(0, A(0))}$ is the price in an Arrow equilibrium of a $(0, A(0))$-dollar in terms of an Arrow-Debreu or period -1 dollar and is defined by the equation

$$q_{(0,A(0))} = \frac{1}{b_{(0,A(0))}}. \tag{7.2}$$

For $t \geq 0$, let $(t+1, A(t+1))$ be a dated event that immediately follows dated event $(t, A(t))$, in the sense that $A(t+1)$ is a subset of $A(t)$. The contingent price of a $(t+1, A(t+1))$-dollar in terms of a $(t, A(t))$-dollar is $q_{(t,A(t)),(t+1,A(t+1))}$ and is defined by the equation

$$q_{(t,A(t)),(t+1,A(t+1))} = \frac{b_{(t,A(t))}}{b_{(t+1,A(t+1))}}. \tag{7.3}$$

A one-period forward contingent contract for unit of account is termed an *Arrow security.*

Let $(\mathbf{P}, \mathbf{q})$ be the full vector of prices

$$p_{(t,A(t)),n},\ q_{(0,A(0))},\ \text{and}\ q_{(t-1,A(t-1)),(t,A(t))}$$

just defined. An equilibrium, $(\mathbf{x}, \mathbf{y}, \mathbf{q}, \mathbf{P})$, with these prices I term an *Arrow equilibrium.* I have derived the Arrow prices from the Arrow-Debreu prices $p_{(t,A(t)),n}$. Conversely, it is possible to calculate the

Arrow-Debreu prices $p_{(t,A(t)),n}$, from the Arrow prices

$$\mathbf{P}_{(t,A(t)),n},\ q_{(0,A(0))},\ \text{and}\ q_{(t-1,A(t-1)),(t,A(t))},$$

by using equations 7.1–7.3.

Throughout what follows, if $\mathbf{x}$ is any vector in $\mathbb{R}^{\Gamma\times N}$ and $(t, A(t))$ is any dated event, then $\mathbf{x}_{(t,A(t))}$ denotes the N-vector $(x_{(t,A(t)),1}, \ldots, x_{(t,A(t)),N})$, and the vector $\mathbf{P}_{(t,A(t))} = (P_{(t,A(t)),1}, P_{(t,A(t)),2}, \ldots, P_{(t,A(t)),N})$ is the vector of current Arrow prices in dated event $(t, A(t))$.

I assume that firms maximize the present value of their profits. In order to define the present value, let

$$\begin{aligned} q_{(t,A(t))} &= \frac{1}{b_{(t,A(t))}} \\ &= q_{(0,A(0))}q_{(0,A(0)),(1,A(1))}q_{(1,A(1)),(2,A(2))}\cdots q_{(t-1,A(t-1)),(t,A(t))} \end{aligned} \tag{7.4}$$

be the price at time -1 of a unit of account in dated event $(t, A(t))$, for $t \geq 0$, where $A(t) \in \mathcal{S}_t$ and where $A(0) \supset A(1) \supset \ldots \supset A(t)$. The present value at time -1 of a production plan $\mathbf{y} \in \mathbb{R}_+^{\Gamma\times N}$ is

$$\sum_{t=0}^{T} \sum_{A(t)\in\mathcal{S}_t} q_{(t,A(t))}\mathbf{P}_{(t,A(t))} \cdot \mathbf{y}_{(t,A(t))}. \tag{7.5}$$

The consumers that own a firm would all agree that it should maximize this present value. In dated event $(t, A(t))$, consumer i receives

$$\Theta_{ij}\mathbf{P}_{(t,A(t))} \cdot \mathbf{y}_{j,(t,A(t))}$$

from firm j, a quantity that could be positive or negative. By using the Arrow one-period forward markets for unit of account, the consumer can transfer this wealth to any other dated event at the rates of exchange among dated events that define the present value.

Before continuing, I collect some useful observations. Because the numbers $b_{(t,A(t))}$ are positive,

$$q_{(t,A(t))} > 0, \tag{7.6}$$

for all t. Equations 7.1–7.4 imply that

$$\begin{aligned} \mathbf{p}_{(t,A(t))} &= q_{(0,A(0))}q_{(0,A(0)),(1,A(1))}q_{(1,A(1)),(2,A(2))} \\ &\quad \cdots q_{(t-1,A(t-1)),(t,A(t))}\mathbf{P}_{(t,A(t))} \\ &= q_{(t,A(t))}\mathbf{P}_{(t,A(t))}, \end{aligned} \tag{7.7}$$

for all $(t, A(t))$, where $A(0) \supset A(1) \supset \cdots \supset A(t)$. Finally, equation 7.4 implies that

$$q_{(t, A(t))} = q_{(t-1, A(t-1))} q_{(t-1, A(t-1)), (t, A(t))}, \tag{7.8}$$

for all $(t, A(t))$.

Expression 7.5 and equation 7.7 imply that in the Arrow model, total profits from $\mathbf{y}$ equal

$$\sum_{t=0}^{T} \sum_{A(t) \in \mathcal{S}_t} \mathbf{P}_{(t, A)} \cdot \mathbf{y}_{(t, A)},$$

which is the formula used for profits in the Arrow-Debreu model. The interpretation differs in the two models, however. In the Arrow-Debreu model, all purchases and sales are made in advance at time -1, before any economic activity occurs. In the Arrow model, purchases and sales are made currently as commodities are needed and become available. The firm calculates the present value in expression 7.5 at time -1, given advance knowledge of what all the prices $q_{(t, A(t))}$ and $P_{(t, A(t)), n}$ will be as the dated events $(t, A(t))$ occur.

I now describe the budget set of a consumer in an Arrow equilibrium. To do so, I must specify the intertemporal pattern of profit distribution to consumers. I make the simple assumption that current expenses or gains are shared among shareholders. That is, firm j pays

$$\Theta_{ij} \mathbf{P}_{(t, A(t))} \cdot \mathbf{y}_{j, (t, A(t))}$$

to consumer i in dated event $(t, A(t))$, where $\mathbf{y}_j \in Y_j$ is the equilibrium production plan of firm j. This quantity may be positive or negative. For each dated event $(t, A(t))$, $a_{(t, A(t))}$ denotes a quantity of $(t, A(t))$-dollars purchased in the immediately preceding dated event as a contingent claim. The vector

$$\mathbf{a} = (a_{(t, A(t))})_{t=0, 1, \ldots, T, A(t) \in \mathcal{S}_t}$$

is a vector of asset holdings. In an Arrow equilibrium, the budget set of consumer i is

$$\beta_i^A(\mathbf{P},\mathbf{q}) = \{(\mathbf{x},\mathbf{a}) \mid \mathbf{x} \in \mathbb{R}_+^{\Gamma\times N}, \mathbf{a} \in \mathbb{R}^{\Gamma}, \sum_{A(0)\in\mathcal{S}_0} q_{(0,A(0))}a_{(0,A(0))} \le 0,$$

$$\mathbf{P}_{(t,A(t))}\cdot\mathbf{x}_{(t,A(t))} + \sum_{\substack{A(t+1)\in\mathcal{S}_{t+1}\text{ and}\\ A(t+1)\subset A(t)}} q_{(t,A(t)),(t+1,A(t+1))}a_{(t+1,A(t+1))}$$

$$\le a_{(t,A(t))} + \mathbf{P}_{(t,A(t))}\cdot\mathbf{e}_{i,(t,A(t))} + \sum_{j=1}^{J}\Theta_{ij}\mathbf{P}_{(t,A(t))}\cdot\mathbf{y}_{j,(t,A(t))}, \tag{7.9}$$

for $t = 0, 1, \ldots, T-1$ and for all $A(t) \in \mathcal{S}_t$, and

$$\mathbf{P}_{(T,A(T))}\cdot\mathbf{x}_{(T,A(T))} \le a_{(T,A(T))} + \mathbf{P}_{(T,A(T))}\cdot\mathbf{e}_{j,(T,A(T))}$$

$$+\sum_{j=1}^{J}\Theta_{ij}\mathbf{P}_{(T,A(T))}\cdot\mathbf{y}_{j,(T,A(T))},$$

for all $A(T) \in \mathcal{S}_T\}$,

where the superscript A on β_i^{A} stands for *Arrow.* In the Arrow equilibrium, each consumer maximizes his or her utility over this budget set, and each firm maximizes the present value of profits.

DEFINITION 7.9 An *Arrow equilibrium* consists of $(\mathbf{x}, \mathbf{y}, \mathbf{a}, \mathbf{P}, \mathbf{q})$ satisfying the following conditions:

1. $(\mathbf{x}, \mathbf{y})$ is a feasible allocation.
2. $\mathbf{a} = (\mathbf{a}_i)_{i=1}^{I}$, where each $\mathbf{a}_i$ is a vector of asset holdings.
3. $(\mathbf{P}, \mathbf{q})$ is a vector of Arrow prices.
4. For each i, $(\mathbf{x}_i, \mathbf{a}_i)$ solves the problem

$$\max_{(\mathbf{x},\mathbf{a})\in\beta_i^A(\mathbf{P},\mathbf{q})} u_i(\mathbf{x}).$$

5. For each j, $\mathbf{y}_j$ solves the problem

$$\max_{\mathbf{y}\in Y_j}\sum_{t=0}^{T}\sum_{A(t)\in\mathcal{S}_t} q_{(t,A(t))}\mathbf{P}_{(t,A(t))}\cdot\mathbf{y}_{(t,A(t))}.$$

6. For each dated event (t, A) and each good n,

$$\mathbf{P}_{(t,A),n} = 0, \text{ if } \sum_{i=1}^{I} x_{i,(t,A),n} < \sum_{i=1}^{I} e_{i,(t,A),n} + \sum_{j=1}^{J} y_{j,(t,A(t)),n}. \tag{7.10}$$

The reader may wonder why the definition of Arrow equilibrium does not include a condition that the markets for Arrow securities clear. Such a condition is not necessary, since asset markets clear automatically if the markets for goods clear and all consumers satisfy their budget constraints, an assertion that is stated as proposition 7.12 below.

As was mentioned earlier in connection with the definition of profit maximization, Arrow equilibrium requires a form of rational expectations. Maximization of consumers' and firms' objective functions in an Arrow equilibrium requires knowledge at time -1 of all the prices, $P_{(t,A(t)),n}$ and $q_{(t,A(t)),(t+1,A(t+1))}$, for all dated events $(t, A(t))$ and for all commodities n. Since inputs bought in one dated event may have repercussions on possible outputs in all succeeding dated events, a firm needs to know all future prices in order to choose inputs rationally. Similarly, future prices may affect the amounts a consumer would want to purchase currently. Knowledge of future prices in each contingency is a form of rational expectations, because the prices are for transactions on markets that are not open at time -1. No such knowledge of the future is needed in an Arrow-Debreu equilibrium, because the prices of all contingent claims are determined simultaneously on markets at time -1. Since no mechanism is proposed in the Arrow model for determining all prices initially, knowledge of the future prices must be assumed.

The Arrow prices for contingent securities bear some relation to interest rates and insurance premiums, though the interpretation should not be pushed too far. The quantity

$$q_{(t,A(t)),t+1} = \sum_{A(t+1)\in \mathcal{S}_{t+1}: A(t+1)\subset A(t)} q_{(t,A(t)),(t+1,A(t+1))} \tag{7.11}$$

is the value in dated event $(t, A(t))$ of an uncontingent unit of account in period $t+1$. We could therefore write

$$q_{(t,A(t)),t+1} = \frac{1}{1 + r(t, A(t))}, \tag{7.12}$$

where $r(t, A(t))$ is the one-period interest rate in dated event $(t, A(t))$. The quantity

$$\alpha_{(t, A(t)), (t+1, A(t+1))} = \frac{q_{(t, A(t)), (t+1, A(t+1))}}{q_{(t, A(t)), t+1}}, \tag{7.13}$$

where $A(t+1) \subset A(t)$, might be thought of as the pure cost in dated event $(t, A(t))$ of insurance on dated event $(t+1, A(t+1))$. The price $\alpha_{(t, A(t)), (t+1, A(t+1))}$ is the cost in dated event $(t, A(t))$ of a unit of account in dated event $(t+1, A(t+1))$ after compensation for the interest earned from dated event $(t, A(t))$ to period $t+1$. The prices $\alpha_{(t, A(t)), (t+1, A(t+1))}$ resemble probabilities in that they are nonnegative and

$$\sum_{A(t+1) \in \mathcal{S}_{t+1} : A(t+1) \subset A(t)} \alpha_{(t, A(t)), (t+1, A(t+1))} = 1.$$

However, the numbers $\alpha_{(t, A(t)), (t+1, A(t+1))}$ bear no necessary relation to the conditional probabilities $\text{Prob}[A(t+1) \mid A(t)]$, because the choice of unit of account in each dated event is arbitrary. If we were to double the value of the unit of account in dated event $(t, A(t+1))$, then we would double $q_{(t, A(t)), (t+1, A(t+1))}$ and increase $\alpha_{(t, A(t)), (t+1, A(t+1))}$, while making no change in the real variables of the equilibrium. There is no money in the Arrow model that fixes the value of the units of account. For the same reason, the interest rates $r(t, A(t))$ are arbitrary and should not be identified with actual interest rates.

An example may clarify this discussion.

EXAMPLE 7.10 The set of dated events is the same as that of example 7.8 (in section 7.1). There are two periods, 0 and 1, two states in the second period, a and b, and the events are $\{a\}$ and $\{b\}$. The dated events are $(0, S)$, $(1, \{a\})$, and $(1, \{b\})$, where $S = \{a, b\}$. There is no production and there is one commodity in each dated event, and there are three consumers, A, B, and C. The initial endowments of the consumers are, respectively,

$$\mathbf{e}_{\text{A}} = (e_{\text{A},(0,S)}, e_{\text{A},(1,a)}, e_{\text{A},(1,b)}) = (0, 4, 0),$$
$$\mathbf{e}_{\text{B}} = (e_{\text{B},(0,S)}, e_{\text{B},(1,a)}, e_{\text{B},(1,b)}) = (0, 0, 4), \text{ and}$$
$$\mathbf{e}_{\text{C}} = (e_{\text{C},(0,S)}, e_{\text{C},(1,a)}, e_{\text{C},(1,b)}) = (4, 0, 0).$$

All three consumers have the same utility function as the consumer in example 7.8, which is

$$u(\mathbf{x}) = u(x_{(0,S)}, x_{(1,a)}, x_{(1,b)}) = \ln(x_{(0,S)}) + \frac{1}{2}\ln(x_{(1,a)}) + \frac{1}{2}\ln(x_{(1,b)}).$$

To calculate an Arrow-Debreu equilibrium in this example, I use equation 4.6 (in section 4.5) to find that

$$x_{\mathrm{A},(1,a)} = 1,\ x_{\mathrm{B},(1,b)} = 1,\ x_{\mathrm{C},(0,S)} = 2.$$

Normalize prices so that

$$p_{(0,S)} = 1.$$

By the symmetry of the example,

$$p_{(1,a)} = p_{(1,b)}, \tag{7.14}$$

and hence

$$x_{\mathrm{A},(1,b)} = x_{\mathrm{A},(1,a)} = 1 \text{ and } x_{\mathrm{B},(1,a)} = x_{\mathrm{B},(1,b)} = 1.$$

The feasibility of the equilibrium allocation now implies that

$$x_{\mathrm{C},(1,a)} = x_{\mathrm{C},(1,b)} = 2.$$

The symmetry of the example implies that

$$x_{\mathrm{A},(0,S)} = x_{\mathrm{B},(0,S)},$$

so that, by feasibility,

$$x_{\mathrm{A},(0,S)} = x_{\mathrm{B},(0,S)} = 1.$$

The budget equation for person C,

$$\begin{aligned} &p_{(0,S)}x_{C,(0,S)} + p_{(1,a)}x_{C,(1,a)} + p_{(1,b)}x_{C,(1,b)} \\ &= p_{(0,S)}e_{C,(0,S)} + p_{(1,a)}e_{C,(1,a)} + p_{(1,b)}e_{C,(1,b)}, \end{aligned}$$

becomes

$$2 + 2p_{(1,a)} + 2p_{(1,b)} = 4,$$

which by equation 7.14 implies that

$$p_{(1,a)} = p_{(1,b)} = \frac{1}{2}.$$

In summary, the Arrow-Debreu equilibrium is

$$((\mathbf{x}_{\mathrm{A}}, \mathbf{x}_{\mathrm{B}}, \mathbf{x}_{\mathrm{C}}), \mathbf{p}) = \left((1, 1, 1), (1, 1, 1), (2, 2, 2), \left(1, \frac{1}{2}, \frac{1}{2}\right)\right).$$

I now compute an Arrow equilibrium with

$$P_{(0,S)} = 1, \text{ and } P_{(1,a)} = P_{(1,b)} = 1.$$

By equation 7.1,

$$b_{(0,S)} = 1, \text{ and } b_{(1,a)} = b_{(1,b)} = 2.$$

By equation 7.3, the prices for contingent claims on unit of account in states $(1, a)$ and $(1, b)$ are, respectively,

$$q_{(0,S),(1,a)} = \frac{b_{(0,S)}}{b_{(1,a)}} = \frac{1}{2} = q_{(0,S),(1,b)}.$$

The Arrow budget conditions in equation 7.9 imply that consumer A's asset holdings are

$$a_{A,(1,a)} = P_{(1,a)}(x_{A,(1,a)} - e_{A,(1,a)}) = 1 - 4 = -3 \text{ and}$$
$$a_{A,(1,b)} = P_{(1,b)}(x_{A,(1,b)} - e_{A,(1,b)}) = 1 - 0 = 1.$$

As a check that the overall budget constraint is satisfied by person A, we calculate that

$$\begin{aligned} a_{A,(0,S)} &= P_{(0,S)}(x_{A,(0,S)} - e_{A,(0,S)}) + q_{(0,S),(1,a)}a_{A,(1,a)} \\ &\quad + q_{(0,S),(1,b)}a_{A,(1,b)} \\ &= 1(1-0) + \frac{1}{2}(-3) + \frac{1}{2}(1) = 0. \end{aligned}$$

Similar calculations show that

$$a_{B,(1,a)} = 1, \ a_{B,(1,b)} = -3, \ a_{B,(0,S)} = 0, \text{ and}$$
$$a_{C,(1,a)} = 2 = a_{C,(1,b)}, \text{ and } a_{C,(0,S)} = 0.$$

As defined by equation 7.11, the uncontingent price of a unit of account in period 1 is

$$q_{(0,S),1} = q_{(0,S),(1,a)} + q_{(0,S),(1,b)} = \frac{1}{2} + \frac{1}{2} = 1,$$

so that $r(0, S)$, the interest rate from period 0 to period 1 defined by equation 7.12, is zero. Therefore, the pure insurance prices defined by equation 7.13 are

$$\alpha_{(0,S),(1,a)} = q_{(0,S),(1,a)} = \frac{1}{2} = \alpha_{(0,S)(1,b)}.$$

Something to notice about the Arrow equilibrium that has just been calculated is that total purchases of Arrow securities for each dated event are zero. That is,

$$a_{A,(1,a)} + a_{B,(1,a)} + a_{C,(1,a)} = -3 + 1 + 2 = 0, \text{ and}$$
$$a_{A,(1,b)} + a_{B,(1,b)} + a_{C,(1,b)} = 1 - 3 + 2 = 0.$$

These equations imply that the markets for Arrow securities clear, as they always do in an Arrow equilibrium.

I now compute another Arrow equilibrium under the assumptions that

$$P_{(0,S)} = 1,\ P_{(1,a)} = 2,\ P_{(1,b)} = \frac{1}{2},$$

so that

$$b_{(0,S)} = 1,\ b_{(1,a)} = 4, \text{ and } b_{(1,b)} = 1.$$

Then,

$$q_{(0,S),(1,a)} = \frac{b_{(0,S)}}{b_{(1,a)}} = \frac{1}{4} \text{ and } q_{(0,S),(1,b)} = \frac{b_{(0,S)}}{b_{(1,b)}} = 1.$$

Proceeding as before, I calculate that

$$a_{A,(1,a)} = P_{(1,a)}(x_{A,(1,a)} - e_{A,(1,a)}) = 2(1-4) = -6,$$
$$a_{A,(1,b)} = P_{(1,b)}(x_{A,(1,b)} - e_{A,(1,b)}) = \frac{1}{2}(1-0) = \frac{1}{2}, \text{ and}$$
$$a_{A,(0,S)} = 0.$$

Similarly,

$$a_{B,(1,a)} = 2,\ a_{B,(1,b)} = -\frac{3}{2},\ a_{B,(0,S)} = 0,$$
$$a_{C,(1,a)} = 4,\ a_{C,(1,b)} = 1, \text{ and } a_{C,(0,S)} = 0.$$

The uncontingent price in period 0 of a unit of account in period 1 is

$$q_{(0,A),1} = q_{(0,S),(1,a)} + q_{(0,S),(1,b)} = \frac{1}{4} + 1 = \frac{5}{4},$$

and the corresponding interest rate is

$$r(0, S) = -\frac{1}{5},$$

and the pure insurance prices are

$$\alpha_{(0,S),(1,a)} = \frac{q_{(0,S),(1,a)}}{q_{(0,S),1}} = \frac{1/4}{5/4} = \frac{1}{5} \text{ and}$$
$$\alpha_{(0,S),(1,b)} = \frac{q_{(0,S),(1,b)}}{q_{(0,S),1}} = \frac{1}{5/4} = \frac{4}{5}.$$

We see that if we change the units of account of each dated event, the Arrow prices may change, though the allocation remains the same.

Example 7.10 illustrates two important functions of markets for Arrow-Debreu or Arrow contingent claims; they allow consumers to move purchasing power through time and across events. Consumer C finances the consumption of the other two consumers in period 1 in return for the ability to consume in period 2. Consumer A finances the consumption of the others in dated event $(1, a)$, and consumer B does the same in dated event $(1, b)$. The movement of purchasing power through time is done in reality by means of lending, borrowing, saving, and dissaving, which are achieved through what are loosely termed capital markets. The movement among events is insurance and is achieved in reality not only by means of insurance, but also through capital market transactions. These two functions of markets for contingent claims can be studied separately by considering static models with uncertainty and intertemporal models with no uncertainty. In the static models, the set of dated events is $\{(0, \{s\}) \mid s \in S\}$. It may be written as $\{s \mid s \in S\}$ and visualized as in the figure 7.2, where there are five states, 1, 2, 3, 4, and 5, and each state is an event. In an Arrow-Debreu model with such a set of dated events, the set of traded contracts may be written as $\{(s, n) \mid s \in S, n = 1, \ldots, N\}$, and consumers can buy in period -1 a contingent claim for any of the N commodities in any of the dated events, $(0, \{s\})$. In an Arrow model, consumers can, at time -1, buy or sell contingent claims for unit of account in each of the dated events $(0, \{s\})$. They then exchange unit of account for the N goods and services in the dated event that occurs. In this way, the Arrow equilibrium enables people to move purchasing power among the states.

In a model with the passage of time and no uncertainty, the set of dated events is $\{(t, S) \mid t = 0, \ldots, T\}$ or simply $\{t \mid t = 0, 1, \ldots, T\}$. If there are four periods, the set of dated events is $\{0, 1, 2, 3\}$ and may be represented as in figure 7.3. With this set of dated events, the set of traded contracts in an Arrow-Debreu model is $\{(t, n) \mid t = 0, 1, 2, \text{and } 3, \text{and } n = 1, 2, \ldots, N\}$. Consumers can buy at time -1 a claim on any of the N goods or services

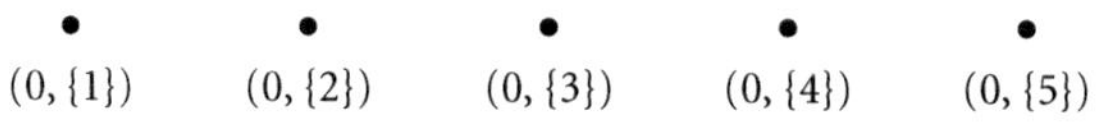

Figure 7.2 A set of dated events with only one date

Finance study
from him

0
1
2
3

Figure 7.3 A set of dated events with no uncertainty

in any period. In the Arrow equilibrium with this set of dated events, consumers can buy or sell in any period t, such that $t = 0, 1, 2, 3$, any of the goods or services deliverable in period t and a claim on unit of account in the succeeding period. In period 3, a consumer can buy goods and services of that period, using unit of account from the sale of endowment, net of repayment of loans arranged in period 2. If there were a market in period -1 for loans to be repaid in period 0, no one would use it, because a consumer earns nothing and needs nothing in period -1. In an Arrow equilibrium, each consumer has a budget constraint in each trading period.

In addition to allowing the shifting of financial resources through time and across events, Arrow-Debreu and Arrow forward prices make possible the efficient planning and coordination of production and consumption. This function is illuminated by the next example.

EXAMPLE 7.11   The set of dated events is as in the previous example. The dated events are $(0, S)$, $(1, \{a\})$, and $(1, \{b\})$, and the dated events $(1, \{a\})$ and $(1, \{b\})$ are equally probable. There is one commodity in each dated event, and there is one consumer with utility function

$$u(x_{(0,S)}, x_{(1,a)}, x_{(1,b)}) = \ln(x_{(0,S)}) + \frac{1}{2}\ln(x_{(1,a)}) + \frac{1}{2}\ln(x_{(1,b)}).$$

The consumer's endowment is

$$\mathbf{e} = (e_{(0,S)}, e_{(1,a)}, e_{(1,b)}) = (1, 0, 0).$$

There is one firm with input-output possibility set

$$Y = \{(y_{(0,S)}, y_{(1,a)}, y_{(1,b)}) \mid y_{(0,S)} \leq 0, \sqrt{y_{(1,a)}^2 + 4y_{(1,b)}^2} \leq -y_{(0,S)}\}.$$

We may think of the one commodity as a grain, which may be eaten or planted in period 0. State a corresponds to wet weather, and state b corresponds to dry weather. Less is produced when the weather is dry. The trade-off between crop sizes in wet or dry weather is determined by the depth of planting. If the firm plants deeply, the seed rots if the weather is wet but does well if it is dry. If planting is shallow, the seed dries out if the weather is dry but does well if it is wet. The firm should choose the depth of planting optimally.

To determine the allocation in an Arrow-Debreu or Arrow equilibrium in this example, I solve the problem

$$\max_{y_{(0,S)},\, y_{(1,a)},\, y_{(1,b)}} \left[\ln(1+y_{(0,S)}) + \frac{1}{2}\ln(y_{(1,a)}) + \frac{1}{2}\ln(y_{(1,b)})\right]$$

$$\text{s.t.} \quad \sqrt{y_{(1,a)}^2 + 4y_{(1,b)}^2} + y_{(0,S)} \leq 0.$$

Using the method of Lagrange multipliers, we find that

$$(y_{(0,S)}, y_{(1,a)}, y_{(1,b)}) = \left(-\frac{1}{2}, \frac{1}{\sqrt{8}}, \frac{1}{2\sqrt{8}}\right).$$

It follows that

$$(x_{(0,S)}, x_{(1,a)}, x_{(1,b)}) = \left(\frac{1}{2}, \frac{1}{\sqrt{8}}, \frac{1}{2\sqrt{8}}\right).$$

Half the grain is planted, and twice as much is produced and consumed in the wet state as in the dry.

In calculating equilibrium Arrow-Debreu prices, let $p_{(0,S)} = 1$. Substitution into the equation

$$\frac{\dfrac{\partial u}{\partial x_{(0,S)}}}{\dfrac{\partial u}{\partial x_{(1,a)}}} = \frac{\dfrac{1}{x_{(0,S)}}}{\dfrac{1}{2x_{(1,a)}}} = \frac{p_{(0,S)}}{p_{(1,a)}}$$

reveals that

$$p_{(1,a)} = \frac{\sqrt{2}}{2}.$$

By a similar calculation,

$$p_{(1,b)} = \sqrt{2},$$

so that the equilibrium Arrow-Debreu price vector is

$$p = \left(1, \frac{\sqrt{2}}{2}, \sqrt{2}\right).$$

I next compute the Arrow equilibrium with

$$P_{(0,S)} = P_{(1,a)} = P_{(1,b)} = 1.$$

Since $P_{(0,S)} = 1$, equations 7.1 and 7.2 imply that $q_{(0,S)} = 1$. Equation 7.7 implies that

$$q_{(0,S),(1,a)} = p_{(1,a)} = \frac{\sqrt{2}}{2}$$

and

$$q_{(0,S),(1,b)} = p_{(1,b)} = \sqrt{2}.$$

In this Arrow equilibrium, the firm solves the profit-maximization problem

$$\max\{y_{(0,S)} + \frac{\sqrt{2}}{2} y_{(1,a)} + \sqrt{2} y_{(1,b)} \mid (y_{(0,S)}, y_{(1,a)}, y_{(1,b)}) \in Y\}.$$

Notice that the firm does not maximize the expected value of profits, which is

$$y_{(0,S)} + \frac{1}{2} y_{(1,a)} + \frac{1}{2} y_{(1,b)},$$

but the present value of profits evaluated using Arrow contingent-claims prices. These prices guide the efficient choice of planting depth. The efficiency of planting depth is not achieved through borrowing, lending, or insurance, none of which are possible in the example because there is only one consumer.

I now prove the assertion mentioned earlier that the markets for Arrow securities clear in equilibrium, though the definition of Arrow equilibrium does not specify that the supply of securities equals the demand.

PROPOSITION 7.12 If $u_i : \mathbb{R}_+^{\Gamma \times N} \to \mathbb{R}$ is locally nonsatiated, for all i, then in any Arrow-Debreu equilibrium, $(\mathbf{x}, \mathbf{y}, \mathbf{a}, \mathbf{P}, \mathbf{q})$,

$$\sum_{i=1}^{I} a_{i,(t,A(t))} = 0,$$

for all $A(t) \in \mathcal{S}_t$ and all t.

Proof. Let $(\mathbf{x}, \mathbf{y}, \mathbf{a}, \mathbf{P}, \mathbf{q})$ be an Arrow equilibrium. From the definition of the Arrow budget set, $\beta_i^{\mathrm{A}}(\mathbf{P}, \mathbf{q})$,

$$\mathbf{P}_{(T,A(T))}\cdot\left(\mathbf{x}_{i,(T,A(T))} - \mathbf{e}_{i,(T,A(T))}\right) \leq a_{i,(T,A(T))} + \sum_{j=1}^{J} \Theta_{ij}\mathbf{P}_{(T,A(T))}\cdot\mathbf{y}_{j,(T,A(T))},$$

for all i. Because u_i is locally nonsatiated, consumer i does not waste any spending power in equilibrium and hence

$$\mathbf{P}_{(T,A(T))}\cdot(\mathbf{x}_{i,(T,A(T))} - \mathbf{e}_{i,(T,A(T))}) = a_{i,(T,A(T))} + \sum_{j=1}^{J} \Theta_{ij}\mathbf{P}_{(T,A(T))}\cdot\mathbf{y}_{j,(T,A(T))},$$

for all i. That is,

$$a_{i,(T,A(T))} = \mathbf{P}_{(T,A(T))}\cdot\left(\mathbf{x}_{i,(T,A(T))} - \mathbf{e}_{i,(T,A(T))}\right) - \sum_{j=1}^{J} \Theta_{ij}\mathbf{P}_{(T,A(T))}\cdot\mathbf{y}_{j,(T,A(T))}, \tag{7.15}$$

for all i. Because the allocation $(\mathbf{x}, \mathbf{y})$ is feasible and because of equilibrium condition 7.10,

$$P_{(t,A(t)),n}\left(\sum_{i=1}^{I}(x_{i,(t,A(t)),n} - e_{i,(t,A(t)),n}) - \sum_{j=1}^{J} y_{j,(t,A(t)),n}\right) = 0,$$

for all t, $A(t)$, and n, so that

$$\mathbf{P}_{(t,A(t))}\cdot\left(\sum_{i=1}^{I}(\mathbf{x}_{i,(t,A(t))} - \mathbf{e}_{i,(t,A(t))}) - \sum_{j=1}^{J} \mathbf{y}_{j,(t,A(t))}\right) = 0, \tag{7.16}$$

for all t and $A(t)$. Summing equation 7.15 over i and using equation 7.16 and the fact that $\sum_{i=1}^{I}\Theta_{ij} = 1$, for all j, we see that

$$\sum_{i=1}^{I} a_{i,(T,A(T))} = \sum_{i=1}^{I}\mathbf{P}_{(T,A(T))}\cdot(\mathbf{x}_{i,(T,A(T))} - \mathbf{e}_{i,(T,A(T))}) - \sum_{j=1}^{J}\mathbf{P}_{(T,A(T))}$$

$$\cdot\mathbf{y}_{j,(T,A(T))} = \mathbf{P}_{(T,A(T))}\cdot\left(\sum_{i=1}^{I}(\mathbf{x}_{i,(T,A(T))} - \mathbf{e}_{i,(T,A(T))}) - \sum_{j=1}^{J}\mathbf{y}_{j,(T,A(T))}\right) = 0$$

for all $A(T) \in \mathcal{S}_T$.

I now proceed by backward induction on t. Suppose that

$$\sum_{i=1}^{I} a_{i,(t+1, A(t+1))} = 0,$$

for all $A(t+1) \in \mathcal{S}_{t+1}$. Because u_i is locally nonsatiated,

$$\mathbf{P}_{(t, A(t))} \cdot \mathbf{x}_{i,(t, A(t))} + \sum_{A(t+1) \in \mathcal{S}_{t+1} \text{ and } A(t+1) \subset A(t)} q_{(t, A(t)),(t+1, A(t+1))} a_{i,(t+1, A(t+1))} \tag{7.17}$$
$$= a_{i,(t, A(t))} + \mathbf{P}_{(t, A(t))} \cdot \mathbf{e}_{i,(t, A(t))} + \sum_{j=1}^{J} \Theta_{ij} \mathbf{P}_{(t, A(t))} \cdot \mathbf{y}_{j,(t, A(t))}.$$

If we sum equation 7.17 over i, substitute from equation 7.16, and use the induction assumption that $\sum_{i=1}^{I} a_{i,(t+1, A(t+1))} = 0$, for all $A(t+1) \in \mathcal{S}_{t+1}$, we find that $\sum_{i=1}^{I} a_{i(t, A(t))} = 0$ as was to be proved. ▪

The next proposition asserts that corresponding Arrow-Debreu and Arrow equilibria have the same allocations. This assertion implies that the set of Arrow equilibrium allocations is the same as the set of Arrow-Debreu equilibrium allocations.

PROPOSITION 7.13 The vector $(\mathbf{x}, \mathbf{y}, \mathbf{a}, \mathbf{P}, \mathbf{q})$ is an Arrow equilibrium, if and only if $(\mathbf{x}, \mathbf{y}, \mathbf{p})$ is an Arrow-Debreu equilibrium, where the Arrow prices $(\mathbf{P}, \mathbf{q})$ are defined from the Arrow-Debreu price vector, $\mathbf{p}$, by equations 7.1–7.3.

Proof. It is clear from the definitions of the two equilibria that $\mathbf{y}_j$ maximizes profits over Y_j in the Arrow-Debreu equilibrium if and only if it maximizes profits over Y_j in the corresponding Arrow equilibrium. It remains to be shown that $\mathbf{x}_i$ maximizes u_i over the Arrow-Debreu budget set, $\beta_i^{\mathrm{AD}}(\mathbf{p})$, if and only if $(\mathbf{x}_i, \mathbf{a}_i)$ maximizes u_i over the Arrow budget set, $\beta_i^{\mathrm{A}}(\mathbf{P}, \mathbf{q})$, for some $\mathbf{a}_i$. To prove this statement, it is sufficient to show that

$$\beta_i^{\mathrm{AD}}(\mathbf{p}) = \{\mathbf{x} \mid (\mathbf{x}, \mathbf{a}) \in \beta_i^{\mathrm{A}}(\mathbf{P}, \mathbf{q}), \text{ for some } \mathbf{a}\}.$$

The budget set of the Arrow-Debreu equilibrium is

$$\beta_i^{AD}(\mathbf{p}) = \left\{ \mathbf{x} \in \mathbb{R}_+^{\Gamma \times N} \mid \sum_{t=0}^{T} \sum_{A \in \mathcal{S}_t} \left(\mathbf{p}_{(t, A(t))} \cdot (\mathbf{x}_{(t, A(t))} - \mathbf{e}_{i, (t, A(t))}) - \sum_{j=1}^{J} \Theta_{ij} \mathbf{p}_{(t, A(t))} \cdot \mathbf{y}_{j, (t, A(t))} \right) \leq 0 \right\}.$$

Let $(\mathbf{x}, \mathbf{a}) \in \beta_i^{A}(\mathbf{P}, \mathbf{q})$. Then,

$$\begin{aligned}
&\sum_{A(0) \in \mathcal{S}_0} q_{(0, A(0))} a_{(0, A(0))} \leq 0, \\
&\mathbf{P}_{(0, A(0))} \cdot \mathbf{x}_{(0, A(0))} + \sum_{A(1) \in \mathcal{S}_1 \text{ and } A(1) \subset A(0)} q_{(0, A(0)), (1, A(1))} a_{(1, A(1))} \\
&\leq a_{(0, A(0))} + \mathbf{P}_{(0, A(0))} \cdot \mathbf{e}_{i, (0, A(0))} + \sum_{j=1}^{J} \Theta_{ij} \mathbf{P}_{(0, A(0))} \cdot \mathbf{y}_{j, (0, A(0))}, \\
&\mathbf{P}_{(1, A(1))} \cdot \mathbf{x}_{(1, A(1))} + \sum_{A(2) \in \mathcal{S}_2 \text{ and } A(2) \subset A(1)} q_{(1, A(1)), (2, A(2))} a_{(2, A(2))} \\
&\leq a_{(1, A(1))} + P_{(1, A(1))} \cdot \mathbf{e}_{i, (1, A(1))} + \sum_{j=1}^{J} \Theta_{ij} P_{(1, A(1))} \cdot \mathbf{y}_{j, (1, A(1))}, \\
&\vdots \\
&\mathbf{P}_{(T-1, A(T-1))} \cdot \mathbf{x}_{(T-1, A(T-1))} \\
&+ \sum_{A(T) \in \mathcal{S}_T \text{ and } A(T) \subset A(T-1)} q_{(T-1, A(T-1)), (T, A(T))} a_{(T, A(T))} \\
&\leq a_{(T-1, A(T-1))} + \mathbf{P}_{(T-1, A(T-1))} \cdot \mathbf{e}_{i, (T-1, A(T-1))} \\
&+ \sum_{j=1}^{J} \Theta_{ij} \mathbf{P}_{(T-1, A(T-1))} \cdot \mathbf{y}_{j, (T-1, A(T-1))}, \\
&\mathbf{P}_{(T, A(T))} \cdot \mathbf{x}_{(T, A(T))} \leq a_{(T, A(T))} \\
&+ \mathbf{P}_{(T, A(T))} \cdot \mathbf{e}_{i, (T, A(T))} + \sum_{j=1}^{J} \Theta_{ij} \mathbf{P}_{(T, A(T))} \cdot \mathbf{y}_{j, (T, A(T))},
\end{aligned} \tag{7.18}$$

for all $A(0), A(1), \ldots, A(T)$, where $A(t) \in \mathcal{S}_t$, for all t. If we multiply the $(t+2)$nd inequality of 7.18 by $q_{(t, A(t))}$, for $t \geq 0$, and use equations 7.7 and 7.8, we see that the inequalities of 7.18 become

$$\sum_{A(0)\in \mathcal{S}_0} q_{(0,A(0))} a_{(0,A(0))} \le 0,$$

$$\mathbf{p}_{(0,A(0))}\cdot \mathbf{x}_{(0,A(0))} + \sum_{A(1)\in \mathcal{S}_1 \text{ and } A(1)\subset A(0)} q_{(1,A(1))} a_{(1,A(1))}$$

$$\le q_{(0,A(0))} a_{(0,A(0))} + \mathbf{p}_{(0,A(0))}\cdot \mathbf{e}_{i,(0,A(0))} + \sum_{j=1}^{J} \Theta_{ij} \mathbf{p}_{(0,A(0))}\cdot \mathbf{y}_{j,(0,A(0))},$$

$$\mathbf{p}_{(1,A(1))}\cdot \mathbf{x}_{(1,A(1))} + \sum_{A(2)\in \mathcal{S}_2 \text{ and } A(2)\subset A(1)} q_{(2,A(2))} a_{(2,A(2))}$$

$$\le q_{(1,A(1))} a_{(1,A(1))} + \mathbf{p}_{(1,A(1))}\cdot \mathbf{e}_{i,(1,A(1))} + \sum_{j=1}^{J} \Theta_{ij} \mathbf{p}_{(1,A(1))}\cdot \mathbf{y}_{j,(1,A(1))}, \tag{7.19}$$

$$\vdots$$

$$\mathbf{p}_{(T-1,A(T-1))}\cdot \mathbf{x}_{(T-1,A(T-1))} + \sum_{A(T)\in \mathcal{S}_T \text{ and } A(T)\subset A(T-1)} q_{(T,A(T))} a_{(T,A(T-1))}$$

$$\le q_{(T-1,A(T-1))} a_{(T-1,A(T-1))} + \mathbf{p}_{(T-1,A(T-1))}\cdot \mathbf{e}_{i,(T-1,A(T-1))}$$

$$+ \sum_{j=1}^{J} \Theta_{ij} \mathbf{p}_{(T-1,A(T-1))}\cdot \mathbf{y}_{j,(T-1,A(T-1))},$$

$$\mathbf{p}_{(T,A(T))}\cdot \mathbf{x}_{(T,A(T))} \le q_{(T,A(T))} a_{(T,A(T))}$$

$$+ \mathbf{p}_{(T,A(T))}\cdot \mathbf{e}_{i,(T,A(T))} + \sum_{j=1}^{J} \Theta_{ij} \mathbf{p}_{(T,A(T))}\cdot \mathbf{y}_{j,(T,A(T))}.$$

Summing these inequalities over all dated events and canceling like terms on both sides of the resulting equation, we obtain

$$\sum_{t=0}^{T} \sum_{A(t)\in \mathcal{S}_t} \mathbf{p}_{(t,A(t))}\cdot \mathbf{x}_{(t,A(t))} \le \sum_{t=0}^{T} \sum_{A(t)\subset \mathcal{S}_t} \left(\mathbf{p}_{(t,A(t))} \mathbf{e}_{i,(t,A(t))} + \sum_{j=1}^{J} \Theta_{ij} \mathbf{p}_{(t,A(t))}\cdot \mathbf{y}_{j,(t,A(t))} \right), \tag{7.20}$$

which is the Arrow-Debreu budget condition. Therefore,

$$\{\mathbf{x} \mid (\mathbf{x}, \mathbf{a}) \in \beta_i^{\mathrm{A}}(\mathbf{P}, \mathbf{q}), \text{ for some } \mathbf{a}\} \subset \beta_i^{\mathrm{AD}}(\mathbf{p}).$$

To prove the reverse inclusion, suppose that $\mathbf{x} \in \beta_i^{AD}(\mathbf{p})$. Then, inequality 7.20 applies. Use the last T inequalities of 7.19 to define the asset holdings $a_{(t, A(t))}$. That is, form the system

$$\begin{aligned}
&\mathbf{p}_{(0, A(0))} \cdot \mathbf{x}_{(0, A(0))} + \sum_{A(1) \in \mathcal{S}_1 \text{ and } A(1) \subset A(0)} q_{(1, A(1))} a_{(1, A(1))} \\
&= q_{(0, A(0))} a_{(0, A(0))} + \mathbf{p}_{(0, A(0))} \cdot \mathbf{e}_{i, (0, A(0))} + \sum_{j=1}^{J} \Theta_{ij} \mathbf{p}_{(0, A(0))} \cdot \mathbf{y}_{j, (0, A(0))}, \\
&\mathbf{p}_{(1, A(1))} \cdot \mathbf{x}_{(1, A(1))} + \sum_{A(2) \in \mathcal{S}_2 \text{ and } A(2) \subset A(1)} q_{(2, A(2))} a_{(2, A(2))} \\
&= q_{(1, A(1))} a_{(1, A(1))} + \mathbf{p}_{(1, A(1))} \cdot \mathbf{e}_{i, (1, A(1))} + \sum_{j=1}^{J} \Theta_{ij} \mathbf{p}_{(1, A(1))} \cdot \mathbf{y}_{j, (1, A(1))}, \\
&\vdots \\
&\mathbf{p}_{(T-1, A(T-1))} \cdot \mathbf{x}_{(T-1, A(T-1))} + \sum_{A(T) \in \mathcal{S}_T \text{ and } A(T) \subset A(T-1)} q_{(T, A(T))} a_{(T, A(T-1))} \\
&= q_{(T-1, A(T-1))} a_{(T-1, A(T-1))} + \mathbf{p}_{(T-1, A(T-1))} \cdot \mathbf{e}_{i, (T-1, A(T-1))} \\
&+ \sum_{j=1}^{J} \Theta_{ij} \mathbf{p}_{(T-1, A(T-1))} \cdot \mathbf{y}_{j, (T-1, A(T-1))}, \\
&\mathbf{p}_{(T, A(T))} \cdot \mathbf{x}_{(T, A(T))} = q_{(T, A(T))} a_{(T, A(T))} + \mathbf{p}_{(T, A(T))} \cdot \mathbf{e}_{i, (T, A(T))} \\
&+ \sum_{j=1}^{J} \Theta_{ij} \mathbf{p}_{(T, A(T))} \cdot \mathbf{y}_{j, (T, A(T))}.
\end{aligned} \tag{7.21}$$

The last or $(T+1)$st of equations 7.21 defines $a_{(T, A(T))}$, for all $A(T) \in \mathcal{S}_T$, because by inequality 7.6, $q_{(T, A(T))} > 0$. I proceed by backward induction on t. Given $a_{(t+1, A(t+1))}$ for all $A(t+1) \in \mathcal{S}_{t+1}$, the $(t+1)$st equation of system 7.21 defines $a_{(t, A(t))}$, for all $A(t) \in \mathcal{S}_t$, since $q_{(t, A(t))} > 0$, by inequality 7.6. It remains to verify that the asset holdings $a_{(0, A(0))}$ satisfy the first inequality of system 7.19, which is

$$\sum_{A(0) \in \mathcal{S}_0} q_{(0, A(0))} a_{(0, A(0))} \leq 0.$$

If we add all the equations of system 7.21 over all dated events and cancel like terms on opposite sides of the resulting equation and use inequality

7.20, we find that

$$\sum_{A(0)\in \mathcal{S}_0} q_{(0,A(0))} a_{(0,A(0))}$$

$$= \sum_{t=0}^{T} \sum_{A(t)\in \mathcal{S}_t} \left(\mathbf{p}_{(t,A(t))} \cdot [\mathbf{x}_{(t,A(t))} - \mathbf{e}_{i,(t,A(t))}] \right.$$

$$\left. - \sum_{j=1}^{J} \Theta_{ij} \mathbf{p}_{(t,A(t))} \cdot \mathbf{y}_{j,(t,A(t))} \right) \le 0.$$

Therefore, the vector $(\mathbf{x}, \mathbf{a})$ satisfies all of the inequalities of system 7.19. We may divide the $(t+2)$nd inequality of system 7.19 by $q_{(t,A(t))}$, for $t \ge 0$, because, by inequality 7.6, $q_{(t,A(t))} > 0$. If we do so, we obtain system 7.18, so that $(\mathbf{x}, \mathbf{a}) \in \beta_i^{\mathrm{A}}(\mathbf{P}, \mathbf{q})$ and therefore

$$\beta_i^{\mathrm{AD}}(\mathbf{p}) \subset \{\mathbf{x} \mid (\mathbf{x}, \mathbf{a}) \in \beta_i^{\mathrm{A}}(\mathbf{P}, \mathbf{q}), \text{ for some } \mathbf{a}\}.$$

This completes the proof that

$$\beta_i^{\mathrm{AD}}(\mathbf{p}) = \{\mathbf{x} \mid (\mathbf{x}, \mathbf{a}) \in \beta_i^{\mathrm{A}}(\mathbf{P}, \mathbf{q}), \text{ for some } \mathbf{a}\}. \quad \blacksquare$$

7.3 Insurance

The main purpose of insurance is to permit people to share or redistribute financial risk. Although it might seem natural to associate insurance with the law of large numbers, it is misleading to do so. What a large provider of automobile insurance earns in premiums each year roughly equals what it pays out in indemnities plus a margin for administrative expenses and profits. This is so because the law of large numbers makes the annual average payment per customer nearly predictable. The law of large numbers so reduces the insurer's risk that it can, in a sense, self-insure. The situation is quite different in the case of damages from large storms or floods, when the losses greatly exceed the flow of premiums and must be paid out of reserves accumulated by insurance companies and by investors who have agreed to bear a share of the risk through reinsurance arrangements. In such circumstances, significant risks are borne by insurance company shareholders and other investors. The Arrow-Debreu and Arrow models are used to analyze the risk-spreading function of insurance rather than its role in making risk disappear through averaging. The models are unrealistic in that they

ask Bewley to elaborate more on this difference

(what models do this?

assume that only consumers buy and sell insurance, whereas in reality, firms are major buyers of insurance as well as its most important providers. I will describe the possible risky outcomes as dated events like those pictured in figure 7.2 in section 7.2. I assume that in each dated event there is only one commodity, which may be thought of loosely as money, and I further simplify the analysis by assuming that consumers maximize the expected value of the utility gained from consumption of the one good. The expected value of utility is termed a von Neumann–Morgenstern utility function.

I introduce appropriate terminology in order to define the domain of von Neumann–Morgenstern utility functions. A function from the set of states to the real numbers, $\mathbf{x}: S \to \mathbb{R}$, is called a *random variable.* In economics, random variables are sometimes referred to as *lotteries,* and the numbers, $x(s)$, are called *outcomes.* Assume that the set of states, S, is finite, let $\mathbb{R}^S = \{\mathbf{x}: S \to \mathbb{R}\}$ be the set of all random variables on S, and let $\mathbb{R}^S_+ = \{\mathbf{x}: S \to [0, \infty)\}$ denote the set of nonnegative random variables. The *expected value* of the random variable $\mathbf{x} \in \mathbb{R}^S$ is

$$E\mathbf{x} = \sum_{s \in S} \pi(s)x(s),$$

where $\pi(s)$ is the probability of state s. The probabilities, $\pi(s)$, may be the objective probabilities of the states, s, or they may be subjective probabilities applied by an individual to the states. A *von Neumann–Morgenstern utility function,* $U: \mathbb{R}^S_+ \to \mathbb{R}$, is a function of nonnegative random variables, $\mathbf{x}$, that has the form

$$U(\mathbf{x}) = \sum_{s \in S} \pi(s)u(x(s)),$$

where $u: [0, \infty) \to (-\infty, \infty)$ is a utility function for the one good; the utility of the random variable or lottery is the expected value of the utilities of the outcomes. The function U is concave if and only if the function u is concave. By a slight abuse of notation, I will write $Eu(x)$ for the expected value $\sum_{s \in S} \pi(s)u(x(s))$, so that $U(\mathbf{x}) = Eu(x)$.

Von Neumann–Morgenstern utility functions have convenient properties. Suppose that an individual has such a utility function with a differentiable function, u, of outcomes. The person's marginal rate of substitution between lotteries in states a and b at the contingent claim vector $\mathbf{x}$ is

$$\mathrm{MRS}_{a,b}(\mathbf{x}) = \frac{\dfrac{\partial U(\mathbf{x})}{\partial x(a)}}{\dfrac{\partial U(\mathbf{x})}{\partial x(b)}} = \frac{\pi(a)\dfrac{du(x(a))}{dx}}{\pi(b)\dfrac{du(x(b))}{dx}},$$

provided $x(a) > 0$ and $x(b) > 0$. If $x(a) = x(b)$, then

$$\frac{du(x(a))}{dx} = \frac{du(x(b))}{dx},$$

so that

$$\mathrm{MRS}_{a,b}(x) = \frac{\pi(a)}{\pi(b)}.$$

If we imagine that there are only two states, a and b, then the utility function U generates indifference curves in the two dimensional space with coordinates $x(a)$ and $x(b)$, and the slope of an indifference curve, I, at the diagonal is $-\pi(a)/\pi(b)$, as shown in figure 7.4 for the case of concave function, u.

The consumer's attitude toward risk is determined by the shape of u.

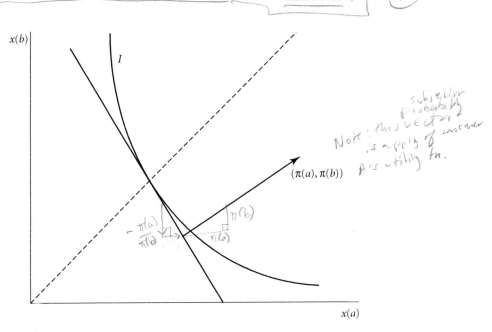

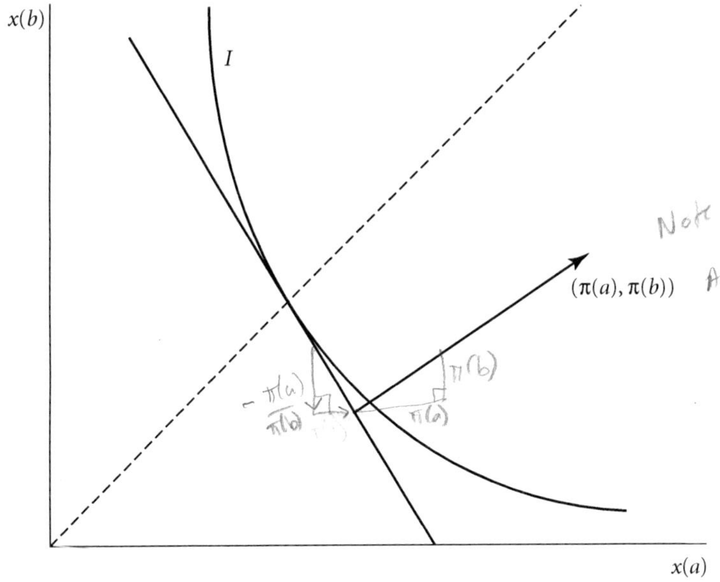

Figure 7.4 An indifference curve of a von Neumann–Morgenstern utility function

DEFINITION 7.14 A consumer with von Neumann–Morgenstern utility function $U(\mathbf{x}) = Eu(x)$ is said to be *risk averse* if u is concave.

DEFINITION 7.15 A consumer with von Neumann–Morgenstern utility function $U(\mathbf{x}) = Eu(x)$ is said to be *risk neutral* if u is affine, where u is affine if

$$u(\alpha\mathbf{x} + (1-\alpha)\mathbf{y}) = \alpha u(\mathbf{x}) + (1-\alpha)u(\mathbf{y}),$$

for all $\mathbf{x}$ and $\mathbf{y}$ in X and for all α such that $0 \leq \alpha \leq 1$.

DEFINITION 7.16 A consumer with von Neumann–Morgenstern utility function $U(\mathbf{x}) = Eu(x)$ is said to be *risk loving* if u is convex.

Recall that $u\colon [0, \infty) \to (-\infty, \infty)$ is concave if and only if $u(\alpha x + (1-\alpha)y) \geq \alpha u(x) + (1-\alpha)u(y)$, for all numbers x and y and for any number α such that $0 \leq \alpha \leq 1$. It follows easily that u is concave if and only if

$$u\left(\sum_{k=1}^{K} \alpha_k x_k\right) \geq \sum_{k=1}^{K} \alpha_k u(x_k),$$

for any finite sequences of numbers $x_1, \ldots, x_K$ and $\alpha_1, \ldots, \alpha_K$, such that $\alpha_k \geq 0$, for all k, and $\sum_{k=1}^{K} \alpha_k = 1$. Hence, if $\mathbf{x}\colon S \to \mathbb{R}$ and u is concave, then

$$u\left(\sum_{s \in S} \pi(s)x(s)\right) \geq \sum_{s \in S} \pi(s)u(x(s)).$$

That is, $u(E\mathbf{x}) \geq Eu(x)$. In other words, we may say that the consumer is risk averse and u is concave if and only if $u(E\mathbf{x}) \geq Eu(x)$, for all random variables $\mathbf{x}$. This assertion means that the consumer finds having for sure the expected value of $\mathbf{x}$ at least as desirable as having the lottery $\mathbf{x}$ itself. For this reason, the consumer is said to be averse to risk.

Similarly, the consumer is risk neutral if and only if $u(E\mathbf{x}) = Eu(x)$, for all random variables $\mathbf{x}$. That is, the consumer is indifferent between having the expected value of $\mathbf{x}$ for sure and having $\mathbf{x}$. Finally, the consumer is risk loving if and only if $u(E\mathbf{x}) \leq Eu(x)$, for all random variables $\mathbf{x}$. That is, the consumer finds having the random variable at least as desirable as having the expected value of the random variable for sure.

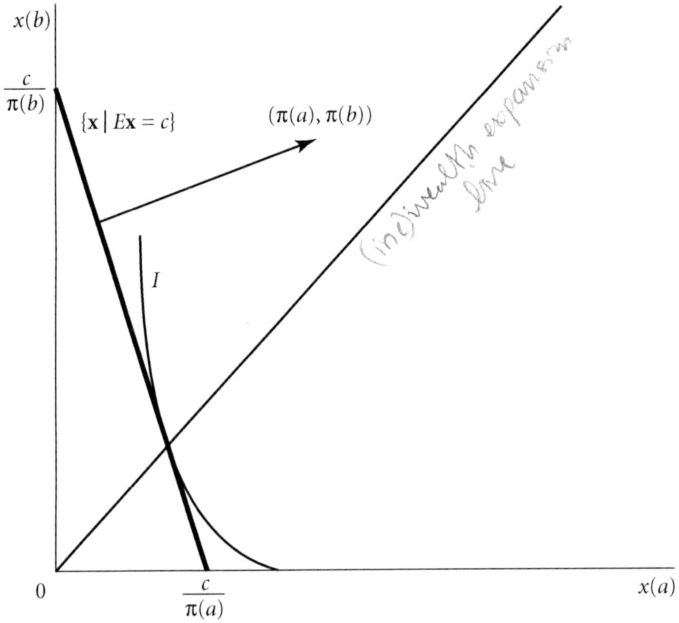

Figure 7.5 Maximization of the expected utility among all random variables with expectation equal to a constant c: The risk-averse case

Another way to see the connection between the concavity of u and the intuitive idea of risk aversion is to consider the problem

$$\begin{aligned} &\max_{\mathbf{x} \in \mathbb{R}^S_+} \; U(\mathbf{x}) \\ &\text{s.t.} \quad E\mathbf{x} = c, \end{aligned} \tag{7.22}$$

where c is a nonnegative constant and U is an increasing function. If U, and hence u, is concave, the solution to this problem is the constant function defined by the equation $x(s) = c$, for all s. If we suppose that there are only two states, a and b, then the solution of the maximization problem 7.22 may be seen in the figure 7.5. The curve in the figure is an indifference curve, I, of the utility function, U, that is tangent to the straight line segment $\{\mathbf{x} \in \mathbb{R}^S_+ \mid E\mathbf{x} = c\}$ at the random variable $\mathbf{x} = c$.

Figure 7.6 is the corresponding diagram in the risk-neutral case. The parallel lines are indifference curves for U. Because u is affine, it has the

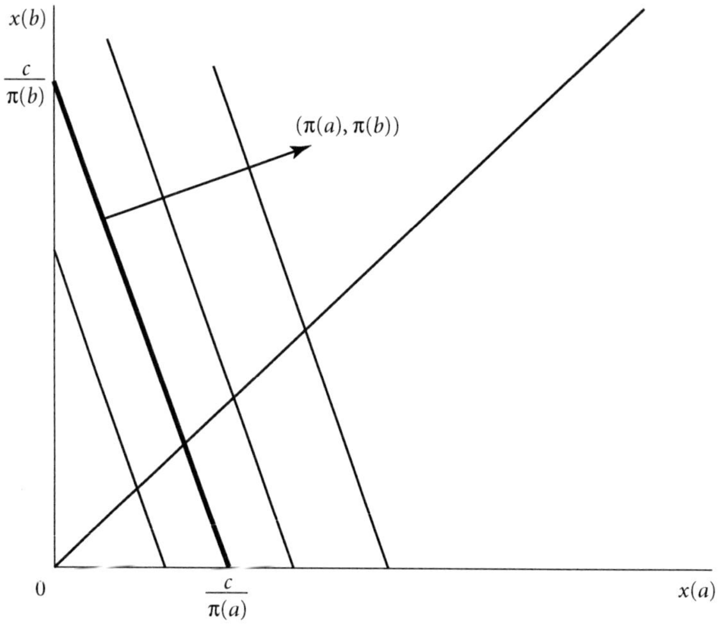

Figure 7.6 Maximization of the expected utility among all random variables with expectation equal to a constant c: The risk-neutral case

form $u(\mathbf{x}) = A\mathbf{x} + B$, where A is a positive number and B is a number. Therefore, $U(\mathbf{x}) = Eu(\mathbf{x}) = AE\mathbf{x} + B$. An indifference curve for U solves the equation $AE\mathbf{x} + B = C$, for some constant C. Therefore, the indifference curve solves the equation $E\mathbf{x} = A^{-1}(C - B)$ and is parallel to the line segment defined by the equation $E\mathbf{x} = c$, which is shown as the thick indifference curve in the figure. It may be seen that any nonnegative random variable $\mathbf{x}$, such that $E\mathbf{x} = c$, solves maximization problem 7.22.

Figure 7.7 describes the risk-loving case. It can be seen that the tangency between an indifference curve and the line $\{\mathbf{x} \mid E\mathbf{x} = c\}$ is not a solution to problem 7.22. Rather, if $\pi(b) \leq \pi(a)$, then a solution, $\mathbf{x}$, is defined by the equation

$$x(s) = \begin{cases} 0, & \text{if } s = a, \text{ and} \\ \frac{c}{\pi(b)}, & \text{if } s = b. \end{cases}$$

In the risk-loving case, the solution to problem 7.22 concentrates all of the gain on the least-probable states.

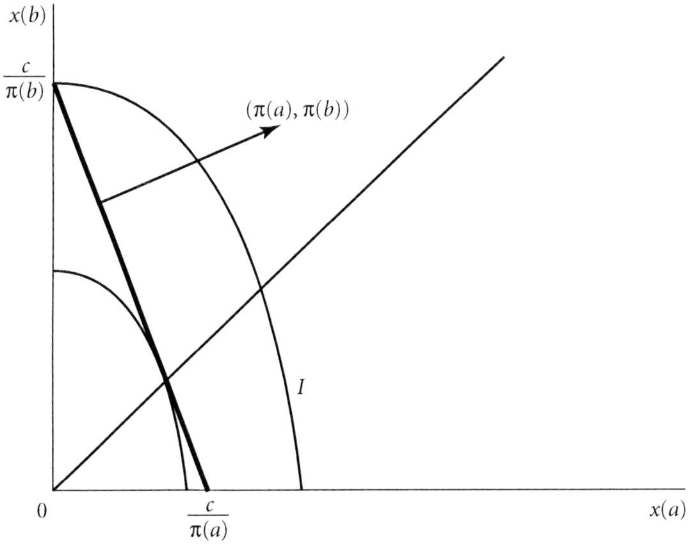

Figure 7.7 Maximization of the expected utility among all random variables with expectation equal to a constant c: The risk-loving case

In studying the connection between Arrow-Debreu or Arrow equilibrium and insurance, I focus on two issues—what insurance does and the relation between the probability of an event and the price of insurance on it. We have already seen in example 7.8 (in section 7.1) that Arrow-Debreu prices need not be proportional to the probabilities of events, and we have seen in example 7.10 (in section 7.2) that there is no fixed relation between the probabilities of events and Arrow contingent-claim prices, because the Arrow prices depend on choice of the unit of account in each dated event.

Suppose we are given $(U_i, \mathbf{e}_i)_{i=1}^{I}$, where, for all i, $\mathbf{e}_i \in \mathbb{R}_+^{\Gamma}$ and $U_i\colon \mathbb{R}_+^{\Gamma} \to \mathbb{R}$ is a von Neumann–Morgenstern utility function of the form $U_i(x) = \sum_{s \in S} \pi_i(s) u_i(x_s)$ and where $\Gamma = S$, where I use s to represent the dated event $(0, \{s\})$. To be consistent with Arrow-Debreu notation, I will use the subscript s on allocation and price variables to refer to the dated event $(0, \{s\})$. An Arrow-Debreu equilibrium for this model consists of $(\overline{\mathbf{x}}, \mathbf{p})$ such that

1. $\overline{\mathbf{x}} = (\overline{\mathbf{x}}_1, \ldots, \overline{\mathbf{x}}_I)$, where $\overline{\mathbf{x}}_i \in \mathbb{R}_+^{\Gamma}$, for all i, and $\sum_i \overline{x}_{is} \leq \sum_i \mathbf{e}_{is}$, for all s
2. $\mathbf{p} \in \mathbb{R}_+^{\Gamma}$ and $\mathbf{p} > 0$

3. for all s, $p_s = 0$, if $\sum_i \overline{x}_{is} < \sum_i e_{is}$
4. for all i, $\overline{\mathbf{x}}_i$ solves the problem

$$\max_{x \in \mathbb{R}^\Gamma_+} U_i(\mathbf{x}) \quad \text{s.t.} \quad p.\mathbf{x} \leq p.\mathbf{e}_i \tag{7.23}$$

In the model just described, there is no point in distinguishing an Arrow from an Arrow-Debreu equilibrium. If $(\overline{\mathbf{x}}, \mathbf{p})$ is an Arrow-Debreu equilibrium, then we can choose as an Arrow equilibrium $(\overline{\mathbf{x}}, \mathbf{a}, \mathbf{P}, \mathbf{q})$, where $a_{is} = q_s(x_{is} - e_{is})$, $P_s = 1$, and $q_s = p_s$, for all s. I discuss only Arrow-Debreu equilibria, since the Arrow equilibrium is notationally more complex.

An important thing to notice is that if the utility functions U_i are locally nonsatiated, then Arrow-Debreu equilibrium allocations are Pareto optimal, even if consumers disagree on the assessment of the probabilities of the events s, that is, even if the probabilities $\pi_i(s)$ change as i varies. Nothing in the statement of the first welfare theorem 5.2 (in section 5.1) requires that the consumers agree on probabilities.

The next proposition describes conditions under which the Arrow-Debreu equilibrium prices are proportional to the probabilities of events.

PROPOSITION 7.17 Suppose that, for all i, the functions u_i are differentiable and $\pi_i(s) = \pi(s)$, for all i and s, so that the consumers agree on the probabilities. Assume that, for all i and x, the first derivative of $u_i(x)$ is a strictly decreasing and positive function x. Assume that $\sum_{i=1}^I e_{is} > 0$ and $\pi(s) > 0$, for all s. In an Arrow-Debreu equilibrium $(\overline{\mathbf{x}}, \mathbf{p})$, the consumption allocations, $\overline{x}_{is}$, are independent of s, for each i, if and only if $\sum_{i=1}^I e_{is}$ is independent of s. Under this condition, $\mathbf{p}$ is proportional to $\boldsymbol{\pi}$, where $\boldsymbol{\pi} = (\pi(s))_{s \in S}$.

Proof. Let $(\overline{\mathbf{x}}, \mathbf{p})$ be an Arrow-Debreu equilibrium. Because the utility functions, u_i, are strictly increasing, $p \gg 0$ and consumer i's marginal utility of wealth, λ_i, is positive, for all i. In order to see that this is so, observe that by the first-order conditions for consumer i's utility-maximization problem,

$$0 < \frac{du_i(\overline{x}_{is})}{dx} \leq \lambda_i p_s,$$

so that both λ_i and p_s are positive. Because all prices are positive, there can be no excess supply in equilibrium. That is,

$$\sum_{i=1}^{I} \overline{x}_{is} = \sum_{i=1}^{I} e_{is}, \tag{7.24}$$

for all s.

If $\overline{x}_{is}$ is independent of s, for all i, then equation 7.24 implies that $\sum_{i=1}^{I} e_{is}$ is independent of s, so that this part of the proposition is correct.

I next show that if $\sum_{i=1}^{I} e_{is}$ is independent of s, then $\overline{x}_{is}$ is independent of s, for all i. The first-order conditions of consumer i's utility-maximization problem are

$$\pi(s)\frac{du_i(\overline{x}_{is})}{dx} \leq \lambda_i p_s, \tag{7.25}$$

for all s, with equality if $\overline{x}_{is} > 0$. Since every state is assumed to have positive probability, we may rewrite inequality 7.25 as

$$\frac{du_i(\overline{x}_{is})}{dx} \leq \lambda_i \frac{p_s}{\pi(s)}, \tag{7.26}$$

for all s, with equality if $\overline{x}_{is} > 0$. Suppose that $\overline{x}_{i\overline{s}} \neq \overline{x}_{i\underline{s}}$, for some i and for two distinct states $\underline{s}$ and $\overline{s}$. Without loss of generality, I may assume that $\overline{x}_{i\overline{s}} > \overline{x}_{i\underline{s}}$ and that $i = 1$. The inequality $\overline{x}_{1\overline{s}} > \overline{x}_{1\underline{s}}$ implies that $\overline{x}_{1\overline{s}} > 0$, so that

$$\lambda_1 \frac{p_{\overline{s}}}{\pi(\overline{s})} = \frac{du_1(\overline{x}_{1,\overline{s}})}{dx} < \frac{du_1(\overline{x}_{1,\underline{s}})}{dx} \leq \lambda_1 \frac{p_{\underline{s}}}{\pi(\underline{s})},$$

where the equation and the second inequality follow from inequality 7.26. The first inequality applies because the first derivative of u_1 is decreasing and $\overline{x}_{1\overline{s}} > \overline{x}_{1\underline{s}}$. Since $\lambda_1 > 0$ we see that

$$\frac{p_{\overline{s}}}{\pi(\overline{s})} < \frac{p_{\underline{s}}}{\pi(\underline{s})}. \tag{7.27}$$

I now show that if $i \geq 2$, then $\overline{x}_{i\overline{s}} \geq \overline{x}_{i\underline{s}}$. Suppose that $\overline{x}_{i\overline{s}} > 0$. If $\overline{x}_{i\underline{s}} = 0$, then clearly $\overline{x}_{i\overline{s}} \geq \overline{x}_{i\underline{s}}$, as was to be proved. If $\overline{x}_{i\underline{s}} > 0$, then inequalities 7.26 and 7.27 imply that

$$\frac{du_i(\overline{x}_{i\overline{s}})}{dx} = \lambda_i \frac{p_{\overline{s}}}{\pi(\overline{s})} < \lambda_i \frac{p_{\underline{s}}}{\pi(\underline{s})} = \frac{du_i(\overline{x}_{i\underline{s}})}{dx} \tag{7.28}$$

and hence that $\overline{x}_{i\overline{s}} > \overline{x}_{i\underline{s}}$. This completes the proof that $\overline{x}_{i\overline{s}} \geq \overline{x}_{i\underline{s}}$, when $\overline{x}_{i\overline{s}} > 0$. It remains to be shown that $\overline{x}_{i\underline{s}} = 0$, when $\overline{x}_{i\overline{s}} = 0$. If $\overline{x}_{i\overline{s}} = 0$, then by inequalities 7.26 and 7.27,

$$\frac{du_i(0)}{dx} = \frac{du_i(\overline{x}_{i\overline{s}})}{dx} \leq \lambda_i \frac{p_{\overline{s}}}{\pi(\overline{s})} < \lambda_i \frac{p_{\underline{s}}}{\pi(\underline{s})}. \tag{7.29}$$

If $\overline{x}_{i\underline{s}} > 0$, then inequalities 7.26 and 7.29 imply that

$$\frac{du_i(0)}{dx} < \lambda_i \frac{p_{\underline{s}}}{\pi(\underline{s})} = \frac{du_i(\overline{x}_{i\underline{s}})}{dx},$$

which is impossible since the first derivative of u_i is decreasing. Therefore, $\overline{x}_{i\underline{s}} = 0$, as was to be proved.

The inequalities $\overline{x}_{i\overline{s}} > \overline{x}_{i\underline{s}}$ and $\overline{x}_{i\overline{s}} \geq \overline{x}_{i\underline{s}}$, for $i \geq 2$, and equation 7.24 together imply that

$$\sum_{i=1}^{I} e_{i\overline{s}} = \sum_{i=1}^{I} \overline{x}_{i\overline{s}} > \sum_{i=1}^{I} \overline{x}_{i\underline{s}} = \sum_{i=1}^{I} e_{i\underline{s}},$$

contrary to hypothesis. This contradiction completes the proof that $\overline{x}_{is}$ is independent of s, for all i, if $\sum_{i=1}^{I} e_{is}$ is independent of s.

It remains to be proved that $\mathbf{p}$ is proportional to $\boldsymbol{\pi}$ if $\sum_{i=1}^{I} e_{is}$ is independent of s. Because $\sum_{i=1}^{I} e_{is} > 0$, for all s, and $\overline{x}_{is}$ is independent of s, for all i, it follows that, for some i, $\overline{x}_{is} > 0$, for all s. For such an i, inequality 7.25 becomes the equation

$$\pi(s)\frac{du_i(\overline{x}_{is})}{dx} = \lambda_i p_s,$$

for all s. Since $\overline{x}_{is}$ is independent of s, it follows that $\frac{du_i(\overline{x}_{is})}{dx}$ is independent of s and therefore $\mathbf{p}$ is proportional to $\boldsymbol{\pi}$. ▪

I now try to make the properties of Arrow-Debreu insurance equilibria more vivid by means of Edgeworth box examples. Let there be two states, states a and b, and two people, consumers A and B. The endowment of consumer A is $\mathbf{e}_{\mathrm{A}} = (e_{\mathrm{A}a}, e_{\mathrm{A}b})$ and that of consumer B is $\mathbf{e}_{\mathrm{B}} = (e_{\mathrm{B}a}, e_{\mathrm{B}b})$. The utility function of consumer A is

$$U_{\mathrm{A}}(\mathbf{x}) = \pi_{\mathrm{A}}(a)u_{\mathrm{A}}(x_a) + \pi_{\mathrm{A}}(b)u_{\mathrm{A}}(x_b)$$

and that of consumer B is

$$U_{\mathrm{B}}(\mathbf{x}) = \pi_{\mathrm{B}}(a)u_{\mathrm{B}}(x_a) + \pi_{\mathrm{B}}(b)u_{\mathrm{B}}(x_b),$$

where $\pi_i(a) > 0$, $\pi_i(b) > 0$, and $\pi_i(a) + \pi_i(b) = 1$, for $i = \mathrm{A}$ and B. Assume that u_{A} and u_{B} are differentiable and are strictly concave, so that the consumers are risk averse.

EXAMPLE 7.18 $(\pi_{\mathrm{A}}(a) = \pi_{\mathrm{B}}(a) = \pi(a)$ and $e_{\mathrm{A}a} + e_{\mathrm{B}a} = e_{\mathrm{A}b} + e_{\mathrm{B}b})$ This example illustrates the conclusions of proposition 7.17. The consumers attach the same probabilities to the two states, and there is no collective risk. There can be individual risk, however, if $e_{\mathrm{A}a} \neq e_{\mathrm{A}b}$ and hence $e_{\mathrm{B}a} \neq e_{\mathrm{B}b}$. At the equilibrium, $(\overline{\mathbf{x}}, \mathbf{p})$, $\overline{x}_{\mathrm{A}a} = \overline{x}_{\mathrm{A}b}$ and $\overline{x}_{\mathrm{B}a} = \overline{x}_{\mathrm{B}b}$, so that all individual risk is absorbed by mutual insurance. Also, $\frac{p_a}{p_b} = \frac{\pi(a)}{\pi(b)}$, so that the equilibrium prices are proportional to the probabilities. Equilibrium is portrayed in figure 7.8.

EXAMPLE 7.19 $(\pi_{\mathrm{A}}(a) = \pi_{\mathrm{B}}(a) = \pi(a)$ and $e_{\mathrm{A}a} + e_{\mathrm{B}a} > e_{\mathrm{A}b} + e_{\mathrm{B}b})$ The consumers attach the same probabilities to the states, but there is collective

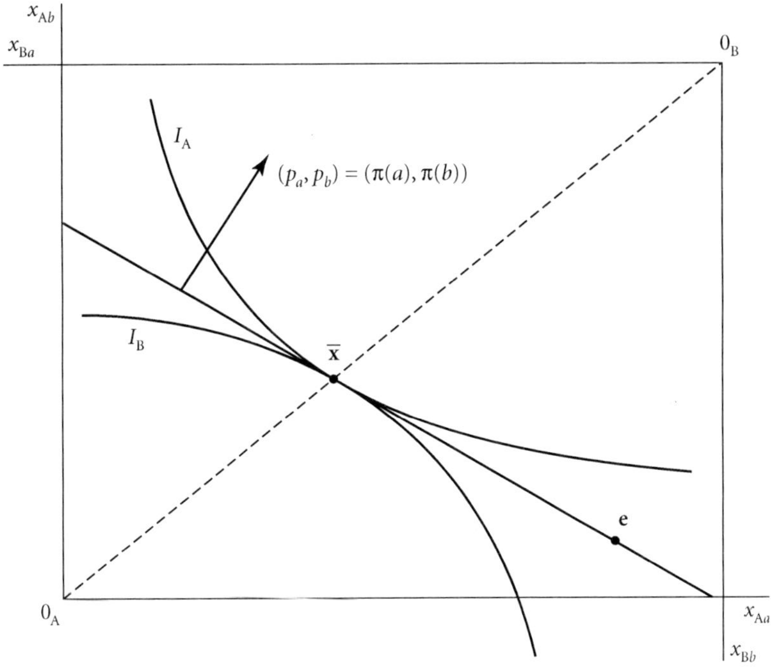

Figure 7.8 The case with common probabilities and no collective risk

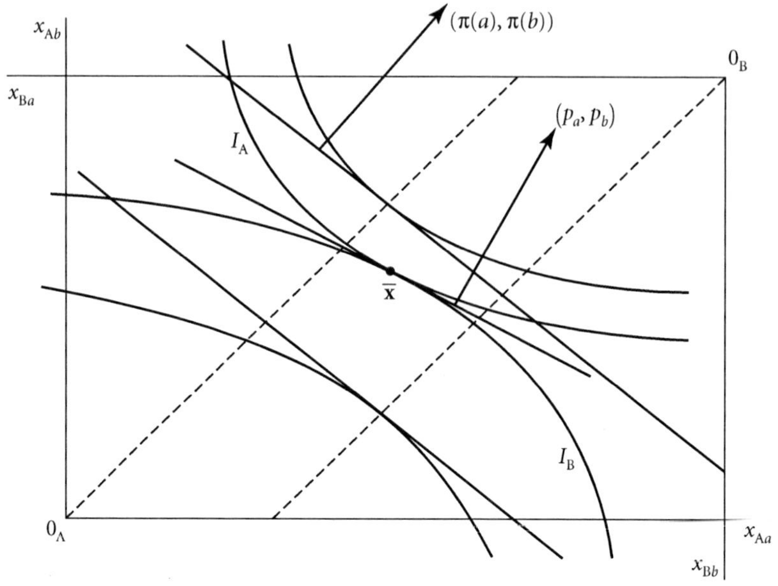

Figure 7.9 The case with common probabilities and collective risk

or uninsurable risk. The example is illustrated in figure 7.9. In the equilibrium $(\overline{\mathbf{x}}, \mathbf{p})$, $\mathbf{p}$ is *not* proportional to $(\pi(a), \pi(b))$, and insurance cannot eliminate risk, though it does redistribute it between the consumers. It is impossible to eliminate the risk through trade alone, for if it were eliminated, then $\overline{x}_{\mathrm{A}a}$ would equal $\overline{x}_{\mathrm{A}b}$ and $\overline{x}_{\mathrm{B}a}$ would equal $\overline{x}_{\mathrm{B}b}$, which is impossible, since then

$$e_{\mathrm{A}a} + e_{\mathrm{B}a} = \overline{x}_{\mathrm{A}a} + \overline{x}_{\mathrm{B}a} = \overline{x}_{\mathrm{A}b} + \overline{x}_{\mathrm{B}b} = e_{\mathrm{A}b} + e_{\mathrm{B}b},$$

contrary to the assumption that $e_{\mathrm{A}a} + e_{\mathrm{B}a} > e_{\mathrm{A}b} + e_{\mathrm{B}b}$. Figure 7.9 represents the equilibrium.

If in example 7.19 $\overline{x}_{is} > 0$, for $i = \mathrm{A}$ and B and $s = a$ and b, then

$$\pi(a)\frac{du_{\mathrm{A}}(\overline{x}_{\mathrm{A}a})}{dx} = \lambda_{\mathrm{A}} p_a \text{ and } \pi(b)\frac{du_{\mathrm{A}}(\overline{x}_{\mathrm{A}b})}{dx} = \lambda_{\mathrm{A}} p_b,$$

so that

$$\frac{\dfrac{du_{\mathrm{A}}(\overline{x}_{\mathrm{A}a})}{dx}}{\dfrac{du_{\mathrm{A}}(\overline{x}_{\mathrm{A}b})}{dx}} = \frac{p_a}{p_b}\frac{\pi(b)}{\pi(a)}.$$

Similarly,

$$\frac{\frac{du_{B}(\overline{x}_{Ba})}{dx}}{\frac{du_{B}(\overline{x}_{Bb})}{dx}} = \frac{p_a}{p_b}\frac{\pi(b)}{\pi(a)},$$

so that

$$\frac{\frac{du_{A}(\overline{x}_{Aa})}{dx}}{\frac{du_{A}(\overline{x}_{Ab})}{dx}} = \frac{\frac{du_{B}(\overline{x}_{Ba})}{dx}}{\frac{du_{B}(\overline{x}_{Bb})}{dx}}.$$

Therefore,

$$\frac{du_{A}(\overline{x}_{Aa})}{dx} < \frac{du_{A}(\overline{x}_{Ab})}{dx},$$

if and only if

$$\frac{du_{B}(\overline{x}_{Ba})}{dx} < \frac{du_{B}(\overline{x}_{Bb})}{dx}.$$

Since u_A and u_B are strictly concave, their derivatives are decreasing functions, and it follows that $\overline{x}_{Aa} > \overline{x}_{Ab}$, if and only if $\overline{x}_{Ba} > \overline{x}_{Bb}$. Since

$$\overline{x}_{Aa} + \overline{x}_{Ba} = e_{Aa} + e_{Ba} > e_{Ab} + e_{Bb} = \overline{x}_{Ab} + \overline{x}_{Bb},$$

it follows that $\overline{x}_{Aa} > \overline{x}_{Ab}$ and $\overline{x}_{Ba} > \overline{x}_{Bb}$; risk is redistributed evenly to this extent.

If $\overline{x}_{Aa} > 0$ and $\overline{x}_{Ab} > 0$, then

$$\frac{p_a}{p_b} = \frac{\pi(a)}{\pi(b)}\frac{\frac{du_{A}(\overline{x}_{Aa})}{dx}}{\frac{du_{A}(\overline{x}_{Ab})}{dx}} < \frac{\pi(a)}{\pi(b)},$$

since $\overline{x}_{Aa} > \overline{x}_{Ab}$ and $\frac{du_A(x)}{dx}$ is a decreasing function of x. The intuition for this result is as follows. In equilibrium, the price of a unit of the good in a state is proportional to the marginal utility of a contingent contract for the good in that state, which in turn is the probability of the state times the marginal utility in the state of consumption of the good. Since each consumer has more of the good in state a than in state b, the marginal utility of consuming the good is less in state a than in state b. Therefore,

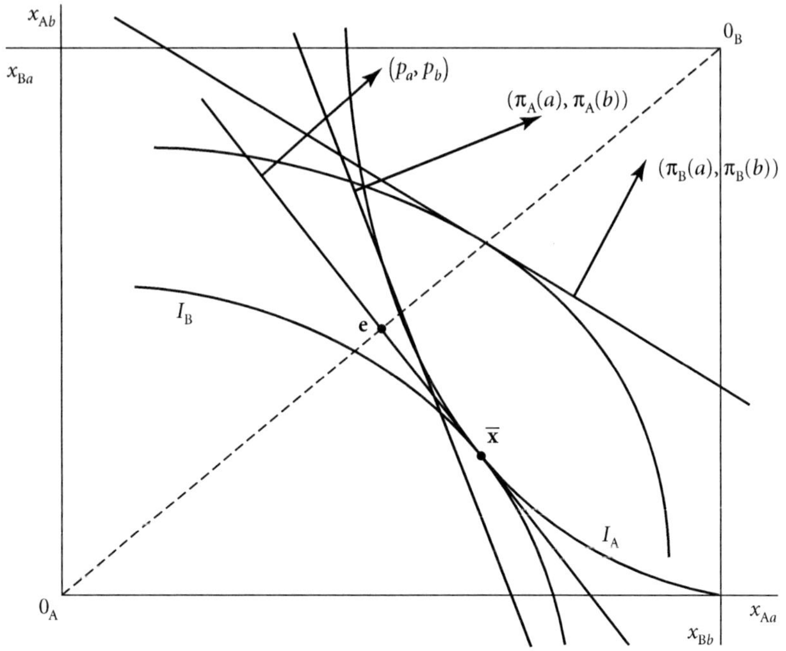

Figure 7.10 The case with differing probabilities and no collective risk

the price of a unit of the good in each state is the probability of the state times a number that is smaller in state a than in state b.

EXAMPLE 7.20 ($\pi_A(a) > \pi_B(a)$ and $e_{Aa} + e_{Ba} = e_{Ab} + e_{Bb}$) There is no collective risk, but consumer A believes that state a is more probable than does consumer B. Figure 7.10 depicts the equilibrium, $(\overline{\mathbf{x}}, \mathbf{p})$. It may be seen that at the equilibrium allocation, $\overline{x}_{Aa} > \overline{x}_{Ab}$ and $\overline{x}_{Ba} < \overline{x}_{Bb}$. It should also be clear that

$$\frac{\pi_A(a)}{\pi_A(b)} > \frac{p_a}{p_b} > \frac{\pi_B(a)}{\pi_B(b)},$$

so that the ratio of the Arrow-Debreu prices lies between the ratios of the probabilities for the two consumers. The Arrow-Debreu insurance markets allow gambling on the state and may create risk, as would be the case if $e_{Aa} = e_{Ab}$ and $e_{Ba} = e_{Bb}$. The consumers redistribute risk Pareto optimally by betting on dated events.

Examples 7.19 and 7.20 illustrate that insurance does not necessarily equalize consumption across states. What it equalizes are the relative marginal utilities of consumption.

To be more precise, insurance may not equalize the quantities x_{is} as the state s varies, where i is the consumer index. However, for each pair of consumers i and j, insurance does equalize the quantities

$$\frac{\pi_i(s)\dfrac{du_i(x_{is})}{dx}}{\pi_j(s)\dfrac{du_j(x_{js})}{dx}}$$

across all states s in which $x_{is} > 0$ and $x_{js} > 0$. These ratios are constant, because in an Arrow-Debreu equilibrium the first-order conditions for a consumer's utility-maximization problem imply that

$$\pi_i(s)\frac{du_i(x_{is})}{dx} = \lambda_i p_s,$$

if $x_{is} > 0$, so that the above ratio equals λ_i/λ_j.

Proposition 7.17 extends to models in which there is more than one commodity in each state. Let $N > 1$ and $\mathbb{R}_+^{S\times N} = \{x: S \to \mathbb{R}_+^N\}$. Suppose that there is no production and that $\mathbf{e}_i \in \mathbb{R}_+^{S\times N}$, for all i. Assume that for each i, $U_i: \mathbb{R}_+^{S\times N} \to \mathbb{R}$ has the form

$$U_i(x) = \sum_{s\in S} \pi(s) u_i(x_{s1}, \ldots, x_{sN}),$$

where u_i is concave and the probabilities, $\pi(s)$, do not depend on i. Prices may be said to be proportional to probabilities in an Arrow-Debreu equilibrium, $(\overline{\mathbf{x}}, \mathbf{p})$, if $\mathbf{p}$ is such that $p_{sn} = \alpha\pi(s)P_n$, for all s and n, where $\alpha > 0$ and $\mathbf{P}$ is an N-vector. Under conditions similar to those of proposition 7.17, this equation is valid, if and only if the N-vector $\sum_{i=1}^{I} \mathbf{e}_{is}$ is independent of s. In a corresponding Arrow equilibrium, $(\mathbf{x}, \mathbf{a}, \mathbf{q}, \mathbf{P})$, we can force $\mathbf{q}$ and $\boldsymbol{\pi}$ to be proportional by choosing a particular normalization of the price vectors $\mathbf{P}_s = (P_{s1}, \ldots, P_{sN})$. This proportionality has no economic meaning, however.

7.4 Incomplete Markets and the Definition of Profit Maximization

An economy is said to have incomplete markets if it does not have a full set of Arrow-Debreu markets, Arrow markets, or equivalent markets. Markets are, of course, incomplete in actual economies. In this section, I show that if markets are incomplete, then shareholders of the same firm may not agree on what its objectives should be. In order to make this point, I define a model in which there are no forward markets.

I define an intertemporal model with no insurance and in which consumers can save an asset I call "money" that earns no interest. Underlying the model is a dated event set, Γ, defined as in definition 7.6 (in section 7.1), with the additional restriction that Γ is a tree in the sense that the only dated event in period 0 is $(0, S)$. This dated event is the root of the tree in that $(0, S)$ precedes all other dated events, (t, A), because $S \supset A$ and $0 \leq t$. Assume that the commodity space for the economy is $\mathbb{R}^{\Gamma \times N}$. That is, the input-output possibility set of each of the J firms is a subset of $\mathbb{R}^{\Gamma \times N}$, and the utility function of each of the I consumers is defined on $\mathbb{R}_+^{\Gamma \times N}$. The current money price of good n in dated event (t, A) is denoted $P_{(t, A), n}$, and $\mathbf{P}$ denotes the vector with components $P_{(t, A), n}$, for $0 \leq t \leq T$, $A \in \mathcal{S}_t$, and $n = 1, \ldots, N$. As in section 7.2, if $\mathbf{x}$ is any vector in $\mathbb{R}^{\Gamma \times N}$ and (t, A) is any dated event in Γ, then $\mathbf{x}_{(t, A)}$ is the N-vector $(x_{(t, A), 1}, \ldots, x_{(t, A), N})$. As before, Θ_{ij} is the ownership share of consumer i in firm j, where $\Theta_{ij} \geq 0$, for all i and j and $\sum_{i=1}^{I} \Theta_{ij} = 1$, for all j. I assume that the profits of each firm are paid to its owners as they are earned. Thus, if $\mathbf{y}_j \in Y_j$ is the input-output vector of firm j, the payment to consumer i in dated event (t, A) is $\Theta_{ij} \mathbf{P}_{(t, A)} \cdot \mathbf{y}_{j, (t, A)}$. This quantity may be positive or negative, as in the Arrow model. The set $\mathbb{R}^{\Gamma}$ denotes $\{M \mid M : \Gamma \to \mathbb{R}\}$. The budget set of consumer i, given price vector $\mathbf{P}$, is $\beta_i(\mathbf{P}) = \{\mathbf{x} \in \mathbb{R}_+^{\Gamma \times N} \mid$ the following three conditions are satisfied$\}$, for some $M_i \in \mathbb{R}^{\Gamma}$:

1. $\mathbf{P}_{(0, S)} \cdot \mathbf{x}_{(0, S)} + M_{i, (0, S)} = \mathbf{P}_{(0, S)} \cdot \mathbf{e}_{i, (0, S)} + \sum_{j=1}^{J} \Theta_{ij} \mathbf{P}_{(0, S)} \cdot \mathbf{y}_{j, (0, S)}$;
2. given $M_{i, (t-1, A(t-1))}$, where $1 \leq t \leq T$ and $A(t-1) \in \mathcal{S}_{t-1}$,

$$\mathbf{P}_{(t, A(t))} \cdot \mathbf{x}_{(t, A(t))} + M_{i, (t, A(t))} = M_{i, (t-1, A(t-1))} + \mathbf{P}_{(t, A(t))} \cdot \mathbf{e}_{i, (t, A(t))} + \sum_{j=1}^{J} \Theta_{ij} \mathbf{P}_{(t, A(t))} \cdot \mathbf{y}_{j, (t, A(t))},$$

   for all $A(t) \in \mathcal{S}_t$ such that $A(t) \subset A(t-1)$;
3. $M_{i, (T, A(T))} \geq 0$, for all $A(T) \in \mathcal{S}_T\}$,

where $\mathbf{y}_j$ is firm j's input-output possibility vector, for all j, and where $M_{i, (t, A(t))}$ is the money holdings or credit balance of consumer i at the end of dated event $(t, A(t))$. The consumer is required to have a nonnegative credit balance only at the end of the last period. In previous periods, he or she could borrow. That is, $M_{i,(t,A(t))}$ could be negative, if $t < T$. Notice that all the constraints defining $\beta_i(\mathbf{P})$ are equations except for the last one. Equations appear because they define the end of period balances, $M_{i,(t,A(t))}$. The overall budget constraint is that the balances at the end of the last period, $M_{i,(T,A(T))}$, be nonnegative.

Equilibrium is defined by having consumers maximize their utility over their budget sets and by having the supply of each commodity be at least as much as the demand for it in every dated event. What has been left out is the description of how firms choose their input-output vectors. The next example shows that owners may disagree as to what their firm should do, so that it is not clear how to define a firm's objectives in equilibrium unless each firm has only one owner.

EXAMPLE 7.21 There are two periods and two equally probable states a and b in the second period. There are three commodities, the first of which is labor. There are three consumers (a worker, W, and two capitalists, A and B), and there are two firms (A and B). Goods 2 and 3 are produced from labor employed in the first period. The production possibility set of both firms is

$$Y = \Big\{(-L, y_{(1,a),2}, y_{(1,a),3}, y_{(1,b),2}, y_{(1,b),3}) \mid L \geq 0,$$

$$y_{(1,a),2} = y_{(1,b),2} = y_2 \geq 0,\ y_{(1,a),3} = y_{(1,b),3} = y_3 \geq 0,\ y_2 + y_3 \leq \sqrt{L}\Big\},$$

where L is the labor input in period 0. Notice that for each of the produced goods, the same amount is produced in the dated events $(1, a)$ and $(1, b)$. The worker is endowed with 200 units of labor in period 0 and with nothing else. Capitalist A is endowed with one unit of good 2 in each of dated events $(1, a)$ and $(1, b)$ and with nothing else. Capitalist B is endowed with one unit of good 3 in each of dated events $(1, a)$ and $(1, b)$ and with nothing else. Capitalist A owns all of firm A, and capitalist B owns all of firm B. The utility function of each of the three consumers is

$$\frac{1}{2}\ln(2x_{(1,a),2} + x_{(1,a),3}) + \frac{1}{2}\ln(x_{(1,b),2} + 2x_{(1,b),3}),$$

so that consumers agree that the probability of each dated event is one-half.

I calculate an equilibrium and show that capitalists A and B choose different production plans for their firms. Since the technologies of the two firms are identical, the capitalists would not agree on production plans if they owned the firms jointly. It is easy to see intuitively why they disagree. Because of the nature of the utility function of all three consumers, the price of good 2 is twice that of good 3 in dated event $(1, a)$ and is half that of good 3 in dated event $(1, b)$. Since capitalist A has an endowment of good 2 in period 1, he or she is relatively richer in dated event $(1, a)$ than in dated event $(1, b)$. Since the capitalist is risk averse, he or she shifts wealth from dated event $(1, a)$ to dated event $(1, b)$ by producing more of good 3 than good 2, thereby producing more of the good that is relatively more valuable in dated event $(1, b)$. Similarly, capitalist B has an endowment that makes him or her relatively richer in dated event $(1, b)$ and so shifts wealth from dated event $(1, b)$ to dated event $(1, a)$ by producing more of good 2 than 3. In the absence of insurance markets, each capitalist uses its firm to shift wealth among dated events in order to offset imbalances in income earned outside the firm.

The equilibrium may be calculated as follows. Normalize prices so that the price of labor in period 0 is 1. From the symmetry of the example, we know that $P_{(1,a),3} = P_{(1,b),2}$ and let this price be p. Then, $P_{(1,a),2} = P_{(1,b),3} = 2p$. The maximization problem of capitalist A is

$$\max_{(x_{(1,a),2}, x_{(1,a),3}, x_{(1,b),2}, x_{(1,b),3}, L, y_2, y_3)} \left[\frac{1}{2}\ln(2x_{(1,a),2} + x_{(1,a),3}) + \frac{1}{2}\ln(x_{(1,b),2} + 2x_{(1,b),3})\right]$$
$$\begin{aligned} \text{s.t.} \quad & 2px_{(1,a),2} + px_{(1,a),3} \leq 2p(y_2 + 1) + py_3 - L, \\ & px_{(1,b),2} + 2px_{(1,b),3} \leq p(y_2 + 1) + 2py_3 - L, \\ & y_2 + y_3 \leq \sqrt{L}. \end{aligned} \tag{7.30}$$

The constraints in problem 7.30 may be rewritten as

$$2x_{(1,a),2} + x_{(1,a),3} \leq 2y_2 + 2 + y_3 - \frac{L}{p},$$

$$x_{(1,b),2} + 2x_{(1,b),3} \leq y_2 + 1 + 2y_3 - \frac{L}{p}, \text{ and}$$

$$y_2 + y_3 \leq \sqrt{L}.$$

Because these constraints are satisfied with equality, problem 7.30 may be rewritten as

$$\max_{(y_2, y_3, L)} \left[\frac{1}{2} \ln\left(2y_2 + 2 + y_3 - \frac{L}{p}\right) + \frac{1}{2} \ln\left(y_2 + 1 + 2y_3 - \frac{L}{p}\right)\right] \tag{7.31}$$

$$\text{s.t.} \quad y_2 + y_3 \leq \sqrt{L}.$$

If we fix $L = L_A$ and solve problem 7.31, we find that

$$y_{A2} = \frac{\sqrt{L_A} - 1}{2} \text{ and } y_{A3} = \frac{\sqrt{L_A} + 1}{2}. \tag{7.32}$$

By symmetry,

$$y_{B2} = \frac{\sqrt{L_B} + 1}{2} \text{ and } y_{B3} = \frac{\sqrt{L_B} - 1}{2}.$$

By symmetry again, $L_A = L_B$. Since there are 200 units of labor available and there is no demand for leisure, $L_A = L_B = 100$ and therefore

$$y_{A2} = \frac{9}{2}, \; y_{A3} = \frac{11}{2}, \; y_{B2} = \frac{11}{2}, \text{ and } y_{B3} = \frac{9}{2}.$$

Therefore, the input-output choice by capitalist A,

$$(-L_A, y_{A2}, y_{A3}) = \left(-100, \frac{9}{2}, \frac{11}{2}\right),$$

is not the same as the input-output choice of capitalist B, which is

$$(-L_B, y_{B2}, y_{B3}) = \left(-100, \frac{11}{2}, \frac{9}{2}\right).$$

In order to find p, substitute equations 7.32 into the objective function of problem 7.31, so that the problem becomes

$$\max_{L_A} \ln\left[\frac{3}{2}\left(\sqrt{L_A} + 1\right) - \frac{L_A}{p}\right].$$

Since the natural logarithm function, ln, is increasing, we may find the optimal value of L_A by solving the problem

$$\max_{L_A} \left[\frac{3}{2}\left(\sqrt{L_A} + 1\right) - \frac{L_A}{p}\right]. \tag{7.33}$$

The first-order condition for the solution of problem 7.33 is

$$p = \frac{4}{3}\sqrt{L_A}.$$

Since $L_A = 100$, we see that $p = \frac{40}{3}$. That is,

$$P_{(1,a),3} = P_{(1,b),2} = \frac{40}{3} \text{ and } P_{(1,a),2} = P_{(1,b),3} = \frac{80}{3}.$$

A similar example can be produced in which the capitalists have the same endowments but disagree about the probabilities of dated events.

Problem Set

1. (a) Compute an Arrow-Debreu equilibrium for an economy with two consumers, A and B, and two states, 1 and 2. Each consumer has a von Neumann–Morgenstern utility function for lotteries of money, and for each consumer the utility of x units of money is $\ln(x)$. Consumer A believes that state 1 occurs with probability 1/4 and state 2 occurs with probability 3/4. Consumer B believes that state 1 occurs with probability 3/4 and state 2 occurs with probability 1/4. Each consumer is endowed with \$1 in each state.

(b) In part (a), suppose that each consumer believes that each state occurs with probability 1/2, that consumer A is endowed with \$2 in state 1 and \$0 in state 2, and that consumer B is endowed with \$0 in state 1 and \$2 in state 2. Recalculate the Arrow-Debreu equilibrium.

2. Consider an economy with two consumers, A and B, and two states, 1 and 2. Each consumer has a von Neumann–Morgenstern utility function for lotteries of money. For each consumer, the utility of x units of money is $\sqrt{x}$, and each consumer believes that each state occurs with probability 1/2. Consumer A is endowed with \$2 in state 1 and \$4 in state 2. Consumer B is endowed with \$1 in state 1 and \$10 in state 2. Compute an Arrow-Debreu equilibrium for this example.

3. Consider the following insurance problem. There are two consumers, A and B, two events, a and b, and one period. The endowment of consumer A is

$$\mathbf{e}_A = (e_{Aa}, e_{Ab}) = (1, 0).$$

The endowment of consumer B is

$$\mathbf{e}_\mathrm{B} = (e_{\mathrm{B}a}, e_{\mathrm{B}b}) = (0, 2).$$

The utility function of consumer A is

$$u_\mathrm{A}(x_a, x_b) = -\frac{1}{3}e^{-x_a} - \frac{2}{3}e^{-x_b}.$$

The utility function of consumer B is

$$u_\mathrm{B}(x_a, x_b) = \frac{1}{3}x_a + \frac{2}{3}x_b.$$

Compute an Arrow-Debreu equilibrium in which the sum of the prices is 1.

4. Consider the following insurance model with two states, a and b, and three consumers, A, B, and C.

$$u_\mathrm{A}(x_a, x_b) = u_\mathrm{B}(x_a, x_b) = u_\mathrm{C}(x_a, x_b) = \frac{1}{3}\ln(x_a) + \frac{2}{3}\ln(x_b).$$

$$\mathbf{e}_\mathrm{A} = (1, 4),\ \mathbf{e}_\mathrm{B} = (2, 1),\ \mathbf{e}_\mathrm{C} = (1, 3).$$

Compute an Arrow-Debreu equilibrium such that the sum of the prices is 1. (Hint: The problem can be solved quickly by noticing that the total endowment is twice as big in state b as in state a and by using the fact that the utility functions are logarithmic.)

5. Consider the following Arrow-Debreu model with production. There are two periods, periods 0 and 1. In period 1, there are two states, a and b, each occurring with probability 1/2. There is one commodity in period 0, which is labor–leisure time. There is one commodity in period 2, which is food. With obvious notation, the utility functions are

$$u_\mathrm{A}(\ell_0, x_{1a}, x_{1b}) = \ln(\ell_0) + \frac{1}{2}\ln(x_{1a}) + \frac{1}{2}\ln(x_{1b}) = u_\mathrm{B}(\ell_0, x_{1a}, x_{1b}).$$

Each consumer is endowed with 15 units of labor–leisure time in period 0 and with nothing else. There is one firm. Its input-output possibility set, again using obvious notation, is

$$Y = \left\{(-L_0, y_{1a}, y_{1b}) \mid L_0 \geq 0,\ y_{1a} \leq 2\sqrt{L_0},\ y_{1b} \leq 20\sqrt{L_0}\right\},$$

where L_0 is labor input in period 0. Each consumer has a share of 1/2 in the profits of the firm. Find an Arrow-Debreu equilibrium where the price of labor–leisure time is 1.

6. Compute an Arrow-Debreu equilibrium for the following example. There are two periods, 0 and 1. There are two states, a and b, in the second period, and one commodity in each period. There are two consumers, A and B, and two firms, A and B. The input-output possibility set of firm A, using obvious notation, is

$$Y_A = \{(y_0, y_{1a}, y_{1b}) = (y_0, -y_0, 0) \mid y_0 \leq 0\}.$$

The input-output possibility set of firm B is

$$Y_B = \{(y_0, y_{1a}, y_{1b}) = (y_0, 0, -2y_0) \mid y_0 \leq 0\}.$$

Because these sets are cones, the firms earn zero profits in equilibrium, and hence there is no need to assign ownership shares in the firms to the consumers.

(a) If the Arrow-Debreu price of the commodity in period 0 is 1, what are the Arrow-Debreu prices, p_{1a} and p_{1b}, respectively, of the commodity in dated events $(1, a)$ and $(1, b)$, if both firms produce positive amounts?

The utility function of consumer A is

$$u_A(x_0, x_{1a}, x_{1b}) = \ln(x_0) + \ln(x_{1a}) + 2\ln(x_{1b}).$$

The utility function of consumer B is

$$u_B(x_0, x_{1a}, x_{1b}) = \ln(x_0) + 2\ln(x_{1a}) + \ln(x_{1b}).$$

The endowment of each consumer is

$$(e_0, e_{1a}, e_{1b}) = (1, 0, 0).$$

(b) Compute an Arrow-Debreu equilibrium,

$$((x_{A0}, x_{A1a}, x_{A1b}), (x_{B0}, x_{B1a}, x_{B1b}),$$
$$(y_{A0}, y_{A1a}, y_{A1b}), (y_{B0}, y_{B1a}, y_{B1b}), (p_0, p_{1a}, p_{1b})),$$

in which the price of the commodity in period 0 is 1.

7. There are two states, 1 and 2, two consumers, A and B, and one good in each state. The two states occur with equal probability. The endowment of consumer A is 2 in state 1 and 0 in state 2. The endowment of consumer B is 0 in state 1 and 1 in state 2. Both consumers have von Neumann–Morgenstern utility functions. Let u_A and u_B be the utility functions of consumers A and B, respectively, for the one good in either state. Suppose that $u_A(x) = \ln(x)$.

(a) Compute an Arrow-Debreu equilibrium if $u_B(x) = \ln(x)$.
(b) Compute an Arrow-Debreu equilibrium if $u_B(x) = x$.
(c) Is there an equilibrium if $u_B(x) = e^x$? If so, calculate it. If not, show why there is no equilibrium. A good drawing would suffice in this case.

8. Compute an Arrow-Debreu equilibrium for the following economy. There are three consumers, A, B, and C, and one good, money. The endowment of each consumer is 1 with probability 1/2 and 0 with probability 1/2. The endowments of the three consumers are independently distributed. Each consumer has a von Neumann–Morgenstern utility function, where the utility of an amount of money, x, in any one state is $\ln(x + 1)$.

9. (a) Compute an Arrow-Debreu equilibrium for the following economy. There is no production. There are two consumers (A and B), two states (1 and 2), one time period, and one consumption good in each state. Each consumer has a von Neumann–Morgenstern utility function. The probability of each state is 1/2. Each consumer's utility of consuming x units of the good in one state is $u(x) = \ln(x)$. The endowment of consumer A is $e_A = (e_{A1}, e_{A2}) = (24, 0)$. The endowment of consumer B is $e_B = (e_{B1}, e_{B2}) = (8, 8)$.

Who bears the risk in this equilibrium?

(b) In the economy of part (a), change the utility function of consumer B for consumption of the good to be $u(x) = x$. Leave the utility function of consumer A as it is in part (a). Compute an Arrow-Debreu equilibrium for the new economy. Who bears the risk in the equilibrium? Why?

(c) Imagine that person A is the victim of a flood in the bad state (state 2) and that the flood may be prevented by constructing a dam. You might believe that there would be no point in building the dam if the consumers were insured against flood damage, as they are in the equilibrium of parts (a) and (b). This problem is meant to contradict this wrong idea. Suppose that if a dam is built, the endowment of consumer A is $e_A = (e_{A1}, e_{A2}) = (20, 20)$ and the endowment of consumer B is $e_B = (e_{B1}, e_{B2}) = (4, 4)$. That is, the dam costs each consumer 4 units of consumption in each state, but prevents the loss of 24 units to consumer A in state 2.

Suppose that the utility functions are as in part (a). Suppose also that consumer A gives c units of the good to consumer B in each state to compensate consumer B for the cost of dam construction. Assume that $0 \leq c \leq 20$.

(i) Compute the equilibrium if the dam is built and consumer A pays c units of the good to consumer B in each state.

(ii) For what values of c, if any, does the equilibrium of part (i) Pareto dominate the equilibrium of part (a)?

10. There are two farmers, A and B, in a valley. There are two states, flood and no flood, and each occurs with probability 1/2. Each farmer has a von Neumann–Morgenstern utility function with the utility of an amount, x, of the crop in any one state being $\ln(x)$. The harvest of farmer A equals 10 if there is no flood and equals 5 if there is a flood. The harvest of farmer B equals 10 whether there is a flood or not.

(a) Compute an Arrow-Debreu equilibrium with the price of the crop being 1 if there is no flood.

Now suppose that a dam can be built that would prevent the flood. That is, if the dam were built, the crop of each farmer would be 10 in both states. The dam would cost a certain amount, say, t, of crop payable after the dam was built and after the harvest, in either state.

(b) Suppose there is no insurance and, hence, no Arrow-Debreu markets, so that each farmer's consumption equals his or her crop in either state. How much would each farmer be willing to pay for the dam, assuming that she or he pays for it alone?

(c) Suppose there is insurance, so that the farmers would consume their allocation under the Arrow-Debreu equilibrium. How much would each farmer be willing to pay for the dam, assuming that he or she pays for it alone? For each farmer, does insurance increase or decrease willingness to pay for the dam?

11. Texas cotton farmers suffer from hail storms. The federal government provides hail insurance. An entrepreneur has discovered a way to seed thunderclouds so as to prevent them from producing hail. The entrepreneur wishes to sell its invention to the government or to a cotton-farmers organization. Both argue that because farmers can buy insurance against hail damage, there is no need to spend money to prevent hail storms. Is this argument correct? Make a case for your answer.

12. Two men agree to insure each other against heart attack, which would incapacitate but not kill them. For simplicity, treat this as a one-period problem. The probability that the first man will have a heart attack is 1/10, as is the probability that the second will have one. For simplicity again, assume that it is impossible for them to have a heart attack simultaneously. Only one, or neither, will have one. Each man earns 100 if healthy and nothing after a heart attack. Each has a von Neumann–Morgenstern utility function, with the utility for money or income, x, being $\ln(x)$.

(a) Compute the Arrow-Debreu equilibrium and the expected utility of the men after trading in insurance but before the state is revealed, that is, before it is known whether either has a heart attack and if so who does. What is the expected utility of each man in this equilibrium?

(b) Suppose that a new medical technology makes it possible to know in advance who will and who will not have a heart attack. This knowledge is available at the time trading in contingent claims occurs. Describe the outcome of Arrow-Debreu trading in the new situation. What are the expected utilities of the two men in this situation, where the expectation is calculated from the point of view of a moment just before the new technology provides the information about who is going to have a heart attack? Does the new medical technology increase their expected utility? Give an intuitive explanation of why or why not.

13. Consider a world with N consumers, with N equally probable states, where $N \geq 2$, and with one good, money. The consumers all have identical von Neumann–Morgenstern utility functions, with the utility for \$$x$ being $2\sqrt{x}$. In state n, for $n = 1, \ldots, N$, the endowment of consumer n is \$0, whereas the endowment of every other consumer is \$1.

(a) Compute the Arrow-Debreu equilibrium with prices that sum to 1.

(b) In the equilibrium, what insurance premium do consumers pay when they have an endowment of \$1? What insurance benefit do they receive when their endowment is \$0?

Suppose that in this world, a public agency can transfer wealth from those with money to the person without any. There is leakage, however, in that if $\$x$ is taken from a wealthy consumer, only $\$x/2$ is given to the needy one. Suppose that the social objective is to maximize the expected utility of a typical consumer.

(c) If there are complete Arrow-Debreu insurance markets, what is the socially optimal transfer by the public agency?
(d) If there is no insurance, what is the socially optimal transfer by the public agency?

Suppose now that it is possible for the government agency to determine and to announce, before the trade in insurance contracts occurs, who is going to have an endowment of $0.

(e) What would be the outcome of Arrow-Debreu trading if the announcement were made?
(f) Would the expected utility of consumers be improved by the announcement, where the expectation is calculated from the point of view of a moment before the announcement was made?

14. Three workers reach a mutual insurance agreement for one period. They know that exactly one of them will be unemployed in that period and each is equally likely to be the one that is unemployed. Each worker earns 10 when employed and nothing when employed. Each worker consumes exactly what they earn in the period plus benefits from or payments for insurance. There are two commodities, leisure and consumption. Each worker has 3 units of leisure if unemployed and 1 unit of leisure if employed. The workers set up Arrow-Debreu markets to insure each other against unemployment. The utility function of each worker has the form

$$Eu(\ell(s), x(s)),$$

where $\ell(s)$ is the consumption of leisure, $x(s)$ is the consumption of income, s is the state of the world, and E is the expected value.

For each of the following functions, u, find an Arrow-Debreu equilibrium and point out whether workers consume more when employed or unemployed or the same in both cases.

(a) $u(\ell, x) = \ell^{1/3}x^{2/3}$.
(b) $u(\ell, x) = \frac{1}{3}\ln(\ell) + \frac{2}{3}\ln(x)$.

(Hint: Make use of symmetry. If you set the problem up with variables for each worker and each state and a price for each state, you will have 12 equations for 12 variables and will waste time. By using symmetry, you can reduce the problem to one involving only two variables, the consumption, x_u, of an unemployed worker and the consumption, x_e, of an employed worker.)

15. One hundred workers in the shipping department of a large factory randomly select one of their members to be their representative to management during the year. Each worker is equally likely to be selected. The job of representative is miserable, as it entails abuse from both management and fellow employees. To induce workers to accept the job, the company pays the representative an income of 10 during the year, whereas every other worker is paid only 1. To further compensate the representative for his or her suffering, the workers consider setting up an Arrow-Debreu insurance market to protect the worker who is chosen. The utility function of a worker for the year has the form

$$Eu(x(s), s),$$

where $x(s)$ is income, s is the state of the world, and E is expected value. Suppose that

$$u(x(s), s) = 2\sqrt{x(s)} - 100,$$

if the worker is selected as representative in state s, and

$$u(x(s), s) = 2\sqrt{x(s)},$$

if the worker is not selected in state s.

Compute an Arrow-Debreu equilibrium. Would the representative be better off with the insurance arrangement or without it, or would it not affect his welfare? Would insurance increase, reduce, or leave unchanged a worker's expected utility for the year, calculated before the selection of a representative? (Hint: Make use of symmetry to reduce the problem to one involving only two variables, the consumption, x_1, of a worker randomly selected to be a representative and the consumption, x_0, of a worker not selected.)

— 8 —

Rational Expectations Equilibrium and the Permanent Income Hypothesis

We have seen that in an ideal world, Arrow-Debreu and Arrow markets for contingent claims make it possible for consumers to move purchasing power across time and events and provide advance knowledge of future prices that can be used for planning investment, production, and consumption. Although actual economies do not have a complete set of Arrow-Debreu markets, their functions are performed to some extent by insurance, borrowing and lending, forward commodity markets, and long-term contracts. The need for markets for contingent claims is further diminished by accumulation of assets for self-insurance and by the use of past experience to predict future prices. I define a notion of rational expectations equilibrium that represents a world in which self-insurance and predictability of future prices are carried to extremes. There are no markets for contingent claims, and goods and services are exchanged only on current markets for current unit of account. The marginal utility of wealth of each consumer remains constant, and people know what prices will be in future dated events and know the probabilities of those events. I apply the term *permanent income hypothesis* to the assumption that the marginal utility of wealth or money is constant. This hypothesis is an idealized version of the more pragmatic permanent income hypothesis introduced by Milton Friedman (1957). Rational expectations refers to knowledge of the probabilities of events and of future prices as functions of dated events. The meanings of the terms *permanent income hypothesis* and *rational expectations,* as used here, are close to those used in the literature on macroeconomics. Both assumptions may be reasonable approximations of reality when applied to short intervals of time during which no major changes occur.

8.1 The Permanent Income Hypothesis

In order to understand the meaning of the permanent income hypothesis, consider an equilibrium model with no production and where consumers can save money but cannot borrow. The dated event set is a tree, $\Gamma = \{(t, A) \mid 0 \le t \le T \text{ and } A \in \mathcal{S}_t, \text{ for all } t\}$ where $\mathcal{S}_0 = \{\mathbf{S}\}$, and $\mathbf{S}$ now denotes the set of states of the world. The tree's root is $(0, \mathbf{S})$. There are I consumers and N commodities in each dated event. The initial endowment and utility function of consumer i are, respectively, $\mathbf{e}_i \in \mathbb{R}_+^{\Gamma\times N}$ and $U_i\colon \mathbb{R}_+^{\Gamma\times N} \to \mathbb{R}$, for $i = 1, \ldots, I$. A price vector is $\mathbf{P} \in \mathbb{R}_+^{\Gamma\times N}$ such that $\mathbf{P} > 0$. Assume that each consumer begins period 0 with a nonnegative quantity, $m_{i,-1}$, of unit of account or money, where $\sum_{i=1}^{I} m_{i,-1} > 0$. The budget set of consumer i at price vector $\mathbf{P}$ is

$\beta_i(\mathbf{P}) = \{\mathbf{x} \in \mathbb{R}_+^{\Gamma\times N} \mid$ there exists $\mathbf{M} \in \mathbb{R}_+^{\Gamma}$ such that the following three conditions are satisfied:

1. $\mathbf{P}_{(0,\mathbf{S})}\cdot\mathbf{x}_{(0,\mathbf{S})} + M_{(0,\mathbf{S})} \le m_{i,-1} + \mathbf{P}_{(0,\mathbf{S})}\cdot\mathbf{e}_{i,(0,\mathbf{S})}$;
2. for t such that $1 \le t \le T$,

$$\begin{aligned} \mathbf{P}_{(t,A(t))}\cdot\mathbf{x}_{(t,A(t))} &+ M_{(t,A(t))} \\ &\le M_{(t-1,A(t-1))} + \mathbf{P}_{(t,A(t))}\cdot\mathbf{e}_{i,(t,A(t))}, \end{aligned} \tag{8.1}$$

   for all $A(t-1) \in \mathcal{S}_{t-1}$ and $A(T) \in \mathcal{S}_t$ such that $A(t) \subset A(t-1)$;
3. $M_{(T,A(T))} \ge m_{i,-1}$, for all $A(T) \in \mathcal{S}_T\}$.

The quantity $M_{i,(t,A(t))}$ is the amount of money consumer i holds at the end of dated event $(t, A(t))$. Notice that $M_{(t,A(t))} \ge 0$, for all $(t, A(t))$, so that the consumer cannot borrow. The purpose of condition (3) in equation 8.1 is to give consumers a reason to hold money at the end of period T. Without such a reason, the model would have no equilibrium.

DEFINITION 8.1 A *monetary equilibrium* consists of $(\overline{\mathbf{x}}_1, \overline{\mathbf{x}}_2, \ldots, \overline{\mathbf{x}}_I, \mathbf{P}) = (\overline{\mathbf{x}}, \mathbf{P})$, where $\overline{\mathbf{x}}_i \in \mathbb{R}_+^{\Gamma\times N}$, for all i, $\mathbf{P} \in \mathbb{R}_+^{\Gamma\times N}$, and these satisfy the following conditions:

1. $\mathbf{P} > 0$.
2. $\sum_{i=1}^{I} \overline{\mathbf{x}}_i \le \sum_{i=1}^{I} \mathbf{e}_i$.
3. For all $(t, A(t))$, and n, $P_{(t,A(t)),n} = 0$, if $\sum_{i=1}^{I} \overline{x}_{i,(t,A(t)),n} < \sum_{i=1}^{I} e_{i,(t,A(t)),n}$.

4. For each i, $\overline{\mathbf{x}}_i$ solves the problem

$$\max_{\mathbf{x} \in \beta_i(P)} U_i(\mathbf{x}).$$

To simplify the analysis of monetary equilibria, assume that the utility functions U_i have the form

$$U_i(\mathbf{x}) = \sum_{t=0}^{T} \sum_{A(t) \in \mathcal{S}_t} \pi(A(t)) u_{i,(t,A(t))}(\mathbf{x}_{(t,A(t))}), \tag{8.2}$$

where $\pi(A(t))$ is the probability of event $A(t)$, and $u_{i(t,A(t))}: \mathbb{R}_+^N \to \mathbb{R}$ is strictly concave and strictly increasing, for all $(t, A(t))$ in Γ. A utility function of this form is said to be *additively separable* with respect to time and uncertainty, because it is a weighted sum of the utilities enjoyed in each dated event. Observe that all consumers have the same subjective probabilities, $\pi(A(t))$.

In a monetary equilibrium $(\overline{\mathbf{x}}, \mathbf{P})$ for an economy with utility functions of the form 8.2, each consumption bundle $\overline{\mathbf{x}}_{i,(t,A(t))}$ solves the problem

$$\max_{\mathbf{x} \in \mathbb{R}_+^N} u_{i,(t,A(t))}(\mathbf{x})$$
$$\text{s.t.} \quad \mathbf{P}_{(t,A(t))}.\mathbf{x} \leq w_{i,(t,A(t))},$$

where $w_{i,(t,A(t))} = \mathbf{P}_{(t,A(t))}.\overline{\mathbf{x}}_{i,(t,A(t))}$. Hence, the Kuhn-Tucker theorem implies that if $\mathbf{P}_{(t,A(t))}.\overline{\mathbf{x}}_{i,(t,A(t))} > 0$, then there exists a nonnegative number $\lambda_{i,(t,A(t))}$ such that $\overline{\mathbf{x}}_{i,(t,A(t))}$ solves the problem

$$\max_{\mathbf{x} \in \mathbb{R}_+^N} \left[u_{i,(t,A(t))}(\mathbf{x}) - \lambda_{i,(t,A(t))} \mathbf{P}_{(t,A(t))}.x \right]. \tag{8.3}$$

I will call $\lambda_{i,(t,A(t))}$ the consumer's marginal utility of money in dated event $(t, A(t))$. Since $u_{i,(t,A(t))}$ is strictly increasing, $\lambda_{i,(t,A(t))} > 0$. The *permanent income hypothesis* is that the $\lambda_{i,(t,A(t))}$ do not depend on $(t, A(t))$. That is, $\lambda_{i,(t,A(t))} = \lambda_i > 0$, for all $(t, A(t))$. If the hypothesis is valid, problem 8.3 becomes

$$\max_{\mathbf{x} \in \mathbb{R}_+^N} \left[u_{i,(t,A(t))}(\mathbf{x}) - \lambda_i \mathbf{P}_{(t,A(t))}.\mathbf{x} \right],$$

so that $\overline{\mathbf{x}}_i = (\overline{\mathbf{x}}_{i,(t,A(t))})_{t=0,A(t)\in\mathcal{S}_t}^{T}$ solves the problem

$$\max_{\mathbf{x}\in\mathbb{R}_+^{\Gamma\times N}} \left[\sum_{t=0}^{T} \sum_{A(t)\in\mathcal{S}_t} \pi(A(t)) u_{i,(t,A(t))}(\mathbf{x}_{(t,A(t))}) \right.$$
$$\left. -\lambda_i \sum_{t=0}^{T} \sum_{A(t)\in\mathcal{S}_t} \pi(A(t))\mathbf{P}_{(t,A(t))}.\mathbf{x}_{(t,A(t))} \right].$$

If we let $\mathbf{p}_{(t,A(t))} = \pi(A(t))\mathbf{P}_{(t,A(t))}$, we may rewrite this problem as

$$\max_{\mathbf{x}\in\mathbb{R}_+^{\Gamma\times N}} \left[\sum_{t=0}^{T} \sum_{A(t)\in\mathcal{S}_t} \pi(A(t)) u_{i,(t,A(t))}(\mathbf{x}_{(t,A(t))}) \right.$$
$$\left. -\lambda_i \sum_{t=0}^{T} \sum_{A(t)\in\mathcal{S}_t} \mathbf{p}_{(t,A(t))}.\mathbf{x}_{(t,A(t))} \right],$$

or in condensed notation as

$$\max_{\mathbf{x}\in\mathbb{R}_+^{\Gamma\times N}} \left[U_i(\mathbf{x}) - \lambda_i \mathbf{p}.\mathbf{x} \right]. \tag{8.4}$$

Since $\overline{\mathbf{x}}_i$ solves problem 8.4, the Kuhn-Tucker theorem implies that $\overline{\mathbf{x}}_i$ solves the problem

$$\max_{\mathbf{x}\in\mathbb{R}_+^{\Gamma\times N}} U_i(\mathbf{x})$$
$$\text{s.t.} \quad \mathbf{p}.\mathbf{x} \leq \mathbf{p}.\mathbf{e}_i - \tau_i,$$

where $\tau_i = \mathbf{p}.(\mathbf{e}_i - \overline{\mathbf{x}}_i)$.

I now show that when the permanent income hypothesis applies, $\tau_i = 0$, for all i, so that $(\overline{\mathbf{x}}, \mathbf{p})$ is an Arrow-Debreu equilibrium. Condition (3) of the definition 8.1 of a monetary equilibrium implies that $\mathbf{p}. \sum_{i=1}^{I}(\overline{\mathbf{x}}_i - \mathbf{e}_i) = 0$, so that $\sum_{i=1}^{I} \tau_i = 0$. I next show that condition (3) of equation 8.1 implies that $\mathbf{p}.\overline{\mathbf{x}}_i \leq \mathbf{p}.\mathbf{e}_i$, for all i, so that $\tau_i \geq 0$, for all i. Let $M_{i,(t,A(t))}$ be the equilibrium money balances that consumer i holds at the end of dated event $(t, A(t))$. By the definition of $M_{i,(t,A(t))}$,

$$M_{i,(T,A(T))} = m_{i,-1} + \sum_{t=0}^{T-1} \mathbf{P}_{(t,A(t))}.(\mathbf{e}_{i,(t,A(t))} - \overline{\mathbf{x}}_{i,(t,A(t))}),$$

where $S = A(0) \supset A(1) \supset \ldots \supset A(T-1) \supset A(T)$. Since

$$M_{i,(T,A(T))} \geq m_{i,-1},$$

by condition (3) of equation 8.1, it follows that

$$\sum_{t=0}^{T} \mathbf{P}_{(t,A(t))}.(\mathbf{e}_{i,(t,A(t))} - \overline{\mathbf{x}}_{i,(t,A(t))}) \geq 0,$$

when $S = A(0) \supset A(1) \supset \ldots \supset A(T-1) \supset A(T)$. Therefore,

$$\pi(A(T)) \sum_{t=0}^{T} \mathbf{P}_{(t,A(t))}.(\mathbf{e}_{i,(t,A(t))} - \overline{\mathbf{x}}_{i,(t,A(t))}) \geq 0,$$

for every $A(T) \in S_T$. Adding over $A(T)$, we see that

$$\begin{aligned} 0 &\leq \sum_{A(T)\in S_T} \pi(A(T)) \sum_{t=0}^{T} \mathbf{P}_{(t,A(t))}.(\mathbf{e}_{i,(t,A(t))} - \overline{\mathbf{x}}_{i,(t,A(t))}) \\ &= \sum_{t=0}^{T} \sum_{A(t)\in S_t} \pi(A(T))\mathbf{P}_{(t,A(t))}.(\mathbf{e}_{i,(t,A(t))} - \overline{\mathbf{x}}_{i,(t,A(t))}) \\ &= \sum_{t=0}^{T} \sum_{A(t)\in S_t} \mathbf{p}_{(t,A(t))}.(\mathbf{e}_{i,(t,A(t))} - \overline{\mathbf{x}}_{i,(t,A(t))}) = \mathbf{p}.(\mathbf{e}_i - \overline{\mathbf{x}}_i). \end{aligned}$$

That is, $\tau_i = \mathbf{p}.(\mathbf{e}_i - \overline{\mathbf{x}}_i) \geq 0$, for all i. Since $\sum_{i=1}^{I} \tau_i = 0$, it follows that $\tau_i = 0$, for all i, and hence that $(\overline{\mathbf{x}}, \mathbf{p})$ is an Arrow-Debreu equilibrium. In summary, if the monetary equilibrium $(\overline{\mathbf{x}}, \mathbf{P})$ satisfies the permanent income hypothesis, then $(\overline{\mathbf{x}}, \mathbf{p})$ is an Arrow-Debreu equilibrium, so that the allocation $\overline{\mathbf{x}}$ is Pareto optimal. The permanent income hypothesis amounts to the assumption that consumers are perfectly self-insuring.

I next give an example to show that the allocation of a monetary equilibrium may not be Pareto optimal if the equilibrium does not satisfy the permanent income hypothesis

EXAMPLE 8.2 There are two consumers, A and B, one commodity in each dated event, two periods, one event in period 0, and two events in period 1. The single dated event of period 0 is (0, **S**). The two dated events of period 1 are $(1, a)$ and $(1, b)$, and they each have probability 1/2. The initial endowments of consumers A and B are

$$\mathbf{e}_{\mathrm{A}} = (e_{\mathrm{A},(0,\mathbf{S})}, e_{\mathrm{A}(1,a)}, e_{\mathrm{B}(1,b)}) = (1, 2, 1)$$

and

$$\mathbf{e}_{\mathrm{B}} = (e_{\mathrm{B},(0,\mathbf{S})}, e_{\mathrm{B}(1,a)}, e_{\mathrm{B}(1,b)}) = (1, 2, 1).$$

The utility of each consumer for consuming x units of consumption in any dated event is $\ln(x)$. Assume that each consumer starts period 0 with one unit of money, so that $m_{A,-1} = m_{B,-1} = 1$.

Let $\mathbf{P} = (P_{(0,S)}, P_{(1,a)}, P_{(1,b)})$ be the equilibrium price system for this example. By the symmetry of the model with respect to the two states, I may assume that $P_{(1,a)} = P_{(1,b)} = P_1$. The equilibrium is such that each consumer carries one unit of money from period 0 into period 1, so that neither consumer saves or dissaves in period 0. Since each consumer must retain at least one unit of money at the end of period 1, neither saves or dissaves in period 1. Therefore $\overline{\mathbf{x}}_A = \mathbf{e}_A$, and $\overline{\mathbf{x}}_B = \mathbf{e}_B$. Since consumers consume something in every dated event, the marginal utilities of money of consumer A in dated events $(1, a)$ and $(1, b)$ are

$$\lambda_{A,(1,a)} = \frac{1}{P_1}\frac{d\ln(\overline{x}_{A,(1,a)})}{dx} = \frac{1}{2P_1}$$

and

$$\lambda_{B,(1,b)} = \frac{1}{P_1}\frac{d\ln(\overline{x}_{B,(1,b)})}{dx} = \frac{1}{P_1}.$$

Similarly, consumer A's marginal utility of money in dated event $(0, S)$ is

$$\lambda_{A,(0,S)} = \frac{1}{P_0}\frac{d\ln(\overline{x}_{A,(0,S)})}{dx} = \frac{1}{P_0}.$$

Since consumer A carries a positive amount of money from period 0 to period 1 and could carry over more by consuming less, his or her marginal utility of money in period 0 equals the expected value of the marginal utility of money in period. That is,

$$\frac{1}{P_0} = \lambda_{A,(0,S)} = \frac{1}{2}\lambda_{A,(1,a)} + \frac{1}{2}\lambda_{A,(1,b)} = \frac{1}{2}\frac{1}{2P_1} + \frac{1}{2}\frac{1}{P_1} = \frac{3}{4}\frac{1}{P_1}.$$

Hence $P_1 = \frac{3}{4}P_0$, and we may choose equilibrium prices to be $P_0 = 4$ and $P_1 = 3$. Then $\lambda_{A,(0,S)} = \frac{1}{4}$, $\lambda_{A,(1,a)} = \frac{1}{6}$, and $\lambda_{A,(1,b)} = \frac{1}{3}$ so that the marginal utility of money is not constant and hence the equilibrium does not satisfy the permanent income hypothesis. The equilibrium allocation is not Pareto optimal, since the allocation equals the endowment, which is Pareto dominated by the allocation $\mathbf{x}_A = \mathbf{x}_B = \left(1, \frac{3}{2}, \frac{3}{2}\right)$.

A question to be examined is whether there are contexts in which it is reasonable to expect that consumers could insure themselves nearly perfectly. You may gain an intuitive understanding of the subject by imagining that you are, say, a car salesperson paid weekly on a commission basis. Your income fluctuates widely because in some weeks you do well and in others you sell nothing. Your weekly expenditures also fluctuate; they are higher when you make your mortgage payments or throw a party. You offset these fluctuations by accumulating enough assets when expenditures are low, relative to income, to pay for excesses of spending over income at other times. In doing so, you are able to maintain a nearly constant marginal utility of money, which is the utility you place on money spent. You are not able to keep the marginal utility of money exactly constant. You may increase it after a run of bad weeks that depletes your savings. The change in the marginal utility of money is sudden when a financial catastrophe uses up most of your assets or if a change in circumstances drastically alters your income or financial needs. For instance, a change in energy prices that was expected to endure could both reduce your sales of cars and increase your expenditures. Nearly perfect self-insurance is plausible only in the context of short-term fluctuations, for over long periods consumers' average incomes and needs may change considerably. Nearly perfect self-insurance is possible only if the probability distribution of the fluctuations remains stable, so that periods of deficit and surplus offset each other on average.

The permanent income hypothesis should make sense in terms of personal experience. When we go shopping, we usually compare the cost of possible purchases with a notion of the value of money to us rather than with the utility of specific alternative items we would like to buy. Our valuation of money normally changes slowly, though it may change a great deal over the course of a lifetime as we become richer or poorer. The value of money to us is indirect; it derives from the utility of other things we could buy now or in the future. Normally, the value of money is insensitive to the purchases we make because the cost of the items we buy at any one time is small relative to our long-run purchasing power. The value of money may not be insensitive to major purchases, such as that of a house.

The intuition just discussed can be made rigorous, though the argument is so complex that I only outline it here. I use a model of a single consumer rather than that of a whole economy, and I assume that the probability distribution of prices is stationary. I also ignore interest earned on assets because the relevant time period is short. I assume that the utility function has the form

$$U(\mathbf{x}_0, \mathbf{x}_1, \ldots, \mathbf{x}_T, \omega_0, \ldots, \omega_T) = E\left[\sum_{t=0}^{T} u(\mathbf{x}_1, \omega_t)\right], \tag{8.5}$$

where E is the expected value and $\mathbf{x}_1$ and ω_t are, respectively, the N-vector of commodity purchases in period t and a random disturbance. The vectors $\mathbf{x}_t$ in equation 8.5 may themselves be random. I choose this form of utility function in order to avoid complications due to links between consumption in different periods arising directly from the utility function. I do not discount future utility, because I am interested in behavior over brief periods of time when the effect of discounting is small.

Because I wish to study the intertemporal control of spending, I work with the indirect utility function for expenditure, not the direct utility function u for consumption bundles. If the price vector in period t is $\mathbf{P}_t$, the indirect utility function in that period is

$$v(c, \mathbf{P}_t, \omega_t) = \max_{\mathbf{x} \in \mathbb{R}_+^N} u(\mathbf{x}, \omega_t)$$
$$\text{s.t.} \quad \mathbf{P}_t.\mathbf{x} \leq c,$$

where c is the amount of money spent on consumption. Assume that the price vectors, $\mathbf{P}_t$, may fluctuate randomly, and let $s_t = (\mathbf{P}_t, \omega_t)$, so that v may be written as $v(c, s_t)$. Consumption at time t depends on $(s_0, s_1, \ldots, s_t)$. The objective function for the consumer is

$$E\left[\sum_{t=0}^{T} v(c_t(s_0, \ldots, s_t), s_t)\right].$$

Let the consumer's income in period t be $y(s_t)$. The consumer's budget set is

$$\beta_T(m_{-1}, s_0) = \{\mathbf{c} = (c_0(s_0), c_1(s_0, s_1), \ldots, c_T(s_0, \ldots, s_T)) \mid \mathbf{c} \geq 0 \text{ and}$$
there is a finite nonnegative sequence
$$(M_0(s_0), M_1(s_0, s_1), \ldots, M_T(s_0, \ldots, s_T))$$
such that $c_0(s_0) + M_0(s_0) \leq m_{-1} + y(s_0)$ and
$$c_t(s_0, \ldots, s_t) + M_t(s_0, \ldots, s_t) \leq M_{t-1}(s_0, \ldots, s_{t-1}) + y(s_t),$$
for t such that $1 \leq t \leq T$, and for all $s_0, \ldots, s_t\}$,

where m_{-1} is the amount of money held at the end of period -1 and $M_t(s_0, \ldots, s_t)$ is the amount of money held at the end of period t, for $t \geq 0$. The consumer's maximization problem is

$$\max_{c \in \beta_T(m_{-1}, s_0)} E\left[\sum_{t=0}^{T} v(c_t(s_0, \ldots, s_t), s_t) \mid s_0\right], \tag{8.6}$$

where $E[. \mid s_0]$ is the conditional expectation, given s_0. The value function for this maximization problem is

$$V_T(m_{-1} + y(s_0), s_0) = \max_{c \in \beta_T(m_{-1}, s_0)} E\left[\sum_{t=0}^{T} v(c_t(s_0, \ldots, s_t), s_t) \mid s_0\right].$$

I describe, informally, properties of the solution of problem 8.6 and of the value function V_T. Rigorous statements and proofs for a more general model may be found in Bewley (1977). Assume that the random variables s_t are independently and identically distributed and take values in a finite set S, so that $y: S \to [0, \infty)$ and $v: [0, \infty) \times S \to (-\infty, \infty)$. In addition, assume that $Ey(s) > 0$, v is twice differentiable, $\frac{dv(c,s)}{dc} > 0$, $\frac{d^2 v(c,s)}{dc^2} < 0$, for all c and s, and that $\frac{dv(0,s)}{dc} < \infty$, for all s. It follows that

$$\frac{dv(c, s)}{dc} \leq \max_{s \in S} \frac{dv(0, s)}{dc} < \infty,$$

for all c and s. Assume also that $\lim_{c \to \infty} \frac{dv(c,s)}{dc} = 0$, for all s.

Given these and other assumptions, problem 8.6 has a solution, and the function V_T is differentiable. Let $\lambda_T(W, s_0) = \frac{dV_T(W, s_0)}{dW}$ be the consumer's marginal utility of money in period 0 when the consumer has W units of money to spend. Let $c_{Tt}(s_0, \ldots, s_t)$ be the optimal period t consumption in problem 8.6, and let $M_{Tt}(s_0, \ldots, s_t)$ be the money balances held at the end of period t under the optimal consumption plan. The first-order conditions for problem 8.6 imply that

$$\frac{dv(c_{T0}(s_0), s_0)}{dc} \leq \lambda_T(m_{-1} + y(s_0), s_0), \tag{8.7}$$

with equality if $c_{T0}(s_0) > 0$.

The consumer's maximization problem from period t on looks just like the problem from period 0 on, except that the horizon is $T - t$ rather than T periods, the initial state is s_t rather than s_0, and the consumer's money balances available for expenditure are $M_{T,t-1}(s_0, \ldots, s_{t-1}) + y(s_1)$ rather than $m_{-1} + y(s_0)$. Therefore,

$$V_{T-t}(M_{T,t-1}(s_0, \ldots, s_{t-1}) + y(s_1), s_1) = \left[\sum_{s=t}^{T} v(c_s(s_0, \ldots, s_s) \mid s_t \right],$$

and the consumer's marginal utility of money at time t is

$$\lambda_{T-t}(M_{T,t-1}(s_0, \ldots, s_{t-1}) + y(s_t), s_t) = \frac{dV_{T-t}(M_{T,t-1}(s_0, \ldots, s_{t-1}) + y(s_t), s_t)}{dW}.$$

The version of condition 8.7 that applies at any time $t > 0$ is

$$\frac{dv(c_{Tt}(s_0, \ldots, s_t), s_t)}{dc} \leq \lambda_{T-t}(M_{T,t-1}(s_0, \ldots, s_{t-1}) + y(s_t), s_t), \quad (8.8)$$

with equality if $c_{Tt}(s_0, \ldots, s_t) > 0$. That is, the marginal utility of money and the money holdings at time t determine consumption at any time t.

The marginal utility of money, $\lambda_T(W, s_0)$, is nondecreasing as a function of T and $\lambda_T(W, s_0) \leq \max_{s \in S} \frac{dv(0,s)}{dc}$, for all W and s_0. Therefore, $\lambda_\infty(W, s_0) = \lim_{T \to \infty} \lambda_T(W, s_0)$ exists and is finite, for all $W \geq 0$. Since the function $V_t(W, s_0)$ is concave and nondecreasing, its derivative, $\lambda_T(W, s_0)$, is a nonnegative and nonincreasing function of W. Similarly, $c_{Tt}(s_0, \ldots, s_t)$ is a nonnegative and nonincreasing function of T, and $M_{Tt}(s_0, \ldots, s_t)$ is a nondecreasing and bounded function of T, for all t and $s_0, \ldots, s_t$, so that $c_{\infty t}(s_0, \ldots, s_t) = \lim_{T \to \infty} c_{Tt}(s_0, \ldots, s_t)$ and $M_{\infty t}(s_0, \ldots, s_t) = \lim_{T \to \infty} M_{Tt}(s_0, \ldots, s_t)$ exist. Passing to the limit in inequality 8.8, we have that

$$\frac{dv(c_{\infty t}(s_0, \ldots, s_t), s_t)}{dc} \leq \lambda_\infty(M_{\infty,t-1}(s_0, \ldots, s_{t-1}) + y(s_t), s_t), \quad (8.9)$$

for all t, with equality if $c_{\infty t}(s_0, \ldots, s_t) > 0$.

I now come to the key findings. Since $\lambda_T(W, s_0)$, is a nonnegative and nonincreasing function of W, $\lambda_\infty(W, s_0) = \lim_{T \to \infty} \lambda_T(W, s_0)$ is a nonnegative and nonincreasing function of W. Hence, $\lambda_\infty(s_0) = \lim_{W \to \infty} \lambda_\infty (W, s_0)$ exists. One main finding is that $\lambda_\infty(s_0)$ does not depend on s_0 and so $\lambda_\infty(s_0) = \overline{\lambda}$, where $\overline{\lambda}$ is a constant.

The number $\overline{\lambda}$ has a special interpretation. The condition

$$\frac{dv(c, s)}{dc} \leq \lambda, \quad (8.10)$$

with equality if $c > 0$, defines c as a nonincreasing function of λ, for all s. Call this function $c(\lambda, s)$. The interpretation of $\bar{\lambda}$ is that

$$Ec(\bar{\lambda}, .) = Ey(.), \tag{8.11}$$

where $c(\bar{\lambda}, .)$ and $y(.)$ are the random variables taking on values $c(\bar{\lambda}, s_0)$ and $y(s_0)$, respectively. Equation 8.11 says that the expected expenditure per period equals the expected income per period, when the marginal utility of money is set equal to $\bar{\lambda}$. The proof of equation 8.11 is an application of the law of large numbers. Equation 8.11 implies that

$$\lim_{T\to\infty} T^{-1} \sum_{t=0}^{T-1} \left[c(\bar{\lambda}, s_t) - y(s_t) = 0 \right],$$

with probability 1, so that if the consumer keeps the marginal utility of money equal to $\bar{\lambda}$, then long-run average expenditure equals long-run average income.

The other main result is that $\lim_{t\to\infty} \lambda_\infty(M_{\infty,t-1}(s_0, \ldots, s_{t-1}) + y(s_t), s_t) = \bar{\lambda}$ with probability 1. Inequality 8.9, therefore, implies that $\lim_{t\to\infty} c_{\infty t}(s_0, \ldots, s_t) = c(\bar{\lambda}, s_t)$ with probability 1. Because of equation 8.11, we see that asymptotically the consumer spends an amount that matches expected expenditure with expected income. If we add the assumption that $c(\bar{\lambda}, s_0) \neq y(s_0)$ with positive probability, then it can be proved that $\lambda_\infty(W, s_0) > \bar{\lambda}$, for all W and s_0, so that $\lim_{t\to\infty}[M_{\infty,t-1}(s_0, \ldots, s_t) + y(s_1)] = \infty$ and hence $\lim_{t\to\infty} M_{\infty t}(s_0, \ldots, s_t) = \infty$ with probability 1.

In order to interpret these results, recall that $\lim_{T\to\infty} c_{Tt}(s_0, \ldots, s_t) = c_{\infty t}(s_0, \ldots, s_t)$ and $\lim_{T\to\infty} M_{Tt}(s_0, \ldots, s_t) = M_{\infty t}(s_0, \ldots, s_t)$. That is, if the finite horizon, T, is large enough, the consumer's optimal consumption and money balances are near those of the limit program, $c_{\infty t}(s_0, \ldots, s_t)$ and $M_{\infty t}(s_0, \ldots, s_t)$, respectively. In addition, if the current period, t, is so large that the consumer has had time to accumulate large money balances, then spending, $c_{Tt}(s_0, \ldots, s_t)$, will be near the level, $c(\bar{\lambda}, s_t)$, that matches expected expenditure to expected income per period. That is, if the horizon, T, and the period, t, are sufficiently large, then the consumer is nearly perfectly self-insuring.

Some examples may make the preceding discussion easier to understand.

EXAMPLE 8.3 The utility from expenditure in one period is

$$v(c) = \begin{cases} 2c, & \text{if } 0 \leq c \leq 1, \\ c+1, & \text{if } 1 \leq c \leq 2, \text{ and} \\ 3, & \text{if } c \geq 2. \end{cases}$$

The income in period t is a random variable, y_t, where the y_t are independently and identically distributed and equal 1 with probability 1/2 and equal 3 with probability 1/2.

Consider problem 8.6 with the above utility function and income and with horizon T and suppose that the consumer has W units of money in some period. If $0 < W < 1$, the consumer spends all of W, because he or she will always have at least that much money in the future. Therefore, the consumer's marginal utility of money is $\lambda_T(W) = 2$. Suppose that $1 \leq W < 2$. The consumer again spends all the money, because in the future he or she will have at least one unit of money and the marginal utility of money will be no greater than the marginal utility of spending it in the present, which is 1. Therefore, $\lambda_T(W) = 1$. Suppose that $n < W < n + 1$, where n is a positive integer bigger than 1. The consumer spends two units of money, for nothing would be gained by spending more and if less were spent, the marginal utility of additional expenditure would be at least 1, which would never be exceeded in the future. As long as the consumer spends exactly two units of money in every period, his or her holdings of money available for expenditure, W_t, follows a random walk such that

$$W_{t+1} = \begin{cases} W_t + 1, & \text{with probability } 1/2, \text{ and} \\ W_t - 1, & \text{with probability } 1/2, \end{cases}$$

until such time as $1 \leq W_t < 2$. At that time, the consumer spends all the money. Additional money is of use to the consumer only when W_t falls in the interval $[1, 2)$, and it then has marginal utility 1. Therefore, the marginal utility of money at time 0, $\lambda_T(W_0)$, equals the probability, $\pi_T(W_0)$, that W_t reaches the interval $[1, 2)$ within T periods. There is no need to calculate this probability. We know from common sense or the theory of random walks that $\pi_T(W_0)$ is nonincreasing in W_0 and that $\lim_{T\to\infty} \pi_T(W_0) = 1$; the probability of reaching $[1, 2)$ declines as the distance of the initial position, W_0, from the interval increases, and eventually the random walk will reach the interval $[1, 2)$. In conclusion,

$$\lambda_T(W) = \begin{cases} 2, & \text{if } 0 \leq W < 1, \\ 1, & \text{if } 1 \leq W < 2, \text{ and} \\ \pi_T(W), & \text{if } W \geq 2, \end{cases}$$

and $\lim_{T\to\infty} \lambda_T(W) = \lambda_\infty(W)$, where

$$\lambda_\infty(W) = \begin{cases} 2, & \text{if } 0 \leq W < 1 \\ 1, & \text{if } W \geq 1. \end{cases}$$

The limit spending policy, $c_\infty(W)$, is defined by the equation

$$c_\infty(W) = \begin{cases} W, & \text{if } 0 \leq W \leq 2 \\ 2, & \text{if } W \geq 2, \end{cases}$$

where W is the amount of money available for expenditure. Since the amount of money available to be spent is at least 1 after period 0, this policy dictates that expenditure be at least 1 in every period after the first.

Since the permanent income hypothesis describes only asymptotic behavior, it can be only approximately accurate. We should not expect that consumers could ever achieve perfect self-insurance, since the models in which consumers achieve perfect self-insurance have infinite horizons, and in such models perfect self-insurance may require infinite money balances, as the next example demonstrates.

EXAMPLE 8.4 The utility from expenditure in one period is $v(c) = \ln(c + 1)$. The consumer's income in period t is a random variable, y_t, and the y_t are independently and identically distributed and equal 0 with probability $\frac{1}{2}$ and 2 with probability $\frac{1}{2}$. If the consumer is perfectly self-insuring, he or she consumes 1 in every period and keeps the marginal utility of money equal to $\frac{1}{1+1} = \frac{1}{2}$. The consumer cannot achieve this result indefinitely by saving and dissaving, for suppose that the consumer starts period 0 with M units of money, where M may be extremely large. Let N be an integer exceeding M. With probability $\frac{1}{2^N}$, the consumer has no income in each of periods 0 through $N - 1$. It is impossible for the consumer to consume 1 in all of these periods, since doing so would require $N > M$ units of money. Perfect self-insurance is therefore impossible.

The above example relies on the consumer's immortality. If the consumer is mortal, another difficulty arises, for he or she may not achieve perfect self-insurance near the end of life, as the next example illustrates.

EXAMPLE 8.5 The example is the same as the previous one, except that the consumer lives only in periods 0, 1, . . . , $T-1$. I show that the consumer cannot perfectly self-insure, no matter what the initial money balance, M, is at the beginning of period 0. If the consumer self-insures perfectly, consumption equals some constant amount c in every period. With probability $\binom{T}{n}\frac{1}{2^t}\frac{1}{2^{T-n}}$, the consumer ends period $T-1$ with money balances of $M+2n-Tc$, where n is the number of periods, t, on or before period $T-1$ in which $y_t=2$. If $M+2n-Tc<0$, the consumer would have violated the budget constraint and so could not have maintained a constant consumption of c. If $M+2n-Tc>0$, the consumer would increase her or his utility by spending the extra cash in period $T-1$ and so consume more than c then. She or he would not, however, be perfectly self-insuring if consumption ever exceeded c.

8.2 Rational Expectations Equilibrium

I now turn to the task of including the permanent income hypothesis in a general equilibrium model. The rational expectations model I describe here is designed to be consistent with the one just used to explain the permanent income hypothesis. All random fluctuations are generated by a sequence of independently and identically distributed random variables, s_t, where s_t belongs to finite set, S, and where t can be any integer, positive, negative, or zero. Consumers' utility functions are additive with respect to time and uncertainty.

ASSUMPTION 8.6 For each i, consumer i has a utility function, $u_i\colon \mathbb{R}^N_+ \times S \to \mathbb{R}$, and evaluates a random stream of consumption from period 0 to T according to the utility function

$$U_i(\mathbf{x}) = u_i(\mathbf{x}(s_0), s_0) + \sum_{t=1}^{T}\sum_{s_t \in S}\pi(s_t)u_i(\mathbf{x}(s_t), s_t),$$

where $\pi(s_t)$ is the probability of s_t.

ASSUMPTION 8.7 The endowment of consumer i is a function $\mathbf{e}_i\colon S \to \mathbb{R}^N_+$, where $i = 1, \ldots, I$.

For the moment, I assume that all production occurs instantaneously, as lags in production complicate the description of a rational expectations equilibrium.

ASSUMPTION 8.8 For $j = 1, \ldots, J$, firm j has an input-output possibility set, $Y_j(s)$, for each $s \in S$, where $Y_j(s)$ is a subset of $\mathbb{R}^N$.

As in the equilibrium models discussed earlier, each consumer i owns a share Θ_{ij} of firm j, where $\Theta_{ij} \geq 0$ and $\sum_{i=1}^{I} \Theta_{ij} = 1$, for all j.

The constituents of a rational expectations equilibrium are as follows.

DEFINITION 8.9 A *stationary consumption plan* consists of $x\colon S \rightarrow \mathbb{R}_+^N$.

DEFINITION 8.10 A *stationary production plan* for firm j consists of $\mathbf{y}_j\colon S \rightarrow \mathbb{R}^N$, such that $\mathbf{y}_j(s) \in Y_j(s)$, for all s.

DEFINITION 8.11 A *stationary allocation* is $(\mathbf{x}, \mathbf{y}) = (\mathbf{x}_1, \ldots, \mathbf{x}_I; \mathbf{y}_1, \ldots, \mathbf{y}_J)$, where $\mathbf{x}_i$ is a stationary consumption plan and $\mathbf{y}_j$ is a stationary production plan for firm j, for all i and j.

The allocation is called stationary, because it represents an allocation that fluctuates according to rules that are invariant with respect to time and yet depend on the random shocks, s_t. If the allocation, $(\mathbf{x}, \mathbf{y})$, is stationary, then the consumption bundle of person i at time t is $\mathbf{x}_i(s_t)$ and the input-output vector of firm j in period t is $\mathbf{y}_j(s_t)$.

DEFINITION 8.12 The stationary allocation $(\mathbf{x}, \mathbf{y})$ is *feasible*, if $\sum_{i=1}^{I} \mathbf{x}_i \leq \sum_{i=1}^{I} \mathbf{e}_i + \sum_{j=1}^{J} \mathbf{y}_j$, that is, if $\sum_{i=1}^{I} \mathbf{x}_i(s) \leq \sum_{i=1}^{I} \mathbf{e}_i(s) + \sum_{j=1}^{J} \mathbf{y}_j(s)$, for all s.

DEFINITION 8.13 A *stationary price system* is a function, $\mathbf{P}\colon S \rightarrow \mathbb{R}_+^N$, such that $\mathbf{P}(s) > 0$, for all s.

Given the stationary price system, $\mathbf{P}$, the price vector at time t is $\mathbf{P}(s_t)$.

DEFINITION 8.14 Given a stationary price system, $\mathbf{P}$, the set of profit-maximizing production plans for firm j is

$$\eta_j(\mathbf{P}) = \{\overline{\mathbf{y}}: S \to \mathbb{R}^N \mid \overline{\mathbf{y}}(s) \in Y(s), \text{ for all } s \text{ and } \sum_{s\in S} \pi(s)\mathbf{P}(s).\overline{\mathbf{y}}(s)$$

$$\geq \sum_{s\in S} \pi(s)\mathbf{P}(s).\mathbf{y}(s), \text{ for all } \mathbf{y}: S \to \mathbb{R}^N \text{ such that } \mathbf{y}(s) \in Y(s), \text{ for all } s\}.$$

Hence, each firm maximizes the expected value of profits in a single period. If prices are determined by the stationary price system $\mathbf{P}$ and a firm adopts a stationary production plan, $\mathbf{y}: S \to \mathbb{R}^N$, then the expected profits of the firm in one period are $\sum_{s\in S} \pi(s)\mathbf{P}(s).\mathbf{y}(s)$. By the law of large numbers, the long-run average profits of the firm, $\lim_{T\to\infty} T^{-1} \sum_{t=0}^{T-1} \mathbf{P}(s_t).\mathbf{y}(s_t)$, equals $\sum_{s\in S} \pi(s)\mathbf{P}(s).\mathbf{y}(s)$. The profits maximized are the same as the long-run average flow of income to the firm.

DEFINITION 8.15 Given a stationary price system $\mathbf{P}$ and a profit maximizing input-output vector, $\overline{\mathbf{y}}_j \in \eta_j(\mathbf{P})$, for each j, the *demand set* of consumer i is the set, $\xi_i(\mathbf{P})$, of solutions of the problem

$$\max_{\mathbf{x}:S\to\mathbb{R}^N_+} \sum_{s\in S} \pi(s)u_i(\mathbf{x}(s), s)$$

$$\text{s.t.} \quad \sum_{s\in S} \pi(s)\mathbf{P}(s).x(s) \leq \sum_{s\in S} \pi(s)\mathbf{P}(s).\mathbf{e}_i(s) + \sum_{j=1}^{J} \Theta_{ij}\pi(s)\mathbf{P}(s).\overline{\mathbf{y}}_j(s). \tag{8.12}$$

The budget constraint of the consumer is that expected expenditure in one period be no greater than expected income. Again by the law of large numbers, the budget constraint can be interpreted as

$$\lim_{T\to\infty} T^{-1} \sum_{t=0}^{T-1} \left[\mathbf{P}(s_1).\mathbf{x}(s_t) - \mathbf{P}(s_t).\mathbf{e}_i(s_t) - \sum_{j=1}^{J} \Theta_{ij}\mathbf{P}(s_t).\mathbf{y}_j(s_t) \right] \leq 0.$$

That is, the consumer must make sure that the long-run average flow of expenditure is no greater than the long-run average flow of income from the sale of endowment and from profits. Given this constraint, the consumer maximizes expected utility per period, which by the law of large numbers is the same as the long-run average flow of utility.

DEFINITION 8.16 A *rational expectations equilibrium* consists of $(\overline{\mathbf{x}}, \overline{\mathbf{y}}, \mathbf{P})$, where

1. $(\overline{\mathbf{x}}, \overline{\mathbf{y}})$ is a feasible stationary allocation
2. $\mathbf{P}$ is a stationary price system

3. for all i, $\overline{\mathbf{x}}_i \in \xi_i(\mathbf{P})$
4. for all j, $\overline{\mathbf{y}}_j \in \eta_j(\mathbf{P})$
5. for all s and n, $P_n(s) = 0$, if

$$\sum_{i=1}^{I} \overline{x}_{in}(s) < \sum_{i=1}^{I} \overline{e}_{in}(s) + \sum_{j=1}^{J} \overline{y}_{jn}(s)$$

If the utility functions $u_i(\mathbf{x}, s)$ are differentiable with respect to $\mathbf{x}$, the first-order conditions of maximization problem 8.12 are that there exists a positive number λ_i, such that

$$\frac{\partial u_i(\overline{\mathbf{x}}_i(s), s)}{\partial x_n} \le \lambda_i \mathbf{P}_n(s),$$

for all s and n, with equality if $\overline{x}_{in}(s) > 0$. Substituting s_t for s in this inequality, we see that

$$\frac{\partial u_i(\overline{\mathbf{x}}_i(s_t), s_t)}{\partial x_n} \le \lambda_i \mathbf{P}_n(s_t),$$

for all t, s_t, and n, with equality if $\overline{x}_{in}(\mathbf{s}_t) > 0$. That is, consumer i's marginal utility of unit of account is constant over time and events; consumers satisfy the permanent income hypothesis. The prices $P_{tn}(s_t)$ are spot prices in terms of current unit of account. They are not forward prices. It should be imagined that all consumers know the prices $P_{tn}(s)$ as functions of t, n, and s. They also know the probability distribution of the random process s_t and so correctly anticipate the joint probability distribution of future prices, $P_{tn}(s_t)$. The accuracy of their predictions explains the use of the term *rational expectations.* The model is meant to apply to conditions in which consumers are able to keep their marginal utilities of unit of account nearly constant and have a good idea of the distribution of future prices and so behave approximately as if they were in a rational expectations equilibrium.

A rational expectations equilibrium can be transformed into an Arrow-Debreu equilibrium with prices $p_n(s) = \pi(s)P_n(s)$, for $n = 1, \ldots, N$ and $s \in S$. It follows from the first welfare theorem 5.2 (in section 5.1), that if the utility functions $u_i(\mathbf{x}, s)$ are locally nonsatiated, then the allocation of a rational expectations equilibrium is Pareto optimal. If we assume that $\pi(s) > 0$, for all s, then we may transform an Arrow-Debreu equilibrium into a rational expectations equilibrium. Hence, we may prove that a rational expectations equilibrium exists by applying theorem 5.25 (in section

5.3) to show that there exists an Arrow-Debreu equilibrium. In order to apply theorem 5.25, I make the assumptions that follow.

ASSUMPTION 8.17 For all i and s, $u_i(\mathbf{x}, s)$ is continuous, strictly increasing, and quasi-concave as a function of $\mathbf{x}$, where quasi-concavity is defined in definition 5.13 (in section 5.2).

ASSUMPTION 8.18 For all j and s, $Y_j(s)$ is closed, convex, and contains the vector 0.

ASSUMPTION 8.19 For all s, $Y(s) \cap \mathbb{R}^N_+ = \{0\}$, where $Y(s) = \sum_{j=1}^J Y_j(s)$.

ASSUMPTION 8.20 For all s, $Y(s) \cap (-Y(s)) = \{0\}$.

ASSUMPTION 8.21 There exists a feasible allocation, $(\mathbf{x}, \mathbf{y})$, such that $\sum_{i=1}^I x_{in}(s) > 0$, for all n and s.

ASSUMPTION 8.22 For all $s \in S$, $\pi(s) > 0$.

The equilibrium existence theorem follows.

THEOREM 8.23 If the economy

$$\mathcal{E} = \left((U_i, \mathbf{e}_i)_{i=1}^I, (Y_j)_{j=1}^J, (\Theta_{ij})_{i=1,}^I{}_{j=1}^J\right)$$

satisfies assumptions 8.6–8.8 and 8.17–8.22, then it has a rational expectations equilibrium $(\overline{\mathbf{x}}, \overline{\mathbf{y}}, \mathbf{P})$.

I now turn to the definition of rational expectations equilibrium when production occurs with lags. The modeling of lags can be simplified by introducing intermediate goods so as to reduce lags of any length to one period. If it takes N periods to manufacture a product, we can introduce $N-2$ intermediate products, where the nth one is the product that results after n periods of production and the $(n+1)$st is produced from the nth.

I introduce a one-period production lag into the rational expectations equilibrium model as follows. The production possibilities for firm j are defined by sets $Y_j(s_0, s_1) \subset \mathbb{R}^N_- \times \mathbb{R}^N$, where there is one such set for every pair of states $(s_0, s_1) \in S \times S$. An input vector at a time t and after a particular history of exogenous states, $(\ldots, s_{t-1}, s_t)$, is a vector $\mathbf{y}_0 \in \mathbb{R}^N_-$, and the output vector in the succeeding state, $\mathbf{y}_1(s_{t+1}) \in \mathbb{R}^N$, depends on s_{t+1}. This vector is feasible for the firm, if $(\mathbf{y}_0, \mathbf{y}_1(s_{t+1})) \in Y_j(s_t, s_{t+1})$, for all s_{t+1}. The vector $\mathbf{y}_0$ consists of inputs and the vectors $\mathbf{y}_1(s_{t+1})$ may include inputs as well as outputs. The introduction of a time lag in production complicates the description of rational expectations equilibrium by allowing output in period t to depend on s_{t-1} as well as on s_t. Therefore, the allocation at time t does not necessarily depend only on the current state, s_t, but may depend on s_{t-1} as well. The allocation at time t may depend on the availability of commodities at time $t-1$ and hence may depend on s_{t-2}. Continuing by backward induction on time, we see that the allocation at time t may depend on s_{t-k}, for all nonnegative integers k. I now describe the notation I use to express this dependence.

The set of all paths of realizations of the random variable s_t is $\mathbf{S} = \{(\ldots, s_{-1}, s_0, s_1, \ldots) \mid s_t \in S$, for all $t\}$, and $\mathbf{s}$ denotes a member of $\mathbf{S}$. Consumption, inputs, and output are functions from $\mathbf{S}$ to $\mathbb{R}$. I restrict attention to functions that are measurable, for only such functions have an expected value. Another advantage of measurability is that it provides a way to express the idea that a function depends only on those s_k such that $k \leq t$, for some fixed t. If k is a fixed integer, let $\mathcal{B}_k$ be the set of all subsets of $\mathbf{S}$ of the form $B = \{\mathbf{s} \in \mathbf{S} \mid s_k \in A\}$, where A is a subset of S. If t is an integer, let $\mathcal{S}_t$ be the smallest set of subsets of $\mathbf{S}$ such that $\mathcal{S}_t$ contains $\mathcal{B}_k$, for $k \leq t$, and $\mathcal{S}_t$ has the following two properties:

1. If E belongs to $\mathcal{S}_t$, then $\mathbf{S}\backslash E$ belongs to $\mathcal{S}_t$, where $\mathbf{S}\backslash E = \{\mathbf{s} \in \mathbf{S} \mid \mathbf{s} \notin E\}$.
2. If E_n belongs to $\mathcal{S}_t$, for $n = 1, 2, \ldots$, then $\bigcap_{n=1}^{\infty} E_n$ belongs to $\mathcal{S}_t$.

It follows from conditions (1) and (2) that if E_n belongs to $\mathcal{S}_t$, for $n = 1, 2, \ldots$, then $\bigcup_{n=1}^{\infty} E_n = \mathbf{S}\backslash \left(\bigcap_{n=1}^{\infty}(\mathbf{S}\backslash E_n)\right)$ belongs to $\mathcal{S}_t$. A set of subsets satisfying conditions (1) and (2) and containing the whole set $\mathbf{S}$ is called a *σ-field*, and $\mathcal{S}_t$ is said to be the σ-field *generated* by $\mathcal{B}_k$, for $k \leq t$. A function $x: \mathbf{S} \to \mathbb{R}$ is said to be *$\mathcal{S}_t$-measurable*, if $x^{-1}([a, b]) = \{\mathbf{s} \in \mathbf{S} \mid a \leq x(\mathbf{s}) \leq b\}$ is a set in $\mathcal{S}_t$, for all numbers a and b. If x is $\mathcal{S}_t$-measurable, then $x(\mathbf{s})$ does not depend on s_k, for $k > t$. That is, $x(\mathbf{s})$ depends only on information available at time t. The smallest σ-field containing $\mathcal{S}_t$, for all t, is denoted $\mathcal{S}$. A function $x: \mathbf{S} \to \mathbb{R}$ is said to be *measurable* if it is $\mathcal{S}$-measurable. A function $x: S \to \mathbb{R}^K$ is said to be $\mathcal{S}_t$-measurable, if each of the component functions $x_k: S \to \mathbb{R}$ is $\mathcal{S}_t$-measurable, for $k = 1, \ldots, K$.

A useful function is the *shift function*, $\sigma: \mathbf{S} \to \mathbf{S}$, where $\sigma(\mathbf{s})$ is defined by the equation $\sigma(\mathbf{s})_t = \mathbf{s}_{t+1}$, for all t. The sequence $\sigma(\mathbf{s})$ is the sequence $\mathbf{s}$ shifted one step to the left, so that what happens at time $t+1$ in $\mathbf{s}$ happens at time t in $\sigma(\mathbf{s})$. If $x: \mathbf{S} \to \mathbb{R}$, then σx is the function defined by the equation $\sigma x(\mathbf{s}) = x(\sigma(\mathbf{s}))$. If x is $\mathcal{S}_t$-measurable, then σx is $\mathcal{S}_{t+1}$-measurable. Similarly, $\sigma^k x$ is $\mathcal{S}_{t+k}$-measurable, for any integer k, whether k be positive, negative, or zero. If $f: \mathbf{S} \to \mathbb{R}$ is $\mathcal{S}_t$-measurable it is sometimes convenient to write $f(\ldots, s_{t-1}, s_t)$ for $f(\mathbf{s})$ and $f(\ldots, s_t, s_{t+1})$ for $\sigma f(\mathbf{s})$.

Recall that the random variables s_t are assumed to be independently and identically distributed, and $\pi(s)$ is the probability that s_t takes on the particular value s in S. These assumptions imply a unique *probability measure* on $\mathcal{S}$ that I again denote by π. A probability measure has the following properties: $\pi: \mathcal{S} \to [0, 1]$, $\pi(\mathbf{S}) = 1$, $\pi(\emptyset) = 0$, and if $B_1, B_2, \ldots$ is a sequence of disjoint sets in $\mathcal{S}$, then $\pi\left(\bigcup_{n=1}^{\infty} B_n\right) = \sum_{n=1}^{\infty} \pi(B_n)$. The *expected value* of a measurable function $x: \mathbf{S} \to \mathbb{R}$ is $Ex = \int_{\mathbf{S}} x(\mathbf{s})\pi(d\mathbf{s})$. If Ex is defined, x is said to be *integrable*. Because the s_t are independently and identically distributed, they form a stationary stochastic process, which means that the shift operator, σ, is *measure preserving*. That is, $\pi(B) = \pi(\sigma B)$, for all B in $\mathcal{S}$, and $Ex = E\sigma x$, for all integrable functions x. An *event* is a set in $\mathcal{S}$. An event A is said to occur *almost surely* or *for almost every* $\mathbf{s}$, if A has probability 1, that is, if $\pi(A) = 1$. For instance, the measurable functions x and y are said to be equal almost surely if $\pi\{\mathbf{s} \mid x(\mathbf{s}) = y(\mathbf{s})\} = 1$. In what follows, I will treat two functions that are equal almost surely as the same function. That is, if $f: \mathbf{S} \to \mathbb{R}^K$ and $g: \mathbf{S} \to \mathbb{R}^K$ are $\mathcal{S}$-measurable, I write $f = g$, if $f(\mathbf{s}) = g(\mathbf{s})$, for almost every $\mathbf{s}$.

I now define stationary allocations.

DEFINITION 8.24 A *stationary consumption plan* consists of a bounded $\mathcal{S}_0$-measurable function $\mathbf{x}: \mathbf{S} \to \mathbb{R}^N_+$. A *stationary production plan* for firm j consists of a bounded $\mathcal{S}_0$-measurable function $\mathbf{y}_0: \mathbf{S} \to \mathbb{R}^N$ and a bounded $\mathcal{S}_1$-measurable function $\mathbf{y}_1: \mathbf{S} \to \mathbb{R}^N$ such that

$$(y_0(\mathbf{s}), y_1(\mathbf{s})) \in Y(s_0, s_1),$$

for almost every $\mathbf{s}$.

DEFINITION 8.25 A *stationary allocation* consists of $(\mathbf{x}, \mathbf{y}) = (\mathbf{x}_1, \ldots, \mathbf{x}_I; \mathbf{y}_1, \ldots, \mathbf{y}_J)$, where $\mathbf{x}_i$ is a stationary consumption plan and $\mathbf{y}_j$ is a stationary production plan for firm j, for all i and j.

As with the stationary allocation defined earlier that depended only on the current state, s_t, a stationary allocation that depends on an entire path, $\mathbf{s} = (\ldots, s_{-1}, s_0, s_1, \ldots)$, fluctuates according to rules that are invariant with respect to time. When the allocation of the economy is governed by a stationary allocation $(\mathbf{x}, \mathbf{y})$, the consumption bundle of person i at time t is $\sigma^t \mathbf{x}_i(\mathbf{s})$ and the period t input-output vector of firm j is $(\sigma^t \mathbf{y}_{j0}(\mathbf{s}), \sigma^t \mathbf{y}_{j1}(\mathbf{s}))$. In the language of probability theory, consumptions and input-output vectors fluctuate according to a stationary stochastic process.

DEFINITION 8.26 The stationary allocation $(\mathbf{x}, \mathbf{y})$ is *feasible* if

$$\sum_{i=1}^{I} \mathbf{x}_i(\mathbf{s}) \le \sum_{i=1}^{I} \mathbf{e}_i(\mathbf{s}) + \sum_{j=1}^{J} \left[\mathbf{y}_{j0}(\mathbf{s}) + \sigma^{-1} \mathbf{y}_{j1}(\mathbf{s})\right],$$

for almost every history $\mathbf{s} \in \mathbf{S}$.

In the definition of feasibility, the vector, $\mathbf{y}_{jt}$, is shifted backward through time by one period, so that the output appears at time 0 rather than at time 1 and the output is from inputs of periods -1 and 0 rather than of periods 0 and 1. The inputs in the vector, $\mathbf{y}_{j0}$, however, contribute to outputs appearing in period 1. The inputs and outputs in definition 8.26 are those that would occur at time 0 if the production allocations were determined by the stationary input-output functions $\mathbf{y}_j = (\mathbf{y}_{j0}, \mathbf{y}_{j1})$, for $j = 1, \ldots, J$. In more succinct notation, $(\mathbf{x}, \mathbf{y})$ is feasible if

$$\sum_{i=1}^{I} \mathbf{x}_i \le \sum_{i=1}^{I} \mathbf{e}_i + \sum_{j=1}^{J} \mathbf{y}_{j0} + \sum_{j=1}^{J} \sigma^{-1} \mathbf{y}_{j1}.$$

I now define the other pieces of a rational expectations equilibrium.

DEFINITION 8.27 A *stationary price system* consists of an integrable and $\mathcal{S}_0$-measurable function, $\mathbf{P}\colon \mathbf{S} \to \mathbb{R}^N_+$, such that

$$\int_S \mathbf{P}(\mathbf{s}) d\pi(\mathbf{s}) > 0.$$

To define profit maximization and the consumers' budget constraints, I must use the expected value of flows of unit of account. For instance, if $\mathbf{x}$ is a stationary consumption plan and $\mathbf{P}$ is a stationary price system, the expected flow of expenditure at time 0 or in any other period is

$$E[\mathbf{P}.x] = \int_S \mathbf{P}(\mathbf{s}).\mathbf{x}(\mathbf{s})d\pi(\mathbf{s}).$$

DEFINITION 8.28 Given a stationary price system $\mathbf{P}$, the set of profit-maximizing stationary input-output vectors for firm j is

$\eta_j(\mathbf{P}) = \{\overline{\mathbf{y}} = (\overline{\mathbf{y}}_0, \overline{\mathbf{y}}_1) \mid \overline{\mathbf{y}}$ is a stationary production plan for firm j and $E[\mathbf{P}.\overline{\mathbf{y}}_0 + \mathbf{P}.\sigma^{-1}\overline{\mathbf{y}}_1] \geq E[\mathbf{P}.\mathbf{y}_0 + \mathbf{P}.\sigma^{-1}\mathbf{y}_1]$, for all stationary production plans, $\mathbf{y}$, for firm $j\}$.

DEFINITION 8.29 Given a stationary price system $\mathbf{P}$ and profit maximizing input-output vectors, $\overline{\mathbf{y}}_j = (\overline{\mathbf{y}}_{j0}, \overline{\mathbf{y}}_{j1}) \in \eta_j(\mathbf{P})$, for all j, the *demand set*, $\xi_1(\mathbf{P})$, of consumer i is the set of all solutions, $\mathbf{x}$, of the problem

$$\max_{\substack{(\mathbf{x})\text{ is a stationary}\\ \text{consumption plan}}} Eu_i(\mathbf{x})$$

$$\text{s.t.}\quad E[\mathbf{P}.\mathbf{x}] \leq E[\mathbf{P}.\mathbf{e}_i] + \sum_{j=1}^{J} \Theta_{ij} E[\mathbf{P}.\overline{\mathbf{y}}_{j0} + \mathbf{P}.\sigma^{-1}\overline{\mathbf{y}}_{j1}].$$

DEFINITION 8.30 A *rational expectations equilibrium* consists of $(\overline{\mathbf{x}}, \overline{\mathbf{y}}, \mathbf{P})$, where

1. $(\overline{\mathbf{x}}, \overline{\mathbf{y}})$ is a feasible stationary allocation
2. $\mathbf{P}$ is a stationary price system
3. for all i, $\overline{\mathbf{x}}_j \in \xi_i(\mathbf{P})$
4. for all j, $\overline{\mathbf{y}}_j \in \eta_j(\mathbf{P})$
5. for all paths $\mathbf{s}$, $P_n(\mathbf{s}) = 0$, if

$$\sum_{i=1}^{I} \overline{x}_{in}(\mathbf{s}) \leq \sum_{i=1}^{I} e_{in}(\mathbf{s}) + \sum_{j=1}^{J} \left[\overline{y}_{j0n}(\mathbf{s}) + \sigma^{-1}\overline{y}_{j1n}(\mathbf{s})\right]$$

This definition is exactly the same as definition 8.16, except for a change in condition (5) made to reflect the one-period lag in production.

It is possible to state and prove versions of the first welfare theorem and of an equilibrium existence theorem for the notion of rational expectations equilibrium just defined and under assumptions much like those of theorem 8.23. The proofs are more difficult than those for the model of theorem 8.23, because there are a continuum of commodities in a model where allocations depend on infinite histories of random shocks. Statements of a first welfare theorem and an existence theorem and their proofs may be found in Bewley (1981a).

8.3 Short-Run Equilibrium

In a rational expectations equilibrium, each consumer matches the long-run flows of expenditures and income and is able, through saving and dissaving, to satisfy the permanent income hypothesis, that is, to keep the marginal utility of unit of account nearly constant. Short-run equilibrium is a snapshot of a rational expectations equilibrium at one moment. Because consumers satisfy the permanent income hypothesis, there is no need to assume that consumers satisfy a budget constraint. This constraint is replaced by the assumption that each consumer's marginal utility of expenditure is constant. The resulting concept of equilibrium is simpler than the Walrasian equilibrium in definition 4.1 (in section 4.1).

The framework of discussion will be a *short-run economy*, $\mathcal{E} = ((u_i, \lambda_i, \mathbf{e}_i)_{i=1}^{I}, (Y_j)_{j=1}^{J}, (\Theta_{ij})_{i=1,\ j=1}^{I\ \ J})$, where, for all i, λ_i is a positive number and is consumer i's marginal utility of unit of account. A price vector is an N-vector $\mathbf{P}$ such that $\mathbf{P} > 0$.

DEFINITION 8.31 Consumer i's *short-run demand* is the set, $\xi_i^S(\mathbf{P})$, of solutions of the problem

$$\max_{\mathbf{x} \in \mathbb{R}_+^N} [u_i(\mathbf{x}) - \lambda_i \mathbf{P}.\mathbf{x}].$$

The demand, $\xi_i^S(\mathbf{P})$, may not be defined for all values of $\mathbf{P}$. If u_i is strictly increasing, $\xi_i^S(\mathbf{P})$ is not defined when any of the components of $\mathbf{P}$ are zero. The short-run demand, $\xi_i^S(\mathbf{P})$, is the instantaneous demand of a consumer who satisfies the permanent income hypothesis. In the background lies a model where consumers have utility functions that are additively separable with respect to time and uncertainty and where the environment fluctuates rapidly according to a stationary stochastic process. The consumer is subject to a budget constraint only in the long run.

Short-run demand functions are used in econometric work, where they are termed *Frisch demand functions,* after work of Ragnar Frisch (1959). The term *Frisch demand* seems to have been introduced by Browning, Deaton, and Irish (1985), who used it in the context of a life-cycle model of consumer demand and labor supply. In their model, utility is additively separable with respect to time and uncertainty, as it is here, and the marginal utility of unit of account may evolve over time. The authors use Frisch demand only in discussing consumer demands and supplies at one moment of time, so that they treat constancy of the marginal utility of unit of account as applying only in the short run, as I do here.

Brown and Calsamiglia (2003) claim that Alfred Marshall had in mind short-run demand in the general equilibrium model he defines in his mathematical appendix to volume I of *Principles of Economics* (1890).

Because $\lambda_i > 0$, $\xi_i^S(\mathbf{P})$ solves the problem

$$\max_{\mathbf{x}\in\mathbb{R}_+^N} \left[\lambda_i^{-1} u_i(\mathbf{x}) - \mathbf{P}.\mathbf{x}\right]. \tag{8.13}$$

The quantity $\lambda_i^{-1} u_i(\mathbf{x}) - \mathbf{P}.\mathbf{x}$ may be thought of as consumer i's surplus, because it represents in terms of unit of account the total benefit to consumer i of consuming bundle $\mathbf{x}$ minus the cost of purchasing the bundle at price vector $\mathbf{P}$. Browning, Deaton, and Irish (1985) call the quantity $\max_{\mathbf{x}\in\mathbb{R}_+^N}[\lambda_i^{-1} u_i(\mathbf{x}) - \mathbf{P}.\mathbf{x}]$ consumer i's profit, as it is analogous to a firm's profit. If we think of consumer i as having utility production possibility set

$$X_i = \{(-\mathbf{x}, v) \mid \mathbf{x} \in \mathbb{R}_+^N \text{ and } v \le u_i(\mathbf{x})\},$$

and if we think of utility as having the value λ_I^{-1} per unit, then the vector $(-\xi_i^S(\mathbf{P}), u_i(\xi_i^S(\mathbf{P})))$ solves the problem

$$\max_{(-\mathbf{x}, v)\in X_i} (\mathbf{P}, \lambda_i^{-1}).(-\mathbf{x}, v).$$

The quantity $(\mathbf{P}, \lambda_i^{-1}).(-\mathbf{x}, v) = \lambda_i^{-1} v - \mathbf{P}.\mathbf{x}$ is the profit in unit of account earned from producing v units of utility from an input consumption bundle $\mathbf{x}$.

In a branch of mathematics called *convex analysis,* the profit function $\pi_i(\mathbf{P}, \lambda_i^{-1}) = \max_{\mathbf{x}\in\mathbb{R}_+^N}[\lambda_i^{-1} u_i(\mathbf{x}) - \mathbf{P}.\mathbf{x}]$ is termed the *conjugate function* of the utility function $\lambda_i^{-1}u_i$. The theory of conjugate functions is explained in Rockafellar (1970, sec. 12).

A monotone transformation of a utility function may change short-run demand, though it has no effect on Walrasian demand. For instance, if $N = 1$, $u(x) = \ln(x)$, and $\lambda = 1$, then the associated short-run demand is $\xi^S(\mathbf{P}) = \mathbf{P}^{-1}$, whereas if $u(x) = 2\ln(x)$ and $\lambda = 1$, then $\xi^S(\mathbf{P}) = 2\mathbf{P}^{-1}$.

Before turning to the study of short-run equilibrium, I discuss the properties of the short-run demand under the following assumption.

ASSUMPTION 8.32 For each i, $u_i\colon \mathbb{R}^N_+ \to \mathbb{R}$ is continuous, strictly increasing, and strictly concave.

To define one important property of the functions ξ_i^S, I require the concept of an open set.

DEFINITION 8.33 If X is a subset of $\mathbb{R}^N$, then a subset U of X is said to be *open in* X if for every $\mathbf{x}$ in U, there is a positive number ε, such that $\mathbf{y}$ belongs to U if $\mathbf{y}$ belongs to X and $\|\mathbf{x} - \mathbf{y}\| < \varepsilon$.

For any set X, the empty set and the entire set X are open in X. If U is a subset of X that is open in X, then U is open in any subset Y of X. A set is said to be *open* if it is open in itself. A set is open if and only if it equals its interior, where the interior is defined in definition 3.28 (in section 3.5).

EXAMPLE 8.34 The open interval, $(0, 1) = \{t \mid 0 < t < 1\}$, is an open set and is open in the set of the real numbers, $\mathbb{R} = (-\infty, \infty)$. It is not open in $\mathbb{R}^2$ if we think of $(0, 1)$ as the set $\{(t, 0) \in \mathbb{R}^2 \mid 0 < t < 1\}$. The open ball, $\{\mathbf{x} \in \mathbb{R}^2 \mid \|\mathbf{x}\| < 1\}$, is an open set in $\mathbb{R}^2$. The half open interval $[0, 1) = \{t \mid 0 \le t < 1\}$ is open in the closed interval $[0, 2] = \{t \mid 0 \le t \le 2\}$ but is not open in $\mathbb{R}$.

Before proceeding, I must prove the following lemma.

LEMMA 8.35 Let B be a nonempty, compact, convex subset of $\mathbb{R}^N_+$, and, for each N-vector $\mathbf{P}$ such that $\mathbf{P} > 0$, let $\mathbf{x}_i(\mathbf{P}, B)$ be the set of solutions of the problem

$$\max_{\mathbf{x} \in B}[u_i(\mathbf{x}) - \lambda_i \mathbf{P}.\mathbf{x}]. \tag{8.14}$$

If assumption 8.32 applies, then $\mathbf{x}_i(\mathbf{P}, B)$ is a continuous function of $\mathbf{P}$.

Proof. Since $u_i(\mathbf{x}) - \lambda_i\mathbf{P}.\mathbf{x}$ is a continuous function of $\mathbf{x}$ and B is compact, problem 8.14 has a solution, for each $\mathbf{P}$. Since $u_i(\mathbf{x}) - \lambda_i\mathbf{P}.\mathbf{x}$ is strictly concave as a function of $\mathbf{x}$, the solution to this problem is unique. Therefore $\mathbf{x}_i(\mathbf{p}, B)$ is a function. I show that it is continuous. Suppose that $\mathbf{P}^k$ is a sequence of nonzero vectors in $\mathbb{R}^N_+$ that converges to $\mathbf{P}$, where $\mathbf{P} > 0$. I must show that $\lim_{k\to\infty} \mathbf{x}_i(\mathbf{P}^k, B) = \mathbf{x}_i(\mathbf{P}, B)$. If $\mathbf{x}_i(\mathbf{P}^k, B)$ does not converge to $\mathbf{x}_i(\mathbf{P}, B)$, then for some positive number ε, $\|\mathbf{x}_i(\mathbf{P}^k, B) - \mathbf{x}_i(\mathbf{P}, B)\| > \varepsilon$, for infinitely many k. Therefore there is a subsequence, which I call $\mathbf{x}_i(\mathbf{P}^k, B)$ again, such that $\|\mathbf{x}_i(\mathbf{P}^k, B) - \mathbf{x}_i(\mathbf{P}, B)\| > \varepsilon$, for all k. Since the vectors $\mathbf{x}_i(\mathbf{P}^k, B)$ all belong to the compact set B, by the Bolzano-Weierstrass theorem (3.12 in section 3.2), I may assume that the sequence $\mathbf{x}(\mathbf{P}^k, B)$ converges to some vector $\overline{\mathbf{x}}$ in B. Passing to the limit in the inequality $\|\mathbf{x}_i(\mathbf{P}^k, B) - \mathbf{x}_i(\mathbf{P}, B)\| > \varepsilon$, we see that $\|\overline{\mathbf{x}} - \mathbf{x}_i(\mathbf{P}, B)\| \geq \varepsilon$, so that $\overline{\mathbf{x}} \neq \mathbf{x}_i(\mathbf{P}, B)$. The definition of $\mathbf{x}_i(\mathbf{P}^k, B)$ implies that

$$u_i(\mathbf{x}_i(\mathbf{P}^k, B)) - \lambda_i\mathbf{P}^k.\mathbf{x}_i(\mathbf{P}^k, B) \geq u_i(\mathbf{x}_i(\mathbf{P}, B)) - \lambda_i\mathbf{P}^k.\mathbf{x}_i(\mathbf{P}, B).$$

Passing to the limit in this inequality, we see that

$$u_i(\overline{\mathbf{x}}) - \lambda_i\mathbf{P}.\overline{\mathbf{x}} \geq u_i(\mathbf{x}_i(\mathbf{P}, B)) - \lambda_i\mathbf{P}.\mathbf{x}_i(\mathbf{P}, B).$$

Since $\overline{\mathbf{x}} \neq \mathbf{x}_i(\mathbf{P}, B)$ and $u_i(\mathbf{x}) - \lambda\mathbf{P}.\mathbf{x}$ is strictly concave in $\mathbf{x}$, it follows that

$$u_i(\overline{\mathbf{x}}) - \lambda_i\mathbf{P}.\overline{\mathbf{x}} < u_i(\mathbf{x}_i(\mathbf{P}, B)) - \lambda_i\mathbf{P}.\mathbf{x}_i(\mathbf{P}, B).$$

The contradiction between the last two inequalities implies that $\mathbf{x}_i(\mathbf{P}^k, B)$ converges to $\mathbf{x}_i(\mathbf{P}, B)$, as was to be proved. ∎

PROPOSITION 8.36 Assumption 8.32 implies that $\{\mathbf{P} \mid \xi_i^S(\mathbf{P}) \neq \emptyset\}$ is an open set in $\mathbb{R}^N$ contained in the interior of $\mathbb{R}^N_+$.

Proof. The proposition is clearly true if $\{P|\xi_i^S(\mathbf{P}) \neq \emptyset\} = \emptyset$. So, suppose that $\xi_i^S(\overline{\mathbf{P}})$ is not empty, for some $\overline{\mathbf{P}} \in \mathbb{R}^N_+$. Because u_i is strictly increasing, $\overline{\mathbf{P}} \gg 0$ and so belongs to the interior of $\mathbb{R}^N_+$.

Let $B = \{\mathbf{x} \in \mathbb{R}^N_+ \mid \|\mathbf{x}\| \leq \|\xi_i^S(\overline{\mathbf{P}})\| + 2\}$ and let $\mathbf{x}_i(\mathbf{P}, B)$ be the set of solutions of problem 8.14. Since B is compact, lemma 8.35 implies that $\mathbf{x}_i(\mathbf{P}, B)$ is continuous as a function of $\mathbf{P}$.

Because $\xi_i^S(\overline{\mathbf{P}})$ solves the problem

$$\max_{\mathbf{x} \in \mathbb{R}^N_+} [u_i(\mathbf{x}) - \lambda_i\overline{\mathbf{P}}],$$

it follows that

$$u_i(\xi_i^S(\overline{\mathbf{P}})) - \lambda_i \overline{\mathbf{P}}.\xi_i^S(\overline{\mathbf{P}}) \geq u_i(\mathbf{x}_i(\overline{\mathbf{P}}, B)) - \lambda_i \overline{\mathbf{P}}.\mathbf{x}_i(\overline{\mathbf{P}}, B).$$

Because $\xi_i^S(\overline{\mathbf{P}})$ belongs to B,

$$u_i(\xi_i^S(\overline{\mathbf{P}})) - \lambda_i \overline{\mathbf{P}}.\xi_i^S(\overline{\mathbf{P}}) \leq u_i(\mathbf{x}_i(\overline{\mathbf{P}}, B)) - \lambda_i \overline{\mathbf{P}}.\mathbf{x}_i(\overline{\mathbf{P}}, B).$$

Therefore,

$$u_i(\xi_i^S(\overline{\mathbf{P}})) - \lambda_i \overline{\mathbf{P}}.\xi_i^S(\overline{\mathbf{P}}) = u_i(\mathbf{x}_i(\overline{\mathbf{P}}, B)) - \lambda_i \overline{\mathbf{P}}.\mathbf{x}_i(\overline{\mathbf{P}}, B).$$

This equation and the strict concavity of u_i imply that

$$\xi_i^S(\overline{\mathbf{P}}) = \mathbf{x}_i(\overline{\mathbf{P}}, B).$$

Because the function $\mathbf{x}_i(\overline{\mathbf{P}}, B)$ is continuous as a function of $\mathbf{P}$, there exists a positive number ε such that

$$\|\mathbf{x}_i(\mathbf{P}, B) - \xi_i^S(\overline{\mathbf{P}})\| = \|\mathbf{x}_i(\mathbf{P}, B) - \mathbf{x}_i(\overline{\mathbf{P}}, B)\| < 1, \tag{8.15}$$

if $\|\mathbf{P} - \overline{\mathbf{P}}\| < \varepsilon$. It is sufficient to show that $\xi_i^S(\mathbf{P}) = \mathbf{x}_i(\mathbf{P}, B)$ and hence that $\xi_i^S(\mathbf{P})$ is not empty, if $\|\mathbf{P} - \overline{\mathbf{P}}\| < \varepsilon$. Suppose that $\|\mathbf{P} - \overline{\mathbf{P}}\| < \varepsilon$ and $\xi_i^S(\mathbf{P}) \neq \mathbf{x}_i(\mathbf{P}, B)$. Then, there exists a vector $\mathbf{x}'$ in $\mathbb{R}_+^N$ such that

$$u_i(\mathbf{x}') - \lambda_i \mathbf{P}.\mathbf{x}' > u_i(\mathbf{x}_i(\mathbf{P}, B)) - \lambda_i \mathbf{P}.\mathbf{x}_i(\mathbf{P}, B). \tag{8.16}$$

By the definitions of B and $\mathbf{x}_i(\mathbf{P}, B)$,

$$\|\mathbf{x}'\| > \|\xi_i^S(\overline{\mathbf{P}})\| + 2.$$

The triangle inequality and inequality 8.15 imply that

$$\|\mathbf{x}_i(\mathbf{P}, B)\| \leq \|\xi_i^S(\overline{\mathbf{P}})\| + \|\mathbf{x}_i(\mathbf{P}, B) - \xi_i^S(\overline{\mathbf{P}})\| < \|\xi_i^S(\overline{\mathbf{P}})\| + 1.$$

Therefore, if the positive number α is sufficiently small,

$$\|\alpha \mathbf{x}' + (1-\alpha)\mathbf{x}_i(\mathbf{P}, B)\| \leq \|\xi_i^S(\overline{\mathbf{P}})\| + 2, \tag{8.17}$$

so that $\alpha \mathbf{x}' + (1-\alpha)\mathbf{x}_i(\mathbf{P}, B) \in B$. We now have that

$$\begin{aligned} &u_i(\alpha \mathbf{x}' + (1-\alpha)\mathbf{x}_i(\mathbf{P}, B)) - \lambda_i \mathbf{P}.(\alpha \mathbf{x}' + (1-\alpha)\mathbf{x}_i(\mathbf{P}, B)) \\ &\geq \alpha[u_i(\mathbf{x}') - \lambda_i P.\mathbf{x}'] + (1-\alpha)[u_i(\mathbf{x}_i(\mathbf{P}, B) - \lambda_i \mathbf{P}.\mathbf{x}_i(\mathbf{P}, B)] \\ &> u_i(\mathbf{x}_i(\mathbf{P}, B)) - \lambda_i \mathbf{P}.\mathbf{x}_i(\mathbf{P}, B), \end{aligned} \tag{8.18}$$

where the first inequality above follows from the concavity of u_i, and the second follows from inequality 8.16. Inequalities 8.17 and 8.18 contradict the definition of $\mathbf{x}_i(\mathbf{P}, B)$, and this contradiction proves that $\xi_i^S(\mathbf{P}) = \mathbf{x}_i(\mathbf{P}, B)$ and hence proves the lemma. ■

PROPOSITION 8.37 If assumption 8.32 applies, then the correspondence ξ_i^S is a continuous function defined on a set of strictly positive N-vectors that is open in $\mathbb{R}^N$.

Proof. Let $U = \{\mathbf{P} \in \mathbb{R}_+^N \mid \xi_i^S(\mathbf{P}) \neq \emptyset\}$. In the course of proving proposition 8.36, it was shown that if $\overline{\mathbf{P}}$ belongs to U, then there is a positive number ε such that if $\|\mathbf{P} - \overline{\mathbf{P}}\| < \varepsilon$ then $\mathbf{P}$ belongs to U and $\xi_i^S(\mathbf{P}) = \mathbf{x}_i(\mathbf{P}, B)$, where $\mathbf{x}_i(\mathbf{P}, B)$ is a continuous function of $\mathbf{P}$. It follows that the function ξ_i^S is everywhere continuous. ■

(Proposition 8.73 at the end of section 8.5 asserts that the domain of definition of ξ_i^S is convex as well as open.)

Before continuing with the analysis of short-run demand, I remark that statements similar to lemma 8.35 and proposition 8.36 apply to production. Although these statements will not be used until section 8.5, I state them here because of the similarity of their proofs to those just given. Recall that the supply set of firm j at price vector $\mathbf{P}$ is the set, $\eta_j(\mathbf{P})$, of solutions of the problem

$$\max_{\mathbf{y} \in Y_j} \mathbf{P}.\mathbf{y}.$$

LEMMA 8.38 Assume that Y_j is a closed and strictly convex subset of $\mathbb{R}^N$. Let B be a compact convex subset of $\mathbb{R}^N$ that intersects Y_j. For each N-vector $\mathbf{P}$ such that $\mathbf{P} > 0$, let $\mathbf{y}_j(\mathbf{P}, B)$ be the set of solutions of the problem

$$\max_{\mathbf{y} \in Y_j \cap B} \mathbf{P}.\mathbf{y}.$$

Then, $\mathbf{y}_j(\mathbf{P}, B)$ is a continuous funcetion of $\mathbf{P}$.

The proof of this lemma is very similar to that of lemma 8.35.

PROPOSITION 8.39 If Y_j is a closed and strictly convex subset of $\mathbb{R}^N$, then the set of N-vectors $\mathbf{P}$ such that $\eta_j(\mathbf{P})$ is not empty is open in $\mathbb{R}_+^N$.

Proof. The demonstration follows from lemma 8.38 in the same way that proposition 8.36 follows from lemma 8.35. ■

PROPOSITION 8.40 If Y_j is a closed and strictly convex subset of $\mathbb{R}^N$, then the correspondence η_j is a continuous function defined on a set of nonnegative N-vectors that is open in $\mathbb{R}^N_+$.

Proof. The proof follows from the full proof of proposition 8.39, just as the proof of proposition 8.37 follows from the proof of proposition 8.36. ■

The market short-run demand, which is the sum of the short-run demands of the individual consumers, may be defined as the short-run demand of a fictitious aggregate consumer. To show that this is so, I use the fact that $\xi_i^S(\mathbf{P})$ solves problem 8.13. Define the welfare function $W: \mathbb{R}^N_+ \to \mathbb{R}$ by the equation

$$W(\mathbf{x}) \quad \max_{\mathbf{x}_i \in \mathbb{R}^N_+, \ldots, \mathbf{x}_I \in \mathbb{R}^N_+} \sum_{i=1}^{I} \lambda_i\ ^{1} u_i(\mathbf{x}_i)$$
$$\text{s.t.} \quad \sum_{i=1}^{I} \mathbf{x}_i = \mathbf{x}. \tag{8.19}$$

Because the utility functions u_i are strictly concave, W is strictly concave as well, and furthermore the following lemma applies.

LEMMA 8.41 If assumption 8.32 applies, then for each $\mathbf{x} \in \mathbb{R}^N_+$ there exists one and only one vector $(\mathbf{x}_1, \ldots, \mathbf{x}_I)$ such that $\mathbf{x} = \sum_{i=1}^{I} \mathbf{x}_i$ and $W(\mathbf{x}) = \sum_{i=1}^{I} \lambda_i^{-1} u_i(\mathbf{x}_i)$.

Proof. Because the function $\sum_{i=1}^{I} \lambda_i^{-1} u_i(\mathbf{x}_i)$ is continuous and $\{(\mathbf{x}_1, \ldots, \mathbf{x}_I) \mid \mathbf{x}_i \in \mathbb{R}^N_+$, for all i, and $\sum_{i=1}^{I} \mathbf{x}_i = \mathbf{x}\}$ is compact, proposition 3.14 (in section 3.2) implies that there exists at least one vector $(\mathbf{x}_1, \ldots, \mathbf{x}_I)$, such that $\mathbf{x} = \sum_{i=1}^{I} \mathbf{x}_i$ and $W(\mathbf{x}) = \sum_{i=1}^{I} \lambda_i^{-1} u_i(\mathbf{x}_i)$. The vector $(\mathbf{x}_1, \ldots, \mathbf{x}_I)$ is unique, for suppose there are two vectors, $(\underline{\mathbf{x}}, \ldots, \underline{\mathbf{x}}_I)$ and $(\overline{\mathbf{x}}, \ldots, \overline{\mathbf{x}}_I)$, where $(\underline{\mathbf{x}}_1, \ldots, \underline{\mathbf{x}}_I) \neq (\overline{\mathbf{x}}_1, \ldots, \overline{\mathbf{x}}_I)$, $\sum_{i=1}^{I} \underline{\mathbf{x}}_i = \mathbf{x} = \sum_{i=1}^{I} \overline{\mathbf{x}}_i$, and $\sum_{i=1}^{I} \lambda_i^{-1} u_i(\underline{\mathbf{x}}_i) = W(\mathbf{x}) = \sum_{i=1}^{I} \lambda_i^{-1} u_i(\overline{\mathbf{x}}_i)$ For each i, let $\mathbf{x}_i = \frac{1}{2}\underline{\mathbf{x}}_i + \frac{1}{2}\overline{\mathbf{x}}_i$. Then, $\sum_{i=1}^{I} \mathbf{x}_i = \mathbf{x}$ and because the u_i are strictly concave, $\sum_{i=1}^{I} \lambda_i^{-1} u_i(\mathbf{x}_i) > \sum_{i=1}^{I} \lambda_i^{-1} u_i(\overline{\mathbf{x}}_i) = W(\mathbf{x})$, which is impossible. This contradiction proves that $(\mathbf{x}_1, \ldots, \mathbf{x}_I)$ is unique. ■

The short-run demand function defined from the welfare function W turns out to be short-run market demand.

DEFINITION 8.42 For any price vector $\mathbf{P}$, let $\Xi^S(\mathbf{P})$ be the set of solutions of the problem

$$\max_{\mathbf{x}\in\mathbb{R}^N_+} [W(\mathbf{x}) - \mathbf{P}.\mathbf{x}].$$

Because W is strictly concave, $\Xi(\mathbf{P})$ is unique, if it exists. The next proposition asserts that $\Xi^S(\mathbf{P})$ is the aggregate short-run demand of all the consumers, so that W may be viewed as the utility function of an aggregate consumer whose short-run demand equals market demand when this consumer's marginal utility of unit of account is 1.

PROPOSITION 8.43 If assumption 8.32 applies, then $\Xi^S(\mathbf{P}) = \sum_{i=1}^I \xi_i^S(\mathbf{P})$, if $\Xi^S(\mathbf{P})$ is defined.

Proof. The statement follows from the following equations and from the fact that, for each i, $\xi_i^S(\mathbf{P})$ is the solution of problem 8.13.

$$\max_{x\in\mathbb{R}^N_+} [W(\mathbf{x}) - \mathbf{P}.\mathbf{x}]$$

$$= \max_{x_1\in\mathbb{R}^N_+} \left[\left(\begin{array}{c} \max_{(x_1\in\mathbb{R}^N_+,\ldots,x_I\in\mathbb{R}^N_+)} \sum_{i=1}^I \lambda_i^{-1} u_i(\mathbf{x}_i) \\ \text{s.t. } \sum_{i=1}^I \mathbf{x}_i = \mathbf{x} \end{array}\right) - \mathbf{P}.\mathbf{x}\right]$$

$$= \max_{x\in\mathbb{R}^N_+} \left[\begin{array}{c} \max_{(x_1\in\mathbb{R}^N_+,\ldots,x_I\in\mathbb{R}^N_+)} \sum_{i=1}^I [\lambda_i^{-1} u_i(\mathbf{x}_i) - \mathbf{P}.\mathbf{x}_i] \\ \text{s.t. } \sum_{i=1}^I \mathbf{x}_i = \mathbf{x} \end{array}\right]$$

$$= \max_{(x_1\in\mathbb{R}^N_+,\ldots,x_I\in\mathbb{R}^N_+)} \sum_{i=1}^I [\lambda_i^{-1} u_i(\mathbf{x}_i) - \mathbf{P}.\mathbf{x}_i]$$

$$= \sum_{i=1}^I \max_{x_i\in\mathbb{R}^N_+} [\lambda_i^{-1} u_i(\mathbf{x}_i) - \mathbf{P}.\mathbf{x}_i] \quad \blacksquare$$

The next proposition asserts that the demand curves generated by $\Xi^S(\mathbf{P})$ are nonincreasing. This behavior of short-run demand contrasts with that of Walrasian demand, for Walrasian demand curves can slope upward, as example 8.63 at the end of this section shows. Let $D_n^S(P_n)$ be the short-run demand function for good n defined by the equation $D_n^S(P_n) = \Xi_n^S(P_1, \ldots, P_n, \ldots, P_N)$, where the prices P_k are held fixed for $k \neq n$. The short-run demand, $D_n^S(P_n)$, depends, of course, on the prices P_k, for $k \neq n$.

PROPOSITION 8.44 Suppose that assumption 8.32 applies. If a is a positive number and $\Xi^S(P_1, \ldots, P_n + a, \ldots, P_N) \neq \Xi^S(P_1, \ldots, P_n, \ldots, P_N)$, then $D_n^S(P_n + a) < D_n^S(P_n)$. Hence $D_n^S(P_n + a) \leq D_n^S(P_n)$.

Proof. Without loss of generality, let $n = 1$. Because W is strictly concave, it follows from the definition of $\Xi^S(\mathbf{P})$ that

$$W(\Xi(\mathbf{P})) - \mathbf{P}.\Xi^S(\mathbf{P}) > W(\mathbf{x}) - \mathbf{P}.\mathbf{x},$$

if $\mathbf{x} \neq \Xi^S(\mathbf{P})$. Therefore,

$$W(\mathbf{x}) < W(\Xi^S(\mathbf{P})) + \mathbf{P}.[\mathbf{x} - \Xi^S(\mathbf{P})], \tag{8.20}$$

if $\mathbf{x} \neq \Xi^S(\mathbf{P})$. Let $\mathbf{P}' = \mathbf{P} + (a, 0, \ldots, 0)$. The reasoning that implies inequality 8.20 also implies that

$$W(\mathbf{x}) < W(\Xi^S(\mathbf{P}')) + \mathbf{P}'.[\mathbf{x} - \Xi^S(\mathbf{P}')], \tag{8.21}$$

if $\mathbf{x} \neq \Xi^S(\mathbf{P}')$. Suppose that $\Xi^S(\mathbf{P}) \neq \Xi^S(\mathbf{P}')$. Then, inequality 8.21 implies that

$$\begin{aligned} W(\Xi^S(\mathbf{P})) &< W(\Xi^S(\mathbf{P}')) + \mathbf{P}'.[\Xi^S(\mathbf{P}) - \Xi^S(\mathbf{P}')] \\ &= W(\Xi^S(\mathbf{P}')) + \mathbf{P}.[\Xi^S(\mathbf{P}) - \Xi^S(\mathbf{P}')] + a[\Xi_1^S(\mathbf{P}) - \Xi_1^S(\mathbf{P}')]. \end{aligned} \tag{8.22}$$

Similarly, inequality 8.20 implies that

$$W(\Xi^S(\mathbf{P}')) < W(\Xi^S(\mathbf{P})) + \mathbf{P}.[\Xi^S(\mathbf{P}') - \Xi^S(\mathbf{P})].$$

By substituting this inequality into inequality 8.22 and simplifying, we see that

$$0 < a\left[\Xi_1^S(\mathbf{P}) - \Xi_1^S(\mathbf{P}')\right],$$

which implies that

$$\Xi_1^S(\mathbf{P}') < \Xi_1^S(\mathbf{P}).$$

That is,

$$D_1^S(P_1 + a) < D_1^S(P_1). \quad \blacksquare$$

If the individual utility functions are not differentiable, short-run demand curves may have flat sections, because the welfare function W may have kinks, as the following example shows.

EXAMPLE 8.45 Let $u: [0, \infty) \to [0, \infty)$ be defined by the equation

$$u(x) = \begin{cases} 2\sqrt{x}, & \text{if } 0 \le x \le 1 \text{ and} \\ 1 + \sqrt{x}, & \text{if } x \ge 1 \end{cases}$$

and let $\lambda = 1$. Then, $\Xi^S(P) = \xi^S(P)$ solves the problem $\max_{x \ge 0}[u(x) - Px]$, so that P is a subgradient of u. Hence,

$$\Xi^S(P) = \begin{cases} \frac{1}{4P^2}, & \text{if } P \ge \frac{1}{2}, \\ 1, & \text{if } \frac{1}{2} \le P \le 1, \text{ and} \\ \frac{1}{P^2}, & \text{if } P \ge 1. \end{cases}$$

We see that $\Xi^S(P)$ is flat over the interval $\frac{1}{2} \le P \le 1$.

The demand $D_n^S(P_n)$ is strictly decreasing if we assume that consumers' utility functions are twice continuously differentiable.

ASSUMPTION 8.46 For all i, u_i is twice continuously differentiable and, for all $\mathbf{x}$, $Du_i(\mathbf{x}) \gg 0$ and $D^2u_i(\mathbf{x})$ is negative definite.

Assumption 8.46 implies assumption 8.32, for u_i is strictly increasing if $Du_i(\mathbf{x}) \gg 0$, for all $\mathbf{x}$, and by lemma 3.38 (in section 3.5) u_i is strictly concave if $D^2u_i(\mathbf{x})$ is negative definite, for all $\mathbf{x}$. To understand the proof that demand curves are strictly decreasing, assume that $\mathbf{P}$ is such that $\xi_i^S(\mathbf{P}) \gg 0$, for all i. Then, $\xi_i^S(\mathbf{P})$ satisfies the equation

$$Du_i(\xi_i^S(\mathbf{P})) = \lambda_i \mathbf{P}. \tag{8.23}$$

The implicit function theorem implies that ξ_i^S is differentiable. Differentiating equation 8.23, we see that

$$D\xi_i^S(\mathbf{P}) = \lambda_i (D^2u_i(\xi_i^S(\mathbf{P})))^{-1},$$

where $(D^2u_i(\xi_i^S(\mathbf{P})))^{-1}$ is the inverse of the matrix $D^2u_i(\xi_i^S(\mathbf{P}))$. Since $D^2u_i(\xi_i^S(\mathbf{P}))$ is negative definite, the matrix $(D^2u_i(\xi_i^S(\mathbf{P})))^{-1}$ is negative definite as well, and hence $D\xi_i^S(\mathbf{P})$ is negative definite. It follows that

$D\Xi(\mathbf{P}) = \sum_{i=1}^{I} D\xi_i^S(\mathbf{P})$ is also negative definite. Since $D\Xi(\mathbf{P})$ is negative definite,

$$\frac{dD_n^S(P_n)}{dP_n} = \frac{\partial \Xi_n^S(\mathbf{P})}{\partial P_n} < 0,$$

for all n.[1] The argument depends on the special assumption that $\xi_i^S(\mathbf{P}) \gg 0$, for all i. If we drop this assumption, $D_n^S(P_n)$ is not necessarily everywhere differentiable, but it is still possible to prove that it is downward sloping. The next proposition says that the market demand curve, $D_n^S(P_n)$, is the sum of individual demand curves, $D_{in}^S(P_n)$, that are downward sloping in a certain sense, though they are not necessarily everywhere differentiable.

PROPOSITION 8.47 Suppose that u_i satisfies assumption 8.46, for all i. Fix P_k for $k \neq n$, let $D_{in}^S(P_n) = \xi_i^S(P_1, P_2, \ldots, P_n, \ldots, P_N)$, and let $U_i = \{P_n \mid D_{in}^S(P_n) > 0\}$. Then, U_i is an open interval of real numbers and is the union of finitely many sets, C, that are closed in U_i and are such that, for each C, the restriction of $D_{in}^S(P_n)$ to C is differentiable and $\frac{dD_{in}^S(P_n)}{dP_n} < 0$, for P_n in C.

Proof. Because u_i is strictly concave and $\xi_i^S(\mathbf{P})$ is the set of solutions of the problem $\max_{\mathbf{x}\in\mathbb{R}_+^N}[\lambda_I^{-1}u_i(\mathbf{x}) - \mathbf{P}.\mathbf{x}]$, $\xi_i^S(\mathbf{P})$ is unique, whenever it is defined. By proposition 8.37, the short-run demand function, ξ_i^S, is continuous and $\xi_i^S(\mathbf{P})$ is defined on an open set of strictly positive N-vectors, $\mathbf{P}$. Therefore, $D_{in}^S(P_n)$ is a continuous function of P_n and is defined on an open subset of $[0, \infty)$. By proposition 8.44, $D_{in}^S(P_n)$ is nonincreasing and is therefore positive on an open interval of prices. It follows that U_i is an open interval of $[0, \infty)$.

Fix n and let $\mathcal{A}$ be the set of subsets, A, of $\{1, 2, \ldots, N\}$ that contain n. For A in $\mathcal{A}$, let $U_{iA} = \{P_n \mid \xi_{ik}^S(P_1, \ldots, P_n, \ldots, P_N) > 0$, for $k \in A$, and $\xi_{ik}^S(P_1, \ldots, P_n, \ldots, P_n) = 0$, for $k \notin A\}$. Then, U_i is the union of all the sets U_{iA} for A in $\mathcal{A}$. For each A in $\mathcal{A}$, let C_{iA} be the closure of U_{iA} in U_i. That is, C_{iA} equals U_{iA} together with all the limits of sequences in U_{iA} that converge to points in U_i. (The closure of a set is defined in definition 3.8 in section 3.2.) Clearly, U_i is contained in the union of the sets C_{iA} as A varies over $\mathcal{A}$. For each P_n in U_{iA},

1. The argument just made may be found in Browning, Deaton, and Irish (1985, 509).

$$\lambda_i^{-1} \frac{\partial u_i(\xi_i^S(P_1, \ldots, P_n, \ldots, P_N))}{\partial P_k} = P_k, \tag{8.24}$$

for all k in A. Since the partial derivatives of u_i are continuous, equation 8.24 applies to every point in C_{iA}. Let $D_A u_i(\xi_i^S(P_1, \ldots, P_n, \ldots, P_N)) = \left(\frac{\partial u_i(\xi_i^S(P_1, \ldots, P_n, \ldots, P_N))}{\partial P_k}\right)_{k \in A}$ and let $\mathbf{P}_A = (P_k)_{k \in A}$. Then, equation 8.24 may be written as

$$\lambda_i^{-1} D_A u_i(\xi_i^S(P_1, \ldots, P_n, \ldots, P_N)) = \mathbf{P}_A. \tag{8.25}$$

Differentiating equation 8.25, we obtain

$$\lambda_i^{-1} D_A^2 u_i(\xi_i^S(P_1, \ldots, P_n, \ldots, P_N)) D_A \xi_i^S(P_1, \ldots, P_n, \ldots, P_N) = I_A, \tag{8.26}$$

where $D_A^2 u_i(\mathbf{x})$ is the square matrix of second partial derivatives with respect to variables x_k, for k in A, $D_A \xi_i^S(\mathbf{P})$ is the vector of partial derivatives of ξ_i^S with respect to variables P_k, for k in A, and I_A is the identity matrix with as many rows and columns as there are members of A. Since the matrix $D^2 u_i(\mathbf{x})$ is negative definite by assumption 8.46, the matrix $D_A^2 u_i(\mathbf{x})$ is negative definite as well and so is invertible. Therefore, equation 8.26 implies that

$$D_A \xi_i^S(P_1, \ldots, P_n, \ldots, P_N) = \lambda_i (D_A^2 u_i(\xi_i^S(P_1, \ldots, P_n, \ldots, P_N)))^{-1},$$

for $P_n \in C_{iA}$. Because n belongs to A by the definition of the sets in $\mathcal{A}$ and because the matrix

$$\lambda_i (D_A^2 u_i(\xi_i^S(P_1, \ldots, P_n, \ldots, P_N)))^{-1}$$

is negative definite, it follows that

$$\frac{\partial \xi_{in}^S(P_1, \ldots, P_n, \ldots, P_N)}{\partial P_n} < 0,$$

for $P_n \in C_{iA}$. This equation is the same as

$$\frac{dD_{in}^S(P_n)}{dP_n} < 0,$$

for $P_n \in C_{iA}$. ▪

The next example shows that the functions D_{in}^S may not be everywhere differentiable, even when u_i satisfies assumption 8.46.

EXAMPLE 8.48 Let $u(x_1, x_2) = 3((1 + x_1)(1 + x_2))^{1/3}$ and let $\lambda = 1$. The function u satisfies assumption 8.46. The matrix $D^2u(x)$ equals

$$\begin{pmatrix} -\frac{2}{3}\frac{(1+x_2)^{1/3}}{(1+x_1)^{5/3}} & \frac{1}{3}\frac{1}{(1+x_1)^{2/3}(1+x_2)^{2/3}} \\ \frac{1}{3}\frac{1}{(1+x_1)^{2/3}(1+x_2)^{2/3}} & -\frac{2}{3}\frac{(1+x_2)^{1/3}}{(1+x_1)^{5/3}} \end{pmatrix}.$$

Since the upper-left-hand entry of this matrix is negative and its determinant,

$$\frac{1}{3}\frac{1}{(1+x_1)^{4/3}(1+x_2)^{4/3}}$$

is positive, the matrix $D^2u(x)$ is negative definite. In this example, the equation $Du(x_1, x_2) = \lambda\mathbf{P}$ defining the short-run demand becomes the two equations

$$P_1 = \frac{(1+x_2)^{1/3}}{(1+x_1)^{2/3}}$$

and

$$P_2 = \frac{(1+x_1)^{1/3}}{(1+x_2)^{2/3}},$$

if $x_1 > 0$ and $x_2 > 0$. Solving these equations for x_1 and x_2, we find that

$$x_1 = \frac{1}{P_1^2 P_2} - 1$$

and

$$x_2 = \frac{1}{P_1 P_2^2} - 1.$$

It follows that $x_1 = 0$, if $P_1^2 P_2 > 1$. If $x_1 = 0$, then utility is $u(0, x_2) = 3(1 + x_2)^{1/3}$, and x_2 is determined by the equation

$$P_2 = \frac{1}{(1+x_2)^{2/3}},$$

and hence

$$x_2 = P_2^{-3/2} - 1.$$

Therefore,

$$\frac{\partial x_2}{\partial P_2} = -\frac{3}{2}P_2^{-5/2}. \tag{8.27}$$

If $x_1 > 0$, that is, if $P_1^2 P_2 < 1$, then

$$\frac{\partial x_2}{\partial P_2} = -\frac{2}{P_1 P_2^3}, \tag{8.28}$$

so that

$$\frac{\partial x_2(1, 1)}{\partial P_2-} = -2,$$

where $\frac{\partial x_2(1,1)}{\partial P_2-}$ is the left-hand derivative of x_2 at $(P_1, P_2) = (1, 1)$. It is computed using equation 8.28. Similarly,

$$\frac{\partial x_2(1, 1)}{\partial P_2+} = -\frac{3}{2},$$

where $\frac{\partial x_2(1,1)}{\partial P_2+}$ is the right-hand derivative of x_2 at $(P_1, P_2) = (1, 1)$ and is computed using equation 8.27. Since the left- and right-hand partial derivatives of $x_2(P_1, P_2)$ with respect to P_2 differ at $(1, 1)$, the function $x_2(1, P_2)$ is not differentiable there. Since $D_2^S(P_1) = x_2(1, P_2)$, it follows that $D_2^S(P_2)$ is not differentiable at $P_2 = 1$.

I now discuss short-run equilibrium, which is what you obtain when you substitute short-run demand for Walrasian demand in the definition of Walrasian equilibrium. Allocations, feasibility of allocations, and firms' set of profit maximizing vectors, $\eta_i(\mathbf{P})$, are defined as before in definitions 2.1 and 2.2 (in section 2.2) and at the beginning of section 4.1.

DEFINITION 8.49 A *short-run equilibrium* for $\mathcal{E}$ consists of $(\overline{\mathbf{x}}, \overline{\mathbf{y}}, \mathbf{P})$ such that

1. $(\overline{\mathbf{x}}, \overline{\mathbf{y}})$ is a feasible allocation, $\mathbf{P} \in \mathbb{R}_+^N$, and $\mathbf{P} > 0$
2. for all $j, \overline{\mathbf{y}}_j \in \eta_j(\mathbf{P})$
3. for all $i, \overline{\mathbf{x}}_i \in \xi_i^S(\mathbf{P})$
4. for all n, $P_n = 0$, if $\sum_{i=1}^I \overline{x}_{in} < \sum_{i=1}^I e_{in} + \sum_{j=1}^J \overline{y}_{jn}$

I make use of the following assumptions.

ASSUMPTION 8.50 For each j, Y_j is closed, convex, and contains the vector 0.

Let $Y = \sum_{j=1}^J Y_j$ be the total production possibility set for the economy.

ASSUMPTION 8.51 $Y \cap \mathbb{R}^N_+ = \{0\}$.

ASSUMPTION 8.52 $Y \cap (-Y) + \{0\}$.

ASSUMPTION 8.53 The economy $\mathcal{E}$ is productive,

where an economy is productive if it can produce a positive amount of every good (definition 3.47 in section 3.6).

I will show that under these assumptions a short-run equilibrium exists and is Pareto optimal. In doing so, I make use of the next lemma. The statement of the lemma is shortened by the following terminology.

DEFINITION 8.54 An *aggregate allocation* for the economy $\mathcal{E}$ consists of $(\mathbf{x}^A, \mathbf{y}^A)$, where $\mathbf{x}^A \in \mathbb{R}^N_+$ and $\mathbf{y}^A \in \mathbb{R}^N$.

DEFINITION 8.55 An aggregate allocation, $(\mathbf{x}^A, \mathbf{y}^A)$, is *feasible* if $\mathbf{x}^A \leq \sum_{i=1}^I \mathbf{e}_i + \mathbf{y}^A$ and $\mathbf{y}^A \in \sum_{j-1}^J Y_j$.

The next lemma is the key to the properties of short-run equilibria. The assertion is that an economy in short-run equilibrium acts as if it were maximizing the utility of the imaginary aggregate consumer.

LEMMA 8.56 Suppose that assumptions 8.46, 8.50, and 8.53 apply. Then, $(\overline{\mathbf{x}}, \overline{\mathbf{y}})$ is the allocation of a short-run equilibrium $(\overline{\mathbf{x}}, \overline{\mathbf{y}}, \mathbf{P})$, if and only if the aggregate allocation $\left(\sum_{i=1}^I \overline{\mathbf{x}}_i, \sum_{j=1}^J \overline{\mathbf{y}}_j\right)$ solves the problem

$$\begin{aligned} &\max_{\substack{(x^A,\, y^A) \text{ is a feasible} \\ \text{aggregate allocation}}} \quad W(\mathbf{x}^A) \\ &\text{s.t.} \quad (\mathbf{x}^A, \mathbf{y}^A), \end{aligned} \tag{8.29}$$

where W is defined by equation 8.19.

Proof. Because assumption 8.50 applies to the sets Y_j, for all j, the aggregate production possibility set, $Y = \sum_{j=1}^J Y_j$, is convex. Problem 8.29 may be written as

$$\begin{aligned} &\max_{\mathbf{x} \in \mathbb{R}^N_+ . \mathbf{y}^A \in Y} \quad W(\mathbf{x}^A) \\ &\text{s.t.} \quad \mathbf{x}^A - \sum_{i=1}^I \mathbf{e}_i - \mathbf{y}^A \leq 0. \end{aligned} \tag{8.30}$$

Because the economy is productive, problem 8.30 satisfies the constraint qualification of the Kuhn-Tucker theorem. That theorem implies that the aggregate allocation $(\overline{\mathbf{x}}^A, \overline{\mathbf{y}}^A)$ solves problem 8.30 if and only if $\overline{\mathbf{y}}^A \in Y$,

$$\overline{\mathbf{x}}^A - \sum_{i=1}^{I} \mathbf{e}_i - \overline{\mathbf{y}}^A \leq 0, \tag{8.31}$$

and there exists a nonnegative N-vector $\mathbf{P}$ such that

$$P_n = 0, \ \text{if}\, \overline{x}_n^A - \sum_{i=1}^{I} e_{in} \overline{y}_n^A < 0, \tag{8.32}$$

for all n, and $(\overline{\mathbf{x}}^A, \overline{\mathbf{y}}^A)$ solves the problem

$$\max_{\mathbf{x} \in \mathbb{R}_+^N, \mathbf{y} \in Y} \left[W(\mathbf{x}) - \mathbf{P}.\left(\mathbf{x} - \sum_{i=1}^{I} \mathbf{e}_i - \mathbf{y} \right) \right]. \tag{8.33}$$

Observe that $(\overline{\mathbf{x}}^A, \overline{\mathbf{y}}^A)$ solves problem 8.33 if and only if $\overline{\mathbf{x}}^A$ solves the problem

$$\max_{\mathbf{x} \in \mathbb{R}_+^N} [W(\mathbf{x}) - \mathbf{P}.\mathbf{x}] \tag{8.34}$$

and $\overline{\mathbf{y}}^A$ solves the problem

$$\max_{\mathbf{y} \in Y} \mathbf{P}.\mathbf{y}. \tag{8.35}$$

Proposition 8.43 implies that $\overline{\mathbf{x}}^A$ solves problem 8.34 if and only if $\overline{\mathbf{x}}^A = \sum_{i=1}^{I} \overline{\mathbf{x}}_i$, where, for each i, $\overline{\mathbf{x}}_i$ solves the problem

$$\max_{\mathbf{x} \in \mathbb{R}_+^N} \left[\lambda_i^{-1} u_i(\mathbf{x}) - \mathbf{P}.\mathbf{x} \right],$$

so that $\overline{\mathbf{x}}_i = \xi_i^S(\mathbf{P})$. By the decentralization theorem (4.10 in section 4.6), $\overline{\mathbf{y}}^A$ solves problem 8.35 if and only if $\overline{\mathbf{y}}^A = \sum_{j=1}^{J} \overline{\mathbf{y}}_j$, where, for each j, $\overline{\mathbf{y}}_j$, solves the problem

$$\max_{\mathbf{y} \in Y_j} \mathbf{P}.\mathbf{y},$$

so that $\overline{\mathbf{y}}_j \in \eta_j(\mathbf{P})$. Inequality 8.31 now becomes

$$\sum_{i=1}^{I} \overline{\mathbf{x}}_i - \sum_{i=1}^{I} \mathbf{e}_i - \sum_{j=1}^{J} \overline{\mathbf{y}} \leq 0,$$

and condition 8.32 becomes

$$P_n = 0, \text{ if } \sum_{i=1}^{I} \overline{x}_{in}^A - \sum_{i=1}^{I} \mathbf{e}_{in} - \sum_{j=1}^{J} \overline{y}_{jn}^A < 0,$$

for all n. In conclusion, we see that $\left(\sum_{i=1}^{I} \overline{\mathbf{x}}_i, \sum_{j=1}^{J} \overline{\mathbf{y}}_i\right)$ solves problem 8.29, if and only if $(\overline{\mathbf{x}}_1, \ldots, \overline{\mathbf{x}}_I; \overline{\mathbf{y}}_1, \ldots, \overline{\mathbf{y}}_J; \mathbf{P})$ satisfies all the conditions of a short-run equilibrium. ▪

It is easy to construct examples of economies with several Walrasian equilibrium allocations and relative price vectors, as was illustrated by figure 4.14 (in section 4.3). In contrast, short-run equilibria are unique under standard assumptions. Not only are the allocations and relative price vectors unique, but the absolute prices are unique as well. The length of a Walrasian equilibrium price vector is not determined, because individual and market excess demand functions are homogeneous of degree 0. The length of a short-run equilibrium price vector is determinate, and short-run demand functions are not homogeneous of degree 0. In the short-run case, a proportional increase in all prices has the same effect on consumer demand as an increase in the marginal utility of unit of account, which decreases or at least does not increase the value of consumer demand. It is easy to see that the value decreases if $\xi_i^S(\mathbf{P}, \lambda_i) \gg 0$ and assumption 8.46 applies. In this case, $\xi_i^S(\mathbf{P}, \lambda_i) \gg 0$ and it satisfies the equation

$$D_x u_i(\xi_i^S(\mathbf{P}, \lambda_i)) = \lambda_i \mathbf{P},$$

where I have made short-run demand, ξ_i^S, a function of λ_i as well as of $\mathbf{P}$. Differentiating this equation implicitly with respect to λ_i, we see that

$$D_x^2 u_i(\xi_i^S(\mathbf{P}, \lambda_i)) \frac{\partial \xi_i^S(\mathbf{P}, \lambda_i)}{\partial \lambda_i} = \mathbf{P},$$

where $\frac{\partial \xi_i^S(\mathbf{P}, \lambda_i)}{\partial \lambda_i}$ is an N-vector. This equation implies that

$$\frac{\partial \xi_i^S(\mathbf{P}, \lambda_i)}{\partial \lambda_i} = (D_x^2 u_i(\xi_i^S(\mathbf{P}, \lambda_i)))^{-1}\mathbf{P}.$$

Multiplying this last equation on the left by $\mathbf{P}^T$, the transpose of $\mathbf{P}$, we see that

$$\frac{\partial \mathbf{P}.\xi_i^S(\mathbf{P}, \lambda_i)}{\partial \lambda_i} = \mathbf{P}.\frac{\partial \xi_i^S(\mathbf{P}, \lambda_i)}{\partial \lambda_i} = \mathbf{P}^T (D_x^2 u_i(\xi_i^S(\mathbf{P}, \lambda)))^{-1}\mathbf{P} < 0,$$

because the matrix $(D_x^2 u_i(\xi_i^S(\mathbf{P}, \lambda_i)))^{-1}$ is negative definite by assumption 8.46.

PROPOSITION 8.57 The consumption allocation, $\overline{\mathbf{x}}$, of a short-run equilibrium $(\overline{\mathbf{x}}, \overline{\mathbf{y}}, \mathbf{P})$ is the same for all short-run equilibria.

Proof. Suppose there are two short-run equilibria, $(\mathbf{x}^1, \mathbf{y}^1, \mathbf{P}^1)$ and $(\mathbf{x}^2, \mathbf{y}^2, \mathbf{P}^2)$. First of all, I show that $\sum_{i=1}^I \mathbf{x}_i^1 = \sum_{i=1}^I \mathbf{x}_i^2$. By lemma 8.56, both $\left(\sum_{i=1}^I \mathbf{x}_j^1, \sum_{j=1}^J \mathbf{y}_j^1\right)$ and $\left(\sum_{i=1}^I \mathbf{x}_i^2, \sum_{j=1}^J \mathbf{y}_j^2\right)$ solve the problem

$$\max_{\substack{(\mathbf{x}^A, \mathbf{y}^A) \text{ is a feasible} \\ \text{aggregate allocation}}} W(\mathbf{x}^A).$$

Suppose that $\sum_{i=1}^I \mathbf{x}_i^1 \neq \sum_{i=1}^I \mathbf{x}_i^2$ and let

$$(\mathbf{x}^A, \mathbf{y}^A) = \frac{1}{2}\left(\sum_{i=1}^I \mathbf{x}_i^1, \sum_{j=1}^J \mathbf{y}_i^1\right) + \frac{1}{2}\left(\sum_{i=1}^I \mathbf{x}_i^2, \sum_{j=1}^J \mathbf{y}_j^2\right).$$

The aggregate allocation $(\mathbf{x}^A, \mathbf{y}^A)$ is feasible, and because W is strictly concave,

$$W(\mathbf{x}^A) > \frac{1}{2} W\left(\sum_{i=1}^I \mathbf{x}_i^1\right) + \frac{1}{2} W\left(\sum_{i=1}^I \mathbf{x}_i^2\right),$$

which is impossible. This contradiction proves that $\sum_{i=1}^I \mathbf{x}_i^1 = \sum_{i=1}^I \mathbf{x}_i^2$.

I finish the proof by showing that $\mathbf{x}_i^1 = \mathbf{x}_i^2$, for all i. Let $\mathbf{x} = \sum_{i=1}^I \mathbf{x}_i^1 = \sum_{i=1}^I \mathbf{x}_i^2$. Then, $(\mathbf{x}_1^1, \mathbf{x}_2^1, \ldots, \mathbf{x}_I^1)$ solves the problem

$$\begin{aligned} &\max_{(\mathbf{x}_1 \in \mathbb{R}_+^N, \ldots, \mathbf{x}_I \in \mathbb{R}_+^N)} \sum_{i=1}^I \lambda_i^{-1} u_i(\mathbf{x}_i) \\ &\text{s.t.} \quad \sum_{i=1}^I \mathbf{x}_i = \mathbf{x}, \end{aligned} \tag{8.36}$$

by the definition of the function W (equation 8.19). According to lemma 8.41, problem 8.36 has a unique solution, so that $\mathbf{x}_i^1 = \mathbf{x}_i^2$, for all i. ▪

If we add the following assumption, the production allocation of a short-run equilibrium is unique as well.

ASSUMPTION 8.58 For each j, Y_j is strictly convex.[2]

PROPOSITION 8.59 If assumptions 8.46, 8.50, 8.53, and 8.58 apply, then the allocation, $(\overline{\mathbf{x}}, \overline{\mathbf{y}})$, is the same for all short-run equilibria.

Proof. By lemma 8.56, the allocation, $(\overline{\mathbf{x}}, \overline{\mathbf{y}})$, of a short-run allocation maximizes the welfare function $\sum_{i=1}^{I} \lambda_i^{-1} u_i(\mathbf{x}_i)$ among all feasible allocations. Because the functions u_i are strictly concave and the sets Y_j are strictly convex, the solution of this maximization problem is unique. ▪

PROPOSITION 8.60 If assumptions 8.46, 8.50, 8.53, and 8.58 apply, then the equilibrium price vector, $\mathbf{P}$, is unique, provided $\sum_{i=1}^{I} \overline{\mathbf{x}}_i \gg 0$, where $\sum_{i=1}^{I} \overline{\mathbf{x}}_i$ is the equilibrium total consumption. Furthermore, $\mathbf{P} \gg 0$.

Proof. If $(\overline{\mathbf{x}}, \overline{\mathbf{y}}, \mathbf{P})$ is a short-run equilibrium, then $\overline{\mathbf{x}} = (\overline{\mathbf{x}}_1, \overline{\mathbf{x}}_2, \ldots, \overline{\mathbf{x}}_I)$ is unique by the previous proposition. Each consumption vector, $\overline{\mathbf{x}}_i$, solves the problem

$$\max_{\mathbf{x} \in \mathbb{R}_+^N} \left[\lambda_i^{-1} u_i(\mathbf{x}) - \mathbf{P}.\mathbf{x}\right].$$

Since by assumption 8.46 the u_i are differentiable, the solution of this maximization problem satisfies the first-order conditions

$$\lambda_i^{-1} \frac{\partial u_i(\overline{\mathbf{x}}_i)}{\partial x_n} \le P_n,$$

for all n, with equality if $\overline{x}_{in} > 0$. Since $\sum_{i=1}^{I} \overline{\mathbf{x}}_i \gg 0$, it follows that $\overline{x}_{in} > 0$, for some i. Therefore, for each n,

$$P_n = \lambda_i^{-1} \frac{\partial u_i(\overline{\mathbf{x}}_i)}{\partial x_n}, \tag{8.37}$$

for any i such that $\overline{x}_{in} > 0$. Since the $\overline{x}_{in}$ are unique, equation 8.37 defines the short-run equilibrium price vector, $\mathbf{P}$, uniquely. Because $\lambda_i^{-1} \frac{\partial u_i(\overline{\mathbf{x}}_i)}{\partial x_n} > 0$, for all n by assumption 8.46, $P_n > 0$, for all n. ▪

I next show that short-run equilibria exist and are Pareto optimal. Recall that proofs of existence of Walrasian equilibrium (theorem 4.14 in section

2. Strict convexity of sets is defined in definition 3.39 (in section 3.5).

4.7 or theorem 4.24 in section 4.8) rely on Walras' law. That law does not apply to short-run market excess demand, $\mathbf{z}^S(\mathbf{P}) = \sum_{i=1}^{I}(\xi_i^S(\mathbf{P}) - \mathbf{e}_i) - \sum_{j=1}^{J} \eta_j(\mathbf{P})$. Fortunately, an argument much simpler than that applying to theWalrasian case shows that short-run equilibria exist.

THEOREM 8.61 If the economy $\mathcal{E}$ satisfies assumptions 8.46, 8.50–8.53, then it has a short-run equilibrium $(\overline{\mathbf{x}}, \overline{\mathbf{y}}, \mathbf{P})$.

Proof. By lemma 8.56, it is sufficient to show that the welfare function $W\left(\sum_{i=1}^{I} \mathbf{x}_i\right)$ has a maximum over the set of feasible allocations $(\mathbf{x}, \mathbf{y})$. It does, because W is continuous and the economy $\mathcal{E}$ satisfies the assumptions of theorem 3.54 (in section 3.7), so that the set of feasible allocations is compact. ▪

THEOREM 8.62 If the economy $\mathcal{E}$ satisfies assumptions 8.46, 8.50, and 8.53, then the allocation of a short-run equilibrium, $(\overline{\mathbf{x}}, \overline{\mathbf{y}}, \mathbf{P})$, is Pareto optimal.

Proof. By lemma 8.56, the allocation $(\overline{\mathbf{x}}, \overline{\mathbf{y}})$ maximizes the welfare function $\sum_{i=1}^{I} \lambda_i^{-1} u_i(\mathbf{x}_i)$ among all feasible allocations, where $\lambda_i > 0$, for all i. It follows from proposition 3.23 (in section 3.5) that $(\overline{\mathbf{x}}, \overline{\mathbf{y}})$ is Pareto optimal. ▪

I now give the example promised earlier of a Walrasian demand curve that slopes upward over part of its range.

EXAMPLE 8.63 (An upward sloping demand curve) There are two commodities, and the utility function of the consumer is

$$u(x_1, x_2) = \min(2x_1 + x_2, x_1 + 10).$$

The consumer's initial endowment is $\mathbf{e} = (5, 0)$. The indifference curves of the utility function are pictured as dashed lines in figure 8.1. The kink in the indifference curves occurs along the line defined by the equation $x_1 + x_2 = 10$, which is shown as a solid line in figure 8.1. The relevant Walrasian demand points are along this line. The utility function u is concave, because it is the minimum of two affine and hence concave functions.

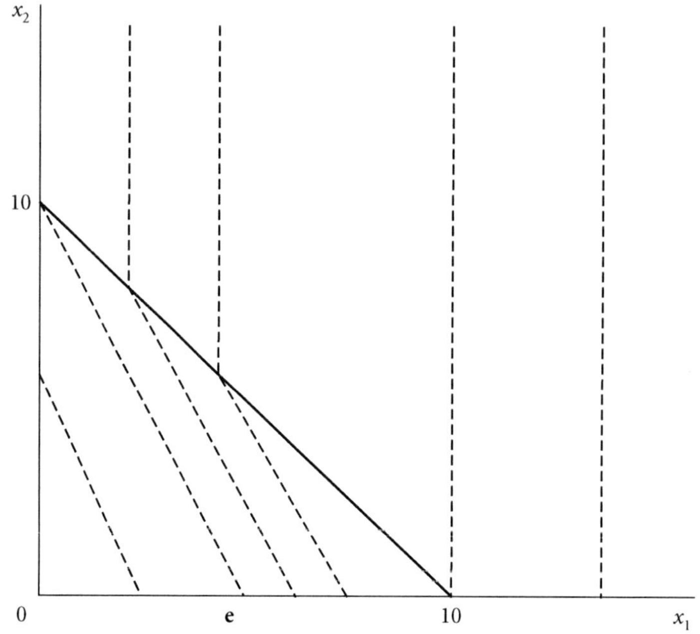

Figure 8.1 Indifference curves for a utility function with an upward sloping demand curve

Let the price of good 1 be 1, so that the consumer's Walrasian demand solves the problem

$$\max_{x_1, x_2} \left[\min(2x_1 + x_2, x_1 + 10) \leq 5\right]$$
$$\text{s.t.} \quad x_1 + p_2 x_2 \leq 5.$$

The Walrasian demand function is

$$\xi(1, p_2) = \begin{cases} \left(\frac{5-10p_2}{1-p_2}, \frac{5}{1-p_2}\right), & \text{if } p_2 \leq \frac{1}{2}, \text{and} \\ \left(0, \frac{5}{p_2}\right), & \text{if } p_2 \geq \frac{1}{2}. \end{cases}$$

Therefore, if $p_2 \leq \frac{1}{2}$, the demand curve for good 2 is

$$D_2(p_2) = \xi_2(1, p_2) = \frac{5}{1 - p_2},$$

and this curve is upward sloping.

The utility function in this example is not differentiable. With more work, it is possible to create an example with a differentiable utility function.

8.4 Consumer Surplus

The concept of consumer surplus is widely used and convenient, but it is hard to make sense of it in the context of Walrasian equilibrium. It does, however, make sense in a short-run equilibrium setting. You may have seen consumer surplus explained in terms of a supply and demand scissors diagram, such as figure 8.2. This shows the supply curve, SS, and demand curve, DD, for a single commodity. The equilibrium price is B. Since the supply curve shows marginal production costs, the area under the curve is the variable cost of production. That is, the variable cost of producing A units is the area of the quadrilateral $0AES$. Since the revenue from sales is

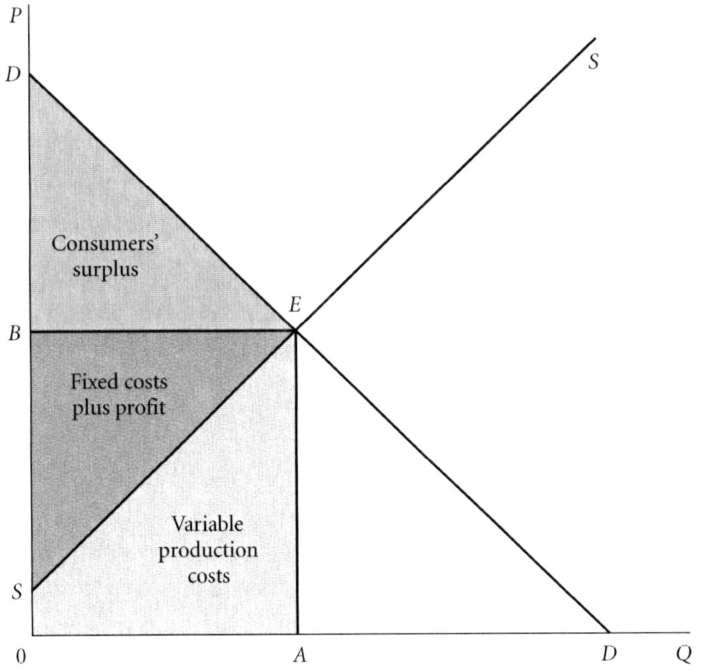

Figure 8.2 Consumer surplus in a scissors diagram

the area of the rectangle $0AEB$, the area of the triangle SEB is fixed costs plus total profit from producing A units. The demand curve DD is the graph of a function $P(Q)$, giving price, P, as a function of the quantity purchased, Q. If consumers have purchased Q units, the monetary value to them of consuming a small amount, ΔQ, more is approximately $P(Q)\Delta Q$. Therefore the total value to them of consuming A units is the area under the demand curve from 0 to A, that is, the area of the quadrilateral $0AED$. Consumers spend money equal to the area of $0AEB$ to buy A units, so that the net gain in money terms from purchasing A units is the area of the triangle BED, a quantity termed *consumers' surplus.* Thus, the total gain to consumers from consuming A units may be divided into the sum of consumers' surplus, fixed costs plus profit, and variable production cost, these being the areas of BED, SEB, and $0AES$, respectively. This way of measuring consumers' gain and its attribution to surplus, fixed costs plus profit, and variable costs provides a convenient tool for estimating the impact of economic policy, public works projects, or any economic change. Although this use of consumers' surplus is of questionable value when demand is Walrasian, it is perfectly reasonable when demand is short run.

The discussion will be in terms of a short-run economy $\mathcal{E} = ((u_i, \lambda_i, \mathbf{e}_i)_{i=1}^{I}, (Y_j)_{j=1}^{J}, (\Theta_{ij})_{i=1, j=1}^{I \ \ J})$, where the consumers' marginal utilities of money, $(\lambda_1, \ldots, \lambda_I)$, are fixed. The following is a strengthening of assumption 8.32.

ASSUMPTION 8.64 For each i, the function $u_i \colon \mathbb{R}_+^N \to \mathbb{R}$ is continuously differentiable, strictly increasing, and strictly concave.[3]

The next assumption is for convenience of presentation.

ASSUMPTION 8.65 For each i, $u_i(\mathbf{0}) = 0$.

Let $W \colon \mathbb{R}_+^N \to \mathbb{R}$ be the welfare function over consumption bundles defined by equation 8.19 (in section 8.3). The function W is differentiable, by proposition 8.68 below. Because the utility functions, u_i, are strictly increasing and concave, the welfare function W is strictly increasing and concave as well. For each price vector $\mathbf{P}$ such that $\mathbf{P} \gg 0$, let $\Xi^S(\mathbf{P})$

3. The terms *strict increasing* and *strictly concave* are defined in definitions 3.36 and 3.37, respectively, in section 3.5.

be the market short-run demand function, that is, the solution to the problem

$$\max_{\mathbf{x}\in\mathbb{R}^N_+} [W(\mathbf{x}) - \mathbf{P}.\mathbf{x}].$$

The first-order conditions for this problem imply that

$$\Xi^S(DW(\mathbf{x})) = \mathbf{x}. \tag{8.38}$$

Let $\mathbf{x}$: $[0, 1] \to \mathbb{R}^N_+$ be a differentiable path in $\mathbb{R}^N_+$ such that $\mathbf{x}(0) = \mathbf{0}$ and $\mathbf{x}(1) = \overline{\mathbf{x}}$. Then,

$$\frac{dW(\mathbf{x}(t))}{dt} = DW(\mathbf{x}(t)).\frac{d\mathbf{x}(t)}{dt},$$

so that

$$W(\overline{\mathbf{x}}) - W(\mathbf{0}) = \int_0^1 DW(\mathbf{x}(t)).\frac{d\mathbf{x}(t)}{dt}. \tag{8.39}$$

Assumption 8.65 implies that $W(\mathbf{0}) = 0$, so that equation 8.39 may be written as

$$W(\overline{\mathbf{x}}) = \int_0^1 DW(x(t)).\frac{d\mathbf{x}(t)}{dt}dt. \tag{8.40}$$

Equation 8.40 is easier to interpret if we let $DW(\mathbf{x}(t)) = \mathbf{P}(t)$. Then equation 8.38 implies that $\mathbf{x}(t) = \Xi^S(\mathbf{P}(t))$, so that $\mathbf{x}(t)$ is the short-run demand at price vector $\mathbf{P}(t)$ and equation 8.40 may be written as

$$W(\overline{\mathbf{x}}) = \int_0^1 \mathbf{P}(t).\frac{d\mathbf{x}(t)}{dt}dt. \tag{8.41}$$

The quantities $\mathbf{P}(t).\frac{d\mathbf{x}(t)}{dt}$ may sometimes be estimated, so that equation 8.41 provides a method for estimating total welfare. It is important that the measure of total welfare does not depend on the paths $\mathbf{x}(t)$ and $\mathbf{P}(t)$, as long as $\mathbf{P}(t) = DW(\mathbf{x}(t))$.

Assumption 8.64 implies that both $u_i(\mathbf{x})$ and $Du_i(\mathbf{x})$ are defined, and hence finite, for every $\mathbf{x}$ in $\mathbb{R}^N_+$. This assumption does not apply to some utility functions commonly used in economics, such as the logarithm function; $\ln(0)$ is not defined. The next example makes clear that the total welfare measured by equation 8.40 may be infinite, if $u_i(0)$ is not defined, for some i.

EXAMPLE 8.66 There is one commodity and one consumer. The utility function of the consumer is $u(x) = \ln(x)$, and the consumer's marginal utility of money is $\lambda = 1$. If we solve the problem $\max_{x \geq 0}[\ln(x) - Px]$, where $P > 0$, we find that $x = \frac{1}{P}$. Let $x(t)$ be the path defined by $x(t) = t$, for $0 \leq t \leq 1$. Then, $P(t) = \frac{1}{t}$ so that welfare at $x(1) = 1$ equals the integral

$$W(1) = \int_0^1 \frac{1}{t} dt = \infty.$$

Thus the integral in equations 8.40 or 8.41 can be meaningless. This difficulty can be avoided by using the integral in these equations to measure changes in welfare along a path, $\mathbf{x}(t)$, such that $\mathbf{x}(t) \gg \mathbf{0}$, for all t, $\mathbf{x}(0) = \underline{\mathbf{x}}$, and $\mathbf{x}(1) = \overline{\mathbf{x}}$. Then, equation 8.41 becomes

$$W(\overline{\mathbf{x}}) - W(\underline{\mathbf{x}}) = \int_0^1 \mathbf{P}(t).\frac{d\mathbf{x}(t)}{dt} dt. \tag{8.42}$$

Suppose that the path $\mathbf{x}(t)$ is such that, for $0 \leq t \leq 1$,

$$x_1(t) = \underline{x}_1 + t(\overline{x}_1 - \underline{x}_1) \text{ and}$$
$$x_n(t) = \underline{x}_n,$$

for $n \geq 1$, where $\overline{x}_1 > \underline{x}_1$. Then, the increase in total welfare, $W(\overline{\mathbf{x}}) - W(\underline{\mathbf{x}})$ given by equation 8.42 is equal to the shaded area under the demand curve shown in figure 8.3.

Of the total increase in welfare, $W(\overline{\mathbf{x}}) - W(\underline{\mathbf{x}})$, the part labeled "CS" in figure 8.4 is enjoyed by consumers as surplus, and the part labeled "Spent" is the money surrendered by the consumer to buy $x_1(1) - x_1(0)$ at the price $P_1(1)$. If the quantity purchased, $x_1(1)$, of good 1 and its price, $P_1(1)$, are part of a competitive equilibrium, then the rectangle labeled "Spent" in figure 8.4 may be split between fixed costs plus profit and variable production cost, as in figure 8.5.

Suppose that total welfare is finite, so that we can measure total welfare as well as welfare changes. In addition, suppose that $\mathbf{P}(1)$ and $\overline{\mathbf{x}} = \Xi^S(\mathbf{P}(1))$ are the price vector and total consumption allocation of a short-run general equilibrium,

$$\left((\overline{\mathbf{x}}_1, \ldots, \overline{\mathbf{x}}_I, \overline{\mathbf{y}}_1, \ldots, \overline{\mathbf{y}}_J), \mathbf{P}(1)\right),$$

with $\overline{\mathbf{x}} = \sum_{i=1}^{I} \overline{\mathbf{x}}_i$. Then $W(\overline{\mathbf{x}})$ corresponds in spirit though not literally to the area of $0AED$ and the total expenditure, corresponds to the area $0AEB$

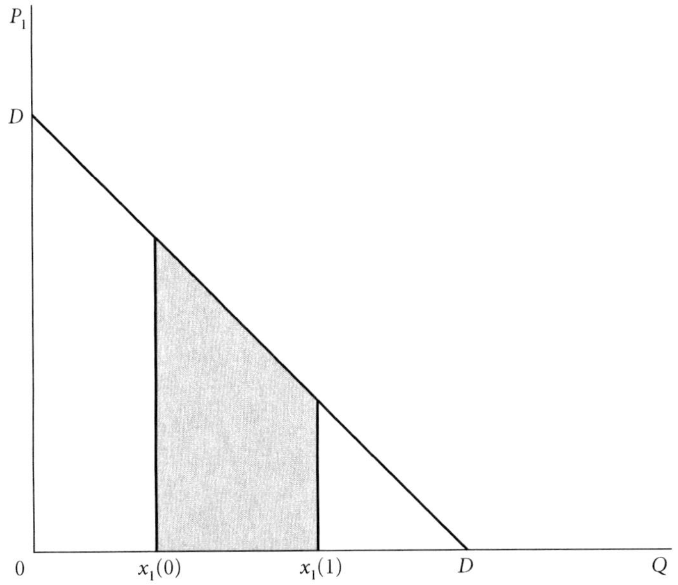

Figure 8.3 Change in total welfare

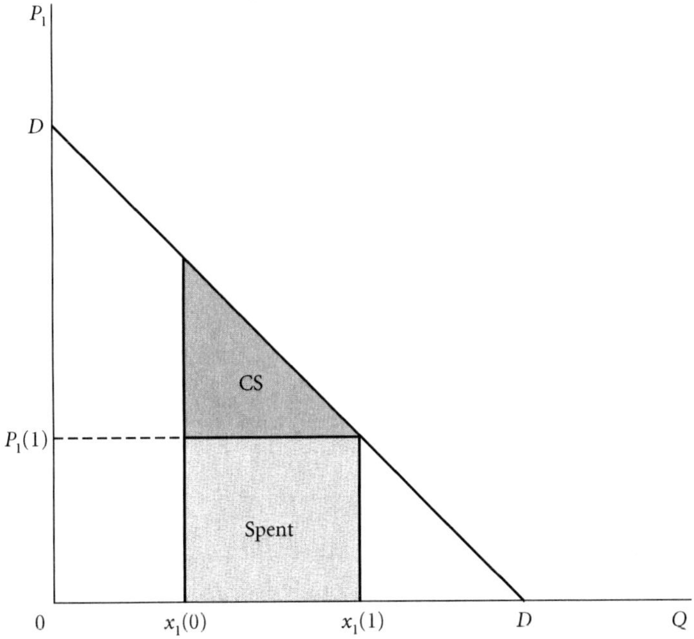

Figure 8.4 The split of the welfare change between surplus and expenditure

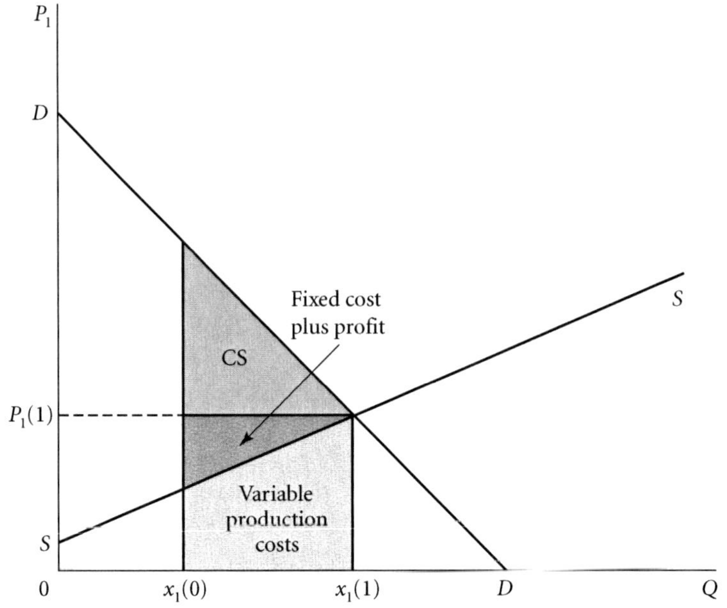

Figure 8.5 The split of the welfare change between profit and production cost

in figure 8.2. Since $\overline{\mathbf{x}} = \sum_{i=1}^{I} \overline{\mathbf{x}}_i = \sum_{i=1}^{I} \mathbf{e}_i + \sum_{j=1}^{J} \overline{\mathbf{y}}_j$, it follows that

$$\mathbf{P}(1).\overline{\mathbf{x}} = \mathbf{P}(1).\sum_{i=1}^{I} \mathbf{e}_i + \mathbf{P}(1).\sum_{j=1}^{J} \overline{\mathbf{y}}_j.$$

The quantities $\mathbf{P}(1).\sum_{i=1}^{I} \mathbf{e}_i$ and $\mathbf{P}(1).\sum_{j=1}^{J} \overline{\mathbf{y}}_j$ are the variable costs of production and total profits, respectively, and correspond in spirit to the areas of 0*AES* and *SEB* in figure 8.2. (There are no fixed costs of production in the model.) In summary,

$$\begin{aligned} W(\overline{\mathbf{x}}) &= (W(\overline{\mathbf{x}}) - \mathbf{P}.\overline{\mathbf{x}}) + \mathbf{P}.\sum_{i=1}^{I} \mathbf{e}_i + \mathbf{P}.\sum_{j=1}^{J} \overline{\mathbf{y}}_j \\ &= \text{consumers' surplus} + \text{value of endowment} + \text{profits}, \end{aligned} \tag{8.43}$$

and these terms correspond to the areas of *BED*, 0*AES*, and *SEB*, respectively, in figure 8.2.

I turn to the proof that the function W is differentiable. Recall that

$$W(\mathbf{x}) = \max_{\mathbf{x}_1 \in \mathbb{R}^N_+, \ldots, \mathbf{x}_I \in \mathbb{R}^N_+} \sum_{i=1}^{I} \lambda_i^{-1} u_i(\mathbf{x}_i)$$
$$\text{s.t.} \quad \sum_{i=1}^{I} \mathbf{x}_i = \mathbf{x}.$$

For each $\mathbf{x}$ in $\mathbb{R}^N_+$ and for each $i = 1, \ldots, I$, let $\mathbf{x}_i(\mathbf{x}) \in \mathbb{R}^N_+$ be such that $\mathbf{x} = \sum_{i=1}^{I} \mathbf{x}_i(\mathbf{x})$ and $W(\mathbf{x}) = \sum_{i=1}^{I} \lambda_i^{-1} u_i(\mathbf{x}_i(\mathbf{x}))$. By lemma 8.41 (in section 8.3), the functions $\mathbf{x}_i(\mathbf{x})$ are uniquely defined. As a step toward proving the differentiability of W, I prove the following.

LEMMA 8.67 If u_i satisfies assumption 8.64, for all i, then the functions $\mathbf{x}_i(\mathbf{x})$ are continuous.

Proof. Let $\mathbf{x}^n$, for $n = 1, 2, \ldots$, be a sequence converging to $\mathbf{x}$ in $\mathbb{R}^N_+$. I must show that $\lim_{n\to\infty} \mathbf{x}_i(\mathbf{x}^n) = \mathbf{x}_i(\mathbf{x})$, for all i. Suppose that $\mathbf{x}_i(\mathbf{x}^n)$ does not converge to $\mathbf{x}_i(\mathbf{x})$, for some i. Without loss of generality, I may assume that $i = 1$, so that $\mathbf{x}_1(\mathbf{x}^n)$ does not converge to $\mathbf{x}_1(\mathbf{x})$. Therefore, there exists a positive number ε and a subsequence $n(k)$ such that

$$\|\mathbf{x}_1(\mathbf{x}^{n(k)}) - \mathbf{x}_1(\mathbf{x})\| \geq \varepsilon,$$

for all k. Because the sequences $\mathbf{x}_i(\mathbf{x}^n)$ are all bounded, for all i, the Bolzano-Weierstrass theorem (3.12 in section 3.2) implies that there is a subsequence of the $n(k)$, call it $n(k(m))$ such that $\mathbf{x}_i(\mathbf{x}^{n(k(m)})$ converges, for all i, as m goes to infinity. For each i, let $\overline{\mathbf{x}}_i = \lim_{m\to\infty} \mathbf{x}_i(\mathbf{x}^{n(k(m))})$. Then by passage to the limit in the above inequality we obtain

$$\|\overline{\mathbf{x}}_1 - \mathbf{x}_1(\mathbf{x})\| \geq \varepsilon. \tag{8.44}$$

For convenience, I denote the sequence $\mathbf{x}_i(\mathbf{x}^{n(k(m))})$ as $\mathbf{x}_i(\mathbf{x}^n)$ again.

I show that $(\overline{\mathbf{x}}_1, \ldots, \overline{\mathbf{x}}_I)$ solves the problem

$$\max_{\mathbf{x}_1 \in \mathbb{R}^N_+, \ldots, \mathbf{x}_I \in \mathbb{R}^N_+} \sum_{i=1}^{I} \lambda_i^{-1} u_i(\mathbf{x}_i)$$
$$\text{s.t.} \quad \sum_{i=1}^{I} \mathbf{x}_i = \mathbf{x}. \tag{8.45}$$

If we pass to the limit with respect to n in the inequality $\sum_{i=1}^{I} \mathbf{x}_i(\mathbf{x}^n) \leq \mathbf{x}^n$, we find that $\sum_{i=1}^{I} \overline{\mathbf{x}}_i \leq \mathbf{x}$. Similarly, $\overline{\mathbf{x}}_i \in \mathbb{R}_+^N$, for all i. Therefore, $(\overline{\mathbf{x}}_1, \ldots, \overline{\mathbf{x}}_I)$ satisfies the constraints of problem 8.45. Suppose $(\overline{\mathbf{x}}_1, \ldots, \overline{\mathbf{x}}_I)$ does not solve problem 8.45, so that

$$\sum_{i=1}^{I} \lambda_i^{-1} u_i(\overline{\mathbf{x}}_i) < \sum_{i=1}^{I} \lambda_i^{-1} u_i(\mathbf{x}_i(\mathbf{x})). \tag{8.46}$$

If $\mathbf{x} = 0$, then $\mathbf{x}_i(\mathbf{x}) = 0$, for all i, so that inequality 8.46 is impossible. So, suppose that $\mathbf{x} > 0$. Because the functions u_i are continuous,

$$\sum_{i=1}^{I} \lambda_i^{-1} u_i(\overline{\mathbf{x}}_i) < \sum_{i=1}^{I} \lambda_i^{-1} u_i((1-\delta)\mathbf{x}_i(\mathbf{x})), \tag{8.47}$$

if δ is a sufficiently small positive number. Also,

$$\sum_{i=1}^{I} (1-\delta)\mathbf{x}_i(\mathbf{x}) = (1-\delta) \sum_{i=1}^{I} \mathbf{x}_i(\mathbf{x}) \leq (1-\delta)\mathbf{x} \leq \mathbf{x}^n, \tag{8.48}$$

if n is sufficiently large, where the last inequality holds because the vectors $\mathbf{x}^n$ are nonnegative and converge to $\mathbf{x}$ as n goes to infinity. Because the $\mathbf{x}_i(\mathbf{x}^n)$ converge to $\overline{\mathbf{x}}_i$ as n goes to infinity and the functions u_i are continuous, inequality 8.47 implies that

$$\sum_{i=1}^{I} \lambda_i^{-1} u_i(\mathbf{x}_i(\mathbf{x}^n)) < \sum_{i=1}^{I} \lambda_i^{-1} u_i((1-\delta)\mathbf{x}_i(\mathbf{x})), \tag{8.49}$$

if n is sufficiently large. Inequality 8.48 implies that if n is large, then the vector $(1-\delta)(\mathbf{x}_1(\mathbf{x}), \ldots, \mathbf{x}_I(\mathbf{x}))$ satisfies the constraints of the problem

$$\max_{\mathbf{x}_1 \in \mathbb{R}_+^N, \ldots, \mathbf{x}_I \in \mathbb{R}_+^N} \sum_{i=1}^{I} \lambda_i^{-1} u_i(\mathbf{x}_i)$$
$$\text{s.t.} \quad \sum_{i=1}^{I} \mathbf{x}_i = \mathbf{x}^n.$$

Inequality 8.49 implies that for large n, the vector $(1-\delta)(\mathbf{x}_1(\mathbf{x}), \ldots, \mathbf{x}_I(\mathbf{x}))$ achieves a higher value of the objective function for this problem than does the optimal vector $(\mathbf{x}_1(\mathbf{x}^n), \ldots, \mathbf{x}_I(\mathbf{x}^n))$, which is impossible. This contradiction proves that $(\overline{\mathbf{x}}_1, \ldots, \overline{\mathbf{x}}_I)$ solves problem 8.45. Lemma 8.41 (in section 8.3) therefore implies that $\overline{\mathbf{x}}_i = \mathbf{x}_i(\mathbf{x})$, for all i, which contradicts inequality 8.44. This last contradiction implies that $\lim_{n\to\infty} \mathbf{x}_i(\mathbf{x}^n) = \mathbf{x}_i(\mathbf{x})$, for all i, as was to be proved. ▪

PROPOSITION 8.68 If u_i satisfies assumption 8.64, for all i, then the function W is differentiable.

Proof. Suppose, first of all, that $\mathbf{x} \gg 0$. Because $\sum_{i=1}^{I} \mathbf{x}_i(\mathbf{x}) = \mathbf{x} \gg 0$, the set $\{1, 2, \ldots, N\}$ may be partitioned into finitely many sets $N_1, N_2, \ldots, N_I$, such that for each i, $x_{in}(x) > 0$, if $n \in N_i$. Some of the sets N_i may be empty. For each i, let $\mathbb{R}^{N_i} = \{\mathbf{x} \in \mathbb{R}^N \mid \mathbf{x}_0 = 0, \text{ if } n \notin N_i\}$ and let $\Pi_i : \mathbb{R}^N \to \mathbb{R}^{N_i}$ be the natural projection defined by the equations

$$\Pi_i(\mathbf{x})_n = \begin{cases} x_n, & \text{if } n \in N_i, \text{ and} \\ 0, & \text{otherwise,} \end{cases}$$

for $n = 1, 2, \ldots, N$, where $\Pi_i(\mathbf{x})_n$ is the nth component of $\Pi_i(\mathbf{x})$. Notice that if $\boldsymbol{\varepsilon} \in \mathbb{R}^N$, then

$$\boldsymbol{\varepsilon} = \sum_{i=1}^{I} \Pi_i(\boldsymbol{\varepsilon}). \tag{8.50}$$

Because $(\mathbf{x}_1(\mathbf{x}), \ldots, \mathbf{x}_I(\mathbf{x}))$ solves problem 8.45, the differentiable Kuhn-Tucker theorem (6.19 in section 6.4) implies that there exists a nonnegative N-vector $\mathbf{p}$ such that, for all i,

$$\lambda_i^{-1} \frac{\partial u_i(\mathbf{x}_i(\mathbf{x}))}{\partial x_n} = p_n, \tag{8.51}$$

if $n \in N_i$, and

$$W(\mathbf{x} + \boldsymbol{\varepsilon}) \leq W(\mathbf{x}) + \mathbf{p}.\boldsymbol{\varepsilon}, \tag{8.52}$$

for any $\boldsymbol{\varepsilon} \in \mathbb{R}^N$ such that $\mathbf{x} + \boldsymbol{\varepsilon} \geq 0$, Because u_i is differentiable, equation 8.51 implies that

$$\lambda_i^{-1} u_i(\mathbf{x}_i(\mathbf{x}) + \Pi_i(\boldsymbol{\varepsilon})) = \lambda_i^{-1} u_i(\mathbf{x}_i(\mathbf{x})) + \mathbf{p}.\Pi_i(\boldsymbol{\varepsilon}) + o(\|\Pi_i(\boldsymbol{\varepsilon})\|), \tag{8.53}$$

where $o(t)$ is a quantity such that $\lim_{t\to\infty} \frac{o(t)}{t} = 0$. Since $\|\Pi_i(\boldsymbol{\varepsilon})\| \leq \|\boldsymbol{\varepsilon}\|$, it follows that

$$\lim_{\|\boldsymbol{\varepsilon}\|\to 0} \frac{o(\Pi_i(\boldsymbol{\varepsilon}))}{\|\boldsymbol{\varepsilon}\|} = 0,$$

so that equation 8.53 implies that

$$\lambda_i^{-1} u_i(\mathbf{x}_i(\mathbf{x}) + \Pi_i(\boldsymbol{\varepsilon})) = \lambda_i^{-1} u_i(\mathbf{x}_i(\mathbf{x})) + \mathbf{p}.\Pi_i(\boldsymbol{\varepsilon}) + o(\|\boldsymbol{\varepsilon}\|). \tag{8.54}$$

Using all this information, we see that

$$\begin{aligned}
&W(\mathbf{x}) + \mathbf{p}.\boldsymbol{\varepsilon} + o(\|\boldsymbol{\varepsilon}\|) \\
&= \sum_{i=1}^{I} \lambda_i^{-1} u_i(\mathbf{x}_i(\mathbf{x})) + \mathbf{p}.\boldsymbol{\varepsilon} + o(\|\boldsymbol{\varepsilon}\|) \\
&= \sum_{i=1}^{I} \left[\lambda_i^{-1} u_i(\mathbf{x}_i(\mathbf{x})) + \mathbf{p}.\Pi_i(\boldsymbol{\varepsilon})\right] + o(\|\boldsymbol{\varepsilon}\|) \\
&= \sum_{i=1}^{I} \lambda_i^{-1} u_i(\mathbf{x}_i(\mathbf{x}) + \Pi_i(\boldsymbol{\varepsilon})) \\
&\leq W(\mathbf{x} + \boldsymbol{\varepsilon}) \\
&\leq W(\mathbf{x}) + \mathbf{p}.\boldsymbol{\varepsilon}.
\end{aligned} \tag{8.55}$$

The first equation in 8.55 follows from the definition of the functions $\mathbf{x}_i(\mathbf{x})$. Equation 8.50 implies the second equation. Equation 8.54 implies the third equation. The first inequality follows from the definition of $W(\mathbf{x} + \boldsymbol{\varepsilon})$ as a maximum. The last inequality is inequality 8.52. Inequality 8.55 implies that

$$o(\|\boldsymbol{\varepsilon}\|) \leq W(\mathbf{x} + \boldsymbol{\varepsilon}) - W(\mathbf{x}) - \mathbf{p}.\boldsymbol{\varepsilon} \leq 0.$$

If we divide these inequalities by $\|\boldsymbol{\varepsilon}\|$, we obtain

$$\frac{o(\|\boldsymbol{\varepsilon}\|)}{\|\boldsymbol{\varepsilon}\|} \leq \frac{W(\mathbf{x} + \varepsilon) - W(\mathbf{x}) - \mathbf{p}.\boldsymbol{\varepsilon}}{\|\boldsymbol{\varepsilon}\|} \leq 0. \tag{8.56}$$

Letting $\|\boldsymbol{\varepsilon}\|$ go to zero in the inequalities in 8.56, we see that

$$\lim_{\|\boldsymbol{\varepsilon}\| \to 0} \frac{| W(\mathbf{x} + \boldsymbol{\varepsilon}) - W(\mathbf{x}) - \mathbf{p}.\boldsymbol{\varepsilon} |}{\|\boldsymbol{\varepsilon}\|} = 0, \tag{8.57}$$

so that W is differentiable at $\mathbf{x}$ and $DW(\mathbf{x}) = \mathbf{p}$.

I now turn to the case where $x_n = 0$, for some n. It is easy to see that all the equations and inequalities in 8.55 apply to this case except for the third equation. I must also show how to define the sets N_i.

For $k = 1, 2, \ldots,$ let $\mathbf{x}^k$ be a sequence of vectors in $\mathbb{R}_+^N$ such that $\mathbf{x}^k \gg 0$, for all k, and $\lim_{k\to\infty} \mathbf{x}^k = \mathbf{x}$. For each k and i, let $N(i, k) = \{n \mid x_{in}(\mathbf{x}^k) > 0\}$. The sets $N(i, k)$ can take only finitely many possible values, so that we can assume, by passing to a subsequence, that the sets $N(i, k)$ do not depend on k. Therefore, we can partition the set $\{1, 2, \ldots, N\}$ into sets

$N_1, N_2, \ldots, N_I$, such that for all i and k, $x_{in}(\mathbf{x}^k) > 0$, for all $n \in N_i$. For each i, define $\mathbb{R}^{N_i}$ and $\Pi_i : \mathbb{R}^N \to \mathbb{R}^{N_i}$ as before.

For each k, let $\mathbf{p}^k$ be an N-vector of Kuhn-Tucker coefficients for the problem

$$W(\mathbf{x}^k) = \max_{\mathbf{x}_1 \in \mathbb{R}^N_+, \ldots, \mathbf{x}_I \in \mathbb{R}^N_+} \sum_{i=1}^{I} \lambda_i^{-1} u_i(\mathbf{x}_i)$$

$$\text{s.t.} \quad \sum_{i=1}^{I} \mathbf{x}_i = \mathbf{x}^k.$$

Then,

$$W(\mathbf{x}^k + \boldsymbol{\varepsilon}) \leq W(\mathbf{x}^k) + \mathbf{p}^k . \boldsymbol{\varepsilon},$$

for all $\boldsymbol{\varepsilon} \in \mathbb{R}^N$, and

$$\lambda_i^{-1} \frac{\partial u_i(\mathbf{x}_i(\mathbf{x}^k))}{\partial x_n} = p_n^k,$$

if $n \in N_i$.

Lemma 8.67 implies that $\lim_{k \to \infty} \mathbf{x}_i(\mathbf{x}^k) = \mathbf{x}_i(\mathbf{x})$, for all i. Since the u_i are continuously differentiable,

$$\lim_{k \to \infty} p_n^k = \lim_{k \to \infty} \lambda_i^{-1} \frac{\partial u_i(\mathbf{x}_i(\mathbf{x}^k))}{\partial x_n} = \lambda_i^{-1} \frac{\partial u_i(\mathbf{x}_i(\mathbf{x}))}{\partial x_n} = p_n, \qquad (8.58)$$

if $n \in N_i$ and where p_n is defined by this equation. Let $\mathbf{p}$ be the N-vector with components p_n. Equation 8.58 implies that equation 8.54 applies, and hence the third equation of the series in 8.55 also applies. Since no new arguments are needed to verify that all the other equations and inequalities of 8.55 apply, we can conclude by the argument used earlier that equation 8.57 applies and hence that W is differentiable at $\mathbf{x}$ and $DW(\mathbf{x}) = \mathbf{p}$. ▪

I now show why consumers' surplus may mean little when demand is Walrasian. Assume that demand is the solution of the problem

$$\max_{\mathbf{x} \in \mathbb{R}^N_+} u(\mathbf{x})$$

$$\text{s.t.} \quad \mathbf{p}.\mathbf{x} \leq w,$$

where w is some positive level of wealth and u is a quasi-concave and continuous function. The next example illustrates the problems that can arise when consumers' surplus is calculated for demands of this form.

EXAMPLE 8.69 Let there be two commodities, and suppose that the consumer's utility function is

$$u(x_1, x_2) = x_2 e^{x_1},$$

This utility function is quasi-concave, because if we take the monotone transformation, $\ln(u)$, of u, we obtain the function $x_1 + \ln(x_2)$, which is the sum of concave functions and therefore is concave. If we solve the problem

$$\begin{aligned} &\max_{x_1 \geq 0, x_2 \geq 0} \; [x_1 + \ln(x_2)] \\ &\text{s.t.} \quad p_1 x_1 + p_2 x_2 \leq w, \end{aligned} \tag{8.59}$$

we find that if $w \geq p_1$, then

$$x_1 = \frac{w}{p_1} - 1,$$

and

$$x_2 = \frac{p_1}{p_2}.$$

If $w < p_1$, then $x_1 = 0$ and $x_2 = \frac{w}{p_2}$.

If we assume that $w \geq p_1$ and solve the above equations for p_1 and p_2, we find that

$$p_1 = \frac{w}{1 + x_1}$$

and

$$p_2 = \frac{w}{(1 + x_1)x_2}.$$

A first difficulty can be seen by calculating the left- and right-hand sides of equation 8.42 along the path $\mathbf{x}(t) = (1, t)$, for $0 \leq t \leq 1$, when welfare is $W(\mathbf{x}) = u(\mathbf{x})$. The right-hand side of equation 8.42 is

$$\int_0^1 p(t).\frac{dx(t)}{dt}dt = \int_0^1 \frac{w}{2t}dt = \infty.$$

The left-hand side is $u(1, 1) - u(1, 0) = e - 0 = e < \infty$. Therefore, the integral does not measure the change in the consumer's welfare along the path.

Another difficulty is that the integral in equation 8.42 depends on the path. Consider the following two paths from consumption bundle (1, 1) to the bundle (2, 2).

$$x^A(t) = \begin{cases} (1+t,\, 1), & \text{if } 0 \le t \le 1, \text{ and} \\ (2,\, t), & \text{if } 1 \le t \le 2. \end{cases}$$

$$x^B(t) = \begin{cases} (1,\, 1+t), & \text{if } 0 \le t \le 1, \text{ and} \\ (t,\, 2), & \text{if } 1 \le t \le 2. \end{cases}$$

The integral along path x^A is

$$\int_0^2 p(t).\frac{dx^A(t)}{dt}dt = \int_0^1 p_1^A(t)dt + \int_1^2 p_2^A(t)dt = \int_0^1 \frac{w}{2+t}dt + \int_1^2 \frac{w}{3t}dt$$

$$= w\left[\ln\left(\frac{3}{2}\right) + \frac{1}{3}\ln(2)\right] = w\ln\left(\frac{3}{2^{2/3}}\right),$$

where

$$p_1^A(t) = \frac{w}{1+x_1^A(t)}$$

and

$$p_2^A(t) = \frac{w}{[1+x_1^A(t)]x_2^A(t)}.$$

Similarly, the integral along path x^B is

$$\int_0^2 p(t).\frac{dx^B(t)}{dt}dt = \int_0^1 p_2^B(t) + \int_1^2 p_1^B(t)dt$$

$$= \int_0^1 \frac{w}{2(1+t)}dt + \int_1^2 \frac{w}{(1+t)}dt$$

$$= w\left[\frac{1}{2}\ln(2) + \ln\left(\frac{3}{2}\right)\right] = w\ln\left(\frac{2}{2^{1/2}}\right).$$

Since the integral differs along the two paths, it cannot represent the change in the consumer's welfare between bundles (1, 1) and (2, 2).

The difficulties just encountered arise because the consumer's marginal utility of unit of account varies as prices change. The use of short-run demand avoids this problem, because the marginal utility of unit of account is assumed to be constant.

8.5 The Stability of Short-Run Equilibrium

Although it is not at all clear how to model the process by which an economy finds equilibrium prices, it is natural to assume that prices of commodities rise if they are in excess demand and fall if they are in excess supply. A process that reflects this intuition is one governed by the differential equation

$$\frac{d\mathbf{p}(t)}{dt} = z(\mathbf{p}(t)), \tag{8.60}$$

where $\mathbf{p}(t)$ is the vector price at time t and $z(\mathbf{p}) = \sum_{i=1}^{I}(\xi_i(\mathbf{p}) - \mathbf{e}_i) - \sum_{j=1}^{J} \eta_j(\mathbf{p})$ is the market excess demand function. Equation 8.60 has been much studied by economists. It is interpreted as approximating Walras' *tâtonnement* process, according to which an auctioneer leads an iterative process in which he or she proposes prices, buyers and seller then say what their demands or supplies would be at those prices, and these reactions guide the auctioneer in the choice of the next round of prices. This process continues until it reaches equilibrium prices, and then trading occurs at these prices. It is well known that if $z(\mathbf{p})$ is obtained from Walrasian demand and supply functions, then the solution of differential equation 8.60 may never converge. I give Scarf's (1960) example of nonconvergence at the end of this section. One might suspect that such instability is possible, since we have already seen in example 8.63 (in section 8.3) that Walrasian demand functions may slope upward, and figure 8.6 shows that if a demand curve, DD, slopes upward less steeply than the supply curve, SS, then an increase in price increases rather than decreases excess demand. Increasing the price in the figure from $p(1)$ to $p(2)$ increases excess demand from zero to AB.

Dynamic system 8.60 is stable, however, if demands and supplies are short run. Short-run demand is probably more appropriate than Walrasian demand for the study of price dynamics, since the convergence of prices to equilibrium levels should occur quickly. It would be inappropriate, however, to use short-run demand to study the stability of the economy over time periods as long as, say, the business cycle.

The idea of the proof of stability is quite simple. It starts from the decomposition, given in equation 8.43 (in section 8.4), of consumer welfare at equilibrium into consumers' surplus, profits, and the value of resources

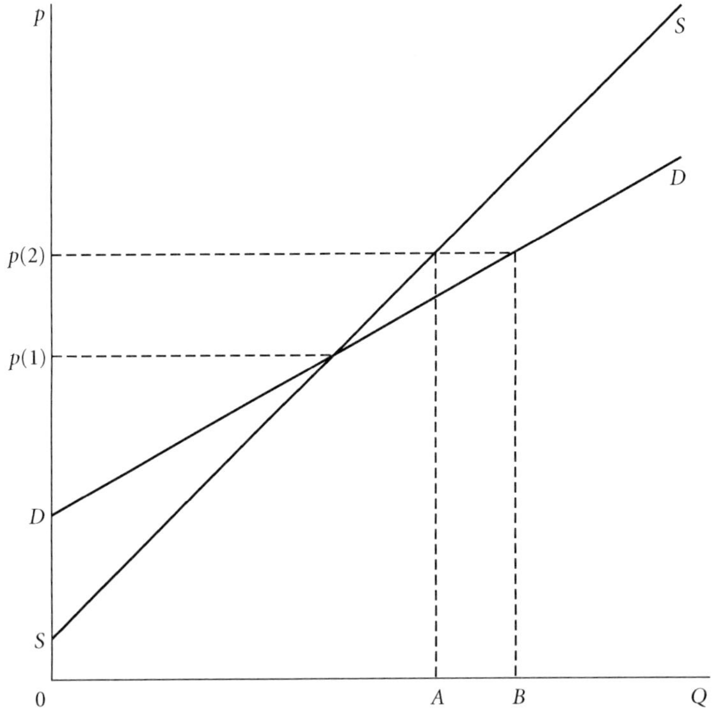

Figure 8.6 A configuration of demand and supply curves that contributes to price instability

or endowments. Inspired by this decomposition, I define for any price vector a total surplus function,

$$
\begin{aligned}
h(\mathbf{P}) &= \sum_{i=1}^{I} \left(\lambda_i^{-1} u_i(\xi_i^S(\mathbf{P})) - \mathbf{P}.\xi_i^S(\mathbf{P}) \right) \\
&\quad + \sum_{j=1}^{J} \pi_j(\mathbf{P}) + \mathbf{P}. \sum_{i=1}^{I} \mathbf{e}_i, \qquad (8.61) \\
&= \sum_{i=1}^{I} \lambda_i^{-1} u_i \left(\xi_i^S(\mathbf{P}) \right) + \sum_{j=1}^{J} \pi_j(\mathbf{P}) - \mathbf{P}. \left(\sum_{i=1}^{I} \xi_i^S(\mathbf{P}) - \sum_{i=1}^{I} \mathbf{e}_i \right),
\end{aligned}
$$

where, for each j, $\pi_j = \max_{y \in Y_j} \mathbf{P}.y = \mathbf{P}.\eta_j(\mathbf{P})$ is the maximum profit of firm j at price vector $\mathbf{P}$. Notice that although $\pi_j(\mathbf{P})$ is defined in section 4.1 to be the supremum of possible profits, it is here defined to be the maximum profits. Hence $\pi_j(\mathbf{P})$ is not necessarily defined for all positive vectors $\mathbf{P}$. The function h turns out to be convex and to achieve a minimum at the unique equilibrium price vector, and, furthermore, the market, short-run, excess demand vector,

$$z^S(\mathbf{P}) = \sum_{i=1}^{I} \left(\xi_i^S(\mathbf{P}) - \mathbf{e}_i \right) - \sum_{j=1}^{J} \eta_j(\mathbf{P}),$$

is everywhere the negative of a subgradient of h. (Convexity of functions is defined in definition 6.1 in section 6.1.) If h is differentiable, then $z^S(\mathbf{P})$ is the negative of the gradient of h, where the gradient of h is its derivative. That is, $z^S(\mathbf{P}) = -Dh(\mathbf{P})$. Therefore, the path solving the differential equation

$$\frac{d\mathbf{P}(t)}{dt} = z^S(\mathbf{P}(t)),$$

in effect, follows the gradient of h backward and downward to the equilibrium price vector at the unique minimum of h. The intuition for this argument may be seen in terms of figures similar to figure 8.2 (in section 8.4). We see, by comparing figure 8.2 with figures 8.7 and 8.8, that the sum of the surpluses, which is $h(\mathbf{P})$, is smallest when the price is at its equilibrium level.

A full and satisfying proof of the convergence of solutions of differential equation 8.60 to the short-run equilibrium requires methods beyond the level of this text. I can, nevertheless, go quite far with the argument. Throughout the discussion, I assume that assumptions 8.46, 8.50–8.53, and 8.58 (in section 8.3) apply. Assumption 8.58, that production possibility sets are strictly convex, is not realistic. In particular, it implies that input-output possibility sets have nonempty interiors and hence are N-dimensional, whereas it seems reasonable that each production process involves only a small number of the many goods and services in an economy. This difficulty can be removed by assuming that production possibility sets are strictly convex only in a lower-dimensional subspace of $\mathbb{R}^N$. The proofs that follow remain valid under this weaker assumption. Even if the input-output possibility sets are of low dimension, the assumption of strict convexity within the lower-dimensional subspace implies decreasing

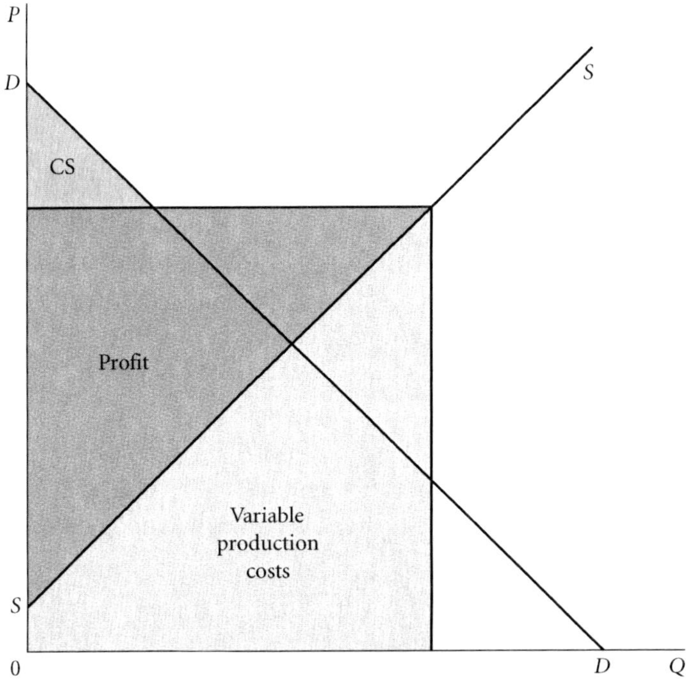

Figure 8.7 Surpluses with excess supply

marginal returns to scale. This assumption is perhaps appropriate in the short-run context appropriate for the theory of price stability, since in the short run a great many productive inputs, such as capital, are fixed or nearly fixed. If the context allows adjustments over a very long run, it would be more appropriate to assume constant returns to scale, that is, that the production possibility sets are cones. (Cones are defined in definition 4.5 in section 4.4.)

By propositions 8.59 and 8.60 and theorem 8.61 (in section 8.3), assumptions 8.46, 8.50–8.53, and 8.58 guarantee that an equilibrium exists and that the equilibrium is unique provided that some of every commodity is consumed in the equilibrium. Recall that assumption 8.46 is that the utility functions, u_i, are strictly increasing and twice continuously differentiable and that, for all $\mathbf{x}$, $Du_i(\mathbf{x}) \gg 0$ and $D^2u_i(\mathbf{x})$ is negative definite. In addition, I make a similar assumption about production.

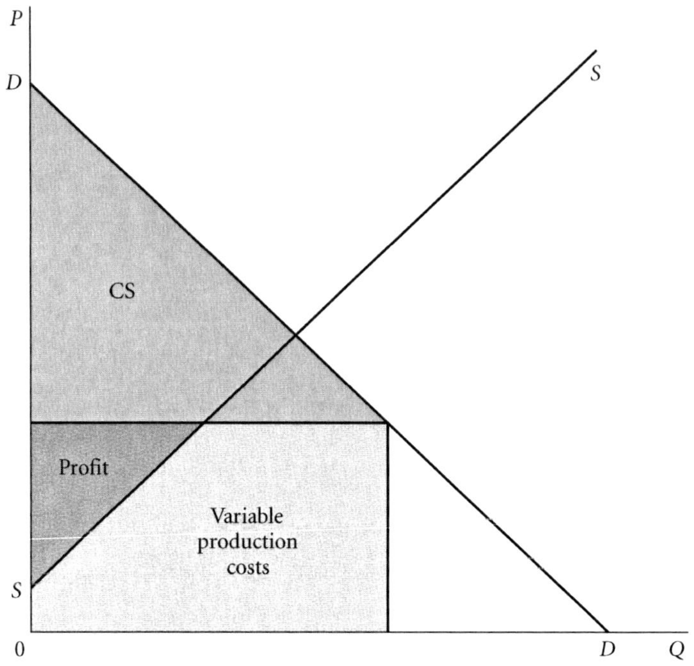

Figure 8.8 Surpluses with excess demand

Before turning to that assumption, I show that profit functions are convex. By proposition 8.73 (at the end of this section), $\pi_j(\mathbf{P})$ is defined on a convex set of price vectors. Since $\pi_j(\mathbf{P}) = \max_{\mathbf{y} \in Y_j} \mathbf{P}.\mathbf{y} = \mathbf{P}.\eta_j(\mathbf{P})$, it follows that for all P^*,

$$\pi_j(\mathbf{P}^*) \geq \mathbf{P}^*.\eta_j(\mathbf{P}) = \pi_j(\mathbf{P}) + (\mathbf{P}^* - \mathbf{P}).\eta_j(\mathbf{P}),$$

so that $\eta_j(\mathbf{P})$ is a subgradient of $\pi_j(\mathbf{P})$ at $\mathbf{P}$. That is, every point on or above the graph of π_j lies in the half space

$$H(\mathbf{P}) = \{(\mathbf{P}^*, t) \mid \mathbf{P}^* \in \mathbb{R}^N_+ \text{ and } t \geq \pi_j(\mathbf{P}) + (\mathbf{P}^* - \mathbf{P}).\eta_j(\mathbf{P})\}.$$

The points on or above the graph of π_j equal the intersection of all the sets $H(\mathbf{P})$, each of which is convex. Since the intersection of convex sets is convex, it follows that all the points on or above the graph of π_j are a convex set and hence that π_j is a convex function.

By proposition 8.39 (in section 8.3), π_j is defined on an open set in $\mathbb{R}^N_+$, so that the following assumption is applicable.

ASSUMPTION 8.70 For each j, the profit function π_j is twice continuously differentiable wherever it is defined.

Because π_j is a convex function, $-\pi_j$ is a concave function, and it follows from lemma 3.30 (in section 3.5) that $D^2\pi_j(\mathbf{P})$ is positive semidefinite, if π_j is defined at $\mathbf{P}$. Furthermore, since $\eta_j(\mathbf{P})$ is a subgradient of π_j at $\mathbf{P}$ and π_j is differentiable, it follows that $\eta_j(\mathbf{P})$ is the derivative of π_j at $\mathbf{P}$. That is,

$$D\pi_j(\mathbf{P}) = \eta_j(\mathbf{P}), \tag{8.62}$$

for all $\mathbf{P}$ such that $\pi_j(\mathbf{P})$ is defined. Because π_j is twice continuously differentiable, η_j is continuously differentiable and

$$D\eta_j(\mathbf{P}) = D^2\pi_j(\mathbf{P}), \tag{8.63}$$

for every $\mathbf{P}$ such that $\pi_j(\mathbf{P})$ and $\eta_j(\mathbf{P})$ are defined.

I now try to give some insight into the proof of stability. To simplify the presentation, I make the following very unrealistic assumption.

ASSUMPTION 8.71 For all i, $\xi_i^S(\mathbf{P}) \gg 0$, for all $\mathbf{P}$ in the domain of definition of the function ξ_i^S.

By the definition of short-run demand, $\xi_i^S(\mathbf{P})$ solves the problem

$$\max\{u_i(\mathbf{P}) - \lambda_i \mathbf{P} \mid \mathbf{P} \in \mathbb{R}_+^N\},$$

for each i. Assumption 8.46 implies that u_i is strictly concave, so that the solution to this maximization problem is unique, if it exists. Because $\xi_i^S(\mathbf{P}) \gg 0$ by assumption, it follows that $\xi_i^S(\mathbf{P})$ satisfies the equation

$$Du_i\left(\xi_i^S(\mathbf{P})\right) = \lambda_i \mathbf{P}, \tag{8.64}$$

whenever it exists. Using the argument following equation 8.23 (in section 8.3), we see from the implicit function theorem that ξ_i^S is differentiable and that

$$D\xi_i^S(\mathbf{P}) = \lambda_i \left[D^2 u_i(\xi_i^S(\mathbf{P}))\right]^{-1}, \tag{8.65}$$

where $[D^2u_i(\xi_i^S(\mathbf{P}))]^{-1}$ is the inverse of the matrix $D^2u_i(\xi_i^S(\mathbf{P}))$. The matrix $\lambda_i[D^2u_i(\xi_i^S(\mathbf{P}))]^{-1}$ is negative definite, because $D^2u_i(\xi_i^S(\mathbf{P}))$ is negative definite.

Suppose that the price vector follows a path $\mathbf{P}(t)$, governed by the differential equation

$$\frac{d\mathbf{P}(t)}{dt} = z^S(\mathbf{P}(t)) = \sum_{i=1}^{I}\left(\xi_i^S(\mathbf{P}) - \mathbf{e}_i\right) - \sum_{j=1}^{J}\eta_j(\mathbf{P}), \tag{8.66}$$

which is the version of equation 8.60 using short-run demand. From equations 8.63 and 8.65, we know that the right-hand side of equation 8.66 is differentiable. By the existence theorem for solutions to ordinary differential equations (Coddington and Levinson 1955, 6; Hartman 1964, 8), given $\mathbf{P}(0)$ in the interior of the domain of definition of z^S, there exists a solution $\mathbf{P}(t)$ of differential equation 8.66 defined at least for small positive values of t. I will presently verify that the domain of definition of z^S is open, so that this existence theorem may be applied.

Let $h(\mathbf{P})$ be defined by equation 8.61. Differentiating $h(\mathbf{P}(t))$ with respect to t, we find that

$$\frac{dh(\mathbf{P}(t))}{dt} = \sum_{i=1}^{I}\lambda_i^{-1}Du_i\left(\xi_i^S(\mathbf{P}(t))\right)D\xi_i^S(\mathbf{P}(t))\frac{d\mathbf{P}(t)}{dt} + \sum_{j=1}^{J}D\pi_j(\mathbf{P}(t))\frac{d\mathbf{P}(t)}{dt}$$
$$-\left(\frac{d\mathbf{P}(t)}{dt}\right)^T\left(\sum_{i=1}^{I}\xi_i^S(\mathbf{P}(t)) - \sum_{i=1}^{I}\mathbf{e}_i\right) - \mathbf{P}(t)^T\left(\sum_{i=1}^{I}D\xi_i^S(\mathbf{P})\right)\frac{d\mathbf{P}(t)}{dt},$$

where $Du_i(\xi_i^S(\mathbf{P}(t)))^T$ is the transpose of the vector $Du_i(\xi_i^S(\mathbf{P}(t)))$. If we now substitute equations 8.62 and 8.64–8.66 into this expression for $\frac{dh(\mathbf{P}(t))}{dt}$ and cancel like terms, we find that

$$\frac{dh(\mathbf{P}(t))}{dt} = -\left(\frac{d\mathbf{P}(t)}{dt}\right)^T\left(\sum_{i=1}^{I}\xi_i^S(\mathbf{P}(t)) - \sum_{i=1}^{I}\mathbf{e}_i - \sum_{j=1}^{J}\eta_j(\mathbf{P}(t))\right)$$
$$= -\left(\sum_{i=1}^{I}\xi_i^S(\mathbf{P}(t)) - \sum_{i=1}^{I}\mathbf{e}_i - \sum_{j=1}^{J}\eta_j(\mathbf{P}(t))\right)^T \tag{8.67}$$
$$\left(\sum_{i=1}^{I}\xi_i^S(\mathbf{P}(t)) - \sum_{i=1}^{I}\mathbf{e}_i - \sum_{j=1}^{J}\eta_j(\mathbf{P}(t))\right)$$
$$= -z^S(\mathbf{P}).z^S(\mathbf{p}) \leq 0,$$

with

$$\frac{dh(\mathbf{P}(t))}{dt} < 0,$$

if $z^S(\mathbf{P}) = \sum_{i=1}^I \xi_i^S(\mathbf{P}(t)) - \sum_{i=1}^I \mathbf{e}_i - \sum_{j=1}^J \eta_j(\mathbf{P}(t)) \neq 0$. That is, the price change determined by differential equation 8.66 tends to decrease the surplus function, h, unless the process has arrived at a short-run equilibrium.

In calculating $\frac{dh(\mathbf{P}(t))}{dt}$, I have at the same time calculated the derivative of h, which is

$$Dh(\mathbf{P}) = -\left(\sum_{i=1}^{I} \xi_i^S(\mathbf{P}) - \sum_{i=1}^{I} \mathbf{e}_i - \sum_{j=1}^{J} \eta_j(\mathbf{P})\right) = -z^S(\mathbf{P}). \quad (8.68)$$

Therefore, differential equation 8.66 is a negative gradient process; the right-hand side of equation 8.66 is the negative of the gradient of h. We may use equations 8.62 and 8.65 to calculate that

$$D^2h(\mathbf{P}) = -\sum_{i=1}^{I} \lambda_i \left[D^2u_i(\xi_i^S(\mathbf{P}))\right]^{-1} + \sum_{j=1}^{J} D^2\pi_j(\mathbf{P}). \quad (8.69)$$

The matrices $D^2u_i(\xi_i^S(\mathbf{P}))$ are negative definite by assumption 8.46, and it has been shown that the functions π_j are convex, so that the matrices $D^2\pi_j(\eta_j(\mathbf{P}))$ are positive semidefinite. Therefore, equation 8.69 implies that $D^2h(\mathbf{P})$ is positive definite. Hence by lemma 3.38 (in section 3.5), h is a strictly convex function, and hence its minimum is unique, if it exists. We see from equation 8.68 that the derivative of h is zero at a short-run equilibrium price vector, so that h does have a minimum. In summary, differential equation 8.66 is a negative gradient process for a strictly convex function with a unique minimum. Because h is convex, its graph may be visualized as a bowl, and the negative gradient process takes the steepest path down the inside of the bowl, just as would a drop of water.

This image, though encouraging, is not a proof. An important step in the proof is to show that $\|z^S(\mathbf{P}(t))\|$ is decreasing as a function of t as long as $\|z^S(\mathbf{P}(t))\| > 0$. (If $z^S(\mathbf{P}(\underline{t}) = 0$, for some $\underline{t}$, then $\frac{d\mathbf{P}(\underline{t})}{dt} = 0$ and so $\mathbf{P}(t) = \mathbf{P}(\underline{t})$, for $t > \underline{t}$ and also $\mathbf{P}(\underline{t})$ is a short-run equilibrium price vector.) Since

$$\|z^S(\mathbf{P}(t))\| = \sqrt{z^S(\mathbf{P}(t)).z^S(\mathbf{P}(t))},$$

it is enough to show that

$$\frac{dz^S(\mathbf{P}(t)).z^S(\mathbf{P}(t))}{dt} < 0, \tag{8.70}$$

for all t such that $z^S(\mathbf{P}(t)) \neq 0$. Calculating this derivative, we see that

$$\frac{dz^S(\mathbf{P}(t)).z^S(\mathbf{P}(t))}{dt} = z^S(\mathbf{P}(t))^T Dz^S(\mathbf{P}(t))z^S(\mathbf{P}(t))$$

$$= z^S(\mathbf{P}(t))^T \left(\sum_{i=1}^{I} D\xi_i^S(\mathbf{P}(t)) - \sum_{j=1}^{J} D\eta_j(\mathbf{P}(t)) \right) z^S(\mathbf{P}(t)),$$

where $z^S(\mathbf{P}(t))^T$ is the transpose of $z^S(\mathbf{P}(t))$. We know from equation 8.65 and assumption 8.46 that $D\xi_i^S(\mathbf{P}(t))$ is negative definite, for all i, and we know from equation 8.63 and the convexity of π_k that $D\eta_j(\mathbf{P}(t))$ is positive semidefinite, for all j. Therefore, the matrix $\sum_{i=1}^{I} D\xi_i^S(\mathbf{P}(t)) - \sum_{j=1}^{J} D\eta_j(\mathbf{P}(t))$ is negative definite, so that

$$z^S(\mathbf{P}(t))^T \left(\sum_{i=1}^{I} D\xi_i^S(\mathbf{P}(t)) - \sum_{j=1}^{J} D\eta_j(\mathbf{P}(t)) \right) z^S(\mathbf{P}(t)) < 0,$$

for all t such that $z^S(\mathbf{P}(t)) \neq 0$. This completes the proof that inequality 8.70 is valid.

I next show that the domain of definition of the function z^S is a nonempty open subset of $\mathbb{R}^N$, so that it is possible to apply to equation 8.66 the standard existence theorem for the solution of a differential equation. (According to proposition 8.73 at the end of this section, the domain of definition of z^S is also convex.) We know that the domain of definition of z^S is nonempty, because it contains the short-run equilibrium price vector. Since the domain of definition of z^S is the intersection of the domains of definition of ξ_i^S, for all i, and of η_j, for all j, it is enough to check that the domain of definition of each of these functions is open in $\mathbb{R}^N_+$ and that at least one domain does not intersect the boundary of $\mathbb{R}^N_+$. Because u_i is continuous, strictly increasing, and strictly concave, proposition 8.36 (in section 8.3) implies that ξ_i^S is a function defined on a set of strictly positive N-vectors that is open in $\mathbb{R}^N$ and contained in the interior of $\mathbb{R}^N_+$. Because Y_j is closed and strictly convex, proposition 8.39

(in section 8.3) implies that η_j is a function defined on a set that is open in $\mathbb{R}^N_+$. Hence, I have shown that the domain of definition of z^S is open in $\mathbb{R}^N$.

The next step in the proof is to check that the solution $\mathbf{P}(t)$ of differential equation 8.66 does not converge to a point that is not in the domain of definition of the function z^S. The key step in this proof is to show that

$$\begin{aligned}&\text{if } z^S(\overline{\mathbf{P}}) \text{ is not defined and } \overline{\mathbf{P}} \text{ belongs to the closure of}\\ &\{\mathbf{P} \mid z^S(\overline{\mathbf{P}}) \text{ is defined}\}, \text{ then } \lim_{\mathbf{P}\to\overline{\mathbf{P}}} \|z^S(\mathbf{P})\| = \infty, \text{ where}\\ &\text{the limit is through any sequence of points } \mathbf{P} \text{ at which } z^S(\mathbf{P}) \text{ is defined.}\end{aligned} \tag{8.71}$$

(The closure of a set is defined in definition 3.8 in section 3.2.)

In order to prove statement 8.71, I prove that $\|\xi_i^S(\mathbf{P})\|$ diverges to infinity as $\mathbf{P}$ converges a point where ξ_i^S is not defined and similarly that $\|\eta_j(\mathbf{P})\|$ diverges to infinity as $\mathbf{P}$ converges to a point where η_j is not defined. These assertions are, respectively, statements 8.72 and 8.74 below.

$$\begin{aligned}&\text{If } \xi_i^S(\overline{\mathbf{P}}) \text{ is not defined and } \overline{\mathbf{P}} \text{ belongs to the closure of}\\ &\{\mathbf{P} \mid \xi_i^S(\overline{\mathbf{P}}) \text{ is defined}\}, \text{ then } \lim_{\mathbf{P}\to\overline{\mathbf{P}}} \|\xi_i^S(\mathbf{P})\| = \infty, \text{ where}\\ &\text{the limit is through any sequence of points } \mathbf{P} \text{ at which } \xi_i^S(\mathbf{P}) \text{ is defined.}\end{aligned} \tag{8.72}$$

Suppose that statement 8.72 is false. Then, there exists a positive number b and a sequence $\mathbf{P}^k$ such that $\lim_{k\to\infty} \mathbf{P}^k = \overline{\mathbf{P}}$ and $\|\xi_i^S(\mathbf{P}^k)\| \le b$, for all k. The problem

$$\begin{aligned}&\max_{\mathbf{x}\in\mathbb{R}^N_+} \left[\lambda_i^{-1} u_i(\mathbf{x}) - \overline{\mathbf{P}}.\mathbf{x}\right]\\ &\text{s.t.} \quad \|x\| \le 2b\end{aligned} \tag{8.73}$$

has a solution, because the function $\lambda_i^{-1} u_i(\mathbf{x}) - \overline{\mathbf{P}}.\mathbf{x}$ is continuous, and the set $\{\mathbf{x} \in \mathbb{R}^N_+ \mid \|\mathbf{x}\| \le 2b\}$ is compact. Call this solution $\overline{\mathbf{x}}$. Because $\|\xi_i^S(\mathbf{P}^k)\| \le b < 2b$, it follows that $\xi_i^S(\mathbf{P}^k)$ solves the problem.

$$\begin{aligned}&\max_{\mathbf{x}\in\mathbb{R}^N_+} \left[\lambda_i^{-1} u_i(\mathbf{x}) - \mathbf{P}^k.\mathbf{x}\right]\\ &\text{s.t.} \quad \|x\| \le 2b,\end{aligned}$$

for all k. Because the function $\lambda_i^{-1}u_i(\mathbf{x}) - \overline{\mathbf{P}}.\mathbf{x}$ is strictly concave with respect to $\mathbf{x}$, it follows that $\lim_{k\to\infty} \xi_i^S(\mathbf{P}^k) = \overline{\mathbf{x}}$. In order to see that this statement is true, assume that the sequence $\xi_i^S(\mathbf{P}^k)$ does not converge to $\overline{\mathbf{x}}$. Then there exists a positive number ε such that $\|\xi_i^S(\mathbf{P}^k) - \overline{\mathbf{x}}\| > \varepsilon$, for infinitely many k. Because the vectors $\xi_i^S(\mathbf{P}^k)$ belong to the compact set $\{\mathbf{x} \mid \|\mathbf{x}\| \leq b\}$, there is a convergent subsequence of the $\xi_i^S(\mathbf{P}^k)$, which I call $\xi_i^S(\mathbf{P}^k)$ again. Let $\underline{\mathbf{x}}$ be the limit of this subsequence. Then $\|\underline{\mathbf{x}}\| \leq b$ and $\|\underline{\mathbf{x}} - \overline{\mathbf{x}}\| \geq \varepsilon$. By the definition of $\xi_i^S(\mathbf{P}^k)$,

$$\lambda_i^{-1}u_i\left(\xi_i^S(\mathbf{P}^k)\right) - \mathbf{P}^k.\xi_i^S(\mathbf{P}^k) \geq \lambda_i^{-1}u_i(\overline{\mathbf{x}}) - \mathbf{P}^k.\overline{\mathbf{x}}.$$

Passage to the limit in this inequality implies that

$$\lambda_i^{-1}u_i(\underline{\mathbf{x}}) - \overline{\mathbf{P}}.\underline{x} \geq \lambda_i^{-1}u_i(\overline{\mathbf{x}}) - \overline{\mathbf{P}}.\overline{\mathbf{x}}.$$

Hence both $\overline{\mathbf{x}}$ and $\underline{\mathbf{x}}$ solve problem 8.73, which is impossible since $\overline{\mathbf{x}} \neq \underline{\mathbf{x}}$ and $\lambda_i^{-1}u_i(\mathbf{x}) - \overline{\mathbf{P}}.\mathbf{x}$ is a strictly concave function of $\mathbf{x}$. This contradiction proves that $\lim_{k\to\infty} \xi_i^S(\mathbf{P}^k) = \overline{\mathbf{x}}$. Since $\|\xi_i^S(\mathbf{P}^k)\| \leq b$, for all k, it follows that $\|\overline{\mathbf{x}}\| \leq b$.

I next show that $\overline{\mathbf{x}} = \xi_i^S(\overline{\mathbf{P}})$. Suppose that $\overline{\mathbf{x}} \neq \xi_i^S(\overline{\mathbf{P}})$. Since $\overline{\mathbf{x}}$ solves problem 8.73, but not the problem

$$\max_{\mathbf{x}\in\mathbb{R}_+^N} \left[\lambda_i^{-1}u_i(\mathbf{x}) - \overline{\mathbf{P}}.\mathbf{x}\right],$$

there exists an $\mathbf{x}$ in $\mathbb{R}_+^N$ such that $\|\mathbf{x}\| > 2b$ and $\lambda_i^{-1}u_i(\mathbf{x}) - \overline{\mathbf{P}}.\mathbf{x} > \lambda_i^{-1}u_i(\overline{\mathbf{x}}) - \overline{\mathbf{P}}.\overline{\mathbf{x}}$. Since $\|\overline{\mathbf{x}}\| < b$, it follows that if α is a sufficiently small number such that $0 < \alpha < 1$,

$$\|\alpha\mathbf{x} + (1-\alpha)\overline{\mathbf{x}}\| \leq 2b.$$

Yet

$$\begin{aligned} &\lambda_i^{-1}u_i(\alpha\mathbf{x} + (1-\alpha)\overline{\mathbf{x}}) - \overline{\mathbf{P}}.(\alpha\mathbf{x} + (1-\alpha)\overline{\mathbf{x}}) \\ &> \alpha(\lambda_i^{-1}u_i(\overline{\mathbf{x}}) - \overline{\mathbf{P}}.\mathbf{x}) + (1-\alpha)(\lambda_i^{-1}u_i(\overline{\mathbf{x}}) - \overline{\mathbf{P}}.\overline{\mathbf{x}}) \\ &> (\lambda_i^{-1}u_i(\overline{\mathbf{x}}) - \overline{\mathbf{P}}.\overline{\mathbf{x}}), \end{aligned}$$

which contradicts the assumption that $\overline{\mathbf{x}}$ solves problem 8.73. This completes the proof that $\overline{\mathbf{x}} = \xi_i^S(\overline{\mathbf{P}})$. The fact that $\xi_i^S(\overline{\mathbf{P}})$ exists contradicts the assumption that $\xi_i^S(\overline{\mathbf{P}})$ is not defined at $\overline{\mathbf{P}}$, and this contraption completes the proof of statement 8.72.

A similar argument proves that

$$\text{if } \eta_j(\overline{\mathbf{P}}) \text{ is not defined and } \overline{\mathbf{P}} \text{ belongs to the closure of } \{\mathbf{P} \mid \eta_j(\overline{\mathbf{P}}) \text{ is defined}\}, \text{ then } \lim_{\mathbf{P}\to\overline{\mathbf{P}}} \|\eta_j(\mathbf{P})\| = \infty, \text{ where} \tag{8.74}$$

the limit is through any sequence of points $\mathbf{P}$ at which $\eta_j(\mathbf{P})$ is defined.

To complete the proof of statement 8.71, recall that assumptions 8.50–8.52 apply. By theorem 3.54 (in section 3.7), these assumptions guarantee that the set of feasible allocations is compact and nonempty. If statement 8.71 is false, then there exist a positive number b and a sequence of price vectors, $\mathbf{P}^k$, for $k = 1, 2, \ldots$, such that $z^S(\mathbf{P}^k)$ is defined and $\|z^S(\mathbf{P}^k)\| \leq b$, for every k and $\lim_{k\to\infty} \mathbf{P}^k = \overline{\mathbf{P}}$. Because $z^S(\overline{\mathbf{P}})$ is not defined, $\xi_i^S(\overline{\mathbf{P}})$ or $\eta_j(\overline{\mathbf{P}})$ are not defined for some i and j. Let $\overline{I}$ be the set of consumers i for which $\xi_i^S(\overline{\mathbf{P}})$ is not defined, and let $\overline{J}$ be the set of firms j for which $\eta_j(\overline{\mathbf{P}})$ is not defined, where either $\overline{I}$ or $\overline{J}$ but not both may be empty. Statements 8.72 and 8.74 imply that $\lim_{k\to\infty} \|\xi_i^S(\mathbf{P}^k)\| = \infty$, for $i \in \overline{I}$, and $\lim_{k\to\infty} \|\eta_j(\mathbf{P}^k)\| = \infty$, for $j \in \overline{J}$. For each k, let

$$M_k = \max_{\substack{i=1,\ldots,I \text{ and} \\ j=1,\ldots,J}} \left(\|\xi_i^S(\mathbf{P}^k)\|, \|\eta_j(\mathbf{P}^k)\|\right).$$

Then, $\lim_{k\to\infty} M_k = \infty$. For each k, $M_k = \|\xi_i^S(\mathbf{P}^k)\|$ or $M_k = \|\eta_j(\mathbf{P}^k)\|$, for some i or j. Since there are only finitely many indices i and j, it follows that for some i or j, $M_k = \|\xi_i^S(\mathbf{P}^k)\|$ or $M_k = \|\eta_j(\mathbf{P}^k)\|$, for infinitely many values of k. By passing to a subsequence and calling it M_k again, I may assume that for some i or j, $M_k = \|\xi_i^S(\mathbf{P}^k)\|$ or $M_k = \|\eta_j(\mathbf{P}^k)\|$, for every value of k. For each i, let $\mathbf{x}_i^k = \frac{\xi_i^S(\mathbf{P}^k)}{M_k}$ and, for each j, let $\mathbf{y}_j^k = \frac{\eta_j(\mathbf{P}^k)}{M_k}$. Because Y_j is convex and contains the zero vector, $\mathbf{y}_i^k \in Y_j$, for all j and k. By assumption, $\|z^S(\mathbf{P}^k)\| \leq b$, for all k, so that

$$\left\|\sum_{i=1}^{I}\left(\mathbf{x}_i^k - \frac{\mathbf{e}_i}{M_k}\right) - \sum_{j=1}^{J}\mathbf{y}_j^k\right\|$$

$$= \frac{\|\sum_{i=1}^{I}(\xi_i^S(\mathbf{P}^k) - \mathbf{e}_i) - \sum_{j=1}^{J}\eta_j(\mathbf{P}^k)\|}{M_k} = \frac{\|z^S(\mathbf{P}^k)\|}{M_k} \leq \frac{b}{M_k},$$

for all k. Therefore,

$$\lim_{k\to\infty}\left\|\sum_{i=1}^{I}\left(\mathbf{x}_i^k-\frac{\mathbf{e}_i}{M_k}\right)-\sum_{j=1}^{J}\mathbf{y}_j^k\right\|=0. \qquad (8.75)$$

Clearly, $\|\mathbf{x}_i^k\|\le 1$ and $\|\mathbf{y}_j^k\|\le 1$, for all i and j. Therefore, the Bolzano-Weierstrass theorem (3.12 in section 3.2) implies that there is a subsequence, which I index by k again, such that the sequences $\mathbf{x}_i^k$ and $\mathbf{y}_j^k$ converge as k goes to infinity. For each i, let $\overline{\mathbf{x}}_i=\lim_{k\to\infty}\mathbf{x}_i^k$ and, for each j, let $\overline{\mathbf{y}}_i=\lim_{k\to\infty}\mathbf{y}_j^k$. Since $\mathbb{R}_+^N$ and Y_j are closed, $\overline{\mathbf{x}}_i\in\mathbb{R}_+^N$ and $\overline{\mathbf{y}}_j\in Y_j$, for all i and j. Since $\lim_{k\to\infty}\frac{\mathbf{e}_i}{M_k}=0$, equation 8.75 implies that

$$\sum_{i=1}^{I}\overline{\mathbf{x}}_i-\sum_{j=1}^{J}\overline{\mathbf{y}}_j=0. \qquad (8.76)$$

Since for some i or j, $M_k=\|\xi_i^S(\mathbf{P}^k)\|$ or $M_k=\|\eta_j(\mathbf{P}^k)\|$, for every value of k, it follows that for some i or j, $\|\mathbf{x}_i^k\|=1$ or $\|\mathbf{y}_j^k\|=1$, for all k. Therefore, for some i or j, $\|\overline{\mathbf{x}}_i\|=1$ or $\|\overline{\mathbf{y}}_j\|=1$ and hence $(\overline{\mathbf{x}},\overline{\mathbf{y}})=(\overline{\mathbf{x}}_1,\ldots,\overline{\mathbf{x}}_I;\overline{\mathbf{y}}_1,\ldots,\overline{\mathbf{y}}_J)\neq 0$. Hence, equation 8.76 implies that $(\overline{\mathbf{x}},\overline{\mathbf{y}})$ is a nonzero feasible allocation with zero endowments. It was shown in the proof of theorem 3.54 (in section 3.7) that there can be no such allocation under assumptions 8.50–8.52. This contradiction proves statement 8.71.

The theory of ordinary differential equations (Coddington and Levinson 1955, 6, 10, 15; Hartman 1964, 12–15) implies that if $\underline{\mathbf{P}}$ belongs to the domain of definition of z^S then there exists $\overline{t}\in(0,\infty]$ and a differentiable function $\mathbf{P}$: $[0,\overline{t})\to\mathbb{R}_+^N$ such that $\frac{d\mathbf{P}(t)}{dt}=z^S(\mathbf{P}(t))$, for all t, $\mathbf{P}(0)=\underline{\mathbf{P}}$, either $\overline{t}=\infty$ or $\overline{t}<\infty$, and, if $\overline{t}<\infty$, either $\{z^S(\mathbf{P}(t))\mid 0\le t<\overline{t}\}$ is unbounded or $\lim_{t\to\overline{t}}\mathbf{P}(t)$ exists and belongs to the boundary of the domain of definition of z^S. Because $\|z^S(\mathbf{P}(t))\|$ is decreasing as a function of t by inequality 8.70, it follows that $\{z^S(\mathbf{P}(t))\mid 0\le t<\overline{t}\}$ is bounded. If $\lim_{t\to\overline{t}}\mathbf{P}(t)$ exists and belongs to the boundary of the domain of definition of z^S, then statement 8.71 implies that $\lim_{t\to\overline{t}}\|z^S(\mathbf{P}(t))\|=\infty$, which is impossible. Therefore, $\overline{t}=\infty$.

Because the function h defined by equation 8.61 is differentiable and strictly convex, equation 8.68, which asserts that $Dh(\mathbf{P})=-z^S(\mathbf{P})$, implies that h achieves a minimum at any price vector $\mathbf{P}$ such that $z^S(\mathbf{P})=0$. A short-run equilibrium price vector satisfies this equation, because, by proposition 8.60 (in section 8.3) and by assumption 8.71, an equilibrium price vector is strictly positive, so that no commodity can be in excess supply. The same proposition implies that the short-run equilibrium price vector is unique. Call it $\mathbf{P}^E$. The objective is to prove that

$$\lim_{t\to\infty} \mathbf{P}(t) = \mathbf{P}^E.$$

A first step of the proof is to show that

$$\lim_{t\to\infty} \|z^S(\mathbf{P}(t))\| = 0. \tag{8.77}$$

Equation 8.77 is valid because

$$\frac{dh(\mathbf{P}(t))}{dt} = -z^S(\mathbf{P}(t)).z^S(\mathbf{P}(t)),$$

by equation 8.67, so that $h(\mathbf{P}(t))$ decreases with t as long as $\mathbf{P}(t)$ does not equal the equilibrium price vector $\mathbf{P}^E$. Furthermore, $z^S(\mathbf{P}(t)).z^S(\mathbf{P}(t))$ decreases with t, by inequality 8.70. Hence, if equation 8.77 is not valid, then $\|z^S(\mathbf{P}(t))\|^2 = z^S(\mathbf{P}(t)).z^S(\mathbf{P}(t))$ remains bounded away from zero, so that $h(\mathbf{P}(t))$ diverges to $-\infty$. Since this implication contradicts the fact that h achieves a finite minimum at $\mathbf{P}^E$, equation 8.77 is valid.

The next task is to prove the statement that

$$\text{for every number } r \text{ such that } r \geq h(\mathbf{P}^E),\ \{\mathbf{P} \mid h(\mathbf{P}) \leq r\} \text{ is bounded.} \tag{8.78}$$

It is sufficient to prove that

$$\text{for every number } r \geq h(\mathbf{P}^E),\ \{\mathbf{q} \in \mathbb{R}^N \mid h(\mathbf{P}^E + \mathbf{q}) \leq r\} \text{ is bounded.} \tag{8.79}$$

Suppose that statement 8.79 is false. Then, there exists a sequence $\mathbf{q}^n$, for $n = 1, 2, \ldots,$ such that $\|\mathbf{q}^n\|$ diverges to infinity as n goes to infinity, and $h(\mathbf{P}^E + \mathbf{q}^n) \leq r$, for all n. Without loss of generality, we may assume that $\|\mathbf{q}^n\| > 1$, for all n. Then,

$$\mathbf{P}^E + \|\mathbf{q}^n\|^{-1}\mathbf{q}^n = (1 - \|\mathbf{q}^n\|^{-1})\mathbf{P}^E + \|\mathbf{q}^n\|^{-1}(\mathbf{P}^E + \mathbf{q}^n),$$

for all n. Because h is a convex function,

$$\begin{aligned} &h\left(\mathbf{P}^E + \|\mathbf{q}^n\|^{-1}\mathbf{q}^n\right) = h\left((1 - \|\mathbf{q}^n\|^{-1})\mathbf{P}^E + \|\mathbf{q}^n\|^{-1}(\mathbf{P}^E + \mathbf{q}^n)\right) \\ &\leq (1 - \|\mathbf{q}^n\|^{-1})h(\mathbf{P}^E) + \|\mathbf{q}^n\|^{-1}h(\mathbf{P}^E + \mathbf{q}^n) \\ &\leq (1 - \|\mathbf{q}^n\|^{-1})h(\mathbf{P}^E) + \|\mathbf{q}^n\|^{-1}r, \end{aligned} \tag{8.80}$$

for all n. Because the sequence $\|\mathbf{q}^n\|^{-1}\mathbf{q}^n$ is bounded, it has a convergent subsequence by the Bolzano-Weierstrass theorem. I index this sequence by n again, so that I may assume that the $\lim_{n\to\infty} \|\mathbf{q}^n\|^{-1}\mathbf{q}^n = \overline{\mathbf{q}}$, where $\|\overline{\mathbf{q}}\| = 1$. If we go to the limit in inequality 8.80 and use the fact that $\lim_{n\to\infty} \|\mathbf{q}^n\| = \infty$ and that h is continuous, we see that

$$h(\mathbf{P}^E + \overline{\mathbf{q}}) \leq h(\mathbf{P}^E).$$

Since h achieves its minimum at $\mathbf{P}^E$, we see that

$$h(\mathbf{P}^E + \overline{\mathbf{q}}) = h(\mathbf{P}^E). \tag{8.81}$$

Since h is minimized at a unique price vector and $\overline{\mathbf{q}} \neq 0$, equation 8.81 is impossible. This contradiction proves statement 8.79 and hence statement 8.78.

I can now prove that

$$\lim_{t\to\infty} \mathbf{P}(t) = \mathbf{P}^E. \tag{8.82}$$

Because $h(\mathbf{P}(t))$ is nonincreasing in t, by inequality 8.67, it follows that $h(\mathbf{P}(t)) \leq h(\underline{\mathbf{P}})$, for all t, where $\underline{\mathbf{P}} = \mathbf{P}(0)$. Hence by statement 8.78, $\{P(t) \mid t \geq 0\}$ is a bounded set. If equation 8.82 is false, then there exists a positive number ε and a sequence of times, t_k, for $k = 1, 2, \ldots$, such that $\lim_{k\to\infty} t_k = \infty$ and $\|\mathbf{P}(t_k) - \mathbf{P}^E\| \geq \varepsilon$, for all k. Because the sequence $\mathbf{P}(t_k)$ is bounded, it has a convergent subsequence, by the Bolzano-Weierstrass theorem. I call this sequence $\mathbf{P}(t_k)$ again. Let $\mathbf{q} = \lim_{k\to\infty} \mathbf{P}(t_k)$. Then,

$$\|\mathbf{P}^E - \mathbf{q}\| \geq \varepsilon. \tag{8.83}$$

By statement 8.77, $\lim_{k\to\infty} \|z^S(\mathbf{P}(t_k))\| = 0$. Since the function z^S is continuous, $z^S(\mathbf{q}) = 0$, so that $\mathbf{q}$ minimizes the function h and

$$\mathbf{q} = \mathbf{P}^E, \tag{8.84}$$

by the uniqueness of the minimizer of h. Since inequality 8.83 contradicts equation 8.84, equation 8.82 must be valid.

I now state in full the theorem that has been proved.

THEOREM 8.72 Assume that the economy satisfies assumptions 8.46, 8.50–8.53, 8.58, 8.70, and 8.71. Then, the function $z^S(\mathbf{P}) = \sum_{i=1}^{I}(\xi_i^S(\mathbf{P}) - \mathbf{e}_i) - \sum_{j=1}^{J} \eta_j(\mathbf{P})$ has a nonempty domain of definition and if $\underline{\mathbf{P}}$ belongs to this domain of definition, the differential equation

$$\frac{d\mathbf{P}(t)}{dt} = z^S(\mathbf{P}(t))$$

with the initial condition $\mathbf{P}(0) = \underline{\mathbf{P}}$ has a solution $\mathbf{P}(t)$, for all $t \geq 0$, such that

$$\lim_{t\to\infty} \mathbf{P}(t) = \mathbf{P}^E,$$

where $\mathbf{P}^E$ is the unique short-run equilibrium price vector.

The major weakness of this theorem is assumption 8.71, that, for all i, $\xi_i^S(\mathbf{P}) \gg 0$, for all $\mathbf{P}$ in the domain of definition of the function ξ_i^S. This assumption may be eliminated at the cost of complicating the argument. The argument for this case may be found in Bewley (1980), though there is no production in that paper.

I now deliver on the promise made earlier to prove that the domain of definition of z^S is convex. The convexity of this domain adds to the orderliness of the dynamic system defined by equation 8.60.

PROPOSITION 8.73 If u_i is continuous and strictly concave, for all i, and Y_j is closed and strictly convex, for all j, then the function z^S is defined on a convex subset of $\mathbb{R}^N_+$.

Proof. Since the domain of definition of z^S is the intersection of the domains of definition of the functions ξ_i^S and η_j, over i and j, it is sufficient to show that each of these sets is convex. It is sufficient to prove that the domain of definition of η_j is convex, since ξ_i^S can be defined in the same way as η_j. In order to see that this last statement is correct, let $X_i = \{(-\mathbf{x}, v) \mid \mathbf{x} \in \mathbb{R}^N_+ \text{ and } v \leq u_i(\mathbf{x})\}$. The set X_i is closed and strictly convex, since u_i is continuous and strictly concave. Then, $\xi_i^S(\mathbf{P})$ solves the problem

$$\max_{(-\mathbf{x}, v)\in X_k} [\lambda_i^{-1} v - \mathbf{P}.\mathbf{x}].$$

That is, $\xi_i^S(\mathbf{P})$ maximizes the linear function $(\mathbf{P}, \lambda_i^{-1}).(-\mathbf{x}, v)$ over the closed and strictly convex set X_i, just as $\eta_j(\mathbf{P})$ maximizes the linear function $\mathbf{P}.y$ over the closed and strictly convex set Y_j.

I show that η_j is defined on a convex set of N-vectors. Let U be the domain of definition of η_j. I must show that if $\mathbf{P}^1$ and $\mathbf{P}^2$ belong to U, then so does $\mathbf{P} = \alpha\mathbf{P}^1 + (1-\alpha)\mathbf{P}^2$, for any α such that $0 < \alpha < 1$. Let $Y_j^T = \{\mathbf{y} \in Y_j \mid \mathbf{P}.\mathbf{y} \geq \mathbf{P}.\eta_j(\mathbf{P}^1) \text{ and } \mathbf{P}.\mathbf{y} \geq \mathbf{P}.\eta_j(\mathbf{P}^2)\}$, where the superscript "T" stands for *truncation*. Since $\eta_j(\mathbf{P}^1)$ and $\eta_j(\mathbf{P}^2)$ both belong to Y_j, $\eta_j(\mathbf{P})$ is the set of solutions of the problem

$$\max_{\mathbf{y}\in Y_j^T} \mathbf{P.y}. \tag{8.85}$$

The set Y_j^T is nonempty, because $\eta_j(\mathbf{P}^1) \in Y_j^T$, if $\mathbf{P}.\eta_j(\mathbf{P}^1) \geq \mathbf{P}.\eta_j(\mathbf{P}^2)$ and $\eta_j(\mathbf{P}^2) \in Y_j^T$, if $\mathbf{P}.\eta_j(\mathbf{P}^2) \geq \mathbf{P}.\eta_j(\mathbf{P}^1)$. I show that if $\mathbf{y} \in Y_j^T$, then

$$\mathbf{P}^1.\mathbf{y} \geq \mathbf{P}^1.\eta_j(\mathbf{P}^2). \tag{8.86}$$

This inequality follows from canceling like terms on the extreme left- and right-hand sides of the following inequalities:

$$\begin{aligned} &\alpha\mathbf{P}^1.\mathbf{y} + (1-\alpha)\mathbf{P}^2.\eta_j(\mathbf{P}^2) \geq \alpha\mathbf{P}^1.\mathbf{y} + (1-\alpha)\mathbf{P}^2.\mathbf{y} = \mathbf{P.y} \\ &\geq \mathbf{P}.\eta_j(\mathbf{P}^2) = \alpha\mathbf{P}^1.\eta_j(\mathbf{P}^2) + (1-\alpha)\mathbf{P}^2.\eta_j(\mathbf{P}^2), \end{aligned}$$

where the first inequality follows from the definition of $\eta_j(\mathbf{P}^2)$ and the second inequality applies because $\mathbf{y} \in Y_j^T$. A similar argument proves that if $\mathbf{y} \in Y_j^T$, then

$$\mathbf{P}^2.\mathbf{y} \geq \mathbf{P}^2.\eta_j(\mathbf{P}^1). \tag{8.87}$$

Let $C_1 = \{\mathbf{y} \in Y_j \mid \mathbf{P}^1.\mathbf{y} \geq \mathbf{P}^1.\eta_j(\mathbf{P}^2)\}$ and $C_2 = \{\mathbf{y} \in Y_j \mid \mathbf{P}^2.\mathbf{y} \geq \mathbf{P}^2.\eta_j(\mathbf{P}^1)\}$. Inequalities 8.86 and 8.87 imply that Y_j^T is contained in $C_1 \cap C_2$. Since $\eta_j(\mathbf{P})$, if it exists, is the set of solutions of problem 8.85, it is also the set of solutions of the problem

$$\max_{\mathbf{y}\in C_1\cap C_2} \mathbf{P.y} \tag{8.88}$$

Because Y_j^T is nonempty, the set $C_1 \cap C_2$ is also nonempty. Because the set Y_j is closed and strictly convex and because $\eta_j(\mathbf{P}^1)$ and $\eta_j(\mathbf{P}^2)$ exist, an argument just like that used to prove statement 8.78 proves that both C_1 and C_2 are bounded and hence compact. Therefore, $C_1 \cap C_2$ is compact and so proposition 3.14 (in section 3.2) implies that problem 8.88 has a solution and therefore that $\eta_j(\mathbf{P})$ is not empty. That is, $\mathbf{P}$ belongs to U, as was to be proved. ▪

As was mentioned earlier, solutions to the differential equation 8.60 may not converge, if market demand is defined using Walrasian rather than short-run demand. Such instability occurs in the next example due to Scarf (1960). Before turning to the example, I note that Walras' law implies that any solution of differential equation 8.60 remains on a sphere of constant radius in the N-space of price vectors. In order to see that this assertion is true, observe that the length squared of the price vector, $\mathbf{p}(t)$, is $\mathbf{p}(t).\mathbf{p}(t) = \sum_{n=1}^{N} p_n^2(t)$. If we take the derivative with respect to t, we find that

$$\frac{d\mathbf{p}(t).\mathbf{p}(t)}{dt} = 2\sum_{n=1}^{N} p_n(t) z_n(\mathbf{p}(t)) = 0,$$

where the second equation follows from Walras' law.

EXAMPLE 8.74 (Scarf's example of instability) There are three commodities, three consumers, and no firm. The utilities and endowments of the three consumers are as follows:

$$u_1(x_1, x_2, x_3) = \min(x_1, x_2), \mathbf{e}_1 = (1, 0, 0),$$
$$u_2(x_1, x_2, x_3) = \min(x_2, x_3), \mathbf{e}_2 = (0, 1, 0),$$
$$u_3(x_1, x_2, x_3) = \min(x_1, x_3), \mathbf{e}_3 = (0, 0, 1).$$

The Walrasian demand function for consumer 1 is

$$\xi_1(\mathbf{p}) = \left(\frac{p_1}{p_1 + p_2}, \frac{p_1}{p_1 + p_2}, 0\right),$$

so that the consumer's excess demand function is

$$\xi_1(\mathbf{p}) - \mathbf{e}_1 = \left(-\frac{p_2}{p_1 + p_2}, \frac{p_1}{p_1 + p_2}, 0\right).$$

Similarly, the excess demand function for consumer 2 is

$$\xi_2(\mathbf{p}) - \mathbf{e}_2 = \left(0, -\frac{p_3}{p_2 + p_3}, \frac{p_2}{p_2 + p_3}\right),$$

and the excess demand function of consumer 3 is

$$\xi_3(\mathbf{p}) - \mathbf{e}_3 = \left(\frac{p_3}{p_1 + p_3}, 0, -\frac{p_1}{p_1 + p_3}\right).$$

The market excess demand function is therefore

$$z(\mathbf{p}) = \left(-\frac{p_2}{p_1 + p_2} + \frac{p_3}{p_1 + p_3}, \frac{p_1}{p_1 + p_2} - \frac{p_3}{p_2 + p_3}, \frac{p_2}{p_2 + p_3} - \frac{p_1}{p_1 + p_3}\right). \tag{8.89}$$

It follows immediately that $z(1, 1, 1) = 0$, so that the $(1, 1, 1)$ is an equilibrium price vector. It is also the unique equilibrium vector of length $\sqrt{3}$, because by elementary algebra the equation $z(\mathbf{p}) = 0$ implies that $p_1, = p_2 = p_3$. Let $\mathbf{p}(t)$ be the solution to differential equation 8.60 with $z(\mathbf{p})$ as just defined, and suppose that $\|\mathbf{p}(0)\| = \sqrt{3}$. Then, $\|\mathbf{p}(t)\| = \sqrt{3}$, for all t, because z satisfies Walras' law. I next verify that $p_1(t)p_2(t)p_3(t) = p_1(0)p_2(0)p_3(0)$, for all t, so that the solution to equation 8.60 stays on the closed curve defined by the two equations $\|\mathbf{p}\| = \sqrt{3}$ and $p_1p_2p_3 = p_1(0)p_2(0)p_3(0)$ and hence cannot converge to the equilibrium $\mathbf{p} = (1, 1, 1)$. To show that $p_1(t)p_2(t)p_3(t) = p_1(0)p_2(0)p_3(0)$, for all t, it is sufficient to check that $\frac{dp_1(t)p_2(t)p_3(t)}{dt} = 0$. If we calculate this derivative, we find by substitution from equation 8.89 that

$$\frac{dp_1p_2p_3}{dt} = p_2p_3\frac{dp_1}{dt} + p_1p_3\frac{dp_2}{dt} + p_1p_2\frac{dp_3}{dt}$$
$$= p_2p_3z_1(\mathbf{p}) + p_1p_3z_2(\mathbf{p}) + p_1p_2z_3(\mathbf{p})$$
$$= p_2p_3\left(-\frac{p_2}{p_1 + p_2} + \frac{p_3}{p_1 + p_3}\right) + p_1p_3\left(\frac{p_1}{p_1 + p_2} - \frac{p_3}{p_2 + p_3}\right)$$
$$+ p_1p_2\left(\frac{p_2}{p_2 + p_3} - \frac{p_1}{p_1 + p_3}\right)$$
$$= -\frac{p_2^2p_3}{p_1 + p_2} + \frac{p_2p_3^2}{p_1 + p_3} + \frac{p_1^2p_3}{p_1 + p_2} - \frac{p_1p_3^2}{p_2 + p_3} + \frac{p_1p_2^2}{p_2 + p_3} - \frac{p_1^2p_3}{p_1 + p_3}$$
$$= \frac{p_3(p_1^2 - p_2^2)}{p_1 + p_2} + \frac{p_2(p_3^2 - p_1^2)}{p_1 + p_3} + \frac{p_1(p_2^2 - p_3^2)}{p_2 + p_3}$$
$$= p_3(p_1 - p_2) + p_2(p_3 - p_1) + p_1(p_2 - p_3) = 0,$$

where for notational convenience I have dropped the variable t from the price functions, $p_n(t)$.

This completes the proof that solutions to differential equation 8.60 do not converge to the unique equilibrium relative price vector unless they start at it.

Scarf's example has the drawback that the utility functions are not differentiable. With more work, it is possible to construct an example of instability with differentiable utility functions. A theorem of Debreu (1974) implies that an example can be made with strictly concave and continuous utility functions. The beauty of Scarf's example is the ease with which it may be understood.

Problem Set

1. For each of the utility functions listed below, compute the short-run demand function, ξ^S, as a function of the price vector. That is, compute the functions $x_1 = \xi_1^S(P_1, P_2)$ and $x_2 = \xi_2^S(P_1, P_2)$ that satisfy the equations

$$\frac{\partial u(x_1, x_2)}{\partial x_1} = \lambda P_1 \text{ and } \frac{\partial u(x_1, x_2)}{\partial x_2} = \lambda P_2,$$

where λ is a positive constant.

(a) $u(x_1, x_2) = a\ln(x_1) + b\ln(x_2)$, where $a > 0$ and $b > 0$.
(b) $u(x_1, x_2) = Ax_1^a x_2^b$, where $A > 0$, $a > 0$, $b > 0$, and $a + b < 1$.
(c) $u(x_1, x_2) = a\sqrt{x_1} + b\sqrt{x_2}$, where $a > 0$, $b > 0$.
(d) $u(x_1, x_2) = ax_1 - bx_1^2 + cx_2 - dx_2^2 + ex_1x_2$, where $a > 0$, $b > 0$, $c > 0$, $d > 0$, and $4bd - e^2 > 0$.

2. For each of the utility functions in problem 1, compute the short-run demand curve for good 1 when $\lambda = P_2 = 1$. That is, calculate the function $\xi_1^S(P_1, 1)$.

3. For each of the utility functions in problem 1, compute the surplus function

$$h(P_1, P_2) = \lambda^{-1}u_i(\xi_1^S(P_1, P_2)) - P_1\left[\xi_1^S(P_1, P_2) - e_1\right] - P_2\left[\xi_2^S(P_1, P_2) - e_2\right],$$

where $\mathbf{e} = (e_1, e_2)$ is a positive endowment vector.

4. Verify that in each of the utility functions of problem 1,

$$\frac{\partial h(P_1, P_2)}{\partial P_k} = e_k - \xi_k^S(P_1, P_2),$$

for $k = 1$ and $k = 2$.

5. Consider a consumer with utility function

$$u(x_1, x_2) = x_1 - \frac{x_1^2}{2} + 5x_2 - \frac{x_2^2}{2}$$

and with endowment $\mathbf{e} = (0, 1)$. Let the price of good 1 be p and the price of good 2 be 1.

(a) Calculate the consumer's Walrasian demand, $x_1(p)$, for good 1 as a function of p.
(b) Calculate the price, $\overline{p}$, such that $x_1(\overline{p}) = \frac{1}{2}$.
(c) Calculate the consumer's surplus when the price is $\overline{p}$, where the surplus is defined using the demand function $x_1(p)$.
(d) Calculate the consumer's marginal utility of money, $\overline{\lambda}$, when $p = \overline{p}$.
(e) Calculate the consumer's short-run demand function, $x_1^S(p)$, when his or her marginal utility of money is $\overline{\lambda}$.
(f) Calculate the consumer's surplus when $p = \overline{p}$ where the surplus is defined using the demand function $x_1^S(p)$.

6. Let $u(x) = ax - \frac{b}{2}x^2$, be the utility of a single consumer for a single commodity, where $a > 0$ and $b > 0$. Let $\lambda = 1$ be the consumer's marginal utility of unit of account.

(a) Compute the consumer's short-run demand function, $\xi^S(P)$, where P is a positive number.
(b) Let e be the consumer's endowment of the single commodity. Compute the equilibrium price, $\overline{P}$, at which $\xi^S(\overline{P}) = e$.
(c) Compute the solution of the differential equation $\frac{dP(t)}{dt} = \xi^S(P(t)) - e$ for an arbitrary initial condition, and show that it converges to $\overline{P}$.

7. Let there be two commodities, let the utility function of a consumer be

$$u(x_1, x_2) = x_1 - x_1^2 + x_2 - x_2^2 + x_1 x_2,$$

let the endowment of the consumer be

$$\mathbf{e} = \left(\frac{1}{2}, \frac{1}{2}\right),$$

and let the consumer's marginal utility of unit of account be $\lambda = 1$.

(a) Compute the consumer's short-run demand function for both commodities,

$$\left(\xi_1^S(P_1, P_2), \xi_2^S(P_1, P_2)\right).$$

(b) Compute the equilibrium price vector $(\overline{P}_1, \overline{P}_2)$ that satisfies the equation

$$\left(\xi_1^S(\overline{P}_1, \overline{P}_2), \xi_2^S(\overline{P}_1, \overline{P}_2)\right) = \left(\frac{1}{2}, \frac{1}{2}\right).$$

(c) Compute the solution to the equations

$$\frac{dP_1(t)}{dt} = \xi_1^S(P_1(t), P_2(t)) - \frac{1}{2}$$

and

$$\frac{dP_2(t)}{dt} = \xi_2^S(P_1(t), P_2(t)) - \frac{1}{2}$$

with arbitrary initial conditions, and show that it converges to $(\overline{P}_1, \overline{P}_2)$.

— 9 —

Samuelson's Overlapping Generations Model

This and the following chapter treat issues that apply only in the long run, namely, capital accumulation and the distribution of consumption between the old and young. In the usual Arrow-Debreu model, there are no births and deaths; new people never appear, and no one disappears from the model. This lack of population turnover may indicate that the model was intended by its creators for the analysis of short time spans. Population renewal is easy to include, though it changes little in the theory unless the time horizon is infinite. An unbounded horizon changes the theory fundamentally. It also complicates the analysis, but the extra complexity can be reduced by considering stationary states. In a finite horizon model with births and deaths, the assertions of standard equilibrium theory remain valid; equilibria exist and are Pareto optimal. When time continues forever, however, equilibria may fail to be Pareto optimal.

The origin of the inefficiency may be visualized with the aid of the following image. Think of a finite group of people in line, all facing in the same direction, with a neighbor to the left and another to the right of everyone except for those at the ends of the line. Suppose that each has two chocolate bars. If each hands one bar to the person on their left, the person on the extreme right ends up with only one bar, the one on the extreme left ends up with three, and everyone else ends up with two. This handing off of chocolates results in no Pareto improvement, since the person on the extreme left gains at the expense of the person on the extreme right. The situation differs if the line goes on forever to the right; after everyone has handed a chocolate to the left, the person on the extreme left gains one bar and no one loses.

To see the connection between this story and the Pareto optimality of equilibria, imagine a model in which time is discrete and unending, there is only one commodity, and one person is born in each period and lives for two periods, so that there is one old and one young person alive at any moment. Each person is endowed with two units of the one commodity in youth and none in old age. All consumers have the same increasing utility function of lifetime consumption, and this function is strictly concave and symmetric with respect to consumption in youth and old age. This is Samuelson's (1958) overlapping generations model. The only possible equilibrium allocation has everyone consume their entire endowment in youth and nothing in old age, for people can trade only with someone who is alive at the same time as they are and old people have nothing to give the young in exchange for some of their endowment. This allocation is not Pareto optimal, for everyone would be better off if each young person gave one unit of consumption to the contemporary old person. If this were done, the old person in the initial period would have one unit to consume rather than none, and everyone else would have one unit in youth and one in old age, which they would prefer to having two units in youth and none in old age because of the symmetry and strict concavity of the utility function. Giving one unit to the old corresponds to passing a chocolate bar to the left in the previous example. Giving one unit to the old would not result in a Pareto improvement if the time horizon were finite, because the youth in the last period would give up one unit of consumption and gain nothing in return.

This analogy with chocolate is to some extent misleading, because it makes it seem that there could be no Pareto optimal allocation in an infinite horizon model, since it is always possible to draw more from the future. The analogy can be improved by having the people start with one chocolate bar in each hand and give the chocolate bar in the left hand to their left neighbor's right hand. The passing to the left then leaves everyone but the person on the extreme left with two bars in their right hand and none in their left. If they have a preference for having a bar in each hand, the change leaves them worse off. The chocolate in the left and right hands corresponds to consumption in youth and old age, respectively.

It is possible to realize equal sharing of endowments as an equilibrium allocation by having a means of payment or money that people can carry from one period to the next. The old could use this money to buy consumption, and the young could save their money and spend it when they were old. In the context of modern societies, it is natural to think of this money as a government obligation or debt, and there is no reason the government could not use tax revenues to pay interest on its obligations. We will see that the allocation of any stationary equilibrium with a nonnegative interest rate is Pareto optimal, provided the taxes are lump sum. The interest rate and taxes may be regarded, respectively, as monetary and fiscal policy that bring the economy to a desired equilibrium. In the Samuelson overlapping generations model, these policies affect only the distribution of welfare between the young and the old; the higher is the interest rate, the higher is the consumption of the old relative to that of the young.

Monetary and fiscal policy become more interesting if capital is introduced into the model, for then the interest rate affects both the rate at which capital is accumulated and the total stock of capital in a stationary equilibrium. The higher the interest rate, the lower the stock of capital in the stationary state. The Samuelson model with production and capital is the model of Diamond (1965) and is the topic of chapter 10. In this chapter, I focus on the Samuelson model, for it provides an uncluttered context in which to introduce new concepts associated with overlapping generations models.[1]

9.1 Overlapping Generations with a Finite Time Horizon

I introduce birth and death into the Arrow-Debreu model. Recall that underlying the model is a set of dated events, Γ, which I assume to be finite. A dated event (t, B) in Γ is said to follow a dated event (s, A), if $t > s$ and B is a subset of A. (Recall that $A \in \mathcal{S}_s$ and $B \in \mathcal{S}_t$, where $\mathcal{S}_t$ refines $\mathcal{S}_s$.)

DEFINITION 9.1 The set of dated events, Γ, is called a *tree* if there is a unique dated event (t, A) in Γ such that every dated event in Γ follows (t, A). The dated event (t, A) may be thought of as the *root* of the tree.

DEFINITION 9.2 If Γ is a set of dated events, a subset, Δ, of Γ is said to be a *subtree* of Γ if Δ is a tree.

EXAMPLE 9.3 The heavily lined part of the tree in figure 9.1 is a subtree of the overall tree of dated events.

Suppose that every consumer i is alive in a set of dated events, Γ_i that is a subtree of Γ. Assume that there are N goods and services in each dated event and that $e_{i,(t,A),n} = 0$ if (t, A) does not belong to Γ_i, where $\mathbf{e}_i \in \mathbb{R}^{\Gamma \times N} = \{\mathbf{x}: \Gamma \rightarrow \mathbb{R}^N\}$ is consumer i's endowment vector. Assume also

1. The point of view toward overlapping generations models presented in this and the succeeding chapter was developed in Bewley (1981b, 1981c).

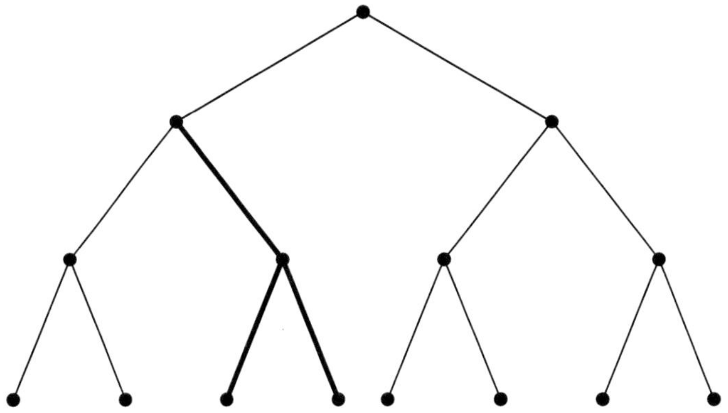

Figure 9.1 Examples of a tree and subtree

that if $\mathbf{x}$ belongs to $\mathbb{R}_+^{\Gamma \times N}$, then $u_i(\mathbf{x})$ does not depend on $x_{i,(t,A),n}$ if (t, A) does not belong to Γ_i. (Another way to say this is that $u_i(\mathbf{x}) = v(\pi_i(\mathbf{x}))$, for some function $v: \mathbb{R}_+^{\Gamma_i \times N} \to \mathbb{R}$, where π_i is the natural projection from $\mathbb{R}_+^{\Gamma \times N}$ to $\mathbb{R}_+^{\Gamma_i \times N} = \{\mathbf{x}: \Gamma_i \to \mathbb{R}^N\}$.) If the utility functions u_i are locally nonsatiated, then any equilibrium allocation for the economy $(u_i, \mathbf{e}_i)_{i=1}^I$ is Pareto optimal. It is also not hard to show that an equilibrium exists provided the utility functions are continuous, strictly increasing, and quasi-concave. This existence theorem may be proved by adapting either the proof of theorem 4.24 (in section 4.8) or that of theorem 5.25 (in section 5.3).

In the above model, an Arrow-Debreu equilibrium can be interpreted as an Arrow equilibrium in which no one is required to trade before they are born. This interpretation as an Arrow equilibrium would be impossible if the sets Γ_i were not trees, for if a Γ_i had no root, then for the equilibrium to be Pareto optimal, consumer i might have to buy insurance before being born on events occurring during his or her initial period of life.

9.2 Inefficiency with an Infinite Horizon

I now describe in detail the example mentioned earlier of an equilibrium with an allocation that is not Pareto optimal. I begin by completing the description of Samuelson's overlapping generations model. It has no uncertainty and has infinitely many time periods, $t = -1, 0, 1, 2, \ldots$. One person, person t, is born in each period t, for $t \geq -1$. Person t dies at the end of period $t + 1$, so that each person lives for two periods and there are one old person and one young person alive at any time. There are N commodities in each period. The consumption vector of person t is $\mathbf{x}_t = (\mathbf{x}_{t0}, \mathbf{x}_{t1})$, where $\mathbf{x}_{t0}$ and $\mathbf{x}_{t1}$ are the consumption vectors in periods t and $t+1$, respectively. Similarly, $\mathbf{e}_t = (\mathbf{e}_{t0}, \mathbf{e}_{t1})$ is person t's endowment, where $\mathbf{e}_{t0}$ and $\mathbf{e}_{t1}$ are the endowment vectors in periods t and $t+1$, respectively. An *allocation* is a nonnegative vector, $\mathbf{x} = (\mathbf{x}_{-1,1}, (\mathbf{x}_{00}, \mathbf{x}_{01}), (\mathbf{x}_{10}, \mathbf{x}_{11}), \ldots)$, with infinitely many components. It is *feasible* if

$$\mathbf{x}_{t-1,1} + \mathbf{x}_{t0} \leq \mathbf{e}_{t-1,1} + \mathbf{e}_{t0},$$

for all $t \geq 0$. The utility function of person t is $u_t(\mathbf{x}_0, \mathbf{x}_1)$, where $\mathbf{x}_0$ and $\mathbf{x}_1$ are the consumption bundles in youth and old age, respectively. The consumption bundle of the youth born in period -1 is assumed to be fixed and to equal $\overline{\mathbf{x}}_{-1,0}$.

Notice that in each period the Samuelson model is like an Edgeworth box model with N commodities. There is no production and there are only two people, the young and old person, alive at that time. In this sense, the Samuelson model is a sequence of Edgeworth box models with the only tie between neighboring ones being that one person lives in both.

Throughout this chapter and the next, I assume that the endowments and utility functions are independent of t. That is, $(\mathbf{e}_{t0}, \mathbf{e}_{t1}) = (\mathbf{e}_0, \mathbf{e}_1)$ and $u_t(\mathbf{x}_0, \mathbf{x}_1) = u(\mathbf{x}_0, \mathbf{x}_1)$, for all t.

DEFINITION 9.4 An *Arrow-Debreu equilibrium* for the Samuelson model consists of $(\overline{\mathbf{x}}, \mathbf{p})$ that satisfies the conditions

1. $\overline{\mathbf{x}}$ is a feasible allocation
2. $\mathbf{p} = (\mathbf{p}_0, \mathbf{p}_1, \ldots)$ is an infinite sequence of nonnegative N-vectors of prices, not all of which are 0,
3. for every $t \geq 0$, $(\overline{\mathbf{x}}_{t0}, \overline{\mathbf{x}}_{t1})$ solves the problem

$$\max_{\mathbf{x}_0 \in \mathbb{R}^N_+, \mathbf{x}_1 \in \mathbb{R}^N_+} u(\mathbf{x}_0, \mathbf{x}_1)$$

$$\text{s.t.} \quad \mathbf{p}_t . \mathbf{x}_0 + \mathbf{p}_{t+1} . \mathbf{x}_1 \leq \mathbf{p}_t . \mathbf{e}_0 + \mathbf{p}_{t+1} . \mathbf{e}_1$$

4. $\overline{\mathbf{x}}_{-1,1}$ solves the problem

$$\max_{\mathbf{x}_1 \in \mathbb{R}^N_+} u(\overline{\mathbf{x}}_{-1,0}, \mathbf{x}_1)$$

$$\text{s.t.} \quad \mathbf{p}_0 . \mathbf{x}_1 \leq \mathbf{p}_0 . \mathbf{e}_1$$

5. for all t and n, $p_{tn} = 0$, if

$$\overline{x}_{t,0,n} + \overline{x}_{t-1,1,n} < e_{0n} + e_{1n}$$

In an Arrow-Debreu equilibrium $(\overline{\mathbf{x}}, \mathbf{p})$, all trading occurs in period -1 and p_{tn} is the price (in terms of the unit of account of period -1) of commodity n delivered in period t.

Arrow-Debreu equilibrium is not believable in the context of an overlapping generations model, because it requires that consumers born after period -1 trade on markets for forward claims that are open only at period -1. We may avoid this difficulty by using Arrow equilibria.

DEFINITION 9.5 An *Arrow equilibrium* consists of $(\overline{\mathbf{x}}, \mathbf{a}, \mathbf{P}, \mathbf{q})$ satisfying the conditions

1. $\overline{\mathbf{x}}$ is a feasible allocation
2. $\mathbf{a} = (a_1, a_2, \ldots)$ is an infinite sequence of asset holdings
3. $\mathbf{P} = (\mathbf{P}_0, \mathbf{P}_1, \ldots)$ is a sequence of N-vectors of nonnegative money prices, not all equal to 0
4. $\mathbf{q} = (q_{0,1}, q_{1,2}, \ldots)$ is a sequence of nonnegative forward prices for unit of account
5. for each $t \geq 0$, $(\overline{\mathbf{x}}_{t0}, \overline{\mathbf{x}}_{t1}, a_{t+1})$, solves the problem
$$\max_{\mathbf{x}_0 \in \mathbb{R}^N_+, \mathbf{x}_1 \in \mathbb{R}^N_+, a \in \mathbb{R}} u(\mathbf{x}_0, \mathbf{x}_1)$$
$$\text{s.t.} \quad \mathbf{P}_t.\mathbf{x}_0 + q_{t,t+1} a \leq \mathbf{P}_t.\mathbf{e}_0 \text{ and}$$
$$\mathbf{P}_{t+1}.\mathbf{x}_1 \leq a + \mathbf{P}_{t+1}.\mathbf{e}_1$$
6. $\overline{\mathbf{x}}_{-1,1}$ solves the problem
$$\max_{\mathbf{x}_1 \in \mathbb{R}^N_+} u(\overline{\mathbf{x}}_{-1,0}, \mathbf{x}_1)$$
$$\text{s.t.} \quad \mathbf{P}_0.\mathbf{x}_1 \leq \mathbf{P}_0.\mathbf{e}_1$$
7. for each t and n, $P_{tn} = 0$, if
$$\overline{x}_{t,0,n} + \overline{x}_{t-1,1,n} < e_{0n} + e_{1n}$$

An Arrow equilibrium is simply an interpretation of an Arrow-Debreu equilibrium. Both equilibria have the same allocations. In an Arrow equilibrium $(\overline{\mathbf{x}}, \mathbf{a}, \mathbf{P}, \mathbf{q})$, the component P_{tn} is the price of commodity n delivered in period t and in terms of the unit of account of that period, a_t is the number of period t units of account purchased in period $t-1$ by the person born in that period, and $q_{t,t+1}$ is the price of period $t+1$ unit of account in terms of period t unit of account. The unborn must trade in an Arrow equilibrium, because in each period the young trade forward contracts in unit of account with the person born in the following period. The unborn are not required to trade, however, if these forward trades are made with an institution, such as a bank or government, that can make intertemporal commitments. A government is incorporated in the model in section 9.3.

I now describe an example, due to Samuelson (1958), of an Arrow-Debreu equilibrium that is not Pareto optimal.

EXAMPLE 9.6 (An inefficient equilibrium) In Samuelson's overlapping generations model, let $N = 1$ and let

$$e_0 = 1,\ e_1 = 0, \text{ and } u(x_0, x_1) = \ln(1 + x_0) + \ln(1 + x_1).$$

I show that the pair $(\overline{\mathbf{x}}, \mathbf{p})$ is an Arrow-Debreu equilibrium for this example, where $\mathbf{p} = (p_0, p_1, p_2, \ldots)$ with $p_t = 2^t$, for all t, and

$$\overline{\mathbf{x}} = (\overline{x}_{-1,1}, (\overline{x}_{00}, \overline{x}_{01}), (\overline{x}_{10}, \overline{x}_{11}), \ldots) = (0, (1, 0), (1, 0), \ldots).$$

The allocation $\overline{\mathbf{x}}$ is feasible, since it equals the endowment allocation. To check that $(\mathbf{p}, \overline{\mathbf{x}})$ is an Arrow-Debreu equilibrium, observe that the old person of period 0 cannot afford to buy anything, so that $\overline{\mathbf{x}}_{-1,1}$ must be zero. The utility maximization problem for the consumer born in period $t \geq 0$ is

$$\max_{x_0 \geq 0, x_1 \geq 0} [\ln(1 + x_0) + \ln(1 + x_1)]$$

$$\text{s.t.} \quad 2^t x_0 + 2^{t+1} x_1 \leq 2^t.$$

Because $(\overline{\mathbf{x}}_{10}, \overline{\mathbf{x}}_{11})$ equals the endowment, it satisfies the budget constraint of this problem. Its first-order conditions are

$$\frac{1}{1 + x_0} = \lambda_t 2^t \text{ and } \frac{1}{1 + x_1} = \lambda_t 2^{t+1},$$

which is true if

$$\frac{1 + x_0}{1 + x_1} = 2.$$

This equation is valid if $x_0 = 1$ and $x_1 = 0$, so that the equilibrium allocation does maximize each consumer's utility in his or her budget set.

The equilibrium allocation $\overline{\mathbf{x}}$ is not Pareto optimal, for the allocation $\underline{\mathbf{x}}$ Pareto dominates it, where $\underline{\mathbf{x}}$ is defined by the equations $\underline{x}_{t0} = \underline{x}_{t-1,1} = 1/2$, for all t. Person -1 is clearly better off with allocation $\underline{\mathbf{x}}$ rather than with $\overline{\mathbf{x}}$ because he or she receives $1/2$ in period 0 under $\underline{\mathbf{x}}$ and nothing under $\overline{\mathbf{x}}$.

People born in periods $t \geq 0$ prefer $\underline{\mathbf{x}}$, because

$$\begin{aligned}\ln(1+\underline{x}_{t0}) + \ln(1+\underline{x}_{t1}) &= \ln\left(\frac{3}{2}\right) + \ln\left(\frac{3}{2}\right) = \ln\left(\frac{9}{4}\right)\\ &> \ln 2 = \ln(1+1) + \ln(1+0) = \ln(1+\overline{x}_{t0}) + \ln(1+\overline{x}_{t1}).\end{aligned}$$

The equilibrium and Pareto dominating allocations just described are stationary in that no one's consumption depends on their date of birth. That is, none of $\overline{x}_{t0}$, $\overline{x}_{t1}$, $\underline{x}_{t0}$, and $\underline{x}_{t1}$ depend on t. Because these allocations are stationary, we may see the relation between them in figure 9.2. The abscissa represents consumption in youth, x_{t0}, by a person born in any period t. The ordinate represents consumption in old age by a person born in periods $t-1$ or t. The line segment with slope -1 represents the feasibility condition $x_{t0} + x_{t-1,1} = 1$. Any feasible stationary allocation must lie on this line, and the underscored allocation, $\underline{x}_{t0} = 0.5$ and $\underline{x}_{t1} = 0.5$, is at its midpoint. The equilibrium allocation, $\overline{x}_{t0} = 1$ and $\overline{x}_{t1} = 0$, lies at the right-hand endpoint of this segment and is labeled **e** for endowment. The flatter line segment with slope -0.5 is the equilibrium budget line of a consumer born in period t, where $t \geq 0$, namely,

$$\{(x_{t0}, x_{t1}) \geq 0 \mid 2^t x_{t0} + 2^{t+1} x_{t1} = 2^t\} = \{(x_{t0}, x_{t1}) \geq 0 \mid x_{t0} + 2x_{t1} = 1\}.$$

The maximum point in this budget set is at the lower right-hand endpoint, **e**. The price vector determining this budget set is proportional to the vector (1, 2). The allocation $\underline{\mathbf{x}}$, where $(x_{t0}, x_{t-1,1}) = (0.5, 0.5)$, for all t, clearly gives higher utility than does the endowment allocation $\overline{\mathbf{x}}$.

The allocation $\underline{\mathbf{x}}$ improves on the equilibrium one by passing some consumption from the young to the old in each period, in effect passing it backward through generations. As was explained in the previous section, such a perpetual backward shift could not be achieved if the time horizon were finite.

The inefficient Arrow-Debreu equilibrium in example 9.6 may be interpreted as an Arrow equilibrium as follows. Let the spot price of the good in every period t, P_t, be the Arrow-Debreu price, $p_t = 2^t$. Then, the price of a $(t+1)$-period dollar in terms of a t-period dollar is $q_{t,t+1} = 1$, for all t, since

$$2^t = p_t = q_{01}q_{12}\ldots q_{t-1,t}P_t = 1(1)\ldots(1)2^t.$$

Asset holdings may be computed from the equation

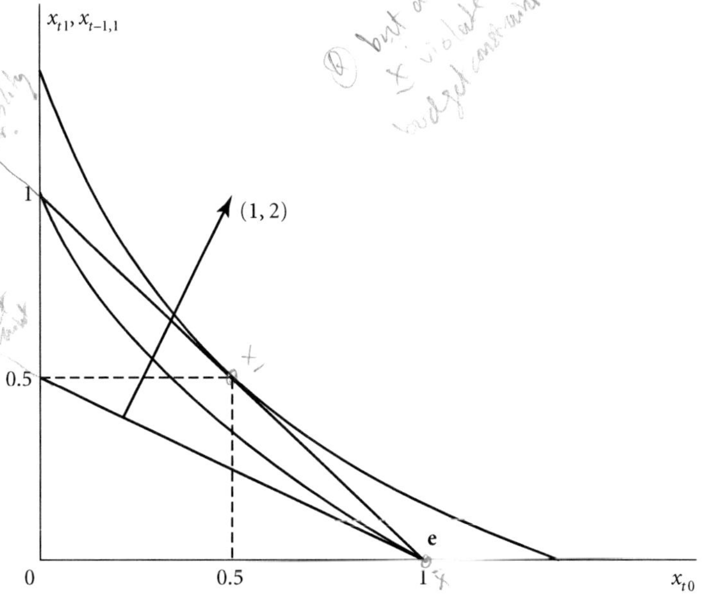

Figure 9.2 An inefficient stationary equilibrium in the Samuelson model

$$P_{t+1}x_{t1} = a_{t+1} + P_{t+1}e_{t1}.$$

Substituting actual values into this equation, we obtain

$$2^t(0) = a_{t+1} + 2^t(0),$$

so that

$$a_{t+1} = 0,$$

for all t. No assets are held, because consumers consume their endowments and do not trade.

The asset prices, $q_{t,t+1}$, may be interpreted as discount factors determined by interest rates. If r_t is the nominal interst rate on money from period t to $t+1$, then

$$q_{t,t+1} = \frac{1}{1+r_t}.$$

Since $q_{t,t+1} = 1$, it follows that $r_t = 0$, for all t.

The Pareto dominating allocation $\underline{\mathbf{x}}$ may be interpreted as the allocation of an Arrow equilibrium if we modify its definition to allow the old person of period 0 to be endowed with positive asset holdings a_0. Such an Arrow equilibrium is $(\underline{\mathbf{x}}, \mathbf{a}, \mathbf{P}, \mathbf{q})$, where $\mathbf{a} = (a_0, a_1, \ldots) = (0.5, 0.5, \ldots)$, and, for all t, $P_t = 1 = q_{t,t+1}$. In this equilibrium, the old person of period 0 uses a half unit of account to buy a half unit of the consumption good from the young person of that period, leaving a half unit of the good to be consumed by the young person. The young person in period 0 earns a half unit of account and saves it for use in period 1, when he or she spends it to buy a half unit of consumption from the young person of that period. The equilibrium perpetuates itself in this manner forever, and we may imagine that the old person of period 0, when young, sold a half unit of endowment in period -1 and used the proceeds to buy forward a half unit of account for period 0.

The Arrow equilibrium just described has the difficulty that the young buy units of account forward to be delivered by people not yet alive. The equilibrium becomes more credible if we think of the unit of account as money or government debt that bears no interest. The old person of period 0 starts the period with a half unit of money, which is used to buy a half unit of the good. The young person saves this half unit of money until old age in period 1, when it is given to the young person of that period in exchange for a half unit of consumption. In this interpretation, forward purchases of unit of account are replaced by the saving of money. This concept of equilibrium is made precise by definition 9.11 of spot price equilibrium (in section 9.3).

It is important to understand why the proof of the first welfare theorem fails in example 9.6. Let us try to repeat the proof of that theorem (theorem 5.2 in section 5.1). Let the allocations $\underline{\mathbf{x}}$ and $\overline{\mathbf{x}}$ be as in the example. Because all consumers prefer $\underline{\mathbf{x}}$ to $\overline{\mathbf{x}}$ and each consumer's allocation under $\overline{\mathbf{x}}$ maximizes utility over his or her budget set, it follows that $p_0\underline{x}_{-1,1} > p_0 e_1$ and $p_t\underline{x}_{t0} + p_{t+1}\underline{x}_{t1} > p_t e_0 + p_{t+1}e_1$, for all $t \geq 0$. Adding these inequalities over t, we obtain

$$p_0\underline{x}_{-1,1} + \sum_{t=0}^{\infty}(p_t\underline{x}_{t0} + p_{t+1}\underline{x}_{t1}) > p_0 e_1 + \sum_{t=0}^{\infty}(p_t e_0 + p_{t+1}e_1). \quad (9.1)$$

Because all the terms in inequality 9.1 are nonnegative, we can change the order of summation and obtain

$$\sum_{t=0}^{\infty} p_t(\underline{x}_{t-1,1} + \underline{x}_{t0}) > \sum_{t=0}^{\infty} p_t(e_1 + e_0). \quad (9.2)$$

Since the allocation $\underline{\mathbf{x}}$ is exactly feasible,

$$\underline{x}_{t-1,1} + \underline{x}_{t0} = e_0 + e_1,$$

for all t, so that inequality 9.2 implies that

$$\sum_{t=0}^{\infty} p_t(e_0 + e_1) > \sum_{t=0}^{\infty} p_t(e_0 + e_1). \tag{9.3}$$

If the numbers on the left- and right-hand sides of inequality 9.3 were finite, we would have the contradiction that proves the first welfare theorem. However, in the example, $e_0 + e_1 = 1$ and $p_t = 2^t$, so that

$$\sum_{t=0}^{\infty} p_t(e_0 + e_1) = \sum_{t=0}^{\infty} 2^t = \infty,$$

and there is no contradiction; $\infty > \infty$ is a valid inequality.

9.3 Pareto Optimal Equilibria

In this section, I present a condition for the Pareto optimality of equilibria and define spot price equilibrium, which is more credible than Arrow or Arrow-Debreu equilibrium and yet has the same allocations as both.

Inequality 9.3 in the previous section would lead to a contradiction if

$$\sum_{t=0}^{\infty} p_t < \infty.$$

This last inequality is, in fact, a sufficient though not necessary condition for the Pareto optimality of equilibrium in the Samuelson model.

In the next proposition, I assume that $u(\mathbf{x}_0, \mathbf{x}_1)$ is locally nonsatiated with respect to $\mathbf{x}_0$ and $\mathbf{x}_1$, separately. By this phrase, I mean that for every $\varepsilon > 0$, there exist $\underline{\mathbf{x}}_0$ and $\underline{\mathbf{x}}_1$, such that $\|\underline{\mathbf{x}}_0 - \mathbf{x}_0\| < \varepsilon$, $\|\underline{\mathbf{x}}_1 - \mathbf{x}_1\| < \varepsilon$, $u(\underline{\mathbf{x}}_0, \mathbf{x}_1) > u(\mathbf{x}_0, \mathbf{x}_1)$, and $u(\mathbf{x}_0, \underline{\mathbf{x}}_1) > u(\mathbf{x}_0, \mathbf{x}_1)$.

PROPOSITION 9.7 The allocation of an Arrow-Debreu equilibrium, $(\overline{\mathbf{x}}, \mathbf{p})$, for the Samuelson model is Pareto optimal if $\sum_{t=0}^{\infty} \mathbf{p}_t < \infty$ and if the utility function, $u(\mathbf{x}_0, \mathbf{x}_1)$, is locally nonsatiated with respect to $\mathbf{x}_0$ and $\mathbf{x}_1$ separately.

Proof. The proof follows the reasoning associated with inequalities 9.1–9.3 in the previous section. Suppose that $\mathbf{x}$ is a feasible allocation that Pareto dominates $\overline{\mathbf{x}}$. Then,

$$u(\overline{\mathbf{x}}_{-1,0}, \mathbf{x}_{-1,1}) \geq u(\overline{\mathbf{x}}_{-1,0}, \overline{\mathbf{x}}_{-1,1})$$

and

$$u(\mathbf{x}_{t0}, \mathbf{x}_{t1}) \geq u(\overline{\mathbf{x}}_{t0}, \overline{\mathbf{x}}_{t1}),$$

for all $t \geq 0$, with "$>$" in at least one inequality. Because u is locally nonsatiated with respect to $\mathbf{x}_0$ and $\mathbf{x}_1$ separately, we may use the argument made in the proof of the first welfare theorem (theorem 5.2 in section 5.1) to demonstrate that

$$\mathbf{p}_0 . \mathbf{x}_{-1,1} \geq \mathbf{p}_0 . \mathbf{e}_1$$

and

$$\mathbf{p}_t . \mathbf{x}_{t0} + \mathbf{p}_{t+1} . \mathbf{x}_{t1} \geq \mathbf{p}_t . \mathbf{e}_0 + \mathbf{p}_{t+1} . \mathbf{e}_1,$$

for all $t \geq 0$, with "$>$" if

$$u(\overline{\mathbf{x}}_{-1,0}, \mathbf{x}_{-1,1}) > u(\overline{\mathbf{x}}_{-1,0}, \overline{\mathbf{x}}_{-1,1})$$

or if

$$u(\mathbf{x}_{t0}, \mathbf{x}_{t1}) > u(\overline{\mathbf{x}}_{t0}, \overline{\mathbf{x}}_{t1}).$$

It follows that

$$\mathbf{p}_0 . \mathbf{x}_{-1,1} + \sum_{t=0}^{\infty} (\mathbf{p}_t . \mathbf{x}_{t0} + \mathbf{p}_{t+1} . \mathbf{x}_{t1}) > \mathbf{p}_0 . \mathbf{e}_1 + \sum_{t=0}^{\infty} (\mathbf{p}_t . \mathbf{e}_0 + \mathbf{p}_{t+1} . \mathbf{e}_1).$$

Because all the terms on both sides of this inequality are nonnegative, I may change the order of summation and obtain

$$\sum_{t=0}^{\infty} \mathbf{p}_t . (\mathbf{x}_{t-1,1} + \mathbf{x}_{t0}) > \sum_{t=0}^{\infty} \mathbf{p}_t . (\mathbf{e}_0 + \mathbf{e}_1). \tag{9.4}$$

Inequality 9.4 is impossible, because the feasibility of the allocation $\mathbf{x}$ implies that

$$\mathbf{x}_{t-1,1} + \mathbf{x}_{t0} \leq \mathbf{e}_0 + \mathbf{e}_1,$$

for all t, so that

$$\mathbf{p}_t . (\mathbf{x}_{t-1,1} + \mathbf{x}_{t0}) \leq \mathbf{p}_t . (\mathbf{e}_0 + \mathbf{e}_1),$$

for all t, since $\mathbf{p}_t \geq 0$. Hence

$$\sum_{t=0}^{\infty} \mathbf{p}_t . (x_{t-1,1} + x_{t0}) \leq \sum_{t=0}^{\infty} \mathbf{p}_t . (e_0 + e_1).$$

Since both sides of this inequality are finite, it contradicts inequality 9.4. ▪

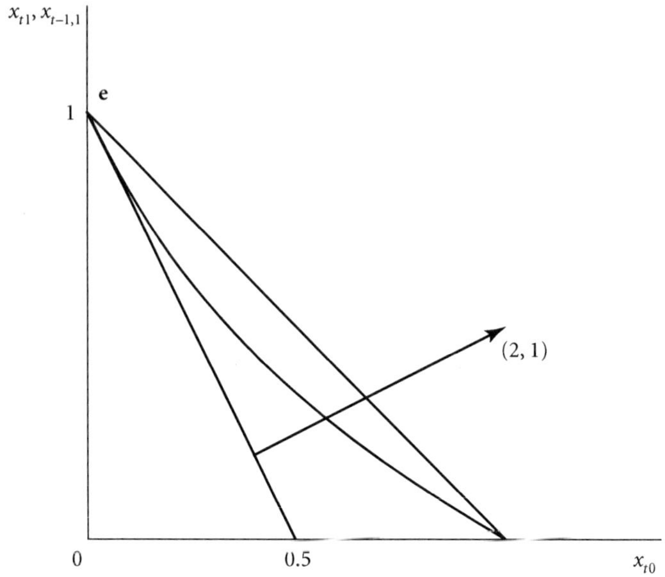

Figure 9.3 A Pareto optimal stationary equilibrium in the Samuelson model

Suppose we change example 9.6 so that consumers have an endowment in old age rather than in youth. That is, $e_0 = 0$ and $e_1 = 1$. It is not hard to check that $(\overline{\mathbf{x}}, \mathbf{p})$ is an Arrow-Debreu equilibrium if $\overline{x}_{t0} = e_0$ and $\overline{x}_{t1} = e_1$, and $p_t = 2^{-t}$, for all t. Because $\sum_{t=0}^{\infty} p_t = \sum_{t=0}^{\infty} 2^{-t} = 2 < \infty$, proposition 9.7 implies that the equilibrium allocation, $\overline{\mathbf{x}}$, is Pareto optimal. This allocation and the budget line are portrayed in figure 9.3. The equilibrium allocation is at the endowment point **e**, and the price vector faced by consumers in their two periods of life is proportional to the vector $\mathbf{p} = (2, 1)$.

The Arrow-Debreu equilibrium $(\overline{\mathbf{x}}, \mathbf{p})$ can be described as an Arrow equilibrium $(\overline{\mathbf{x}}, \mathbf{a}, \mathbf{P}, \mathbf{q})$ by letting $a_t = 0$, $P_t = 1$, and $q_{t,t+1} = \frac{1}{2}$, for all t. The forward prices $q_{t,t+1}$ equal $\frac{1}{1+r_t}$, where r_t is the interest rate from period t to $t+1$ and $r_t = 1$, for all t. We could just as well think of the equilibrium as having no forward trade in unit of account but with consumers able to hold interest-bearing government debt that earns interest at rate 1. In the equilibrium of figure 9.3, consumers happen to hold no debt.

Let us pursue the idea of holding interest-bearing debt and return to example 9.6, where the endowment is at the lower right-hand corner of the feasibility line. That is, the endowment of any consumer is $(e_0, e_1) = (1, 0)$. Imagine a stationary equilibrium with government debt bearing interest at rate $r = 1$ and where the price of the one commodity is 1 in every period. This is a spot price, because it is in terms of the current unit of account, not the unit of account of period -1. Then the present value of the cost to a youth of consumption in old age is $\frac{1}{1+r} = \frac{1}{2}$, so that the marginal rate of substitution between consumption in youth and old age is 1 divided by $\frac{1}{2}$, which is 2. Then the equilibrium allocation satisfies the equation

$$\frac{\dfrac{\partial u(x_0, x_1)}{\partial x_0}}{\dfrac{\partial u(x_0, x_1)}{\partial x_1}} = 2,$$

where x_0 and x_1 are consumption in youth and old age, respectively, in the equilibrium and where $u(x_0, x_1) = \ln(1 + x_0) + \ln(1 + x_1)$. We also have the equation for feasibility

$$x_0 + x_1 = e_0 + e_1,$$

where e_0 and e_1 are the endowments in youth and old age, respectively. Substituting the values for u, e_0, and e_1 from example 9.6, we obtain the following equations

$$\frac{1 + x_1}{1 + x_0} = 2$$

and

$$x_0 + x_1 = 1.$$

Solving these equations, we obtain

$$x_0 = 0 \text{ and } x_1 = 1.$$

The youth spends nothing but saves all of his or her earnings for old age. Since the price of the one good is 1, the young consumer earns one unit of account, all of which is invested in government debt, which earns interest at rate 1. Therefore, an old consumer has two units of government debt, but there is only one unit of the good available for purchase at price 1. There can be no equilibrium, unless the consumer pays a tax. Suppose young consumers pay a tax of a half unit. They then have a half unit of account to invest and after earning interest have one unit of government debt in old age to spend on the one unit of good. The tax of a half unit allows the economy to reach equilibrium. The tax equals exactly the interest paid on government debt, so that it serves to keep the government's budget in balance; the government's tax receipts equal the disbursement of interest on its debt. The equilibrium also requires that the old consumer of period 0 start that period with one unit of government debt with which to buy one unit of consumption.

A similar stationary equilibrium can be defined for any interest rate r between 0 and 1. A consumer's utility maximization problem is

$$\max_{x_0 \geq 0,\, x_1 \geq 0} [\ln(1+x_0) + \ln(1+x_1)]$$

$$\text{s.t.} \quad x_0 + (1+r)^{-1} x_1 \leq 1.$$

The first-order conditions for this problem imply that

$$\frac{1/(1+x_0)}{1/(1+x_1)} = 1 + r.$$

This equation together with the feasibility condition

$$x_0 + x_1 = 1$$

imply that

$$x_0 = \frac{1-r}{2+r} \text{ and } x_1 = \frac{1+2r}{2+r}.$$

If we assume that each consumer pays a tax of T when young, then the budget constraint is

$$x_0 + (1+r)^{-1} x_1 = 1 - \mathsf{T},$$

so that

$$\mathsf{T} = \frac{r(1+2r)}{(2+r)(1+r)}.$$

A young person's savings must be held as government debt, G, and these savings are

$$1 - x_0 - \mathsf{T} = 1 - \frac{1-r}{2+r} - \frac{r(1+2r)}{(2+r)(1+r)} = \frac{1+2r}{(2+r)(1+r)} = G.$$

We see that $rG = \mathsf{T}$, so that the tax pays for the interest on the government debt. The old person of period 0 must start the period with enough government debt to buy x_1. However, $x_1 = (1+r)G$, which is the amount of government debt held by every old consumer before they buy consumption. Figure 9.4 may help you visualize this equilibrium graphically. It is important to realize that the interest rate, r, is arbitrary, as long as the appropriate tax, T, is chosen together with r. The interest rate and tax are not determined by the equilibrium but may be thought of as instruments of monetary and fiscal policy, respectively. Because the equilibrium is stationary, r is the real as well as the nominal interest rate.

Let us express this equilibrium as an Arrow-Debreu equilibrium. It is natural to let the Arrow-Debreu price of the good in period t be the present value of the spot price of period t from the point of view of period 0 and when the interest rate is 1. Then, the Arrow-Debreu price is $p_t = (1+r)^{-t}$. The young consumer of period t pays a tax of T, which in present-value terms is $\tau_t = (1+r)^{-t}\mathsf{T} = (1+r)^{-t} rG$. In addition, the old consumer of period 0 must have a subsidy of $(1+r)G$ in order to purchase one unit of consumption. Call this subsidy a tax of $\tau_{-1} = -(1+r)G$, the tax being negative because it is a subsidy. We can think of these taxes, τ_t, as lump-sum transfer payments. Furthermore, they add up to zero, because

$$\sum_{t=-1}^{\infty} \tau_t = -(1+r)G + \sum_{t=0}^{\infty} (1+r)^{-t} rG = 0.$$

It is easy to check that with these transfer payments and with Arrow-Debreu prices p_t, every consumer chooses to buy none of the good in youth and one unit in old age. We can, therefore, say that $(\overline{\mathbf{x}}, \mathbf{p}, \boldsymbol{\tau})$ is an Arrow-Debreu equilibrium with transfer payments, where $\overline{\mathbf{x}}$ is the allocation defined by the equations $\overline{x}_{t0} = \frac{1-r}{2+r}$ and $\overline{x}_{t1} = \frac{1+2r}{2+r}$, for all t, and where $\mathbf{p} = (p_t)_{t=0}^{\infty}$ and $\boldsymbol{\tau} = (\tau_t)_{t=0}^{\infty}$ are as just defined. We see that there is a close connection between Arrow-Debreu equilibria with transfer payments on the one hand and, on the other hand, equilibria with no forward trading and with taxes and interest-bearing government debt.

In order to make these ideas more precise, I define the new concepts of equilibrium. The next definition differs from definition 9.4 only by the inclusion of transfer payments.

DEFINITION 9.8 An *Arrow-Debreu equilibrium with transfer payments* for the Samuelson model consists of $(\overline{\mathbf{x}}, \mathbf{p}, \boldsymbol{\tau})$ that satisfies the conditions

1. $\overline{\mathbf{x}}$ is a feasible allocation
2. $\mathbf{p} = (p_0, p_1, \ldots)$ is an infinite sequence of nonnegative N-vectors of prices, not all of which are 0

3. $\boldsymbol{\tau} = (\tau_{-1}, \tau_0, \tau_1, \ldots)$ is a sequence of numbers, where τ_t is the lump-sum tax paid by the consumer born in period t
4. for every $t \geq 0$, $(\overline{\mathbf{x}}_{t0}, \overline{\mathbf{x}}_{t1})$ solves the problem

$$\max_{\mathbf{x}_0 \in \mathbb{R}^N_+, x_1 \in \mathbb{R}^N_+} u(\mathbf{x}_0, \mathbf{x}_1)$$
$$\text{s.t.} \quad \mathbf{p}_t.\mathbf{x}_0 + \mathbf{p}_{t+1}.\mathbf{x}_1 \leq \mathbf{p}_t.\mathbf{e}_0 + \mathbf{p}_{t+1}.\mathbf{e}_1 - \tau_1$$

5. $\overline{\mathbf{x}}_{-1,1}$ solves the problem

$$\max_{\mathbf{x}_1 \in \mathbb{R}^N_+} u(\overline{\mathbf{x}}_{-1,0}, \mathbf{x}_1)$$
$$\text{s.t.} \quad \mathbf{p}_0.\mathbf{x}_1 \leq \mathbf{p}_0.\mathbf{e}_1 - \tau_{-1}$$

6. for all t and n, $p_{tn} = 0$, if

$$\overline{x}_{t,0,n} + \overline{x}_{t-1,1,n} < e_{0n} + e_{1n}$$

A consequence of the summability of prices is that if u is locally nonsatiated, then the taxes, τ_t, are transfer payments in that they sum to 0. The taxes are transfers only in a virtual sense, since they are carried out at time -1 among the person born in that period and the ghosts of the as-yet unborn.

PROPOSITION 9.9 Assume that the utility function u is locally nonsatiated with respect to each of $\mathbf{x}_0$ and $\mathbf{x}_1$ separately and that $\sum_{t=0}^{\infty} \mathbf{p}_t < \infty$. Then $\sum_{t=-1}^{\infty} |\tau_t| < \infty$ and $\sum_{t=-1}^{\infty} \tau_t = 0$, for any Arrow-Debreu equilibrium with transfer payments, $(\overline{\mathbf{x}}, \mathbf{p}, \boldsymbol{\tau})$.

Proof. Because u is locally nonsatiated with respect to each of $\mathbf{x}_0$ and $\mathbf{x}_1$ separately,

$$\mathbf{p}_0.\overline{\mathbf{x}}_{-1,1} = \mathbf{p}_0.\mathbf{e}_1 - \tau_{-1},$$

and

$$\mathbf{p}_t.\overline{\mathbf{x}}_{t0} + \mathbf{p}_{t+1}.\overline{\mathbf{x}}_{t1} = \mathbf{p}_t.\mathbf{e}_0 + \mathbf{p}_{t+1}.\mathbf{e}_1 - \tau_t,$$

for all $t \geq 0$. Therefore,

$$\sum_{t=-1}^{\infty} \tau_t = \mathbf{p}_0.(\mathbf{e}_1 - \overline{\mathbf{x}}_{-1,1}) + \sum_{t=0}^{\infty} [\mathbf{p}_t.(\mathbf{e}_0 - \overline{\mathbf{x}}_{t0}) + \mathbf{p}_{t+1}.(\mathbf{e}_1 - \overline{\mathbf{x}}_{t1})]. \quad (9.5)$$

Because $0 \leq \overline{\mathbf{x}}_{t0} \leq \mathbf{e}_0 + \mathbf{e}_1$ and $0 \leq \overline{\mathbf{x}}_{t1} \leq \mathbf{e}_0 + \mathbf{e}_1$, for all t, the definition of τ_t and the condition that $\sum_{t=0}^{\infty} \mathbf{p}_t < \infty$ imply that

$$\sum_{t=-1}^{\infty} |\tau_t| = |\mathbf{p}_0.(\mathbf{e}_1 - \overline{\mathbf{x}}_{-1,1})| + \sum_{t=0}^{\infty} |\mathbf{p}_t.(\mathbf{e}_0 - \overline{\mathbf{x}}_{t0}) + \mathbf{p}_{t+1}.(\mathbf{e}_1 - \overline{\mathbf{x}}_{t1})| < \infty.$$

Therefore the infinite series on the right-hand side of equation 9.5 converges absolutely,[2] so that we may reorder its terms to obtain the equation

$$\sum_{t=-1}^{\infty} \tau_t = \sum_{t=0}^{\infty} \mathbf{p}_t.(\mathbf{e}_0 + \mathbf{e}_1 - \overline{\mathbf{x}}_{t0} - \overline{\mathbf{x}}_{t-1,1}). \tag{9.6}$$

The feasibility of the allocation $\overline{\mathbf{x}}$ implies that $\mathbf{e}_0 + \mathbf{e}_1 - \overline{\mathbf{x}}_{t0} - \overline{\mathbf{x}}_{t-1,1} \geq 0$, for all t, so that condition (6) of definition 9.8 implies that $\mathbf{p}_t.(\mathbf{e}_0 + \mathbf{e}_1 - \overline{\mathbf{x}}_{t0} - \overline{\mathbf{x}}_{t-1,1}) = 0$. Therefore equation 9.6 implies that

$$\sum_{t=-1}^{\infty} \tau_t = 0. \quad \blacksquare$$

We have the following analogue of proposition 5.7 (in section 5.2).

PROPOSITION 9.10 The allocation of an Arrow-Debreu equilibrium with transfer payments, $(\overline{\mathbf{x}}, \mathbf{p}, \boldsymbol{\tau})$, for the Samuelson model is Pareto optimal if $\sum_{t=0}^{\infty} p_t < \infty$ and if u is locally nonsatiated with respect to each of $\mathbf{x}_0$ and $\mathbf{x}_1$ separately.

Proof. The proof is much like that of proposition 9.7. If $\overline{\mathbf{x}}$ is not Pareto optimal, there exists a feasible allocation $\mathbf{x}$ such that

$$u(\overline{\mathbf{x}}_{-1,0}, \mathbf{x}_{-1,1}) \geq u(\overline{\mathbf{x}}_{-1,0}, \overline{\mathbf{x}}_{-1,1})$$

and

$$u(\mathbf{x}_{t0}, \mathbf{x}_{t1}) \geq u(\overline{\mathbf{x}}_{t0}, \overline{\mathbf{x}}_{t1}),$$

for all $t \geq 0$, with ">" in at least one inequality. Because u is locally nonsatiated with respect to $\mathbf{x}_0$ and $\mathbf{x}_1$ separately, we know that

$$\mathbf{p}_0.\mathbf{x}_{-1,1} \geq \mathbf{p}_0.\mathbf{e}_1 - \tau_{-1}$$

and

$$\mathbf{p}_t.\mathbf{x}_{t0} + \mathbf{p}_{t+1}.\mathbf{x}_{t1} \geq \mathbf{p}_t.\mathbf{e}_0 + \mathbf{p}_{t+1}.\mathbf{e}_1 - \tau_t,$$

2. An infinite series, $\sum_{n=0}^{\infty} z_n$, is said to converge absolutely if the series $\sum_{n=0}^{\infty} |z_n|$ converges. If an infinite series converges absolutely, its total does not depend on the order in which its terms are summed.

for all $t \geq 0$, with ">" if

$$u(\overline{\mathbf{x}}_{-1,0}, \mathbf{x}_{-1,1}) > u(\overline{\mathbf{x}}_{-1,0}, \overline{\mathbf{x}}_{-1,1})$$

or if

$$u(\overline{\mathbf{x}}_{t0}, \mathbf{x}_{t1}) > u(\overline{\mathbf{x}}_{t0}, \overline{\mathbf{x}}_{t1}).$$

Therefore,

$$\mathbf{p}_0.\mathbf{x}_{-1,1} + \sum_{t=0}^{\infty}(\mathbf{p}_t.\mathbf{x}_{t0} + \mathbf{p}_{t+1}.\mathbf{x}_{11}) > \mathbf{p}_0.\mathbf{e}_1 + \sum_{t=0}^{\infty}(\mathbf{p}_t.\mathbf{e}_0 + \mathbf{p}_{t+1}.\mathbf{e}_1).$$

Since $\sum_{t=0}^{\infty} \mathbf{p}_t < \infty$ and $\sum_{t=-1}^{\infty} |\tau_t| < \infty$, the infinite sums in this inequality converge absolutely, and the totals do not depend on the order of summation. Therefore,

$$\sum_{t=0}^{\infty} \mathbf{p}_t.(\mathbf{x}_{t-1,1} + \mathbf{x}_{t0}) > \sum_{t=0}^{\infty} \mathbf{p}_t.(\mathbf{e}_0 + \mathbf{e}_1) - \sum_{t=-1}^{\infty} \tau_t = \sum_{t=0}^{\infty} \mathbf{p}_t.(\mathbf{e}_0 + \mathbf{e}_1),$$

since $\sum_{t=-1}^{\infty} \tau_t = 0$ by proposition 9.9. This inequality is impossible since both of its sides are finite and, for all t, $\mathbf{p}_t \geq 0$, and $\mathbf{x}_{t-1,1} + \mathbf{x}_{t0} \leq \mathbf{e}_0 + \mathbf{e}_1$. This contradiction proves the theorem. ▪

I now define a notion of equilibrium that is much like an Arrow equilibrium with lump-sum taxes and subsidies.

DEFINITION 9.11 A *spot price equilibrium* for the Samuelson model consists of $(\overline{\mathbf{x}}, \mathbf{P}, \mathbf{r}, G, \mathsf{T})$ that satisfies the conditions

1. $\overline{\mathbf{x}}$ is a feasible allocation
2. $\mathbf{P} = (\mathbf{P}_0, \mathbf{P}_1, \ldots)$ is an infinite sequence of nonnegative N-vectors of prices, not all of which are zero
3. $\mathbf{r} = (r_{-1}, r_0, r_1, \ldots)$ is an infinite sequence of numbers, where r_t is the nominal interest rate paid in period $t+1$ on government debt held from period t to period $t+1$ and $r_t > -1$, for all t
4. $\mathsf{T} = (\mathsf{T}_0, \mathsf{T}_1, \ldots)$ is a sequence of numbers, where T is the lump-sum tax paid by the young consumer of period t
5. $(1 + r_{-1})G$ is the amount of government debt held by the old consumer of period 0 at the beginning of that period
6. for every $t \geq 0$, $(\overline{\mathbf{x}}_{t0}, \overline{\mathbf{x}}_{t1})$ solves the problem

$$\max_{\mathbf{x}_0\in\mathbb{R}_+^N,\,\mathbf{x}_1\in\mathbb{R}_+^N} u(\mathbf{x}_0,\mathbf{x}_1)$$

$$\text{s.t.}\quad \mathbf{P}_t.\mathbf{x}_0 + (1+r_t)^{-1}\mathbf{P}_{t+1}.\mathbf{x}_1 \le \mathbf{P}_t.\mathbf{e}_0 + (1+r_t)^{-1}\mathbf{P}_{t+1}.\mathbf{e}_1 - \mathsf{T}_t$$

7. $\overline{\mathbf{x}}_{-1,1}$ solves the problem

$$\max_{\mathbf{x}_1\in\mathbb{R}_+^N} u(\overline{\mathbf{x}}_{-1,0},\mathbf{x}_1)$$

$$\text{s.t.}\quad \mathbf{P}_0.\mathbf{x}_1 \le \mathbf{P}_0.\mathbf{e}_1 + (1+r_{-1})G$$

8. for all t and n, $P_{tn} = 0$, if

$$\overline{x}_{t,0,n} + \overline{x}_{t-1,1,n} < e_{0n} + e_{1n}$$

A spot price equilibrium differs from an Arrow equilibrium with lump-sum taxes and subsidies only in that the definition of a spot price equilibrium does not have explicit forward purchases and sales of unit of account. The form of the consumer's budget constraint in the spot price equilibrium implies, however, that such purchases and sales occur; they are equivalent to saving and borrowing, respectively. The Arrow forward price, $q_{t,t+1}$, in period t of a unit of account in period $t + 1$ becomes $(1+r_t)^{-1}$ in a spot price equilibrium.

In a spot price equilibrium, consumers have perfect foresight in that the young consumer in period t knows the spot commodity prices P_{tn} that will occur in period $t + 1$. Without this knowledge, the consumer could not maximize utility over a two-period budget set.

As was mentioned earlier in connection with an example, the taxes and interest rates in a spot price equilibrium are not determined by equilibrium forces but are exogenous and may be associated with fiscal and monetary policy.

In the definition of spot price equilibrium, there is no requirement that the government satisfy a budget constraint, because it does so automatically in equilibrium provided the utility function, $u(\mathbf{x}_0,\mathbf{x}_1)$, is locally nonsatiated with respect to each of the variables $\mathbf{x}_0$ and $\mathbf{x}_1$ separately. The government's budget constraint for period $t + 1$, where $t \ge 0$, is

$$G_{t+1} = (1+r_t)G_t - \mathsf{T}_{t+1},\tag{9.7}$$

where G_t is the government's debt at the end of period t. Since this debt equals the savings of the young person at the end of period t, we have the equation

$$G_t = \mathbf{P}_t.(\mathbf{e}_0 - \overline{\mathbf{x}}_{t0}) - \mathsf{T}_t,\tag{9.8}$$

$$T_{t+}\,G_t = P_t(e_0 - \overline{x}_{t0})$$

$$(1+r_{t-1})G_{t-1} =$$

where G_t is the government's debt at the end of period t. I will now verify that the government's budget constraint, equation 9.7, is satisfied in equilibrium. This verification will, to some extent, justify the interpretation of the quantity G_t defined by equation 9.8 as government debt.

To verify equation 9.7, notice that by condition (8) of the definition 9.11 of a spot price equilibrium, the feasibility condition,

$$\overline{\mathbf{x}}_{t1} + \overline{\mathbf{x}}_{t+1,0} \leq \mathbf{e}_0 + \mathbf{e}_1,$$

implies that

$$\mathbf{P}_{t+1}.(\overline{\mathbf{x}}_{t1} + \overline{\mathbf{x}}_{t+1,0}) = \mathbf{P}_{t+1}.(\mathbf{e}_0 + \mathbf{e}_1),$$

which in turn implies that

$$\mathbf{P}_{t+1}.(\overline{\mathbf{x}}_{t1} - \mathbf{e}_1) = \mathbf{P}_{t+1}.(\mathbf{e}_0 - \overline{\mathbf{x}}_{t+1,0}). \tag{9.9}$$

Another equation required is the budget constraint for the person born at timc t,

$$\mathbf{P}_t.\overline{\mathbf{x}}_{t0} + \frac{\mathbf{P}_{t+1}}{1+r_t}.\overline{\mathbf{x}}_{t1} = \mathbf{P}_t.\mathbf{e}_0 + \frac{\mathbf{P}_{t+1}}{1+r_r}.\mathbf{e}_1 - \mathsf{T}_t,$$

which implies that

$$(1+r_t)[\mathbf{P}_t.(\mathbf{e}_0 - \overline{\mathbf{x}}_{t0}) - \mathsf{T}_t] = \mathbf{P}_{t+1}.(\overline{\mathbf{x}}_{t1} - \mathbf{e}_1). \tag{9.10}$$

This budget constraint holds with equality because the utility function is locally nonsatiated. From these equations, we see that

$$\begin{aligned}(1+r_t)G_t &= (1+r_t)[\mathbf{P}_t.(\mathbf{e}_0 - \overline{\mathbf{x}}_{t0}) - \mathsf{T}_t] = \mathbf{P}_{t+1}.(\overline{\mathbf{x}}_{t1} - \mathbf{e}_1) \\ &= \mathbf{P}_{t+1}.(\mathbf{e}_0 - \overline{\mathbf{x}}_{t+1,0}) = G_{t+1} + \mathsf{T}_{t+1},\end{aligned} \tag{9.11}$$

where the first equation is equation 9.8, the second is equation 9.10, the third is equation 9.9, and the last equation follows from equation 9.8 again. Equality between the extreme left and right of equations 9.11 is equation 9.7. The government's budget equation for period 0 is

$$G_0 = (1+r_{-1})G - \mathsf{T}_0, \tag{9.12}$$

because $(1+r_{-1})G$ is the government's debt at the beginning of period 0 and G_0 is its debt at the end of the period. To see that equation 9.12 is valid, notice that the budget constraint of the old person of period 0 is

$$(1+r_{-1})G = \mathbf{P}_0.(\overline{\mathbf{x}}_{-1,1} - \mathbf{e}_1), \tag{9.13}$$

where the constraint holds with equality because the utility function is locally nonsatiated with respect to $\mathbf{x}_1$. Using equation 9.13, we see that

$$(1+r_{-1})G = \mathbf{P}_0.(\overline{\mathbf{x}}_{-1,1} - \mathbf{e}_1) = \mathbf{P}_0.(\mathbf{e}_0 - \overline{\mathbf{x}}_{00}) = G_0 + \mathsf{T}_0, \quad (9.14)$$

where the second equation holds by equation 9.9 and the third equation follows from equation 9.8. Equality between the extreme left and right of equations 9.14 is equation 9.12.

Satisfaction of the government's budget equation does not imply that this budget is in balance. The government's budget may be said to be balanced in period $t+1$ if $G_{t+1} = G_t$, so that $r_t G_t = \mathsf{T}_{t+1}$.

The next proposition asserts that spot price equilibria are really another form of Arrow-Debreu equilibria.

PROPOSITION 9.12 Suppose that $(\overline{\mathbf{x}}, \mathbf{P}, \mathbf{r}, G, \mathbf{T})$ is a spot price equilibrium and let $1 + R_t = (1+r_0)(1+r_1)\ldots(1+r_t)$, for $t \geq 0$. Then, $(\overline{\mathbf{x}}, \mathbf{p}, \boldsymbol{\tau})$ is an Arrow-Debreu equilibrium with transfer payments, where

$$\mathbf{p}_0 = \mathbf{P}_0,$$

$$\tau_{-1} = -(1+r_{-1})G,$$

$$\tau_0 = \mathsf{T}_0,$$

$$\mathbf{p}_t = \frac{\mathbf{P}_t}{1+R_{t-1}},$$

and

$$\tau_t = \frac{\mathsf{T}_t}{1+R_{t-1}},$$

for $t \geq 1$.

I give no proof of this proposition, as it is easy to check that $(\overline{\mathbf{x}}, \mathbf{p}, \boldsymbol{\tau})$ satisfies all the conditions of an Arrow-Debreu equilibrium.

When relating the theory to actual economies, spot price equilibrium is probably the equilibrium concept of most interest, because it is fairly realistic and contains clear instruments of fiscal and monetary policy. It is more realistic than Arrow-Debreu equilibrium, because it contains no forward trading. It does, however, have the unrealistic requirement of perfect foresight about prices one period ahead. Arrow-Debreu equilibrium is of interest mainly as a tool of analysis. For instance, there is an easy criterion for the Pareto optimality of an Arrow-Debreu equilibrium allocation, the summability of prices. The next corollary says that this criterion carries over to spot price equilibrium.

COROLLARY 9.13 Suppose that the utility function in the Samuelson model is locally nonsatiated with respect to each of $\mathbf{x}_0$ and $\mathbf{x}_1$ separately and that $(\overline{\mathbf{x}}, \mathbf{P}, \mathbf{r}, G, \mathbf{T})$ is a spot price equilibrium that satisfies the condition

$$\mathbf{P}_0 + \sum_{t=1}^{\infty} \frac{\mathbf{P}_t}{1+R_{t-1}} < \infty,$$

where $1 + R_t = (1 + r_0)(1 + r_1) \ldots (1 + r_t)$, for $t \geq 0$. Then, the allocation $\overline{\mathbf{x}}$ is Pareto optimal and

$$G = \frac{\mathsf{T}_0}{1+r_{-1}} + \sum_{t=1}^{\infty} \frac{\mathsf{T}_t}{(1+r_{-1})(1+R_{t-1})}.$$

Proof. When $(\overline{\mathbf{x}}, \mathbf{P}, \mathbf{r}, G, \mathbf{T})$ is converted to an Arrow-Debreu equilibrium, $(\overline{\mathbf{x}}, \mathbf{p}, \boldsymbol{\tau})$, as in proposition 9.12, then the condition

$$\mathbf{P}_0 + \sum_{t=1}^{\infty} \frac{\mathbf{P}_t}{1+R_{t-1}} < \infty$$

implies that $\sum_{t=0}^{\infty} \mathbf{p}_t < \infty$, so that $\overline{\mathbf{x}}$ is Pareto optimal by proposition 9.10 and the transfer payments sum to 0 by proposition 9.9. The sum of the transfer payments is

$$-(1 + r_{-1})G + \mathsf{T}_0 + \sum_{t=1}^{\infty} \frac{\mathsf{T}_t}{1+R_{t-1}}.$$

If we set this last quantity equal to 0, we obtain the last equation of the corollary. ∎

The last equation of the corollary means that government debt at the end of period -1 equals the total present value of all future taxes.

This corollary in turn implies a sufficient condition for the Pareto optimality of stationary spot price equilibria. These equilibria are defined as follows.

DEFINITION 9.14 A *stationary* spot price equilibrium is a spot price equilibrium, $(\overline{\mathbf{x}}, \mathbf{P}, \mathbf{r}, G, \mathbf{T})$, such that $\overline{\mathbf{x}}_{t0} = \overline{\mathbf{x}}_0$, $\overline{\mathbf{x}}_{t1} = \overline{\mathbf{x}}_1$, $\mathbf{P}_t = \mathbf{P}_0$, $r_t = r$, and $\mathsf{T}_t = \mathsf{T}$, for all t.

I denote a stationary spot price equilibrium by $(\overline{\mathbf{x}}_0, \overline{\mathbf{x}}_1, \mathbf{P}_0, r, G, \mathsf{T})$, where, for all t, $\overline{\mathbf{x}}_{t0} = \overline{\mathbf{x}}_0$, $\overline{\mathbf{x}}_{t1} = \overline{\mathbf{x}}_1$, $\mathbf{P}_t = \mathbf{P}_0$, $r_t = r$, and $\mathsf{T}_t = \mathsf{T}$. Similarly, I denote a stationary allocation by $(\mathbf{x}_0, \mathbf{x}_1)$. Notice that in a stationary equilibrium, $G_{t+1} = G_t = G$, for all t, so that the government's budget always balances and $\mathsf{T} = rG$.

In a stationary equilibrium, either the interest rate r or the ratio T/P_0 may be thought of as exogenous. If the interest rate is fixed exogenously, then the ratio T/P_0 is determined by the requirement that the government's budget balance in a stationary equilibrium. Similarly, if T/P_0 is fixed exogenously, there may be only certain interest rates that allow a stationary equilibrium, or there may be no such interest rate.

COROLLARY 9.15 The allocation of a stationary spot price equilibrium with a positive interest rate, r, is Pareto optimal, provided u is locally nonsatiated with respect to each of $\mathbf{x}_0$ and $\mathbf{x}_1$ separately.

I now characterize stationary spot price equilibria, $(\overline{x}_0, \overline{x}_1, P_0, r, G, \mathsf{T})$, when there is only one commodity in each period and where $r > -1$. Assume that the utility function, u, is differentiable, quasi-concave, and increasing. (Quasi-concavity is defined in definition 5.13 in section 5.2.) Let the endowment of each consumer be (e_0, e_1). As a price normalization, let $P_0 = 1$. Because u is increasing, the feasibility constraint holds with equality in an equilibrium. That is,

$$\overline{x}_0 + \overline{x}_1 = e_0 + e_1. \tag{9.15}$$

For simplicity, assume that $\overline{x}_0 > 0$ and $\overline{x}_1 > 0$ in the stationary equilibrium. To a young person, the price of consumption in youth is 1 and the price of consumption in old age is $\frac{1}{1+r}$. Hence, the first-order conditions for utility maximization subject to a budget constraint imply that

$$\frac{\dfrac{\partial u(\overline{x}_0, \overline{x}_1)}{\partial x_0}}{\dfrac{\partial u(\overline{x}_0, \overline{x}_1)}{\partial x_1}} = \frac{1}{\dfrac{1}{1+r}} = 1 + r.$$

This equation simplifies to

$$(1+r)\frac{\partial u(\overline{x}_0, \overline{x}_1)}{\partial x_1} = \frac{\partial u(\overline{x}_0, \overline{x}_1)}{\partial x_0}. \tag{9.16}$$

Since equations 9.15 and 9.16 have two unknowns, they are normally enough to determine the stationary equilibrium allocation $(\overline{x}_0, \overline{x}_1)$. The other parameters of the equilibrium are G and T_0. Government debt, G, is determined by equation 9.13, which becomes

$$(1+r)G = \overline{x}_1 - e_1. \tag{9.17}$$

The government's budget constraint, equation 9.7, becomes

$$rG = \mathsf{T}. \tag{9.18}$$

Equations 9.15–9.18 determine all the parameters of the equilibrium, and corollary 9.15 implies that the equilibrium allocation is Pareto optimal, provided $r > 0$.

Figure 9.4 shows a typical equilibrium with positive interest rate r when the initial endowment is $\mathbf{e} = (e_0, e_1) = (e_0, 0)$. The point $\overline{\mathbf{x}}$ is the stationary optimal allocation. The line $A\mathbf{e}$ is the set of feasible stationary allocations. The line HC through $\overline{\mathbf{x}}$ and tangent to the indifference curve through $\overline{\mathbf{x}}$ is the budget line of a consumer. The vector perpendicular to this line, $(1, (1+r)^{-1})$, is the vector of prices of current and next period consumption faced by a young consumer. The tax, T, is equal to the distance from C to the endowment point, $\mathbf{e}$, along the abscissa. Government debt, G, at the end of any period equals the distance from $\overline{x}_0$ to C. The government debt, $(1+r)G$, at the beginning of any period equals $\overline{x}_1$. This quantity equals the total assets of an old person at the beginning of any period.

An equilibrium like that just portrayed can be constructed for any stationary allocation on the interval AB along the feasibility line $A\mathbf{e}$. The allocations at points in line segment AB and not including B belong to stationary equilibria with a positive interest rate and so are Pareto optimal by corollary 9.15.

The stationary allocation at point B corresponds to a stationary equilibrium with interest rate 0 and with government debt equal to the distance from D to B or from D to $\mathbf{e}$. Because the interest rate is 0, this equilibrium does not satisfy the summability condition on prices of corollary 9.13. Nevertheless, the stationary allocation at point B is Pareto optimal, as is implied by corollary 9.45 (in section 9.7).

Stationary allocations along the feasibility line from B to $\mathbf{e}$ and not including B are not Pareto optimal, though they are the allocations of stationary spot price equilibria. These equilibria have negative interest rates. Consider the stationary allocation at the point E in this interval and suppose that the economy switches at time 0 from the allocation at E to that at

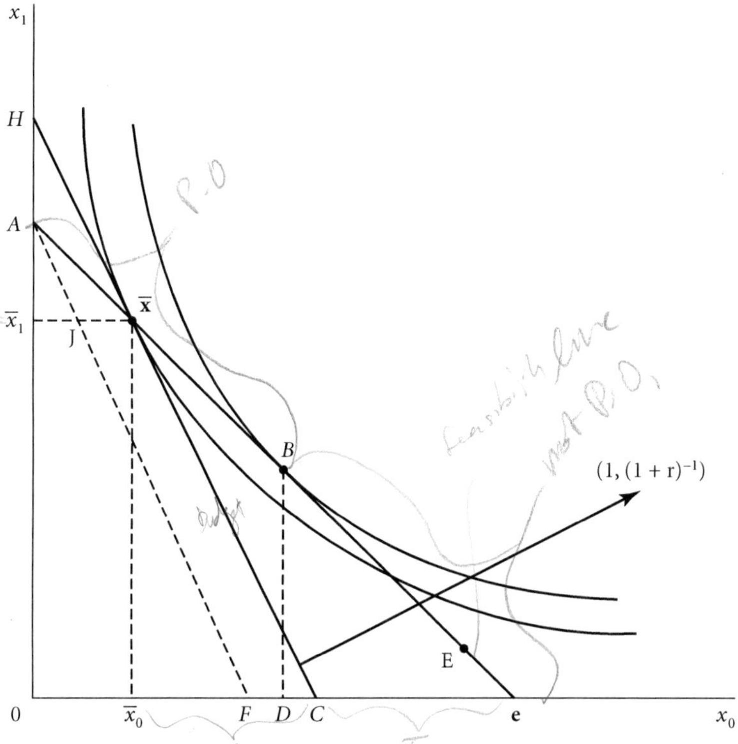

Figure 9.4 A Pareto optimal stationary equilibrium

B and stays at B forever. Every consumer born in period 0 or later would be better off, because the lifetime utility enjoyed at B exceeds that enjoyed at E. The old person of period 0 would also be better off, because the consumption of the old at B exceeds that at E. Since no changes occur before period 0 and the welfare of everybody alive in period 0 or later is increased by the switch, it leads to a Pareto improvement. The same reasoning was used to show that the equilibrium of example 9.6 (in section 9.2) was not Pareto optimal.

You may be curious as to why a similar switch from the allocation $\overline{\mathbf{x}}$ to that at B does not lead to a Pareto improvement, because the lifetime utility of every consumer is higher at B than at $\overline{\mathbf{x}}$. A transition from allocation $\overline{\mathbf{x}}$ to B is not a Pareto improvement, because it requires that the old person alive at the time of transition make a sacrifice. He or she would consume no more in youth and less in old age.

The Pareto optimality of stationary allocations along the feasibility line in figure 9.4 does not depend on where the initial endowment point is on this line. The position of this line and the set of Pareto optimal allocations depends only on the total endowment $e_0 + e_1$. If the individual endowment of consumer t were (e_{t0}, e_{t1}) and fluctuated over time, the set of Pareto optimal stationary allocations would be as described, as long as the total, $e_{t0} + e_{t-1,1}$, remained constant.

The position of the endowment point does, however, affect the size of government debt and taxes. If in figure 9.4 the endowment were at point A rather than $\mathbf{e}$, then the tax, T, would be negative and $-\mathsf{T}$ would equal the distance from point F to C along the horizontal axis. The tax would be a subsidy that moved the consumer's budget line from AF to the line through $\overline{\mathbf{x}}$ and C. The subsidy would return to consumers the interest earned by the government on a negative government debt. The negative debt would be loans to young consumers, analogous to government loans to college students. Youths would finance consumption through loans from the government that they would pay off with interest when old. In figure 9.4, $-(1+r)G$ is the distance from $\overline{x}_1$ to A, $-G$ is the distance from 0 to $\overline{x}_0$ minus the distance from F to C, which is the distance from $\overline{x}_1$ to J.

I now turn to the proposition that characterizes stationary allocations (such as that at point B in figure 9.4) as the allocations of equilibria. To state the proposition, I must define a concept of equilibrium with noninterest-bearing government debt or money.

DEFINITION 9.16 A *spot price equilibrium with interest rate 0*, denoted $(\overline{\mathbf{x}}, \mathbf{P}, G)$, is a spot price equilibrium, $(\overline{\mathbf{x}}, \mathbf{P}, \mathbf{r}, G, \mathbf{T})$, such that $r_t = \mathsf{T}_t = 0$, for all t.

In a spot price equilibrium with interest rate 0, the quantity of government debt remains constant and equals G in all periods, provided the utility function is locally nonsatiated with respect to each of $\mathbf{x}_0$ and $\mathbf{x}_1$ separately, for all t. Because interest rates and taxes are 0, the government budget equations 9.12 and 9.7, respectively, become

$$G_0 = G \text{ and } G_{t+1} = G_t,$$

for all $t \geq 0$, and these equations imply that

$$G_t = G,$$

for all $t \geq 0$.

DEFINITION 9.17 A *stationary* spot price equilibrium with interest rate 0, $(\overline{\mathbf{x}}, \mathbf{P}, G)$, is a spot price equilibrium with interest rate 0 such that $\overline{\mathbf{x}}_{t0} = \overline{\mathbf{x}}_0$, $\overline{\mathbf{x}}_{t1} = \overline{\mathbf{x}}_1$, and $\mathbf{P}_t = \mathbf{P}_0$, for all $t \geq 0$.

I will denote such an equilibrium by the vector $(\overline{\mathbf{x}}_0, \overline{\mathbf{x}}_1, \mathbf{P}_0, G)$, where, for all t, $\overline{\mathbf{x}}_{t0} = \overline{\mathbf{x}}_0$, $\overline{\mathbf{x}}_{t1} = \overline{\mathbf{x}}_1$, and $\mathbf{P}_t = \mathbf{P}_0$.

The next proposition shows that stationary spot price equilibrium allocations solve the same maximization problem as does the point B in figure 9.4.

PROPOSITION 9.18 If u is continuous, strictly concave, and locally nonsatiated and if $\mathbf{e}_0 + \mathbf{e}_1 \gg 0$, then there exists a stationary spot price equilibrium with interest rate 0, $(\overline{\mathbf{x}}_0, \overline{\mathbf{x}}_1, \mathbf{P}_0, G)$. All such equilibria have the same allocation, and that allocation solves the problem

$$\begin{aligned} &\max_{\mathbf{x}_0 \in \mathbb{R}^N_+, \mathbf{x}_1 \in \mathbb{R}^N_+} \quad u(\mathbf{x}_0, \mathbf{x}_1) \\ &\text{s.t.} \quad \mathbf{x}_0 + \mathbf{x}_1 \leq \mathbf{e}_0 + \mathbf{e}_1. \end{aligned} \tag{9.19}$$

Proof. By proposition 3.14 (in section 3.2), problem 9.19 has a solution, $(\overline{\mathbf{x}}_0, \overline{\mathbf{x}}_1)$. Because $\mathbf{e}_0 + \mathbf{e}_1 \gg 0$, this problem satisfies the constraint qualification of the Kuhn-Tucker theorem (theorem 6.3 in section 6.1). That theorem implies that there exists a nonnegative N-vector $\mathbf{P}_0$ such that $(\overline{\mathbf{x}}_0, \overline{\mathbf{x}}_1)$ solves the problem

$$\max_{\mathbf{x}_0 \in \mathbb{R}^N_+, \mathbf{x}_1 \in \mathbb{R}^N_+} [u(\mathbf{x}_0, \mathbf{x}_1) - \mathbf{P}_0.(\mathbf{x}_0 + \mathbf{x}_1)]$$

and, for all n, $\mathbf{P}_{0n} = 0$, if $\overline{x}_{0n} + \overline{x}_{1n} < e_{0n} + e_{1n}$. Since $\overline{\mathbf{x}}_0 + \overline{\mathbf{x}}_1 \leq \mathbf{e}_0 + \mathbf{e}_1$, it follows that $\mathbf{P}_0.(\overline{\mathbf{x}}_0 + \overline{\mathbf{x}}_1) = \mathbf{P}_0.(\mathbf{e}_0 + \mathbf{e}_1)$. Hence, the sufficiency part of the Kuhn-Tucker theorem (with $\lambda = 1$) implies that $(\overline{\mathbf{x}}_0, \overline{\mathbf{x}}_1)$ solves the problem

$$\begin{aligned} &\max_{\mathbf{x}_0 \in \mathbb{R}^N_+, \mathbf{x}_1 \in \mathbb{R}^N_+} \quad u(\mathbf{x}_0, \mathbf{x}_1) \\ &\text{s.t.} \quad \mathbf{P}_0.(\mathbf{x}_0 + \mathbf{x}_1) \leq \mathbf{P}_0.(\mathbf{e}_0 + \mathbf{e}_1). \end{aligned} \tag{9.20}$$

Since $\overline{\mathbf{x}}_0 + \overline{\mathbf{x}}_1 \leq \mathbf{e}_0 + \mathbf{e}_1$, it follows that $(\overline{\mathbf{x}}_0, \overline{\mathbf{x}}_1, \mathbf{P}_0, G)$ is a stationary spot price equilibrium with interest rate 0, where $G = \mathbf{P}_0.(\overline{\mathbf{x}}_1 - \mathbf{e}_1)$. This proves that stationary equilibria with interest rate 0 exist.

I now show that all such stationary equilibria have the same allocation and that it solves problem 9.19. Let $(\overline{\mathbf{x}}_0, \overline{\mathbf{x}}_1, \mathbf{P}_0, G)$ be a stationary spot price equilibrium with interest rate 0. Then by the definition of the equilibrium, $\overline{\mathbf{x}}_0 + \overline{\mathbf{x}}_1 \leq \mathbf{e}_0 + \mathbf{e}_1$, $P_{0n} = 0$, if $\overline{x}_{0n} + \overline{x}_{1n} < e_{0n} + e_{1n}$, for all n, and $(\overline{\mathbf{x}}_0, \overline{\mathbf{x}}_1)$

solves problem 9.20. Since $\mathbf{e}_0 + \mathbf{e}_1 \gg 0$, it follows that $\mathbf{P}_0.(\mathbf{e}_0 + \mathbf{e}_1) > 0$, and so problem 9.20 satisfies the constraint qualification of the Kuhn-Tucker theorem and there exists $\lambda \geq 0$, such that $\lambda = 0$ if $\mathbf{P}_0.(\overline{\mathbf{x}}_0 + \overline{\mathbf{x}}_1) < \mathbf{P}_0.(\mathbf{e}_0 + \mathbf{e}_1)$ and $(\overline{\mathbf{x}}_0, \overline{\mathbf{x}}_1)$ solves the problem

$$\max_{\mathbf{x}_0 \in \mathbb{R}^N_+, \mathbf{x}_1 \in \mathbb{R}^N_+} [u(\mathbf{x}_0, \mathbf{x}_1) - \lambda \mathbf{P}_0.(\mathbf{x}_0 + \mathbf{x}_1)].$$

Since u is locally nonsatiated, this problem has no solution if $\lambda = 0$, so that $\lambda > 0$. Since $\lambda P_{0n} = 0$, if $\overline{x}_{0n} + \overline{x}_{1n} < e_{0n} + e_{1n}$, the Kuhn-Tucker theorem implies that $(\overline{\mathbf{x}}_0, \overline{\mathbf{x}}_1)$ solves problem 9.19. Since u is strictly concave, this problem can have only one solution. ■

Example 9.26 (in section 9.5) shows that the allocation of a stationary spot price equilibrium with a positive interest rate may not be unique.

9.4 Stationary Discounted Optima and Equilibria

In a general equilibrium model without production and with finitely many consumers, if utility functions are concave, then any equilibrium allocation maximizes a weighted sum of the consumers' utilities and any allocation that does that is the allocation of an equilibrium with transfer payments. Similar assertions apply to the Samuelson model and appear in section 9.6. I introduce these ideas here in the context of stationary equilibria, which are much simpler than nonstationary ones.

DEFINITION 9.19 Let $r > 0$. A *stationary r-discounted optimum*, $(\overline{\mathbf{x}}_0, \overline{\mathbf{x}}_1)$, is a stationary solution, $\overline{\mathbf{x}} = (\overline{\mathbf{x}}_1, (\overline{\mathbf{x}}_0, \overline{\mathbf{x}}_1), (\overline{\mathbf{x}}_0, \overline{\mathbf{x}}_1), \ldots)$, to the optimization problem

$$\max_{\substack{\mathbf{x}_{t0} \in \mathbb{R}^N_+, \mathbf{x}_{t-1,1} \in \mathbb{R}^N_+, \\ \text{for all } t}} \left[(1+r)u(\overline{\mathbf{x}}_{-1,0}, \mathbf{x}_{-1,1}) + \sum_{t=0}^{\infty} (1+r)^{-t} u(\mathbf{x}_{t0}, \mathbf{x}_{t1})\right]$$
$$\text{s.t.} \quad \mathbf{x}_{t0} + \mathbf{x}_{t-1,1} \leq \mathbf{e}_0 + \mathbf{e}_1, \ \text{for } t \geq 0, \qquad (9.21)$$

where $\overline{\mathbf{x}}_{-1,0} = \overline{\mathbf{x}}_0$.

If the allocation $\overline{\mathbf{x}} = (\overline{\mathbf{x}}_{-1,1}, (\overline{\mathbf{x}}_{00}, \overline{\mathbf{x}}_{01}), (\overline{\mathbf{x}}_{10}, \overline{\mathbf{x}}_{11}), \ldots)$ solves problem 9.21, then for each nonnegative integer T, $(\overline{\mathbf{x}}_{T0}, \overline{\mathbf{x}}_{T-1,1})$ solves the problem

$$\max_{\mathbf{x}_0 \in \mathbb{R}^N_+, \mathbf{x}_1 \in \mathbb{R}^N_+} [(1+r)u(\overline{\mathbf{x}}_{T-1,0}, \mathbf{x}_1) + u(\mathbf{x}_0, \overline{\mathbf{x}}_{T1})]$$
$$\text{s.t.} \quad \mathbf{x}_0 + \mathbf{x}_1 \leq \mathbf{e}_0 + \mathbf{e}_1. \qquad (9.22)$$

To see that this is so, fix $\mathbf{x}_{t0}$ to equal $\overline{\mathbf{x}}_{t0}$ and fix $\mathbf{x}_{t-1,1}$ to equal $\overline{\mathbf{x}}_{t-1,1}$, for $t \neq T$ in the objective function of problem 9.21. Then that problem becomes

$$\max_{\mathbf{x}_{T0}\in\mathbb{R}^N_+,\, \mathbf{x}_{T-1,1}\in\mathbb{R}^N_+} \Bigg[(1+r)u(\overline{\mathbf{x}}_{-1,0}, \overline{\mathbf{x}}_{1,1}) + \sum_{t=0}^{T-2}(1+r)^{-1}u(\overline{\mathbf{x}}_{t0}, \overline{\mathbf{x}}_{t1})$$
$$+(1+r)^{-T+1}u(\overline{\mathbf{x}}_{T-1,0}, \mathbf{x}_{T-1,1}) + (1+r)^{-T}u(\mathbf{x}_{T0}, \overline{\mathbf{x}}_{T1})$$
$$+\sum_{t=T+1}^{\infty}(1+r)^{-t}u(\overline{\mathbf{x}}_{t0}, \overline{\mathbf{x}}_{t1})\Bigg]$$
$$\text{s.t.}\quad \mathbf{x}_{T0} + \mathbf{x}_{T-1,1} \leq \mathbf{e}_0 + \mathbf{e}_1.$$

If we eliminate constant terms from the objective function of this maximization problem and multiply that function by $(1+r)^T$, we obtain problem 9.22.

If $\overline{\mathbf{x}}$ is stationary, then $(\overline{\mathbf{x}}_{t0}, \overline{\mathbf{x}}_{t-1,1}) = (\overline{\mathbf{x}}_0, \overline{\mathbf{x}}_1)$, for all t, so that if $\overline{\mathbf{x}}$ is a stationary r-discounted optimum, then problem 9.22 becomes

$$\max_{\mathbf{x}_0\in\mathbb{R}^N_+,\, \mathbf{x}_1\in\mathbb{R}^N_+} [(1+r)u(\overline{\mathbf{x}}_0, \mathbf{x}_1) + u(\mathbf{x}_0, \overline{\mathbf{x}}_1)]$$
$$\text{s.t.}\quad \mathbf{x}_0 + \mathbf{x}_1 \leq \mathbf{e}_0 + \mathbf{e}_1. \tag{9.23}$$

In this maximization problem, the vector $(\overline{\mathbf{x}}_0, \overline{\mathbf{x}}_1)$ is held fixed, and if it is a stationary optimum, then the solution to the problem is $(\overline{\mathbf{x}}_0, \overline{\mathbf{x}}_1)$ again.

I show that stationary prices may be associated with a stationary r-discounted optimum so as to form stationary spot price equilibrium.

THEOREM 9.20 Assume that u is differentiable, concave, and strictly increasing, that $\mathbf{e}_0 + \mathbf{e}_1 \gg 0$, and that $r > 0$. If $(\overline{\mathbf{x}}_0, \overline{\mathbf{x}}_1)$ is a stationary r-discounted optimum or if it solves problem 9.23, then there exists an N-vector $\mathbf{P}_0$, such that $\mathbf{P}_0 \gg 0$ and $(\overline{\mathbf{x}}_0, \overline{\mathbf{x}}_1, \mathbf{P}_0, r, G, \mathsf{T})$ is a stationary spot price equilibrium, where $G = (1+r)^{-1}\mathbf{P}_0.(\overline{\mathbf{x}}_1 - \mathbf{e}_1)$.

Proof. We know that $(\overline{\mathbf{x}}_0, \overline{\mathbf{x}}_1)$ solves problem 9.23, either by assumption or because stationary r-discounted optima do so. Because $\mathbf{e}_0 + \mathbf{e}_1 \gg 0$, that problem satisfies the constraint qualification of the Kuhn-Tucker theorem (theorem 6.3 in section 6.1). Because u is strictly increasing, $\overline{\mathbf{x}}_0 + \overline{\mathbf{x}}_1 = \mathbf{e}_0 + \mathbf{e}_1$. The Kuhn-Tucker theorem therefore implies that there exists a nonnegative N-vector, $\mathbf{P}_0$, such that $(\overline{\mathbf{x}}_0, \overline{\mathbf{x}}_1)$ solves the problem

$$\max_{\mathbf{x}_0 \in \mathbb{R}^N_+, \mathbf{x}_1 \in \mathbb{R}^N_+} [(1+r)u(\overline{\mathbf{x}}_0, \mathbf{x}_1) + u(\mathbf{x}_0, \overline{\mathbf{x}}_1) - \mathbf{P}_0.(\mathbf{x}_0 + \mathbf{x}_1)].$$

Since u is differentiable, it follows from calculus or from proposition 6.18 (in section 6.4) that for all n,

$$\frac{\partial u(\overline{\mathbf{x}}_0, \overline{\mathbf{x}}_1)}{\partial x_{0n}} \leq P_{0n},$$

with equality if $\overline{\mathbf{x}}_{0n} > 0$, and

$$(1+r)\frac{\partial u(\overline{\mathbf{x}}_0, \overline{\mathbf{x}}_1)}{\partial x_{1n}} \leq P_{0n}, \tag{9.24}$$

with equality if $\overline{x}_{1n} > 0$. I may now apply theorem 6.19 (in section 6.4) with $K = 1$ and $\lambda_1 = 1$ to see that $(\overline{\mathbf{x}}_0, \overline{\mathbf{x}}_1)$ solves the problem

$$\begin{aligned} &\max_{\mathbf{x}_0 \in \mathbb{R}^N_+, \mathbf{x}_1 \in \mathbb{R}^N_+} u(\mathbf{x}_0, \mathbf{x}_1) \\ &\text{s.t.} \quad \mathbf{P}_0.\mathbf{x}_0 + (1+r)^{-1}\mathbf{P}_0.\mathbf{x}_1 \leq \mathbf{P}_0.\mathbf{e}_0 + (1+r)^{-1}\mathbf{P}_0.\mathbf{e}_0 - \mathsf{T}, \end{aligned} \tag{9.25}$$

where

$$\mathsf{T} = \mathbf{P}_0.(\mathbf{e}_0 - \overline{\mathbf{x}}_0) + (1+r)^{-1}\mathbf{P}_0.(\mathbf{e}_1 - \overline{\mathbf{x}}_1).$$

Let G be defined by the equation

$$(1+r)G = \mathbf{P}_0.(\overline{\mathbf{x}}_1 - \mathbf{e}_1).$$

Inequality 9.24 and proposition 6.18 (in section 6.4) imply that $\overline{\mathbf{x}}_1$ solves the problem

$$\begin{aligned} &\max_{\mathbf{x}_1 \in \mathbb{R}^N_+} u(\overline{\mathbf{x}}_0, \mathbf{x}_1) \\ &\text{s.t.} \quad \mathbf{P}_0.\mathbf{x}_1 \leq \mathbf{P}_0.\mathbf{e}_1 + (1+r)G. \end{aligned} \tag{9.26}$$

Since u is strictly increasing, $\mathbf{P}_0 \gg 0$, for otherwise, neither problem 9.25 nor problem 9.26 has a solution. This completes the verification that $(\overline{\mathbf{x}}_0, \overline{\mathbf{x}}_1, \mathbf{P}_0, r, G, \mathsf{T})$ has all the properties of a stationary spot price equilibrium. ▪

It is possible to make a counterexample to this theorem if u is not differentiable. I do not give one for lack of space. This theorem implies that a stationary optimum may be realized as the allocation of a stationary spot price equilibrium. It remains to prove the converse—that the allocation of a stationary spot price equilibrium with positive interest rate r is an r-discounted stationary optimum.

THEOREM 9.21 Assume that u is continuous, concave, and strictly increasing and that $\mathbf{e}_0 + \mathbf{e}_1 \gg 0$ and $r > 0$. If $(\overline{\mathbf{x}}_0, \overline{\mathbf{x}}_1, \mathbf{P}_0, r, G, \mathrm{T})$ is a stationary spot price equilibrium, then $(\overline{\mathbf{x}}_0, \overline{\mathbf{x}}_1)$ is a stationary r-discounted optimum.

Proof. By the definition of a stationary spot price equilibrium, $(\overline{\mathbf{x}}_0, \overline{\mathbf{x}}_1)$ solves problem 9.25. Because u is strictly increasing, it follows that $\mathbf{P}_0 \gg 0$, for otherwise, problem 9.25 would not have a solution. Therefore, $\overline{\mathbf{x}}_0 + \overline{\mathbf{x}}_1 = \mathbf{e}_0 + \mathbf{e}_1$, by condition (8) of definition 9.11 of a spot price equilibrium. Since $\overline{\mathbf{x}}_0 + \overline{\mathbf{x}}_1 = \mathbf{e}_0 + \mathbf{e}_1 \gg 0$ and $\mathbf{P}_0 \gg 0$, it follows that

$$\mathbf{P}_0.\overline{\mathbf{x}}_0 + (1+r)^{-1}\mathbf{P}_0.\overline{\mathbf{x}}_1 > 0,$$

so that problem 9.25 satisfies the conditions of proposition 6.14 (in section 6.3). Therefore, by that proposition there exists a positive number λ such that $(\overline{\mathbf{x}}_0, \overline{\mathbf{x}}_1)$ solves the problem

$$\max_{\mathbf{x}_0 \in \mathbb{R}^N_+, \mathbf{x}_1 \in \mathbb{R}^N_+} \left[u(\mathbf{x}_0, \mathbf{x}_1) - \lambda\left(\mathbf{P}_0.\mathbf{x}_0 + (1+r)^{-1}\mathbf{P}_0.\mathbf{x}_1\right)\right].$$

It follows that $\mathbf{x}_{-1,1} = \overline{\mathbf{x}}_1$ solves the problem

$$\max_{\mathbf{x}_{-1,1} \in \mathbb{R}^N_+} [(1+r)u(\overline{\mathbf{x}}_0, \mathbf{x}_{-1,1}) - \lambda \mathbf{P}_0.\mathbf{x}_{1,1}].$$

Similarly, $(\mathbf{x}_{t0}, \mathbf{x}_{t1}) = (\overline{\mathbf{x}}_0, \overline{\mathbf{x}}_1)$ solves the problem

$$\max_{\mathbf{x}_{t0} \in \mathbb{R}^N_+, \mathbf{x}_{t1} \in \mathbb{R}^N_+} \{(1+r)^{-t}u(\mathbf{x}_{t0}, \mathbf{x}_{t1}) - \lambda[(1+r)^{-t}\mathbf{P}_0.\mathbf{x}_{t0} + (1+r)^{-t-1}\mathbf{P}_0.\mathbf{x}_{t1}]\},$$

for any $t \geq 0$, and $\mathbf{x}_{T0} = \overline{\mathbf{x}}_0$ solves the problem

$$\max_{\mathbf{x}_{T0} \in \mathbb{R}^N_+} [(1+r)^{-T}u(\mathbf{x}_{T0}, \overline{\mathbf{x}}_1) - \lambda(1+r)^{-T}\mathbf{P}_0.\mathbf{x}_{T0}],$$

for any $T > 0$. Adding the objective functions of these maximization problems, we see that $(\mathbf{x}_{t0}, \mathbf{x}_{t-1,1})_{t=0}^T = (\overline{\mathbf{x}}_0, \overline{\mathbf{x}}_1)_{t=0}^T$ solves the problem

$$\max_{\mathbf{x}_{t0} \in \mathbb{R}^N_+, \mathbf{x}_{t-1,1} \in \mathbb{R}^N_+} \left[(1+r)u(\overline{\mathbf{x}}_0, \mathbf{x}_{-1,1}) + \sum_{t=1}^{T-1}(1+r)^{-t}u(\mathbf{x}_{t0}, \mathbf{x}_{t1}) + (1+r)^{-T}u(\mathbf{x}_{T0}, \overline{\mathbf{x}}_1) - \lambda\sum_{t=0}^{T}(1+r)^{-t}\mathbf{P}_0.(\mathbf{x}_{t-1,1} + \mathbf{x}_{t0})\right].$$

The Kuhn-Tucker theorem 6.3 (in section 6.1) implies that the allocation $(\mathbf{x}_{t0}, \mathbf{x}_{t-1,1})_{t=0}^{T} = (\overline{\mathbf{x}}_0, \overline{\mathbf{x}}_1)_{t=0}^{T}$ solves the problem

$$\max_{\substack{\mathbf{x}_{t0}\in\mathbb{R}_+^N,\, \mathbf{x}_{t-1,1}\in\mathbb{R}_+^N,\\ \text{for } t=0,\ldots,T}} \Big[(1+r)u(\overline{\mathbf{x}}_0, \mathbf{x}_{-1,1}) + \sum_{t=1}^{T-1}(1+r)^{-t}u(\mathbf{x}_{t0}, \mathbf{x}_{t1}) + (1+r)^{-T}u(\mathbf{x}_{T0}, \overline{\mathbf{x}}_1)\Big] \tag{9.27}$$
$$\text{s.t.}\quad \mathbf{x}_{t-1,1} + \mathbf{x}_{t0} \le \mathbf{e}_0 + \mathbf{e}_1, \text{ for } t = 0, \ldots, T.$$

I now show that the stationary allocation $\overline{\mathbf{x}} = (\overline{\mathbf{x}}_1, (\overline{\mathbf{x}}_0, \overline{\mathbf{x}}_1), (\overline{\mathbf{x}}_0, \overline{\mathbf{x}}_1), \ldots)$ solves problem 9.21. Suppose that it does not. Then there exists a feasible allocation $(\underline{\mathbf{x}}_{t-1,1}, \underline{\mathbf{x}}_{t0})_{t=0}^{\infty}$ such that for some positive number ε,

$$(1+r)u(\overline{\mathbf{x}}_0, \underline{\mathbf{x}}_{-1,1}) + \sum_{t=0}^{\infty}(1+r)^{-t}u(\underline{\mathbf{x}}_{t0}, \underline{\mathbf{x}}_{t1})$$
$$> (1+r)u(\overline{\mathbf{x}}_0, \overline{\mathbf{x}}_1) + \sum_{t=0}^{\infty}(1+r)^{-t}u(\overline{\mathbf{x}}_0, \overline{\mathbf{x}}_1) + \varepsilon.$$

I now derive a contradiction. Since feasible allocations are bounded, there is a positive number b such that for any feasible allocation $(\mathbf{x}_{t-1,1}, \mathbf{x}_{t0})_{t=0}^{\infty}$, $x_{t0n} \le b$ and $x_{t1n} \le b$, for all t and n. Let $B = \max(|u(0, 0, \ldots, 0)|, |u(b, b, \ldots, b)|)$. Choose a positive integer T such that

$$\frac{4B(1+r)^{-T}}{\min(1, r)} < \varepsilon.$$

Notice that if $(\mathbf{x}_{t-1,1}, \mathbf{x}_{t0})_{t=0}^{\infty}$ is any feasible allocation, then

$$\left|\sum_{t=T+1}^{\infty}(1+r)^{-t}u(\mathbf{x}_{t0}, \mathbf{x}_{t1})\right| \le \sum_{t=T+1}^{\infty}(1+r)^{-t}\left|u(\mathbf{x}_{t0}, \mathbf{x}_{t1})\right|$$
$$\le B\sum_{t=T+1}^{\infty}(1+r)^{-t} = \frac{B(1+r)^{-T}}{r} < \frac{\varepsilon}{4},$$

and similarly

$$(1+r)^{-T}|u(\mathbf{x}_{T0}, \mathbf{x}_{T1})| \le (1+r)^{-T}B < \frac{\varepsilon}{4}.$$

Therefore,

$$(1+r)u(\bar{\mathbf{x}}_0, \underline{\mathbf{x}}_{-1,1}) + \sum_{t=0}^{T-1}(1+r)^{-t}u(\underline{\mathbf{x}}_{t0}, \underline{\mathbf{x}}_{t1}) + (1+r)^{-T}u(\underline{\mathbf{x}}_{T0}, \bar{\mathbf{x}}_1)$$

$$+ 2B(1+r)^{-T} + \frac{B(1+r)^{-T}}{r}$$

$$\geq (1+r)u(\bar{\mathbf{x}}_0, \underline{\mathbf{x}}_{-1,1}) + \sum_{t=0}^{T-1}(1+r)^{-t}u(\underline{\mathbf{x}}_{t0}, \underline{\mathbf{x}}_{t1}) + (1+r)^{-T}u(\underline{\mathbf{x}}_{T0}, \bar{\mathbf{x}}_1)$$

$$+ (1+r)^{-T}[u(\underline{\mathbf{x}}_{T0}, \underline{\mathbf{x}}_{T1}) - u(\underline{\mathbf{x}}_{T0}, \bar{\mathbf{x}}_1)] + \sum_{t=T+1}^{\infty}(1+r)^{-t}u(\underline{\mathbf{x}}_{t0}, \underline{\mathbf{x}}_{t1})$$

$$= (1+r)u(\bar{\mathbf{x}}_0, \underline{\mathbf{x}}_{-1,1}) + \sum_{t=0}^{\infty}(1+r)^{-t}u(\underline{\mathbf{x}}_{t0}, \underline{\mathbf{x}}_{t1})$$

$$> (1+r)u(\bar{\mathbf{x}}_0, \bar{\mathbf{x}}_1) + \sum_{t=0}^{\infty}(1+r)^{-t}u(\bar{\mathbf{x}}_0, \bar{\mathbf{x}}_1) + \varepsilon$$

$$> (1+r)u(\bar{\mathbf{x}}_0, \bar{\mathbf{x}}_1) + \sum_{t=0}^{T}(1+r)^{-t}u(\bar{\mathbf{x}}_0, \bar{\mathbf{x}}_1) + \varepsilon - \frac{B(1+r)^{-T}}{r}.$$

Therefore,

$$(1+r)u(\bar{\mathbf{x}}_0, \underline{\mathbf{x}}_{-1,1}) + \sum_{t=0}^{T-1}(1+r)^{-t}u(\underline{\mathbf{x}}_{t0}, \underline{\mathbf{x}}_{t1}) + (1+r)^{-T}u(\underline{\mathbf{x}}_{T0}, \bar{\mathbf{x}}_1)$$

$$> (1+r)u(\bar{\mathbf{x}}_0, \bar{\mathbf{x}}_1) + \sum_{t=0}^{T}(1+r)^{-t}u(\bar{\mathbf{x}}_0, \bar{\mathbf{x}}_1) + \varepsilon - \frac{2B(1+r)^{-T}}{r}$$

$$- 2B(1+r)^{-T} > (1+r)u(\bar{\mathbf{x}}_0, \bar{\mathbf{x}}_1) + \sum_{t=0}^{T}(1+r)^{-t}u(\bar{\mathbf{x}}_0, \bar{\mathbf{x}}_1),$$

where the last inequality follows from the choice of ε. The strict inequality between the extreme left- and right-hand sides is impossible, because the allocation $(\mathbf{x}_{t0}, \mathbf{x}_{t-1,1})_{t=0}^{T} = (\bar{\mathbf{x}}_0, \bar{\mathbf{x}}_1)_{t=0}^{T}$ solves problem 9.27. This contradiction proves that the stationary allocation $\bar{\mathbf{x}} = (\bar{\mathbf{x}}_1, (\bar{\mathbf{x}}_0, \bar{\mathbf{x}}_1), (\bar{\mathbf{x}}_0, \bar{\mathbf{x}}_1), \ldots)$ solves problem 9.21. ▪

We know that an r-discounted optimum solves problem 9.23. Theorems 9.20 and 9.21 imply that if u is differentiable, concave, and strictly increasing and if $\mathbf{e}_0 + \mathbf{e}_1 \gg 0$ and $r > 0$, then a solution of problem 9.23 is an r-discounted optimum, so that a stationary allocation is an r-discounted optimum if and only if it solves this problem. If in addition there is only one commodity, so that $N = 1$, and if $\overline{x}_0 > 0$ and $\overline{x}_1 > 0$, then $(\overline{x}_0, \overline{x}_1)$ solves problem 9.23 if and only if

$$\overline{x}_0 + \overline{x}_1 = e_0 + e_1$$

and

$$(1+r)\frac{\partial u(\overline{x}_0, \overline{x}_1)}{\partial x_1} = \frac{\partial u(\overline{x}_0, \overline{x}_1)}{\partial x_0},$$

which are the equations 9.15 and 9.16 (in section 9.3) that characterize the allocation of a stationary equilibrium.

I now prove that stationary r-discounted optima exist.

THEOREM 9.22 Assume that u is differentiable, strictly concave, and strictly increasing and that $\mathbf{e}_0 + \mathbf{e}_1 \gg 0$ and $r > 0$. Then there exists a stationary allocation $(\overline{\mathbf{x}}_0, \overline{\mathbf{x}}_1)$ that solves problem 9.23, and this allocation is a stationary r-discounted optimum.

Proof. By theorem 9.20, any solution $(\overline{\mathbf{x}}_0, \overline{\mathbf{x}}_1)$ of problem 9.23 is the allocation of a stationary spot price equilibrium $(\overline{\mathbf{x}}_0, \overline{\mathbf{x}}_1, \mathbf{P}_0, r, G, \mathsf{T})$. By theorem 9.21, the allocation of such an equilibrium is a stationary r-discounted optimum. Therefore, it is sufficient to prove that there is an $(\overline{\mathbf{x}}_0, \overline{\mathbf{x}}_1)$ that solves problem 9.23.

The objective function, $(1+r)u(\overline{\mathbf{x}}_0, \mathbf{x}_1) + u(\mathbf{x}_0, \overline{\mathbf{x}}_1)$, of problem 9.23 is continuous and strictly concave with respect to all variables. Furthermore, the maximization is over the nonempty, compact, and convex set, $\Delta = \{(\mathbf{x}_0, \mathbf{x}_1) \in \mathbb{R}^N_+ \times \mathbb{R}^N_+ \mid \mathbf{x}_0 + \mathbf{x}_1 \le e_0 + e_1\}$. I will show that the maximizing value, $(\mathbf{x}_0, \mathbf{x}_1)$, in problem 9.23, is a well-defined and continuous function, $f(\overline{\mathbf{x}}_0, \overline{\mathbf{x}}_1)$, of the variables $(\overline{\mathbf{x}}_0, \overline{\mathbf{x}}_1)$. Hence, f has a fixed point by the Brouwer fixed point theorem. That is, there is a vector $(\overline{\mathbf{x}}_0, \overline{\mathbf{x}}_1) \in \Delta$ such that $f(\overline{\mathbf{x}}_0, \overline{\mathbf{x}}_1) = (\overline{\mathbf{x}}_0, \overline{\mathbf{x}}_1)$. Such a fixed point is a stationary r-discounted optimum by the argument of the previous paragraph.

To prove that f is well defined, observe that since u is continuous and Δ is compact and nonempty, it follows from proposition 3.14 (in section 3.2) that problem 9.23 has at least one solution. Suppose that there are two distinct solutions, $(\mathbf{x}_0^1, \mathbf{x}_1^1)$ and $(\mathbf{x}_0^2, \mathbf{x}_1^2)$. Then,

$$(1+r)u(\overline{\mathbf{x}}_0, \mathbf{x}_1^1) + u(\mathbf{x}_0^1, \overline{\mathbf{x}}_1) = (1+r)u(\overline{\mathbf{x}}_0, \mathbf{x}_1^2) + u(\mathbf{x}_0^2, \overline{\mathbf{x}}_1).$$

Let $(\mathbf{x}_0, \mathbf{x}_1) = \frac{1}{2}(\mathbf{x}_0^1, \mathbf{x}_1^1) + \frac{1}{2}(\mathbf{x}_0^2, \mathbf{x}_1^2)$. Then $(\mathbf{x}_0, \mathbf{x}_1) \in \Delta$, and because u is strictly concave,

$$\begin{aligned}(1+r)&u(\overline{\mathbf{x}}_0, \mathbf{x}_1) + u(\mathbf{x}_0, \overline{\mathbf{x}}_1)\\ &> \frac{1}{2}[(1+r)u(\overline{\mathbf{x}}_0, \mathbf{x}_1^1) + u(\mathbf{x}_0^1, \overline{\mathbf{x}}_1)] + \frac{1}{2}[(1+r)u(\overline{\mathbf{x}}_0, \mathbf{x}_1^2) + u(\mathbf{x}_0^2, \overline{\mathbf{x}}_1)]\\ &= (1+r)u(\overline{\mathbf{x}}_0, \mathbf{x}_1^1) + u(\mathbf{x}_0^1),\end{aligned}$$

which is impossible since $(\mathbf{x}_0^1, \mathbf{x}_1^1)$ solves problem 9.23. This proves that f is a function.

It remains to prove that f is continuous. Let $(\overline{\mathbf{x}}_0^k, \overline{\mathbf{x}}_1^k)$, for $k = 1, 2, \ldots,$ be a sequence in Δ such that $(\overline{\mathbf{x}}_0^k, \overline{\mathbf{x}}_1^k)$ converges to $(\overline{\mathbf{x}}_0, \overline{\mathbf{x}}_1)$ in Δ as k goes to infinity. I must show that $f(\overline{\mathbf{x}}_0^k, \overline{\mathbf{x}}_1^k)$ converges to $f(\overline{\mathbf{x}}_0, \overline{\mathbf{x}}_1)$. If $f(\overline{\mathbf{x}}_0^k, \overline{\mathbf{x}}_1^k)$ does not converge to $f(\overline{\mathbf{x}}_0, \overline{\mathbf{x}}_1)$, then there exists a positive number ε and a subsequence, $(\overline{\mathbf{x}}_0^{k(m)}, \overline{\mathbf{x}}_1^{k(m)})$ of $(\overline{\mathbf{x}}_0^k, \overline{\mathbf{x}}_1^k)$, such that

$$\| f(\overline{\mathbf{x}}_0^{k(m)}, \overline{\mathbf{x}}_1^{k(m)}) - f(\overline{\mathbf{x}}_0, \overline{\mathbf{x}}_1)\| > \varepsilon, \tag{9.28}$$

for all m. Since the $f(\overline{\mathbf{x}}_0^{k(m)}, \overline{\mathbf{x}}_1^{k(m)})$ belong to the compact set Δ, the Bolzano-Weierstrass theorem (3.12 in section 3.2) implies that there is a subsequence of $(\overline{\mathbf{x}}_0^{k(m)}, \overline{\mathbf{x}}_1^{k(m)})$, which I call $(\overline{\mathbf{x}}_0^{k(m)}, \overline{\mathbf{x}}_1^{k(m)})$ again, such that $f(\overline{\mathbf{x}}_0^{k(m)}, \overline{\mathbf{x}}_1^{k(m)})$ converges. Let $(\underline{\mathbf{x}}_0, \underline{\mathbf{x}}_1) = \lim_{m\to\infty} f(\overline{\mathbf{x}}_0^{k(m)}, \overline{\mathbf{x}}_1^{k(m)})$. Then $(\underline{\mathbf{x}}_0, \underline{\mathbf{x}}_1) \in \Delta$, and passage to the limit in inequality 9.28 implies that $\|(\underline{\mathbf{x}}_0, \underline{\mathbf{x}}_1) - f(\overline{\mathbf{x}}_0, \overline{\mathbf{x}}_1)\| \geq \varepsilon$, so that $(\underline{\mathbf{x}}_0, \underline{\mathbf{x}}_1) \neq f(\overline{\mathbf{x}}_0, \overline{\mathbf{x}}_1)$. Let $f(\overline{\mathbf{x}}_0, \overline{\mathbf{x}}_1) = (\mathbf{x}_0^*, \mathbf{x}_1^*)$. Because $(\mathbf{x}_0^*, \mathbf{x}_1^*)$ is the unique solution of problem 9.23, it follows that

$$(1+r)u(\overline{\mathbf{x}}_0, \underline{\mathbf{x}}_1) + u(\underline{\mathbf{x}}_0, \overline{\mathbf{x}}_1) < (1+r)u(\overline{\mathbf{x}}_0, \mathbf{x}_1^*) + u(\mathbf{x}_0^*, \overline{\mathbf{x}}_1). \tag{9.29}$$

Let $(\underline{\mathbf{x}}_0^{k(m)}, \underline{\mathbf{x}}_1^{k(m)}) = f(\overline{\mathbf{x}}_0^{k(m)}, \overline{\mathbf{x}}_1^{k(m)})$. Then,

$$\lim_{m\to\infty} f(\overline{\mathbf{x}}_0^{k(m)}, \overline{\mathbf{x}}_1^{k(m)}) = \lim_{m\to\infty} (\underline{\mathbf{x}}_0^{k(m)}, \underline{\mathbf{x}}_1^{k(m)}) = (\underline{\mathbf{x}}_0, \underline{\mathbf{x}}_1). \tag{9.30}$$

By assumption,

$$\lim_{m\to\infty} (\overline{\mathbf{x}}_0^{k(m)}, \overline{\mathbf{x}}_1^{k(m)}) = (\overline{\mathbf{x}}_0, \overline{\mathbf{x}}_1). \tag{9.31}$$

Equations 9.30 and 9.31 and the continuity of u imply that

$$\lim_{m\to\infty}[(1+r)u(\overline{\mathbf{x}}_0^{k(m)}, \underline{\mathbf{x}}_1^{k(m)}) + u(\underline{\mathbf{x}}_0^{k(m)}, \overline{\mathbf{x}}_1^{k(m)})] \\ = (1+r)u(\overline{\mathbf{x}}_0, \underline{\mathbf{x}}_1) + u(\underline{\mathbf{x}}_0, \overline{\mathbf{x}}_1). \tag{9.32}$$

Equation 9.31 and the continuity of u imply that

$$\lim_{m\to\infty}[(1+r)u(\overline{\mathbf{x}}_0^{k(m)}, \mathbf{x}_1^*) + u(\mathbf{x}_0^*, \overline{\mathbf{x}}_1^{k(m)})] = (1+r)u(\overline{\mathbf{x}}_0, \mathbf{x}_1^*) + u(\mathbf{x}_0^*, \overline{\mathbf{x}}_1). \tag{9.33}$$

Inequality 9.29 and equations 9.32 and 9.33 imply that, for m sufficiently large,

$$(1+r)u(\overline{\mathbf{x}}_0^{k(m)}, \underline{\mathbf{x}}_1^{k(m)}) + u(\underline{\mathbf{x}}_0^{k(m)}, \overline{\mathbf{x}}_1^{k(m)}) < (1+r)u(\overline{\mathbf{x}}_0^{k(m)}, \underline{\mathbf{x}}_1^*) \\ + u(\mathbf{x}_0^*, \overline{\mathbf{x}}_1^{k(m)}),$$

and this inequality contradicts the definition of the function f and the fact that $(\underline{\mathbf{x}}_0^{k(m)}, \underline{\mathbf{x}}_1^{k(m)}) = f(\overline{\mathbf{x}}_0^{k(m)}, \overline{\mathbf{x}}_1^{k(m)})$. This contradiction proves that $\lim_{k\to\infty} f(\overline{\mathbf{x}}_0^k, \overline{\mathbf{x}}_1^k) = f(\overline{\mathbf{x}}_0, \overline{\mathbf{x}})$ and hence that f is continuous. ∎

This theorem implies that there exists a stationary spot price equilibrium, for it implies that there is a stationary allocation $(\overline{\mathbf{x}}_0, \overline{\mathbf{x}}_1)$ that solves problem 9.23, and by theorem 9.20, such solutions are allocations of stationary spot price equilibria.

How are we to interpret the previous three theorems? We may think of the interest rate in a stationary spot price equilibrium $(\overline{\mathbf{x}}_0, \overline{\mathbf{x}}_1, \mathbf{P}_0, r, G, \mathsf{T})$ as determined by monetary policy, and we may think of the tax rate, T, as an instrument of fiscal policy. Loosely speaking, the interest and tax rate determine the equilibrium. Whether the government is aware of its influence or not, its policy determines interest rates, price levels, and a path for the economy that maximizes some welfare function, provided the economy is such that the model applies. Similarly, the government may act so as to maximize a given welfare function. This result is proved here only for stationary equilibria and welfare functions, but we will see (theorem 9.28 in section 9.6) that it applies to nonstationary ones as well.

If u is differentiable, then a stationary spot price equilibrium may be characterized by conditions 9.34–9.38 below, which correspond to conditions 9.15–9.18 (in section 9.3).

$$\frac{\partial u(\overline{\mathbf{x}}_0, \overline{\mathbf{x}}_1)}{\partial \overline{x}_{0n}} \le P_{0n}, \tag{9.34}$$

with equality if $\overline{x}_{0n} > 0$, for $n = 1, 2, \ldots, N$.

$$(1+r)\frac{\partial u(\overline{\mathbf{x}}_0, \overline{\mathbf{x}}_1)}{\partial \overline{x}_{1n}} \leq P_{0n}, \tag{9.35}$$

with equality if $\overline{x}_{1n} > 0$, for $n = 1, 2, \ldots, N$. Because u is strictly increasing, feasibility holds with equality rather than inequality, and so

$$\overline{x}_{0n} + \overline{x}_{1n} = e_{0n} + e_{1n}, \tag{9.36}$$

for $n = 1, 2, \ldots, N$.

$$G = (1+r)^{-1}\mathbf{P}_0.(\overline{\mathbf{x}}_1 - \mathbf{e}_1), \tag{9.37}$$

and

$$\mathsf{T} = rG. \tag{9.38}$$

These make $3N + 2$ conditions on the $3N + 2$ variables G, T, and ($\overline{x}_{0n}$, $\overline{x}_{1n}$, P_{0n}), for $n = 1, 2, \ldots, N$. Notice that the consumer's marginal utility of unit of account in this equilibrium equals 1, so that utility is, in a sense, the unit of account.

When $N = 1$, stationary spot price equilibria may be visualized as in figure 9.4 (in section 9.3). This figure helps us to consider the uniqueness of stationary equilibria and optima. A glance at the figure should indicate that there is no reason that the indifference curve through $\mathbf{x}$ should not have the same slope at many points $\mathbf{x}$ along the feasibility line between A and B. Example 9.26 (in section 9.5) shows that this possibility is real and that stationary equilibria and optima may not be unique, even if u is strictly concave. The next proposition points out that no such example can be constructed, however, if the utility function u is additively separable.

PROPOSITION 9.23 If u is strictly concave and additively separable in the sense that $u(\mathbf{x}_0, \mathbf{x}_1) = u_0(\mathbf{x}_0) + u_1(\mathbf{x}_1)$, then there is at most one stationary solution to welfare maximization problem 9.21.

Proof. We know that $\overline{\mathbf{x}}$ is a stationary solution to welfare maximization problem 9.21 if and only if $(\overline{\mathbf{x}}_0, \overline{\mathbf{x}}_1)$ solves problem 9.23. If u is additively separable, this problem takes the form

$$\max_{\mathbf{x}_0 \in \mathbb{R}^N_+, \mathbf{x}_1 \in \mathbb{R}^N_+} [(1+r)[u_0(\overline{\mathbf{x}}_0) + u_1(\mathbf{x}_1)] + u_0(\mathbf{x}_0) + u_1(\overline{\mathbf{x}}_1)]$$

$$\text{s.t.} \quad \mathbf{x}_0 + \mathbf{x}_1 \leq \mathbf{e}_0 + \mathbf{e}_1,$$

which has the same solutions as the problem

$$\max_{\mathbf{x}_0 \in \mathbb{R}^N_+, \mathbf{x}_1 \in \mathbb{R}^N_+} [(1+r)u_1(\mathbf{x}_1) + u_0(\mathbf{x}_0)] \quad \text{s.t.} \quad \mathbf{x}_0 + \mathbf{x}_1 \le \mathbf{e}_0 + \mathbf{e}_1. \tag{9.39}$$

Since u is strictly concave, u_0 and u_1 are strictly concave, so that $(1+r)u_1(\mathbf{x}_1) + u_0(\mathbf{x}_0)$ is strictly concave and the solution to problem 9.39 is unique. ■

Another consequence of the additive separability of u is that it eliminates the need to assume that u is differentiable in theorem 9.20.

PROPOSITION 9.24 Assume that $\mathbf{e}_0 + \mathbf{e}_1 \gg 0$ and that u is strictly concave, strictly increasing, and is additively separable in the sense that $u(\mathbf{x}_0, \mathbf{x}_1) = u_0(\mathbf{x}_0) + u_1(\mathbf{x}_1)$. If $(\overline{\mathbf{x}}_0, \overline{\mathbf{x}}_1)$ is a stationary solution to welfare maximization problem 9.21, then there exists an N-vector, $\mathbf{P}_0$, such that $P_0 \gg 0$ and $(\overline{\mathbf{x}}_0, \overline{\mathbf{x}}_1, \mathbf{P}_0, r, G, \mathsf{T})$ is a stationary spot price equilibrium, where $G = (1+r)^{-1}\mathbf{P}_0.(\overline{\mathbf{x}}_1 - \mathbf{e}_1)$ and $\mathsf{T} = rG$.

Proof. From the proof of the previous proposition, we know that $(\overline{\mathbf{x}}_0, \overline{\mathbf{x}}_1)$ solves problem 9.39. Application of the Kuhn-Tucker theorem directly to this maximization problem yields a price vector $\mathbf{P}_0$ such that $(\overline{\mathbf{x}}_0, \overline{\mathbf{x}}_1)$ solves the problem

$$\max_{\mathbf{x}_0 \in \mathbb{R}^N_+, \mathbf{x}_1 \in \mathbb{R}^N_+} [(1+r)u_1(\mathbf{x}_1) + u_0(\mathbf{x}_0) - \mathbf{P}_0.(\mathbf{x}_0 + \mathbf{x}_1)].$$

This problem, in turn, decomposes into two problems,

$$\max_{\mathbf{x}_0 \in \mathbb{R}^N_+} [u_0(\mathbf{x}_0) - \mathbf{P}_0.\mathbf{x}_0] \tag{9.40}$$

and

$$\max_{\mathbf{x}_1 \in \mathbb{R}^N_+} [(1+r)u_1(\mathbf{x}_1) - \mathbf{P}_0.\mathbf{x}_1].$$

The latter problem has the same solutions as the problem

$$\max_{\mathbf{x}_1 \in \mathbb{R}^N_+} [u_1(x_1) - (1+r)^{-1}\mathbf{P}_0.\mathbf{x}_1]. \tag{9.41}$$

Problems 9.40 and 9.41 may be consolidated into the single problem

$$\max_{\mathbf{x}_0 \in \mathbb{R}^N_+, \mathbf{x}_1 \in \mathbb{R}^N_+} [u_0(\mathbf{x}_0) + u_1(\mathbf{x}_1) - \mathbf{P}_0.\mathbf{x}_0 + (1+r)^{-1}\mathbf{P}_0.\mathbf{x}_1)].$$

Since $(\overline{\mathbf{x}}_0, \overline{\mathbf{x}}_1)$ solves this last problem, by the Kuhn-Tucker theorem it solves the problem

$$\max_{\mathbf{x}_0 \in \mathbb{R}^N_+, \mathbf{x}_1 \in \mathbb{R}^N_+} [u_0(\mathbf{x}_0) + u_1(\mathbf{x}_1)]$$

$$\text{s.t.} \quad \mathbf{P}_0.\mathbf{x}_0 + (1+r)^{-1}\mathbf{P}_0.\mathbf{x}_1 \le \mathbf{P}_0.\mathbf{e}_0 + (1+r)^{-1}\mathbf{P}_0.\mathbf{e}_1 - \mathsf{T},$$

where

$$\mathsf{T} = \mathbf{P}_0.(\mathbf{e}_0 - \overline{\mathbf{x}}_0) + (1+r)^{-1}\mathbf{P}_0.(\mathbf{e}_1 - \overline{\mathbf{x}}_1).$$

This is the problem solved by a consumer in a stationary spot price equilibrium. The rest of the proof is just like that of theorem 9.20. ▪

According to the next theorem, additive separability of the utility function eliminates the influence of the initial consumption $\overline{\mathbf{x}}_{-1,0}$ on the solution of welfare maximization problem 9.21.

PROPOSITION 9.25 If the utility function u is additively separable and strictly concave, then welfare maximization problem 9.21 has a unique solution and it is stationary.

Proof. Any solution $\overline{\mathbf{x}}$ to problem 9.21 solves the problem

$$\max_{\mathbf{x}_0 \in \mathbb{R}^N_+, \mathbf{x}_1 \in \mathbb{R}^N_+} [(1+r)u(\overline{\mathbf{x}}_{t-1,0}, \mathbf{x}_1) + u(\mathbf{x}_0, \overline{\mathbf{x}}_{t1})]$$

$$\text{s.t.} \quad \mathbf{x}_0 + \mathbf{x}_1 \le \mathbf{e}_0 + \mathbf{e}_1,$$

for each t. Since u is additively separable, this problem becomes

$$\max_{\mathbf{x}_0 \in \mathbb{R}^N_+, \mathbf{x}_1 \in \mathbb{R}^N_+} [(1+r)(u_0(\overline{\mathbf{x}}_{t-1,0}) + u_1(\mathbf{x}_1)) + u_0(\mathbf{x}_0) + u_1(\overline{\mathbf{x}}_{t1})]$$

$$\text{s.t.} \quad \mathbf{x}_0 + \mathbf{x}_1 \le \mathbf{e}_0 + \mathbf{e}_1.$$

After elimination of the constant terms $u_0(\overline{\mathbf{x}}_{t-1,0})$ and $u_1(\overline{\mathbf{x}}_{t,1})$ from the objective function, this problem becomes problem 9.39, which has only one solution because u is strictly concave. Therefore, problem 9.21 has a unique solution and it is stationary. ▪

The use of an additively separable utility function for consumption makes clear how the discounting of the welfare of future generations influences the distribution of consumption between young and old consumers. If u is additively separable, then a solution, $\overline{\mathbf{x}}$, of problem 9.21 is such that

$(\overline{\mathbf{x}}_{t-1,1}, \overline{\mathbf{x}}_{t0})$ solves problem 9.39, for each t. The objective function of this problem, $(1+r)u_1(\mathbf{x}_1) + u_0(\mathbf{x}_0)$, clearly gives greater weight to the utility of the old than that of the young. Assume that u is strictly concave, so that the solution of problem 9.39 is unique. Call this solution $(\overline{\mathbf{x}}_1, \overline{\mathbf{x}}_0)$, so that $(\overline{\mathbf{x}}_{t-1,1}, \overline{\mathbf{x}}_{t0}) = (\overline{\mathbf{x}}_1, \overline{\mathbf{x}}_0)$, for all t. It should be clear that if u is also increasing, then $u_1(\overline{\mathbf{x}}_1)$ is a nondecreasing function of r and that $u_0(\overline{\mathbf{x}}_0)$ is a nonincreasing function of r.

9.5 Nonuniqueness of Equilibrium

In this section, I give two examples of Samuelson models with more than one equilibrium. The first example shows that stationary equilibrium allocations and hence r-discounted optima may not be unique when the discount rate is positive, even if the utility function is strictly concave.

EXAMPLE 9.26 (Multiple stationary optima and equilibrium allocations) Consider the stationary Samuelson model with one commodity and where $e_0 = 1$ and $e_1 = 0$ and the utility function is

$$u(x_0, x_1) = \min(4x_0 + 2x_1, 3x_0 + x_1 + 1) - \frac{1}{3(1+x_0)} - \frac{1}{3(1+x_1)}.$$

I claim that any stationary allocation is the allocation of a stationary equilibrium if the nominal interest rate, r, is such that

$$\frac{27}{25} \leq r \leq \frac{21}{16}. \tag{9.42}$$

An example of such an interest rate is $r = 1.2$.

The function $\min(4x_0 + 2x_1, 3x_0 + x_1 + 1)$ is concave and strictly increasing, because it is the minimum of two concave and strictly increasing functions. The utility function u is strictly concave and strictly increasing, since the function $-\frac{1}{3(1+x_0)} - \frac{1}{3(1+x_1)}$ is strictly concave and strictly increasing and the function $\min(4x_0 + 2x_1, 3x_0 + x_1 - 1)$ is concave and increasing. This function is not differentiable, however. If we set $4x_0 + 2x_1$ equal to $3x_0 + x_1 + 1$, we obtain the equation $x_0 + x_1 = 1$, and the indifference curves of u have a kink along this line. I compute the slope of this indifference curve on each side of the line. The slope above the line is

$$-\frac{\dfrac{\partial u(x_0, 1-x_0)}{\partial x_0+}}{\dfrac{\partial u(x_0, 1-x_0)}{\partial x_1+}} = -\frac{3+\dfrac{1}{3(1+x_0)^2}}{1+\dfrac{1}{3(2-x_0)^2}} < -\frac{3+\dfrac{1}{3(4)}}{1+\frac{1}{3}} = -\frac{37}{16},$$

where the inequality holds because $0 \le x_0 \le 1$ and for x_0 in this interval the numerator of the fraction

$$\frac{3+\dfrac{1}{3(1+x_0)^2}}{1+\dfrac{1}{3(2-x_0)^2}}$$

is decreasing in x_0 and the denominator is increasing in x_0 and hence the whole fraction is decreasing in x_0. The slope below the line is

$$-\frac{\dfrac{\partial u(x_0, 1-x_0)}{\partial x_0-}}{\dfrac{\partial u(x_0, 1-x_0)}{\partial x_1-}} = -\frac{4+\dfrac{1}{3(1+x_0)^2}}{2+\dfrac{1}{3(2-x_0)^2}} > -\frac{4+\dfrac{1}{3}}{2+\dfrac{1}{3(4)}} = -\frac{52}{25},$$

where the inequality holds for reasons similar to those just given for the previous inequality. Any feasible allocation along the line $x_0 + x_1 = 1$ is that of a stationary equilibrium with interest rate r if

$$-\frac{37}{16} \le -(1+r) \le -\frac{52}{25},$$

which is the same as inequality 9.42.

The next example, due to Gale (1973), shows that there may be many spot price equilibria corresponding to one time path of taxes and interest rates.

EXAMPLE 9.27 (Indeterminacy of spot price equilibrium in the Samuelson model) Consider the stationary Samuelson model with $N = 1$, $e_0 = \frac{3}{4}$, $e_1 = \frac{1}{4}$, and $u(x_0, x_1) = \ln(1+x_0) + \ln(1+2x_1)$.

It is easy to calculate that if $P_0 = 1$, then the offer curve is $\{(\frac{3}{8}P_1 - \frac{1}{8}, \frac{7}{8P_1} - \frac{1}{8}) \mid P_1 \ge 0\}$ and is as pictured in figure 9.5, where the axes are labeled as in figure 9.2 (in section 9.2). The offer curve goes through the initial endowment point, $\mathbf{e} = (\frac{3}{4}, \frac{1}{4})$, when $P_1 = \frac{7}{3}$. The offer curve

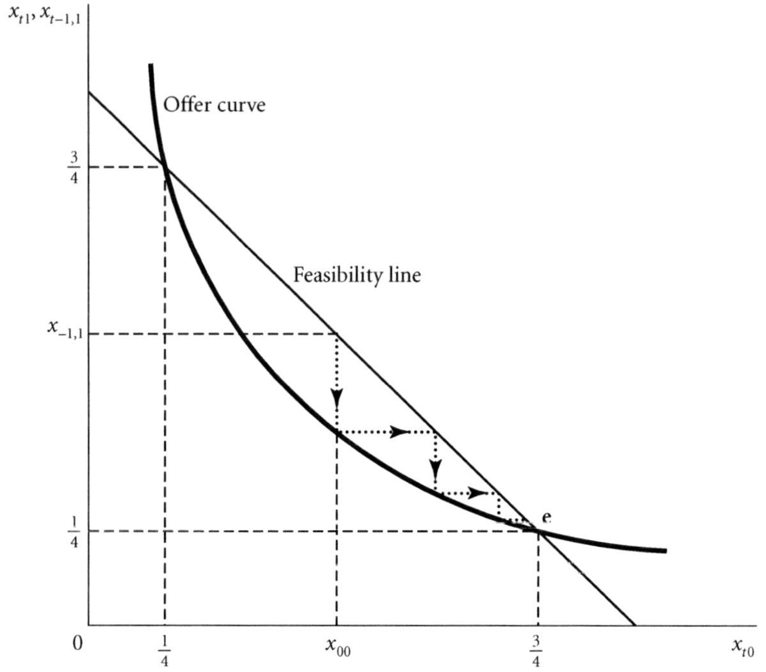

Figure 9.5 Multiplicity of equilibria in the Samuelson model

intersects the feasibility line again at the point $(\frac{1}{4}, \frac{3}{4})$. This point corresponds to a Pareto optimal stationary spot price equilibrium with allocation $(\overline{x}_{t0}, \overline{x}_{t1}) = (\overline{x}_0, \overline{x}_1) = (\frac{1}{4}, \frac{3}{4})$ and price $P_t = 1 = P_0$, for every t. In this equilibrium, the government debt is $G = P_0(\overline{x}_1 - e_1) = \frac{3}{4} - \frac{1}{4} = \frac{1}{2}$. I will show that when $G = 1/2$ there is a distinct equilibrium, $(x_{t-1,0}, x_{t0}, P_t)_{t=0}^{\infty}$, for every initial price vector P_0 such that $P_0 > 1$. The consumption of the old person of period 0 is

$$x_{-1,1} = \frac{G}{P_0} + e_1 = \frac{1}{2P_0} + \frac{1}{4},$$

so that $\frac{1}{4} < x_{-1,1} < \frac{3}{4}$, if $P_0 > 1$. Then, the consumption of the young person of period 0 is $x_{00} = e_0 + e_1 - x_{-1,1} = 1 - (\frac{1}{2P_0} + \frac{1}{4}) = \frac{3}{4} - \frac{1}{2P_0}$. Since the point (x_{00}, x_{01}) must be on the offer curve, we know that $\frac{3}{4} - \frac{1}{2P_0} = x_{00} = \frac{3}{8}\frac{P_1}{P_0} - \frac{1}{8}$, so that $P_1 = \frac{7}{3}P_0 - \frac{4}{3}$. Since government debt G remains equal to 1/2 in all periods, we can use the same reasoning to show that

$P_{t+1} = \frac{7}{3}P_t - \frac{4}{3}$, for all $t \geq 0$. Therefore,

$$P_t = \left(\frac{7}{3}\right)^t P_0 - \left(\frac{7}{3}\right)^{t-1}\frac{4}{3} - \left(\frac{7}{3}\right)^{t-2}\frac{4}{3} - \cdots - \frac{4}{3}$$

$$= \left(\frac{7}{3}\right)^t P_0 - \frac{4}{3}\left[\frac{\left(\frac{7}{3}\right)^t - 1}{\frac{7}{3} - 1}\right]$$

$$= \left(\frac{7}{3}\right)^t (P_0 - 1) + 1,$$

for all $t \geq 1$, so that P_t diverges to infinity as t goes to infinity, since $P_0 > 1$. Therefore, $x_{t-1,1} = e_1 + \frac{G}{P_{t+1}} = \frac{1}{4} + \frac{1}{2P_{t+1}}$, converges to $\frac{1}{4}$ as t goes to infinity. Similarly, $x_{t0} = e_0 + e_1 - x_{t-1,1} = 1 - x_{t-1,1}$, converges to $\frac{3}{4}$ as t goes to infinity. The evolution of x_{t0} and x_{t1} is portrayed by the zigzag dotted line in figure 9.5. The allocation converges to the inefficient stationary allocation equal to the initial endowment, and the real value of government debt converges to 0 as the price level diverges to infinity. The equilibrium allocation is itself inefficient, because a jump at any time to the stationary allocation $(\overline{x}_0, \overline{x}_1) = (\frac{3}{4}, \frac{1}{4})$ would be a Pareto improvement. The significance of the example, however, has nothing to do with economic efficiency but is that the initial price level, P_0, is indeterminate.

The possibility of indeterminacy demonstrated by this example calls into question the assertion made in section 9.4 that monetary and fiscal policy can control the economy so as to maximize any desired welfare function.

9.6 Discounted Optimality and Equilibrium

You may recall from theorem 3.31 (in section 3.5) that equilibrium allocations maximize a weighted sum of the consumers' utility functions, when utility functions are concave and production possibility sets are convex. Furthermore, proposition 3.23 (in section 3.5) and the second welfare theorem (5.14 in section 5.2) imply that an allocation that maximizes such a weighted sum is the allocation of an equilibrium with transfer payments. The same statements apply to equilibria in the Samuelson model. These assertions reinforce the view that monetary and fiscal policy influence the distribution of welfare between the young and the old.

I first show that an Arrow-Debreu equilibrium allocation maximizes a welfare function.

THEOREM 9.28 Assume that u is continuous, concave, and strictly increasing. If $(\overline{\mathbf{x}}, \mathbf{p}, \boldsymbol{\tau})$ is an Arrow-Debreu equilibrium with transfer payments such that $\overline{\mathbf{x}}_{-1,1} > 0$ and $\overline{\mathbf{x}}_{t0} + \overline{\mathbf{x}}_{t1} > 0$, for all t, and

$$\sum_{t=0}^{\infty} \mathbf{p}_t < \infty, \tag{9.43}$$

then the allocation $\overline{\mathbf{x}}$ solves the problem

$$\max_{\substack{\mathbf{x} \text{ is a feasible} \\ \text{allocation}}} [\lambda_{-1}^{-1} u(\overline{\mathbf{x}}_{-1,0}, \mathbf{x}_{-1,1}) + \sum_{t=0}^{\infty} \lambda_t^{-1} u(\mathbf{x}_{t0}, \mathbf{x}_{t1})], \tag{9.44}$$

where λ_t is consumer t's marginal utility of unit of account in the equilibrium, $\lambda_t > 0$, for all t, and $\sum_{t=-1}^{\infty} \lambda_t^{-1} < \infty$.

Proof. First of all, I show that the λ_t exist, for all t, and that

$$\sum_{t=-1}^{\infty} \lambda_t^{-1} < \infty.$$

By definition 9.8 (in section 9.3) of an Arrow-Debreu equilibrium with transfer payments, $(\overline{\mathbf{x}}_{t0}, \overline{\mathbf{x}}_{t1})$ solves the problem

$$\begin{aligned} &\max_{\mathbf{x}_0 \in \mathbb{R}_+^N, \mathbf{x}_1 \in \mathbb{R}_+^N} \quad u(\mathbf{x}_0, \mathbf{x}_1) \\ &\text{s.t.} \quad \mathbf{p}_t.\mathbf{x}_0 + \mathbf{p}_{t+1}.\mathbf{x}_1 \leq \mathbf{p}_t.\mathbf{e}_0 + \mathbf{p}_{t+1}.\mathbf{e}_1 - \tau_t, \end{aligned} \tag{9.45}$$

for all $t \geq 0$. Because u is strictly increasing, it follows that $\mathbf{p}_t \gg 0$, for all t, for otherwise problem 9.45 would not have a solution. Since $\overline{\mathbf{x}}_{t0} + \overline{\mathbf{x}}_{t1} > 0$ and $\mathbf{p}_t \gg 0$, for all t, it follows that $0 < \mathbf{p}_t.\overline{\mathbf{x}}_{t0} + \mathbf{p}_{t+1}.\overline{\mathbf{x}}_{t1} \leq \mathbf{p}_t.\mathbf{e}_0 + \mathbf{p}_{t+1}.\mathbf{e}_1 - \tau_t$, for all t, so that problem 9.45 satisfies the constraint qualification of the Kuhn-Tucker theorem (6.3 in section 6.1). Therefore, all the assumptions of proposition 6.14 (in section 6.3) apply, so that $(\overline{\mathbf{x}}_{t0}, \overline{\mathbf{x}}_{t1})$ solves the problem

$$\max_{\mathbf{x}_0 \in \mathbb{R}_+^N, \mathbf{x}_1 \in \mathbb{R}_+^N} [u(\mathbf{x}_0, \mathbf{x}_1) - \lambda_t(\mathbf{p}_t.\mathbf{x}_0 + \mathbf{p}_{t+1}.\mathbf{x}_1)], \tag{9.46}$$

where $\lambda_t \geq 0$.

Because u is strictly increasing, $\lambda_t > 0$, for otherwise problem 9.46 would not have a solution. I now obtain an upper bound on λ_t^{-1}. Because $(\overline{\mathbf{x}}_{t0}, \overline{\mathbf{x}}_{t1})$ solves problem 9.46, it follows that

$$\begin{aligned} &u(2\mathbf{e}_0 + 2\mathbf{e}_1, 2\mathbf{e}_0 + 2\mathbf{e}_1) - \lambda_t(\mathbf{p}_t + \mathbf{p}_{t+1}).(2\mathbf{e}_0 + 2\mathbf{e}_1) \\ &\quad \leq u(\overline{\mathbf{x}}_{t0}, \overline{\mathbf{x}}_{t1}) - \lambda_t(\mathbf{p}_t.\overline{\mathbf{x}}_{t0} + \mathbf{p}_{t+1}.\overline{\mathbf{x}}_{t1}). \end{aligned} \tag{9.47}$$

Because u is increasing, $\overline{\mathbf{x}}_{t0} \leq \mathbf{e}_0 + \mathbf{e}_1$, $\overline{\mathbf{x}}_{t1} \leq \mathbf{e}_0 + \mathbf{e}_1$, and $\lambda_t \geq 0$, it follows that

$$u(\overline{\mathbf{x}}_{t0}, \overline{\mathbf{x}}_{t1}) - \lambda_t(\mathbf{p}_t.\overline{\mathbf{x}}_{t0} + \mathbf{p}_{t+1}.\overline{\mathbf{x}}_{t1}) \leq u(\mathbf{e}_0 + \mathbf{e}_1, \mathbf{e}_0 + \mathbf{e}_1). \tag{9.48}$$

Inequalities 9.47 and 9.48 together imply that

$$u(2\mathbf{e}_0 + 2\mathbf{e}_1, 2\mathbf{e}_0 + 2\mathbf{e}_1) - \lambda_t(\mathbf{p}_t + \mathbf{p}_{t+1}).(2\mathbf{e}_0 + 2\mathbf{e}_1) \leq u(\mathbf{e}_0 + \mathbf{e}_1, \mathbf{e}_0 + \mathbf{e}_1). \tag{9.49}$$

Because u is strictly increasing and $\mathbf{e}_0 + \mathbf{e}_1 > 0$, it follows that

$$u(2\mathbf{e}_0 + 2\mathbf{e}_1, 2\mathbf{e}_0 + 2\mathbf{e}_1) > u(\mathbf{e}_0 + \mathbf{e}_1, \mathbf{e}_0 + \mathbf{e}_1),$$

so that inequality 9.49 implies that

$$\lambda_t^{-1} \leq \frac{(\mathbf{p}_t + \mathbf{p}_{t+1}).(2\mathbf{e}_0 + 2\mathbf{e}_1)}{u(2\mathbf{e}_0 + 2\mathbf{e}_1, 2\mathbf{e}_0 + 2\mathbf{e}_1) - u(\mathbf{e}_0 + \mathbf{e}_1, \mathbf{e}_0 + \mathbf{e}_1)} < \infty.$$

Therefore,

$$\sum_{t=0}^{\infty} \lambda_t^{-1}$$
$$\leq 2[u(2\mathbf{e}_0 + 2\mathbf{e}_1, 2\mathbf{e}_0 + 2\mathbf{e}_1) - u(\mathbf{e}_0 + \mathbf{e}_1, \mathbf{e}_0 + \mathbf{e}_1)]^{-1}(\mathbf{e}_0 + \mathbf{e}_1) \tag{9.50}$$
$$.\sum_{t=0}^{\infty}(\mathbf{p}_t + \mathbf{p}_{t+1}) < \infty,$$

where the last inequality follows from the assumed summability of the sequence of price vectors $\mathbf{p}_t$.

Again, by the definition of Arrow-Debreu equilibrium, $\overline{\mathbf{x}}_{-1,1}$ solves the problem

$$\max_{\mathbf{x}_1 \in \mathbb{R}_+^N} u_t(\overline{\mathbf{x}}_{-1,0}, \mathbf{x}_1)$$
$$\text{s.t.} \quad \mathbf{p}_0.\mathbf{x}_1 \leq \mathbf{p}_0.\mathbf{e}_1 - \tau_{-1}.$$

Since $\mathbf{p}_0 \gg 0$ and $\overline{\mathbf{x}}_{-1,1} > 0$, it follows that $\mathbf{p}_0.\overline{\mathbf{x}}_{-1,1} > 0$. Therefore, all the assumptions of proposition 6.14 (in section 6.3) apply and $\overline{\mathbf{x}}_{-1,1}$ solves the problem

$$\max_{\mathbf{x}_1 \in \mathbb{R}_+^N} [u(\overline{\mathbf{x}}_{-1,0}, \mathbf{x}_1) - \lambda_{-1}\mathbf{p}_0.\mathbf{x}_1], \tag{9.51}$$

for some nonnegative number λ_{-1}. Because u is strictly increasing, it now follows that

$$\lambda_{-1} > 0. \tag{9.52}$$

Inequalities 9.50 and 9.52 imply that $\sum_{t=-1}^{\infty} \lambda_t^{-1} < \infty$, as was to be proved.

I use the value loss method to prove that $\overline{\mathbf{x}}$ solves problem 9.44. For $t \geq 0$, define the value loss function, $\mathcal{L}_{-1} : \mathbb{R}_+^N \times \mathbb{R}_+^N \to \mathbb{R}$, by the equation

$$\mathcal{L}_{-1}(\mathbf{x}_{-1,1}) = [\lambda_{-1}^{-1} u(\overline{\mathbf{x}}_{-1,0}, \overline{\mathbf{x}}_{-1,1}) - \mathbf{p}_0 . \overline{\mathbf{x}}_{-1,1}]$$
$$- [\lambda_{-1}^{-1} u(\overline{\mathbf{x}}_{-1,0}, \mathbf{x}_{-1,1}) - \mathbf{p}_0 . \mathbf{x}_{-1,1}].$$

For $t \geq 0$, define the value loss function, $\mathcal{L}_{t1} : \mathbb{R}_+^N \times \mathbb{R}_+^N \to \mathbb{R}$, by the equation

$$\mathcal{L}_t(\mathbf{x}_{t0}, \mathbf{x}_{t1}) = \left[\lambda_t^{-1} u(\overline{\mathbf{x}}_{t0}, \overline{\mathbf{x}}_{t1}) - \mathbf{p}_t . \overline{\mathbf{x}}_{t0} - \mathbf{p}_t . \overline{\mathbf{x}}_{t1}\right]$$
$$- \left[\lambda_t^{-1} u(\mathbf{x}_{t0}, \mathbf{x}_{t1}) - \mathbf{p}_t . \mathbf{x}_{t0} - \mathbf{p}_t . \mathbf{x}_{t1}\right].$$

Because $\overline{\mathbf{x}}_{-1,1}$ solves problem 9.51, $\mathcal{L}_{-1}(\mathbf{x}_1) \geq 0$, for all $\mathbf{x}_1 \in \mathbb{R}_+^N$. Similarly, because $(\overline{\mathbf{x}}_{t0}, \overline{\mathbf{x}}_{t1})$ solves problem 9.46, $\mathcal{L}_t(\mathbf{x}_0, \mathbf{x}_1) \geq 0$, for all $(\mathbf{x}_0, \mathbf{x}_1)$ and for all $t \geq 0$. Let $\mathbf{x}$ be any feasible allocation. Then,

$$\begin{aligned}
0 &\leq \mathcal{L}_{-1}(\mathbf{x}_{-1,1}) + \sum_{t=0}^{\infty} \mathcal{L}_t(\mathbf{x}_{t0}, \mathbf{x}_{t1}) \\
&= \lambda_{-1}^{-1}[u(\overline{\mathbf{x}}_{-1,0}, \overline{\mathbf{x}}_{-1,1}) - u(\overline{\mathbf{x}}_{-1,0}, \mathbf{x}_{-1,1})] \\
&+ \sum_{t=0}^{\infty} \lambda_t^{-1}[u(\overline{\mathbf{x}}_{t0}, \overline{\mathbf{x}}_{t1}) - u(\mathbf{x}_{t0}, \mathbf{x}_{t1})] \\
&+ \sum_{t=0}^{\infty} \mathbf{p}_t.(\mathbf{x}_{t0} + \mathbf{x}_{t-1,1} - \overline{\mathbf{x}}_{t0} - \overline{\mathbf{x}}_{t-1,1}) \\
&\leq \lambda_{-1}^{-1} u(\overline{\mathbf{x}}_{-1,0}, \overline{\mathbf{x}}_{-1,1}) + \sum_{t=0}^{\infty} \lambda_t^{-1} u(\overline{\mathbf{x}}_{t0}, \overline{\mathbf{x}}_{t1}) - [\lambda_{-1}^{-1} u(\overline{\mathbf{x}}_{-1,0}, \mathbf{x}_{-1,1}) \\
&+ \sum_{t=0}^{\infty} \lambda_t^{-1} u(\mathbf{x}_{t0}, \mathbf{x}_{t1})].
\end{aligned} \tag{9.53}$$

Because $\sum_{t=-1}^{\infty} \lambda_t^{-1} < \infty$ and $\sum_{t=0}^{\infty} \mathbf{p}_t < \infty$, the terms in the infinite sum $\mathcal{L}_{-1}(\mathbf{x}_{-1,1}) + \sum_{t=0}^{\infty} \mathcal{L}_t(\mathbf{x}_{t0}, \mathbf{x}_{t1})$ converge absolutely, so that the infinite sum does not change when the order of summation is changed. This reasoning explains the equation in 9.53. The second inequality is valid, because

$$\sum_{t=0}^{\infty} \mathbf{p}_t.(\mathbf{x}_{t0} + \mathbf{x}_{t-1,1} - \overline{\mathbf{x}}_{t0} - \overline{\mathbf{x}}_{t-1,1})$$
$$= \sum_{t=0}^{\infty} \mathbf{p}_t.(\mathbf{x}_{t0} + \mathbf{x}_{t-1,1} - \mathbf{e}_0 - \mathbf{e}_1) + \sum_{t=0}^{\infty} \mathbf{p}_t.(\mathbf{e}_0 + \mathbf{e}_1 - \overline{\mathbf{x}}_{t0} - \overline{\mathbf{x}}_{t-1,1})$$
$$= \sum_{t=0}^{\infty} \mathbf{p}_t.(\mathbf{x}_{t0} + \mathbf{x}_{t-1,1} - \mathbf{e}_0 - \mathbf{e}_1) \leq 0.$$

The second equation here follows from the feasibility of the allocation $\overline{\mathbf{x}}$ and condition (6) in definition 9.8 (in section 9.3) of an Arrow-Debreu equilibrium with transfer payments. The inequality follows from the feasibility of the allocation $\mathbf{x}$ and from the nonnegativity of the price vectors $\mathbf{p}_t$. Inequality 9.53 proves that allocation $\overline{\mathbf{x}}$ solves problem 9.44. ■

Any allocation that solves a welfare maximization problem of the form of 9.44 is Pareto optimal.

The next corollary is the application of the previous theorem to spot price equilibria.

COROLLARY 9.29 Assume that u is continuous, concave, and strictly increasing and that $(\overline{\mathbf{x}}, \mathbf{P}, \mathbf{r}, G, \mathbf{T})$ is a spot price equilibrium such that $\overline{\mathbf{x}}_{-1,1} > 0$ and $\overline{\mathbf{x}}_{t0} + \overline{\mathbf{x}}_{t1} > 0$, for all t, and

$$\mathbf{P}_0 + \sum_{t=1}^{\infty} \frac{\mathbf{P}_t}{1 + R_{t-1}} < \infty,$$

where $1 + R_t = (1 + r_0)(1 + r_1) \ldots (1 + r_t)$, for $t \geq 0$. For each t, let Λ_t be the marginal utility of unit of account of consumer t in the equilibrium $(\overline{\mathbf{x}}, \mathbf{P}, \mathbf{r}, G, \mathbf{T})$, where Λ_{-1} is measured from the point of view of period -1. Then, the allocation $\overline{\mathbf{x}}$ solves the welfare maximization problem

$$\max_{\substack{\mathbf{x} \text{ is a feasible} \\ \text{allocation}}} \Big[(1 + r_{-1})\Lambda_{-1}^{-1} u(\overline{\mathbf{x}}_{-1,0}, \mathbf{x}_{-1,1}) + \Lambda_0^{-1} u(\mathbf{x}_{00}, \mathbf{x}_{01}) + \sum_{t=1}^{\infty} (1 + R_{t-1})^{-1} \Lambda_t^{-1} u(\mathbf{x}_{t0}, \mathbf{x}_{t1})\Big] \quad (9.54)$$

and

$$(1 + r_{-1})\Lambda_{-1}^{-1} + \Lambda_0^{-1} + \sum_{t=1}^{\infty} (1 + R_{t-1})^{-1} \Lambda_t^{-1} < \infty.$$

Proof. By proposition 9.12 (in section 9.3), the equilibrium $(\overline{\mathbf{x}}, \mathbf{P}, \mathbf{r}, G, \mathbf{T})$ may be converted to an Arrow-Debreu equilibrium with transfer payments, $(\overline{\mathbf{x}}, \mathbf{p}, \boldsymbol{\tau})$, where $\mathbf{p}_0 = \mathbf{P}_0$ and $\mathbf{p}_t = \frac{\mathbf{P}_t}{1+R_{t-1}}$, for $t \geq 1$. It follows from these equations for the Arrow-Debreu prices that $\lambda_0 = \Lambda_0$, and $\lambda_t = (1 + R_{t-1})\Lambda_t$, for $t \geq 1$, where λ_t is the marginal utility of unit of account of consumer t in the Arrow-Debreu equilibrium. Notice that λ_{-1} is the marginal utility of unit of account for person -1 measured from the point of view of period -1, when prices are $\mathbf{p}_0 = \mathbf{P}_0$. Similarly, Λ_{-1} is the same marginal utility measured from the point of view of period -1, when the present value of prices for period 0 are $(1 + r_{-1})^{-1}\mathbf{P}_0$, so that $\lambda_{-1} = (1 + r_{-1})^{-1}\Lambda_{-1}$. Theorem 9.28, therefore, implies that the allocation $\overline{\mathbf{x}}$ solves problem 9.54 and that

$$(1 + r_{-1})\Lambda_{-1}^{-1} + \Lambda_0^{-1} + \sum_{t=1}^{\infty}(1 + R_{t-1})^{-1}\Lambda_t^{-1} < \infty,$$

as was to be proved. ■

The previous corollary is easier to interpret when prices are normalized so that every consumer's marginal utility of unit of account is 1. The next proposition says that such a normalization is possible and that, in fact, we may choose any normalization for the price vectors P_t in a spot price equilibrium.

PROPOSITION 9.30 Let $(\overline{\mathbf{x}}, \mathbf{P}, \mathbf{r}, G, \mathbf{T})$ be a spot price equilibrium and, for $t \geq -1$, let b_t be an arbitrary sequence of positive numbers. Let $\underline{\mathbf{P}}_t = b_t\mathbf{P}_t$, for $t \geq 0$. Then, $(\overline{x}, \underline{\mathbf{P}}, \underline{\mathbf{r}}, \underline{G}, \underline{\mathbf{T}})$ is also a spot price equilibrium, where $\underline{r}_t = \frac{b_{t+1}}{b_t}(1 + r_t) - 1$, $\underline{G} = \frac{b_{-1}}{1+r_{-1}}G$, and $\underline{\mathrm{T}}_t = b_t\mathrm{T}_t$, for all t. If Λ_t is the marginal utility of unit of account for consumer t in period t in the equilibrium $(\overline{\mathbf{x}}, \mathbf{P}, \mathbf{r}, G, \mathbf{T})$, then in the equilibrium $(\overline{x}, \underline{\mathbf{P}}, \underline{\mathbf{r}}, \underline{G}, \underline{\mathbf{T}})$, the marginal utility of unit of account for consumer t in period t is $\frac{\Lambda_t}{b_t}$, for all $t \geq -1$. If

$$\mathbf{P}_0 + \sum_{t=1}^{\infty} \frac{\mathbf{P}_t}{1 + R_{t-1}} < \infty,$$

then

$$\underline{\mathbf{P}}_0 + \sum_{t=1}^{\infty} \frac{\underline{\mathbf{P}}_t}{1 + \underline{R}_{t-1}} < \infty$$

as well, where $1 + \underline{R}_t = (1 + \underline{r}_0)(1 + \underline{r}_1) \ldots (1 + \underline{r}_t)$, for $t \geq 0$.

Proof. To see that the equation for $\underline{r}_t$ is correct for $t \geq -1$, notice that in the spot price equilibrium $(\overline{\mathbf{x}}, \mathbf{P}, \mathbf{r}, G, \mathbf{T})$, person t faces price vector $\mathbf{P}_t$ in youth and, in present-value terms from the point of view of youth, faces price vector $\frac{\mathbf{P}_{t+1}}{1+r_t}$ in old age. Let $\underline{\Lambda}_t$ be the marginal utility of consumer t in the equilibrium $(\overline{x}, \underline{\mathbf{P}}, \underline{\mathbf{r}}, \underline{G}, \underline{\mathbf{T}})$. If we are to have $\underline{\Lambda}_t$ equal $\frac{\Lambda_t}{b_t}$, then we must have $\frac{\underline{\mathbf{P}}_{t+1}}{1+\underline{\mathbf{r}}_t} = \frac{b_t \mathbf{P}_{t+1}}{1+r_t}$ as well as $\underline{\mathbf{P}}_t = b_t \mathbf{P}_t$. However, $\frac{b_t \mathbf{P}_{t+1}}{1+r_t} = \frac{b_{t+1}\mathbf{P}_{t+1}}{b_t^{-1} b_{t+1}(1+r_t)} = \frac{\underline{\mathbf{P}}_{t+1}}{1+\underline{r}_t}$, so that $\underline{r}_t$ is correct in that it yields the equation $\underline{\Lambda}_t = \frac{\Lambda_t}{b_t}$.

To see that the price summability condition of corollary 9.29 applies to the equilibrium $(\overline{x}, \underline{\mathbf{P}}, \underline{\mathbf{r}}, \underline{G}, \underline{\mathbf{T}})$, notice that

$$\begin{aligned}(1+\underline{R}_{T-1}) &= (1+\underline{r}_0)(1+\underline{r}_1)\ldots(1+\underline{r}_{T-1})\\ &= \frac{b_1}{b_0}(1+r_0)\frac{b_2}{b_1}(1+r_1)\ldots\frac{b_T}{b_{T-1}}(1+r_{T-1}) = \frac{b_T}{b_0}(1+R_{T-1}),\end{aligned}$$

so that

$$\frac{\underline{\mathbf{P}}_T}{1+\underline{R}_{T-1}} = \frac{b_T \mathbf{P}_T}{b_0^{-1} b_T (1+R_{T-1})} = \frac{b_0 \mathbf{P}_T}{(1+R_{T-1})}.$$

Therefore,

$$\underline{\mathbf{P}}_0 + \sum_{t=1}^{\infty} \frac{\underline{\mathbf{P}}_t}{1+\underline{R}_{t-1}} = b_0 \left[\mathbf{P}_0 + \sum_{t=1}^{\infty} \frac{\mathbf{P}_t}{1+R_{t-1}}\right] < \infty. \quad \blacksquare$$

This proposition makes it possible to express corollary 9.29 as follows.

COROLLARY 9.31 Assume that u is continuous, concave, and strictly increasing and that $(\overline{\mathbf{x}}, \mathbf{P}, \mathbf{r}, G, \mathbf{T})$ is a spot price equilibrium such that $\overline{\mathbf{x}}_{-1,1} > 0$ and $\overline{\mathbf{x}}_{t0} + \overline{\mathbf{x}}_{t1} > 0$, for all t, and

$$\mathbf{P}_0 + \sum_{t=1}^{\infty} \frac{\mathbf{P}_t}{1+R_{t-1}} < \infty,$$

where $1+R_t = (1+r_0)(1+r_0)(1+r_1)\ldots(1+r_t)$, for $t \geq 0$. Then, the spot equilibrium price vectors may be normalized to create a spot price equilibrium $(\overline{x}, \underline{\mathbf{P}}, \underline{\mathbf{r}}, \underline{G}, \underline{\mathbf{T}})$ in which the marginal utility of unit of account in youth of every consumer is 1 and the allocation $\overline{\mathbf{x}}$ solves the welfare maximization problem

$$\max_{\substack{\mathbf{x} \text{ is a feasible} \\ \text{allocation}}} \left[(1+\underline{r}_{-1})u(\overline{\mathbf{x}}_{-1,0}, \mathbf{x}_{-1,1}) + u(\mathbf{x}_{00}, \mathbf{x}_{01}) + \sum_{t=1}^{\infty}(1+\underline{R}_{t-1})^{-1}u(\mathbf{x}_{t0}, \mathbf{x}_{t1})\right] \tag{9.55}$$

and

$$(1+\underline{r}_{-1}) + 1 + \sum_{t=1}^{\infty}(1+\underline{R}_{t-1})^{-1} < \infty,$$

where $1+\underline{R}_t = (1+\underline{r}_0)(1+\underline{r}_1)\ldots(1+\underline{r}_t)$, for $t \geq 0$.

Proof. For $t \geq -1$, let Λ_t be the marginal utility of unit of account of consumer t in youth in the equilibrium $(\overline{\mathbf{x}}, \mathbf{P}, \mathbf{r}, G, \mathbf{T})$ and apply proposition 9.30 to $(\overline{\mathbf{x}}, \mathbf{P}, \mathbf{r}, G, \mathbf{T})$ with $b_t = \Lambda_t$. ▪

If the equilibrium of corollary 9.31 is stationary, then that corollary implies theorem 9.21 (in section 9.4).

I now turn to a converse of theorem 9.28 that is analogous to the second welfare theorem.

THEOREM 9.32 Assume that u is continuous, concave, and strictly increasing and that $\mathbf{e}_0 + \mathbf{e}_1 \gg 0$. Suppose that the allocation $\overline{\mathbf{x}}$ solves the problem

$$\max_{\substack{\mathbf{x} \text{ is a feasible} \\ \text{allocation}}} [\lambda_{-1}^{-1}u(\overline{\mathbf{x}}_{-1,0}, \mathbf{x}_{-1,1}) + \sum_{t=0}^{\infty}\lambda_t^{-1}u(\mathbf{x}_{t0}, \mathbf{x}_{t1})], \tag{9.56}$$

where $\lambda_t > 0$, for all t, and $\sum_{t=-1}^{\infty}\lambda_t^{-1} < \infty$. Then, $\overline{\mathbf{x}}$ is the allocation of an Arrow-Debreu equilibrium with transfer payments, $(\overline{\mathbf{x}}, \mathbf{p}, \boldsymbol{\tau})$, satisfying the conditions $\mathbf{p}_t \gg 0$, for all t, and $\sum_{t=0}^{\infty}\mathbf{p}_t < \infty$. For each t, the number λ_t is consumer t's marginal utility of unit of account in the equilibrium.

Proof. This theorem is a consequence of theorem 9.49 (in section 9.9), which asserts that $\overline{\mathbf{x}}_{t0} + \overline{\mathbf{x}}_{t-1,1} = \mathbf{e}_0 + \mathbf{e}_1$, for all t, and that there exists a sequence of N-vectors, $\mathbf{p}_t$, for $t = 0, 1, \ldots,$ such that $\mathbf{p}_t \gg 0$, for all t, and $\sum_{t=0}^{\infty}\mathbf{p}_t < \infty$, and the allocation $\overline{\mathbf{x}}$ solves the problem

$$\max_{\substack{\mathbf{x} \text{ is a bounded} \\ \text{allocation}}} [\lambda_{-1}^{-1} u(\overline{\mathbf{x}}_{-1,0}, \mathbf{x}_{-1,1}) + \sum_{t=0}^{\infty} \lambda_t^{-1} u(\mathbf{x}_{t0}, \mathbf{x}_{t1})$$
$$- \sum_{t=0}^{\infty} \mathbf{p}_t.(\mathbf{x}_{t0} + \mathbf{x}_{t-1,1})].$$

Hence, for any bounded allocation $\mathbf{x}$,

$$\begin{aligned} &\lambda_{-1}^{-1} u(\overline{\mathbf{x}}_{-1,0}, \overline{\mathbf{x}}_{11}) + \sum_{t=0}^{\infty} \lambda_t^{-1} u(\overline{\mathbf{x}}_{t0}, \overline{\mathbf{x}}_{11}) - \sum_{t=0}^{\infty} \mathbf{p}_t.(\overline{\mathbf{x}}_{t0} + \overline{\mathbf{x}}_{t-1,1}) \\ &\geq \lambda_{-1}^{-1} u(\overline{\mathbf{x}}_{-1,0}, \mathbf{x}_{11}) + \sum_{t=0}^{\infty} \lambda_t^{-1} u(\mathbf{x}_{t0}, \mathbf{x}_{11}) - \sum_{t=0}^{\infty} \mathbf{p}_t.(\mathbf{x}_{t0} + \mathbf{x}_{t-1,1}). \end{aligned} \tag{9.57}$$

I show that for $t \geq 0$, $(\overline{\mathbf{x}}_{t0}, \overline{\mathbf{x}}_{t1})$ solves the problem

$$\begin{aligned} &\max_{\mathbf{x}_0 \in \mathbb{R}_+^N, \mathbf{x}_1 \in \mathbb{R}_+^N} u(\mathbf{x}_0, \mathbf{x}_1) \\ &\text{s.t. } \mathbf{p}_t.\mathbf{x}_0 + \mathbf{p}_{t+1}.\mathbf{x}_1 \leq \mathbf{p}_t.\mathbf{e}_0 + \mathbf{p}_{t+1}.\mathbf{e}_1 - \tau_t, \end{aligned} \tag{9.58}$$

where $\tau_t = \mathbf{p}_t.(\mathbf{e}_0 - \overline{\mathbf{x}}_{t0}) + \mathbf{p}_{t+1}.(\mathbf{e}_1 - \overline{\mathbf{x}}_{t1})$. Let all the unbarred consumption variables in inequality 9.57 equal the corresponding barred values, except $\mathbf{x}_{t0}$ and $\mathbf{x}_{t1}$. By canceling like terms on both sides of the inequality, we see that

$$\begin{aligned} &\lambda_t^{-1} u(\overline{\mathbf{x}}_{t0}, \overline{\mathbf{x}}_{t1}) - \mathbf{p}_t.\overline{\mathbf{x}}_{t0} - \mathbf{p}_{t+1}.\overline{\mathbf{x}}_{t1} \\ &\geq \lambda_t^{-1} u(\mathbf{x}_{t0}, \mathbf{x}_{t1}) - \mathbf{p}_t.\mathbf{x}_{t0} - \mathbf{p}_{t+1}.\mathbf{x}_{t1}. \end{aligned} \tag{9.59}$$

If $(\overline{\mathbf{x}}_{t0}, \overline{\mathbf{x}}_{t1}) > 0$, then $\mathbf{p}_t.\overline{\mathbf{x}}_{t0} + \mathbf{p}_{t+1}.\overline{\mathbf{x}}_{t1} > 0$, since $\mathbf{p}_t \gg 0$ and $\mathbf{p}_{t+1} \gg 0$. Therefore, the constraint qualification of proposition 6.14 (in section 6.3) applies. Since all the other assumptions of that proposition apply, $(\overline{\mathbf{x}}_{t0}, \overline{\mathbf{x}}_{t1})$ solves problem 9.58. If $(\overline{\mathbf{x}}_{t0}, \overline{\mathbf{x}}_{t1}) = 0$, then the budget set of problem 9.58 contains only the zero vector, since $\mathbf{p}_t \gg 0$ and $\mathbf{p}_{t+1} \gg 0$, and therefore $(\overline{\mathbf{x}}_{t0}, \overline{\mathbf{x}}_{t1}) = 0$ solves that problem.

I next show that $\overline{\mathbf{x}}_{-1,1}$ solves the problem

$$\begin{aligned} &\max_{\mathbf{x}_1 \in \mathbb{R}_+^N} u(\overline{\mathbf{x}}_{-1,0}, \mathbf{x}_1) \\ &\text{s.t. } \mathbf{p}_0.\mathbf{x}_1 \leq \mathbf{p}_0.\mathbf{e}_1 - \tau_{-1}, \end{aligned} \tag{9.60}$$

where $\tau_{-1} = \mathbf{p}_0.(\mathbf{e}_0 - \overline{\mathbf{x}}_{-1,1})$. Set all the unbarred consumption variables in inequality 9.57 equal to the corresponding barred values, except $\mathbf{x}_{-1,1}$. Then, after canceling like terms on both sides of that inequality, we see that

$$\lambda_{-1}^{-1} u(\overline{\mathbf{x}}_{-1,0}, \overline{\mathbf{x}}_{-1,1}) - \mathbf{p}_0.\overline{\mathbf{x}}_{-1,1} \geq \lambda_{-1}^{-1} u(\overline{\mathbf{x}}_{-1,0}, \mathbf{x}_{-1,1}) - \mathbf{p}_0.\mathbf{x}_{-1,1}. \tag{9.61}$$

Arguing as in the previous paragraph, we see that inequality 9.61 implies that $\overline{\mathbf{x}}_{-1,1}$ solves problem 9.60.

Since $\overline{\mathbf{x}}$ is a feasible allocation, $(\overline{\mathbf{x}}, \mathbf{p}, \boldsymbol{\tau})$ satisfies all the conditions of an Arrow-Debreu equilibrium with transfer payments. Inequalities 9.59 and 9.61 imply that for each $t \geq -1$, λ_t is the marginal utility of unit of account of consumer t in the Arrow-Debreu equilibrium. ■

The welfare maximization problem 9.56 has a solution, by theorem 9.50 (in section 9.9). Therefore, theorem 9.32 implies that there exists an Arrow-Debreu equilibrium with transfer payments in the Samuelson model. I now turn to converses of corollary 9.31.

COROLLARY 9.33 Assume that u is continuous, concave, and strictly increasing and that $\mathbf{e}_0 + \mathbf{e}_1 \gg 0$. Suppose that the allocation $\overline{\mathbf{x}}$ solves the problem

$$\max_{\substack{\mathbf{x} \text{ is a feasible} \\ \text{allocation}}} \left[(1 + r_{-1})u(\overline{\mathbf{x}}_{-1,0}, \mathbf{x}_{-1,1}) + u(\mathbf{x}_{00}, \mathbf{x}_{01}) + \sum_{t=1}^{\infty}(1 + R_{t-1})^{-1}u(\mathbf{x}_{t0}, \mathbf{x}_{t1})\right], \tag{9.62}$$

where

$$(1 + r_{-1}) + 1 + \sum_{t=1}^{\infty}(1 + R_{t-1})^{-1} < \infty, \tag{9.63}$$

$1 + R_t = (1 + r_0)(1 + r_1) \ldots (1 + r_t)$, for $t \geq 0$, and $r_t > -1$, for $t \geq -1$. Then, $\overline{\mathbf{x}}$ is the allocation of a spot price equilibrium, $(\overline{\mathbf{x}}, \mathbf{P}, \mathbf{r}, G, \mathbf{T})$, in which the marginal utility of unit of account of every consumer is 1 and the interest rates are $\mathbf{r} = (r_{-1}, r_0, \ldots)$. This equilibrium satisfies the condition

$$\mathbf{P}_0 + \sum_{t=1}^{\infty} \frac{\mathbf{P}_t}{1 + R_{t-1}} < \infty.$$

Proof. Let $\lambda_{-1} = (1 + r_{-1})^{-1}$, $\lambda_0 = 1$, and $\lambda_t = 1 + R_t$. Inequality 9.63 implies that $\sum_{t=-1}^{\infty} \lambda_t^{-1} < \infty$, so that theorem 9.32 implies that $\overline{\mathbf{x}}$ is the allocation of an Arrow-Debreu equilibrium with transfer payments, $(\overline{\mathbf{x}}, \mathbf{p}, \boldsymbol{\tau})$, such that $\sum_{t=0}^{\infty} \mathbf{p}_t < \infty$ and, for all t, $\mathbf{p}_t \gg 0$, and λ_t is the marginal utility of unit of account of consumer t. Define the spot price equilibrium,

$(\overline{\mathbf{x}}, \mathbf{P}, \mathbf{r}, G, \mathbf{T})$, by the equations

$$\mathbf{P}_0 = \mathbf{p}_0, \mathbf{P}_t = (1 + R_{t-1})\mathbf{p}_t, \text{ for } t > 0,$$
$$\mathsf{T}_0 = \tau_0, \mathsf{T}_t = (1 + R_{t-1})\tau_t, \text{ for } t > 0, \text{ and}$$
$$G + -(1 + r_{-1})^{-1}\tau_{-1}.$$

I begin by showing that prices and interest rates in $(\overline{\mathbf{x}}, \mathbf{P}, \mathbf{r}, G, \mathbf{T})$ are such that the marginal utility of every consumer is 1. From the point of view of each consumer, the Arrow-Debreu equilibrium, $(\overline{\mathbf{x}}, \mathbf{p}, \boldsymbol{\tau})$, is the same as a spot price equilibrium with interest rate always equal to 0, with price vector $\mathbf{p}_t$ and tax τ_t in period t, and with $G = -\tau_{-1}$. The above formulas for the parameters of the spot price equilibrium $(\overline{\mathbf{x}}, \mathbf{P}, \mathbf{r}, G, \mathbf{T})$ can be obtained by applying proposition 9.30 to $(\overline{\mathbf{x}}, \mathbf{p}, \boldsymbol{\tau})$ with $b_t = \lambda_t$, for $t \geq -1$, where λ_t is as defined above. Proposition 9.30 implies that the marginal utility of unit of account of every consumer is 1 in the equilibrium $(\overline{\mathbf{x}}, \mathbf{P}, \mathbf{r}, G, \mathbf{T})$.

Since the equilibrium $(\mathbf{x}, \mathbf{p}, \boldsymbol{\tau})$ satisfies the condition $\sum_{t=0}^{\infty} \mathbf{p}_t < \infty$, it follows that

$$\mathbf{P}_0 + \sum_{t=1}^{\infty} \frac{\mathbf{P}_t}{1 + R_{t-1}} < \infty. \quad ■$$

If we assume that $r_t = r > 0$, for all t, in corollary 9.33, we obtain the following assertion.

COROLLARY 9.34 Assume that u is continuous, concave, and strictly increasing and that $\mathbf{e}_0 + \mathbf{e}_1 \gg 0$. Suppose that the allocation $\overline{\mathbf{x}}$ solves the problem

$$\max_{\substack{\mathbf{x} \text{ is a feasible} \\ \text{allocation}}} \left[(1 + r)u(\overline{\mathbf{x}}_{-1,0}, \mathbf{x}_{-1,1}) + \sum_{t=0}^{\infty}(1 + r)^{-t}u(\mathbf{x}_{t0}, \mathbf{x}_{t1})\right], \quad (9.64)$$

where $r > 0$. Then, $\overline{\mathbf{x}}$ is the allocation of a spot price equilibrium, $(\overline{\mathbf{x}}, \mathbf{P}, \mathbf{r}, G, \mathbf{T})$, in which the marginal utility of unit of account of every consumer is 1 and where $r_t = r$, for all t. This equilibrium satisfies the condition

$$\sum_{t=0}^{\infty}(1 + r)^{-t}\mathbf{P}_t < \infty.$$

The equilibrium of the corollary may not be stationary. Its allocation is stationary only if the initial consumption $\overline{\mathbf{x}}_{-1,0}$ is chosen correctly. If $\overline{\mathbf{x}}$ is stationary, then theorem 9.20 (in section 9.4) implies that $\overline{\mathbf{x}}$ is the allocation of a stationary spot price equilibrium, provided that u is differentiable.

It is important that this initial consumption is held fixed in optimization problem 9.64. It is not true that a stationary optimal allocation solves the problem

$$\max_{\substack{\mathbf{x} \text{ is a feasible} \\ \text{stationary allocation}}} [(1+r)u(\overline{\mathbf{x}}_{-1,0}, \mathbf{x}_{-1,1}) + \sum_{t=0}^{\infty}(1+r)^{-t}u(\mathbf{x}_{t0}, \mathbf{x}_{t1})], \quad (9.65)$$

for if we restrict choice to feasible stationary allocations, we do not hold the initial consumption $\mathbf{x}_{-1,0}$ fixed. If $(\mathbf{x}_{t0}, \mathbf{x}_{t1}) = (\mathbf{x}_0, \mathbf{x}_1)$, for all t, then the discounted welfare function of problem 9.65 becomes

$$\frac{(1+r)^2}{r}u(\mathbf{x}_0, \mathbf{x}_1),$$

so that the stationary allocation that maximized this welfare function would be the one that maximized the welfare of a typical consumer. That is, it would be the stationary allocation that solved the problem

$$\max_{\mathbf{x}_0 \in \mathbb{R}^N_+, \mathbf{x}_1 \in \mathbb{R}^N_+} u(\mathbf{x}_0, \mathbf{x}_1)$$
$$\text{s.t.} \quad \mathbf{x}_0 + \mathbf{x}_1 \leq \mathbf{e}_0 + \mathbf{e}_1.$$

Although this allocation maximizes the utility of a typical consumer, it does not maximize the discounted sum of consumer utilities, given a fixed initial consumption $\overline{\mathbf{x}}_{-1,0}$. When the utility of future generations is discounted, the welfare of a typical consumer is sacrificed to some extent in order to favor the old over the young at each moment in time.

The welfare maximization problems studied in this section can be understood better if we focus on the maximization that occurs in one time period. The maximization at time t in problem 9.62 (in corollary 9.33) is

$$\max_{\mathbf{x}_0 \in \mathbb{R}^N_+, \mathbf{x}_1 \in \mathbb{R}^N_+} [(1+R_{t-2})^{-1}u(\overline{\mathbf{x}}_{t-1,0}, \mathbf{x}_1) + (1+R_{t-1})^{-1}u(\mathbf{x}_0, \overline{\mathbf{x}}_{t1})]$$
$$\text{s.t.} \quad \mathbf{x}_0 + \mathbf{x}_1 \leq \mathbf{e}_0 + \mathbf{e}_1.$$

If we multiply the objective function of this problem by $1 + R_{t-1}$, we obtain the problem

$$\max_{\mathbf{x}_0 \in \mathbb{R}^N_+, \mathbf{x}_1 \in \mathbb{R}^N_+} [(1+r_{t-1})u(\overline{\mathbf{x}}_{t-1,0}, \mathbf{x}_1) + u(\mathbf{x}_0, \overline{\mathbf{x}}_{t1})]$$
$$\text{s.t.} \quad \mathbf{x}_0 + \mathbf{x}_1 \leq \mathbf{e}_0 + \mathbf{e}_1.$$

From the objective function of this problem, we see that the greater the discount rate, r_{t-1}, the greater is the weight given in period t to the utility of the old person relative to that of the young person, so that the old person receives a larger share of the total endowment $\mathbf{e}_0 + \mathbf{e}_1$.

How are we to interpret the results of this section? The theorems that have to do with Arrow-Debreu equilibrium, 9.28 and 9.32, are useful only as technical tools. The assertions of economic interest are those having to do with spot price equilibria, namely, corollaries 9.29, 9.31, 9.33, and 9.34. We may interpret the interest rates, r_t, in a spot price equilibrium $(\overline{\mathbf{x}}, \mathbf{P}, \mathbf{r}, G, \mathsf{T})$ as determined by monetary policy, and we may think of the tax rates, T_t, as instruments of fiscal policy. Loosely speaking, these interest and tax rates determine the equilibrium. In actual economies, monetary and fiscal policy interact with uncertain market forces to determine interest rates and the price level. There is the theoretical possibility, demonstrated by example 9.27 (in section 9.5), that many equilibria may correspond to any one time path of policy variables, so that policy makers may not be able to control the economy. In interpreting the results of this section, one must set aside this difficulty.

Corollaries 9.29 and 9.31 assert that the allocation of any spot price equilibrium maximizes some welfare function that discounts the utility of future generations at a rate that may vary over time. Asymptotic conditions on the summability of discounted prices must be satisfied by the equilibria, although these conditions are without practical significance since they apply only as time goes to infinity. Hence, whether the government is aware of its influence or not, its policy determines interest rates, price levels, and a path for the economy that maximizes some welfare function. In the model, there is no natural rate of interest determined by economic fundamentals, unless by natural one means the interest rate that applies when government policy is fixed at some particular level.

Corollaries 9.33 and 9.34 assert that government policy can maximize any welfare function that discounts the utility of future generations at a perhaps varying rate. (The proof of this statement is completed by theorem 9.50 [in section 9.9], which asserts that there is an allocation that maximizes the welfare function.) The results offer hope that policy could achieve a desired outcome.

The practical significance of these results might be questioned on the grounds that consumers' utility functions are improperly formulated in the model because they do not take account of people's desire to save in order to enrich their heirs. Barro (1974) has proposed that people incorporate the welfare of their heirs into their own utility function. If in the overlapping generations model, the young person of each period is the child and heir of that period's old person, then, following Barro, we might let the utility of the person born in period t be $u(\mathbf{x}_{t0}, \mathbf{x}_{t1}, U_{t+1})$, where $U_t = u(\mathbf{x}_{t0}, \mathbf{x}_{t1}, U_{t+1})$ is the utility level of consumer t, for all t. If consumers were modeled in this way and had perfect foresight, then they would, in effect, behave as if they were immortal, and the government would not be able to influence real interest rates through fiscal and monetary policy. Consumer saving behavior would offset the effects of government policy, because the saving would be so elastic with respect to the interest rate that government policy could not affect it. It is doubtful that this possibility is realistic, since actual saving seem to be little affected by interest rates. The interest elasticity of saving has been studied extensively, and this literature is surveyed in Bernheim (2002, sec. 3).

9.7 Undiscounted Optimality and Equilibrium[3]

I now introduce an optimality criterion that does not discount the utility of future generations but treats them all equally. Care must be exercised in formulating this criterion. Although it might be tempting to use the infinite sum,

$$u(\overline{\mathbf{x}}_{-1,0}, \mathbf{x}_{-1,1}) + \sum_{t=0}^{\infty} u(\mathbf{x}_{t0}, \mathbf{x}_{t1}),$$

as a welfare measure, this sum may not converge. Another possibility is the long-run average,

$$\limsup_{T\to\infty} T^{-1} \sum_{t=0}^{T-1} u(\mathbf{x}_{t0}, \mathbf{x}_{t1}),$$

but this criterion is a blunt tool, because a change in any finite number of consumption vectors in the allocation $(\mathbf{x}_{t0}, \mathbf{x}_{t-1,1})_{t=0}^{\infty}$ does not alter this average. A more useful device is von Weizäcker's (1965) catching up criterion.

DEFINITION 9.35 Given a fixed initial consumption, $\overline{\mathbf{x}}_{-1,0}$, the allocation $(\overline{\mathbf{x}}_{t0}, \overline{\mathbf{x}}_{t-1,1})_{t=0}^{\infty}$ *catches up* to the allocation $(\mathbf{x}_{t0}, \mathbf{x}_{t-1,1})_{t=0}^{\infty}$ if for every positive number ε, there exists a number $T(\varepsilon)$ such that

$$[u(\overline{\mathbf{x}}_{-1,0}, \mathbf{x}_{-1,1}) + \sum_{t=0}^{T} u(\mathbf{x}_{t0}, \mathbf{x}_{t1})] - [u(\overline{\mathbf{x}}_{-1,0}, \overline{\mathbf{x}}_{-1,1}) + \sum_{t=0}^{T} u(\overline{\mathbf{x}}_{t0}, \overline{\mathbf{x}}_{t1})] < \varepsilon,$$

for $T \geq T(\varepsilon)$.

3. Many of the arguments in this section are inspired by the work of McKenzie (1976).

DEFINITION 9.36 Given a fixed initial consumption, $\overline{\mathbf{x}}_{-1,0}$, the feasible allocation $(\overline{\mathbf{x}}_{t0}, \overline{\mathbf{x}}_{t-1,1})_{t=0}^{\infty}$ is *optimal,* according to the catching up criterion, if it catches up to every other feasible allocation.

The catching up criterion does not provide a complete ordering of allocations; only some pairs of programs can be compared. It may be that neither $(\overline{\mathbf{x}}_{t0}, \overline{\mathbf{x}}_{t-1,1})_{t=0}^{\infty}$ nor $(\mathbf{x}_{t0}, \mathbf{x}_{t-1,1})_{t=0}^{\infty}$ catches up to the other. When future utility is discounted, a sufficient condition for optimality is that the Arrow-Debreu equilibrium prices be summable. As the catching up criterion treats all generations equally, it is to be expected that an Arrow-Debreu price system associated with a catching up optimal allocation would have prices that summed to infinity. An Arrow-Debreu equilibrium may be interpreted as a spot price equilibrium with interest rate 0, and we will see that an allocation is optimal with respect to the catching up criterion if and only if it is the allocation of such a spot price equilibrium with interest rate 0 and in which the prices are bounded and all consumers have the same marginal utility of unit of account.

It is possible to use the catching up criterion to treat generations inequitably by multiplying the utility of generation t by λ_t^{-1} and applying the catching up criterion to the partial sums $\lambda_{-1}^{-1}u(\overline{\mathbf{x}}_{-1,0}, \mathbf{x}_{-1,1}) + \sum_{t=0}^{T} \lambda_t^{-1}u(\mathbf{x}_{t0}, \mathbf{x}_{t1})$. The optima so defined are associated with spot price equilibria in which the marginal utility of consumer t is λ_t. If $\sum_{t=0}^{\infty} \lambda_t^{-1} < \infty$, then a catching up optimal allocation maximizes the welfare function $\lambda_{-1}^{-1}u(\overline{\mathbf{x}}_{-1,0}, \mathbf{x}_{-1,1}) + \sum_{t=0}^{\infty} \lambda_t^{-1}u(\mathbf{x}_{t0}, \mathbf{x}_{t1})$, so that catching up optimality is consistent with the concept of optimality used in section 9.6.

By corollary 9.52 (in section 9.9), there exists an allocation that is optimal according to the catching up criterion, for any choice of $\overline{\mathbf{x}}_{-1,0}$, provided u is continuous, strictly concave, and strictly increasing.

Allocations that are optimal with respect to the catching up criterion are also Pareto optimal, just as are allocations that maximize a welfare function that is a discounted sum of the utilities of all consumers.

THEOREM 9.37 The feasible allocation $\overline{\mathbf{x}}$ is Pareto optimal, if it is optimal with respect to the catching up criterion.

Proof. If $\overline{\mathbf{x}}$ is not Pareto optimal, then there exists a feasible allocation $\mathbf{x}$ such that $u(\overline{\mathbf{x}}_{-1,0}, \mathbf{x}_{-1,1}) \geq u(\overline{\mathbf{x}}_{-1,0}, \overline{\mathbf{x}}_{-1,1})$ and $u(\mathbf{x}_{t,0}, \mathbf{x}_{t,1}) \geq (\overline{\mathbf{x}}_{t,0}, \overline{\mathbf{x}}_{t,1})$, for $t \geq 0$, with ">" in at least one of these inequalities. It follows that there is a positive number ε such that

$$u(\overline{\mathbf{x}}_{-1,0}, \mathbf{x}_{-1,1}) + \sum_{t=0}^{T} u(\mathbf{x}_{t0}, \mathbf{x}_{t1}) > u(\overline{\mathbf{x}}_{-1,0}, \overline{\mathbf{x}}_{-1,1}) + \sum_{t=0}^{T} (\overline{\mathbf{x}}_{t0}, \overline{\mathbf{x}}_{t1}) + \varepsilon,$$

for T that are sufficiently large. Therefore, the allocation $\overline{\mathbf{x}}$ cannot catch up to the allocation $\mathbf{x}$ and hence $\overline{\mathbf{x}}$ is not optimal according to the catching up criterion, contrary to hypothesis. ▪

The next task is to state conditions under which the allocation of a spot price equilibrium is optimal according to the catching up criterion.

DEFINITION 9.38 A *spot price equilibrium with interest rate 0* for the Samuelson model, denoted $(\overline{\mathbf{x}}, \mathbf{P}, G, \mathbf{T})$, is a spot price equilibrium, $(\overline{\mathbf{x}}, \mathbf{P}, \mathbf{r}, G, \mathbf{T})$, such that $r_t = 0$, for all t.

If the utility function is locally nonsatiated, the government debt at the end of period t, G_t, satisfies the equations

$$G_t = \mathbf{P}_t.(\mathbf{e}_0 - \overline{\mathbf{x}}_{t0}) - \mathsf{T}_t = \mathbf{P}_t.(\overline{\mathbf{x}}_{t1} - \mathbf{e}_1)$$

and the budget equations

$$G_{t+1} = G_t - \mathsf{T}_{t+1},$$

for $t \geq 1$. Similarly,

$$G_0 = G - \mathsf{T}_0.$$

The validity of the last two equations follows from the government budget equations 9.7 and 9.12 (in section 9.3) by setting the interest rates r_t equal to 0.

THEOREM 9.39 Assume that u is continuous, strictly concave, and strictly increasing and that $\mathbf{e}_0 + \mathbf{e}_1 \gg 0$. The allocation, $\overline{\mathbf{x}}$, of a spot price equilibrium, $(\overline{\mathbf{x}}, \mathbf{P}, G, \mathbf{T})$, with interest rate 0 is optimal according to the catching up criterion, if in the equilibrium all consumers have same the marginal utility of unit of account and if $\overline{\mathbf{x}}_{-1,1} > 0$ and $(\overline{\mathbf{x}}_{t0}, \overline{\mathbf{x}}_{t1}) > 0$, for all $t \geq 0$. In such an equilibrium, the price vectors $\mathbf{P}_t$ are bounded.

The assumptions that $\overline{\mathbf{x}}_{-1,1} > 0$ and $(\overline{\mathbf{x}}_{t0}, \overline{\mathbf{x}}_{t1}) > 0$ are made so that the Kuhn-Tucker theorem guarantees that all consumers have a marginal utility of unit of account.

Proof of Theorem 9.39. If the marginal utility of every consumer equals Λ, we may replace every price vector $\mathbf{P}_t$ by $\Lambda\mathbf{P}_t$ and obtain an equilibrium in which the marginal utility of unit of account of every consumer is 1. So, I will assume that the marginal utility of unit of account is 1.

Because u is strictly increasing, $\mathbf{P}_t \gg 0$, for $t \geq 0$, for otherwise the problem

$$\begin{aligned} &\max_{\mathbf{x}_0 \in \mathbb{R}^N_+, \mathbf{x}_1 \in \mathbb{R}^N_+} \quad u(\mathbf{x}_0, \mathbf{x}_1) \\ &\text{s.t.} \quad \mathbf{P}_t.\mathbf{x}_0 + \mathbf{P}_{t+1}.\mathbf{x}_1 \leq \mathbf{P}_t.\mathbf{e}_0 + \mathbf{P}_{t+1}.\mathbf{e}_1 - \mathsf{T}_t, \end{aligned} \tag{9.66}$$

satisfied by $(\overline{\mathbf{x}}_{t0}, \overline{\mathbf{x}}_{t1})$, would not have a solution.

I next show that the price vectors, $\mathbf{P}_t$, are bounded. Because $\mathbf{P}_t \gg 0$ and $(\overline{\mathbf{x}}_{t0}, \overline{\mathbf{x}}_{t1}) > \mathbf{0}$, for all $t \geq 0$, it follows that $\mathbf{P}_t.\overline{\mathbf{x}}_{t0} + \mathbf{P}_{t+1}.\overline{\mathbf{x}}_{t1} > 0$ and therefore problem 9.66 satisfies the constraint qualification of the Kuhn-Tucker theorem, so that consumer t's marginal utility of unit of account is well defined. Because u is concave and the marginal utility of unit of account is 1, the Kuhn-Tucker theorem (6.3 in section 6.1) implies that $(\overline{\mathbf{x}}_{t0}, \overline{\mathbf{x}}_{t1})$ solves the problem

$$\max_{\mathbf{x}_0 \in \mathbb{R}^N_+, \mathbf{x}_1 \in \mathbb{R}^N_+} [u(\mathbf{x}_0, \mathbf{x}_1) - \mathbf{P}_t.\mathbf{x}_0 - \mathbf{P}_{t+1}.\mathbf{x}_1].$$

Therefore,

$$u(\overline{\mathbf{x}}_{t0}, \overline{\mathbf{x}}_{t1}) - \mathbf{P}_t.\overline{\mathbf{x}}_{t0} - \mathbf{P}_{t+1}.\overline{\mathbf{x}}_{t1} \geq u(\mathbf{0}, \overline{\mathbf{x}}_{t1}) - \mathbf{P}_{t+1}.\overline{\mathbf{x}}_{t1}.$$

Canceling $\mathbf{P}_{t+1}.\overline{\mathbf{x}}_{t1}$ from both sides of this inequality, we see that

$$\mathbf{P}_t.\overline{\mathbf{x}}_{t0} \leq u(\overline{\mathbf{x}}_{t0}, \overline{\mathbf{x}}_{t1}) - u(\mathbf{0}, \overline{\mathbf{x}}_{t1}) \leq u(\mathbf{e}_0 + \mathbf{e}_1, \mathbf{e}_0 + \mathbf{e}_1) - u(\mathbf{0}, \mathbf{0}), \tag{9.67}$$

for all $t \geq 0$, where the second inequality is valid because u is increasing and $\overline{\mathbf{x}}_{t0} \leq \overline{\mathbf{x}}_{t0} + \overline{\mathbf{x}}_{t-1,1} \leq \mathbf{e}_0 + \mathbf{e}_1$ and similarly $\overline{\mathbf{x}}_{t1} \leq \mathbf{e}_0 + \mathbf{e}_1$. A similar argument using the assumption that $\overline{\mathbf{x}}_{-1,1} > \mathbf{0}$ implies that

$$\mathbf{P}_t.\overline{\mathbf{x}}_{t-1,1} \leq u(\mathbf{e}_0 + \mathbf{e}_1, \mathbf{e}_0 + \mathbf{e}_1) - u(\mathbf{0}, \mathbf{0}), \tag{9.68}$$

for all $t \geq 0$. Adding inequalities 9.67 and 9.68, we find that

$$\mathbf{P}_t.(\overline{\mathbf{x}}_{t0} + \overline{\mathbf{x}}_{t-1,1}) \leq 2[u(\mathbf{e}_0 + \mathbf{e}_1, \mathbf{e}_0 + \mathbf{e}_1) - u(\mathbf{0}, \mathbf{0})],$$

for all $t \geq 0$. Since $\mathbf{P}_t \gg 0$, $\overline{\mathbf{x}}_{t0} + \overline{\mathbf{x}}_{t-1,1} = \mathbf{e}_0 + \mathbf{e}_1$, so that the previous inequality implies that

$$\mathbf{P}_t.(\mathbf{e}_0 + \mathbf{e}_1) \leq 2[u(\mathbf{e}_0 + \mathbf{e}_1, \mathbf{e}_0 + \mathbf{e}_1) - u(\mathbf{0}, \mathbf{0})].$$

Since $\mathbf{e}_0 + \mathbf{e}_1 \gg 0$, it follows that $e_{0n} + e_{1n} > 0$, for all n, and hence

$$P_{tn} \leq (e_{0n} + e_{1n})^{-1} 2[u(\mathbf{e}_0 + \mathbf{e}_1, \mathbf{e}_0 + \mathbf{e}_1) - u(\mathbf{0}, \mathbf{0})] < \infty,$$

for all t and n. This proves that the vectors $\mathbf{P}_{tn}$ are bounded.

Suppose that $(\overline{\mathbf{x}}_{t0}, \overline{\mathbf{x}}_{t-1,1})_{t=0}^{\infty}$ is not optimal. Then, there is a feasible allocation $(\mathbf{x}_{t0}, \mathbf{x}_{t-1,1})_{t=0}^{\infty}$ and a positive number ε such that for infinitely many values of T,

$$u(\overline{\mathbf{x}}_{-1,0}, \mathbf{x}_{-1,1}) + \sum_{t=0}^{T} u(\mathbf{x}_{t0}, \mathbf{x}_{t1}) - [u(\overline{\mathbf{x}}_{-1,0}, \overline{\mathbf{x}}_{-1,1}) + \sum_{t=0}^{T} u(\overline{\mathbf{x}}_{t0}, \overline{\mathbf{x}}_{t1})] \geq \varepsilon.$$

In order to arrive at a contradiction, I make use of the value loss, used earlier in the proof of theorem 9.28 (in section 9.6). For $t \geq 0$, let the value loss of person t be

$$\mathcal{L}_t(\mathbf{x}_0, \mathbf{x}_1) = u(\overline{\mathbf{x}}_{t0}, \overline{\mathbf{x}}_{t1}) - \mathbf{P}_t.\overline{\mathbf{x}}_{t0} - \mathbf{P}_{t+1}.\overline{\mathbf{x}}_{t1} - [u(\mathbf{x}_0, \mathbf{x}_1) - \mathbf{P}_t.\mathbf{x}_0 - \mathbf{P}_{t+1}.\mathbf{x}_1].$$

Similarly, for $t = -1$, let

$$\mathcal{L}_{-1}(\mathbf{x}_1) = u(\overline{\mathbf{x}}_{-1,0}, \overline{\mathbf{x}}_{-1,1}) - \mathbf{P}_0.\overline{\mathbf{x}}_{-1,1} - [u(\overline{\mathbf{x}}_{-1,0}, \mathbf{x}_1) - \mathbf{P}_0.\mathbf{x}_1].$$

Because $(\overline{\mathbf{x}}_{t0}, \overline{\mathbf{x}}_{t1})$ solves problem 9.66 and u is concave and every consumer's marginal utility of unit of account is 1, it follows that $\mathcal{L}(\mathbf{x}_0, \mathbf{x}_1) \geq 0$, for all $(\mathbf{x}_0, \mathbf{x}_1)$ and for all $t \geq 0$. Because u is strictly concave, $\mathcal{L}_t$ is strictly convex and $\mathcal{L}_t(\mathbf{x}_0, \mathbf{x}_1) > 0$, if $(\mathbf{x}_0, \mathbf{x}_1) \neq (\overline{\mathbf{x}}_{t0}, \overline{\mathbf{x}}_{t1})$, for $t \geq 0$. Similar arguments imply that $\mathcal{L}_{-1}(\mathbf{x}_1) \geq 0$, for all $\mathbf{x}_1$, and $\mathcal{L}_{-1}(\mathbf{x}_1) > 0$, if $\mathbf{x}_1 \neq \overline{\mathbf{x}}_{-1,1}$.

The argument now hinges on the following string of equations and inequalities:

$$\begin{aligned}
0 &\leq \mathcal{L}_{-1}(\mathbf{x}_{-1,1}) + \sum_{t=0}^{T} \mathcal{L}_t(\mathbf{x}_{t0}, \mathbf{x}_{t1}) \\
&= [u(\overline{\mathbf{x}}_{-1,0}, \overline{\mathbf{x}}_{-1,1}) - u(\overline{\mathbf{x}}_{-1,0}, \mathbf{x}_{-1,1})] + \sum_{t=0}^{T} [u(\overline{\mathbf{x}}_{t,0}, \overline{\mathbf{x}}_{t1}) - u(\mathbf{x}_{t0}, \mathbf{x}_{t1})] \\
&\quad - \sum_{t=0}^{T} \mathbf{P}_t.(\overline{\mathbf{x}}_{t-1,1} + \overline{\mathbf{x}}_{t0} - \mathbf{x}_{t-1,1} - \mathbf{x}_{t0}) - \mathbf{P}_{T+1}.(\overline{\mathbf{x}}_{T1} - \mathbf{x}_{T1}) \\
&= [u(\overline{\mathbf{x}}_{-1,0}, \overline{\mathbf{x}}_{-1,1}) - u(\overline{\mathbf{x}}_{-1,0}, \mathbf{x}_{-1,1})] + \sum_{t=0}^{T} [u(\overline{\mathbf{x}}_{t,0}, \overline{\mathbf{x}}_{t1}) - u(\mathbf{x}_{t0}, \mathbf{x}_{t1})]
\end{aligned} \tag{9.69}$$

$$
\begin{aligned}
&-\sum_{t=0}^{T} \mathbf{P}_t.(\overline{\mathbf{x}}_{t-1,1} + \overline{\mathbf{x}}_{t0} - \mathbf{e}_0 - \mathbf{e}_1) \\
&-\sum_{t=0}^{T} \mathbf{P}_t.(\mathbf{e}_0 + \mathbf{e}_1 - \mathbf{x}_{t-1,1} - \mathbf{x}_{t0}) - \mathbf{P}_{T+1}.(\overline{\mathbf{x}}_{T1} - \mathbf{x}_{T1}) \\
&\leq [u(\overline{\mathbf{x}}_{-1,0}, \overline{\mathbf{x}}_{-1,1}) - u(\overline{\mathbf{x}}_{-1,0}, \mathbf{x}_{-1,1})] \\
&+\sum_{t=0}^{T} [u(\overline{\mathbf{x}}_{t0}, \overline{\mathbf{x}}_{t1}) - u(\mathbf{x}_{t0}, \mathbf{x}_{t1})] - \mathbf{P}_{T+1}.(\overline{\mathbf{x}}_{T1} - \mathbf{x}_{T1}),
\end{aligned}
$$

for all T. The first inequality above is a consequence of the nonnegativity of the value losses. The first equation is obtained by substituting the formulas for the value losses and rearranging terms. The second equation follows by adding and subtracting $\mathbf{P}_t.(\mathbf{e}_0 + \mathbf{e}_1)$, for all t. The last inequality follows from the facts that $\mathbf{P}_t(\overline{\mathbf{x}}_{t0} + \overline{\mathbf{x}}_{t-1,1} - \mathbf{e}_0 - \mathbf{e}_1) = 0$, and that $\mathbf{x}_{t0} + \mathbf{x}_{t-1,1} \leq \mathbf{e}_0 + \mathbf{e}_1$, for all t, and from the nonnegativity of the vectors $\mathbf{P}_t$. Because

$$
u(\overline{\mathbf{x}}_{-1,0}, \overline{\mathbf{x}}_{-1,1}) + \sum_{t=0}^{T} u(\overline{\mathbf{x}}_{t0}, \overline{\mathbf{x}}_{t1}) - u(\overline{\mathbf{x}}_{-1,0}, \mathbf{x}_{-1,1}) + \sum_{t=0}^{T} u(\mathbf{x}_{t0}, \mathbf{x}_{t1}) \leq -\varepsilon,
$$

for infinitely many values of T, it follows from inequalities 9.69 that

$$
0 \leq -\varepsilon - \mathbf{P}_{T+1}.(\overline{\mathbf{x}}_{T1} - \mathbf{x}_{T1}),
$$

for infinitely many values of T. Replacing T by t, we see that

$$
\mathbf{P}_{t+1}.(\mathbf{x}_{t1} - \overline{\mathbf{x}}_{t1}) \geq \varepsilon, \tag{9.70}
$$

for infinitely many values of t.

I now show that inequality 9.70 implies that $\mathbf{x}_{t1}$ and $\overline{\mathbf{x}}_{t1}$ must differ by at least a certain amount. Since the price vectors $\mathbf{P}_t$ are bounded, there is a positive number b such that $\|\mathbf{P}_t\| \leq b$, for all t. Then,

$$
\|\mathbf{x}_{t1} - \overline{\mathbf{x}}_{t1}\| \geq \frac{\varepsilon}{b},
$$

if $\mathbf{P}_{t+1}.(\mathbf{x}_{t1} - \overline{\mathbf{x}}_{t1}) \geq \varepsilon$. This last inequality holds, because

$$
\varepsilon \leq \mathbf{P}_{t+1}.(\mathbf{x}_{t1} - \overline{\mathbf{x}}_{t1}) \leq \|\mathbf{P}_{t+1}\| \|\mathbf{x}_{t1} - \overline{\mathbf{x}}_{t1}\| \leq b\|\mathbf{x}_{t1} - \overline{\mathbf{x}}_{t1}\|.
$$

In summary, inequality 9.70 implies that

$$
\|\mathbf{x}_{t1} - \overline{\mathbf{x}}_{t1}\| \geq \frac{\varepsilon}{b}, \tag{9.71}
$$

for infinitely many values of t.

I next show that there exists a positive number δ such that, for any t, $\mathcal{L}_t(\mathbf{x}_{t0}, \mathbf{x}_{t1}) \geq \delta$, if $\|\mathbf{x}_{t1} - \overline{\mathbf{x}}_{t1}\| \geq \frac{\varepsilon}{b}$. Suppose that this assertion is false. Then, there is a sequence $t(k)$, for $k = 1, 2, \ldots$, such that $\lim_{k\to\infty} \mathcal{L}_{t(k)}(\mathbf{x}_{t(k),0}, \mathbf{x}_{t(k),1}) = 0$ and $\|\mathbf{x}_{t(k),1} - \overline{\mathbf{x}}_{t(k),1}\| \geq \frac{\varepsilon}{b}$, for all k. Since the sequences $\mathbf{x}_{t(k),0}$, $\mathbf{x}_{t(k),1}$, $\overline{\mathbf{x}}_{t(k),0}$, $\overline{\mathbf{x}}_{t(k),1}$, $\mathbf{P}_{t(k)}$, and $\mathbf{P}_{t(k)+1}$ are all bounded, the Bolzano-Weierstrass theorem (3.12 in section 3.2) implies that there is a subsequence, call it $t(k)$ again, such that all six of the sequences $\mathbf{x}_{t(k),0}$, $\mathbf{x}_{t(k),1}$, $\overline{\mathbf{x}}_{t(k),0}$, $\overline{\mathbf{x}}_{t(k),1}$, $\mathbf{P}_{t(k)}$, and $\mathbf{P}_{t(k)+1}$ converge. Let their limits be $\underline{\mathbf{x}}_0$, $\underline{\mathbf{x}}_1$, $\overline{\mathbf{x}}_0$, $\overline{\mathbf{x}}_1$, $\overline{\mathbf{P}}_0$, and $\overline{\mathbf{P}}_1$, respectively. Then, $\|\underline{\mathbf{x}}_1 - \overline{\mathbf{x}}_1\| \geq \frac{\varepsilon}{b}$, so that $\overline{\mathbf{x}}_1 \neq \underline{\mathbf{x}}_1$. Because $\mathcal{L}_{t(k)}(\mathbf{x}_0, \mathbf{x}_1) \geq 0$, for all k and for all $\mathbf{x}_0$ and $\mathbf{x}_1$, we have that

$$\begin{aligned} &u(\overline{\mathbf{x}}_{t(k),0}, \overline{\mathbf{x}}_{t(k),1}) - \mathbf{P}_{t(k)}.\overline{\mathbf{x}}_{t(k),0} - \mathbf{P}_{t(k)+1}.\overline{\mathbf{x}}_{t(k),1} \\ &\quad \geq u(\mathbf{x}_0, \mathbf{x}_1) - \mathbf{P}_{t(k)}.\mathbf{x}_0 - \mathbf{P}_{t(k)+1}.\mathbf{x}_1, \end{aligned}$$

for all k. Passing to the limit in this inequality, we obtain that

$$\begin{aligned} &u(\overline{\mathbf{x}}_0, \overline{\mathbf{x}}_1) - \overline{\mathbf{P}}_0.\overline{\mathbf{x}}_0 - \overline{\mathbf{P}}_1.\overline{\mathbf{x}}_1 \\ &\quad \geq u(\mathbf{x}_0, \mathbf{x}_1) - \overline{\mathbf{P}}_0.\mathbf{x}_0 - \overline{\mathbf{P}}_1.\mathbf{x}_1. \end{aligned} \tag{9.72}$$

Putting all this information together and using the continuity of the function u, we have that

$$\begin{aligned} 0 &= \lim_{k\to\infty} \mathcal{L}_{t(k)}(\mathbf{x}_{t(k),0}, \mathbf{x}_{t(k),1}) \\ &= \lim_{k\to\infty} \left\{\left[u(\overline{\mathbf{x}}_{t(k),0}, \overline{\mathbf{x}}_{t(k),1}) - \mathbf{P}_{t(k)}.\overline{\mathbf{x}}_{t(k),0} - \mathbf{P}_{t(k)+1}.\overline{\mathbf{x}}_{t(k),1}\right]\right. \\ &\qquad \left. - \left[u(\mathbf{x}_{t(k),0}, \mathbf{x}_{t(k),1}) - \mathbf{P}_{t(k)}.\mathbf{x}_{t(k),0} - \mathbf{P}_{t(k)+1}.\mathbf{x}_{t(k),1}\right]\right\} \\ &= \left[u(\overline{\mathbf{x}}_0, \overline{\mathbf{x}}_1) - \overline{\mathbf{P}}_0.\overline{\mathbf{x}}_0 - \overline{\mathbf{P}}_1.\overline{\mathbf{x}}_1\right] - \left[u(\underline{\mathbf{x}}_0, \underline{\mathbf{x}}_1) - \overline{\mathbf{P}}_0.\underline{\mathbf{x}}_0 - \overline{\mathbf{P}}_1.\underline{\mathbf{x}}_1\right]. \end{aligned}$$

This equation is impossible, because the function

$$\mathcal{L}(\mathbf{x}_0, \mathbf{x}_1) = \left[u(\overline{\mathbf{x}}_0, \overline{\mathbf{x}}_1) - \overline{\mathbf{P}}_0.\overline{\mathbf{x}}_0 - \overline{\mathbf{P}}_1.\overline{\mathbf{x}}_1\right] - \left[u(\mathbf{x}_0, \mathbf{x}_1) - \overline{\mathbf{P}}_0.\mathbf{x}_0 - \overline{\mathbf{P}}_1.\mathbf{x}_1\right]$$

is strictly convex and inequality 9.72 implies that $\mathcal{L}(\mathbf{x}_0, \mathbf{x}_1)$ has a minimum of zero at $(\mathbf{x}_0, \mathbf{x}_1) = (\overline{\mathbf{x}}_0, \overline{\mathbf{x}}_1)$. Because $\mathcal{L}$ is strictly convex, the minimum is unique, yet we know that $\overline{\mathbf{x}}_1 \neq \underline{\mathbf{x}}_1$. This completes the proof that there exists a $\delta > 0$ such that, for any t, $\mathcal{L}_t(\mathbf{x}_{t0}, \mathbf{x}_{t1}) \geq \delta$, if $\|\mathbf{x}_{t1} - \overline{\mathbf{x}}_{t1}\| \geq \frac{\varepsilon}{b}$.

I now finish the argument. Since, by inequality 9.71, $\|\mathbf{x}_{t1} - \overline{\mathbf{x}}_{t1}\| \geq \frac{\varepsilon}{b}$, for infinitely many values of t, it follows from what has just been shown that there exists a positive number δ such that $\mathcal{L}_t(\mathbf{x}_{t0}, \mathbf{x}_{t1}) \geq \delta$, for infinitely many values of t. Since $\mathcal{L}_t(\mathbf{x}_{t0}, \mathbf{x}_{t1}) \geq 0$, for all values of t, we see that

$$\lim_{T\to\infty} [\mathcal{L}_{-1}(\mathbf{x}_{-1,1}) + \sum_{t=0}^{T} \mathcal{L}_t(\mathbf{x}_{t0}, \mathbf{x}_{t1})] = \infty.$$

By inequality 9.69,

$$\begin{aligned}
&\mathcal{L}_{-1}(\mathbf{x}_{-1,1}) + \sum_{t=0}^{T} \mathcal{L}_t(\mathbf{x}_{t0}, \mathbf{x}_{t1}) \\
&\quad \le [u(\overline{\mathbf{x}}_{-1,0}, \overline{\mathbf{x}}_{-1,1}) - u(\overline{\mathbf{x}}_{-1,0}, \mathbf{x}_{-1,1})] \\
&\quad + \sum_{t=0}^{T} [u(\overline{\mathbf{x}}_{t,0}, \overline{\mathbf{x}}_{t1}) - u(\mathbf{x}_{t0}, \mathbf{x}_{t1})] + \mathbf{P}_{T+1}.(\mathbf{x}_{T1} - \overline{\mathbf{x}}_{T1}).
\end{aligned}$$

Since $[u(\overline{\mathbf{x}}_{-1,0}, \overline{\mathbf{x}}_{-1,1}) - u(\mathbf{x}_{-1,0}, \mathbf{x}_{-1,1})] + \sum_{t=0}^{T} [u(\overline{\mathbf{x}}_{t,0}, \overline{\mathbf{x}}_{t1}) - u(\mathbf{x}_{t0}, \mathbf{x}_{t1})]$ $\le -\varepsilon$, for infinitely many values of T, we have that

$$\mathbf{P}_{T+1}.(\mathbf{x}_{T1} - \overline{\mathbf{x}}_{T1}) \ge \varepsilon + \mathcal{L}_{-1}(\mathbf{x}_{-1,1}) + \sum_{t=0}^{T} \mathcal{L}_t(\mathbf{x}_{t0}, \mathbf{x}_{t1}),$$

for infinitely many values of T. Therefore,

$$\limsup_{T\to\infty} \mathbf{P}_{T+1}.(\mathbf{x}_{T1} - \overline{\mathbf{x}}_{T1}) = \infty.$$

However,

$$\mathbf{P}_{T+1}.(\mathbf{x}_{T1} - \overline{\mathbf{x}}_{T1}) \le \mathbf{P}_{T+1}.(\mathbf{e}_0 + \mathbf{e}_1) \le \|\mathbf{P}_{T+1}\| \|\mathbf{e}_0 + \mathbf{e}_1\| \le b\|\mathbf{e}_0 + \mathbf{e}_1\| < \infty,$$

for all t. The contradiction between the last two inequalities proves that $(\overline{\mathbf{x}}_{t0}, \overline{\mathbf{x}}_{t-1,1})_{t=0}^{\infty}$ catches up to $(\mathbf{x}_{t0}, \mathbf{x}_{t-1,1})_{t=0}^{\infty}$ and hence that $(\overline{\mathbf{x}}_{t0}, \overline{\mathbf{x}}_{t-1,1})_{t=0}^{\infty}$ is optimal. ∎

The following example shows that it is necessary to assume in theorem 9.39 that all consumers have the same the marginal utility of unit of account.

EXAMPLE 9.40 The utility function is $u(x_0, x_1) = \ln(x_0) + \ln(x_1)$, and the endowment is $(e_0, e_1) = \left(\frac{1}{3}, \frac{2}{3}\right)$.

The endowment is itself the allocation of a spot price equilibrium with interest rate equal to 1, as may be seen as follows. The first-order conditions for maximization of utility over the budget set imply that

$$(1 + r)\frac{1}{\overline{\mathbf{x}}_1} = \frac{1}{\overline{\mathbf{x}}_0},$$

where r is the interest rate. Feasibility implies that

$$\overline{\mathbf{x}}_0 + \overline{\mathbf{x}}_1 = 1.$$

These two equations together imply that

$$\overline{\mathbf{x}}_0 = \frac{1}{2+r} \text{ and } \overline{\mathbf{x}}_1 = \frac{1+r}{2+r}.$$

If $r = 1$, then

$$\overline{\mathbf{x}}_0 = \frac{1}{3} \text{ and } \overline{\mathbf{x}}_1 = \frac{2}{3}.$$

Let the price of the single commodity be 1 in every period, so that every consumer's marginal utility of unit of account is 3. Since the endowment equals the consumption allocation, there is no government debt and there are no taxes in this equilibrium. Therefore, the endowment is also the allocation for a spot price equilibrium with interest rate 0 and with price $P_t = \frac{1}{2^t}$, for all t. In this deflationary equilibrium, the marginal utility of unit of account of the consumer born in period t is $3(2^t)$ and so is not constant. The endowment allocation is clearly not optimal according to the catching up criterion, for consider the allocation $(x_{t0}, x_{t-1,1})_{t=0}^{\infty} = \left(\frac{1}{2}, \frac{1}{2}\right)_{t=0}^{\infty}$ and assume that the initial consumption is $\overline{x}_{-1,0} = \frac{1}{3}$. The total utility of the consumers -1 to T under the endowment allocation $(x_{t0}, x_{t-1,1})_{t=0}^{\infty} = \left(\frac{1}{3}, \frac{2}{3}\right)_{t=0}^{\infty}$ is

$$\ln\left(\frac{1}{3}\right) + \ln\left(\frac{2}{3}\right) + (T+1)\left[\ln\left(\frac{1}{3}\right) + \ln\left(\frac{2}{3}\right)\right] = \ln\left(\frac{2}{9}\right) + (T+1)\ln\left(\frac{8}{36}\right).$$

The total utility of the consumers -1 to T under the allocation $(x_{t0}, x_{t-1,1})_{t=0}^{\infty} = \left(\frac{1}{2}, \frac{1}{2}\right)_{t=0}^{\infty}$ is

$$\ln\left(\frac{1}{3}\right) + \ln\left(\frac{1}{2}\right) + (T+1)\left[\ln\left(\frac{1}{2}\right) + \ln\left(\frac{1}{2}\right)\right] = \ln\left(\frac{1}{6}\right) + (T+1)\ln\left(\frac{9}{36}\right).$$

Since

$$\lim_{T\to\infty}\left[\ln\left(\frac{1}{6}\right) + (T+1)\ln\left(\frac{9}{36}\right) - \ln\left(\frac{2}{9}\right) - (T+1)\ln\left(\frac{8}{36}\right)\right] = \infty,$$

the endowment allocation $(x_{t0}, x_{t-1,1})_{t=0}^{\infty} = \left(\frac{1}{3}, \frac{2}{3}\right)_{t=0}^{\infty}$ cannot catch up to the allocation $(x_{t0}, x_{t-1,1})_{t=0}^{\infty} = \left(\frac{1}{2}, \frac{1}{2}\right)_{t=0}^{\infty}$.

The next task is to prove that if $(\overline{\mathbf{x}}_{t0}, \overline{\mathbf{x}}_{t-1,1})_{t=0}^{\infty}$ is optimal according to the catching up criterion, then it is the allocation of a spot price equilibrium with bounded prices and in which the interest rate is 0 and all consumers have the same marginal utility of unit of account.

LEMMA 9.41 If the allocation $(\overline{\mathbf{x}}_{t0}, \overline{\mathbf{x}}_{t-1,1})_{t=0}^{\infty}$ is optimal according to the catching criterion, then for each $T \geq 0$, $(\overline{\mathbf{x}}_{t0}, \overline{\mathbf{x}}_{t-1,1})_{t=0}^{\infty}$ solves the problem

$$\max_{\substack{\mathbf{x}_{t0} \in \mathbb{R}_+^N,\, \mathbf{x}_{t-1,1} \in \mathbb{R}_+^N \\ \text{for all } t}} \left[u(\overline{\mathbf{x}}_{-1,0}, \mathbf{x}_{-1,1}) + \sum_{t=0}^{T-1} u(\mathbf{x}_{t0}, \mathbf{x}_{t1}) + u(\mathbf{x}_{T0}, \overline{\mathbf{x}}_{T1})\right] \tag{9.73}$$

$$\text{s.t.} \quad \mathbf{x}_{t-1,1} + \mathbf{x}_{t0} \leq \mathbf{e}_0 + \mathbf{e}_1, \quad \text{for } t = 0, \ldots, T.$$

Proof. Suppose that for some $\overline{T}$, $(\overline{\mathbf{x}}_{t0}, \overline{\mathbf{x}}_{t-1,1})_{t=0}^{\overline{T}}$ does not solve problem 9.73. Then there exists a positive number ε and an allocation $(\underline{\mathbf{x}}_{t0}, \underline{\mathbf{x}}_{t-1,1})_{t=0}^{\overline{T}}$ such that

$$\left[u(\overline{\mathbf{x}}_{-1,0}, \underline{\mathbf{x}}_{-1,1}) + \sum_{t=0}^{\overline{T}-1} u(\underline{\mathbf{x}}_{t0}, \underline{\mathbf{x}}_{t1}) + u(\underline{\mathbf{x}}_{\overline{T}0}, \overline{\mathbf{x}}_{\overline{T}1})\right]$$
$$- \left[u(\overline{\mathbf{x}}_{-1,0}, \overline{\mathbf{x}}_{-1,1}) + \sum_{t=0}^{\overline{T}-1} u(\overline{\mathbf{x}}_{t0}, \overline{\mathbf{x}}_{t1}) + u(\overline{\mathbf{x}}_{\overline{T}0}, \overline{\mathbf{x}}_{\overline{T}1})\right] > \varepsilon.$$

Let $(\mathbf{x}_{t0}, \mathbf{x}_{t-1,1})_{t=0}^{\infty}$ be the allocation defined by $(\mathbf{x}_{t0}, \mathbf{x}_{t-1,1}) = (\underline{\mathbf{x}}_{t0}, \underline{\mathbf{x}}_{t-1,1})$, if $0 \leq t \leq \overline{T}$, and $(\mathbf{x}_{t0}, \mathbf{x}_{t-1,1}) = (\overline{\mathbf{x}}_{t0}, \overline{\mathbf{x}}_{t-1,1})$, if $t > \overline{T}$. Then, if $T > \overline{T}$,

$$\left[u(\overline{\mathbf{x}}_{-1,0}, \mathbf{x}_{-1,1}) + \sum_{t=0}^{T} u(\mathbf{x}_{t0}, \mathbf{x}_{t1})\right] - \left[u(\overline{\mathbf{x}}_{-1,0}, \overline{\mathbf{x}}_{-1,1}) + \sum_{t=0}^{T} u(\overline{\mathbf{x}}_{t0}, \overline{\mathbf{x}}_{t1})\right] > \varepsilon,$$

so that $(\overline{\mathbf{x}}_{t0}, \overline{\mathbf{x}}_{t-1,1})_{t=0}^{\infty}$ cannot catch up to $(\mathbf{x}_{t0}, \mathbf{x}_{t-1,1})_{t=0}^{\infty}$. This is impossible, since $(\overline{\mathbf{x}}_{t0}, \overline{\mathbf{x}}_{t-1,1})_{t=0}^{\infty}$ is optimal according to the catching up criterion. The contradiction proves that $(\overline{\mathbf{x}}_{t0}, \overline{\mathbf{x}}_{t-1,1})_{t=0}^{T}$ solves problem 9.73, for all T. ■

This lemma implies that an allocation that is optimal with respect to the catching up criterion solves problem 9.22 (in section 9.4) with $r = 0$.

COROLLARY 9.42 If $(\overline{\mathbf{x}}_{t0}, \overline{\mathbf{x}}_{t-1,1})_{t=0}^{\infty}$ is optimal according to the catching up criterion, then, for each $t \geq 0$, $(\overline{\mathbf{x}}_{t0}, \overline{\mathbf{x}}_{t-1,1})$ solves the problem

$$\max_{\mathbf{x}_0 \in \mathbb{R}_+^N, \mathbf{x}_1 \in \mathbb{R}_+^N} [u(\overline{\mathbf{x}}_{t-1,0}, \mathbf{x}_1) + u(\mathbf{x}_0, \overline{\mathbf{x}}_{t1})]$$
$$\text{s.t.} \quad \mathbf{x}_0 + \mathbf{x}_1 \leq \mathbf{e}_0 + \mathbf{e}_1.$$

I now state and prove a converse to theorem 9.39.

THEOREM 9.43 Assume that u is continuous, concave, and strictly increasing and that $\mathbf{e}_0 + \mathbf{e}_1 \gg 0$. If the feasible allocation $\overline{\mathbf{x}}$ is optimal according to the catching up criterion, then $\overline{\mathbf{x}}$ is the allocation of a spot price equilibrium with interest rate 0, $(\overline{\mathbf{x}}, \mathbf{P}, G, \mathbf{T})$, such that every consumer's marginal utility of unit of account is 1 and prices are bounded.

Proof. By lemma 9.41, for each $T \geq 0$, $(\overline{\mathbf{x}}_{t0}, \overline{\mathbf{x}}_{t-1,1})_{t=0}^{T}$ solves problem 9.73. Since $\mathbf{e}_0 + \mathbf{e}_1 \gg 0$, this problem satisfies the constraint qualification of the Kuhn-Tucker theorem. Since u is concave, that theorem implies that there exist N-vectors, $\mathbf{P}_t^T$, for $t = 0, 1, \ldots, T$, such that $(\overline{\mathbf{x}}_{t0}, \overline{\mathbf{x}}_{t-1,1})_{t=0}^{T}$ solves the problem

$$\max_{\substack{\mathbf{x}_{t0} \in \mathbb{R}_+^N, \mathbf{x}_{t-1,1} \in \mathbb{R}_+^N \\ \text{for all } t=0,\ldots,T}} \left[u(\overline{\mathbf{x}}_{-1,0}, \mathbf{x}_{-1,1}) + \sum_{t=0}^{T-1} u(\mathbf{x}_{t0}, \mathbf{x}_{t1}) + u(\mathbf{x}_{T0}, \overline{\mathbf{x}}_{T1}) - \sum_{t=0}^{T} \mathbf{P}_t^T . (\mathbf{x}_{t-1,1} + \mathbf{x}_{t0}) \right]. \tag{9.74}$$

I prove that the vectors $\mathbf{P}_t^T$ are uniformly bounded. Because $(\overline{\mathbf{x}}_{t0}, \overline{\mathbf{x}}_{t-1,1})_{t=0}^{T}$ solves problem 9.74, it follows that, for t such that $0 \leq t \leq T$,

$$u(\overline{\mathbf{x}}_{t0}, \overline{\mathbf{x}}_{t-1,1}) + u(\overline{\mathbf{x}}_{t0}, \overline{\mathbf{x}}_{t1}) - \mathbf{P}_t^T . (\overline{\mathbf{x}}_{t-1,1} + \overline{\mathbf{x}}_{t0})$$
$$\geq u(\overline{\mathbf{x}}_{t-1,0}, \mathbf{x}_1) + u(\mathbf{x}_0, \overline{\mathbf{x}}_{t1}) - \mathbf{P}_t^T . (\mathbf{x}_1 + \mathbf{x}_0),$$

for any $\mathbf{x}_0$ and $\mathbf{x}_1$ in $\mathbb{R}_+^N$. If we set $\mathbf{x}_0 = \mathbf{x}_1 = 0$ in this inequality, we find that

$$u(\overline{\mathbf{x}}_{t0}, \overline{\mathbf{x}}_{t-1,1}) + u(\overline{\mathbf{x}}_{t0}, \overline{\mathbf{x}}_{t1}) - \mathbf{P}_t^T . (\overline{\mathbf{x}}_{t-1,1} + \overline{\mathbf{x}}_{t0})$$
$$\geq u(\overline{\mathbf{x}}_{t-1,0}, \mathbf{0}) + u(\mathbf{0}, \overline{\mathbf{x}}_{t1}),$$

so that

$$\mathbf{P}_t^T . (\overline{\mathbf{x}}_{t-1,1} + \overline{\mathbf{x}}_{t0}) \leq u(\overline{\mathbf{x}}_{t0}, \overline{\mathbf{x}}_{t-1,1}) + u(\overline{\mathbf{x}}_{t0}, \overline{\mathbf{x}}_{t1}) - u(\overline{\mathbf{x}}_{t-1,0}, \mathbf{0}) - u(\mathbf{0}, \overline{\mathbf{x}}_{t1})$$
$$\leq 2[u(\mathbf{e}_0 + \mathbf{e}_1, \mathbf{e}_0 + \mathbf{e}_1) - u(\mathbf{0}, \mathbf{0})].$$

Since u is strictly increasing, $\overline{\mathbf{x}}_{t-1,1} + \overline{\mathbf{x}}_{t0} = \mathbf{e}_0 + \mathbf{e}_1$, so that the previous inequality implies that

$$\mathbf{P}_t^T.(\mathbf{e}_0 + \mathbf{e}_1) \leq 2[u(\mathbf{e}_0 + \mathbf{e}_1, \mathbf{e}_0 + \mathbf{e}_1) - u(\mathbf{0}, \mathbf{0})].$$

Since $\mathbf{e}_0 + \mathbf{e}_1 \gg 0$, there exists a positive number ε such that $e_{0n} + e_{1n} \geq \varepsilon$, for all n. Therefore, the previous inequality implies that

$$0 \leq P_{tn}^T \leq 2\varepsilon^{-1}[u(\mathbf{e}_0 + \mathbf{e}_1, \mathbf{e}_0 + \mathbf{e}_1) - u(\mathbf{0}, \mathbf{0})],$$

for all t and n.

Since the sequence $\mathbf{P}_0^T$ is bounded, the Bolzano-Weierstrass theorem implies that it has a convergent subsequence, call it $\mathbf{P}_0^{T_1(k)}$, for $k = 1, 2, \ldots$. Since the sequence $\mathbf{P}_1^{T_1(k)}$ is bounded, it also has a convergent subsequence, call it $\mathbf{P}_1^{T_2(k)}$. Since a subsequence of a convergent sequence converges, the sequence $\mathbf{P}_0^{T_2(k)}$ also converges. Continuing by induction on m, suppose that there is a sequence $T_m(k)$ such that $\mathbf{P}_t^{T_m(k)}$ converges as k goes to infinity, for $t = 0, 1, \ldots, m$. Since the sequence $\mathbf{P}_{m+1}^{T_m(k)}$ is bounded, it has a convergent subsequence, call it $\mathbf{P}_{m+1}^{T_{m+1}(k)}$. Then, $\mathbf{P}_t^{T_{m+1}(k)}$ converges for $t = 0, 1, \ldots, m$ as well. This inductive argument proves that for every positive integer m, there exists a subsequence of T, call it $T_m(k)$, such that $\mathbf{P}_t^{T_m(k)}$ converges for $t = 0, 1, \ldots, m$. Let $T(k)$ be the sequence defined by the formula $T(k) = T_k(k)$. The vector $\mathbf{P}_t^{T(k)}$ is defined for t such that $0 \leq t \leq T(k)$. For all t, the sequence $\mathbf{P}_t^{T_t(k)}$ converges as k goes to infinity, and, for $k \geq t$, the sequence $T(k)$ is a subsequence of $T_t(k)$. Hence $\mathbf{P}_t^{T(k)}$ converges, for all t. Let $\mathbf{P}_t = \lim_{k\to\infty} \mathbf{P}_t^{T(k)}$. Since

$$P_{tn} \leq 2\varepsilon^{-1}[u(\mathbf{e}_0 + \mathbf{e}_1, \mathbf{e}_0 + \mathbf{e}_1) - u(0, 0)],$$

for all t and n, the sequence $\mathbf{P}_t$ is bounded. Let $G = \mathbf{P}_0.(\overline{\mathbf{x}}_{-1,1} - \mathbf{e}_1)$ and, for all t, let $\mathsf{T}_t = \mathbf{P}_t.(\mathbf{e}_0 - \overline{\mathbf{x}}_{t0}) + \mathbf{P}_{t_1}.(\mathbf{e}_1 - \overline{\mathbf{x}}_{t1})$. I claim that $(\overline{\mathbf{x}}, \mathbf{P}, G, \mathsf{T})$ is a spot price equilibrium with interest rate 0, where $\mathbf{P} = (\mathbf{P}_0, \mathbf{P}_1, \ldots)$ and $\mathsf{T} = (\mathsf{T}_0, \mathsf{T}_1, \ldots)$.

It is sufficient to show that every consumer solves his or her utility maximization problem at the allocation $\overline{\mathbf{x}}$ when the prices and lump-sum taxes are $\mathbf{P}$ and T, respectively. Because $(\overline{\mathbf{x}}_{t0}, \overline{\mathbf{x}}_{t-1,1})_{t=0}^T$ solves problem 9.74, it follows that, for t such that $0 \leq t \leq T - 1$, $(\overline{\mathbf{x}}_{t0}, \overline{\mathbf{x}}_{t1})$ satisfies

$$u(\overline{\mathbf{x}}_{t0}, \overline{\mathbf{x}}_{t1}) - \mathbf{P}_t^T.\overline{\mathbf{x}}_{t0} - \mathbf{P}_{t+1}^T.\overline{\mathbf{x}}_{t1} \geq u(\mathbf{x}_0, \mathbf{x}_1) - \mathbf{P}_t^T.\mathbf{x}_0 - \mathbf{P}_{t+1}^T.\mathbf{x}_1,$$

for all $\mathbf{x}_0$ and $\mathbf{x}_1$ in $\mathbb{R}^N_+$. Hence, if k is such that $T(k) \geq t$, then

$$u(\overline{\mathbf{x}}_{t0}, \overline{\mathbf{x}}_{t1}) - \mathbf{P}_t^{T(k)}.\overline{\mathbf{x}}_{t0} - \mathbf{P}_{t+1}^{T(k)}.\overline{\mathbf{x}}_{t1} \geq u(\mathbf{x}_0, \mathbf{x}_1) - \mathbf{P}_t^{T(k)}.\mathbf{x}_0 - \mathbf{P}_{t+1}^{T(k)}.\mathbf{x}_1,$$

Passing to the limit in this inequality, we find that

$$u(\overline{\mathbf{x}}_{t0}, \overline{\mathbf{x}}_{t1}) - \mathbf{P}_t.\overline{\mathbf{x}}_{t0} - \mathbf{P}_{t+1}.\overline{\mathbf{x}}_{t1} \geq u(\mathbf{x}_0, \mathbf{x}_1) - \mathbf{P}_t.\mathbf{x}_0 - \mathbf{P}_{t+1}.\mathbf{x}_1, \tag{9.75}$$

for all $t \geq 0$. The sufficiency part of the Kuhn-Tucker theorem now implies that for each $t \geq 0$, $(\overline{\mathbf{x}}_{t0}, \overline{\mathbf{x}}_{t1})$ solves the problem

$$\max_{\mathbf{x}_0 \in \mathbb{R}^N_+, \mathbf{x}_1 \in \mathbb{R}^N_+} u(\mathbf{x}_0, \mathbf{x}_1)$$
$$\text{s.t.} \quad \mathbf{P}_t.\mathbf{x}_0 + \mathbf{P}_{t+1}.\mathbf{x}_1 \leq \mathbf{P}_t.\mathbf{e}_0 + \mathbf{P}_{t+1}.\mathbf{e}_1 - \mathsf{T}_t,$$

where $\mathsf{T}_t = \mathbf{P}_t.(\mathbf{e}_0 - \overline{\mathbf{x}}_{t0}) + \mathbf{P}_{t+1}.(\mathbf{e}_1 - \overline{\mathbf{x}}_{t1})$. Inequality 9.75 implies that consumer t's marginal utility of unit of account is 1.

A similar argument shows that $\overline{\mathbf{x}}_{-1,1}$ solves the problem

$$\max_{\mathbf{x}_1 \in \mathbb{R}^N_+} u(\overline{\mathbf{x}}_{-1,0}, \mathbf{x}_1)$$
$$\text{s.t.} \quad \mathbf{P}_0.\mathbf{x}_1 \leq \mathbf{P}_0.\mathbf{e}_1 + G,$$

where $G = \mathbf{P}_0.(\overline{\mathbf{x}}_{-1,1} - \mathbf{e}_1)$, and also shows that consumer -1's marginal utility of unit of account is 1. ■

The core of the above proof is the argument extracting the sequence $T(k)$ from a sequence of sequences, $T_m(k)$. This argument is an example of a Cantor diagonal argument, which is often used to prove the existence of a sequence of vectors with certain properties. The argument will be used again in section 9.9.

The next corollary deals with the obvious candidate for a stationary allocation that is optimal with respect to the catching up criterion. This candidate is the stationary allocation that maximizes the utility of a typical consumer.

COROLLARY 9.44 Assume that u is continuous, strictly concave, and strictly increasing and that $\mathbf{e}_0 + \mathbf{e}_1 \gg 0$. Then, the unique stationary allocation, $(\overline{\mathbf{x}}_0, \overline{\mathbf{x}}_1)$, that solves the problem

$$\max_{\mathbf{x}_0 \in \mathbb{R}^N_+, \mathbf{x}_1 \in \mathbb{R}^N_+} u(\mathbf{x}_0, \mathbf{x}_1)$$
$$\text{s.t.} \quad \mathbf{x}_0 + \mathbf{x}_1 \leq \mathbf{e}_0 + \mathbf{e}_1$$

is optimal with respect to the catching up criterion. Furthermore, $(\overline{\mathbf{x}}_0, \overline{\mathbf{x}}_1)$ is the allocation of a stationary spot price equilibrium, $(\overline{\mathbf{x}}_0, \overline{\mathbf{x}}_1, \mathbf{P}_0, G)$, with interest rate 0.

Proof. By proposition 9.18 (in section 9.3), $(\overline{\mathbf{x}}_0, \overline{\mathbf{x}}_1)$ is the allocation of a stationary spot price equilibrium with interest rate 0, $(\overline{\mathbf{x}}_0, \overline{\mathbf{x}}_1, \mathbf{P}_0, G)$. I apply theorem 9.39 to this equilibrium. Since the equilibrium is stationary, all consumers have the same marginal utility of unit of account in the equilibrium, if they have one. Since $\mathbf{e}_0 + \mathbf{e}_1 \gg 0$ and u is strictly increasing, $\overline{\mathbf{x}}_0 + \overline{\mathbf{x}}_1 = \mathbf{e}_0 + \mathbf{e}_1 \gg 0$, so that all consumers have positive income in the stationary equilibrium and therefore have a well-defined marginal utility of unit of account. In theorem 9.39, it is assumed that $\overline{\mathbf{x}}_{-1,1} > 0$ in order to guarantee that consumer -1 has a marginal utility of unit of account. Because the equilibrium $(\overline{\mathbf{x}}_0, \overline{\mathbf{x}}_1, \mathbf{P}_0, G)$ is stationary, it is not necessary to make that assumption. Theorem 9.39, therefore, implies that $(\overline{\mathbf{x}}_0, \overline{\mathbf{x}}_1)$ is optimal according to the catching up criterion. ■

The next corollary together with corollary 9.15 (in section 9.3) show, with the qualification $\mathbf{e}_0 + \mathbf{e}_1 \gg 0$, that the stationary spot price equilibria that are Pareto optimal are those with nonnegative interest rates.

COROLLARY 9.45 If u is continuous, strictly concave, and strictly increasing and if $\mathbf{e}_0 + \mathbf{e}_1 \gg 0$, then the allocation, $(\overline{\mathbf{x}}_0, \overline{\mathbf{x}}_1)$, of any stationary spot price equilibrium, $(\overline{\mathbf{x}}_0, \overline{\mathbf{x}}_1, \mathbf{P}_0, G)$, with interest rate 0 is Pareto optimal.

Proof. By proposition 9.18, the allocation $(\overline{\mathbf{x}}_0, \overline{\mathbf{x}}_1)$ solves problem 9.19 (both in section 9.3), so that corollary 9.44 implies that it is optimal according to the catching up criterion and hence by theorem 9.37 is Pareto optimal. ■

Corollary 9.44 implies that if $\overline{\mathbf{x}}_{-1,0}$ is chosen correctly, then the unique allocation with this initial consumption that is optimal, with respect to the catching up criterion, is stationary. The reader may wonder whether any allocation that is optimal with respect to the catching up criterion converges over time to the unique stationary optimal allocation, no matter what the choice of initial consumption may be. The answer is that it does so if u is strictly concave and increasing and if $\mathbf{e}_0 + \mathbf{e}_1 \gg 0$. This assertion is an example of a turnpike theorem, where the origin of the term *turnpike* is explained in section 10.12. Although I do not prove such a theorem for the N-commodity Samuelson model, it is true.

9.8 Uniqueness of Optimal Allocations

I show that optimal allocations are unique in both the discounted and undiscounted models, provided the utility function is strictly concave. The statement for the discounted case is as follows.

PROPOSITION 9.46 If u is strictly concave and $\lambda_t > 0$, for all $t \geq -1$, and $\sum_{t=-1}^{\infty} \lambda_t^{-1} < \infty$, then there is at most one solution to the problem

$$\max_{\substack{\mathbf{x} \text{ is a feasible} \\ \text{allocation}}} [\lambda_{-1}^{-1} u(\overline{\mathbf{x}}_{-1,0}, \mathbf{x}_{-1,1}) + \sum_{t=0}^{\infty} \lambda_t^{-1} u(\mathbf{x}_{t0}, \mathbf{x}_{t1})] \tag{9.76}$$

for any choice of $\overline{x}_{-1,0}$ in $\mathbb{R}_+^N$.

Proof. Suppose that problem 9.76 has two distinct solutions, $(\overline{\mathbf{x}}_{t-1,1}, \overline{\mathbf{x}}_{t0})_{t=0}^{\infty}$ and $(\underline{\mathbf{x}}_{t-1,1}, \underline{\mathbf{x}}_{t0})_{t=0}^{\infty}$. Then,

$$\begin{aligned} &\lambda_{-1}^{-1} u(\overline{\mathbf{x}}_{-1,0}, \overline{\mathbf{x}}_{-1,1}) + \sum_{t=0}^{\infty} \lambda_t^{-1} u(\overline{\mathbf{x}}_{t0}, \overline{\mathbf{x}}_{t1}) \\ &= \lambda_{-1}^{-1} u(\overline{\mathbf{x}}_{-1,0}, \underline{\mathbf{x}}_{-1,1}) + \sum_{t=0}^{\infty} \lambda_t^{-1} u(\underline{\mathbf{x}}_{t0}, \underline{\mathbf{x}}_{t1}). \end{aligned} \tag{9.77}$$

Let

$$(\mathbf{x}_{t-1,1}, \mathbf{x}_{t0})_{t=0}^{\infty} = \frac{1}{2}(\overline{\mathbf{x}}_{t-1,1}, \overline{\mathbf{x}}_{t0})_{t=0}^{\infty} + \frac{1}{2}(\underline{\mathbf{x}}_{t-1,1}, \underline{\mathbf{x}}_{t0})_{t=0}^{\infty}.$$

Then $(\mathbf{x}_{t-1,1}, \mathbf{x}_{t0})_{t=0}^{\infty}$ is feasible, because

$$\begin{aligned} \mathbf{x}_{t-1,1} + \mathbf{x}_{t0} &= \frac{1}{2}(\overline{\mathbf{x}}_{t-1,1} + \overline{\mathbf{x}}_{t0}) + \frac{1}{2}(\underline{\mathbf{x}}_{t-1,1} + \underline{\mathbf{x}}_{t0}) \\ &\leq \frac{1}{2}(\mathbf{e}_1 + \mathbf{e}_0) + \frac{1}{2}(\mathbf{e}_1 + \mathbf{e}_0) = \mathbf{e}_1 + \mathbf{e}_0, \end{aligned}$$

for all t. Because u is strictly concave and $(\overline{\mathbf{x}}_{t-1,1}, \overline{\mathbf{x}}_{t0})_{t=0}^{\infty} \neq (\underline{\mathbf{x}}_{t-1,1}, \underline{\mathbf{x}}_{t0})_{t=0}^{\infty}$, it follows that

$$\lambda_{-1}^{-1}u(\overline{\mathbf{x}}_{-1,0}, \mathbf{x}_{-1,1}) + \sum_{t=0}^{\infty} \lambda_t^{-1}u(\mathbf{x}_{t0}, \mathbf{x}_{t1}) > \frac{1}{2}[\lambda_{-1}^{-1}u(\overline{\mathbf{x}}_{-1,0}, \overline{\mathbf{x}}_{-1,1})$$

$$+ \sum_{t=0}^{\infty} \lambda_t^{-1}u(\overline{\mathbf{x}}_{t0}, \overline{\mathbf{x}}_{t1})]$$

$$+ \frac{1}{2}[\lambda_{-1}^{-1}u(\overline{\mathbf{x}}_{-1,0}, \underline{\mathbf{x}}_{-1,1}) + \sum_{t=0}^{\infty} \lambda_t^{-1}u(\underline{\mathbf{x}}_{t0}, \underline{\mathbf{x}}_{t1})]$$

$$= \lambda_{-1}^{-1}u(\overline{\mathbf{x}}_{-1,0}, \overline{\mathbf{x}}_{-1,1}) + \sum_{t=0}^{\infty} \lambda_t^{-1}u(\overline{\mathbf{x}}_{t0}, \overline{\mathbf{x}}_{t1}),$$

where the equation follows from equation 9.77. This inequality contradicts the optimality of $(\overline{\mathbf{x}}_{t-1,1}, \overline{\mathbf{x}}_{t0})_{t=0}^{\infty}$. This contradiction completes the proof. ■

The corresponding assertion for the undiscounted case follows.

PROPOSITION 9.47 If u is strictly concave, then there is at most one allocation that is optimal according to the catching up criterion for any choice of $\overline{\mathbf{x}}_{-1,0}$.

Proof. Suppose that there are two distinct allocations, $(\overline{\mathbf{x}}_{t-1,1}, \overline{\mathbf{x}}_{t0})_{t=0}^{\infty}$ and $(\underline{\mathbf{x}}_{t-1,1}, \underline{\mathbf{x}}_{t0})_{t=0}^{\infty}$, that are optimal with respect to the catching up criterion, and let $(\mathbf{x}_{t-1,1}, \mathbf{x}_{t0})_{t=0}^{\infty} = \frac{1}{2}(\overline{\mathbf{x}}_{t-1,1}, \overline{\mathbf{x}}_{t0})_{t=0}^{\infty} + \frac{1}{2}(\underline{\mathbf{x}}_{t-1,1}, \underline{\mathbf{x}}_{t0})_{t=0}^{\infty}$. By the argument given in the proof of proposition 9.46, $(\mathbf{x}_{t-1,1}, \mathbf{x}_{t0})_{t=0}^{\infty}$ is feasible. Since $(\overline{\mathbf{x}}_{t-1,1}, \overline{\mathbf{x}}_{t0})_{t=0}^{\infty}$ and $(\underline{\mathbf{x}}_{t-1,1}, \underline{\mathbf{x}}_{t0})_{t=0}^{\infty}$ are distinct, $(\overline{\mathbf{x}}_{t-1,1}, \overline{\mathbf{x}}_{t0})_{t=0}^{T} \neq (\underline{\mathbf{x}}_{t-1,1}, \underline{\mathbf{x}}_{t0})_{t=0}^{T}$, if T is sufficiently large. Because u is strictly concave, it follows that there is a positive number ε such that

$$u(\overline{\mathbf{x}}_{-1,0}, \mathbf{x}_{-1,1}) + \sum_{t=0}^{T} u(\mathbf{x}_{t0}, \mathbf{x}_{t1}) - \varepsilon > \frac{1}{2}[u(\overline{\mathbf{x}}_{-1,0}, \underline{\mathbf{x}}_{-1,1})$$

$$+ \sum_{t=0}^{T} u(\underline{\mathbf{x}}_{t0}, \underline{\mathbf{x}}_{t1})] + \frac{1}{2}[u(\overline{\mathbf{x}}_{-1,0}, \overline{\mathbf{x}}_{-1,1}) + \sum_{t=0}^{T} u(\overline{\mathbf{x}}_{t0}, \overline{\mathbf{x}}_{t1})] \qquad (9.78)$$

$$\geq \min\left[u(\overline{\mathbf{x}}_{-1,0}, \underline{\mathbf{x}}_{-1,1}) + \sum_{t=0}^{T} u(\underline{\mathbf{x}}_{t0}, \underline{\mathbf{x}}_{t1}), u(\overline{\mathbf{x}}_{-1,0}, \overline{\mathbf{x}}_{-1,1}) + \sum_{t=0}^{T} u(\overline{\mathbf{x}}_{t0}, \overline{\mathbf{x}}_{t1})\right],$$

for any T such that $T \geq \overline{T}$, where $\overline{T}$ is so large that $(\overline{\mathbf{x}}_{t-1,1}, \overline{\mathbf{x}}_{t0})_{t=0}^{\overline{T}} \neq (\underline{\mathbf{x}}_{t-1,1}, \underline{\mathbf{x}}_{t0})_{t=0}^{\overline{T}}$. One of $u(\overline{\mathbf{x}}_{-1,0}, \underline{\mathbf{x}}_{-1,1}) + \sum_{t=0}^{T} u(\underline{\mathbf{x}}_{t0}, \underline{\mathbf{x}}_{t1})$ or $u(\overline{\mathbf{x}}_{-1,0}, \overline{\mathbf{x}}_{-1,1}) + \sum_{t=0}^{T} u(\overline{\mathbf{x}}_{t0}, \overline{\mathbf{x}}_{t1})$ equals the minimum of these two numbers for infinitely many values of T. Say that $u(\overline{\mathbf{x}}_{-1,0}, \underline{\mathbf{x}}_{-1,1}) + \sum_{t=0}^{T} u(\underline{\mathbf{x}}_{t0}, \underline{\mathbf{x}}_{t1})$ equals the minimum infinitely often, and let $T(k)$, for $k = 1, 2, \ldots$, be an increasing sequence of numbers all greater than $\overline{T}$, such that

$$u(\overline{\mathbf{x}}_{-1,0}, \underline{\mathbf{x}}_{-1,1}) + \sum_{t=0}^{T(k)} u(\underline{\mathbf{x}}_{t0}, \underline{\mathbf{x}}_{t1}) \leq u(\overline{\mathbf{x}}_{-1,0}, \overline{\mathbf{x}}_{-1,1}) + \sum_{t=0}^{T(k)} u(\overline{\mathbf{x}}_{t0}, \overline{\mathbf{x}}_{t1})$$

for every k. Then, inequality 9.78 implies that

$$u(\overline{\mathbf{x}}_{-1,0}, \mathbf{x}_{-1,1}) + \sum_{t=0}^{T(k)} u(\mathbf{x}_{t0}, \mathbf{x}_{t1}) - \varepsilon > u(\overline{\mathbf{x}}_{-1,0}, \underline{\mathbf{x}}_{-1,1}) + \sum_{t=0}^{T(k)} u(\underline{\mathbf{x}}_{t0}, \underline{\mathbf{x}}_{t1}),$$

for every k. It follows that the allocation $(\underline{\mathbf{x}}_{t-1,1}, \underline{\mathbf{x}}_{t0})_{t=0}^{\infty}$ cannot catch up to the allocation $(\mathbf{x}_{t-1,1}, \mathbf{x}_{t0})_{t=0}^{\infty}$, which contradicts the optimality of $(\underline{\mathbf{x}}_{t-1,1}, \underline{\mathbf{x}}_{t0})_{t=0}^{\infty}$. ■

9.9 Existence of Optimal Allocations

This section extends to the Samuelson model theorems that are already familiar from finite dimensional contexts, namely, the Kuhn-Tucker theorem and assertions on the existence of welfare optima. The demonstrations rely on the Cantor diagonal argument, used earlier when proving theorem 9.43 (in section 9.7).

DEFINITION 9.48 The allocation $\mathbf{x} = (\mathbf{x}_{t0}, \mathbf{x}_{t-1,1})_{t=0}^{\infty}$ is *bounded,* if there is a positive number b such that $\|\mathbf{x}_{t0}\| \leq b$ and $\|\mathbf{x}_{t-1,1}\| \leq b$, for all $t \geq 0$.

Clearly, an allocation $\mathbf{x}$ is bounded, if it is feasible, because then $0 \leq \mathbf{x}_{t0} + \mathbf{x}_{t-1,1} \leq \mathbf{e}_0 + \mathbf{e}_1$, for all t.

KUHN-TUCKER THEOREM FOR THE SAMUELSON MODEL THEOREM 9.49 Assume that u is continuous, concave, and strictly increasing and that $\mathbf{e}_0 + \mathbf{e}_1 \gg 0$. Let λ_t, for $t = -1, 0, 1, \ldots$, be positive numbers such that $\sum_{t=-1}^{\infty} \lambda_t^{-t} < \infty$. Then, the allocation $(\overline{\mathbf{x}}_{t0}, \overline{\mathbf{x}}_{t-1,1})_{t=0}^{\infty}$ solves the problem

$$\max_{\substack{\mathbf{x} \text{ is a feasible} \\ \text{allocation}}} [\lambda_{-1}^{-1} u(\overline{\mathbf{x}}_{-1,0}, \mathbf{x}_{-1,1}) + \sum_{t=0}^{\infty} \lambda_t^{-1} u(\mathbf{x}_{t0}, \mathbf{x}_{t1})], \tag{9.79}$$

if and only if $(\overline{x}_{t0}, \overline{x}_{t-1,1})_{t=0}^{\infty}$ is feasible and

1. for all t, $\overline{\mathbf{x}}_{t0} + \overline{\mathbf{x}}_{t-1,1} = \mathbf{e}_0 + \mathbf{e}_1$,

and there exist N-vectors, $\mathbf{p}_t$, for $t \geq 0$, such that $\mathbf{p}_t \gg 0$ and

2. $(\overline{\mathbf{x}}_{t0}, \overline{\mathbf{x}}_{t-1,1})_{t=0}^{\infty}$ solves the problem

$$\max_{\substack{\mathbf{x} \text{ is a bounded} \\ \text{allocation}}} [\lambda_{-1}^{-1} u(\overline{\mathbf{x}}_{-1,0}, \mathbf{x}_{-1,1}) + \sum_{t=0}^{\infty} \lambda_t^{-1} u(\mathbf{x}_{t0}, \mathbf{x}_{t1}) - \sum_{t=0}^{\infty} \mathbf{p}_t . (\mathbf{x}_{t0} + \mathbf{x}_{t-1,1})]$$

3. $\sum_{t=0}^{\infty} \mathbf{p}_t < \infty$

Proof. I begin by proving that a feasible allocation, $\overline{\mathbf{x}}$, is optimal if it and the sequence of nonnegative Kuhn-Tucker coefficient vectors, $\mathbf{p}_t$, for $t = 0, 1, 2, \ldots$, satisfy conditions (1)–(3) of the theorem. I must show that if $\mathbf{x}$ is any other feasible allocation, then

$$\begin{aligned} &\lambda_{-1}^{-1} u(\overline{\mathbf{x}}_{-1,0}, \overline{\mathbf{x}}_{-1,1}) + \sum_{t=0}^{\infty} \lambda_{-1}^{-1} u(\overline{\mathbf{x}}_{t0}, \overline{\mathbf{x}}_{t1}) \\ &\geq \lambda_{-1}^{-1} u(\overline{\mathbf{x}}_{-1,0}, \mathbf{x}_{-1,1}) + \sum_{t=0}^{\infty} \lambda_{-1}^{-1} u(\mathbf{x}_{t0}, \mathbf{x}_{t1}). \end{aligned} \tag{9.80}$$

Because $\mathbf{x}$ is feasible, it is bounded. It follows that since $\overline{\mathbf{x}}$ solves the maximization problem in condition (2),

$$\begin{aligned} &\lambda_{-1}^{-1} u(\overline{\mathbf{x}}_{-1,0}, \overline{\mathbf{x}}_{-1,1}) + \sum_{t=0}^{\infty} \lambda_{-1}^{-1} u(\overline{\mathbf{x}}_{t0}, \overline{\mathbf{x}}_{t1}) - \sum_{t=0}^{\infty} \mathbf{p}_t . (\overline{\mathbf{x}}_{t0} + \overline{\mathbf{x}}_{t-1,1}) \\ &\geq \lambda_{-1}^{-1} u(\overline{\mathbf{x}}_{-1,0}, \mathbf{x}_{-1,1}) + \sum_{t=0}^{\infty} \lambda_{-1}^{-1} u(\mathbf{x}_{t0}, \mathbf{x}_{t1}) - \sum_{t=0}^{\infty} \mathbf{p}_t . (\mathbf{x}_{t0} + \mathbf{x}_{t-1,1}). \end{aligned} \tag{9.81}$$

All the infinite sums in inequality 9.81 converge, because $\sum_{t=0}^{\infty} \mathbf{p}_t < \infty$ and $\sum_{t=-1}^{\infty} \lambda_t^{-1} < \infty$ and the allocations $\overline{\mathbf{x}}$ and $\mathbf{x}$ are bounded. (The allocation

$\overline{\mathbf{x}}$ is bounded because it is feasible.) Inequality 9.81 may be rewritten as

$$\begin{aligned}
&\lambda_{-1}^{-1}u(\overline{\mathbf{x}}_{-1,0}, \overline{\mathbf{x}}_{-1,1}) + \sum_{t=0}^{\infty} \lambda_{-1}^{-1}u(\overline{\mathbf{x}}_{t0}, \overline{\mathbf{x}}_{t1}) \\
&\geq \lambda_{-1}^{-1}u(\overline{\mathbf{x}}_{-1,0}, \mathbf{x}_{-1,1}) + \sum_{t=0}^{\infty} \lambda_{-1}^{-1}u(\mathbf{x}_{t0}, \mathbf{x}_{t1}) \qquad (9.82) \\
&+ \sum_{t=0}^{\infty} \mathbf{p}_t.(\overline{\mathbf{x}}_{t0} + \overline{\mathbf{x}}_{t-1,1}) - \sum_{t=0}^{\infty} \mathbf{p}_t.(\mathbf{x}_{t0} + \mathbf{x}_{t-1,1}).
\end{aligned}$$

Condition (1) implies that

$$\sum_{t=0}^{\infty} \mathbf{p}_t.(\overline{\mathbf{x}}_{t0} + \overline{\mathbf{x}}_{t-1,1}) = \sum_{t=0}^{\infty} \mathbf{p}_t.(\mathbf{e}_0 + \mathbf{e}_1). \qquad (9.83)$$

Since the allocation $\mathbf{x}$ is feasible and the Kuhn-Tucker coefficient vectors $\mathbf{p}_t$ are nonnegative, it follows that

$$\sum_{t=0}^{\infty} \mathbf{p}_t.(\mathbf{x}_{t0} + \mathbf{x}_{t-1,1}) \leq \sum_{t=0}^{\infty} \mathbf{p}_t.(\mathbf{e}_0 + \mathbf{e}_1). \qquad (9.84)$$

Inequalities 9.83 and 9.84 imply that

$$\sum_{t=0}^{\infty} \mathbf{p}_t.(\overline{\mathbf{x}}_{t0}, \overline{\mathbf{x}}_{t-1,1}) - \sum_{t=0}^{\infty} \mathbf{p}_t.(\mathbf{x}_{t0} + \mathbf{x}_{t-1,1}) \geq 0.$$

This inequality and inequality 9.82 imply inequality 9.80. This completes the proof that conditions (1)–(3) are sufficient for optimality.

I now prove that if $\overline{\mathbf{x}}$ solves problem 9.79, then there exist Kuhn-Tucker coefficient vectors $\mathbf{p}_t$ such that $\overline{\mathbf{x}}$ and the $\mathbf{p}_t$ satisfy conditions (1)–(3). First of all, I may assume that $u(\mathbf{0}, \mathbf{0}) = 0$, for the solution to maximization problem 9.79 remains unchanged if I replace u by the function $u - u(\mathbf{0}, \mathbf{0})$.

Because $\overline{\mathbf{x}}$ solves problem 9.79, it follows that, for each $T \geq 0$, $(\overline{\mathbf{x}}_{t0}, \overline{\mathbf{x}}_{t-1,1})_{t=0}^{T}$ solves the problem

$$\max_{(\mathbf{x}_{t0}, \mathbf{x}_{t-1,1})_{t=0}^{T}} [\lambda_{-1}^{-1}u(\overline{\mathbf{x}}_{-1,0}, \mathbf{x}_{-1,1}) + \sum_{t=0}^{T-1} \lambda_t^{-1}u(\mathbf{x}_{t0}, \mathbf{x}_{t1}) + \lambda_T^{-1}u(\mathbf{x}_{T0}, \overline{\mathbf{x}}_{T1})]$$

$$\text{s.t.} \quad \mathbf{x}_{t0} + \mathbf{x}_{t-1,1} \leq \mathbf{e}_0 + \mathbf{e}_1, \quad \text{for } t \text{ such that } 0 \leq t \leq T.$$

Since $\mathbf{e}_0 + \mathbf{e}_1 \gg 0$, this problem satisfies the constraint qualification of the Kuhn-Tucker theorem. Since u is concave, all the assumptions of that theorem are satisfied, and it implies that there exist nonnegative N-vectors, $\mathbf{p}_t^T$, for $t = 1, 2, \ldots, T$, such that

$$\begin{aligned}\sum_{t=-1}^{T} \lambda_t^{-1} u(\overline{\mathbf{x}}_{t0}, \overline{\mathbf{x}}_{t1}) - \sum_{t=0}^{T} \mathbf{p}_t^T.(\overline{\mathbf{x}}_{t0} + \overline{\mathbf{x}}_{t-1,1}) \\ \geq \lambda_{-1}^{-1} u(\overline{\mathbf{x}}_{-1,0}, \mathbf{x}_{-1,1}) + \sum_{t=0}^{T-1} \lambda_t^{-1} u(\mathbf{x}_{t0} + \mathbf{x}_{t1}) \\ + \lambda_T^{-1} u(\mathbf{x}_{T0}, \overline{\mathbf{x}}_{T1}) - \sum_{t=0}^{T} \mathbf{p}_t^T.(\mathbf{x}_{t0} + \mathbf{x}_{t-1,1}),\end{aligned} \tag{9.85}$$

for any nonnegative $(\mathbf{x}_{t0}, \mathbf{x}_{t-1,1})_{t=0}^{T}$. Let S be an integer such that $0 \leq S < T$. In inequality 9.85, let $(\mathbf{x}_{t0}, \mathbf{x}_{t1}) = (\overline{\mathbf{x}}_{t0}, \overline{\mathbf{x}}_{t1})$, for $t > S$, and cancel like terms on the right and left sides. We then obtain

$$\begin{aligned}\sum_{t=-1}^{S} \lambda_t^{-1} u(\overline{\mathbf{x}}_{t0}, \overline{\mathbf{x}}_{t1}) - \sum_{t=0}^{S} \mathbf{p}_t^T.(\overline{\mathbf{x}}_{t0} + \overline{\mathbf{x}}_{t-1,1}) \\ \geq \lambda_{-1}^{-1} u(\overline{\mathbf{x}}_{-1,0}, \mathbf{x}_{-1,1}) + \sum_{t=0}^{S} \lambda_t^{-1} u(\mathbf{x}_{t0} + \mathbf{x}_{t1}) \\ - \sum_{t=0}^{S} \mathbf{p}_t^T.(\mathbf{x}_{t0} + \mathbf{x}_{t-1,1}) + \mathbf{p}_{S+1}^T.(\overline{\mathbf{x}}_{S1} - \mathbf{x}_{S1}),\end{aligned} \tag{9.86}$$

for any nonnegative $(\mathbf{x}_{t0}, \mathbf{x}_{t-1,1})_{t=0}^{S}$ and $\mathbf{x}_{S1}$.

I next obtain a bound on the vectors $\mathbf{p}_t^T$, for $t = 0, 1, \ldots, T$. Let $s = 0, 1, \ldots,$ or T. In inequality 9.85, set $\mathbf{x}_{t0} = \overline{\mathbf{x}}_{t0}$ and $\mathbf{x}_{t-1,1} = \overline{\mathbf{x}}_{t-1,1}$, for all variables except $\mathbf{x}_{s-1,1}$, and cancel like terms on both sides of the inequality. We then find that

$$\lambda_{s-1}^{-1} u(\overline{\mathbf{x}}_{s-1,0}, \overline{\mathbf{x}}_{s-1,1}) - \mathbf{p}_s^T.\overline{\mathbf{x}}_{s-1,1} \geq \lambda_{s-1}^{-1} u(\overline{\mathbf{x}}_{s-1,0}, \mathbf{x}_{s-1,1}) - \mathbf{p}_s^T.\mathbf{x}_{s-1,1}.$$

If we set $\mathbf{x}_{s-1,1} = 0$ in this inequality, we see that

$$\begin{aligned}\mathbf{p}_s^T.\overline{\mathbf{x}}_{s-1,1} &\leq \lambda_{s-1}^{-1}[u(\overline{\mathbf{x}}_{s-1,0}, \overline{\mathbf{x}}_{s-1,0}) - u(\overline{\mathbf{x}}_{s-1,0}, \mathbf{0})] \\ &\leq \lambda_{s-1}^{-1}[u(\mathbf{e}_0 + \mathbf{e}_1, \mathbf{e}_0 + \mathbf{e}_1) - u(\mathbf{0}, \mathbf{0})] = \lambda_{s-1}^{-1} u(\mathbf{e}_0 + \mathbf{e}_1, \mathbf{e}_0 + \mathbf{e}_1),\end{aligned} \tag{9.87}$$

where the second inequality is valid because u is strictly increasing and the allocation $\overline{\mathbf{x}}$ is feasible. Similarly, inequality 9.85 implies that

$$\lambda_s^{-1} u(\overline{\mathbf{x}}_{s0}, \overline{\mathbf{x}}_{s1}) - \mathbf{p}_s^T.\overline{\mathbf{x}}_{s0} \geq \lambda_s^{-1} u(\mathbf{x}_{s0}, \overline{\mathbf{x}}_{s1}) - \mathbf{p}_s^T.\mathbf{x}_{s0},$$

so that

$$\begin{aligned} \mathbf{p}_s^T.\overline{\mathbf{x}}_{s0} &\leq \lambda_s^{-1}[u(\overline{\mathbf{x}}_{s0}, \overline{\mathbf{x}}_{s1}) - u(\mathbf{0}, \overline{\mathbf{x}}_{s1})] \\ &\leq \lambda_s^{-1} u(\mathbf{e}_0 + \mathbf{e}_1, \mathbf{e}_0 + \mathbf{e}_1). \end{aligned} \tag{9.88}$$

By adding inequalities 9.87 and 9.88, we obtain

$$\mathbf{p}_s^T.(\overline{\mathbf{x}}_{s0} + \overline{\mathbf{x}}_{s-1,1}) \leq (\lambda_{s-1}^{-1} + \lambda_s^{-1}) u(\mathbf{e}_0 + \mathbf{e}_1, \mathbf{e}_0 + \mathbf{e}_1). \tag{9.89}$$

The complementary slackness condition of the Kuhn-Tucker theorem implies that

$$\mathbf{p}_s^T.(\overline{\mathbf{x}}_{s0} + \overline{\mathbf{x}}_{s-1,1}) = \mathbf{p}_s^T.(\mathbf{e}_0 + \mathbf{e}_1),$$

for all s, so that inequality 9.89 implies that

$$\mathbf{p}_s^T.(\mathbf{e}_0 + \mathbf{e}_1) \leq (\lambda_{s-1}^{-1} + \lambda_s^{-1}) u(\mathbf{e}_0 + \mathbf{e}_1, \mathbf{e}_0 + \mathbf{e}_1). \tag{9.90}$$

Since $\mathbf{e}_0 + \mathbf{e}_1 \gg \mathbf{0}$, $\varepsilon = \min_n(e_{0n} + e_{1n}) > 0$. Therefore, inequality 9.90 implies that

$$p_{sn}^T \leq \varepsilon^{-1}(\lambda_{s-1}^{-1} + \lambda_s^{-1}) u(\mathbf{e}_0 + \mathbf{e}_1, \mathbf{e}_0 + \mathbf{e}_1), \tag{9.91}$$

for all s and n.

I now pass to the limit using the Cantor diagonal argument. Because the sequence $\mathbf{p}_0^T$, for $T = 1, 2, \ldots$, is bounded, it has a convergent subsequence $\mathbf{p}_0^{T_0(k)}$, for $k = 0, 1, 2, \ldots$, by the Bolzano-Weierstrass theorem. The sequence $\mathbf{p}_1^{T_0(k)}$ is also bounded and hence has a convergent subsequence, $\mathbf{p}_1^{T_1(k)}$, for $k = 0, 1, \ldots$. Because a subsequence of a convergent sequence converges, it follows that the sequence $\mathbf{p}_1^{T_1(k)}$, converges as k goes to infinity. I proceed by induction on t. Suppose we have found a subsequence of T, call it $T_t(k)$, such that $\mathbf{p}_s^{T_t(k)}$ converges for $s = 0, 1, \ldots, t$. Because $\mathbf{p}_{t+1}^{T_t(k)}$ is bounded, there is a subsequence of $T_t(k)$, call it $T_{t+1}(k)$, such that $\mathbf{p}_s^{T_{t+1}(k)}$ converges for $s = 0, 1, \ldots, t+1$, as k goes to infinity. By induction on t, I have defined a sequence $T_t(k)$ of sequences $T_t(1), T_t(2), \ldots$, such that, for each t, $\lim_{k\to\infty} \mathbf{p}_s^{T_t(k)}$ exists, for $\mathbf{s} = 0, 1, \ldots, t$. Let $T(k)$ be the subsequence of T defined by $T(k) = T_k(k)$. For $k \geq t$, the sequence $T(k)$ is a subsequence of $T_t(k)$, so that $\mathbf{p}_t = \lim_{k\to\infty} \mathbf{p}_t^{T(k)}$ exists, for all $t \geq 0$.

Since inequality 9.86 applies for each k and $S < T(k)$, we find (by passage to the limit with respect to k in that inequality) that for any nonnegative integer S,

$$\sum_{t=-1}^{S} \lambda_1^{-1} u(\overline{\mathbf{x}}_{t0}, \overline{\mathbf{x}}_{t1}) - \sum_{t=0}^{S} \mathbf{p}_t \cdot (\overline{\mathbf{x}}_{t0} + \overline{\mathbf{x}}_{t-1,1})$$
$$\geq \lambda_{-1}^{-1} u(\overline{\mathbf{x}}_{-1,0}, \mathbf{x}_{-1,1}) + \sum_{t=0}^{S} \lambda_t^{-1} u(\mathbf{x}_{t0}, \mathbf{x}_{t1}) \tag{9.92}$$
$$- \sum_{t=0}^{S} \mathbf{p}_t \cdot (\mathbf{x}_{t0} + \mathbf{x}_{t-1,1}) + \mathbf{p}_{S+1} \cdot (\overline{\mathbf{x}}_{S1} - \mathbf{x}_{S1}),$$

for any nonnegative $(\mathbf{x}_{t0}, \mathbf{x}_{t-1,1})_{t=0}^{S}$ and $\mathbf{x}_{S1}$. I use this inequality to prove that the allocation $\overline{\mathbf{x}}$ and the price vector $\mathbf{p}_t$ satisfy condition (2). That is, I show that if $\mathbf{x}$ is a bounded but not necessarily feasible allocation, then

$$\sum_{t=-1}^{\infty} \lambda_1^{-1} u(\overline{\mathbf{x}}_{t0}, \overline{\mathbf{x}}_{t1}) - \sum_{t=0}^{\infty} \mathbf{p}_t \cdot (\overline{\mathbf{x}}_{t0} + \overline{\mathbf{x}}_{t-1,1})$$
$$\geq \lambda_{-1}^{-1} u(\overline{\mathbf{x}}_{-1,0}, \mathbf{x}_{-1,1}) + \sum_{t=0}^{\infty} \lambda_t^{-1} u(\mathbf{x}_{t0}, \mathbf{x}_{t1}) - \sum_{t=0}^{\infty} \mathbf{p}_t \cdot (\mathbf{x}_{t0} + \mathbf{x}_{t-1,1}). \tag{9.93}$$

This inequality follows immediately from inequality 9.92 if the infinite sums in inequality 9.93 converge and if

$$\lim_{S \to \infty} \mathbf{p}_{S+1} \cdot (\overline{\mathbf{x}}_{S1} - \mathbf{x}_{S1}) = 0. \tag{9.94}$$

To complete the argument, I develop some bounds. Because the allocation $\mathbf{x}$ is bounded, there exists an N-vector $\mathbf{B}$ such that $\mathbf{x}_{t0} \leq \mathbf{B}$ and $\mathbf{x}_{t-1,1} \leq \mathbf{B}$, for all t. I may assume that $\mathbf{B}$ is so large that $\mathbf{e}_0 + \mathbf{e}_1 \leq \mathbf{B}$ and $\overline{\mathbf{x}}_{-1,0} \leq \mathbf{B}$. Because u is increasing, we know that $0 \leq u(\overline{\mathbf{x}}_{t0}, \overline{\mathbf{x}}_{t1}) \leq u(\mathbf{e}_0 + \mathbf{e}_1, \mathbf{e}_0 + \mathbf{e}_1) \leq u(\mathbf{B}, \mathbf{B})$ and $0 \leq u(\mathbf{x}_{t0}, \mathbf{x}_{t1}) \leq u(\mathbf{B}, \mathbf{B})$, for all t, and also $0 \leq u(\overline{\mathbf{x}}_{-1,0}, \overline{\mathbf{x}}_{-1,1}) \leq u(\mathbf{B}, \mathbf{B})$. Since $\sum_{t=-1}^{\infty} \lambda_t^{-1} < \infty$ by assumption, it follows that

$$0 \leq \sum_{t=-1}^{\infty} \lambda_t^{-1} u(\overline{\mathbf{x}}_{t0}, \overline{\mathbf{x}}_{t1}) \leq u(\mathbf{B}, \mathbf{B}) \sum_{t=-1}^{\infty} \lambda_t^{-1} < \infty \tag{9.95}$$

and

$$0 \leq \lambda_{-1}^{-1} u(\overline{\mathbf{x}}_{-1,0}, \overline{\mathbf{x}}_{-1,1}) + \sum_{t=0}^{\infty} \lambda_t^{-1} u(\mathbf{x}_{t0}, \mathbf{x}_{t1}) \leq u(\mathbf{B}, \mathbf{B}) \sum_{t=-1}^{\infty} \lambda_t^{-1} < \infty. \tag{9.96}$$

Turning to the terms involving price vectors, by inequality 9.91,

$$p_{sn}^{T(k)} \leq \varepsilon^{-1}(\lambda_{s-1}^{-1} + \lambda_s^{-1})u(\mathbf{e}_0 + \mathbf{e}_1, \mathbf{e}_0 + \mathbf{e}_1),$$

for all k. Passage to the limit with respect to k in this inequality implies that

$$p_{tn} \leq \varepsilon^{-1}(\lambda_{t-1}^{-1} + \lambda_t^{-1})u(\mathbf{e}_0 + \mathbf{e}_1, \mathbf{e}_0 + \mathbf{e}_1),$$

for all n, so that

$$\sum_{t=0}^{\infty} p_{tn} \leq \varepsilon^{-1}u(\mathbf{e}_0 + \mathbf{e}_1, \mathbf{e}_0 + \mathbf{e}_1)\sum_{t=0}^{\infty}(\lambda_{t-1}^{-1} + \lambda_t^{-1}) < \infty. \tag{9.97}$$

Since the vectors $\overline{\mathbf{x}}_{t0} + \overline{\mathbf{x}}_{t-1,1}$ and $\mathbf{x}_{t0} + \mathbf{x}_{t-1,1}$ are bounded from above by the vector 2**B**, for all t, it follows that

$$\sum_{t=0}^{\infty} \mathbf{p}_t.(\overline{\mathbf{x}}_{t0} + \overline{\mathbf{x}}_{t-1,1}) < \infty \tag{9.98}$$

and

$$\sum_{t=0}^{\infty} \mathbf{p}_t.(\mathbf{x}_{t0} + \mathbf{x}_{t-1,1}) < \infty, \tag{9.99}$$

for all t.

Inequality 9.97 implies that

$$\lim_{t\to\infty} \mathbf{p}_t = 0.$$

This equation in turn implies equation 9.94, since the vectors $\overline{\mathbf{x}}_{S1} - \mathbf{x}_{S1}$ are bounded. Equation 9.94 and inequalities 9.95, 9.96, 9.98, and 9.99 imply that inequality 9.93 follows from inequality 9.92 and hence that $\overline{\mathbf{x}}$ and $\mathbf{p} = (\mathbf{p}_0, \mathbf{p}_1, \ldots)$ satisfy condition (2) of the theorem.

Inequality 9.97 implies that $\sum_{t=0}^{\infty} \mathbf{p}_t < \infty$, which is condition (3) of the theorem. Condition (1) is an immediate consequence of the optimality of $\overline{\mathbf{x}}$ and of the assumption that u is strictly increasing. It remains to prove that $\mathbf{p}_t \gg 0$, for all t. Since $\mathbf{p}_t \geq 0$, for all t, it is sufficient to show that no component of $\mathbf{p}_t$ can be zero, for any t. If some component of $\mathbf{p}_t$ were zero, for some t, then because u is strictly increasing, $\mathbf{p} = (\mathbf{p}_0, \mathbf{p}_1, \ldots)$ and $\overline{\mathbf{x}}$ could not satisfy condition (2), which is false. ■

I now show that there exists an allocation that maximizes an infinite weighted sum of the consumers' utility functions, where the weights are positive and summable.

THEOREM 9.50 (Existence of a welfare optimum) Assume that u is continuous and let λ_t, for $t = -1, 0, 1, \ldots,$ be positive numbers such that $\sum_{t=-1}^{\infty} \lambda_t^{-1} < \infty$. Then, for every initial consumption $\overline{\mathbf{x}}_{-1,0}$, there exists a solution, $\overline{\mathbf{x}}$, to the problem

$$\max_{\substack{\mathbf{x} \text{ is a feasible} \\ \text{allocation}}} [\lambda_{-1}^{-1} u(\overline{\mathbf{x}}_{-1,0}, \mathbf{x}_{-1,1}) + \sum_{t=0}^{\infty} \lambda_t^{-1} u(\mathbf{x}_{t0}, \mathbf{x}_{t1})]. \quad \blacksquare \tag{9.100}$$

Proof. I first show that I may assume that $u(\mathbf{x}_0, \mathbf{x}_1) \geq 0$, if $(\mathbf{x}_0, \mathbf{x}_1)$ is such that $\mathbf{0} \leq \mathbf{x}_0 \leq \mathbf{e}_0 + \mathbf{e}_1 + \overline{\mathbf{x}}_{-1,0}$ and $\mathbf{0} \leq \mathbf{x}_0 \leq \mathbf{e}_0 + \mathbf{e}_1$. Since u is continuous,

$$\begin{aligned} &\min_{\mathbf{x}_0 \in \mathbb{R}_+^N, \mathbf{x}_1 \in \mathbb{R}_+^N} u(\mathbf{x}_0, \mathbf{x}_1) \\ &\text{s.t.} \quad 0 \leq \mathbf{x}_0 \leq \mathbf{e}_0 + \mathbf{e}_1 + \overline{\mathbf{x}}_{-1,0} \\ &\qquad \text{and } 0 \leq \mathbf{x}_1 \leq \mathbf{e}_0 + \mathbf{e}_1, \end{aligned}$$

exists and is finite by proposition 3.14 (in section 3.2). Let this minimum be m. The solution of problem 9.100 remains unchanged if we replace u by $u - m$, and this function clearly has the assumed property.

If $(\mathbf{x}_{t0}, \mathbf{x}_{t-1,1})_{t=0}^{\infty}$ is a feasible allocation, then $\mathbf{0} \leq \mathbf{x}_{t0} \leq \mathbf{e}_0 + \mathbf{e}_1$ and $\mathbf{0} \leq \mathbf{x}_{t1} \leq \mathbf{e}_0 + \mathbf{e}_1$, for all $t \geq 0$, and clearly $\mathbf{0} \leq \overline{\mathbf{x}}_{-1,0} \leq \mathbf{e}_0 + \mathbf{e}_1 + \overline{\mathbf{x}}_{-1,0}$, so that under the assumption just made about u, $u(\overline{\mathbf{x}}_{-1,0}, \mathbf{x}_{-1,1}) \geq 0$ and $u(\mathbf{x}_{t0}, \mathbf{x}_{t1}) \geq 0$, for all $t \geq 0$.

For each positive integer T, let $(\mathbf{x}_{-1,1}^T, (\mathbf{x}_{t0}^T, \mathbf{x}_{t1}^T)_{t=0}^T)$ solve the problem

$$\begin{aligned} &\max_{(\mathbf{x}_{-1,1}, (\mathbf{x}_{t0}, \mathbf{x}_{t1})_{t=0}^T) \geq 0} [\lambda^{-1} u(\overline{\mathbf{x}}_{-1,0}, \mathbf{x}_{-1,1}) + \sum_{t=0}^{T} \lambda_t^{-1} u(\mathbf{x}_{t0}, \mathbf{x}_{t1})] \\ &\text{s.t.} \quad \mathbf{x}_{t0} + \mathbf{x}_{t-1,1} \leq \mathbf{e}_0 + \mathbf{e}_1, \ \text{for } t \text{ such that } 0 \leq t \leq T, \\ &\qquad \text{and } \mathbf{x}_{T1} \leq \mathbf{e}_0 + \mathbf{e}_1, \end{aligned} \tag{9.101}$$

and let $M(T) = \lambda_{-1}^{-1} u(\overline{\mathbf{x}}_{-1,0}, \mathbf{x}_{-1,1}^T) + \sum_{t=0}^{T} \lambda_t^{-1} u(\mathbf{x}_{t0}^T, \mathbf{x}_{t1}^T)$ be the maximum value of this problem.

I show that for each positive integer S, $M(S+1) \geq M(S)$. Let $(\mathbf{x}_{t0}, \mathbf{x}_{t-1,1})_{t=0}^{S+1}$ be defined by the equations $\mathbf{x}_{-1,1} = \mathbf{x}_{-1,1}^S$, $(\mathbf{x}_{t0}, \mathbf{x}_{t1}) = (\mathbf{x}_{t0}^S, \mathbf{x}_{t1}^S)$, for $0 \leq t \leq S$, and $(\mathbf{x}_{S+1,0}, \mathbf{x}_{S+1,1}) = (\mathbf{0}, \mathbf{e}_0 + \mathbf{e}_1)$. Since $(\mathbf{x}_{t0}, \mathbf{x}_{t-1,1})_{t=0}^{S+1}$ is a feasible allocation for problem 9.101 with $T = S + 1$,

$$M(S+1) \geq \lambda_{-1}^{-1} u(\overline{\mathbf{x}}_{-1,0}, \mathbf{x}_{-1,1}) + \sum_{t=0}^{S+1} \lambda_t^{-1} u(\mathbf{x}_{t0}, \mathbf{x}_{t1})$$
$$\geq \lambda_{-1}^{-1} u(\overline{\mathbf{x}}_{-1,0}, \mathbf{x}_{-1,1}) + \sum_{t=0}^{S} \lambda_t^{-1} u(\mathbf{x}_{t0}, \mathbf{x}_{t1}) = M(S),$$

where the second inequality is valid because $u(\mathbf{x}_{S+1,0}, \mathbf{x}_{S+1,1}) = u(\mathbf{0}, \mathbf{e}_0 + \mathbf{e}_1) \geq 0$.

I next show that the sequence $M(T)$ converges as T goes to infinity. Since this sequence is nondecreasing, it is sufficient to show that it is bounded from above. By proposition 3.14 (in section 3.2),

$$\overline{U} = \max_{(\mathbf{x}_0, \mathbf{x}_1) \geq 0} u(\mathbf{x}_0, \mathbf{x}_1)$$
$$\text{s.t.} \quad 0 \leq \mathbf{x}_0 \leq \mathbf{e}_0 + \mathbf{e}_1 + \overline{\mathbf{x}}_{-1,0}$$
$$\text{and } 0 \leq \mathbf{x}_1 \leq \mathbf{e}_0 + \mathbf{e}_1$$

exists and is finite. Clearly,

$$M(T) \leq \overline{U} \sum_{t=-1}^{\infty} \lambda_t^{-1},$$

for all T, so that $\overline{M} = \lim_{T\to\infty} M(T)$ exists.

I next show that if $\mathbf{x} = (\mathbf{x}_{t0}, \mathbf{x}_{t-1,1})_{t=0}^{\infty}$ is a feasible allocation, then

$$\lambda_{-1}^{-1} u(\overline{\mathbf{x}}_{-1,0}, \mathbf{x}_{-1,1}) + \sum_{t=0}^{\infty} \lambda_t^{-1} u(\mathbf{x}_{t0}, \mathbf{x}_{t1}) \leq \overline{M}. \tag{9.102}$$

Suppose that $\lambda_{-1}^{-1} u(\overline{\mathbf{x}}_{-1,0}, \mathbf{x}_{-1,1}) + \sum_{t=0}^{\infty} \lambda_t^{-1} u(\mathbf{x}_{t0}, \mathbf{x}_{t1}) - \overline{M} = \varepsilon > 0$, for some feasible allocation $\mathbf{x} = (\mathbf{x}_{t0}, \mathbf{x}_{t-1,1})_{t=0}^{\infty}$. Let T be such that $\overline{U} \sum_{t=T+1}^{\infty} \lambda_t^{-1} < \varepsilon$. Then, $\sum_{t=T+1}^{\infty} \lambda_t^{-1} u(\mathbf{x}_{t0}, \mathbf{x}_{t1}) < \varepsilon$, so that

$$0 < \lambda_{-1}^{-1} u(\overline{\mathbf{x}}_{-1,0}, \mathbf{x}_{-1,1}) + \sum_{t=0}^{T} \lambda_t^{-1} u(\mathbf{x}_{t0}, \mathbf{x}_{t1}) - \overline{M}$$
$$\leq \lambda_{-1}^{-1} u(\overline{\mathbf{x}}_{-1,0}, \mathbf{x}_{-1,1}) + \sum_{t=0}^{T} \lambda_t^{-1} u(\mathbf{x}_{t0}, \mathbf{x}_{t1}) - M(T).$$

Since $(\mathbf{x}_{-1,1}, (\mathbf{x}_{t0}, \mathbf{x}_{t1})_{t=0}^{T})$ is a feasible allocation for problem 9.101, we know that

$$M(T) \geq \lambda_{-1}^{-1} u(\overline{\mathbf{x}}_{-1,0}, \mathbf{x}_{-1,1}) + \sum_{t=0}^{T} \lambda_t^{-1} u(\mathbf{x}_{t0}, \mathbf{x}_{t1}).$$

The contradiction between the previous two inequalities establishes inequality 9.102.

I next apply a Cantor diagonal argument to the allocations $(\mathbf{x}_{-1,1}^T, (\mathbf{x}_{t0}^T, \mathbf{x}_{t1}^T)_{t=0}^T)$ in order to define an allocation $\overline{\mathbf{x}} = (\overline{\mathbf{x}}_{t0}, \overline{\mathbf{x}}_{t-1,1})_{t=0}^{\infty}$ such that

$$\lambda_{-1}^{-1} u(\overline{\mathbf{x}}_{-1,0}, \overline{\mathbf{x}}_{-1,1}) + \sum_{t=0}^{T} \lambda_t^{-1} u(\overline{\mathbf{x}}_{t0}, \overline{\mathbf{x}}_{t1}) = \overline{M}. \tag{9.103}$$

All the components of $(\mathbf{x}_{-1,1}^T, (\mathbf{x}_{t0}^T, \mathbf{x}_{t1}^T)_{t=0}^T)$ are bounded below by zero and above by the corresponding components of $\mathbf{e}_0 + \mathbf{e}_1$. Therefore, I may use a Cantor diagonal argument to show that there exists a subsequence, $T(k)$, of T such that $(\mathbf{x}_{t-1,1}^{T(k)}, \mathbf{x}_{t0}^{T(k)})$ converges, for all t, as k goes to infinity. Let $(\overline{\mathbf{x}}_{t-1,1}, \overline{\mathbf{x}}_{t0}) = \lim_{k\to\infty}(\mathbf{x}_{t-1,1}^{T(k)}, \mathbf{x}_{t0}^{T(k)})$, for $t \geq 0$.

I now show that the allocation $\overline{\mathbf{x}} = (\overline{\mathbf{x}}_{t0}, \overline{\mathbf{x}}_{t-1,1})_{t=0}^{\infty}$ satisfies equation 9.103. Inequality 9.102 will then imply that $\overline{\mathbf{x}}$ solves problem 9.100. Since $\mathbf{x}_{t0}^{T(k)} + \mathbf{x}_{t-1,1}^{T(k)} \leq \mathbf{e}_0 + \mathbf{e}_1$, for all t, it follows by passage to the limit that $\overline{\mathbf{x}}_{t0} + \overline{\mathbf{x}}_{t-1,1} \leq \mathbf{e}_0 + \mathbf{e}_1$, for all t, so that $\overline{\mathbf{x}}$ is feasible. Therefore, inequality 9.102 implies that

$$\sum_{t=-1}^{\infty} \lambda_t^{-1} u(\overline{\mathbf{x}}_{t0}, \overline{\mathbf{x}}_{t1}) \leq \overline{M}.$$

Hence, it is sufficient to show that for every positive number ε,

$$\sum_{t=-1}^{\infty} \lambda_t^{-1} u(\overline{\mathbf{x}}_{t0}, \overline{\mathbf{x}}_{t1}) > \overline{M} - \varepsilon. \tag{9.104}$$

Let T be so large that $\overline{U} \sum_{t=T+1}^{\infty} \lambda_i^{-1} < \frac{\varepsilon}{3}$ and $\overline{M} - M(T) < \frac{\varepsilon}{3}$. Let k be so large that $T(k) \geq T$ and

$$\left| \sum_{t=-1}^{T} \lambda_t^{-1} u(\overline{\mathbf{x}}_{t0}, \overline{\mathbf{x}}_{t1}) - \left[\lambda_{-1}^{-1} u(\overline{\mathbf{x}}_{-1,0}, \mathbf{x}_{-1,1}^{T(k)}) + \sum_{t=0}^{T} \lambda_t^{-1} u(\mathbf{x}_{t0}^{T(k)}, \mathbf{x}_{t1}^{T(k)}) \right] \right| < \frac{\varepsilon}{3}. \tag{9.105}$$

It follows that

$$
\begin{aligned}
&\sum_{t=-1}^{\infty} \lambda_t^{-1} u(\overline{\mathbf{x}}_{t0}, \overline{\mathbf{x}}_{t1}) \\
&\geq \lambda_{-1}^{-1} u(\overline{\mathbf{x}}_{-1,0}, \overline{\mathbf{x}}_{-1,1}) + \sum_{t=0}^{T} \lambda_t^{-1} u(\overline{\mathbf{x}}_{t0}, \overline{\mathbf{x}}_{t1}) \\
&> \lambda_{-1}^{-1} u(\overline{\mathbf{x}}_{-1,0}, \mathbf{x}_{-1,1}^{T(k)}) + \sum_{t=0}^{T} \lambda_t^{-1} u(\mathbf{x}_{t0}^{T(k)}, \mathbf{x}_{t1}^{T(k)}) - \frac{\varepsilon}{3} \\
&> \lambda_{-1}^{-1} u(\overline{\mathbf{x}}_{-1,0}, \mathbf{x}_{-1,1}^{T(k)}) + \sum_{t=0}^{T(k)} \lambda_t^{-1} u(\mathbf{x}_{t0}^{T(k)}, \mathbf{x}_{t1}^{T(k)}) - \frac{2\varepsilon}{3} \\
&= M(T(k)) - \frac{2\varepsilon}{3} > \overline{M} - \varepsilon,
\end{aligned}
$$

where the second inequality follows from inequality 9.105, the third inequality follows from the fact that $\overline{U} \sum_{i=T+1}^{\infty} \lambda_i^{-1} < \frac{\varepsilon}{3}$, and the fourth inequality follows from the facts that $\overline{M} - M(T) < \frac{\varepsilon}{3}$, that $T(k) \geq T$, and that $M(T)$ is nondecreasing in T. This completes the proof of inequality 9.104 and hence of the assertion that the allocation $\overline{\mathbf{x}} = (\overline{\mathbf{x}}_{t0}, \overline{\mathbf{x}}_{t-1,1})_{t=0}^{\infty}$ is optimal. ∎

The last assertion to be proved is that there exists an allocation that is optimal according to the catching up criterion. I will establish this statement by proving that there exists a spot price equilibrium with interest rate 0 in which all consumers have the same marginal utility of unit of account. It will then follow from theorem 9.39 (in section 9.7) that the allocation of this equilibrium is optimal according to the catching up criterion.

THEOREM 9.51 Assume that u is continuous, concave, and strictly increasing and that $\mathbf{e}_0 + \mathbf{e}_1 \gg 0$. Then, for every initial consumption $\overline{\mathbf{x}}_{-1,0}$, there exists a spot price equilibrium with interest rate 0 in which the marginal utility of unit of account of every consumer equals 1.

Proof. For each positive integer T, let $(\mathbf{x}_{-1,1}^T, (\mathbf{x}_{t0}^T, \mathbf{x}_{t-1,1}^T)_{t=0}^T)$ solve the problem

$$
\begin{aligned}
&\max_{(\mathbf{x}_{-1,1}, (\mathbf{x}_{t0}, \mathbf{x}_{t1})_{t=0}^{T}) \geq 0} \left[u(\overline{\mathbf{x}}_{-1,0}, \mathbf{x}_{-1,1}) + \sum_{t=0}^{T} u(\mathbf{x}_{t0}, \mathbf{x}_{t1})\right] \\
&\text{s.t.}\quad \mathbf{x}_{t0} + \mathbf{x}_{t-1,1} \leq \mathbf{e}_0 + \mathbf{e}_1, \ \text{for } t \text{ such that } 0 \leq t \leq T, \text{ and} \\
&\qquad \mathbf{x}_{T1} \leq \mathbf{e}_0 + \mathbf{e}_1.
\end{aligned}
\tag{9.106}
$$

Since $\mathbf{e}_0 + \mathbf{e}_1 \gg 0$, problem 9.106 satisfies the constraint qualification of the Kuhn-Tucker theorem, and that theorem implies that there exist N-vectors, $\mathbf{P}_0^T, \mathbf{P}_1^T, \ldots, \mathbf{P}_{T+1}^T$, such that $(\mathbf{x}_{-1,1}^T, (\mathbf{x}_{t0}^T, \mathbf{x}_{t-1,1}^T)_{t=0}^T)$ solves the problem

$$\max_{(\mathbf{x}_{-1,1}, (\mathbf{x}_{t0}, \mathbf{x}_{t1})_{t=0}^T) \geq 0} \left[u(\overline{\mathbf{x}}_{-1,0}, \mathbf{x}_{-1,1}) + \sum_{t=0}^{T} u(\mathbf{x}_{t0}, \mathbf{x}_{t1}) \right.$$
$$\left. - \sum_{t=0}^{T} \mathbf{P}_t^T . (\mathbf{x}_{t0} + \mathbf{x}_{t-1,1}) - \mathbf{P}_{T+1}^T . \mathbf{x}_{T1} \right]. \tag{9.107}$$

Because u is strictly increasing, $\mathbf{P}_t^T \gg 0$, for all t, for otherwise problem 9.107 would not have a solution. By varying only $\mathbf{x}_{t0}$ and $\mathbf{x}_{t1}$ in this problem, we see that $(\mathbf{x}_{t0}^T, \mathbf{x}_{t1}^T)$ solves the problem

$$\max_{\mathbf{x}_0 \in \mathbb{R}_+^N, \mathbf{x}_1 \in \mathbb{R}_+^N} [u(\mathbf{x}_0, \mathbf{x}_1) - \mathbf{P}_t^T . \mathbf{x}_0 - \mathbf{P}_{t+1}^T . \mathbf{x}_1], \tag{9.108}$$

for t such that $0 \leq t \leq T$. Similarly, $\mathbf{x}_{-1,1}^T$ solves the problem

$$\max_{\mathbf{x}_1 \in \mathbb{R}_+^N} [u(\overline{\mathbf{x}}_{-1,0}, \mathbf{x}_1) - \mathbf{P}_0^T . \mathbf{x}_1]. \tag{9.109}$$

By an argument used at the beginning of the proof of theorem 9.43 (in section 9.7),

$$0 \leq P_{tn}^T \leq 2\varepsilon^{-1}[u(\mathbf{e}_0 + \mathbf{e}_1, \mathbf{e}_0 + \mathbf{e}_1) - u(\mathbf{0}, \mathbf{0})],$$

for all T, t, and n, where ε is a positive number such that $e_{0n} + e_{1n} \geq \varepsilon$, for all n. Since the price vectors $\mathbf{P}_t^T$ and the allocation vectors $(\mathbf{x}_{t0}^T, \mathbf{x}_{t1}^T)$ are uniformly bounded, I can apply a Cantor diagonal argument to them to show that there exists a subsequence, $T(k)$, of T such that $\mathbf{P}_t^{T(k)}$, $\mathbf{x}_{t0}^{T(k)}$, and $\mathbf{x}_{t1}^{T(k)}$ converge, for all t, as k goes to infinity. Let $\mathbf{P}_t$, $\overline{\mathbf{x}}_{t0}$, and $\overline{\mathbf{x}}_{t1}$ be the respective limits of these sequences.

Because $(\mathbf{x}_{t0}^T, \mathbf{x}_{t1}^T)$ solves problem 9.108, for all $T > t$, it follows that

$$u(\mathbf{x}_{t0}^{T(k)}, \mathbf{x}_{t1}^{T(k)}) - \mathbf{P}_t^{T(k)} . \mathbf{x}_{t0}^{T(k)} - \mathbf{P}_{t+1}^{T(k)} . \mathbf{x}_{t1}^{T(k)}$$
$$\geq u(\mathbf{x}_0, \mathbf{x}_1) - \mathbf{P}_t^{T(k)} . \mathbf{x}_0 - \mathbf{P}_{t+1}^{T(k)} . \mathbf{x}_1,$$

for all $\mathbf{x}_0$ and $\mathbf{x}_1$, if $k > t$, so that $T(k) > t$. Passing to the limit with respect to k in this inequality, we see that

$$u(\overline{\mathbf{x}}_{t0}, \overline{\mathbf{x}}_{t1}) - \mathbf{P}_t . \overline{\mathbf{x}}_{t0} - \mathbf{P}_{t+1} . \overline{\mathbf{x}}_{t1} \geq u(\mathbf{x}_0, \mathbf{x}_1) - \mathbf{P}_t . \mathbf{x}_0 - \mathbf{P}_{t+1} . \mathbf{x}_1, \tag{9.110}$$

for all $\mathbf{x}_0$ and $\mathbf{x}_1$. Similarly, because $\mathbf{x}^T_{-1,1}$ solves problem 9.109, for all T, it follows that

$$u(\overline{\mathbf{x}}_{-1,0}, \overline{\mathbf{x}}_{-1,1}) - \mathbf{P}_0.\overline{\mathbf{x}}_{-1,1} \geq u(\overline{\mathbf{x}}_{-1,0}, \mathbf{x}_1) - \mathbf{P}_0\mathbf{x}_1, \qquad (9.111)$$

for all $\mathbf{x}_1$. By proposition 6.14 (in section 6.3), inequality 9.110 implies that $(\overline{\mathbf{x}}_{t0}, \overline{\mathbf{x}}_{t1})$ solves the problem

$$\max_{\mathbf{x}_0, \mathbf{x}_1 \in \mathbb{R}^N_+} u(\mathbf{x}_0, \mathbf{x}_1)$$

$$\text{s.t.} \quad \mathbf{P}_t.\mathbf{x}_0 + \mathbf{P}_{t+1}.\mathbf{x}_1 \leq \mathbf{P}_t.\mathbf{e}_0 + \mathbf{P}_{t+1}.\mathbf{e}_1 - \mathsf{T}_t,$$

for $\mathsf{T}_t = \mathbf{P}_t.(\mathbf{e}_0 - \overline{\mathbf{x}}_{t0}) + \mathbf{P}_{t+1}.(\mathbf{e}_1 - \overline{\mathbf{x}}_{11})$. Similarly, inequality 9.111 implies that $\overline{\mathbf{x}}_{-1,1}$ solves the problem

$$\max_{\mathbf{x}_1 \in \mathbb{R}^N_+} u(\overline{\mathbf{x}}_{-1,0}, \mathbf{x}_1)$$

$$\text{s.t.} \quad \mathbf{P}_0.\mathbf{x}_1 \leq \mathbf{P}_0.\mathbf{e}_0 + G,$$

for $G = \mathbf{P}_0.(\overline{\mathbf{x}}_{-1,1} - \mathbf{e}_0)$. Because the allocations $(\mathbf{x}^{T(k)}_{-1,1}, (\mathbf{x}^{T(k)}_{t0}, \mathbf{x}^{T(k)}_{t1})^{T(k)}_{t=0})$ are feasible, it follows that the allocation $\overline{\mathbf{x}} = (\overline{\mathbf{x}}_{t0}, \overline{\mathbf{x}}_{t-1,1})^{\infty}_{t=0}$ is feasible by passage to the limit in the inequalities defining feasibility. Therefore, $(\overline{\mathbf{x}}, \mathbf{P}, G, \mathbf{T})$ satisfies all the conditions of a spot price equilibrium with interest rate 0, where $\overline{\mathbf{x}} = (\overline{\mathbf{x}}_{t0}, \overline{\mathbf{x}}_{t-1,1})^{\infty}_{t=0}$, $\mathbf{P} = (\mathbf{P}_0, \mathbf{P}_1, \ldots)$, G is the government debt already defined, and $\mathbf{T} = (\mathsf{T}_0, \mathsf{T}_1, \ldots)$. Inequalities 9.110 and 9.111 imply that the marginal utility of unit of account of every consumer is 1 in this equilibrium. ▪

COROLLARY 9.52 If in addition to the assumptions of theorem 9.51, it is assumed that u is strictly concave, then for every initial consumption, $\overline{\mathbf{x}}_{-1,0}$, there exists an allocation that is optimal with respect to the catching up criterion.

Proof. By theorem 9.51, there exists a spot price equilibrium, $(\overline{\mathbf{x}}, \mathbf{P}, G, \mathbf{T})$, with interest rate 0 in which the marginal utility of account of every consumer is 1. Theorem 9.39 (in section 9.7) implies that the allocation $\overline{\mathbf{x}}$ is optimal according to the catching up criterion. ▪

Problem Set

1. Consider a Samuelson model with one commodity in which consumers are endowed with one unit of good in youth and none in old

age and where their utility functions are

$$u(x_0, x_1) = \ln(x_0) + (0.5)\ln(x_1).$$

(a) Compute formulas for a stationary spot price equilibrium, $(\overline{x}_0, \overline{x}_1, P, r, G, \mathsf{T})$, with nonnegative interest rate r and with $P = 1$.

(b) Show on a diagram all feasible stationary allocations and those allocations that are Pareto optimal. Show in similar diagrams the allocations and budget sets for the equilibria with interest rates $r = 0$ and $r = 1$. Indicate the tax payments on the diagrams for each of these equilibria.

2. Consider a Samuelson model with one commodity in each period and where the endowment of every consumer is $e = (1, 0)$. Let the utility function of every consumer be

$$u(x_0, x_1) = x_0 + 2x_1.$$

(a) Draw a diagram that shows the set of feasible stationary allocations, the endowment, and sample indifference curves.

(b) Indicate on a second copy of the diagram which of the feasible stationary allocations are Pareto optimal.

(c) Compute a stationary spot price equilibrium, $(\overline{x}_0, \overline{x}_1, P, r, G, \mathsf{T})$, for this economy with positive interest rate r and with $P = 1$.

(d) State a social welfare maximization problem that is solved by the allocation of the stationary spot price equilibrium that you just found.

3. Consider a Samuelson model with one commodity in each period and where each consumer is endowed with one unit of the commodity in youth and none in old age. The utility function of each consumer is

$$u(x_0, x_1) = 2\sqrt{x_0} + 2\sqrt{x_1}.$$

(a) Compute a stationary spot price equilibrium, $(\overline{x}_0, \overline{x}_1, P, r, G, \mathsf{T})$, with $r = P = 1$.

(b) Compute a stationary spot price equilibrium, $(\overline{x}_0, \overline{x}_1, P, r, G, \mathsf{T})$, with $P = 1$ and $r = 0$.

(c) Show that the allocation of the equilibrium of part (a) is Pareto optimal.

(d) Compute the utility of a typical consumer in each of the equilibria of parts (a) and (b).
(e) Why is the allocation of the equilibrium of part (a) not Pareto dominated by that of part (b)?
(f) Show the equilibrium allocations of parts (a) and (b) in a two-dimensional diagram.

4. Consider a Samuelson model with one commodity in each period and where each consumer has utility function

$$u(x_0, x_1) = 2\sqrt{x_0 x_1}$$

and endowment

$$e = (10, 0).$$

(a) Show the set of feasible stationary allocations in a diagram.
(b) Indicate which of these are Pareto optimal.
(c) Find a stationary spot price equilibrium, $(\overline{x}_0, \overline{x}_1, P, r, G, \mathsf{T})$, the allocation of which maximizes the social welfare function

$$(1.1)u(x_{-1,0}, x_{-1,1}) + \sum_{t=0}^{\infty}(1.1)^{-t}u(x_{t0}, x_{t1})$$

among feasible allocations and with $x_{-1,0}$ given. Notice that you have to choose $x_{-1,0}$, so that the equilibrium is stationary.
(d) Is the allocation of this equilibrium Pareto optimal? Why or why not?

5. Consider the Samuelson overlapping generations model with one commodity and with

$$u(x_0, x_1) = 4x_0^{1/3} + x_1^{1/3} \text{ and } (e_0, e_1) = (1, 8).$$

(a) Draw a diagram showing the set of feasible stationary allocations and indicate on the diagram which of these are Pareto optimal. In addition, give a precise formula for the set of Pareto optimal stationary allocations.
(b) Define a stationary spot price equilibrium, $(\overline{x}_0, \overline{x}_1, P, r, G, \mathsf{T})$, such that $P = 1$ and the endowment allocation, $(x_0, x_1) = (e_0, e_1) = (1, 8)$, is the equilibrium allocation. Be sure to state the equilibrium interest rate.

6. Consider the following one-commodity Samuelson model.

$$\mathbf{e} = (1, 1), \quad u(x_0, x_1) = \min(3x_0 + x_1, 2x_0 + 5x_1).$$

(a) Show the set of feasible stationary allocations in a diagram. Show indifference curves in the diagram.
(b) Show in a separate copy of the same diagram which of the feasible stationary allocations is Pareto optimal.
(c) Find a stationary spot price equilibrium, $(\overline{x}_0, \overline{x}_1, P, r, G, \mathsf{T})$, in which $P = 1$, where the endowment is the equilibrium allocation.
(d) Find a stationary spot price equilibrium, $(\overline{x}_0, \overline{x}_1, P, r, G, \mathsf{T})$, such that $P = 1$ and the stationary allocation $(\overline{x}_0, \overline{x}_1) = (0, 2)$ is the equilibrium allocation.
(e) What social welfare function is maximized by the endowment allocation?

7. Consider a Samuelson model with one commodity in each period, where each consumer is endowed with one unit of the commodity in youth and none in old age and has utility function

$$u(x_0, x_1) = \min(2x_0 + x_1, x_0 + 2x_1).$$

Compute all the stationary spot price equilibria, $(\overline{x}_0, \overline{x}_1, P, r, G, \mathsf{T})$, in which $P = r = 1$.

8. Consider a Samuelson model with two commodities, 1 and 2, respectively, in each period. Each consumer is endowed with one unit of each commodity in youth and none in old age. The utility function of each consumer is

$$u(x_{01}, x_{02}, x_{11}, x_{12}) = 2\ln(x_{01}) + \ln(x_{02}) + \ln(x_{11}) + 2\ln(x_{12}).$$

(a) Compute a stationary spot price equilibrium, $(\overline{\mathbf{x}}_0, \overline{\mathbf{x}}_1, \mathbf{P}(r), r, G, \mathsf{T})$, with nonnegative interest rate r and with $P_1(r) + P_2(r) = 1$.
(b) Does the ratio $P_1(r)/P_2(r)$ increase, decrease, or remain constant as r increases? Give an intuitive explanation for what occurs.

9. We know that the allocation of a stationary spot price equilibrium in the Samuelson model is Pareto optimal if its sequence of equilibrium prices is summable when discounted to period 0 at market interest rates. This fact might lead you to suspect that stationary equilibrium allocations would be Pareto optimal if some asset were present that yielded a fixed positive return indefinitely, for then the price of the asset would be finite and equal to the discounted present value of its future returns. The following problem tests this idea.

Consider a Samuelson model with one commodity in every period and where each consumer has endowment $(e_0, e_1) \in \mathbb{R}^2_+$ and utility function $u\colon \mathbb{R}^2_+ \to \mathbb{R}$. Suppose that there is an asset that yields i units of the single commodity in every period, where $i > 0$. This problem concerns stationary equilibria, $(\overline{x}_0, \overline{x}_1, P, r, G, \mathsf{T})$, for this model, where $P = 1$ and $G = \mathsf{T} = 0$. The feasibility equation for the model is

$$\overline{x}_0 + \overline{x}_1 \leq e_0 + e_1 + i. \tag{9.112}$$

Assume that $P = 1$ and $\mathsf{T} = 0$, so that there are no taxes and the budget constraint is

$$\overline{x}_0 + \frac{\overline{x}_1}{1+r} \leq e_0 + \frac{e_1}{1+r}. \tag{9.113}$$

Assume that the utility function is strictly increasing and that $e_1 = 0$. Because $e_1 = 0$, the young cannot have negative savings. That is, they cannot borrow against future income. They can only invest, lend, or buy land.

(a) Show that if a stationary equilibrium with no taxes exists, then its interest rate is positive, so that its allocation is Pareto optimal.

(b) Calculate a stationary spot price equilibrium with no taxes when

$$u(x_0, x_1) = \ln(x_0) + \ln(x_1) \text{ and } e_0 = 1.$$

The equilibrium will depend on the asset yield i.

(c) Make a drawing showing the set of feasible stationary allocations and the budget set of a consumer in a stationary equilibrium with no taxes and when $e_0 = i = 1$.

(d) Prove that if $e_0 = 0$, then no stationary spot price equilibrium without taxes exists.

— 10 —

The One-Sector Growth and Diamond Overlapping Generations Models

The Diamond model is obtained from the Samuelson overlapping generations model by including production and capital and requiring that there be only one produced good and one primary input. This model provides a natural setting for the study of economic growth and social security. Many of the results proved in this chapter are extensions of corresponding ones proved in chapter 9. For instance, I show that equilibrium allocations maximize a welfare function that is a discounted sum of the consumers' utility functions, and any allocation that maximizes such a welfare function is the allocation of an equilibrium with government debt and lump-sum taxes.

10.1 The One-Sector Diamond and Optimal Growth Models

In the Diamond model, there are two commodities, a produced good and labor. One person is born in each period and lives two periods, and each person is endowed with one unit of labor in youth, no labor in old age, and with none of the produced good in either period of life. People consume only the produced good, so that there is no disutility of labor. The utility function of a typical consumer is $u(x_0, x_1) = u_0(x_0) + u_1(x_1)$, where x_0 and x_1 are consumption of the produced good in youth and old age, respectively. Output in period $t + 1$ is produced from labor in that period and capital absorbed in the previous period, where capital is the produced good used as an input into production. If K_t and L_{t+1} are the capital used in period t and the labor input in period $t + 1$, respectively, then the output in period $t + 1$ is $y_{t+1} = f(K_t, L_{t+1})$, where $f : \mathbb{R}^2_+ \to [0, \infty)$ is a production function. The assumptions listed below apply to f and the utility functions, and I follow the convention used in economics that a function $g : [0, \infty) \to$

$(-\infty, \infty)$ may be said to be differentiable at 0 if its derivative there is infinite.

ASSUMPTION 10.1 f is homogeneous of degree 1.

ASSUMPTION 10.2 There exists a positive number $\underline{K}$ such that $f(\underline{K}, 1) - \underline{K} > 0$.

ASSUMPTION 10.3 $f(K, 0) = 0 = f(0, L)$, for all $K \geq 0$ and $L \geq 0$.

ASSUMPTION 10.4 f is continuous and is continuously differentiable at every point (K, L) such that $(K, L) \neq \mathbf{0}$, and it is twice differentiable at points (K, L) such that $K > 0$ and $L > 0$. At all such points, $D^2 f(K, L)$ is negative semidefinite, $\frac{\partial^2 f(K,L)}{\partial K^2} < 0$, and $\frac{\partial^2 f(K,L)}{\partial L^2} < 0$. If $L > 0$, then $\frac{\partial f(K,L)}{\partial K} > 0$, for all $K \geq 0$. If $K > 0$, then $\frac{\partial f(K,L)}{\partial L} > 0$, for all $L \geq 0$.

ASSUMPTION 10.5 The utility functions $u_0 : [0, \infty) \to [0, \infty)$ and $u_1 : [0, \infty) \to [0, \infty)$ are differentiable and strictly concave. Their first derivatives are everywhere positive and $u_0(0) = 0 = u_1(0)$.

Assumption 10.1 guarantees that there are constant returns to scale in production, so that equilibrium profits are 0. This assumption is made in order to avoid having to specify the distribution of profits to consumers. Assumption 10.2 guarantees that the economy is productive. Assumption 10.3 means that both capital and labor are necessary for production. Assumption 10.4 guarantees that the production function is increasing and concave. I assume it is differentiable solely to simplify the exposition. It is possible for all these assumptions to be satisfied, as is illustrated by the functions $f(K, L) = \sqrt{KL}$ and $f(K, L) = L \ln(KL^{-1} + 1)$. More generally, the following is true.

PROPOSITION 10.6 Assume that $F : [0, \infty) \to [0, \infty)$ is continuously differentiable and on $(0, \infty)$ is twice differentiable. Assume, in addition, that $F(0) = 0$, $\frac{dF(0)}{dk} > 1$, $\frac{dF(k)}{dk} > 0$, for all nonnegative k, that $\frac{d^2F(k)}{dk^2} < 0$, for all positive k, and that $\lim_{k\to\infty} \frac{dF(k)}{dk} = 0$. Let

$$f(K, L) = \begin{cases} LF(KL^{-1}), & \text{if } L > 0, \text{ and} \\ 0, & \text{if } L = 0. \end{cases}$$

Then f satisfies assumptions 10.1–10.4.

Proof. Since it is obvious that f satisfies assumptions 10.1–10.3, I show only that f satisfies assumption 10.4. First, I show that f is continuous. It is clearly continuous at points (K, L), where $L > 0$. To show that it is continuous at points $(K, 0)$, for $K \geq 0$, suppose that (K_n, L_n) is a sequence such that $\lim_{n\to\infty}(K_n, L_n) = (K, 0)$. I must show that $\lim_{n\to\infty} f(K_n, L_n) = 0$. Let ε be an arbitrarily small positive number and let $\underline{k}$ be a positive number that is so large that $\frac{dF(\underline{k})}{dk} < \frac{\varepsilon}{2(K+1)}$. Since F is concave and differentiable,

$$F(k) \leq F(\underline{k}) + \frac{dF(\underline{k})}{dk}(k - \underline{k}).$$

Therefore, if $L_n > 0$,

$$0 \leq f(K_n, L_n) = L_n F(K_n L_n^{-1}) \leq L_n F(\underline{k}) + L_n \frac{dF(\underline{k})}{dk}(K_n L_n^{-1} - \underline{k})$$

$$= L_n\left(F(\underline{k}) - \frac{dF(\underline{k})}{dk}\underline{k}\right) + K_n \frac{dF(\underline{k})}{dk} \leq \frac{\varepsilon}{2} + (K+1)\frac{\varepsilon}{2(K+1)} = \varepsilon,$$

if n is sufficiently large. If $L_n = 0$, then $f(K_n, L_n) = 0$. In conclusion, $\lim_{n\to\infty} f(K_n, L_n) = 0$.

The first and second derivatives of f when $L > 0$ are

$$\frac{\partial f(K, L)}{\partial K} = \frac{dF}{dk}(KL^{-1}), \quad \frac{\partial f(K, L)}{\partial L} = F(KL^{-1}) - KL^{-1}\frac{dF}{dk}(KL^{-1}),$$

$$\frac{\partial^2 f(K, L)}{\partial K^2} = L^{-1}\frac{d^2F}{dk^2}(KL^{-1}), \quad \frac{\partial^2 f(K, L)}{\partial L \partial K} = -KL^2\frac{d^2F}{dk^2}(KL^{-1})$$

$$= \frac{\partial^2 f(K, L)}{\partial K \partial L}, \text{ and } \frac{\partial^2 f(K, L)}{\partial L^2} = K^2L^{-3}\frac{d^2F}{dk^2}(KL^{-1}).$$

Because $\frac{dF}{dk}(KL^{-1}) > 0$, it follows that $\frac{\partial f(K,L)}{\partial K} > 0$. Because $F(0) = 0$ and F is strictly concave, $\frac{\partial f(K,L)}{\partial L} > 0$, if $K > 0$. Because $\frac{d^2F}{dk^2}(KL^{-1}) < 0$, it follows that $\frac{\partial^2 f(K,L)}{\partial K^2} < 0$ and $\frac{\partial^2 f(K,L)}{\partial L^2} < 0$. The second derivative matrix of f is

$$\frac{d^2F}{dk^2}(KL^{-1})\begin{pmatrix} L^{-1} & -KL^{-2} \\ -KL^{-2} & K^2L^{-3} \end{pmatrix}.$$

The upper-left entry of this matrix is negative, and its determinant is zero because the second column is $-KL^{-1}$ times the first column. Therefore the matrix is negative semidefinite.

I show that f is continuously differentiable at every point (K, L) such that $(K, L) \neq \mathbf{0}$. It is clear from the formulas for the first derivatives that they are continuous on $\{(K, L) \mid L > 0\}$. Since $f(K, 0) = 0$, for all K, it follows that $\frac{\partial f(K,0)}{\partial K} = 0$. If $\lim_{n\to\infty}(K_n, L_n) = (K, 0)$, where $K > 0$ and $L_n > 0$, for all n, then $\lim_{n\to\infty} K_n L_n^{-1} = \infty$, so that $\lim_{n\to\infty} \frac{\partial f(K_n, L_n)}{\partial K} = \lim_{n\to\infty} \frac{dF}{dK}(K_n L_n^{-1}) = 0$. Therefore $\frac{\partial f(K,L)}{\partial K}$ is continuous at every (K, L) such that $(K, L) \neq \mathbf{0}$.

To show that $\frac{\partial f(K,L)}{\partial L}$ is continuous at every $(K, L) \neq \mathbf{0}$, observe that because f is continuous and $\frac{\partial^2 f(K,L)}{\partial L^2} < 0$ when $K > 0$ and $L > 0$, it follows that $f(K, L)$ is a concave function of L for $K > 0$. Since in addition $f(K, 0) = 0$, it follows that

$$\frac{f(K, \Delta L) - f(K, 0)}{\Delta L}$$

is a nonincreasing function of ΔL, so that

$$\lim_{\Delta L\to 0} \frac{f(K, \Delta L) - f(K, 0)}{\Delta L}$$

exists, though it may be infinite. Call this limit $\frac{\partial f(K,0)}{\partial L}$. Furthermore the mean value theorem implies that

$$\frac{\partial f(K,0)}{\partial L} = \lim_{\Delta L\to 0} \frac{\partial f(K, \Delta L)}{\partial L} =$$

$$\lim_{L\to 0}\left[F(KL^{-1}) - KL^{-1}\frac{dF}{dk}(KL^{-1})\right] = \lim_{k\to\infty}\left[F(k) - k\frac{dF(k)}{dk}\right].$$

If $\lim_{n\to\infty}(K_n, L_n) = (K, 0)$, where $K > 0$, and $L_n > 0$, for all n, then

$$\lim_{n\to\infty} \frac{\partial f(K_n, L_n)}{\partial L} = \lim_{n\to\infty}\left[F(K_n L_n^{-1}) - K_n L_n^{-1}\frac{dF}{dk}(K_n L_n^{-1})\right] =$$

$$\lim_{k\to\infty}\left[F(k) - k\frac{dF(k)}{dk}\right] = \frac{\partial f(K,0)}{\partial L},$$

so that $\frac{\partial f(K,L)}{\partial L}$ is continuous at every (K, L) such that $(K, L) \neq \mathbf{0}$. ▪

Assumption 10.4 implies that f is concave, for suppose that $(\underline{K}, \underline{L}) \geq 0$ and $(\overline{K}, \overline{L}) \geq 0$ and that $0 \leq \alpha \leq 1$. Then, there are sequences $(\underline{K}_n, \underline{L}_n)$ and $(\overline{K}_n, \overline{L}_n)$ such that $(\underline{K}_n, \underline{L}_n) \gg 0$ and $(\overline{K}_n, \overline{L}_n) \gg 0$, for all n, $\lim_{n\to\infty} (\underline{K}_n, \underline{L}_n) = (\underline{K}, \underline{L})$, and $\lim_{n\to\infty}(\overline{K}_n, \overline{L}_n) = (\overline{K}, \overline{L})$. Because $D^2 f(K, L)$ is negative semidefinite on the set of (K, L) such that $(K, L) \gg 0$, it follows that f is concave there, so that

$$f(\alpha \underline{K}_n + (1-\alpha)\overline{K}_n, \alpha \underline{L}_n + (1-\alpha)\overline{L}_n) \geq \alpha f(\underline{K}_n, \underline{L}_n) + (1-\alpha) f(\overline{K}_n, \overline{L}_n).$$

Passing to the limit in this inequality, we see that because f is continuous,

$$f(\alpha \underline{K} + (1-\alpha)\overline{K}, \alpha \underline{L} + (1-\alpha)\overline{L}) \geq \alpha f(\underline{K}, \underline{L}) + (1-\alpha) f(\overline{K}, \overline{L}),$$

so that f is everywhere concave.

The production function can be interpreted as including depreciation on capital, for suppose that the input of K units of capital and L units of labor results in δK units of capital and $h(K, L)$ units of output in the following period, where $0 < \delta < 1$. Then, we can let $f(K, L) = \delta K + h(K, L)$.

The assumption that $u_0(0) = 0 = u_1(0)$ is simply a normalization. If this assumption does not apply, the utility functions u_0 and u_1 may be replaced by $u_0 - u_0(0)$ and $u_1 - u_1(0)$, respectively, without changing the properties of any equilibrium or allocation.

Assumption 10.5 excludes the utility function $\ln(x)$, because it is not defined at zero. It is possible to modify the assumption to include $\ln(x)$, but at a considerable cost in the complexity of proofs. I will, nevertheless, use this function in examples.

An *allocation* consists of $(\mathbf{x}, \mathbf{K}, \mathbf{L}) = (x_{t0}, x_{t-1,1}, K_t, L_t)_{t=0}^{\infty}$, where x_{t0} and $x_{t-1,1}$ are the consumptions of the produced good in period t by the young and old person, respectively, and K_t and L_t are, respectively, the input of capital and input of labor in period t. All the components of $(\mathbf{x}, \mathbf{K}, \mathbf{L})$ are nonnegative. The allocation $(\mathbf{x}, \mathbf{K}, \mathbf{L})$ is *feasible*, given an initial input of capital, $\overline{K}_{-1}$, if

$$L_t \leq 1 \quad \text{and}$$
$$x_{t0} + x_{t-1,1} + K_t \leq f(K_{t-1}, L_t),$$

for all $t \geq 0$, where $K_{-1} = \overline{K}_{-1}$.

It is quite easy to see that under the above assumptions, feasible allocations are bounded.

DEFINITION 10.7 The allocation $(\mathbf{x}, \mathbf{K}, \mathbf{L}) = (x_{t0}, x_{t-1,1}, K_t, L_t)_{t=0}^{\infty}$ is *bounded*, if there is a positive number b such that every component of $(\mathbf{x}, \mathbf{K}, \mathbf{L})$ is less than or equal to b. A set of allocations, A, is *uniformly bounded* if the bound b applies to every component of every allocation in A.

PROPOSITION 10.8 If assumptions 10.1–10.4 apply, then the allocations that are feasible, given the initial capital $\overline{K}_{-1}$, are uniformly bounded.

Proof. Because f is homogeneous of degree 1,

$$f(K, 1) - K = K[f(1, K^{-1}) - 1]. \tag{10.1}$$

Since f is continuous,

$$\lim_{K\to\infty} f(1, K^{-1}) = f(1, 0) = 0,$$

where the second equation follows from assumption 10.3. Therefore, equation 10.1 implies that $f(K, 1) - K < 0$, if K is sufficiently large, so that the graph of the function $y = f(K, 1)$ is below the diagonal line, $y = K$, for K large, as in figure 10.1. By assumption 10.2, $f(\underline{K}, 1) - \underline{K} > 0$, for some positive capital $\underline{K}$. Since f is continuous, the intermediate value theorem implies that there exists a positive number $\hat{K}$, such that $f(\hat{K}, 1) - \hat{K} = 0$. By assumption 10.4, the function $f(K, 1)$ is strictly concave, so that there is only one value, $\hat{K}$, satisfying this equation, as in the figure.

The figure makes it easy to see why feasible allocations are bounded. If the initial capital equals K^*, where $K^* \leq \hat{K}$, then even if no output is ever consumed and all of it is invested, the economy cannot accumulate more than $\hat{K}$ units of capital. If no output is consumed, the capital stock and output follow the dotted path to the left of $\hat{K}$ in figure 10.1. Similarly if the economy starts with an initial capital K^{**}, where $K^{**} > \hat{K}$, then the capital stock shrinks toward $\hat{K}$, even if no output is ever consumed. In this case, output and capital follow the dotted path to the right of $\hat{K}$. Therefore, the amounts of output and capital in any period $t \geq 0$ in any feasible allocation are bounded by the maximum of $\hat{K}$ and $f(\overline{K}_{-1}, 1)$, where $\overline{K}_{-1}$ is the initial capital stock. Since consumptions are bounded above by outputs, they too cannot ever exceed $\max(K, f(\overline{K}_{-1}, 1))$. ▪

I now turn to the definition of an Arrow-Debreu equilibrium. An Arrow-Debreu *price system* consists of sequences of nonnegative numbers, $\mathbf{p} = (p_0, p_1, \ldots)$ and $\mathbf{w} = (w_0, w_1, \ldots)$, where p_t is the price of the produced good and w_t is the wage of labor in period t and not all of these are 0. Both of these prices are forward prices from the point of view of period -1. Given a price system (p, w) and an allocation $(\mathbf{x}, \mathbf{K}, \mathbf{L})$, the lifetime expenditure of consumer t is $p_t x_{t0} + p_{t+1} x_{t1}$ and the profits from production from period t to period $t+1$ are $p_{t+1} f(K_t, L_{t+1}) - p_t K_t - w_{t+1} L_{t+1}$.

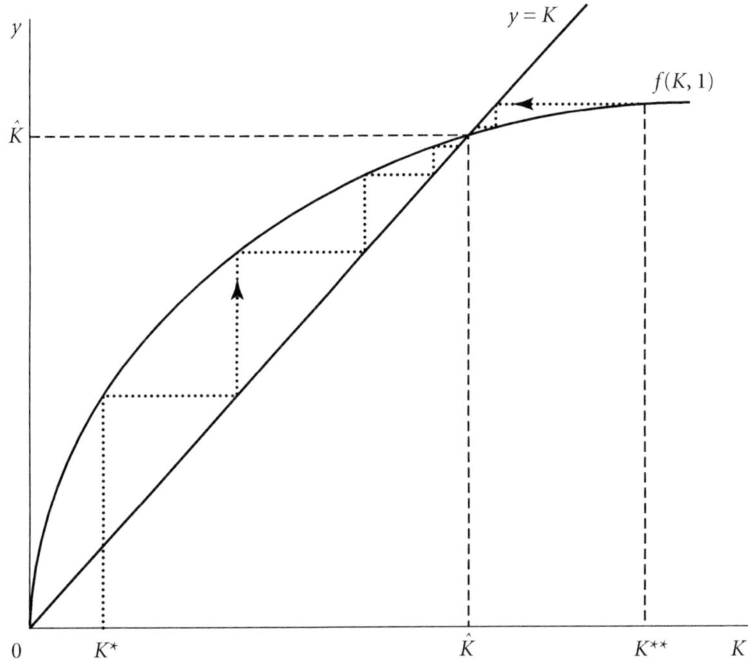

Figure 10.1 Boundedness of output

DEFINITION 10.9 An *Arrow-Debreu equilibrium with transfer payments* consists of $(\overline{\mathbf{x}}, \overline{\mathbf{K}}, \overline{\mathbf{L}}, \mathbf{p}, \mathbf{w}, \boldsymbol{\tau})$ such that

1. $(\overline{\mathbf{x}}, \overline{\mathbf{K}}, \overline{\mathbf{L}})$ is a feasible allocation, given initial capital $\overline{K}_{-1}$
2. $(\mathbf{p}, \mathbf{w})$ is a price system
3. $\boldsymbol{\tau} = (\tau_{-1}, \tau_0, \tau_1, \ldots)$ is a sequence of numbers, where τ_t is the lump-sum tax paid by the consumer born in period t
4. $\overline{L}_0$ solves the problem

$$\max_{L_0 \geq 0} [p_0 f(\overline{K}_{-1}, L_0) - w_0 L_0]$$

5. For all $t \geq 0$, $(\overline{K}_t, \overline{L}_{t+1})$ solves the problem

$$\max_{K_t \geq 0, L_{t+1} \geq 0} [p_{t+1} f(K_t, L_{t+1}) - p_t K_t - w_{t+1} L_{t+1}]$$

6. $\overline{x}_{-1,1}$ solves the problem

$$\max_{x_1 \geq 0} u_1(x_1)$$
$$\text{s.t.} \quad p_0 x_1 \leq p_0 f(\overline{K}_{-1}, \overline{L}_0) - w_0 \overline{L}_0 - \tau_{-1}$$

7. For all $t \geq 0$, $(\overline{x}_{t0}, \overline{x}_{t1})$ solves the problem

$$\max_{x_0 \geq 0, x_1 \geq 0} [u_0(x_0) + u_1(x_1)]$$
$$\text{s.t.} \quad p_t x_0 + p_{t+1} x_1 \leq w_t - \tau_t$$

8. For all t, $p_t = 0$, if

$$\overline{x}_{t0} + \overline{x}_{t-1,1} < f(\overline{K}_{t-1}, \overline{L}_t) - \overline{K}_t$$

and $w_t = 0$, if $\overline{L}_t < 1$

An explanation is required for the budget constraint appearing in condition (6). Production occurring in period 0 earns positive profits, because the capital used to produce the output has already been paid for in period -1. This profit must be assigned to someone, and I assign it to the old person of period 0. There are no profits to assign in any period other than period 0, for since f is homogeneous of degree 1, equilibrium profits are 0 for output appearing in every period after period 0. That is,

$$p_{t+1} f(\overline{K}_t, \overline{L}_{t+1}) - p_t \overline{K}_t - w_{t+1} \overline{L}_{t+1} = 0,$$

for all $t \geq 0$. The value of net output in period 0, $p_0 f(\overline{K}_{-1}, \overline{L}_0) - w_0 \overline{L}_0$, is not offset by a quantity $p_{-1}\overline{K}_{-1}$, because period -1 is not in the model. The value $p_{-1}\overline{K}_{-1}$ must be owned by somebody, and it makes sense to assign it to the old person of period 0 if we imagine that the young consumer in each period t provides the firm with funds equal to $p_t \overline{K}_t$ for the purchase of capital in exchange for receiving in old age the value, $p_{t+1} f(\overline{K}_{t,1}, \overline{L}_{t+1}) - w_{t+1}\overline{L}_{t+1}$, of output net of labor cost. This discussion of the provision of funds will make more sense in the context of a spot price model, where financial transfers occur when goods and services are delivered. In an Arrow-Debreu model, of course, all transfers of unit of account occur at time -1.

The transfer payments in an Arrow-Debreu equilibrium sum to 0, provided the prices are summable. In order to prove this assertion, I need the following lemma.

LEMMA 10.10 If assumptions 10.1–10.5 apply and $\sum_{t=0}^{\infty} p_t < \infty$, then $\sum_{t=0}^{\infty} w_t < \infty$.

Proof. Because u_0 and u_1 are strictly increasing, $p_t > 0$, for all t, for if $p_t = 0$, for some t, then the maximization problem in condition (7) of definition 10.9 of an Arrow-Debreu equilibrium has no solution.

Suppose that $\overline{K}_{t-1} > 0$. Then assumption 10.4 implies that $\frac{\partial f(\overline{K}_{t-1}, L)}{\partial L} > 0$, for all $L \geq 0$. Therefore $w_t > 0$, for if $w_t = 0$, then, since $p_t > 0$, the profit maximization problem in condition (5) of definition 10.9 of an Arrow-Debreu equilibrium has no solution. Since $w_t > 0$, it follows from condition (8) of definition 10.9 that $\overline{L}_t = 1$. Because profits are maximized at $\overline{L}_t = 1$, it follows that

$$w_t = p_t \frac{\partial f(\overline{K}_t, 1)}{\partial L}.$$

Let b be an upper bound on the components of a feasible allocation. By assumption 10.4, $\frac{\partial f(K, 1)}{\partial L}$ is a continuous function of K, so that by proposition 3.14 (in section 3.2), there exists a positive number B such that $\left|\frac{\partial f(K, 1)}{\partial L}\right| \leq B$, for all K such that $0 \leq K \leq b$. The previous inequality now implies that $w_t \leq Bp_t$.

Suppose that $\overline{K}_{t-1} = 0$. Then by assumption 10.3, no output can be produced in period t. It follows that $w_t = 0$, for if $w_t > 0$, then the profit maximizing level of labor input in period t is $\overline{L}_t = 0$. In this case, condition (8) of definition 10.9 of an Arrow-Debreu equilibrium implies that $w_t = 0$, a contradiction that proves $w_t = 0$.

It now follows that $\sum_{t=0}^{\infty} w_t \leq B \sum_{t=0}^{\infty} p_t < \infty$. ■

The next proposition is completely analogous to proposition 9.9 (in section 9.3) and has the same interpretation.

PROPOSITION 10.11 Suppose that assumptions 10.1–10.5 apply and that $\sum_{t=0}^{\infty} p_t < \infty$. Then in any Arrow-Debreu equilibrium, $(\overline{\mathbf{x}}, \overline{\mathbf{K}}, \overline{\mathbf{L}}, \mathbf{p}, \mathbf{w}, \boldsymbol{\tau})$, with transfer payments, $\sum_{t=-1}^{\infty} |\tau_t| < \infty$ and $\sum_{t=-1}^{\infty} \tau_t = 0$.

Proof. Because u_0 and u_1 are increasing, they are locally nonsatiated and so consumers spend all their wealth. Hence

$$p_0 \overline{x}_{-1,1} = p_0 f(\overline{K}_{-1}, \overline{L}_0) - w_0 \overline{L}_0 - \tau_{-1} \tag{10.2}$$

and

$$p_t\overline{x}_{t0} + p_{t+1}\overline{x}_{t1} = w_t - \tau_t,$$

for $t \geq 0$. Since equilibrium profits are 0,

$$0 = p_{t+1} f(\overline{K}_t, \overline{L}_{t+1}) - p_t \overline{K}_t - w_{t+1}\overline{L}_{t+1},$$

for all $t \geq 0$. If we add the previous two equations, we obtain

$$p_t\overline{x}_{t0} + p_{t+1}\overline{x}_{t1} = w_t - p_t\overline{K}_t - w_{t+1}\overline{L}_{t+1} + p_{t+1} f(\overline{K}_t, \overline{L}_{t+1}) - \tau_t. \quad (10.3)$$

Equations 10.2 and 10.3 may be rewritten as

$$\tau_{-1} = -w_0\overline{L}_0 + p_0[f(\overline{K}_{-1}, \overline{L}_0) - \overline{x}_{-1,1}]$$

and

$$\tau_t = w_t - w_{t+1}\overline{L}_{t+1} - p_t(\overline{x}_{t0} + \overline{K}_t) + p_{t+1}[f(\overline{K}_t, \overline{L}_{t+1}) - \overline{x}_{t1}],$$

for $t \geq 0$. By assumption, $L_t \leq 1$, for all t, and $\sum_{t=0}^{\infty} p_t < \infty$. By lemma 10.10, $\sum_{t=0}^{\infty} w_t < \infty$, and by proposition 10.8, the sequences x_{t0}, x_{t1}, and K_t are bounded. Therefore

$$\sum_{t=-1}^{\infty} |\tau_t| = \left|-w_0\overline{L}_0 + p_0[f(\overline{K}_{-1}, \overline{L}_0) - \overline{x}_{-1,1}]\right|$$
$$+ \sum_{t=0}^{\infty} \left|w_t - w_{t+1}\overline{L}_{t+1} - p_t(\overline{x}_{t0} + \overline{K}_t) + p_{t+1}[f(\overline{K}_t, \overline{L}_{t+1}) - \overline{x}_{t1}]\right| < \infty.$$

Since the infinite series below converge absolutely, we may change the order of summation in order to obtain the second equation.

$$\sum_{t=-1}^{\infty} \tau_t = -w_0\overline{L}_0 + p_0[f(\overline{K}_{-1}, \overline{L}_0) - \overline{x}_{-1,1}]$$
$$+ \sum_{t=0}^{\infty} \{w_t - w_{t+1}\overline{L}_{t+1} - p_t(\overline{x}_{t0} + \overline{K}_t) + p_{t+1}[f(\overline{K}_t, \overline{L}_{t+1}) - \overline{x}_{t1}]\} \quad (10.4)$$
$$= \sum_{t=0}^{\infty} w_t(1 - \overline{L}_t) + \sum_{t=0}^{\infty} p_t[f(\overline{K}_{t-1}, \overline{L}_t) - \overline{K}_t - \overline{x}_{t0} - \overline{x}_{t-1,1}] = 0.$$

The third equation follows from condition (8) of definition 10.9 of an Arrow-Debreu equilibrium. ■

The most realistic equilibrium concept is that of a spot price equilibrium.

DEFINITION 10.12 A *spot price equilibrium* consists of $(\overline{\mathbf{x}}, \overline{\mathbf{K}}, \overline{\mathbf{L}}, \mathbf{P}, \mathbf{W}, \mathbf{r}, G, \mathbf{T})$ that satisfies the conditions

1. $(\overline{\mathbf{x}}, \overline{\mathbf{K}}, \overline{\mathbf{L}})$ is a feasible allocation, given initial capital $\overline{K}_{-1}$
2. $\mathbf{P} = (P_0, P_1, \ldots)$ and $\mathbf{W} = (W_0, W_1, \ldots)$ are infinite sequences of nonnegative spot prices and not all of the P_t and W_t are zero
3. $\mathbf{r} = (r_{-1}, r_0, r_1, \ldots)$ is an infinite sequence of numbers, where $r_t > -1$, for all t, and r_t is the nominal interest rate paid in period $t+1$ on government debt held from period t to period $t+1$
4. $\mathsf{T} = (\mathsf{T}_0, \mathsf{T}_1, \ldots)$ is a sequence of numbers, where T_t is the lump-sum tax paid by the young consumer of period t
5. G is a number such that $(1+r_{-1})G$ is the amount of government debt held by the old consumer of period 0 at the beginning of that period
6. $\overline{L}_0$ solves the problem

$$\max_{L_0 \geq 0} [P_0 f(\overline{K}_{-1}, L_0) - W_0 L_0]$$

7. For all $t \geq 0$, $(\overline{K}_t, \overline{L}_{t+1})$ solves the problem

$$\max_{K_t \geq 0,\, L_{t+1} \geq 0} \{(1+r_t)^{-1}[P_{t+1} f(K_t, L_{t+1}) - W_{t+1} L_{t+1}] - P_t K_t\}$$

8. $\overline{x}_{-1,1}$ solves the problem

$$\max_{x_1 \geq 0} u_1(x_1)$$

$$\text{s.t.} \quad P_0 x_1 \leq P_0 f(\overline{K}_{-1}, \overline{L}_0) - W_0 \overline{L}_0 + (1+r_{-1})G$$

9. For every $t \geq 0$, $(\overline{x}_{t0}, \overline{x}_{t1})$ solves the problem

$$\max_{x_0 \geq 0,\, x_1 \geq 0} [u_0(x_0) + u_1(x_1)]$$

$$\text{s.t.} \quad P_t x_0 + (1+r_t)^{-1} P_{t+1} x_1 \leq W_t - \mathsf{T}_t$$

10. For all t, $P_t = 0$, if

$$\overline{x}_{t0} + \overline{x}_{t-1,1} < f(\overline{K}_{t-1}, \overline{L}_t) - \overline{K}_t$$

and $W_t = 0$, if $\overline{L}_t < 1$.

The budget constraint in condition (8) has an explanation similar to that of the same constraint in condition (6) of definition 10.9 of an Arrow-Debreu equilibrium. It is assumed that young consumers invest their savings in government debt and in loans to the firm that finance purchases of capital. Since the firm earns no profits, the lender in period t has a claim to the entire value of the input-output vector of the succeeding period made possible by the input of capital in period t. Therefore, if consumer -1 in youth finances the purchase of the capital stock K_{-1} in period -1, he or she in effect owns the entire net value of output, $P_0 f(\overline{K}_{-1}, \overline{L}_0) - W_0 L_0$, of period 0. Consumer -1 also holds government debt, G, purchased in period -1 and earns interest on it. Therefore, the purchasing power of consumer -1 in period 0 is $P_0 f(\overline{K}_{-1}, \overline{L}_0) - W_0 L_0 + (1 + r_{-1})G$.

It is easy to verify that in the Diamond model any spot price equilibrium can be converted to an Arrow-Debreu equilibrium, using formulas similar to those of proposition 9.12 (in section 9.3). If $(\overline{\mathbf{x}}, \overline{\mathbf{K}}, \overline{\mathbf{L}}, \mathbf{P}, \mathbf{W}, \mathbf{r}, G, \mathbf{T})$ is a spot price equilibrium, then $(\overline{\mathbf{x}}, \overline{\mathbf{K}}, \overline{\mathbf{L}}, \mathbf{p}, \mathbf{w}, \boldsymbol{\tau})$ is an Arrow-Debreu equilibrium where $p_0 = P_0$, $w_0 = W_0$, $\tau_{-1} = -(1 + r_{-1})G$, $\tau_0 = \mathsf{T}_0$, $p_t = \frac{P_t}{1+R_{t-1}}$, $w_t = \frac{W_t}{1+R_{t-1}}$, and $\tau_t = \frac{\mathsf{T}_t}{1+R_{t-1}}$, for $t \geq 1$, where $1 + R_t = (1 + r_0)(1 + r_1) \ldots (1 + r_t)$, for $t \geq 0$.

Transfer payments sum to 0 just as they do in Arrow-Debreu equilibria.

COROLLARY 10.13 Suppose that assumptions 10.1–10.5 apply and that

$$\mathbf{P}_0 + \sum_{t=1}^{\infty} \frac{\mathbf{P}_t}{1 + R_{t-1}} < \infty,$$

where $1 + R_t = (1 + r_0)(1 + r_1) \ldots (1 + r_t)$, for $t \geq 0$. Then,

$$|\mathsf{T}_0| + \sum_{t=1}^{\infty} \frac{|\mathsf{T}_t|}{1 + R_{t-1}} < \infty$$

and

$$G = \frac{\mathsf{T}_0}{1 + r_{-1}} + \sum_{t=1}^{\infty} \frac{\mathsf{T}_t}{(1 + r_{-1})(1 + R_{t-1})}.$$

Proof. This corollary is proved by applying proposition 10.11 to the spot price equilibrium after it has been converted to an Arrow-Debreu equilibrium by the formulas given above. ▪

Since the utility functions u_0 and u_1 are locally nonsatiated, the government meets a budget constraint in spot price equilibria, just as in the case of the Samuelson model. We must, however, be careful how we define government debt. The total savings of consumers at the end of period t is that of the young person, which is

$$W_t - P_t\overline{x}_{t0} - \mathsf{T}_t.$$

This wealth may be held as government debt, G_t, or as loans to business to finance the purchase of capital in period t. The loans equal $P_t\overline{K}_t$. Therefore, $G_t + P_t\overline{K}_t = W_t - P_t\overline{x}_{t0} - T_t$, so that

$$G_t = W_t - P_t(\overline{x}_{t0} + \overline{K}_t) - \mathsf{T}_t, \tag{10.5}$$

for $t \geq 0$.

I now verify that the government budget equation

$$G_{t+1} = (1 + r_t)G_t - \mathsf{T}_{t+1}, \tag{10.6}$$

applies. As in the case of the Samuelson model, this equation lends force to the interpretation of G_t as government debt. Because the allocation $(\overline{\mathbf{x}}, \overline{\mathbf{K}}, \overline{\mathbf{L}})$ is feasible,

$$\overline{x}_{t-1,1} + \overline{x}_{t0} \leq f(\overline{K}_{t-1}, \overline{L}_t) - \overline{K}_t,$$

for all $t \geq 0$. Condition (10) of definition 10.12 of spot price equilibrium implies that

$$P_t(\overline{x}_{t-1,1} + \overline{x}_{t0}) = P_t[f(\overline{K}_{t-1}, \overline{L}_t) - \overline{K}_t] \tag{10.7}$$

and

$$W_t\overline{L}_t = W_t, \tag{10.8}$$

for all $t \geq 0$. Equation 10.7 may be rewritten as

$$P_t[\overline{x}_{t-1,1} - f(\overline{K}_{t-1}, \overline{L}_t)] = -P_t(\overline{x}_{t0} + \overline{K}_t), \tag{10.9}$$

for all $t \geq 0$. Because u_0 and u_1 are locally nonsatiated, each consumer satisfies his or her budget condition with equality, so that

$$P_t\overline{x}_{t0} + \frac{P_{t+1}}{1 + r_t}\overline{x}_{t1} = W_t - \mathsf{T}_t,$$

for $t \geq 0$. This equation implies that

$$(1 + r_t)(W_t - P_t\overline{x}_{t0} - \mathsf{T}_t) = P_{t+1}\overline{x}_{t1}, \tag{10.10}$$

for $t \geq 0$. Finally because firms earn zero profits in equilibrium,

$$P_t \overline{K}_t = (1 + r_t)^{-1}[P_{t+1} f(\overline{K}_t, \overline{L}_{t+1}) - W_{t+1}\overline{L}_{t+1}], \tag{10.11}$$

for all $t \geq 0$. All these equations together imply that

$$\begin{aligned}(1 + r_t)G_t &= (1 + r_t)[W_t - P_t.(\overline{x}_{t0} + \overline{K}_t) - \mathsf{T}_t] \\ &= (1 + r_t)(W_t - P_t\overline{x}_{t0} - \mathsf{T}_t) - P_{t+1} f(\overline{K}_t, \overline{L}_{t+1}) + W_{t+1}\overline{L}_{t+1} \\ &= P_{t+1}[\overline{x}_{t1} - f(\overline{K}_t, \overline{L}_{t+1})] + W_{t+1}\overline{L}_{t+1} \\ &= W_{t+1} - P_{t+1}(\overline{x}_{t+1,0} + \overline{K}_{t+1}) \\ &= G_{t+1} + \mathsf{T}_{t+1},\end{aligned}$$

where the first equation follows from equation 10.5, the second from equation 10.11, the third from equation 10.10, the fourth from equations 10.8 and 10.9, and the last equation follows from equation 10.5 again. This completes the verification of equation 10.6.

The government budget equation for period 0 is

$$G_0 = (1 + r_{-1})G - \mathsf{T}_0. \tag{10.12}$$

Because u_1 is locally nonsatiated and $\overline{x}_{-1,1}$ solves the utility maximization problem of condition (8) of definition 10.12, it follows that

$$P_0\overline{x}_{-1,1} = P_0 f(\overline{K}_{-1}, \overline{L}_0) - W_0\overline{L}_0 + (1 + r_{-1})G. \tag{10.13}$$

Therefore,

$$\begin{aligned}(1 + r_{-1})G &= P_0[\overline{x}_{-1,1} - f(\overline{K}_{-1}, \overline{L}_0)] + W_0\overline{L}_0 \\ &= W_0 - P_0.(\overline{x}_{00} + \overline{K}_0) = G_0 + \mathsf{T}_0,\end{aligned}$$

where the first equation follows from equation 10.13, the second from equations 10.8 and 10.9, and the third from equation 10.5. This completes the verification of equation 10.12.

As the transactions in a spot price equilibrium may be confusing, I describe them during one period T. Imagine that in each period t a firm t invests capital in period t and that in the succeeding period it uses labor to produce output. In period T, the young consumer earns $W_T\overline{L}_T$ in wages from firm $T - 1$ and pays the same firm $P_T\overline{x}_{T0}$ for consumption and pays the government a lump-sum tax of T_T. The young consumer invests the residual, $W_T\overline{L}_T - P_T\overline{x}_{T0} - \mathsf{T}_T$, in G_T units of government debt and in a loan to firm T of $P_T\overline{K}_T$. The old consumer receives the value of his or her investments in the previous period plus interest, which is $(1 + r_{T-1})G_{T-1}$, from the government and $(1 + r_{T-1})P_{T-1}\overline{K}_{T-1}$ from firm $T - 1$. The old consumer pays $P_T\overline{x}_{T-1,1}$ to firm $T - 1$ for consumption. Firm $T - 1$ receives $P_T(\overline{x}_{T0} + \overline{x}_{T-1,1})$ in revenues from sales to consumers and $P_T\overline{K}_T$ in sales of capital to firm T. Firm $T - 1$ pays the young consumer $W_T\overline{L}_T$ in wages and pays the old consumer $(1 + r_{T-1})P_{T-1}\overline{K}_{T-1}$ for its loan plus interest. Firm T pays firm $T - 1$ the amount $P_T\overline{K}_T$ for capital goods and borrows the same amount from the young consumer. The government receives T_T as a lump-sum tax paid by the young consumer and borrows G_T from the young consumer. The government pays $(1 + r_{T-1})G_{T-1}$ to the old consumer for its loan plus interest. These payments must be thought of as all happening simultaneously, as in a 1-period general equilibrium model. It is impossible for the transactions to occur sequentially, for no one can be the first to pay. For instance, firm $T - 1$ cannot pay wages and repay its debt plus interest before it sells its output, and consumers cannot buy the firm's output before they receive payment for wages and loans.

I state a few other definitions that should be familiar from the Samuelson model.

DEFINITION 10.14 A *spot price equilibrium with interest rate 0*, $(\overline{\mathbf{x}}, \overline{\mathbf{K}}, \overline{\mathbf{L}}, \mathbf{P}, \mathbf{W}, G, \mathbf{T})$, for the Diamond model, is a spot price equilibrium, $(\overline{\mathbf{x}}, \overline{\mathbf{K}}, \overline{\mathbf{L}}, \mathbf{P}, \mathbf{W}, \mathbf{r}, G, \mathbf{T})$, such that $r_t = 0$, for all t.

If we set $r_t = 0$ in equations 10.6 and 10.12, we obtain the following government budget equations:

$$G_{t+1} = G_t - \mathsf{T}_{t+1},$$

for $t \geq 0$, and

$$G_0 = G - \mathsf{T}_0.$$

DEFINITION 10.15 A *stationary* spot price equilibrium for the Diamond model is a spot price equilibrium, $(\overline{\mathbf{x}}, \overline{\mathbf{K}}, \overline{\mathbf{L}}, \mathbf{P}, \mathbf{W}, \mathbf{r}, G, \mathbf{T})$, such that none of the variables depends on the time index t.

Similarly a *stationary* allocation is an allocation, $(\overline{\mathbf{x}}, \overline{\mathbf{K}}, \overline{\mathbf{L}})$, such that none of the variables depends on t. A stationary spot price equilibrium is denoted by $(\overline{x}_0, \overline{x}_1, \overline{K}, \overline{L}, P, W, r, G, \mathsf{T})$, where, for all t, $(\overline{x}_{t0}, \overline{x}_{t1}) =$

$(\overline{x}_0, \overline{x}_1)$, $\overline{K}_t = \overline{K}$, $\overline{L}_t = \overline{L}$, $P_t = P$, $W_t = W$, $r_t = r$, and $\mathsf{T}_t = \mathsf{T}$. A stationary spot price equilibrium with interest rate 0 is denoted by $(\overline{x}_0, \overline{x}_1, \overline{K}, \overline{L}, P, W, G)$, since $r = \mathsf{T} = 0$ in such an equilibrium. A stationary allocation is denoted by $(\overline{x}_0, \overline{x}_1, \overline{K}, \overline{L})$.

I now show how to transform the Diamond overlapping generations model into a one-sector optimal growth model. A growth model is a simplification of the Diamond model that makes it possible to focus on the trade-off between current and future consumption, undistracted by consumer budgets and taxes or intergenerational transfer payments. Let the utility function of a consumer be $u(x_0, x_1)$, as in chapter 9. If we discount future utility at a constant positive rate, r, and translate into the Diamond framework the welfare optimization problem already studied in the Samuelson model, we obtain the problem

$$\begin{aligned} \max_{(x_{t0}, x_{t-1,1}, K_t, L_t)_{t=0}^{\infty} \geq 0} \quad & \left[(1+r)u(\overline{x}_{-1,0}, x_{-1,1}) + \sum_{t=0}^{\infty}(1+r)^{-t}u(x_{t0}, x_{t1})\right] \\ \text{s.t.} \quad & x_{t0} + x_{t-1,1} + K_t \leq f(K_{t-1}, L_t) \text{ and} \\ & L_t \leq 1, \text{ for } t \geq 0, \text{ and } K_{-1} = \overline{K}_{-1}, \end{aligned} \tag{10.14}$$

where $\overline{x}_{-1,0}$ and $\overline{K}_{-1}$ are fixed and $r > 0$. If we substitute the utility function $u(x_0, x_1) = u_0(x_0) + u_1(x_1)$ into the objective function of problem 10.14, change the order of summation, and drop the constant term $(1+r)u_0(\overline{x}_{-1,0})$, we obtain the problem

$$\begin{aligned} \max_{(x_{t0}, x_{t-1,1}, K_t, L_t)_{t=0}^{\infty} \geq 0} \quad & \sum_{t=0}^{\infty}(1+r)^{-t}[u_0(x_{t0}) + (1+r)u_1(x_{t-1,1})] \\ \text{s.t.} \quad & x_{t0} + x_{t-1,1} + K_t \leq f(K_{t-1}, L_t) \text{ and} \\ & L_t \leq 1, \text{ for } t \geq 0, \text{ and } K_{-1} = \overline{K}_{-1}, \end{aligned} \tag{10.15}$$

where $\overline{K}_{-1}$ is fixed. It is permissible to change the order of summation in the objective function when going from problem 10.14 to problem 10.15, because the utilities appearing in the infinite sum are nonnegative. Define the utility function v by the equation

$$v(C) = \max_{x_0 : 0 \leq x_0 \leq C} [u_0(x_0) + (1+r)u_1(C - x_0)]. \tag{10.16}$$

Since f, u_0, and u_1 are nondecreasing by assumptions 10.4 and 10.5, it follows that $\overline{L}_t = 1$, for all t, if $(\overline{x}, \overline{K}, \overline{L})$ is an optimal allocation for problem 10.15 with $\overline{K}_t > 0$, for all t. It therefore makes sense to suppress the labor variable and to replace f by the function $F(K) = f(K, 1)$. I may use the functions v and F to rewrite problem 10.15 as

$$\begin{aligned} \max_{(C_t, k_t)_{t=0}^{\infty} > 0} \quad & \sum_{t=0}^{\infty} (1+r)^{-t} v(C_t) \\ \text{s.t.} \quad & C_t + K_t \leq F(K_{t-1}), \ \text{for } t \geq 0, \\ & \text{and } K_{-1} = \overline{K}_{-1}, \end{aligned} \tag{10.17}$$

and $\overline{K}_{-1}$ is fixed. Problem 10.17 is the central problem of the one-sector growth model in optimal growth theory.[1] I will always use the letter "C" to indicate consumption in a growth model in order to distinguish it from the consumptions, x_0 and x_1, in the overlapping generations model. The quantity $v(C_t)$ is the maximum welfare that can be generated in period t by making C_t units of output available to the old and young persons. The pair of functions (v, F) that has just been defined will be said to correspond to the triple (u_0, u_1, f) at interest rate r.

The allocations of overlapping generations models are called *programs* in growth models. A program consists of $(\mathbf{C}, \mathbf{K}) = (C_t, K_t)_{t=0}^{\infty}$, where each of the components, C_t and K_t, is a nonnegative number. The program is *feasible*, given the initial capital stock $\overline{K}_{-1}$, if

$$C_t + K_t \leq F(K_{t-1}),$$

for all $t \geq 0$, where it is understood that $K_{-1} = \overline{K}_{-1}$. A feasible program is *optimal* if it solves problem 10.17. The program $(\mathbf{C}, \mathbf{K})$ and the allocation $(\mathbf{x}, \mathbf{K}, \mathbf{L})$ are said to correspond to each other at interest rate r if $v(C_t) = u_0(x_{t0}) + (1+r)u_1(x_{t-1,1})$, $C_t = x_{t0} + x_{t-1,1}$, and $L_t = 1$, for all t. The next proposition says that a program is optimal if and only if the corresponding allocation is optimal. I give no formal proof of this assertion as it is almost self-evident.

PROPOSITION 10.16 If the allocation $(\overline{\mathbf{x}}, \overline{\mathbf{K}}, \overline{\mathbf{L}})$ and the program $(\overline{\mathbf{C}}, \overline{\mathbf{K}})$ correspond at the positive interest rate r, then $(\overline{\mathbf{x}}, \overline{\mathbf{K}}, \overline{\mathbf{L}})$ solves problem 10.15 if and only if $(\overline{\mathbf{C}}, \overline{\mathbf{K}})$ solves problem 10.17, where, in these problems, (F, v) corresponds to (f, u_0, u_1) at interest rate r.

1. This growth model is known as the *Ramsey model* or the *Ramsey-Solow growth model*, as it was introduced in Ramsey (1928) and again in Solow (1956).

The next lemma aids in the passage back and forth between Diamond models and growth models.

LEMMA 10.17 If assumption 10.5 applies and $r \geq 0$, then the equation

$$v(C) = \max_{x_0 : 0 \leq x_0 \leq C} [u_0(x_0) + (1+r)u_1(C - x_0)]$$

defines x_0 and $x_1 = C - x_0$ as continuous functions of C.

Proof. It is sufficient to prove the lemma for x_0. First of all, I prove that x_0 is a function of C. Suppose that

$$u_0(\underline{x}_0) + (1+r)u_1(C - \underline{x}_0) = v(C) = u_0(\overline{x}_0) + (1+r)u_1(C - \overline{x}_0),$$

where $\underline{x}_0 \neq \overline{x}_0$. Then, because u_0 and u_1 are strictly concave,

$$\begin{aligned}
&u_0\left(\tfrac{1}{2}\underline{x}_0 + \tfrac{1}{2}\overline{x}_0\right) + (1+r)u_1\left(\tfrac{1}{2}(C - \underline{x}_0) + \tfrac{1}{2}(C - \overline{x}_0)\right)\\
&> \tfrac{1}{2}u_0(\underline{x}_0) + \tfrac{1}{2}u_0(\overline{x}_0) + \tfrac{1}{2}(1+r)u_1(C - \underline{x}_0) + \tfrac{1}{2}(1+r)u_1(C - \overline{x}_0)\\
&= \tfrac{1}{2}[u_0(\underline{x}_0) + (1+r)u_1(C - \underline{x}_0)] + \tfrac{1}{2}[u_0(\overline{x}_0) + (1+r)u_1(C - \overline{x}_0)]\\
&= \tfrac{1}{2}v(C) + \tfrac{1}{2}v(C) = v(C),
\end{aligned}$$

which contradicts the definition of $v(C)$. Therefore, we may write $x_0 = x_0(C)$ and $x_1 = x_1(C) = C - x_0(C)$.

I now show that the function $x_0(C)$ is continuous. Suppose that the sequence C_n converges to C, where $n = 1, 2, \ldots$. I must show that $x_0(C_n)$ converges to $x_0(C)$. I may assume that $C > 0$, for if $C = 0$, then clearly $x_0(C_n)$ converges to zero, since $0 \leq x_0(C_n) \leq C_n$, for all n. Suppose that $x_0(C_n)$ does not converge to $x_0(C)$. Then, there exists a positive number ε and a subsequence $n(k)$ such that $|x_0(C_{n(K)}) - x_0(C)| \geq \varepsilon$, for all k. By the Bolzano-Weierstrass theorem, we may assume that the subsequence $x_0(C_{n(k)})$ converges to some number $\overline{x}_0$, as k goes to infinity. By passage to the limit in the inequality $|x_0(C_{n(k)}) - x_0(C)| \geq \varepsilon$, we see that $|\overline{x}_0 - x_0(C)| \geq \varepsilon$. Because $x_0(C)$ is the unique value of x_0 that solves problem 10.16, it follows, that for some positive number δ,

$$\begin{aligned}
&u_0(x_0(C)) + (1+r)u_1(C - x_0(C)) >\\
&\quad u_0(\overline{x}_0) + (1+r)u_1(C - \overline{x}_0) + 2\delta.
\end{aligned} \tag{10.18}$$

Because $C > 0$ and u_0 and u_1 are continuous, there exists a number α such that $\alpha < 1$ and α is so close to 1 that

$$\begin{aligned}
&u_0(\alpha x_0(C)) + (1+r)u_1(\alpha C - \alpha x_0(C)) >\\
&\quad u_0(x_0(C)) + (1+r)u_1(C - x_0(C)) - \delta.
\end{aligned} \tag{10.19}$$

If k is so large that $C_{n(k)} > \alpha C$, then

$$\begin{aligned}
&u_0(x_0(C_{n(k)})) + (1+r)u_1(C_{n(k)} - x_0(C_{n(k)})) = v(C_{n(k)}) \\
&\geq u_0(x_0(\alpha C)) + (1+r)u_1(C_{n(k)} - x_0(\alpha C)) \\
&> u_0(x_0(\alpha C)) + (1+r)u_1(\alpha C - x_0(\alpha C)) = v(\alpha C) \\
&\geq u_0(\alpha x_0(C)) + (1+r)u_1(\alpha C - \alpha x_0(C)) \\
&> u_0(x_0(C)) + (1+r)u_1(C - x_0(C)) - \delta \\
&> u_0(\overline{x}_0) + (1+r)u_1(C - \overline{x}_0) + \delta,
\end{aligned} \tag{10.20}$$

where the first inequality is true because of the definition of v. The second inequality is true because the function u_1 is increasing. The third inequality is a consequence of the definition of the function v. The fourth inequality is inequality 10.19, and the last inequality follows from inequality 10.18. Because the sequences $C_{n(k)}$ and $x_0(C_{n(k)})$ converge to C and $\overline{x}_0$, respectively, it follows that for k that is large enough,

$$\begin{aligned}
&u_0(x_0(C_{n(k)})) + (1+r)u_1(C_{n(k)} - x_0(C_{n(k)})) \\
&\qquad < u_0(\overline{x}_0) + (1+r)u_0(C - \overline{x}_0) + \delta.
\end{aligned} \tag{10.21}$$

The contradiction between inequalities 10.20 and 10.21 proves that $x_0(C_n)$ converges to $x_0(C)$, as n goes to infinity. ▪

I make the following assumptions about the optimal growth model.

ASSUMPTION 10.18 $F(0) = 0$, and there exists a positive number $\underline{K}$ such that $F(\underline{K}) - \underline{K} > 0$.

ASSUMPTION 10.19 F is continuously differentiable on $[0, \infty)$, twice differentiable on $(0, \infty)$, $\frac{dF(K)}{dK} > 0$, for $K \geq 0$, and $\frac{d^2F(K)}{dK^2} < 0$, for $K > 0$.

ASSUMPTION 10.20 $\lim_{K\to\infty} K^{-1}F(K) = \lim_{K\to\infty} \frac{dF(K)}{dK} = 0$.

ASSUMPTION 10.21 The utility function v is differentiable and strictly concave, and its derivative is everywhere positive.

It is easy to see that assumptions 10.18 and 10.19 are implied by assumptions 10.1–10.4 and the definition of F. I show that these assumptions imply assumption 10.20. Because f is homogeneous of degree 1,

$$\frac{F(K)}{K} = K^{-1}f(K, 1) = f(1, K^{-1}),$$

and $f(1, K^{-1})$ converges to $f(1, 0) = 0$, as K goes to infinity. Because $F(0) = 0$ and F is concave and increasing,

$$0 \leq \frac{dF(K)}{dK} \leq \frac{F(K)}{K}.$$

Since $\frac{F(K)}{K}$ converges to 0 as K goes to infinity, $\frac{dF(K)}{dK}$ must do so as well.

It is easy to see that assumptions 10.18–10.20 imply that feasible programs are bounded. I now prove that assumption 10.21 is implied by assumption 10.5 and the definition of v. To do so, I need the following lemma.

LEMMA 10.22 If $v : [0, \infty) \to (-\infty, \infty)$ is an increasing and concave function, then v has a positive subgradient at every positive member of its domain.

Proof. This statement was already proved in the course of proving the Kuhn-Tucker theorem (in section 6.5). Let $\overline{C}$ be greater than 0. I must show that there is a positive number p such that for all nonnegative numbers C

$$v(C) \leq v(\overline{C}) + p(C - \overline{C}). \tag{10.22}$$

I apply the Minkowski separation theorem to the sets

$$B = \{(C, t) \mid C \leq \overline{C} \text{ and } t \geq v(\overline{C})\}$$

and

$$Z = \{(C, t) \mid C \geq 0 \text{ and } t \leq v(C)\}.$$

The set B is clearly convex, and the concavity of v implies that Z is convex. The sets are portrayed in figure 10.2.

Because v is strictly increasing, B and Z intersect solely at the point $(\overline{C}, v(\overline{C}))$. Since both sets have nonempty interiors, we may apply the Minkowski separation theorem to prove that there is a nonzero vector (r, s) such that

$$(r, s).(C, t) \geq (r, s).(\underline{C}, \underline{t}), \tag{10.23}$$

for all (C, t) in B and $(\underline{C}, \underline{t})$ in Z. The nature of the set B implies that $r \leq 0$ and $s \geq 0$. I show that $s > 0$. Suppose that $s = 0$. Since $(r, s) \neq 0$, it follows that $r < 0$. Since $(\overline{C}, v(\overline{C})) \in B$, inequality 10.23 implies that $r\overline{C} \geq rC$, for all $C \geq 0$, so that $\overline{C} \leq C$, for all $C \geq 0$. Since $\overline{C} > 0$, this inequality is

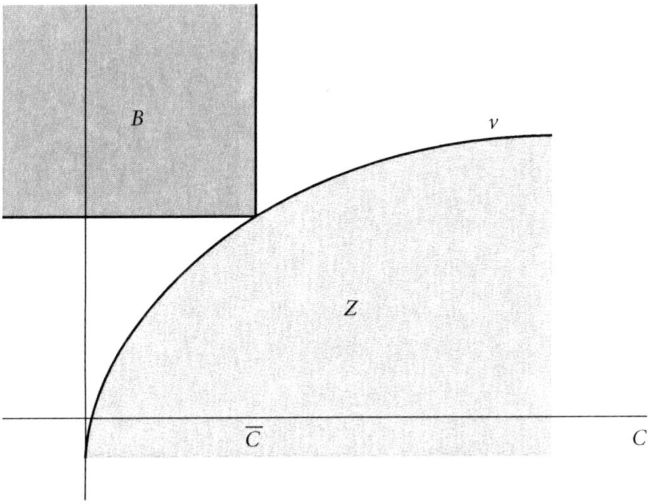

Figure 10.2 The sets to be separated

impossible. Hence $s > 0$. Let $p = -r/s$. If we divide inequality 10.23 by s, it becomes

$$(-p, 1).(C, t) \geq (-p, 1).(\underline{C}, \underline{t}),$$

for all (C, t) in B and $(\underline{C}, \underline{t})$ in Z. Since $(\overline{C}, v(\overline{C}))$ belongs to B and $(C, v(C))$ belongs to Z, for all $C \geq 0$, we have that

$$(-p, 1).(\overline{C}, v(\overline{C})) \geq (-p, 1).(C, v(C)),$$

for all $C \geq 0$. When expanded and rearranged, this inequality becomes inequality 10.22.

It remains to be shown that $p > 0$. If we substitute $\overline{C} + 1$ for C in inequality 10.22, we find that

$$p \geq v(\overline{C} + 1) - v(\overline{C}).$$

Since v is strictly increasing, $v(\overline{C} + 1) - v(\overline{C}) > 0$ and therefore $p > 0$. ■

LEMMA 10.23 If u_0 and u_1 are strictly concave and differentiable and have positive derivatives, then the function v defined by equation 10.16 has the same properties and

$$\frac{dv(C)}{dC} = \frac{du_0(x_0(C))}{dx}, \tag{10.24}$$

if $x_0(C) > 0$. Similarly,

$$\frac{dv(C)}{dC} = (1+r)\frac{du_1(x_1(C))}{dx}, \tag{10.25}$$

if $x_1(C) > 0$.[2] Finally,

$$\frac{dv(0)}{dc} = \max\left(\frac{du_0(0)}{dx}, (1+r)\frac{du_1(0)}{dx}\right). \tag{10.26}$$

Proof. It should be obvious that v is strictly increasing because u_0 and u_1 are strictly increasing. I next show that v is concave. Let $\underline{x}$ and $\overline{x}$ be such that $0 \leq \underline{x} < \overline{x}$, and suppose that $0 < \alpha < 1$. Let $\underline{x}_0$ be such that $0 \leq \underline{x}_0 \leq \underline{x}$ and $v(\underline{x}) = u_0(\underline{x}_0) + u_1(\underline{x} - \underline{x}_0)$. Similarly, let $\overline{x}_0$ be such that $0 \leq \overline{x}_0 \leq \overline{x}$ and $v(\overline{x}) = u_0(\overline{x}_0) + u_1(\overline{x} - \overline{x}_0)$. Then, by the definition of v and because u_0 and u_1 are strictly concave

$$\begin{aligned}
&v(\alpha\underline{x} + (1-\alpha)\overline{x}) \geq u_0(\alpha\underline{x}_0 \\
&+ (1-\alpha)\overline{x}_0) + (1+r)u_1((\alpha\underline{x} + (1-\alpha)\overline{x}) - (\alpha\underline{x}_0 + (1-\alpha)\overline{x}_0)) \\
&= u_0(\alpha\underline{x}_0 + (1-\alpha)\overline{x}_0) + (1+r)u_1(\alpha(\underline{x} - \underline{x}_0) + (1-\alpha)(\overline{x} - \overline{x}_0)) \\
&> \alpha u_0(\underline{x}_0) + (1-\alpha)u_0(\overline{x}_0) + \alpha(1+r)u_1(\underline{x} - \underline{x}_0) \\
&+ (1-\alpha)(1+r)u_1(\overline{x} - \overline{x}_0) \\
&= \alpha v(\underline{x}) + (1-\alpha)v(\overline{x}),
\end{aligned}$$

so that v is strictly concave.

I now show that v is differentiable and that its derivative satisfies equations 10.24–10.26. Suppose, first of all, that $C > 0$ and $x_0(C) > 0$. Because v is concave and increasing, lemma 10.22 implies that v has a positive subgradient, p, at C. If ΔC is a small change in C, then

$$v(C + \Delta C) \leq v(C) + p\Delta C,$$

so that

$$\begin{aligned}
p\Delta C &\geq v(C + \Delta C) - v(C) \\
&\geq u_0(x_0(C) + \Delta C) + (1+r)u_1(C + \Delta C - x_0(C) - \Delta C) \\
&\quad - u_0(x_0(C)) - (1+r)u_1(C - x_0(C)) \\
&= u_0(x_0(C) + \Delta C) - u_0(x_0(C)).
\end{aligned} \tag{10.27}$$

2. Equations 10.24 and 10.25 are implied by what is known in mathematical economics as the envelope theorem. See Varian (1992, 490–1).

Therefore, if $\Delta C > 0$, then

$$p \geq \frac{v(C + \Delta C) - v(C)}{\Delta C} \geq \frac{u_0(x_0(C) + \Delta C) - u_0(x_0(C))}{\Delta C}. \qquad (10.28)$$

The right-hand side of inequality 10.28 converges to $\frac{du_0(x_0(C))}{dx}$ as ΔC converges to zero, so that

$$p \geq \frac{du_0(x_0(C))}{dx}.$$

Inequality 10.27 implies that if $\Delta C < 0$, then

$$p \leq \frac{v(C + \Delta C) - v(C)}{\Delta C} \leq \frac{u_0(x_0(C) + \Delta C) - u_0(x_0(C))}{\Delta C}, \qquad (10.29)$$

so that

$$p \leq \frac{du_0(x_0(C))}{dx}.$$

We may conclude, therefore, that

$$p = \frac{du_0(x_0(C))}{dx}. \qquad (10.30)$$

Inequalities 10.28 and 10.29 and equation 10.30 imply that

$$\lim_{\Delta C - 0} \frac{v(C + \Delta C) - v(C)}{\Delta C} = p = \frac{du_0(x_0(C))}{dx},$$

so that

$$\frac{dv(C)}{dC} = \frac{du_0(x_0(C))}{dx}.$$

A similar argument proves that

$$\frac{dv(C)}{dC} = (1 + r)\frac{du_1(x_1(C))}{dx},$$

if $x_1(C) > 0$. This proof of the differentiability of v is illustrated in figure 10.3.

Suppose now that $C = 0$. Because $C = 0$, $\Delta C \geq 0$, and because v is concave, the ratio

$$\frac{v(\Delta C) - v(0)}{\Delta C}$$

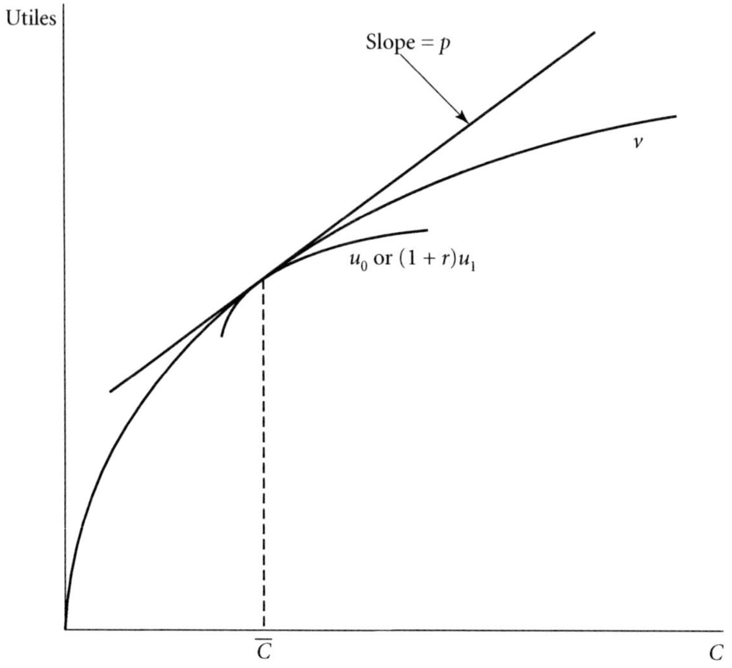

Figure 10.3 Proving the differentiability of v by trapping its graph between those of two differentiable functions

is nonincreasing in ΔC for $\Delta C \geq 0$. Therefore,

$$\lim_{\Delta C \to \infty} \frac{v(\Delta C) - v(0)}{\Delta C}$$

exists, though it may be infinite. I call this limit $\frac{dv(0)}{dC}$. (This argument was already used in proving proposition 10.6.) By the definition of v,

$$\frac{v(\Delta C) - v(0)}{\Delta C} \geq \frac{u_0(\Delta C) + (1+r)u_1(0) - [u_0(0) + (1+r)u_1(0)]}{\Delta C}$$
$$= \frac{u_0(\Delta C) - u_0(0)}{\Delta C},$$

so that

$$\frac{dv(0)}{dC} \geq \frac{du_0(0)}{dC}.$$

A similar argument implies that

$$\frac{dv(0)}{dC} \geq (1+r)\frac{du_1(0)}{dC}.$$

These last two inequalities imply equation 10.26 if either $\frac{du_0(0)}{dx} = \infty$ or $\frac{du_1(0)}{dx} = \infty$. Suppose that $\frac{du_0(0)}{dx} < \infty$ and $\frac{du_1(0)}{dx} < \infty$. The definition of v implies that

$$\begin{aligned}
&\frac{v(\Delta C) - v(0)}{\Delta C} \\
&= \frac{u_0(x_0(\Delta C)) + (1+r)u_1(x_1(\Delta C)) - [u_0(0) + (1+r)u_1(0)]}{\Delta C} \\
&= \frac{u_0(x_0(\Delta C)) - u_0(0)}{\Delta C} + (1+r)\frac{u_1(x_1(\Delta C)) - u_1(0)}{\Delta C} \\
&= \frac{x_0(\Delta C)}{\Delta C}\frac{du_0(0)}{dx} + o(x_0(\Delta C)) + \frac{x_1(\Delta C)}{\Delta C}(1+r)\frac{du_0(0)}{dx} + o(x_1(\Delta C)),
\end{aligned}$$

where the symbol "$o(y)$" means a quantity such that

$$\lim_{y \to 0} \frac{o(y)}{y} = 0.$$

Because $0 \leq x_0(\Delta C) \leq \Delta C$ and $0 \leq x_1(\Delta C) \leq \Delta C$ and $x_0(\Delta C) + x_1(\Delta C) = \Delta C$, it follows that for small ΔC, $\frac{v(\Delta C) - v(0)}{\Delta C}$ is, to within an asymptotically vanishing error, a weighted average of $\frac{du_0(0)}{dx}$ and $(1+r)\frac{du_1(0)}{dx}$. By the definition of v, the weights are chosen so as to maximize the average, so that if these two derivatives differ, all the weight is put on the larger one. This completes the proof of equation 10.26. ▪

Given functions v and F that satisfy assumptions 10.18–10.21, there exist functions u_0, u_1, and f that satisfy assumptions 10.1–10.5 and such that v and F correspond to u_0, u_1, and f in the manner that has been described. The functions u_0 and u_1 are defined by the equations $u_0(x) = \frac{1}{2}v(2x)$ and $u_1(x) = \frac{1}{2(1+r)}v(2x)$, respectively. The function f is defined by the equations $f(K, L) = LF\left(\frac{K}{L}\right)$, if $L > 0$ and $f(K, 0) = 0$. Proposition 10.6 implies that f satisfies assumptions 10.1–10.4.

10.2 Inefficiency

We have seen in section 9.2 that Arrow-Debreu equilibria in the Samuelson model can allocate consumption inefficiently between young and old consumers by giving too much to the young. An additional form of inefficiency occurs in the Diamond model if the real rate of interest is persistently negative, for then the economy acquires so much capital that reducing it would make it possible for all consumers from some time onward to consume more. In such a case, the economy is said to have overaccumulated capital. I give an example of an economy that has spot price and Arrow-Debreu equilibria that exhibit this inefficiency as well as the excessive favoring of the young discussed in section 9.2.

Instead of describing the example as if it came from nowhere, I show how to arrive at it. I seek a stationary spot price equilibrium in which the stationary interest rate is negative and there are no taxes, so that the corresponding Arrow-Debreu equilibrium has no transfer payments. Transfer payments would make the Arrow-Debreu equilibrium seem dubious, since they would grow exponentially along with prices and so would not be summable.

Euler's equation for homogeneous functions (equation 4.3 in section 4.4) implies that

$$f(K, 1) = K\frac{\partial f(K, 1)}{\partial K} + \frac{\partial f(K, 1)}{\partial L}, \tag{10.31}$$

where K and 1 are the stationary equilibrium levels of the capital and labor inputs, respectively. In the stationary spot price equilibrium, let P, W, and r be the price of the produced good, the wage, and the interest rate, respectively, and suppose that prices are normalized so that $P = 1$. The profit to be maximized in equilibrium is $(1+r)^{-1}[f(K, L) - WL] - K$. Since $L = 1$ in equilibrium, the first order conditions for profit maximization are

$$\frac{\partial f(K, 1)}{\partial K} = 1 + r \tag{10.32}$$

and

$$\frac{\partial f(K, 1)}{\partial L} = W, \tag{10.33}$$

assuming that $K > 0$. Substituting these two equations into equation 10.31, we find that

$$f(K, 1) = K(1 + r) + W. \tag{10.34}$$

If x_0 and x_1 are the stationary equilibrium levels of consumption in youth and old age, respectively, then feasibility implies that

$$x_0 + x_1 = f(K, 1) - K. \tag{10.35}$$

Since there are no taxes in the equilibrium, a typical consumer's budget equation is

$$x_0 + \frac{x_1}{1+r} = W. \tag{10.36}$$

Substituting equations 10.35 and 10.36 into equation 10.34 and simplifying, we find that

$$x_1 = (1+r)K.$$

If we substitute this equation into the budget equation 10.36, we find that

$$x_0 = W - K.$$

Therefore, in order to construct an example, we need a production function such that $W > K$, for some r between -1 and 0. One such production function is

$$f(K, L) = 4K^{1/4}L^{3/4},$$

for if $r = -1/2$, then equations 10.32 and 10.33 imply that $W = 3(2^{1/3}) > 2(2^{1/3}) = K$. Let $x_0 = 2^{1/3} = x_1$. We can check that the allocation $(x_0, x_1, K) = (2^{1/3}, 2^{1/3}, 2(2^{1/3}))$ is feasible, for $f(K, 1) = 4(2^{1/3}) = 2^{1/3} + 2^{1/3} + 2(2^{1/3}) = x_0 + x_1 + K$. In order to finish the example, all that remains to be done is to find a utility function such that a consumer chooses $x_0 = 2^{1/3} = x_1$ when the interest rate is $-1/2$ and the total expenditure is $W = 3(2^{1/3})$. One possibility is the Cobb-Douglas utility function $u_0(x_0) + u_1(x_1) = \frac{1}{3}\ln(x_0) + \frac{2}{3}\ln(x_1)$. In conclusion, we have the following.

EXAMPLE 10.24 (Inefficient equilibrium) Let $f(K, L) = 4K^{1/4}L^{3/4}$, $u_0(x_0) = \frac{1}{3}\ln(x_0)$, and $u_1(x_1) = \frac{2}{3}\ln(x_1)$. Then the following defines a stationary spot price equilibrium that has no taxes: $\overline{K} = 2(2^{1/3})$, $\overline{x}_0 = 2^{1/3} = \overline{x}_1$, $P = 1$, $W = 3(2^{1/3})$, and $r = -1/2$. This equilibrium may be expressed as an Arrow-Debreu equilibrium with no transfer payments by letting $p_t = 2^t$ and $w_t = 3(2^{1/3})2^t$, for all t.

I show that the equilibrium allocation of this example is not Pareto optimal. Call the spot price equilibrium just calculated the old situation, and imagine that at time 0 the economy switches to a new regime by reducing the capital stock from $2(2^{1/3})$ to 1 and keeping it there forever. Because of this change, the amount of output available for consumption in period 0 is $f(2(2^{1/3}), 1) - 1 = 4(2^{1/3}) - 1$. Suppose that the young person of period 0, consumes one unit of this output, so that the old person of that period consumes $4(2^{1/3}) - 2$, which exceeds the amount $2^{1/3}$ consumed in the old situation. Hence he or she is better off in the new situation. Suppose that the level of capital in the new regime equals 1 from period 0 onward, so that from that period onward, total output is $f(1, 1) = 4$ and output net of capital input is $f(1, 1) - 1 = 3$. Let the young consume one unit of output from period 0 onward and the old consume two units from period 1 onward. This consumption pattern is feasible, since the total consumption (3) in each period equals output net of capital input. In the new situation, the lifetime utility of a consumer born in period 0 or thereafter is $\frac{1}{3}\ln(1) + \frac{2}{3}\ln(2) = \frac{2}{3}\ln(2)$, which exceeds the lifetime utility,

$$\frac{1}{3}\ln(2^{1/3}) + \frac{2}{3}\ln(2^{1/3}) = \frac{1}{3}\ln(2),$$

of consumers in the old situation. Since everyone gains by the shift to the new allocation, the equilibrium allocation of the old situation was not Pareto optimal.

There are two causes of inefficiency. One cause is the overaccumulation of capital in the old situation. The capital stock in that allocation, $2(2^{1/3})$, was so large that the output left over for consumption after providing for capital, $4(2^{1/3}) - 2(2^{1/3}) = 2(2^{1/3})$, was less than the stationary level of 3 that can be maintained with the lower capital stock of 1.

Not only was there a deficient quantity of output available for consumption in the old situation, but the allocation of that output between the young and old was inefficient, for suppose that no change is made in capital inputs, so that only $2(2^{1/3})$ units of output can be consumed in every period. Then, just as in the Samuelson model, a Pareto improvement can be obtained by switching to a regime in which the old consume $(4/3)(2^{1/3})$ and the young consume $(2/3)(2^{1/3})$ units of the produced good in every period. In the old situation, the old consumed too little relative to the young.

The inefficiencies are illustrated in figure 10.4, which shows the allocation of consumption between typical old and young consumers. Given the stationary equilibrium investment in capital, the feasibility line for the sta-

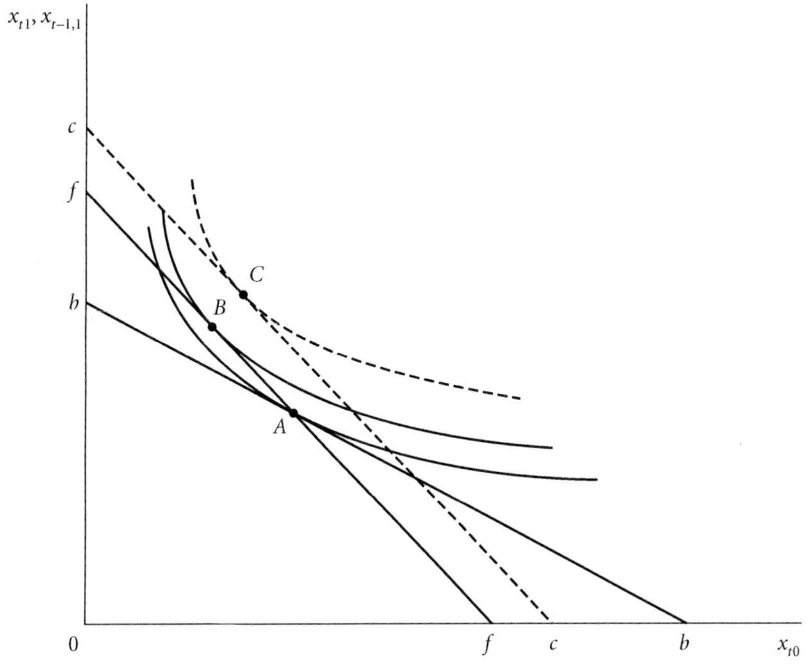

Figure 10.4 Inefficiencies in the equilibrium

tionary allocation of consumption between young and old is the line ff. The equilibrium allocation is at point A on the line ff where the indifference curve of a typical consumer is tangent to the budget line, bb. The best feasible allocation of consumption along ff is at point B, which is preferred to the equilibrium point A. The superiority of B to A results from the misallocation of consumption between the young and the old. If the investment in capital is reduced, the feasible consumption line moves out to cc, and the best allocation of consumption on this line is at point C, which is preferred to both B and A. The superiority of C over B results from the overaccumulation of capital at B. Such overaccumulation is the form of inefficiency typically studied in growth theory and occurs as an equilibrium when the real interest rate is eventually negative and remains so indefinitely, as in the above example.

Overaccumulation may be visualized with the help of figure 10.5. The figure shows the graph of the production function $y = f(K, 1)$ and the

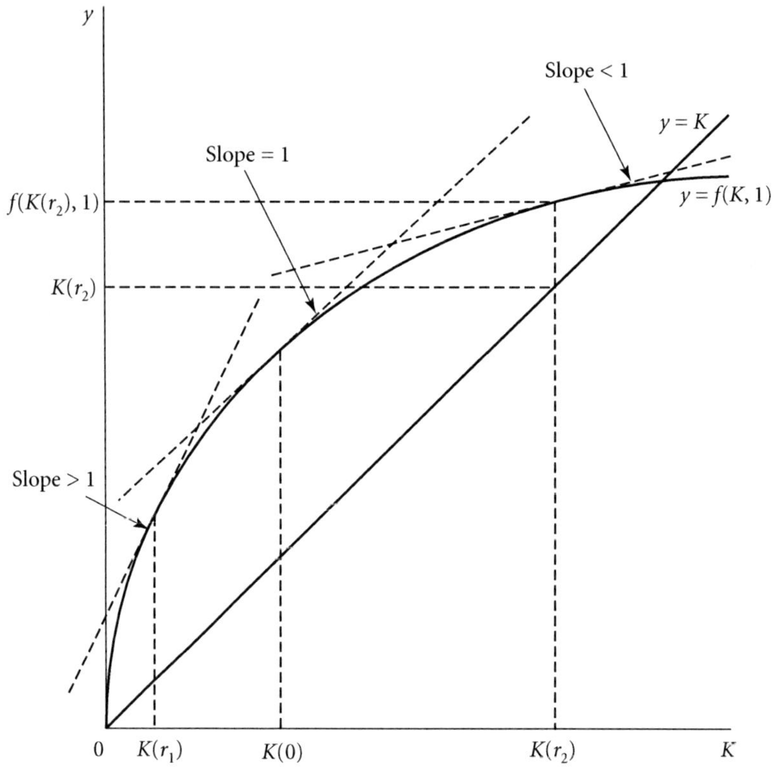

Figure 10.5 Output, net output, and capital input

graph of the line $y = K$. The difference between these two graphs is the amount of produced good available for consumption in a stationary allocation, namely, $f(K, 1) - K$, for in a stationary equilibrium with allocation $(\overline{x}, \overline{K}, \overline{L})$ and where $\overline{L} = 1$, feasibility implies that $\overline{x}_0 + \overline{x}_1 \leq f(\overline{K}, 1) - \overline{K}$. Let $K(r)$ be the capital input that solves the equation

$$\frac{\partial f(K(r), 1)}{\partial K} = 1 + r.$$

The difference $f(K(r), 1) - K(r)$ is maximized when $r = 0$, as is shown in the figure. The difference is less than the maximum when $r < 0$, as at r_2, or when $r > 0$, as at r_1. If the stationary interest rate, r, is negative, then

$$\frac{\partial f(K, 1)}{\partial K} = 1 + r < 1,$$

when $K = K(r)$, so that

$$\frac{\partial}{\partial K}[f(K, 1) - K] < 0,$$

at $K = K(r)$, and there would be more output net of capital input left over for consumption if the stationary capital stock were reduced. If the reduction were made at time 0, the consumers of that period could consume the extra amount of produced good thereby made available, and in every period thereafter there would be more output net of capital available for consumption. The reduction in capital input would lead to a Pareto improvement, so that it is not efficient to have the large capital stock generated by an equilibrium with a negative interest rate. If $r > 0$, then

$$\frac{\partial f(K, 1)}{\partial K} = 1 + r > 1,$$

when $K = K(r)$, so that

$$\frac{\partial}{\partial K}[f(K, 1) - K] > 0,$$

at $K = K(r)$, and more output net of capital input would be available for consumption if the capital input were increased. This change would not necessarily lead to a Pareto improvement, because it could not take place without reducing consumption at the time the increase was initiated. It will be shown in section 10.3 that the allocations of stationary spot price equilibria with positive interest rates are Pareto optimal.

The capital stock $K(0)$ is known as the *golden rule capital stock,* for the stationary allocation with that capital stock maximizes the net output, $f(K, 1) - K$, available for consumption.

10.3 Pareto Optimal Equilibria

The theory of Pareto optimal equilibria is nearly the same in the Diamond and Samuelson models.

PROPOSITION 10.25 If assumptions 10.1–10.5 apply, then the allocation, $(\overline{\mathbf{x}}, \overline{\mathbf{K}}, \overline{\mathbf{L}})$, of an Arrow-Debreu equilibrium, $(\overline{\mathbf{x}}, \overline{\mathbf{K}}, \overline{\mathbf{L}}, \mathbf{p}, \mathbf{w}, \boldsymbol{\tau})$, with transfer payments is Pareto optimal if

$$\sum_{t=0}^{\infty} p_t < \infty.$$

Proof. If $(\overline{\mathbf{x}}, \overline{\mathbf{K}}, \overline{\mathbf{L}})$ is not Pareto optimal, it is Pareto dominated by an allocation $(\mathbf{x}, \mathbf{K}, \mathbf{L})$ that is feasible with the same initial capital $\overline{K}_{-1}$. Because $(\mathbf{x}, \mathbf{K}, \mathbf{L})$ Pareto dominates $(\overline{\mathbf{x}}, \overline{\mathbf{K}}, \overline{\mathbf{L}})$ and u_0 and u_1 are locally nonsatiated, it follows from arguments used in the proof of the first welfare theorem 5.2 (in section 5.1) that

$$p_0 x_{-1,1} \geq p_0 f(\overline{K}_{-1,1}, \overline{L}_0) - w_0 \overline{L}_0 - \tau_{-1}$$

and

$$p_t x_{t0} + p_{t+1} x_{t1} \geq w_t - \tau_t,$$

for $t \geq 0$, with strict inequality for those people who prefer $(\mathbf{x}, \mathbf{K}, \mathbf{L})$ to $(\overline{\mathbf{x}}, \overline{\mathbf{K}}, \overline{\mathbf{L}})$. The right-hand sides of these inequalities are the income of the consumers in the equilibrium. Adding these inequalities, we find that

$$\begin{aligned} p_0 x_{\ 1,1} + \sum_{t=0}^{\infty} (p_t x_{t0} + p_{t+1} x_{t1}) > \\ \sum_{t=0}^{\infty} (w_t - \tau_t) + p_0 f(\overline{K}_{-1}, \overline{L}_0) - w_0 \overline{L}_0 - \tau_{-1}. \end{aligned} \tag{10.37}$$

By lemma 10.10 (in section 10.1), $\sum_{t=0}^{\infty} w_t < \infty$, and by proposition 10.11 in the same section, $\sum_{t=-1}^{\infty} \tau_t = 0$ and $\sum_{t=-1}^{\infty} |\tau_t| < \infty$. Hence the infinite series in inequality 10.37 all converge absolutely, so that the values of the left- and right-hand sides are not changed by reordering the terms. Therefore

$$\begin{aligned} &\sum_{t=0}^{\infty} p_t (x_{t0} + x_{t-1,1}) > \\ &\sum_{t=0}^{\infty} w_t - \sum_{t=-1}^{\infty} \tau_t + p_0 f(\overline{K}_{-1}, \overline{L}_0) - w_0 \overline{L}_0 = \\ &\sum_{t=0}^{\infty} w_t + p_0 f(\overline{K}_{-1}, \overline{L}_0) - w_0 \overline{L}_0 \geq \\ &\sum_{t=0}^{\infty} w_t L_t + p_0 f(\overline{K}_{-1}, \overline{L}_0) - w_0 \overline{L}_0, \end{aligned} \tag{10.38}$$

where the last inequality follows from the fact that $L_t \leq 1$, for all t. Profit maximization implies that

$$p_0 f(\overline{K}_{-1}, L_0) - w_0 L_0 \leq p_0 f(\overline{K}_{-1}, \overline{L}_0) - w_0 \overline{L}_0 \tag{10.39}$$

and

$$\begin{aligned} &p_t f(K_{t-1}, L_t) - w_t L_t - p_{t-1} K_{t-1} \leq \\ &p_t f(\overline{K}_{t-1}, \overline{L}_t) - w_t \overline{L}_t - p_{t-1} \overline{K}_{t-1} = 0, \end{aligned} \tag{10.40}$$

for $t \geq 1$, where the equation follows from the fact that f is homogeneous of degree 1. Inequality 10.40 implies that

$$w_t L_t \geq p_t f(K_{t-1}, L_t) - p_{t-1} K_{t-1}, \tag{10.41}$$

for $t \geq 1$. Substituting inequalities 10.39 and then 10.41 into inequality 10.38, we see that

$$\begin{aligned} \sum_{t=0}^{\infty} p_t (x_{t0} + x_{t-1,1}) &> \sum_{t=0}^{\infty} w_t L_t + p_0 f(\overline{K}_{-1}, L_0) - w_0 L_0 \\ &= \sum_{t=1}^{\infty} w_t L_t + p_0 f(\overline{K}_{-1}, L_0) \\ &\geq \sum_{t=1}^{\infty} [p_t f(K_{t-1}, L_t) - p_{t-1} K_{t-1}] + p_0 f(\overline{K}_{-1}, L_0), \end{aligned}$$

so that

$$\sum_{t=0}^{\infty} p_t (K_t + x_{t0} + x_{t-1,1}) > p_0 f(\overline{K}_{-1}, L_0) + \sum_{t=1}^{\infty} p_t f(K_{t-1}, L_t).$$

This inequality is impossible, since $p_t \geq 0$, for all $t \geq 0$, and the feasibility of $(\mathbf{x}, \mathbf{K}, \mathbf{L})$ implies that $K_0 + x_{00} + x_{-1,1} \leq f(\overline{K}_{-1}, L_0)$ and $K_t + x_{t0} + x_{t-1,1} \leq f(K_{t-1}, L_t)$, for all $t \geq 1$. This contradiction proves the proposition. ▪

Because a spot price equilibrium may be converted to an Arrow-Debreu equilibrium with transfer payments, we have the following two corollaries.

COROLLARY 10.26 Assume that assumptions 10.1–10.5 apply. If the spot price equilibrium, $(\overline{\mathbf{x}}, \overline{\mathbf{K}}, \overline{\mathbf{L}}, \mathbf{P}, \mathbf{W}, \mathbf{r}, G, \mathbf{T})$, satisfies the condition

$$P_0 + \sum_{t=1}^{\infty} \frac{P_t}{1 + R_{t-1}} < \infty,$$

where $1 + R_t = (1 + r_0)(1 + r_1) \ldots (1 + r_t)$, for $t \geq 0$, then the equilibrium allocation, $(\overline{\mathbf{x}}, \overline{\mathbf{K}}, \overline{\mathbf{L}})$, is Pareto optimal.

Proof. When $(\overline{\mathbf{x}}, \overline{\mathbf{K}}, \overline{\mathbf{L}}, \mathbf{P}, \mathbf{W}, \mathbf{r}, G, \mathbf{T})$ is converted to an Arrow-Debreu equilibrium, $(\overline{\mathbf{x}}, \overline{\mathbf{K}}, \overline{\mathbf{L}}, \mathbf{p}, \mathbf{w}, \boldsymbol{\tau})$, with transfer payments, then the condition

$$P_0 + \sum_{t=1}^{\infty} \frac{P_t}{1 + R_{t-1}} < \infty$$

implies that $\sum_{t=0}^{\infty} p_t < \infty$, so that the allocation $(\overline{\mathbf{x}}, \overline{\mathbf{K}}, \overline{\mathbf{L}})$ is Pareto optimal by proposition 10.25. ▪

The next corollary is an immediate consequence of the previous one.

COROLLARY 10.27 If assumptions 10.1–10.5 apply, then the allocation of a stationary spot price equilibrium with a positive interest rate is Pareto optimal.

I now describe the set of stationary spot price equilibria, $(\overline{x}_0, \overline{x}_1, \overline{K}, \overline{L}, P, W, r, G, \mathsf{T})$ when $r > -1$. Assume that assumptions 10.1–10.5 apply. Because f, u_0, and u_1 are nondecreasing, we may assume that

$$\overline{L} = 1. \tag{10.42}$$

Because u_0 and u_1 are strictly increasing, we know that

$$\overline{x}_0 + \overline{x}_1 + \overline{K} = f(\overline{K}, 1) \tag{10.43}$$

and $P > 0$. I normalize P to be 1. Assume that $\overline{x}_0 > 0$ and $\overline{x}_1 > 0$, so that by the first order conditions for utility maximization over a typical consumer's budget set

$$(1+r)\frac{du_1(\overline{x}_1)}{dx_1} = \frac{du_0(\overline{x}_0)}{dx_0}. \tag{10.44}$$

Since profit from one period's production is $(1+r)^{-1}[f(\overline{K}, \overline{L}) - W\overline{L}] - \overline{K}$, the first order conditions for profit maximization are

$$\frac{\partial f(\overline{K}, 1)}{\partial K} = 1 + r \tag{10.45}$$

and

$$\frac{\partial f(\overline{K}, 1)}{\partial L} = W. \tag{10.46}$$

The budget equation for the typical consumer is

$$\overline{x}_0 + (1+r)^{-1}\overline{x}_1 = W - \mathsf{T}. \tag{10.47}$$

Government debt is defined by the equation

$$G = W - \overline{x}_0 - \mathsf{T} - \overline{K}. \tag{10.48}$$

Equations 10.42–10.45 determine the real variables, $(\overline{x}_0, \overline{x}_1, \overline{K}, \overline{L})$. Equations 10.46–10.48 determine the monetary variables W, G, and T. The interest rate, r, is fixed in advance. It may be checked that G and T satisfy the government budget constraint

$$rG = \mathsf{T}. \tag{10.49}$$

The stationary equilibrium has no output and no consumption if $r > \frac{\partial f(0,1)}{\partial K} - 1$, and there exists no stationary equilibrium if $r < \frac{\partial f(\hat{K},1)}{\partial K} - 1$, where $\hat{K}$ is the unique positive solution of the equation $f(\hat{K}, 1) = \hat{K}$.

Because of the concavity properties of the functions f, u_0, and u_1, equations 10.43–10.45 determine $\overline{x}_0$, $\overline{x}_1$, and $\overline{K}$ uniquely, and we may write the stationary equilibrium allocation as $(x_0(r), x_1(r), K(r))$. This allocation is unique because u is additively separable with respect to time. By imitating example 9.26 (in section 9.5), it is not hard to make up an example for the Diamond model with a nonseparably additive utility function and with more than one stationary equilibrium allocation.

To visualize this equilibrium graphically, recall from equations 10.34 and 10.35 (in section 10.2) that

$$\overline{x}_0 + \overline{x}_1 = f(\overline{K}, 1) - \overline{K} = r\overline{K} + W.$$

This equation determines the feasibility line from $W + r\overline{K}$ to $W + r\overline{K}$ in figures 10.6 and 10.7, and equation 10.47 determines the budget line through $\overline{x}$ and C in the same figures. The tax, T, equals the distance from C to W in figure 10.6. It is not possible to see the amount of government debt in the figure, because $G = W - \overline{x}_0 - \mathsf{T} - \overline{K}$ and there is no easy way to represent the capital stock, $\overline{K}$. The tax may be negative, as in figure 10.7 where $-\mathsf{T}$ equals the distance from W to C.

It is easy to make up examples in which the tax may be either positive or negative. For instance, suppose that the utility function is $u(x_0, x_1) = \ln(x_0) + \ln(x_1)$. Then, equation 10.44 implies that $\overline{x}_1 = (1 + r)\overline{x}_0$, where r is the interest rate. Since $\overline{x}_0 + \overline{x}_1 = W + r\overline{K}$, it follows that $\overline{x}_0 = (2 + r)^{-1}(W + r\overline{K})$ and $\overline{x}_1 = (1 + r)(2 + r)^{-1}(W + r\overline{K})$. If we substitute these formulas for $\overline{x}_0$ and $\overline{x}_1$ into the consumer's budget equation, $\overline{x}_0 + (1 + r)^{-1}\overline{x}_1 = W - \mathsf{T}$, we see that $2(2 + r)^{-1}(W + r\overline{K}) = W - \mathsf{T}$. Solving this equation for T, we find that $\mathsf{T} = r(2 + r)^{-1}(W - 2\overline{K})$, which is positive if

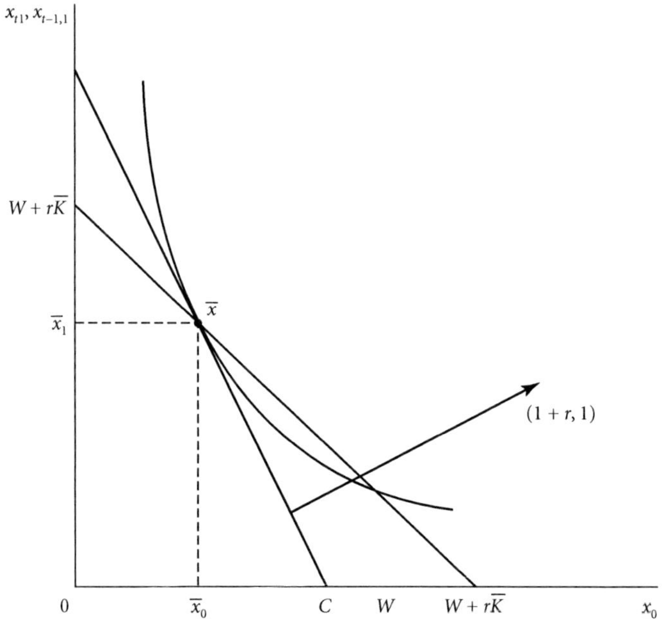

Figure 10.6 Stationary equilibrium in the Diamond model with a positive tax

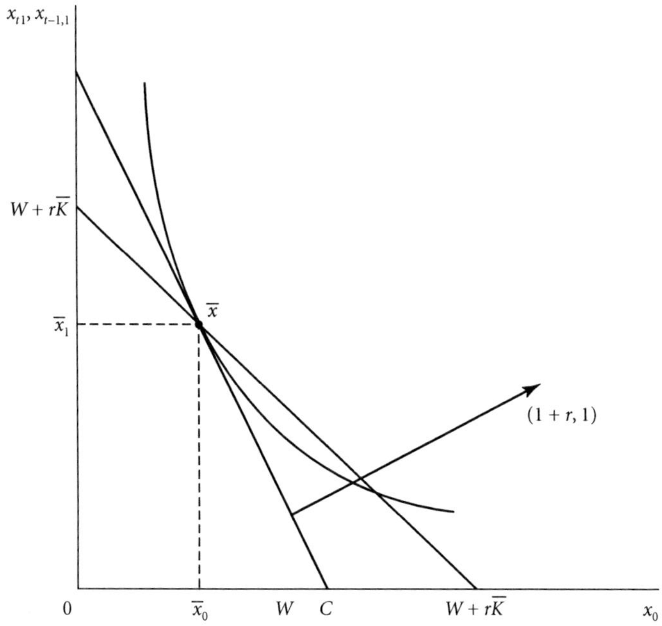

Figure 10.7 Stationary equilibrium in the Diamond model with a negative tax

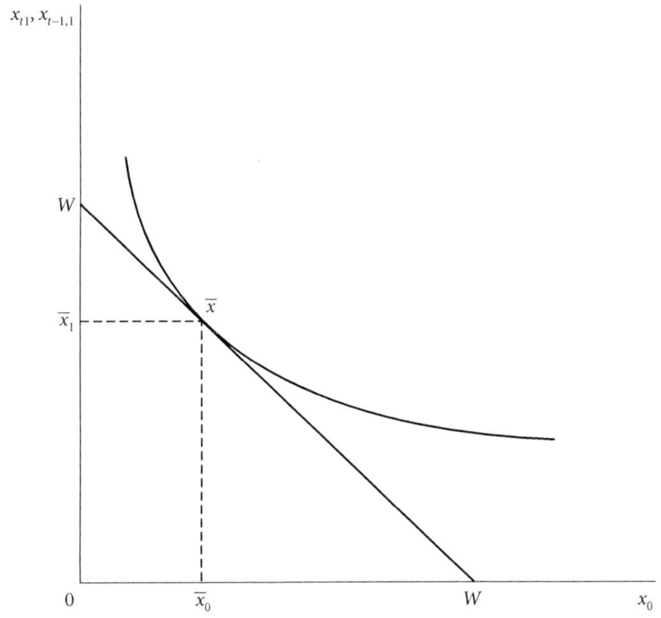

Figure 10.8 Stationary equilibrium in the Diamond model with interest rate 0

and only if $W > 2\overline{K}$. If we let $f(K, L) = \alpha^{-1}K^{\alpha}L^{1-\alpha}$, where $0 < \alpha < 1$, then the equation $\frac{\partial f(\overline{K},1)}{\partial K} = 1 + r$ implies that $\overline{K} = (1+r)^{-\frac{1}{1-\alpha}}$ and hence $W = \frac{\partial f(\overline{K},1)}{\partial L} = \alpha^{-1}(1-\alpha)(1+r)^{-\frac{\alpha}{1-\alpha}}$. Substituting these equations into the inequality $W > 2\overline{K}$, we find that $\mathsf{T} > 0$, if and only if $\frac{1-\alpha}{\alpha} > \frac{2}{1+r}$. It follows that if $r = 1$, then $\mathsf{T} > 0$, $= 0$, or < 0 if $\alpha < \frac{1}{2}$, $\alpha = \frac{1}{2}$, or $\alpha > \frac{1}{2}$, respectively.

If $r = 0$, then the term $r\overline{K}$ disappears from the equation $\overline{x}_0 + \overline{x}_1 = W + r\overline{K}$ and the picture of a stationary equilibrium is as in figure 10.8. This is the stationary equilibrium that maximizes the utility of a typical consumer. Since $W = f(\overline{K}, 1) - \overline{K}$, when $r = 0$, this stationary allocation solves the problem

$$\begin{aligned}&\max_{(x_0, x_1, K, L) \geq 0} [u_0(x_0) + u_1(x_1)]\\ &\text{s.t.}\quad x_0 + x_1 + K \leq f(K, L) \text{ and}\\ &L \leq 1.\end{aligned}$$

Corollary 10.68 (in section 10.13) implies that this allocation is Pareto optimal.

10.4 Stationary Discounted Optima and Equilibria

This section is similar to section 9.4 on the Samuelson model. I consider stationary allocations that are optimal with respect to a welfare function that discounts the utility of future generations at a constant rate. I show that these allocations are optimal if and only if they are the allocations of a stationary spot price equilibrium.

DEFINITION 10.28 Let $r > 0$. A *stationary r-discounted optimum*, $(\overline{x}_0, \overline{x}_1, \overline{K}, \overline{L})$, is a stationary solution to the optimization problem

$$\max_{\substack{x_{t0}\geq 0,\, x_{t-1,1}\geq 0,\\ K_t\geq 0,\, L_t\geq 0,\ \text{for } t=0,1,\ldots}} \left\{(1+r)u_1(x_{-1,1}) + \sum_{t=0}^{\infty}(1+r)^{-t}[u_0(x_{t0}) + u_1(x_{t1})]\right\} \tag{10.50}$$

$$\text{s.t.}\quad x_{00} + x_{-1,1} + K_0 \leq f(\overline{K}_{-1}, L_0),$$

$$x_{t0} + x_{t-1,1} + K_t \leq f(K_{t-1}, L_t), \quad \text{for } t > 0,$$

$$L_t \leq 1, \quad \text{for } t \geq 0,$$

such that $\overline{x}_0 + \overline{x}_1 > 0$, where $\overline{K}_{-1} = \overline{K}$ is given and where a solution, $(x_{t0}, x_{t-1,1}, K_t, L_t)_{t=0}^{\infty}$, is stationary if, for all t, $(x_{t0}, x_{t-1,1}, K_t, L_t) = (x_0, x_1, K, L)$, for some (x_0, x_1, K, L), and if $\overline{K}_{-1} = K$.

THEOREM 10.29 Suppose that assumptions 10.1–10.5 apply. Then any stationary r-discounted optimum is the allocation of a stationary spot price equilibrium with interest rate r.

Proof. Let $(\overline{x}_0, \overline{x}_1, \overline{K}, \overline{L})$ be the stationary r-discounted optimum. By the definition of an optimum, $\overline{x}_0 + \overline{x}_1 > 0$. Because $\overline{x}_0 + \overline{x}_1 > 0$, it follows that $\overline{K} > 0$ and $\overline{L} > 0$, for otherwise, by assumption 10.3, nothing could be produced and so $\overline{x}_0 + \overline{x}_1$ would be 0. Therefore $\frac{\partial f(\overline{K}, \overline{L})}{\partial K} > 0$ and $\frac{\partial f(\overline{K}, \overline{L})}{\partial L} > 0$, by assumption 10.4. By assumption 10.5, u_0, and u_1 are increasing. Therefore $(\overline{x}_0, \overline{x}_1, \overline{K}, \overline{L})$ could not solve problem 10.50 unless $\overline{L} = 1$ and $\overline{x}_0 + \overline{x}_1 + \overline{K} = f(\overline{K}, 1)$.

Assume that $\overline{x}_0 > 0$. An argument similar to what follows applies if $\overline{x}_0 = 0$ and $\overline{x}_1 > 0$.

In problem 10.50, hold all variables fixed at their values in the optimum, except x_{00}, K_0, and x_{10}. Then problem 10.50 reduces to

$$\max_{x_{00}}[u_0(x_{00}) + (1+r)^{-1}u_0(f(\overline{K} + \overline{x}_0 - x_{00}, 1) - \overline{x}_1 - \overline{K})].$$

Since this problem is solved by $x_{00} = \overline{x}_0$ and $\overline{x}_0 > 0$ and $\overline{K} > 0$, it follows that

$$\frac{du_0(\overline{x}_0)}{dx} = (1+r)^{-1}\frac{du_0(\overline{x}_0)}{dx}\frac{\partial f(\overline{K}, 1)}{\partial K},$$

where I have used the fact that $f(\overline{K}, 1) - \overline{x}_1 - \overline{K} = \overline{x}_0$. Since $\frac{du_0(\overline{x}_0)}{dx} > 0$, it follows that $\frac{\partial f(\overline{K}, 1)}{\partial K} = 1 + r$.

Now hold all variables fixed in problem 10.50 except x_{00} and $x_{-1,1}$. Then the problem reduces to

$$\max_{\substack{x_{00}\geq 0,\\ x_{-1,1}\geq 0}} [u_0(x_{00}) + (1+r)u_1(x_{-1,1})]$$

$$\text{s.t.} \quad x_{00} + x_{-1,1} \leq f(\overline{K}, 1) - \overline{K}.$$

Since this problem is solved by $(x_{00}, x_{-1,1}) = (\overline{x}_0, \overline{x}_1)$ and $\overline{x}_0 > 0$ and u_0 and u_1 are concave, the first order conditions for its solution are that for some positive number λ,

$$\frac{du_0(\overline{x}_0)}{dx} = \lambda \text{ and } \frac{du_1(\overline{x}_1)}{dx} \leq \frac{\lambda}{1+r},$$

with equality if $\overline{x}_1 > 0$. Theorem 6.19 (in section 6.4) implies that $(\overline{x}_0, \overline{x}_1)$ solves the problem

$$\max_{x_0\geq 0, x_1\geq 0} [u_0(x_0) + u_1(x_1)]$$

$$\text{s.t.} \quad x_0 + \frac{x_1}{1+r} \leq W - \mathsf{T},$$

where $W = \frac{\partial f(\overline{K}, 1)}{\partial K}$ and $\mathsf{T} = W - \overline{x}_0 - \frac{\overline{x}_1}{1+r}$. Let $G = r^{-1}\mathsf{T}$.

I have shown that $(\overline{x}_0, \overline{x}_1, \overline{K}, \overline{L}, P, W, r, G, \mathsf{T})$ satisfies all the conditions of a stationary spot price equilibrium, where $\overline{L} = 1$ and $P = 1$. In particular, $(K, L) = (\overline{K}, 1)$ solves the profit maximization problem

$$\max_{K\geq 0, L\geq 0} [(1+r)^{-1}(f(K, L) - WL) - K]. \quad \blacksquare$$

Next I show that the allocations of stationary spot price equilibria are r-discounted optima, provided the interest rate is positive.

THEOREM 10.30 Assume that assumptions 10.1–10.5 apply. If a stationary spot price equilibrium, $(\overline{x}_0, \overline{x}_1, \overline{K}, \overline{L}, P, W, r, G, \mathsf{T})$, is such that $r > 0$ and $\overline{x}_0 + \overline{x}_1 > 0$, then $(\overline{x}_0, \overline{x}_1, \overline{K}, \overline{L})$ is a stationary r-discounted optimum.

Proof. First of all, the assumption that $\overline{x}_0 + \overline{x}_1 > 0$ implies that $\overline{K} > 0$ and $\overline{L} > 0$, since $\overline{x}_0 + \overline{x}_1 = f(\overline{K}, \overline{L}) - \overline{K}$ and, by assumption 10.3, $f(\overline{K}, \overline{L}) = 0$, if $\overline{K} = 0$ or $\overline{L} = 0$.

I next show that $P > 0$ and $W > 0$. By the definition of a spot price equilibrium, $(P, W) > 0$ and $(\overline{K}, \overline{L})$ solves the profit maximization problem

$$\max_{K \geq 0, L \geq 0} \{(1+r)^{-1}[Pf(K, L) - WL] - PK\}. \tag{10.51}$$

If $P = 0$, then $W > 0$ and $(\overline{K}, \overline{L})$ can solve this problem only if $\overline{L} = 0$, in which case $\overline{L} < 1$, so that $W = 0$. This contradiction proves that $P > 0$. It now follows that $W > 0$, for if $W = 0$, then problem 10.51 has no solution.

By the definition of a spot price equilibrium, $(\overline{x}_0, \overline{x}_1)$ solves the problem

$$\max_{x_0 \geq 0, x_1 \geq 0} [u_0(x_0) + u_1(x_1)]$$

$$\text{s.t.} \quad Px_0 + (1+r)^{-1}Px_1 \leq W - \mathsf{T}.$$

Since $\overline{x}_0 + \overline{x}_1 > 0$, it follows that $0 < P\overline{x}_0 + (1+r)^{-1}P\overline{x}_1 \leq W - \mathsf{T}$, so that this problem satisfies the positive income condition of proposition 6.14 (in section 6.3). Therefore, that proposition implies that for some positive number λ, $(\overline{x}_0, \overline{x}_1)$ solves the problem

$$\max_{x_0 \geq 0, x_1 \geq 0} [u_0(x_0) + u_1(x_1) - \lambda Px_0 - (1+r)^{-1}\lambda Px_1].$$

Hence $(\overline{x}_0, \overline{x}_1)$ solves

$$\max_{x_0 \geq 0, x_1 \geq 0} [\lambda^{-1}u_0(x_0) + \lambda^{-1}u_1(x_1) - Px_0 - (1+r)^{-1}Px_1]. \tag{10.52}$$

Similarly $\overline{x}_1$ solves

$$\max_{x_1 \geq 0} [\lambda^{-1}(1+r)u_1(x_1) - Px_1]. \tag{10.53}$$

Adding the objectives of problems 10.51 and 10.52, we find that $(x_0, x_1, K, L) = (\overline{x}_0, \overline{x}_1, \overline{K}, 1)$ solves the problem

$$\max_{\substack{x_0 \geq 0, x_1 \geq 0, \\ K \geq 0, L \geq 0}} \{\lambda^{-1}u_0(x_0) + \lambda^{-1}u_1(x_1) - Px_0 - (1+r)^{-1}Px_1 + (1+r)^{-1}[Pf(K, L) - WL] - PK\}. \tag{10.54}$$

Similarly $(x_1, L) = (\overline{x}_1, 1)$ solves the problem

$$\max_{x_1 \geq 0, L \geq 0} [\lambda^{-1}(1+r)u_1(x_1) - Px_1 + Pf(\overline{K}, L) - WL]. \tag{10.55}$$

Let $(x_{t0}, x_{t-1,1}, K_t, L_t)_{t=0}^{\infty}$ be an allocation that is feasible given initial capital $\overline{K}_{-1} = \overline{K}$. I use the value loss method first introduced in proving theorem 9.28 (in section 9.6) to show that

$$\begin{aligned} &(1+r)u_1(\overline{x}_1) + \sum_{t=0}^{\infty}(1+r)^{-t}[u_0(\overline{x}_0) + u_1(\overline{x}_1)] \\ &\geq (1+r)u_1(x_{-1,1}) + \sum_{t=0}^{\infty}(1+r)^{-t}[u_0(x_{t0}) + u_1(x_{t1})]. \end{aligned} \tag{10.56}$$

Let

$$\begin{aligned} \mathcal{L}_{-1}(x_{-1,1}, L_0) &= [(1+r)\lambda^{-1}u_1(\overline{x}_1) - P\overline{x}_1 + Pf(\overline{K}, 1) - W] \\ &- [(1+r)\lambda^{-1}u_1(x_{-1,1}) - Px_{-1,1} + Pf(\overline{K}, L_0) - WL_0]. \end{aligned}$$

Similarly, let

$$\begin{aligned} &\mathcal{L}(x_{t0}, x_{t1}, K_t, L_{t+1}) \\ &= \{\lambda^{-1}[u_0(\overline{x}_0) + u_1(\overline{x}_1)] - P\overline{x}_0 - (1+r)^{-1}P\overline{x}_1 \\ &+ (1+r)^{-1}[Pf(\overline{K}, 1) - W] - P\overline{K}\} \\ &- \{\lambda^{-1}[u_0(x_{t0}) + u_1(x_{t1})] - Px_{t0} - (1+r)^{-1}Px_{t1} \\ &+ (1+r)^{-1}[Pf(K_t, L_{t+1}) - WL_{t+1}] - PK_t\}. \end{aligned}$$

Because $(x_1, L) = (\overline{x}_1, 1)$ solves problem 10.55, it follows that

$$\mathcal{L}_{-1}(x_{-1,1}, L_0) \geq \mathcal{L}_{-1}(\overline{x}_1, 1) = 0. \tag{10.57}$$

Similarly, because $(\overline{x}_0, \overline{x}_1, \overline{K}, 1)$ solves problem 10.54, it follows that

$$\mathcal{L}(x_{t0}, x_{t1}, K_t, L_{t+1}) \geq \mathcal{L}(\overline{x}_0, \overline{x}_1, \overline{K}, 1) = 0. \tag{10.58}$$

Adding inequality 10.57 and 10.58, for all t, we find that

$$
\begin{aligned}
0 &\le \mathcal{L}_{-1}(x_{-1,1}, L_0) + \sum_{t=0}^{\infty}(1+r)^{-t}\mathcal{L}(x_{t0}, x_{t1}, K_t, L_{t+1}) \\
&= \{(1+r)\lambda^{-1}u_1(\overline{x}_1) + \sum_{t=0}^{\infty}(1+r)^{-t}\lambda^{-1}[u_0(\overline{x}_0) + u_1(\overline{x}_1)]\} \\
&\quad - \{(1+r)\lambda^{-1}u_1(x_{-1,1}) + \sum_{t=0}^{\infty}(1+r)^{-t}\lambda^{-1}[u_0(x_{t0}) + u_1(x_{t1})]\} \\
&\quad + P[x_{00} + x_{-1,1} + K_0 - f(\overline{K}, L_0)] \\
&\quad - P[\overline{x}_0 + \overline{x}_1 + \overline{K} - f(\overline{K}, 1)] \\
&\quad + \sum_{t=1}^{\infty}(1+r)^{-t}P[x_{t0} + x_{t-1,1} + K_t - f(K_{t-1}, L_t)] \qquad (10.59) \\
&\quad - \sum_{t=1}^{\infty}(1+r)^{-t}P[\overline{x}_0 + \overline{x}_1 + \overline{K} - f(\overline{K}, 1)] \\
&\quad + \sum_{t=0}^{\infty}(1+r)^{-t}W(L_t - 1) \\
&\le \{(1+r)\lambda^{-1}u_1(\overline{x}_1) + \sum_{t=0}^{\infty}(1+r)^{-t}\lambda^{-1}[u_0(\overline{x}_0) + u_1(\overline{x}_1)]\} \\
&\quad - \{(1+r)\lambda^{-1}u_1(x_{-1,1}) + \sum_{t=0}^{\infty}(1+r)^{-t}\lambda^{-1}[u_0(x_{t0}) + u_1(x_{t1})]\},
\end{aligned}
$$

where the equation follows because the allocations are bounded, so that all the series converge absolutely and their sums do not depend on the order of summation. The second inequality follows in part from the feasibility of the allocation $(x_{t0}, x_{t-1,1}, K_t, L_t)_{t=0}^{\infty}$, so that

$$
\begin{aligned}
&P[x_{00} + x_{-1,1} + K_0 - f(\overline{K}, L_0)] \le 0, \\
&\sum_{t=1}^{\infty}(1+r)^{-t}P[x_{t0} + x_{t-1,1} + K_t - f(K_{t-1}, L_t) \le 0,
\end{aligned}
$$

and

$$\sum_{t=0}^{\infty}(1+r)^{-t}W(L_t - 1) \le 0.$$

Also condition (10) of the definition of a spot price equilibrium (definition 10.12 in section 10.1) implies that

$$P[\overline{x}_0 + \overline{x}_1 + \overline{K} - f(\overline{K}, 1)] = 0$$

and

$$\sum_{t=0}^{\infty}(1+r)^{-t} P[\overline{x}_0 + \overline{x}_1 + \overline{K} - f(\overline{K}, 1)] = 0.$$

If we multiply the extreme left- and right-hand sides of inequality 10.59 by λ, we obtain inequality 10.56, and the verification of that inequality completes the proof of the theorem. ▪

It is easy to see that stationary spot price equilibria exist for interest rates in a certain interval.

THEOREM 10.31 There exist $\underline{r}$ and $\overline{r}$, where $-1 < \underline{r} < 0 < \overline{r} \leq \infty$, and there exists a unique stationary spot price equilibrium $(\overline{x}_0, \overline{x}_1, \overline{K}, \overline{L}, P, W, r, G, \mathsf{T})$ with $P = 1$ and $\overline{x}_0 + \overline{x}_1 > 0$, for any r such that $\underline{r} < r < \overline{r}$. No such equilibrium exists if $r \leq \underline{r}$ or $r \geq \overline{r}$.

Proof. From the proof of proposition 10.8 (in section 10.1), we know that there exists a positive number $\hat{K}$ such that $f(\hat{K}, 1) = \hat{K}$, $f(K, 1) > K$, if $0 < K < \hat{K}$, and $f(K, 1) < K$, if $K > \hat{K}$. Let $\overline{r} = \frac{\partial f(0,1)}{\partial K} - 1$. Since $f(K, 1)$ is concave by assumption 10.4 and $f(K, 1) > K$, for some K, it follows that $\overline{r} > 0$. Let $\underline{r} = \frac{\partial f(\hat{K},1)}{\partial K} - 1$, and let $K(0)$ be the value of K that solves the problem

$$\max_{K \geq 0}[f(K, 1) - K].$$

By assumption 10.2, $f(K(0), 1) - K(0) > 0$, so that $K(0) < \hat{K}$. Since $f(K, 1)$ is a strictly concave function and $\frac{\partial f(K(0),1)}{\partial K} - 1 = 0$, it follows that $\underline{r} < 0$. If $r > -1$, let $K(r)$ be the unique capital stock such that $\frac{\partial f(K(r),1)}{\partial K} \leq 1 + r$, with equality if $K(r) > 0$. Then $0 < K(r) < \hat{K}$, if and only if $\underline{r} < r < \overline{r}$.

If $\underline{r} < r < \overline{r}$, let $\overline{K} = K(r)$ and let $(\overline{x}_0, \overline{x}_1)$ solve the problem

$$\max_{x_0 \geq 0, x_1 \geq 0} [u_0(x_0) + (1+r)u_1(x_1)]$$

$$\text{s.t.} \quad x_0 + x_1 = f(\overline{K}, 1) - \overline{K}.$$

Since u_0 and u_1 are continuous and strictly concave, $(\overline{x}_0, \overline{x}_1)$ exists and is unique. Since $f(\overline{K}, 1) - \overline{K} > 0$, it follows that $\overline{x}_0 + \overline{x}_1 > 0$. Let

$$W = \frac{\partial f(\overline{K}, 1)}{\partial L},$$

and let $G = (1+r)^{-1}\overline{x}_1 - \overline{K}$ and $\mathsf{T} = rG$. Then $(\overline{x}_0, \overline{x}_1, \overline{K}, \overline{L}, P, W, r, G, \mathsf{T})$ is a stationary spot price equilibrium with $P = 1$ and where $\overline{L} = 1$. It is not hard to see that all variables are uniquely defined, given the choice of P.

If $r \leq \underline{r}$ or $r \geq \overline{r}$, then $f(K(r), 1) - K(r) \leq 0$, so that it is not possible to define a stationary spot price equilibrium with interest rate r and such that $\overline{x}_0 + \overline{x}_1 > 0$. ▪

An immediate consequence of the previous two theorems is that there exists a unique stationary r-discounted optimal allocation, $(\overline{x}_0, \overline{x}_1, \overline{K}, \overline{L})$, with $\overline{x}_0 + \overline{x}_1 > 0$, provided $\underline{r} < r < \overline{r}$.

10.5 Social Security

Social security may be included in the Diamond model by introducing lump-sum payments that are made or received by both young and old consumers. A spot market equilibrium with social security and a constant positive interest rate, r, is $(\overline{\mathbf{x}}, \overline{\mathbf{K}}, \overline{\mathbf{L}}, \mathbf{P}, \mathbf{W}, \mathbf{r}, G, \mathbf{T})$, where

$$\mathbf{T} = (\mathsf{T}_{-1,1}, (\mathsf{T}_0 + \mathsf{T}_{00}, \mathsf{T}_{01}), (\mathsf{T}_1 + \mathsf{T}_{10}, \mathsf{T}_{11}), \ldots),$$

the budget set of consumer -1 is

$$\{x_1 \geq 0 \mid P_0 x_1 \leq P_1 f(\overline{K}_{-1}, \overline{L}_0) - W_0 \overline{L}_0 + (1+r)G - \mathsf{T}_{-1,1}\},$$

and the budget set of consumer t, for $t \geq 0$, is

$$\{(x_0, x_1) \geq 0 \mid P_t x_0 + (1+r)^{-1} P_{t+1} x_1 \leq W_t - \mathsf{T}_t - \mathsf{T}_{t0} - (1+r)^{-1}\mathsf{T}_{t1}\}.$$

Consumer t pays, when young, a regular lump-sum tax of T_t and a social security lump-sum contribution of T_{t0} and receives, when old, a lump-sum social security benefit of $-\mathsf{T}_{t1}$.

You might assume that social security discourages saving, investment, and economic growth because it reduces the need for young people to provide for their old age, a point of view advanced by Feldstein (1974). We will see that theoretically this intuition is not necessarily valid. I test the idea by comparing stationary equilibria with and without social security. If the introduction of social security increases the steady state interest rate, it decreases the steady state capital stock and has the contrary effect if it increases the interest rate. I could consider the impact of social security on nonstationary growth paths, but conclusions would be harder to derive and more ambiguous. Stationary equilibria are, to some extent, made more relevant by the turnpike theorem introduced in section 10.12, for this theorem suggests that a modern economy may be close to an optimal steady state.

Before considering social security directly, I show that the interest rate in a stationary spot price equilibrium may be thought of as depending on total tax collections. Let $(x_0(r), x_1(r), K(r), W(r), r, G(r), \mathsf{T}(r))$ be a stationary spot price equilibrium of the Diamond model in which the price of the produced good is normalized to be 1 and there is no social security. Since the price level is fixed to be 1, $W(r)$ is the real wage, r is the real interest rate, and $\mathsf{T}(r)$ is the tax rate in real terms. The budget equation of a consumer may be written as

$$\mathsf{T}(r) = W(r) - x_0(r) - (1+r)^{-1}x_1(r).$$

I treat $\mathsf{T}(r)$ as the function $W(r) - x_0(r) - (1+r)^{-1}x_1(r)$. If we assume that the tax is fixed and equals T, then r satisfies the equation

$$\mathsf{T}(r) = T.$$

Think of T as the level of the regular lump-sum tax before the introduction of social security. Although the equation $\mathsf{T}(r) = T$ may have multiple solutions for one value of T, we can imagine that it implicitly defines r as a function of T, for T near some particular value. Suppose that the function $\mathsf{T}(r)$ is continuously differentiable and that for a particular value of r, say, $\overline{r}$,

$$\frac{d\mathsf{T}(\overline{r})}{dr} \neq 0.$$

Let $\overline{T} = \mathsf{T}(\overline{r})$ and assume that if T is changed a little bit from its initial value, $\overline{T}$, then the value of r in the new stationary equilibrium will equal the differentiable function $r(T) = \mathsf{T}^{-1}(T)$, for values of T close to $\overline{T} = \mathsf{T}(\overline{r})$. Since

$$\frac{dr(\overline{T})}{dT} = \left(\frac{d\mathsf{T}(\overline{r})}{dr}\right)^{-1},$$

it follows that $\frac{dr(\overline{T})}{dT}$ and $\frac{d\mathsf{T}(\overline{r})}{dr}$ have the same sign.

Suppose that a social security program is introduced that obliges young consumers to pay an additional lump-sum tax of T_0 and pays old consumers a lump-sum benefit of $-\mathsf{T}_1$, where $\mathsf{T}_0 > 0$ and $\mathsf{T}_1 < 0$. Suppose that before the introduction of social security, the interest rate is $\overline{r}$ and the regular lump-sum tax paid by young consumers is $\overline{T} = \mathsf{T}(\overline{r})$. Assume that this tax is held fixed at $\overline{T}$ after social security is instituted. In the resulting new stationary equilibrium with consumption vector (x_0, x_1) and interest rate r, a consumer's budget equation is

$$x_0 + (1+r)^{-1}x_1 = W - \overline{T} - \mathsf{T}_0 - (1+r)^{-1}\mathsf{T}_1$$
$$= W - [\overline{T} + \mathsf{T}_0 + (1+r)^{-1}\mathsf{T}_1].$$

It can be seen from this equation that social security has the same impact on the budget constraint as increasing the regular tax, $\overline{T}$, by the amount $\mathsf{T}_0 + (1+r)^{-1}\mathsf{T}_1$. That is,

$$W(r) - x_0(r) - (1+r)^{-1}x_1(r) = \mathsf{T}(r) = \overline{T} + \mathsf{T}_0 + (1+r)^{-1}\mathsf{T}_1.$$

Social security may be said to be a fair investment or *fully funded* if

$$\mathsf{T}_0 + (1+r)^{-1}\mathsf{T}_1 = 0.$$

For social security satisfying this condition, it is as if the social security contribution, T_0, paid by the young was invested at the going interest rate, r, and the revenue plus interest were returned to the payers in their old age. Such social security has no impact on the steady state interest rate and allocation because it has no impact on consumer budgets. Fully funded social security does, however, affect government debt. The government debt without social security, G, satisfies the equation

$$\overline{r}G = \overline{T},$$

so that

$$G = \overline{r}^{-1}\overline{T},$$

where $\overline{T}$ is the level of the regular tax in the stationary equilibrium without social security. Government debt with social security, G_S, satisfies the equation

$$\overline{r}G_S = \overline{\mathsf{T}} + \mathsf{T}_0 + \mathsf{T}_1 = \overline{T} + \mathsf{T}_0 - (1+\overline{r})\mathsf{T}_0 = \overline{T} - \overline{r}\mathsf{T}_0,$$

so that

$$G_S = \bar{r}^{-1}\overline{T} - \mathsf{T}_0 = G - \mathsf{T}_0,$$

where these equations are valid because fully funded social security does not change the interest rate. Fully funded social security replaces government debt on a dollar for dollar basis, because every dollar paid as a social security tax in youth reduces by a dollar the youth's need to save and buy government debt.

We can imagine that the transition in period 0 from an equilibrium with no social security to one with fully funded social security occurs as follows. In period 0, no benefit is paid to the old person of that period, as he or she paid no social security tax when young. However, a tax of T_0 is collected from the young person in that period, who receives a benefit of $-\mathsf{T}_1$ in period 1 when old. There is no change in either consumer's spending or in the interest rate. The payment of T_0 by the young person of period 0 reduces the government debt by T_0 in period 0, and this reduction in the government debt is permanent. The reduction in government debt by T_0 decreases government expenditures by $\bar{r}\mathsf{T}_0$ in every period, exactly offsetting the increase in government net expenditures resulting directly from social security. This increase is $-\mathsf{T}_0 - \mathsf{T}_1 = \bar{r}\mathsf{T}_0$ and occurs in period 1 and in every period thereafter.

Social security is said to be *pay-as-you-go* if

$$\mathsf{T}_0 + \mathsf{T}_1 = 0.$$

If social security is pay as you go, then

$$\mathsf{T}_0 + \frac{1}{1+r}\mathsf{T}_1 = \frac{r}{1+r}\mathsf{T}_0 > 0.$$

Hence, pay-as-you-go social security has the same effect as an increase in the regular lump-sum tax paid in youth. To calculate the impact of pay-as-you-go social security on the interest rate, hold the regular tax fixed at the level $\overline{T}$. Then

$$\mathsf{T}(r) = \overline{T} + \mathsf{T}_0 + \frac{\mathsf{T}_1}{1+r} = \overline{T} + \frac{r}{1+r}\mathsf{T}_0,$$

so that

$$T(r) - \frac{r}{1+r}\mathsf{T}_0 = \overline{T}. \tag{10.60}$$

Suppose we start with $\mathsf{T}_0 = 0$. To calculate the impact of a small increase in T_0 on the stationary equilibrium interest rate r, I differentiate equation 10.60 implicitly with respect to T_0, obtaining

$$\frac{d\mathsf{T}(r)}{dr}\frac{dr}{d\mathsf{T}_0} - \frac{1}{(1+r)^2}\mathsf{T}_0\frac{dr}{d\mathsf{T}_0} - \frac{r}{1+r} = 0.$$

Because $\mathsf{T}_0 = 0$, this equation implies that

$$\frac{dr}{d\mathsf{T}_0} = \left(\frac{d\mathsf{T}(r)}{dr}\right)^{-1}\frac{r}{1+r},$$

so that $\frac{d\mathsf{T}(r)}{dr}$ and $\frac{dr}{d\mathsf{T}_0}$ have the same sign, provided r is positive.[3]

With pay-as-you-go social security, government debt with social security, G_S, satisfies the equation

$$G_S = r^{-1}(\overline{T} + \mathsf{T}_0 + \mathsf{T}_1) = r^{-1}\overline{T}.$$

Therefore, G_S varies inversely with r, so that $\frac{dG_S}{d\mathsf{T}_0}$ and $\frac{dr}{d\mathsf{T}_0}$ have opposite signs, provided r is positive.

Three important things to notice about social security are as follows:

1. Although social security can influence the interest rate, the direction of the influence is ambiguous.
2. No matter what this influence may be, the stationary equilibrium that occurs with social security is Pareto optimal as long as the equilibrium interest rate is nonnegative; the new equilibrium is Pareto optimal even if social security increases the interest rate and hence reduces investment and the capital stock.
3. The regular tax, T, can be changed so as to offset any impact that social security might have on the interest rate. That is, if the interest rate is $\overline{r}$ and the regular tax, T, is changed from the level $\overline{T}$ to

$$\underline{T} = \overline{T} - \left[\mathsf{T}_0 + \frac{\mathsf{T}_1}{1+\overline{r}}\right]$$

3. Blanchard and Fischer (1989) discuss the effects of a fully funded and pay-as-you-go social security on pages 110–114. They do their analysis in the context of an overlapping generations model with population growth and also for a model with a bequest motive. Another interesting paper on the topic is Diamond and Geanakoplos (2003).

at the same time that social security is introduced, then social security has no effect on the interest rate.

There will, however, be an impact on the steady state level of government debt. The government debt before social security is

$$G = \overline{r}^{-1}\overline{T}.$$

After the introduction of social security and adjustment of the lump-sum tax to equal $\underline{T}$, the government debt in a stationary equilibrium becomes $\underline{G}$, where

$$\overline{r}\underline{G} = \underline{T} + \mathsf{T}_0 + \mathsf{T}_1 = \overline{T} - \mathsf{T}_0 - \frac{\mathsf{T}_1}{1+\overline{r}} + \mathsf{T}_0 + \mathsf{T}_1 = \overline{T} + \frac{\overline{r}}{1+\overline{r}}\mathsf{T}_1,$$

so that

$$\underline{G} = \overline{r}^{-1}\overline{T} + \frac{\mathsf{T}_1}{1+\overline{r}} = G + \frac{\mathsf{T}_1}{1+\overline{r}}.$$

Because $\mathsf{T}_1 < 0$, the above equation implies that the introduction of social security reduces government debt by $-\frac{\mathsf{T}_1}{1+\overline{r}}$. It does so because it reduces the need for personal saving by this amount.

An example may clarify the analysis.

EXAMPLE 10.32 Consider the Diamond model in which

$$f(K, L) = 2\sqrt{KL}$$

and

$$u(x_0, x_1) = \ln(x_0) + \ln(x_1).$$

I calculate a stationary equilibrium with a positive interest rate r with no social security and with a fixed lump-sum tax paid by youth. The equation $\frac{\partial f(K(r), 1)}{\partial K} = 1 + r$ implies that

$$K(r) = \frac{1}{(1+r)^2}.$$

Using equations 10.43, 10.44, and 10.46–10.48 (in section 10.3), it is easy to calculate that

$$x_0(r) = \frac{1+2r}{(2+r)(1+r)^2} \text{ and } x_1(r) = \frac{1+2r}{(2+r)(1+r)},$$

$$W(r) = \frac{1}{1+r},$$

$$G(r) = \frac{-1+r}{(2+r)(1+r)^2},$$

and

$$T(r) = \frac{-r+r^2}{(2+r)(1+r)^2}.$$

From the last formula above, it follows that

$$\frac{d\mathsf{T}(r)}{dr} = \frac{-2+6r+3r^2-r^3}{(2+r)^2(1+r)^3}.$$

If $r = 0.25$, then

$$x_0 = 0.42666,\ x_1 = 0.5333,\ K = 0.64,\ W = 0.8,\ G = -0.21333,$$
$$T = -0.05333,$$

and

$$\frac{d\mathsf{T}(0.25)}{dr} = -0.033185.$$

Notice that equation $\mathsf{T}(r) = T$ has multiple solutions for some values of T, since the function $\mathsf{T}(r)$ is decreasing for small values of r and increasing for larger values.

If we start from the steady state equilibrium with $\overline{r} = 1/4$ and $\overline{T} = -12/225$, and introduce pay-as-you-go social security with $\mathsf{T}_0 = 0.1 = -\mathsf{T}_1$, then equation 10.60 becomes

$$\frac{-r+r^2}{(2+r)(1+r)^2} - \frac{r}{1+r}\frac{1}{10} = -\frac{12}{225},$$

which reduces to the cubic equation

$$48 - 420r + 411r^2 - 21r^3 = 0.$$

A solution of this equation is $r = 0.131$, which is less than 0.25, the interest rate before social security. The fact that pay-as-you-go social security could reduce the interest rate is consistent with the fact that

$$\frac{d\mathsf{T}(0.25)}{dr} = -0.033185 < 0.$$

10.6 Population Growth

There has been increased public awareness in recent years of the impact of population growth on the ease of paying for social security pension benefits. Reduced population growth in wealthy countries has increased the proportion of the population receiving benefits and so has increased the social security tax burden on the working population. The overlapping generations model provides a convenient framework for considering the impact of population growth on the burden of social security as well as on social welfare. I briefly discuss the impact of population growth on social security in a stationary equilibrium and then turn to the impact on welfare. In both cases, I consider only stationary equilibrium allocations that maximize per capita utility among all stationary allocations. In the model, the maximum can be achieved with or without social security by appropriate fiscal and monetary policy.

Consider a Diamond model that satisfies assumptions 10.1–10.4 (in section 10.1) and assume that population grows at rate g, where $g > -1$. That is, if there are N identical young people in one generation, there are $(1+g)N$ identical young people in the succeeding one. Let K be the stationary amount of capital input in one period per young person of that period, and let x_0 and x_1 be the stationary consumption of a young and an old person, respectively. By a stationary allocation, I mean one in which these quantities do not depend on time. Because of population growth, if K units of capital per current young person are invested in production in each period, then $\frac{K}{1+g}$ units of capital per period t young person are used in production in period $t-1$. Therefore the amount of production in the current period per current young person is $f(K/(1+g), 1)$. Similarly the consumption by the old per young person in any period is $x_1/(1+g)$. Therefore, the feasibility condition for a stationary allocation is

$$x_0 + \frac{x_1}{1+g} + K = f\left(\frac{K}{1+g}, 1\right).$$

The stationary allocation that maximizes the utility of a typical consumer solves the problem

$$\begin{aligned} &\max_{x_0 \geq 0,\, x_1 \geq 0,\, K \geq 0} \quad u_0(x_0, x_1) \\ &\text{s.t.} \quad x_0 + \frac{x_1}{1+g} + K \leq f\left(\frac{K}{1+g}, 1\right), \end{aligned} \qquad (10.61)$$

where $u(x_0, x_1)$ is the lifetime utility of a consumer. The solution to this problem can be thought of as the golden rule allocation with constant population growth. Assume that u is twice continuously differentiable and everywhere has positive first derivatives and a negative definite second derivative.

You can see by inspecting problem 10.61 that the maximizing allocation is realized by the allocation, $(x_0, x_1, K, L) = (\overline{x}_0, \overline{x}_1, \overline{K}, 1)$, of a stationary equilibrium with interest rate g. I show that there is no lump-sum tax in this golden rule equilibrium. Profit maximization implies that

$$\frac{\partial f\left(\frac{K}{1+g}, 1\right)}{\partial L} = W,$$

where W is the wage, and

$$\frac{\partial f\left(\frac{K}{1+g}, 1\right)}{\partial k} = 1 + g,$$

where k represents the first variable in the function $f(k, L)$. Because f is homogeneous of degree 1 by assumption 10.1, Euler's equation implies that

$$f\left(\frac{K}{1+g}, 1\right) = \left(\frac{\partial f\left(\frac{K}{1+g}, 1\right)}{\partial k}\right)\left(\frac{K}{1+g}\right) + \frac{\partial f\left(\frac{K}{1+g}, 1\right)}{\partial L} = K + W,$$

so that feasibility implies that

$$x_0 + \frac{x_1}{1+g} = f\left(\frac{K}{1+g}, 1\right) - K = W. \qquad (10.62)$$

This last equation implies that when the lump-sum tax is 0, a consumer satisfies his or her budget constraint in the stationary equilibrium.

Suppose that there is social security in the above equilibrium and that the social security taxes are T_0 and T_1 in youth and old age, respectively. Since there are $1 + g$ times more youths than old people in each period, the social security is pay as you go if

$$\mathsf{T}_0 + \frac{\mathsf{T}_1}{1+g} = 0. \qquad (10.63)$$

The budget constraint for a consumer in a stationary equilibrium with interest rate g and this social security system is

$$x_0 + \frac{x_1}{1+g} \leq W - \left(\mathsf{T}_0 + \frac{\mathsf{T}_1}{1+g}\right). \tag{10.64}$$

Equations 10.62 and 10.63 imply that equation 10.64 is satisfied in the equilibrium with interest rate g as long as social security is pay as you go.

Imagine that the economy is in a stationary equilibrium with interest rate and population growth rate equal to g and with lump-sum social security taxes $\overline{\mathsf{T}}_0$ and $\overline{\mathsf{T}}_1$. Suppose that the population growth rate declines to $\underline{g}$, where $\underline{g} < g$ and that after this decline the economy reaches a new stationary equilibrium with interest rate $\underline{g}$. If the government wishes to maintain pay-as-you-go social security with a benefit level of $-\overline{\mathsf{T}}_1$, then it will have to increase the level of social security contributions from $\overline{\mathsf{T}}_0 = -\frac{\overline{\mathsf{T}}_1}{1+g}$ to $\mathsf{T}_0 = -\frac{\overline{\mathsf{T}}_1}{1+\underline{g}}$. The decrease in population growth increases the tax burden on the young, though pay-as-you-go social security itself has no effect on economic welfare in the stationary golden rule equilibrium.

I now turn to the impact of population growth on the maximum per capita welfare achievable by a stationary allocation. The effect is easiest to see in the Samuelson model with only one good. Suppose that each young person is endowed with one unit of the good and each old person is endowed with none. In order to maximize the utility of a typical person in a stationary allocation with population growing at rate g, society must solve the problem

$$\begin{aligned} &\max_{x_0 \geq 0, x_1 \geq 0} \quad u(x_0, x_1) \\ &\text{s.t.} \quad x_0 + \frac{x_1}{1+g} \leq 1. \end{aligned} \tag{10.65}$$

The form of this problem is the same as that of utility maximization by a consumer who has an income of one unit and buys two goods with prices 1 and $(1+g)^{-1}$, respectively. An increase in g reduces the price of the second good and therefore increases the maximum utility. The utility maximization problem may be visualized in figure 10.9, which shows the effect of an increase in the growth rate from g to $\overline{g}$. Clearly, an increase in the rate of population growth increases the lifetime utility of a typical consumer.

This conclusion may not be valid when there is capital. Consider the one-sector Diamond model in which each consumer's sole endowment is one unit of labor in youth and a consumer's lifetime utility is $u(x_0, x_1)$. If

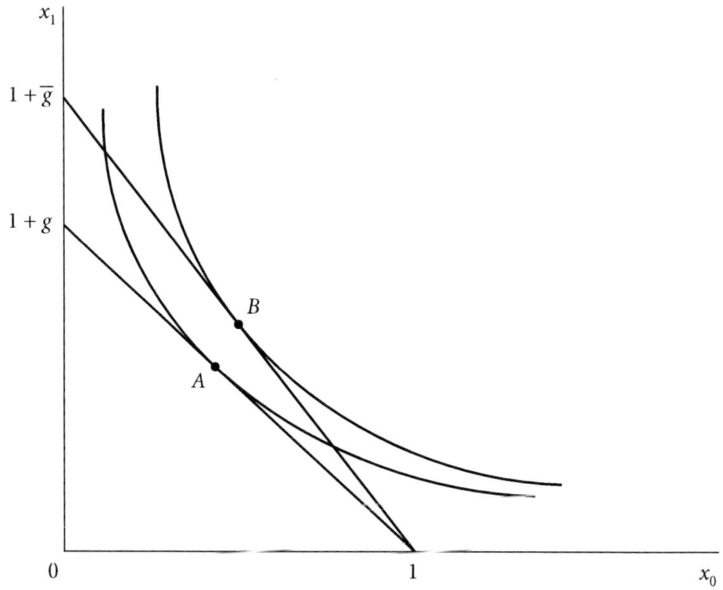

Figure 10.9 The impact of population growth on welfare in the Samuelson model

population grows at the rate g, the stationary allocation that maximizes the utility of a typical consumer is the solution of problem 10.61. This problem may be decomposed into two problems, one involving the choice of capital and the other involving the choice of consumption. The capital choice problem is

$$\max_{K\geq 0}\left[f\left(\frac{K}{1+g},1\right)-K\right]. \tag{10.66}$$

Let $K(g)$ be the optimal value of K in this problem and let

$$C(g)=f\left(\frac{K(g)}{1+g},1\right)-K(g)$$

be the optimal level of output available per young person in a period for consumption by young and old. The consumption choice problem is

$$\begin{aligned}&\max_{x_0\geq 0,x_1\geq 0} \quad u(x_0,x_1)\\ &\text{s.t.}\quad x_0+\frac{x_1}{1+g}\leq C(g),\end{aligned} \tag{10.67}$$

which resembles problem 10.65 for the Samuelson model. The capital choice problem may be simplified by letting

$$k = \frac{K}{1+g}$$

and letting $F(k) = f(k, 1)$. Problem 10.66 then becomes

$$\max_{K \geq 0}[F(k) - (1+g)k]. \tag{10.68}$$

Let $k(g)$ be the optimal value of k in this problem, so that $C(g) = F(k(g)) - (1+g)k(g)$. The task, therefore, is to study the impact of changes in g on the solution of problems 10.67 and 10.68.

To simplify the analysis, assume that u is twice differentiable, that $Du(x_0, x_1) \gg 0$, and that $D^2u(x_0, x_1)$ is negative definite, for all (x_0, x_1). Assume also that F is twice differentiable and that the first derivative is everywhere positive and that the second is everywhere negative. Suppose that $k(g) > 0$ in the relevant range of g. The first order condition for the solution of problem 10.68 is

$$\frac{dF(k(g))}{dk} = 1 + g. \tag{10.69}$$

Under the stated assumptions, $k(g)$ is a differentiable function of g and

$$\begin{aligned} \frac{dC(g)}{dg} &= \frac{dF(k(g))}{dk}\frac{dk(g)}{dg} - (1+g)\frac{dk(g)}{dg} - k(g) \\ &= -k(g) = -\frac{K(g)}{1+g}, \end{aligned} \tag{10.70}$$

where the second equation follows from equation 10.69 (or from the envelope theorem). Therefore, the total amount of output per young person available for consumption decreases as population growth increases. This decrease occurs, because greater population growth dilutes the amount of capital per person inherited from the past or increases the amount that must be invested to maintain a given level of capital per person. That the function $C(g)$ is decreasing may be seen in figure 10.10, where the variable y is output per young person. When the population growth rate increases from g to $\overline{g}$, the amount of output available for consumption per youth decreases from the distance AB to the distance CD.

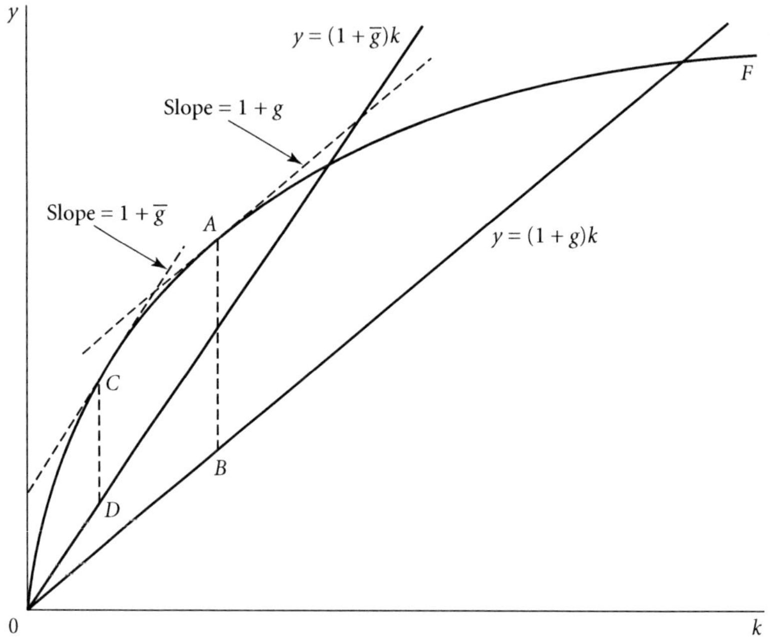

Figure 10.10 The impact of an increase in population growth on total consumption per young person

I use the Slutsky equation to calculate a formula for the total impact on lifetime utility in the stationary golden rule allocation of a change in the rate of population growth. I write the solution of the problem

$$\max_{(x_0, x_1)\geq 0} \quad u(x_0, x_1)$$
$$\text{s.t.} \quad x_0 + p_1 x_1 \leq w$$

as $(x_0(p_1, w), x_1(p_1, w))$, where p_1 is the price of consumption in old age. If we substitute $C(g)$ for w, then the Slutsky equation implies that

$$\frac{dx_i(g)}{dg} = \left[\left. \frac{\partial x_i}{\partial p_1} \right|_{u(x_0, x_1)=\overline{u}} - x_1(g)\frac{\partial x_i}{\partial w} \right] \frac{dp_1}{dg} + \frac{\partial x_i}{\partial w}\frac{dC(g)}{dg} \qquad (10.71)$$

for $i = 0$ or 1, where $\overline{u}$ equals $u(x_0(g), x_1(g))$ at the level of g where the derivative is taken. The first term inside the brackets in equation 10.71 is the substitution effect, and the second term is the income effect. Using this equation, I obtain

$$\frac{du(x_0(g), x_1(g))}{dg} = \frac{\partial u(x_0(g), x_1(g))}{\partial x_0}\frac{dx_0(g)}{dg} + \frac{\partial u(x_0(g), x_1(g))}{\partial x_1}\frac{dx_1(g)}{dg}$$

$$= \left[\frac{\partial u}{\partial x_0}\frac{\partial x_0}{\partial p_1}\bigg|_{u=\bar{u}} + \frac{\partial u}{\partial x_1}\frac{\partial x_1}{\partial p_1}\bigg|_{u=\bar{u}}\right]\left(\frac{dp_1}{dg}\right)$$

$$- x_1(g)\left(\frac{\partial u}{\partial x_0}\frac{\partial x_0}{\partial w} + \frac{\partial u}{\partial x_1}\frac{\partial x_1}{\partial w}\right)\left(\frac{dp_1}{dg}\right) \tag{10.72}$$

$$+ \left(\frac{\partial u}{\partial x_0}\frac{\partial x_0}{\partial w} + \frac{\partial u}{\partial x_1}\frac{\partial x_1}{\partial w}\right)\frac{dC(g)}{dg}.$$

Since the substitution effects are calculated while keeping utility constant, it follows that

$$\frac{\partial u}{\partial x_0}\frac{\partial x_0}{\partial p_1}\bigg|_{u=\bar{u}} + \frac{\partial u}{\partial x_1}\frac{\partial x_1}{\partial p_1}\bigg|_{u=\bar{u}} = 0. \tag{10.73}$$

If we let $p_1 = \frac{1}{1+g}$, we see that

$$\frac{dp_1}{dg} = -\frac{1}{(1+g)^2}. \tag{10.74}$$

In addition,

$$\frac{\partial u}{\partial x_0}\frac{\partial x_0}{\partial w} + \frac{\partial u}{\partial x_1}\frac{\partial x_1}{\partial w} = \frac{du(x_0, x_1)}{dw}. \tag{10.75}$$

By substituting equations 10.70 and 10.73–10.75 into equation 10.72, we see that

$$\frac{du(x_0(g), x_1(g))}{dg} = \frac{du(x_0, x_1)}{dw}\left(\frac{x_1(g)}{(1+g)^2} - \frac{K(g)}{1+g}\right)$$

$$= \frac{1}{(1+g)^2}\frac{du(x_0, x_1)}{dw}[x_1(g) - (1+g)K(g)].$$

Since

$$\frac{du(x_0, x_1)}{dw} > 0,$$

the utility of a typical consumer in the golden rule allocation increases with increased population growth if and only if

$$x_1(g) - (1+g)K(g) > 0.$$

The term $x_1(g)$ stems from the positive effect of population growth on utility that was seen in the Samuelson model. The term $-(1+g)K(g)$

stems from the negative effect of population growth on $C(g)$, which is the output that is available for consumption per young person.

The optimum rate of population growth is discussed in Samuelson (1975, 1976) and Deardorff (1976).[4]

10.7 Discounted Optimal and Equilibrium Allocations

The welfare optimization problem analogous to problem 9.44 (in section 9.6) is

$$\max_{\substack{(x,\,y)\text{ is a feasible}\\ \text{allocation with initial capital } \overline{K}_{-1}}} \left\{\lambda_{-1}^{-1} u_1(x_{-1,1}) + \sum_{t=0}^{\infty} \lambda_t^{-1}[u_0(x_{t0}) + u_1(x_{t1})]\right\}, \quad (10.76)$$

where $\lambda_t > 0$, for all t, $\sum_{t=-1}^{\infty} \lambda_t^{-1} < \infty$, and $\overline{K}_{-1}$ is fixed. From the analysis of problem 9.44, we expect a theorem saying that if $(\overline{\mathbf{x}}, \overline{\mathbf{K}}, \overline{\mathbf{L}}, \mathbf{p}, \mathbf{w}, \boldsymbol{\tau})$ is an Arrow-Debreu equilibrium with transfer payments such that $\sum_{t=0}^{\infty} p_t < \infty$, then its allocation solves problem 10.76, where λ_t is consumer t's marginal utility of unit of account in the equilibrium and $\sum_{t=-1}^{\infty} \lambda_t^{-1} < \infty$. We also expect that if $(\overline{\mathbf{x}}, \overline{\mathbf{K}}, \overline{\mathbf{L}})$ solves problem 10.76, then $(\overline{\mathbf{x}}, \overline{\mathbf{K}}, \overline{\mathbf{L}})$ is the allocation of an Arrow-Debreu equilibrium, $(\overline{\mathbf{x}}, \overline{\mathbf{K}}, \overline{\mathbf{L}}, \mathbf{p}, \mathbf{w}, \boldsymbol{\tau})$, such that $\sum_{t=0}^{\infty} p_t < \infty$. The second statement is much harder to demonstrate than the first one. The difficulty has to do with the behavior of consumption. The proof of the corresponding statement in theorem 9.32 (in section 9.6) depends on the fact that total consumption equals the total endowment and so is bounded away from 0. Because consumption is bounded away from 0, it is possible to prove that $\sum_{t=0}^{\infty} p_t < \infty$ if $\sum_{t=-1}^{\infty} \lambda_t^{-1} < \infty$. In a model with capital, we must prove that optimal consumption is bounded away from 0. The next theorem is the assertion that $(\overline{\mathbf{x}}, \overline{\mathbf{K}}, \overline{\mathbf{L}})$ is the allocation of an Arrow-Debreu equilibrium; it says nothing about the summability of prices.

THEOREM 10.33 Assume that assumptions 10.1–10.5 (in section 10.1) apply. If the allocation $(\overline{\mathbf{x}}, \overline{\mathbf{K}}, \overline{\mathbf{L}})$ solves problem 10.76 and $\overline{K}_{-1} > 0$, then $(\overline{\mathbf{x}}, \overline{\mathbf{K}}, \overline{\mathbf{L}})$ is the allocation of an Arrow-Debreu equilibrium with transfer payments, $(\overline{\mathbf{x}}, \overline{\mathbf{K}}, \overline{\mathbf{L}}, \mathbf{p}, \mathbf{w}, \boldsymbol{\tau})$, where, for each t, the number λ_t is consumer t's marginal utility of unit of account in the equilibrium.

4. I owe these references to Daniel Mulino, a graduate student at Yale University.

Proof. Because $(\overline{\mathbf{x}}, \overline{\mathbf{K}}, \overline{\mathbf{L}})$ solves problem 10.76, the finite horizon allocation $(\overline{x}_{t0}, \overline{x}_{t-1,1}, \overline{K}_t, \overline{L}_t)_{t=0}^T$ solves the problem

$$\max_{\substack{x_{t0}\geq 0,\, x_{t-1,1}\geq 0,\, K_t\geq 0,\, L_t\geq 0,\\ \text{for } t=0,1,\ldots,T}} \sum_{t=0}^{T}[\lambda_t^{-1}u_0(x_{t0}) + \lambda_{t-1}^{-1}u_1(x_{t-1,1})]$$
$$\text{s.t.}\quad L_t \leq 1 \text{ and} \tag{10.77}$$
$$x_{t0} + x_{t-1,1} + K_t \leq f(K_{t-1}, L_t),\ \text{for } t = 0, \ldots, T,$$
$$\text{where } K_{-1} = \overline{K}_{-1},\ \text{and } K_T \geq \overline{K}_T,$$

for each T. I must verify that this problem satisfies the constraint qualification of the Kuhn-Tucker theorem, if T is sufficiently large. By assumption, $\overline{K}_{-1} > 0$. Then, $\overline{x}_{t0} + \overline{x}_{t-1,1} > 0$, for some t, for suppose that $\overline{x}_{t0} + \overline{x}_{t-1,1} = 0$, for all t. Then, the objective function of problem 10.77 could be increased by consuming all the capital stock, $\overline{K}_0$, in period 0 and letting $x_{00} = x_{-1,1} = \frac{f(\overline{K}_{-1}, 1)}{2}$. If T is so large that $\overline{x}_{t0} + \overline{x}_{t-1,1} > 0$, for some $t \leq T$, then by reducing this consumption, it is possible to meet the constraints of problem 10.77 and waste a little labor and a little of the produced good in every period, s, such that $0 \leq s \leq T$. Therefore, the problem satisfies the constraint qualification in this case as well.

Because problem 10.77 satisfies the constraint qualification, the Kuhn-Tucker theorem implies that there exist nonnegative prices $(p_t, w_t)_{t=0}^T$ and q_T that are not all 0 and are such that $(\overline{x}_{t0}, \overline{x}_{t-1,1}, \overline{K}_t, \overline{L}_t)_{t=0}^T$ solves the problem

$$\max_{\substack{x_{t0}\geq 0,\, x_{t-1,1}\geq 0,\, K_t\geq 0,\, L_t\geq 0,\\ \text{for } t=0,\ldots,T}} \sum_{t=0}^{T}\Big[\lambda_t^{-1}u_0(x_{t0}) + \lambda_{t-1}^{-1}u_1(x_{t-1,1}) - w_t L_t$$
$$- p_t x_{t0} - p_t x_{t-1,1} - p_t K_t + p_t f(K_{t-1}, L_t)\Big] + q_T K_T,$$

where $K_{-1} = \overline{K}_{-1}$. Also,

$$p_t = 0,\ \text{if}\, \overline{x}_{t0} + \overline{x}_{t-1,1} < f(\overline{K}_{t-1}, \overline{L}_t) \tag{10.78}$$

$$w_t = 0,\ \text{if}\, \overline{L}_t < 1. \tag{10.79}$$

It follows that

$$\frac{du_0(\overline{x}_{t0})}{dx} \leq \lambda_t p_t, \tag{10.80}$$

with equality if $\overline{x}_{t0} > 0$,

$$\frac{du_1(\overline{x}_{t-1,1})}{dx} \leq \lambda_{t-1} p_t, \tag{10.81}$$

with equality if $\overline{x}_{t-1,1} > 0$,

$$p_t \frac{\partial f(\overline{K}_{t-1}, \overline{L}_t)}{\partial L} \leq w_t, \tag{10.82}$$

with equality if $\overline{L}_t > 0$, for $t = 0, 1, \ldots, T$, and

$$p_t \frac{\partial f(\overline{K}_{t-1}, \overline{L}_t)}{\partial K} \leq p_{t-1}, \tag{10.83}$$

with equality if $\overline{K}_{t-1} > 0$, for $t = 1, \ldots, T$.

If $\overline{K}_t = 0$, for some t, and $T \geq t$ in problem 10.77, then by assumption 10.3 there is no consumption or production after period T, so that it is trivial to specify equilibrium wages and prices for these periods. If we define the transfers to be

$$\tau_t = w_t - p_t \overline{x}_{t0} - p_{t+1} \overline{x}_{t1}, \tag{10.84}$$

then, conditions 10.78–10.84 guarantee that $(\overline{x}_{t0}, \overline{x}_{t-1,1}, \overline{K}_t, \overline{L}_t, p_t, w_t, \tau_t)_{t=0}^{T}$ forms an Arrow-Debreu equilibrium for the economy with $T+1$ periods.

Suppose that $\overline{K}_t > 0$, for all t. Since $\frac{\partial f(\overline{K}_{t-1}, L)}{\partial L} > 0$, for all $L \geq 0$, by assumption 10.4, it follows that $\overline{L}_t = 1$, for all t. In addition, $\overline{x}_{t0} + \overline{x}_{t-1,1} > 0$, for infinitely many t, for otherwise there exists a positive integer S such that $\overline{x}_{t0} + \overline{x}_{t-1,1} = 0$, for all $t \geq S$. Then, the objective function of problem 10.77 could be increased by consuming all the capital stock $\overline{K}_S$ in period S and producing nothing thereafter. Let T be so large that $\overline{x}_{t0} + \overline{x}_{t-1,1} > 0$, for some t such that $t \leq T$, and let $t(T)$ be the largest t such that $t \leq T$ and $\overline{x}_{t0} + \overline{x}_{t-1,1} > 0$. I show that p_t and w_t do not depend on T, for $t \leq t(T)$. Either $\overline{x}_{t(T),0} > 0$ or $\overline{x}_{t(T)-1,1} > 0$. If $\overline{x}_{t(T),0} > 0$, then

$$p_{t(T)} = \lambda_{t(T)}^{-1} \frac{du_0(\overline{x}_{t(T),0})}{dx},$$

and if $\overline{x}_{t(T)-1,1} > 0$, then

$$p_{t(T)} = \lambda_{t(T)}^{-1} \frac{du_1(\overline{x}_{t(T)-1,1})}{dx},$$

so that $p_{t(T)}$ does not depend on T. I show by backward induction on t that p_t is determined independently of T, for $t \leq t(T)$. We know that $p_{t(T)}$ is so determined. Suppose by induction that p_t is determined, where $t \leq t(T)$. Because $\overline{K}_{t-1} > 0$,

$$p_{t-1} = p_t \frac{\partial f(\overline{K}_{t-1}, 1)}{\partial K},$$

so that p_{t-1} is determined. Hence, p_t is determined independently of T, for all $t \leq t(T)$. The wages, w_t, are also determined, for $t \leq t(T)$, since

$$w_t = p_t \frac{\partial f(\overline{K}_{t-1}, 1)}{\partial L},$$

for $t \leq t(T)$.

It now follows that p_t, w_t, and hence τ_t, are defined for any nonnegative t, for let $t \geq 0$. Then, there exists a $\bar{t}$ such that $\bar{t} \geq t$ and $\overline{x}_{\bar{t}0} + \overline{x}_{\bar{t}-1,1} > 0$. Let T be such that $T \geq \bar{t}$. Then application of the Kuhn-Tucker theorem to problem 10.77 with this value of T determines p_t and w_t independently of T. The entire sequence $(p_t, w_t, \tau_t)_{t=0}^{\infty}$ satisfies conditions 10.78–10.84, where the τ_t are defined by equation 10.84. These conditions are enough to guarantee that $(x_{t0}, x_{t-1,1}, K_t, L_t, p_t, w_t, \tau_t)_{t=0}^{T}$ is an Arrow-Debreu equilibrium. ▪

The next theorem includes a condition that guarantees that the prices are summable in the equilibrium of theorem 10.33. The condition is that total consumption be bounded away from 0 in periods t, for t sufficiently large. I will later use the turnpike theorem to guarantee that this condition applies in the case where the $\lambda_t^{-1} = (1+r)^{-t}$, for all t, and where $r > 0$. (See theorem 10.54 in section 10.12.)

THEOREM 10.34 Assume that assumptions 10.1–10.5 apply and that the allocation $(\overline{\mathbf{x}}, \overline{\mathbf{K}}, \overline{\mathbf{L}})$ solves problem 10.76, where $\sum_{t=-1}^{\infty} \lambda_t^{-1} < \infty$. Suppose that there is a positive number ε such that

$$\overline{x}_{t0} + \overline{x}_{t-1,1} \geq \varepsilon,$$

for t sufficiently large. Then $(\overline{\mathbf{x}}, \overline{\mathbf{K}}, \overline{\mathbf{L}})$ is the allocation of an Arrow-Debreu equilibrium with transfer payments, $(\overline{\mathbf{x}}, \overline{\mathbf{K}}, \overline{\mathbf{L}}, \mathbf{p}, \mathbf{w}, \boldsymbol{\tau})$, where, for each t, the number λ_t is consumer t's marginal utility of unit of account in the equilibrium and where $\sum_{t=0}^{\infty} p_t < \infty$ and $\sum_{t=0}^{\infty} w_t < \infty$.

Proof. Because $\overline{x}_{t0} + \overline{x}_{t-1,1} \geq \varepsilon$ for large t, it must be that $\overline{K}_{-1} > 0$, for if $\overline{K}_{-1}$ were 0, then no output could ever be produced. Therefore theorem 10.33 implies that $(\overline{\mathbf{x}}, \overline{\mathbf{K}}, \overline{\mathbf{L}})$ is the allocation of an Arrow-Debreu equilibrium with transfer payments $(\overline{\mathbf{x}}, \overline{\mathbf{K}}, \overline{\mathbf{L}}, \mathbf{p}, \mathbf{w}, \boldsymbol{\tau})$, where, for each t, the number λ_t is consumer t's marginal utility of unit of account in the equilibrium. It remains to be shown that $\sum_{t=0}^{\infty} p_t < \infty$ and $\sum_{t=0}^{\infty} w_t < \infty$.

Let T be such that $\overline{x}_{t0} + \overline{x}_{t-1,1} \geq \varepsilon$, if $t \geq T$. Then, $\overline{x}_{t0} \geq \varepsilon/2$ or $\overline{x}_{t-1,1} \geq \varepsilon/2$ if $t \geq T$, so that

$$p_t = \lambda_t^{-1} \frac{du_0(\overline{x}_{t0})}{dx} \leq \lambda_t^{-1} \frac{du_0(\varepsilon/2)}{dx}$$

or

$$p_t = \lambda_{t-1}^{-1} \frac{du_1(\overline{x}_{t-1,1})}{dx} \leq \lambda_{t-1}^{-1} \frac{du_1(\varepsilon/2)}{dx}.$$

Let

$$b = \max\left(\frac{du_0(\varepsilon/2)}{dx}, \frac{du_1(\varepsilon/2)}{dx}\right).$$

Then, $p_t \leq b(\lambda_{t-1}^{-1} + \lambda_t^{-1})$, for $t \geq T$. Since $\sum_{t=-1}^{\infty} \lambda_t^{-1}$, it follows that $\sum_{t=0}^{\infty} p_t < \infty$.

Lemma 10.10 (in section 10.1) implies that $\sum_{t=0}^{\infty} w_t < \infty$. ■

No lower bound on consumption is required to prove a converse to the previous theorem.

THEOREM 10.35 Suppose that assumptions 10.1–10.5 apply and let $(\overline{\mathbf{x}}, \overline{\mathbf{K}}, \overline{\mathbf{L}}, \mathbf{p}, \mathbf{w}, \boldsymbol{\tau})$ be an Arrow-Debreu equilibrium with transfer payments such that $\sum_{t=0}^{\infty} p_t < \infty$ and $\overline{K}_{-1} > 0$. Then, the equilibrium allocation $(\overline{\mathbf{x}}, \overline{\mathbf{K}}, \overline{\mathbf{L}})$ solves the problem

$$\max_{\substack{(\mathbf{x}, \mathbf{K}, \mathbf{L}) \text{ is a feasible allocation} \\ \text{with initial capital } \overline{K}_{-1}}} \{\lambda_{-1}^{-1} u_1(x_{-1,1}) + \sum_{t=0}^{\infty} \lambda_t^{-1}[u_0(x_{t0}) + u_1(x_{t1})]\}$$

where, for all t, λ_t is consumer t's marginal utility of unit of account in the equilibrium and λ_t is a positive number or is infinite and is less than infinity if the equilibrium consumption of consumer t is not 0. Furthermore, $0 < \sum_{t=-1}^{\infty} \lambda_t^{-1} < \infty$.

Proof. By lemma 10.10 (in section 10.1), $\sum_{t=0}^{\infty} w_t < \infty$. By assumption 10.5, the utility functions are strictly increasing, so that $p_t > 0$, for all t. If $\overline{x}_{-1,1} > 0$, then by the Kuhn-Tucker theorem, there exists a unique positive number, λ_{-1}, such that $\overline{x}_{-1,1}$ solves the problem

$$\max_{x_1 \geq 0} [u_1(x_1) - \lambda_{-1} p_0 x_1].$$

Similarly, if, for $t \geq 0$, $(\overline{x}_{t0}, \overline{x}_{t1}) > 0$, then there exists a unique positive number, λ_t, such that $(\overline{x}_{t0}, \overline{x}_{t1})$ solves the problem

$$\max_{x_0 \geq 0, x_1 \geq 0} [u_0(x_0) + u_1(x_1) - \lambda_t (p_t x_0 - p_{t+1} x_1)].$$

If $\overline{x}_{-1,1} = 0$, let $\lambda_{-1} = \infty$, and if $(\overline{x}_{t0}, \overline{x}_{t1}) = 0$, let $\lambda_t = +\infty$. It follows from these definitions that

$$\lambda_{-1} \geq p_0^{-1} \frac{du_1(\overline{x}_{-1,1})}{dx}, \tag{10.85}$$

with equality if $\overline{x}_{-1,1} > 0$, and, for all $t \geq 0$,

$$\lambda_t \geq p_t^{-1} \frac{du_0(\overline{x}_{t0})}{dx}, \tag{10.86}$$

with equality if $\overline{x}_{t0} > 0$, and

$$\lambda_t \geq p_{t+1}^{-1} \frac{du_1(\overline{x}_{t1})}{dx}, \tag{10.87}$$

with equality if $\overline{x}_{t1} > 0$. The definition of the λ_t also implies that $\overline{x}_{-1,1}$ solves the problem

$$\max_{x_1 \geq 0} [\lambda_{-1}^{-1} u_1(x_1) - p_0 x_1], \tag{10.88}$$

and that, for $t \geq 0$, $(\overline{x}_{t0}, \overline{x}_{t1})$ solves the problem

$$\max_{x_0 \geq 0, x_1 \geq 0} [\lambda_t^{-1}(u_0(x_0) + u_1(x_1)) - p_t x_0 - p_{t+1} x_1], \tag{10.89}$$

for $t \geq 0$, where $\lambda_t^{-1} = 0$, if $\lambda_t = \infty$.

Because profits are maximized in equilibrium, $(\overline{K}_t, \overline{L}_{t+1})$ solves the problem

$$\max_{K\geq 0, L\geq 0} [p_{t+1}f(K, L) - p_t K - w_{t+1}L], \tag{10.90}$$

for all $t \geq 0$, and $\overline{L}_0$ solves the problem

$$\max_{L\geq 0}[p_0 f(\overline{K}_{-1}, L) - w_0 L]. \tag{10.91}$$

I show that $\sum_{t=-1}^{\infty} \lambda_t^{-1} < \infty$. Because feasible allocations are bounded by proposition 10.8 (in section 10.1), there is a positive number B such that $\overline{x}_{t0} \leq B$ and $\overline{x}_{t1} \leq B$, for all t. Inequalities 10.86 and 10.87 imply that

$$\lambda_t^{-1} \leq \min\left[p_t\left(\frac{du_0(\overline{x}_{t0})}{dx}\right)^{-1}, p_{t+1}\left(\frac{du_1(\overline{x}_{t1})}{dx}\right)^{-1}\right] \leq b^{-1}(p_t + p_{t+1}),$$

for $t \geq 0$, where

$$b = \min\left(\frac{du_0(B)}{dx}, \frac{du_1(B)}{dx}\right).$$

By assumption 10.5, $b > 0$. Similarly, inequality 10.85 implies that

$$\lambda_{-1}^{-1} \leq b^{-1}p_0.$$

Therefore,

$$\sum_{t=-1}^{\infty} \lambda_t^{-1} < b^{-1}\left[p_0 + \sum_{t=0}^{\infty}(p_t + p_{t+1})\right] < \infty.$$

Let $(\mathbf{x}, \mathbf{K}, \mathbf{L})$ be a feasible allocation. I will use the value loss method to show that

$$\begin{aligned}\lambda_{-1}^{-1}u_1(\overline{x}_{-1,1}) &+ \sum_{t=0}^{\infty} \lambda_t^{-1}[u_0(\overline{x}_{t0}) + u_1(\overline{x}_{t1})] \\ &\geq \lambda_{-1}^{-1}u_1(x_{-1,1}) + \sum_{t=0}^{\infty} \lambda_t^{-1}[u_0(x_{t0}) + u_1(x_{t1})].\end{aligned} \tag{10.92}$$

Let

$$\begin{aligned}\mathcal{L}_{-1}(x_{-1,1}, L_0) = {} & [\lambda_{-1}^{-1}u_1(\overline{x}_{-1,1}) - p_0\overline{x}_{-1,1} + p_0 f(\overline{K}_{-1}, \overline{L}_0) - w_0\overline{L}_0] \\ & - [\lambda_{-1}^{-1}u_1(x_{-1,1}) - p_0 x_{-1,1} + p_0 f(\overline{K}_{-1}, L_0) - w_0 L_0].\end{aligned}$$

Similarly, let

$$\begin{aligned}
&\mathcal{L}_t(x_{t0}, x_{t1}, K_t, L_{t+1}) \\
&\quad = \{\lambda_t^{-1}[u_0(\overline{x}_{t0}) + u_1(\overline{x}_{t1})] - p_t\overline{x}_{t0} - p_{t+1}\overline{x}_{t1} + p_{t+1}f(\overline{K}_t, \overline{L}_{t+1}) \\
&\quad - p_t\overline{K}_t - w_{t+1}\overline{L}_{t+1}\} \\
&\quad - \{\lambda_t^{-1}[u_0(x_{t0}) + u_1(x_{t1})] - p_t x_{t0} - p_{t+1}x_{t1} + p_{t+1}f(K_t, L_{t+1}) \\
&\quad - p_t K_t - w_{t+1}L_{t+1}\},
\end{aligned}$$

for $t \geq 0$. Because $\overline{x}_{-1,1}$ solves problem 10.88 and $\overline{L}_0$ solves problem 10.91, it follows that $\mathcal{L}_{-1}(x_{-1,1}, L_0) \geq 0 = \mathcal{L}_{-1}(\overline{x}_{-1,1}, \overline{L}_0)$. Similarly because $(\overline{x}_{t0}, \overline{x}_{t1})$ solves problem 10.89 and $(\overline{K}_t, \overline{L}_{t+1})$ solves problem 10.90, it follows that $\mathcal{L}_t(x_{t0}, x_{t1}, K_t, L_{t+1}) \geq 0 = \mathcal{L}_t(\overline{x}_{t0}, \overline{x}_{t1}, \overline{K}_t, \overline{L}_{t+1})$, for all t. Therefore,

$$\begin{aligned}
0 &\leq \mathcal{L}_{-1}(x_{-1,1}, L_0) + \sum_{t=0}^{\infty} \mathcal{L}_t(x_{t0}, x_{t1}, K_t, L_{t+1}) \\
&= \{\lambda_{-1}^{-1}u_1(\overline{x}_{-1,1}) + \sum_{t=0}^{\infty} \lambda_t^{-1}[u_0(\overline{x}_{t0}) + u_1(\overline{x}_{t1})]\} \\
&- \{\lambda_{-1}^{-1}u_1(x_{-1,1}) + \sum_{t=0}^{\infty} \lambda_t^{-1}[u_0(x_{t0}) + u_1(x_{t1})]\} \\
&+ p_0[x_{00} + x_{-1,1} + K_0 - f(\overline{K}_{-1}, L_0)] \\
&- p_0[\overline{x}_{00} + \overline{x}_{-1,1} + \overline{K}_0 - f(\overline{K}_{-1}, \overline{L}_0)] \\
&+ \sum_{t=1}^{\infty} p_t[x_{t0} + x_{t-1,1} + K_t - f(K_{t-1}, L_t)] \\
&- \sum_{t=1}^{\infty} p_t[\overline{x}_{t0} + \overline{x}_{t-1,1} + \overline{K}_t - f(\overline{K}_{t-1}, \overline{L}_t)] \\
&+ \sum_{t=0}^{\infty} w_t(L_t - 1) - \sum_{t=0}^{\infty} w_t(\overline{L}_t - 1) \\
&\leq \{\lambda_{-1}^{-1}u_1(\overline{x}_{-1,1}) + \sum_{t=0}^{\infty} \lambda_t^{-1}[u_0(\overline{x}_{t0}) + u_1(\overline{x}_{t1})]\} \\
&- \{\lambda_{-1}^{-1}u_1(x_{-1,1}) + \sum_{t=0}^{\infty} \lambda_t^{-1}[u_0(x_{t0}) + u_1(x_{t1})]\},
\end{aligned}$$

where the equation follows because the allocations are bounded and $\sum_{t=0}^{\infty} p_t < \infty$, $\sum_{t=0}^{\infty} w_t < \infty$, and $\sum_{t=-1}^{\infty} \lambda_t^{-1} < \infty$, so that the infinite series converge absolutely and hence their sums do not depend on the order of summation. The second inequality follows from the nonnegativity of prices and wages, the feasibility of the allocations $(\mathbf{x}, \mathbf{K}, \mathbf{L})$ and $(\overline{\mathbf{x}}, \overline{\mathbf{K}}, \overline{\mathbf{L}})$, and condition (8) of definition 10.9 (in section 10.1) of an Arrow-Debreu equilibrium with transfer payments. This completes the verification of inequality 10.92.

It remains to be shown that $\sum_{t=0}^{\infty} \lambda_t^{-1} > 0$. If $\sum_{t=0}^{\infty} \lambda_t^{-1} = 0$, then $\lambda_t = \infty$, for all t, so that no consumer consumes anything in the equilibrium. Since $\overline{K}_{-1} > 0$ by assumption, there is a feasible allocation that gives the consumer born in period -1 a positive consumption in period 0, and this allocation would Pareto dominate the equilibrium allocation. This implication contradicts the assertion of proposition 10.25 (in section 10.3) that the equilibrium allocation is Pareto optimal. Hence $\sum_{t=0}^{\infty} \lambda_t^{-1} > 0$. ▪

The next three corollaries are obtained by applying theorems 10.34 and 10.35 to spot price equilibria.

COROLLARY 10.36 Suppose that assumptions 10.1–10.5 apply and that $(\overline{\mathbf{x}}, \overline{\mathbf{K}}, \overline{\mathbf{L}}, \mathbf{P}, \mathbf{W}, \mathbf{r}, G, \mathbf{T})$ is a spot price equilibrium such that

$$P_0 + \sum_{t=1}^{\infty} \frac{P_t}{1 + R_{t-1}} < \infty$$

where $1 + R_t = (1 + r_0)(1 + r_1) \ldots (1 + r_t)$, for $t \geq 0$. Let Λ_t be the marginal utility of unit of account of consumer t in the equilibrium if his or her consumption is positive. Otherwise, let Λ_t be infinite. Assume that Λ_{-1} is measured from the point of view of period -1. Then, the allocation $(\overline{\mathbf{x}}, \overline{\mathbf{K}}, \overline{\mathbf{L}})$ solves the welfare maximization problem

$$\max_{\substack{(\mathbf{x},\mathbf{K},\mathbf{L}) \text{ is a feasible allocation} \\ \text{with initial capital } \overline{K}_{-1}}} \Bigg\{ (1 + r_{-1})\Lambda_{-1}^{-1} u_1(x_{-1,1}) + \Lambda_0^{-1}(u_0(x_{00}) + u_1(x_{01})) + \sum_{t=1}^{\infty} (1 + R_{t-1})^{-1} \Lambda_t^{-1} [u_0(x_{t0}) + u_1(x_{t1})] \Bigg\}, \quad (10.93)$$

and furthermore

$$(1 + r_{-1})\Lambda_{-1}^{-1} + \Lambda_0^{-1} + \sum_{t=1}^{\infty} (1 + R_{t-1})^{-1} \Lambda_t^{-1} < \infty.$$

Proof. The equilibrium $(\overline{\mathbf{x}}, \overline{\mathbf{K}}, \overline{\mathbf{L}}, \mathbf{P}, \mathbf{W}, \mathbf{r}, G, \mathbf{T})$ may be converted to an Arrow-Debreu equilibrium with transfer payments, $(\overline{\mathbf{x}}, \overline{\mathbf{K}}, \overline{\mathbf{L}}, \mathbf{p}, \mathbf{w}, \boldsymbol{\tau})$ where $p_0 = P_0$ and $p_t = \frac{P_t}{1+R_{t-1}}$, for $t \geq 1$. It follows from these equations for the Arrow-Debreu prices that $\lambda_0 = \Lambda_0$, and $\lambda_t = (1 + R_{t-1})\Lambda_t$, for $t \geq 1$, where λ_t is the marginal utility of unit of account of consumer t in the Arrow-Debreu equilibrium. Arguing as in the proof of corollary 9.29 (in section 9.6), we see that $\lambda_{-1} = (1 + r_{-1})^{-1}\Lambda_{-1}$. Theorem 10.35 implies that the allocation $\overline{x}$ solves problem 10.93 and that

$$(1 + r_{-1})\Lambda_{-1}^{-1} + \Lambda_0^{-1} + \sum_{t=1}^{\infty}(1 + R_{t-1})^{-1}\Lambda_t^{-1} < \infty,$$

as was to be proved. ▪

COROLLARY 10.37 Suppose that assumptions 10.1–10.5 apply and that $(\overline{\mathbf{x}}, \overline{\mathbf{K}}, \overline{\mathbf{L}}, \mathbf{P}, \mathbf{W}, \mathbf{r}, G, \mathbf{T})$ is a spot price equilibrium such that $\overline{x}_{-1,1} > 0$ and $\overline{x}_{t0} + \overline{x}_{t1} > 0$, for all t, and

$$P_0 + \sum_{t=1}^{\infty} \frac{P_t}{1 + R_{t-1}} < \infty,$$

where $1 + R_t = (1 + r_0)(1 + r_1) \ldots (1 + r_t)$, for $t \geq 0$. New units of account can be chosen so as to obtain a new spot price equilibrium, $(\overline{\mathbf{x}}, \overline{\mathbf{K}}, \overline{\mathbf{L}}, \underline{\mathbf{P}}, \underline{\mathbf{W}}, \underline{\mathbf{r}}, \underline{G}, \underline{\mathbf{T}})$, in which the marginal utility of unit of account in youth of every consumer is 1 and the allocation $(\overline{\mathbf{x}}, \overline{\mathbf{K}}, \overline{\mathbf{L}})$ solves the welfare maximization problem

$$\max_{\substack{(\mathbf{x}, \mathbf{K}, \mathbf{L}) \text{ is a feasible allocation} \\ \text{with initial capital } \overline{K}_{-1}}} \Big\{ (1 + \underline{r}_{-1})u_1(x_{-1,1}) + u_0(x_{00}) + u_1(x_{01}) + \sum_{t=1}^{\infty}(1 + \underline{R}_{t-1})^{-1}[u_0(x_{t0}) + u_1(x_{t1})] \Big\}$$

and

$$(1 + \underline{r}_{-1}) + 1 + \sum_{t=1}^{\infty}(1 + \underline{R}_{t-1})^{-1} < \infty,$$

where

$$1 + \underline{R}_T = (1 + \underline{r}_0)(1 + \underline{r}_1) \ldots (1 + \underline{r}_T), \text{ for } T \geq 0.$$

Proof. The assumption that all consumers consume something guarantees that every consumer t's marginal utility of unit of account in the equilibrium, Λ_t, is finite. The corollary is proved just as was corollary 9.31 (in section 9.6) by replacing P_t by $\underline{P}_t = \Lambda_t P_t$, for all t, and making corresponding adjustments in the other nominal variables and interest rates. ▪

If we require that the interest rates be constant in the previous corollary, it becomes the following.

COROLLARY 10.38 Suppose that assumptions 10.1–10.5 apply and that $(\overline{\mathbf{x}}, \overline{\mathbf{K}}, \overline{\mathbf{L}}, \mathbf{P}, \mathbf{W}, \mathbf{r}, G, \mathbf{T})$ is a spot price equilibrium such that every consumer's marginal utility of unit of account equals the same positive number and $r_t = r > 0$, for all t. Suppose also that

$$\sum_{t=0}^{\infty}(1+r)^{-t}P_t < \infty.$$

Then, the allocation $(\overline{\mathbf{x}}, \overline{\mathbf{K}}, \overline{\mathbf{L}})$ solves the welfare maximization problem

$$\max_{\substack{(\mathbf{x},\mathbf{K},\mathbf{L}) \text{ is a feasible allocation} \\ \text{with initial capital } \overline{K}_{-1}}} \left\{(1+r)u_1(x_{-1,1}) + \sum_{t=0}^{\infty}(1+r)^{-t}[u_0(x_{t0}) + u_1(x_{t1})]\right\}.$$

Notice that in this corollary, I do not require that $\overline{x}_{-1,1} > 0$ and $\overline{x}_{t0} + \overline{x}_{t1} > 0$, for all t, but assume that the marginal utilities of unit of account are all 1.

The following two corollaries are consequences of theorem 10.34.

COROLLARY 10.39 Suppose that assumptions 10.1–10.5 apply and that the allocation $(\overline{\mathbf{x}}, \overline{\mathbf{K}}, \overline{\mathbf{L}})$ solves the problem

$$\max_{\substack{(\mathbf{x},\mathbf{K},\mathbf{L}) \text{ is a feasible allocation} \\ \text{with initial capital } \overline{K}_{-1}}} \left\{(1+r_{-1})u_1(x_{-1,1}) + u_0(x_{00}) + u_1(x_{01}) + \sum_{t=1}^{\infty}(1+R_{t-1})^{-1}[u_0(x_{t0}) + u_1(x_{t1})]\right\},$$

where

$$(1+r_{-1}) + 1 + \sum_{t=1}^{\infty}(1+R_{t-1})^{-1} < \infty,$$

$1 + R_t = (1 + r_0)(1 + r_1) \ldots (1 + r_t)$, for $t \geq 0$, and $r_t > -1$, for $t \geq -1$. Suppose that there is a positive number ε such that

$$\overline{x}_{t0} + \overline{x}_{t-1,1} \geq \varepsilon,$$

for sufficiently large t. Then, $(\overline{\mathbf{x}}, \overline{\mathbf{K}}, \overline{\mathbf{L}})$ is the allocation of a spot price equilibrium, $(\overline{\mathbf{x}}, \overline{\mathbf{K}}, \overline{\mathbf{L}}, \mathbf{P}, \mathbf{W}, \mathbf{r}, G, \mathbf{T})$, in which the marginal utility of unit of account of every consumer is 1 and $\mathbf{r} = (r_{-1}, r_0, \ldots)$. This equilibrium satisfies the condition

$$P_0 + \sum_{t=1}^{\infty} \frac{P_t}{1 + R_{t-1}} < \infty.$$

Proof. This corollary follows from theorem 10.34 in the same way that corollary 9.33 follows from theorem 9.32 (in section 9.6). ▪

If we let $r_t = r > 0$, for all t, in this corollary, it becomes the following.

COROLLARY 10.40 Suppose that assumptions 10.1–10.5 apply and that the allocation $(\overline{\mathbf{x}}, \overline{\mathbf{K}}, \overline{\mathbf{L}})$ solves the problem

$$\max_{\substack{(\mathbf{x}, \mathbf{K}, \mathbf{L}) \text{ is a feasible allocation} \\ \text{with initial capital } \overline{K}_{-1}}} \left\{(1 + r)u_1(x_{-1,1}) + \sum_{t=0}^{\infty} (1 + r)^{-t} [u_0(x_{t0}) + u_1(x_{t1})]\right\} \tag{10.94}$$

where $r > 0$. Suppose that there is a positive number ε such that

$$\overline{x}_{t0} + \overline{x}_{t-1,1} \geq \varepsilon,$$

for sufficiently large t. Then, $(\overline{\mathbf{x}}, \overline{\mathbf{K}}, \overline{\mathbf{L}})$ is the allocation of a spot price equilibrium, $(\overline{\mathbf{x}}, \overline{\mathbf{K}}, \overline{\mathbf{L}}, \mathbf{P}, \mathbf{W}, \mathbf{r}, G, \mathbf{T})$, in which the marginal utility of unit of account of every consumer is 1 and where $r_t = r$, for all t. This equilibrium satisfies the condition

$$\sum_{t=0}^{\infty} (1 + r)^{-t} P_t < \infty.$$

This corollary extends theorem 10.30 (in section 10.4) to nonstationary allocations and equilibria.

The economic significance of the above corollaries, as with similar ones in section 9.6, is that manipulation of fiscal and monetary policy can maximize any welfare function that is a weighted sum of the utilities of the different generations, and any fiscal and monetary policy using lump-sum taxes maximizes such a welfare function, provided the equilibrium satisfies the asymptotic condition that $\sum_{t=-1}^{\infty} \lambda_t^{-1} < \infty$. Of course, there is no way of knowing in practice whether this condition is satisfied since the future can be only vaguely foreseen. These results imply that the model has no truly natural rate of interest. They are more significant than those in section 9.6, for in the Diamond model, fiscal and monetary policy determine the accumulation of capital as well as the distribution of consumption between young and old. If the government wished to do so, it could drive output down to zero or up to a high level.

10.8 Discounted Optimal and Equilibrium Programs

I now turn to the study of optimal economic growth, which is also known as *Ramsey growth theory.* The terminology of this subject was introduced in section 10.1, where I defined programs and the feasibility and optimality of programs. The first task is to obtain a criterion for optimality based on an equilibrium concept analogous to Arrow-Debreu equilibrium.

DEFINITION 10.41 A *program equilibrium* consists of $(\overline{\mathbf{C}}, \overline{\mathbf{K}}, r, \mathbf{p})$, where

1. $(\overline{\mathbf{C}}, \overline{\mathbf{K}})$ is a feasible program
2. $\mathbf{p} = (p_0, p_1, \ldots)$ is a sequence of nonnegative prices, not all of which are 0
3. r is a number exceeding -1
4. for each $t \geq 0$, $\overline{C}_t$ solves the problem

$$\max_{C \geq 0} [(1+r)^{-t} v(C) - p_t C]$$

5. for each t, $\overline{K}_t$ solves the problem

$$\max_{K \geq 0} [p_{t+1} F(K) - p_t K]$$

6. for each t, $p_t = 0$, if

$$\overline{C}_t + \overline{K}_t < F(\overline{K}_{t-1})$$

Condition (4) implies that the marginal utility of unit of account at time t of a virtual consumer is $(1+r)^t$, for each t. It also implies that $p_t > 0$, for all t, for otherwise the problem

$$\max_{C \geq 0}[(1+r)^{-t}v(C) - p_t C]$$

would have no solution. In a model with only one consumption good, the sole function of condition (4) is to provide a normalization for prices.

There is a natural correspondence between program equilibria and spot price equilibria with interest rate r and marginal utility of money equal to 1.

THEOREM 10.42 Suppose that assumptions 10.1–10.5 apply to the Diamond model (u_0, u_1, f) and let $(\overline{\mathbf{x}}, \overline{\mathbf{K}}, \overline{\mathbf{L}}, \mathbf{P}, \mathbf{W}, \mathbf{r}, G, \mathsf{T})$ be a spot price equilibrium for this model in which $r_t = r$, for all t, where $r > -1$. Suppose that the marginal utility of unit of account for every consumer equals 1. Then $(\overline{\mathbf{C}}, \overline{\mathbf{K}}, r, \mathbf{p})$ is a program equilibrium for the growth model corresponding to (u_0, u_1, f), where $p_t = (1+r)^{-t}P_t$, for all t, and where $(\overline{\mathbf{C}}, \overline{\mathbf{K}})$ is the program corresponding to the allocation $(\overline{\mathbf{x}}, \overline{\mathbf{K}}, \overline{\mathbf{L}})$ at interest rate r.

Suppose that assumptions 10.18–10.21 (in section 10.1) apply to the growth model (v, F), and let $(\overline{\mathbf{C}}, \overline{\mathbf{K}}, r, \mathbf{p})$ be a program equilibrium for this model. Then, there is a spot price equilibrium, $(\overline{\mathbf{x}}, \overline{\mathbf{K}}, \overline{\mathbf{L}}, \mathbf{P}, \mathbf{W}, \mathbf{r}, G, \mathsf{T})$, with $r_t = r$, for all t, and for a corresponding Diamond model, (u_0, u_1, f), that satisfies assumptions 10.1–10.5 (in section 10.1). The spot price equilibrium is such that $(\overline{\mathbf{x}}, \overline{\mathbf{K}}, \overline{\mathbf{L}})$ corresponds to $(\overline{\mathbf{C}}, \overline{\mathbf{K}})$ at interest rate r, $P_t = (1+r)^t p_t$, for all t, and the marginal utility of unit of account of each consumer is 1.

Proof. Let $(\overline{\mathbf{x}}, \overline{\mathbf{K}}, \overline{\mathbf{L}}, \mathbf{P}, \mathbf{W}, \mathbf{r}, G, \mathsf{T})$ be a spot price equilibrium for the Diamond model with $r_t = r$, for all t, and with the marginal utility of unit of account of every consumer equal to 1. Because this marginal utility equals 1, it follows that, for each t, $(\overline{x}_{t0}, \overline{x}_{t1})$ solves the problem

$$\max_{(x_0, x_1) \geq 0}[u_0(x_0) + u_1(x_1) - P_t x_0 - (1+r)^{-1}P_{t+1}x_1].$$

Hence, $P_t > 0$, for all t, for otherwise this problem would have no solution. For each t, $\overline{L}_t$ solves the problem

$$\max_{L \geq 0}[P_t f(\overline{K}_{t-1}, L) - W_t L].$$

Since $P_t > 0$, it follows that $W_t > 0$, for otherwise this problem would have no solution. Therefore, $\overline{L}_t = 1$, by condition (10) of definition 10.12 (in section 10.1) of a spot price equilibrium. Therefore, for every $t \geq 0$, $\overline{K}_t$ solves the problem

$$\max_{K \geq 0}[(1+r)^{-1}P_{t+1}f(K_t, 1) - P_t K],$$

which implies that $\overline{K}_t$ solves the problem

$$\max_{K \geq 0}[p_{t+1}f(K, 1) - p_t K],$$

where $p_t = (1+r)^{-t}P_t$, for all t. Since, for all $t \geq 0$, $\overline{x}_{t-1,1}$ solves the problem

$$\max_{x_1 \geq 0}[u_1(x_1) - (1+r)^{-1}P_t x_1],$$

$\overline{x}_{t1}$ solves the problem

$$\max_{x_1 \geq 0}[(1+r)u_1(x_1) - P_t x_1].$$

Similarly, $\overline{x}_{t0}$ solves the problem

$$\max_{x_0 \geq 0}[u_0(x_0) - P_t x_0],$$

for all $t \geq 0$. Suppose that $C \geq 0$ and $C = x_0 + x_1$, where $v(C) = u_0(x_0) + (1+r)u_1(x_1)$. Then

$$\begin{aligned}
&(1+r)^{-t}v(\overline{C}_t) - p_t\overline{C}_t \\
&= (1+r)^{-t}[u_0(\overline{x}_{t0}) + (1+r)u_1(\overline{x}_{t-1,1}) - P_t\overline{x}_{t0} - P_t\overline{x}_{t-1,1}] \\
&\geq (1+r)^{-t}[u_0(x_0) + (1+r)u_1(x) - P_t x_0 - P_t x_1] \\
&= (1+r)^{-t}v(C) - p_t C.
\end{aligned}$$

Since the allocation $(\overline{\mathbf{C}}, \overline{\mathbf{K}})$ is feasible, $(\overline{\mathbf{C}}, \overline{\mathbf{K}}, r, \mathbf{p})$ satisfies all the conditions of a program equilibrium.

Suppose that $(\overline{\mathbf{C}}, \overline{\mathbf{K}}, r, \mathbf{p})$ is a program equilibrium for the growth model (v, F). Let $u_0(x) = \frac{1}{2}v(2x)$, $u_1(x) = \frac{1}{2(1+r)}v(2x)$, and let f be defined by the equations $f(K, L) = LF\left(\frac{K}{L}\right)$, if $L > 0$, and $f(K, 0) = 0$. Proposition 10.6 (in section 10.1) implies that f satisfies assumptions 10.1–10.4, and it is clear that u_0 and u_1 satisfy assumption 10.5. For each t, let $P_t = (1+r)^t p_t$ and $W_t = P_t\frac{\partial f(\overline{K}_{t-1}, 1)}{\partial L}$. Because f is concave and differentiable and $\overline{K}_t$ solves the problem

$$\max_{K\geq 0}[p_{t+1}F(K) - p_t K],$$

it follows that $(\overline{K}_t, 1)$ solves the problem

$$\max_{(K,L)\geq 0}[(1+r)^{-t}P_{t+1}f(K,L) - P_t K - W_{t+1}L].$$

Similarly, $L = 1$ solves the problem

$$\max_{L\geq 0}[P_0 f(\overline{K}_{-1}, L) - W_0 L].$$

Since $\overline{C}_t$ solves the problem

$$\max_{C\geq 0}[(1+r)^{-t}v(C) - p_t C],$$

for all t, it follows that if C is such that $C = x_0 + x_1$ and $v(C) = u_0(x_0) + (1+r)u_1(x_1)$, then

$$\begin{aligned} u_0(\overline{x}_{t0}) &+ (1+r)u_1(\overline{x}_{t-1,1}) - P_t(\overline{x}_{t0} + \overline{x}_{t-1,1}) \\ &= v(\overline{C}_t) - (1+r)^t p_t \overline{C}_t \\ &\geq v(C) - (1+r)^t p_t C \\ &= u_0(x_0) + (1+r)u_1(x_1) - P_t(x_0 + x_1). \end{aligned}$$

Letting $x_1 = \overline{x}_{t-1,1}$ in this inequality, we see that, for all $t \geq 0$,

$$u_0(\overline{x}_{t0}) - P_t\overline{x}_{t0} \geq u_0(x_0) - P_t x_0,$$

for all $x_0 \geq 0$. Letting $x_0 = \overline{x}_{t0}$, we see that, for all $t \geq 0$,

$$u_1(\overline{x}_{t-1,1}) - (1+r)^{-1}P_t\overline{x}_{t-1,1} \geq u_1(x_1) - (1+r)^{-1}P_t x_1,$$

for $x_t \geq 0$. Therefore,

$$\begin{aligned} u_0(\overline{x}_{t0}) &+ u_1(\overline{x}_{t1}) - P_t\overline{x}_{t0} - (1+r)^{-1}P_{t+1}\overline{x}_{t1} \\ &\geq u_0(x_0) + u_1(x_1) - P_t x_0 - (1+r)^{-1}P_{t+1}x_1. \end{aligned}$$

Therefore, for $t \geq 0$, $(\overline{x}_{t0}, \overline{x}_{t1})$ solves the problem

$$\begin{aligned} &\max_{(x_0,x_1)\geq 0}[u_0(x_0) + u_1(x_1)] \\ &\text{s.t.}\quad P_t x_0 + (1+r)^{-1}P_{t+1}x_1 \leq W_t - \mathsf{T}_t, \end{aligned}$$

for a suitable choice of T_t. Similarly, $\overline{x}_{-1,1}$ solves the problem

$$\max_{x_1 \geq 0} u_1(x)$$
$$\text{s.t.} \quad P_0 x_1 \leq P_0 f(\overline{K}_{-1}, 1) - W_0 + (1+r)G,$$

for a suitable choice of G. Since $(\overline{\mathbf{x}}, \overline{\mathbf{K}}, \overline{\mathbf{L}})$ is a feasible allocation, where $\overline{L}_t = 1$, for all t, it follows that $(\overline{\mathbf{x}}, \overline{\mathbf{K}}, \overline{\mathbf{L}}, \mathbf{P}, \mathbf{W}, \mathbf{r}, G, \mathsf{T})$, where $r_t = r$, for all t, is a spot price equilibrium for a suitable choice of G and T. ■

Theorem 10.42 can be used to derive assertions about program equilibria from corresponding assertions about equilibria for the Diamond model. For instance, we have the following.

THEOREM 10.43 Suppose that assumptions 10.18–10.21 (in section 10.1) apply to a growth model and that $(\overline{\mathbf{C}}, \overline{\mathbf{K}}, r, \mathbf{p})$ is a program equilibrium such that $\sum_{t=0}^{\infty} p_t < \infty$. Then the program $(\overline{\mathbf{C}}, \overline{\mathbf{K}})$ solves the problem

$$\max_{\substack{(\mathbf{C}, \mathbf{K}) \text{ is a feasible program} \\ \text{with initial capital } \overline{K}_{-1}}} \sum_{t=0}^{\infty} (1+r)^{-t} v(C_t). \tag{10.95}$$

Proof. By theorem 10.42, there is a spot price equilibrium, $(\overline{\mathbf{x}}, \overline{\mathbf{K}}, \overline{\mathbf{L}}, \mathbf{P}, \mathbf{W}, r, G, \mathsf{T})$, for a corresponding Diamond model, (u_0, u_1, f), that satisfies assumptions 10.1–10.5 and where $(\overline{\mathbf{x}}, \overline{\mathbf{K}}, \overline{\mathbf{L}})$ corresponds to $(\overline{\mathbf{C}}, \overline{\mathbf{K}})$ at interest rate r and $P_t = (1+r)^t p_t$, for all t, and the marginal utility of unit of account of every consumer is 1. Therefore,

$$\sum_{t=0}^{\infty} (1+r)^{-t} P_t = \sum_{t=0}^{\infty} p_t < \infty.$$

By corollary 10.38 (in section 10.7), $(\overline{\mathbf{x}}, \overline{\mathbf{K}}, \overline{\mathbf{L}})$ solves the problem

$$\max_{\substack{(\mathbf{x}, \mathbf{K}, \mathbf{L}) \text{ is a feasible allocation} \\ \text{with initial capital } \overline{K}_{-1}}} \left\{(1+r)u_1(x_{-1,1}) + \sum_{t=0}^{\infty} (1+r)^{-t} [u_0(x_{t0}) + u_1(x_{t1})]\right\}.$$

By proposition 10.16 (in section 10.1), it follows that $(\overline{\mathbf{C}}, \overline{\mathbf{K}})$ solves problem 10.95. ■

The converse of this theorem requires that consumption be eventually bounded away from 0, as in the analogous result for the Diamond model, corollary 10.40 (in section 10.7).

THEOREM 10.44 Assume that assumptions 10.18–10.21 (in section 10.1) apply and that the program $(\overline{C}, \overline{K})$ solves problem 10.95. Suppose that there is a positive number ε such that $\overline{C}_t \geq \varepsilon$, for t sufficiently large. Then, there exists a sequence of prices, $\mathbf{p} = (p_0, p_1, \ldots)$, such that $(\overline{\mathbf{C}}, \overline{\mathbf{K}}, r, \mathbf{p})$ is a program equilibrium and

$$\sum_{t=0}^{\infty} p_t < \infty.$$

Proof. Let (u_0, u_1, f) be the Diamond model corresponding to the growth model (v, F), where $u_0(x) = \frac{1}{2}v(2x)$, $u_1(x) = \frac{1}{2(1+r)}v(2x)$, $f(K, L) = LF\left(\frac{K}{L}\right)$, if $L > 0$, and $f(K, 0) = 0$. Let $(\overline{\mathbf{x}}, \overline{\mathbf{K}}, \overline{\mathbf{L}})$ be the allocation for this model that corresponds to the program $(\overline{\mathbf{C}}, \overline{\mathbf{K}})$. By proposition 10.16 (in section 10.1), $(\overline{\mathbf{x}}, \overline{\mathbf{K}}, \overline{\mathbf{L}})$ solves the problem

$$\max_{\substack{(\mathbf{x}, \mathbf{K}, \mathbf{L}) \text{ is a feasible allocation} \\ \text{with initial capital } \overline{K}_{-1}}} \left\{(1+r)u_1(x_{-1,1}) + \sum_{t=0}^{\infty}(1+r)^{-t}[u_0(x_{t0}) + u_1(x_{t1})]\right\}.$$

Because $\overline{x}_{t0} + \overline{x}_{t-1,1} \geq \varepsilon$, for sufficiently large t, corollary 10.40 (in section 10.7) implies that $(\overline{\mathbf{x}}, \overline{\mathbf{K}}, \overline{\mathbf{L}})$ is the allocation of a spot price equilibrium, $(\overline{\mathbf{x}}, \overline{\mathbf{K}}, \overline{\mathbf{L}}, \mathbf{P}, \mathbf{W}, \mathbf{r}, G, \mathbf{T})$, in which the marginal utility of unit of account of every consumer is 1 and $r_t = r$, for all t, and

$$\sum_{t=0}^{\infty}(1+r)^{-t}P_t < \infty.$$

Theorem 10.42 implies that $(\overline{\mathbf{C}}, \overline{\mathbf{K}}, r, \mathbf{p})$ is a program equilibrium for the growth model with $p_t = (1+r)^{-1}P_t$, for all t. Therefore,

$$\sum_{t=0}^{\infty} p_t = \sum_{t=0}^{\infty}(1+r)^{-t}P_t < \infty. \quad \blacksquare$$

A program $(\overline{\mathbf{C}}, \overline{\mathbf{K}})$ is stationary if $\overline{C}_t = C$ and $\overline{K}_t = K$, for all t. It is natural to say that a program equilibrium $(\overline{\mathbf{C}}, \overline{\mathbf{K}}, \mathbf{p})$ is stationary if $(\overline{\mathbf{C}}, \overline{\mathbf{K}})$ is stationary and the ratios of successive price, $\frac{p_t}{p_{t+1}}$, do not depend on t. If we let $\frac{p_t}{p_{t+1}} = 1 + r$, we can write a stationary program equilibrium as

(C, K, r), where $r > -1$. A stationary program equilibrium satisfies the conditions

$$\frac{dF(K)}{dK} = 1 + r$$

and

$$C + K = F(K).$$

I let $C(r)$ and $K(r)$ denote the values for C and K that satisfy these two equations. If assumption 10.19 applies, so that F is strictly concave, then $K(r)$ and hence $C(r)$ are uniquely defined and $(C(r), K(r), r)$ defines a unique stationary program equilibrium, where the price of the good at time t is $p_t = (1+r)^{-t}$, for all t. If $r > 0$ and $C(r) > 0$, then theorem 10.43 implies that the stationary allocation $(C(r), K(r))$ is optimal in that it solves problem 10.95. It will be shown (in section 10.13) that the program $(C(0), K(0))$ is optimal with respect to the catching up criterion. If $r < 0$, the program $(C(r), K(r))$ is not optimal according to any reasonable criterion, because it is possible to have more consumption in every period by decreasing the amount of capital invested in period 0. This point is illustrated in figure 10.5 (in section 10.2). The steady state quantity of consumption, $F(K) - K$, is maximized when $K = K(0)$. If $r < 0$, $K(r) > K(0)$, and a decrease in capital invested in period 0 makes available $K(r) - K(0)$ units of output for consumption at that time. If $r > 0$, $K(r) < K(0)$, and it would require a sacrifice of current consumption to build up capital to the level $K(0)$. For this reason, $(C(r), K(r))$ can be optimal, even though it provides less than the maximum amount of consumption per period. The stationary program $(C(0), K(0))$ is called the *golden rule program*. If $r > 0$, the stationary program $(C(r), K(r))$ is called the *modified golden rule program*. The modified golden rule and golden rule programs correspond to the Pareto optimal stationary equilibria discussed at the end of section 10.3. A specific example may clarify these concepts.

EXAMPLE 10.45 Let $F(K) = 3K^{1/3}$. The equation $\frac{dF(K(r))}{dK} = 1 + r$ implies that

$$K(r) = \left(\frac{1}{1+r}\right)^{3/2} = \frac{1}{1+r}\sqrt{\frac{1}{1+r}},$$

$$C(r) = F(K(r)) - K(r) = \left(3 - \frac{1}{1+r}\right)\sqrt{\frac{1}{1+r}}.$$

The golden rule stationary program is

$$(C(0), K(0)) = (2, 1).$$

An example of a modified golden rule is

$$(C(1), K(1)) = \left(\frac{5}{2}\sqrt{\frac{1}{2}}, \frac{1}{2}\sqrt{\frac{1}{2}}\right) = \left(\frac{5\sqrt{2}}{4}, \frac{\sqrt{2}}{4}\right).$$

An example of a nonoptimal stationary program is

$$(C(-1/2), K(-1/2)) = (\sqrt{2}, 2\sqrt{2}).$$

The triple $(C(r), K(r), r) = (C(0), K(0), 0)$ defines a program equilibrium where the price in every period is 1. The triple $(C(1), K(1), 1)$ defines a program equilibrium where the price in period t is 2^{-t}. The triple $(C(-1/2), K(-1/2), -1/2)$ defines a program equilibrium where the price in period t is 2^t; prices grow forever.

The stationary program $(C(r), K(r))$ corresponds to the stationary allocation $(x_0(r), x_1(r), K(r))$ in the Diamond model. Both are unique for any nonnegative value of r. If $r > 0$, then both optimize an infinite sum of utilities discounted at rate r. If $r = 0$, then both are optimal according to the catching up criterion, as will be proved in corollaries 10.68 and 10.78 (in section 10.13). I call the stationary allocation $(x_0(0), x_1(0), K(0))$ the *golden rule allocation* for the Diamond model, and if $r > 0$, I call $(x_0(r), x_1(r), K(r))$ a *modified golden rule allocation.*

10.9 Program Efficiency and the Hahn Problem

Efficiency is the concept in growth theory that corresponds to Pareto optimality in the general equilibrium theory of overlapping generations models.

DEFINITION 10.46 A feasible program $(\overline{\mathbf{C}}, \overline{\mathbf{K}})$ is *efficient* if there exists no other feasible program $(\mathbf{C}, \mathbf{K})$ such that $C_t \geq \overline{C}_t$, for all t, and $C_t > \overline{C}_t$, for some t.

There is no need for the definition of efficiency to involve the utility of consumption, unless there is more than one produced good. When there is only one commodity, the utility function is relevant only to the choice between current and future consumption, and this choice does not bear on efficiency.

A program $(\overline{\mathbf{C}}, \overline{\mathbf{K}})$ is automatically efficient if $\overline{C}_t + \overline{K}_t = F(\overline{K}_{t-1})$, for all t, and $\overline{C}_t = 0$ and $\overline{K}_t = 0$, for $t \geq T$, where T is some positive integer. When the program is confined within a finite horizon, more consumption can be had in one period only by giving up consumption in some other period. Efficiency when there is only one commodity has to do with the behavior of $\overline{C}_t$ and $\overline{K}_t$ as t goes to infinity.

It should be clear that a program is efficient if it is optimal in the sense that it solves a problem of the form

$$\max_{\substack{(\overline{\mathbf{C}}, \overline{\mathbf{K}}) \text{ is a feasible program} \\ \text{with initial capital } \overline{K}_{-1}}} \sum_{t=0}^{\infty} (1+r)^{-t} v(C_t)$$

where $r > 0$ and the utility function v is strictly increasing. Therefore, theorem 10.43 (in section 10.8) implies that the feasible program, $(\overline{\mathbf{C}}, \overline{\mathbf{K}})$, is efficient if there is a sequence of prices, $\mathbf{p} = (p_0, p_t, \ldots)$, such that $\sum_{t=0}^{\infty} p_t < \infty$ and $(\overline{\mathbf{C}}, \overline{\mathbf{K}}, \mathbf{p})$ is a program equilibrium. The condition that $\sum_{t=0}^{\infty} p_t < \infty$ is stronger than is needed to guarantee efficiency. Malinvaud (1953) has provided the following weaker criterion for efficiency.

PROPOSITION 10.47 Suppose that assumptions 10.18–10.20 (in section 10.1) apply. If $(\overline{\mathbf{C}}, \overline{\mathbf{K}}, r, \mathbf{p})$ is a program equilibrium, then $(\overline{\mathbf{C}}, \overline{\mathbf{K}})$ is efficient if $\inf_t p_t K_t = 0$.

Proof. It is sufficient to show that if $(\overline{\mathbf{C}}, \overline{\mathbf{K}})$ is not efficient, then $p_t K_t$ is bounded away from 0. If $K_T = 0$, for some T, then $K_t = 0$ and $C_t = 0$, for $t > T$, and the program $(\overline{\mathbf{C}}, \overline{\mathbf{K}})$ is efficient. So, we may suppose that $\overline{K}_t > 0$, for all t.

It follows from profit maximization that $p_t > 0$, for all t, for we know from definition 10.41 (in section 10.8) of a program equilibrium that $p_T > 0$, for some T. If $p_{T+1} = 0$, then profit maximization implies that $\overline{K}_T = 0$, contrary to hypothesis. Therefore, $p_{T+1} > 0$, and, continuing by induction on t, we see that $p_t > 0$, for all $t > T$. If $p_{T-1} = 0$, then the problem $\max_{K \geq 0}[p_T F(K) - p_{T-1} K]$ has no solution, contrary to the definition of a program equilibrium. Therefore, $p_{T-1} > 0$, and continuing by backward induction on t, we see that $p_t > 0$, for all $t < T$.

By the definition of a program equilibrium, the positiveness of the prices p_t implies that $\overline{C}_t = F(\overline{K}_{t-1}) - \overline{K}_t$, for all t.

If $(\overline{\mathbf{C}}, \overline{\mathbf{K}})$ is not efficient, it is dominated by some feasible program $(\mathbf{C}, \mathbf{K})$. Therefore, for every t,

$$F(K_t) - K_{t+1} \geq C_{t+1} \geq \overline{C}_{t+1} = F(\overline{K}_t) - \overline{K}_{t+1},$$

with strict inequality, for some t. Hence

$$\overline{K}_{t+1} - K_{t+1} \geq F(\overline{K}_t) - F(K_t) \geq (\overline{K}_t - K_t)\frac{dF(\overline{K}_t)}{dK} = (\overline{K}_t - K_t)\frac{p_t}{p_{t+1}},$$

where the second inequality follows from the concavity of F, and the equation follows from profit maximization and from the assumption that $\overline{K}_t > 0$, for all t. It follows that

$$p_{t+1}(\overline{K}_{t+1} - K_{t+1}) \geq p_t(\overline{K}_t - K_t),$$

for all t. Let T be the smallest value of t such that $K_t \neq \overline{K}_t$. Since the initial capital, $\overline{K}_{-1}$, is fixed $T > -1$. Since $C_t > \overline{C}_t$, for some t, it follows that $K_t \neq \overline{K}_t$, for some t, and hence, $T < \infty$. Then $K_{T-1} = \overline{K}_{T-1}$, and, because $(\mathbf{C}, \mathbf{K})$ dominates $(\overline{\mathbf{C}}, \overline{\mathbf{K}})$,

$$F(\overline{K}_{T-1}) - K_T = F(K_{T-1}) - K_T = C_T \geq \overline{C}_T = F(\overline{K}_{T-1}) - \overline{K}_T.$$

Therefore, $\overline{K}_T - K_T \geq 0$. Since $\overline{K}_T \neq K_T$, it follows that $\overline{K}_T - K_T > 0$. Therefore,

$$0 < p_T(\overline{K}_T - K_T) \leq p_t(\overline{K}_t - K_t) \leq p_t\overline{K}_t,$$

for all $t > T$. Since $p_t\overline{K}_t > 0$, for $t \leq T$, it follows that $p_t\overline{K}_t$ is bounded away from 0. ▪

The Malinvaud condition is sufficient but not necessary for efficiency. A golden rule stationary program equilibrium, $(C(0), K(0), 0)$, with $K(0) > 0$ is an example that violates the condition $\inf_t p_t\overline{K}_t = 0$ and yet has an efficient stationary program, $(C(0), K(0))$. The price, p, in this equilibrium is constant and positive, so that $p_t K_t = pK(0)$ is bounded away from 0 as t varies. By corollary 10.78 (in section 10.13), this golden rule program is optimal with respect to the catching up criterion and hence is efficient.

An example of a program that violates the Malinvaud condition and is inefficient is the program of the stationary program equilibrium $(C(r), K(r), r)$, where $-1 < r < 0$ and provided $K(r) > 0$. In this case,

$p_t K(r) = (1+r)^{-1}K(r)$, which diverges to $+\infty$ as t goes to infinity. The inefficiency of program equilibria is attributable to an overaccumulation of capital. Hahn (1966) was the first to point out that equilibrium programs need not be efficient. This finding surprised many economists, because program equilibria resemble Arrow-Debreu equilibria. The puzzle posed by the existence of inefficient program equilibria is known in the literature as the *Hahn problem.* Inefficient program equilibria are similar to non-Pareto optimal Arrow-Debreu equilibria in the Diamond overlapping generations model.

10.10 Euler's Equation

Euler's equation is a necessary condition for optimality in the growth problem

$$\begin{aligned} &\max_{\substack{C_t \geq 0,\, K_t \geq 0,\\ \text{for } t \geq 0}} \sum_{t=0}^{\infty} (1+r)^{-1} v(C_t) \\ &\text{s.t.} \quad C_t + K_t \leq F(K_{t-1}), \ \text{for } t \geq 0, \\ &\text{and } K_{-1} = \overline{K}_{-1}, \end{aligned} \tag{10.96}$$

where $\overline{K}_{-1}$ is fixed and positive and $r > 0$. Euler's equation is useful for calculating optima and deriving their properties. To derive the equation, I assume that assumptions 10.18–10.21 (in section 10.1) apply.

Euler's equation may be derived as follows. Let $(\overline{\mathbf{C}}, \overline{\mathbf{K}})$ be a program that solves the above problem. Assume in addition that $\overline{C}_t > 0$ and $\overline{K}_t > 0$, for all t. Fix all the variables in the problem, except for C_t, K_t, and C_{t+1}, at their values in this optimal program, and multiply the objective function by $(1+r)^t$. When constant terms are removed from the objective function, the problem becomes

$$\begin{aligned} &\max_{C_t \geq 0,\, K_t \geq 0,\, C_{t+1} \geq 0} [v(C_t) + (1+r)^{-1} v(C_{t+1})] \\ &\text{s.t.} \quad C_t + K_t \leq F(\overline{K}_{t-1}), \ \text{and} \\ &C_{t+1} + \overline{K}_{t+1} \leq F(K_t). \end{aligned} \tag{10.97}$$

Because $\overline{C}_t > 0$ and $\overline{K}_t > 0$, the constraint qualification of the Kuhn-Tucker theorem applies to this problem. Because both F and v are strictly increasing, the feasibility constraints hold with equality at an optimum. That is,

$$\overline{C}_t + \overline{K}_t = F(\overline{K}_{t-1}),$$

for all t, so that the complementary slackness conditions hold automatically for problem 10.97. The Kuhn-Tucker theorem implies that there exist non-negative numbers P_t and P_{t+1} such that $(\overline{C}_t, \overline{K}_t, \overline{C}_{t+1})$ solves the problem

$$\max_{C_t \geq 0, K_t \geq 0, C_{t+1} \geq 0} \Big\{ v(C_t) + (1+r)^{-1} v(C_{t+1}) - P_t(C_t + K_t) \\ -(1+r)^{-1} P_{t+1}[C_{t+1} - F(K_t)] \Big\}.$$

Since $(\overline{C}_t, \overline{K}_t, \overline{C}_{t+1}) \gg 0$ by assumption, the first order conditions of this problem are

$$P_t = \frac{dv(\overline{C}_t)}{dC},$$

$$P_{t+1} = \frac{dv(\overline{C}_{t+1})}{dC},$$

and

$$P_t = (1+r)^{-1} P_{t+1} \frac{dF(\overline{K}_t)}{dK}.$$

Upon substitution, these equations give rise to the single equation

$$\frac{dv(\overline{C}_t)}{dC} = \frac{1}{1+r} \frac{dv(\overline{C}_{t+1})}{dC} \frac{dF(\overline{K}_t)}{dK}, \tag{10.98}$$

which is *Euler's equation.*

The equation determines the entire path of an optimal program once a single initial condition is fixed. To see why this is so, notice that $\overline{K}_{-1}$ is fixed by assumption, so that $F(\overline{K}_{-1})$ is known. Fix C_0 as an initial condition. Then we know that $K_0 = F(\overline{K}_{-1}) - C_0$ and hence we know $F(K_0)$. The Euler equation then determines the derivative of v at C_1 by the equation

$$\frac{dv(C_1)}{dC} = (1+r)\frac{dv(C_0)}{dC}\left(\frac{dF(K_0)}{dK}\right)^{-1}.$$

Since v is strictly concave, its derivative is a strictly decreasing function, and therefore this equation determines C_1. Suppose by induction on t that we have determined C_s, for $s \leq t$, and K_s, for $s \leq t-1$. Then by the same steps we can determine C_{t+1} and K_t. This process can be continued indefinitely or until in some period t, $K_t < 0$, which is infeasible. If the process can be continued indefinitely, it is not certain that the resulting program is optimal; there may be many feasible programs that can be generated in this way. I give an example to illustrate the use of Euler's equation and the existence of nonoptimal feasible programs that satisfy it.

EXAMPLE 10.48 Let $F(K) = 2\sqrt{K}$, $v(C) = \log C$, and $r > 0$.

Euler's equation for this example is

$$\frac{1}{C_t} = \frac{1}{1+r}\frac{1}{C_{t+1}}\frac{1}{\sqrt{K_t}},$$

which is the same as

$$C_{t+1} = \frac{1}{1+r}\frac{C_t}{\sqrt{K_t}}. \tag{10.99}$$

To solve this problem, assume that

$$K_t = sF(K_{t-1}) = s2\sqrt{K_{t-1}}, \tag{10.100}$$

for all $t \geq 0$, where $0 < s < 1$ and s is independent of t. Then, for all $t \geq 0$

$$C_t = (1-s)2\sqrt{K_{t-1}},$$

since $C_t + K_t = 2\sqrt{K_{t-1}}$. By substituting this last equation into the Euler equation 10.99 and simplifying, we obtain the equation

$$K_t = \frac{1}{1+r}\sqrt{K_{t-1}}. \tag{10.101}$$

This equation gives us the value of the constant savings rate, s, appearing in equation 10.100, namely,

$$s = \frac{1}{2(1+r)}. \tag{10.102}$$

The difference equation 10.101 converges, and the limit is $(1+r)^{-2}$. That is, if K_t evolves according to equation 10.101 then

$$\lim_{t\to\infty} K_t = \frac{1}{(1+r)^2}.$$

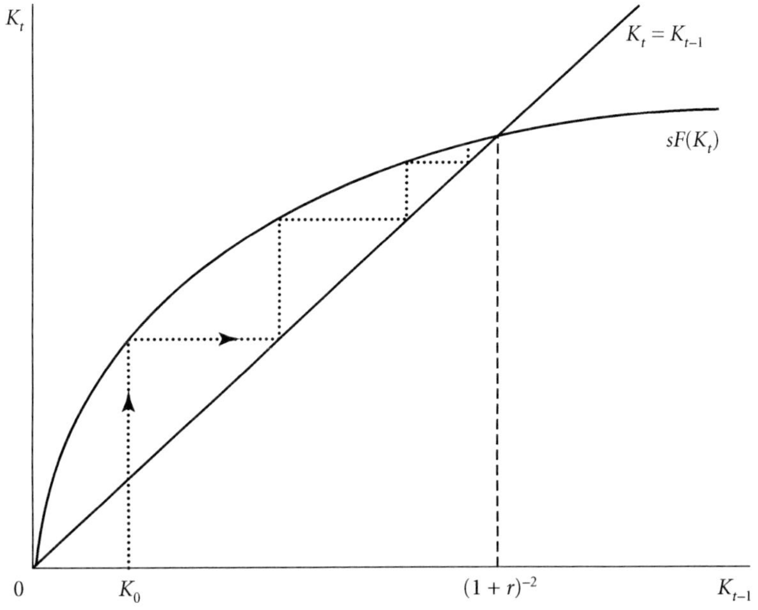

Figure 10.11 Convergence of the optimal capital stock to the optimal steady state

The convergence may be seen in figure 10.11. The straight line in the diagram is the diagonal $K_t = K_{t-1}$. The curve, labeled $sF(K_t)$, is the graph of the function $\frac{1}{1+r}\sqrt{K_{t-1}}$. Because the sequence K_t converges, so does the sequence C_t, and its limit is a positive number, namely, $\frac{1+2r}{(1+r)^2}$.

There is another way to see that the sequence K_t converges that is more closely related to the proof of the turnpike theorem, to be explained in section 10.12. Let

$$y_t = 2\sqrt{K_{t-1}} \tag{10.103}$$

be total output in period t. Then, according to equations 10.100 and 10.102,

$$K_t = sy_t = \frac{1}{2(1+r)} y_t. \tag{10.104}$$

The function sy_t appearing in this equation is called a policy function. Equations 10.103 and 10.104 define the evolution of y_t and K_t. The graphs of these two functions are shown in figure 10.12, and the dotted line indicates how y_t and K_t evolve. In the diagram, the straight line labeled *Policy*

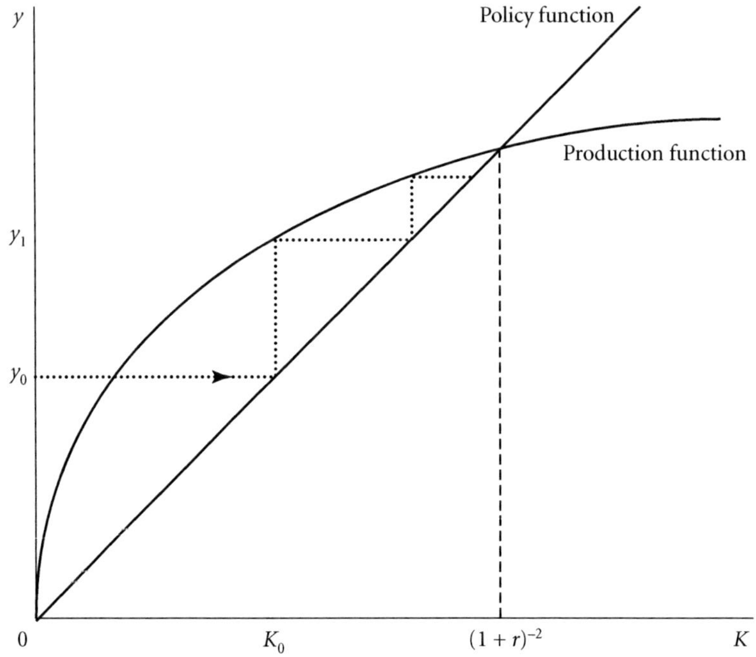

Figure 10.12 Convergence seen via policy and production functions

function represents equation 10.104, where the independent variable for the policy function is on the vertical, not the horizontal, axis. The curve labeled *Production function* represents equation 10.103.

I now explore what happens in the example if we start with the wrong initial condition. Define the number a_t by the equation

$$C_t = a_t 2\sqrt{K_{t-1}}.$$

For the consumption C_t to be feasible, we must have that $0 \leq a_t \leq 1$. If we substitute this equation for consumption into the Euler equation 10.99 and simplify, we obtain

$$a_{t+1} K_t = (1+r)^{-1} a_t \sqrt{K_{t-1}}. \tag{10.105}$$

If we substitute $(1 - a_t)2\sqrt{K_{t-1}}$ for K_t in equation 10.105 and simplify, we obtain the difference equation

$$a_{t+1} = f(a_t) = \frac{1}{2(1+r)} \frac{a_t}{1 - a_t}.$$

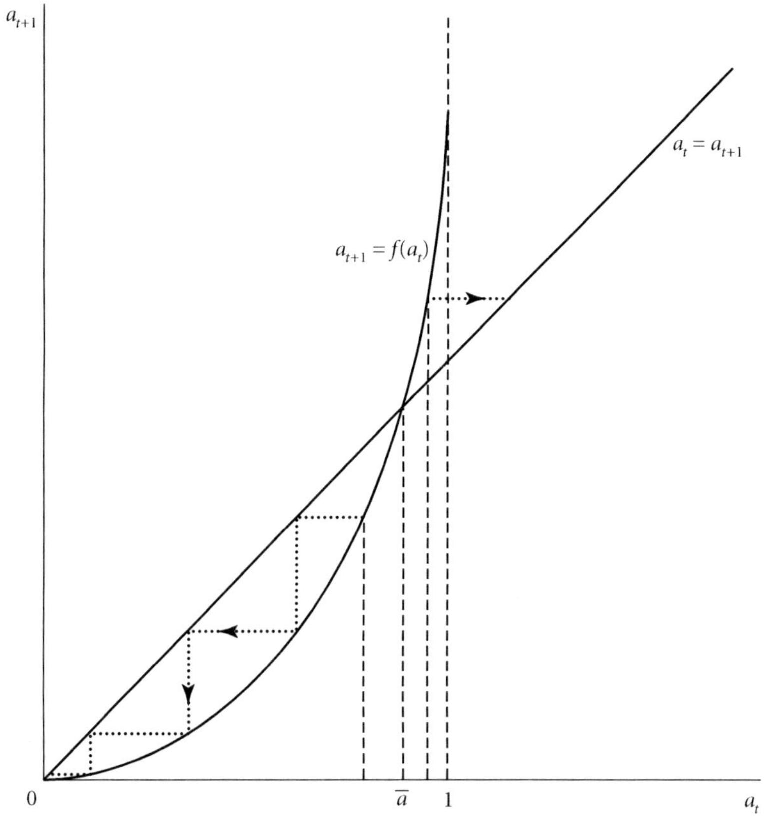

Figure 10.13 Solutions that do not converge to the optimum

Figure 10.13 indicates that this difference equation has an unstable steady state at $\overline{a} = \frac{1+2r}{2(1+r)}$. If the initial value of a_t exceeds $\overline{a}$, that is, if initial consumption exceeds the optimal value, then Euler's equation and feasibility force consumption to evolve in such a way that the program becomes infeasible. If the initial value of a_t is less than $\overline{a}$, then Euler's equation and feasibility force consumption to converge to 0 while remaining forever positive.

The case just described of a path where consumption converges to 0 is another instance of the Hahn problem mentioned in section 10.9. In this case, the overaccumulation of capital is so exaggerated that consumption asymptotically disappears. Such a program is clearly inefficient as well as suboptimal, because more consumption could be had from some time onward by stopping the decline in consumption and keeping capital at a constant level from that point on.

Although it has been assumed throughout the discussion of the use of Euler's equation that all the components of the program, $(\overline{\mathbf{C}}, \overline{\mathbf{K}})$, generated by the equation are positive, the same idea can be applied even if some components are 0. The Kuhn-Tucker theorem can be applied to problem 10.97 as long as capital input remains positive and hence the constraint qualification applies. The first-order conditions generated by that theorem are

$$\frac{dv(\overline{C}_t)}{dC} \le P_t,$$

with equality if $\overline{C}_t > 0$,

$$\frac{dv(\overline{C}_{t+1})}{dC} \le P_{t+1},$$

with equality if $\overline{C}_{t+1} > 0$, and

$$(1+r)^{-1}P_{t+1}\frac{dF(\overline{K}_t)}{dK} \le P_t,$$

with equality if $\overline{K}_t > 0$. Assume that $\overline{K}_{-1} > 0$. The appropriate initial condition is P_0, and suppose that some value for P_0 has been chosen. If $\frac{dv(0)}{dC} \le P_0$, let $\overline{C}_0 = 0$. Otherwise let $\overline{C}_0$ be the unique solution of the equation $\frac{dv(\overline{C}_0)}{dC} = P_0$ and let $\overline{K}_0 = F(\overline{K}_{-1}) - \overline{C}_0$. If $\overline{K}_0 < 0$, then the choice of P_0 is incorrect, because the program generated from it is infeasible. If $\overline{K}_0 = 0$, let $P_1 = (1+r)\left(\frac{dF(0)}{dK}\right)^{-1} P_0$, if $\frac{dF(0)}{dK} < \infty$ and let $P_1 = 0$, if $\frac{dF(0)}{dK} = \infty$. If $\frac{dv(0)}{dC} \le P_1$, let $\overline{C}_t = 0$ and $\overline{K}_t = 0$, for $t \ge 1$. In this case, the continuation stops, and the program solves problem 10.96 by the Kuhn-Tucker theorem. If $\frac{dv(0)}{dC} > P_1$, let $\overline{C}_1$ be the unique solution of the equation $\frac{dv(\overline{C}_1)}{dC} = P_1$. Since $\overline{C}_1 > 0 = F(\overline{K}_0)$, the program is infeasible and the choice of P_0 was incorrect. Similarly, the choice of P_0 was incorrect if $\frac{dF(0)}{dK} = \infty$, so that $P_1 = 0$ and hence $\overline{C}_1 = \infty$.

If $\overline{K}_0 > 0$, let $P_1 = \left(\frac{dF(\overline{K}_0)}{dK}\right)^{-1} P_0$ and let $\overline{C}_1$ be the unique solution of the relation $\frac{dv(\overline{C}_1)}{dC} \le P_1$, with equality if $\overline{C}_1 > 0$. If $\overline{C}_1 > F(\overline{K}_0)$, the choice of P_0 was incorrect, because the program generated is infeasible in period 1. Otherwise, the process may be continued. The same construction may be continued in each successive period until it is found that the program is infeasible or it is found that $\overline{K}_t = \overline{C}_t = 0$ in some period t. If $\overline{K}_t = \overline{C}_t = 0$ for some t, the program is optimal by the Kuhn-Tucker theorem. If the construction can be continued indefinitely, then $(\overline{\mathbf{C}}, \overline{\mathbf{K}}, \mathbf{p})$ is a program equilibrium, where the price sequence $\mathbf{p} = (p_0, p_1, \ldots)$ is defined by the equations $p_t = (1+r)^{-t} P_t$, for all t, and theorem 10.43 (in section 10.8) implies that the program $(\overline{\mathbf{C}}, \overline{\mathbf{K}})$ is optimal if $\sum_{t=0}^{\infty} p_t < \infty$, that is, if $\sum_{t=0}^{\infty} (1+r)^{-t} P_t < \infty$.

Optimal allocations for the Diamond model may be generated by the same process if we substitute $u_0(x_{t0}) + (1+r)u_1(x_{t-1,1})$ for $v(C_t)$, where x_{t0} and $x_{t-1,1}$ solve the problem

$$\max_{x_0 \geq 0,\, x_t \geq 0} \; [u_0(x_0) + (1+r)u_1(x_1)]$$

$$\text{s.t.} \quad x_0 + x_1 \leq C_t,$$

and if we substitute $f(K, 1)$ for $F(K)$. In this case, if we assume that assumptions 10.1–10.5 (in section 10.1) apply, the construction described in the previous paragraph generates a sequence of capital stocks $\overline{K}_t$, consumptions $\overline{x}_{t0}$ and $\overline{x}_{t-1,1}$, and spot prices P_t, for $t = 0, 1, \ldots$. The prices P_t are such that

$$\frac{du_0(\overline{x}_{t0})}{dx} \leq P_t,$$

with equality if $\overline{x}_{t0} > 0$, and

$$(1+r)\frac{du_1(\overline{x}_{t-1,1})}{dx} \leq P_t,$$

with equality if $\overline{x}_{t-1,1} > 0$, for all t. Spot wages, W_t, are defined by the equation $W_t = P_t \frac{\partial f(\overline{K}_{t-1}, 1)}{\partial L}$, for all t. Recall that u_0 and u_1 are strictly increasing and that $f(K, L)$ is increasing in L if $K > 0$. We may, therefore, assume that the entire stock of labor is used and $\overline{L}_t = 1$, for all t such that $\overline{K}_t > 0$. Lump-sum taxes, T_t, are defined by the equation $\mathrm{T}_t = W_t - P_t \overline{x}_{t0} - P_{t+1} \overline{x}_{t1}$, for all t. The initial government debt, G, is defined by the equation $G = (1+r)^{-1}[P_0 \overline{x}_{-1,1} + W_0 - P_0 f(\overline{K}_{-1}, 1)]$. If the construction can be continued indefinitely and if $\sum_{t=0}^{\infty} (1+r)^{-t} P_t < \infty$, then corollary 10.38 (in section 10.7) implies that the allocation, $(\overline{\mathbf{x}}, \overline{\mathbf{K}}, \overline{\mathbf{L}})$, of the spot price equilibrium, $(\overline{\mathbf{x}}, \overline{\mathbf{K}}, \overline{\mathbf{L}}, \mathbf{P}, \mathbf{W}, \mathbf{r}, G, \mathbf{T})$, is optimal in that it solves the problem

$$\max_{\substack{(\mathbf{x}, \mathbf{K}, \mathbf{L}) \text{ is a feasible allocation} \\ \text{with initial capital } \overline{K}_{-1}}} \sum_{t=0}^{\infty} (1+r)^{-t} [u_0(x_{t0}) + (1+r)u_1(x_{t-1,1})].$$

10.11 Policy Functions and the Value Function

I now develop tools to be used in proving the turnpike theorem in section 10.12. A first important result is that optimal programs are unique and hence are functions of the initial capital.

PROPOSITION 10.49 If assumptions 10.18–10.21 (in section 10.1) apply, then there is at most one solution to the optimal growth problem

$$\begin{aligned} &\max_{C_t \geq 0,\, K_t \geq 0} \sum_{t=0}^{\infty} (1+r)^{-t} v(C_t) \\ &\text{s.t.} \quad C_t + K_t \leq F(K_{t-1}), \text{ for } t \geq 0, \\ &\qquad \text{and } K_{-1} = \overline{K}_{-1}. \end{aligned} \tag{10.106}$$

Proof. The proof is by contradiction. Suppose that there are two distinct solutions $(\underline{\mathbf{C}}, \underline{\mathbf{K}})$ and $(\overline{\mathbf{C}}, \overline{\mathbf{K}})$. Because the programs are optimal and v is strictly increasing,

$$\underline{C}_t + \underline{K}_t = F(\underline{K}_{t-1}) \text{ and } \overline{C}_t + \overline{K}_t = F(\overline{K}_{t-1}), \tag{10.107}$$

for all $t \geq 0$. Because the programs $(\underline{\mathbf{C}}, \underline{\mathbf{K}})$ and $(\overline{\mathbf{C}}, \overline{\mathbf{K}})$ are distinct, it follows that $\underline{C}_t \neq \overline{C}_t$ or $\underline{K}_t \neq \overline{K}_t$, for some t. Because the programs $(\underline{\mathbf{C}}, \underline{\mathbf{K}})$ and $(\overline{\mathbf{C}}, \overline{\mathbf{K}})$ satisfy equation 10.107 and start with the same initial capital stock, $\overline{K}_{-1}$, it follows that if $C_t = \overline{C}_t$, for all t, then $K_t = \overline{K}_t$, for all t. Therefore, $\underline{C}_t \neq \overline{C}_t$, for some t. The program (C, K) defined by the equation

$$(C_t, K_t) = \frac{1}{2}(\underline{C}_t, \underline{K}_t) + \frac{1}{2}(\overline{C}_t, \overline{K}_t),$$

for all t, is feasible, since

$$\begin{aligned} C_t + K_t &= \frac{1}{2}\underline{C}_t + \frac{1}{2}\overline{C}_t + \frac{1}{2}\underline{K}_t + \frac{1}{2}\overline{K}_t \\ &= \frac{1}{2}(\underline{C}_t + \underline{K}_t) + \frac{1}{2}(\overline{C}_t + \overline{K}_t) \\ &= \frac{1}{2}F(\underline{K}_{t-1}) + \frac{1}{2}F(\overline{K}_{t-1}) \leq F\left(\frac{1}{2}\underline{K}_{t-1} + \frac{1}{2}\overline{K}_{t-1}\right) = F(K_{t-1}), \end{aligned}$$

where the inequality follows from the concavity of F. Since $(\underline{\mathbf{C}}, \underline{\mathbf{K}})$ and $(\overline{\mathbf{C}}, \overline{\mathbf{K}})$ both have initial capital $\overline{K}_{-1}$, $(\mathbf{C}, \mathbf{K})$ is feasible with the same initial capital. By the definition of $(\underline{\mathbf{C}}, \underline{\mathbf{K}})$,

$$\sum_{t=0}^{\infty}(1+r)^{-t}v(C_t) = \sum_{t=0}^{\infty}(1+r)^{-t}v\left(\frac{1}{2}\underline{C}_t + \frac{1}{2}\overline{C}_t\right).$$

Because v is strictly concave and $\underline{C}_t \neq \overline{C}_t$, for some t, it follows that

$$\begin{aligned}
&\sum_{t=0}^{\infty}(1+r)^{-t}v\left(\frac{1}{2}\underline{C}_t + \frac{1}{2}\overline{C}_t\right) \\
&\quad > \frac{1}{2}\sum_{t=0}^{\infty}(1+r)^{-t}v(\underline{C}_t) + \frac{1}{2}\sum_{t=0}^{\infty}(1+r)^{-t}v(\overline{C}_t) \qquad (10.108)\\
&\quad = \sum_{t=0}^{\infty}(1+r)^{-t}v(\underline{C}_t),
\end{aligned}$$

where the equation holds because

$$\sum_{t=0}^{\infty}(1+r)^{-t}v(\underline{C}_t) = \sum_{t=0}^{\infty}(1+r)^{-t}v(\overline{C}_t),$$

since $(\underline{\mathbf{C}}, \underline{\mathbf{K}})$ and $(\overline{\mathbf{C}}, \overline{\mathbf{K}})$ are both optimal. Since inequality 10.108 contradicts the optimality of $(\underline{\mathbf{C}}, \underline{\mathbf{K}})$, there is only one optimal program. ▪

By theorem 10.84 (in section 10.14), optimal programs exist under assumptions 10.18–10.21. Since optimal programs are also unique, they are functions of the initial capital $\overline{K}_{-1}$. It is more convenient to think of the initial condition as $\overline{y}_0 = F(\overline{K}_{-1})$, so that the optimal program is a function of $\overline{y}_0$. Specifically, $\overline{C}_0 = c(\overline{y}_0)$, and $\overline{K}_0 = k(\overline{y}_0)$, where the optimal program is $(\overline{\mathbf{C}}, \overline{\mathbf{K}})$. Because the optimization problem from any time t onward is just like that from time 0 onward, it follows that $\overline{C}_t = c(\overline{y}_t)$, and $\overline{K}_t = k(\overline{y}_t)$, for any t, where $\overline{y}_t = F(\overline{K}_{t-1})$. The functions c and k are called *policy functions,* and they can be used to define any optimal program iteratively.

To derive properties of the policy functions, I use the *value function,* V, which gives the optimal value, $V(y)$, of the objective function in problem 10.106, given that $F(\overline{K}_{-1}) = y$. That is,

$$V(y) = \max_{\substack{C_t \geq 0,\, K_t \geq 0, \\ \text{for } t=0,\,1,\,\ldots}} \sum_{t=0}^{\infty} (1+r)^{-t} v(C_t)$$

$$\text{s.t.} \quad C_0 + K_0 \leq y, \text{ and}$$

$$C_{t+1} + K_{t+1} \leq F(K_t), \text{ for } t \geq 0.$$

The value function is useful in large part because of the Bellman equation, which I now derive. Suppose that in this maximization problem we optimize first with respect to C_t and K_t, for $t \geq 1$, and then maximize with respect to C_0 and K_0. We then see that the maximization problem may be rewritten as

$$\max_{\substack{C_0 \geq 0,\, K_0 \geq 0: \\ C_0 + K_0 \leq y}} [v(C_0) + \max_{\substack{C_t \geq 0,\, K_t \geq 0: \\ C_t + K_t \leq F(K_{t-1}) \\ \text{for } t=1,\,2,\,\ldots}} \sum_{t=1}^{\infty} (1+r)^{-t} v(C_t)],$$

which is the same as

$$\max_{\substack{C_0 \geq 0,\, K_0 \geq 0: \\ C_0 + K_0 \leq y}} \{v(C_0) + (1+r)^{-1} [\max_{\substack{C_t \geq 0,\, K_t \geq 0: \\ C_t + K_t \leq F(K_{t-1}) \\ \text{for } t=1,\,2,\,\ldots}} \sum_{t=0}^{\infty} (1+r)^{-t} v(C_{t+1})]\}.$$

Since the second maximum in this problem is $V(F(K_0))$, this last problem is seen to be the same as

$$\max_{C_0 \geq 0,\, K_0 \geq 0} [v(C_0) + (1+r)^{-1} V(F(K_0))]$$

$$\text{s.t.} \quad C_0 + K_0 \leq y,$$

so that

$$V(y) = \max_{C_0 \geq 0,\, K_0 \geq 0} [v(C_0) + (1+r)^{-1} V(F(K_0))]$$

$$\text{s.t.} \quad C_0 + K_0 \leq y.$$

Equations of this type are known as *Bellman equations* in the literature on dynamic programming. The idea of the equation is that the optimization problem from time 1 on is the same as the optimization problem from time 0 on with the initial stock of goods equal to $F(K(y))$ rather than y.

Useful properties of the value function are that it is concave, increasing, and differentiable.

PROPOSITION 10.50 If assumptions 10.18–10.21 apply, then the value function, V, is concave.

Proof. Let $\underline{y}$ and $\overline{y}$ be initial stocks and let $0 < \alpha < 1$. I show that

$$V(\alpha \underline{y} + (1-\alpha)\overline{y}) \geq \alpha V(\underline{y}) + (1-\alpha)V(\overline{y}).$$

Let $(\underline{\mathbf{C}}, \underline{\mathbf{K}})$ and $(\overline{\mathbf{C}}, \overline{\mathbf{K}})$ be optimal programs beginning with initial stocks $\underline{y}$ and $\overline{y}$, respectively. That is,

$$V(\underline{y}) = \sum_{t=0}^{\infty} v(\underline{C}_t) \text{ and } V(\overline{y}) = \sum_{t=0}^{\infty} v(\overline{C}_t).$$

Let $(\mathbf{C}, \mathbf{K})$ be the program defined by the equations

$$C_t = \alpha \underline{C}_t + (1-\alpha)\overline{C}_t \text{ and}$$
$$K_t = \alpha \underline{K}_t + (1-\alpha)\overline{K}_t.$$

This program is feasible if the initial stock of goods equals $\alpha \underline{y} + (1-\alpha)\overline{y}$, since

$$\begin{aligned} C_0 + K_0 &= \alpha \underline{C}_0 + (1-\alpha)\overline{C}_0 + \alpha \underline{K}_0 + (1-\alpha)\overline{K}_0 \\ &= \alpha(\underline{C}_0 + \underline{K}_0) + (1-\alpha)(\overline{C}_0 + \overline{K}_0) \\ &\leq \alpha \underline{y} + (1-\alpha)\overline{y}, \end{aligned}$$

and, for $t \geq 1$,

$$\begin{aligned} C_t + K_t &= \alpha \underline{C}_t + (1-\alpha)\overline{C}_t + \alpha \underline{K}_t + (1-\alpha)\overline{K}_t \\ &= \alpha(\underline{C}_t + \underline{K}_t) + (1-\alpha)(\overline{C}_t + \overline{K}_t) \\ &\leq \alpha F(\underline{K}_{t-1}) + (1-\alpha)F(\overline{K}_{t-1}) \leq F(\alpha \underline{K}_{t-1} + (1-\alpha)\overline{K}_{t-1}) \\ &= F(K_{t-1}), \end{aligned}$$

where the last inequality follows from the concavity of F.

The proof of the concavity of V is completed by observing that

$$\begin{aligned} \alpha V(\underline{y}) + (1-\alpha)V(\overline{y}) &= \alpha \sum_{t=0}^{\infty} v(\underline{C}_t) + (1-\alpha) \sum_{t=0}^{\infty} v(\overline{C}_t) \\ &\leq \sum_{t=0}^{\infty} v(\alpha \underline{C}_t + (1-\alpha)\overline{C}_t) \\ &= \sum_{t=0}^{\infty} v(C_t) \leq V(\alpha \underline{y} + (1-\alpha)\overline{y}), \end{aligned}$$

where the next to last inequality follows from the concavity of v and the last inequality follows from the definition of $V(\alpha \underline{y} + (1-\alpha)\overline{y})$. ■

PROPOSITION 10.51 If assumptions 10.18–10.21 apply, then the value function, V, is strictly increasing.

Proof. Because any increase in the initial stock can be consumed in period 0, it follows that if $\Delta y > 0$, then

$$V(y + \Delta y) \geq V(y) + v(c(y) + \Delta y) - v(c(y)) > V(y),$$

where the last inequality is valid because v is strictly increasing. ▪

PROPOSITION 10.52 If assumptions 10.18–10.21 apply, then the value function, V, is differentiable and

$$\frac{dV(y)}{dy} = \frac{dv(c(y))}{dC}, \tag{10.109}$$

if $c(y) > 0$.

Proof. The proof is very much like the proof of lemma 10.23 (in section 10.1), which is the statement that v is differentiable. If $c(y) > 0$, I prove that V is differentiable by trapping it between two differentiable functions. If $c(y) > 0$, a small enough increase or decrease in y can be absorbed in a change in C_0 with no change in any other variable. Therefore

$$v(c(y) + \Delta y) - v(c(y)) + V(y) \leq V(y + \Delta y), \tag{10.110}$$

for Δy so small that $y + \Delta y \geq 0$ and $c(y) + \Delta y \geq 0$. Inequality 10.110 may be rewritten as

$$v(c(y) + \Delta y) - v(c(y)) \leq V(y + \Delta y) - V(y). \tag{10.111}$$

Because $c(y) > 0$, it follows that $y > 0$. Therefore, by lemma 10.22 (in section 10.1), there is a positive number b such that

$$V(y + \Delta y) \leq V(y) + b\Delta y.$$

This inequality may be rewritten as

$$V(y + \Delta y) - V(y) \leq b\Delta y. \tag{10.112}$$

Inequalities 10.111 and 10.112 assert that $V(y + \Delta y) - V(y)$ lies between two differentiable functions of Δy, that are both equal to 0 when $\Delta y = 0$, namely, the functions $b\Delta y$, and $v(c(y) + \Delta y) - v(c(y))$. It follows, as in the proof of lemma 10.23, that V is differentiable at y and that

$$\frac{dV(y)}{dy} = \frac{dv(c(y))}{dC}.$$

Suppose now that $y > 0$ but that $c(y) = 0$. Since all of y may be consumed in period 0, we know that $V(y) > 0$. Therefore, $C_t(y) > 0$, for some $t > 0$, where $(\mathbf{C}(y), \mathbf{K}(y))$ is the optimal program with the stock of output in period 0 equal to y. Let T be the smallest value of t such that $C_t(y) > 0$. Since $C_T(y) > 0$, V is differentiable at $F(K_{T-1}(y))$, which is the stock of output available for consumption or investment in period T. Since $C_t(y) = 0$, for $t = 0, 1, \ldots, T-1$,

$$F(K_{T-1}(y)) = F^{T-1}(K_0(y)),$$

where F^{T-1} is F composed with itself $T-1$ times. Since $C_0(y) = 0$, it follows that $K_0(y) = y$. Since F is differentiable by assumption 10.19, it follows that

$$\frac{dV(y)}{dy} = \frac{dF(y)}{dK}\frac{dF(K_1(y))}{dK}\cdots\frac{dF(K_{T-1}(y))}{dK}\frac{dV(F(K_{T-1}))}{dz},$$

where z represents the dependent variable of the function V. Since $C_T(y) > 0$, $\frac{dV(F(K_{T-1}))}{dz}$ exists by the argument of the previous paragraph. Therefore, V is differentiable at y.

Because V is concave, it is differentiable at 0, though the derivative may be infinite. This argument was explained in the proof of lemma 10.23. ▪

Euler's equation may be rewritten using the value function and the Bellman equation. Recall that Euler's equation is

$$\frac{dv(\overline{C}_t)}{dC} = \frac{1}{1+r}\frac{\partial F(\overline{K}_t)}{\partial K}\frac{dv(\overline{C}_{t+1})}{dC},$$

where $(\overline{\mathbf{C}}, \overline{\mathbf{K}})$ is an optimal program. Using policy functions, Euler's equation may be rewritten as

$$\frac{dv(c(y))}{dC} = \frac{1}{1+r}\frac{dF(k(y))}{dK}\frac{dv(c(F(k(y))))}{dC}.$$

A useful form, obtained by substitution from equation 10.109, is

$$\frac{dV(y)}{dy} = \frac{1}{1+r}\frac{dF(k(y))}{dK}\frac{dV(F(k(y)))}{dy}. \tag{10.113}$$

I now prove properties of the policy functions, c and k, that will be used in proving the turnpike theorem.

PROPOSITION 10.53 The functions $c(y)$ and $k(y)$ are continuous and nondecreasing functions of the initial stock, y.

Proof. Because V is concave, $\frac{dV(y)}{dy}$ is a nonincreasing function of y. Therefore, equation 10.109 implies that if y increases, $\frac{dv(c(y))}{dy}$ does not increase. Because $\frac{dv(C)}{dC}$ is a strictly decreasing function of C by assumption 10.21, it follows that $c(y)$ does not decrease when y increases.

I next show that the function $k(y)$ is nondecreasing. Suppose that the function k is decreasing at some point y and that y increases. Because V is concave, $\frac{dV(y)}{dy}$ does not increase. The number $k(y)$ decreases, and so $F(k(y))$ decreases, since the function F is increasing by assumption 10.19. Therefore, $\frac{dV(F(k(y)))}{dy}$ does not decrease. Similarly, $\frac{dF(k(y))}{dK}$ increases, because $\frac{dF(K)}{dK}$ is a decreasing function of K by assumption 10.19. Therefore, if $k(y)$ decreases when y increases, the right-hand side of equation 10.113 increases whereas the left-hand side does not increase. This contradiction proves that $k(y)$ cannot decrease.

Because $c(y) + k(y) = y$ and both $c(y)$ and $k(y)$ are nondecreasing, it follows that for any positive number ε,

$$c(y) \le c(y+\varepsilon) \le c(y) + \varepsilon \text{ and}$$
$$k(y) \le k(y+\varepsilon) \le k(y) + \varepsilon,$$

and so both of the functions c and k are continuous. ▪

10.12 The Turnpike Theorem

The term *turnpike theorem* arose early in work on optimal growth theory. We may visualize the turnpike in a model in which the initial and terminal capital stocks are held fixed. Suppose that the initial and terminal periods are -1 and T, respectively, so that $\underline{K}_{-1}$ and $\underline{K}_T$ are the initial and terminal capital stocks. Radner (1961) showed that if T was large, then the optimal path of capital approaches a unique optimal stationary level, stays close to it for a large fraction of the $T+2$ periods, and veers away toward the terminal stock only in the final periods. The picture is like that in figure 10.14, where time is on the horizontal axis. The image resembles a map of an interstate highway or turnpike with entrance and exit ramps. In other work, researchers assume that the horizon is infinite, so that there is only an entrance ramp, and the theorem says that optimal paths asymptotically approach the unique stationary optimal path. The term *turnpike theorem* refers to any such assertion. Turnpike theorems give structure to optimal

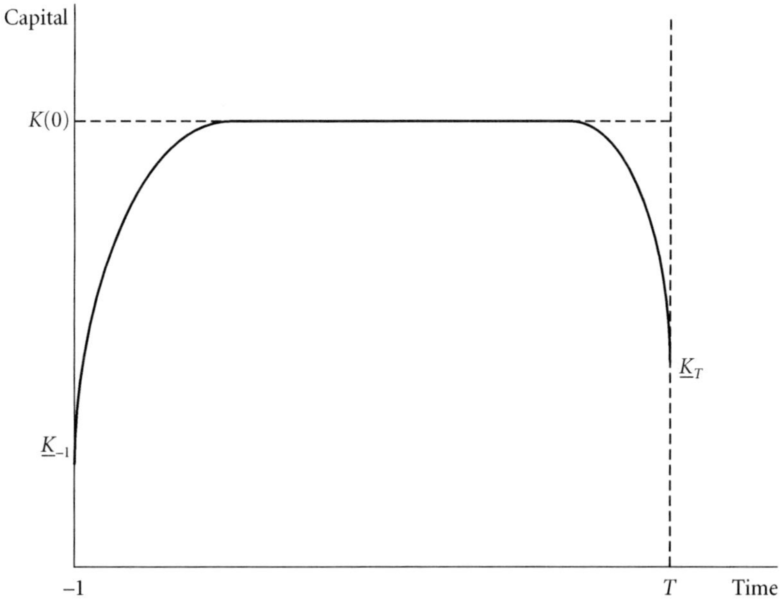

Figure 10.14 The turnpike

paths and focus attention on the stationary optimal one. Since convergence to the unique optimal stationary path is quite rapid in most fully specified examples, we are encouraged to think of modern economies as always near the stationary optimal state.[5]

It is easy to prove a turnpike theorem for the one-sector growth model using the results of the previous section.

TURNPIKE THEOREM 10.54 Suppose that assumptions 10.18–10.21 apply. Let $(\overline{\mathbf{C}}, \overline{\mathbf{K}})$ be the optimal program that solves the problem

$$\max_{\substack{C_t \geq 0,\, K_t \geq 0, \\ \text{for } t=0,1,\ldots}} \sum_{t=0}^{\infty} (1+r)^{-t} v(C_t)$$
$$\text{s.t.} \quad C_t + K_t \leq F(K_{t-1}), \ \text{for } t \geq 0,$$
$$\text{and } K_{-1} = \overline{K}_{-1}, \tag{10.114}$$

5. The analogy just described with a turnpike highway was, according to McKenzie (1976, 841), first made by Dorfman, Samuelson, and Solow (1958, 331).

where $\overline{K}_{-1}$ is fixed, $\overline{K}_{-1} > 0$, and where $r > 0$. Let $(C(r), K(r))$ be the modified golden rule program with interest rate r. Then, $\lim_{t\to\infty}(\overline{C}_t, \overline{K}_t) = (C(r), K(r))$.

A disappointing feature of growth theory is that this turnpike theorem does not generalize fully to models with many commodities or with uncertainty. The turnpike theorem with a positive discount rate, r, seems to require special assumptions in these interesting settings, and the generalizations are true only when r is sufficiently small. The turnpike theorems with $r = 0$, theorems 10.79 and 10.80 (in section 10.13), do generalize to models with many commodities and with uncertainty. For this reason, they probably should be thought of as the true turnpike theorems.

Proof.[6] Let $k(y)$ be the optimal policy function defined in section 10.11. Because the stationary program $(C(r), K(r))$ is optimal if the initial stock of produced good is $y(r) = F(K(r))$, it follows that

$$k(F(K(r))) = K(r). \tag{10.115}$$

Consider figures 10.15 and 10.16 showing the functions $y = F(K)$ and $K = k(y)$, where the production function F is read from the horizontal to the vertical axis and the policy function, k, is read from the vertical to the horizontal axis. Equation 10.115 implies that the graphs of the two functions intersect at the point $(K(r), y(r))$. In the figures, the evolution of the capital stock, K_t, and total output, y_t, follow the dotted paths. That is, $K_0 = k(y_0)$, $y_1 = F(K_0)$, $K_1 = k(y_1)$, $y_2 = F(K_1)$, and so on. We see that if the curves k and F are as in the diagrams, then K_t converges to $K(r)$ as t goes to infinity. I have already shown that the function k is continuous and nondecreasing. The function F is continuous and increasing by assumption 10.19. I must show that the graph of k lies to the right of the graph of F for values of y less than $y(r)$ and that the graph of k lies to the left of the graph of F for values of y exceeding $y(r)$.

First of all, the graphs of k and F intersect only at the origin and at the point $(K(r), y(r))$. If y is the output coordinate of an intersection point and y is positive, then $y = F(k(y))$, and by Euler's equation 10.113 (in section 10.11), $\frac{dF(k(y))}{dK} = 1 + r$, and hence $k(y) = K(r)$, and $y = F(k(y)) = F(K(r)) = y(r)$. I next show that if $0 < y < y(r)$, then $k(y) > F^{-1}(y)$. Let

6. The following proof is based on section 2 of Brock and Mirman (1972).

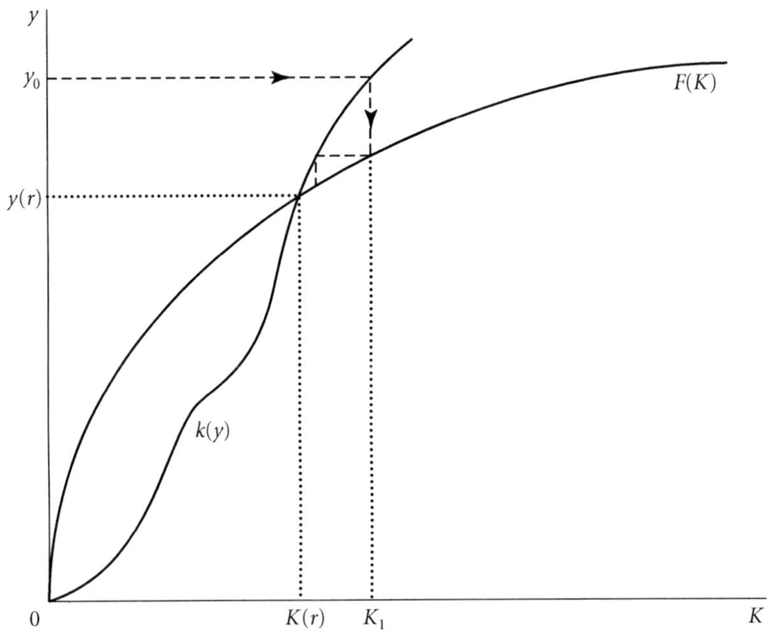

Figure 10.15 The policy and production functions

$y < y(r)$ and suppose that $k(y) \leq F^{-1}(y)$. I derive a contradiction. Because $k(y) \leq F^{-1}(y)$ and F is increasing, $F(k(y)) \leq y$. Because V is concave, the function $\frac{dV(y)}{dy}$ is nonincreasing in y, so that

$$\frac{dV(F(k(y)))}{dy} \geq \frac{dV(y)}{dy}.$$

This inequality and Euler's equation 10.113 (in section 10.11) imply that

$$\frac{1}{1+r}\frac{dF(k(y))}{dK} \leq 1,$$

which is the same as

$$\frac{dF(k(y))}{dK} \leq 1+r.$$

Because $\frac{dF(K)}{dK}$ is a decreasing function of K and $\frac{dF(K(r))}{dK} = 1+r$, it follows that

$$k(y) \geq K(r). \tag{10.116}$$

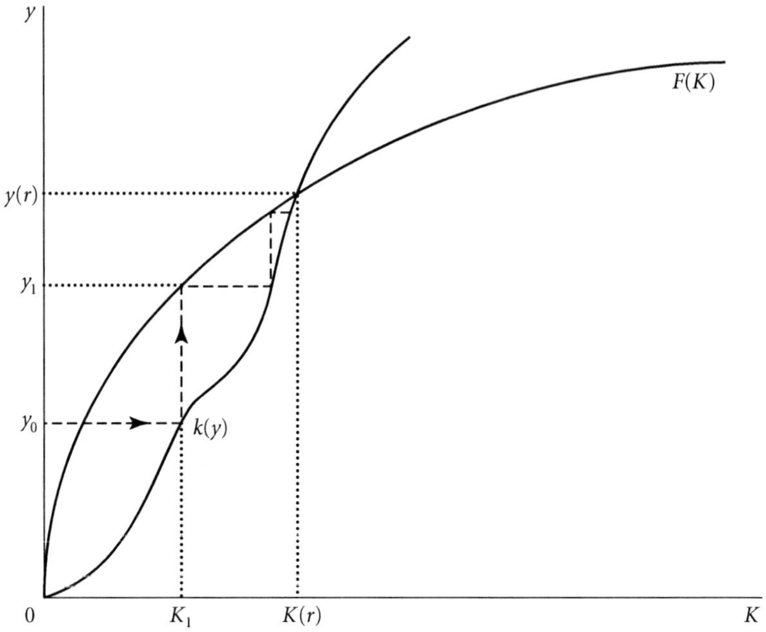

Figure 10.16 The policy and production functions

Recall that $k(y) \leq F^{-1}(y)$ and $y < y(r)$, by hypothesis. Since $F^{-1}(y)$ is an increasing function of y, it follows that

$$k(y) \leq F^{-1}(y) < F^{-1}(y(r)) = K(r). \qquad (10.117)$$

The contradiction between inequalities 10.116 and 10.117 implies that $k(y) > F^{-1}(y)$ when $0 < y < y(r)$.

A similar argument implies that $k(y) < F^{-1}(y)$ when $y > y(r)$. ∎

THEOREM 10.55 Suppose that the Diamond model presented in section 10.1 satisfies assumptions 10.1–10.5 and that the allocation $(\overline{x}, \overline{K}, \overline{L})$ solves the problem

$$\max_{\substack{(\mathbf{x}, \mathbf{K}, \mathbf{L}) \text{ is a feasible} \\ \text{allocation with initial capital } \overline{K}_{-1}}} \sum_{t=0}^{\infty} (1+r)^{-t}[u_0(x_{t0}) + (1+r)u_1(x_{t-1,1})] \qquad (10.118)$$

where $\overline{K}_{-1}$ is fixed, $\overline{K}_{-1} > 0$, and $r > 0$. Then,

$$\lim_{t\to\infty} (\overline{x}_{t0}, \overline{x}_{t1}, \overline{K}_t) = (x_0(r), x_1(r), K(r)),$$

where $(x_0(r), x_1(r), K(r), L(r))$ is the modified golden rule allocation.

Proof. For all t, let $\underline{L}_t = 1$. Because f is nondecreasing, the allocation $(\overline{\mathbf{x}}, \overline{\mathbf{K}}, \underline{\mathbf{L}})$ is feasible and therefore optimal. That is, it solves problem 10.118.

Let (F, v) correspond to (f, u_0, u_1) at interest rate r in the manner that was described after definition 10.15 (in section 10.1). Let $\overline{C}_t = \overline{x}_{t0} + \overline{x}_{t-1,1}$, for all t. By proposition 10.16 (in section 10.1), the optimality of $(\overline{\mathbf{x}}, \overline{\mathbf{K}}, \underline{\mathbf{L}})$ implies that the program $(\overline{\mathbf{C}}, \overline{\mathbf{K}})$ solves problem 10.114. Therefore, the turnpike theorem 10.54 implies that $\lim_{t\to\infty}(\overline{C}_t, \overline{K}_t) = (C(r), K(r))$. By lemma 10.17 (in section 10.1), we can write $\overline{x}_{t0} = x_0(\overline{C}_t)$ and $\overline{x}_t = x_1(\overline{C}_t)$, for all t, where the functions x_0 and x_1 are continuous. Similarly, $x_0(r) = x_0(C(r))$, and $x_1(r) = x_1(C(r))$. It follows that

$$\begin{aligned}\lim_{t\to\infty} (\overline{x}_{t0}, \overline{x}_{t1}) &= \lim_{t\to\infty} (x_0(\overline{C}_t), x_1(\overline{C}_t)) = (x_0(C(r)), x_1(C(r)) \\ &= (x_0(r), x_1(r)). \quad \blacksquare\end{aligned}$$

The turnpike theorem makes it possible to eliminate the special condition in corollary 10.40 (in section 10.7). This condition is that when t is large enough, total consumption in period t is bounded away from 0.

THEOREM 10.56 Suppose that the Diamond model presented in section 10.1 satisfies assumptions 10.1–10.5. Suppose also that r is positive and so small that $K(r) > 0$. Then the feasible allocation $(\overline{x}, \overline{K}, \overline{L})$ solves problem 10.118 if and only if there exist sequences of spot prices and wages, $\mathbf{P} = (P_0, P_1, \ldots)$ and $\mathbf{W} = (W_0, W_1, \ldots)$, a sequence of lump-sum taxes, $\mathsf{T} = (\mathsf{T}_0, \mathsf{T}_1, \ldots)$, and an initial quantity of government debt, G, such that $(\overline{\mathbf{x}}, \overline{\mathbf{K}}, \overline{\mathbf{L}}, \mathbf{P}, \mathbf{W}, \mathbf{r}, G, \mathsf{T})$ is a spot price equilibrium in which $r_t = r$, for all t, and

$$P_0 + \sum_{t=1}^{\infty}(1+r)^{-t}P_t < \infty,$$

and the marginal utility of unit of account of every consumer is 1.

Theorem 10.56 implies that the modified golden rule allocation is optimal in that it solves problem 10.118. The turnpike theorem 10.55 implies that the modified golden rule is the unique stationary allocation with positive capital that is optimal when utility is discounted at a positive interest rate, since any other stationary allocation with positive capital converges to the modified golden rule, and one stationary allocation can converge to another only if they are equal.

In proving theorem 10.56, I use the following lemma.

LEMMA 10.57 Suppose that the Diamond model satisfies assumptions 10.1–10.5 and that $r > 0$. If $(x_0(r), x_1(r), K(r), L(r))$ is the optimal stationary allocation that solves problem 10.118 with $\overline{K}_{-1} = K(r)$, and if $K(r) > 0$, then $x_0(r) + x_1(r) > 0$.

Similarly, if $(C(r), K(r))$ is the optimal stationary program that solves problem 10.114 with $\overline{K}_{-1} = K(r)$ and $K(r) > 0$, then $C(r) > 0$.

Proof. I prove the lemma only for the Diamond model, since the proof for the growth model is similar. Since $x_0(r) + x_1(r) = f(K(r), 1) - K(r)$, it is sufficient to show that $f(K(r), 1) - K(r) > 0$. Assumption 10.3 implies that $f(0, 1) - 0 = 0$. Since, in addition,

$$\frac{\partial[f(K, 1) - K]}{\partial K} = \frac{\partial f(K, 1)}{\partial K} - 1 > 0,$$

if $K < K(0)$, it follows that $f(K, 1) - K > 0$, if $0 < K < K(0)$. Since $0 < K(r) < K(0)$, it follows that $f(K(r), 1) - K(r) > 0$. ■

Proof of Theorem 10.56. First of all, $K(r) > 0$, if r is sufficiently small and positive, since $K(r)$ satisfies the relation

$$\frac{\partial f(K(r), 1)}{\partial K} \leq 1 + r,$$

with equality if $K > 0$, and because assumptions 10.2–10.4 imply that $\frac{\partial f(0,1)}{\partial K} > 1$.

Suppose that $(\overline{\mathbf{x}}, \overline{\mathbf{K}}, \overline{\mathbf{L}})$ solves problem 10.118. By theorem 10.55,

$$\lim_{t\to\infty} (\overline{x}_{t0}, \overline{x}_{t1}, \overline{K}_t) = (x_0(r), x_1(r), K(r)).$$

Since $x_0(r) + x_1(r) > 0$ by lemma 10.57 and since $\lim_{t\to\infty}(\overline{x}_{t0}, \overline{x}_{t1}) = (x_0(r), x_1(r))$, it follows that there exists a positive number ε such that if t is sufficiently large, then $x_0(r) + x_1(r) \geq \varepsilon$. Therefore, corollary 10.40 (in section 10.7) implies that $(\overline{\mathbf{x}}, \overline{\mathbf{K}}, \overline{\mathbf{L}})$ is the allocation of a spot price equilibrium, $(\overline{\mathbf{x}}, \overline{\mathbf{K}}, \overline{\mathbf{L}}, \mathbf{P}, \mathbf{W}, \mathbf{r}, G, \mathbf{T})$, in which the marginal utility of unit of account of every consumer is 1 and where $r_t = r$, for all t, and

$$\sum_{t=0}^{\infty} (1+r)^{-t} P_t < \infty.$$

Suppose that $(\overline{\mathbf{x}}, \overline{\mathbf{K}}, \overline{\mathbf{L}}, \mathbf{P}, \mathbf{W}, \mathbf{r}, G, \mathbf{T})$ is a spot equilibrium in which the marginal utility of unit of account of every consumer is 1 and $r_t = r$, for all t, and

$$P_0 + \sum_{t=1}^{\infty}(1+r)^{-t} P_t < \infty.$$

Then, by corollary 10.38 (in section 10.7), the allocation $(\overline{\mathbf{x}}, \overline{\mathbf{K}}, \overline{\mathbf{L}})$ solves problem 10.118. ■

The analogue of theorem 10.56 applies to the growth model.

COROLLARY 10.58 Suppose that the one-sector growth model satisfies assumptions 10.18–10.21, that $r > 0$ and r is so small that $K(r) > 0$, where $K(r)$ satisfies the equation

$$\frac{\partial f(K(r), 1)}{\partial K} = 1 + r.$$

Then, the program $(\overline{\mathbf{C}}, \overline{\mathbf{K}})$ solves problem 10.114 if and only if there is a sequence of $\mathbf{p} = (p_0, p_1, \ldots)$ such that $\sum_{t=0}^{\infty} p_t < \infty$ and $(\overline{\mathbf{C}}, \overline{\mathbf{K}}, r, \mathbf{p})$ is a program equilibrium.

Proof. This assertion is an immediate consequence of theorem 10.56, theorem 10.42 (in section 10.8), and proposition 10.16 (in section 10.1). ■

Corollary 10.58 implies that the modified golden rule program is optimal in that it solves problem 10.114, and the turnpike theorem 10.54 implies that the modified golden rule is the unique stationary program with positive capital that is optimal when utility is discounted, since any other stationary optimal program with positive capital converges to the modified golden rule.

Recall that at the end of section 10.10 I explained how to generate an entire feasible program, $(\overline{\mathbf{C}}, \overline{\mathbf{K}})$, and equilibrium prices for it, $(1+r)^{-t} P_t$, from the initial condition, P_0. It is now possible to show that this process has one and only one correct initial condition.

COROLLARY 10.59 Suppose that the one-sector growth model satisfies assumptions 10.18–10.21 and that $r > 0$ and r is so small that $K(r) > 0$. If $\overline{K}_{-1} > 0$, then there exists one and only initial choice of P_0 such that a program equilibrium, $(\overline{\mathbf{C}}, \overline{\mathbf{K}}, r, \mathbf{p})$, can be constructed iteratively from this choice, where, for all t, the price at time t is $p_t = (1+r)^{-t}P_t$, $\overline{C}_t$ solves the relation $\frac{dv(\overline{C}_t)}{dC} \le P_t$, with equality if $\overline{C}_t > 0$, and the sequence P_t is bounded and bounded away from 0. The program so obtained, $(\overline{\mathbf{C}}, \overline{\mathbf{K}})$, is the unique program that solves the problem

$$\max_{\substack{(\mathbf{C},\,\mathbf{K}) \text{ is a feasible program} \\ \text{with initial capital } \overline{K}_{-1}}} \sum_{t=0}^{\infty} (1+r)^{-t} v(C_t).$$

Proof. Theorem 10.84 (in section 10.14) implies that there exists an optimal program, $(\overline{\mathbf{C}}, \overline{\mathbf{K}})$, starting from $\overline{K}_{-1}$. The turnpike theorem 10.54 implies that $\lim_{t\to\infty}(\overline{C}_t, \overline{K}_t) = (C(r), K(r))$. By lemma 10.57, $C(r) > 0$, so that $\overline{C}_t > 0$, for t sufficiently large. If $\overline{C}_t > 0$, then $P_t = \frac{dv(\overline{C}_t)}{dC}$, by the construction of the spot prices P_t. Therefore, $\lim_{t\to\infty} P_t = \frac{dv(C(r))}{dC}$, so that the sequence P_t is bounded and bounded away from 0. By proposition 10.49 (in section 10.11), the optimal allocation, $(\overline{\mathbf{C}}, \overline{\mathbf{K}})$, is unique, so that the spot prices, P_t, are uniquely defined if t is so large that $\overline{C}_t > 0$. Let T be so large that $\overline{C}_T > 0$. Then, $\overline{K}_t > 0$, for $t < T$, so that $P_t = (1+r)^{-1}P_{t+1}\frac{dF(\overline{K}_t)}{dK}$, for $t < T$, and hence P_t is uniquely defined for all $t < T$, by backward induction on t. Let $p_t = (1+r)^{-t}P_t$, for all t. Then $(\overline{\mathbf{C}}, \overline{\mathbf{K}}, r, \mathbf{p})$ is a program equilibrium, and it has been shown that it is the only one with the stated properties.

It remains to be shown that if a program equilibrium, $(\overline{\mathbf{C}}, \overline{\mathbf{K}}, r, \mathbf{p})$, has the stated properties, then the program $(\overline{\mathbf{C}}, \overline{\mathbf{K}})$ is optimal. If the sequence P_t is bounded, then $\sum_{t=0}^{\infty} p_t = \sum_{t=0}^{\infty}(1+r)^{-t}P_t < \infty$ and so theorem 10.43 (in section 10.8) implies that $(\overline{\mathbf{C}}, \overline{\mathbf{K}})$ is optimal. ■

A similar result for the Diamond model follows from the previous corollary because of the equivalence between optimal programs for the growth model and optimal allocations for the Diamond model. This equivalence is stated as proposition 10.16 (in section 10.1).

COROLLARY 10.60 Suppose that the Diamond model satisfies assumptions 10.1–10.5, that $r > 0$, and r is so small that $K(r) > 0$. If $\overline{K}_{-1} > 0$, then there exists one and only one initial choice of P_0 such that a spot price equilibrium, $(\overline{\mathbf{x}}, \overline{\mathbf{K}}, \overline{\mathbf{L}}, \mathbf{P}, \mathbf{W}, \mathbf{r}, G, \mathbf{T})$, can be constructed iteratively from this choice, where the sequence P_t is bounded and bounded away from 0 and, for all t, $\overline{x}_{t0}$ and $\overline{x}_{t1}$ solve the relations

$$\frac{du_0(\overline{x}_{t0})}{dx} \le P_t,$$

with equality if $\overline{x}_{t0} > 0$, and

$$\frac{du_1(\overline{x}_{t-1,1})}{dx} \le P_t,$$

with equality if $\overline{x}_{t-1,1} > 0$. The allocation so obtained, $(\overline{\mathbf{x}}, \overline{\mathbf{K}}, \overline{\mathbf{L}})$, is the unique allocation that solves the problem

$$\max_{\substack{(\mathbf{x},\, \mathbf{K},\, \mathbf{L}) \text{ is a feasible} \\ \text{allocation with initial capital } \overline{K}_{-1}}} \sum_{t=0}^{\infty} (1+r)^{-t}[u_0(x_{t0}) + (1+r)u_1(x_{t-1,1})].$$

10.13 Equilibrium, Optimality, and the Turnpike Theorem in the Undiscounted Case

Although the theory of optimal allocations and programs becomes more difficult when utility is not discounted, the theory does become more robust. For instance, the turnpike theorem does not apply fully when there is more than one commodity and future utility is discounted, but it does apply when there are multiple commodities and there is no discounting.[7] Since the total utility over an infinite horizon may be infinite, it is common practice to use von Weizäcker's (1965) catching up criterion to define optimality when there is no discounting, as was done with the Samuelson model in section 9.7. The main goal of this section is to prove that an allocation or program is optimal if and only if it belongs to an equilibrium with bounded prices. The proof uses the turnpike theorem. The main arguments rely on the value loss method and are based on the work of McKenzie (1976).

Optimality according to the catching up criterion is defined for the Diamond and optimal growth models just as it was defined for the Samuelson model. An allocation $(\underline{\mathbf{x}}, \underline{\mathbf{K}}, \underline{\mathbf{L}})$ *catches up* to an allocation $(\mathbf{x}, \mathbf{K}, \mathbf{L})$ if for any positive number ε there exists a number $T(\varepsilon)$ such that

$$[u_1(x_{-1,1}) - u_1(\underline{x}_{-1,1})] + \sum_{t=0}^{T} [u_0(x_{t0}) + u_1(x_{t1}) - u_0(\underline{x}_{t0}) - u_1(\underline{x}_{t1})] < \varepsilon,$$

7. Because of space limitations, I do not prove these assertions about the theory with multiple commodities.

for $T \geq T(\varepsilon)$. A program $(\underline{\mathbf{C}}, \underline{\mathbf{K}})$ catches up to a program $(\mathbf{C}, \mathbf{K})$ if for any positive number ε there exists a number $T(\varepsilon)$ such that

$$\sum_{t=0}^{T} [v(C_t) - v(\underline{C}_t)] < \varepsilon,$$

for $T \geq T(\varepsilon)$. A feasible program or allocation is *optimal* if it catches up to any feasible program or allocation, respectively, with the same initial capital. Throughout this section, I assume that assumptions 10.1–10.5 (in section 10.1) apply to the Diamond model and assumptions 10.18–10.21 apply to the optimal growth model.

For many of the arguments, it is important that allocations waste no labor or produced good.

DEFINITION 10.61 The allocation $(\mathbf{x}, \mathbf{K}, \mathbf{L})$ is *strongly feasible* if $L_t = 1$ and $x_{t0} + x_{t-1,1} + K_t = f(K_{t-1,1}, 1)$, for all t. The program $(\mathbf{C}, \mathbf{K})$ is strongly feasible if $C_t + K_t = F(K_{t-1})$, for all t.

The following lemma will prove useful.

LEMMA 10.62 If $\overline{K}_{-1} > 0$ and the allocation $(\overline{\mathbf{x}}, \overline{\mathbf{K}}, \overline{\mathbf{L}})$ is optimal according to the catching up criterion, then $\overline{K}_t > 0$, for all t, and $(\overline{\mathbf{x}}, \overline{\mathbf{K}}, \overline{\mathbf{L}})$ is strongly feasible. If the program $(\overline{\mathbf{C}}, \overline{\mathbf{K}})$ is optimal according to the catching up criterion, then $\overline{K}_t > 0$, for all t, and $(\overline{\mathbf{C}}, \overline{\mathbf{K}})$ is strongly feasible.

Proof. I present the proof only for the case of an optimal allocation, $(\overline{\mathbf{x}}, \overline{\mathbf{K}}, \overline{\mathbf{L}})$. I begin by showing that $\overline{K}_t > 0$, for all t. If $\overline{K}_s = 0$, for some s, then assumption 10.3 implies that $f(\overline{K}_s, \overline{L}_{s+1}) = 0$, so that $\overline{x}_{s+1,0} = \overline{x}_{s1} = \overline{K}_{s+1} = 0$. Proceeding by induction on t, we see that $\overline{x}_{t0} = \overline{x}_{t-1,1} = \overline{K}_t = 0$, for all $t > s$. Hence, there exists a finite positive number B such that

$$u_1(\overline{x}_{-1,1}) + \sum_{t=0}^{T} [u_0(\overline{x}_{t0}) + u_1(\overline{x}_{t1})] < B, \tag{10.119}$$

for all T. I now show that this inequality implies that $(\overline{\mathbf{x}}, \overline{\mathbf{K}}, \overline{\mathbf{L}})$ is not optimal.

By assumption 10.2, there exists a positive number K such that $f(K, 1) - K > 0$. Let $\underline{K} = \min(K, \overline{K}_{-1})$, so that $f(\underline{K}, 1) - \underline{K} > 0$. Let $\underline{x}_0 = f(\underline{K}, 1) - \underline{K}$ and $\underline{x}_1 = 0$. The stationary allocation $(\underline{x}_0, \underline{x}_1, \underline{K}, 1)$ is feasible given initial capital $\overline{K}_{-1}$. By assumption 10.5, $u_0(0) = u_1(0) = 0$ and u_0 and u_1 are strictly increasing. Since $\overline{x}_0 > 0$, it follows that $u_0(\underline{x}_0) + u_1(\underline{x}_1) > 0$, and so

$$\lim_{t\to\infty} \left\{ u_1(\underline{x}_1) + \sum_{t=0}^{T} [u_0(\underline{x}_0) + u_1(\underline{x}_1)] \right\} = \infty. \qquad (10.120)$$

Inequalities 10.119 and 10.120 imply that $(\overline{\mathbf{x}}, \overline{\mathbf{K}}, \overline{\mathbf{L}})$ cannot catch up to the stationary allocation $(\underline{x}_0, \underline{x}_1, \underline{K}, 1)$ and hence that $(\overline{\mathbf{x}}, \overline{\mathbf{K}}, \overline{\mathbf{L}})$ is not optimal. This completes the proof that $\overline{K}_t > 0$, for all t.

Since $\overline{K}_t > 0$, assumption 10.4 implies that $f(\overline{K}_t, L)$ is strictly increasing in L, for all t. Since u_0 and u_1 are strictly increasing, it now follows easily from the optimality of $(\overline{\mathbf{x}}, \overline{\mathbf{K}}, \overline{\mathbf{L}})$ that $\overline{L}_t = 1$ and $\overline{x}_{t0} + \overline{x}_{t-1,1} + \overline{K}_t = f(\overline{K}_{t-1}, 1)$, for all t, so that $(\overline{\mathbf{x}}, \overline{\mathbf{K}}, \overline{\mathbf{L}})$ is strongly feasible. ▪

Optimal allocations and programs are unique and are Pareto optimal or efficient just as they are for the Samuelson model.

PROPOSITION 10.63 Suppose that $\overline{K}_{-1} > 0$. Then there is at most one allocation, $(\overline{\mathbf{x}}, \overline{\mathbf{K}}, \overline{\mathbf{L}})$, in the Diamond model that is optimal according to the catching up criterion and there is at most one program, $(\overline{\mathbf{C}}, \overline{\mathbf{K}})$, in the optimal growth model that is optimal according to the catching up criterion.

Proof. I make the argument only for the case of the Diamond model. By lemma 10.62, $\overline{L}_t = 1$, for all t. Since u_0 and u_1 are strictly concave and $f(K, 1)$ is strictly concave in K, an argument used in the proof of proposition 9.47 (in section 9.8) shows that there can be only one optimal allocation with initial capital $\overline{K}_{-1}$. ▪

THEOREM 10.64 If the allocation $(\overline{\mathbf{x}}, \overline{\mathbf{K}}, \overline{\mathbf{L}})$ is optimal according to the catching up criterion, it is Pareto optimal, and if the program $(\overline{\mathbf{C}}, \overline{\mathbf{K}})$ is optimal according to the catching up criterion, it is efficient.

The proof of this theorem is nearly identical to that of theorem 9.37 (in section 9.7) and so will not be given. Similarly, the proof of the following lemma is similar to that of lemma 9.41 (in the same section).

LEMMA 10.65 If the allocation $(\overline{\mathbf{x}}, \overline{\mathbf{K}}, \overline{\mathbf{L}})$ is optimal according to the catching up criterion, then for each $T \geq 0$, $(\overline{x}_{t0}, \overline{x}_{t-1,1}, \overline{K}_t, \overline{L}_t)_{t=0}^T$ solves the problem

$$\max_{\substack{x_{t0}\geq 0,\, x_{t-1,1}\geq 0,\, K_t\geq 0,\, L_t\geq 0,\\ \text{for } t=0,1,\ldots,T}} \sum_{t=0}^{T} [u_0(x_{t0}) + u_1(x_{t-1,1})]$$

$$\text{s.t.}\quad x_{t-1,1} + x_{t0} + K_t \leq f(K_{t-1}, L_t), \text{ and}$$

$$L_t \leq 1, \text{ for } t = 0, \ldots, T,$$

$$K_{-1} = \overline{K}_{-1} \text{ and } K_T \geq \overline{K}_T.$$

If the program $(\overline{\mathbf{C}}, \overline{\mathbf{K}})$ is optimal according to the catching up criterion, then for each $T \geq 0$, $(\overline{C}_t, \overline{K}_t)_{t=0}^T$ solves the problem

$$\max_{\substack{C_t\geq 0,\, K_t\geq 0,\\ \text{for } t=0,1,\ldots,T}} \sum_{t=0}^{T} v(C_t)$$

$$\text{s.t.}\quad C_t + K_t \leq F(K_{t-1}), \text{ for } t = 0, \ldots, T,$$

$$K_T \geq \overline{K}_T, \text{ and } K_{-1} = \overline{K}_{-1}.$$

Lemmas 10.62 and 10.65 allow us to construct candidate programs or allocations that may be optimal according to the catching up criterion. The construction process is exactly the same as that described at the end of section 10.10 in connection with programs that maximize a discounted sum of utilities; it is sufficient to set r equal to 0 in the formulas given there. When applied to the growth model, this process generates a sequence $(\overline{C}_t, \overline{K}_t, P_t)$, for $t = 0, 1, 2, \ldots$, which either terminates at some time T or continues indefinitely. I show at the end of this section that for the correct choice of P_0, the process may be continued indefinitely and that for only one such choice does the sequence, P_t, remain bounded, and in this case the corresponding program $(\overline{\mathbf{C}}, \overline{\mathbf{K}})$ is optimal according to the catching up criterion. A similar process may be used to generate optimal allocations for the Diamond model.

THEOREM 10.66 Suppose that $\overline{K}_{-1} > 0$ and that $(\overline{\mathbf{x}}, \overline{\mathbf{K}}, \overline{\mathbf{L}}, \mathbf{P}, \mathbf{W}, \mathbf{r}, G, \mathbf{T})$ is a spot price equilibrium with interest rate 0 such that the prices P_t are bounded and every consumer has the same positive and finite marginal utility of unit of account. Then the allocation $(\overline{\mathbf{x}}, \overline{\mathbf{K}}, \overline{\mathbf{L}})$ is optimal according to the catching up criterion.

In proving this theorem, I use the next lemma. To state the lemma, I need new notation. Let

$$M = \Big\{(\overline{x}_0, \overline{x}_1, \overline{K}, P_0, P_1) \in \mathbb{R}^5_+ \big| u_0(\overline{x}_0) + u_1(\overline{x}_1) - P_0\overline{x}_0 - P_1\overline{x}_1$$
$$\geq u_0(x_0) + u_1(x_1) - P_0x_0 - P_1x_1, \text{ for all } (x_0, x_1) \in \mathbb{R}^2_+, \text{ and}$$
$$P_1 f(\overline{K}, 1) - P_0\overline{K} \geq P_1 f(K, 1) - P_0K, \text{ for all } K \geq 0\Big\}.$$

For $(\overline{x}_0, \overline{x}_1, \overline{K}, P_0, P_1) \in M$ and $(x_0, x_1, K) \in \mathbb{R}^3_+$, let

$$\begin{aligned}&\mathcal{L}(\overline{x}_0, \overline{x}_1, \overline{K}, P_0, P_1; x_0, x_1, K)\\ &\quad= [u_0(\overline{x}_0) + u_1(\overline{x}_1) - P_0\overline{x}_0 - P_1\overline{x}_1 + P_1 f(\overline{K}, 1) - P_0\overline{K}]\\ &\quad- [u_0(x_0) + u_1(x_1) - P_0x_0 - P_1x_1 + P_1 f(K, 1) - P_0K].\end{aligned}$$

LEMMA 10.67 Let b be any positive number. For every positive number ε, there exists a positive number δ such that if $(\overline{x}_0, \overline{x}_1, \overline{K}, P_0, P_1) \in M$, $(x_0, x_1, K) \in \mathbb{R}^3_+$, and all the components of $(\overline{x}_0, \overline{x}_1, \overline{K}, P_0, P_1)$ and (x_0, x_1, K) are less than or equal to b and $P_1 \geq b^{-1}$, then $\|(\overline{x}_0, \overline{x}_1, \overline{K}) - (x_0, x_1, K)\| < \varepsilon$, if $\mathcal{L}(\overline{x}_0, \overline{x}_1, \overline{K}, P_0, P_1; x_0, x_1, K) < \delta$.

Proof. If the lemma is false, then there exists a positive number ε and a sequence $(\overline{x}^n_0, \overline{x}^n_1, \overline{K}^n, P^n_0, P^n_1, x^n_0, x^n_1, K^n)$ in $\mathbb{R}^8_+$, all the components of which are bounded above by b and are such that, for all n, $P^n_1 \geq b^{-1}$, $(\overline{x}^n_0, \overline{x}^n_1, \overline{K}^n, P^n_0, P^n_1) \in M$, $\mathcal{L}(\overline{x}^n_0, \overline{x}^n_1, \overline{K}^n, P^n_0, P^n_1; x^n_0, x^n_1, K^n) < \frac{1}{n}$, and $\|(\overline{x}^n_0, \overline{x}^n_1, \overline{K}^n) - (x^n_0, x^n_1, K^n)\| \geq \varepsilon$. Because the components of the sequence $(\overline{x}^n_0, \overline{x}^n_1, \overline{K}^n, P^n_0, P^n_1, x^n_0, x^n_1, K^n)$ are bounded, we may, by the Bolzano-Weierstrass theorem (3.12 in section 3.2), assume that this sequence converges. Let

$$(\overline{x}_0, \overline{x}_1, \overline{K}, P_0, P_1, \underline{x}_0, \underline{x}_1, \underline{K}) = \lim_{n\to\infty}(\overline{x}^n_0, \overline{x}^n_1, \overline{K}^n, P^n_0, P^n_1; x^n_0, x^n_1, K^n).$$

Then $P_1 \geq b^{-1} > 0$. Since

$$u_0(\overline{x}^n_0) + u_1(\overline{x}^n_1) - P^n_0\overline{x}^n_0 - P^n_1\overline{x}^n_1 \geq u_0(x_0) + u_1(x_1) - P^n_0x_0 - P^n_1x_1,$$

for all n and for all $(x_0, x_1) \in \mathbb{R}^2_+$, it follows by passage to the limit that

$$u_0(\overline{x}_0) + u_1(\overline{x}_1) - P_0\overline{x}_0 - P_1\overline{x}_1 \geq u_0(x_0) + u_1(x_1) - P_0x_0 - P_1x_1,$$

for all $(x_0, x_1) \in \mathbb{R}^2_+$. Similarly, since

$$P_1^n f(\overline{K}^n, 1) - P_0^n \overline{K}^n \geq P_1^n f(K, 1) - P_0^n K,$$

for all $K \geq 0$, it follows that

$$P_1 f(\overline{K}, 1) - P_0 \overline{K} \geq P_1 f(K, 1) - P_0 K,$$

for all $K \geq 0$. Therefore,

$$\mathcal{L}(\overline{x}_0, \overline{x}_1, \overline{K}, P_0, P_1; x_0, x_1, K) \geq 0,$$

for all $(x_0, x_1, K) \in \mathbb{R}^3_+$, and

$$\mathcal{L}(\overline{x}_0, \overline{x}_1, \overline{K}, P_0, P_1; \overline{x}_0, \overline{x}_1, \overline{K}) = 0.$$

Because u_0 and u_1 are strictly concave and $P_1 f(K, 1)$ is a strictly concave function of K, it follows that $\mathcal{L}(\overline{x}_0, \overline{x}_1, \overline{K}, P_0, P_1; x_0, x_1, K)$ is a strictly convex function of (x_0, x_1, K) and hence that $\mathcal{L}(\overline{x}_0, \overline{x}_1, \overline{K}, P_0, P_1; x_0, x_1, K) > 0$, if $(x_0, x_1, K) \neq (\overline{x}_0, \overline{x}_1, \overline{K})$. Since $\mathcal{L}$ is a continuous function and $\mathcal{L}(\overline{x}_0, \overline{x}_1, \overline{K}, P_0, P_1; \underline{x}_0, \underline{x}_1, \underline{K})$ is the limit of the sequence $(\overline{x}_0^n, \overline{x}_1^n, \overline{K}^n, P_0^n, P_1^n, x_0^n, x_1^n, K^n)$, it follows that

$$\lim_{n\to\infty} \mathcal{L}(\overline{x}_0^n, \overline{x}_1^n, \overline{K}^n, P_0^n, P_1^n; x_0^n, x_1^n, K^n)$$
$$= \mathcal{L}(\overline{x}_0, \overline{x}_1, \overline{K}, P_0, P_1; \underline{x}_0, \underline{x}_1, \underline{K}).$$

Since $0 \leq \mathcal{L}(\overline{x}_0^n, \overline{x}_1^n, \overline{K}^n, P_0^n, P_1^n; x_0^n, x_1^n, K^n) < \frac{1}{n}$, for all n, it follows that

$$\mathcal{L}(\overline{x}_0, \overline{x}_1, \overline{K}, P_0, P_1; \underline{x}_0, \underline{x}_1, \underline{K}) = 0.$$

This equation is impossible, however, because passage to the limit in the inequality

$$\|(\overline{x}_0^n, \overline{x}_1^n, \overline{K}^n) - (x_0^n, x_1^n, K^n)\| \geq \varepsilon$$

implies that

$$\|(\overline{x}_0, \overline{x}_1, \overline{K}) - (x_0, x_1, K)\| \geq \varepsilon$$

and hence that

$$\mathcal{L}(\overline{x}_0, \overline{x}_1, \overline{K}, P_0, P_1; \underline{x}_0, \underline{x}_1, \underline{K}) > 0. \quad \blacksquare$$

Proof of Theorem 10.66. I may assume that the marginal utility of unit of account of every consumer is 1, because if it equals the positive number λ, it becomes 1 if $\mathbf{P}$, G, and $\mathbf{T}$ are replaced by $\lambda\mathbf{P}$, λG, and $\lambda\mathbf{T}$, respectively.

I begin by showing that $\overline{K}_t > 0$, for all t. Suppose that $\overline{K}_t = 0$, for some t. Then, $\overline{K}_s = 0 = x_{s0} = x_{s-1,1}$ for $s > t$, by an argument made in the proof of lemma 10.62. Since the firm produces no output in any period after t, it earns no profits in those periods. Because the marginal utility of unit of account of every consumer is 1,

$$P_s = \frac{du_0(x_{s0})}{dx} = \frac{du_0(0)}{dx} = Q,$$

for $s > t$, where Q is defined by this equation and Q must be finite by the definition of a spot price equilibrium. Therefore profit maximization implies that $\overline{K}_s$ solves the problem

$$\max_{K \geq 0}[Qf(K, \overline{L}_s) - QK],$$

for $s > t$. By assumption 10.3, $f(0, \overline{L}_s) = 0$, and by assumption 10.2, $f(K, \overline{L}_s) - K > 0$, for some $K > 0$, if $\overline{L}_s > 0$. Since $f(K, \overline{L}_s)$ is concave as a function of K by assumption 10.4, it follows that

$$\frac{\partial f(0, \overline{L}_s)}{\partial K} > 1.$$

It now follows that if $s > t$ and $\overline{L}_{s+1} > 0$, then $\overline{K}_s$ must be positive, which is impossible. Therefore, $\overline{L}_{s+1} = 0$, which implies by condition (10) of definition 10.12 of a spot price equilibrium (in section 10.1) that $W_{s+1} = 0$. In this case, it is clearly possible for the firm to earn positive profits from period s to $s+1$ by using one unit of labor and $\underline{K}$ units of capital, where $\underline{K}$ is as in assumption 10.2. Since this assertion contradicts the hypothesis that $\overline{K}_s = 0$, it must be that $\overline{K}_t > 0$, for all t.

Because the functions u_0 and u_1 are strictly increasing, $P_t > 0$, for all t, for otherwise $(\overline{x}_{t0}, \overline{x}_{t1})$ would not maximize consumer t's utility over his or her budget set. It follows that $\overline{L}_t = 1$, for all t, for if $\overline{L}_1 < 1$, then $W_t = 0$. Since $\overline{K}_{t-1} > 0$, it follows that $P_t \frac{\partial f(\overline{K}_{t-1}, L)}{\partial L} > 0$, for any L, and so the firm's profit maximization problem has no solution, contrary to the definition of a spot price equilibrium. This contradiction proves that $\overline{L}_1 = 1$. Profit maximization now implies that

$$W_t = P_t \frac{\partial f(\overline{K}_{t-1}, 1)}{\partial L}, \tag{10.121}$$

for all t. Since the allocation $(\overline{\mathbf{x}}, \overline{\mathbf{K}}, \overline{\mathbf{L}})$ is feasible, it is bounded by proposition 10.8 (in section 10.1). Since by assumption 10.4 the function f is continuously differentiable except at **0**, the partial derivatives, $\frac{\partial f(\overline{K}_{t-1}, 1)}{\partial L}$, are bounded by proposition 3.14 (in section 3.2). Because the spot prices, P_t, are bounded, it follows from equation 10.121 that the spot wages, W_t, are bounded.

Since every consumer's marginal utility of unit of account is 1,

$$P_t \geq \frac{du_0(\overline{x}_{t0})}{dx} \geq \frac{du_0(b)}{dx} > 0, \qquad (10.122)$$

for all t, where b is an upper bound on the components of the allocation $(\overline{\mathbf{x}}, \overline{\mathbf{K}}, \overline{\mathbf{L}})$.

The proof of optimality is by contradiction. If $(\overline{\mathbf{x}}, \overline{\mathbf{K}}, \overline{\mathbf{L}})$ is not optimal, then there exists a feasible allocation $(\mathbf{x}, \mathbf{K}, \mathbf{L})$ with the same initial capital $\overline{K}_{-1}$ such that $(\overline{\mathbf{x}}, \overline{\mathbf{K}}, \overline{\mathbf{L}})$ does not catch up to $(\mathbf{x}, \mathbf{K}, \mathbf{L})$. We may assume that $L_t = 1$, for all t, for if $L_t < 1$, for some t, we can, by increasing L_t to 1, create a new program that would be even harder to catch up to than $(\mathbf{x}, \mathbf{K}, \mathbf{L})$. Define value losses as follows. Let

$$\mathcal{L}_{-1}[u_1(\overline{x}_{-1,1}) - P_0\overline{x}_{-1,1}] - [u_1(x_{-1,1}) - P_0x_{-1,1}].$$

For $t \geq 0$, let

$$\begin{aligned}\mathcal{L}_t = {} & [u_0(\overline{x}_{t0}) + u_1(\overline{x}_{t1}) - P_t\overline{x}_{t0} - P_{t+1}\overline{x}_{t1} + P_{t+1}f(\overline{K}_t, 1) - P_t\overline{K}_t] \\ & - [u_0(x_{t0}) + u_1(x_{t1}) - P_tx_{t0} - P_{t+1}x_{t1} + P_{t+1}f(K_t, 1) - P_tK_t].\end{aligned}$$

Because every consumer's marginal utility of unit of account is 1 in the equilibrium, $\overline{x}_{-1,1}$, solves the problem $\max_{x_1 \geq 0}[u_1(x_1) - P_0x_1]$ and, for $t \geq 0$, $(\overline{x}_{t0}, \overline{x}_{t1})$ solves the problem $\max_{x_0 \geq 0, x_1 \geq 0}[u_0(x_0) + u_1(x_1) - P_tx_0 - P_{t+1}x_1]$. By profit maximization, $K = \overline{K}_t$ solves the problem $\max_{K \geq 0}$ $[P_{t+1}f(K, 1) - P_tK]$, for $t \geq 0$. It follows that $\mathcal{L}_t \geq 0$, for all t. I may now apply lemma 10.67, because the allocations $(\overline{\mathbf{x}}, \overline{\mathbf{K}}, \overline{\mathbf{L}})$ and $(\mathbf{x}, \mathbf{K}, \mathbf{L})$ and the sequences P_t and W_t are bounded and the prices P_t are bounded away from 0 by inequality 10.122. Hence, for every positive number ε, there exists a positive number δ such that

$$\|(x_{t0}, x_{t1}, K_t) - (\overline{x}_{t0}, \overline{x}_{t1}, \overline{K}_t)\| < \varepsilon, \text{ if } \mathcal{L}_t < \delta, \qquad (10.123)$$

for $t \geq 0$.

By algebraic rearrangement,

$$
\begin{aligned}
0 \le \sum_{t=-1}^{T} \mathcal{L}_t &= [u_1(\overline{x}_{-1,1}) - u_1(x_{-1,1})] \\
&+ \sum_{t=0}^{T} \{u_0(\overline{x}_{t0}) + u_1(\overline{x}_{t1}) - [u_0(x_{t0}) + u_1(x_{t1})]\} \\
&+ \sum_{t=0}^{T} \{P_t[x_{t0} + x_{t-1,1} + K_t - f(K_{t-1}, 1)] - P_t[\overline{x}_{t0} + \overline{x}_{t-1,1} \\
&+ \overline{K}_t - f(\overline{K}_{t-1}, 1)]\} \\
&+ P_{T+1}[f(\overline{K}_T, 1) - f(K_T, 1)] + P_{T+1}(x_{T1} - \overline{x}_{T1}) \\
&\le [u_1(\overline{x}_{-1,1}) - u_1(x_{-1,1})] + \sum_{t=0}^{T} [u_0(\overline{x}_{t0}) + u_1(\overline{x}_{t1}) - (u_0(x_{t0}) + u_1(x_{t1}))] \\
&+ P_{T+1}[f(\overline{K}_T, 1) - f(K_T, 1)] + P_{T+1}(x_{T1} - \overline{x}_{T1}),
\end{aligned}
\tag{10.124}
$$

for all $T \ge 0$, where the second inequality follows, because 1) $P_t \ge 0$, for all t; 2) the feasibility of the allocation $(\mathbf{x}, \mathbf{K}, \mathbf{L})$ implies that

$$x_{t0} + x_{t-1,1} + K_t - f(K_{t-1}, 1) \le 0,$$

for all t; and 3) condition (10) of definition 10.12 of a spot price equilibrium (in section 10.1) implies that

$$P_t[\overline{x}_{t0} + \overline{x}_{t-1,1} + \overline{K}_t - f(\overline{K}_{t-1}, 1)] = 0,$$

for all t.

Since $(\overline{\mathbf{x}}, \overline{\mathbf{K}}, \overline{\mathbf{L}})$ does not catch up to $(\mathbf{x}, \mathbf{K}, \mathbf{L})$, there exists a positive number ε such that

$$[u_1(x_{-1,1}) - u_1(\overline{x}_{-1,1})] + \sum_{t=0}^{T} \{u_0(x_{t0}) + u_1(x_{t1}) - [u_0(\overline{x}_{t0}) + u_1(\overline{x}_{t1})]\} \ge \varepsilon,$$

for infinitely many values of T, so that

$$
\begin{aligned}
&[u_1(\overline{x}_{-1,1}) - u_1(x_{-1,1})] \\
&\quad + \sum_{t=0}^{T} \{u_0(\overline{x}_{t0}) + u_1(\overline{x}_{t1}) - [u_0(x_{t0}) + u_1(x_{t1})]\} \le -\varepsilon,
\end{aligned}
\tag{10.125}
$$

for infinitely many values of T. Since $\mathcal{L}_t \ge 0$, for all t, and the sequences $P_{T+1}[f(\overline{K}_T, 1) - f(K_T, 1)]$ and $P_{T+1}(x_{T1} - \overline{x}_{T1})$ are bounded, for all t, inequalities 10.124 and 10.125 imply that the infinite sum $\sum_{t=-1}^{\infty} \mathcal{L}_t$ exists and is finite, so that $\lim_{t\to\infty} \mathcal{L}_t = 0$. Therefore, statement 10.123 implies that $\lim_{t\to\infty} |K_t - \overline{K}_t| = 0$ and $\lim_{t\to\infty} |x_{t1} - \overline{x}_{t1}| = 0$. Hence, inequality 10.124 implies that

$$[u_1(\overline{x}_{-1,1}) - u_1(x_{-1,1})] + \sum_{t=0}^{T} [u_0(\overline{x}_{t0}) + u_1(\overline{x}_{t1}) - (u_0(x_{t0}) + u_1(x_{t1}))] > -\varepsilon,$$

if T is sufficiently large. This contradiction of inequality 10.125 establishes that $(\overline{\mathbf{x}}, \overline{\mathbf{K}}, \overline{\mathbf{L}})$ is optimal according to the catching up criterion. ■

These theorems imply that any stationary spot price equilibrium allocation with interest rate 0 is optimal according to the catching up criterion.

COROLLARY 10.68 The unique stationary allocation, $(\overline{x}_0, \overline{x}_1, \overline{K}, \overline{L})$, that solves the problem

$$\begin{aligned} &\max_{x_0\geq 0,\, x_1\geq 0,\, K\geq 0,\, L\geq 0} [u_0(x_0) + u_1(x_1)] \\ &\text{s.t.} \quad x_0 + x_1 + K \leq f(K, L) \text{ and} \\ &L \leq 1 \end{aligned} \tag{10.126}$$

is optimal according to the catching up criterion and hence is Pareto optimal. All stationary spot price equilibria with interest rate 0 have the same allocation, and it solves problem 10.126. Furthermore, in any such stationary equilibrium $(\overline{x}_0, \overline{x}_1, \overline{K}, \overline{L}, P, W, G)$, $P > 0$ and $W > 0$.

Proof. I begin by showing that $\overline{K} > 0$ and $\overline{L} = 1$. If $\overline{K} = 0$, then $\overline{x}_0 = \overline{x}_1 = 0$. By assumption 10.2, there exists a stationary allocation $(x_0, x_1, K, 1)$ such that $x_0 + x_1 > 0$. Since u_0 and u_1 are strictly increasing and $(\overline{x}_0, \overline{x}_1, \overline{K}, \overline{L})$ solves problem 10.126, it must be that $\overline{K} > 0$. Hence assumption 10.4 implies that $f(\overline{K}, L)$ is increasing in L, so that $\overline{L} = 1$.

Because $u_0(x_0)$, $u_1(x_1)$, and $f(K, 1)$ are strictly concave functions, the solution to problem 10.126 is unique. Assumption 10.2 implies that problem 10.126 satisfies the constraint qualification of the Kuhn-Tucker theorem. Therefore, this theorem implies that there exists a positive 2-vector

(P, W) such that $(\overline{x}_0, \overline{x}_1, \overline{K}, \overline{L})$ solves the problem

$$\max_{x_0 \geq 0, x_1 \geq 0, K \geq 0, L \geq 0} \{u_0(x_0) + u_1(x_1) - P[x_0 + x_1 + K - f(K, L)] - WL\}.$$

Let $G = W - P(\overline{x}_0 + \overline{K})$. Then, $(\overline{x}_0, \overline{x}_1, \overline{K}, \overline{L}, P, W, G)$ is a stationary spot price equilibrium with interest rate 0. Theorem 10.66 implies that the stationary allocation $(\overline{x}_0, \overline{x}_1, \overline{K}, \overline{L})$ is optimal according to the catching up criterion. Hence, $(\overline{x}_0, \overline{x}_1, \overline{K}, \overline{L})$ is Pareto optimal, by theorem 10.64.

Let $(\overline{x}_0, \overline{x}_1, \overline{K}, \overline{L}, P, W, G)$ be a stationary spot price equilibrium with interest rate 0. Because $(\overline{x}_0, \overline{x}_1)$ solves the problem

$$\begin{aligned} &\max_{x_0 \geq 0, x_1 \geq 0} [u_0(x_0) + u_1(x_1)] \\ &\text{s.t.} \quad Px_0 + Px_1 \leq W, \end{aligned} \tag{10.127}$$

and u_0 and u_1 are strictly increasing, $P > 0$, for, otherwise, problem 10.127 would have no solution.

I show that $W > 0$ and $\overline{L} = 1$. By profit maximization, $(\overline{K}, \overline{L})$ solves the problem

$$\max_{K \geq 0, L \geq 0} [Pf(K, L) - PK - WL\}. \tag{10.128}$$

Assumption 10.2 implies that there is a positive number $\underline{K}$ such that $Pf(\underline{K}, 1) - P\underline{K} > 0$. Since $\underline{K} > 0$, $f(\underline{K}, L)$ is an increasing function of L, so that if $W = 0$, then problem 10.128 has no solution, which is false. This contradiction implies that $W > 0$ and hence that $\overline{L} = 1$ by condition (10) of definition 10.12 of a spot price equilibrium (in section 10.1).

Since $W > 0$, problem 10.127 satisfies the constraint qualification. Because $(\overline{x}_0, \overline{x}_1)$ solves this problem, the Kuhn-Tucker theorem implies that there exists a nonnegative number λ such that $(\overline{x}_0, \overline{x}_1)$ solves the problem

$$\max_{x_0 \geq 0, x_1 \geq 0} [u_0(x_0) + u_1(x_1) - \lambda P(x_0 + x_1)].$$

Then, $\lambda > 0$, for if $\lambda = 0$, this problem has no solution since u_0 and u_1 are strictly increasing. Since $(\overline{K}, 1)$ solves problem 10.128, it follows that $(\overline{x}_0, \overline{x}_1, \overline{K}, 1)$ solves the problem

$$\begin{aligned} \max_{x_0 \geq 0, x_1 \geq 0, K \geq 0, L \geq 0} &\{u_0(x_0) + u_1(x_1) - \lambda P[x_0 + x_1 + K - f(K, L)] \\ &- \lambda WL\}. \end{aligned}$$

The sufficiency part of the Kuhn-Tucker theorem implies that $(\overline{x}_0, \overline{x}_1, \overline{K}, 1)$ solves problem 10.126. ∎

The stationary allocation $(\overline{x}_0, \overline{x}_1, \overline{K}, \overline{L})$ defined in the previous corollary is the *golden rule allocation* discussed previously at the end of section 10.8. The stationary spot price equilibrium, $(\overline{x}_0, \overline{x}_1, \overline{K}, \overline{L}, P, W, G)$, with interest rate 0 is unique provided that every consumer's marginal utility of unit of account is 1, and I call this equilibrium the *golden rule equilibrium.*

I now develop a condition for optimality according to the catching up criterion that will enable me to prove that an allocation for the Diamond model is optimal if and only if the corresponding program for the growth model is optimal. The condition is inspired by Brock's (1970) proof of the existence of an optimal growth program. Let $(\overline{x}_0, \overline{x}_1, \overline{K}, \overline{L}, P, W, G)$ be the golden rule equilibrium, and let $\mathcal{L}_{-1} : [0, \infty) \to (-\infty, \infty)$ be the function

$$\mathcal{L}_{-1}(x) = [u_1(\overline{x}_1) - P\overline{x}_1] - [u_1(x) - Px].$$

Similarly, let

$$\begin{aligned}\mathcal{L}(x_0, x_1, K) = {}& [u_0(\overline{x}_0) + u_1(\overline{x}_1) - P(\overline{x}_0 + \overline{x}_1) + Pf(\overline{K}, 1) - P\overline{K}] \\ & - [u_0(x_0) + u_1(x_1) - P(x_0 + x_1) + Pf(K, 1) - PK].\end{aligned}$$

Because profits are maximized and the marginal utility of every consumer is 1, in the golden rule equilibrium,

$$\mathcal{L}_{-1}(x) \geq 0$$

and

$$\mathcal{L}(x_0, x_1, K) \geq 0,$$

for all x_0, x_1, and K. It follows that

$$\mathcal{L}_{-1}(x_{-1,1}) + \sum_{t=0}^{\infty} \mathcal{L}(x_{t0}, x_{t1}, K_t)$$

is defined for any allocation $(\mathbf{x}, \mathbf{K}, \mathbf{L})$, though the sum may be infinite.

THEOREM 10.69 The feasible allocation, $(\underline{\mathbf{x}}, \underline{\mathbf{K}}, \underline{\mathbf{L}})$, with positive initial capital $\overline{K}_{-1}$ is optimal according to the catching up criterion if and only if

$(\underline{\mathbf{x}}, \underline{\mathbf{K}}, \underline{\mathbf{L}})$ solves the problem

$$\min_{\substack{(\mathbf{x}, \mathbf{K}, \mathbf{L}) \text{ is a strongly feasible} \\ \text{allocation with initial} \\ \text{capital } \overline{K}_{-1}}} [\mathcal{L}_{-1}(x_{-1,1}) + \sum_{t=0}^{\infty} \mathcal{L}(x_{t0}, x_{t1}, K_t)], \tag{10.129}$$

and this limit is finite.

This theorem provides an alternative proof of the assertion of corollary 10.68 that the golden rule allocation is optimal according to the catching up criterion, for the sum

$$\mathcal{L}_{-1}(x_{-1,1}) + \sum_{t=0}^{\infty} \mathcal{L}(x_{t0}, x_{t1}, K_t)$$

equals 0 if $(x_{t0}, x_{t-1,1}, K_t, L_t) = (\overline{x}_0, \overline{x}_1, \overline{K}, \overline{L})$, for all t, where $(\overline{x}_0, \overline{x}_1, \overline{K}, \overline{L})$ is the golden rule allocation.

I need the next two lemmas in order to prove theorem 10.69.

LEMMA 10.70 If $\overline{K}_{-1} > 0$, then there exists a strongly feasible allocation, $(\underline{\mathbf{x}}, \underline{\mathbf{K}}, \underline{\mathbf{L}})$, with initial capital $\overline{K}_{-1}$ and such that

$$\mathcal{L}_{-1}(\underline{x}_{-1,1}) + \sum_{t=0}^{\infty} \mathcal{L}(\underline{x}_{t0}, \underline{x}_{t1}, \underline{K}_t) < \infty. \tag{10.130}$$

Proof. Let $(\overline{x}_0, \overline{x}_1, \overline{K}, \overline{L})$ be the golden rule allocation. If $\overline{K}_{-1} \geq \overline{K}$, let

$$\underline{x}_{00} = \underline{x}_{-1,1} = \frac{f(\overline{K}_{-1}, 1) - \overline{K}}{2},$$

and let $\underline{K}_0 = \overline{K}$. For $t > 0$, let $\underline{x}_{t0} = \overline{x}_0$, $\underline{x}_{t-1,1} = \overline{x}_1$, and let $\underline{K}_t = \overline{K}$. If $\overline{K}_{-1} < \overline{K}$, let $\delta = f(\overline{K}_{-1}, 1) - \overline{K}_{-1}$ and let $\underline{K}_0 = f(\overline{K}_{-1}, 1)$ and $\underline{x}_{00} = \underline{x}_{-1,1} = 0$. Since f is concave and $f(0, 1) = 0$ and

$$f(\overline{K}, 1) - \overline{K} = \max_{K \geq 0}[f(K, 1) - K] > 0,$$

it follows that $\delta > 0$. Observe that $\underline{K}_0 - \overline{K}_{-1} = f(\overline{K}_{-1}, 1) - \overline{K}_{-1} = \delta > 0$. Continue by induction on t. If $\underline{K}_t < \overline{K}$, let $\underline{K}_t = f(\underline{K}_{t-1}, 1)$ and let $\underline{x}_{t0} = \underline{x}_{t-1,1} = 0$. Then, $\underline{K}_t - \underline{K}_{t-1} = f(\underline{K}_{t-1}, 1) - \underline{K}_{t-1} > f(\overline{K}_{-1}, 1) - \overline{K}_{-1} =$

$\delta > 0$, where the first inequality applies because $\underline{K}_{t-1} < \overline{K}$ and $\frac{\partial f(K,1)}{\partial K} > 1$, if $K < \overline{K}$. Because $\underline{K}_{s+1} - \underline{K}_s > \delta$, for each s, there is a smallest t such that $\underline{K}_t \geq \overline{K}$. Let T be this value of t. Let $\underline{K}_{T+1} = \overline{K}$, and let

$$\underline{x}_{T+1,0} = \underline{x}_{T1} = \frac{f(\underline{K}_T, 1) - \overline{K}}{2}.$$

For $t > T + 1$, let $\underline{K}_t = \overline{K}$, $\underline{x}_{t0} = \overline{x}_0$, and $\underline{x}_{t-1,1} = \overline{x}_1$. The allocation $(\underline{\mathbf{x}}, \underline{\mathbf{K}}, \underline{\mathbf{L}})$ is strongly feasible by definition. It satisfies inequality 10.130, because it equals the stationary allocation $(\overline{x}_0, \overline{x}_1, \overline{K}, \overline{L})$ from some time onward. ▪

LEMMA 10.71 Let b be a positive number. For every positive number ε, there exists a positive number δ such that $\|(x_0, x_1, K) - (\overline{x}_0, \overline{x}_1, \overline{K})\| < \varepsilon$, if $\mathcal{L}(x_0, x_1, K) < \delta$ and all the components of (x_0, x_1, K) are less than or equal to b.

Proof. This lemma is an immediate consequence of lemma 10.67, since the price P of a golden rule equilibrium is positive. ▪

Proof of Theorem 10.69. I first prove that if the allocation $(\underline{\mathbf{x}}, \underline{\mathbf{K}}, \underline{\mathbf{L}})$ solves problem 10.129, then it is optimal. I must show that if $(\mathbf{x}, \mathbf{K}, \mathbf{L})$ is a feasible allocation with initial capital $\overline{K}_{-1}$, then $(\underline{\mathbf{x}}, \underline{\mathbf{K}}, \underline{\mathbf{L}})$ catches up to $(\mathbf{x}, \mathbf{K}, \mathbf{L})$. I may assume that $(\mathbf{x}, \mathbf{K}, \mathbf{L})$ is strongly feasible, for if it were not, I could define a new allocation with more consumption in some periods and no less in any period and the new allocation would be harder to catch up to than $(\mathbf{x}, \mathbf{K}, \mathbf{L})$.

By lemma 10.70,

$$\min_{\substack{(\mathbf{x},\mathbf{K},\mathbf{L})\text{ is a strongly feasible}\\ \text{allocation with initial}\\ \text{capital }\overline{K}_{-1}}} \left[\mathcal{L}_{-1}(x_{-1,1}) + \sum_{t=0}^{\infty} \mathcal{L}(x_{t0}, x_{t1}, K_t)\right] < \infty,$$

so that

$$\mathcal{L}_{-1}(\underline{x}_{-1,1}) + \sum_{t=0}^{\infty} \mathcal{L}(\underline{x}_{t0}, \underline{x}_{t0}, \underline{K}_t) < \infty.$$

By algebraic manipulation, we see that

$$[\mathcal{L}_{-1}(x_{-1,1}) - \mathcal{L}_{-1}(\underline{x}_{-1,1})] + \sum_{t=0}^{T}[\mathcal{L}(x_{t0}, x_{t1}, K_t) - \mathcal{L}(\underline{x}_{t0}, \underline{x}_{t1}, \underline{K}_t)]$$
$$= \{[u_1(\overline{x}_1) - P\overline{x}_1] - [u_1(x_{-1,1}) - Px_{-1,1}]\}$$
$$- \{[u_1(\overline{x}_1) - P\overline{x}_1] - [u_1(\underline{x}_{-1,1}) - P\underline{x}_{-1,1}]\}$$
$$+ \sum_{t=0}^{T}\Big\{[u_0(\overline{x}_0) + u_1(\overline{x}_1) - P(\overline{x}_0 + \overline{x}_1) + Pf(\overline{K}, 1) - P\overline{K}]$$
$$-[u_0(x_{t0}) + u_1(x_{t1}) - P(x_{t0} + x_{t1}) + Pf(K_t, 1) - PK_t]$$
$$-[u_0(\overline{x}_0) + u_1(\overline{x}_1) - P(\overline{x}_0 + \overline{x}_1) + Pf(\overline{K}, 1) - P\overline{K}]$$
$$+[u_0(\underline{x}_{t0}) + u_1(\underline{x}_{t1}) - P(\underline{x}_{t0} + \underline{x}_{t1}) + Pf(\underline{K}_t, 1) - P\underline{K}_t]\Big\}$$
$$= [u_1(\underline{x}_{-1,1}) - u_1(x_{-1,1})] + \sum_{t=0}^{T}\{[u_0(\underline{x}_{t0}) + u_1(\underline{x}_{t1})] - [u_0(x_{t0}) + u_1(x_{t1})]\}$$
$$- P[\underline{x}_{00} + \underline{x}_{-1,1} + \underline{K}_0 - f(\overline{K}_{-1}, 1)] - \sum_{t=1}^{T} P[\underline{x}_{t0} + \underline{x}_{t-1,1} + \underline{K}_t - f(\underline{K}_{t-1}, 1)]$$
$$+ P[x_{00} + x_{-1,1} + K_0 - f(\overline{K}_{-1}, 1)] + \sum_{t=1}^{T} P[x_{t0} + x_{t-1,1} + K_t - f(K_{t-1}, 1)]$$
$$+ P[f(\underline{K}_T, 1) - f(K_T, 1)] + P(x_{T1} - \underline{x}_{T1})$$
$$= [u_1(\underline{x}_{-1,1}) - u_1(x_{-1,1})] + \sum_{t=0}^{T}[u_0(\underline{x}_{t0}) + u_1(\underline{x}_{t1}) - u_0(x_{t0}) - u_1(x_{t1})]$$
$$+ P[f(\underline{K}_T, 1) - f(K_T, 1)] + P(x_{T1} - \underline{x}_{T1}), \tag{10.131}$$

where the last equation follows, because

$$P[\underline{x}_{00} + \underline{x}_{-1,1} + \underline{K}_0 - f(\overline{K}_{-1}, 1)] + \sum_{t=1}^{T} P[\underline{x}_{t0} + \underline{x}_{t-1,1}$$
$$+ \underline{K}_t - f(\underline{K}_{t-1}, 1)] = 0,$$

by the strong feasibility of the allocation $(\underline{\mathbf{x}}, \underline{\mathbf{K}}, \underline{\mathbf{L}})$, and

$$P[x_{00} + x_{-1,1} + K_0 - f(\overline{K}_{-1}, 1)] + \sum_{t=1}^{T} P[x_{t0}$$
$$+ x_{t-1,1} + K_t - f(K_{t-1}, 1)] = 0,$$

by the strong feasibility of the allocation $(\mathbf{x}, \mathbf{K}, \mathbf{L})$. Since feasible allocations are bounded by proposition 10.8 (in section 10.1), the sequence $P[f(\underline{K}_T, 1) - f(K_T, 1)] + P(x_{T1} - \underline{x}_{T1})$ is bounded.

The sum $\mathcal{L}_{-1}(x_{-1,1}) + \sum_{t=0}^{\infty} \mathcal{L}(x_{t0}, x_{t1}, K_t)$ is either finite or infinite. Suppose that it is infinite. Then,

$$[\mathcal{L}_{-1}(x_{-1,1}) - \mathcal{L}_{-1}(\underline{x}_{-1,1})] + \sum_{t=0}^{T} [\mathcal{L}(x_{t0}, x_{t1}, K_t) - \mathcal{L}(\underline{x}_{t0}, \underline{x}_{t1}, \underline{K}_t)]$$

diverges to infinity as T goes to infinity. Therefore, equation 10.131 and the boundedness of the sequence $P[f(\underline{K}_T, 1) - f(K_T, 1)] + P(x_{T1} - \underline{x}_{T1})$ imply that the sum

$$[u_1(\underline{x}_{-1,1}) - u_1(x_{-1,1})] + \sum_{t=0}^{T} [u_0(\underline{x}_{t0}) + u_1(\underline{x}_{t1}) - u_0(x_{t0}) - u_1(x_{t1})]$$

diverges to infinity so that $(\underline{\mathbf{x}}, \underline{\mathbf{K}}, \underline{\mathbf{L}})$ catches up to $(\mathbf{x}, \mathbf{K}, \mathbf{L})$. Suppose that $\mathcal{L}_{-1}(x_{-1,1}) + \sum_{t=0}^{\infty} \mathcal{L}(x_{t0}, x_{t1}, K_t) < \infty$. Then,

$$\lim_{t\to\infty} \mathcal{L}(x_{t0}, x_{t1}, K_t) = 0.$$

Since the allocation $(\mathbf{x}, \mathbf{K}, \mathbf{L})$ is bounded, lemma 10.71 implies that

$$\lim_{t\to\infty} (x_{t0}, x_{t1}, K) = (\overline{x}_0, \overline{x}_1, \overline{K}).$$

Similarly, since $\mathcal{L}_{-1}(\underline{x}_{-1,1}) + \sum_{t=0}^{\infty} \mathcal{L}(\underline{x}_{t0}, \underline{x}_{t1}, \underline{K}_t) < \infty$, it follows that

$$\lim_{t\to\infty} \mathcal{L}(\underline{x}_{t0}, \underline{x}_{t1}, \underline{K}_t) = 0$$

and therefore

$$\lim_{t\to\infty} (\underline{x}_{t0}, \underline{x}_{t1}, \underline{K}_t) = (\overline{x}_0, \overline{x}_1, \overline{K}),$$

so that

$$\lim_{T\to\infty} \{P[f(\underline{K}_T, 1) - f(K_T, 1)] + P(x_{T1} - \underline{x}_{T1})\} = 0. \quad (10.132)$$

Since $(\underline{\mathbf{x}}, \underline{\mathbf{K}}, \underline{\mathbf{L}})$ solves problem 10.129, it follows that

$$\mathcal{L}_{-1}(\underline{x}_{-1,1}) + \sum_{t=0}^{\infty} \mathcal{L}(\underline{x}_{t0}, \underline{x}_{t1}, \underline{K}_t) \le \mathcal{L}_{-1}(x_{-1,1}) + \sum_{t=0}^{\infty} \mathcal{L}(x_{t0}, x_{t1}, K_t),$$

so that

$$\lim_{T\to\infty}\{[\mathcal{L}_{-1}(x_{-1,1}) - \mathcal{L}_{-1}(\underline{x}_{-1,1})] + \sum_{t=0}^{T}[\mathcal{L}(x_{t0}, x_{t1}, K_t)$$
$$- \mathcal{L}(\underline{x}_{t0}, \underline{x}_{t1}, \underline{K}_t)]\} \geq 0.$$

Therefore, equations 10.131 and 10.132 imply that

$$\lim_{T\to\infty}\{[u_1(\underline{x}_{-1,1}) - u_1(x_{-1,1})] + \sum_{t=-1}^{T}[u_0(\underline{x}_{t0}) + u_1(\underline{x}_{t1})$$
$$- u_0(x_{t0}) - u_1(x_{t1})]\} \geq 0.$$

It follows that $(\underline{\mathbf{x}}, \underline{\mathbf{K}}, \underline{\mathbf{L}})$ catches up to $(\mathbf{x}, \mathbf{K}, \mathbf{L})$. This completes the proof that an allocation is optimal if it solves problem 10.129. I now prove the converse.

Let $(\underline{\mathbf{x}}, \underline{\mathbf{K}}, \underline{\mathbf{L}})$ be an optimal allocation with initial capital $\overline{K}_{-1}$. I must show that $(\underline{\mathbf{x}}, \underline{\mathbf{K}}, \underline{\mathbf{L}})$ solves problem 10.129. By lemma 10.62, $(\underline{\mathbf{x}}, \underline{\mathbf{K}}, \underline{\mathbf{L}})$ is strongly feasible, so that it is a candidate for a solution of problem 10.129. Suppose it does not solve this problem. Then there is another strongly feasible allocation $(\mathbf{x}, \mathbf{K}, \mathbf{L})$ such that

$$\mathcal{L}_{-1}(\underline{x}_{-1,1}) + \sum_{t=0}^{\infty}\mathcal{L}(\underline{x}_{t0}, \underline{x}_{t1}, \underline{K}_t) > \mathcal{L}_{-1}(x_{-1,1}) + \sum_{t=0}^{\infty}\mathcal{L}(x_{t0}, x_{t1}, K_t).$$

By lemma 10.70, I may assume that

$$\mathcal{L}_{-1}(x_{-1,1}) + \sum_{t=0}^{\infty}\mathcal{L}(x_{t0}, x_{t1}, K_t) < \infty.$$

Equation 10.131 applies to the allocations $(\underline{\mathbf{x}}, \underline{\mathbf{K}}, \underline{\mathbf{L}})$ and $(\mathbf{x}, \mathbf{K}, \mathbf{L})$ and because these allocations are feasible, the sequence $P[f(\underline{K}_T, 1) - f(K_T, 1)] + P(x_{T1} - \underline{x}_{T1})$ is bounded. If

$$\mathcal{L}_{-1}(\underline{x}_{-1,1}) + \sum_{t=0}^{\infty}\mathcal{L}(\underline{x}_{t0}, \underline{x}_{t1}, \underline{K}_t) = \infty,$$

then equation 10.131 implies that

$$[u_1(\underline{x}_{-1,1}) - u_1(x_{-1,1})] + \sum_{t=-1}^{T}[u_0(\underline{x}_{t0}) + u_1(\underline{x}_{t1}) - u_0(x_{t0}) - u_1(x_{t1})]$$

diverges to negative infinity, so that $(\underline{\mathbf{x}}, \underline{\mathbf{K}}, \underline{\mathbf{L}})$ cannot catch up to $(\mathbf{x}, \mathbf{K}, \mathbf{L})$. This implication contradicts the optimality of $(\underline{\mathbf{x}}, \underline{\mathbf{K}}, \underline{\mathbf{L}})$. If

$$\mathcal{L}_{-1}(\underline{x}_{-1,1}) + \sum_{t=0}^{\infty} \mathcal{L}(\underline{x}_{t0}, \underline{x}_{t1}, \underline{K}_t) < \infty,$$

then equation 10.132 applies and

$$\lim_{T\to\infty} \{[\mathcal{L}_{-1}(x_{-1,1}) - \mathcal{L}_{-1}(\underline{x}_{-1,1})] + \sum_{t=0}^{T} [\mathcal{L}(x_{t0}, x_{t1}, K_t) - \mathcal{L}(\underline{x}_{t0}, \underline{x}_{t1}, \underline{K}_t)]\} < 0.$$

Therefore, equation 10.131 implies that

$$\lim_{T\to\infty} \{[u_1(\underline{x}_{-1,1}) - u_1(x_{-1,1})] + \sum_{t=-1}^{T} [u_0(\underline{x}_{t0}) + u_1(\underline{x}_{t1}) - u_0(x_{t0}) - u_1(x_{t1})]\} < 0$$

and hence $(\underline{\mathbf{x}}, \underline{\mathbf{K}}, \underline{\mathbf{L}})$ cannot catch up to $(\mathbf{x}, \mathbf{K}, \mathbf{L})$. Since we have again contradicted the optimality of $(\underline{\mathbf{x}}, \underline{\mathbf{K}}, \underline{\mathbf{L}})$, it must be that $(\underline{\mathbf{x}}, \underline{\mathbf{K}}, \underline{\mathbf{L}})$ solves problem 10.129. ■

Theorem 10.69 implies the following.

COROLLARY 10.72 The feasible allocation, $(\underline{\mathbf{x}}, \underline{\mathbf{K}}, \underline{\mathbf{L}})$, with positive initial capital $\overline{K}_{-1}$ is optimal according to the catching up criterion if and only if $(\underline{\mathbf{x}}, \underline{\mathbf{K}}, \underline{\mathbf{L}})$ solves the problem

$$\min_{\substack{(\mathbf{x}, \mathbf{K}, \mathbf{L}) \text{ is a strongly feasible} \\ \text{allocation with initial} \\ \text{capital } \overline{K}_{-1}}} \sum_{t=0}^{\infty} \mathcal{L}(x_{t0}, x_{t-1,1}, K_t).$$

Proof. By theorem 10.69, $(\underline{\mathbf{x}}, \underline{\mathbf{K}}, \underline{\mathbf{L}})$ is optimal according to the catching up criterion if and only if it solves the problem

$$\min_{\substack{(\mathbf{x}, \mathbf{K}, \mathbf{L}) \text{ is a strongly feasible} \\ \text{allocation with initial} \\ \text{capital } \overline{K}_{-1}}} [\mathcal{L}_{-1}(x_{-1,1}) + \sum_{t=0}^{\infty} \mathcal{L}(x_{t0}, x_{t1}, K_t)].$$

Lemma 10.70 implies that this minimum is finite, if it exists. Therefore, if $(\underline{\mathbf{x}}, \underline{\mathbf{K}}, \underline{\mathbf{L}})$ is optimal or achieves the minimum, then it is strongly feasible and

$$\mathcal{L}_{-1}(\underline{x}_{-1,1}) + \sum_{t=0}^{\infty} \mathcal{L}(\underline{x}_{t0}, \underline{x}_{t1}, \underline{K}_t) < \infty.$$

It follows that

$$\begin{aligned}
&\mathcal{L}_{-1}(\underline{x}_{-1,1}) + \sum_{t=0}^{\infty} \mathcal{L}(\underline{x}_{t0}, \underline{x}_{t1}, \underline{K}_t) \\
&= \{[u_1(\overline{x}_1) - P\overline{x}_1] - [u_1(\underline{x}_{-1,1}) - P\underline{x}_{-1,1}]\} \\
&\quad + \sum_{t=0}^{\infty} \Big\{[u_0(\overline{x}_0) + u_1(\overline{x}_1) - P(\overline{x}_0 + \overline{x}_1) + Pf(\overline{K}, 1) - P\overline{K}] \\
&\quad - [u_0(\underline{x}_{t0}) + u_1(\underline{x}_{t1}) - P(\underline{x}_{t0} + \underline{x}_{t1}) + Pf(\underline{K}_t, 1) - P\underline{K}_t]\} \\
&= \{[u_1(\overline{x}_1) - P\overline{x}_1] - [u_1(\underline{x}_{-1,1}) - P\underline{x}_{-1,1}]\} \\
&\quad + \sum_{t=0}^{\infty} \{\big[[u_0(\overline{x}_0) - P\overline{x}_0] - [u_0(\underline{x}_{t0}) - P\underline{x}_0]\big] \\
&\quad + \big[[u_1(\overline{x}_1) - P\overline{x}_1] - [u_1(\underline{x}_{t1}) - P\underline{x}_{t1}]\big] \\
&\quad + \Big[[Pf(\overline{K}, 1) - P\overline{K}] - [Pf(\underline{K}_t, 1) - P\underline{K}_t]\Big]\Big\} \\
&= \sum_{t=0}^{\infty} \{\big[[u_0(\overline{x}_0) - P\overline{x}_0] - [u_0(\underline{x}_{t0}) - P\underline{x}_{t0}]\big] \\
&\quad + \Big[[u_1(\overline{x}_1) - P\overline{x}_1] - [u_1(\underline{x}_{t-1,1}) - P\underline{x}_{t-1,1}]\Big] \\
&\quad + \Big[[Pf(\overline{K}, 1) - P\overline{K}] - [Pf(\underline{K}_t, 1) - P\underline{K}_t]\Big]\Big\} \\
&= \sum_{t=0}^{\infty} \Big\{u_0(\overline{x}_0) + u_1(\overline{x}_1) - P(\overline{x}_0 + \overline{x}_1) + Pf(\overline{K}, 1) - P\overline{K} \\
&\quad - u_0(\underline{x}_{t0}) - u_1(\underline{x}_{t-1,1}) + P(\underline{x}_{t0} + \underline{x}_{t-1,1}) - Pf(\underline{K}_t, 1) + P\underline{K}_t\Big\} \\
&= \sum_{t=0}^{\infty} \mathcal{L}(\underline{x}_{t0}, \underline{x}_{t-1,1}, \underline{K}_t).
\end{aligned}$$

The third equation above is valid, because all the terms in the large square brackets in the sum on the left-hand side of this equation are nonnegative, so that the order of summation of these terms does not affect the total. We obtain the fourth equation by adding the three terms in large brackets on the left-hand side that refer to the same time period. The last equation follows from the definition of $\mathcal{L}(\underline{x}_{t0}, \underline{x}_{t-1,1}, \underline{K}_t)$.

The same reasoning applies to any strongly feasible allocation, $(\mathbf{x}, \mathbf{K}, \mathbf{L})$, such that $\sum_{t=0}^{\infty} \mathcal{L}(x_{t0}, x_{t-1,1}, K_t) < \infty$, so that for any such allocation

$$\mathcal{L}_{-1}(x_{-1,1}) + \sum_{t=0}^{\infty} \mathcal{L}(x_{t0}, x_{t1}, K_t) = \sum_{t=0}^{\infty} \mathcal{L}(x_{t0}, x_{t-1,1}, K_t).$$

Therefore, $(\mathbf{x}, \mathbf{K}, \mathbf{L})$ minimizes the sum $\mathcal{L}_{-1}(x_{-1,1}) + \sum_{t=0}^{\infty} \mathcal{L}(x_{t0}, x_{t1}, K_t)$ if and only if it minimizes the sum $\sum_{t=0}^{\infty} \mathcal{L}(x_{t0}, x_{t-1,1}, K_t)$ and hence theorem 10.69 implies that $(\mathbf{x}, \mathbf{K}, \mathbf{L})$ is optimal according to the catching up criterion if and only if it minimizes the sum $\sum_{t=0}^{\infty} \mathcal{L}(x_{t0}, x_{t-1,1}, K_t)$. ■

To discuss the equivalence of optimality in the Diamond and growth models, I describe how to make a correspondence between the two types of models. If a Diamond model has utility functions u_0 and u_1 and a production function f, the corresponding growth model has a utility function v and a production function F, where

$$v(C) = \max_{x_0 : 0 \le x_0 \le C} [u_0(x_0) + u_1(C - x_0)]$$

and $F(K) = f(K, 1)$. If an optimal growth model is defined by functions v and F, a corresponding Diamond model may be defined with functions u_0, u_1, and f, where

$$u_0(x) = u_1(x) = \frac{v(2x)}{2}$$

and

$$f(K, L) = \begin{cases} LF(KL^{-1}), & \text{if } L > 0, \\ \text{and } 0, & \text{if } L = 0. \end{cases}$$

The original functions v and F then correspond to these functions u_0, u_1, and f. An allocation, $(\mathbf{x}, \mathbf{K}, \mathbf{L})$, and a program, $(\mathbf{C}, \mathbf{K})$, correspond if $L_t = 1$, $x_{t0} + x_{t-1,1} = C_t$, and $v(C_t) = u_0(x_{t0}) + u_1(x_{t-1,1})$, for all t.

A version of theorem 10.69 applies to the optimal growth model. In order to state this version, I introduce appropriate terminology. Let $(\overline{C}, \overline{K})$ be the golden rule program described at the end of section 10.8. The capital stock $\overline{K}$ solves the problem $\max_{K \ge 0}[F(K) - K]$, and $\overline{C} = F(\overline{K}) - \overline{K}$. Then $(\overline{C}, \overline{K})$ is the allocation of a stationary program equilibrium with interest rate 0, and we may let the constant price level in this equilibrium be $P = \frac{dv(\overline{C})}{dC}$, so that $\overline{C}$ solves the problem $\max_{C \ge 0}[v(C) - PC]$. Of course, $\overline{K}$

solves the problem $\max_{K\geq 0}[PF(K) - PK]$. The appropriate value loss is

$$\mathcal{L}(C, K) = [v(\overline{C}) - P\overline{C} + PF(\overline{K}) - P\overline{K}] - [v(C) - PC + PF(K) - PK].$$

THEOREM 10.73 The program $(\underline{\mathbf{C}}, \underline{\mathbf{K}})$ is optimal, according to the catching up criterion, if and only if $(\underline{\mathbf{C}}, \underline{\mathbf{K}})$ solves the problem

$$\min_{\substack{(\mathbf{C},\,\mathbf{K}) \text{ is a strongly feasible} \\ \text{program with initial} \\ \text{capital } \overline{K}_{-1}}} \sum_{t=0}^{\infty} \mathcal{L}(C_t, K_t).$$

The proof of this theorem requires the following analogues of lemmas 10.70 and 10.71.

LEMMA 10.74 There exists a strongly feasible program $(\underline{\mathbf{C}}, \underline{\mathbf{K}})$, such that

$$\sum_{t=0}^{\infty} \mathcal{L}(\underline{C}_t, \underline{K}_t) < \infty.$$

Proof. By lemma 10.70, there exists a strongly feasible allocation, $(\underline{\mathbf{x}}, \underline{\mathbf{K}}, \underline{\mathbf{L}})$, for a Diamond model corresponding to the given growth model such that

$$\mathcal{L}_{-1}(\underline{x}_{-1,1}) + \sum_{t=0}^{\infty} \mathcal{L}(\underline{x}_{t0}, \underline{x}_{t1}, \underline{K}_t) < \infty.$$

Let $(\underline{\mathbf{C}}, \underline{\mathbf{K}})$ be the program corresponding to the allocation $(\underline{\mathbf{x}}, \underline{\mathbf{K}}, \underline{\mathbf{L}})$. Since

$$\underline{C}_t + \underline{K}_t = \underline{x}_{t0} + \underline{x}_{t-1,1} + \underline{K}_t = f(\underline{K}_{t-1}, 1) = F(\underline{K}_{t-1}),$$

it follows that $(\underline{\mathbf{C}}, \underline{\mathbf{K}})$ is strongly feasible. By an argument given in the proof of corollary 10.72,

$$\mathcal{L}_{-1}(\underline{x}_{-1,1}) + \sum_{t=0}^{\infty} \mathcal{L}(\underline{x}_{t0}, \underline{x}_{t1}, \underline{K}_t) = \sum_{t=0}^{\infty} \mathcal{L}(\underline{x}_{t0}, \underline{x}_{t-1,1}, \underline{K}_t).$$

When $x_0 + x_1 = C$ and $u_0(x_0) + u_1(x_1) = v(C)$, the value loss functions for the corresponding Diamond and growth models are equal in that

$$\begin{aligned}\mathcal{L}(x_0, x_1, K) &= [u_0(\overline{x}_0) + u_1(\overline{x}_1) - P(\overline{x}_0 + \overline{x}_1) + Pf(\overline{K}, 1) - P\overline{K}] \\ &\quad - [u_0(x_0) + u_1(x_1) - P(x_0 + x_1) + Pf(K, 1) - PK] \\ &= [v(\overline{C}) - P\overline{C} + PF(\overline{K}) - P\overline{K}] - [v(C) \\ &\quad - PC + PF(K) - PK] = \mathcal{L}(C, K).\end{aligned}$$

Therefore,

$$\sum_{t=0}^{\infty} \mathcal{L}(\underline{C}_t, \underline{K}_t) = \sum_{t=0}^{\infty} \mathcal{L}(\underline{x}_{t0}, \underline{x}_{t-1,1}, \underline{K}_t) < \infty. \quad \blacksquare$$

LEMMA 10.75 For every positive number ε, there exists a positive number δ such that $\|(C, K) - (\overline{C}, \overline{K})\| < \varepsilon$, if $\mathcal{L}(C, K) < \delta$.

Proof. If the lemma is false, then there exists a positive number ε and a sequence (C^n, K^n) such that, for all n, $\mathcal{L}(C^n, K^n) < \frac{1}{n}$ and $\|(C^n, K^n) - (\overline{C}, \overline{K})\| \geq \varepsilon$. I may assume that $\|(C^n, K^n) - (\overline{C}, \overline{K})\| = \varepsilon$, for all n, for suppose that $\|(C^n, K^n) - (\overline{C}, \overline{K})\| > \varepsilon$, for some n. Let

$$\alpha = \frac{\varepsilon}{\|(C^n, K^n) - (\overline{C}, \overline{K})\|},$$

so that $0 < \alpha < 1$, and let

$$(\underline{C}^n, \underline{K}^n) = \alpha(C^n, K^n) + (1 - \alpha)(\overline{C}, \overline{K}).$$

Then

$$\|(\underline{C}^n, \underline{K}^n) - (\overline{C}, \overline{K})\| = \alpha\|(C^n, K^n) - (\overline{C}, \overline{K})\| = \varepsilon,$$

and, because the function $\mathcal{L}$ is convex,

$$\begin{aligned} \mathcal{L}(\underline{C}^n, \underline{K}^n) &\leq \alpha\mathcal{L}(C^n, K^n) + (1 - \alpha)\mathcal{L}(\overline{C}, \overline{K}) \\ &= \alpha\mathcal{L}(C^n, K^n) < \alpha\frac{1}{n} < \frac{1}{n}. \end{aligned}$$

Since $\|(C^n, K^n) - \overline{C}, \overline{K})\| = \varepsilon$, for all n, the sequence (C^n, K^n) is bounded and so I may, by the Bolzano-Weierstrass theorem (3.12 in section 3.2), assume that it converges. Let

$$(\underline{C}, \underline{K}) = \lim_{n\to\infty} (C^n, K^n).$$

Because the function $\mathcal{L}$ is continuous and $\mathcal{L}(C^n, K^n) < \frac{1}{n}$, for all n, it follows that $\mathcal{L}(\underline{C}, \underline{K}) = 0$. Therefore, $(\underline{C}, \underline{K}) = (\overline{C}, \overline{K})$, because $\mathcal{L}$ is a strictly convex function. This equation contradicts the equation

$$\|(\underline{C}, \underline{K}) - (\overline{C}, \overline{K})\| = \varepsilon,$$

obtained by passing to the limit in the equation $\|(C^n, K^n) - (\overline{C}, \overline{K})\| = \varepsilon$, for all n. $\blacksquare$

Proof of Theorem 10.73. The proof is very similar to that of theorem 10.69. The central part of that proof is equation 10.131, and the corresponding equation here is

$$\sum_{t=0}^{T} [\mathcal{L}(C_t, K_t) - \mathcal{L}(\underline{C}_t, \underline{K}_t)]$$

$$= \sum_{t=0}^{T} \Big\{ [v(\overline{C}) - P\overline{C} - PF(\overline{K}) - P\overline{K}]$$

$$- [v(C_t) - PC_t + PF(K_t) - PK_t]$$

$$- [v(\overline{C}) - P\overline{C} - PF(\overline{K}) - P\overline{K}]$$

$$+ [v(\underline{C}_t) - P\underline{C}_t + PF(\underline{K}_t) - P\underline{K}_t] \Big\}$$

$$= \sum_{t=0}^{T} [v(\underline{C}_t) - v(C_t)]$$

$$- P[\underline{C}_0 + \underline{K}_0 - F(\overline{K}_{-1})] - \sum_{t=1}^{T} P[\underline{C}_t + \underline{K}_t - F(\underline{K}_{t-1})]$$

$$+ P[C_0 + K_0 - F(\overline{K}_{-1})] + \sum_{t=1}^{T} P[C_t + K_t - F(K_{t-1})]$$

$$+ P[F(\underline{K}_T) - F(K_T)]$$

$$= \sum_{t=0}^{T} [v(\underline{C}_t) - v(C_t)] + P[F(\underline{K}_T) - F(K_T)].$$

The rest of the proof of theorem 10.69 applies with hardly any changes. Lemma 10.74 replaces lemma 10.70 and lemma 10.75 replaces lemma 10.71 in the argument. ▪

THEOREM 10.76 An allocation $(\underline{\mathbf{x}}, \underline{\mathbf{K}}, \underline{\mathbf{L}})$ is optimal with respect to the catching up criterion if and only if the corresponding program $(\underline{\mathbf{C}}, \underline{\mathbf{K}})$ is optimal with respect to the catching up criterion in the corresponding growth model.

Proof. By theorem 10.69, $(\underline{\mathbf{x}}, \underline{\mathbf{K}}, \underline{\mathbf{L}})$ is optimal if and only if it solves the problem

$$\min_{\substack{(\mathbf{x}, \mathbf{K}, \mathbf{L}) \text{ is a strongly feasible} \\ \text{allocation with initial} \\ \text{capital } \overline{K}_{-1}}} [\mathcal{L}_{-1}(x_{-1,1}) + \sum_{t=0}^{\infty} \mathcal{L}(x_{t0}, x_{t1}, K_t)].$$

By corollary 10.72, $(\underline{\mathbf{x}}, \underline{\mathbf{K}}, \underline{\mathbf{L}})$ solves this problem if and only if it solves the problem

$$\min_{\substack{(\mathbf{x}, \mathbf{K}, \mathbf{L}) \text{ is a strongly feasible} \\ \text{allocation with initial} \\ \text{capital } \overline{K}_{-1}}} \sum_{t=0}^{\infty} \mathcal{L}(x_{t0}, x_{t-1,1}, K_t). \tag{10.133}$$

The golden rule stationary allocation $(\overline{x}_0, \overline{x}_1, \overline{K}, 1)$ and the golden rule stationary program $(\overline{C}, \overline{K})$ correspond in that they have the same stationary capital stock, $\overline{C} = \overline{x}_0 + \overline{x}_1$, and $v(\overline{C}) = u_0(\overline{x}_0) + u_1(\overline{x}_1)$. We know from the proof of lemma 10.74 that when $x_0 + x_1 = C$ and $u_0(x_0) + u_1(x_1) = v(C)$, then the value loss functions for the corresponding Diamond and growth models are equal. Therefore, $(\underline{\mathbf{x}}, \underline{\mathbf{K}}, \underline{\mathbf{L}})$ solves problem 10.133 if and only if $(\underline{\mathbf{C}}, \underline{\mathbf{K}})$ solves the problem

$$\min_{\substack{(\mathbf{C}, \mathbf{K}) \text{ is a strongly feasible} \\ \text{program with initial} \\ \text{capital } \overline{K}_{-1}}} \sum_{t=0}^{\infty} \mathcal{L}(C_t, K_t).$$

Hence, theorem 10.73 implies that $(\underline{\mathbf{x}}, \underline{\mathbf{K}}, \underline{\mathbf{L}})$ is optimal if and only if $(\underline{\mathbf{C}}, \underline{\mathbf{K}})$ is optimal. ■

I define a *program equilibrium with interest rate 0,* $(\overline{\mathbf{C}}, \overline{\mathbf{K}}, \mathbf{p})$, to be a program equilibrium, $(\overline{\mathbf{C}}, \overline{\mathbf{K}}, r, \mathbf{p})$, as in definition 10.41 (in section 10.8), but with $r = 0$. Theorem 10.76 implies that the conclusion of theorem 10.66 applies to growth models as well as Diamond models.

THEOREM 10.77 If $(\overline{\mathbf{C}}, \overline{\mathbf{K}}, \mathbf{p})$ is a program equilibrium with interest rate 0 such that the prices p_t are bounded and, for every t, $\overline{C}_t$ solves the problem $\max_{C \geq 0}[v(C) - p_t C]$, then the program $(\overline{\mathbf{C}}, \overline{\mathbf{K}})$ is optimal according to the catching up criterion.

Proof. Let $(\overline{\mathbf{x}}, \overline{\mathbf{K}}, \overline{\mathbf{L}})$ be the allocation that corresponds to the program $(\overline{\mathbf{C}}, \overline{\mathbf{K}})$ and is an allocation for the Diamond model, (u_0, u_1, f), corresponding at interest rate 0 to the growth model (v, F). By theorem 10.42 (in section 10.8), there is a spot price equilibrium with interest rate 0 and transfer payments, $(\overline{\mathbf{x}}, \overline{\mathbf{K}}, \overline{\mathbf{L}}, \mathbf{P}, \mathbf{W}, G, \mathbf{T})$, where, for all t,

$$P_t = p_t,$$

$$W_t = P_t \frac{\partial f(\overline{K}_{t-1}, 1)}{\partial L},$$

$$\mathsf{T}_t = W_t - P_t \overline{x}_{t0} - P_{t+1} \overline{x}_{t1},$$

and

$$G = P_0[\overline{x}_{-1,1} - f(\overline{K}_{-1}, 1)] + W_0\overline{L}_0.$$

Because the prices P_t are bounded and every consumer's marginal utility of unit of account is 1, theorem 10.66 implies that the allocation $(\overline{\mathbf{x}}, \overline{\mathbf{K}}, \overline{\mathbf{L}})$ is optimal according to the catching up criterion. Hence, theorem 10.76 implies that the program $(\overline{\mathbf{C}}, \overline{\mathbf{K}})$ is optimal according to the catching up criterion. ▪

COROLLARY 10.78 The golden rule stationary program, $(\overline{C}, \overline{K})$, is optimal according to the catching up criterion and is therefore efficient. It is the unique program of a stationary program equilibrium with interest rate 0.

Proof. Let $p = \frac{dv(\overline{C})}{dC}$. Then, the stationary program equilibrium $(\overline{C}, \overline{K}, p)$ with interest rate 0 satisfies the conditions of theorem 10.77, so that the stationary allocation $(\overline{C}, \overline{K})$ is optimal according to the catching up criterion. If $(\underline{C}, \underline{K}, \underline{p})$ is any stationary program equilibrium with interest rate 0, then because the equilibrium is stationary,

$$\frac{dF(\underline{K})}{dK} = 1,$$

so that the $\underline{K}$ solves the problem

$$\max_{K \geq 0}[F(K) - K].$$

Since F is strictly concave, this problem has a unique solution. Since $\underline{C} = F(\underline{K}) - \underline{K}$, it follows that $\underline{C}$ is uniquely defined as well. ▪

I now turn to the turnpike theorem for allocations or programs that are optimal with respect to the catching up criterion.

THEOREM 10.79 (Turnpike theorem) If the allocation $(\mathbf{x}, \mathbf{K}, \mathbf{L})$ is optimal according to the catching up criterion and if the initial capital, $\overline{K}_{-1}$, is positive, then $\lim_{t\to\infty}(x_{t0}, x_{t1}, K_t, L_t) = (\overline{x}_0, \overline{x}_1, \overline{K}, \overline{L})$, where $(\overline{x}_0, \overline{x}_1, \overline{K}, \overline{L})$ is the golden rule stationary optimal allocation that solves the problem

$$\max_{x_0\geq 0, x_1\geq 0, K\geq 0, L\geq 0} [u_0(x_0) + u_1(x_1)]$$
$$\text{s.t. } x_0 + x_1 + K \leq f(K, L) \text{ and}$$
$$L \leq 1.$$

Proof. By lemma 10.62, $L_t = 1 = \overline{L}$, for all t, so that it is only necessary to show that $\lim_{t\to\infty}(x_{t0}, x_{t1}, K_t) = (\overline{x}_0, \overline{x}_1, \overline{K})$.

Because the allocation $(\mathbf{x}, \mathbf{K}, \mathbf{L})$ is feasible, there is a positive number b such that all the components of $(\mathbf{x}, \mathbf{K}, \mathbf{L})$ are less than or equal to b. I may assume that this bound applies to the components of $(\overline{x}_0, \overline{x}_1, \overline{K})$ as well. The bound enables me to apply lemma 10.71.

By lemma 10.70, there exists a strongly feasible allocation $(\underline{\mathbf{x}}, \underline{\mathbf{K}}, \underline{\mathbf{L}})$, such that

$$\mathcal{L}_{-1}(\underline{x}_{-1,1}) + \sum_{t=0}^{\infty} \mathcal{L}(\underline{x}_{t0}, \underline{x}_{t1}, \underline{K}_t) < \infty.$$

I show that if $\lim_{t\to\infty}(x_{t0}, x_{t1}, K_t) \neq (\overline{x}_0, \overline{x}_t, \overline{K})$, then the allocation $(\mathbf{x}, \mathbf{K}, \mathbf{L})$ cannot catch up to $(\underline{\mathbf{x}}, \underline{\mathbf{K}}, \underline{\mathbf{L}})$, which contradicts the optimality of $(\mathbf{x}, \mathbf{K}, \mathbf{L})$. If (x_{t0}, x_{t1}, K_t) does not converge to $(\overline{x}_0, \overline{x}_t, \overline{K})$, then because the components of $(\mathbf{x}, \mathbf{K}, \mathbf{L})$ are bounded above by b, lemma 10.71 implies that $\mathcal{L}(x_{t0}, x_{t1}, K_t)$ does not converge to 0, so that $\sum_{t=0}^{\infty} \mathcal{L}(x_{t0}, x_{t1}, K_t) = \infty$. Since $\sum_{t=0}^{\infty} \mathcal{L}(\underline{x}_{t0}, \underline{x}_{t1}, \underline{K}_t) < \infty$, it follows that

$$[\mathcal{L}_{-1}(x_{-1,1}) - \mathcal{L}_{-1}(\underline{x}_{-1,1})] + \sum_{t=0}^{T} [\mathcal{L}(x_{t0}, x_{t1}, K_t) - \mathcal{L}(\underline{x}_{t0}, \underline{x}_{t1}, \underline{K}_t)]$$

diverges to infinity as T goes to infinity. Equation 10.131 applies, so that

$$\begin{aligned}
&[\mathcal{L}_{-1}(x_{-1,1}) - \mathcal{L}_{-1}(\underline{x}_{-1,1})] + \sum_{t=0}^{T} [\mathcal{L}(x_{t0}, x_{t1}, K_t) - \mathcal{L}(\underline{x}_{t0}, \underline{x}_{t1}, \underline{K}_t)] \\
&= [u_1(\underline{x}_{-1,1}) - u_1(x_{-1,1})] + \sum_{t=0}^{T} [u_0(\underline{x}_{t0}) + u_1(\underline{x}_{t1}) - u_0(x_{t0}) - u_1(x_{t1})] \\
&\quad + P[f(\underline{K}_T, 1) - f(K_T, 1)] + P(x_{T1} - \underline{x}_{T1}).
\end{aligned}$$

Since the sequence $P[f(\underline{K}_T, 1) - f(K_T, 1)] + P(x_{T1} - \underline{x}_{T1})$ is bounded, the fact that

$$[\mathcal{L}_{-1}(x_{-1,1}) - \mathcal{L}_{-1}(\underline{x}_{-1,1})] + \sum_{t=0}^{T} [\mathcal{L}(x_{t0}, x_{t1}, K_t) - \mathcal{L}(\underline{x}_{t0}, \underline{x}_{t1}, \underline{K}_t)]$$

diverges to infinity implies that $[u_1(\underline{x}_{-1,1}) - u_1(x_{-1,1})] + \sum_{t=0}^{T} [u_0(\underline{x}_{t0}) + u_1(\underline{x}_{t1}) - u_0(x_{t0}) - u_1(x_{t1})]$ also diverges to $+\infty$, as T goes to infinity. Therefore, $(\mathbf{x}, \mathbf{K}, \mathbf{L})$ cannot catch up to $(\underline{\mathbf{x}}, \underline{\mathbf{K}}, \underline{\mathbf{L}})$. ■

A similar theorem applies to optimal programs in the growth model.

THEOREM 10.80 If the feasible program, $(\mathbf{C}, \mathbf{K})$, for the optimal growth model has positive initial capital $\overline{K}_{-1}$ and is optimal according to the catching up criterion, then $\lim_{t\to\infty}(C_t, K_t) = (\overline{C}, \overline{K})$, where $(\overline{C}, \overline{K})$ is the golden rule program.

Proof. Let $(\mathbf{x}, \mathbf{K}, \mathbf{L})$ be the allocation that corresponds to $(\mathbf{C}, \mathbf{K})$ in the corresponding Diamond model. Theorem 10.76 implies that $(\mathbf{x}, \mathbf{K}, \mathbf{L})$ is optimal according to the catching up criterion and by theorem 10.79, $\lim_{t\to\infty}(x_{t0}, x_{t1}, K_t) = (\overline{x}_0, \overline{x}_1, \overline{K})$, where $(\overline{x}_0, \overline{x}_1, \overline{K})$ is the stationary golden rule allocation. Since $C_t = x_{t0} + x_{t-1,1}$ and $\overline{C} = \overline{x}_0 + \overline{x}_1$, it follows that $\lim_{t\to\infty}(C_t, K_t) = (\overline{C}, \overline{K})$. ∎

The two previous theorems imply that the golden rule allocation or program is the unique stationary allocation or program with positive capital that is optimal with respect to the catching up criterion, since any other stationary optimal allocation or program with positive capital converges to the golden rule.

As was explained in section 10.12, turnpike theorems 10.79 and 10.80 rather than theorem 10.54 probably ought to be thought of as the true turnpike theorems in that they generalize to models with many produced goods or with uncertainty.

The turnpike theorem for the Diamond model makes it possible to prove a converse to theorem 10.66 that allocations are optimal if they belong to spot price equilibria with interest rate 0 and constant marginal utility of unit of account.

THEOREM 10.81 If the allocation $(\underline{\mathbf{x}}, \underline{\mathbf{K}}, \underline{\mathbf{L}})$ is optimal according to the catching up criterion and if the initial capital, $\overline{K}_{-1}$, is positive, then $(\underline{\mathbf{x}}, \underline{\mathbf{K}}, \underline{\mathbf{L}})$ is the allocation of a spot price equilibrium with interest rate 0, $(\underline{\mathbf{x}}, \underline{\mathbf{K}}, \underline{\mathbf{L}}, \mathbf{P}, \mathbf{W}, G, \mathbf{T})$, where the prices P_t are bounded and every consumer's marginal utility of unit of account is 1.

Proof. By lemma 10.62, $(\underline{\mathbf{x}}, \underline{\mathbf{K}}, \underline{\mathbf{L}})$ is strongly feasible and $\underline{K}_t > 0$, for all t. By the turnpike theorem 10.79, $\lim_{t\to\infty}(\underline{x}_{t0}, \underline{x}_{t1}, \underline{K}_t, \underline{L}_t) = (\overline{x}_0, \overline{x}_1, \overline{K}, 1)$, where $(\overline{x}_0, \overline{x}_1, \overline{K}, 1)$ is the golden rule allocation. Assumption 10.2 implies that $f(\overline{K}, 1) - \overline{K} > 0$, so that $\overline{x}_0 + \overline{x}_1 > 0$. Therefore, there is a positive integer T such that $\underline{x}_{t0} > 0$, for $t \geq T$, or $\underline{x}_{t-1,1} > 0$, for $t \geq T$. For $t \geq T$, let $P_t = \frac{du_0(\underline{x}_{t0})}{dx}$, if $\underline{x}_{t0} > 0$, and let $P_t = \frac{du_1(\underline{x}_{t-1,1})}{dx}$, if $\underline{x}_{t-1,1} > 0$. Lemma 10.65 implies that $\frac{du_0(\underline{x}_{t0})}{dx} = \frac{du_0(\underline{x}_{t+1,0})}{dx}\frac{\partial f(\underline{K}_t, 1)}{\partial K}$, if $\underline{x}_{t0} > 0$ and

$\underline{x}_{t+1,0} > 0$, and similar equations apply if $\underline{x}_{t-1,1} > 0$ and $\underline{x}_{t1} > 0$, Therefore, $P_t = P_{t+1}\frac{\partial f(\underline{K}_t, 1)}{\partial K}$, for $t \geq T$. Let $W_t = P_t\frac{\partial f(\underline{K}_{t-1}, 1)}{\partial L}$, for $t \geq T$. By lemma 10.65, the allocation $(\underline{x}_{t0}, \underline{x}_{t-1,1}, \underline{K}_t, \underline{L}_t)_{t=0}^T$ solves the problem

$$\max_{\substack{x_{t0}, \geq 0, x_{t-1,1} \geq 0, K_t \geq 0, L_t \geq 0, \\ \text{for } t=0, 1, \ldots, T}} \sum_{t=0}^{T} [u_0(x_{t0}) + u_1(x_{t-1,1})]$$

$$\text{s.t.} \quad x_{t-1,1} + x_{t0} + K_t \leq f(K_{t-1}, L_t) \text{ and}$$

$$L_t \leq 1, \text{ for } t = 0, \ldots, T,$$

$$K_{-1} = \overline{K}_{-1}, \text{ and } K_T \geq \underline{K}_T,$$

where $\underline{K}_T$ is given. Because $\overline{K}_{-1} > 0$, this problem satisfies the constraint qualification of the Kuhn-Tucker theorem, so that there exist prices $P_0, \ldots, P_T$ and wages $W_0, \ldots, W_T$ and a nonnegative number Q such that $(\underline{x}_{t0}, \underline{x}_{t-1,1}, \underline{K}_t, \underline{L}_t)_{t=0}^T$ solves the problem

$$\max_{\substack{x_{t0}, \geq 0, x_{t-1,1} \geq 0, K_t \geq 0, L_t \geq 0, \\ \text{for } t=0, 1, \ldots, T}} \Big\{[u_0(x_0) + u_1(x_{-1,1}) - P_t(x_{00} + x_{-1,1}$$

$$+ K_0 - f(\overline{K}_{-1}, L_0)) - W_0 L_0]$$

$$\sum_{t=1}^{T-1}[u_0(x_{t0}) + u_1(x_{t-1,1}) - P_t(x_{t0} + x_{t-1,1} + K_t - f(K_{t-1}, L_t)) - W_t L_t]$$

$$[u_0(x_{T0}) + u_1(x_{T-1,1}) - P_T(x_{T0} + x_{T-1,1}$$

$$+ \overline{K}_T - f(K_{T-1}, L_T)) - W_T L_T + Q K_T]\Big\}.$$

It follows that for $t < T$, $\frac{du_0(\underline{x}_{t0})}{dx} \leq P_t$, with equality if $\underline{x}_{t0} > 0$, and $\frac{du_1(\underline{x}_{t-1,1})}{dx} \leq P_t$, with equality if $\underline{x}_{t-1,1} > 0$. Since $\underline{K}_t > 0$, for all $t < T$, $P_t = P_{t+1}\frac{\partial f(\underline{K}_t, 1)}{\partial K}$, for $t < T$. Similarly, $W_t = P_t\frac{\partial f(\underline{K}_{t-1}, 1)}{\partial L}$, for $t < T$.

Let $G = P_0\underline{x}_{-1,1} - [P_0 f(\underline{K}_{-1}, 1) - W_0]$ and $\mathsf{T}_t = W_t - P_t\underline{x}_{t0} - P_{t+1}\underline{x}_{t1}$, for all t. Then, $(\mathbf{x}, \mathbf{K}, \mathbf{L}, \mathbf{P}, \mathbf{W}, G, \mathsf{T})$ satisfies all the conditions of a spot price equilibrium with interest rate 0.

I now show that the sequence P_t is bounded. Since $\overline{x}_0 + \overline{x}_1 > 0$, it follows that $\overline{x}_0 > 0$ or $\overline{x}_1 > 0$. Suppose that $\overline{x}_0 > 0$. (A similar argument applies if $\overline{x}_0 = 0$ and $\overline{x}_1 > 0$.) Since $\lim_{t\to\infty} \underline{x}_{t0} = \overline{x}_0$, there exists a positive integer T such that $\underline{x}_{t0} \geq \frac{\overline{x}_0}{2} > 0$, if $t \geq T$. Therefore,

$$P_t = \frac{du_0(\underline{x}_{t0})}{dx} \leq \frac{du_0(\overline{x}_0/2)}{dx},$$

if $t \geq T$. This completes the proof that the sequence P_t is bounded and hence the proof of the theorem. ▪

A similar statement applies to optimal programs.

THEOREM 10.82 If the feasible program $(\mathbf{C}, \mathbf{K})$ is optimal according to the catching up criterion and if the initial capital, $\overline{K}_{-1}$, is positive, then there is a price sequence $\mathbf{p} = (p_0, p_1, \ldots)$ such that $(\mathbf{C}, \mathbf{K}, \mathbf{p})$ is a program equilibrium with interest rate 0, where the prices p_t are bounded.

Proof. Let $(\mathbf{x}, \mathbf{K}, \mathbf{L})$ be the allocation corresponding to the program $(\mathbf{C}, \mathbf{K})$. By theorem 10.76, $(\mathbf{x}, \mathbf{K}, \mathbf{L})$ is optimal with respect to the catching up criterion. By theorem 10.81, $(\mathbf{x}, \mathbf{K}, \mathbf{L})$ is the allocation of a spot price equilibrium with interest rate 0, $(\mathbf{x}, \mathbf{K}, \mathbf{L}, \mathbf{p}, \mathbf{W}, G, \mathbf{T})$ and such that every consumer's marginal utility of unit of account is 1. By theorem 10.42 (in section 10.8), $(\mathbf{C}, \mathbf{K}, \mathbf{p})$ is a program equilibrium with interest rate 0. ▪

It is now possible to show that the construction process mentioned after lemma 10.65 may be continued indefinitely for one and only one initial condition and generates an optimal program or allocation. Consider the Diamond model. Let the initial capital $\overline{K}_{-1}$ be given and positive, and choose a positive initial price P_0. Let $\overline{x}_{00}$ be the unique solution of the conditions $\frac{du_0(x_0)}{dx} \leq P_0$, with equality if $x_0 > 0$, and similarly let $\overline{x}_{-1,1}$ be the unique solution of the conditions $\frac{du_1(x_1)}{dx} \leq P_0$, with equality if $x_0 > 0$. Let

$$W_0 = P_0 \frac{\partial f(\overline{K}_{-1}, 1)}{\partial L},$$

$$G = P_0 \overline{x}_{-1,1} - [P_0 f(\overline{K}_{-1}, 1) - W_0],$$

$$\overline{K}_0 = f(\overline{K}_{-1}, 1) - \overline{x}_{00} - \overline{x}_{-1,1},$$

and let

$$P_1 = \left(\frac{\partial f(\overline{K}_{-1}, 1)}{\partial K} \right)^{-1} P_0.$$

Given P_1, we can define $\overline{x}_{10}$ and $\overline{x}_{01}$ from P_1 just as $\overline{x}_{00}$ and $\overline{x}_{-1,1}$ were defined from P_0. Let

$$\mathsf{T}_0 = W_0 - P_0 \overline{x}_{00} - P_1 \overline{x}_{01}.$$

Continuing by induction on t, we can construct P_t, W_t, T_t, $\overline{x}_{t0}$, $\overline{x}_{t-1,1}$, and $\overline{K}_t$, for all t or until the allocation becomes infeasible.

I now show that there is a unique choice of P_0 such that the construction process just described can be continued indefinitely and yields a bounded sequence of prices. This construction, therefore, defines an optimal allocation. By theorem 10.85 (in section 10.14), there exists a feasible allocation $(\overline{\mathbf{x}}, \overline{\mathbf{K}}, \overline{\mathbf{L}})$ that has initial capital $\overline{K}_{-1}$ and is optimal with respect to the catching up criterion. By theorem 10.81, $(\overline{\mathbf{x}}, \overline{\mathbf{K}}, \overline{\mathbf{L}})$ is the allocation of a spot price equilibrium with interest rate 0, $(\overline{\mathbf{x}}, \overline{\mathbf{K}}, \overline{\mathbf{L}}, \mathbf{P}, \mathbf{W}, G, \mathbf{T})$, such that every consumer's marginal utility of unit of account is 1 and the sequence of prices, P_t, is bounded. By proposition 10.63, $(\overline{\mathbf{x}}, \overline{\mathbf{K}}, \overline{\mathbf{L}})$ is the only optimal allocation with initial capital $\overline{K}_{-1}$. There is at most one price sequence $\mathbf{P} = (P_0, P_1, \ldots)$ for this allocation that makes every consumer's marginal utility of unit of account equal to 1. By theorem 10.66, a feasible allocation is optimal if it is the allocation of a spot price equilibrium with interest rate 0 such that the prices are bounded and every consumer's marginal utility of unit of account is 1. In conclusion, the equilibrium $(\overline{\mathbf{x}}, \overline{\mathbf{K}}, \overline{\mathbf{L}}, \mathbf{P}, \mathbf{W}, G, \mathbf{T})$ can be obtained by the continuation process, and any other equilibrium so obtained equals this one, if it has bounded prices and its marginal utilities of unit of account equal 1. An exactly parallel and simpler argument applies to optimal growth programs.

10.14 Existence of Optimal Allocations and Programs

I now prove that there exist allocations and programs that maximize a discounted sum of consumer utilities or are optimal with respect to the catching up criterion.

THEOREM 10.83 If assumptions 10.1–10.5 (in section 10.1) apply to the Diamond model, then the problem

$$\max_{\substack{(\mathbf{x}, \mathbf{K}, \mathbf{L}) \text{ is a feasible allocation} \\ \text{with initial capital } \overline{K}_{-1}}} \{\lambda_{-1}^{-1} u_1(x_{-1,1}) + \sum_{t=0}^{\infty} \lambda_t^{-1}[u_0(x_{t0}) + u_1(x_{t1})]\}$$

has a solution, where $\overline{K}_{-1}$ is given and $\lambda_t > 0$, for all t, and $\sum_{t=-1}^{\infty} \lambda_t^{-1} < \infty$.

Proof. There exists at least one feasible allocation with initial capital $\overline{K}_{-1}$. An example is the zero allocation, $(\mathbf{x}, \mathbf{K}, \mathbf{L})$, where $x_{t0} = x_{t-1,1} = K_t = L_t = 0$, for all $t \geq 0$.

Because feasible allocations are bounded by proposition 10.8 (in section 10.1), there is a positive number B such that if $(\mathbf{x}, \mathbf{K}, \mathbf{L})$ is any feasible allocation, then $x_{t0} \leq B$ and $x_{t1} \leq B$, for all t. Because u_0 and u_1 are increasing by assumption 10.5, it follows that

$$\begin{aligned} &\lambda_{-1}^{-1} u_1(x_{-1,1}) + \sum_{t=0}^{\infty} \lambda_t^{-1}[u_0(x_{t0}) + u_1(x_{t1})] \\ &\leq \lambda_{-1}^{-1} u_1(B) + \sum_{t=0}^{\infty} \lambda_t^{-1}[u_0(B) + u_1(B)] < \infty. \end{aligned} \tag{10.134}$$

Let

$$A = \sup_{\substack{(\mathbf{x}, \mathbf{K}, \mathbf{L}) \text{ is a feasible allocation} \\ \text{with initial capital } \overline{K}_{-1}}} \{\lambda_{-1}^{-1} u_1(x_{-1,1}) + \sum_{t=0}^{\infty} \lambda_t^{-1}[u_0(x_{t0}) + u_1(x_{t1})]\}.$$

Inequality 10.134 implies that $A < \infty$. Because there exists at least one feasible allocation and u_0 and u_1 are nonnegative functions, it follows that $A \geq 0$.

For each positive integer N, let (x^N, K^N, L^N) be a feasible allocation with initial capital $\overline{K}_{-1}$ such that

$$\lambda_{-1}^{-1} u_1(x_{-1,1}^N) + \sum_{t=0}^{\infty} \lambda_t^{-1}(u_0(x_{t0}^N) + u_1(x_{t1}^N)) > A - \frac{1}{N}. \tag{10.135}$$

By the Cantor diagonal argument first used in proving theorem 9.43 (in section 9.7), there exists a subsequence $(x^{N(k)}, K^{N(k)}, L^{N(k)})$, for $k = 1, 2, \ldots,$ such that $(x_{t0}^{N(k)}, x_{t-1,1}^{N(k)}, K_t^{N(k)}, L_t^{N(k)})$ converges, for every t, as k goes to infinity. Let

$$(\overline{x}_{t0}, \overline{x}_{t-1,1}, \overline{K}_t, \overline{L}_t) = \lim_{t \to \infty} (x_{t0}^{N(k)}, x_{t-1,1}^{N(k)}, K_t^{N(k)}, L_t^{N(k)}),$$

for all $t \geq 0$. By passage to the limit, the allocation $(\overline{\mathbf{x}}, \overline{\mathbf{K}}, \overline{\mathbf{L}})$ is feasible with initial capital $\overline{K}_{-1}$.

I show that

$$\lambda_{-1}^{-1} u_1(\overline{x}_{-1,1}) + \sum_{t=0}^{\infty} \lambda_t^{-1}[u_0(\overline{x}_{t0}) + u_1(\overline{x}_{t1}) = A.$$

Since

$$\lambda_{-1}^{-1} u_1(\overline{x}_{-1,1}) + \sum_{t=0}^{\infty} \lambda_t^{-1}[u_0(\overline{x}_{t0}) + u_1(\overline{x}_{t1}) \leq A$$

by the definition of A, it is sufficient to show that for every positive number ε,

$$\lambda_{-1}^{-1} u_1(\overline{x}_{-1,1}) + \sum_{t=0}^{\infty} \lambda_t^{-1}[u_0(\overline{x}_{t0}) + u_1(\overline{x}_{t1})] > A - \varepsilon.$$

Let T be a positive integer so large that

$$\sum_{t=T+1}^{\infty} \lambda_t^{-1}[u_0(B) + u_1(B)] < \frac{\varepsilon}{3}. \tag{10.136}$$

Let k be a positive integer so large that

$$N(k) > \frac{3}{\varepsilon} \tag{10.137}$$

and, for all $t = 0, 1, \ldots, T$,

$$\lambda_t^{-1}|u_0(x_{t0}^{N(k)}) - u_0(\overline{x}_{t0})| \leq \frac{\varepsilon}{6(T+1)+3} \tag{10.138}$$

and

$$\lambda_t^{-1}|u_0(x_{t-1,1}^{N(k)}) - u_1(\overline{x}_{t-1,1})| \leq \frac{\varepsilon}{6(T+1)+3}. \tag{10.139}$$

Then,

$$\begin{aligned}
&\lambda_{-1}^{-1} u_1(\overline{x}_{-1,1}) + \sum_{t=0}^{\infty} \lambda_t^{-1}[u_0(\overline{x}_{t0}) + u_1(\overline{x}_{t1})] \\
&\geq \lambda_{-1}^{-1} u_1(\overline{x}_{-1,1}) + \sum_{t=0}^{T} \lambda_t^{-1}[u_0(\overline{x}_{t0}) + u_1(\overline{x}_{t1})] \\
&\geq \lambda_{-1}^{-1} u_1(x_{-1,1}^{N(k)}) + \sum_{t=0}^{T} \lambda_t^{-1}[u_0(x_{t0}^{N(k)}) + u_1(x_{t1}^{N(k)})] - \frac{\varepsilon}{3} \\
&\geq \lambda_{-1}^{-1} u_1(x_{-1,1}^{N(k)}) + \sum_{t=0}^{\infty} \lambda_t^{-1}[u_0(x_{t0}^{N(k)}) + u_1(x_{t1}^{N(k)})] - \frac{2\varepsilon}{3} \\
&> A - \frac{1}{N(k)} - \frac{2\varepsilon}{3} > A - \varepsilon,
\end{aligned}$$

where the first inequality holds because u_0 and u_1 are nonnegative functions, the second inequality holds by inequalities 10.138 and 10.139, the third holds by inequality 10.136, the fourth holds by inequality 10.135, and the last holds by inequality 10.137. ▪

A similar argument proves the corresponding theorem for optimal growth programs.

THEOREM 10.84 If assumptions 10.18–10.21 (in section 10.1) apply to the optimal growth model, then

$$\max_{\substack{(\mathbf{C},\mathbf{K}) \text{ is a feasible program} \\ \text{with initial capital } \overline{K}_{-1}}} \sum_{t=0}^{\infty} \lambda_t^{-1} v(C_t)$$

has a solution, where $\overline{K}_{-1}$ is fixed, $\lambda_t > 0$, for all t, and $\sum_{t=-1}^{\infty} \lambda_t^{-1} < \infty$.

I now prove that there exist an allocation and a program that are optimal with respect to the catching up criterion.

THEOREM 10.85 If assumptions 10.1–10.5 apply to the Diamond model and assumptions 10.18–10.21 apply to the optimal growth model, then there exist a feasible allocation, $(\mathbf{x}, \mathbf{K}, \mathbf{L})$, for the Diamond model and a feasible program, $(\mathbf{C}, \mathbf{K})$, for the growth model that are optimal with respect to the catching up criterion.

Proof.[8] If the initial capital, $\overline{K}_{-1}$, is 0, then the only feasible allocation or program is the one that has zero output and consumption in every period, so that this allocation or program is optimal according to the catching up criterion. So assume that $\overline{K}_{-1} > 0$.

By theorem 10.76 (in section 10.13), it is sufficient to show that there exists an optimal program, $(\mathbf{C}, \mathbf{K})$. By theorem 10.73 (in the same section), there exists an optimal program if the following problem has a solution:

$$\min_{\substack{(\mathbf{C},\mathbf{K}) \text{ is a strongly feasible} \\ \text{program with initial capital } \overline{K}_{-1}}} \sum_{t=0}^{\infty} \mathcal{L}(C_t, K_t).$$

8. This proof is based on an argument of Brock (1970).

Let

$$A = \inf_{\substack{(\mathbf{C},\,\mathbf{K}) \text{ is a strongly feasible} \\ \text{program with initial capital } \overline{K}_{-1}}} \sum_{t=0}^{\infty} \mathcal{L}(C_t, K_t).$$

I show that there exists a strongly feasible program $(\mathbf{C}, \mathbf{K})$ such that $\sum_{t=0}^{\infty} \mathcal{L}(C_t, K_t) = A$. By lemma 10.74 (in section 10.13), there exists a strongly feasible program $(\mathbf{C}, \mathbf{K})$ such that $\sum_{t=0}^{\infty} \mathcal{L}(C_t, K_t) < \infty$, so that $A < \infty$. For each positive integer N, let $(\mathbf{C}^N, \mathbf{K}^N)$ be a strongly feasible program with initial capital $\overline{K}_{-1}$ such that

$$\sum_{t=0}^{\infty} \mathcal{L}(C_{t0}^N, K_t^N) < A + \frac{1}{N}.$$

Since feasible programs are bounded by proposition 10.8 (in section 10.1), I may use the Cantor diagonal argument to prove that there exists a subsequence $(\mathbf{C}^{N(k)}, \mathbf{K}^{N(k)})$, for $k = 1, 2, \ldots$, such that, for all t, $(C_t^{N(k)}, K_t^{N(k)})$ converges as k goes to infinity. Let $(C_t, K_t) = \lim_{k\to\infty}(C_t^{N(k)}, K_t^{N(k)})$, for all t. Because each of the programs $(\mathbf{C}^{N(k)}, \mathbf{K}^{N(k)})$ is strongly feasible, the limit program $(\mathbf{C}, \mathbf{K})$ is so as well. I prove that $\sum_{t=0}^{\infty} \mathcal{L}(C_t, K_t) = A$. Since $\mathcal{L}(C_t, K_t) \geq 0$, for all t, the infinite sum $\sum_{t=0}^{\infty} \mathcal{L}(C_t, K_t)$ exists. Since $\sum_{t=0}^{\infty} \mathcal{L}(C_t, K_t) \geq A$ by the definition of A, it is sufficient to show that for every positive number ε, $\sum_{t=0}^{\infty} \mathcal{L}(C_t, K_t) < A + \varepsilon$. To show that $\sum_{t=0}^{\infty} \mathcal{L}(C_t, K_t) < A + \varepsilon$, it is sufficient to show that for every positive integer T, $\sum_{t=0}^{T} \mathcal{L}(C_t, K_t) < A + \varepsilon$. So fix the positive integer T and the positive number ε. Because $(C_t, K_t) = \lim_{k\to\infty}(C_t^{N(k)}, K_t^{N(k)})$, for all t, there exists a positive integer k such that

$$|\mathcal{L}(C_t^{N(k)}, K_t^{N(k)}) - \mathcal{L}(C_t, K_t)| < \frac{\varepsilon}{2(T+1)},$$

for $t = 0, \ldots, T$. I may assume that k is so large that $N(k) > \frac{2}{\varepsilon}$. Therefore,

$$\sum_{t=0}^{T} \mathcal{L}(C_t, K_t) \leq \sum_{t=0}^{T} \mathcal{L}(C_t^{N(k)}, K_t^{N(k)}) + \frac{\varepsilon}{2} \leq \sum_{t=0}^{\infty} \mathcal{L}(C_t^{N(k)}, K_t^{N(k)}) + \frac{\varepsilon}{2}$$
$$< A + \frac{1}{N(k)} + \frac{\varepsilon}{2} < A + \varepsilon.$$

This completes the proof that

$$\sum_{t=0}^{\infty} \mathcal{L}(C_t, K_t) = A = \inf_{\substack{(\underline{\mathbf{C}},\,\underline{\mathbf{K}}) \text{ is a strongly feasible} \\ \text{program with initial capital } \overline{K}_{-1}}} \sum_{t=0}^{\infty} \mathcal{L}(\underline{C}_t, \underline{K}_t). \quad ■$$

Problem Set

1. Consider the Diamond model with utility function

$$u(x_0, x_1) = \ln(1 + x_0) + \ln(1 + x_1)$$

and with production function

$$f(K_t, L_{t+1}) = \sqrt{L_t K_{t-1}},$$

for all time periods t. (Recall that the supply of labor equals 1 in the Diamond model.)

(a) What is the set of feasible stationary allocations?
(b) Which of these are Pareto optimal?
(c) Find a stationary spot price equilibrium, $(\overline{x}_0, \overline{x}_1, \overline{K}, \overline{L}, P, W, r, G, \mathsf{T})$, with $\mathsf{T} = 0$.
(d) Is the allocation of this equilibrium Pareto optimal?
(e) Find the stationary spot price equilibrium, $(\overline{x}_0, \overline{x}_1, \overline{K}, \overline{L}, P, W, r, G, \mathsf{T})$, with $P = 1$ and such that its allocation maximizes the social welfare function

$$(1.1)u(x_{-1,0}, x_{-1,1}) + \sum_{t=0}^{\infty}(1.1)^{-t}u(x_{t0}, x_{t1})$$

among feasible allocations, where $x_{-1,0}$ and K_{-1} are given. Notice that you have to choose $x_{-1,0}$ and K_{-1}, so that the equilibrium is stationary. Is the allocation of this equilibrium Pareto optimal?
(f) Answer part (e) with the social welfare function equal to

$$2u(x_{-1,0}, x_{-1,1}) + \sum_{t=0}^{\infty} 2^{-t}u(x_{t0}, x_{t1}).$$

(g) Compare the capital stocks in parts (e) and (f). Which is bigger?

2. Consider a Diamond model with the price of the produced good equal to 1, when the production function is

$$f(K, L) = 2\sqrt{KL}$$

and the utility function of each consumer is

$$u(x_0, x_1) = 2\ln(x_0) + \ln(x_1).$$

Remember that the only endowment consumers have is one unit of labor in youth.

(a) Compute a stationary spot price equilibrium

$$(x_0(r), x_1(r), K(r), L(r), P, W(r), r, G(r), \mathsf{T}(r)),$$

where $P = 1$ and $r > -1$.

(b) Graph the function $\mathsf{T}(r)$.

(c) How many values of r satisfy the equation

$$\mathsf{T}(r) = -\frac{1}{32}?$$

(d) Over what range of values of r is the utility of a typical consumer increasing in r, and over what range is the utility of a typical consumer decreasing in r?

(e) For what values of r is the equilibrium allocation Pareto optimal?

(f) Suppose that the lump-sum tax is maintained at level $\mathsf{T}(\overline{r})$ and that an infinitesimal amount of pay-as-you-go social security is introduced. Social security changes the equilibrium interest rate to r. Will r exceed $\overline{r}$ or be less than $\overline{r}$, when

(i) $\overline{r} = 0$?

(ii) $\overline{r} = 2$?

3. Consider the Diamond model with utility function

$$u(x_0, x_1) = \ln(x_0) + \ln(x_1)$$

and with production function

$$f(K, L) - 4K^{1/4}L^{3/4}.$$

(a) Compute a spot price equilibrium,

$$(x_0(r), x_1(r), K(r), L(r), P, W(r), r, G(r), \mathsf{T}(r)),$$

when $r \geq 0$ and $P = 1$.

(b) What is the stationary equilibrium interest rate when the lump-sum tax on youth, T, equals 0.15? What are the levels of capital and of consumption in youth and old age?

(c) Suppose that a social security program is introduced that taxes youth 0.1 and pays a benefit of 0.1 to the old. The lump-sum tax of 0.15 on youth is continued after the social security is introduced, so that youths pay 0.25 in total taxes. What is the stationary equilibrium interest rate? What are the levels of capital and consumption in youth and old age?

(d) Suppose that when the social security program of part (c) is introduced, the lump-sum tax of 0.15 paid by youth is changed to a new level, T, so that the introduction of social security does not change the interest rate. What is this new level of the lump-sum tax?

4. Consider the Diamond model with

$$u(x_0, x_1) = \ln(x_0) + \ln(x_1)$$

and $f(K, L) = \frac{4KL}{K+L}$.

(a) Compute the stationary spot price equilibrium,

$$(x_0(r), x_1(r), K(r), L(r), P, W(r), r, G(r), \mathsf{T}(r)),$$

with $P = 1$ and for those nonnegative interest rates, r, for which the stationary capital stock exists and is positive. For which interest rates is the stationary equilibrium capital stock defined and positive?

(b) Compute the equilibrium for $r = 1$.

(c) Suppose the economy is in a stationary spot price equilibrium with a nonnegative interest rate for which the capital stock is positive and that a small amount of pay-as-you-go social security, $(\mathsf{T}_0, \mathsf{T}_1)$, is introduced. Will the new stationary capital stock be higher or lower? Does the answer depend on the interest rate?

5. One might imagine that if the government fixed the lump-sum tax to be equal to T, then the economy would eventually settle into a stationary equilibrium,

$$(x_0(r), x_1(r), K(r), L(r), P, W(r), r, G(r), \mathsf{T}(r)),$$

with an interest rate, r, determined by the equation $\mathsf{T}(r) = T$. In this statement, I am assuming that the price of the produced good is 1, so that T is the real value of the tax. The following problem is meant to show that we cannot necessarily assume that the stationary equilibrium interest rate is a function, $r(T)$, of the tax, T.

Let production function $f(K, L)$ satisfy assumptions 10.1–10.5 (in section 10.1), and let the utility function $u(x_0, x_1)$ satisfy assumption 10.5. Let

$$(x_0(r), x_1(r), K(r), L(r), P, W(r), r, G(r), \mathsf{T}(r))$$

be a stationary spot price equilibrium for the Diamond model with production function f and utility function u and where $r > 0$ and $P = 1$.

(a) Show that $f(K(r), 1) = (1 + r)K(r) + W(r)$.

(Hint for parts (b)–(e): Use the equation of part (a) as well as the equations

$$\mathsf{T}(r) = W(r) - x_0(r) - \frac{x_1(r)}{1+r} \text{ and}$$
$$x_0(r) + x_1(r) = f(K(r), 1) - K(r).)$$

(b) Show that $T(0) = 0$.

(c) Show that $\lim_{r\to\infty}(1 + r)K(r) = 0$, $\lim_{r\to\infty} f(K(r), 1) = 0$, and $\lim_{r\to\infty} W(r) = 0$.

(d) Show that $\lim_{r\to\infty} \mathsf{T}(r) = 0$.

(e) Show that $\mathsf{T}(r)$ is a continuous function of r.

(f) Show that if from some positive number r, $\mathsf{T}(r) \neq 0$, then for some value of T, the equation $\mathsf{T}(r) = T$ has more than one positive solution.

6. Let $(\overline{C}_t, \overline{K}_t)_{t=0}^{\infty}$ be a solution of the problem

$$\max_{\substack{C_t\geq 0,\, K_t\geq 0,\\ \text{for } t=0,\,1,\,\ldots}} \sum_{t=0}^{\infty} \beta^t \gamma^{-1} C_t^{\gamma}$$
$$C_t + K_t = \alpha^{-1} K_{t-1}^{\alpha},$$

where $\overline{K}_{-1}$ is a given positive number and where $0 < \alpha < 1, 0 < \beta < 1$, and $0 < \gamma < 1$.

(a) Show that $\lim_{t\to\infty} K_t$ and $\lim_{t\to\infty} C_t$ exist.

(b) Calculate $\lim_{t\to\infty} K_t$ and $\lim_{t\to\infty} C_t$ in terms of α, β, and γ.

7. In an optimal growth model, let the production function be

$$y_{t+1} = 20\sqrt{K_t}$$

and let the one-period utility function be

$$u(C_t) = 3C_t^{1/3},$$

for all t.

(a) Find the golden rule allocation for this model.

(b) Let $(C_t, K_t)_{t=0}^{\infty}$ be a program that has initial capital $K_{-1} = 1$ and is optimal with respect to the catching up criterion. What is the first period t such that $|K_t - \overline{K}| \leq 10$, where $\overline{K}$ is the golden rule capital stock?

8. Consider the growth model with

$$u(C_t) = \ln(C_t)$$

and

$$F(K_t) = \min((1+a)K_t, b),$$

where $a > 0$ and $b > 0$. Find a program that is optimal with respect to the overtaking criterion given an arbitrary, positive, initial capital stock $\overline{K}_{-1}$.

(Hint: The answer depends on whether

$$(1+a)\overline{K}_{-1} \geq b$$

or

$$(1+a)\overline{K}_{-1} < b.)$$

The harder case is where $(1+a)\overline{K}_{-1} < b$. For this case, you may use Euler's equation, feasibility, the production function, and backward induction on time to calculate an optimal program with initial capital equal to any one of an infinite decreasing sequence of stocks, where the sequence starts with $(1+a)^{-1}b$ and converges asymptotically to 0. The capital of an optimal program starting at one of these points reaches $(1+a)^{-1}b$, after finitely many periods, and then stays at this level forever. If the initial capital is between two points in this sequence, then relative to the smaller of these two points, there is an extra amount of output to be consumed and invested over finitely many periods until the capital stock reaches $(1+a)^{-1}b$. Again use Euler's equation, feasibility, and the production function to see how this extra consumption and capital should evolve. Verify that the program that you calculate in this manner is optimal by showing that it is part of a program equilibrium with interest rate 0.

— 11 —

A Critical Assessment

I now evaluate the practical significance of what has been presented in this book. The main results are the two welfare theorems applied to static and intertemporal contexts. In a static model, the interpretation of the first welfare theorem is fairly straightforward: an equilibrium allocation is economically efficient provided preferences are locally nonsatiated and there are no external effects. The first of these conditions seems reasonable, and the second surely does not apply strictly, since external effects are there to be seen by all. The pertinence of this theorem therefore depends on our judgment as to the importance of external effects. The second welfare theorem is more problematic because its application requires special knowledge that no government is likely to have. Although the theorem's assertion may seem innocuous—that any Pareto optimal allocation can be achieved as the allocation of an equilibrium with transfer payments—no government could make a reasonable selection of a Pareto optimal allocation without knowing consumer preferences and having a way to compare different individuals' welfare. The government would also need to know a great deal about demand and supply functions of both firms and consumers in order to calculate the appropriate lump-sum transfers.

The infinite horizon of the overlapping generations model makes the interpretation of both welfare theorems more dubious. In order to be sure that an equilibrium is Pareto optimal, the prices should be summable or at least bounded after being normalized, so that all consumers have the same marginal utility of unit of account. These requirements could never be verified, because they require knowledge of prices indefinitely far in the future. Another difficulty is that prices can be normalized so that the marginal utility of unit of account is constant only if individual utility functions are known and there is some way to select units of utility for different people. We can imagine that this problem might be met by some standardized procedure for approximating consumers' utility functions, so that consumers' marginal utility of unit of account could be held roughly constant. A further difficulty is that consumers must anticipate correctly the prices that will obtain later in their lives. This is an especially demanding requirement in the context of a nonstationary equilibrium, such as one for a growing economy. Still another complication is that some mechanism might be needed to avoid inefficient perfect foresight equilibria such as those occurring in Gale's example (example 9.27 in section 9.5). This example shows that market clearance and perfect foresight may not determine the price level. Perhaps some means of economic control is required to avoid such perverse equilibria, or perhaps actual expectations are formed in such a way that the perverse equilibria never occur. Very little is known, however, about how economic agents form expectations of future prices.

Despite these reservations, it would be a mistake to throw up one's hands and say, "All this rigorous formalism is useless." The theory indicates what we need to know in order to have more useful models, and rigor helps the theory serve this function. If the theory were vague and informal, we might not know whether it was loose thinking or lack of empirical knowledge that caused our confusion or, worse, we might fool ourselves by believing we understood what we do not understand.

References

Arrow, Kenneth. 1953. "Le rôle des valeurs boursières pour la répartition la meilleure des risques," *Econométrie*. Paris: Centre National de la Recherche Scientifique. Trans. Kenneth Arrow. 1964. "The Role of Securities in the Optimal Allocation of Risk-Bearing." *Review of Economic Studies* 31: 91–96.

Ballard, Charles L., Don Fullerton, John B. Shoven, and John Whalley. 1985. *A General Equilibrium Model for Tax Policy Evaluation.* Chicago: University of Chicago Press.

Barro, Robert J. 1974. "Are Government Bonds Net Wealth?" *Journal of Political Economy* 82 (November/December): 1095–1117.

Barro, Robert J., and Xavier Sala-i-Martin. 1999. *Economic Growth.* Cambridge, MA: MIT Press.

Bernheim, B. Douglas. 2002. "Taxation and Saving." In Alan J. Auerbach and Martin Feldstein, eds., vol. 3, chap. 18, *Handbook of Public Economics.* Amsterdam: Elsevier.

Bewley, Truman. 1977. "The Permanent Income Hypothesis: A Theoretical Formulation." *Journal of Economic Theory* 16 (December): 252–292.

——— 1980. "The Permanent Income Hypothesis and Short-Run Price Stability." *Journal of Economic Theory* 23 (December): 323–333.

——— 1981a. "Stationary Equilibrium." *Journal of Economic Theory* 24 (April): 265–295.

——— 1981b. "The Indeterminacy of Interest Rates." Discussion Paper 491, the Center for Mathematical Studies in Economics and Management Science, Northwestern University, Evanston, IL.

——— 1981c. "The Relation between Social Security, Saving, and Investment in a Life- Cycle Model." Discussion Paper 492, the Center for Mathematical Studies in Economics and Management Science, Northwestern University, Evanston, IL.

Blanchard, Oliver J., and Stanley Fischer. 1989. *Lectures on Macroeconomics.* Cambridge, MA: MIT Press.

Blaug, Mark. 1980. *The Methodology of Economics.* Cambridge: Cambridge University Press.

Brock, William A. 1970. "On the Existence of Weakly Maximal Programs in a Multisector Economy." *Review of Economic Studies* 37 (April): 275–280.

Brock, William A., and Leonard J. Mirman. 1972. "Optimal Economic Growth and Uncertainty: The Discounted Case." *Journal of Economic Theory* 4 (June): 479–513.

Brown, Donald J., and Rosa L. Matzkin. 1996. "Testable Restrictions on the Equilibrium Manifold." *Econometrica* 64 (6): 1249–1262.

Brown, Donald J., and Caterina Calsamiglia. 2003. "The Strong Law of Demand." Discussion Paper, Cowles Foundation, Yale University, February.

Browning, Martin, Angus Deaton, and Margaret Irish. 1985. "A Profitable Approach to Labor Supply and Commodity Demands over the Life-Cycle." *Econometrica* 53 (May): 503–542.

Coddington, Earl A., and Normal Levinson. 1955. *Theory of Ordinary Differential Equations.* New York: McGraw-Hill.

Deardorff, Alan V. 1976. "The Optimum Growth Rate of Population: Comment." *International Economic Review* 17 (June): 510–525.

Debreu, Gerard. 1959. *Theory of Value.* New York: Wiley.

——— 1974. "Excess Demand Functions." *Journal of Mathematical Economics* 1 (March): 15–21.

Dervis, Kemal, Jaime de Melo, and Sherman Robinson. 1982. *General Equilibrium Models for Development Policy.* Cambridge: Cambridge University Press.

Diamond, Peter. 1965. "National Debt in a Neoclassical Growth Model." *American Economic Review* 55 (December): 1126–1150.

Diamond, Peter, and John Geanakoplos. 2003. "Social Security Investment in Equities." *American Economic Review* 93 (September): 1047–1074.

Dorfman, Robert, Paul Samuelson, and Robert Solow. 1958. *Linear Programming and Economic Analysis.* New York: McGraw-Hill.

Edgeworth, Francis Y. 1881. *Mathematical Psychics; An Essay on the Application of Mathematics to the Moral Sciences.* London: C. K. Paul and Company.

Feldstein, Martin. 1974. "Social Security, Induced Retirement, and Aggregate Capital Accumulation." *Journal of Political Economy* 82 (September/October): 905–926.

Fossati, Amedeo, and Wolfgang Wiegard, eds. 2002. *Policy Evaluation with Computable General Equilibrium Models.* New York: Routledge.

Friedman, Milton. 1953. "The Methodology of Positive Economics." In *Essays in Positive Economics*, pt. I. Chicago: Chicago University Press.

——— 1957. *A Theory of the Consumption Function.* Princeton, NJ: Princeton University Press.

Frisch, Ragnar. 1959. "A Complete Scheme for Computing All Direct and Cross Demand Elasticities in a Model with Many Sectors." *Econometrica* 27 (April): 177–196.

Gale, David. 1973. "Pure Exchange Equilibrium of Dynamic Economic Models." *Journal of Economic Theory* 6 (February): 12–36.

Ginzburgh, Victor, and Michiel Keyzer. 1997. *The Structure of Applied General Equilibrium Models.* Cambridge, MA: MIT Press.

Hahn, Frank H. 1966. "Equilibrium Dynamics with Heterogeneous Capital Goods." *Quarterly Journal of Economics* 80 (November): 633–646.

Hartman, Philip. 1964. *Ordinary Differential Equations.* New York: John Wiley and Sons.

Hausman, Daniel M. 1992. *The Inexact and Separate Science of Economics.* Cambridge: Cambridge University Press

Hildenbrand, Werner. 1994. *Market Demand: Theory and Empirical Evidence.* Princeton, NJ: Princeton University Press.

Kehoe, Patrick J., and Timothy J. Kehoe, eds. 1995. *Modeling North American Economic Integration.* Boston, MA: Kluwer Academic Publishers.

Keller, Wouter J. 1980. *Tax Incidence: A General Equilibrium Approach.* Amsterdam: North Holland.

Koopmans, Tjalling C. 1957. *Three Essays on the State of Economic Science.* New York: McGraw-Hill.

Kuhn, A. W., and A. W. Tucker. 1951. "Nonlinear Porgramming." In *Proceedings of the Second Berkeley Symposium on Mathematical Statistics and Probability,* 481–492. Berkeley: University of California Press.

Malinvaud, Edmund. 1953. "Capital Accumulation and Efficient Allocation of Resources." *Econometrica* 21 (April): 233–267.

Marshall, Alfred. 1890. *Principles of Economics.* Vol. 1. London: MacMillan and Company.

McKenzie, Lionel. 1976. "Turnpike Theory." *Econometrica* 44 (September): 841–865.

Mercenier, Jean, and T. N. Srinivasan, eds. 1994. *Applied General Equilibrium and Economic Development: Present Achievements and Future Trends.* Ann Arbor, MI: University of Michigan Press.

Mill, John S. 1836. "On the Definition of Political Economy and the Method of Investigation Proper to It." In *Collected Works of John Stuart Mill.* 1967, vol. 4. Toronto: University of Toronto Press.

Negishi, Takashi. 1960. "Welfare Economics and Existence of an Equilibrium for a Competitive Economy." *Metroeconomica* 12: 92–97.

Pigott, John and John Whaller eds. 1985. *New Developments in Applied General Equilibrium Analysis*. Cambridge, UK: Cambridge University Press.

Radner, Roy. 1961. "Paths of Economic Growth That Are Optimal with Regard Only to Final States: A Turnpike Theorem." *Review of Economic Studies* 28 (February): 98–104.

Ramsey, F. 1928. "A Mathematical Theory of Saving." *Economic Journal* 38: 543–549.

Rockafellar, R. Tyrell. 1970. *Convex Analysis*. Princeton, NJ: Princeton University Press.

Samuelson, Paul A. 1951. "Abstract of a Theorem Concerning Substitutability in Open Leontief Models." In Tjalling Koopmans, ed., *Activity Analysis of Production and Allocation*. New York: Wiley.

——— 1954. "The Pure Theory of Public Expenditure" *Review of Economics and Statistics* 36: 387–389.

——— 1955. "Diagrammatic Exposition of a Pure Theory of Public Expenditure." *Review of Economics and Statistics* 37: 350–356.

——— 1958. "An Exact Consumption-Loan Model of Interest without the Social Contrivance of Money." *Journal of Political Economy* 66 (December): 467–482.

——— 1975. "The Optimum Growth Rate of Population." *International Economic Review* 16 (October): 531–538.

——— 1976. "The Optimum Growth Rate of Population: Agreement and Evaluations." *International Economic Review* 17 (June): 516–525.

Scarf, Herbert. 1960. "Some Examples of Global Instability of the Competitive Equilibrium." *International Economic Review* 1 (September): 157–172.

Scarf, Herbert E. and John B. Shoven eds. 1984. *Applied General Equilibrium Analysis*. Cambridge, UK: Cambridge University Press.

Shoven, John B. and John Whalley. 1992. *Applying General Equilibrium*. Cambridge, UK: Cambridge University Press.

Solow, Robert M. 1956. "A Contribution to the Theory of Economic Growth." *Quarterly Journal of Economics* 70: 65–94.

Srinivasan, T. N. and John Whalley eds. 1986. *General Equilibrium Trade Policy Modeling*. Cambridge, MA: MIT Press.

von Weizäcker, Carl C. 1965. "Existence of Optimal Programs of Accumulation for an Infinite Time Horizon" *Review of Economic Studies* 32 (April): 85–104.

Index

Harvard University Press is a member of Green Press Initiative
(greenpressinitiative.org), a nonprofit organization working to
help publishers and printers increase their use of recycled paper
and decrease their use of fiber derived from endangered forests.
This book was printed on recycled paper containing 30%
post-consumer waste and processed chlorine free.